POWER, STATE, AND SOCIETY
An Introduction to Political Sociology

W. Lawrence Neuman
University of Wisconsin at Whitewater

Boston   Burr Ridge, IL   Dubuque, IA   Madison, WI   New York   San Francisco   St. Louis
Bangkok   Bogotá   Caracas   Kuala Lumpur   Lisbon   London   Madrid   Mexico City
Milan   Montreal   New Delhi   Santiago   Seoul   Singapore   Sydney   Taipei   Toronto

Higher Education

POWER, STATE, AND SOCIETY: AN INTRODUCTION TO POLITICAL SOCIOLOGY
Published by McGraw-Hill, a business unit of The McGraw-Hill Companies, Inc., 1221 Avenue of the Americas, New York, NY, 10020. Copyright © 2005 by The McGraw-Hill Companies, Inc. All rights reserved. No part of this publication may be reproduced or distributed in any form or by any means, or stored in a database or retrieval system, without the prior written consent of The McGraw-Hill Companies, Inc., including, but not limited to, in any network or other electronic storage or transmission, or broadcast for distance learning.
Some ancillaries, including electronic and print components, may not be available to customers outside the United States.

This book is printed on acid-free paper.

1 2 3 4 5 6 7 8 9 0 QPF/QPF 0 9 8 7 6 5 4

ISBN   0-07-285380-8

Publisher: *Phillip A. Butcher*
Senior sponsoring editor: *Carolyn Henderson Meier*
Senior marketing manager: *Daniel M. Loch*
Project manager: *Richard Hecker*
Associate production supervisor: *Jason Huls*
Associate designer: *Srdjan Savanovic*
Associate media project manager: *Meghan Durko*
Permissions editor: *Marty Granahan*
Cover and interior design: *Kay Fulton*
Cover photo credit: *Farinaz Taghavi/Getty Images*
Typeface: *10/12 Palatino*
Compositor: *Carlisle Communications, Ltd.*
Printer: *Quebecor World Fairfield Inc.*

Library of Congress Cataloging-in-Publication Data

Neuman, William Lawrence, 1950–
    Power, state, and society : an introduction to political sociology / W. Lawrence Neuman.
      p. cm.
    Includes bibliographical references and index.
    ISBN 0-07-285380-8 (alk. paper)
    1. Political sociology. I. Title
JA76.N417 2005
306.2—dc22

                                                               2004057928

www.mhhe.com

CONTENTS

CHAPTER 12

Conclusion *555*

LIST OF BOXES AND CHARTS

If you are like most people, on nearly a daily basis you encounter public issues, concerns, disputes, and controversies, or you learn about them in the news or through other media. The issues can assume many forms and can vary widely in intensity. Many involve who will get to have a say in some decision and who will be ignored. Others involve people of a particular race, gender, or sexual identity, or a group with shared economic interests, a common outlook on life, or strongly-held religious, moral, or cultural values trying to defend interests or beliefs.

Some public concerns and issues are fairly minor, such as whether to allow smoking in restaurants or where to locate a new city park. Others are weightier, such as stopping toxic pollution that is seeping into drinking water, getting health care for a sick child, deciding who will pay for local schools, or changing the legal definition of marriage. Such issues can affect how people live and make decisions in their everyday lives. For example, should a farmer plant tobacco or another crop? Can a person buy a gun without a special permit or a long waiting period? Can a pregnant woman and her partner chose abortion as an option? Should parents send their child to a public or private school? How much is taken out of a person's paycheck for

taxes? Will a family lose its health care coverage when a company closes its local factory and moves production overseas? What can a person do when he/she is turned away from renting an apartment simply because of racial-ethnic background? Many personal or family concerns and decisions are linked to larger public issues, and these larger issues might expand into serious disputes over fundamental beliefs and values about morality, freedom, justice, fairness, or equality.

People respond differently to the public issues and debates around them. Some people become very involved with an issue and develop a strong position on it; they may join organizations, attend meetings, write letters, and donate their time or money to support the position. Other people watch and listen to issues from the sidelines; talk about the issue with family, friends, neighbors, or co-workers; and use the issues to help them make choices when voting. Still other people seem to be totally unconcerned and apathetic.

The development of such public issues, people's reactions and responses to them, and resolution of the issues in the public arena are central in political sociology, a field at the intersection of politics and sociology. The politics in political sociology includes electing candidates, voting, and government, but it is also much more. The sociology in political sociology includes the formation and operation of social relations in families, groups, organizations, and society at large, but the focus is on the dynamics of power and influence in the social relations. Political sociologists look at who has power, who does not, and why. They also consider the difference that having power makes and how the power balance might change. Political sociology is simultaneously a mode of inquiry, an analytic perspective, an evolving set of topics, and a growing body of knowledge. It helps reveal the dynamics of power relations as they operate in personal concerns, in defending basic rights and freedoms, and in society-wide change.

ORGANIZATION OF THIS BOOK

The 12 chapters of this book begin with an overview of political sociology as a field.

- Chapter 1 addresses questions such as: What is political sociology? How do political sociology and political science differ? Where did political sociology come from and where is it going? What are the problems or topics that political sociologists wrestle with and try to explain? What major ideas or concepts do political sociologists use when making an explanation?
- In Chapter 2 you will see how political sociologists approach core concepts such as democracy, citizenship, nationalism, and the nation-state.
- Chapter 3 provides an outline of the major models and theories that political sociologists use to study political life. This chapter provides a foundation for using the rest of the book, because the same models and theories are applied to specific questions and topics in Chapters 4 through 12.

- The focus in Chapter 4 is on the polity of the United States. The term *polity* includes a great deal—institutions, organizations, people, processes, rules, and symbols. Beyond exploring the structure and development of the American polity, you will see how some people, groups, or ideas get included in or are excluded from the national polity.
- Chapter 5 explores how people participate in the political life of a polity. It specifically looks at conventional politics, such as voting and elections and discusses who does or does not vote in elections and why, forms of political involvement by different sectors of society, and periodic historic shifts in overall pattern of electoral politics.
- After examining conventional forms of political participation in Chapter 5, we turn to unconventional forms in Chapter 6. These include organized collective actions, political protest, and social movements, or what some have called contentious politics, stretching from small-scale riots to national revolutions.

Chapters 7 and 8 shift to the realm of ideas, beliefs, symbols, and culture.

- In Chapter 7, we examine the importance of symbols in politics, political ideology, and so-called "culture wars."
- Our examination of the role of ideas and symbols continues in Chapter 8, with a focus on two major cultural institutions— the schools and the mass media. We also look at why and when some people are willing to defend, or try to restrict, the civil liberties and free expression of other people, groups, or ideas.
- Chapter 9 is concerned with law, crime, social control, and government surveillance. In this chapter we see how law, justice, and crime are closely intertwined topics that reflect the distribution and use of power in a society.

Chapters 10 and 11 discuss what governments do, or don't do, in the larger economy and society. We examine economic and social policy in these chapters.

- Business and economic issues such as taxes, jobs, corporate lobbying, regulation, and pork barrel politics, are explored in Chapter 10.
- Chapter 11 is about social policies, or what is called the welfare state. In this chapter we look at the term *"welfare"* and see how the form and operation of social programs (such as child care, family leave, health insurance, unemployment insurance, and retirement pensions), shape many areas of personal and family life. You also will see that there is great variation in the social programs and policies across the advanced industrial nations. We look at the causes and consequences of nations adopting different kinds of social policies and programs.
- The last chapter is divided into three parts. The first part explores a number of topics that cross-reference major themes found in more than one of the earlier chapters. The second part looks at topics or themes likely to have a growing impact on how we understand power relations and politics in the future. The last section re-evaluates the models of political sociology that were first introduced in Chapter 3 and that were used to explain many specific topics in the book.

PEDAGOGICAL AIDS

A brief outline appears at the beginning of each chapter to orient you to topics that will be covered. Skimming the outline before you read the chapter gives you a quick idea of its major sections and their sequence. Key terms introduced in each chapter are highlighted in the text, listed at the end of the chapter, and also appear in a glossary section of the book along with their definitions. There are several types of terms. Some refer to specific political sociological theories or propositions, others are major concepts described in a chapter, and some are terms that come from historical events or are used in public debates. If you master all of the key terms, you will have a solid working vocabulary and set of ideas for following, understanding, and even contributing to discussions about political sociology and political life.

You will also see review questions at the end of each chapter. These are general essay-type questions about the chapter's broad themes and topics. It is good practice to read and to try to answer all of these questions. If you have difficulty answering any of them, reread the associated chapter section. Each chapter also comes with a list of recommended readings. The list is limited to book-length works. Some of the books listed are classics in the field, others reflect recent advances, and still others are introductions to complex topics. These are offered for students who want to study particular topics in greater depth.

Lastly, within each chapter, you will find various types of boxes and charts, as well as tables and figures. Do not overlook them; they are important. Some of them provide a global or international focus, others are case studies or in-depth examinations of a concrete example, and still others provide condensed summaries of the points discussed in the text.

ACKNOWLEDGMENTS

This book began with my initiation to political sociology over 30 years ago when I was fortunate as an undergraduate to be under the tutelage of the late Marvin Olsen and others including Alan Grimshaw, Lawrence

Hazelrigg, Bud Mehan, the late Nick Mullins, David Sallach, Shel Stryker, and Austin Turk. As a graduate student, I continued to learn from Michael Aiken, Robert Alford, Ron Aminzade, Nick Danigelis, Joe Elder, Manuel Castels, Marshall Clinard, Jerry Hage, Warren Hagstrom, Chuck Halaby, Bill Hauser, Leon Lindberg, Jim O'Connor, Jane Piliavin, Ed Silva, Ivan Szelenyi, Erik Wright, and Maurice Zeitlin as well as the late Aage Sorensen and Richard Havens. These scholars contributed directly or indirectly to my understanding of political sociology. Graduate students often learn as much from peers as faculty, and I was lucky to have fellow students of the caliber of Vern Baxter, Bill Bielby, David Bills, Kathy Blee, John Campbell, Bill Canak, Richard Colignon, Sandy Danziger, Nancy DiTomasso, Betty Dobratz, Gösta Esping-Andersen, Roger Friedland, Al Gedicks, Alexander Hicks, David Hachen, Randy Hodson, Greg Hooks, David James, Robin Stryker, Andy Szasz, Neil Fligstein, Roger Friedland, Jim Kruegel, John Myles, Richard Radcliff, Mike Radelet, Nancy Randall, Rachel Rosenberg, Mike Soref, Paul Schervish, Mike Schulman, Joey Sprague, Julia Wrigley, Glenn Yago, and Pete Yeager. These student-colleagues and others helped me develop the principles and ideas found in this book. Others who influenced my thinking include Pat Akard, Michael Allen, Joel Best, Beth Clements, Jim Davis, Bill Domhoff, Craig Jenkins, Rhonda Levine, Marty Marger, Scott McNall, Mark Mizruchi, Carol McClurg Mueller, Beth Mintz, Ann Shola Orloff, Bill Roy, Tony Orum, Claus Offe, Harlan Prechel, Mitch Sato, Bill Sewell, Jr., Randy Stoecker, Mike Useem, and Fred Wiel. And there are others whose names I have forgotten.

Lastly, I wish to thank the reviewers at Mayfield Publishing, which became part of McGraw Hill, and those at McGraw Hill who read draft chapters of this book. Their careful comments and criticisms helped me to improve this book. All of the shortcomings of this book are entirely mine alone.

POWER, THE STATE, HEGEMONY, AND STRUGGLE

INTRODUCTION

Political activism seems to be at a low level around the world. A 1998 survey found that only 20 percent of Americans were satisfied with the state of the nation and only 34 percent trusted the government. That year about one in three eligible voters went to the polls in the congressional election. A 1997 annual survey of U.S. college freshmen found interest in politics was the lowest recorded in 30 years, and few reported discussing politics.[1] In the close, hotly contested November 2000 U.S. presidential election, only about half of Americans voted.

The election was plagued by voting irregularities, and due to the U.S. system of selecting presidents, the candidate favored by a majority of voters did not become the president. The percentage of people voting reached a historical low in the 1990s as people became disgusted and frustrated with politics. In many nations, more people seem to admire film stars or sports heroes than their national political leaders.

Yet this picture of political apathy is incomplete. Even before the September 11, 2001 World Trade Center terrorist attack that triggered political interest, American college students' interest in politics grew. The percentage of students saying they frequently discussed politics jumped from 16.4 to 20.9 percent in 2001; this was the largest 1-year increase since 1992. In addition, the percentage of students saying it is essential to keep up-to-date with political events rose to 31.4 percent, marking the largest 1-year increase since 1972.[2]

Despite a general lack of interest in politics, many people are politically active. They put flags on their cars, stand with protest signs in front of abortion clinics, fight against mandatory standardized tests in schools, join marches to demand money for breast cancer research, form parents' support groups for their gay sons and lesbian daughters, or sign petitions to stop shipping nuclear waste through their towns. People engage in politics when they voice concerns about the direction of events and join together to influence powerful organizations or other people.

This broader view of politics is what political sociologists study to learn about power relations. For example, many thousands of homeless people live in the streets of major cities in America, Britain, Canada, France, and Japan. Observers may feel anger, pity, or disgust, but few ask, Why are there so many homeless? Some rely on self-righteous moral condemnation and call the homeless "lazy bums," while others call it bad luck. Few understand how the homeless situation grew due to political decisions and contests for power. A political sociologist explores how changing societal power relationships and specific political actions combined to create the national homeless situation. Another example is street crime. In many nations newspapers and television news programs report murder, rape, and robbery. Opinion polls show that crime is a top public concern and politicians make speeches and enact laws to control crime. In the United States, public funding to build prisons and hire new police officers skyrocketed in the 1990s, and criminal justice became one of the fastest growing college majors. At the same time, public attention and government action became more disconnected from changes in the actual incidence of criminal behavior. If the crime rates changed little, why was there an increase in the media attention, more money spent, and more people sent to prison? The answer is politics and power. For example, changes in the number of people imprisoned in the United States are closely related to the political party in power and the timing of elections.[3] Fighting crime is an easy political issue that functions like a morality play; it excites emotions, contains drama, pits good against evil, offers simple answers, and uni-

"We don't talk about Larry . . .
he went into politics."

fies people to feel self-righteous. It organizes the complexity of social reality into the simple categories of right and wrong and promises to restore social order and reaffirm authority as it diverts public attention from difficult, irresolvable issues such as racial divisions or people feeling they have little say in government.[4] Political sociologists probe into thorny issues, ask tough questions, and reveal unpleasant truths, and often what they learn is neither simple nor comforting. By studying political sociology you will not become rich overnight, win instant fame, or become wildly popular, but you may begin to see the world in new ways and ask questions that go to the core of vital local, national, and global concerns. Political sociology can help you understand why some people prevail in major public issues, while others do not and are baffled as to why. ■

What Is Political Sociology?

Political sociology is the study of power and relationships between society and politics. Power is a pervasive, barely visible force. It is a fundamental dimension in all human relations and social institutions. Politics is a process by which social groups (i.e., classes, genders, races, and so forth) acquire, extend, apply, maintain, and struggle over power. A political sociologist sees politics as a lot more than voting once every few years. Politics takes many forms (see Case in Point 1.1). It occurs when you enter the voting booth and when you put a Save the Earth bumper sticker on your car. It occurs when you honor a national flag and national anthem. Politics is present when you visit the public library to borrow a

CASE IN POINT 1.1 — Being Chased Offstage for Defending the U.S. Constitution

The president and publisher of a major U.S. newspaper gave a speech in which she praised political values and patriotism in the United States. She praised freedom of press, argued for protecting basic constitutionally protected rights, and expressed concerns over the government wiretaps of innocent citizens, unlawful detention, and expanded racial profiling. The crowd's response after just 5 minutes was intense booing, chanting, and heckling. The crowd's anger was so fierce that the speaker was forced to stop her speech and flee the stage in fear of bodily harm. Did this occur in some nondemocratic nation? No, it was Sacramento, California. Did it happen in the distant past? No, it was in 2001. Was the crowd a group of uneducated, political extremists? No, it was graduating college students and their families who were attending a graduation ceremony at the California State University. The speech came 3 months after the attack of September 11, 2001, and many in the audience were still full of raw political rage and could not bear to hear someone question their government's actions. The event illustrates political life beyond elections: It includes due process with protected constitutional rights, people's beliefs and emotional response to events, and the impact of several months of one-sided media coverage during which the U.S. government's actions were praised and dissent was virtually absent.

Sources: See "Network Coverage a Target of Fire from Conservatives," *New York Times*, November 7, 2001; "Opponents of War Are Scarce on Television," *New York Times*, November 9, 2001; "In Sacramento, a Publisher's Questions Draw the Wrath of the Crowd," *New York Times*, December 21, 2001.

book; when a police officer stops you for a traffic violation; or when you join friends and coworkers to discuss issues such as war, immigration, affirmative action, tax rates, or illegal drug use. Politics includes most issues—gun control, inner city decay, racial tensions, same-sex marriages, public health care, retirement, and terrorism—that connect people's deeply felt values and abstract ideals (e.g., citizenship, justice, freedom, repression, or democracy) to their everyday experiences.

The Relevance of Political Sociology

Political sociology is relevant because it will help you make sense of your situation by allowing you to better see the political forces around you and situate those forces in a broader context. It is relevant if you want to gain greater control over events, improve the quality of life for family members, and exert influence over the direction of your community. Political sociology can help you to recognize how power relations are constantly shaping many areas of your daily life. Its ideas shape public debates over a growing sense of social isolation (e.g., Putnam's 1995 "Bowling Alone") or the sources of international conflicts (e.g., Huntington's 1992 "Clash of Civilizations").

To make real progress on public issues, such as achieving racial justice, improving the environment, providing quality day care for working mothers, lowering crime rates, or reducing violence on television, we must first ask the right questions. Without the right questions, meaningful answers are impossible.

Political sociology points to important questions; ones that once asked alter the entire direction of a discussion and open up new ways to see issues, make connections, and find solutions.

The relevance of political sociology resides in its capacity to generate new ideas and analyze power relations. It is a dynamic field that has periodically reinvented itself. As Anthony Orum (1996, 142) remarked, "Political sociology in the past fifteen years or so has come to look vastly different from a generation ago." Indeed, a new political sociology emerged in the past decade.[5] Other fields borrow from political sociology, and it provides a vocabulary and perspective that connects diverse fields of study.[6] In this way, political sociology can help you to better recognize the linkages among a range of seemingly disconnected public issues.

Political Sociology versus Political Science

Students and friends often ask me how political sociology differs from political science. Political sociology is an interdisciplinary field where political science and sociology overlap. Like other interdisciplinary areas (e.g., social psychology, historical sociology, political philosophy), the line between political science and sociology is permeable, and their interchange fosters creativity. Both fields study voting patterns, public policy, law enactment, and protest movements. At times, political scientists and political sociologists will study the same topic in similar ways. More often, they focus on different issues, ask different questions, and apply different theoretical perspectives.[7]

Political scientists tend to focus on how political institutions operate (empirical political science) or on ideal forms of governing (normative political science). They examine the committee structure of the legislature, look at how alternative voting rules affect election outcomes, or consider what makes a law just or fair. A political scientist concentrates on the more visible aspects of the "game of politics" in various levels of government (e.g., local, national, international) and maps out the operations at each level (e.g., voting in elections, passing new laws, administering a policy). By contrast, a political sociologist emphasizes the interaction of society and politics, investigates power relations, and explores political dynamics occurring in many arenas of society (e.g., sexual politics, cultural politics, racial politics, religious politics, educational politics, and environmental politics).

Political scientists and political sociologists both study government but from different perspectives. A political scientist focuses on the government's internal structure (unified or divided, centralized or decentralized, tall or flat hierarchy) and its mechanics (who gets elected, how laws are passed, which agency budget grew). A political sociologist views government as a key site in society where power is concentrated and consolidated. Both study elections. The political scientist sees them as central and focuses on who won and who voted for which candidate, while the political sociologist asks questions such as: What does voting actually mean? Does the election's outcome affect the daily lives of most people? How much can elections significantly change the distribution of power in society?

Political sociologists differ from other sociologists in three ways. First, because they operate in an interdisciplinary area, political sociologists tend to borrow ideas, issues, and research techniques from outside of sociology or synthesize them with traditional sociology. Second, sociologists focus on the human relationships, group processes, and social institutions of a society, while political sociologists focus on the power dimension wherever it appears, sometimes outside the boundaries of traditional sociology. Lastly, some parts of political sociology are applied (e.g., voting outcomes), but usually the focus is on developing a critical understanding of power dynamics. Although some sociologists concentrate on achieving a critical understanding, many work in applied areas (e.g., criminal justice, family, schooling, health care) where they are oriented more toward achieving the equitable or efficient operation of existing social or governmental organizations/programs.

How Did We Get to Where We Are?

The history of political sociology reveals how its core ideas evolved. It grew from writings by German and Italian thinkers of the late nineteenth and early twentieth century. Major contributors include Karl Marx (1818–1883), Vilfredo Pareto (1848–1923), Gaetano Mosca (1858–1941), Max Weber (1864–1920), Robert Michels (1876–1936), and Antonio Gramsci (1891–1937). These men sought to explain the advance of industrialization, growth of class conflict, and the spread of participatory democracy across Western Europe—issues that were the foundation of political sociology.

The Classic Era

By 1950 most activity in political sociology moved to the United States, and the 20 years that followed World War II mark the classic era of political sociology. With the defeat of fascism, the onset of the Cold War, and the demise of colonialism, Americans saw their nation as the world leader of democracy and freedom. Domestically, strong economic growth and social stability fostered a general mood of optimism and self-assurance.

A primary question in classic-era political sociology was, Why do some societies become democratic while others become totalitarian (either fascist [e.g., 1930s Germany, Japan, Italy, and Spain] or communist [e.g., the Soviet Union, Cuba, China, and North Korea])? As Morris Janowitz (1968, 306) summarized, "political sociology has come to be linked to the analysis of the economic, social, and psychological preconditions for political democracy." Major studies in this era reflected this focus. They outlined the conditions that supported democracy and the type of society that reinforced or threatened it.[8] To oversimplify, the studies held that democracy is coincident with the rise of a modern industrial capitalist economy, an expanding educated middle class, and a division in or the defeat of traditional ruling elites. Political sociologists argued that democracy requires open institutions and a value system that favors popular participation, rule of law, and tolerance for dissent. Democracy could only exist where a large middle class was committed to modern values and certain types of political institutions. Lewis Coser (1967, 203–205) remarked, "Democracy has historically been highly correlated with relatively high standards of living, with urbanization, industrialization, and education. However, the correlation is not automatic . . . if there are no local, religious, or class forces independently pushing in the same direction, then democratic revolutions are unlikely. . . ."

Classic-era political sociologists also explored the social bases of voting. This arose from a belief that formal democratic processes, and specifically elections, peacefully resolved tensions and conflicts among contenting social groups. Political sociologists studied how people from different parts of society (e.g., different classes, regions, religions, races) voted and asked, Do they support the same or different political parties? Two major studies found that America lacked deep, irreparable social divisions or a strong commitment to an ideology.[9] Instead, most people had a modest interest in politics and voted to advance their own social group's interests. A related issue was to explain why social programs expanded in democratic industrial societies. Most political sociologists believed that industrialization created new needs, and governments expanded social programs to address the evolving needs of the population.[10] In sum, a modern industrial society had a democratic government that gave people the basics of a middle-class lifestyle.

A third central question of the classic era was, How can freedom and democratic politics prevail even if some people supported right-wing or left-wing political extremism? Political sociologists examined why people supported fascism, communism, and other forms of extremism. In addition to studying people who were attracted to antidemocratic movements, they explored why other people remained politically tolerant and vigorously defended basic civil liberties (e.g., freedom of speech).[11] In the classic era, many political sociologists distrusted the mass of uneducated, low income, marginal members of society who did not embrace establishment norms. William Kornhauser (1959, 228) worried about this and warned that, "the main danger to political order and civil liberty is the domination of elites by masses." Robert Lane (1962) found that most people were not greatly involved in politics and accepted basic democratic values, except for a few marginal people outside the mainstream. Many feared that "marginal" members of society were not strong supporters of democracy. By implication, they saw well-educated, middle-class, professional, white-collar workers; business owners; and upper-level managers as the bastion of a stable democratic society.

A related issue grew from the writings of a founder of political sociology, Robert Michels. He presented the Iron Law of Oligarchy that held that as large-scale bureaucratic organizations spread in modern industrial society, they produced antidemocratic tendencies. This posed a problem to political sociologists who saw modern societies as becoming more democratic. In a famous study, *Union Democracy*, Lipset, Trow, and Coleman (1956) examined blue-collar workers in a bureaucratic setting and discovered that the workers ran a large bureaucratic union on democratic principles. Their discovery seemed to contradict both the Iron Law of Oligarchy and distrust of marginal blue-collar workers. Yet, the particular union they studied was atypical. The workers were well-educated and highly skilled with strong professional values and a strong sense of community. Thus, the *Union Democracy* findings reinforced the idea that schooling and middle-class values were essential to sustain democratic politics.

A central assumption of classic-era political sociology was that Americans shared a broad agreement or consensus on basic values. Daniel Bell (1960) in the *End of Ideology* argued that rising living standards, a growing middle class, and increased levels of schooling would eliminate ideological thinking and expand democracy. Other studies found that few Americans were well-informed or involved in politics, and that most people lacked consistent, stable political views.[12] Political sociologists reconciled these contradictory findings by arguing that most Americans were politically uninvolved because they were politically satisfied. They felt that as more people became more educated and joined the middle class, they would embrace democratic values more strongly. Slow progress was preferable because rapid change might create social strains and disruptions in the smooth-functioning social system.[13]

A few political sociologists in the classic era rejected the mainstream view. Three controversial studies of power structure questioned the prevailing positive image of American politics.[14] These studies found that powerful elites made most major political decisions.

Defenders of the mainstream view reinterpreted the critical findings and said the elites were the staunchest supporters of democratic rights. They said mass apathy was positive and perhaps a necessary condition for a stable democracy. Dye and Zeigler (1970, 328, 339) concluded, "The future of American democracy depends on the wisdom, responsibility and resourcefulness of the nation's elite. . . . the survival of democracy depends upon the commitment of elites to democratic ideals rather than upon broad support for democracy by the masses." Thus, democracy worked because a small minority of informed, wise, and tolerant elites governed, while most people were apathetic. Likewise, America's two-party system limited choice, but it created stable politics and avoided the chaos of many ideological parties.[15]

Two other issues in the classic era grew into major developments by the 1990s. One issue was how "things are not always what they appear," and how political symbols can be important in power relations. Murray Edelman (1964) argued for looking beyond what people say directly. He noted that political actors use emotional appeals and manipulate symbols to distract people and advance their own political goals. Joseph Gusfield (1963) showed that the Prohibition movement was actually a power contest between competing status groups in which a high status group dominated low-status recent immigrants by packaging their quest for power in symbolic, moral terms. The second issue was the difficulty of achieving collective goals when each individual pursues his or her own self-interest. Anthony Downs and Marcur Olson borrowed assumptions about rationally calculated behavior and applied precise quantitative models from economics.[16] They showed why collective behavior was difficult to achieve and predicted how people who followed individual self-interest alone could sometimes produce collective political behaviors.

By the mid-1960s, political sociology had become a firmly established academic field with a sophisticated theory, key questions to address, and a well-established body of knowledge.[17]

Rupture and Redirection

Political sociology dramatically changed direction during the late 1960s and early 1970s because it had failed to anticipate and was unable to explain a major turn in political events. During these years, television screens were filled with images of Southern police officers beating and attacking African Americans who peacefully tried to exercise their democratic right to vote. Southern Blacks and Northern White allies who joined to demand equal citizenship rights were murdered in schools, churches, or along the roadside in the South. Summer after summer, armed U.S. soldiers in armored vehicles patrolled large U.S. cities after massive riots destroyed dozens of city blocks. Hundreds of thousands of people who opposed a national foreign policy found that their free speech rights lacked real legal protection. Scholars and journalists published revelations showing how U.S. foreign policy backed brutal dictators who suppressed their citizens requesting basic democratic rights. Television showed planes dropping napalm bombs on villages populated by women, old men, and children as American teenage soldiers were killing others and being killed. But when people ask why, many came to believe that their political leaders were lying to them. The image of America as a great defender of peace, stability, and democracy at home and abroad seemed to be an illusion. At the same time, protest movements for freedom and democracy spread across most nations of the advanced industrial world.

As tear gas clouds drifted across many college campuses and students caught sight of police in riot gear marching past classroom windows, the textbooks of classic era political sociologists who had described a stable world of consensus and democracy looked out of touch with reality. Social change, political unrest, and theoretical breakthroughs quickly transformed the field of political sociology. Simultaneously, graduate programs rapidly grew, producing a flood of new scholars and researchers who questioned the ideas of classic era political sociology.

In the 1970s, political sociologists studied the new protest movements. Classic era political sociology rarely discussed movements and tended to view protest actions as irrational outbursts by isolated malcontents who threatened democracy. New research on the protest of the 1960s contradicted the classic era views and documented that most protesters were well-integrated members of society who deeply believed in democratic values. Political sociologists now saw protest as a form of politics used by dispossessed people to wrestle power from entrenched elites.[18] Other studies showed how parts of the American government engaged in antidemocratic spying and activities against its own citizens who questioned the authority of political elites and their decisions.[19]

Looking into the causes of revolutions and repressive military dictatorships in less-developed nations, political sociologists found that rise of democracy did not depend on whether the public embraced American values. Instead, active competition among a wide range of social groups was needed.[20] Others, such as Immanuel Wallerstein (1976), questioned the view that all nations progressed toward industrialism and democracy. He instead saw conflict-filled relationships among nations based on their position in a capitalist world system. In this view, rich first world nations grew powerful by extracting resources from and exploiting people in less-developed nations. Multinational corporations, first world governments, and local dictators collaborated to suppress attempts by grass-roots movements to oppose first world nations and achieve local democracy.

Still other political sociologists asked, Does America have a ruling class? They questioned the classic-era assumption that in America the government always represents the majority's wishes. For example, Richard Hamilton (1972, 1) presented evidence that, "in the United States the accomplishments of the legislative and executive branches fall well short of the current desires of a majority of the population." Political sociologists compiled evidence showing that wealthy, upper-class people had vast influence over the government at all levels.[21] At the same time, many new European theorists tried to explain the current political events and their debates over the relationship between social classes and government under capitalism stimulated many new studies.[22]

Others questioned the classic-era view that industrialized society automatically created social welfare programs and found that the programs only appeared if workers and the poor organized politically and demanded better conditions.[23] Historical political sociologists discovered that businesses controlled government regulation in the Progressive Era, corporations dominated U.S. foreign policy, and elites quashed a democratic populist movement during the 1890s.[24]

The classic-era political sociologists did not disappear but moved into the background and longed for a return to the quiet 1950s. In one revealing commissioned study for top leaders of large corporations and first world government officials, Crozier, Huntington, and Watanuki (1975) argued that too much political involvement by ordinary citizens, or excessive democracy, caused the protest and social disorder of the 1960s. Thus, widespread apathy was not the problem, it was the solution. In their view, "problems of governance in the United States stem from an excess of democracy . . . expertise, experience and special talents may override the claims of democracy as a way of constituting authority . . . the effective operation of a democratic political system requires some measure of apathy and noninvolvement on the part of some individuals and groups."[25]

Dispersion and Fragmentation

By the early 1980s, political–social unrest had faded and the national mood in America and elsewhere shifted toward the political right. The U.S. government and private foundations cut funding for social science research, social science graduate programs shrank, and student interest shifted. New academic fields, such as environmental studies, urban studies, race and ethnic studies, cultural studies, or women's studies, grew, borrowed from political sociology, and blurred old distinctions. By the 1990s, political sociology was going in several directions, until as Anthony Orum (1996, 132) observed, "there no longer is any kind of coherent paradigm that guides the work of political sociology in America." The field fragmented as did sociology as a whole.[26]

At the dawn of the twenty-first century, a new political sociology is emerging. "There has been 'a paradigm shift' in political sociology . . . toward an understanding of politics as potential in all social experiences. . . ."[27] Continuing to focus on power relations, a revitalized political sociology has five major features.

- It is sensitive to historical change/conflict, including worldwide changes (e.g., the process of globalization) and social movements.
- It sees culture (e.g., language, symbols, and the media) as central to the exercise of power.
- It draws linkages among the global, society-wide, organizational, and group levels.
- It takes the formation of social identity and new social movements as key concerns.
- It integrates structure (stable institutions) with agency (thinking, conscious social actors).

KEY CONCEPTS: POWER, THE STATE, HEGEMONY, AND STRUGGLE

Every academic field has a few core ideas that people repeatedly use to anchor discussions on key questions. Four such core, orienting ideas that you will encounter throughout this book and in most readings in political sociology are power, state, hegemony, and struggle.

Power

Power is the very heart of political sociology. It is an essentially contested concept.[28] This means it is an idea that people frequently dispute because it is tied to fundamental assumptions about the nature of reality and how to study it. Power is also value dependent (i.e., it contains values and assumptions that are embedded within its definition).[29] Power has enigmatic connotations and is often invisible, but it pervades social life. We can say a person, group, or organization has *power over* another, *holds power*, has *power to do* something, or has *more power* than another. Those with power are free to achieve or impose their desires

CLOSER LOOK 1.1   **Four Definitions of Power**

Weber: "the probability that one actor within a social relationship will be in a position to carry out his own will despite resistance, regardless of the basis on which this probably rests."

Etzioni: "a capacity to overcome part or all of the resistance, to introduce changes in the face of opposition."

Olsen and Margar: "the ability to affect the actions or ideas of others."

Wrong: "the capacity of some persons to produce intended and foreseen effects on others."

on others. Those without power feel great pressure to do what they do not desire and follow the demands of others. Power is defined in several ways (see Closer Look 1.1).[30]

We can see four aspects of power present in these definitions: **Power is a *relationship* between two or more people (or groups); it is a *capacity* or ability to influence others; it *can be possessed, accumulated, or held*; and it is *unequal* in that one person or group has more than the other.** Power takes multiple forms and exists at multiple levels—the levels of individual people, organizations, social movements, racial or ethnic groups, social classes, and nations. The primary focus is on political power, but power comes in many forms. Below we look at several types of power.

Coercion

The most visible, direct type of power is coercion. Some people do not even consider it to be power. **Coercion is the use or threat to use force (e.g., physical injury to oneself or loved ones, imprisonment, confiscation of property) to compel compliance** (i.e., to get someone to do something she/he would not otherwise chose to do). It occurs when military forces, police, gangsters, thugs, bandits, terrorists, or guerrilla fighters threaten or impose harm on people. It is the crudest type of power and is based on a fear of personal injury or loss. While it may achieve immediate results, it tends to be an unstable and inefficient type of power for governing large groups, complex organizations, or an entire country.

A continuum with three levels or dimensions illustrates noncoercive forms of power.[31] The three dimensions move away from the visible, physical, and direct form of power (i.e., raw coercion) toward forms that are barely visible, nonphysical, and very indirect.[32]

First Dimension of Power

The first dimension of power involves observable conflict among competing interests. People exercise this form of power in formal settings (e.g., elections, public hearings, committee meetings, and legislative sessions) to decide policy preferences or which rules to use. Unlike coercion, it is based on a passive acceptance of the rules rather than a direct threat. For example, rules may specify the number of supporters needed to advance a ballot, who can vote, or who can speak at a public meeting.

The first dimension of power is easy to see. You may find it in newspaper or television reports. For example, the city council where I live held a public hearing on whether to expand bus service. About 50 people showed up, and almost all spoke against the proposal. Most of them came from a high-income area and objected to the noise, extra traffic, and "undesirable" people who might come to their neighborhoods. They had little use for buses, since most families owned two cars. Based on public input, the city council delayed expanding bus service. The anti-bus people demonstrated their power in this situation.

The first dimension of power is also called decision-making or behavioral power. Its visibility in the decision-making process makes it easy to measure (e.g., how many voted for position X, whether the proposed policy passed, or how much was allocated to program Y). In the decision-making process, people take formal votes, rationally discuss factual information, respond to emotional appeals, and trade favors (you vote for my bill and I'll support yours).

The first dimension of power involves a visible process operating under fair, explicit rules. The first dimension is pushed to its limits if decision-making rules are altered to influence an outcome. Tactics to alter rules may include scheduling votes when opposing members are absent, manipulating parliamentary procedure to avoid taking a vote, referring a decision to a committee (then stacking a committee with people on one side of an issue), packing a public hearing with the supporters of an issue, or using vote fraud and irregular ballots.

Second Dimension of Power

The second dimension of power involves barely visible processes that limit or shape the operation of the first dimension of power. This form of power only occasionally makes it into news reports and usually occurs behind the scenes. The second dimension of power is the ability to control the issues (or candidates) to be considered or that will appear on a ballot. For example, decision-makers may not make a formal, open decision on issues or candidates. An issue (or candidate) may be eliminated because key decision-makers see it as irrelevant, unimportant, unrealistic, unable to win, or too technical. The second dimension of power often occurs at an early stage in the process, before the visible first dimension of power begins. For example, leading financial backers of a political party decide that a specific presidential candidate is undesirable and do not donate money to the campaign. As a result, the candidate cannot enter primaries or gain public office. The second dimension of power can also occur after a formal decision is made. It can be used to block, derail, or quietly kill a decision made in the first dimension of power.

Second dimensional power comes in two major forms—agenda-setting and nondecision-making.[33] **Agenda-setting is when alternative options or issues** exist but are prevented from entering the formal decision-making process or are assigned a very low priority. It occurs when a small group of people blocks certain points of view, policy alternatives, or other people from entering the formal decision-making process or when key gatekeepers to the path of decision-making selectively derail issues, candidates, or positions. The gatekeepers are more successful when an alternative policy position is poorly developed or when a challenging group is disorganized.

Nondecisions are situations that occur when a policy alternative is not formulated, people do not mobilize, or candidates do not advance because of the overwhelming odds of failure. The two types of second dimensional power often overlap. For example, a challenging group may say that public immunization for a disease is a public responsibility and public health funds should pay for it, but officials say it is a private issue. The officials call it an illegitimate public policy concern and say each person should seek and pay for her/his own immunization. The officials can use a variety of tactics to delay or stall the issue, alter it (e.g., merge it with another issue or cut out vital parts of it), deny that they have the authority to deal with it, or ask a higher authority to kill it.

Second dimensional power is difficult to measure. It asks us to consider something that did not happen. Nonetheless, studies have examined second dimensional power.[34] In one study, a city had terrible air pollution, but air quality never became a public issue because the city's entire economy heavily depended on one major company that was also the biggest polluter. Air pollution was not a public issue because of the company's central role in the local economy. Another example of this power is when a company locates trash incinerators or toxic waste dumps in areas where low-income, minority people live. The location is rarely a public issue because high-income areas have high land costs and well-informed, politically active residents who loudly object. The land in low-income areas is cheaper, organized opposition is rare, and local residents might welcome the creation of new low-skilled jobs.

Opposing or resisting second dimensional power requires an unmasking or debunking tactic that raises awareness, redefines a situation, and calls attention to an issue. Depending on how people come to understand an issue, it can be ignored, or it can grow into a major controversy. Challengers to second dimensional power must attract widespread attention, create new ways to discuss a situation, elaborate on alternative views, and present the alternatives as realistic options.

Third Dimension of Power

The third dimension of power involves invisible influence and domination that is built into patterns of thought, terms and categories of language, and the very way that activities are organized. The third dimension, or systemic power, is so insidious and subtle that most people are unaware of it. While agenda-setting or nondecisions imply censorship or blocking a course of action on an issue, in the third dimension of power the "bias of the system can be mobilised, recreated and reinforced in ways that are neither consciously chosen nor the intended result of particular individuals' choices."[35]

The third dimension of power is built into relationships, institutional structure, and cultural patterns. It censors and disorganizes people's very wants, needs, and thoughts. The third dimension of power makes it difficult for people to formulate an alternative point of view, locate an enemy or target to oppose, or express their grievances. This is because it operates deep within their assumptions, motivations, perceptions, and preferences. It is such an integral aspect of daily practice and the fabric of institutions and social life that people rarely recognize it as being power.

Systemic power implies that people can decide to or consent to being put in a powerless position. However, since it is invisible and built into the surroundings, people comply or continue their subordination without being aware of it. Because it is beyond awareness, people believe they are acting freely, while in reality, they are under another's power. The third dimension of power is difficult to grasp, especially in a culture in which individualism, autonomy, and free choice are prominent. A cultural emphasis on freedom of choice actually tends to accentuate the potency of the third dimension of power.

The second dimension of power also undermines a simple notion of free choice, but it only does so by narrowing the range of choices or blocking alternatives from political discussion. The third dimension of power goes a step further. More than blocking alternatives from reaching the agenda, it implies that people are unable to develop alternatives or have thoughts about them. It says there are limits to what people consider to be possible, so people cannot even imagine alternatives. Chart 1.1 outlines differences among the three dimensions of power.

The French post-modernist philosopher, Michel Foucault (1926–1984), offered a version of the third dimension of power. He said that power is built into how we create knowledge and the categories we use when we think and talk. Thus, power "can be identified better by what it does than what it is."[36] Power becomes real in its use, or when or where it is felt. Foucault's main ideas can be summarized into three points:

1. Power is conflated with what people consider to be true or valid knowledge.
2. Power takes a multitude of forms and arises in many areas of life, not just in government or politics.
3. How people apply, exercise, or use power reveals a great deal about it.[37]

Feminist theory also offers a version of the third dimension of power. Feminist theorists argue that the domination/subordination relations between the genders are often unconscious, and that people recreate or reenact them in the course of ordinary, everyday events. They also note that political sociologists have largely used masculine metaphors for power—unequal strength, opposition, domination, and hierarchy. Yet, ". . . such definitions overlook power as it is experienced by women. Traditional definitions of power, which focus on antagonism and competition, fail to take into account power embedded in the normative order and they do not encompass power that is generative, cooperative, or based on a communal model of human interaction."[38] A masculine view of

chart 1.1
THE THREE DIMENSIONS OF POWER

Characteristic	First Dimension	Second Dimension	Third Dimension
How visible are power relations?	Highly visible in people's political behaviors and actions.	Partly visible; the powerless have only limited expression and ability to act.	Nearly invisible. Often there is only limited and indirect evidence, except during periods of great conflict.
What is the main source of power?	Activated political resources (i.e., votes, knowledge, organizational skill).	Organizational control (i.e., control over information and access to decision sites).	Symbolic meanings and understandings (i.e., assumptions, ideas, patterns of thought and action).
How aware are people of their grievances?	Almost everyone is fully aware of and able to act on their grievances.	The powerless are partly aware and often cannot act on their grievances.	The powerless are usually unaware; they do not even think of acting on their grievances.
Where is "real politics"?	It occurs in the formal decision-making arenas and in elections.	It occurs outside formal arenas when the agenda is determined.	It occurs in media, language, cultural institutions, and daily social practices.
Who do participants in formal decision-making represent?	They represent most of society's diverse social interests and groups.	They are greatly unbalanced in favor of the powerful, with others having some limited say.	They include only the powerful with a few token others. Large parts of society are excluded and their views unheard.
What are policy decisions and outcomes?	They are the result of open and fair votes, compromises, and negotiations among participants.	They are the result of constrained and biased processes that are weighed to favor the powerful.	They reflect the interests of the powerful, but promote an illusion of fairness, consensus, and participation.
What is the meaning of the absence of protest?	It indicates consent. People are satisfied or else lazy and uninterested.	It indicates that the powerless are repressed, or their attempts to act and express demands have been frustrated.	It indicates that the powerless are being repressed, or they have acquiesced into a "culture of silence."

power is apparent when someone external to us (often a stranger) compels us to behave or think in certain ways.[39] In a feminine view of power, it is embedded within a web of interpersonal relationships; it is rooted in relationships of dependence, obligation, creation, affection, and protection. For example, a feminine view of power includes a pull to fulfill mutual obligations, a compulsion to care and nurture someone linked by ties of affection, or pressures to contribute to the collective well-being of family and community. It is a sticky power that comes from being caught up in a dense network of human connections. For example, power can originate in feelings of admiration and commitment when given an unexpected, generous gift, in a strong desire to maintain the esteem and respect of friends in a social network, or in a feeling of pride and loyalty based sharing intimate confidences. A feminine view of power includes pressures that arise from a sense of duty to care for a dying parent or the pressure when a crying infant pulls a parent out of a warm bed in the middle of the night.

It is extremely difficult to fight or resist the third dimension of power because it requires that people develop alternative identities, social practices, cultural beliefs, and institutions. The alternatives are similar to "collectives" or utopian communes or intentional communities (e.g., religious groups such as the Amish). By avoiding and rejecting conventional norms, mainstream forms of organization, and dominant systems of authority, the alternatives can short circuit the third dimension of power and offer people a totally different vision of society.

State

Most political sociologists put the state–society relationship at the center of their field, yet, "Defining the state is a notoriously difficult task."[40] People often confuse "the state" with government. They are not far off; the state is a more abstract and general idea. For practical purposes, **the state is all the government, or the public sector, plus much of what immediately surrounds it, connects it to society, and holds to it together.** Anthony Giddens (1987, 17) observed, "State' has two senses in ordinary language. . . . Sometimes means an apparatus of government or power and sometimes the overall social system subject to that government or power. . . ." In other words, at times it means organizations of government, while at other times it is all aspects of society affected by the government.

Americans particularly have a difficult time understanding the state. Theirs is one of the weakest and sparsest states among advanced capitalist nations. America's political traditions and rhetoric downplay or denounce the state. As David Held (1989, 11) remarked, "the nature of the state is hard to grasp. . . . There is nothing more central to political and social theory than the nature of the state, and nothing more contested." Yet we are in daily contact with the state and sense its power and authority. Consider some visible manifestations of the state's presence in Summary 1.1.

The state touches your life when you go to a public school, use the postal system, get a marriage or driver's license, or drive on a public road. It is everywhere.

SUMMARY 1.1   Some Visible Indicators of the State

Symbols and artifacts—flags, statues, national anthems, coins, stamps, and passports

Physical property—land, parks, lakes, buildings, bridges, roads, airports, trucks, tanks

People—police, teachers, soldiers, postal carriers, politicians, judges, dogcatchers

Institutions—schooling, postal service, bank regulations, criminal justice system, social welfare

Services—clean streets, deliver mail, patrol borders, dispose of sewage, and protect air quality

Events—holidays, parades, elections, official celebrations

Borders—signs and fences corresponding to lines on maps and areas of legal authority

Taxes—income, excise, property and sales taxes; user or license fees; import tariffs; tolls

Laws—formal laws and official regulations that tell people what they cannot do or must do

Eat at a restaurant and the state is there; it defines building codes, oversees working conditions, and sets food safety standards. Pay the bill and you use money printed and controlled by the state. Get in a plane and the state oversees the airport, security, and air traffic. Turn on a television, and the state regulates the airwaves and what can be shown. Few areas of life are untouched by the state.

The state is an essentially contested concept. Its meaning involves fundamental, long-standing differences in how people see and understand the world. If we trace word origins, *state* comes from Latin words meaning to stand or a condition. The condition or stand of a king or ruler evolved into today's term, "the state."[41] Scholars have over 100 definitions of the state.[42] Forty years ago some political scientists suggested dropping the term altogether, while others claimed it obscured or concealed power.[43] More recently, Weiss (1998, 2) claimed, "we have entered a new era of 'state denial'," while Steinmetz (1999, 11) observed that since the mid-1980s, "anti-statism came to dominate mainstream political discourse." Lastly, Mitchell (1999) suggests dropping the state as a free-standing concept, because there is no clear boundary between state and society.

"The state is undeniably a messy concept."[44] Observers define it as an institution, a set of functions, a site or place where specific people make decisions and conflicts occur, or a set of effects on other people or events. The state is a collective actor; that is, it is an organized, coordinated collection of people and roles operating together (with failings at doing this). The purpose of the state is complex; it "is to promote the commonwealth or common good."[45] It is easiest to see the state as an institution, with people acting on its behalf in specific situations. For example, a state official (i.e., a mayor, elected representative, military general, clerk, police officer) acts for the state, but there are less clear situations. Is it a state action when a librarian checks out a book for a patron at a public library or a store clerk collects a sales tax on purchases?

As an institution, the state includes all branches, divisions and agencies of government at all levels, local through national. Yet, it is more. The state also includes the social roles, rules and laws, land and buildings, jobs, military weapons, and jails indirectly associated with government. Some people divide organizations and activities into the public or private sector, then equate the state with the public sector, but this is problematic. The public sector refers to legal ownership. My house, the local pizza restaurant, the telephone company, and the oil corporation that ships gasoline to the local gas station are part of the private sector. Legally, a person or voluntary collection of people (i.e., a company) own and operate them based on market forces (supply and demand). The street, the public library, and the police force are parts of the public sector because the government owns and controls them. Yet, the public and private blur together. Many quasi-governmental organizations or situations are neither fully public nor private. For example, the American Red Cross is an independent nongovernment, nonprofit agency. Yet a political official appoints its leader and most of its funds come from government sources. Are a volunteer mayor, firefighter, or crossing guard part of the state?

Private people or organizations often act for or inside the state. State programs or policies can be a substitute for companies in the private sector. For example, a governor appoints corporate executives to serve as the regents or trustees of a public university. Their primary occupation and income sources are private, yet as regents, their decisions create public policy. In their public role, they mandate what public employees can do in their jobs and how government-owned property is used. They are private citizens, but they act as parts or agents of the state. On the other hand, the government has tourist agencies that operate as private advertising agencies for private companies, sells lottery tickets like a private gambling company, makes loans like a private bank, and provides camping sites like a private company.

Being private does not remove people or property from the state. For example, privately operated prisons are part of the state. The state identifies and passes a sentence on the prisoners; the prison must follow state-created rules, and it depends wholly on state funds for its operation. A prison operated by a private corporation does not remove it from the state; it is a private company acting in a quasi-state capacity. The same is true of military contractors who sell goods solely to the government. The state determines all their income, services, and products. They are neither in the state nor separate from it. Many functions (e.g., airlines, phone service, health care) are performed by the government in some nations but by a private organization in others.

Another example is the law. Law is part of the state, yet most lawyers are not public employees.[46] Abstract law that exists in law books and in the minds of lawyers is a part of the state, but the business operation and daily activity of a law office is private. One cannot exist without the other. The state registers births, deaths, marriages, and adoptions; it regulates the highways, broadcast airwaves, air traffic, major bodies of water, air and water quality, food safety, and medical care. The state reinforces or reshapes relations throughout society, including the family, childcare, sexual orientation, and even gender. As R.W. Connell remarked, "The state is the main organizer of the power relations of gender."[47]

No fixed, clear line divides state and society.[48] Society and state are interdependent and interconnected. A state cannot exist without a society, and modern society cannot exist without a state. Rather than fixed, clear boundaries, the state has a core and a series of layers that get thinner as they fade into society. It is not a single seamless, consistent, and closed system. Some areas are central to the state and undeniably within it (e.g., supreme court, military), but others barely touch it (e.g., birth certificates, barber licensing). In addition, the state is layered with parts that are loosely held together, and with some parts that may oppose or contradict other parts.[49] Political sociologists try to identify the number, types, and functions of state parts and explain their origins, operation, and relationships.[50] Making this task more complex is a variety of types of states, as Peter Evans (1995, 11) remarked, "States are not generic. They vary dramatically in their internal structure and relations to society."

If we look at the state as a variable—something that varies in intensity—we can then ask about the degree of "stateness" in an organization or relationship.[51] The speed and degree of state penetration into social–economic life has expanded or contracted in various historical periods with a long-term trend of expansion, at least through the end of the twentieth century. The rise of globalization may signal the end of this trend or a major change in its form.

Where does this discussion leave us? The state is a central concern for political sociology, and government is at its core, but the state has multiple meanings. Recall the elephant in the well-known story about the blind men. Different scholars describe parts of it, but no one sees the whole. There are multiple perspectives on the state, and "no single usage of the concept is self-evidently correct, nor does any one usage necessarily exclude others."[52] Because the state is an abstraction that summarizes many components, we can consider its component parts[53] (see Summary 1.2 for a list).

In this book we focus on the modern nation state; that is, a form of state that appeared about 300 years ago and has since spread across the globe. The state in advanced capitalist countries has grown in size (as measured by public spending as a percentage of the gross national product) and in terms of its jurisdiction over society. For example, at the onset of the twentieth century, public spending was about 10 percent of the economy in advanced nations. By the end of the twentieth century, it was closer to 40 percent, and the state expanded into cultural and symbolic aspects of life.[54] As the state grew, it standardized a national language, created a system of schooling, introduced a monetary system, and instituted controls over the movement of people across borders.[55]

Another way to view the state is as capacity. It is a *capacity* to do things (i.e., potential ability to affect change). Possessing capacity is distinct from using it or applying the capacity (i.e., the policy objectives pursued).[56] When something fails to happen it can be because the state lacks capacity, or because it has capacity but withheld action. For example, an official says class size in elementary schools cannot be reduced. This could be because of a lack of capacity (i.e., a

SUMMARY 1.2   Characteristics of the Contemporary State

1. The state is historically conditioned; it developed in particular places and times. It emerged in Western Europe with the dissolution of feudal society and rise of industrial capitalism. Its form and function changed over time. Indeed, "The whole concept of state might well prove to be temporally determined" (Nettl 1968, 587).

2. The state represents, or claims to represent, the entire society. The state is the premier institution that looks out for, or speaks for, the collectivity as a whole. "The state is an arena, the condensation, the crystallization, the summation of the social relations in its territory" (Mann 1988, 26). The degree of autonomy of the state from society is a central issue in political sociology. It involves how much the state shapes society and how various groups control or use the state.

3. The state consolidates power from society into one location and brings forward new powers (See Badie and Birnbaum 1983, 56). It absorbs and unites power from various parts of society and condenses it in one organization.

4. The state secures, defends, and maintains both physical (territory) and cultural–social (a national culture) boundaries. A state's role is "maintaining the boundaries between collectivities, and in particular, with protecting each collectivities'

cultural identity from outside threats" (Poggi 1978, 6).

5. The state gives people an identity and helps to define a people (Thomas and Meyer 1984, 476). Through processes such as schooling, national history, and citizenship, the state constructs who we are. As it helps form identity, people accept the state as morally legitimate.

6. The state has a monopoly over the means of violence in its territory and society. It has sovereignty or ultimate control in its land. Control over the means of violence (e.g., armies, police, border guards, prisons) is a key function. Failure to maintain control signals that the state is breaking apart or is losing control over parts of its territory.

7. The state operates within a system of other states. It has control over a territory, but it interacts with other states. The strength of a state, as an entity, depends in part on its role in the larger global system (see Meyer et al. 1997).

8. Other features of the state include, developing an administrative bureaucracy; creating laws and operating by rule of law; defending territorial borders; extracting resources or taxes to maintain itself; maintaining infrastructure (e.g., coinage, roads and rivers, communication, measures); upholding social order; and redistributing services, benefits or selective favors to citizens (Mann 1988).

school cannot collect sufficient funds to build more rooms and hire additional teachers), or it could occur when funds are available and authority exists, but the government official decides not to reduce class size. Officials may say they lack capacity when, in reality, they simply want to avoid taking responsibility for making an unpopular decision.

The amount of land and number of people under a state can be large or small. Some states, such as Singapore, are concentrated in just one city and are very powerful (see World View 1.1). Other states may cover vast expanses of land or large amounts of people (e.g., India) but are weak compared to other groups and institutions.

WORLD VIEW 1.1   The Global City-State of Singapore

The city-state of Singapore is located on a small, tropical island just off the coast of the Malay peninsula in Southeast Asia. There is no agricultural land of note, and geographically, Singapore is very small—about three times the size of Washington DC. It was a British colony from 1819 until it achieved independence in 1963. At first part of the Malay Federation, Singapore separated from Malaysia to be a separate country in 1965. Today, with a population of roughly 4 million, all living in the one city, Singapore is one of the world's most high-tech, advanced countries. With gleaming skyscrapers, a sleek subway system, busy and crowded shopping centers, a large and updated international airport, and huge modern shipping port, Singapore is a hub of international trade, commerce, and finance in Pacific Asia. Its well-educated, English-speaking population of Chinese, Malay, and Indian people get along peacefully. There is low unemployment, and people share a high standard of living. For example, Singapore's 2000 per capita income exceeded that of Australia, Canada, and Italy. Thirty years after independence, most people of Singapore have a higher standard of living than people in Great Britain, the country that had owned it as a colony.

Things have not always been this way. At the time of independence, Singapore was a poor, remote, run-down port city. It was dirty and disease-ridden, and torn by violent political conflict and ethnic strife. A strong, systematic state-directed program of economic growth and social control imposed for three decades has been highly suc-cessful. The state closely monitors and encourages business and banking activities. Working conditions and wages are strictly state-controlled and are good. Although it is officially democratic, Singapore has been ruled by one political party, the People's Action Party, since its independence. For the first 25 years, the man who led the independence movement, Lee Kuan Yew, was firmly in control, and he has remained powerful since his retirement. There is strict censorship, limited press freedom, and very little public dissidence is allowed. Yet this is no brutal dictatorship, and people are free to leave if they wish. So long as one avoids engaging in organized political opposition and does not voice serious disagreement with state policy, life can be comfortable.

Singapore's authoritarian state directs most aspects of daily social life, city development, political activity, and the economy. The state requires that everyone save for retirement and gives benefits to educated women who have children. The state provides and closely monitors schooling, and it provides everyone with quality housing and health care. Multiethnic relations are watched and regulated. The state supervises and seriously limits anti-social activities. For example, it imposes large fines for jaywalking, failing to flush a public toilet, possessing pornography, littering, driving on city streets during rush hour, or chewing gum. The powerful state, through its police/social control agencies, ensures that Singapore remains clean, neat, and orderly. A powerful state imposes hegemony and limits overt struggle.

Sources: Chua (1995, 1997), Hefner (2001), Mauzy and Milne (2002), Murray and Perera (1996), Perry et al. (1997), Purushotam (1997), Rodan (2001), and Tremewan (1996).

Hegemony

Of the four core concepts, hegemony is the least well-known. It comes from the Greek word for leadership, *hegemonia*. In international relations, it refers to a powerful leading nation or set of nations. In political sociology, **hegemony is moral and ideational leadership of society attained with the consent of major social groups.**[57] It includes a coherent, integrated worldview of widely shared ideas about what is right and wrong, good or bad, fair or unjust held by most people of a society. It is similar to the third dimension of power. A form of the idea comes from Marxian social theory. In a famous passage in the *German Ideology*, Karl Marx and Frederick Engles (1947, 39) wrote,

> The ideas of the ruling class are in every epoch the ruling ideas: i.e., the class, which is the ruling material force of society, is at the same time its ruling intellectual force . . . among other things [they] rule also as thinkers, as producers of ideas, and regulate the production and distribution of ideas of their age; thus their ideas are the ruling ideas of the epoch.

Others expanded on this observation, especially the Italian, Antonio Gramsci and members of the Frankfurt School of social–political theory.[58] In contrast to orthodox Marxist thinkers who emphasized the material forces of production, economics, and revolution, these thinkers drew from a humanistic or idealistic side of Marx's writings.

The leading theorist on hegemony, Gramsci, spent much of his adult life in Mussolini's prisons and wrote in a way that could pass prison censors.[59] This makes his writings difficult to read, and they were not available in English until the 1970s. Gramsci, like Max Weber, emphasizes looking at long-term historical change. He also says that moral values, ideas, worldviews, and subjective motivation are essential parts of any explanation of social or political life.

Gramsci assumed that each society contains a more or less coherent worldview or a set of leading ideas. Hegemony is the dominant way of thinking about or seeing the world. In periods of dramatic, rapid change, this worldview breaks down and another replaces it, but this is rare. Gramsci accepted Marx's thesis that capitalists exploit workers, but he asked, Why haven't workers risen up and rebelled as Marx predicted? Why do they voluntarily accept the rule by the capitalist or owning class—their enemy? On the surface, this appears irrational. Gramsci examined the paradox of workers obeying an enemy who rarely used threats of force. He observed that people rule by means of controlling the leading ideas. This control is rarely explicit or direct; rather, it is so subtle that even the ruling group may not be aware of it. If every society has a system of leading ideas, the ruling group shapes the ideas, and most people embrace the ideas as natural, then the workers' behavior is not irrational.

Hegemony implies consent, or acceptance by most people who embrace the ideas without a threat of force. People accept the leading ideas, or the dominant outlook, and use it to understand the events around them. It includes basic assumptions about human nature and is embedded in language, religion, schooling, academic theory, and the mass media. The outlook is so widely accepted that people rarely notice it, even as they reproduce it in their daily conversations, activities, rituals, and symbols. They believe it is simply the way things are. Robert Bocock (1986, 63) summarized, "Hegemony, in its most complete form, occurs when the intellectual, moral and philosophical leadership provided by the class which is ruling . . . provides the fundamental outlook for the whole of society."

Hegemony is embedded within language, values, and culture. It is hidden, but it shapes how schools operate, what museums display, the content of movies and television shows, and architectural design.[60] It is how events, physical space, or arrangements shape people's thinking and experience. For example, a building's spatial design can express hegemonic power. A major insurance office building may channel people to enter one way as security cameras watch. The entrance directs one's visual attention to one wall but not to others. One can "read" doorways, room sizes, corridor width, lighting, and elevator placement to say, this is important and that is not. The building obscures some activities in a cramped, windowless, poorly lighted basement (e.g., cleaning service) as it elevates and glorifies others (e.g., the top corporate officers) with spacious rooms, prominent positioning, and expansive views. An attentive, sensitive person may feel such control. No one person actively exercises the control; it is built into how the space is organized. Hegemony is an outlook and a way of thinking that is built into the organized routines, practices, and hierarchies of mainstream daily life.

Hegemony is similar to ideology, but ideology has connotations of something untrue or deceptive. By contrast, hegemony refers to ideas and actual practices that appear throughout society. Instead of being false consciousness, hegemony refers to the very organization of daily activities and outlooks. The daily activities and outlooks are not neutral; they contain a slant or bias with real political effects.[61]

Struggles over the prevailing outlook in society can occur on a battlefield, at a street barricade, or in a voting booth. They also can occur in church basements, club gatherings, school classrooms, trade union halls, corporate board meetings, and company cafeterias. Struggles over hegemony determine how people will define events, what they place value on, and the line between moral and immoral conduct. Struggles occur when people decide to spend their time getting rich instead of becoming an artist or musician, to devote time to a career instead of having another child, or to stay at a job instead of enriching their spiritual lives.

Struggles for hegemony also take place in newspaper editorial pages, policy think tanks, and university research centers. The ideas of intellectuals do not have to be "dead" on the pages of books or sterile in academic debates. For example, a philosopher, economist, politician, or news reporter writes on the virtues of the individual choice and free markets. This contributes to hegemony if two conditions hold. First, if the ideas favor one class or group and reinforce continued dominance by that class. Second, if the ideas diffuse to become part of common sense and unquestioned daily activity, shaping thought and action. Hegemony depends not on direct control (domination), but on diffusion. "It is not a mode of mystification, producing 'false consciousness'. . . but a disseminated form of self-evidence of common sense that regulates subjects. . . ."[62]

So long as one class or group holds unchallenged hegemonic control and its outlook dominates thought and social life, conflict will be minimal. The ruling hegemony extinguishes real alternatives, and it makes thinking of alternatives nearly impossible. However, once the ruling hegemony breaks apart, and counter-hegemonic ideas sprout and spread, overt struggle will erupt over fundamentally opposing outlooks. This can rapidly escalate into open, violent conflict across society.

Struggle

Politics is a struggle among groups for power as they try to gain control over resources, outlooks, symbols, or the state. As a verb *struggle* means to contend with an opponent, to put forth a great effort, or to make one's way through a difficult situation. As a noun, it means a great effort, a contest, or a contention among people. Political sociologists study these meanings. **Struggle includes the peaceful and nonpeaceful actions by a group or coalition of people to expand or defend their position of power that meets with opposition from others.** Struggles can occur in the courtroom or at the ballot box. They may involve violent conflict with death, destruction, and imprisonment or attempts to alter the thoughts, emotions, and beliefs of others.

In the classic era, two approaches were in contention, order (or consensus) and conflict. They were not equal. As Lewis Coser (1956, 16) observed, "Even a cursory examination of the contemporary work of American sociologists clearly indicates that conflict has been very much neglected indeed as a field of investigation." The debate between the two approaches is beyond this book, but it bears on political sociology today.[63]

Until the 1970s, structural functionalism was the reigning sociological theory. It focuses on order, consensus, and social system equilibrium with society a system of interdependent parts, each performing distinct functions. Society slowly evolves into a more complex system, and conflict is a secondary concern that arises from short-term strains until society adjusts. Normal political conflict is a peaceful competition for votes or interest groups negotiating within formal democratic institutions.

During the late 1960s through the 1970s, political sociologists turned away from structural functionalism and toward conflict theories. In conflict theories, society is comprised of antagonistic groups that try to dominate one another, and conflict is a basic, built-in feature of social relations. Significant disagreements are "normal" as various groups, classes, or parts of society with fundamentally opposing interests fight to express them through politics. Gianfranco Poggi (1978, 111) observed, "Conflict, however bounded; controversy, however regulated—these are features not incidental but essential to the operation of the political system."

Struggle does not always require a direct confrontation, physical force, or acts of violence. It can vary in form and intensity; and it can include peaceful negotiation in which each party tries to advance their position, end limits on their free expression (e.g., prejudice, lack of organization, no resources), or improve their quality of life. Struggles can continue for many decades or last an hour. They can be visible or hidden beneath the surface. Their resolution may be temporary or permanent, and it can be a full win, partial win, or a stalemate. Political sociologists examine struggles among organized groups, classes, institutions, movements, organizations, or nations, but rarely among specific individuals.

ISSUES IN CONTEMPORARY POLITICAL SOCIOLOGY

In the remainder of this book, we will examine the topics of contemporary political sociology. In Chapter 2 we consider the question of how the modern nation state developed and why it took the form it did. We also consider the ideas of democracy, nationhood, and citizenship. In Chapter 3 we look at competing explanations for how power and politics operate. In particular, we will see how the various theories of political sociology see power, the state, hegemony, and the struggle. We will use these explanations in subsequent chapters as we encounter other issues. Chapter 4 considers political institutions in the United States and democracy in the institutions. We also look at the national polity and why and how different social groups have been included in or excluded from it. In Chapter 5 we turn to political participation in the U.S. polity and look at, who does or does not participate in specific forms of political activity in the United States and why.

The next three chapters extend into the state–society interface. In Chapter 6 we investigate the cultural dimension of politics, including issues of symbolic politics, and ideology. In Chapter 7 we specifically consider schooling and the mass media to see how values and ideas are a part of politics. We continue to the legal system, crime, and issues of repression and social control in Chapter 8.

In Chapter 9 we look at revolution, protest, and movements. Next, we look at state policies and political agendas. In Chapter 10 we examine economic policies and programs, including taxes, business regulation, and government controls of the economy. We take up the issue of the warfare and welfare state in Chapters 11 and 12. In the last chapter, we look forward to a future that political sociology can help us understand.

CONCLUSION

Political sociologists study power and the relationship between society and politics. Power is pervasive and barely visible but a fundamental dimension in human relations and social institutions. Political sociologists give politics a broad meaning—it is primarily about how groups, classes, genders, races, and so forth acquire, extend, use, maintain, and struggle over power. Political sociology is relevant because it helps people make sense of and see their situation in a larger, often unnoticed context and ask critical questions. Political sociology and political science overlap a great deal. The main difference between them is that political science focuses on

government, while political sociology looks at how power and inequality are translated into political power and how that power can reinforce or reduce inequality.

Modern political sociology began after World War II. During the classic era (1950s–1960s), political sociologists studied the basis of democratic society but often idealized the United States as a democratic nation. After the 1960s, this view changed sharply as the United States and other nations experienced civil turmoil that was unexpected and poorly explained by classic era political sociology. In the 1970s and 1980s, political sociologists created a wave of new theories and conducted many studies to explain the political events. By the late 1980s, political sociology fragmented as other fields adopted many of its ideas. Since then, political sociologists continued to refine their analysis of current and past power relations, and by the early twenty-first century, they had revitalized the field.

Four central, orienting concepts of political sociology are power, state, hegemony, and struggle. Each has been controversial. Power is an unequal relationship in which one party can realize or impose its interests on others. The visibility and directness of the unequal relationship varies in the three dimensions of power. A great deal of political sociology focus on the state. It is a broader idea than government and represents the place where organized power is consoli-

dated in contemporary society. The state has multiple definitions that reflect its complex and diverse nature, and its boundary with society is blurred or fuzzy.[64] Hegemony is similar to the third dimension of power because both are subtle and difficult to see. Hegemony refers to the leading ideas or outlook that prevails throughout a society and operates in its major institutions and daily events or activities. People accept it although it is not neutral and reinforces the dominance of the leading social class or group. Political sociology also examines struggle or conflict. This includes peaceful and nonpeaceful actions to alter or defend power relations that meet with opposition. A great deal of politics is people in opposition over unequal power relations. This means that a struggle for power is central to politics.

KEY TERMS

Agenda-Setting	Nondecisions	State
Coercion	Political Sociology	Struggle
First Dimension of Power	Power	Third Dimension of Power
Hegemony	Second Dimension of Power	

REVIEW QUESTIONS

1. What is the central focus of political sociology? How does it see politics?

2. How does political sociology differ from political science? What is its relevance?

3. What was the primary issue for classic era political sociology? What were two other issues of this era?

4. Why was the study, *Union Democracy*, by Lipset, Trow and Coleman important?

5. What core assumption guided classic era political sociology? How did this core

assumption fit with the finding that many Americans were not highly political?

6. What factors or events caused the direction of political sociology to change around 1970? What new issues or questions became the focus of the field due to the change?

7. What does it mean to say that power is an "essentially contested" concept?

8. What four aspects of power are in most definitions of it?

9. Describe the differences between coercion and the first dimension of power. Why is it called decision-making power?

10. Describe the two types of second dimensional power and explain how each illustrates the core idea in this dimension of power.

11. Give an example of the third dimension of power and distinguish it from the second dimension.

12. What is the difference among the state, the government, and the public sector?

What does it mean to say that the state has layers or that there is a degree of "stateness"?

13. What is a major assumption of hegemony? Can it ever change? What does it mean to say that hegemony is embedded in culture?

14. In what ways is hegemony similar to the third dimension of power?

15. What do political sociologists mean by "struggle"? Why is this idea important to them?

RECOMMENDED READINGS

Bocock, Robert. 1986. *Hegemony*. New York: Travistock.

Cousins, Mark and Athar Hussain. 1984. *Michel Foucault*. New York: St. Martins.

Kornhauser, William. 1959. *The Politics of Mass Society*. New York: Free Press.

Lipset, Seymour Martin. 1960. *Political Man: The Social Bases of Politics*. New York: Doubleday.

Lukes, Steven. 1974. *Power: A Radical View*. London: Macmillan.

Mann, Michael. 1988. *States, War and Capitalism: Studies in Political Sociology*. Cambridge, MA: Basil Blackwell.

Markhoff, John. 1996. *Waves of Democracy*. Thousand Oaks, CA: Pine Forge Press.

Poggi, Gianfranco. 1978. *The Development of the Modern State: A Sociological Introduction*. Stanford University Press.

ENDNOTES

1. See Seelye (1998) on trust in government and Clymer (2000) on student opinions.

2. Higher Education Research Institute (January 2002). "2001 CIRP Press Release: CIRP Freshman Survey" http://www.gseis.ucla.edu/heri/heri.html

3. The study is by Jacobs and Helms (1996).

4. See Steingold (1995).

5. For a discussion of new political sociology see Nash (2000).

6. Cappell and Guterbock (1992) and Ennis (1992) discuss subfields in sociology.

7. See Hicks (1995) for four areas of political science from which sociology can benefit.

8. Almond and Verba (1963), Bendix (1964), Lipset (1963), Moore (1966), and Huntington (1968).

9. The two 1960 works are Lipset's *Political Man* and *The American Voter* by Campbell et al.

10. See Wilensky and Lebeaux (1958).

11. Two major studies by Stouffer (1955) and Bell (1964) build on Adorno et al. (1950).

12. See Berelson et al. (1954), Campbell et al. (1960), and Converse (1964).

13. From Smelser (1963).

14. The three studies are Hunter (1953), Mills (1956), and Domhoff (1967).

15. See Lipset (1960).

16. See Downs (1957) and Olson (1965) as major works in this tradition.

17. Bendix (1968), Bendix and Lipset (1957), Janowitz (1968), and Lipset (1959a) offer "state of the field" statements. Also see Hall (1981), Poggi (1973), and Zafirovski (1999a) for overviews.

18. See Piven and Cloward (1977) and Tilly (1978).

19. See especially Wolfe (1973).

20. See Paige (1975), Skocpol (1979), Tilly (1975), and Wolf (1969).

21. See Domhoff (1970) and O'Connor (1973).

22. Leaders in the debate included Miliband (1969), Poulantzas (1973), and Therborn (1978).

23. A good example is Korpi (1978).

24. Important works include Kolko (1963), Williams (1964), and Goodwyn (1976).

25. From Crozier et al. (1975, 113–14).

26. The fragmentation of sociology and borrowing by other areas is discussed in Becker and Rau (1992), Calhoun (1992), Crane and Small (1992), D'Antonio (1992), Gans (1989), Horowitz (1993), and Turner and Turner (1990).

27. Quote is from Nash (2000, 2–3).

28. See Barrow (1993, 10), Lukes (1974, 9), and Vincent (1987, 42) on the state as an essentially contested idea.

29. See discussion of "value-dependent" in Lukes (1974, 26).

30. The sources for the quotes in Closer Look 1.1 are Weber (1968, 53), Etzioni (1993, 18), Olsen and Margar (1993, 1), and Wrong (1979, 2).

31. See Lukes (1974) and Garventa (1980).

32. On multiple dimensions see Whitt (1979).

33. On nondecisions see (Bachrach and Baratz 1963).

34. For empirical studies of two-dimensional power see Crenson (1971), Gaventa (1980), Richard Smith (1979), and Zelditch, Harris, Thomas, and Walker (1983).

35. Quote is from Lukes (1974, 21).

36. Quote is from Fiske (1993, 11).

37. For more on Foucault and his theory of power, see Cousins and Hussian (1984), Gordon (1980), Poster (1984), Sheridan (1980), and Smart (1985).

38. Quote is from Margolis (1989, 387).

39. From Mitchell (1990).

40. Quote is from Faulks (2000, 20).

41. Vincent (1987, 16) discussed the origins of the word *state*.

42. For various definitions of the state see Caporaso (1989).

43. Almond et al. (1988) and Easton (1981) suggest dropping the term, while Abrams (1988) says it obscures more than it reveals.

44. Quote is from Mann (1988, 4).

45. Quote is from Vincent (1987, 21).

46. See Nettl (1968, 584–86) on the state and law distinction. Also see Chapter 8 on law.

47. Quote is from Connell (1990, 520).

48. On the blurring of state and society, see Connell (1990, 509) and Mitchell (1991, 1999).

49. Haney (2000) discusses the concept of "layered" parts in her review of Feminist State Theory.

50. See Rose (1983) for a discussion of the many aspects or parts of contemporary governments.

51. Nettl (1968) discusses viewing "stateness" as a variable.

52. Quote is from Barrow (1993, 10).

53. The list of characteristics of the state comes from Badie and Birnbaum (1983, 14–15, 21–22, 55–58, 65), Giddens (1987, 18), Hall and Inkenberry (1989, 1–2), Held (1995, 48–49), Lentner (1984), Mann (1988, 4–28), Pierson (1996, 6–32), Poggi (1978, 1–9, 88–100), Weber (1968, 14, 56, 905, 1393), and Weiss (1998, 9).

54. See Barkey and Parikh (1991).

55. These major features of a state are reviewed by Calhoun (1993a, 217).

56. On state capacity see Barkey and Parikh (1991), Mayntz (1975a), and Markoff (1996, 15).

57. This definition is borrowed from Bocock (1986, 11).

58. See Held (1980) and Slater (1977) on the Frankfurt School and critical theory.

59. An introduction to Gramsci is in Femia (1981), Joll (1977), Sasson (1987), and Simon (1982).

60. On hegemony as embedded in the structure of life and objects, see Mitchell (1990).

61. See Mouffe (1979) on the difference between ideology and hegemony and Bocock (1986) on hegemony.

62. Quote is from Lloyd and Thomas (1998, 19).

63. Collins (1968) introduces this debate as it applies to political sociology.

64. See discussion in Poggi (1978, 120–31).

DEMOCRACY, NATIONALISM, AND THE NATION STATE

INTRODUCTION

Are you a patriotic citizen? What does it mean to be patriotic? Is it waving flags and total obedience to government, or questioning the government and defending fundamental political values and rights, including rights for dissenters? Patriotism is love of one's country or nation and is closely associated with nationalism.

Nationalism is a belief system and movement that emphasizes the supremacy of the nation-state. Nationalism has been a basis for both great achievements and sacrifices that people made for the nation and horrible oppression committed in the name of the nation. Citizenship is how an individual relates to his/her nation.

In Chapter 1, you encountered the four core ideas of political sociology. Here, we focus on the state. It is a highly abstract and general idea, so we will examine the contemporary nation-state, looking at its historical development as well as two closely related issues—nationalism and citizenship. Most people say that a democracy is the best type of state or national government. Almost everyone believes in it as an ideal, even if it is not fully realized in practice. People use the term, *democracy*, to discuss politics, power, struggles, or the state, but it is not a simple idea. For centuries, people have struggled and continue to struggle for democracy, often spilling blood in the process. American colonialists in 1776, Mexican peasants in 1910, Hungarians facing Russian tanks in 1956, black South Africans in Soweto in 1976, Chinese students in Tiananmen Square in 1989, and the people of East Timor in 1999 all struggled and died pursuing democracy. Democracy is central to the contemporary nation-state, so we begin by examining it. ■

DEMOCRACY

The Changing Meaning of Democracy

The idea of democracy is over 2,000 years old. The term comes from two Greek words, *demos* meaning the whole people or lower orders of society, and *krators*, meaning power or to rule.[1] Today everyone seems to favor democracy, but 250 years ago it was a pejorative term because ordinary people who participated in it were held in distain.[2] Democracy is a claim about who should have a say in ruling and a share in government power.[3] It has many meanings—a philosophic ideal, a widely used symbol, and specific types of political processes. In addition, there are many kinds of democracy. For our purposes, **democracy is a type of collective decision-making, or a process, by which people reach decisions together that will apply to all.** Robert Dahl tried to substitute polyarchy for democracy in political science.[4] **Polyarchy means rule by many; it refers to contemporary representative democratic institutions that have elected officials, universal suffrage, fair elections, free speech, and so forth.**

Instead of being all or nothing, we can think of democracy as a variable operating along a continuum with greater or lesser degrees of democracy.[5] Some people see it as specific political mechanisms, especially in an American context.[6] Yet, the idea has undergone continual redefinition, often involving social and political struggle, and "democracy can move forward or backward, but it cannot stand still."[7] As with other core ideas, it is an essentially contested concept.[8]

Forms of Participation and Majority Rule

In its simplest form, democracy is the opposite of a dictatorship or monarchy, which are forms of one-person rule. Young children learn about democracy when they participate in decision-making by voting, often by raising their hands, and they learn that the majority's choice wins. These two ideas—people participating in the decisions that affect them, or self-rule, and the majority's decision prevails—are fundamental to democracy, but democracy involves much more!

Short of complete agreement, people can participate in a process to reach a collective decision in three ways: they can debate and argue until some persuade others, they can bargain and exchange favors (sometimes called "horse trading"), or they can vote. Democratic participation can include all three processes. In a *debate* the goal is to transform others' thinking through informed, rational deliberation. People freely consider views and evidence in an open exchange; they present logically connected statements or reasons to explain their positions and persuade others. An example of this process is a courtroom or public hearing. People present various sides and consider evidence and reasons before reaching a decision. *Bargaining* involves making offers and counteroffers about things of value. The people negotiate and use resources to make their promises or threats credible. Instead of complete agreement, the goal is compromised in which each side gets something it wants. An example is a collective bargaining situation in which employees and management negotiate over work conditions and how to distribute a firm's income. *Voting* is the quickest and least involved collective decision-making process. It does not require a discussion, but simply aggregates each individual's preference. In a democracy, people often use a combination of these three types of processes.[9]

Many advocates of greater democracy favor combining voting with debate or **deliberative democracy.**[10] **Deliberative democracy is decision-making based on a conversation among rational, open-minded equals who gather to discuss, present arguments, and listen to various positions before they vote to make a collective decision.** The process assumes that those involved are rational and impartial, and that they will avoid persuasion by pure eloquence, propaganda (i.e., misrepresentation), or threats during the conversation phase. The deliberation process equalizes information across participants and stimulates them to seek innovative solutions. It rests on the assumption that free, open debate and discussion are essential to a full, effective democracy. This is in contrast to silent, isolated individuals who vote without discussion and situations in which not participating implies consent or agreement with the final decision.

For example, the Texas Public Utility Commission used a form of deliberative democracy called deliberative polling. As an alternative to opinion polls or public hearings, the Commission accessed citizen views by inviting representative samples of citizens to spend a weekend at a hotel where they learned about a policy issue from readings and lectures and engaged in open debates before expressing a choice. This experiment yielded three findings: citizens were actively engaged and highly attentive, everyone participated equally, and the final choices differed from the results of simple voting or opinion polls. Simple voting or opinion polls showed that only a minority of the people was willing to pay extra for renewable energy sources or greater energy efficiency. After deliberative polling with fellow citizens, a large majority favored the renewable energy option. In another example from Britain, a group of 300 persons gathered to deliberate crime policy. Again, the outcome differed from that of simple voting. More people favored a more humane, rehabilitative approach toward crime after a discussion process, and the percentage who favored "sending more people to prison" as a way to control crime dropped from 57 to 38 percent.[11]

The second major idea, majority rule, is easy to grasp. Paradoxically, following it totally will harm democracy and limiting it can expand democracy. The majority might decide to punish someone whom they dislike or to take away another's right to vote. Does majority rule mean that 50.1 percent can impose unjust conditions on others or deny basic rights to the minority? **The tyranny of the majority occurs when government facilitates or permits the majority's (or a powerful vocal minority's) religious, ideological, or cultural beliefs to be imposed on all people and suppresses minority dissent.** Democracy is not absolute power to the majority; it also includes protecting the basic rights of minorities. The tyranny of the majority occurs when a nation tries to assimilate everyone to a common culture or present a strong, unified front against an external threat. The political philosopher, John Stuart Mill in *On Liberty* (1859), expressed greater fear of intolerant, uninformed public opinion that became a tyranny than of a powerful state.[12] The tyranny occurs when the majority act like tyrants and impose their will on everyone.

When I asked my students about tyranny, they were familiar with religious tyranny in certain Islamic nations, but few recognized a milder, but similar, tyranny in their own country. In the United States, a large majority of people believe in a Judeo-Christian god and only a small minority do not. In 1954 federal politicians inserted "under God" into the Pledge of Allegiance, and a year later, they mandated the phrase "In God We Trust" be added on all coins and paper currency. Conservative activists had wanted to add the phrases for decades, but they only succeeded in heightening tension and national conformity to the Cold War when they portrayed the ideological-political division between the Soviet Union and the West as a war between Judeo-Christian civilization and godless communism. Individuals who were upset or offended were in the minority and were overruled. After the September 11, 2001 terrorist attacks, the phrases "In God We Trust" and "One Nation Under God" were widely promoted to symbolize the Judeo-Christian majority's hostility toward the terrorists' Islamic religious beliefs.

What Makes a Democracy?

Obviously, one-person rule by a military dictatorship in which the police threaten people is not democratic, but democracy requires more than the absence of a dictator. A critical issue is *who participates*? Joseph Schumpeter (1950, 250) held democracy is, "that institutional arrangement for arriving at political decisions which realizes the common good by making the people itself decide issues through the elections of individuals who are assembled to carry out its will." Historically, "the people itself" has not always included *all* people. For example, the United States claims to be one of the oldest democracies. Yet early in its history only property-owning, white males over 21 years old could vote. This excluded a large majority of people, including low-income individuals, slaves, American Indians, women, and anyone under 21. Even today, aliens, convicted felons, seriously mentally ill people, and children cannot vote. Many democratic nations did not permit women to vote until the mid-twentieth century, despite a century of arguments to allow it.[13] A democracy includes not only the assumption that everyone participates, but also the assumption that each person's vote, or voice, will count the same. Early in U.S. history, slaves did not count as whole people for electoral purposes, and a common form of electoral fraud has been for some people to vote more than once. Charles Tilly (1997, 276) noted, "a polity is undemocratic to the degree that citizens' political rights and obligations vary by gender, race, religion, national origin, wealth or any other general set of categories . . . [and] to the extent that large numbers of people subject to the state's jurisdiction lack citizenship." The issues of political exclusion/inclusion and different participation are central in political sociology.

Two other issues relevant for democracy are the directness of decision-making and the range or types of decisions. Directness varies from direct democracy at one end of a continuum (i.e., each person makes all decisions unmediated by others) to representative democracy at the opposite end (i.e., people elect others and delegate their decision-making authority to others). A referendum allows for a direct expression of the public's choice between alternatives, but such direct democracy is rare and may actually undermine equality.[14] Most governments are representative democracies. Each person does not vote on every issue; the voters delegate or assign authority to their elected representatives. A related concern is that voters get to decide on some issues but not on others or they may be overruled (see Case in Point 2.1).

CASE IN POINT 2.1 | **Congress Tries to Stop Voters from Voicing Their Views**

Direct ballot initiatives, or public referendums, are a form of direct democracy and a way to express "the people's will" unmediated by formal representative political institutions, although some studies suggest that initiatives do not always produce more populist policy. In 1999 the District of Columbia conducted a referendum, called Initiative 59, on whether to legalize the use of marijuana for medical purposes (e.g., cancer, AIDS, glaucoma) with a medical doctor's prescription. Several members of the U.S. Congress objected to letting voters have a voice in such an issue, and some members of Congress tried to block the ballot count after people had voted by blocking funds for an election board. After a judge ruled that blocking a count of legitimate voter ballots was illegal, Congress passed a law that specifically prohibited the District of Columbia law from taking effect. By the way, 69 percent of the voters had supported permitting medical uses of marijuana.

Sources: Camobreco (1998) and "Judge Permits Washington to Count Vote on Marijuana," *New York Times,* September 18, 1999.

Representative democracy is widespread. In the United States and many other nations, voters do not directly select the chief political official. The electoral college selects the U.S. president, and in a parliamentary system, the parliament selects the chief official. In most representative democracies, most government officials never face an election but are appointed by elected politicians. Also, elected officials depend on large bureaucracies of nonelected employees to accomplish most tasks. Three issues about the operation of a representative democracy are: (1) Who can become an elected representative?, (2) How long do they serve?, and (3) Can they be removed from office? (see Summary 2.1).

Democracy implies giving people a range of choices or candidates. At first, the range of choices seems simple—more choices equal more democracy, but it is more complex than that. For example, in the last election for the governor of my state I could choose among candidates from four political parties. In the previous election, I had two choices—the Democratic or Republican Party. The two-

---

SUMMARY 2.1   Three Mechanics of Representative Democracy

Who Can Be a Representative?   Some limits on who can run for public office are legal requirements (e.g., age, residence, criminal record), while others are practical (e.g., being physically attractive and articulate, being of a race or religion most voters accept, having a lot of money or supporters with money). In general, fewer limitations on who can run for office mean more democracy.

Length of Terms of Office   Terms of political offices vary from one, two, four, six, or eight years to a lifetime appointment. A candidate might serve repeatedly as long as voters reelect him/her or within fixed term limits. For example, some U.S. states passed term limits to control the number of times a politician can serve, and since Franklin Roosevelt, U.S. presidents have been limited to a maximum of two four-year terms. Limits on term length and reelection help force elected officials to be responsive to voters and effective in office. Short term lengths or term limits create high levels of responsiveness but reduce effectiveness because officials often have to be in office for several years to fully understand and enact significant policy.

People who are reelected to the same office build up inside knowledge and can be more effective, but they may use their name recognition and incumbency to block alterative candidates or new ideas. Related issues are the pay and duties of public office. Full-time positions with high pay will attract and retain top quality candidates much more than part-time positions with low pay. Part-time positions and low pay attract people who have personal wealth or who hold jobs that permit extra part-time work. Yet high pay and a full-time position may distance politicians from ordinary voters.

Removal from Office   After being elected, laws may allow voters or other politicians to remove an official before the term expires. If removing an official from office is very difficult or impossible, the ideal of holding politicians accountable is weakened. Yet if voters can easily recall and remove officials, the official's ability to function without being subjected to voters' short-term mood swings and to be an effective leader is limited. Again, democracy requires a balance between competing goals.

party tradition in the United States offers fewer choices than are offered in many countries. Recent elections in Australia and France involved four political parties; in Canada five political parties; in Germany, Japan, and Russia six political parties; and in Denmark and Sweden seven large political parties won seats in the national legislative body.

The number of alternatives is important, but the degree of difference among the alternatives is equally relevant. Are six parties that differ very little on policies more democratic than three parties that offer huge differences? And how viable are the alternatives (i.e., can they do the job or fulfill expectations)? Choices are real only if the alternative candidates can follow through. In my state's election for governor, the Green and Libertarian Party candidates got a tiny fraction of the votes. Since the government was set up by the two major parties, the smaller party choices were not very viable. Likewise, fringe parties may not be viable as the leading party, but if they get enough votes, they can join in a coalition with others to influence policy. So when the Greens in Germany got 50 seats out of 656, they could play a role.

A related issue is the number of elections and the number of offices open to voting. On the surface, it may appear that more opportunities to vote for more offices will yield more democracy. Yet too many decisions can trivialize voting and weaken democracy. Imagine an election in which each voter selects candidates for 65 public offices. With so many candidates, voters cannot learn where each candidate stands, and many offices may have minor duties (e.g., town dog catcher, street sweeper). Also, the person elected needs to have actual authority and not be someone who is only in a ceremonial position while someone else makes the real decisions. For example, voting for a mayor who only attends school openings or cuts ribbons is meaningless if nonelected city officials make all the real decisions on major policies and budgets.

Democracy requires a fair, open presentation of all choices so people can learn about the alternatives. Presenting alternatives takes time, and voters should fully understand all the alternatives. Giving three candidates 30 minutes to explain their positions, but allowing two of the candidates only 1 minute to speak is clearly unfair. People need to choose fairly without outside pressures. Real democracy means honest voting and a fair process, not confusion, long lines at polling places, turning people away, and rejecting some ballots, as happened in Florida in the 2000 U.S. presidential election.

Democratic Society

So far we have focused on *democratic politics,* which is not the same as a *democratic society.*[15] Many political sociologists believe that a democratic society is a precondition to full, true democratic politics.[16] **A democratic society has a lively civil society in which people organize themselves into groups outside of government control based on their shared interests or beliefs (e.g., churches, labor**

"People who need people, Jason, are usually democrats."

unions, clubs) and democratic processes prevail throughout all institutions and collective social activities (see Closer Look 2.1). A democratic society provides public space or settings where people can easily engage in free, open, and equal discussions of all ideas and issues. Consistent with deliberative democracy, the discussions are without fear or domination by a few people who possess greater resources. A democratic society implies that all people can participate in multiple ways (e.g., petitions, demonstrations, recalls, or protests), that everyone is protected from abuse or infringement of their rights by the government or others, and that minorities (e.g., individuals with disabilities, of different races or ethnicities, or different religions) do not face discrimination. A full democratic society has a well-informed population with high levels of active participation.

Elected politicians may enact laws and allocate budgets, but administrative agencies and public bureaucracies carry out most ongoing government functions. In a fully democratic society, the people who are most directly affected by governmental actions have an influence on how policies are implemented. For example, before building a new road, officials seek input on road design and location from drivers and people who live nearby. A fully democratic society also extends self-rule to the nongovernmental organizations of civil society. For example, parents of school children, church members, and a business's employees democratically decide the major issues affecting them.

A Model of Ideal Democracy

An ideal democracy includes multiple, reinforcing features (see Chart 2.1). A basic precondition is that forces of organized violence (e.g., military, police, or

| CLOSER LOOK 2.1 | Civil Society and Democratic Politics |

Political sociology is positioned at the intersection of state and society. Chapter 1 defined the state. But defining what a society is can be difficult. A society consists of interacting individuals, groups, organizations, and institutions that tend to share patterns of behavior and thought; act with similar processes, beliefs, or values (i.e., a culture); and persist over time. **Civil society is the "space" in society beyond the state occupied by voluntary, semi-autonomous, citizen-based groups.** The Center for Civil Society at the London School of Economics defines civil society as "the set of institutions, organizations and behaviour situated between the state, the business world, and the family. Specifically, this includes voluntary and non-profit organisations of many different kinds, philanthropic institutions, social and political movements, other forms of social participation and engagement and the values and cultural patterns associated with them." Civil society is populated by informal voluntary or membership-based organizations such as labor unions, social or recreational clubs, service organizations, or churches that may operate at the neighborhood, community, national, regional, and international levels (e.g., Greenpeace, Girl Scouts, Red Cross, World Council of Churches). Edwards (2001) observed that civil society is "the arena in which people come together to advance the interests they hold in common, not for profit or political power, but because they care enough about something to take collective action."

Civil society is a contested term. Some people who distrust and fear the state define civil society as all parts of society that are outside the state, including the family and private business. They advocate using civil society actions or solutions to address most of society's needs, concerns, and problems. Others want to exclude private for-profit businesses and the patriarchal family, limiting civil society to nongovernment, voluntary citizen organizations. Still others are concerned that status and power relations and other structures that create racial and gender inequality and similar differences among people cause the nongovernment organizations of civil society to fail to include everyone's voice or embrace all citizens equally.

Since the French observer, Alexis de Tocqueville (1805–1859) published *Democracy in America* in 1831, people have seen the United States as having an extensive civil society that supports a vibrant democracy. In the United States, citizens formed many formal and informal voluntary associations to counterbalance state power or fill in for a weak state. In addition, the organizations of civil society temper the excessive individualism of U.S. culture. In his article, "Bowling Alone," Robert Putnam (1995) argued that in the past few decades, U.S. civil society has weakened, and this harms American democracy as excessive individualism and self-interest prevail. Others say Putnam presents a romanticized reading of de Tocqueville and implies that in the past, local voluntary groups sprung up from below. In his view, individuals freely and spontaneously decided to associate together and created associations in small geographic areas to accomplish tasks outside the scope of government. Yet this is both naive and historically inaccurate. As Theda Skocpol (1996, 25) remarked, "Organized civil society in the United States has never flourished apart from active government and inclusive democratic politics. Civic vitality has also depended on vibrant ties across classes and localities. If we want to repair civil society, we must first and foremost revitalize political democracy."

Sources: Edwards (2001), Putnam (1995), Skocpol (1996), and Tarrow (1998a), and http://www.lse.ac.uk/collections/CCS/what_is_civil_society.htm.

paramilitary) do not interfere in politics. Other features of an ideal democracy include the free selection of political representatives who have real authority, inclusive participation (i.e., universal suffrage), and fair voting (e.g., secret ballots, no vote fraud or intimidation) without burdens (e.g., no poll taxes, easy access to polling places). It includes competitive elections for a reasonable number of positions with diverse alternatives, equal information on all alternatives, and few barriers to creating a new political party or becoming a political candidate. A list like the one provided in Chart 2.1 is the ideal. As C. Pierson (1996, 24) observed, "If democracy is defined as a political order in which all the people themselves rule and rule themselves directly, no contemporary state can qualify as democratic."

Beyond the mechanics of democratic decision-making and an active civil society, an effective democracy requires a stable social environment (e.g., no rioting or mass arrests) under the rule of law in which all people are treated fairly by the police and courts, have equal rights to a fair trial with equal defense, and have freedom from arbitrary penalties or favors. In addition to the threat to democracy by the government, the very wealthy of a society can also threaten

chart 2.1

FEATURES OF AN IDEAL DEMOCRACY

1. The military, police, or paramilitary is restricted from influence over and intervention in politics.

2. There is open participation to select political representatives who have real authority.

3. All citizens and residents are included and fully participate (universal suffrage, equal treatment).

4. Voting is fair and effortless (i.e., secret ballot elections without burdens, vote fraud, or intimidation).

5. The number of positions filled by elections and regular turnover in public office are balanced.

6. There is a competitive contest for votes in elections with diverse and balanced choices among the alternatives (e.g., equal resources for the alternatives).

7. People are free to form political parties/movements and become political candidates.

8. There is a "civil society" that has the right to organize groups outside government control based on interests or beliefs (e.g., churches, labor unions, clubs).

9. People are educated and informed, and they have "public space" for open and equal expression (e.g., free speech, media access) with multiple sources of information.

10. People have the right to use nonelectorial politics (e.g., petitions, demonstrations, recalls, or protests).

11. Minorities are protected by the rule of law and from discrimination by the government or others.

12. Public participation in policy implementation or bureaucratic decision-making is encouraged.

democracy and undermine civil society by buying up all mass media outlets and using them to shape public debate, a criticism of Prime Minister Silvio Berlusconi in Italy, or by donating vast sums of money to certain candidates, as is common in the United States. Likewise, democracy is weakened when government officials use their positions to retain power and to influence others, as when major political parties enact laws that make it harder to form a new party that might challenge them.

The rhetoric of democracy is widespread. Few rulers claim that their right to govern is based on a mandate from heaven, a divine right, or an inherited birthright. Most say they rule for the people and that the people have a say in that rule. Paradoxically, even when democracy is limited *in practice* to letting ordinary people select among competing elites, the *moral right* of elites to govern rests on democratic ideals of self-rule by ordinary people.[17]

Democratic Elitism versus Participatory Democracy

Some political scientists and political sociologists have narrowed the idea of democracy to democratic elitism.[18] **Democratic elitism says rule by multiple, competing elites, while the mass of ordinary people have limited participation, is inevitable, if not desirable.** The social-economic theorist Joseph Schumpeter (1883–1950) argued for democratic elitism. He said that people have unequal abilities or talents, and large-scale organizations require a few to lead the many. This means that a talented few, or the elites, have always ruled and will continue to do so. Multiple, competing elites are better than a single, unified elite that will become inflexible and nonresponsive. Moreover, elites have the resources, talent, and time to acquire refined tastes and consider the needs of the entire society, while most ordinary people tend to be apathetic, intolerant, and ignorant. Widespread activism or political involvement by the masses will only result in a dictatorship or totalitarian regime. But if the masses are given some small voice, then elites can address their concerns. This can also release built-up social tension and reduce outbursts of unrest by the masses. For these reasons, the masses should have some voice in selecting their rulers from among the multiple, competing elites. As Carole Pateman (1970, 1) argued, in democratic elitism "participation has only a minimal role" and "the emphasis [is] placed on the dangers inherent in wide popular participation in politics." Some political sociologists expressed this view when they blamed unrest in the 1960s on excessive democracy. In practice, few governments are fully democratic, even with a restricted definition of democracy (see Chart 2.2).

The contrast between ideal democracy and democratic elitism illustrates the changing meaning of democracy. Two hundred years ago, democracy meant a type of society, not a form of government. According to Anthony Arblaster (1994, 42), "A democratic society was one in which the mass of people played an active rather than a passive role, and in which old traditions . . . had been replaced by a sense of equality among the people."

---

c h a r t   2 . 2

THE WORLD'S MOST DEMOCRATIC GOVERNMENTS

This chart shows 41 governments that were classified as polyarchies as of 1985.

Argentina	Finland	Nauru	Sweden*
Australia*	France	Netherlands*	Switzerland*
Austria*	Germany (West)	New Zealand*	Tivalu*
Barbados*	Grenada	Norway*	Trinidad & Tobago*
Belgium*	Honduras	Papua New Guinea	United Kingdom*
Belize	Iceland*	Portugal	United States*
Brazil	Ireland*	Saint Christopher	Uruguay
Canada*	Italy*	Saint Lucia	Venezuela
Colombia*	Japan*	Saint Vincent	
Costa Rica*	Kiribati	San Marino	
Denmark*	Luxembourg*	Spain	

Each government listed has all of the following four characteristics:

1. Elections without significant or routine fraud or coercion.

2. No restrictions on purely political organization, although some trade unions or interest groups may be harassed or banned.

3. Citizens can express their views on all topics without fear of punishment.

4. Alternative sources of information exist and are protected by law. If significant government ownership of the media exists, it is effectively controlled by truly independent or multiparty government.

---

*Indicates that the government is also ranked as having a high level of political rights and civil liberties in 1988 (see Gastil 1991).
Source: Adapted from Coppedge and Reinicke (1991). For a similar listing see Birch (1993, 46).

Participatory Democracy

A participatory theory of democracy is close to the ideal of democracy.[19] **Participatory democracy theory holds that active, equal participation by all people in nonpolitical institutions (e.g., civic organizations, workplace, churches) has a powerful educational function that fosters, and may be a critical precondition for, a genuine political democracy.** Participatory democracy delivers three benefits:

1. Social responsibility—People recognize that their individual freedom depends on working with others.
2. Political efficacy—People gain self-confidence and understand that they have a role in decision-making.
3. Social integration—People develop a feeling of community or common membership.

While democratic elitism suggests that widespread public apathy is inevitable and that well-schooled, "properly" socialized elite rulers are best, participatory democracy moves toward ideal democracy by focusing on the relationship between ordinary individuals and the state, or citizenship, which is our next topic.[20]

CITIZENSHIP

Many years ago when I was in high school, I read a story titled, the "Man without a Country." For cursing his country, a man spent the remainder of his life traveling on a ship, unable to get off and call anywhere home.[21] This widely read work, written over 100 years ago, asks What does it mean to be a citizen? Such situations don't occur only in the distant past. Today Russians in Latvia are noncitizens. Latvians do not recognize them as citizens, and Russia does not accept them. Because of the rapid breakup of the Soviet Union and the many ethnic Russians living in Latvia when it became an independent nation, these Russians became a people without a country.

Citizenship is the tie or relationship between an individual and the state. Few people think about citizenship unless they travel outside their own nation, try to become citizens of another nation, or interact with many noncitizens. Schools teach citizenship, but usually it is a mix of patriotism and nationalism (discussed later in this chapter). Political sociologists define citizenship in several ways, and as Charles Tilly noted (1996b, 8), "No standard definition of citizenship has yet gained scholarly consensus." Citizenship has become a major topic in political sociology in recent years.[22]

Defining Citizenship

Citizenship is defined in three ways: (1) a membership status, (2) a collection of rights, and (3) a set of practices. Citizenship can mean membership in the national collectivity. "Citizenship is a status bestowed on those who are full members of a national community."[23] Membership can be defined by three principles, the soil or *jus soli* (i.e., place of birth and permanent residence), blood or *jus sanguinis* (i.e., descent with a clear racial-ethnic heritage), or residence with naturalization *jus domicili* (i.e., living in a nation and affirmatively adopting its culture), which can include religious identity.[24] Membership creates a social boundary; it includes some categories of people and excludes others and can cause social closure, a social stratification term. C. Pierson (1996, 31) explains that with membership comes exclusion. "There are a number of ways we might seek to explain these formal mechanisms of membership and social closure in the modern nation-state. In part, there is a fear among more affluent nations that an influx of migrants from less prosperous regions . . . might dilute their wealth." Often this fear is rather poorly disguised from a more general cultural and ethnic prejudice against varyingly defined "outsiders." The citizenship boundary can change over time or can be applied unequally.[25] It is usually an ascribed social status and can define one's social identity and feelings of belonging.

Citizenship is also defined as a collection of rights. In the United States, citizenship provides membership and rights.[26] Citizenship assigns protections, offers access to opportunities, and entitles citizens to benefits that noncitizens do not receive. Next we examine the three kinds of rights that citizens in a democracy receive: civil, political, and social-economic.

Americans tend to view civil rights narrowly in terms of the struggles African Americans and other racial minorities have experienced for equal treatment. In a broad sense, **civil citizenship rights are rights attached to being a full member of society and receiving equal treatment regardless of factors such as race or ethnicity, gender, age, disability, sexual orientation, marital status, or income level.** David Held explained this idea (1995, 67), "By 'civil rights' is meant those rights which are necessary for the establishment of personal autonomy, including liberty of the person, freedom of speech, thought and faith, and the right to own property and to enter into contracts, and the right to be treated equally with others before the law." For Americans, civil citizenship rights are enshrined in the Bill of Rights, which protects individuals from state action and originated with ideas that emerged from the breakup of feudalism 300 years ago.

Political citizenship rights are a citizen's rights to participate in governance or rule, including the right to vote, to run for public office, to form a political party, to circulate petitions, and to recall elected officials. Political rights depend on supporting or secondary conditions (e.g., the secret ballot, election districts of approximately equal size) that ensure fair elections and on the idea that elected officials represent the voters. Political and civil citizenship rights are tied to social-economic rights, but such rights are often controversial. **Social-economic citizenship rights are a citizen's rights to a minimal standard of living (e.g., a right not to starve or freeze to death), including the right to safe working conditions, a healthy environment, decent housing, medical care, schooling, maternity leave and child care, and a pension.**

Conditions of extreme social and economic inequality can undermine formal citizenship rights. Those seriously disadvantaged by social class, race, gender, or other social statuses may find it difficult to participate fully as citizens. Despite one's legal status as a citizen, the conditions of daily life may "render the possession of citizenship ineffective, if not worthless."[27] Without the necessary education, economic, and other resources to exercise civil and legal rights, "citizenship remains empty for all practical purposes."[28] Thus, basic social-economic rights may be a precondition to realize civil and political rights and participate fully as a citizen. For example, how meaningful is the legal right to vote, to speak at a public hearing, to hold public office, or to express a view in the media if a person cannot afford transportation across town, cannot get time off from work, cannot read or write, or has a mouth of rotting teeth because she/he cannot afford basic medical care?

Citizenship rights often take the form of protections (e.g., people cannot enslave you, you are free to speak what you think, your property cannot be taken without due process). Duties are the flip side of rights (e.g., you must pay taxes, you must serve in the military if drafted, you must serve on a jury if called, you must obey laws). Rights and duties imply an exchange or contract, but citizenship is not a contract. A citizen is obligated to pay taxes, obey laws, or serve in the military whether or not he/she receives all citizenship rights. Citizenship is not a voluntary agreement between two equal parties, and the tie between duties and rights is rarely direct (e.g., you must pay so much in taxes to vote). For most people, the citizenship "contract" is entered into involuntarily when they are born.

T. H. Marshall and Citizenship Rights

Political sociological debate over citizenship began with influential lectures delivered at Cambridge University by T. H. Marshall (1893–1981) in 1947.[29] Marshall's ideas are summarized in three main points:

1. Citizenship has evolved over time though the expansion of rights backed by the state.
2. Rights expanded in a particular sequence—civil, then political, and finally social-economic.
3. The development of capitalism created inequality that has driven the expansion of rights.

Marshall's theory was a foundation, but political sociologists moved beyond it (see Chart 2.3).

---

c h a r t   2 . 3

T. H. MARSHALL'S MODEL OF THE GROWTH OF CITIZENSHIP

Topic	Civil Rights	Political Rights	Social Rights	Workplace Rights[*]
Time period	Eighteenth century	Nineteenth century	Early twentieth century	Late twentieth century
Defining principle	Individual freedom	Political participation	Social welfare and security	Employment protection
Typical measures	Habeas corpus, free speech, freedom to move, freedom of worship	Right to vote, fair elections, paid professional politicians, limits on patronage and favoritism	Right to a public education, public pensions, unemployment insurance, consumer protection, health care, child care	Right to organize unions, right to strike, vacation time, a voice in workplace conditions or corporate governance

[*]Marshall does not include, but critics have added (see Barbalet 1988, 9, 22–26; Giddens 1982, 172).
Source: Adapted from Marshall (1950) and C. Pierson (1996, 136).

Some political sociologists criticize Marshall's thesis that citizenship expanded smoothly and the evolution of rights is inevitable. They note that citizenship rights expanded only as the result of struggles by people at the lower end of society, divisions among elites, warfare, a diffusion of ideas across national borders, or international migration.[30] They note that political rights, especially the right to vote, expanded irregularly in several waves. First, property ownership as a requirement for citizenship was removed, next gender distinctions, then family ties or age requirements, and lastly, citizenship rights have moved to include the environment (e.g., animals and clean air).[31] In addition, social rights often conflict with other rights or with demands of the capitalist economic system.[32] For example, a worker's right to join a union conflicts with an employer's right to have a union-free workplace, the right to have clean air conflicts with the right to smoke tobacco or with a company's right to make profits by polluting. As J. M. Barbalet (1988, 10) noted, "class conflict is likely to be an expression of the struggle for rights and especially citizenship rights." Citizenship rights are often compromises. For example, workers could not get all employers to provide pensions, but they gained the social citizenship right of a minimum public pension (i.e., Social Security).

Citizenship is also defined as a set of practices, negotiated relations, or a series of transactions.[33] Marshall concentrated on **formal citizenship—the official, legal definition of a citizen in political–legal theory.** Many note that formal legal rights are not always enforced, or they may be upheld selectively. These critics say we should focus on **substantive citizenship—the actual practices, conditions, and experiences of various citizens in specific situations.** Citizenship requires that we examine how the formal laws or rules are applied in concrete social settings with real people. Substantive citizenship depends on a specific historical and cultural context. For example, people may possess official legal protections that are violated in practice (e.g., in the People's Republic of China, police can severely beat retarded citizens without penalty).[34]

Limits to Citizenship: Gender and Race

Formal citizenship implies equality among all people in the state's territory, but in practice, citizenship builds on preexisting inequalities, including patriarchy, racial-ethnic hierarchies, and dominant sexual practices.[35] In most nations, male heads of households of the dominant racial-ethnic group who were property owners and potential soldiers were first to get citizenship. Women and racial-ethnic minorities only gained it later after a century of struggling for it, and they only achieved full, formal citizenship rights (e.g., equal access to education, the right to join the police) in democratic nations in the second half of the twentieth century. Formal citizenship rights are for an abstract individual, but that individual often includes an embedded, hidden assumption. In the United States, that assumption is that an individual is a white, heterosexual male. People outside this assumption may find that they are not accorded full citizenship rights. In this way, citizenship reinforces social inequalities rooted in power relations, such as patriarchy or a racial-ethnic hierarchy.

Citizenship rights are gendered (i.e., the rights reflect and reinforce social distinctions between men and women). As Sylvia Walby (1994, 379) observed, "Gender is absent from many discussions of citizenship." The delay in women receiving the right to vote is only the most obvious way that gender relates to citizenship.[36] It extends to other legal rights as well (e.g., the right to own property, serve on a jury, or leave a marriage). Between 1907 and the 1930s an American woman lost her citizenship if she married a foreign-born noncitizen, but the reverse was not true for a man.[37] Also, most social citizenship rights (e.g., social security benefits, unemployment insurance, aid for the poor) assume that the citizen is a male head of a household. For example, public pensions that are based on paid work in the labor force devalue women's unpaid household labor and restricted public maternity rights and public services that treat pregnancy as a disability instead of a natural condition all reflect the assumption that the individual is male.

Citizenship is also gendered if it stops at the door of private family life in patriarchal society, and leaves family life as a site of unquestioned male authority. Citizenship protections have rarely crossed into the family domain. Until recent decades, males could beat or rape their wives without legal interference. Gender-neutral citizenship rights might include protecting a woman's capacity to form and maintain an autonomous household without men by providing access to training, employment, and support services (e.g., childcare) that would allow a woman to live as a fully independent person (i.e., not force her into a marriage if she wants children or compel her to stay in a heterosexual marriage).[38]

Racial divisions also shaped citizenship expansion. For example, until the 1960s, U.S. citizenship and immigration policy was based on a person's race.[39] Bryan Turner (1990, 197) argued that, "The debate about citizenship in the United States cannot take place without an analysis of the historical impact of the black South . . . ." Racial minorities struggled for political civil rights (e.g., the right to vote) and social citizenship rights.[40] The uneven expansion of social citizenship along racial-ethnic lines illustrates the interrelation among various citizenship rights. For example, decades later southern blacks had less access to public schools in areas where blacks lost the right to vote in the 1890s than in areas where they retained the right to vote or where political party competition for their vote existed.[41]

Citizenship Issues and Expansion

The changing meaning of citizenship is shaped by three central ideas: (1) participatory citizenship, (2) a reversal of citizenship rights, and (3) citizenship beyond the nation-state. First, paralleling participatory democracy, **participatory citizenship argues that authentic citizenship requires that all citizens participate and engage in political and civil life; it is more than a set of rights passively attached to people.**[42] Like a muscle, citizenship atrophies if people do not exercise it. As Angus Stewart (1995, 65) argued, "citizens are political actors *constituting* political communities" (emphasis in original). People actively create and continually redefine citizenship, because being a citizen means being a full member of society who can actively participate in the full breadth of political and social institutions.[43] This expands T. H. Marshall's ideas to a wider range of economic rights (see Chart 2.4).[44]

Second, citizenship expansion over time was not inevitable, and instead of a constant progressive expansion over time, citizenship rights have been withdrawn, reduced, redefined, or reversed.[45] Keith Faulks (2000, 135) observed, ". . . citizenship is never a fixed status. Its fortunes fluctuate according to social change." Also, Marshall's model assumed a society with equal people who shared values and lacked social divisions.[46] Yet, states have distributed citizenship rights unequally and "at minimum distinguishing between minors and adults, prisoners and free persons, naturalized and native-born."[47] Instead of expanding evenly, citizenship is better viewed as a changing, flexible relationship between the state and specific categories of people. Citizenship rights have expanded or contracted unevenly across categories of people depending on the outcome of political events and struggles.

Lastly, citizenship has been traditionally understood as the relationship between an individual and the nation-state, but as globalization weakens the nation-state, citizenship may become a relationship between an individual and the state *or other political institutions or communities.*[48] As Christopher Pierson (1996, 204) argued, "our citizenship can no longer be exhaustively defined by membership in the nation-state, nor democracy by participation in purely national political processes." Citizenship may mean membership, identity, rights, practices, and participation with regard to smaller political units (e.g., towns, cities)

---

c h a r t   2 . 4

AN EXPANDED TYPOLOGY OF CITIZENSHIP RIGHTS

Right/Domain	Personal Domain	Organizational Domain	Access and Enforcement Domain
Legal/civil rights	Freedom of speech Equal treatment	Business incorporation Political party formation	Access to courts (legal aid) Fair law enforcement
Political rights	Right to vote Secret ballots	Lobby political officials Form protest organization	Monitor elections Control lobbying
Social rights	Health care Child care	Education Job training	Old-age pension Work injury insurance
Participatory rights	Job placement Job creation	Affirmative action Collective bargaining	Antitrust laws Capital escape laws

Source: Adapted from Janoski (1990, 210).

or nongovernment organizations (e.g., schools, workplaces).[49] It is becoming an individual's relationship with larger political units (e.g., European Union, United Nations, world community). The concept of world citizenship is growing with the belief that people have basic human rights no matter where they reside.[50] "We need to remind ourselves that citizenship is not reducible to membership in the modern nation-state. It is not primarily definable as 'national citizenship' . . . citizenship is mainly definable in terms of the existence of a political community, civil society and public sphere, whether or not that is codeterminous with a nation-state."[51]

Democracy and citizenship historically expanded via diverse routes, and the expansion routes illuminate how citizenship relates to democracy.[52] Democracy and citizenship grew as continuous processes reflecting shifts in the distribution of power. "Democratization represents first and foremost an increase in political equality"[53] and "citizenship cannot be explained by looking for rights granted 'ready made' by states."[54] Political sociologists use two theories to explain the expansion of democracy and citizenship historically—modernization theory and political-conflict theory.

Modernization Theory

Social scientists developed modernization theory during the classic era. In this theory, democracy and citizenship are viewed as complementary parts of a broader evolutionary process that operates in similar ways in most countries.[55] As industrialization spread, levels of education and urbanization grew and a new modern form of society emerged. For modernization theorists, society was an integrated system in which some parts could not change without affecting all others, and industrialization triggered most other changes. As industrialization broke down the traditional social order, it ushered in a new economy (i.e., free trade with market-determined prices), social relations (i.e., achievement-based), forms of work (i.e., nonagricultural), types of knowledge (i.e., secular, scientific, rational), and structure of classes (i.e., open mobility). Improving health conditions spawned population growth and people migrated from the countryside to cities. Traditional social institutions, forms of wealth, and sources of power eroded, and an educated middle class emerged demanding a voice in politics. Modernizing elites created new democratic institutions and expanded citizenship to incorporate more people into the political process and broaden their base of support.

Modernization theorists placed societies on a continuum with traditional societies at one end and modern societies at the other (usually the United States, United Kingdom, France, Germany). They felt that all nations would move through the following distinct stages eventually to reach a similar form: traditional, take-off, drive to maturity, mass consumption, and post-mass consumption.[56] Modernization encouraged a modern value system or a "civic culture" that provided the psychological, political, and cultural factors needed to support democracy (e.g., openness to change, merit-based reward, tolerance, need–achievement psychology, faith in progress). As Seymour Martin Lipset (1994, 3) argued, "Democracy requires a supportive culture, the acceptance by the citizenry and political elites of principles underlying freedom of speech, media, assembly, religion, of the rights of opposition parties, of the rule of law, of human rights, and the like." Democracy and citizenship grew together and diffused with rising educational levels and greater mass communication. Old elites only slowly and reluctantly admitted new people into governing. Once a nation attained a sufficient level of wealth to sustain a large middle class that embraced modern cultural values and formed the requisite institutions (e.g., schooling, mass communication), it would achieve modern democracy and citizenship.

Political Conflict Theory

Other political sociologists criticized the modernization theorists for failing to study the specific historical conditions and places where democracy and citizenship grew.[57] Political-conflict theorists rejected the simple evolutionary model of modernization theory. They held that different nations took various paths to democracy. They observed that citizenship rights expanded unevenly across the population or parts of a nation and expanded in different nations under different conditions.[58] Charles Tilly (1997, 281) observed, "We have absolutely no *a priori* reason to believe that only one set of circumstances produces and sustains democracy . . . ." For example, in England, citizenship rights were tied to the political and economic conditions of different parts of the country. Areas with small farms and a strong village life advocated for and won citizenship rights sooner.[59] The theorists held that democracy and citizenship do not expand on a blank slate but rather build on what preceded them. For example, social citizenship rights (e.g., health care, housing) are weak in nations where the core working class gained civic and political rights easily and early, such as in the United States. "In comparison with Canada and most Western European countries, social citizenship rights in the United States are less developed and less intertwined with political and civil citizenship."[60] In the United States, white working-class males acquired political and civic rights with little struggle. Since they acquired civic and political citizenship rights quickly, other citizenship rights expanded slower than in countries where workers had a long struggle for citizenship. Michael Mann (1988, 194) noted, "If civil and political citizenship could be attained early, before the class struggles of industrialism, then social citizenship need not follow." This is because political-civil citizenship gets disconnected from social-economic citizenship. "U.S. political culture . . . combines a richly elaborated discourse about 'civic citizenship' with a near total absence of discourse about 'social citizenship.'"[61] Early and easy political citizenship for white males explains a continued reluctance to expand social citizenship to all people—giving full access for the disabled, the underclass, marginalized groups, and the indigent.[62] In the political conflict theory, six enabling factors explain the spread of democracy and citizenship. Let us look at each of them.

Civil Wars and Revolutions that Pushed Out the Old, Established Elites   At the end of the Middle Ages, democracy and citizenship spread in Western Europe where kings or monarchs were weak and new elites based in towns and cities arose to oppose the established feudal aristocracy. New economic conditions, including the breakup of the feudal manors, the commercialization of agriculture, and new technology, which especially improved communication and transportation, helped destroy the economic and social structure of feudalism. An expansion of market-based economic relations and international trade undermined the social and economic structure on which the old political structure had been built. Conflict between the rising merchant class and an entrenched nobility discredited traditional forms of political legitimacy, or the "right to rule." It had been based on ancient traditions, landlord–serf relations, royal privilege, and divine rights. Slowly a new system of legitimacy emerged, one that emphasized individual rights (e.g., property rights, freedom to move, work for wages) and a reciprocal relationship between the state and its people. This new form of legitimacy sped the expansion of emerging capitalist economic forces. Thus, democracy and citizenship spread in a way that co-existed with and protected an emerging capitalist economic system.[63]

A Shortage of Skilled Labor or the Emigration of Labor   A shortage or surplus of workers and emigration or immigration affected when and how democracy and citizenship rights expanded.[64] Where laborers were in short supply, political and legal rights expanded faster because expanded rights reduced emigration and garnered worker loyalty. Where workers were abundant or could not leave easily, rights rarely expanded beyond the property-owning elite. J. M. Barbalet (1988, 18) observed it was because "Rights are thus much more significant for those without social and political power than they are for the powerful."

Warfare and a Mass Conscription Army   During wartime, the state must collect more taxes and recruit soldiers, especially for the mass citizen armies that had developed by the late nineteenth century. As the state levied a heavier tax burden and conscripted sons or fathers to fight for the nation, citizenship rights expanded as a way to lessen popular resistance. Basically, in exchange for soldiers and tax revenues, political elites gave a bigger stake in the government to a wider section of the population. Thus, we find citizenship expanding based on the demands of modern forms of warfare.[65]

Disunity Among the Elites of a Society   When and where a society's elites were highly unified and held tight political control, they restricted the lower classes. But when and where elites were divided, weakened, and fought among one another, they were less able to resist the demands of ordinary people to expand citizenship. At times among various competing elites, one of the elite groups would promise more democratization to gain popular support in its fight against the other elites.

Challenges by Mobilized People at the Bottom of Society   Political elites expanded citizenship and democracy both as a concession to well-organized challengers and as a preemptive strategy to detract from their opponents. Democracy did not spread automatically, it was won in struggle.[66] Citizenship rights and democracy slowly extended downward from the most privileged and wealthy levels of society, but only under duress. As Charles Tilly (1997, 275) noted, "durable democratic institutions emerged out of repeated, long-term struggles in which workers, peasants, and other ordinary people were much involved. . . ." Citizenship struggles, especially over social citizenship rights, were rooted in fights for greater equality. Bryan Turner (1986, 11–12) explained, "citizenship is a consequence of real and popular struggles against various forms of hierarchy, patriarchy, class exploitation and political oppression. . . . The political achievement of full citizenship, where it involves significant social rights, is a direct challenge to capitalism, but it is also a challenge to authoritarian forms of political rule."

The Diffusion of Models of Government and Ideas Across International Borders and Following Other Nations   Democracy and citizenship also grew because people were agitated by rights and ideas from abroad, and because elites borrowed ideas from other countries or adopted their methods to resolve domestic conflicts.[67] In addition to the social learning or diffusion of ideas, greater international contact also disrupted established social and economic patterns, creating new opportunities for change.

In sum, the political conflict theorists see democracy and citizenship spreading because of social struggles, divided elites, international military competition, and ideas that cross national borders (see World View 2.1). Democracy spread when the established aristocratic landed class split and the working class joined an alliance with small farmers or small business owners to struggle for more rights. For example, in a study of Western European, Latin America, and Caribbean nations as well as the United States, Canada, Australia, and New Zealand, Rueschemeyer and colleagues (1992, 8) observed, "The working class was the most consistently prodemocratic force." The middle class was an inconsistent democratic supporter. Large landlords, especially those most dependent on low-wage peasants or tenants, were consistently antidemocratic.

By contrast, the modernization theorists see the middle class (small business owners, investors, professionals, white-collar employees) as being the foundation of democracy and the workers as inconsistent supporters of it. For modernization theorists, social movements, raising citizen armies, or international conflicts do not promote democracy. By contrast, political conflict theorists like Rueschemeyer, et. al. (1992, 277) argued that, "Transnational power relations—war, the structure effects of economic dependency, and . . . interventions of foreign powers—profoundly affected changes in democratization." Being dependent on another country for economic or military support decreases a country's democratization, but wartime mobilization with a citizen army tends to expand democratization because ruling elites need to win broad popular support to advance the war effort.

Democracy and Capitalism

Both modernization and political conflict theorists see industrialization and market capitalism as preconditions for democratic expansion but insufficient

WORLD VIEW 2.1   Why Did Portugal Become Democratic?

Schwartzman (1998) identified six factors that increased a wave of democracy around the world in the 1970s–1980s and applied them to the case of Portugal. The six factors follow.

1. **Favorable International Climate**—Success in some parts of the world encourages others to look to democratization as an appropriate solution for their domestic problems.
2. **Global Industrialization**—Global industrialization creates technological change in communication and transportation, fosters the growth of a middle class and an industrial working class (both often supporters of democratization), lessens the previous gap between industrialized and nonindustrialized countries, and thereby alters the relationship that the state has with upper classes. For example, elites in South Africa and Brazil, who had cooperated with the previous authoritarian state and depended upon it for protection and support, began to challenge the state and to accept workers' demands when conditions changed.
3. **Global Shocks**—Any economic or other shock may trigger a legitimacy crisis that upsets the political regime. For example, the second major world oil crisis in 1979 fueled political changes in nondemocratic states and also caused voters to throw out the political party in power in many democratic nations of Western Europe and North America.
4. **Foreign Intervention**—International agencies and, at times, the United States, promoted democracy. For example in 1991, the U.S. Congress tied guidelines regarding democracy and human rights to foreign aid. In addition, the United States and the Paris Club declared a moratorium on aid to Kenya

and to Malawi pending the implementation of political reforms such as multiparty democracy and cessation of politically motivated torture and imprisonment.
5. **Shifting Global Power Center**—When a major world empire collapses or powerful nation's position in the international system shifts, current domestic alliances that support nondemocratic rulers may be reconfigured.
6. **World-System Cycles**—According to a world-system model, the world economy develops through cycles of growth followed by periods of consolidation, then decline. This cycle can create economic instability that can upset the rigid economic systems on which antidemocratic governments depend.

CASE OF PORTUGAL

After being a world power in the fifteenth and sixteenth centuries, Portugal lost much of its wealth and status after a major earthquake in 1755, it was occupied by France from 1807–1808, and Brazil won its independence from Portugal in 1822. A dictatorship replaced the monarchy in 1910 and nondemocratic governments ran the country for six decades. Portugal had no free elections, political parties, or free trade unions; the press was censored, and the political police were repressive. Even after World War II, Portugal continued to derive wealth by exploiting its remaining colonies in Africa and Asia, although it had to fight wars to retain its colonies in the 1960s. Then in 1974, Portugal became the first country in the worldwide third wave of democratization, and it relinquished all of its colonies. Democratization quickly followed in Spain, Greece, across Latin America, in South Korea and Taiwan, then in Eastern Europe and the former Soviet Union.

Many say that in the 1970s a new phase of a *world-system cycle* began. By the late 1960s, with

Continued on page 54

Continued from page 53

high wages in the advanced nations, multinational firms began to invest in less-industrialized countries, such as Portugal, where low wages and greater labor exploitation could yield higher profits. As *global industrialization* spread, corporations and investors from advanced nations increasingly introduced simple technology and returned the profits to their home nations. For example, foreign investors entered Portugal in 1960 and greatly accelerated industrial growth. Over time, the origin of foreign investment shifted from the United States to Europe. By 1972, United States dominance was weakening and a *shifting global power center* allowed West German capital investments in Portugal to overtake those of the United States. Portugal's percentage of trade with the European Union grew faster than its trade with the United States. About this time, a *global shock*, the first oil crisis of 1973, sent world oil prices up four-fold.

The Portuguese retention of overseas colonies had a political parallel at home. There were few industrial workers, and they were politically weak; small business owners were tied to a large national government; and the wealthy landowning oligarchy depended on trade that was tied to exploiting the colonies. As foreign investment expanded domestic industries, a new class of Portuguese owners/managers developed. The rising

owners/managers who were connected to new economic activity sought state assistance and protection from international competition. However, the old Portuguese regime continued to allocate resources to fight expensive colonial wars and to try to hold onto their colonial system. Also *foreign intervention* in the form of international pressure from most of the industrial world encouraged an end to the remaining colonial rule worldwide.

The new groups of Portuguese owners/ managers sought political weight equal to their new economic weight, but deep conflicts erupted among the nation's power elites. At the same time, the Portuguese peasants increasingly moved to cities to work in newly established factories, but they faced low wages and harsh factory conditions. Labor unions were illegal under the dictatorship, so economic struggles became highly politicized. A *favorable international climate* helped to create a prodemocracy coalition among new domestic investors/managers and unhappy industrial workers. The investors/managers cooperated with factory workers because they needed the mobilized workers to advance their own interests and could not end the dictatorship alone. Thus, a tactical convergence of domestic interests developed between investors/managers and workers, and they replaced the dictatorship with a democratic regime.

alone for democracy and citizenship. Note that not all capitalist economic systems are democratic (e.g., Nazi Germany, one-party nations such as Singapore). The two theories specify different dynamics. For modernization theorists, efficient market capitalism requires private property rights, a free flow of information, and personal freedoms. These are key factors to expand democracy. A government that protects property rights for the market will build a foundation of individual political rights and the rule of law. In addition, capitalism encourages civil society, which fosters a diversity of social-economic interests and alternative sources of power to counterbalance concentrated government power. Market competition also stimulates multiple elites, ensuring that no one will have total control, and it weakens traditional sources of power. Capitalism encourages openness to new ideas, greater contacts with people in other nations, innovation, technological change, and modern education. By contrast, political-conflict theorists hold that

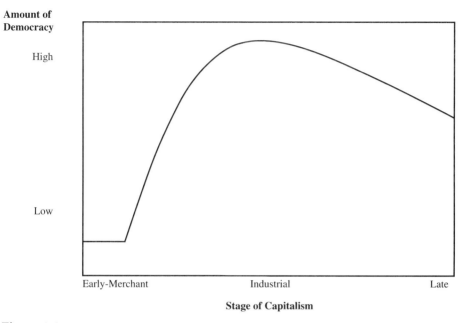

Amount of Democracy

High

Low

Early-Merchant   Industrial   Late

Stage of Capitalism

Figure 2.1
Relationship between capitalism and democracy in political conflict theory.

industrial capitalism generates conditions—a conflict among social classes, a stronger state, and international pressures—that stimulate prodemocracy struggles, and that these struggles are critical for expanding citizenship.[68] As Göran Therborn (1997, 135) argued, "the fact that democracy . . . did not appear anywhere prior to capitalism; that some capitalist countries have experienced a purely internal development of democracy; and that all major advanced bourgeois states are today democracies—these naturally call for some elucidation of the tendencies inherit within capitalism."

If pushed to their limits, capitalism and democracy are incompatible. In its early stages, capitalism is a prodemocracy force because it breaks down traditional social controls and political restrictions. Bryan Turner (1986, 23) explained this process, "Capitalism undermines hierarchical, particularistic, patriarchal, and religious institutions and values, while promoting a society based simply on the cash nexus where there are no traditional or moral assumptions about social relationships . . . capitalism promotes the growth of a universalistic culture . . . ." Yet as it continues and further develops, capitalism generates great social and economic inequality and emphasizes the pursuit of private, individual interests. Often, a powerful capitalist class emerges that will try to control the state, intensifying the conflict between the major social classes. These factors tend to operate against a full participatory democracy (see Figure 2.1).

Political-conflict theorists argue that capitalism can only sustain a limited, incomplete form of democracy. It does not support full, equal participation by everyone in all social, political, and economic activities. Limited democracy strengthens capitalism by fostering the rule of law, protecting private property, and guaranteeing abstract individual liberties (for those who can afford to exercise them). Full democracy only occurs when workers and others struggle for it; elites will grant it only under duress (e.g., the need to raise a large army or to defuse social unrest). Nonproperty owners can expand democratic political rights but will be limited to expanding them in ways that do not threaten core features of capitalism, such as private property ownership or the market economy. Capitalism limits democracy to a nonthreatening form. See Chart 2.5 for a

---

chart 2.5
WHY/HOW MODERN DEMOCRATIC CITIZENSHIP DEVELOPED

Modernization Theory

Major Factors

1. Shift to a market economy, capitalism, and greater societal wealth

2. Expansion of literacy and the secular (rational/scientific) education system

3. Growth of a large middle class (small business owners, professionals)

4. Creation of new social/political institutions (e.g., law, mass media)

5. Change in cultural value orientation (i.e., less traditional, prochange)

6. Industrial technology, modern communication/transportation, urbanization

Prodemocratic Groups: Most of the educated middle class (professionals, business owners), some "enlightened" among the aristocracy
Antidemocratic Groups: Traditional landed elites, most of the very poor and blue collar workers

Political Conflict Theory

Major Factors

1. Defeat or breakdown of old landed aristocracy or powerful monarchy

2. Need to tax or recruit the masses into new conscription armies for wars

3. A labor shortage or possible large-scale emigration of workers/farmers

4. Political struggles by people in bottom half of society for a greater voice or rights

5. A major split among the elites at the top of society

6. A diffusion of models and ideas of democracy and citizenship from other nations

Prodemocratic Groups: Many in the middle class (small business owners, independent farmers), most blue-collar workers, minority groups, some professionals
Antidemocratic Groups: Traditional landed elites, almost all aristocracy, traditional religious leaders, many large business owners

summary of the two theories. One of the most significant ideas of the nineteenth century that spread from country to country around the world was nationalism. We will now examine this concept.

NATIONALISM

Nationalism has been a central organizing force in politics, social change, and international relations for over two centuries. Conflicts over nationalism caused World War I; the violent conflicts in Bosnia, Serbia and Croatia (what was once Yugoslavia); and the 1999 bloodbath in East Timor. **Nationalism is a mode of discourse, a movement, and an emotional sentiment about the nation.** Michael Mann (1988, 184) noted, "The nation has become the main symbolic identity of the modern world, the community, the 'we of social life'." Craig Calhoun (1997) went further to argue that it is a master framework used in the world today to talk about, think about, and see social units. Nationalism and patriotism are interrelated. Nationalism is a belief by people that they are distinct and have a common culture; it includes a desire for self-rule and pride in one's people or culture. Patriotism, sometimes called positive nationalism, is more narrow and specific; it is a person's loyalty to or love of her/his own country. Patriotism signals a person's commitment to his/her own nation-state.

At its core, nationalism is a sense of affiliation or communality with other people of the same nation.[69] Self-identification as a nation is, "the dominant form of modern self-understanding and the central organizing principle of modern politics. . . ."[70] Nationalism includes an awareness of belonging and a unity with others that generates a feeling of common destiny and membership; it has an intense psychological dimension similar to religiosity.[71] Elites have used nationalism to consolidate, defend, or promote separate states. Nationalist thinking assumes the world contains many separate, naturally distinct peoples, or nations, and that each nation should rule itself. Nationalism includes efforts to protect a group's separate political, social, and economic autonomy through self-government and to justify autonomy by claiming status as a nation, thus fusing ideological and political dimensions.[72]

Nationalism has political, economic, and cultural forms (see Summary 2.2). From an early twenty-first century perspective, nations appear as natural, inevitable divisions in the world that always existed. Yet nation-states appeared only about 300 years ago and are historical creations that have since reordered social–political reality. They changed politics, altered how we see the world, strengthened forms of collective identity and integration, and advanced types of economic activity.

A nation is a collection of people with a common culture, and by implication, a common territory. Culture is a slippery term that means a shared heritage, customs and traditions, language, religious beliefs, food, family lineage or living patterns, value systems, and so forth. The term *nation* (from *natio*, Latin for something born) initially meant foreigners or outsiders who shared a place of origin, and it had derogatory connotations.[73] In early Medieval Europe, the nation meant a collection of university students from other lands. In the twelfth century, its derogatory meaning declined, and it began to mean a community of shared opinion. When scholars appeared before church officials in Rome in the thirteenth century to present positions, the term meant the political or social elites from a land. In sixteenth century England, the term changed to mean a people. Liah Greenfeld (1992, 6) noted, "This semantic transformation signaled the emergence of the first nation in the world, in the sense in which the word is understood today, and launched the era of nationalism."

A major development was combining ordinary people, or the rabble, with the elite into a single entity. In an era of constant warfare, *nation* shifted to have a positive connotation and implied sovereignty. *Nation* increasingly came to mean a unique or distinctive people, or the population residing in a unified territory. In twentieth century anticolonial movements, the ideals of democracy and self-rule blended with the idea of nation. "Democracy was born with the sense of nationality. The two are inherently linked .... Nationalism was the form in which democracy appeared in the world .... But as nationalism spread in different conditions the idea of the nation moved from the sovereign character to the uniqueness of the people, the original equivalence between it and democratic principles was lost" (Greenfeld 1992, 10).

SUMMARY 2.2   Three Types of Nationalism

Political nationalism defends national interests and strengthens institutions of national sovereignty, including the military. While demanding respect for national symbols and institutions (e.g., the founding fathers, the Constitution), political nationalism advocates strong national governmental authority relative to nongovernmental organizations, other levels of government, and other nations. An example of political nationalism is when political leaders withhold dues owed to an international agency like the United Nations, limit participation in international treaties (e.g., the 1998 Kyoto Accord on global warming), or refuse to follow international law or human rights standards, because they believe that the national interest should be an absolute priority.

Economic nationalism defends and strengthens the economic position of one nation relative to other nations. Economic nationalism rests on the assumption of a unity between the national interest and a national economy. Economic nationalists favor public subsidies or tax breaks for domestic private industry, protectionist trade policies (i.e., high tariffs on imported goods), and domestic production (e.g., Buy American campaigns, domestic content rules, being self-sufficient in food or oil production). They align a nation's international trade, military, and foreign aid policies to benefit its domestic financial institutions and industry.

Cultural nationalism defends and strengthens the cultural identity and institutions of a nation. Led by a nation's cultural elites and intellectuals, this form of nationalism emphasizes the uniqueness of a nation, defines its distinct features and people, and works to preserve or fortify one nation's culture (e.g., art, music, history, literature, language). For example, defenders of French culture advocate using only the French language and want to limit the number of non-French films shown in theatres or non-French music played on radio stations in France.

Nation as Ethnic Group

People develop a sense of identity of being a single nation from a real or imagined racial-ethnic heritage. Therefore, as Katherine See (1986, 5) observed, "the nation constitutes a politicized ethnic group." When a group occupies the same territory over time and intermarries, it develops shared customs, traditions, and myths. Thus, a nation can be an ethnic group with a sense of territory, shared cultural practices, and a common language (see Closer Look 2.2).

Ethnic identity can be a basis for nationhood.[74] Ethnicity is a social–political creation, not a natural feature of human life, and it is diffused with seventeenth- and eighteenth-century empire building and international contact.[75] Anthony D. Smith (1986, 50) elaborated the idea of ethnicity (or ethnicism) and said, "Ethnicism is more than a heightened and active sense of ethnocentrism . . . [It] is more of a collective movement, whose activities and efforts are aimed at resisting perceived threats from outside and corrosion within, at renewing a community's forms and traditions, and at reintegrating a community's members and strata which have become dangerously divided by conflicting pressures . . . ethnicist movements are by no means confined to the pre-modern world." In the last sentence, Smith rejects the idea that ethnic identity or tribalism is primitive. Primitive, preliterate people are not alone in needing a sense of collective membership. Individuals in industrialized, rational-scientific societies also need this sense of belonging. This need to be part of a collectivity may be universal. It is important to recognize that, "ethnicity, language, or religion may help define the people of the nation, but the framework of nationalism and the role of the state shape how these forms play out in peoples lives. . . . State-seeking nationalisms also suppress some aspects of a people/nation and promote others."[76]

The competition for scarce resources and power can strengthen feelings of in-group solidarity. Many racial, religious, and cultural conflicts in advanced societies are struggles over cultural identity and the boundaries of group membership.[77] Nationalism gives people a shared identity; this identity can assume a highly moral or quasi-sacred significance.[78] Yet, as Hutchinson and Smith (1994, 5) remarked, "Nationalism, as an ideological movement, did not emerge

 CLOSER LOOK 2.2   **Ways to Understand the Meaning of a Nation**

- The nation is a primordial or racial-ethnic identity with ancient roots. It arises from basic human needs and desires to affiliate with others who are similar and to create exclusive social boundaries.
- The nation is a feeling of membership in a collectivity. It developed from two sources as an unintended consequence: (1) from power struggles among early states to define borders and separate themselves and (2) from economic-social integration within state boundaries with industrial capitalism.
- The nation is a created cultural identity. Nation-building elites actively constructed, disseminated, and maintained it in the process of gaining and consolidating power.

without antecedents." It grew out of earlier forms of identity. Ethnic identity can be defined in three ways:

1. Primordial—Members share either a biological heritage (through ancestors or physical appearance), psychological group membership, or a strong cultural attachment.
2. Constructed—In-group elites create a common or a myth of a common past.
3. Instrumental—Outsiders, such as intellectuals or government officials assign membership.

Ethnicity is a socially-created identity that is based on maintaining social boundaries between "us" and "them." It is a relational concept (i.e., it requires an outsider against whom insiders can contrast a sense of self). Joanne Nagel (1994, 154) argued, "Ethnic boundaries determine who is a member and who is not and designate which ethnic categories are available for individual identification. . . ." Ethnicity and the nation also imply a shared memory or history as an ethnic group. People create stories or select past events to define themselves; they construct monuments and museums to highlight their values and events, both real and invented.

Nationalism can contribute to racist thinking, especially if national identity includes the idea of being a biologically distinct people or race.[79] Racism arises when people assume that the world is inhabited by fundamentally different types of people, and this assumption is combined with a conviction that some types are superior to others. Racist ideologies mix ethnocentrism with ethnic-national pride to support a classification system that ranks physical-cultural types of people. The ideologies defend racial purity from contamination and justify exploiting those viewed as being inferior.

People often grow emotionally attached to a collectivity and develop intense feelings of loyalty and belonging. Such feelings contribute to social conditions (e.g., friendship, intermarriage) and institutions (e.g., clubs, neighborhoods) that reinforce mutual interaction and strengthen relationships among people who think that they are alike. Those who believe they are alike will overlook internal differences and accentuate disparities between themselves and others. As Anthony D. Smith (1986, 147) noted, for political leaders, "ethnic homogeneity and cultural unity are paramount considerations. Even where their societies are genuinely plural and there is an ideological commitment to pluralism and cultural toleration, the elites of the new states find themselves compelled, by their own ideals and the logic of the ethnic situation to forge new myths and symbols of their emergent nations. . . ." Elites who want to build a nation emphasize shared ideals, lifestyles, and culture to reinforce feelings of oneness and belonging. This strengthens national homogeneity and promotes the idea of being a special people. It also appears in national symbols such as flags, monuments, and anthems, and in official museums that celebrate a people's greatness, history, and collective myths.

The Nation Grows within State Boundaries

Nations were formed more for political organization than from any innate desire in the human species to separate itself into distinct peoples. Ernest Gellner

(1983, 6, 48) argued that the nation is "not an inherent attribute of humanity, but it has now come to appear as such" and "nationalism is not the awakening of an old, latent, dormant force, though that is how it does indeed present itself. It is in reality the consequence of a new form of social organization, based on deeply internalized, education-dependent high cultures, each protected by its own state." The social–cultural unit, or nation, was an unanticipated outcome of forming a new political organization.[80] Feudal elites emphasized specific traditions, language, or parentage to win mass loyalty during their competitive struggles for power. By doing this, they indirectly strengthened the idea that a collectivity of people were a distinct unit or nation. Thus, changes in the state gave birth to two powerful ideas: (1) people belong to culturally homogenous communities (the nation), and (2) political authority rests with the people of a nation who should rule themselves.[81]

In late feudalism, the state was a war-making machine that sought constantly to expand its territorial control. As states grew, they engaged in violent conflicts with other states. Clashes with other states helped create more visible, fixed borders between the territories each state controlled. Within the borders, the states homogenized the people and cultures (i.e., a common language, legal procedures, tax policies). Elites did not unify local regional areas and standardize language out of some grand scheme to create a nation but rather for basic, pragmatic reasons—it strengthened the state's capacity to tax and wage war.[82] To mobilize larger, stronger armies for the purpose of war, the state in late feudalism organized and consolidated resources (e.g., possible soldiers, food for armies, taxes) within their territorial borders. Thus, interstate conflicts set into motion processes that unified the nation, and international processes beyond the evolving nation stimulated the formation of the nation.[83] Craig Calhoun (1993a, 216) argued that, "Claims to nationhood . . . are also claims to distinctiveness vis-à-vis other nations, claims to at least some level of autonomy and self-sufficiency, and claims to certain rights within the world-system of states."

As elites built a stronger state with a uniform political–legal system, they promoted beliefs in a common history and shared traditions and spread these beliefs among the ordinary people. They fostered institutions that would subjugate local institutions that might provide competing loyalties or alternative forms of authority. Critical institutions in this process were tax collection, the mass conscription army, and mass schooling. States advanced mass schooling in the late nineteenth century to create a unified national consciousness and homogenize a secular culture.[84] Schooling spread a shared national identity and strengthened the state, and it also contributed to social and economic advancement.[85]

Thus, nationhood, a capitalist economic system, industrial production, and the self-governing state developed together as one mutually reinforcing process. Industrial capitalism weakened local identities and allegiances to a traditional family-based village in which one was born, lived, and died. It encouraged geographic mobility and weakened the religious-based idea of community common in the Middle Ages, and as Greenfeld (1996, 171) noted, "nationalism has replaced religion as the main cultural mechanism of social integration."

Capitalism transformed social and economic relations, and in so doing, it indirectly fed a growing sense of nationhood. When the population was scattered in tiny, isolated villages, people were separated by petty, local distinctions; their customs, language, interactions, and trade were all localized. As industrial capitalism stimulated trade, exchange, and communication, people traveled, moved to towns or cities, and increasingly encountered others. As they mixed and interacted with others who had different dialects, customs, and ways of living, they felt more affinity for people with a familiar language and customs. Shared systems of law, money, and religion that grew up with territorial boundaries also helped to forge a sense of unity of being a single people or nation.

Paradoxically, imperialism, a system in which a powerful state controls and exploits distant colonies, promoted the spread of nationalism. During the sixteenth through nineteenth centuries, Western European powers conquered the lands and peoples of Africa, Asia, and the Americas. They collected diverse peoples who had separate languages and cultures into a single colony and built transportation and communication systems that internally integrated the colonies so they could better exploit natural riches and native peoples. They also incorporated the goods and peoples from colonies into a larger international system of trade and political domination. As the diverse colonial peoples came into contact with one another and struggled together against their imperial overlords, many developed a feeling of being one people in opposition to the imperial power. In addition, improved communication and transportation gave them contact with the outside world, which introduced new ideas, often from the imperial states, including the idea of self-government. For example, what is now Indonesia once contained hundreds of separate ethnic groups scattered across an archipelago of over 13,000 islands in an area 3,000 miles by 1,000 miles. The people were at different technological levels, lacked common origins, held diverse religious beliefs, practiced distinct customs, and spoke different languages. For over the 300 years that they were under foreign domination, these different peoples increasingly interacted with one another as colonial subjects and were a single political unit created for the exploitation of resources by a single foreign power. By working together in an integrated economy under a single oppressor, and by learning Western ideas of self-determination, they constructed the identity of being one people or nation.

At the onset of the twenty-first century, some observers foresaw the dissolution of the nation-state. Past attempts to create transnational or international identities based on a political ideology (e.g., the communist "workers of the world unite") or religion (all Christians or Muslims of the world unite) have been unsuccessful. Some observers see globalization as a new threat to nationalism that will create a new, unified global identity. **Globalization is the rapid growth of internationally connected economic, social, and cultural relations spurred by new communication, transportation technology, and shifts in the world economy.**[86] Globalization may not replace nationalism and national identity with a single transnational identity because it simultaneously fragments national identity into smaller parts as it builds identities across national borders. Weakening nationalism has increased demands for local autonomy; fostered separatist movements; and renewed ethnic, religious, and regional divisions within nations. For example, separatist movements have grown within European borders (e.g., Spain, the United Kingdom, France, and Italy), not to mention bloody ethnic subnationalist conflicts in the former Yugoslavia. Simultaneous with the formation of the European Union, which supercedes the nation with a transnational identity, is the assertion of subnational identities and demands for greater local autonomy. In addition, as national borders weaken the boundaries that define cultural or ethnic identity are expanding. The diaspora of people with a shared cultural identity who have spread into many nations, such as the Chinese, creates transnational identities.[87] In nations that attract many immigrants who do not fully assimilate but rather retain a separate cultural identity, new hybrid cultural or ethnic identities are emerging that increasingly traverse national borders.

The Nation as a Cultural Construction

As we have seen, the nation did not develop naturally; it was the byproduct of international competition born during the rise of capitalism and self-conscious movements by elites. Cultural elites also created a sense of nationhood in the realm of writing, culture, and ideas. Highly educated people selected elements from the local culture and promoted them as representing a shared, common heritage that would define a separate people. Religious, political, and cultural elites selected and amplified distinctions among people and invented a sense of oneness. As they strengthened traditions, myths, symbols, and rituals, an imagined community and a sense of solidarity arose.[88] Thus, a unified national identity was the outcome of the process of consolidating elite power.[89] Elites invested resources in schooling, museums, history, art and music forms, and so forth to reinforce national identity and secure their positions of power. National heritage, history as taught in public schools, and displays in national museums all cultivated and disseminated a national identity. National identity is still at stake in public disputes over historical monuments (e.g., the U.S. Vietnam War memorial).[90] When people honor and venerate national symbols, they are defining the "we" of a nation, but such symbols can be redefined and their meanings contested.[91] We further examine these issues in Chapter 7.

THE NATION-STATE

In the early twenty-first century, the nation-state is the prevailing form of the state, and nation-states cover the globe. **The nation-state is a joining of political organization (the sovereign state) with a distinct cultural community (the nation or people).** At one time, Cobban (1994, 249) reminded us, "there had been no necessary connection between the state as a political unit and the nation as a cultural one, the combination of these two elements into a single conception was the significant fact . . . in the history of the nation-state."

Feudalism and the Absolutist State

The modern nation-state arose in a specific historical time (the late feudal period) and geographic location (Western Europe) in response to specific conditions.[92] The state in feudal society differed from today's nation-state. European feudal states were small and loosely ruled. Contacts among them typically took the form of military conflict or strategic alliances. Ruling elites interacted with ruling classes elsewhere and had limited interaction with the culture and activities of the ordinary people of the country they ruled. In a feudal society economy, land was the most valued resource, so acquiring more territory was the primary objective. Areas between states were frontier zones with unclear and disputed borders. Because central state authority (or the ruler's authority since they were the same) weakened quickly with distance from the political center, a ruler's orders could be ignored easily in areas distant from the political center.[93]

Feudalism was a system of politics, economy, and society based on agriculture. The same person (or family) held economic power and "political power was located in the manors of feudal lords."[94] Local lords coerced, ruled over, and extracted resources from serfs and peasants who could not freely leave the manor. Serfs had to stay in one place and deliver much of what they grew to their local lord. Each lord held almost total political, economic, and social power over a separate local area. As Poggi (1978, 27, 31) observed, "the main trend through most (but not all) of the feudal period was the fragmenting of each large system of rule into many smaller, and increasingly autonomous, systems that differed widely in how they carried out the business of rule . . . the center of political gravity shifted towards even narrower and more locally rooted centers of rule, which grew increasingly independent from one another."

Border disputes and primitive systems of transportation, trade, and communication meant that anarchic violence was frequent in the countryside. Relations of caste, personal loyalty, pride in patrimony, and particularistic lineages prevailed, not the rule of law or rational-universal principles that applied to all people. Stratification was an estate, or "stand" system that divided society into estates. The members of each estate (e.g., clergy, town merchants, nobility) had a distinct set of duties, privileges, legal capacities, and obligations. The estates came together to bargain with and cooperate with the ruler. This system excluded the vast majority of serfs and peasants who made up 80–90 percent of the population. They were little more than a form of property that the lord owned as part of the land.

In various periods and countries, representatives of the estates met together as assemblies. Over time, these grew into more institutionalized arrangements and became the basis of a new kind of relationship between subject and ruler. They evolved into a system in which the ruler (e.g., prince, duke, baron) remained apart and above the estate but increasingly ruled with its cooperation, especially since the estates helped the ruler to raise funds for warfare.[95] Gradually, rulers gathered a large permanent household staff, including clerics, lawyers, and educated persons, to help with the complex business of ruling. Slowly the feudal pattern of a specific individual's relationship to the ruler moved toward a set of general expectations and rights between the estates and the ruler.

In late feudalism, towns or cities grew. The towns and cities were semi-independence zones outside the feudal system. Town dwellers, who would otherwise be powerless in feudal society, held political rights within the town. Town dwellers developed a sense of freedom and pooled their resources as a fellowship of "individually powerless equals" (Poggi 1978, 38). City walls and the urban militia defended a city's autonomy and property. By living in a social–political space outside the feudal system, townspeople gained self-rule and some freedom to pursue their livelihoods (e.g., craft production, trade). The towns

"At last! After all the debates and polls, it's back to <u>real</u> politics!"

depended on trade with the surrounding hinterland and with distant towns. Over time, collections of towns that regularly traded formed political and military alliances with one another.

By the sixteenth century, the feudal state was evolving into a new form—the absolutist state. **The absolutist state was a hybrid or a transitional form that laid the foundation for the modern nation-state. The nobility or feudal aristocracy continued to rule, but elements of a modern nation-state started to appear and the nation had not yet developed**. The absolutist state arose in a highly competitive system that required clear territorial borders and a strong military (see Summary 2.3). Indeed, Perry Anderson (1974, 33) argued, "the virtual permanence of international armed conflict is one of the hallmarks of the whole climate of Absolutism."[96] The absolutist state consolidated power and absorbed other political units. For example, in 1500 Europe had more than 500 political units; by 1900 there were just 25.[97] A major paradox of European Absolutism is that rulers and the aristocracy modified the state as they attempted to protect their social positions and privileges in the face of rapidly changing conditions. But their actions had the unanticipated effect of accelerating the breakdown of the feudal social and economic system and ushering in an entirely new social and economic system we now know as capitalism.[98] Anderson (1974, 18–19) observed, "Absolutism was essentially . . . *a redeployed and recharged apparatus of feudal domination*, designed to clamp the peasant masses back into their traditional social position . . . it was the new political carapace of a threatened nobility . . . with the gradual disappearance of serfdom [it was] a *displacement* of political-legal coercion upwards towards a centralized, militarized summit—the Absolutist State" (emphasis in original).

SUMMARY 2.3   Features of the Absolutist State

- Borders or territories became more clearly defined and defended than in feudalism. The state became part of a system of states, each touching one another at the borders.
- The idea of sovereignty penetrated to most of the territory (i.e., supreme rule over a territory that overrides other political power; the king or monarch's power is superior to all others in the territory).
- Power was taken away from many feudal lords, barons, dukes and the like and centralized with a supreme ruler or court. Internal barriers were reduced, increasing the flow of people and commerce within national borders.

- A centralized bureaucracy for the whole territory became important in administering political rule and public finance (taxation). The supreme ruler delegated authority to it.
- A consolidated system of law developed and applied impersonally to most of the population. It included private property rights, use of written contracts, and a system of criminal law that superseded local community practices.
- The absolutist state's military became a large, permanent, standing army that was much better organized and equipped with the latest weapons technology.

The Nation-State Appears

Increased trade and emerging capitalist economic relations contributed to the rise of the modern nation-state, but ruling elites also had a role. In response to repeated economic, demographic, and other crises of feudalism, ruling elites modified the form of the state, and a new form of state and capitalism mutually developed. To deal with recurrent crises, feudal rulers increasingly centralized state power, tried to raise efficiency by using more rational scientific techniques, and granted freedoms to people who engaged in new economic activities that produced more taxes for their wars. Their actions strengthened capitalist social-economic relations and weakened those of feudalism.[99]

The nation-state developed in an international context; thus many nation-states appeared together. Hall and Ikenberry (1989, 39) noted that, "Individual states did not exist in a vacuum. They were rather part of a competing state system." Internationally, each state was in fierce military competition trying to defend and extend its territories, and warfare was the primary force shaping the nation-state.[100] In short, as a form of political organization, the nation-state diffused because it was successful in international competition. Other states tried to mimic or adopt similar patterns, so, there was a demonstration effect.[101] The nation-state was thus a successful political model that diffused.

To carry out warfare, states required huge quantities of human, material, and financial resources. In late feudal Europe, towns in which merchants and traders were creating early capitalism formed the most dynamic, fastest-growing economic sector. Yet, the towns were semidetached from feudal society and townspeople had greater freedom of movement. Feudal rulers faced a dilemma: If they imposed too many controls or excessive taxes to pay for their wars, they would frighten off the merchants or destroy the vibrant economic activity, killing the flow of loans and investments that they needed to finance the wars. So rulers allowed townspeople to retain freedoms. Rulers also departed from traditional feudal practices to create more efficient (i.e., more rational and bureaucratic) forms of state organization. These factors had the effect of creating a stable, predicable social-political and legal climate that also fostered the expanding capitalist market economy.[102]

The new social conditions, property relations, industrial production, technologies (for warfare, communication, and transportation), and ideas (in science, democracy, nationalism, and rule of law) combined to erode the system of feudalism. So, the nation state triumphed because it was successful at conducting war, promoting new economic growth, and winning loyalty.[103] Four factors helped it grow: (1) the ideas and ideology of classical liberalism, (2) the rule of law, (3) sovereignty (i.e., a state having supreme control over its territory), and (4) defining the people of a territory as citizens of the state. Let us briefly examine each factor.

Liberal Ideology

Here liberalism refers to liberty from state authority, or specifically limiting state authority and protecting individual freedoms by maintaining a sphere in society free from direct state control. The ideology of liberalism supports a market economy or capitalism, because it emphasizes the values of individual free choice, the application of reason, and tolerance of dissent. It holds that people have individual rights (including property rights), the state should rule only with the consent of those it governs, and the state's primary purpose is to regulate society and protect people and their property. Liberalism sharply differed from the prevailing thinking of feudalism and absolutism. Under an absolutist state, the populace owed the all-powerful ruler unquestioned obedience, and no area was beyond his/her reach. Its guiding principles were to obey traditional authority (i.e., the king, the church), preserve social hierarchy, and conform to custom.

Liberalism grew out of the experiences of merchants, traders, and small manufacturers who lived in towns. It became a way to explain, justify, and guide the emergent nation-state. One finds such ideas in major works of political theory and philosophy of the eighteenth century that were part of the Enlightenment movement, (such as John Locke (1632–1704), David Hume (1711–1776), Tom Paine (1737–1809), Jean-Jacques Rousseau (1712–1778), Adam Smith (1723–1790). Their writings influenced political, economic, and social thought for two centuries and recently have been revived.

The Rule of Law

Under feudalism, rights, social obligations, or duties were based on land ownership, birth into a caste, religious tradition, and personal relations. By contrast, the nation-state extended legal ideas of the contract and rights, often reviving ancient Roman legal concepts. As the capitalist market expanded, strangers began to create complex banking and finance agreements, and trade grew across greater distances or for longer time periods. A system of abstract law, written contracts, and formal rules replaced the traditional norms, informal oral agreements, and personal trust that had worked for small-scale, simple, feudal economic relations. In addition, European states borrowed ideas from Christian religious beliefs about the individual soul. Badie and Birnbaum (1983, 86) argued, "It is beyond doubt that Christianity played a major role in the 'invention' of the state and in the state building process." Christian theology held that each individual had a soul, and after the Protestant Reformation, ideas of personal worship and autonomy spread. Such ideas combined with liberalism to promote the principle of individual rights granted by the state and protected under law.[104]

During the late Middle Ages, the Catholic Church ended the ability of kings and princes to interfere in its affairs and drew a clear distinction between its control over the spiritual realm and the rest of society. This separation indirectly encouraged growth of the nation-state. The religious courts increasingly specialized in religious law and spiritual matters, leaving other legal matters to the secular state. Political rulers began to justify their right to rule less on purely religious grounds and increasingly turned to justifications based on abstract principles (e.g., freedom, justice) and an administrative capacity with a rational-bureaucratic-legal system of formal rules, abstract laws, and written procedures.

International factors also contributed to the rise of law. As ships sailed further and discovered new lands, traders and explorers encountered more diverse people and cultures. This weakened tradition and opened them to experimental thinking. The movement of people and goods also encouraged abstract universal principles and rules—ones that could be portable and detached from specific people and places.

Sovereignty

Sovereignty is unquestioned state authority to rule over a specific territory. It permits the coexistence of one state among others and is a basis of international law. According to Biersteker and Weber (1996, 1–2), sovereignty allows states to "interact as an international system of societies, while at the same time, the mutual recognition of claims to sovereignty is an important element in the construction of states themselves." Internally, sovereignty developed as the absolutist state consolidated power over its territory. This has been called "unitary internal sovereignty" (Poggi 1978, 92), "internal pacification" (Giddens 1987, 172), or "state social control" (Migdal 1988, 22). As state control over the population increased, people ceased to follow norms or engage in behaviors prescribed by social–political units other than the state. Joel Migdal (1988, 23) explained that it meant "getting the population to obey the rules of the state rather than the rules of the local manor, class, or any other organizations." For example, families had to give up local customs and marry off children at ages that differed from the minimum marriage age set by the state.[105] National rules and laws took priority over local rules or laws, and the nation-state became the preeminent organization displacing other units. It issued supreme directives that applied across the entire national territory. As the nation-state consolidated power, it absorbed the rule-based systems of alternative types of organization (e.g., churches, families, corporations, villages).

The nation state created a police force, established courts, suppressed rebellions, and disseminated beliefs and symbols. As the national authority overrode competing local authority, it provided a uniform system for understanding and regulating behavior to all residing within its borders.[106] As Anthony Giddens (1987, 120–121) observed, "A nation-state is, therefore, a bordered power-container . . . the pre-eminent power-container of the modern era. [It] . . . is a set of institutional forms of governance maintaining an administrative monopoly over a territory with demarcated boundaries (borders), its rule being sanctioned by law and direct control over the means of internal and external violence."

Citizenship in a Nation

Nationalizing elites fostered a single nation by creating a unified system of justice, morality, or retribution that borrowed from the existing culture and added new elements. They standardized the language and the writing system, built an apparatus of police, judges, prisons, social workers, official censors, and morals police, and supported nationwide systems of transportation and communication. The idea of citizenship replaced the old feudal relationship of the individual subject who was wholly subservient to the ruler. The citizen was an individual who held rights that the state guaranteed. The state provided its citizens with legal protection, military defense, and services (e.g., money system, postal system), and the citizens gave the state taxes, sons and fathers for military service, and loyalty.[107] Citizenship was very different in the nation-state than in the feudal or absolutist forms of the state (see Chart 2.6).

The Neoliberal Alternative

Some antistate intellectuals advocated a neoliberal explanation of nation-state development in recent years.[108] It tends to be ahistorical and decontextualized; it says little about the initial appearance of the nation-state, expanding citizenship,

---

chart 2.6

A COMPARISION OF FEUDAL, ABSOLUTIST, AND NATION FORMS OF THE STATE

	Feudal State	Absolutist State	Nation State
Territory	Unclear borders; lands of different rulers run into one another; uncontrolled frontiers	Slowly defined fixed boundaries to separate the lands controlled by different states	Clearly mapped and defended borders in a global system of nation-states
Sovereignty	Disputed and contested among multiple rulers, institutions, and areas	Centralized authority expands to cover all ruled land/people	Relatively unchallenged at national government level
Power	Dispersed among many in the nobility and other institutions (e.g., church)	King or monarch consolidates control from all others	Concentrated at national level in the state apparatus
Bureaucracy	Barely exists; instead the ruler has many servants, assistants, and counselors	Supreme ruler delegates authority to an emerging bureaucracy of appointed personnel	Complex system with written records, set procedures, and a trained civil service
Legal System	Almost none; instead a ruler's personal decisions are applied, but unequally	Abstract, systematic principles develop with an educated staff, and decisions are codified	A highly developed, written system operated by autonomous professionals
Military	Many local armies, war lords, and local bandit groups	Monarch builds a large and permanent standing army	State has monopoly use of force; citizen armies, international treaties
Citizenship	Attachment is to the local town or village	Local ties weaken and loyalty shifts to the supreme ruler	Unified in the nation, standardized rights

or state functions.[109] The basic argument is that the modern nation-state developed due to natural factors within the state itself—it grew out of rulers' selfish desires for personal gain or power and an inherent drive in all bureaucracies to grow. The focus is on the growing size of state bureaucracies (e.g., number of rules and regulations over persons or businesses) and the rising public expenditures (with a corresponding rise in taxation). Neoliberals argue that the state can only thrive by extracting resources from the private sector (e.g., taxes, confiscation). They conceptualize state actions (e.g., raising armies, delivering public services, and issuing laws) as state intervention into (with connotations of interference) a prior and separate natural world. Hard-core neoliberals view the state as a parasitic organization that feeds on private individuals and their property.

The neoliberals assume that humans have a natural selfishness, and they make the desire to acquire power, money, or status the prime causal force. They assume that everyone, including state officials, are rational, self-interested, and acquisitive, and that officials can only gain status, wealth, and power by enacting laws, imposing regulations, and spending public money. For example, in a democracy, the elected politicians have an incentive to offer more public services or benefits so they will attract votes. Empirical support for the theory is limited. Studies show that state spending growth varies greatly by country and time period.[110] For example, increased government spending, especially on social-welfare programs, is associated with people voting for political parties advocating the programs. When few in the population can vote, spending for welfare and education decline, and when more can vote, these expenditures grow.[111] We examine state expenditures in later chapters.[112]

FORMS OF THE NATION-STATE

While the state existed prior to the modern era of the nation-state, the nation-state existed in several forms.[113] Instead of reviewing all possible forms, we consider four here: (1) liberal-market, (2) totalitarian, (3) corporatist, and (4) developmental. All are found in major, advanced industrial societies as well as in several rapidly industrializing societies. These forms are ideal types, or models, and in reality, a specific country might have overlapping forms of the state.

The Liberal-Market State

The meaning of *liberal* here is associated with liberal ideology as discussed previously with the rise of the nation-state and not the late twentieth-century American meaning of the term. Sometimes people use the term liberal-democratic to emphasize the connection between a specific state-society relationship and democratic processes, but the other forms can be democratic as well. The liberal-market form of the nation-state usually has two or more competitive political parties, and regular open, free elections. Its civil society tends to be large and extensive with autonomous, diverse, and decentralized groups that are unequal in power and resources. Because the state's involvement in the market economy is limited, it sometimes appears to be chaotic and freewheeling. The state sets the rules for the economy and may give some particular groups special help, but there is little state planning or control of the economy. Instead, market forces rule. This extends to other areas, such as the mass media. People will have well-developed citizenship rights and duties, but the conditions of citizenship might be contested and undergo changes. Compared to the other forms of the state, the United States fits the liberal-market model well with its low-capacity, noninterventionist state. Despite a lot of political rhetoric about big government or government interference in the United States, in reality, the U.S. state is smaller, intervenes in the market less, and provides fewer social welfare services than most other advanced nations.[114]

The Totalitarian State

In democratic nation-states, there is an independent civil society, citizens can freely express ideas and associate together, and the public participates in the competitive selection of political leaders. By contrast, the **totalitarian state is nondemocratic with a controlled and very restricted civil society, limited public expression, and little or no real popular participation in selecting leaders.**[115] The term *totalitarian* comes from total and implies complete control over all aspects of society. The totalitarian state operates with either a socialist/planned or a capitalist/free-market economy.[116] Because capitalism and democracy are closely associated in theory and practice, many people falsely assume that all capitalist economies have a liberal-market (democratic) state. Totalitarian states are usually one-party states; that is, a single political party is the only real political organization. The party's ideology and beliefs are the only ones permitted, and its loyalists hold all the top government posts. Alternative parties are often illegal and are banned, or they are so weakened and restricted that they are ineffective. Often the ruling political party seized power through a violent revolution, civil war, military coup, or with rigged elections. Totalitarian states tightly control mass communication (including books, film, and newspapers), schooling, and other institutions where ideas are developed and expressed (e.g., religion, art). Censoring ideas, activities, and forms of expression that oppose or contradict the ruling party is common in totalitarian societies. The state, sometimes working with religious, business, or other institutions, excludes views that threaten or oppose the rulers. It creates special agencies to observe and regulate the flow of ideas and expression, monitor public meetings and publications, and restrict interchanges with people from other nations. Political sociologists study reasons for the totalitarian party's success in gaining power, the social base of its loyalists, how leaders organize the state to maintain control, and potential sources of opposition or resistance. Two forms of the totalitarian state are the communist and the fascist states.[117]

Communist states have included the Soviet Union, most Central European nations, China, Laos, North Korea, Vietnam, Cuba, and others. From the end of World War II until the widespread dissolution of communist rule around 1990, the Cold War between leading capitalist nations and communist countries dominated international relations. Today, several communist states remain, and some have initiated significant change or economic reform since the mid-1980s, with China being the most prominent. The term *communist* is confusing because it has so many meanings (see Summary 2.4).

SUMMARY 2.4   Multiple Meanings of Communism

Communism is the name of a political movement and party, a particular social and political philosophy, an ideology, an idealized utopian society, and a type of economic system.

- As a political movement, it is an association of people who claim to be committed to the ideals of helping the poor and downtrodden and see this as only possible by radically reorganizing society to equalize wealth and end private property ownership.
- As a political party, it can be similar to other parties that typically have organized labor as a base of support and that regularly run for office in democratic countries such as France, or it can be the party in control of a totalitarian state.

- As a philosophy, it is a theory of human nature, social relations, and the historical development of humankind that opposes private property and advocates equality.
- As an ideology, it is a set of beliefs and values that questions tradition, property, and hierarchy, and favors social and economic equality, international unity, and fulfilling human potential.
- As a utopia, it refers to a near perfect society in which there is equality, justice, harmony, and the absence of private property.
- As an economic system, it is an extreme form of a command, planned, or socialist economy in which business enterprise and all employment is under direct state control.

Communist states vary in their intensity of totalitarianism and form of economy. North Korea, at one extreme, is a highly totalitarian state with a planned economy in which the entire population works for the state. Market exchange, private property, or profits are forbidden. There is no civil society, and the state controls all aspects of people's lives. Other communist states, such as the People's Republic of China, are less totalitarian or have introduced some features of a private market economy.

Fascist states are strongly anticommunist. Communism and fascism are on opposite ends of the ideological continuum—communism is an extreme left-wing ideology, and fascism is an extreme right-wing ideology.[118] The National Socialist or Nazi party of Germany in the 1930s and early 1940s may be the best known fascist state, but fascist governments also arose in Argentina, Spain, Italy, and Japan. Fascist movements and parties tend to be very nationalistic, promilitarist, and violent; they emphasize total obedience to the state and centralized power. Fascist states modify capitalism, subordinating business activity to ensure that it operates to advance national military–political goals. Fascistlike or neofascist movements exist today. In the United States they work with right-wing extremist groups such as the Ku Klux Klan, White Aryan Nation, and Christian Identity. In many countries (e.g., Austria, France, Germany, Great Britain), neofascist parties advocate racist and nationalist-traditional values while opposing immigrants and labor unions.

The totalitarian state shows how a powerful, disciplined political movement or party can take control of the state under conditions of conflict and use state autonomy and control over communication to crush opposing beliefs. It also highlights the importance of the state's systematic use of surveillance and organized violence (e.g., police, military, prisons) to maintain social–political control. (We will examine these topics in Chapter 9.)

The Corporatist State

A corporatist state can be democratic or nondemocratic. The democratic corporatist state is common in continental Western Europe and Scandinavia.[119] Other nations have a degree of corporatism, and countries outside Western Europe have borrowed the corporatist model (especially in Latin America). **Corporatism describes a state–society relationship in which society is divided into pillars or sectors that are recognized by the state.** Major sectors include business, labor, farmers, clergy, and occupational or interest groups (e.g., medical doctors). Civil society is organized into sectors that provide stable, predictable channels of political representation. The corporatist model views society-state as an organic whole, with society divided into sectors that work closely under state supervision to produce stable, negotiated compromises. Corporatist states often have well-regulated union-management relations, high rates of unionization, and high levels of social services. The state encourages sector self-organization and assigns rights and duties to reach. Most citizens belong to a sector organization that provides its members with a formal channel of political representation, benefits, and services (e.g., mutual-aid societies, social services). There are often specialized media and programs by sector. Government agencies address specific sector needs and many state agencies have reserved seats for sector representation. Sector leaders negotiate with one another under state aegis to set public policy. People participate politically in a corporate-sector organization and as individual voting citizens.

Corporatist states tend to be centralized with high levels of capacity. Compared to the liberal-market form (sometimes called Anglo-American), corporatism appears to be very organized and somewhat inflexible. In the liberal-market form, many atomistic individuals and groups rise and fall around issues or interests, forming temporary alliances or coalitions in a free-for-all of open competition, while the state stands apart and is rarely involved. Except for a few regulatory agencies and experiments during the 1920s and 1930s, the United States has avoided corporatism.[120]

The corporatist state arose from specific historical and cultural conditions. It developed out of the feudal estate system and was based on a model of society as having major parts that fit together into an organic whole. It is a compromise among competing groups and sectors of approximately equal strength to avoid violent conflict. The corporatist state highlights patterned divisions in civil society and the state's role in organizing society and the economy.

The Developmental State

Chalmers Johnson (1982) outlined the developmental state, or state-directed capitalism, in a study of post-war Japanese industrialization; others applied it to other states, especially in East Asia.[121] **The developmental state thesis says**

that a high capacity, relatively autonomous state can coordinate and direct private industrial expansion to build an internationally competitive economy. It links a form of state with rapid industrial expansion, a system of business–government relations, and a nation's position in the world economy. Like the corporatist state, a developmental state has a strong, centralized government and state supervised negotiation among major parts of society. The strong executive branch deploys its political authority to plan, direct, and coordinate national human and material resources around vision of the national interest. As Samuels (1994, 4) observed, "ideology and institutions are linked, shaping strategic choices on different conceptions of national interest than are widely accepted in the United States." The national interest has included building a technologically advanced and vibrant national economy that will have international influence.

The developmental state is capitalist, but the state overrides the market mechanism to force private businesses to align with its national goals. Formal (e.g., government directives) and informal (e.g., favorable loans, persuasion) mechanisms pressure private banks and large companies to invest and grow in areas determined by government planning experts. Labor unions are usually weak or government controlled, and political parties may be restricted. The state pressures capitalists and coordinates other institutions (e.g., schooling, mass media, labor unions) and even civil society to work together for the national interest. The development state only rarely uses overt force, direct censorship, or totalitarian measures. Instead, it relies on a nationalist ideology, cultural values, and cooperative institutions. Technocratic leaders convince the population that their personal standard of living, long-term business profitability, and the strength of the nation in the world require that they bend to the state's policy directives.

Many observers attributed Japan's rapid economic success in the 1950s–1970s and the rapid growth of Pacific Asian nations in the 1980s–1990s to the developmental state. Japan's central government bureaucracy, especially the Ministry of International Trade and Industry, directed national economic growth in cooperation with leading industrial firms and banks. State officials drew up plans and decided which industries should grow and which should not, then allocated public funds and loans to specific firms or industries, funded scientific research, enacted favorable business regulation, and promoted cooperation among firms. Compared to the developmental state, the liberal-market state looks weak and chaotic. Instead of government plans and coordinated business growth, each business firm makes its own decisions. Instead of state direction, there is an open, free-for-all competitive environment, with major decisions about investments, bank loans, or research priorities in private capitalist hands. The developmental state thesis suggests incorporating more of a nation's international and historical context into theories of the state. It cautions us against overemphasizing domestic power relations (e.g., interest groups, elites or classes). Lastly, it points out the interdependence of the nation-state form and the pattern of capitalist industrial growth, linking patterns of economic expansion to forms of the state. As Chart 2.7 illustrates, the contemporary nation-state takes several forms.

chart 2.7

FORMS OF THE NATION-STATE

| Feature | Form of Nation-State | | | |
	Liberal-Market	Corporatist	Totalitarian	Developmental
Overall image	Chaotic, free-wheeling, and competitive	An integrated, organic whole with well-coordinated, clearly defined parts	Tightly directed from the top with little freedom	State technocrats direct carefully planned progress toward national goals
Type of civil society	Autonomous, diverse, and decentralized	Comprehensive, organized and directly tied into the state	Very limited and tightly controlled by the state	Organized but subordinate to state goals and plans of technocrats
Citizen rights	Highly developed but contested and changing	Well-developed but tied to membership in a social group	None or almost none	Developed but limited for national goal of economic growth
Strength of state bureaucracy	Limited to Weak	Strong	Strong and centralized	Strong and centralized
Character of political dynamics	Competition among many diverse interests with unequal power and resources	Formal, rule-governed negotiation among recognized sectors	Totally state-directed	Negotiation among diverse interests, but state has great oversight and the final say
State-economy relationship	Limited state involvement; no state planning	State oversees business cooperation and business–worker relations	Complete state control and direction	Target areas are strongly influenced by state planning
Mass media	Free and open; shaped by market forces	Free but organized along social sectors	Censorship and total state control	Free but some limits based on state goals
Number of political parties	Multiple	Multiple often aligned with social sectors	One	Several but with bounded competition
Example country	United States	Germany	Cuba	Japan

CONCLUSION

In this chapter, we examined democracy, citizenship, nationalism, and the nation-state. Democracy is the active participation by people in self-rule, but a full and effective democracy requires many conditions. Democracy's meaning has changed over time and continues to evolve. Participatory and deliberative forms of democracy are closer to the ideal of a system of fair and equal self-rule by everyone. Indirect or representative democracy, polyarchy, and democratic elitism are compromises that depart from the ideal.

Citizenship is the individual's relationship to the nation-state. It is membership in a society, a collection of rights, and particular practices. Citizenship developed historically in tandem with spreading democracy. Following T. H. Marshall, civil, political, and social rights of citizenship expanded sequentially to more of the population. Yet the process was not always peaceful and many sectors of society lacked full citizenship in nations that claimed to be democratic. Citizenship continues to expand globally and appears more complex than T. H. Marshall's model. Citizenship rights arose and spread unevenly, are distributed unequally across society, and may be reversed or rescinded.

Political life across the globe over the past two centuries has been organized based on nation-states. The nation refers to people with a shared identity and a desire for self-rule. The modern idea of a nation appeared in Europe about 300 years ago. Nationalism, a people's deep emotional attachment to being a part of a nation, can be based on ethnicity or a shared culture, or it can be invented by nation-building elites. A people's belief that they constitute a nation is among the most powerful political forces in the contemporary world.

The modern form of the state developed simultaneous with the formation of a system of nations, giving rise to the nation-state. It grew as part of an international system of nation-states. The nation-state arose out of the dissolution of feudal society and its absolutist state, and it ascended with the advance of market capitalism. It appeared in the eighteenth century, matured in the nineteenth century, and diffused around the world in the twentieth century. The modern nation-state takes several forms, including liberal-market, totalitarian, corporatist, and developmental. A great deal of the attention in political sociology is devoted to studying the activities, features, and consequences of the nation-state. We will continue to discuss the nation-state throughout this book.

KEY TERMS

Absolutist State

Citizenship

Civil Citizenship Rights

Civil Society

Corporatism

Cultural Nationalism

Deliberative Democracy

Democracy

Democratic Elitism

Democratic Society

Developmental State Thesis

Economic Nationalism

Formal Citizenship

Globalization

Nation

Nation-State	Political Citizenship Rights	Substantive Citizenship
Nationalism	Polyarchy	Totalitarian State
Participatory Citizenship	Social-Economic Citizenship Rights	Tyranny of the Majority
Participatory Democracy	Sovereignty	
Political Nationalism		

REVIEW QUESTIONS

1. In what three ways do people reach agreement for political decisions, and how are they related to the idea of democracy? Which one is most closely related to the idea of deliberative democracy?

2. What are the major issues or questions one should ask to evaluate the effectiveness or fullness of a democratic process? Why does having numerous candidates running for offices and elections every year not always increase democracy?

3. What are the advantages and disadvantages of term limits for politicians? Does it always increase democracy? Why does "majority rule" not equal democracy?

4. Contrast the theory of democratic elitism with that of participatory democracy. Explain the relationship between the ideas of democratic society and that of participatory citizenship.

5. Explain T. H. Marshall's theory of citizenship and the different types of citizenship rights. What are limitations or criticisms of his theory of citizenship?

6. What does it mean to say that citizenship has been limited by race and gender? How does the way that citizenship expanded over time clarify the limitations?

7. Compare and contrast the modernization and political conflict theories of citizenship and democracy expansion. What is the relationship between the rise of capitalism and the expansion of democracy in each?

8. What does nationalism do? What are the differences between political, economic, and cultural nationalism?

9. What is the relationship between race/ethnicity and nationalism and the idea of a nation? How can nationalism contribute to racist thinking?

10. How did the attempts by feudal elites to protect their rule actually help to bring about the nation-state? What conflicts and processes in feudal society help to create the absolutist state?

11. What is globalization and will it destroy the nation-state?

12. What does it mean to call the state a "cultural construction" or say that it was "invented"?

13. How does the idea of hegemony apply or not apply to the totalitarian state?

14. Contrast the model of society found in countries with a corporatist state with a pluralist model.

15. What is a developmental state? How does it differ from the state in the United States today?

RECOMMENDED READINGS

Anderson, Benedict. 1991. *Imagined Communities: Reflections on the Origin and Spread of Nationalism.* New York: Verso.

Anderson, Perry. 1974. *Lineages of the Absolutist State.* London: New Left Books.

Calhoun, Craig. 1997. *Nationalism.* Minneapolis: University of Minnesota Press.

Gellner, Ernest. 1983. *Nations and Nationalism.* Ithaca, NY: Cornell University Press.

Pateman, Carole. 1970. *Participation and Democratic Theory.* New York: Cambridge University Press.

Rueschemeyer, Dietrich, et. al. 1992. *Capitalist Development and Democracy.* Chicago: University of Chicago Press.

Tilly, Charles, ed. 1996. *Citizenship, Identity and Social History.* New York: Cambridge University Press.

ENDNOTES

1. See Arblaster (1994, 13) and Birch (1993, 45).
2. See Arblaster (1994), Elster (1998), and Markoff (1996, 2–3).
3. From Markoff (1996, 13).
4. See Dahl (1971, 1998) for a discussion of the concept.
5. See Bollen (1991).
6. See Coppedge and Reinicke (1991).
7. Quote is from Dryzek (1996b, 5).
8. See Arblaster (1994, 6) and Dryzek (1996b, 4).
9. See Elster (1998).
10. For discussion of deliberative democracy, see Arblaster (1994, 88–95), Cohen (1988, 1998), and Warren (1996).
11. See Fishkin (1996) and Hibbing and Theiss-Morse (2001). Also see "Democracy in Texas 1998: The Frontier Spirit," *Economist*, May 16, 1998, p. 31.
12. See Arblaster (1994, 45).
13. Strong philosophical arguments for including women go back to Mary Wollstonecraft's (1792) *Vindication of the Rights of Women* and John Stuart Mill's *The Subjection of Women* (1869), but mainstream debates largely ignored such arguments (see Held 1987, 79–87, 97–100).
14. See Camobreco (1998), Papadopoulos (1995), and "How far can you trust the people," *Economist*, August 15, 1998.
15. See Dryzek (1996b, 54–70) for discussion.
16. More on the democratic and civil society can be found in Cohen and Rogers (1992); Dahl (1982); Ferree, Gamson, Gerhards, and Rucht (2002); and Putnam (1993).
17. On the moral right of popular participation, see Arblaster (1994, 61).
18. Democratic elitism in Schumpeter is discussed in Arblaster (1994, 49) and Pateman (1970, 3–5). For other representatives of this position see Dahl (1971), Kornhauser (1959), Lipset (1960).
19. See Pateman (1970) and Birch (1993, 81–88) for a more detailed discussion.
20. See Pateman (1970) on democracy and Giddens (1987, 200) for a discussion of citizenship rights.
21. To read this famous story see Hale (1886).
22. See Nash (2000, 156) on recent interest in citizenship.
23. Quote is from Barbalet (1988, 18).
24. See Tilly 1996b, 9–11. Kashiwazaki (1998a, 1998b), and Nash (2000, 180–182) also discuss citizenship.
25. See Shanahan (1997).
26. See Glenn (2000).
27. Quote is from Barbalet (1988, 2).
28. Quote is from Barbalet (1988, 69).
29. See Marshall (1950) for the lecture. See Heater (1999, 12–25) for an analysis of Marshall.
30. The relationship between class conflict and citizenship is discussed in Barbalet (1988, 34–42), Cohen and Hanagan (1996), Giddens (1982, 166–179), Mann (1988, 188–198), and Turner (1986).
31. See Turner (1986, 97–98).
32. See Barbalet (1988, 9, 22).
33. Somers (1993) and Turner (1993a) discuss practices; Ikegami (1996) and Tilly (1996b) emphasize negotiated relations or transactions.
34. Heater (1999) discussed formal versus substantive citizenship. See Kristof and Wudunn (1994, 95) for an incident.
35. See (Richardson 1998).
36. On gender and citizenship see Fraser and Gordon (1994), Haney (2000), Orloff (1993a, 1993b), Pateman (1989), Pierson (1996, 146–149), Roche (1995), Turner (1986, 18), Walby (1994), and Vogel (1991, 1994).

37. See Kerber (1997).

38. Ann Orloff (1993) provides a strong statement of this point.

39. See Kerber (1997).

40. See Quadagno (1994).

41. See Walters, et al. (1997).

42. See Habermas (1994, 24–28). Also see Kalberg (1993) and Kerber (1997).

43. Hobson and Lindholm (1997) discuss this idea.

44. For discussions of extending citizenship to include workplace and economic decisions beyond traditional ideas of citizenship, sometimes called "industrial citizenship," see Fleurbaey (1993), Janoski (1990), Hanagan (1997), Roche (1987), Rothstein (1992).

45. Hanagan (1997, 398) is quoted source. Heisler (1991) provides additional discussion of citizenship expansion.

46. See Hindess (1993).

47. Quote is from Tilly (1997, 601).

48. Forms of citizenship beyond the nation-state are discussed in Stewart (1995), Roche (1995), Turner (1993a, 1993b), Weale (1991), and Wendt (1994). Heater (1999) describes the concept of multiple citizenship and sees citizenship as a mosaic of rights and duties, not as a unitary concept.

49. For citizenship in the city see Holston and Appadurai (1999) and Solinger (1999).

50. See Falk (1994), Meyer, et al. (1997), Turner (1993b), and van Steenbergen (1994).

51. Quote is from Roche (1995, 726).

52. For discussions of nationalism, democracy, and citizenship development in various nations, see Anderson (1974), Greenfeld (1992), Hall and Ikenberry (1989), Moore (1966), and Rueschemeyer et al. (1992).

53. Quote is from Rueschemeyer, et al. (1992, 5).

54. Quote is from Somers (1993, 611).

55. The modernization approach here draws on works by Almond and Verba (1963), Apter (1965), Cutright (1963), Deutsch (1966), Hagan (1962), Huntington (1991), Inkeles and Smith (1974), Lenski (1966), Lipset (1959b, 1994), McCelland (1961), and Pye (1971). Crenshaw (1995) updates evolutionary modernization theory using "proto-modernity"; that is a preindustrial demographic and institutional heritage of prodemocratic features.

56. See Rostow (1960) for a classic modernization statement on stages of development.

57. The political economy section draws on Bowles and Gintis (1986), Held (1989, 1995), Mann (1988), Markoff (1996), Moore (1966), Therborn (1997), and Tilly (1975, 1996a, 1997).

58. See Ikegami (1996).

59. See Somers (1993).

60. Quote is from Turner (1986, 55).

61. Quote is from Fraser and Gordon (1994, 91).

62. See Dahrendorf (1994), Heisler (1991), Roche (1992), Turner (1986), and Wilson (1994).

63. See Bowles and Gintis (1986), Held (1995, 69–70), Therborn (1997), and Turner (1986).

64. Cohen and Hanagan (1996) provide a discussion.

65. The importance of warfare and military service for the expansion of citizenship is discussed in Barbalet (1988, 37–40), Giddens (1987), Held (1995), Mann (1987, 1988), Therborn (1977, 1997), Tilly (1975, 73), and Turner (1986, 70). The threat of a war can erode existing democratic accomplishments and civil rights, but the actuality of war, when the state must mobilize a whole nation, can expand democracy and citizenship (Dryzek 1996b, 74–76). Defeat in war can spread democracy and citizenship rights.

66. See Arblaster (1994, 14) who says democracy ". . . has never been achieved without a struggle, and that struggle has always been, in good part, a class struggle."

67. See Ikegami (1996), Markoff (1996), Meyer (1999), and Meyer et al. (1997), Ramirez et al. (1997).

68. See Turner (1986, 26) on the role of violent struggle.

69. See Armstrong (1982), Seton-Watson (1977), Greenfeld (1992), Hall (1995), Anthony Smith (1979), and Tilly (1996a).

70. Quote is from Friedman (1996, 166).

71. On religiosity and nation see Greenfeld (1996), Markoff (1996), Tilly (1996a) and Turner (1986, 16–17).

72. This is based on Brevilly (1994, 110), See (1986, 4). Also see Puri (2004).

73. This is from Greenfeld (1992, 4–9).

74. Further arguments of how ethnicity relates to nationhood and nationalism can be found in Barth (1969), See (1986) and Smith (1986). Brass (1994), Calhoun (1993), and Eley and Suny (1996) provide useful reviews and criticisms.

75. See Brown (1994) for discussion.

76. Quote is from Puri (2004, 35).

77. See Shanahan (1997).

78. See Greenfeld (1996).

79. Marx (1998) discusses ideas about racism and national-ethnic identity in nation building.

80. As Balibar (1996, 134) stated, ". . . non-national state apparatuses aiming at quite other (for example, dynastic) objectives have progressively produced the elements of the nation-state . . . they have been involuntarily 'nationalized' and have begun to nationalize society."

81. See Gellner (1987, 9).

82. On the important of warfare and the military, see Michael Mann (1995).

83. See Greenfeld (1992, 14).

84. See Gellner (1983).

85. See Smith (1986, 134)

86. See Albrow (1997), Held et al. (1999), Schaeffer (1997), and Waters (1995) on globalization. Anthony Smith (1990) discusses globalism will supercede nationalism.

87. On Chinese diaspora, see Tu (1994) and Ong and Nonini (1997). The topic of diasporas is discussed in Cohn (1997) and Van Hear (1998).

88. As Brass (1994, 87) states, "whether or not the culture of the group is ancient or is newly-fashioned, the study of ethnicity and nationality is in large part the study of politically induced cultural change . . . the process by which elites and counter-elites within ethnic groups select aspects of the group's culture, attach new meaning and value to them, and use them as symbols to mobilize the group, to defend its interests, and to compete with other groups."

89. Anderson's (1991) famous study of Indonesia, studies of Africa and Britain (Hobsbawm [1983], Ranger [1983]), of Japan (Garon 1997, Gluck 1985, Yoshino 1992), and the United States (Gillis 1994; Wagner-Pacifici and Schwartz 1991; Schwartz 1995b, 1996) document how political leaders created cultural myths, symbols and interpretations of history to unify people. Also see Robinson (1993) on the concept of cultural nationalism.

90. See Wagner-Pacifici and Schwartz (1991).

91. As Duara (1996, 163, 168) stated, "the nation . . . is hardly the realization of an original essence, but a historical configuration which is designed to include certain groups and exclude or marginalize others—often violently . . . the manner in which a nation is created is not the result of a natural process of accumulating cultural commonalities. Rather the process reveals the imposition of a historical narrative of descent and/or dissent. . . ."

92. See Badie and Birnbaum (1983, 65, 68, 79) for discussion.

93. See Giddens (1987, 85–90).

94. Quote is from Hall and Ikenberry (1989, 35).

95. This is discussed in Poggi (1978, 52).

96. On the absolutist state, see Anderson (1974), Giddens (1987, 83–121), Mann (1988, 113–118), and Poggi (1978, 60–85).

97. From Tilly (1975, 15).

98. See Anderson (1974, 40).

99. Badie and Birnbaum (1983, 21, 135–136) provide a discussion.

100. See Howard (1994, 256).

101. See Badie and Birnbaum (1983, 93–94) and Meyer et al. (1997).

102. See Hall and Ikenberry (1989).

103. From Held (1995, 71).

104. See Badie and Birnbaum (1993, 87–89) on the role of religious doctrine in European state formation.

105. From Migdal (1988, 31).

106. See Migdal (1988, 27).

107. See Held (1989, 11–49).

108. See Fraser and Gordon (1994).

109. For a critique of the neoliberal, rational choice position, see Adams (1999).

110. See Peters and Heisler (1983) and Schmidt (1983).

111. See Kohl (1983, 214).

112. See Gould (1983), Nordlinger (1981, 53–56), and Taylor (1983).

113. See Giddens (1987, 267–276).

114. See Badie and Birnbaum (1983, 129) and Nettl (1968).

115. On totalitarianism, see Arendt (1958).

116. For discussion of the relationship between totalitarian and corporatist states, see Zhang (1994).

117. Johnson (1997) argues that contemporary communist China is a "soft" totalitarian state.

118. On fascism, see Laquerur (1976), Neumann (1944), Mosse (1966, 1979), Paxton (1998), and Payne (1980). Also, see Berezin (1991, 1994) for a study of how the arts and culture were controlled under Italian fascism.

119. For more on corporatism see Almond (1983), Birnbaum (1982), Collier and Collier (1979), Cox (1981), Diamat (1981), Hearn (1984), Hicks (1988), Lehmbruch (1979), Maier (1984), Malloy (1977), Martin (1983), Panitch (1979), Schmitter (1974), Shonfield (1965), Williamson (1985), and Winkler (1976).

120. American experiments with corporatism and the low level of American corporatism are discussed in Brand (1983), Cuff (1973), Gitelman (1984), Hawley (1974a, 1974b), Neuman (1988a), and Salisbury (1979).

121. See Amsden (1989), Evans (1995), Samuels (1994), Wade (1990), Waldner (1999), and Woo-Cummings (1991, 1999).

3

THEORETICAL FRAMEWORKS IN POLITICAL SOCIOLOGY

INTRODUCTION

We all carry around a mental picture of how politics operates (i.e., who has power, how they use it, power relations in society). For example, you may say that politics in advanced democracies is about citizens voting to express their desires and competing interest groups seeking input into government. People with different desires—some want lower taxes; others want better roads, cleaner air, and quality day care; while still others seek justice in race relations or prayer in schools—vote and use other political processes (e.g., petition drives, letter-writing campaigns, or marches) to express their desires. In addition, organizations, such as clubs, churches, unions, and corporations, mobilize members, advertise, lobby, or make campaign donations to candidates to advance their interests. The government, or the state, balances out all the competing demands. If this is your mental image of how politics operates, you are using a simplified version of a political sociological theory.

G. William Domhoff (1998) presented an alternative mental image when he asked, Who rules America? More specifically, does America have a ruling class? Some people are uneasy with this question because it contradicts the official picture taught in schools and pronounced by government officials. It suggests that ordinary people have little say about how their nation is ruled, and it implies that voting and democratic processes are fraudulent, while real power lies elsewhere. While few people are naive enough to think that the picture of democracy taught to children works all the time, many people do not accept the idea that a monolithic ruling class operates behind the scenes, pulling all the strings of power. Domhoff is a leading thinker of an alternative theory in political sociology.

The mental images of politics that most people have are loose and fuzzy, and their thinking tends to be incomplete, contradictory, and a bit confused. Political sociologists want to avoid confusion and systematically study politics to build precise, reliable knowledge. To do so, they have developed several coherent, internally consistent theoretical explanations to guide their empirical research and address major questions about politics.

In Chapter 2, we looked at the nation-state, democracy, and citizenship. We now look at how political sociologists use ideas such as power, hegemony, and struggle to explain and analyze political events, relationships, and structures. The many specific theories (e.g., of voting behavior or political influence) that political sociologists test and use in explanations fit into a few major theoretical frameworks. Each framework offers a set of assumptions, key orienting ideas, and a basic model of politics. Political sociologists draw on these frameworks, instead of classical political philosophy, when thinking about politics and identifying variables or factors for hypotheses, explanations, and predictions.[1]

When describing alternative theoretical approaches to issues, political sociologists often discuss competing "theories of the state." This term can be confusing for two reasons. First, the word *theory* has multiple meanings. Sometimes it means a simple hypotheses and narrow explanation about specific events (e.g., Why do more women now vote for the Democratic rather than the Republican Party?). It also can mean a broader set of intergrated ideas and abstract model of relationships (e.g., Society contains numerous, competing interest groups that express citizen desires, but because no one group is overpowering, they are the key to sustaining a democratic form of government.). It also can refer to an entire orientation or large collection of specific theories (e.g., Root economic-material forces are the foundation of social and political life). Second, the theories of the state explain and differ on much more than the state. Each is linked to different comprehensive social theories that contain implicit assumptions and moral or political values; each also provides one or more models of society and politics. Instead of theories of the state, for consistency in this book I will use the terms "framework" for three major orientations that provide basic assumptions and key concepts, "model" for a few major idealized representations of the state and the power workings within each of the three frameworks, and "theory" for the more specific explanations of areas of politics, political processes, events, and so forth. ■

THREE FRAMEWORKS OF POLITICAL SOCIOLOGY

Here you will learn about political sociology's three broad frameworks. The core features of each framework—its basic assumptions, key concepts, and the definitions that shape its understanding of politics—are emphasized to avoid getting embroiled in the heated and ongoing debates that rage within each. Adherents of different frameworks often define and use the same term very differently. This can be confusing and can cause opponents to "talk past" one another. It occurs because the definition conforms to a framework's underlying assumptions about social relations, main values, and beliefs about human nature.

The best strategy for learning about the frameworks is to see that each offers something of value, rather than trying to pick the best or single correct one. The frameworks are in active competition, with leading scholars and many studies behind each. Each tries to offer a complete explanation but tends to be stronger on different levels of analysis (e.g., the individual, organization, or society) or for specific areas of politics.[2] As Robert Alford and Roger Friedland (1985, 3) argued, "each theoretical perspective on the state has a home domain of description and explanation. That is, the meaning of 'state' depends upon whether the vantage point for analysis is individuals, organizations, or societies, and also upon the fundamental assumptions made about the relationships among those levels of analysis."

Do not be surprised if you find some frameworks or models easier to grasp than others. No one begins with a blank slate, devoid of past knowledge. Ideas from the first two frameworks are often used in the mass media. "Public definition of issues by the mass media is almost exclusively based on pluralist or managerial perspectives . . . the taken-for-granted vocabulary and assumptions of underlying political discourse are drawn from either pluralist or managerial perspectives."[3] In contrast, the third framework is less publicized and claims to be "counter hegemonic" (i.e., it contradicts the prevailing outlook of most people and most institutions in contemporary society). As you saw in Chapter 1, hegemony means that certain assumptions, ideas, and ways of thinking are built into how we see and understand the world—they are part of common sense and what everyone knows. So a framework that opposes the prevailing outlook is not only less publicized, but it also may be a bit more difficult to grasp at first.

The frameworks are organized and presented in the following five key questions:

1. What is its general view of society and politics?
2. How does it see the nation-state?

3. How does it define democracy and citizenship?
4. How does it understand power, hegemony, and struggle?
5. What are its most critical questions or issues?

Pluralist Framework: Individuals and a Competing Plurality of Interest Groups

Pluralism (also known as democratic, market, individual, or behavioral theory) is the most well known framework.[4] Up through the classic era, it was widely accepted. Today many political sociologists question it, but it is more accepted in political science. **Pluralism is a framework that understands politics primarily in terms of many competing interest groups, concentrates on the first dimension of power, and views the state as a neutral mechanism that balances and responds to citizen demands.**

A Pluralist View of Society and Politics

The individual and interest groups are core units in pluralist theory. Pluralists see society as comprised of individuals and groups, each with desires, objectives, and resources. Politics is the competition among individuals and groups who use their resources (e.g., votes, public relations, donations, lobbying) to advance their desires or interests. Politicians and bureaucrats in the state respond to and serve the demands expressed by a majority of the people, or sometimes the best organized and most vocal groups. Interest group leaders do not always hold public office themselves but can have political influence by mobilizing followers. For example, in the United States two ministers, Jerry Farwell (of the Moral Majority) and Jesse Jackson (of Operation Push), are recognized national political leaders who never held a political office.

Pluralists recognize inequalities by individual or group characteristics (e.g., income, race, education, cultural belief, region, religion, age, gun ownership, urban/rural residence), but they say that these are not fundamental divisions of society. All three frameworks recognize interest groups, but the pluralists place them at the center of politics and their vision of society.

Interest groups originate in diverse roles and activities that arise from the division of labor, specialization, and differentiation in a complex, industrialized society. Borrowing from the French sociologist Emile Durkheim (1858–1917), a society's division of labor, or its structural specialization, also creates functional interdependence. Modern industrial society fosters many specialized role/activities, and from these arise interests/preferences. Individuals associate with and form groups around shared interests. As society changes and individuals acquire new preferences, the interest groups develop, expand, decline, and disappear. People act politically as individuals and through their voluntary interest groups. For pluralists, the civil society is a major source of the diverse interest groups that shape politics. Individuals vote, make donations, attend rallies, or write letters to politicians both as individuals and as members of various civic organizations, such as a local parent teacher association, church, garden club, chamber of commerce, labor union, environmental organization, or dog owners club. In pluralism, the business of politics is balancing the competing demands made by the many diverse interest groups to forge an outcome for the common good of society as a whole.

A Pluralist View of the Nation-State

Pluralists rarely discuss the state per se but favor terms such as "political system" or "polity."[5] They see the state as a neutral, nonmarket mechanism that stands apart from the rest of society. Its essential functions are to gather and balance the preferences of citizens and interest groups, provide a fair and stable arena for decision-making, and deliver the services and resources desired by the public. By doing this, the state integrates the parts of society. Pluralists also use the modernization approach to explain state development (discussed in Chapter 2). As outlined by Seymour Martin Lipset (1959b), market-based economic development creates a type of political culture and social structure that supports stable democratic politics. Rising education contributes to tolerance and feelings of trust, while economic growth builds a large middle class that helps to civilize and moderate social, economic, and political conflicts.

Pluralists believe that the contemporary democratic state has little autonomy, or independence, from society. This is because public officials face many constraints (e.g., elections, impeachment, court rulings, media criticism) and must follow public opinion and demands expressed by interest groups. State officials may have their own ideas about what is in the public interest, but ultimately they must do what the voters and organized interests in society demand. At best, autonomy of the state means officials are creative leaders, or they are just another interest in a fluid process of pluralism.[6]

A Pluralist View of Democracy and Citizenship

Democracy is a major focus of pluralists. They conceptualize democracy as a process of equal representation that operates within a set of well-recognized, fair procedures and in a context of shared values. The pluralist image of democracy is a collection of rules or a machinelike apparatus that, if properly functioning, prevents rigid bureaucratic control, domination by a small minority, or violent conflicts. Short-term, minor deviations from democratic ideals can occur in real politics, but democracy includes a system of checks and balances to maintain social and political equilibrium. Democratic institutions also prevent demand overload. **Demand overload occurs when each interest group or individual person vigorously participates and expresses a separate interest, and chaos results because the government cannot respond to all the disparate demands**. Institutions of representative democracy contain demand overload with indirect governance that restricts excessive political mobilization and limits overzealous mass participation that could undermine social and political stability. Also, institutions such as political parties channel and manage popular participation. A political party consolidates and organizes a set of interest groups; develops a platform, policies, and programs to express the preferences and demands of the interest groups; and competes in elections to have its supporters occupy government posts. Parties also nurture people who will serve as candidates, provide leadership for running government, act as a "loyal opposition" to criticize the regime in power, and check excessive power. For example, the Democratic and Republican parties in the United States merge specific diverse interests (e.g., young mothers, small business owners, dairy farmers) into grand coalitions. In doing this, they temper political extremism and appeal to the moderate center of society.

For pluralists, citizenship is a collection of civil and political rights. Citizenship incorporates people into formal politics and helps to channel interests, disagreements, and concerns into political institutions where they are peacefully resolved. Citizenship is a cause of democracy, because as citizenship spreads, governance includes popular participation by most people who have clearly defined rights. Citizenship is also a consequence of democracy, because once people exercise basic rights to express themselves democratically, they pressure for a continued expansion of citizenship.

A Pluralist View of Power, Hegemony, and Struggle

Pluralists focus on the first dimension of power (see Chapter 1) and on visible political behaviors, such as voting, lobbying, or military force. For example, a natural resource and parks agency holds public hearings on proposed new rules for hunting. People who favor and oppose the rules speak. After listening to diverse opinions, the agency officials vote on new rules. Pluralists see the public exercising its power through discussion at the hearing, and the agency using its power in the decisions that officials made after the public hearing.

Hegemony is an alien concept for pluralists. Instead, they tend to emphasize value consensus, public opinion, and the public interest. Pluralists assume that most democratic societies have a consensus, or voluntarily agreement, on basic core values. An individual tends to have multiple interests and these counterbalance one another to prevent deep cleavages and polarization. For example, a person may be low income, Catholic, rural, and white. She agrees with other lower-income people on some issues, but she disagrees with non-Catholic, urban, unskilled, low-income people on other issues, and she may share only some ideas with people of different races. For pluralists, values (also called preferences, tastes, or desires) arise naturally out of daily experiences in the economy, family, community, or religion. Such values and interests explain how people vote, why they form or join interest-group organizations, and how they make political choices.

Pluralists believe that individuals can freely form preferences or opinions on public issues, and that public policy in a democracy will reflect the majority's preferences almost all the time. For example, if most people feel that smoking is undesirable in public places, then government officials will enact rules and laws to limit smoking. For pluralists, a major issue to analyze is how the many diverse interests are aggregated into a common, widely accepted public interest. This occurs as representative political institutions gather diverse demands and channel them through a system that spreads the division of power among branches of the government. Thus, the legislative branch responds to shifts in popular opinion, the executive branch tempers popular demands with a need for administrative efficiency and practicality, and the judicial branch protects basic legal rights and upholds formally fair procedures.

Instead of focusing on the struggle, pluralists emphasize stable and orderly competition within established institutions. They see armed struggles or violent conflicts as being abnormal and a threat to social–political stability. They see intense conflict, such as the massive riots in Los Angles in 1992 over the Rodney King jury verdict, or the antiglobalization street battles in Seattle in 1999 and Genoa, Italy in 2001, as being a breakdown of normal politics and social control. Pluralists emphasize the need for governments to ensure social control through procedures (e.g., elections), rules, and self-regulation instead of deception, manipulation, or repression. To pluralists, protest movements indicate a failure of normal politics. Since people can express legitimately their demands and affect government through interest groups and responsive political parties, protest or unrest arise when established democratic political channels have not responded properly or quickly enough. Very rapid social change, rigid and inflexible prejudice, or unusual conditions might prevent democratic mechanisms from responding to interest groups. Under normal conditions, candidates offer choices to voters in the "political marketplace," voters (like consumers) make choices, and government combines voter choices and converts them into policy. In this way, struggle or unrest is unnecessary and people's interests can be addressed through peaceful electoral competition.

What Are the Most Critical Questions for the Pluralist Framework?

1. How do people develop party loyalty? How are party leaders recruited? How do divisions develop in parties and how are they bridged? What are the social bases of party support?
2. Who (what groups) participates by voting? How does public opinion change? Does public policy reflect public opinion?
3. How widespread is political apathy? What causes it? What creates intense extremist political involvement that might threaten democratic politics?
4. Who is tolerant or intolerant? What institutions reinforce tolerance and democratic values?
5. How do people form interest groups? On what basis do interest groups become more or less influential? When and how do they form coalitions or alliances with one another? How do interest groups exercise influence on government agencies?

Managerial Framework: Elite Rule and the State's Organizational Capacity

The origins of the managerial framework (also called elite, institutional, statist, state capacity or state-autonomy rule) can be found with the Italian political thinker Niccolò Machiavelli (1469–1527) and classical elite theorists.[7] They argued that a small elite will inevitably rule.[8] Parry (1969, 34–35) noted, "'classical elitists' held that the existence of a ruling elite was a necessary feature of all societies . . . [and] predict the futility of egalitarian attempts. . . . Elites were not merely features of all hitherto existing societies but of every society that might conceivably exist in the future." The sociologist C. Wright Mills (1916–1962) applied these ideas to the United States in the 1950s.[9] In *The Power Elite* (1956), he questioned the American creed of a pluralist democracy. He argued that an interconnected set of business, military, and political elites ruled America (see Figure 3.1).

The managerial framework contains two more specific models. The oldest and best known is the **elite-managerial model in which society is divided into powerful elites and powerless masses, with the elite in control of politics**. In its weakest form, it overlaps with pluralism and accepts a plurality of many strategic elites, each with relatively equal power. The elites are separate from the vast majority or masses, but competing elites represent diverse interest groups.[10] In its radical form, the model overlaps with a class-analysis framework (to be discussed later in this chapter). It asserts that one rich, powerful elite forms a ruling class that hides its power and controls the government. In its conservative or aristocratic form, the model extols elite rule and argues that rule by a small number of talented, refined leaders with high moral standards is preferred over sharing power with the unstable rabble of ordinary, ill-educated and uncouth people (i.e., the masses).[11]

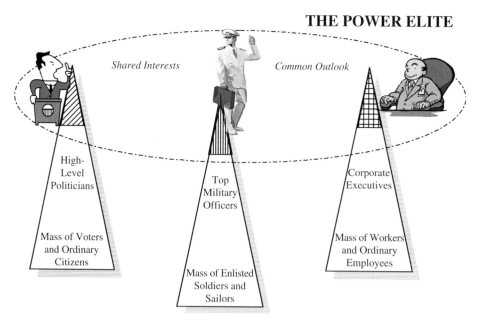

THE POWER ELITE

Shared Interests   *Common Outlook*

High-Level Politicians

Top Military Officers

Corporate Executives

Mass of Voters and Ordinary Citizens

Mass of Enlisted Soldiers and Sailors

Mass of Workers and Ordinary Employees

Figure 3.1
A representation of C. Wright Mills's Power Elite.

The statist-managerial model is an updating of the managerial approach.[12] **A statist-managerial model views the state as an institution with autonomy that develops its own interests** and **is insulated from pressures in the larger society, especially when it has high capacity.** This model focuses more on the structure of the state's organization and less on the individual rulers. In the model, state activities (e.g., providing social services, building bridges, regulating the money supply) depend on bureaucracies that have established procedures, trained employees, and many written laws, policies, and regulations. These institutional factors create powerful constraints and interests that are beyond and separate from what the individuals who serve as officials or rulers may desire.

A Managerial View of Society and Politics

Early thinkers within a managerial framework claimed that elites gained power based on a naturally unequal distribution of talent, a natural desire that people had to dominate/control others, and a natural psychological dependence of weak people on strong leaders. Later thinkers shifted the argument. They said that elite rule was due to a greater efficiency of communication among a small minority and inevitable concentrated decision-making in an organizational hierarchy. The approach builds on the ideas of Max Weber (1864–1920). He saw rationalization as a master historical trend in modern societies. *Rationalization* is applying human reason and careful calculation to more areas of life. In the past, people relied on tradition, folk wisdom, superstition, or religion to make decisions; today they rely on scientific reason, bureaucratic legal processes, and experts who maximize efficiency. For example, rationalization organizes large-scale, complex human activities into bureaucracies that have centralized decision-making, a clear chain of command authority structure, and rule-governed activities. Bureaucracies are pervasive in many areas of contemporary society, including business, government, religion, education, and so forth. They necessarily concentrate power at the top, reduce local control, and lessen lower-level participation in decision-making. In the managerial view, a small cadre of people from the top levels of large bureaucratic organizations are an elite that has great power. Beneath the elites are a huge mass of relatively powerless people. The elites cooperate and work with one another to rule over the masses. Two critical processes in this model are: recruiting new people into the elite, and keeping the elite cohesive or unified.

Recruiting New People into the Elite   A persistent danger is that individuals of the elite will try to perpetuate their power and that of their offspring. A heredity-based elite tends to grow rigid and stagnant. Despite many advantages and superior training for their children, members of the elite cannot continually produce a highly skilled and vibrant next generation of rulers. Of course, some families produce multiple leaders, such as the Bush, Kennedy, or Roosevelt families in America. In addition, the masses may find inherited power offensive in contemporary societies because old hereditary-based legitimacy has been replaced by the ideal of meritocracy (i.e., authority based on a person's merit or skill). To refresh itself, the elite recruits from the masses by selecting and encouraging a few with outstanding talent or achievement to join them in ruling. The process of allowing a few talented people from the masses to join the elite and co-opting them also serves as a safety value that deprives the masses of potential leaders who might challenge elite rule. In short, it both revitalizes the elite with fresh blood and selects the most talented people from the masses. For example, a talent search program sends scouts out among disadvantaged minority youth and offers them scholarships so that a few very bright, hard-working students can attend elite universities. After progressing though exclusive schooling, they join prestigious law, banking, or investment firms, or enter top-level government service. By conforming to elite values and beliefs, they are able to earn large salaries and hold positions of power within the elite. The minority community is deprived of potential rebellious leaders, the elite gains fresh talent, and as added benefit, the elite now has a few token minorities so it looks less closed and exclusive.

Keeping the Elite Unified   The second issue of elite unity has two positions: plural elite and power elite. **A plural elite position holds that each sector of society, such as business, government, mass media, labor, or religion, has its own separate elite, and that the elites are of nearly equal importance and compete with one another.**[13] This draws on Emile Durkheim's theory that a growing population, occupational specialization, and greater diversity creates multiple bases for elites. For example, Lerner, et. al. (1996, 136) studied beliefs of the elites in twelve sectors of U.S. society and concluded, "The image of a unified American elite . . . is of limited relevance today. . . ." The plural elite view rejects the idea from the class-analysis framework (discussed later in this chapter) that power is concentrated in a capitalist class that owns and controls the banks and corporations. While capitalists were important in the nineteenth or early twentieth century, today they have been replaced by highly trained expert managers who have the technical skills needed to run large-scale business bureaucracies.[14] Today's corporate managers rose through the ranks based on their hard work and merit. Unlike the old-style, "robber baron" capitalists of the past, they are more socially responsible. By contrast, **the power elite position holds that there is a tightly interconnected, overlapping single network of elites who have shared interests and rule society.**[15] This view argues that significant elite unity arises from similar socialization, selective recruitment from a narrow sector of society, and a community of interest that develops among top leaders. Members of the elite live in exclusive residential areas; send their children to private schools; intermarry with one another; and intermingle socially in fashionable, private clubs. People in top-level government posts travel in the same social circles as the upper-tier executives of the major banks and corporations; they come to share the same values and see the world in the same way.

Power elite and power structure theorists (discussed later in this chapter) both study the social origins and backgrounds of elites as a means of understanding political power.[16] They argue that a similar social background and shared outlook that arise from occupying top posts in large-scale organizations (i.e., business, government, the military, universities) creates a sense of self-importance that sets members of the elite apart. In simple terms, power corrupts; holding power alters one's values and view of events. As elite members accumulate power, control organizations, and command others, they grow apart from the mass of ordinary people. Perhaps a few are malevolent, greedy, and only seek self-preservation, but many in the elite sincerely believe that they are doing good. Based on their experience and self-confidence, they develop a conviction that they can accomplish more good deeds than others and have a moral responsibility to act on behalf of society. This conviction justifies their desire to hold onto power, rule others, and keep the masses almost powerless.

A Managerial View of the Nation-State

In the managerialist framework, the state is a collection of bureaucratic organizations that perform administrative, taxing, policing, military, and other functions. The state defends national borders, maintains social control, supports economic development, and preserves the national culture. All these duties require significant central coordination and planning. It places the state, especially the executive branch, at the center of power in society. Managerialists tend to embrace the political conflict theory of state development (see Chapter 2).

The two specific models in the managerial framework offer slightly different views on the nation-state. In the elite-managerial model, the state is very important but is basically a neutral tool or instrument used by rulers. In the statist-managerial model, state capacity and state autonomy are critical factors that shape state action.[17] **State capacity is the state's ability to effectively mobilize resources to carry out tasks.**[18] For example, a state with ample financial resources, well-prepared armies, and a highly efficient bureaucracy can better perform tasks than one with few resources; it is a stronger state.[19] State capacity varies over time and by policy area (e.g., economic regulation, policing). A state with little capacity tends to have minimal authority; powerful domestic groups or other nations can easily dominate it. State capacity increases with financial resources and four kinds of nonfinancial resources: (1) policy legacy, (2) professionalized staff, (3) ideological unity, and (4) organizational efficiency (see Summary 3.1).

States vary in capacity. Some states (e.g., France, Germany, Japan) possess more capacity than others, (e.g., Australia, Canada, United States, the United Kingdom). As Linda Weiss (1998, 26) observed, "Britain and the United States are paired as 'weak states' marked by incoherent or fragmented administrative structures. At the other extreme are France and Japan, both classified as 'strong' states for their highly centralized, insulated bureaucracies staffed by a technocratic elite, able to resist and transform private preferences." State capacity shaped how countries industrialized. In low-capacity states, powerful private economic elites controlled the form and direction of industrialization. In high-capacity states, top-level state managers decisively directed the industrialization processes, and private economic elites were secondary (e.g., the East Asian developmental state).[20] State autonomy refers to state independence from external or non-state interests. In the statist-managerial model the state

SUMMARY 3.1   **Nonfinancial Sources of State Capacity**

1. **Policy Legacy. A policy legacy is a body of preexisting law, past policy actions, procedures and rules, or bureaucratic agencies and staff that influence subsequent action**. A state's capacity increases if a body of preexisting laws, rules, and well-developed policies is in place. As Theda Skocpol (1985, 18) argued, administrative rules and processes in operation that can continue with minor or no changes are resources that allow the state to undertake tasks easier and more quickly. A policy legacy can be a resource, but it can also slow shifting to a dramatically different direction and tends to insulate the state from external pressures because it is an infrastructure for ongoing tasks. For example, Gregg Hooks (1990a) discovered that the legacy of bureaucratic structures in the U.S. agriculture policy shaped state action in the 1930s farm crisis. The policy legacy insulated the agricultural agency from the demands of angry farmers and allowed expert officials to create an innovative policy that was consistent with preexisting policies and programs.

2. **Professionalized Staff.** Capacity increases if a state recruits people with the highest quality technical training, extensive social networks, and high social status. For example, in the United States, top graduates from the most prestigious universities rarely seek government jobs but instead join high paying Wall Street firms, while in France, Germany, and Japan, the best and brightest typically seek government jobs.

3. **Ideological Unity.** State capacity increases with ideological unity and decreases when people inside and outside the state adhere to diverse, conflicting value positions. Without unity, the state must devote time, resources, personnel, and energy to negotiation, compromise, or conflict resolution, resulting in delays and low commitment. By contrast, unity of belief created by a national crisis, effective authority structures, a strong state-reinforced ideology, or rigorous and uniform socialization fosters dedication and increases capacity.

4. **Organizational Efficiency.** The state's internal organization affects capacity. A state with many small agencies that have overlapping jurisdictions, vague mandates, and conflicting objectives will have less capacity than one with well-organized, coordinated agencies that have clear, consistent, and coherent goals and lines of authority. Capacity grows when state administration is efficient with smooth-operating agencies, excellent channels of communication, little corruption, and abundant resources (e.g., the latest technology, large budgets, extra personnel).

is an institution with autonomy that develops its own interests and is insulated from pressures in the larger society, especially when it has high capacity.

A Managerial View of Democracy and Citizenship

In the managerialist framework, democracy is seen less as a mechanism that facilitates popular participation in governance than as an elite strategy for winning mass acceptance and holding onto power. For the elite-managerial model, a strong, "real" democracy is impractical and inefficient for running a complex, advanced society. Elites only extended citizenship and democratic process to gain control over a nation's resources (e.g., the military, tax revenues) and to defuse mass rebellion. In late feudalism and early capitalism, new economic elites expanded citizenship to sections of the masses as a way to strengthen their position against the old aristocracy. Since popular participation by uninformed, nonexpert masses would be hazardous to national defense, economic growth, and social stability, elites promoted formal not substantive citizenship. They touted the rhetoric but not the reality of democracy, and initiated government programs. For example, the conservative German Chancellor Otto von Bismarck (1815–1898) offered limited citizenship rights in a conscious attempt to preempt and quiet more radical demands by workers (see Chapter 11).

In the statist-managerial model, citizenship expanded as part of growing state institutional power and capacity. As political leaders building a nation-state acquired control over more people and territory, they formulated a national interest that went beyond the immediate demands expressed by traditional elites or by the masses through electoral processes. They needed to operate in an international arena and "stand at the intersections between domestic sociopolitical orders and the transnational relations within which they must maneuver for survival and advantage in relation to other states."[21] The leaders created a national interest of the state that was separate from, or sometimes even opposed to, what specific domestic groups demanded. Stephen Krasner (1978, 35) described the process.

> A statist approach must begin by defining the goals sought by central decision
> makers. These can be called the national interest. . . . If their preferences meet two
> basic criteria, they can be called the national interest. First, the actions of leaders
> must be related to general objectives, not the preferences or needs of any particular
> group or class, or to the private power drives of officeholders. Second, the
> ordering of preference must persist over time.

A Managerial View of Power, Hegemony, and Struggle

The managerial framework focuses on the second dimension of power (see Chapter 1). It locates power in organizational authority, communication, and technical expertise. This places real decision-making "behind the scenes" of formal democratic processes. For example, political sociologists operating within this framework asked whether new telecommunication technologies of the 1990s altered the balance of power among elites or intensified elite competition. A study found that the rise of a new area of administration and expertise—financial departments with budget, accounting, and expenditure controls—shifted power within corporations to the financial managers.[22]

In the managerial framework, attention is on both interelite and elite-mass struggles. Interelite struggle develops out of competition within the elite community, among elites inside and outside of the state. For example, leaders of a major business organization (e.g., National Association of Manufacturers) many disagree with other business elites (e.g., the Business Roundtable or the U.S. Chamber of Commerce) over trade policy, or elites in different parts of the state, such as the Departments of Education and Defense, may conflict with one another. Elite-mass struggle grows from the division between the elite and the masses. Elites often divide, confuse, and manipulate the masses to prevent the masses from directly challenging their rule. On occasion, the masses, or sections of it, rise up to challenge the elites, in demonstrations, riots, or protests. The two types of struggle can overlap. One elite faction might activate a section of the masses to oppose other elites. Competing elites may also use political parties and elections to stimulate mass interest and gain power relative to other elites.

The classic elite theorist, Vilfredo Pareto, observed that elites can rarely hold onto power for long periods, so there is a **circulation of elites in which, over time, various conditions trigger the rise or fall of different social groups into elite positions.** The basic structure of the elite at the top and the masses at the bottom remains; only the occupants of the elite or the mass positions change. Conditions that can trigger a circulation of elites include changes in climate, shifts in technology, new ideas, or differences in the willingness to use force. In addition, over time, members of the elite tend to grow soft, or lose their aggressive, ruthless desire to dominate and advance. They become rentiers who live off their past glory or investments. As they become soft, more aggressive and ambitious people rise up to replace them. This involves the tendency for members of the elite to promote their own children. By the second or third generation, the offspring often lack the necessary talent, aggressiveness, and motivation, so they fall from power and are replaced.

Instead of hegemony, managerialists tend to focus on how the elite manipulate beliefs and ideas. Classical elite theorists emphasized how elites used irrational, emotional, symbolic, or ideological aspects of life for continued rule. For example, Robert Mosca (1939) noted that elites need a **political formula that is a myth they create and disseminate to justify their rule.** It is based on religion, stories of national honor, racial ideology (e.g., the Nazi's idea of Aryan superiority), and so forth. Pareto offered a similar idea of *residues*, which are deeply held beliefs (e.g., justice, freedom, progress) that elites manipulate to control the masses. Where the pluralists see a societywide consensus, the managerialists instead, see pressure on the masses to conform while elites control information, public relations, advertising campaigns, and the mass media. In the elite-managerial model, the emphasis is on the manipulation of mass opinion. By contrast the statist-managerial model recognizes that state managers are themselves influenced by ideology, so autonomous state actions may not be based on rational considerations alone.[23]

What Are the Most Critical Questions for the Managerial Framework?

1. What are sources of state capacity? How does state capacity affect the ability of elites, both inside and outside the state, to realize their desires? How does the state's institutional form and legacy of past policy or conflicts, continue to constrain the actions of state managers?
2. How autonomous or independent are state managers from outside interests? What causes autonomy to vary over time and by agency?
3. How do elites use cultural symbols and the mass media to shape or manipulate public opinion?

4. What are the major elite divisions? How does the elite maintain rule in the face of internal and external threats? How politically organized are elites? How are people recruited into the elite?

Class-Analysis Framework: A Capitalist Mode of Production and the Ruling Class

As in the managerial framework, political sociologists who use a class-analysis framework question the reality of democracy and believe that a small, powerful group of people truly rules in advanced industrial nations. This framework borrows ideas from Karl Marx (1818–1883), but studying Marx's writing is of limited help because he wrote little directly on the state. Plus, conditions have changed over the past 150 years since he wrote. This framework contains three specific models. One is similar to the elite model, one is similar to the statist model, and the last one emphasizes the idea of struggle.

A Class-Analysis View of Society and Politics

Recall that pluralists focus on the individual or group levels, and managerialists focus on the organizational or institutional levels. In the class-analysis framework, the focus is more on society as a whole. This macro-level orientation influences the framework's views on society and politics. Adherents of the class-analysis framework note that contemporary advanced societies are fundamentally capitalist, and they are organized on the basis of a capitalist mode of production. A *mode of production* is a key concept. It is more than just the economy; it is the overriding, master organizing system of a society. It summarizes how people and organizations produce and exchange goods and services. It historically evolves through stages and may last for a century or longer. As Marx summarized in *A Contribution to the Critique of Political Economy* ([1869] 1970, 20–21), "The mode of production in material life determines the general character of the social, political, and spiritual processes of life."

The mode of production has two main, interdependent parts: the forces of production and the relations of production. The forces of production are how things (e.g., food, televisions, clothing, accounting services) get made or produced, including technology (e.g., factories, fast food restaurants, computers, tractors). The relations of production are the relationships that people have with one another socially, including how work fits into people's lives (e.g., overwork, child care, gender relations), and at the workplace (e.g., relations with owners and coworkers; levels of training, hierarchy, and authority). Both the forces and relations of production profoundly shape social and political relationships (e.g., law, religion, media, family).[24] In this way, the capitalist mode of production generates the fundamental structure of a society and determines its basic contours, sets its main direction, and holds it together. The mode of production is like a steel framework that is buried inside a large building.

The basic laws of the capitalist mode of production include the primacy of private property ownership, a right to earn and keep profits, paying for labor with money wages (versus slavery), and the market determination of prices and distribution (i.e., supply and demand). These laws reinforce and nurture particular types of social relations and cultural values (e.g., individualism, pursuit of self-interest, acquisitiveness). The capitalist mode of production also divides the people into a few major social classes, which makes social class society's most fundamental division.

In the class-analysis framework, the various areas of a society (e.g., religion, mass media, business, labor, education) are not equally important. Earning a living and producing goods and services outweighs all the other areas. For example, the investors and executives who run major U.S. corporations make decisions that influence more people and control more wealth than many of the world's nations even have. Their position is qualitatively different from other types of elites (e.g., university presidents, church leaders, newspaper editors). A person's social class is based on his/her relationship to the means of production. Note that this differs from popular and mass media presentations of class (e.g., ownership of consumer goods such as houses or cars, taste and speech pattern, social reputation) and from some social stratification research (e.g., individual characteristics such as income, education level, occupational status). In a class-analysis framework, a person's consumption, lifestyle, or subjective awareness are not her/his social class, they are a result of social class. Moreover, a person can be unaware of, or outright wrong about, his/her true, objective social class position.

A capitalist mode of production generates two basic types of available positions—the capitalist and the worker—and these are the basis of social classes. A person's class position profoundly shapes most aspects of her/his life. While most people focus on their daily concerns and believe they have great freedom, in reality, their choices and life chances are largely shaped by their class position. Few people fully recognize the enormous impact and source of such economic forces. Instead, they tend to accept the economic forces as being natural, inevitable, or unchangeable. Since they cannot imagine alternatives, they mistake the laws of a capitalist mode of production for the laws of nature. This explains why few people seriously question capitalism.

In addition to the two basic classes, a class-analysis framework recognizes other minor classes in capitalist societies. The two main classes contain internal factions or segments. The historical stage of development of a mode of production and specific historical and cultural factors determine the specific mix of classes in a society. The capitalist class (i.e., large investors, owners of medium and large businesses, top executives) is a tiny percentage of the population, usually 1–2 percent. Its members own and control the means of production (i.e., most businesses, real estate, stock and bond investments). Their position in the mode of production provides them with great wealth and economic power.[25] Members of this class control and direct the major profit-generating organizations (i.e., large corporations, financial firms).[26] The capitalist class is divided by size of firm, sector (e.g., manufacturing, banking), source of profits (e.g., speculative investing, retail sales) and other factors (e.g., international versus local orientation).

Most people (50–80 percent of the population) hold positions in the working class. They sell their labor power (i.e., time, sweat, skills, ideas, work effort) to capitalists or serve as helpers or assistants to the capitalists (i.e., managers, supervisors). In the early stages of capitalism, most workers were unskilled or semiskilled. They held manual labor or blue-collar jobs. In advanced stages of capitalism, most workers hold service sector jobs (e.g., retail clerks, secretaries, janitors, engineers, computer programmers). Factors such as skill level, formal schooling, work conditions (e.g., office worker versus truck driver), and nonclass factors (e.g., gender, race, age) divide the working class. In wealthy nations, many people confuse their lifestyle and consumer spending with their social class, and they fail to recognize their true class position. As Alford and Friedland (1985, 283) remarked, "members of the working class tend to see themselves in the cultural categories produced by capitalism: as individual workers and citizens." Classes other than capitalists and workers include the "lumpen proletariat" (i.e., an impoverished lower or underclass of the unemployed, homeless, welfare dependents, prostitutes, criminals, etc.), the "petite bourgeoisie" (i.e., small-scale family farmers, self-employed small business owners), state workers (e.g., civil servants, public employees), and the supervisory-managerial sector that helps capitalists.[27]

In the class-analysis framework, politics is primarily about struggles among classes or parts of classes over the operation of capitalism. Class politics is the heart of all politics. Divisions within a class, such as the racial or religious divisions within the working class, often distract people from recognizing society's true, central class divisions.

A Class-Analysis View of the Nation-State

In the class-analysis framework, the primary role of state is to protect capitalism and uphold and advance the power of the capitalist class. The state does this by defending capitalist economic relations and suppressing or disorganizing those who resist or oppose capitalism. The state's basic form evolved simultaneous with the rise of capitalism, and the nation-state and capitalism are mutually interdependent. For this reason, political sociologists who use a class-analysis framework call it the "capitalist state." Under capitalism, the state is formally separate from the private, market economy. It has the legal and political authority to perform functions that private businesses cannot perform but that the market's operation requires. For example, the state provides police and courts, prints money and oversees banking, and defends a nation's territory.

The issue of **state autonomy, or state independence from external or nonstate interests**, is hotly debated in the class-analysis framework.[28] A key idea is the **relative autonomy of the state, where the state has limited room to maneuver, but it cannot violate the basic tenets of capitalism or oppose the long-term interests of the capitalist class.** Depending on the political organization and activism of social classes and geopolitical conditions, state managers are semi-insulated from immediate capitalist pressures. As Fred Block (1987, 87) noted, "There are . . . certain historical periods in which the capitalist context changes, allowing state managers more freedom of action in relation to capitalists. In the twentieth century, [there have included] periods of war, depression, and postwar reconstruction. . . ." There are three bases for state autonomy (see Summary 3.2)

Political sociologists who apply a class-analysis framework use three more specific models of it: power structure, structuralism, and class struggle. All three

| SUMMARY 3.2 | Three Sources of the Capitalist State's Relative Autonomy |

1. **Structural Dependence. The structural dependence thesis says that the state depends on a healthy private economy for its resources** (Swank 1992). Under capitalism, income growth, price stability, and employment depend on capitalists investing their money or private capital. Capitalists and businesses invest because they expect future profits. When capitalists expect high and stable profits (i.e., a good return on their investments), they invest in productive activities that provide goods and services, keeping the entire market economy growing. Positive economic performance provides political leaders with popular approval and helps them win reelection. The state, as an institution, also gets its revenue from the private economy via taxes. If the private economy has serious problems, or if the state threatens to confiscate their property, capitalists will stop investing and try to hide, store (i.e., in gold), or move their wealth (i.e., money capital) to other nations. This "capital strike" is rational from an individual perspective, but a mass refusal to invest will bring down the entire economy. As tax revenue drops and unemployment rises, the state will be unable to perform (e.g., build roads, pay state employees, buy tanks) and voters will become unhappy. Thus, state managers must protect and help capitalism to thrive, whether or not they personally favor capitalism.

2. **Illusion of Neutrality.** The state's separation from the private economy fosters an illusion that the state operates in the general public interest, or for all in the entire society, and that it is not directly under capitalist class control. Capitalists gain their wealth in private markets through market exchanges of buying and selling and through negotiating wages and working conditions in labor markets. Thus, class

oppression, or economic exploitation, occurs in the private market sphere. The state is outside the market relationships where exploitation takes place and does not directly exploit workers. Yet it indirectly permits, supports, and reinforces private exploitation. Separation from the private market veils the exploitation, allowing the state to appear to protect all citizens. The illusion of a neutral state promotes social–political stability. If people saw that the state was directly exploiting them, it would politicize the conflict between classes and the mass of working people would distrust the state and act against it. For example, in areas with a "company town," where the state and private economy are fused together, political radicalism, violent outbursts, and unrest are frequent.

3. **Steering Mechanism. The state has a unique position in society; it distills and advances general capitalist class interests and stands apart from the narrow, short-term, conflicting, and incomplete interests that individual capitalists express.** In capitalism, the state and the private economy are formally separate. Capitalist market relations require a legal system and other structures with rules that are semi-independent from private economic power. This also helps the state look after the interests of capitalism as an entire system and fend off anticapitalist threats (Offe 1974). The class analysis framework calls the state the "executive committee of the capitalist class." This means that the state distills and advances general class interests, standing above narrow, short-term capitalist views. Particular capitalists complain loudly about big government and antibusiness acts, but in reality, the state tends to advance the long-term interests of the capitalist class as a whole.

models assume the primacy of the capitalist mode of production, accept the centrality of class in society, and see the state as upholding capitalism. They differ regarding exactly how the state supports capitalism.

Power-Structure Model

The power structure model (also called an instrumental, plain Marxist, or ruling class model) focuses on the organization and political actions of capitalist class members.[29] In this model the state is an instrument or tool used by self-aware, cohesive, and socially interacting capitalists. This model is similar to the managerialist position and agrees that a powerful economic elite rules society, but it differs in two critical points. First, the model holds that a ruling class is far more than the elite. A ruling class is a socially interacting and self-conscious collective whose members share a common relationship to the means of production and whose wealth, position, and power depend on continuing a system that exploits workers. Second, the model holds that despite intraclass divisions, capitalists agree that their survival as a class is crucial; they will unite to defend ferociously their common class interest in the capitalist system if it is challenged. Political sociologists have conducted many studies that documented aspects of this model in the United States, including the following:[30]

- A large percentage of top government officials have come from capitalist class social backgrounds.
- Large investors and top corporate executives have great influence over national policy decisions.
- Capitalist organizations provide informal contacts and advice that shape most major public policies.
- There is an inner circle of the most politically active groups among the top corporate leaders.

The inner circle is a subset of capitalists in a network of interlocking positions among top corporate and bank boards of directors who (1) occupy positions on several different boards of directors, (2) have a family background in or marry into old upper-class wealth, and (3) interact socially with one another.[31] Power structure researchers documented support for the corporate liberal thesis in U.S. history. **The corporate liberal thesis states that a group of farsighted, class-conscious capitalists became politically organized and had a direct, active role in introducing liberal reforms during periods of social–political crisis.** The corporate capitalists advocated liberal reforms (e.g., antitrust regulation, Social Security), to save capitalism.[32]

In the power-structure model, capitalists directly enter government service and take charge of, or colonize, areas of the state. Political sociologists who embrace this model recognize that the, "colonization of certain key positions is merely one weapon, albeit an important one, in the arsenal of ruling-class domination."[33] Beyond occupying top posts, capitalists use an array of lobbyists, policy advisory boards, think tanks, and private advisory organizations to influence government (see Closer Look 3.1).[34] We will examine such influence in greater depth in later chapters.

CLOSER LOOK 3.1   **The Power-Structure Model and American Politics**

Intraclass organization or class-wide cohesion is a major issue for political sociologists who adopt the power-structure model. For example, in a study of political action campaign contributions from large U.S. corporations to candidates for Congress in 1980, Alan Neustalt and Dan Clawson (1988) found little support for pluralism. Instead, the authors found that large businesses worked together for classwide political cooperation. They (1988, 186) concluded that "corporations were able to transcend their short-term interests [and] this class conscious activity rests on more than ideology; shared material interests and a set of formal and informal organizations *enforce and coerce* behavior in the interests of the class as a whole" (emphasis in original). Another study of American corporate

contributions to political parties by Val Burris (1987) compared various divisions in the capitalist class's political organization. He found that despite general unity, capitalists also organized around specific regulatory agencies (e.g., polluting industries act together) and around regional interests (Northeast Yankees versus Sunbelt Cowboys). In a third study, Patrick Akard (1992, 611) examined political lobbying around specific laws and found that from the late 1970s to early 1980s, the business community was politically united and ". . . a relatively unified business lobby was successful in turning back major legislative initiatives by labor and liberal interest groups. . . ." These three studies illustrate how power structure theorists conduct research into contemporary American politics.

Structuralist Model

The structural model (also called the Marxist functionalist model) emphasizes that the state is first and foremost a capitalist state with a primary function of steering and protecting capitalism.[35] The state is not a neutral tool or instrument that one class can control. Control is not up to individual people; it is built in as structural dependence and as a steering mechanism (see Summary 3.2). One of the characteristics of capitalism is that it is an unstable economic system that has periodic crises or periods of rapid growth followed by economic recessions or even traumatic depressions. Capitalism, as a system, needs an independent state to manage it. Likewise, capitalism is fundamentally an economic system of exploitation and inequality; it needs external forces to maintain social peace and cohesion. The state, due to its structural position in society must protect capitalism, whether or not individual capitalists occupy key positions in the organizational apparatus of the state.[36] State managers have no alternative but to support capitalism. Capitalists themselves do not have to join the government to protect capitalism. In fact, individual capitalists are often too narrowly focused, selfish, and shortsighted to make decisions that would be best for the long-term health of the entire capitalist system.

According to the structuralist model, the capitalist mode of production is comprised of a set of mutually reinforcing economic, political, and ideological structures. The economic structure is the source of production (i.e., goods and services), employment, profits and wealth accumulation, and flow of income. The political structure includes the coercive, organizational, and symbolic-ideological parts of the state. It maintains national borders, oversees the economy, imposes social control, and defuses disruptive domestic conflict. The ideological structure maintains general social hegemony. It extends beyond the state to include religion, family and gender relations, the culture industry (e.g., art and music, schooling, mass media), and the legal system. At each historical stage of capitalism, the mode of production requires a slightly different set of interlocking structures for its vitality. A specific form of structure interdependence at a given stage creates a "social structure of accumulation" that supports the patterns of social relations, urban growth, production, finance and international trade, popular beliefs and ideology, public policies, and state institutions. Early in the twenty-first century, the capitalist mode of production was in the monopoly-financial stage. The structures of this stage differ somewhat from earlier stages (e.g., the financial-investment sector is more central, global transportation and communication advances increased international independence, systems of social control are more sophisticated, and so forth).

The structuralist model also emphasizes the internal contradictions of capitalism. A contradiction means that the same activities that are central to capitalism's continuation produce consequences or conditions that, over time, will oppose or go against those very activities. One such contradiction arises in the state-economy relationship. The state operates to keep capitalism running and to protect the capitalist class, but to do this, the state must constrain the freedoms of specific capitalists. Fred Block (1977b, 358), noted, "The corporations depend on the regulatory agencies to stabilize the business environment, but dependence makes the corporations potentially vulnerable to undesired interference." As capitalism becomes increasingly complex and less stable, the state's role in managing capitalism also expands and becomes more complicated. The state increasingly must develop actions to stabilize and protect capitalism, but this causes the state to grow larger and become more powerful. Yet a larger, more powerful state absorbs more resources and becomes a drag on capitalist economic growth. At the same time, capitalists oppose a larger and more powerful state because they resent a large, powerful, nonmarket force in society that is outside their direct control. So, the very forces that stimulate a larger, more powerful state (i.e., managing the economy and protecting capitalists) are the same ones that will try to limit it.

The capitalist state has two functions: to promote capital accumulation and to legitimate the system of capitalism. For example, the state imposes business regulations to guide and stabilize business activity in ways that will encourage capitalist accumulation (i.e., economic growth). As Bob Jessop (1982, 80) noted, "state intervention is not just a secondary activity aimed at modifying the effects of a self-sufficient market, but is absolutely essential to sustain the operation of capitalist production and market relations." The state also redistributes some wealth through programs such as Social Security or welfare, and it provides public schooling. These maintain a peaceful, productive working class. Over time, capitalism stimulates advances in technology and production that make job skills obsolete and result in people being unemployed, it encourages improved sanitation and health that results in retired people living longer, and it requires more years of schooling that remove people from contributing to a productive economy. All these factors affect the level of public spending and mean that the state must extract resources (e.g., taxes, people) from the society, making them no longer available to the private economy. As a result, spending by the state, as a percentage of the entire economy, tends to grow over time and compete with private, profitable investments. State social spending then slows economic growth and lowers profits, triggering a "fiscal crisis of the state."[37] An added problem is that state managers do not always know exactly what capitalism really needs in the long run. They can make mistakes. So even as they try to uphold capitalism, with imperfect knowledge and limited power, state officials might unintentionally pursue policies that weaken or undermine capitalism.

Class-Struggle Model

The class-struggle model (also called the power resource mobilization model) holds that capitalists are not all-powerful and that the state does not always automatically advance capitalism.[38] Instead, struggles over power shape the state's form and actions in specific sociohistorical settings. Usually the capitalists win and most of the state actions advance capitalism, but this is not inevitable. A crucial variable is the balance of power in particular situations. The state develops structural selectivity as it manages the economic and social crises of capitalism. **Structural selectivity means that state agencies create coherent policies or programs based on rationality, law, and science that are more than simply reflections of immediate political pressures in society.**[39] The state usually selects procapitalist growth principles and avoids harmful or anticapitalist ideas or actions, but imperfect knowledge can produce actions inimical to capitalism. Yet there is uncertainty and flexibility. In addition, the noncapitalist classes and various fractions of classes are always trying to influence specific state actions (e.g., laws, tax policies, social programs). This means that specific state actions can be victories or losses for the various classes or class fractions. For example, a policy on gasoline supply and pricing must balance two fractions of capitalists, transportation, and the oil industry. The long-term best interest for capitalism as an entire system is not clear, and each class fraction will try to get a policy favoring its specific interests. This makes the state an arena of class struggle and an object over which classes or class fractions struggle.

As the various classes and class fractions struggle for control over state actions (e.g., laws, policies, and programs), some are successful. They penetrate and colonize (i.e., occupy and gain direct control over) specific policy areas (e.g., agencies, bureaus), while others lose out. In this way, conflicts within the state (e.g., between different branches or agencies) can become a form of class struggle. For example, the Departments of Energy and Transportation fight for jurisdiction over a new fuel program. One will lose and may be reduced in size or influence. Intragovernment conflicts often express struggles among various fractions of social classes.

In developing an explanation, political sociologists who use the class-struggle model take into consideration several factors—the degree of organization of capitalists and workers, the ideas and beliefs of various classes, alliances formed among classes or quasi-class groups, and specific outcomes of conflicts. In certain periods or under specific conditions, individual capitalists may move into top state positions, but in other periods or under different conditions, this may not occur. In some periods or places, workers may join into an alliance with other classes (e.g., farmers) to gain power and push the state in a noncapitalist direction. For example, the working class of Western European nations organized into political parties and won in elections, they shortened the work week, lengthened paid vacation time for everyone, and expanded social welfare programs (e.g., day care, public pensions, subsidized housing, education, health care, unemployment benefits, parks and recreation).[40] Such programs redistributed wealth away from capitalists and toward workers; it slowed the growth of, but did not entirely destroy, capitalism. By contrast, when class-conscious capitalists and their allies formed or led political parties and gained electoral power, they pursued policies to weaken the working class (i.e., enacted antiunion laws, imposed mandatory overtime rules, cut the minimum wage). They redistributed wealth toward their own class (i.e., reduced taxes on capital gains and high incomes, eliminated inheritance tax, cut social spending, reduced unemployment benefits), and increased repressive social control over workers (e.g., more police and prisons). In other words, the class-struggle model sees conflicts between social classes taking a wide range of forms, but the outcome of the conflicts are not always known and depend on specific conditions. Moreover, winning or losing one conflict at one time and place can alter conditions and have implications for the shape and outcome of future struggles.

A Class-Analysis View of Democracy and Citizenship

In the class-analysis framework, democracy and citizenship are seen as concessions that workers and their allies won through struggles. Democratic politics and citizenship expansion can have contradictory effects. On the one hand, they reduce the intensity of class conflict by channeling discontent into electoral or bureaucratic forms and by spreading ideas about acting as separate individuals rather than as a united class. On the other hand, workers have used democratic processes and citizenship rights to expand their rights, to organize politically, and to improve their living conditions.

As workers use political democracy to improve their living and working conditions, they run up against the limitations of capitalism. Citizenship rights can be expanded, especially compared to what was possible in feudalism, but only within the confines of capitalist principles. If ordinary people demand government actions that seriously harm profits or slow economic growth (e.g., costly public services, very generous pensions and early retirement), they fail. This shows that politics cannot be fully democratic under capitalism; a capitalist democracy is always a limited democracy. A capitalist democracy provides capitalists with opportunities and avenues to influence politics that are not open to people in other classes; it limits attacks on capitalism and blocks truly radical alternatives. The laws and beliefs of a capitalist democracy treat people as separate, isolated individuals not members of classes, and it discourages the formation of massive class-based political movements with anticapitalist demands. Lastly, a capitalist democracy encourages divisions among people on cultural issues (e.g., abortion, drugs, racial differences) instead of along class lines, and few of these nonclass divisions directly threaten capitalism.

A Class-Analysis View of Power, Hegemony, and Struggle

The class-analysis framework embraces all three dimensions of power. The power structure and class struggle models focus more on the first two dimensions but recognize the third dimension of power. A critical factor for gaining political power is to mobilize people as classes, or to get them to act as a class. In this sense, the rhetoric of democracy works as a smokescreen that hides true class power. Repression and overt social control (i.e., police, private security forces, military) are essential to maintaining and protecting the capitalist system.

Recall that the third dimension of power means that power is evident more as a pattern of consequences than as overt intentions by those who perpetuate it. For example, the U.S. tax code rewards behavior that conforms to running a for-profit private business. You can get a reduction in taxes (i.e., tax deductions) for a home office if you operate a for-profit business at home, when you drive a car for specific business purposes, or when you pay someone to photocopy for your profit-producing business. You cannot legally take tax deductions for devoting a room to your hobby, daily commuting to a job, or paying someone to photocopy letters to your friends and family. Thus, the tax code offers a reward if you organize your personal life around for-profit business activities but not for enjoying your hobbies and spending time with family and friends. In this way, the tax law contains third-dimensional procapitalist power by providing you with systematic benefits for capitalist behaviors and imposing costs (i.e., you may owe more in taxes) if you do not. This kind of hegemonic power encourages an individualistic, self-interested orientation in one's personal relationships. Likewise, this form of power is pervasive in a highly commercialized culture. Commercials on television, billboards across the landscape, and T-shirts and hats with corporate logos, promote the messages that "you are what you buy" (or drink or drive), "everything is for sale," "being rich is glorious," become "cool and popular" just by wearing clothing that advertises a company's logo, and "profits are supreme." Most people accept such commercialism and see it as a normal, natural part of daily life. Alternative ways of organizing your life or creating a self-identity become almost inconceivable or feel alien.

While pluralists concentrate on public opinion, and managerialists examine how elites manipulate symbols to mislead the masses, political sociologists who use the class-analysis framework tend to focus on hegemony. They see capitalism as shaping daily living patterns and modifying people's consciousness in ways that expand acceptance of the dominant class's power. Beliefs and values that reinforce capitalism are embedded in consciousness during early childhood socialization (e.g., competition, obedience to authority), in daily workplace patterns (e.g., individual achievement, profit motive), and in the activities of everyday life (e.g., consumerism). A procapitalist outlook is infused throughout the larger culture. It is institutionalized in the hierarchies of status, honor, and morality.

Class-analysis theorists use hegemony when they analyze isolated, self-destructive behavior that is labeled as individual deviance. They note that working class and lower class people who become frustrated and enraged based on their class situation but who feel fragmented, disorganized, and without political awareness, do not join together politically to struggle as a class. Instead, they engage in violent or destructive behaviors. The state controls and represses many such behaviors, treating them as individual actions of crime, and thus masks its true character based in social class.[41]

In the class-analysis framework, struggles among classes are viewed as normal and unavoidable; they are a built-in feature of social relations and the motor of significant societal change. Nonetheless, struggles around issues of class may be distorted, suppressed, or hidden by ideologies or repression. Even if they are not manifested, deep-seated class antagonisms do not disappear; they only get rechanneled into other forms (e.g., vandalism, road rage) or self-destructive behavior (e.g., excessive drinking, addictive drug use, suicide).

Theorists who synthesized the statist and class-struggle models argue that state capacity and class struggle combine to produce state actions with specific combinations of capacity and struggle yielding different state actions.[42] This makes the context in which class struggle occurs critical. State action can itself affect the ability of social classes to mobilize and engage in struggle.[43] For example, a politically active capitalist class under conditions of weak state capacity produces short-term programs to benefit specific capitalists but not to help capitalism as a whole. One study found that policies to provide private businesses with funds to stimulate economic growth occurred under the following conditions: unions compromised with business, business leaders were unified, state capacity was high, and the state needed more business tax revenues.[44]

Political sociologists who use a class analysis framework frequently examine the conditions that facilitate collective action by oppressed people and explore how the state and dominant classes subdue, suppress, and contain struggle. Unlike pluralist or managerial political sociologists, they do not fear all the struggles of oppressed people, but instead see them as inevitable and a necessary part of the process of positive social change.

What Are the Most Critical Questions for the Class-Analysis Framework?

1. Under what conditions do nondominant classes mobilize into movements to struggle for power? How do the class and nonclass divisions in society reinforce or counterbalance one another?
2. How have struggles among classes and dominant class repression shaped state policies? How do the specific organizational features, laws, and polices of the state affect struggles and manifestations of class power?
3. How do specific state actions operate to maintain the capitalist economic system? How does the state resolve (or displace) the contradictions of

capitalism? How do attempts to contain the crises of capitalism contribute to other problems and demands for state action?

4. How does the ruling class rule? What mechanisms are used by the ruling class to resolve its internal divisions, develop cohesion, and govern?

POLITICAL SOCIOLOGY BEYOND THE THREE FRAMEWORKS

Each of the major frameworks offers an integrated set of assumptions, key concepts, and major questions to guide research (see Chart 3.1 for a review of features).

One limitation of the frameworks is that political sociologists who use different ones can easily "talk past" one another. This happens because each uses different assumptions and key concepts and seeks the answers to different critical questions. Each framework has sophisticated and vulgar versions. Advocates of a framework tend to defend its sophisticated versions and criticize the vulgar versions of alternative frameworks. A second limitation is that the frameworks generally concentrate on the domestic side of the state and politics and relatively neglect the state's external or international side.[45] Since contemporary nation-states operate in a global system of other states, nondomestic factors may affect the state's structure, allocation of resources, and domestic policies. Third, the frameworks are built around the experiences of a small number of stable, advanced nation-states. The frameworks do not seriously explore the conditions under which revolution, political movements, or civil wars have transformed the state's basic form. Lastly, because the frameworks focus on the state, they rarely explore the features of the civil society and the interrelationship between civil society and the state.

Three perspectives that first developed outside of political sociology have a growing influence on how political sociologists think about and explain politics, constructionism, rational choice, and new institutionalism. Next, we briefly look at each.

Constructionist Theory

Constructionist theory developed outside of political sociology in the areas of social problems, deviance, race relations, gender identity, schooling, and social movements.[46] It is part of a cultural turn in the social sciences that began around 1990, and as George Steinmetz (1999, 3) remarked, "the cultural study of the state is still relatively underdeveloped." Its core idea is that humans create cultural meaning (i.e., beliefs, religion, ideology), and that these creations influence their subsequent behavior. Constructionist theorists see culture, symbols, language, ideas, and communication as major forces that shape the state and produce political behaviors.

The frameworks discussed previously developed in the 1970s–1980s. All took individual, group, or class interests and desires as preexisting or treated them as starting points. By contrast, constructionist theorists focus on processes by which people construct interests. Thus, the constructionists take what the others assume and turn it into a question for investigation—How are

chart 3.1

A COMPARISON OF POLITICAL SOCIOLOGY FRAMEWORKS AND MODELS

Framework and Model	Critical Social-Political Units	Form of Conflict	Basis of Political Power	Nature of the State	State Autonomy
Pluralist Framework	Interest groups, political parties	Competition among interest groups	Elections, public opinion, lobbying	Government	Little, highly responsive to public
Managerial Framework, Elite Model	Elites and masses	Elite competition, domination of or co-opt the masses	Hold top positions, elite coordination, control agendas and mass media	Bureaucratic organization, control over means of violence	Significant, elites face few limits
Managerial Framework, Statist Model	Organizations, institutions	Competition among interest groups and for institutional resources	Organizational capacity, economic and legal resources	Organization and a unit in a system of nation-states	Significant but varies by state capacity
Class-Analysis Framework, Power-Structure Model	Social classes, class fractions or segments, quasi-class groups	Intraclass divisions, and repression of subordinate classes	Economic resources, social networks and intraclass cohesion	Executive committee of dominant class	Little but greater in crisis situations
Class-Analysis Framework, Structuralist Model	Class positions and structures (economic, political, ideological)	Economic, political, and ideological repression/resistance, contradiction	Functional role in the mode of production, position in the global economy	Organizer of class dominance, steering function of capitalism	Limited, relative, within basic capitalist principles
Class-Analysis Framework, Class-Struggle Model	Politically active movements, isolated apolitical individuals, nonclass cultural divisions (e.g., race, religion)	State-based repression (police, army), mass protests, battle of ideas	Capacity to organize, use of violence, movement frame, form of institution	Site of battle and object of struggles among classes	Relative, varies by issue and historical situation

interests created? Constructionist theorists also question what others consider to be objective facts and view such facts as the outcomes of dynamic cultural processes. Likewise, social groupings (e.g., races, genders, nations), are not fixed, natural categories but rather evolving cultural–political processes. Constructionists also emphasize a diversity of worldviews and argue that people often hold fundamentally different understandings of key ideas or events and apply different standards to determine what is reasonable. Thus, what one set of people consider to be universal ideas, common sense, or rational action, others might see as irrational or unreasonable. Culture is not located in an individual's cognitive framework; rather, it is built into social practices and institutionalized as a shared logic. Culture emerges from specific historic events, and it shapes state priorities and actions. For example, culture shapes what state managers define as important or unimportant crises and what they understand to be acceptable or unacceptable alternative political solutions. As Frank Dobbin (1994, 23) argued, "the core logic of political culture was woven through state institutions . . . permeated such diverse state attributes as the locus of political authority, the concentration of powers, the nature of the legal system, the system of office holding and public expertise and public fiscal capacities. "For constructionist studies, culture is integral to politics, not a backdrop (see World View 3.1).

Rational Choice Theory

In some respects, constructionist theory and rational choice theory are polar opposites. Rational choice theory (also called public choice or social choice theory) is often associated with pluralism and a conservative ideology, but some Marxist theorists use it as well. It has been around for many years and presents itself as a general theory that can unify all social science. Rational choice theory often expresses its arguments and predictions in formal symbolic or mathematiclike

---

 WORLD VIEW 3.1   **Culture in the Study of Politics**

In Frank Dobbin's (1994) study of nineteenth-century state policy in France, England, and the United States to develop railroads, the critical factor that explained state policy was rational political culture, not interest group competition, elite desires, institutional development, or class power. Likewise, John Campbell (1998) found that interest group competition, institutional structure, and class mobilization did not explain shifts in economic policy to market-based solutions in 1980s. Instead, the prevailing cultural ideas, values, and beliefs were critical in shaping public opinion, popular acceptance, and policymaker thinking. In her study of U.S. housing policy, Jill Quadagno (1992) argued that class politics were important, but that racial ideologies built into American culture were the vital factor. Joachim Savelsberg (1994) explained U.S. and German crime policy by looking at differences in national institutions, beliefs about the proper role of the state, and cultural understanding of what crime means. In each study, cultural assumptions and ideas are central to the explanation.

models. Many people are attracted to its great logical rigor and ability to yield precise predictions with quantitative data. Johnson (1996, 77) argued, "Rational choice theory consists primarily of formal, deductive models of interactions among strategically rational agents. It is among the most firmly established research traditions in contemporary political science."

Rational choice theory is based on ideas from economics, but it can explain most political and social behavior, and it has become influential in political science.[47] Its core assumption is that individuals are rational and make decisions based on what they understand to be the most effective way to achieve objectives. People calculate costs and benefits, consider alternatives, and select what they believe will maximize their desires, position, wealth, or status.

Rational choice theory is similar to exchange theory in sociology. In exchange theory, all human interaction is seen as an exchange between two or more people and social life involves individuals giving one another tangible goods (e.g., money, property, grades, specific favors) or intangible goods (e.g., affection, praise, honor, esteem, approval, obedience, sympathy). Each person tries to maximize what he or she will receive. People's perceptions of fairness and their expectations of others' behaviors are important factors in decision-making.[48] Rational choice theory also shares assumptions with behavioral psychology (e.g. the theory of B. F. Skinner). Behaviorism focuses on people's external, observable behaviors (versus the unseen, internal forces in a person's mind) and assumes that overt stimuli cause specific behaviors or responses. The assumptions of rational choice theory go back to late nineteenth-century utilitarian philosophy and neoclassical economics. Neoclassical economics emphasized the virtues of an unlimited pursuit of individual self-interest. It held that as each person pursues his or her own interest, the "invisible hand of the marketplace" will ensure that society as a whole benefits.

Most rational choice theorists define the general social good as maximum economic growth with many consumer choices and rapid technological change. They extend the law of supply and demand and centrality of competition from economics to all social relations (e.g., the marriage market). For example, if a small town has 1 intelligent, beautiful unmarried woman and 15 unmarried males looking for a mate, then the woman will be better able to bargain for what she desires (e.g., physical strength, money, power) than if there were 10 other equal women in the town.

The theory argues that institutional actions and society-wide change are the result of numerous individuals behaving rationally. For example, crime is explained by saying an individual commits a crime if it is rational to do so from his/her point of view. A radical choice or opportunity approach to criminology states that crimes occur when a person has a goal or need (e.g., wants money or a car) and there are easy opportunities (e.g., an unlocked car on an empty street) and few costs (e.g., the odds of getting caught are very small).[49] So crime is rational for some people under certain conditions, and reducing crime requires changing these conditions so that people will rationally chose alternative, noncriminal behaviors.

Rational choice theorists sometimes use game theory—predicting the choices people will make among alternative actions. The purpose of game theory is not to play games but to understand how rational decision-making operates when a person encounters a complex situation. Game theory predicts strategies that people use and possible outcomes. Three classic examples of game theory are the *prisoner's dilemma*, the *free rider problem*, and the *tragedy of the commons*. The prisoner's dilemma is powerful at predicting outcomes; it has direct parallels to many social situations. Hundreds of studies with dozens of variations used this game (see Closer Look 3.2). The free rider problem in collective behavior occurs in voluntary organizations when it is rational for an individual to cheat (e.g., not pay dues, not contribute time) and still receive benefits from the organization. For example, all workers in a unionized firm share in benefits whether or not they pay union dues. It is rational self-interested behavior to pay no dues but to enjoy the benefits or get a "free ride." This only works for the individual, because if everyone engaged in the same action, then everyone would lose. If no one paid dues, the union and the benefits would disappear. The tragedy of the commons applies to environmental issues where it is individually rational for an individual to use as much of "free" shared resources (e.g., water, air, land) as possible. This is not a problem so long as very few do it, but if everyone acts the same way, it will destroy the shared resources, making things worse for everyone.

Game theory calculations enable rational choice theorists to explain many collective decisions (e.g., votes in Congress). For example, elected representatives care greatly about a subset of all issues. They exchange votes on issues unimportant to them (e.g., world trade rules) to get other representatives to support an issue that they do care about (e.g., lower taxes to help farmers). As in a game, players trade useless votes for useful power by forming coalitions. The more votes traded, the more coalitions win on particular issues. As they participate in a series of decisions over time, stable relationships are built. When individuals play the game repeatedly with the same players, they cooperate and keep their word because the relationships extend to future games. Players who make

CLOSER LOOK 3.2   The Prisoner's Dilemma

The classic version of the prisoner's dilemma is as follows:

1. If you confess and your companion does not, he gets 9 years, and you go free.
2. If you confess and he confesses, you each get 5 years.
3. If neither of you confess, you each get 2 years.
4. If you do not confess, and he does, you get 9 years, and he goes free.

The worst choice for both of the prisoners option is 2, yet in experiments, it is the most frequent outcome. In most situations, both prisoners end up confessing, even though both know that they would be better off if they worked together and neither confessed. Pursuing individual self-interest over cooperation hurts both. This outcome explains a type of unintended consequence called *perverse effects*. Perverse effects are those which neither party desires, but which each nonetheless freely chooses. In other words, the combination of individual decisions does not automatically produce the best outcome. Each individual acts rationally and in her/his best interest, but the resulting outcome is irrational for the larger society.

promises but fail to keep them soon find that others lose trust in them. So under these conditions in the long run, trust and cooperation are rational behavior, and new group norms emerge that alter the rational calculation of individual choices. Rational choice theory has been applied to a wide range of other decisions, including voting (see World View 3.2).

Critics charge that rational choice theory's multi-level explanations fail to include social forces, social structure, culture, and group norms. Although individual choices occur in a context of social norms, forces, and structures, the theory rarely examines the source of the context. Michael Hector and Satoshi Kanazawa (1997, 208) admitted that, "Rational choice has been mute on the origin and nature of individual values . . . rational choice theorists usually impute values to actors by assumption." It is a theory of "mid-range mechanisms" that clarifies key political patterns and as Julia Adams (1999, 99) observed, "cannot capture individual

WORLD VIEW 3.2   Rational Choice and Voting for Fascists

Rational choice theory is what William Brustein (1996, xiii) called, "a model of political behavior founded on the assumption that political affiliation is based on self-interest." He applied the theory to analyze the social basis of voting for the Nazi Party in Germany in 1925–1933 and the Italian Fascist Party in 1921. Brustein (1996, 22) found that, "individuals who joined the Nazi Party calculated that the benefits of joining would exceed the costs" and (1991, 652) that "support for Italian fascism can be attributed to voter's rational calculations of their material interests."

In Germany, Brustein found that individuals supported the Nazis because of a self-awareness of their personal interest (possibly based on distorted or false information); it offered them more compared to the available alternatives. Thus, Nazism did not arise out of irrational, emotional appeals to anti-Semitism or deep-seated German authoritarianism. It grew because the Nazi party offered a program that most closely matched individual economic interests, and it offered people concrete incentives (e.g., jobs, subsidies, tax cuts) that outweighed the disincentives for joining (e.g., ostracism, violence). Specific incentives matched the material interests of the traditional small business owners (old middle class), married white-collar males, and skilled workers in industries weakened by imports. Millions joined

the Nazi Party out of a rational self-interest because, "in the depth of Germany's economic depression, the Nazi Party's positions answered the demands of various social groups better than those of any competing party" (Brustein 1996, 180).

Similarly, support for the Italian Fascist Party was based on a rational calculation of individual material interests more than on an often cited explanation—an emotional fear of rising socialist and communist strength (called the "Red Menace"). Many of the people who had previously voted for the Socialist Party switched to the Fascists once their economic situation changed. "After World War I, many farm tenants became owners and many aspired to acquire more land. . . . The Fascists could satisfy the aspirations of those who wanted land as well as those who wanted more land" (Brustein 1991, 662). Initially, the Socialist Party had improved tenant farmer conditions and enabled many of them to become land owners. Yet, once they were landowners, they opposed Socialist Party plans to nationalize their land and switched their support to the party that promised to protect their land and help them to get more, the Fascists. Thus, the Socialist Party's initial success contributed to its later failure and to the subsequent rise of the Fascists.

motivations or institutional or cultural conditions." Instead of examining traditions, religious beliefs, values or morals, social norms, legal systems, relations of production, social structures, and so forth, the theory assumes that people's interests are stable, unambiguous, and consistent.[50] The theory is best suited for situations where individual self-interest guides action, not values, identities, or emotions,[51] and its assumptions and values tend to mirror American cultural values (e.g., individualism, freedom).[52] Yet, the theory remains controversial (see Summary 3.3).[53]

There are several rational choice views of the nation-state.[54] The minimalist state is associated with neoclassical economics and conservative or libertarian political ideologies. It treats individualism as an ultimate value or moral good and the private market as a just and natural way to order society. In this view, the state is a necessary evil that people tolerate only because it performs essential functions (e.g., collective defense, printing money, protection, neutral law enforcement). The state tends to expand into inappropriate areas beyond what is minimally necessary because self-interested, rational state officials try to accumulate power. The purpose of the state is to protect individual rights, allow people to be free from violence by others, and to enjoy one's property. People agree to a state based on an ideal or myth of the social contract. Rational individuals in a pure, imaginary natural condition without a state would never

SUMMARY 3.3   **Criticisms of Rational Choice Theory**

- It fails to explain the origins of preferences, values, tastes, norms. These are recognized as critical for shaping choices and what is rational.
- It assumes human beings are individualistic, atomistic, isolated and self-centered. While that description may fit some people, especially traditional males in modern Western society, it is not universal to all humans.
- It cannot easily explain acts of kindness, caring, or altruism. It has no place for the subconscious or emotions.
- It is strongest when discussing small group interaction and is weak when explaining behaviors of large organizations, social institutions, and entire societies.
- It assumes that there are fixed basic, universal principles that can explain all human behavior, but there is no evidence that these principles exist or are even possible.

- The theory is tautological. It says people make rational choices. When asked about specific, very odd choices, the theory states they are also "rational," at least to the person who made them. This means no individual choice can be irrational; the theory would say it is rational in that particular person's view.
- The theory assumes a great range of individual freedom of choice or volition. In reality most people's alternatives are limited by habit, custom, lack of awareness, timidity, lack of knowledge, and so forth.
- Institutional power and historical social change are not well recognized by the theory.
- Societywide, long-term organizational behavior, institutional structures, and macro-issues are not discussed (e.g., Why does a society have an army? Why do certain racial groups face discrimination in some societies but not others?).

create a state, since the state abridges individual freedom which is what rational choice theory assumes to be the highest value for all people. People only accept a state when it allows them maximum individual freedom. From such assumptions, state action beyond the bare minimum is not what rational, free individuals would voluntarily choose, so it is illegitimate. Rational choice theory often relies on "natural law" arguments (both theological and nonreligious). It treats unequal power, exploitation, and inequality as morally acceptable if they are produced by operations of the "natural" free market; by contrast, any unequal power, exploitation, or inequality created by the state is treated as being a moral evil. This is because the theory assumes that the state is artificial, not natural.[55]

New Institutionalism Theory

New institutionalism theory emerged first in organizational sociology and has been developed in both economics and political science.[56] Its theorists synthesized parts of statist, rational choice, and constructionist theories. Some new institutional theorists emphasize historical-comparative analysis, others emphasize the "bounded rationality" of organizational decision-makers, and a third group incorporates rational choice ideas from microeconomic theory.[57] Paul DiMaggio and Walter Powell (1991, 8) noted that, "The new institutionalism . . . comprises a rejection of rational-actor models, an interest in institutions as independent variables, a turn toward cognitive and cultural explanations, and an interest in . . . units of analysis that cannot be reduced to aggregations or direct consequences of individuals' attributes or motives." Some versions of new institutionalism do not reject rational choice theory but try to integrate its ideas with social institutions.[58] Victor Nee (1998, 1–2) argued that, "The new institutionalism paradigm involves integrating the assumptions of purposive action with comparative institutional analysis central to the sociological tradition. . . ."

Institutional explanations had been used across the social sciences for a long time. Several features distinguish the new from the previous or old institutionalism. Old institutionalism was highly descriptive, assigned rational goals or objectives to organizations, did not question the normative structure of society (i.e., norms, beliefs, values) as a determinate of individual behavior, and emphasized formal organizational structures. Compared to new institutionalism, it gave little attention to power relations. It did not fully appreciate the importance of the context or broader field of similar organizations or institutions in shaping an organization and its direction; it did not stress how significant the legacy of past actions and decisions were for present conditions; and it did not recognize the great importance of symbols, beliefs and ideology. In addition, it did not use formal models of rational calculation.[59]

The *institution* of new institutionalism is defined as a mixture of formal rules, traditional procedures, routines, financial and personnel resources, and bureaucratic organization as well as informal norms, idea systems, symbols, and cultural conventions. It is less the product of conscious, rational design than the outcome of a web of formal and informal norms that govern people's relationships. Institutions fix limits and create pressures on people, and this is how the theory explains social and political outcomes. According to Douglas North

(1998, 248), "Institutions are humanly devised constraints that structure human interaction." New institutionalism weds the cultural–historical context with other explanations of state action.

New institutionalism theorists reject the ahistorical, atomized, and individualist assumptions often found in rational choice theory. Instead of individual interests that flow automatically from group membership, social class location, position in an organization, or rational self-interest, new institutionalists see human behavior and political action as firmly embedded within a system of emotions, norms, customs, and feelings of obligation. In short, human desires emerge from within a context of institutional factors (i.e., influenced by rules or procedures). New institutional theorists borrow the constructionist idea that people create interests out of fluid interactions with others in specific historical–cultural settings. Emotions, irrational thinking, routines, and habits all shape people's interests. For example, a class or pluralist theorist may see a person's interests originating in objective class position or interest group membership, and then explain the person's political actions based on those interests. A new institutional theorist first explains how people create and define interests, then examines how specific situations intensify, divert, or suppress those interests and their impacts on political actions.

For new institutional theorists, institutions are simultaneously cultural-symbolic and material-objective. Moreover, as March and Olsen (1989, 52) have argued, "the symbolic consequences of political decision-making are at least as important as the substantive consequences." This is because people operate within a worldview and institutional context, although they may falsely attribute constraints on their actions to "natural law" rather than to political or social conditions.[60] For example, many people see the market as a neutral, technical resource allocation mechanism. They cannot recognize it as a human-constructed system for generating and measuring value.[61] This implies that a person's choice on a policy issue, such as paying for college education, is not really market (e.g., private savings) versus public (e.g., high taxes for scholarships) because markets and public funds are interwoven (e.g., savings depend on tax policy and a government banking system).

An institution may have inertia and persist long after it serves the specific interests or purpose for its creation; it has traditions, beliefs, routines, and informal norms that continue to shape behavior. Political actions can be influenced by institutional forces, such as following organizational norms or models. For example, civil service reforms in America were caused by one set of factors, but in a later period, government agencies adopted the same reforms to mimic other areas of government. Institutions shape action indirectly and the effects can be unexpected, unintentional, or indirect. People negotiate, reinterpret, and struggle over the symbolic dimension of life, but material conditions are also important. Roger Friedland and Robert Alford (1991, 249) reminded us, "The central institutions of contemporary Western societies—capitalism, family, bureaucratic state, democracy, and Christianity—are simultaneously symbolic systems and material practices."

New institutional theorists dissolve simple dichotomies between state and society, politics and markets, and symbolic and material; they see these as interrelated and mutually reinforcing dimensions, not as opposites. Instead of saying that a class, interest group, or elite causes political action, they argue that outcomes flow from the interdependence or mutual influence of state and society. Thus, state action does not autonomously affect society, nor does the market autonomously affect the state. Instead the market emerged along with the state in particular places and times, and the state and market are linked together with local patterns, values, and ways of life.[62] It views the state as a process, not as a fixed structure.[63]

New institutional theorists also argue that "selling ideas," or ways to understand events, can be a significant factor in many political struggles.[64] According to Jill Quadagno (1992, 619) we should see new policies and state agencies as arising through conflict "in the context of negotiation over cultural symbols that legitimate the structural change." Political movements battle over the framing, or ways to think about an issue. The frame that wins, or becomes most popular, sets the basic parameters for public policy. This theme is related to struggles over hegemony. In sum, new institutionalism may be "one of the most creative and promising new paradigms of the social sciences."[65] Yet it is very new, and its development has been outside the major theories of the state.

CONCLUSION

We began this chapter with a consideration of the modern nation-state and examined major frameworks used by political sociologists. Political sociologists developed and applied the frameworks to study politics and the state in advanced capitalist democracies. Each of the three major frameworks (pluralist, managerial, class analysis) offers an entire analytic framework, including a theory of society and approaches to key political ideas such as democracy, citizenship, power, hegemony, and struggle. Each also directs attention to different major issues. Several of the frameworks contain more than one specific model of politics, leaving us with a total of six contrasting models of how politics works.

Despite the many differences, there is much agreement across the frameworks. First, all three view the state's form and type of economy as being closely related. This means that

understanding the economy advances understanding about the form of state, and vice versa. Second, all three recognize that various groups, or sectors of society, possess different forms and amounts of power. This means that it is essential to understand power relations in civil society to understand the state. Lastly, all three agree that the amount of state autonomy, or independence of state from groups in society, is a key factor. This means that investigating the sources and degree of state autonomy has implications beyond any one framework.

Lastly, we briefly considered three theories beyond the three major frameworks that are having an influence in political sociology: constructionist, rational choice, and new institutionalism. Each offers a theoretical perspective that originated in a field outside of political sociology but has implications for thinking about the nation-state.

The abstract, general frameworks are most useful when we apply them to the development of a specific political issue. In Chapter 4 we will examine the political institutions and historical development of one nation-state—the United States. It will enable us to apply the ideas and insights from frameworks to the contours of American politics.

KEY TERMS

Circulation of Elites

Corporate Liberal Thesis

Demand Overload

Elite-Managerial Model

Inner Circle

Plural Elite

Pluralism

Policy Legacy

Political Formula

Power Elite

Relative Autonomy of the State

Steering Mechanism (state as)

State Autonomy

State Capacity

Statist-Managerial Model

Structural Dependence Thesis

Structural Selectivity

REVIEW QUESTIONS

1. What makes the study of "theories of the state" confusing and difficult for many people?

2. Explain the pluralist framework. How does it see society, the nation-state, citizenship, democracy, and struggle?

3. Explain the managerial framework. How does it see society, the nation-state, citizenship, democracy, and struggle?

4. Explain the class-analysis framework. How does it see society, the nation-state, citizenship, democracy, and struggle?

5. Compare and contrast how the three major frameworks understand the concept of hegemony.

6. What are the major similarities and differences between two different models in the managerial framework?

7. Compare the elite model in the managerial framework with the power-structure model in the class analysis framework.

8. Compare the statist model in the managerial framework with the structuralist model in the class analysis framework.

9. Discuss how the concepts of state capacity and relative autonomy of the state are viewed by the three main frameworks.

10. Explain how the structural dependence thesis might affect political election campaigns in the United States.

11. Class-analysis theorists discuss social class most extensively, but it appears in other theories as well. Explain how each theory uses the concept of social class and economic inequality more generally.

12. What limitations are shared by the three main frameworks and how might they be overcome or corrected?

RECOMMENDED READINGS

Alford, Robert R. and Roger Friedland. 1985. *Powers of Theory: Capitalism, the State and Democracy.* New York: Cambridge University Press.

Brinton, Mary C. and Victor Nee, eds. 1998. *The New Institutionalism in Sociology.* New York: Russell Sage Foundation.

Domhoff, G. William. 1998. *Who Rules America? 3rd ed.* Mountain View, CA: Mayfield Publishing Company.

Evans, Peter. 1995. *Embedded Autonomy: States and Industrial Transformation.* Princeton, NJ: Princeton University Press.

Evans, Peter, D. Rueschemeyer, and T. Skocpol, eds. 1985. *Bringing the State Back In.* New York: Cambridge University Press.

Jessop, Bob. 1990. *State Theory: Putting the Capitalist State in its Place.* University Park, PA: Pennsylvania State University Press.

Mills, C. Wright. 1956. *The Power Elite.* New York: Oxford University Press.

ENDNOTES

1. Classical approaches are discussed in Vincent (1987).
2. See Alford and Friedland (1985).
3. Quote is from Alford and Friedland (1985, 403).
4. For pluralist approaches, see Dahl (1961), Polsby (1963), Rose (1967), and Wolfinger (1974).
5. See Dahl (1961) and Rose (1967). Mitchell (1991) describes the abandonment of the concept of the state by pluralists and its replacement by polity or political system.
6. For example, see Nordlinger (1981).
7. Classical elite theorists include Gaetano Mosca (1858–1941), Vilfredo Pareto (1848–1923), and Robert Michels (1876–1936).
8. For a discussion of classical elite theorists see Meisel (1965) and Parry (1969). Also, see Burnham (1970 [1943]) on American elite theory.
9. See Mills (1956).
10. Theorists of American elites include Burch (1980), Dye (1986), Keller (1991 [1963]), and Lerner et al. (1996). For a discussion of a diversity of views among plural elites, also see Verba and Orren (1985).
11. Keller (1991 [1963]) argues that powerful elites are essential to uphold "moral ideals" in modern society.
12. For examples and elaboration on the statist or state capacity theory see Amenta and Carruthers (1988), Amenta and Parikh (1991), Amenta and Zylan (1991), Amenta, Cattruthers, and Zylan (1992), Amenta, Dunleavy, and Bernstein (1994), Hooks (1990a, 1990b, 1991a, 1991b, 1993), Finegold and Skocpol (1995), Krasner (1978), Skocpol (1985, 1992a, 1992b), Skocpol and Amenta (1985, 1986), Skowronek (1982), and Weir, Orloff, and Skocpol (1988). Krasner (1984) and Mitchell (1991) offer a review of theories and discuss the statist approach.
13. For example, see Keller (1991 [1963]).
14. See Zeitlin (1974) on the managerialist debate.
15. See Dye (1986).
16. This is explained in Kerbo and Della Fave (1979). For studies of social interaction within the capitalist class in elite colleges, boarding schools and clubs, see Domhoff (1974a, 1975b). Also see Cookson and Persell (1985), Higley (1995), Ostrander (1984), and Zweigenhaft and Domhoff (1991).
17. Barkey and Parikh (1991, 525–526) define these ideas, "Autonomy refers to the state's ability to formulate interests of its own, independent or against the will of divergent societal interests. Autonomy is not necessarily a characteristic of the state in totality; a state can be autonomous in certain domains and dependent in others. Capacity is the state's ability to implement strategies to achieve its economic, political or social goals. . . ."
18. For an elaboration on state capacity, see Skocpol and Finegold (1982), Skocpol (1985) and Evans (1995).
19. See Evans (1995), Migdal (1988), and Weiss (1998) on the relationship of state strength and capacity.
20. See Amsdsen (1989), Evans (1995), Wade (1990), Weiss (1998), and Woo-Cummings (1991, 1999) on development and the state. For an alternative view see Bollen and Jackman (1985) and Muller (1995).
21. Quote is from Skocpol (1985, 8).
22. See Fligstein (1987).
23. Krasner (1978) provides a useful discussion.
24. See Bottomore (1983).

25. This contrasts with popular definitions of capitalists or entrepreneurs in which they are presented (or see themselves) as individuals who achieve high levels of success and create businesses.

26. There is an argument over whether ownership of corporations and control are identical (Zeitlin 1974).

27. On the special position of state employees in class theory, see Wright and Cho (1992).

28. See Poulantzas (1973, 1974, 1975, 1976), Jessop (1982, 1985, 1990), Miliband (1969, 1977, 1982), and Valocchi (1989) for discussions of relative autonomy in class theory. Akard (1992) applies the concept to recent U.S. political experience.

29. The power structure approach is discussed in Domhoff (1967, 1970, 1975a, 1976, 1978, 1980, 1983, 1990, 1996), Johnson and Mintz (1988), Lo (1982b), Mintz and Schwartz (1981, 1985, 1986), Mizruchi (1982, 1989, 1990a), Mizruchi and Koenig (1986), Neustadtl and Clawson (1988), M. Useem (1980), and Zeitlin (1980).

30. For studies of interlocking directorates, see Mizruchi and Stearns (1988) and Roy and Bonacich (1988).

31. The networks are discussed in Jessop (1982, 106–109) and Offe (1974, 37–40), but see Useem (1984) for a detailed discussion of the inner circle.

32. For examples of a corporate liberal approach, see Beck (1991), Block (1977b), Burris and Salt (1990), Kolko (1963), Lustig (1982), and Weinstein (1968). See Jenkins and Brents (1989) modified version applied to the Social Security Act.

33. Quote is from Barrow (1993, 27).

34. For related studies of capitalist class power and American political campaign funding see Allen and Broyles (1989, 1991), Boies (1989), Clawson and Su (1990), and Mizruchi (1990b).

35. For discussion of structuralist theory of the state, see Barrow (1993), Block (1977a, 1987), Clark and Dear (1984), Jessop (1985), and Poulantzas (1973, 1974, 1975, 1976, 1978, 1979).

36. See Jessop (1982, 15).

37. On the fiscal crisis of the state, see Block (1981) and O'Connor (1973, 1984, 1987).

38. Huber and Stephens (2001a, 17–32) provide a useful overview.

39. Offe (1972a, 1973, 1974, 1976) and O'Connor (1984, 1987) discuss indeterminate state selection processes. Also see Zeitlin, Neuman, and Ratcliff (1976) for an example of politics and upper class divisions in Chile.

40. For discussions of welfare states and class power see Esping-Anderson (1990), Hicks (1999), Hicks and Misra (1993), Hicks, Misra, and Ng (1995), Huber and Stephens (2001a), Hicks and Swank (1992), King (1987), Korpi (1978, 1989), Korpi and Shalev (1980), Quadagno (1988, 1990), Schneider (1982), Shalev (1983), Skocpol and Ikenberry (1983), and Offe (1972b).

41. The idea that individual crime or deviance is class oppression can be found in Balkan, Berger, and Schmidt (1980), Chambliss (1975), Greenberg (1993), Quinney (1977), and Spitzer (1975).

42. Examples include Hicks and Mistra (1993) and Leicht and Jenkins (1998).

43. For discussion, see Gilbert and Howe (1991).

44. See the study by Leicht and Jenkins (1998) for details.

45. See Held (1989, 46).

46. Studies using constructionist perspective include Best (1989, 1993), Dobbin (1993), Neuman (1998), Spector and Kituse (1977), and Williams (1995).

47. For discussions of rational choice theory, see Becker (1976, 1985, 1996), Brogan (1996), Coleman (1990), Elster (1986), Finkel and Muller (1998), Ostrom (1998), and Simon (1986). The journal *Rationality and Society* is a major outlet of rational choice research. The percent of leading political science articles using the theory rose from 0 in the 1950s to 40 percent by 1992 (Hechter and Kanazawa 1996, 192).

48. For an overview of rational choice theory in sociology, see Hechter and Kanazawa (1997).

49. The opportunity approach in criminology is described in Neuman and Berger (1988). On crime and rational choice theory, see Becker and Landes (1974), Moran (1996), and Short (1997).

50. See March and Olsen (1989, 6) for additional comment and criticism. Also see March and Olsen (1995).

51. See Kiser (1996, 265).

52. See Smelser (1992).

53. For criticisms see Blau (1997), Denzin (1990), Green and Ian Shapiro (1994), O'Neill (1995), Stretton and Orchard (1994), Smelser (1992), and Yee (1997).

54. See Chai and Hechter (1997) and North (1998).

55. This version of a rational-choice approach to the state is found in Barzel (2002), Friedman (1963), Nozick (1974, 1995), and von Hayek (1994).

56. New institutionalism is discussed by Bielby and Bielby (1994), Brinton and Nee (1998), Campbell (1997), Christensen, Karnøe, Pederson, and Dobbin (1997), Clemens and Cook (1999), DiMaggio and Powell (1991), and Rockman (1994). The study of rationality, democracy, and city planning by Flyvbjerg (1998) also fits into the institutional approach. Skocpol (1995a) calls herself a historical intuitionalist.

57. For discussion of types of new institutionalism, see Hall and Taylor (1996), Immergut (1998), and Rockman (1994).

58. Rational choice and interpretative approaches of constructionism are largely incompatible (Kiser 1996, 260), but Bates, Figueiredo and Weingast (1998) and Weingast (1995) argue for integrating them.

59. For defenders of old institutionalism, see Selznick (1996) and Stinchcombe (1997).

60. From Dowd and Dobbin (1997).

61. From Friedland and Alford (1991, 234).

62. See Hopcroft (1998) and Lie (1993) on the construction of markets. Also see Tolbert and Zucker (1983).

63. The "state as process" is discussed by Broadbent (1988).

64. See Fligstein (1997) for discussion.

65. Quote is from Christensen, Karnøe, Pedersen, and Dobbin (1997, 392).

THE POLITY OF THE UNITED STATES

INTRODUCTION

Have you ever felt frustrated by a barrier, such as a rule or law, that prevented you from participating in an activity causing you to stand by watching while others get the red carpet treatment? Political institutions can include or exclude certain people, ideas, and activities in politics. In this chapter, we look at political institutions and the boundaries of politics, specifically we look at the development of political institutions in the United States. We will see how political processes, such as elections, developed and how people gained or lost rights to participate in them.

A central idea in this chapter is the polity. It is a term with which you may not be familiar. It goes back to Aristotle's notion of the body politic, or *polis*, in ancient Greece. Compared to other conceptions, it included the widest range of people and, if it operated properly, had rules and procedures to insure fair and extensive participation. The term also means political community, but it is not restricted to the government; it is the public sphere.[1] Updating this idea, **the polity is the people, institutions, organizations, processes, rules, beliefs, and symbols that operate together (loosely or tightly) as the politics of a specific nation-state.** It includes the state plus the people (i.e., the citizens, voters, elected officials), institutions (e.g., levels of government, party system), organizations (e.g., courts, administrative agencies, armies), processes (e.g., voting, jury service, public debate), rules (i.e., laws, regulations), beliefs (e.g., justice, democracy, freedom), and symbols (e.g., flags, national anthem) that surround it.

A second central idea of this chapter is the institution. **An institution is a coherent system or framework of people, organizations, and ideas that operate together in a patterned, or rule-governed, manner across time.** It is a very abstract but critical idea that encompasses coherence, patterns, and continuity to organize human activities. Institutions are everywhere. As DiMaggio and Powell (1991, 9) said, "from handshakes to marriages to strategic-planning departments." Our concern here is with a nation's major political institutions that lie at the heart of its polity.

Sometimes the term *political system* is used for polity. However, a system assumes that the polity's parts are tightly intermeshed and work smoothly together as a unit. Rather than assume unity, we need to ask these key questions: How integrated are the polity's parts? How did the parts develop? Has their interconnection changed over time? What are its boundaries? What is polity's shape and structure, its major institutions and dynamics? How and why are certain groups, ideas, or activities included or excluded/expelled from the polity?[2] ∎

MODELS OF POLITICAL SOCIOLOGY

You learned the models and frameworks of political sociology in Chapter 3. Each provides alternative views of the polity. *Pluralists* define the polity as government agencies, formal political participation, and the first dimension of power. They see formal democracy as promoting polity expansion and inclusion. In a democracy, virtually everyone is included. Exclusion is rare and limited to groups or behaviors that threaten to cause serious harm to the social order. Only in a totalitarian state is inclusion highly restricted and exclusion widespread. The *elite-managerial model* shares the pluralist's definition of the polity but focuses more on the processes of inclusion and exclusion. The model holds that elites narrowly include themselves and allies but actively exclude most others. Politics largely are processes of elite strategies to exclude, control, and contain opponents or potential enemies. The elites form inclusive coalitions to gain power and retain privileged advantages. They marginalize and exclude the masses from the polity through a mixture of idea/symbol manipulation and outright repression. In the *statist-managerial model,* a broader definition of the polity is used. It includes organizational arrangements to open up or close off access to the state. The emphasis is on how the polity's very structure selectively facilitates or inhibits entry into the polity by specific groups, actions, or ideas. An *open polity* is similar to a set of buildings, each has many large entrances and handicapped-accessible ramps, allowing a constant flow of many people to move freely back and forth. Entry is easy and encouraged, and access barriers have been dismantled. A *closed polity* is similar to a large building with one entrance that has a checkpoint. Few are allowed in and they must go up a single, long, very narrow stairway. The building's arrangement or structure indirectly limits entry. According to a *power-structure model,* the polity includes the capitalist class at the polity's very center. This class sets the basic rules for inclusion and exclusion of all others in society. Capitalists protect their social, economic, and political position by strategically including certain parts of society while excluding others, especially opposing classes. A *structuralist model* defines the polity as a set of integrated and mutually reinforcing economic and social relations. Direct exclusion (e.g., arresting someone, passing a law prohibiting a group from voting, banning a book) is less significant than indirect exclusion. Similar to the statist-managerial model, exclusion and inclusion are built into the structure of institutions. Bob Jessop (1990, 367) argued that state structures "offer unequal chances to different forces within and outside the state to act for different political purposes." The polity weakens or excludes anticapitalist actions and includes activities supportive of capitalism. The most powerful forms of exclusion maintain relations of power by making the exclusion appear to be natural so it is not questioned. The *class-struggle model* of the polity emphasizes inclusion and exclusion as central issues over which classes and groups struggle. Constant struggles erupt over the line that separates who is included or excluded. In power struggles, the polity's boundaries are negotiated or redefined in many ways. For example, as one group tries to stretch boundaries to include some people or behaviors, another group fights to tighten, raise, or defend the polity's boundaries to keep a group outside or limited. Keeping these models in mind, we can examine the political institutions of the United States.

AMERICAN POLITICAL INSTITUTIONS

A polity's political institutions develop in processes of state formation or state-building. Specific conditions and historical events shape their features. Institutions have three characteristics: (1) a past legacy, (2) a field of interrelated organizations, and (3) a web of symbolic meaning and understanding (see Summary 4.1). Most political institutions of the United States today acquired their basic form during their development in the late nineteenth and early twentieth centuries.

SUMMARY 4.1	Three Major Characteristics of Institutions

1. Historical Legacy—Institutions grow and change slowly, carrying the weight of past events, ideas, and decisions built up over many years that constrain current action. Past decisions affect present ones and "history is encoded into institutions" (March and Olsen 1989, 56).

2. Field of Organizations—An institution is a set of organizations (e.g., government agencies, newspaper companies, political parties, schools) that are in a web of relations (i.e., a field) with others. Together, the organizations are interconnected and mutually affect one another.

3. Symbolic Dimension—Institutions contain routines, symbols, emotional appeals, beliefs, factual knowledge, and legal or moral principles. Beliefs, interests, and preferences develop within and are parts of the institution.

A System of Courts and Parties

During the nineteenth century, the United States operated under a **system of courts and parties in which courts and political parties had greater significant influence than today, while the national government and administrative bureaucracy was small and weak.** The state emerged from a violent revolution against the monarchy in England, and its early leaders borrowed heavily from Enlightenment Era liberal-democratic ideals that opposed the absolutist state. Most people distrusted central government authority; this feeling shaped the formation of political institutions and remains a pervasive theme in American political discourse. The state grew from a collection of separate colonies, each with its own local interests and culture. Early leaders adopted a federal structure for the national government (i.e., an organized federation of semi-independent government units). Other nation-states have a federal system (e.g., Canada and Germany), but many do not. **Federalism is a system that divides the nation-state's political authority between the central national government and other localized levels of government.** Federalism is a major feature of the American polity.

Demographic and geographic conditions affect how institutions develop. The United States had a huge land area over which people were thinly spread. Today it remains the world's third largest country in land area with most of the land arable. Throughout the nineteenth century, the United States was much less densely populated than Europe or Asia. For example, it had about 3.2 people per square kilometer, whereas France, the United Kingdom, Italy, and Germany had 50–100 people per square kilometer, and China, Japan, and India had 45–68 people per square kilometer.[3] Small groups of elites were concentrated in a narrow area along the Eastern coast. They controlled the small, weak national government that was physically distant from most people. Before the 1820s, electoral participation was very low. Only white males over age 21 who owned property were eligible to vote and only 9 percent of those eligible voted in 1820.

Between 1820 and 1840, the adult white males politically mobilized, and by 1828, over 55 percent of those eligible voted; this rose to 80 percent by the 1840 elections. The rise of political parties stimulated this mobilization. Parties were coalitions of local officials and elites who actively sought voter support and rewarded friends and followers after they took office.[4]

Before 1860, the national government remained very small. It had little impact on local affairs, and taxes were minimal because the government owned vast amounts of land and natural resources (e.g., timber, rivers, minerals). It was a distributive state. **The distributive state is one in which the government controls vast resources that it gives to favored individuals and businesses. It also gives them tax waivers and the right to collect tolls and taxes foreign goods to protect local industry.** Officials at the village, town, or county level made most routine political decisions with little interference from a distant state capitol or the national government. State and federal government lacked the capacity (e.g., laws, officials, bureaucracy) to do much. When individuals came into conflict, they went to the local courts. Charles Bright (1984, 139) noted that, "The role of the courts was crucial, for it worked both to promote competition and innovation in the market place and to restrict the power of political parties in the legislative branch to intervene in economic affairs." The courts were highly decentralized, used jury trials that drew on local citizens, and applied a case law approach in which judges based their decisions on a review of past cases. As state government legislatures granted special concessions, monopolies, and privileges to specific businesses, the local courts would limit the privileges that a state legislature could distribute.[5] Thus, politics up to the Civil War era was a system of courts and parties. Steven Skowronek (1982, 29) summarized the situation: "Together, courts and parties formed the bulwark of the early American state."

As immigrants, business owners, and farmers expanded onto vast frontier areas, economic growth was rapid, unregulated, and volatile. The business owners faced little interference, except for a few local farm or settler interests, and they often used political influence or bribery to advance their interests. Electoral and legislative politics largely operated on a **spoils system in which the winning political party distributed jobs and favors (i.e., the spoils) to its followers and loyalists.** The party that won enriched itself and its followers by awarding government jobs, allowing friends to build or operate public works projects at inflated rates, and favoring party supporters in law cases or in tax assessments. People were very locally oriented and had little contact with the rest of the country. Nearly half the population resided on farms or tiny villages thinly scattered over a huge expanse of land. Standard time zones had not yet been established and travel or communication time was counted in months, weeks, or days.

Decentralization remains a major feature of American political institutions. Public policies decided at the central government level in most nations (e.g., schooling, unemployment insurance, and taking care of the poor) are placed at the state or local level in the United States. The federal government establishes broad guidelines and collects taxes for public service (e.g., roads and bridges), but it transfers funds to the state or local governments that decide specific ways to spend the money and how to implement the guidelines.

The division of powers among levels of government is highly inconsistent. One level may enact a program while another pays for it. For example, the federal government gathers taxes for roads, and state government builds them; state government requires recycling, but a local government designs a program and pays for it; the federal government mandates special education programs, but local governments collect taxes to pay for it. As James (1988, 194) noted, "This fragmentation of sovereignty provides differential access to state power for various agents and interest groups and makes uneven policy implementation . . . . Local autonomy in the U.S. results not just from decentralization and fragmentation, but also from the local state's capacity to control the recruitment of personnel to local offices and power to tax . . . ." An important dynamic of the American polity is that decision-making authority and responsibility for payment are pushed back and forth among the various levels of government.

Patronage and Party Systems

Between the beginning of the Civil War in 1860 and the end of World War I in 1918, the U.S. was transformed from an underpopulated, second-rate, agricultural nation to a leading military and financial–industrial global power. Political institutions shaped this transformation and were altered in the process.[6] The Civil War that ended slavery and the Southern plantation system also accelerated Northern manufacturing and financial power and created a deep, lasting regional divide.[7] After the Civil War, the South, with one-fourth of the national population, operated as a single political block while the Mountain and Pacific West regions remained a remote frontier. American political institutions retain a strong strain of regionalism. The Civil War also upset the old party system and activated political parties. "The party system," Silberman (1993, 250) observed, "emerged strengthened rather than weakened from the Civil War." The two-party system was firmly established in the period between the Civil War and World War I—the "party period" of American history (see Chart 4.1).[8] In this era, 80 percent of the eligible population voted, and most voted a straight party ticket. The intensity and form of partisanship was a loud, boisterous public spectacle (see Case in Point 4.1)

Into the early twentieth century, public sector jobs were largely filled by **political patronage, in which party loyalists received government jobs as a reward for political support.** Appointees often made a "voluntary contribution" of a percentage of their salaries to the party. For example, the largest federal government agency was the U.S. Post Office. It employed 72 percent of all federal workers in 1871, and all postal workers were political appointees. In a patronage system, when the party holding power changes, thousands of people lose their jobs. For example, President Benjamin Harrison (1889–1893) changed 31,000 postmasters in one year. Patronage brought ordinary citizens into government, but at the cost of career instability and inefficiency because party loyalty or contributions were the primary criteria for appointment, not technical expertise. Expertise was not a

c h a r t   4 . 1

THE BASIS OF "TWO-PARTYISM" IN THE UNITED STATES

1. A decentralized government with local party organizations that are only loosely connected to national party organizations

2. Social diversity and divisions based on region or ethnic–religious difference

3. Parties that are nonideological coalitions that quickly absorb new issues or movements

4. Entrenched party power from patronage, awarding public projects, and the need to raise campaign money

5. Electoral rules (i.e., winner takes all and single-member districts instead of proportionate representation) and rules restricting getting onto the ballot

6. An early franchise, since party divisions did not arise over fights for the right to vote

 CASE IN POINT 4.1   **Party Politics in Nineteenth-Century America**

Early one evening in October 1876 groups of young men wearing military-style caps and carrying kerosene torches in the shape of rifles gathered in the six wards . . . marching companies were formed for the presidential campaign that year. . . . The members of the marching companies, mostly Irish immigrants and the sons of immigrants, lived and worked as day-laborers and factory operators in the poorest sections. . . . By seven o'clock the companies had formed into line and lit their torches. On the orders from the commanding officers, the men set off, a brass band at their head, through the darkened streets. Several blocks away, in the first ward, the process was joined by the "Deutsche Feger" or "German Sweepers," carrying brooms. . . . As the companies marched and counter marched, the band played and fireworks lit the sky. . . . (quote from McGerr 1986, 3–4)

significant basis for government employment until the Pendleton Act (1883) guaranteed an open competition for federal jobs based on merit, without regard to politics, religion, race, or national origin. The law initially covered only 10 percent of federal jobs. As late as 1910, politicians still filled nearly half of all federal jobs by appointment.[9] A very large number of government political appointees still remains a distinctive feature of U.S. political institutions.

The U.S. has had several party systems (see Chart 4.2). **A party system has a level of voter activity, key issues, major social divisions, and patterns of party behavior.** "A competitive party system," according to Chambers (1967, 6), is "a pattern of interaction in which two or more political parties compete for office and power in government and for the support of the electorate, and therefore take one another into account . . . . This pattern . . . is marked by durability and thus relative predictability of consequences . . . ." Parties operate within a party system, and it is difficult to understand them outside of the system in which they operate.

---

c h a r t   4 . 2

AMERICAN PARTY SYSTEMS

Political parties mobilize voters for election campaigns, adjust interest group coalitions, supply candidates and appointees, and provide policy direction. The two major parties in the United States have retained the same names for over 120 years but have operated within five or six distinct party systems, each with different major issues and social divisions.

1. Experimental System (1789–1820)

Major Issues: Degree of independence from Europe, amount of public input into politics, type of foreign defense, level/type of government promotion of business/trade

Social Divisions: Elite coalitions, merchants, plantation owners

2. Democratizing System (1820–1860)

Major Issues: Openness of government offices, expansion of who could vote, increasing local control, and enlarging the spoils system, slavery (last stages)

Social Divisions: Small farmers and craftspeople, merchants, New England, Deep South

3. Civil War System (1860–1893)

Major Issues: Supporting the development of banking, industry, and railroads; tariff policy; land grants to small farmers; expanding the patronage system

Social Divisions: Southerners, workers and farmers, new wealthy, ethnic-religious identities

4. Industrial System (1896–1932)

Major Issues: Building a national administrative bureaucracy, regulating new corporations, resolving social problems and unrest created by rapid industrial urban expansion, reducing patronage

Social Divisions: New immigrants, established residents, ethnic-religious groups, urban/rural, Southerners

5. New Deal System (1932–1976?)

Major Issues: Instituting union/worker rights, building social welfare programs, creating a "mixed" economy, expanding the military, guaranteeing civil rights (last stages)

Social Divisions: Urban immigrant/working class, white Southerners, small-town and suburban whites

6. Not Clear (1980–?)

Major Issues: Moral-religious issues, race, crime/social control, taxes, decentralization

Social Divisions: Blacks, urban professionals with liberal ideologies, low income people, feminists vs. traditionalists, new Christian right, and upper middle class suburban whites, Mountain/Pacific West regions

---

Sources: American party systems are discussed in Burnham (1970, 1967), Chambers (1967), McCormick (1981a, 1986) and Shefter (1979).

Administrative Bureaucracy

Government bureaucracies deliver the mail, register marriages, collect taxes, defend borders, print money, clear snow from roads, and enforce criminal law. Bureaucracy gets a lot of bad press and is not very popular, but all large organizations (e.g., corporations, hospitals, schools, military) are bureaucracies. Bureaucracies may seem cold and impersonal, but they are the most efficient method for getting large numbers of people to work together. A bureaucracy follows preplanned rules (i.e., not rules invented on the spot), keeps careful written records (i.e., it does not depend on someone's memory), uses impersonal procedures (i.e., does not show favoritism), uses specialized, trained experts, and operates with clear lines of authority (i.e., knows who is in charge). Public bureaucracies in advanced nations follow either an adaptive or coordinated pattern.[10]

In the **adaptive pattern, the government hires independent professionals who move back and forth between the private and public sector, and top positions are held by political appointees instead of permanent government staff, who are often held in low regard.** In the United States and Great Britain high-level state workers with general professional training (e.g., law, medicine, accounting, or personnel management) and credentials controlled by independent professional associations enter public sector jobs all along the administrative hierarchy, and they easily move back and forth between the public and private sectors. Politicians appoint many top-level officials who direct the lower-status career public employees.

In the **coordinated pattern, the government hires people specially trained to be government officials, people stay with public service for an entire career, and bureaucrats who worked their way up hold top positions and are highly respected.** In this pattern, found in France and Japan, experts receive similar, intense education at a few highly competitive schools specialized to train people for government service. State workers make an early commitment to become a civil servant, begin in an entry-level position, and advance within the bureaucracy based on competence and seniority. Career moves between the private and public sectors are rare. A few top officials are politically appointed; most rise up from within the ranks of public service (see Chart 4.3).

Patterns of public bureaucracy shape institutions. A weak, permeable administration run by professionals who are independent of the government has long dominated in the United States.[11]

Progressive Era Expansion

Martin Sklar (1992, 38) noted there is ". . . agreement among scholars that the 1890s marked a turning point in the nation's history." The rise of a corporate form of capitalism altered the structure of the industrial economy and social relations. It ushered in large-scale corporations that employed thousands of people, coordinated dozens of factories, operated across an entire continent, and generated billions of dollars in profits. It was part of a larger transformation

---

chart 4.3

A COMPARISON OF TWO PATTERNS OF PUBLIC BUREAUCRACY FORMATION

Adaptive Pattern (e.g., United States and Britain)	Coordinated Pattern (e.g., France and Japan)
Decentralized, divided authority	Centralized national authority
Staff turnover, moves in/out of government	Lifetime career path within government
Staff come from independent professions	Staff are experts trained for public service
Political appointees are most powerful	Career government officials most influential
Public service gets modest respect	Public civil servants get high prestige/respect

Source: Silberman (1993).

from an agricultural economy with small-scale manufacturing to an industrial-urban economy. The transition generated widespread social unrest, an economic downturn rivaling the Great Depression of the 1930s, radical political movements, and repeated bloody clashes between striking workers and troops.[12]

The transformation of the economy and society both shaped political institutions and was shaped by them. New technologies and business-economic relations do not automatically or inevitably arise; they are shaped by a political–institutional context of laws, policy, and procedures.[13] Something paradoxical often occurs—once technologies and economic patterns develop to a certain stage they trigger changes in the institutional features that first facilitated their emergence, and the changes are ones that, if they had been in place, would have inhibited the new technology/economic relations. For example, large land grants to private interests, decentralized political authority, unstable and speculative financing, and an absence of business regulation all created huge profits and spurred a vast nineteenth century railroad transportation system. Yet after the railroad industry developed, cutthroat competition, public outrage over unfair rates, violent labor unrest, and terrible train accidents produced political agitation that demanded worker safety rules, financial controls, limits on fare increases, and regulations on train routes.[14] If such a system of rules and regulations had been present early on, railroads would not have expanded rapidly.

Similar patterns of institutional change affected the emerging large corporation. In response to mounting public pressure, governments passed new laws and created administrative regulatory agencies that specialized in overseeing the economic relations. This displaced the power of political parties, although the courts retained a role, and held back public demands for more regulatory action.[15] The economy grew in size and the population urbanized. The percentage of people in rural areas dropped from three-fourths in 1880 to under one-half by 1920; and from 1880 to 1930, manufacturing output grew tenfold and the gross national product (GNP) grew 900 percent. Federal employment grew sixfold

CASE IN POINT 4.2   **Political Institutions and Asylum Expansion**

In 1880 there were 40,000 inmates in U.S. insane asylums. This number grew rapidly to 263,000 by 1923. Was there a vast increase in madness across America? Sutton (1991) says no. He argues that the huge expansion varied greatly by state and is best explained in the context of political institutions. Early in this era, families, private charities, or local governments provided the very little care that existed for the old, poor, disabled, or severely ill. The elderly had no pensions or retirement plans. The major exception were elderly Civil War veterans who received regular federal pensions. At the time, the profession of psychiatry was just beginning and definitions of mental problems were loose and applied inconsistently. The construction and staffing of asylums provided many jobs and were funded by the state government.

Sutton noted that asylum construction and the inmate population grew fastest in states where (1) the population living in almshouses, local public housing for the very poor and elderly, declined the fastest, (2) the economy was strong with growing tax revenues, (3) few of the elderly received federal veteran pensions, and (4) patronage-oriented party machines faced intense electoral competition. He argued that political parties in the states that had tax revenue undertook a large-scale asylum construction program to house large numbers of elderly and disabled people in poverty, created few other facilities to care for them, and channeled jobs to party loyalists. The asylums provided care for the very poor, the elderly, and disabled, irrespective of their mental health, and were a form of state expansion "conditioned and compounded by the peculiarities of the American state-building process" (p. 675).

from about 100,000 to 600,000; as a percentage of the total national population it doubled. Nonmilitary spending by the federal government grew tenfold, but as a percentage of the gross national product, it changed little. In comparison to the accumulation of private wealth, federal government spending actually declined. For each $1 the federal government spent, private individuals and companies held $2 more in banks in 1930 than in 1880.[16] Government expanded even more at the state and local levels. Between 1902 and 1927, state and local government spending grew from $1.92 to $2.21 for each $1 spent by the national government. For example, the proportion of orphaned or delinquent children cared for by government agencies doubled, but this occurred at the local and state levels, not at the national level.[17] Often, state governments initiated a new program or service that later became part of the federal government, but overall, social welfare programs expanded little.[18] While federal government authority and power grew, state government expansion retained old-style party politics and shaped government growth (see Case in Point 4.2). In a search for order, politicians and political movements of the early twentieth century reorganized institutions to respond to rapidly expanding wealth and major population shifts.[19]

   The great increase in wealth in the late nineteenth century was accompanied by widespread poverty, child labor, unsafe working conditions, and erratic financial markets. Protest movements and third political parties pressed for ending rule by corrupt party bosses and instituting a more open, fair system for ordinary citizens with the direct primary, direct election of senators (rather than by state legislatures), the referendum, and recall elections. Reformists pressed for government regulation of railroads and public utilities, laws to prevent child labor and protect women workers, penal reform, expanded services for the poor and disabled, and accident insurance for injured workers and their families.[20] Old-style newspapers that had been closely aligned with the political parties were replaced by new ones that pointed out social ills and corruption to a national audience.[21] Institutional reorganization took many forms (see Chart 4.4), state capacity expanded, and public administration became more rational.

As the older power center, the political party in the legislative branch, weakened, a new branch of government emerged—administrative agencies. They were staffed by nonpatronage professionals who specialized in legal–administrative rulemaking. This shift dramatically altered patterns of interest group influence. Organized interest groups (e.g., trade associations), corporations, and national-level elites shifted their focus from locally based political parties to the new national-level administrative agencies. This illustrates how new political institutions alter (inhibit or facilitate) the ability of specific groups to make political demands. For example, after major strikes and widespread unrest, the U.S. Bureau of Labor Statistics was established in 1884. Employers and workers fought over the agency's size, its degree of centralization, the types of data it collected, and the types of reports it issued. In 1902, employer groups succeeded in having the agency absorbed into the Department of Commerce, where it received only 2 percent of the department's budget. Agitation by worker groups and pressure by the Progressive and Socialist parties in the 1912 election caused government officials to reorganize it in 1913 into a separate cabinet-level agency, the Department of Labor. Employer groups continued pressure and kept the department decentralized, isolated from other agencies, and ineffectual. It

chart 4.4

PROGRESSIVE ERA CHANGES IN AMERICAN POLITICAL INSTITUTIONS (1885–1920)

1. The country became more fully integrated and national-level political institutions expanded and grew in importance.

2. Many new laws, government agencies, and public policies were developed to respond to social problems created by rapid industrialization and urbanization.

3. Alternating periods of mass unrest mobilization and repression demobilization moved large numbers of citizens in and out of electoral politics.

4. A layer of people and organizations with vast economic power and a national scope emerged with the rise of large corporations and financial organizations that created great amounts of new and concentrated wealth.

remained one of the smallest cabinet departments. The organizational situation of the Department of Labor weakened the ability of organized labor to mount national collective action.[22] This example shows how organizational forms are not neutral. As Elisabeth Clemens (1997, 98) observed, "The organizational logic of a political regime privileges some groups while marginalizing others."

A highly decentralized, federal structure enhances the bargaining position of organizations that operate across many states. They can avoid government actions they dislike by playing local or state governments against one another and threatening to relocate. For example, if one state imposes high business taxes, a company relocates to a state where the government is unwilling, or too weak, to impose taxes. This happened on a large scale in the late 1800s. New Jersey passed laws with few restrictions and gave corporations many advantages, including the ability to be a "holding company" and buy/own other companies. As the governments of other states tried to impose limits on large corporations, many large corporations, trusts, and monopolies incorporated in New Jersey to avoid the other states' rules, regulations, and taxes.[23] They were New Jersey companies but operated nationally.

After World War I, a highly conservative period in U.S. history began with Prohibition laws, strict limits on immigration, new antiforeigner and antiunion laws, a revival of the Ku Klux Klan, and a hands off probusiness policy that rolled back government oversight of large banks and corporations.[24] This party system and pattern of national policy remained intact until the 1930s. Thus, developments from the 1880s to the mid-1930s highlight a major lesson about political institutions: Institutional development occurs in spurts. Periods of continuity are interspersed with short transition periods of very rapid change when some parts of existing institutional structures remain unchanged, but many others are rearranged or displaced, and new parts added (see Closer Look 4.1).

The state-building process involves a sequence of "regimes which substantially alter the substantive content and operations of federalism and the separation of powers . . . revamping constitutional relationships and installing new government agendas."[25] **A political regime is an interwoven mode of governance that includes a party system, relations among levels of government, the central policy divisions, and organizational structure of national government.** A sequence of overlapping regimes arose across two centuries of U.S. history, each lasting over a decade. Shifting between regimes, or realignment, is what Richard McCormick (1986, 12) called "America's surrogate for revolutions." **Realignment theory states that periods of regime stability are punctuated by transition periods, during which several areas of a regime, particularly the party system, national policies, and the organizational form of the national government, experience rapid, significant change.** The most common trigger event to a transition period is the critical election. **Critical elections are unusual elections in which many blocks of voters change party affiliation, voter turnout is very high, and parties are more ideologically polarized.** Regime transition is not a simple one-way flow from the wishes of citizens to new policy and government agencies, in which parties, voters, movements, lobbying,

CLOSER LOOK 4.1   Critical Elections and Partisan Realignments

Most elections are predictable, low-pressure events. Stable coalitions of interest groups and sectors of society tend to support one or the other party. For example, the film and entertainment industry has backed Democrats and the National Rife Association has supported Republicans for decades. Major sectors of society rarely shift from strong support for one party to the other (e.g., as urban African Americans did in the 1930s or as Southern whites did in the 1990s). Only rarely does a major new hot issue emerge that divides parties and persists for years (e.g., legalized abortion). Many areas (i.e., election districts, counties, states) show regular and high levels of support for one party, while a few others are very competitive and frequently switch party support. In some states, one party wins the governorship, controls the state legislature, and gets presidential electoral votes year after year, while other states are divided and switch parties. For example, between 1876 and 1944, eleven Southern states were almost totally controlled by the Democratic Party. As virtual one-party states, electoral influence

was limited to intraparty factions and primary elections. A few American elections are critical elections that trigger a shift in the party system. There is a great deal of debate about when and why they occur. They have these characteristics:

- Competition between parties increases, with many more close races.
- The impact spreads across different levels of government and regions.
- The configuration of the social base of support for parties shifts.
- There is increased ideological polarization over new issues.
- Voter participation increases due to the following:

1. A conversion of voters to support a new party
2. Adding many new voters who vote for one party
3. The withdrawal of previous voters who supported one party

Sources: Andersen (1979), Clubb et al. (1980), Key (1955), Burnham (1967, 1970), Sundquist (1973).

and so forth carry popular feelings or ideas into new government policy. This might occur, but the regime realignment is often more complex. The relationship among electoral politics, party, state organization, and policy is not tight or seamless. Moreover, new voting patterns do not produce an immediate, automatic shift in public policy. For example, electoral realignment in the late 1890s took nearly 20 years to affect many public policies.[26]

The direction of change is not only from the electorate to government policy. Party leaders, top officials, or organized elite groups can perceive and seize new opportunities to push policy changes that affect other regime parts, including electoral politics. Political officials use new openings to advocate change. For example, the public demanded a response to the severe economic crisis of the 1930s. Two alternative models of how the government could manage the economy were available—fiscal policy (i.e., controlling the money supply and government spending), advocated by officials in the Bureau of Budget, and developmental policy (i.e., negotiating to control labor costs, plan production, and control natural resources), advocated by officials in the National Resources

Planning Board (NRPB). In 1939, NRPB was a larger agency and the developmental plan looked stronger. Six years later, the developmental plan had disappeared, the NRPB was dismantled, and the fiscal policy option was adopted. The Bureau of Budget had won. This was not the result of voter demand; rather, certain political elites and their allied organized interests inside and outside of government had pressured for the fiscal policy option. Only after political elites had adopted the fiscal policy option did the political parties shift to correspond to it.[27]

A realignment period can last as little as a year or as long as a decade. During this period, the relative power of social and political forces can profoundly shape the direction of regime change and the reconfiguration of major institutions. Powerful organized groups, social classes, or organizations active during the transition period when institutions are most fluid and being reconstructed can fix organizational arrangements, rules and procedures, and personnel that can persist long afterwards. Even if the political forces that had been active during the transition period weaken, their activism during a critical historical juncture may endure as divisions and hostilities among government agencies or avenues of influence. Their imprint can last for decades and become self-perpetuating.

Next we examine the regime realignment of the 1930s that restructured institutions, conflicts, and policies, creating a regime that lasted into the 1980s. Its impact can be still seen on U.S. political institutions today.

The New Deal Regime

The Great Depression of the 1930s and World War II brought about a "New Deal" domestic political system and a military-industrial complex that reorganized institutions and provided a structure of politics that lasted 50 years.[28] The New Deal was triggered by a major social and economic crisis and political unrest that seriously threatened the nation's stability. The regime shift was preceded by massive protest movements, severe economic dislocation, and a groundswell of electoral support. The New Deal was more than a set of new government agencies and programs; in an attempt to save the democratic-capitalist system and restore political legitimacy, it redirected institutions, changed numerous economic and social policies, reoriented government's role in society, and realigned the political parties.

The size and reach of the federal government grew significantly under the New Deal regime. Throughout the 1920s and into the early 1930s, federal employment rarely exceeded 2 percent of the civilian, nonfarm labor force, and it dropped to just 1.6 percent in the mid-1920s. During the New Deal, it increased to 3 percent of the labor force. The national government grew faster than state and local governments. Annual federal expenditures grew from about $1.3 billion in the 1920s to $6 billion in 1940. As a percentage of the entire economy, this was substantial since the economy had slowed. For example, in the 1920s annual federal government expenditures averaged 1.55 percent of the GNP, but between

1933 and 1940, they averaged 6.65 percent. The impact was huge in specific sectors of the economy. For example, by 1933 new housing starts had dropped to one-tenth of their pre-Depression level, but after New Deal programs stimulated a housing recovery, they rose to 70 percent of the pre-Depression level. Federal housing aid went from 0 to about 30 percent of all private housing starts while, for public assistance, spending grew tenfold from levels in the 1920s. The entire public-national government relationship changed as more ordinary citizens came into closer contact with the federal government. Increasingly, the population came to believe the national government had an obligation to deal with major adversity and improve or alleviate many social ills. As a result, the nature of citizenship changed and social citizenship rights expanded.

The national government also redefined business–government relationships and assumed an active role in regulating private business activities with a flurry of new laws, agencies, policies, and court decisions. Federal oversight of banking, labor relations, marketing, communication, and transportation grew, and most of today's economic regulatory agencies began during the New Deal period. For example, the farm sector was in terrible condition, and three program options were being considered: (1) limit the amount that farmers produced, (2) control and plan agricultural land use, or (3) provide social programs for farmers. The main farm program today, production controls, was selected over alternatives based on the political strength of its advocates in the 1930s. The advocates had pre-existing organizations, a national communication system, allies or friends inside government agencies, and significant resources (i.e., money, people, symbols). Backed by large farmers with more resources and who had cultivated significant support within the U.S. Agricultural Department, a New Deal agricultural policy was formed. It set the basic parameters that remained in place for over six decades.[29] The specific impact of many social programs depended on the local structure of political institutions (i.e., the state-level party system and political rights) (see Closer Look 4.2).

The best-known New Deal program, Social Security, became solidly entrenched after World War II as did an enlarged federal role in health care provision, occupational safety, support for the disabled and poor, education, transportation, and housing. Before the New Deal, the federal government had a minimal role in these areas, and many of the social programs were just getting underway when World War II began.

The Welfare–Warfare State

World War II reshaped U.S. political institutions more than any war since the Revolutionary War. Its long-term consequence was to solidify public support for an enlarged federal domestic role and for a large, permanent military establishment to back an expanded U.S. international role. In the United States, as elsewhere, a wartime crisis that threatens the people, ideals and sovereignty triggered rapid state growth and expansion into new areas of society under the directive of protecting and preserving the nation-state. Hegemony was reconfigured around a mixture of patriotism, militarism, and nationalist

Political Institutions and Social Program Expansion

In the United States as a whole, political institutions are fragmented and the executive branch has weak administrative capability. Amenta and Halfmann (2000, 506) refined the idea that, "fragmented political institutions make it easy for anti-social spending groups to block social legislation and a weak executive makes social policy difficult to implement . . . ." They also argued that political institutions vary, and the degree of democracy they permit affects social policy expansion. Two factors shape the degree of democracy in a polity: the openness of political rights (e.g., the degree of restrictions on the right to vote, free speech) and the party system (e.g., the degree to which it is ideological program-based or patronage-based and distributes individualized benefits). Amenta and Halfmann classified the polity in each state in the United States during the New Deal era into one of four categories based on these two factors (see table), but no state was in the underdemocratic-patronage polity category. They believed that the polity of a state would vary in allowing political activists who favored social programs (e.g., unions, left-leaning parties, protest movements) to be successful. They predicted lower success in winning social programs where political rights were less open because politicians did not need to appeal to lower-income voters and largely relied on the economically privileged for support. They also predicted lower success in areas with patronage-based parties, because such parties avoided pro-

fessional bureaucracies that provided social benefits to all qualified people and instead preferred to control benefits so they could direct the benefits to their supporters on a nonuniversal basis. Amenta and Halfmann (2000) tested their ideas by looking at the Works Progress Administration (WPA). The WPA began in 1935 and lasted until 1939, and it was one of the largest social programs of the New Deal. The WPA provided good paying, public-sector jobs to the unemployed for a variety of public works (e.g., public buildings, highway and park improvements). The WPA was a federal program but delegated social program implementation to the state level. Amenta and Halfmann found that WPA varied by state depending on the state's political institutional context and degree of pressure from prosocial program activists. The highest WPA benefits were in states with an open polity and strong pro-benefit political pressure. Somewhat lower levels of benefits occurred in states with an open polity but little political pressure or in a patronage-based polity with strong political pressure, and even lower social benefits occurred in patronage-based policy states with little political pressure. The lowest social benefit levels were in undemocraticized polity states. In sum, at the height of New Deal mobilization for social programs, political–institutional conditions shaped the state-level polity, and the type of polity either allowed or inhibited political activists from pressuring for an expansion of social programs.

Type of Polity of States in the New Deal Era (Number of States)

Party System	Political System	
	Extensive Rights	Restricted Rights
Program Oriented	Open polity (24)	Underdemocratic polity (11)
Patronage Oriented	Patronage based polity (13)	Underdemocratic patronage (0)

symbols. Dissent was limited; social control increased; and ethnic, religious, and racial minorities were incorporated into the polity around wartime goals. Executive branch power rapidly expanded and intervention into the private economy increased (e.g., rationing, property confiscation, curtailed economic activity that did not contribute to war production). World War II created a new national direction that lasted nearly 50 years as the Cold War period that followed the war reinforced the newly created or reorganized institutions. The Cold War era (1949–1989) reshaped policies and institutions (e.g., domestic science policy, industrial production policy, natural resource policy, transportation and education policy, international policy). Once the United States became the world leader in economic, political, and military affairs, a tension grew between the nation's international role as the premier global power and the domestic concerns of ordinary citizens (also discussed in Chapter 12).

Having examined political institutions of the polity, we next turn to inclusion within or exclusion from the polity.

INCLUSION WITHIN OR EXCLUSION FROM THE POLITY

Beyond the polity's basic structure, a second major issue is its boundaries and inclusion in or exclusion from those boundaries. Inclusion and exclusion involve movement into or out of specific areas of the polity. For example, we can ask whether inclusion is at the core or the fringe of the polity. In addition, inclusion and exclusion operate at all three dimensions of power. Inclusion and exclusion determine who is in or out of polity boundaries, and what behaviors and ideas are permitted or prohibited.

We can see the idea of inclusion in politically correct jokes. This is not the place to review controversies about political correctness, but such jokes typically involve insensitivity over the inclusion of a social group that had been blocked or excluded from full, equal involvement. **Inclusion is bringing people, groups, ideas, or behaviors into the polity.** Minimal inclusion is crossing into the polity; maximum inclusion is to be an insider who calls the shots. Inclusion may involve making special deals to speed the way for specific groups. For example, a political official may offer certain business firms special tax breaks if they move into a depressed area. Here inclusion uses incentives to bring the businesses "inside." Many people accept the myth is that there has been continuous, expanding inclusion in the United States. This is only partly true; there are major exceptions and reversals. **Exclusion means denying full integration into the polity (e.g., not letting people or groups vote, speak, or express views or denying use of public services).** The term *second class citizen* indicates exclusion—that some people lack full rights and do not receive the same treatment as others.

Inclusion and exclusion take many forms and vary along a continuum. Exclusion ranges from barriers or discrimination to explicit restrictions on access (including censorship or legal prohibitions) to violent repression. Inclusion ranges from removing barriers to actively encouraging entry to granting special, or privileged, access. In addition, people or actions excluded in the past may be included now and may be excluded again in the future.

Three Forms of Inclusion: Privideged Access, Encouragement, and Removal of Direct Barriers

Below we examine three forms of inclusion—privileged access, encourage-ment, and barrier removal. Two examples from U.S. politics illustrate each type of inclusion.

Privileged Access

Privileged access occurs when some people or groups have significant ad-vantages compared to others in selecting candidates, having a voice in elec-tions, placing items on the public agenda, or influencing policymaking.

Financing Political Campaigns   Campaign finance is a large, complex area with many legal issues and debates. The mass media concentrates on the quan-tities of money involved, who gives whom money, and how money is spent. Most reform proposals try to limit the amounts of money spent, control meth-ods of collecting money, or advocate replacing privately donated money with public funds. Such reform proposals miss many issues of inclusion.

"Campaign finance" is a misnomer. A small part of campaign finance is about the flow of money into a candidate's election campaign. Most involves buying ac-cess to influence politicians, so "influence buying" may be a better term. Contrib-utors make large donations—often hundreds of thousands of dollars—in years when no elections are held, to candidates without an opponent, and for elections in far distant districts. National advocacy organizations may donate more than the total from all the citizens, organizations, and supporters within a district, even to opposing sides in an election. Such actions are nonsensical if the goal is only to help a candidate win, but they make perfect sense if the goal is to foster gratitude and indebtedness from elected politicians.

Advocacy organizations buy "issue advertising" during an election without a candidate's approval. The advertising does not directly ask voters to support a specific candidate, but after making a one-sided presentation on an issue, it mentions a candidate's stand. Technically it educates, informs, and persuades voters on an issue. In 1995–1996, $135 million to $150 million was spent on such advertising, while this figure jumped from $275 million to $340 million in 1997–1998.[30] A federal reform law passed in 2002 slightly limited the advertis-ing and shifted fund-raising to the unregulated state level; it had been weak-ened already to allow corporate and union donations.[31] State elections are a major growth area. Donations to judicial candidates in the eleven states with state Supreme Court elections grew by 61 percent from 1998 to 2000.[32]

Campaign money from advocacy groups, individuals, or organizations to candidates, politicians, or a political party buys three related kinds of inclusion: (1) candidate selection by encouraging a person to run for office; (2) politician selection by affecting who can win an election; and (3) policy selection by accessing elected politicians as they draft laws, formulate policy, allocate budget money, and vote on pending legislation. The money convinces friendly candidates to run for office, helps them win, keeps them sensitive to a donor's ideas, information, issues, and disapproval, and influences a politician's priorities and decision-making.

"A <u>very</u> special interest to see you, Senator."

In an ideal democracy, each citizen has equal and full participation and an equal vote. Large campaign donations create inequality and give groups, organizations, or individuals with more money a greater impact. They undermine the democratic principle that each citizen has an equal voice. The relationship between wealth and exercising political rights is not limited to elections. A citizen's capacity to use, defend, and enforce other legal–political rights (e.g., divorced parent visitation of children, complaints over bad products, race or sex discrimination) often depends on the person's ability to pay for a lawyer and litigation costs.

Some say that a campaign donation is simply a form of "political speech" that uses money instead of words. Yet, it is like saying anyone can make a speech in a public park. Person A stands on a soap box and speaks in a normal voice for 20 minutes. Person B sets up a 50-foot stage with spotlights, hires a band to play, provides free food and drinks, uses a microphone with a powerful amplifier and 12-foot speakers, and speaks for an entire day. Both have equal rights to deliver a message, but their impact is not equal. Privileged inclusion occurs when some groups attain major advantages that others lack. Unequal access to the polity creates a de facto privilege.

Large campaign donations come from a tiny percentage of the population. About .25 percent of the population gives $200 or more, which accounts for 80 percent of all campaign donations. Donation rates vary geographically and by race. For example, in the 26 zip codes with high campaign donation rates (and almost no racial minorities), 4.34 percent of people made donations versus .08 percent in the areas where 50 percent of the people are racial minorities.[33]

Really large donations come from corporations and organized interests to affect policy. For example, in 2000 the National Academy of Sciences announced after years of study that raising the auto fuel efficiency standards would reduce global warming and dependence on foreign oil using existing technology without harming auto safety or performance. That year General Motors, Ford, Daimler-Chrysler, and the United Auto Workers donated $4.8 million to federal candidates and political parties and opposed improving fuel economy standards. Then in August 2001, 10 months after the election, Congress voted against improving fuel economy standards.[34]

Candidates and potential candidates also get money indirectly. A donor might pay a candidate a large fee ($20,000) for a speech, lend him/her a private jet, or buy land or other items from the candidate for far more than its true value.[35] One senator described how he was invited to a luxury apartment and introduced as "someone who helped with copyright issues." He gave a very short speech to some total strangers and walked out with $46,000.[36]

Large donations do not automatically win elections; voters not money decide elections. Yet large amounts of money influence what voters know about candidates and how they think about issues. Most campaign finance debates remain at the first dimension of power and focus on winning elections. Yet it reaches the second dimension of power when donations decide who can become a candidate, the issues discussed in a campaign, and the policies politicians vote on after an election. Large donations can drown out or silence points of view that are not backed with money. The third dimension of power involves how many people feel "nothing can be done" about campaign finance and how free speech is redefined to mean political speech equal to using private wealth. It elevates property rights over the principle that limiting property rights is essential to protect basic democratic processes.

Policy Planning Networks   Public policy begins with processes of formulating, refining, and elaborating ideas about a concern (e.g., taxes, welfare, schooling, immigration). Such ideas support specific interests, ideological–philosophical values, and assumptions (e.g., the market is best, individual choice is good, unions are bad). Each country has its own forms of priviledged access (see World View 4.1). For example, in the United States school vouchers and school choice originated with elite concerns about public schools and developed into a serious policy option. These policies give tax money to parents to send their children to private or public schools based on an assumption that free competition among schools will reward good schools, punish bad ones, and raise the quality of education (see also Chapter 8).[37]

New policy ideas can originate from a constituent's letter, a politician consulting with her/his staff, an academic report, the news media, or a civil servant in the government. Yet as Anker et. al. (1987, 106) noted, the "lonely chief executive working late at night . . . has little to do with reality: every important political policy is the result of careful research, multiple authorship, collective judgment, and in most cases, a long period of incubation." Today, many new ideas originate in a network of nongovernment organizations—independent, nonprofit think tanks that are barely visible. Clawson and Clawson (1987, 205) observed, "Think tanks are crucial to the policy formation process, providing information, ideas, and proposals to be considered by the government, mass

WORLD VIEW 4.1   Descent from Heaven, Iron Triangles, and Political Tribes in Japan

Each nation has its own forms of privileged access and policy planning. The polity of Japan has some interesting features. First, its current democratic constitution, which was adopted after the country's defeat in World War II and has not been amended since, was written and imposed by American Occupation forces. Second, one political party, the Liberal Democratic Party (LDP), has held power in its parliamentary system since 1955, except for about 2 years, despite numerous and repeated bribery and influence-peddling scandals. Third, the national government bureaucracy and large corporations are tightly coordinated. This has been cited both as the source of Japan's economic miracle in the 1970s–1980s, and as the cause of its economic recession that lasted from 1991 to 2003. While Japanese politics appears quiet and is based on cultural values of cooperation and group harmony, before World War II, the country was racked by violent clashes and the assassination of political leaders. Even after the war, until 1980 it saw violent strikes, assassinations of politicians, massive violent street demonstrations and rioting, and domestic terrorist attacks.

The center of the current Japanese power structure is a close relationship (sometimes called an Iron Triangle) among the executives of major corporations, high-level government bureaucrats, and leading LDP officials. A central institution of privileged access in Japan's developmental state (see Chapter 2) is *amakudari*. It translates as "descent from heaven" and refers to a system of re-employing top government bureaucrats in major corporations or as elected/appointed politicians after they retire (at an early age) from public office. In the United States it is sometimes called "parachuting." Amakudari solidifies a system of close ties and alliances among leading bureaucrats, politicians, and business. It is a channel of influence and communication among corporations, state officials, and politicians, because the retired exgovernment officials have extensive insider knowledge, maintain personal contacts

and friendships, and still have great influence in government. Throughout their government careers, the officials know that high pay and status as a top corporate official await them if they are careful to protect big business interests. Of course other nations have a "revolving door" in which people move back and forth between high-level corporate posts and top government positions (see Chapter 10). In the United States this is seen in the careers of Vice President Richard Cheney and Secretary of Defense Donald Rumsfeld, or in France in graduates of the *grande ecoles*. Yet few nations reach the scale, extent, or closeness of Japan's deeply embedded informal influence system, and it is largely hidden from public view. As Colignon and Usui (2003, 4) observed, "The social institution of amakudari is pervasive, unique, and enigmatic."

Each year over 1,700 of Japan's upper-level government officials retire and move into business positions, so it is a very large system. One report noted that 90 percent of the officials who retired in 2000 assumed new private industry jobs within 3 months of leaving government office (Colignon and Usui 2003, 82). Japan has a law against taking such positions shortly after leaving public office, but the law is very weak and limited, and it misses most of the amakudari system. In addition, ex-officials often move from one top corporate position to another after retirement, pursuing a 15- to 20-year career leading Japan's largest companies. For example, one or more retired government officials are top executives in over one-half of the 100 largest companies in Japan and in 621 of the 2,220 largest firms. Most served in a few key government ministries (e.g., tax, investment, finance, construction). Beyond cementing a very close relationship between big business and government, the institution of amakudari contributes to raising the barriers to accessing Japan's polity. It contributes to a restriction of political alternatives by reinforcing a system with minimal political party competition, a nonaggressive media (ex-officials lead major media corporations and public media companies), limited public access to information, and vague laws and administrative rules that only a few political insiders can interpret.

Another related feature of Japanese politics is the political *zoku,* a term that translates as "tribe" or "group." It refers to a set of members of parliament in conjunction with counterparts in government ministries, think tanks, companies, and so forth that exercise great control over policy areas (e.g., education, railroads, defense). For example, the zoku around tobacco would include interested members of parliament, executives from tobacco companies, and officials from the Ministry of Health and the Ministry of Finance. The Japanese Ministry of Finance owns 67 percent of Japan Tobacco (JT), the world's third largest tobacco company that controls 80 percent of Japan's domestic market. Not surprisingly, 50–60 percent of Japanese men smoke—one of the highest rates in the world. Cigarette machines are everywhere in public, cigarette advertising is almost

unrestricted, and cigarette taxes and prices are about 60–70 percent of those found in other industrialized countries.

The LDP is generally conservative and probusiness, but much of its success has been its nonideological extensive use of "pork barrel" politics (see Chapter 10). Essentially, the national government funds many expensive, large-scale public works projects (e.g., new bridges, highways) to keep construction companies busy (a major source of political donations) and boost specific local communities. It also enacts legal protections or grants subsidies to targeted groups (i.e., farmers, residents of small towns) that have a much larger weight in elections than their actual share of the population because of election laws. Although it has retained power by sustaining a strong economy with low unemployment and by skillfully awarding distributive favors to specific groups, LDP has enacted few laws to advance the basic rights or social conditions of most ordinary Japanese citizens.

Sources: Colignon and Usui (2001, 2003), Kerbo and McKinstry (1995), Schlesinger (1999), and Stockwin (1999).

media and capitalists themselves." **A think tank is an organization (usually nonprofit, nongovernment) in which one or more researchers, writers, journalists, or others develop, refine, elaborate, and publicize ideas about policy issues.**[38] Most are legal nonprofit, nongovernment organizations funded by private donations. A network of such organizations has become the Policy Planning Network (PPN), a critical part of the polity. The **Policy Planning Network is a collection of overlapping think tanks, private foundations, advocacy groups, and individuals that supply ideas, arguments, justifications, and models for public policy on contemporary issues.** The PPN has been around for a century but has greatly expanded in size and influence in four phases, each with its own style—the Progressive Era, the New Deal, the post-World War II period, and the Conservative Backlash.

During the Progressive Era, the policy organizations were few, small, and limited. Often they advocated a middle position between a radical-socialist and rigid-conservative polarization, or they opposed urban machines (see below). The organizations (e.g., National Civic Federation) brought together leading bankers and business executives, academics, lawyers, and others (e.g., religious leaders, moderate labor leaders) in conferences on public issues that politicians attended to learn ideas and hear advice. During the 1930s, corporate leaders and academics joined discussion groups or "advisory councils" to advise the executive branch. Again, the context was a growing ideological polarization between radical and conservative positions. Government officials and corporate leaders together developed policy solutions in a collaboration that formed a basis for cooperative planning during World War II. In the 1950s–1960s, a new few organizations appeared, such as the Rand Corporation and the Brookings Institute. They hired professional social scientists with technical training and developed ties to specific government agencies. They received a mix of private and government funding, including funds to conduct policy studies and for consulting with government agencies. By the late 1970s, a conservative mobilization against late-1960s social movements and Great Society policies transformed the PPN landscape. Numerous new organizations were created at the state and national levels. Many had much better funding and were very ideologically combative. Unlike the organizations in the 1950s and 1960s that employed social scientists, they were staffed with people from public relations, law, or journalism. The new organizations advised the executive and legislative branches, distributed press releases to media outlets, and supplied politicians with lists of ideologically committed political appointees. For example, the Heritage Foundation, founded in 1973, is oriented toward conservative ideological advocacy (also see Case in Point 4.3).[39]

The PPN is a private branch of the polity that operates outside, but beside, government and the media. It operates with political institutions that have "the constitutional separation of powers; a party system historically grounded in electoral political ambitions, rather than ideology; and a civil service tradition that gives leeway to numerous political appointees."[40] Policy debates and discussions that occur in the PPN in the United States, take place among strong ideologically oriented parties in a parliamentary system and in coordination with an expert-based administrative bureaucracy in Western Europe. The U.S. Policy Planning Network has five kinds of organizations (see Chart 4.5).[41]

Some parts of the PPN are small, low cost affairs. A task force might be all volunteer labor and involve a half dozen people meeting six times operating on a budget of less than the cost of a new luxury automobile. While other parts, such as some think tanks or foundations, have multi-million dollar annual budgets and are like small colleges without students. They own buildings in prominent locations; maintain large professional and clerical staffs; have public relations; publications; and research departments, libraries, and lavish conference centers. Many pay well. They may give an author over $100,000 to write a book that expounds the group's ideological position.

Organizations in the PPN represent a range of ideology and opinions, but they are unbalanced with regard to political position and funding. In terms of the left-liberal versus right-conservative ideology continuum, there are about four on the ideological right for each on the liberal left, with a funding ratio of about 100:1. The largest one on the right, the Heritage Foundation, had a 2000 budget of $38 million, a fine large building in the center of Washington D.C., and a staff over 200 people. Its corporate sponsors include General Motors, Ford Mo-

CASE IN POINT 4.3   **The Manhattan Institute**

The conservative think tank, the Manhattan Institute, was founded in 1978 when Anthony Fisher, the intellectual mentor of British Prime Minister Margaret Thatcher, convinced American businessmen to provide funding. It was first led by William Casey, whom Ronald Reagan later appointed to head the Central Intelligence Agency. It now has a $6 million a year budget, about one-third of which is funded by corporations (including Chase Manhattan, Proctor and Gamble, State Farm Insurance, American Express), two-fifths by right-wing foundations (such as the Lynde and Harry Bradley, John M. Olin, and Scaife foundations) and the remainder by individual contributors. It publishes a quarterly magazine with a circulation of 10,000, and supports twenty "fellows" who include former city officials, ex-state government executives, journalists, and professors. Leading business executives and conservative professors from Harvard University and the University of Chicago sit on its board of trustees.

The institute has had national impact on state policies (e.g., New Jersey governor Christie Whitman's proposals), and especially on the Mayor Rudolph Giuliani's administration in New York City. In New York it is opposes open admissions for the city university system and rent control, and it pushed for the privatization of public hospitals. It helped Charles Murray, a leading right-wing intellectual, publish an influential book that attacked the welfare state, and it provided, $100,000 to support a book attacking affirmative action by the Thernstroms. It also supported a book by Myron Magnet attacking policies of the 1960s that was influential in George W. Bush's presidential bid in 2000.

The institute's goal is to develop policy-relevant pro-free market ideas and get them into the "media food chain" so they reach mainstream discourse. It does this by publishing books and articles, providing congressional testimony, and sponsoring lavish lunches at private clubs for journalists, politicians and top government officials several times each month. It is neither the largest nor most publicized think tank, but it has been influential in shaping public debate in several key issue areas.

Sources: See: Kaplan (1998), Mitchell (2000), Rubin (1996), Scott (1997), James Smith (1990), Solomon (1998), and Taub (1994). Also see the Manhattan Institute homepage http://www.manhattan-institute.org.

tors, Proctor and Gamble, Chase Manhattan Bank, Dow Chemical, the Reader's Digest Association, Mobil Oil, and Smith Kline Corporation. The largest one on the left, the Institute for Policy Studies, had a $650,000 annual budget. Much of the imbalance is due to the values and beliefs of wealthy individuals—both those who control major foundations and corporate executives. For example, one wealthy individual, Richard Mellon Scaife, heir to a Pittsburgh banking and oil fortune, has donated about $300 million to ultraconservative organizations over the past 30 years. The Joseph Coors family (makers of Coors beer) is a founding supporter of the ultraconservative Heritage Foundation.[42]

Think tanks produce a stream of reports, testimony, newsletters, magazines, policy-issue books, and press releases for journalists that steer the direction of public policy. "The product of a non-profit public policy organization" Alpert and Markusen (1980, 179) observed, "is ideology and suggestions for policy. It is not policy as such." In addition, PPN organizations supply people for political appointments and to appear on public issues television programs or at

---

chart   4 . 5

ORGANIZATIONS OF AMERICA'S POLICY PLANNING NETWORK

Task forces are temporary, single-issue groups that bring together experts, community leaders, and politicians to analyze, discuss, reach conclusions, and offer policy recommendations on an issue. Often a private foundation or government agency provides funding, but participants may volunteer their time. For example, at the local level, a school principal, a small business owner, a retired corporate executive, a wealthy homemaker who serves on the board of several charities, a police official, a social service agency director, a religious minister, and a representative of the mayor's office join to discuss youth drug problems. They recommend a drug-testing program for youths in city recreation programs.

Policy discussion groups (e.g., Council on Foreign Relations, Conference Board, Trilateral Commission) are ongoing collections of business leaders, government officials, and academics that meet to discuss and evaluate broad policy options. They have very small staffs and serve in an important coordination and consensus-building role.

Foundations (e.g., Ford, Carnegie, Rockefeller, Pew, Mellon) are major sources of funding for the PPN. Some have their internal staff to develop new ideas. Less than a dozen major foundations, with $300 million to $3 billion in assets, influence the entire network. Most are legacies of the vast fortunes accumulated during the robber baron era of American history; wealthy individuals or top managers of corporations created the rest. Each has priorities or an agenda to advance and does so by directing donations and gifts. Foundations that are connected to large corporations tend to have more moderate politics compared to those funded by wealthy individuals.

"Think tanks" (e.g., Brookings Institute, Heritage Foundation, American Enterprise Institute, Manhattan Institute, Cato Institute, Economic Policy Institute) are the main players in today's PPN. They bring together people who discuss, refine, and generate ideas and have a twofold purpose: to support people who formulate and elaborate ideas, and to communicate those ideas to promote a policy. They range across the ideological continuum, and major ones had a large influence over national political debates (see Case in Point 4.3).

Academic policy research centers (Center for the Study of Human Rights at Columbia University, the Woodrow Wilson Center, the Peace Institute) are small and minor players in the PPN. Sometimes they are no more than an endowed chair at a university (i.e., part or all of a single professor's salary and funds for supplies and a secretary) or a tiny government-funded agency to conduct academic research. One reason for their fringe position is that other parts of the network can hire experts or professors on an as-needed basis as consultants. For example, the consulting fees of one Yale professor were $40,000 to $50,000 per year for 4 years. In fact, professors or university presidents often sit on the boards of directors of think tanks and serve on policy discussion groups.

Sources: Domhoff (1990, 113–144) and Shoup and Minter (1977) give a detailed discussion of the Council on Foreign Relations. Also see Sklar (1980) on the Trilateral Commission. On foundations, see Allen (1992), Brown (1979), Burris (1992b), Domhoff (1998, 142), and Dunn (1980). Domhoff (1996, 117–176) provides a case of the Rockefeller Foundation and original Social Security legislation. On think tanks, see Callahan (1998), Denham (1996), and Easterbrook (1986). The case of the Yale Professor's fees was taken from Domhoff (1998, 138).

---

conferences. Donors to think tanks exercise the second dimension of power, because the ideas, reports and so forth flow into a barely visible layer of lobbyists, advocacy groups, the mass media, congressional hearings, campaign committees, and politicians who shape the policy agenda. Recommendations and ideas from think tanks fill television reports and newspaper articles, but this is almost unseen. American journalists increasingly rely on reports from advocacy think tanks but rarely give the source, and if they name a think tank, few identify its political orientation or source of funding. Many in the public have a false impression that the think tanks offer disinterested ideas from neutral experts. Think tank ideas have become accepted in mainstream public discourse, showing that they also operate on the third dimension of power.[43]

In sum, the PPN is an inclusion mechanism that enables a tiny sector of society to influence the political agenda, and it largely operates at the second and third dimensions of power where few others have access.

Encouragement

Encouragement includes government and nongovernment programs that target parts of the population and provide incentives to facilitate their participation in the polity. Encouragement differs from privileged access in three ways:

1. Privileged access originates with an individual, group, or organization that seeks greater input and anticipates direct benefits. Encouragement originates with the state or a third party to facilitate other individuals', groups', or organizations' involvement in the polity.
2. Groups already firmly within the polity use privileged access, while encouragement expands the involvement of those not yet fully included.
3. Individuals, groups, or organizations use privileged access to acquire more influence than their opponents, to make input unavailable to others, or to block others from access. Encouragement tries to raise and equalize the basic level of effective involvement in the polity for all groups.

Affirmative Action   The U.S. federal government, other levels of government, and many large organizations have affirmative action programs to expand opportunities for qualified racial minorities and women in job hiring, admission to higher education, and awarding government contracts. **Affirmation action is a set of policies, programs, and procedures designed to improve the employment and educational opportunities for minority group members and women**. The program suggests that if two equally capable and qualified candidates are available, an employer should give preference to candidates from an underrepresented group that faced past discrimination. For example, a fire department should promote a racial minority firefighter over an equally qualified majority-group, white firefighter if the department has very few racial minorities in management positions.

Affirmative action grew out of the civil rights movement and unrest in the late 1960s. While civil rights laws ended existing racial discrimination (i.e., they removed barriers), affirmative action policy was designed as an interim policy to remedy the legacy of past discrimination by creating extra opportunities for members of groups that had experienced unjust treatment. In theory, the representation of minorities would increase until it reached a proportion equal to their numbers in society, then affirmative action would no longer be necessary. Over time, the federal government extended affirmative action from African Americans to women, American Indians, Latinos, and other minorities, and from employment to higher education settings. The government also created programs to encourage the creation and growth of minority-owned businesses by earmarking or setting aside a percentage of government spending (e.g., to build a new highway) for minority-owned businesses. Affirmative action grew because specific groups demanded social justice and greater legal–political rights, and it seemed rational to use fully the talents of all people.

Shortly after affirmative action began, social conservatives and others attacked the policy and initiated legal actions to end it. They said that racial quotas and set-asides were reverse discrimination against white males. In a major case (*Regents of the University of California v. Bakke*, 1978), the U.S. Supreme Court outlawed quotas but said that schools could consider race as one factor among others. In the 1980s the Court further restricted affirmative action and gave weight to claims of reverse discrimination, outlawed minority set-asides unless past racial discrimination was proven, and limited state government use of racial preferences. In 1996, California voters approved Proposition 209, which prohibited giving preferences based on race or sex in any state government program or in university admissions. The U.S. Supreme Court upheld its legality. In 2003, the Court again upheld the principle of affirmative action but ruled that explicit quotas were illegal.

At first affirmative action was backed by a broad political coalition. By the late 1970s, the coalition weakened, the political climate shifted, and affirmative action fueled a backlash against blacks. It also weakened part of the Democratic Party's base of support.[44] Critics claimed that instead of encouraging access by well-qualified people, the program was providing government-enforced privileged access for racial minorities. National surveys revealed racial divisions over it (see Table 4.1) with a majority of all groups except blacks opposing it.

Opponents of affirmative action rarely oppose other forms of preference (e.g., low cost loans for veterans, college admissions for the children of alumni, jobs for friends in a company). Other forms such as preferential hiring and admissions are not explicitly race based, are not government mandated (except veterans), and do not try to bring disadvantaged people into the polity. Instead, they help people who are already in the polity and who possess other forms of privilege. The debate over affirmative action is complex and largely involves symbolic politics (see Chapter 7). The battles for and against it operate across all three dimensions of power.[45] It has generated overt political battles, voting divisions, attempts to control the public agenda, and resentments over core cultural beliefs.

Public Schooling   While affirmative action is hotly controversial, another form of encouragement, access to schooling, is not. Two centuries ago, schools were private and limited to children of the elite. Today, a worldwide consensus exists that mass schooling is desirable for national well-being. Most nations offer citizens free or nearly free schooling. As Brint (1998, 7) recognized, "Schooling has become strongly associated with interests of the nation-state in the development of a trained workforce and well-disciplined citizenry." No one

TABLE 4.1	Support for Affirmative Action by Race				
	Non-Hispanic White	Non-Hispanic Black	Non-Hispanic American Indian	Non-Hispanic Asian/Pacific Islander	Hispanic All Races
Favor	9.8%	53.1%	9.1%	20.0%	30.1%
Oppose	85.0%	38.6%	81.8%	60.0%	58.8%
Other	3.2%	3.4%	0.0%	0.0%	2.9%
Don't Know	2.0%	4.8%	9.1%	20.0%	8.1%
TOTAL	957	145	11	15	136

This question was asked: "Some people say that because of past discrimination, blacks should be given preference in hiring and promotion. Others say that such preference in hiring and promotion is wrong because it gives blacks advantages they haven't earned. What is your opinion? Are you for or against preferential hiring and promotion for blacks?"

Source: Calculated from 1998 National Election Studies Data. http://www.umich.edu/~nes/.

debates schooling; they debate the number of years of free schooling, its quality, teacher preparation, and the content of what is taught.

When a person sends his/her children to school, it signals full membership in the polity, and getting the children of an entire population to attend school for many years is a major inclusion issue. In the United States, the last major barriers to inclusion based on sex or race were removed after the *Brown v. Board of Education* decision in 1954 and the 1964 Civil Rights Act. A few parents expend huge amounts of money and great effort to get their children into exclusive private schools and selective colleges in hopes of advancing the family's class position, while the state must use compulsory attendance and truancy laws to force a few parents to educate their children. For the vast majority, simple encouragement is enough. Although some American urban schools resemble prisons, there is a range of encouragement actions, including a safe, clean physical environment with recreational facilities and services; periodic revisions in curriculum; upgrades in teacher preparation; innovative teaching methods; scholarships and tuition waivers; free transportation and meals; free health or social services to students; and services for special needs and non-English-speaking children. Other policies (e.g., laws that limit the working hours for youth and prohibit child labor) make the alternatives to attending school undesirable.

The main form of encouragement is to make schooling a very low-cost service. In much of Western Europe, schooling is free through the university level. The United States has a mixed system: Most students attend free public schools through grade 12, and about two-thirds attend public universities, where taxes usually pay over half the costs, or community colleges with a larger public subsidy. In other nations, such as Japan, compulsory schooling ends at junior high. Although it is not compulsory, Japan has a higher proportion of students attending high school than in the United States. Rates for attending higher education institutions are about the same, but most Japanese students attend private universities. Cultural beliefs and a tight linkage between employment and higher education explains the differences.[46]

Public polices encourage school attendance, but schooling has inequalities, barriers, and conflicts. There is a contradiction between encouragement and inequalities because schooling has multiple purposes: It socializes the youth to a culture, transfers skills and knowledge, and sorts out people for further job opportunities. Encouragement emphasizes the first two of these, while inequalities involve the last one. Conflicts rarely arise over general school attendance. They erupt over controlling the school curriculum (e.g., the values to which youth are socialized) and maintaining built-in inequalities by income and race (e.g., tracking students by ability, lines between school districts, paying for school). In the highly decentralized U.S. system, with deep racial and class divisions, schooling for all is not controversial so long as it is not too expensive, teaches the proper subjects, and does not force students from different racial or class backgrounds to mix together. Implicitly, the system of schooling also allows parents who have money or who want an alternative to the public school system to send their children to private schools, or to home school their children.

Schooling operates at all three dimensions of power. At the first dimension, laws enforce attendance, people vote for school board members, parents attend public meetings, and schools have official curriculum guides. At the second dimension of power, school district boundaries avoid some groups and include other groups and funding formulas keep some schools impoverished and others luxurious. At the third dimension of power, public schooling is coordinated with private economic demands, it promotes certain cultural–political values, and wealthy parents have a right to buy superior schooling for their children (schooling is discussed further in Chapter 8).

Removal of Direct Barriers
Removal of Direct Barriers is an inclusion mechanism that ends blockages to a group's entrance to the polity and expands access for a group that is not fully included in the polity. It differs from the other types of inclusion because the excluded group seeks full participation but cannot achieve it due to specific, recognized barriers. The initiative to remove barriers can originate with the affected group, a third party, or the state itself.

Women's Suffrage   Virtually every democratic nation today includes both genders in the polity through the fundamental right of voting. A century ago, women could only vote in the national elections of three countries—Australia (1902), Finland (1906), and New Zealand (1893). World War I sped women's enfranchisement in Europe and North America. Often, women could first vote in local or state elections, and only later in national elections. Shortly after World War II, women gained the vote in China, France, Italy, Japan, and in many other nations (see Table 4.2). Many ex-colonies granted women equal rights when they gained independence (e.g., India, Indonesia, Singapore, most of Africa). Only a handful of nations still deny women equal voting rights today.[47]

TABLE 4.2	**Women's Suffrage Acquisition by Country**

(grouped by decade and alphabetically within decade)

Before 1910		Costa Rica	1949	Ethiopia	1955
Australia	1902	Cuba	1942	Gabon	1956
Finland	1906	Dominican Republic	1942	Ghana	1955
New Zealand	1893	France	1944	Greece	1952
1909–1919		Guatemala	1945	Guinea	1956
Austria	1919	Hungary	1945	Haiti	1957
Czechoslovakia	1919	India	1949	Honduras	1957
Denmark	1915	Indonesia	1945	Iraq	1958
Germany	1919	Israel	1948	Ivory Coast	1956
Luxembourg	1919	Italy	1945	Jamaica	1953
Netherlands	1917	Japan	1945	Kampuchea	1956
Norway	1915	Liberia	1946	Laos	1956
Poland	1919	Malta	1947	Lebanon	1957
U.S.S.R.	1917	North Korea	1948	Madagascar	1956
1920–1929		Panama	1946	Malaysia	1957
Canada	1920	Philippines	1947	Mali	1956
Ecuador	1929	Romania	1946	Mauritania	1956
Iceland	1920	South Korea	1948	Mauritius	1959
Ireland	1922	Syria	1949	Mexico	1953
Mongolia	1924	Trinidad/Tobago	1946	Morocco	1959
Sweden	1920	Venezuela	1947	Nepal	1951
United Kingdom	1928	Vietnam	1947	Nicaragua	1955
United States	1920	Yugoslavia	1946	Niger	1956
1930–1939		**1950–1959**		Pakistan	1956
Brazil	1932	Albania	1958	Peru	1955
Burma	1935	Algeria	1958	Senegal	1956
South Africa	1930	Barbados	1950	Somalia	1958
Spain	1931	Benin	1956	Sudan	1956
Sri Lanka	1934	Bolivia	1952	Taiwan	1953
Thailand	1932	Burkina Faso	1956	Togo	1956
Turkey	1934	Cameroon	1956	Tunisia	1959
Uruguay	1932	Central African	1956	**1960–1969**	
1940–1949		Republic		Afghanistan	1964
Argentina	1947	Chad	1956	Botswana	1965
Belgium	1948	Columbia	1954	Burundi	1961
Bulgaria	1947	Congo	1956	Gambia	1961
Chile	1949	Cyprus	1959	Guyana	1966
China	1947	Egypt	1956	Iran	1963

Continued on page 152

TABLE 4.2	*Continued from page 151*				
Kenya	1963	Swaziland	1968	Jordan	1974
Lesotho	1966	Tanzania	1961	Portugal	1976
Libya	1963	Uganda	1962	South Africa	1993
Malawi	1964	Yemen, PDR	1967	Switzerland	1971
Nigeria	1960	Zambia	1964	**None**	
Paraguay	1961	Zimbabwe	1961	Kuwait, Oman, Qatar,	
Rwanda	1961	**1970–present**		Saudi Arabia, United Arab	
Sierra Leone	1961	Bangladesh	1972	Emirates	
Singapore	1965	Fiji	1970		

Source: Ramirez, Soysal, and Shanahan (1997, 743–744).

A movement for women's suffrage in the U.S. began early in the nineteenth century during antislavery agitation. When Wyoming became a state in 1890, its constitution gave women voting rights, and during the next 25 years, 15 other states enfranchised women. Women and their allies engaged in hard-fought protests, marches, petition drives, and political battles to win the vote nationally. Women were divided by class and race-ethnicity over the issue. Traditionalist Anglo-Protestant, upper class women, who feared giving immigrants, the poor, or working-class women political power, opposed the franchise for women.[48]

By 1918, both political parties backed women's suffrage, a Constitutional amendment carried in Congress, and over the next two years two-thirds of the states approved it. A legacy of disenfranchisement is that several decades later, women in the states that had not granted them the franchise earlier still had lower women's voting participation rates.[49] Often when barriers fall and subordinates can advance, those who defended the barriers become resentful, fueling backlash and attempts to reinstate barriers. This occurred with an antiwomen backlash.[50]

The battle for women's suffrage was fought along all three dimensions of power. It involved the visible level of marches, petitions, and getting votes in legislatures, behind the scenes fights to get the issue of woman's inclusion in the polity on the public agenda, and shifts in basic understandings about male-female roles and gender identity. These are third-dimension fights that continue today.

Sexual Orientation   As discussed in Chapter 2, full citizenship is more than a right to vote, it means equal access to public expression, basic living conditions, and the ability to participate fully in a community's public life. First-class citizenship means few or no barriers prevent the free expression of opinions openly in public or limit access to equal education, public services, employment, or housing. Conflict over sexual orientation in the contemporary United States, specifically denying equal rights to openly gay or lesbian people, illustrates how the politics of barrier removal operates. At issue is whether gays and lesbians are included in the polity as full citizens, or whether heterosexuality is a de facto requirement for full inclusion in the American polity.

Although few legal barriers now prohibit consenting adults from engaging in private sexual acts or operating a bar or business with a homosexual clientele, in most of the United States, gays and lesbians face legal and social barriers that block them from equal access to rental housing, retaining a job, obtaining insurance, getting married, and so forth. The barriers are not the harsh antihomosexual repression that occurred in Germany in the 1940s when the Nazis rounded up homosexuals and put them in death camps; nonetheless, they receive less than first-class citizenship. For example, a gay couple has few legal rights in a deportation hearing or to visit a hospitalized same-sex partner.[51]

The sexual orientation barrier illustrates how entry into the polity arises from cultural-moral-religious beliefs. Most of the barriers faced by homosexuals are forms of social discrimination, such as verbal harassment, jokes, expressions of disgust, or subtle refusals for equal treatment. The issue's volatility was apparent in 1993 when President Clinton sparked a national uproar over a proposal to allow openly gay people to stay in the military. Despite the controversy, survey data in 2000 showed that 75 percent of the U.S. population supported allowing homosexuals in the military, and 67 percent favored laws to prohibit job discrimination based on sexual orientation.[52] Direct acts of violence against homosexuals are no longer acceptable. For example, when a young gay man was tortured and killed in Wyoming, all but a tiny, extreme minority failed to condemn it. At the same time, the U.S. Congress refuses to pass a national hate crime law to protect gays from harassment.[53] **Hate crime laws are laws designed to provide legal protection from hostile acts based solely on a person's race, gender, religion, or sexual orientation.** FBI statistics from the few state and local governments that have their own hate crime laws show that 1,019 hate crime incidents were reported nationally to police in 1995 based on sexual orientation (the most recent data available). This is about equal to religious hate crimes.[54]

Most remaining barriers are subtle, such as censoring the expression of opinions, beliefs, or ideas, and they operate at the second or third dimensions of power. For example, in 1998 a television station refused to broadcast a program produced by a church with a majority of gay and lesbian members. The thirty-minute program contrasted antigay demonstrations with homosexual people quietly living in a positive way (e.g., warm, happy, religious, stable, family-oriented). An exclusionary barrier was revealed when the Chicago television station that had signed a contract to air the program backed out saying, "It is not appropriate."[55] Full citizenship also includes the ability to hold public office. Openly gay men and lesbians hold elected political posts at the local, state, and national levels. Yet a group of U.S. Senators rejected James Hormel, a gay man nominated to become an ambassador in 1998 solely based on his sexual orientation.[56] Historical comparisons with other groups that faced similar kinds of barriers in the United States in the past (e.g., Catholics, Jews, Blacks, women, the disabled) suggest that removing barriers and full inclusion takes several decades of political mobilizing, court battles, and other political action.

Three Forms of Exclusion: Creating Indirect Barriers, Explicit Restrictions, and Repression

Next we consider exclusion. As with inclusion, exclusion is dynamic, and its form and intensity vary as the height and density of barriers rise and fall over time. Like inclusion, exclusion operates at all three dimensions of power. Overt attacks and explicit denials are exclusion at the first dimension of power. Exclusion at the second dimension is keeping people from participating in setting public agendas. At the third dimension of power, exclusion means banishing ideas, values, or beliefs from acceptable public discourse. It also means structuring laws, procedures, and administrative organizations to keep out or remove a group from the polity without explicitly naming or singling out the excluded group. Following we consider three forms of exclusion and look at two examples of each.

Creating Indirect Barriers

Sometimes a group plans to exclude another from the polity, while at other times exclusion is an indirect or an unintended consequence. Distinguishing between the two can be difficult. Advocates of barriers may be divided or unclear about their intentions. Some may believe that exclusion is a justified cost for a higher purpose. In addition, people may not foresee or be aware of consequences, or they may make miscalculations. We next consider two examples, one past and one present, of denying voting rights.

Urban Political Machines   Large-scale immigration and rural migration in late nineteenth-century America fed rapid urban growth, but often city governments were weak and could not provide adequate public services. In response, political parties built a loyal following, especially among recent immigrants, by providing services (e.g., jobs, housing) to specific groups and created the urban political machine, such as Tammany Hall in New York City. **The political machine was a disciplined organization of party followers that reached down to the ward or neighborhood level and responded to specific neighborhood or family needs in exchange for loyalty at election time.** Voters elected candidates and city hall enacted laws with machinelike predictability, hence the term *machine politics*. Party followers delivered votes in exchange for patronage jobs, and business owners made donations in exchange for tax reductions, zoning deals, or lucrative public works contracts. The machine government reinforced competition based on ethnic solidarity within blue-collar neighborhoods of supporters.[57]

In the 1890s, reform organizations (e.g., the National Municipal League, formed in 1894) allied with the Progressive Movement mounted a campaign against political machines. Reformers (i.e., upper middle and upper class white men) claimed to want fair taxes, improved housing, better schools, expanded social services, an end to vote fraud, and efficient public administration. They demanded new "clean" city governments and the end of a strong mayor and city ward government structure. Strong mayors with ward-based elections gave well-organized ethnic and blue-collar districts significant electoral power. Hays (1998, 127) remarked, "Reformers loudly proclaimed a new structure of municipal government was more moral, more rational, and more efficient and, before it was so, self-evidently more desirable." Behind their calls for greater efficiency, reformers also wanted to remove political control from working class immigrants and shift it to a coalition of upper-income business owners and white-collar professionals. Reformers also wanted to block the growing influence of the Socialist Party and proworker, proegalitarian candidates.[58] The reformers advocated changing the rules of the game by: (1) forbidding political parties from running for city government and instituting nonpartisan elections, (2) shifting city elections so they are not the same days as presidential or other high turnout elections, (3) eliminating salaries for city council members, (4) replacing ward or distinct elections for city council posts with citywide elections.

Reformers were successful in certain types of cities—those that had greater legal restrictions on who could vote (aimed at lower income people and recent arrivals), those with a politically strong and organized local business community, those that had people without strong attachments to the political parties and a population mix containing fewer immigrants relative to long-term residents or Anglos. In addition, many newer cities in the Western United States needed to provide city services quickly (e.g., electric, and water utilities) but had limited tax revenue. Utility corporations were more willing to invest in a city and provide the services if it had a reform government.[59]

By 1920, most midsized cities had adopted one of two forms of reform government and the machine-style governments remained only in a few major Eastern and Midwestern cities. A *commission form* gave all the responsibility for running the city to a small group of commissioners, each responsible for a single department. A *city manager form* had a professionally trained expert who oversaw city administration. The citizens did not directly elect the "expert" or manager; an elected city council selected the manager.

The new forms of city government had the intended effect of reducing vote fraud and political patronage and increasing a businesslike administration for delivering public services. They also had the effect of excluding some people from the polity while including others, and public participation in city politics declined. "The municipal reform movement was," Bridges and Kronick (1999, 697) observed, "from its beginnings in the middle of the 19th century, associated with efforts to restrict popular participation in politics." The reforms insulated city government from working class demands as they consolidated the political control in the hands of local coalitions of bankers, real estate developers, and middle-class professionals.[60]

One legacy of the reform movement is that today 75 percent of American cities have nonpartisan elections, 59 percent use citywide elections instead of districts, and 52 percent have a city manager or commission form of government. Equally important, the reform movement introduced a new vocabulary that dominates how people talked and thought about urban politics.[61]

"Municipal reform" has positive connotations while "political machine" has negative connotations.

Another legacy of the reform movement has been the rise of urban growth coalitions or "growth machines" in most cities.[62] **An urban growth coalition is a cooperative political arrangement between the local business community and city officials to promote private economic expansion.** Local bankers, real estate developers, apartment and office building owners, construction firms, hospitals, newspapers and television stations, and store owners all reap financial benefits when the population in a city grows. City government officials gain prestige, tax revenues, and employees. The city grows when the local economy grows, especially when corporate investments increase and new businesses relocate to it. Growth coalition policies bring jobs to a city, but they also bring greater traffic congestion, air and water pollution, a degradation of traditional neighborhoods, a strain on city services, and overcrowded schools. To attract new businesses, city officials grant tax breaks and expand urban services (e.g., roads, water system, fire stations), but this increases the tax burden on local residents. Growth coalition policies encourage demolishing unsightly older housing and stores that produce little tax revenue. They encourage new freeways and high-rent buildings for upscale retail stores, office complexes, and luxury condominiums. Often federal urban development funds pay for the new roads and housing demolition. Unfortunately, low-income residents are displaced, old neighborhoods destroyed, and local taxes on residences rise.

Urban growth coalitions were strongest in cities that had a well-organized local business community that contributed heavily to the election campaigns of city politicians. City officials find they must balance the demands of powerful private development interests with the wishes of the voting public. Growth coalition politics increase land values, shape how a city develops, redirect urban projects, and affect public service delivery. For example, Whitt (1982) found that the San Francisco Bay area's BART urban rail transit system was the product of a strong growth coalition. Local citizen groups were excluded from BART's conception and planning, and it did not improve most local people's mobility or reduce traffic congestion. A network of banks, corporations, and business leaders controlled the agenda of BART's creation, system design, and taxation scheme. He noted, their "paramount goal was to preserve and extend the economic development of downtown San Francisco" (p. 51) by helping upper-income people commute from the suburbs. The growth coalition's success is an example of the second dimension of power.

Criminal Records and Voting Rights   In the past, voting barriers were removed as women gained the right to vote (discussed previously in this chapter) or instituted as African Americans in the South lost their right to vote (discussion follows). Today, people convicted of a crime are excluded from the polity, and as Uggen and Manza (2002, 778) observed, "the United States is unique in restricting the rights of non-incarcerated felons." Nationally, 1.4 million black men, or about 13 percent, lost their right to vote because of a criminal record. In the decentralized U.S. political system, state-level law determines the voting rights. In four states (Maine, Massachusetts, Utah, and Vermont) anyone can vote, including those in prison. In 13 states, anyone convicted of a felony (a definition that keeps expanding) loses the right to vote for life. For example, a black man in Mississippi lost his right to vote for life for writing a bad $150 check.[63] In some states, one in four black men can never vote, and in six states, over 15 percent of the black population has been disenfranchised.[64] Uggen and Manza (2002) suggest that if these people had been allowed to vote, it probably would have changed the outcome of six U.S. Senate elections and two presidential elections.

The number of states banishing those with criminal records from the polity has grown over time, from 44 percent in 1860 to 88 percent by 1970.[65] As a group, young African American males are most likely to be convicted of crimes and incarcerated. This is due to many factors—poverty, community living conditions, police practices, and unequal treatment in the criminal justice system. Similar to legal restrictions that took away black voting rights in the 1890s South, today's laws do not explicitly mention race, but the consequence is to remove many blacks from the polity.

This example offers us three lessons. First, a law's actual result reveals more about power and politics than an exclusive focus on its formal justification or rationale. Second, laws, rights, and policies in diverse issue areas, such as criminal justice policy and citizenship rights, are interconnected. A "get tough on crime" policy might translate into political disempowerment in practice. Third, there are powerful analogies between the actions of the past and the present. The states that denied black men voting rights and terrorized them with lynching in 1904 are the same ones most likely to bar black men from voting on other grounds in 2004. The issue of denying 1 million black men the right to vote is not on the political agenda. It remains at the second dimension and third dimension of power.

Explicit Restrictions

Often when people see other people threatening their social position, privileges, and way of life, they reinterpret the ideals of democracy to include people like themselves but to exclude others. They embrace beliefs and ideas that justify or rationalize actions that devalue and exclude others while protecting their own position. People appear confused by the symbols and rhetoric and fail to see the connection between defending their own privileged position and denying the political rights of other people.

Mass Disenfranchisement of the 1890s Before the reform of American electoral politics in the 1890s–1910s, McCormick (1997, 4) observed, "To a greater degree than today, the ballot symbolized the 'democracy' of American society, and its possession signified inclusion within the political community . . . virtually every segment of the electorate mobilized in nearly equal proportions—rich and poor, immigrant and native-born alike. Most of those who voted probably cast their ballot for the same party in election and after election." Established elites concentrated in Eastern states feared full popular democracy and felt that only "proper" people who had a stake in the social-economic order and who paid taxes deserved to have a voice in politics. They argued that low-income people who paid few or no taxes did not deserve a voice in politics and should not be allowed to vote. Echoes of this sentiment are heard today. "Taxpayer" has replaced "citizens" or "the people" in political appeals. A candidate promises to work for "the taxpayers" or a politician says that "taxpayers" will not accept a policy. Saying taxpayers instead of all the people is a way of excluding people similar to explicit nineteenth-century restrictions that based voting on property owned or taxes paid.[66]

Massive exclusion from the polity occurred when state governments across the South denied African Americans basic rights just 25 years after they won freedom from slavery. At the time, 89 percent of all black Americans lived in the South where they were one-third of the population.[67] After the Civil War, the Southern economic and social system was in ruins. Many young men had been killed, and the South's railways, towns, and farms were destroyed. Systems of tenant farming and sharecropping replaced slave labor. Poor farmers, some whites but most blacks, rented land and housing, borrowed money and paid a landowner with half or more of the crops they grew. Slavery ended in the Reconstruction Era (1865–1877) as Northern troops occupied the South and controlled local Southern government. After Southern agitation, Northern discontent, and the 1877 Uprising in the North, Northern and Southern politicians agreed to withdraw troops and a return to local home rule in 1877. Local Southern politicians initiated the Jim Crow era and passed local laws to enforce white supremacy.[68]

Southern white elites did not immediately disfranchise blacks because they feared that Northern troops might return and they could achieve many goals through fraud and intimidation. Black voters were embroiled in a political contest between small-scale white farmers and a coalition of white business owners and rich planters, often helping the former hold power. A massive populist movement swept across the South in the late 1880s. It mobilized poor white farmers and drew in many blacks. The Third Party Populist movement intensified electoral competition and made political parties compete for black votes. After the Populists lost in 1892–1896, white elites mounted a campaign to ensure that blacks could never again threaten white elite control of state and local governments in the South.[69]

Beginning with Mississippi in 1890 and continuing through the ex-Confederacy, by 1908 each state disfranchised blacks. The U.S. Constitution forbade laws that explicitly mentioned race, so they used other devices that had the same effect, such as grandfather clauses, poll taxes, residency restrictions, literacy requirements, and polling station locations. Seven states passed a grandfather clause between 1895 and 1910 that exempted a person from literacy, property, or tax requirements if their descents had voted before slaves were freed, effectively excluding all blacks (see Summary 4.2). The Ku Klux Klan and White Cap movement waged campaigns of terror and lynching to quell black opposition to the election law manipulation and the Jim Crow white supremacy system (discussion follows). Many of these techniques con-

SUMMARY 4.2   **Techniques Used to Prevent Voting by African Americans in the South**

Grandfather clause*—People who had not voted in previous elections or whose parents did not vote, could not begin voting. Adopted in Mississippi (1890), South Carolina (1895), Louisiana (1898), North Carolina (1900), Alabama (1901), Virginia (1902), Georgia (1908), Oklahoma (1910).

Poll tax**—A tax that had to be paid before a person could vote. Sometimes a person had to pay "past due" taxes for previous elections. Adopted in 12 states.

Literacy test***—A test selectively given to assess a person's reading/writing ability.

Sometimes the test would require knowing political information as well.

Residency requirements*—The length of time a person lived in the same place.

Limiting the number of polling places*—Locating polling places far from certain voters.

*Continues in some form today.
**Also outlawed by Twenty-fourth Amendment to the U.S. Constitution.
***Outlawed in 1915; test removed between 1964 and 1970 by civil rights legislation.

Source: See Crotty (1977).

tinued until the civil rights movement and federal government forced their end in the 1960s.[70]

Explicit disenfranchisement, backed by violence and coercion, was first-dimension power. Second- and third-dimensional power reinforced it. After whites had expelled blacks from the polity, blacks could not move their concerns onto the public agenda. This protected a white supremacist culture, mind-set, and way of life. For generations, Southern whites grew up in a culture in which white superiority over blacks was part of the hegemony.

Anti-Immigrant Exclusion   America is a land of immigrants, but its history of immigration is full of repeated exclusion attempts. To protect their social and economic position, people who arrived earlier tried to limit further immigration or exclude newer immigrants, often combining self-protection with racial and religious prejudice. Beginning with the 1840s Know Nothing Party that advocated anti-immigrant and anti-Roman Catholic actions, many white Protestants tried to limit immigration. Native-born Protestants felt threatened by the many immigrants, mostly Germans, in the Midwest and Irish in the East. When asked about their semisecret, nativist organization, members replied that they "knew nothing," hence the party's name. The party tried to exclude the foreign-born from voting or holding public office and tried to impose a 21-year residency requirement for citizenship. By 1852, the Know Nothing Party did well in state and local elections. At its peak in 1855, the party had 43 representatives in the United States Congress. The party later split along regional lines over the slavery issue and disappeared by the Civil War.[71]

Twenty years later, whites on the Pacific Coast rioted and attacked Chinese immigrants imported as low-wage agricultural and railroad workers. They achieved a total ban with the Chinese Exclusion Act of 1888. The anti-Catholic, anti-immigrant group, the American Protection Association, which was founded in 1887, had 2 million members in the 1890s. Strongest in rural areas and small towns, it played on fears of city immigrants. By 1911, it had disappeared.

During the 1920s, immigration laws were tightened and racially based quotas were imposed to favor Western Europeans. Elites tied to the Eugenics Movement (advocates of controlled human breeding/sterilization for racial improvement) sought to keep America white and halt the inflow of "inferior races". The racially based immigration limits remained in effect for almost 50 years.

After Chinese exclusion, Japanese people migrated to Hawaii and the West Coast to become agricultural workers. They faced similar discrimination there, and Japanese immigration slowed. An agreement between the U.S. and Japanese governments and improved conditions in Japan ended the flow by 1920. The Japanese were successful farmers but whites along the Pacific coast objected to the Japanese competition and enacted racially based state laws to limit Japanese land ownership.[72] This racial prejudice was a backdrop for the World War II internment episode. In the mass hysteria that followed the Japanese military attack on Pearl Harbor (December 7, 1941), the U.S. government created the War Relocation Authority. It forcibly relocated everyone of Japanese ancestry on the West Coast, including citizens born in the United States, to ten relocation centers in Eastern California, Arizona, Idaho, Utah, Wyoming, and Arkansas. Forced to sell all property quickly and suddenly end schooling or careers, the Japanese-Americans suffered great financial loss and personal hardship.[73] Not one of the approximately 110,000 Japanese-Americans imprisoned for 4 years was ever convicted of committing espionage. It took over 40 years for the U.S. government to apologize and offer financial repatriations.

Anti-immigrant sentiments resurfaced in the mid-1980s in the largest upsurge of nativism since the 1920s. National political leaders called for tighter immigration laws and expanded border patrols. States enacted legislation making English the official language, limiting public services for recent immigrants, and abolishing bilingual education. Renewed exclusion symbolically began in 1986 with California Proposition 63, a law to make English the official state language. Other states passed similar laws, and in 1996, the U.S. House of Representatives passed a version which the Senate failed to take up.[74] Most Americans (78 percent) support a law to make English the official language.[75] Immigrants are learning English as fast now as ever before, but the exclusion movement encourages discrimination: Employers restrict non-English conversation at workplaces, cities outlaw non-English commercial signs or stop printing non-English election ballots, and courts prohibit testimony in languages other than English.[76]

In 1994, California voters approved Proposition 187 by 59 to 41 percent. It required state and local law enforcement, social service, health care, and public education personnel to detect persons in violation of immigration laws; report them to government officials; and deny them social services, health care, and education. After its passage, the law fueled widespread discrimination against citizens, legal residents, and others who looked like immigrants (mostly dark-skinned people and Asians). In March 1998, federal courts ruled against many provisions in Proposition 187. Four months later California voters passed a referendum to abolish bilingual education and to require that all public school students be taught primarily in English, even though bilingual education can be highly effective. Because of its huge immigrant population, one-fourth of California students are not proficient in English, and Latino children have the lowest test scores and the highest dropout rates (40 percent) in the state.

To become a U.S. citizen requires a person to live in the country for 5 years, have no criminal record, not be affiliated with an organization that advocates overthrowing the government, pass a U.S. civics test (see Summary 4.3), and take an English language test during a 15-40 minute interview. The criteria to become a citizen have changed many times. Between World War I and World War II there was no English language test, a prospective citizen only had to know 40 words in any language. The language test was added in 1952 and expanded into a knowledge test in 1986 to be given orally in English. Today it is more difficult to become a naturalized citizen than ever before in U.S. history.[77]

Media reports and politicians fuel anti-immigrant stereotypes. For example, studies show no relationship between immigration and crime rates. Yet in a 2000 national survey, 73 percent of Americans believed that increased immigration produces higher crime rates.[78] After the September 11, 2001 terrorist attack, immigrants from Islamic nations were demonized and treated as suspects in media reports, government actions, and by many ordinary people.

Explicit anti-immigrant restrictions involve the first dimension of power. Like the mass disenfranchisement of the 1890s (discussed previously in this

---

| SUMMARY 4.3 | Could You Pass the Citizenship Test? |

Here is a sample of 15 of the 100 questions used by the U.S. Immigration and Naturalization Service since 1986. Interviewers can ask several or all 100 questions; they can rephrase questions and use their judgment about a correct answer.

1. What are the colors of our flag?
2. What do the stripes in the flag mean?
3. What is the Constitution?
4. What are the duties of Congress?
5. How many senators are there in Congress?
6. What Immigration and Naturalization Service form is used to apply to become a naturalized citizen?
7. Who helped the Pilgrims in America?
8. Which president freed the slaves?
9. What is the introduction to the Constitution called?
10. Name one benefit of becoming a U.S. citizen.
11. What were the 49th and 50th states to join the union?
12. In what year was the Constitution written?
13. How many changes or amendments are there to the Constitution?
14. What is the Chief Justice of the Supreme Court?
15. Who said, "Give me liberty or give me death?"

Source: Sachs (1999).

chapter), they reinforce the second dimension of power by keeping immigrant concerns off the political agenda and fortify the third dimension of power by endorsing what some define as an American way of life (e.g., speaking English, adopting certain Western customs), although their definition excludes many American citizens.

Repression

Repression is the use of organized violence to maintain social order. It is the most blatant and extreme form of exclusion. Genocide, the most severe type of repression, often took place in the twentieth century, such as the attempted extermination of Muslims in Bosnia in 1995, the Tutsi minority in Rwanda in 1994, the Kurds in Iraq in 1988, the educated, urban population in Cambodia from 1975 to 1979, the Jews in Germany in the 1940s, or the Armenians in Turkey in 1915. Less extreme forms of repression include threats of violence, up to and including death, to keep people under control, such as the treatment of women in Afghanistan under the Taliban or in Saudi Arabia today. U.S. political history has many instances of repression, including the 1877 Uprising, the aftermath of the Haymarket Riot in Chicago (1886), the Palmer raids (1919), and the McCarthy Era (early 1950s).[79] Below we examine the lynching and anticommunist "white terror" of the Palmer Raids and the McCarthy Era.

Lynching Lynching is an extra-legal act, usually by a vigilante mob, with the tacit consent of local law enforcement officials, in which a person is tracked down and publicly killed. Lynching is a form of vigilantism (i.e., when unofficial volunteers engage in organized violence to enforce a social code, moral principle, or law). Death was usually by hanging, often accompanied by torture or mutilation (cutting off or burning body parts). These were not the secretive, isolated acts of a few individuals; rather, they were collective public actions that people accepted as normal or natural. Lynching was widely practiced in Southern states between 1890 and 1930. During its peak (1890–1919), 1,748 black men, women, and children were lynched, about one every 6 days.[80] Most of the victims were African American males who were accused of disrespect toward whites or immoral acts. It often supplemented and reinforced other legal forms of exclusion from the polity (e.g., Jim Crow laws).

Lynching was the use of violence to uphold the political–social order and was tacitly allowed by the state when it was officially unable or unwilling to uphold the order.[81] In addition to terrorizing blacks, lynching provided an outlet for white anger and frustration over increased economic competition.[82] Lynching was associated with black-white economic competition, and whites used it to protect their social and economic position.[83] Tolnay, Deane and Beck (1996, 789–90) called lynching "a form of state-tolerated terrorism aimed at the black community—it was the instrumental use of violence to preserve white hegemony and maintain caste boundary." Beyond the first dimension of power, lynching was rarely challenged (second dimension), and it fortified an entire way of life (third dimension).

The Red Scares   America hosts a diversity of political beliefs, but government officials and some political groups periodically have mounted campaigns to narrow the range of acceptable opinions. They primarily target the political left (i.e., people who questioned unlimited property rights, traditional values, and social–economic inequality). The campaigns defined certain ideas to be illegitimate and sought to expel people who held them from the polity. Believing they were defending the American way of life, they labeled (correctly or not) their opponents as alien and hostile. Officials used real or imagined threats from tiny groups of dissenters to justify denying many more people their legal rights and jobs. They also used imprisonment, beatings, deportation or exile, and executions.

The impact of Red Scare campaigns went beyond the specific targeted organizations or people. They tainted the political climate and narrowed the range of public debate for a decade. For example during World War I, patriotism was redefined narrowly and dissent was suppressed; this left a lingering distrust of foreigners. Shortly after the war, conservative politicians and advocacy groups used the Russian Revolution (1917) to incite public fear about the growing influence of leftists or anarchists. A postwar economic recession, anti-black race riots and labor unrest, large violent strikes, and a wave of anarchist bombings in 1919, led federal officials to believe there was a coordinated communist-inspired attack. They initiated a full-scale "Red Scare."[84] Backed by a climate of fear and antiforeign prejudice, law enforcement officials along with local vigilante groups detained, arrested, and imprisoned thousands of people who had engaged in prounion activities or advocated prosocialist ideas. During a yearlong campaign, government officials raided homes and offices, closed newspapers, stopped speeches, and deported innocent foreigners. Before this period, the Socialist Party was growing in popularity. It had grown from 75,000 members in 1918 to 108,000 in 1919. After attacks by the federal government, local officials, and vigilante groups, its membership dropped to 26,000 in 1920, and by 1928, only 8,000 remained. The Communist Party declined from 27,000 in October 1919 to about 8,200 by April 1920.

An organized, powerful "open shop" movement began in 1919 and joined the Red Scare to target unionized blue-collar workers. Associated with local business groups (e.g., National Association of Manufacturers, U.S. Chamber of Commerce), Hicks (1961, 60) noted, "open shop associations appeared in nearly every sizeable city." Employers used labor spies and operated 300 open shop associations in eight states. As Faulkner (1951, 73) observed, "Just as 1920 witnessed the greatest increase in the membership of organized labor since 1903, so 1922 showed the greatest decrease yet recorded. The depression of 1920–1921 threw multitudes out of work, and the open shop movement drive of employer's associations smashed hundreds of [union] locals." Right-wing organizations ended mass unionization for 10 years,[85] and a distrust of foreigners, liberal reformers, and unions lingered through the 1920s.[86]

A second major Red Scare erupted in the 1950s and is associated with Senator Joseph McCarthy, but it went far beyond him. Despite President Truman's strong anticommunist foreign policy and a Federal Employee Loyalty Program

in 1947 that caused hundreds of federal workers to be fired and thousands to resign, a group of right-wing politicians sought to gain power by advancing a
campaign to purge leftist ideas from the country. They had opposed the New
Deal policies of late 1930s and a growth in union strength in the 1930s and 1940s,
and they mounted a backlash.

The campaign merged conservative hostility toward domestic leftist policies
and ideas that had grown under the New Deal with international Cold War fears.
After the Korean War began and the Soviet Union tested its first A-bomb, emotions went wild. Campaign leaders claimed communist spies in the federal government weakened the United States and were aiding communist China and the
Soviet Union. A few actual cases of disloyalty or espionage existed, but the campaign spread to claim a massive conspiracy among thousands of federal government employees. The colorful leader of the Red Scare campaign, Senator Joseph
R. McCarthy, held that the Roosevelt and Truman administrations amounted to
"20 years of treason." In 1950 Senator McCarthy claimed to have a list of State Department employees who were loyal to the Soviet Union. He never had firm evidence and revealed only one name (someone who was not even in the State
Department and was never convicted). Despite a lack of evidence, he won a large
public following. During the decadelong Red Scare, few people were convicted
of any crime but tens of thousands of government employees, teachers, scholars,
and people in the mass media lost their jobs. Trials and legal evidence were not
necessary. Suspicion of insufficient loyalty was enough to cause a person to lose
her or his job and be disgraced. Having suspected friends or refusing to cooperate fully with Red Scare officials were also grounds for dismissal.[87]

A climate of apprehension spread. Politicians, scholars, entertainers, publishers, and people in the media were afraid to say anything that Red Scare leaders might call leftist since it was treated as support for communism that equaled
subversion and disloyalty. Physical violence was rare, but ideas that had been
widely accepted in the 1930s and 1940s and that were openly debated in other
democratic-capitalist nations were censored by the Red Scare leaders.

PROCESSES OF INCLUSION AND EXCLUSION

Inclusion and exclusion take many forms (see Chart 4.6). Forms that involve an
identifiable group of people, such as women getting the right to vote, are easiest
to see. More difficult to see are forms that involve a program, idea, or activity.
Also, a program, idea, or activity may not be clearly inside or outside the polity
but on an ambiguous borderline. Some programs are fully within the polity, others are in between (i.e., publicly funded but privately decided or privately
funded but publicly decided), and some are fully outside (entirely without any
state involvement).[88] Four issues are involved: (1) legal ownership, (2) funding,
(3) managerial authority, and (4) ultimate authority.

For example, a public park is part of the polity—a city legally owns it, taxes
pay for it, employees on the public payroll manage it, and democratically

c h a r t   4 . 6

EXCLUSION AND INCLUSION

Major Types of Exclusion

- **Creating an indirect barrier** occurs when the state permits the intentional or unintentional denial of equal access for some citizens to what is available to other citizens, thus limiting their full participation in public life. For example, a local official in Alabama refused to give recent immigrants tax credits they were due because they had difficulty speaking English. (See "Don't Speak English? No Tax Break, Alabama Official Declares," *New York Times*, June 4, 1999.)

- **Explicit restriction** is intentionally limiting or preventing of a targeted group from full access and participation in the polity though law, procedure, or a denial of equal services. It occurred in 1963 when Governor George C. Wallace stood in the doorway of the University of Alabama and blocked qualified students from access to an education solely on the basis of their race.

- **Repression** can be nonviolent or violent. It includes the systematic denial of employment, confiscation of property, imprisonment, beatings and injury, and death threats. An example of violent repression was the 1999 forced expulsion of one-million ethnic Albanians from Kosovo, a province in the Serbian Republic of Yugoslavia.

Major Types of Inclusion

- The **removal of barriers** begins by identifying existing barriers and then reducing or eliminating them. Suppose a library is not wheelchair accessible and does not accommodate a person in a wheelchair who wants to borrow a book. The library could remove physical barriers (e.g., provide ramps, elevators, wider doorways) to help include the person in a wheelchair.

- **Active encouragement** is providing a service or access to public resources in a manner that reaches out and makes it easier for more people. An example would be a government agency that wants to offer services to more elderly people. It mails announcements to housing for the elderly, extends its hours two days a week to coordinate with bus service, and provides instructions in large print.

- **Privileged inclusion** occurs when certain people or groups are given advantages over others in access. Consider the situation of a business owner who wants a low-cost government loan to expand his/her business. The owner socializes with important politicians at a country club where both are members and donates money to candidates and the political party in power. Politicians then invite the owner to review and comment on early drafts of a new program for business loans. Once it is passed and funds appropriated, and the politicians call on agency bureaucrats if the loan approval process for the owner is slow. The business owner is included in the system, and she/he has complete access and fully participates in political decisions. Another example of privileged inclusion occurs when veterans who wish to work for the government get bonus points for their military service added to their scores in competitive civil service examinations.

elected officials decide park policy. Issues of inclusion or exclusion arise when people who play loud music, drink beer, or sleep overnight cannot use the park. Such actions define boundaries of the polity. At various times in U.S. history, women or blacks could not enter public parks. It indicated their second-class citizenship. Two issues are involved in this example: potential access and use of public facilities. Some are denied access (e.g., the homeless), others have access but rarely use public parks (because they have large private yards and vacation homes). When rules about exclusion are developed, socially marginal groups (welfare recipients, homeless, recent immigrants, the disabled) are rarely asked their opinions, are not invited to public meetings, and are left out of the policy development process even for policy decisions that directly affect them. Others (e.g., concerned citizens, experts, officials) assume to know what is best and make rules for them.

Five rules operate in conflicts over boundaries and inclusion or exclusion processes: (1) *Group size is unrelated to inclusion.* For example, a PPN think tank places its items on the policy agenda without large numbers of supporters. A majority of the population was female but not able to vote in democratic nations. (2) *Having allies is essential for inclusion.* For example, most of the gains gay and lesbian people have made in removing barriers depended on outsiders or heterosexual supporters. (3) *The loudest and most active may not be the main beneficiaries.* For example, most of the people who benefit from English-only laws and immigration restrictions are unaware of or uninvolved in the political actions to exclude other people. (4) *Shifting venue is a common strategy.* If one cannot win or succeed in one arena (e.g., policy area, level of government), energies are redirected to a different area where it is possible to win. For example, women could not win the right to vote nationally, but they could win it in some states before gaining it nationally. (5) *Actions may have unintended consequences that may work against a person's goals.* For example, the goals of affirmative action were to increase the equality of opportunity and improve race relations, but it may have increased racial tensions. As Scattschneider (1960, 102, 103) observed, "The struggle is no longer about the right to vote, but about the organization of politics. . . . We get confused because we assume that the fight for democracy was won a long time ago. We would find it easier to understand if we assumed that the battle for democracy is still going on but assumed new forms."

The models of political sociology apply to both the social groups being included or excluded and in the scope and primary mechanism used for inclusion or exclusion (see Chart 4.7). For example, pluralists see very little exclusion (only extremists), and consistent with their focus on the first dimension of power, emphasize explicit barriers. In sharp contrast, in the class-analysis power structure model, capitalists are narrowly included and most others excluded. Capitalists get privileged access while others are excluded by explicit restrictions and repression. The class struggle model is least specific because it emphasizes the processes of struggle that can have indeterminate outcomes.

chart 4.7

POLITICAL SOCIOLOGY MODELS AND POLITY INCLUSION/EXCLUSION

Political Sociology Models	Parts of Society		Scope and Primary Mechanisms	
	Inclusion	Exclusion	Inclusion	Exclusion
Pluralist	Almost everyone	Few extremists	Broad; removal of direct barriers	Narrow; explicit restrictions
Elite	Elites	Masses	Narrow; privileged access	Broad; explicit restrictions and repression
Statist	Varies; wealthy and higher status groups	Varies; poor, lower-status groups, minorities	Varies; encouragement and removal of direct barriers	Varies; creates indirect barriers
Power-Structure	Capitalist class and allies	Other classes	Narrow; privileged access	Broad; explicit restrictions, and repression
Structuralist	Capitalist class and allies	Noncapitalist classes	Narrow; encouragement and removal of direct barriers	Broad; creates indirect barriers
Class-Struggle	Varies; usually capitalist class and allies	Varies; usually noncapitalist classes	Varies; all	Varies; all

CONCLUSION

In this chapter we looked at the polity—the institutions, people, organizations, processes, rules, and symbols of politics. The U.S. polity operates under a federal system with a state that began as very small, weak, and decentralized in a vast geographical area. It is marked by a tension between national and local government and geographic-regional divisions. U.S. polity has an adaptive model of administrative bureaucracy that is a legacy of state-building processes with a system of courts and parties. The state expanded in a fragmented array of agencies with uncoordinated, overlapping, or contradictory purposes. Since the New Deal regime and World War II, a tension has developed between the state's domestic and international roles that continues into the twenty-first century.

We also examined boundaries that separate people and organizations from the polity, and ways some are included or excluded from it. People, organizations, or ideas can be included into or excluded from specific levels or parts of the polity. Inclusion or exclusion can involve the center of political power (e.g., the Policy Planning Network) or merely permission to cling to the margins (recent immigrants, gay and lesbians). Some social classes or groups are encamped securely at the center of the polity, while other classes or groups cling tenuously to the margins of the polity, and they could be quickly expelled if conditions changed.

Inclusion and exclusion occur at all three dimensions of power and operate along a continuum. We looked at three points along the continuum and two examples of each from American political history and contemporary events. The degree of exclusion ranges from indirect barriers (e.g., municipal reform government, denial of voting for convicted criminals), to explicit restrictions on access (e.g., disenfranchisement of African Americans, anti-immigrant laws), to repression (e.g., lynching, Red Scares). The degree of inclusion ranges from removing barriers (e.g., women's franchise, sexual orientation), to encouragement (e.g., affirmative action programs, public schooling), to privileged access (e.g., the campaign finance system, the Policy Planning Network).

In Chapter 5, we look at people included within the polity to see how differences in political involvement by various parts of society, even among those who are formally included, reinforces and extends the dynamics of inclusion and exclusion discussed in this chapter.

KEY TERMS

Adaptable Pattern	Hate Crime Laws	Polity
Affirmative Action	Inclusion	Privileged Access
Coordinated Pattern	Institution	Realignment Theory
Critical Election	Lynching	Removal of Direct Barriers
Distributive State	Party System	Repression
Encouragement (form of inclusion)	Policy Planning Network	Spoils System
Exclusion	Political Machine	System of Courts and Parties
Federalism	Political Patronage	Think Tank
	Political Regime	Urban Growth Coalition

REVIEW QUESTIONS

1. What is the polity and why is it important?

2. Identify four features of nineteenth century America that shaped U.S. political institutions.

3. What is the basis of a two-party system in the United States?

4. What are the major features of the two paths of developing a state bureaucracy?

5. What are the consequences of a highly decentralized pattern of government authority?

6. What was the New Deal and its significance for American politics?

7. Explain why large donations to a political campaign are inclusion.

8. How is the Policy Planning Network similar to large campaign donations, and how do they differ?

9. How do hate crime laws protect or extend citizenship rights?

10. Using the municipal reform movement, explain how calls for efficiency in government can reduce democracy. How are current urban growth coalitions similar to politics of the municipal reform era?

11. In what ways were the movement to take away the right to vote from African Americans in the 1890s and lynching similar processes? How are they related to the concept of a democratic polity?

12. Immigration policy and anti-immigrant actions are central to the process of defining a citizen. Has U.S. immigration policy been consistent over time? What does it say about citizenship?

RECOMMENDED READINGS

Bensel, Richard Franklin. 1984. *Sectionalism and American Political Development, 1880–1980.* Madison, WI: University of Wisconsin Press.

Burnham, Walter Dean. 1970. *Critical Elections and the Mainsprings of American Politics.* New York: Norton.

McCormick, Richard L. 1997. *Public Life in Industrial America, 1877–1917,* revised and expanded. Washington DC: American Historical Association.

McGerr, Michael E. 1986. *The Decline of Popular Politics: The American North, 1865–1928.* New York: Oxford University Press.

Silberman, Bernard S. 1993. *Cages of Reason: The Rise of the Rational State in France, Japan, the United States and Great Britain.* Chicago: University of Chicago Press.

Sklar, Martin J. 1991. *The United States as a Developing Country.* New York: Cambridge University Press.

Skowronek, Stephen. 1982. *Building a New American State: The Expansion of National Administrative Capacities, 1877–1920.* New York: Cambridge University Press.

Wiebe, Robert H. 1967. *The Search for Order, 1877–1920.* New York: Hill and Wang.

ENDNOTES

1. See Orum (2001, 92–94) for a brief description of Aristotle's ideas. Also see Calhoun (1994) who links the idea to both the meaning of civil society and Habermas's theorizing on the "public sphere."

2. For an excellent general discussion of inclusion and exclusion in the polity, see Dryzek (1996a).

3. See Rogowski (1989, 26) and World Bank at http://www.worldbank/org/data.

4. The Jackson Era and increased voting is discussed in McCormick (1986).

5. On the Courts and Parties system see Skowronek (1982). Also see Bright (1984), Hattam (1992), and Keller (1977).

6. On nineteenth century political parties see Baker (1983), Kleppner (1979), McCormick (1981a), and McGerr (1986).

7. In different ways, Bensel (1984), Quadango (1988), and Sanders (1986) emphasize regional divisions.

8. See discussion by Formisano (1999).

9. The continuing role of party patronage is discussed in McCormick (1986, 1997) and is also emphasized by Orloff and Skocpol (1984).

10. See Silberman (1993).

11. See Balough (1991) and Clemens (1997).

12. On conflict in the late 1890s and early 1900s see Destler (1946), Fusfeld (1984), and Ramirez (1978).

13. See Campbell and Lindberg (1990), Dobbin and Dowd (2000), and Roy (1997).

14. Berk (1994) discusses railway regulation. Also see Dobbin (1994), Skowronek (1981), and Zunz (1990).

15. The continuing importance of courts in the early Progressive Era is discussed by Keller (1990) and Pavalko (1989). Also see Hattam (1992).

16. From United States Census Bureau 1975, *Historical Statistics of the United States.*

17. See Balough (1991, 144).

18. On nationalizing local initiatives see Clemens (1997), McDonagh (1992a, 1992b), and Orloff and Skocpol (1984).

19. Wiebe (1967) discusses a "Search for Order." On Progressive Era politics see Brady and Althoff (1974), Buenker (1978), Crotty (1977), Kleppner (1987), McDonagh (1992), Neuman (1998), and Sklar (1991).

20. Clemens (1997, 27–28) provides a useful list.

21. McCormick (1981b) argues for the importance of the "discovery" that big business corrupted politics.

22. See DiTomasso (1980) on the Department of Labor. A similar idea can be found in Amenta and Zylan (1991), Colignon (1997), and Hattam (1992) in different contexts.

23. For more on New Jersey incorporation law see Parker-Gwin and Roy (1996) and Noble (1997).

24. For an overview of the 1920s see Murray, (1973).

25. Quote is from Orren and Skowronek (1999, 690).

26. Critical elections and realignment are discussed in Andersen (1979), Brady (1981), Burnham (1970), Clubb et al. (1980), Ginsberg (1972), Key (1955), Lichtman (1976, 1983), Nardulli (1995), Orren and Skowronek (1999), Shafter (1979), and Sundquist (1973). For a related discussion on policy effects see McFarland (1991).

27. Katznelson and Pietrykowsi (1991) provide the basis of the example. The idea is also discussed in Colignon (1997), McCormick (1986, 75–88), and Swenson (1997).

28. For more on political sociological discussions of the New Deal see Allen (1991), Amenta, Dunleavy, and Bernstein (1994), Finegold and Skocpol (1995), Gilbert and Howe (1991), Goldfield, (1989), Hooks (1990a), Jenkins and Brent (1989), Levine (1988), Manza (1993), Skocpol (1980), and Swenson (1997).

29. Gilbert and Howe (1991) discuss the Department of Agriculture during the New Deal.

30. The figures come from Stanger and Rivlin (1998).

31. See "Panel Allows Solicitation of Soft Money at Fund-Raisers," *New York Times,* June 21, 2002 and "Election Panel Eases A Soft-Money Rule," *New York Times,* July 25, 2003.

32. See "Gifts in State Judicial Races are Up Sharply," *New York Times,* February 14, 2002.

33. "Color of Money" http://www.publicampaign.org/ColorOfMoney/index.html. Downloaded November 30, 2001.

34. From "OUCH! #82—August 13, 2001", http://www.publicampaign.org/ouch8_13_01.html. Downloaded November 30, 2001.

35. See Domhoff (1998, 217–221).

36. From Drinkard (1995).

37. Witte (2000) outlines major school choice/voucher ideas.

38. Think tanks are discussed in Callahan (1998, 1999a, 1999b), Denham (1996), Easterbrook (1986), Kuttner (2002), McGann and Weaver (2000), Rich and Weaver (2000), and James Smith (1990).

39. See James Smith (1990). Also see Peschek (1987).

40. Quote is from James Smith (1990, xv).

41. See Domhoff (1998, 129) and Domhoff (1996, 29–40).

42. For discussion, see Bellent and Berlet (1992), Dolny (2000), Kaplan (1998), Soley (1998), Solomon (1998b). The information on Mr. Scaife comes from Domhoff (1998, 142). Information for the Heritage Foundation came from its web site. Also see interview with a staff member from the Heritage Foundation in D. Jacobs (1999, 107–137).

43. From Dolny (1998).

44. See Gilens, Sniderman, and Kuklinski (1998).

45. Taylor (1995) found that whites working in firms with affirmative action policies are less likely to be hostile to the policies than those who did not. See Hochshild (1999) who argues that affirmative action debate is a "cultural war" in which the two sides talk past one another.

46. Brint (1998) provides a good summary of schooling issues. Guttmann (1988b) describes the place of public schooling in a democracy.

47. For a history of women's rights and struggles for the right to vote see Flexner (1968), Kraditor, (1981), McGlen and O'Connor (1983), and Sochen (1981). Also see Klein (1984) and Freeman (1975). Ramirez, Soysal, and Shanahan (1997) provide data on women's suffrage worldwide and explain it as the global institutionalization of more inclusive citizenship.

48. See Marshall (1986, 1998).

49. On women's voting patterns, see Firebaugh and Chen (1995).

50. See Faludi (1991) on antifeminist backlash and Lo (1982a) and Mottl (1980) on countermovements.

51. See A. Jacobs (1999).

52. Calculated from National Election Survey data (2000).

53. See Brooke (1998, 1999b), Grattet, Jennes and Curry (1998), Ireland (1998), Jennes (1995), and Jennes and Garett (2001) on hate crime.

54. From U.S. Department of Justice, Federal Bureau of Investigation, Uniform Crime Reports 1995. For differences in how some states oppose hate crime laws see Brooke (1999a).

55. See Belluck (1998).

56. See Shenon (1998) on the case of Mr. Hormel.

57. Urban machine politics are discussed in Ansell and Burris (1997), DiGaetano (1988), Katznelson (1981a), and Shefter (1985, 1993).

58. At its peak in 1912, the Socialist Party elected 79 mayors in 24 states (from Domhoff 1998, 212).

59. See Bridges (1992) and Bridges and Kronick (1999). Also see Gimpel (1993).

60. For details on the municipal reform movement, see Buenker (1978), Hays (1998), Rice (1977), Schiesl (1977), Weinstein (1962). Also see Alford and Lee (1968) on voter turnout declines, Knoke (1982) on regional distribution, and Gordon (1968) on immigrant populations.

61. Bridges (1994) discusses the new discourse that became dominant and its impact.

62. The urban growth coalition is discussed in Logan and Molotch (1987), Logan et al. (1997), Mollenkopf (1983), and Ratcliff (1980). Also see Domhoff (1998, 214) on current city types.

63. See the *Economist,* "Disenfranchised for Life" 349:30 (October 24, 1998).

64. See Butterfield (1997) and Lewin (1998). Data by Uggen and Manza (2002).

65. Crotty (1977, 40–41).

66. See McGerr (1986, 42–68).

67. From United States Census 1970. Historical Statistics of the United States, Colonial Times to 1970.

68. See Cooper (1977) and Valelly (1993).

69. Kousser (1974) and Young and Burstein (1995).

70. See Harding (1984).

71. For discussions of the Know Nothing Party and movement see Anbinder (1992) and Billington (1964).

72. See Daniels (1964, 1971, 1988) on the early history of the Japanese in California. Olzak (1989) also discusses conflict over immigration in this period.

73. For more discussion see Daniels (1989), Drinnon (1987), Weglyn (1976), and Yasui (1989).

74. See Schmitt (1996) and Tatalovich (1995).

75. Calculated from the 2000 General Social Survey.

76. See Madrid (1990), Ojito (1997), Santoro (1999), and Terry (1998). Also see "Don't Speak English? No Tax Break, Alabama Official Declares," *New York Times,* June 4, 1999.

77. See Sachs (1999).

78. Survey data was calculated from the 2000 General Social Survey. On crime rate comparisons see Butcher and Piehl (1998) and Hagen and Palloni (1999).

79. For a discussion of incidents, see Fusfeld (1984), Goldstein (1978), and Preston (1963).

80. See Tolnay, Deane, and Beck (1996, 789).

81. See Culberson (1990, 8) and Rosenbaum and Sederbert (1976) on vigilante politics.

82. Brundage (1993) provides a good overview of lynching.

83. For studies on how economic competition and other factors affect lynching, see Beck and Tolnay (1990), Clarke (1998), Corzine, Creech, and Corzine (1983), Crozine, Huff-Crozine, and Creech (1988), Inverarity (1976), Olzak (1990), Soule (1992), Tolnay and Beck (1992), Tolnay, Beck, and Massey (1992), Tolnay, Dean, and Beck (1996), and Wolf (1992).

84. See Neuman (1982, 838–842) for discussion and historical works.

85. Adapted from Neuman (1982, 842).

86. The best single work is by Murray (1955). Also see Preston (1963) and Faulkner (1951).

87. This overview is based on Neuman (1982, 1090–1098). Also see Bergesen (1977).

88. See Steinberger (1999) who argues that the public-private distinction is misconceived.

POLITICAL INVOLVEMENT AND CONFLICT IN THE UNITED STATES

INTRODUCTION

Do you vote? Voting is the first form of political involvement/participation that comes to mind for most people, but it is just one of many types. In Chapter 4, we looked at inclusion into or exclusion from the U.S. polity. We now consider how those who are included participate in conventional politics. As DeSipio (1996, 2) observed, "Formal inclusion, however, does not guarantee equal levels of political participation." Political involvement ranges from local concerns, such as opposing the building of a new road through a neighborhood, to global issues, such as ending international human rights violations. It covers mild actions, such as signing a petition for an environmental group, speaking at a public meeting on a school policy, writing a letter to the editor, or hanging a flag on a national holiday, to intense actions, such as going to jail for refusing to serve in the military, getting tear-gassed and arrested for blocking the entrance to a World Trade Organization meeting, or joining a terrorist group committed to armed conflict. In this chapter we focus on participation in conventional politics. **Conventional politics refers to legal, open influence to affect government agencies, elected officials, or other citizens about recognized political issues.** As Kourvetaris and Dobratz (1982, 303) noted, it looks at who participates and trends of electoral politics. ■

Democracy and Participation

Citizen involvement in conventional politics is central in an ideal representative, participatory democracy. Yet, the ideal rarely matches reality (see Summary 5.1).

SUMMARY 5.1	Ideal Versus Real American Political Participation

IDEAL MODEL OF PARTICIPATORY DEMOCRACY

1. Citizens engage in many forms of political participation, but elections are of central importance. They give each citizen an equal voice in selecting politicians and affecting the direction of government policy.
2. All citizens have the right to vote and exercise that right regularly in elections.
3. People vote in ways that express their social and economic ideals, interests, or desires. They elect politicians who represent those interests and balance the interest against basic democratic rights and the general national interest.
4. Political parties organize and coordinate voters, candidates, and public issues. The voters support the party that advocates their ideals, interests, and desires.
5. Voters are knowledgeable about the political system and informed about issues and the candidates' positions, which enables them to vote to advance their ideals, interests, and desires.
6. Citizens' views and public opinions not only shape elections but also continue to influence parties, politicians, and policy decisions between elections.

REALITY OF AMERICAN POLITICS

1. Most people are uninvolved or only participate ritually in elections, but a small, nonrepresentative minority is highly active in politics. Elections are modestly important as a form of participation.
2. Almost half of the citizens feel discouraged about voting and do not vote or vote irregularly.
3. Voters can only express some of their ideals, interests, and desires by voting. They are limited by their political awareness, mobilization, and the choices offered by elites. Elected representatives reflect the demands of a tiny minority of political activists who claim to represent all the citizens.
4. American political parties only represent some divisions or alternatives. Many people are "independents" and are not attached to a party. Party leaders have made the parties polarized on a few issues.
5. Most voters are poorly informed and easily misled on major public issues.
6. Citizens' views and opinions can affect parties, politicians, and policy, but people are confused and act in contradictory ways. Elites try to manipulate public opinion and are sometimes successful.

We need to look at who participates, why, and the consequences in real, not ideal, political settings. Democracy implies citizen participation in politics, but "the widely accepted theory of democracy is one in which the concept of participation has only a minor role" (Pateman 1970, 1). Indeed, many "modern theorists suggest that *participatory democracy* is anathema to stable democratic government and by default seemingly accept unrepresentation or under-representation as a natural, if not necessary condition" (emphasis in original, Cobb and Elder 1983, 8). Paradoxically, some political sociologists say that noninvolvement, or citizen apathy, helps democracy operate more effectively.[1] This is confusing because they are calling situations in which citizens are uninvolved democratic, while most others say that such cases violate the core principle of what democracy means.

Models of Political Sociology

The models of political sociology view participation (and nonparticipation) differently (see Chart 5.1). *Pluralists* put a great emphasis on citizen participation. They say democracy involves the voluntary participation by most citizens who make informed, rational choices among clear political alternatives which influence public policy. Pluralists become concerned when citizens are uninformed, apathetic, distrust government, and fail to participate; they favor improved voter information, high trust in government, and widespread participation. One leading pluralist, Robert Dahl (1998, 37), said, "Before a policy is developed . . . all members must have equal and effective opportunities for making their views known . . . every member must have an equal and effective opportunity to vote, and all votes must be counted as equal . . . each member must have equal and effective opportunities for learning about the relevant alternative polices and their likely consequences."

By contrast, in the *elite model*, nonparticipation is considered inevitable and even desirable, because in a large, complex society, only a tiny percentage of the population is well-informed and motivated to follow public issues. Only the elites, within and outside of government, have the knowledge, time, resources, and interest necessary to be well-informed participants. Apathy and minimal participation by the mass of uninformed, confused citizens ensures a stable, peaceful society. If the masses become seriously involved, it could be dangerous and spill beyond the confines of conventional politics. Electoral participation itself can generate feelings of involvement without real power, and elections may allow elites to control citizens as much as they let citizens select rulers.[2]

In the *statist model*, the focus shifts to the ways institutional arrangements influence the levels and kinds of participation. For example, how do voter registration rules influence who participates in elections, and how does greater participation by some social groups affect policy outcomes? The model recognizes that nonelectoral channels of participation (e.g., lobbying, shaping the agenda) may be more significant than voting.

Political sociologists using a *power-structure model* see a systematic, persistent class bias in conventional participation. The capitalist class dominates forms of

> ### chart 5.1
>
> ## SUMMARY OF POLITICAL SOCIOLOGICAL MODELS OF PARTICIPATION IN CONVENTIONAL POLITICS

Model	Conventional Political Participation
Pluralist	Citizens voluntarily participate in established electoral channels and make informed, reasonable choices among a range of political alternatives.
Elite	In a complex society, only elites have the knowledge, time, resources, and interest to be informed participants. Mass apathy and minimal participation in elections help to ensure a stable and peaceful society.
Statist	Different institutional arrangements greatly influence both the levels and kinds of participation by people in various parts of society. Specific electoral and nonelectoral channels may vary in their significance for real political power.
Power-Structure	The capitalist class dominates all forms of political participation that really matter. They control political and other institutions and discourage participation by the poor. In elections, citizens can only choose among competing segments of the established ruling class.
Structuralist	Election rituals in conventional politics only serve to legitimate class dominance. Conventional political participation perpetuates a myth of citizen power and provides an illusion to back the rhetoric of democracy. It can also serve as an early warning system for popular unrest.
Class-Struggle	Real power struggles can take place in conventional channels of political participation. Struggles among opposing groups often arise when one group imposes limits on participation by opponents while expanding their own influence into new forms of participation.

participation that matter most (e.g., campaign contributions, policy planning organizations, candidate selection, lobbying). In elections, ordinary citizens can only show support for one or another segment of the ruling class. The ruling class's control over political and other institutions (e.g., schools, media), combined with implicitly discouraging the poor to participate, creates a serious class bias. In any case, the impact of elections is limited. As Alford and Friedland (1975, 432) observed, "electoral participation is not highly correlated with power as measured by public expenditures or other measures of state responsiveness."

The *structuralist model* views the ritual of elections as legitimating and justifying class inequality. Social–economic stability in capitalist societies depends on political institutions that encourage apathy and deactivate citizens. Participation helps perpetuate an illusion of involvement and gives a veneer of plausibility to the rhetoric of democracy. It is both a safety valve that releases pent-up popular pressure for real, large-scale social change and an early warning system that signals growing anger that could develop into a serious challenge. Elections help the rulers adjust and smooth over popular concerns as they help keep rulers in charge.

In the *class-struggle model*, conventional participation can be a real power struggle, and forms of involvement today reflect the results of past struggles. Struggles arise over symbols, policies, and forms of participation. Competing groups try to limit, restrict, or deactivate opponents as they expand, enhance, and increase their own participation and influence. In power struggles, the intensity and forms of participation constantly shift as contending groups devise new types of political participation and discard ineffective types.

POLITICAL PARTICIPATION AND NONPARTICIPATION

A widely used definition of political participation says it includes citizen actions "aimed at influencing the election of government personnel and/or the actions they take" (Verba and Nie 1972, 2–3). Others (Cobb and Elder 1983) found this definition restrictive because it omits four factors: (1) influence over nongovernmental power and resources, (2) decisions about what becomes a public issue, (3) symbolic displays of support or displeasure, and (4) challenges to core principles (e.g., the division between public and private). For our purposes, political participation includes three factors: (1) deliberate acts designed to influence others' political behavior or state policy through elections or otherwise, (2) acts to affirm or deny membership in the polity, and (3) expressions of ideas and beliefs to influence political outcomes. Thus, participation shapes specific outcomes, the polity's boundaries, and ideas. Individuals, organizations (e.g., hospitals, corporations), collections of people (e.g., real estate agents, nurses, Latinos), and advocacy groups (e.g., National Rifle Association, Sierra Club, Teamster's Union, National Manufacturer's Association) can all participate in politics.

Forms, Intensities, and Channels of Participation

Forms of Participation

Participation in the electoral and nonelectoral arenas takes three forms: instrumental, symbolic, and communal (see Summary 5.2). These three forms can operate separately or together. The form of a specific action (e.g., voting) depends on the context in which it occurs. For example, John votes to change who is in office and decides policy (instrumental); Maria votes to support a candidate who is expected to win, but she wants to push the majority higher to send a message (symbolic); and Jian cares little about the winner but votes to express feelings of belonging with others in the neighborhood and do the right thing (communal).

Intensity of Participation

Participation varies by level of involvement, intensity of commitment, and amount of energy or resources expended. Low-intensity participation might

SUMMARY 5.2   **Three Forms of Political Participation**

1. Instrumental political participation is when a person or organization deliberately tries to affect politics to accomplish a specific goal (i.e., influence a policy or obtain a personal benefit). It depends on a rational calculation of costs and benefits, having a clear goal, a strong desire to achieve the goal, and a belief that politics can achieve the goal. Consider the following two situations. In the first situation, I feel strongly about an issue, and in an election, the candidates offer real alternatives on the issue. It is easy to go to the polls and vote. I believe my vote will make a difference. Once in office, the elected official has the authority to change policy on the issue. In the second situation, I do not feel strongly about the issue, and candidates do not differ on it. Going to the polls and voting is difficult, and I believe my vote makes no difference. Even if elected, the candidate cannot affect policy on the issue. Instrumental participation makes sense in the first situation but not in the second. Beyond voting, instrumental participation can be particularistic contact. **Particularistic political contact is when a person contacts a government official or office to obtain a particular material benefit for herself/himself or his/her family or business.** This is participation only to obtain something specific. For example, a bank president visits a government agency for

permission to allow the bank to be exempt from certain banking regulations.

2. Symbolic political participation occurs when a person or organization affirms (or rejects) political ideas or processes in an attempt to influence others. Symbolic participation is a kind of expression or speech. For example, someone publicly burns the American flag to express his/her objection to a government action. The nonviolent act of burning cloth harms no one, but it sends a defiant symbolic message designed to influence others (see Welch 2000, and Welch and Bryan 1996, on flag burning).

3. Communal political participation occurs when a person or organization displays her/his membership in the polity (or a subgroup within it). It is rooted in feelings of belonging or identity. Although it can overlap with other participation, the primary motivation is a desire to be a part of collectivity not to accomplish a goal or send a message. Communal behavior affirms connections with other people, certain ideas, or political institutions. Examples include going to a fireworks display on the Fourth of July with others, volunteering for combat duty in the armed forces, flying the national flag, passively complying with laws, and showing deference towards government officials (see Shingles 1981, 79).

include voting, signing a petition, flying a flag, or attaching a bumper sticker to your car, while intense participation would be running as a candidate for a public office, forming a new political party, or organizing a patriotic rally. About one-half of Americans are inactive, and 15 percent are very active in electoral politics (i.e., working in campaigns, contacting officials) (see Closer Look 5.1). Most of the time, a small minority participates beyond voting, but this can grow dramatically and quickly under certain conditions.

Channels of Participation

People and organizations can participate via electoral and nonelectoral channels. Participation in the electoral channel can be direct (e.g., voting, working on a

CLOSER LOOK 5.1	Levels of Individual Involvement in Elections

45% Active

Complete activist	10%	Highly active; aware, and powerful in all ways
Campaigner	15%	Votes; active in campaigns
Communalist	20%	Voter; regularly participates in community events

55% Inactive

Ritual voter	20%	Usually votes but does little else
Deactivated	15%	Rarely votes; might become interested
Disengaged	20%	Withdrawn; never votes or engages in other activity

Participation beyond Voting (1952–1990)

	Presidential Election	Midterm Election
Tried to influence others	32%	20%
Contributed money to party or candidate	10%	9%
Attended political meeting or rally	8%	8%
Worked for a party or candidate	4%	5%

Nonelectoral Participation (1973–2002)

Signed petition	35%
Attended a public meeting on town or school issues	18–33%
Wrote congressional representative or senator	15–24%
Attended political rally or speech	6–9%
Wrote letter to newspaper	5%
Made a public speech	5%

Sources: Adapted from Verba and Nie (1972, 79) and Rosenstone and Hanson (1993, 42–43). Supplemented with National Election Survey (NES) data from various years to 2002.

campaign, donations) or indirect (e.g., following a candidate's television advertising, joining a political party). It is usually narrowly focused (e.g., selecting a candidate, passing a referendum), open to most people on a regular schedule, and highly visible. It operates according to explicit, written rules or procedures. By contrast, the nonelectoral channel is diffuse, irregularly open to only a few, and barely visible. It rarely follows fixed, written rules. The nonelectoral channel includes attempts to influence government actions or the beliefs and behaviors of others. Both individuals and organizations use the nonelectoral channel. For example, my father-in-law wanted to get a stop sign installed at an intersection in front of his house. He wrote to city hall, talked to neighbors, and met with transportation officials. He used intense, instrumental participation in the nonelectoral channel. Organizations tend to use nonelectoral channels. For example, a newspaper investigates and prints articles on the failure of a government office to enforce a pollution law, resulting in unsafe drinking water. At times nonelectoral participation becomes controversial because some people want to avoid labeling their actions as "politics" so they can win wider acceptance. For example, 10 homeowners want to stop a social service agency from locating a homeless shelter in their neighborhood. They call their actions economic (i.e., protecting their investment in a house) or personal (i.e., defending family life), not political. It is really low-intensity, nonelectoral, instrumental political participation. Another example is a local official who issues parade permits and calls a high school band that carries the national flag a community or family event, not politics. It is really low-intensity, nonelectoral, communal-symbolic political participation. That same official may call an activist who distributes leaflets to oppose a proposed toxic waste dump "political." The activist may say her/his actions are not politics but a family or town concern.[3] Contending groups try to control how their actions will be labeled to exercise control over the boundaries of political participation and to gain advantages.

Nonparticipation

Not participating in politics can be as important as participating and ranges from passive disengagement to conscious, active refusal. Nonparticipation operates in various forms, intensities, and channels like participation does. For example, a person may decide not to vote (instrumental), fail to identify with a nation or learn its national anthem (communal), or substitute a sports team's flag for the national flag (symbolic). Examples of active nonparticipation include not standing for the playing of the national anthem, refusing to serve on a jury, or avoiding the military draft. Passive nonparticipation is tuning out or withdrawing from politics. Yet as Eliasoph (1998, 6) remarked, "apathy takes work to produce."

Labeling all nonparticipation as "apathy" is a mistake, because it assumes that all people are aware and free and that all actions are voluntary and unrestricted. History is full of cases of blocked citizen participation. To call all nonparticipation apathy may be blaming the victim. For example, the southern white power structure designed and implemented a system of intimidation, threats of violence, and legal barriers to block participation by African Americans (see Chapter 4). As Michael Avey (1989, 3) noted, "The exclusion of major segments of the U.S. population from political participation is not a rare occurrence, but in fact was a general policy in American politics from at least 1890." Many factors can discourage participation (see Summary 5.3)

SUMMARY 5.3	**Direct and Indirect Barriers to Political Participation**

In addition to the forms of exclusion discussed in Chapter 4 (e.g., urban political machines, voting rules that bar people with criminal records), other barriers exist that discourage participation, include the following:

- Laws, rules, and regulations that may make participation very difficult for some people. (Avey 1989, Highton 1997, Jackman 1987, Jackman and Miller 1995, Kleppner and Baker 1980, Lijphart 1997, Myles 1979, Nagler 1991, Powell 1986, Rosenstone and Hanson 1993, Rusk 1970, Squire et al. 1987, Teixeira 1987, 1992, Wolfinger and Rosenstone 1980).
- A public agenda that excludes or denies the entry of issues that concern people (Cobb and Ross 1997a, Gamson 1992b).
- A lack of alternatives or real competition between political parties (Crepaz 1990,

Hill and Leighley 1996, Kaempfer and Lowenberg 1993, Rosenstone, et al. 1984, Rosenstone and Hansen 1993, and Zipp 1985).

- A lack of political efficacy (i.e., a person feels that he/she makes a difference) (House and Mason 1975, Piven and Cloward 1988, Southwell 1986, 1987, 1995).
- Cultural settings that create social disapproval for openly discussing politics and public issues (Eliasoph 1998 and Noelle-Neumann 1984).
- Mass media coverage that trivializes public issues and treats politics as boring or irrelevant (see Chapter 8).
- Cultural discourse that says public issues are private, personal problems to be solved by individual therapy or coping strategies (Cloud 1998 and Eliasoph 1998).

---

c h a r t   5 . 2

TYPOLOGY OF FOUR KINDS OF NONPARTICIPATION IN POLITICS

Pressures on a Person to Not Participate	A Person's Conscious, Deliberate Decision to Not Participate	
	Yes	**No**
High	Strategic withdrawal	Forced silence
Low	Active rejection	Oblivious disengagement (Apathy)

External pressures on a person combine with voluntary individual decisions to create different types of nonparticipation. If we cross-classify the degree of individual, voluntary participation by external constraints, we create a typology with four kinds of nonparticipation (see Chart 5.2). For example, people who feel that participation is dangerous may strategically withdraw, while others may choose noninvolvement for ethical reasons. Some people may be aware and want to participate, but they may be locked out by legal or other barriers.

Explaining Participation

Political sociologists developed five overlapping explanations of political participation and nonparticipation. According to the *civic virtue* thesis, people participate because they are socialized to the values of good citizenship. People who are most socially integrated (e.g., are married; have regular jobs; belong to clubs, parent-teacher associations, churches) are socialized to democratic norms that include being politically active. By contrast, socially isolated, disengaged, alienated people tend to show little interest in politics, do not follow political events, withdraw from conventional politics, or are attracted to extremist movements outside democratic norms.[4]

The *individual resource* argument says participation varies along a continuum. The amount of resources, such as money, time, information, organizational skills (e.g., running a meeting, taking notes) determine how likely a person is to participate. Overall U.S. voter turnout has declined since the 1980s, but most educated people still tend to vote (see Table 5.1). The assumption is that individuals rationally decide to participate when it is easier (e.g., they have the time, money, skills), and when they expect benefits from participating. People with few resources, who face difficulties (e.g., low education, no money, cannot register to vote), or who expect few benefits, decide not to participate and withdraw due to rational ignorance.[5] **Rational ignorance says people rationally decide not to invest the time and effort into following and participating in politics if they expect it to have little impact.**[6]

In the *mobilization* proposition, people participate when an organization (e.g., political party, interest group, advocacy organization) offers them a cause or ideological reason to participate, contacts potential supporters, and encourages involvement.[7] Some types of mobilization (e.g., a phone call from a political party) have immediate effects (voting in one election), while other types build an "electoral mobilization infrastructure" (i.e., volunteers, potential candidates, a communication network, and many local organizations) that can influence participation

TABLE 5.1	Percentages of Eligible Voting Population Reporting They Voted in Select U.S. Presidential and Congressional Elections (1980–2000) By Level of Schooling					
	Presidential Election			**Off-Year Congressional Election**		
Schooling	**1980**	**1992**	**2000**	**1986**	**1994**	**1998**
Under 8 Years	42.6	35.1	26.8	32.7	27.7	24.6
1–3 Years of High School	45.6	41.2	33.6	33.8	30.9	25.0
High School Graduate	58.9	57.5	49.4	44.1	42.2	37.1
4+ Years of College	79.9	81.0	72.0	62.5	62.5	57.2

Source: Compiled from *Statistical Abstract of the United States, 2001,* Table 401.

for many years. Andrews (1997, 815) found, "Civil rights mobilization shaped electoral outcomes 10 to 20 years after the peak of the movement." Just as mobilization increases participation, demobilization may foster disengagement. Thus, beliefs, values, and norms in contemporary popular culture may inhibit expression and involvement for all but a tiny activist elite, creating a culture of political silence that evaporates politics and depoliticizes issues.[8]

The *group solidarity* hypothesis states that people who feel a strong sense of group membership—in a racial-ethnic group, a religious community, or labor union—will participate to defend or advance group interests. Their collective solidarity is a basis of political action, and they express their identities through participation. Likewise, people who lack group identity or collective consciousness, and who feel isolated as individuals, participate less.[9] For example, people who feel an intense identity toward their ethnic group (e.g., Irish Catholic) might be very motivated to campaign and vote for an Irish Catholic candidate (e.g., John F. Kennedy).

A *social network* explanation is that people with whom one has regular contact in a social network (e.g., neighbors, friends, coworkers, family members) provide information, assistance, and social–emotional support to promote participation. The network is "social capital" or a web of social relations with whom one can discuss politics. Political parties often rely on preexisting social networks to mobilize voters.[10] As Huckfeldt et al. (1993, 380) argued, "People locate themselves in neighborhoods, churches, workplaces, clubs and associations . . . in this process they also define—even if indirectly and unintentionally—the dimensions of their social experience. This social experience . . . defines the composition of political preferences to which an individual is exposed." Sustained, intense participation requires a supportive social network, and people lacking a network rarely engage in intense participation.[11]

The five explanations of political participation overlap (see Chart 5.3). For example, rational choice theories see voting as a general case of generating collective action with solidarity and selective incentives where norms (i.e., civic virtue, group solidarity, mobilization) motivate rational choice.[12] Factors in the explanations can compound one another. As one study found, ". . . processes in the United States tended to be individual ones, resulting in a disproportion of upper-status individuals in the participant population. Group-based processes—with the exception of those associated with black Americans—tended to increase the participation disparity between the haves and the have nots, largely because upper status individuals in America also have more group-based resources" (Verba, Nie, and Kim 1978, 15).

THE ELECTORAL CHANNEL

Americans extol elections and majority rule, yet most presidents are elected by a numerical minority. Since 1936, only three presidents received votes from more than one-third of the eligible voters. In eight elections, about one-fourth of people chose the winner (see Table 5.2). This occurs because the winner needs

chart 5.3

FIVE EXPLANATIONS OF POLITICAL PARTICIPATION

Explanation	Major Cause of Political Participation	Who Participates in Conventional Politics?	Who Does Not Participate?
Civic virtue	Strong commitment to democratic norms	People who are highly socially integrated	People who are isolated and alienated
Individual resource	Individual cost/benefit decision	People who have social–economic resources	People lacking resources
Mobilization	Direct encouragement by organized activists	People who were directly contacted and encouraged	People who were not contacted
Social network	Being embedded in a web of social ties with others who participate	Most tightly interconnected people	People who are disconnected or have few links to others
Group solidarity	Desires to express and defend group interests	People with strong group consciousness and identity	People with weak group identity

TABLE 5.2 — Voter Turnout, Percentage of Votes to Winner, and Percentage of Population for Winner in U.S. Presidential Elections (1936–2000)

Presidential Election Year	Percentage of Eligible Population Voting	Percentage of Votes Going to the Winner	Percentage of Population Voting for Winner
1936	56.9	60.8	34.6
1940	58.9	54.7	32.2
1944	56.0	53.7	29.9
1948	51.1	49.6	25.3
1952	61.6	55.1	33.9
1956	59.3	57.4	34.0
1960	62.8	49.7	31.2
1964	61.9	61.1	37.8
1968	60.9	43.4	26.4
1972	55.2	60.7	33.5
1976	53.5	50.1	26.8
1980	52.8	50.7	26.8
1984	53.3	58.8	31.3
1988	50.3	53.4	26.9
1992	55.1	43.0	23.7
1996	49.0	49.2	24.1
2000	51.3	50.0	25.5

Source: Compiled from *Statistical Abstract of the United States* and *U.S. Election Commission,* various years.

only half the votes but since only half of eligible voters vote, one-fourth actually select the winner (50 percent eligible × 50 percent voting = 25 percent). When voter turnout is lower, as in congressional elections, a smaller percentage of the eligible population selects the winner.

Who Does and Does Not Vote?

Why do some people vote and others do not? Compared to other advanced industrial democracies, the United States has one of the lowest voter turnout rates, beating only Switzerland (see Table 5.3). The United States also has the highest differences in voting based on social class.[13] The U. S. turnout rate declined sharply after the 1890s and after the 1960s, and is now near its lowest point in 100 years.[14] Such an international comparative focus directs our attention to the impact of institutional factors on turnout.

Several factors affect voter turnout rates (see Summary 5.4).[15] Three mutually supporting, additive factors are: (1) individual social characteristics that distinguish nonvoters from voters, (2) structural factors in the political system that encourage or discourage voting, (3) contextual factors or social situations that encourage or discourage voting. Such factors operate within the explanations of participation, but there is no one-to-one correspondence. For example, the resource and civic virtues emphasize individual factors, but contextual factors can be a resource; group solidarity and social network emphasize contextual factors, while mobilization emphasizes structural factors.

Individual Factors

Two main individual factors are demographic and attitudinal. Most demographic studies simply list correlates of voting and rely on a resource (also called

**"I don't vote. They've got machines
that do that now."**

TABLE 5.3 Voter Turnout Rates in 35 Selected Countries (1960–2000)

Country	Year 1960	1970	1980	1990	2000	FH Rating
Argentina*	69.8	72.9	77.5	79.8	n/a	5
Australia	84.0	85.3	84.0	82.1	81.7	2
Austria*	92.7	91.7	86.7	75.7	68.6	2
Belgium	88.0	88.6	94.3	85.1	83.2	2
Brazil*	n/a	n/a	n/a	76.9	81.0	7
Canada	73.3	71.3	64.5	68.3	54.6	2
Costa Rica*	71.4	75.7	79.0	85.1	73.7	3
Czech Republic	n/a	n/a	n/a	93.1	76.6	3
Denmark	85.9	87.3	86.3	80.4	83.1	2
Finland*	81.8	69.3	88.1	81.4	76.8	2
France*	74.9	72.4	77.0	72.3	n/a	3
Germany	86.9 (W)	88.7 (W)	81.8 (W)	73.1	75.3	3
Greece	86.3	82.7	84.5	85.6	89.0	4
Hungary	n/a	n/a	n/a	75.9	59.0	3
Iceland*	n/a	91.1	91.7	87.0	n/a	2
India	54.4	57.2	61.9	57.2	65.5	5
Ireland*	65.7	47.7	n/a	n/a	47.7	2
Israel	80.4	81.8	79.9	81.7	84.4	3
Italy	95.3	94.7	91.8	92.3	84.9	3
Japan	71.4	73.9	74.7	74.9	59.0	3
Netherlands	87.9	77.8	85.2	75.2	70.1	2
New Zealand	85.6	85.3	88.9	78.6	76.1	2
Norway	77.7	80.1	82.3	74.5	73.1	2
Poland*	n/a	n/a	n/a	55.1	62.6	3
Portugal*	n/a	n/a	86.7	69.8	57.2	2
Singapore	n/a	73.8	45.9	43.5	35.4	10
Slovakia	n/a	n/a	n/a	93.1	78.9	4
South Korea	n/a	74.8	78.4	74.6	55.7	4
Spain	n/a	n/a	83.1	77.4	73.8	3
Sweden	82.8	87.3	88.6	82.8	77.7	2
Switzerland	53.5	97.3	40.8	39.7	34.9	2
Turkey	75.1	56.7	75.5	79.8	80.4	9
Thailand	n/a	46.0	46.9	58.4	70.1	7
United Kingdom	75.1	71.2	71.7	75.4	56.6	3
United States*	63.1	55.2	52.6	55.2	49.3	2

* Indicates a presidential election, all others are for parliament.

Turnout rate is percentage of valid votes divided by the voting age population in the country.

Year = Election year indicated or closest following year. For 2000, most are 1998 or 1999 because it is the most recent year with the most accurate total population data.

(W) = West Germany only.

n/a = Data not available or no democratic election held.

FH = Freedom House indicator for levels of a country's political system. Range is 2 to 14, where 2 is the highest level of rights and freedoms and 14 is the lowest. Score is for year of most recent election only.

Source: International Institute for Democracy and Electoral Assistance (http://www.idea.int/vt/survey/voter_turnout2.cfm).

| SUMMARY 5.4 | Factors Favoring Voter Turnout |

INDIVIDUAL FACTORS

Demographic: Compared to nonvoters, regular voters tend to be more educated, older, have higher incomes, be married, and belong to voluntary organizations (e.g., clubs, churches, unions)

Attitudinal: People who vote regularly are more likely to trust government and other people, be informed and knowledgeable about politics, and have political efficacy (a person feels that he/she can make a difference and is listened to). They are less likely to feel alienated, feel involved in society, more likely to think in ideological terms, and have strong feelings of racial-ethnic group solidarity.

STRUCTURAL FACTORS

Settings that promote higher rates of voting do not have voter registration requirements; they are likely to have compulsory voting laws, election days that are holidays, highly competitive election contests, a multi-party system, parliamentary system, and a system of proportionate representation. Low rates of voting are associated with the characteristics of the United States system. They include voter registration requirements, individualistic and voluntary voting, elections held on work days, low levels of competition in many districts, a two-party system, primary elections, elections for non-major positions held on separate days than other elections, and a "single-district, winner-take-all" electoral representation system.

CONTEXTUAL FACTORS

Compared to nonvoters, regular voters tend to live in neighborhoods of similar ethnic-racial background, have been contacted by a political party or advocacy organization, discuss politics with friends and neighbors, and see ideological differences among political parties and candidates.

the capacity, or socioeconomic status [SES]) approach.[16] **A resource theory of voter turnout says that individuals who have more social and economic resources (e.g., money, time, civic skills) are more likely to vote.**[17] Researchers differ on the impact of social class on voter turnout in the 1960–1990 period.[18] Yet all agree that people who have few social or economic resources (e.g., the unemployed, the poor) are least likely to vote.[19] Other researchers focus on attitudes, feelings, knowledge, and rational calculations. They say a person's outlook generates an attachment to or detachment from politics. Some explain nonvoting in terms of voter ignorance, while others emphasize disaffection or disenchantment with politics and frustration over the absence of real electoral choices. **A rational choice theory of voter turnout holds that individuals make instrumental decisions about whether to invest time and effort into voting, and they vote if or when they believe it is likely to make a difference for their immediate personal situation**[20] (also see Chapter 3).

Structural Factors

The "rules of the game" or the "machinery of elections" also affect voter turnout. Electoral system design can encourage certain people to vote but not others or can discourage most of the public. Certain procedural features, such as elections held on working days, required voter registration, and inconveniently located polling stations, make it more difficult for citizens to vote. Other features, such as winner-takes-all elections with single-politician districts, many separate elections for political offices scheduled at different times, and little real party competition, also depress voter turnout.[21] Nations with very high turnout often have compulsory voting laws (e.g., it goes on a person's police record or fines for not voting) and schedule elections for Sundays or holidays so they do not interfere with working.

Americans are familiar with a winner-takes-all system with single-representative districts. This means that a candidate receiving 50.1 percent of the votes, or less in multi-candidate races, wins and alone will represent a district. It reduces the incentive for voters who favor a candidate who is unlikely to get 50 percent of the votes. Alternatives, such as a proportional representation system with multiple seats per district, raise the incentive for all voters to participate because all candidates who get substantial votes (e.g., 25 percent) will represent a district. For example, a district elects three representatives with winners based on the proportion of votes received; all winners can be from one party or each from a different party.

A parliamentary system also seems to increase turnout. Unlike most leading democracies, the United States does not have a parliamentary system. U.S. political institutions, along with a strong separation of powers and a system of checks and balances, weakens party power. It also divides power; the chief executive officer (e.g., president, governor) can be from one party while another controls the legislature. Weak political parties and divided state power tend to lower turnout.[22] Voter turnout is greatest for a high stakes contest between strong, disciplined, and unified parties that will win control of the entire government.

Paradoxically, numerous elections can reduce democracy. Asking citizens to vote in many elections creates voter fatigue and depresses turnout. For example, voters are likely to go to the polls when they elect the local school board, city mayor, state governor, president, and Congressional representatives all at once. They are less likely to vote if there is a separate election for each on a different day. The trend in the United States has been away from consolidated elections in which voters elect many public officials at once. For example, in 1952 nearly one-half of state governor elections were tied with the presidential election. By 1990 this dropped to 12 percent. The ostensive reason was to insulate state politics from national politics and to lessen outside influence.[23] Primary elections, especially contested ones, reduce turnout in the main election. The number of states with presidential primaries more than doubled since the 1960s.[24]

Voter turnout is lower when two nonideological political parties compete, or the parties do not compete, in all districts. Countries with tighter elections among multiple political parties that offer markedly different policies tend to have higher turnout. In "safe districts," where one party is very strong and party competition is unbalanced, turnout declines. Nearly one-half of U.S. districts are safe districts.[25] Most state and local, and many national, districts are noncompetitive (i.e., a candidate faces no challenger or repeatedly wins by a large margin).[26] For example in the 2000 election, almost two-thirds of Congressional elections were landslides where the winner got 60 percent or more of the votes. In the six largest states (by population), 80 percent of districts were noncompetitive, and not a single incumbent lost in California, Illinois, Massachusetts, Michigan, Pennsylvania, or Wisconsin.[27]

Gerrymandering also restricts voter participation. **Gerrymandering is the practice of drawing election district boundaries in a way that favors one political party or another.**[28] It occurs when officials draw legislative districts to exclude or include specific areas based on party registration or demographic characteristics associated with stable party support, creating a strange-looking coiled snake image on a map. For example, officials will split a section with a concentration of low-income people and racial minorities who favor the Democratic Party into four parts. They will join three parts with white, high-income Republican areas to dilute the Democratic electoral impact to under 40 percent, and then they put the remaining voters in a 90 percent Democratic area to create three majority Republican districts and one Democratic area. Often a small shift in district lines can change the balance to a strenghten the party in a neighboring district's party, without it losing control in the home district. In almost every United States state, elected politicians and political party leaders—the people most directly affected in future elections—draw district lines. While blatant, extreme cases of bias can be brought to the courts, shaping districts to favor a party is common practice. Once in place, districts remain the same for a decade, until the next census (see Case in Point 5.1).

Complex voter registration rules lower turnout. Among major democracies, the United States has some of the most complex, cumbersome voter registration rules. In the decentralized U.S. system, each state sets its own rules. These can require long periods of residence, showing photo identification, and completing long forms months before an election. Locales that don't require prior registration—they have instant registration—have higher turnout. Complex voter registration rules especially depress voting among lower-income, highly mobile, and less educated people.[29] As Piven and Cloward (1988, 17,119) argued, "the linchpin of distorted American democracy in the contemporary period is the distinctive system of voter registration procedures . . . . Legal and administrative barriers to voting impinge less on the well-off and well-educated than they do on the poor and the uneducated." Also, legal disenfranchisement in the past has a "legacy effect" that persists to depress voting rates for subsequent decades.[30] In addition, the percentage of the total population that is eligible to vote has declined since 1972 due to new requirements, felon disenfranchisement, and immigration (also see Case in Point 5.2).[31]

Contextual Factors

Settled, socially well-connected people vote more than transient or isolated people.[32] Being engaged in civil society (i.e., being married; a member of a union, club, or church; or a long-time resident) promotes voting (see World View 5.1).[33] One's

CASE IN POINT 5.1   Political Representation and the U.S. Census

An angry public debate erupted in 1998 over what is usually a dull, routine, and technical topic that only interests statisticians and demographers—how to conduct a census. The issue was whether to conduct the 2000 U.S. Census using a total count of all people or only a scientific sampling. The debate began when studies revealed that past censuses had serious undercounts and some overcounts. They missed as much as 4 percent of the population. The scientists agreed that carefully designed random sampling techniques would yield much more accurate results than the old method and would cost less money.

The government conducts a census every ten years to determine how many political representatives each district can elect. It also uses results to allocate funds for public programs, since the amount of money is based on the population in an area. Past errors suggested that a dozen elected politicians and tens of millions of dollars could be geographically reallocated if the count was more accurate.

Certain types of people tend to be overcounted and other types undercounted. High-income whites in the suburbs who own two or more homes are most likely to be counted twice; they tend to vote for the Republican Party. Low-income people, especially racial minorities and recent immigrants in inner cities and remote rural areas, are most likely to be undercounted; they tend to support the Democratic Party.

At first both parties favored scientific adjustment for greater accuracy. Then a 1997 memo by a Republican expert pointed out how Republicans benefited from past practice and projected they could lose up to 24 Congressional seats if undercounts ended. Despite its inaccuracy and greater cost, Republicans switched to argue in favor of the traditional method. Scientists, Democrats, and people in many areas that might get more funds with a more accurate count argued for sampling. In January 1999 the U.S. Supreme Court gave opponents of a more accurate census a victory with a 4–5 ruling in favor of tradition in deciding a suit brought by the right-wing Southeastern Legal Foundation on behalf of 16 individuals in states that might lose seats in Congress and then-Speaker Newt Gingrich on behalf of Republicans in the House of Representatives.

Politicization of the census intensified when within less than 1 month after taking office, President George W. Bush removed final authority over the census from the professional scientists and put it in the hands of a highly partisan political appointee, Mr. Donald Evans, who had chaired President Bush's 2000 presidential election campaign. After 2 weeks in office, he ruled that no type of adjustment for accuracy was necessary.

Sources: Anderson and Fienberg (1999); Skerry (2000); "U.S. Census Bureau Rejects Revision to Nation's Tally," *New York Times,* March 2, 2001; "Census Makes Gains in Reducing Number of People Not Counted," *New York Times,* February, 14, 2001; "Census Officials Ponder Adjustments Crucial to Redistricting," *New York Times,* February 12, 2001; "Some Counted Twice in Census, Officials Say," *New York Times,* January 12, 2001; "Census Bills Advance in House Despite the Bureau's Protests," *New York Times,* March 18, 1999; "Partisan Fighting Flares Anew Over Handling of the Census," *New York Times,* March 9, 2000; "The Path to the Next Census Has Been Far From Routine," *New York Times,* February 1, 1999; "Justices Express Misgivings Over Reviewing Census Plan," *New York Times,* December 1, 1998; "Fight Over Statistical Sampling in 2000 Is Postponed," *New York Times,* October 16, 1998; "High Court to Hear Case on Sampling for Census," *New York Times,* September 11, 1998; "House Republicans Plan to Keep a Tight Rein on 2000 Census," *New York Times,* February 9, 1998; "Weary of Political Sniping, the Census Bureau Chief Resigns," *New York Times,* January 13, 1998.

immediate social setting, including feelings of efficacy and following the news, contribute to voting.[34] In addition, mobilization efforts increase voting, especially labor-intensive personal contact (e.g., door-to-door, telephone calling). Many researchers believe U.S. civil society is weakening.[35] U.S. political parties have moved away from using volunteers who directly contact potential voters and toward

CASE IN POINT 5.2   ## "Ballot Security"—Curtailing Voting by Racial Minorities

After the Florida ballot fiasco during the 2000 presidential election, Congress enacted the Help America Vote Act to avoid its recurrence. The act offers states federal funds to replace their old voting systems with modern and reliable technology. The act also contains provisions that could increase the harassment and intimidation of racial minorities through ballot-security programs. Presented as "good government" measures to stop alleged voter fraud, they may be used to suppress voting by racial minorities and for targeted partisan purposes. For example, shortly before the November 2002 election, the Republican attorney general announced a "voting integrity initiative" to curtail voter fraud. It began by investigating alleged voter fraud in South Dakota counties that had significant American-Indian populations. Coincidently, this was shortly after the Democratic Party had a voter registration and get-out-the-vote campaign on South Dakota's Indian reservations. Under the initiative, state and federal agents questioned 2,000 new Native-American registrants, many of whom were first time voters. New registrations in other counties that had few American-Indian residents were not examined, although those counties contained most of the new voter registrations. At the end of the investigation, only one Native American was charged with violating voting rules. Similar antifraud actions surfaced before the 2002 elections in Pine Bluff, Arkansas. There Republican poll watchers drove away black voters by taking photos of them and demanding their identification.

New rules in the Help America Vote Act require anyone who has registered by mail and has not previously voted to present a photo ID, bank statement, government check, or utility bill with her/his name and address on election day. One problem with the ID requirement is that minorities are less likely than other people to have photo IDs. A study in Louisiana found that whites are five times more likely than blacks to have a driver's license or other picture identification. Also, there is no evidence that the new ID requirement reduces voter fraud. States without ID requirements have no record of more voter fraud than ones that have them. The requirement also allows aggressive poll officials to single out minority voters and interrogate them, asking humiliating questions such as, "Where's your government check?" and "Why don't you have a bank statement?"

Such minority voter harassment is not new. As part of an antifraud initiative before the 1981 New Jersey gubernatorial election, the Republican National Committee mailed letters to registered Democrats in predominantly black or Hispanic areas. Letters returned as undeliverable to the address listed were then used to challenge voters and remove them from the voter lists. On election day, a security force of armed, off-duty police officers wearing official-looking armbands went to heavily black (and Democratic) precincts, and Republican Party activists posted signs warning that the polls were being patrolled by a security force and offered a $1,000 reward for anyone giving information leading to the arrest and conviction of election-law violators. Although the Republican Party lost a lawsuit in New Jersey, similar tactics were used in Louisiana in 1986 and in North Carolina in 1990. In both cases, after the election, the Republican Party was sued. They admitted no wrongdoing and entered into a decree promising not to conduct similar ballot-security programs in the future. Existing federal laws make intimidating or harassing minority voters illegal, but the law is barely enforced and protecting voter rights depends on someone bringing a lawsuit. The impact of the new ID requirement may have less to do with ending fraud than it does with making it more difficult for members of disadvantaged groups to vote.

Source: McDonald, Laughlin. "The New Poll Tax." *The American Prospect* (December 20, 2002), pp. 26–28.

WORLD VIEW 5.1   Campaign Finance and Influence in Western European Democracies

Some Europeans criticize the U.S. system of campaign finance and corporate lobbying as being corrupt, and even cite it when they face scandals over illegal political donations and business influence (Walker 2000). Each European nation regulates its campaigns somewhat differently, but they use a combination of limits on donation size, free media access, public financing, and restricted election spending. Generally, political party funding falls into three patterns: (1) extensive state control over party financing (in Austria, Belgium, France, Greece, Ireland, the Netherlands, and Switzerland), (2) a market approach with little or no state funding (in the United Kingdom and the United States), and (3) a mix of public–private funding (in Germany, Italy, Spain, and Sweden). Some countries also give subsidies, such as free postage, to political parties.

For example, France and Britain limit campaign spending, ban paid political advertising, and provide free airtime. Campaign spending for French presidential candidates is limited to $16 million during the 12 months prior an election, and the parties cannot accept corporate donations. The French government reimburses a proportion of campaign spending depending on election results. In Britain, the party spending is capped at $28 million per party (that amounts to $1.65 per eligible voter, compared to $13.50 per eligible voter spent by Democratic and Republican parties in the 2000 U.S. election). The spending limits apply both to individual candidates and to the national parties. Both France and Britain ban radio and television political advertising. The French allot each candidate and political party equal amounts of free radio and television time to discuss the issues. In Britain, parties are allowed to have five 5-minute television and radio broadcasts during the campaign.

In addition, corporate lobbyists in Europe face more controls due to less of a "free market" tradition and a history of more state control over business activity than is the case in the United States. For example, Europeans discussed banning all television commercials aimed at children because young children cannot differentiate entertainment from merchandising. This gets serious attention and receives broad support in Europe. In the United States, major media and advertising corporations (e.g., Disney, Viacom, Coca-Cola) have argued that American freedom includes a basic right to view advertising, making such a ban beyond the realm of possibility. Likewise, in Europe, the environmental, health, and consumer movements are very powerful, comparable to antiabortion or progun movements in the United States. This makes them more potent counterforces to major corporations in lobbying that occurs in the United States.

Another important difference is that European governments operate at both the national and European Union (EU) levels. The EU is relatively new. This means its ruling-making and law-enactment processes are not under the control of established politicians who dominate legislative committees and who have been conditioned to pay close attention to corporate lobbyists after many years of campaign donations and lobbying. Each member nation of the EU has substantial veto power and represents a sovereign state that represents a distinct ideological position and set of economic interests. All of this does not mean that campaign donations and lobbying are unimportant as a source of corporate political influence in Europe, but it does illustrate different ways nations wrestle with similar issues.

Sources: Basham (2002), Loewenberg (2002), Walker (2000) and "Is Europe corrupt?," the *Economist*, January 27, 2000.

indirect capital-intensive techniques—such as hired public relations experts, professional opinion polling, television advertising, and mass mailings. The switch to expensive media-based techniques has increased the dependence of parties on large financial contributions from wealthy donors or organized interests.[36] Another factor lowering turnout, especially among the poor, is an economic recession.[37]

Does Turnout Matter?

If people who vote and those who do not vote think and act identically, then nonvoting may indicate low political enthusiasm, but it will make little difference in election outcomes or public policy choices. We know that voters differ little from nonvoters in ideological self-identification and in political party identification.[38] Yet they differ in other respects. Voters and nonvoters differ demographically; voters are older and have higher incomes. Voters and nonvoters hold different positions on public issues that reinforce class differences. Nonvoters favor a proactive government that will provide social welfare programs and aid racial minorities, while voters tend to be less supportive of government social programs.[39] As Verba and associates (1993, 303) observed, on certain economic issues, such as public sector jobs for the unemployed, the "voters are slightly more conservative than the public as a whole." Since elected officials are most attentive to politically active people, "it matters not only how participants differ from nonparticipants in their opinions (whether they want higher or lower taxes, greater or lesser attention to social welfare) but who they are" (1993, 304). Also, high income people have greater access to elected officials.[40] In the United States, "where political activity is clearly stratified by socioeconomic level, there is a clear gap between those active in political life and those inactive . . . . Political leaders paying attention to the participant population would underestimate the extent to which such needs [of low income people] exist . . . the class basis of political activity is very strong—the participant population is heavily biased in the direction of those who are more affluent and better educated . . . " (Verba, Nie, and Kim 1978, 307).

We can reconcile the finding that voters and nonvoters do not differ by party or ideological label, but they differ on several policy issues by noting that nonvoters feel the parties are alike and rarely use ideological labels. This supports the **Piven and Cloward turnout proposition which states that the American voting system operates in a way that silences citizens who desire a more activist government and who advocate left-liberal social policies.**[41] Many left-liberal citizens feel that the Democratic Party represents many other interests, and it has failed to be a strong, consistent advocate for egalitarian policies at the local and national levels.

Low voter turnout weakens public confidence in government and increases political alienation, and it further reduces turnout because nonvoters see government as distant and unresponsive. Politicians ignore nonvoters and promote policies to favor voters. Because the nonvoters have lower education and income levels, nonvoting reinforces the power of those with social-economic resources.

Partisanship

Partisanship means attachment to a political party. The political parties in the United States are loose coalitions of diverse interests that join together to try to win power. They have been criticized for being indistinguishable and lacking distinct, coherent ideologies. Beyond the short-term game of elections that generates heated rhetoric, the parties tend to promote a national consensus, avoid divisive issues, and disregard the powerless. Without a large difference between the major parties and without a third party challenge, partisanship is weak in the United States.

The two major political parties defend individual private property rights and support the capitalist economic system for three reasons.

1. Simple self-interest—Both depend on financial and popular support from people who are successful in the existing social-economic order.
2. Structural dependence—The structural dependence thesis (see Chapter 3) notes that healthy capitalism prevents a government revenue shortfall and avoids mass unemployment.
3. Entrenched powerholders—People who have great wealth or who run corporate America have privileged access to top-level political party decisions; they can mobilize vast resources if they sense the possibility of a serious threat to their continued power and control.

American parties differ on cultural issues (e.g., racial equality, abortion, gun control), on regional concerns (e.g., Western mountain versus East coast urban), and on policy implementation (e.g., block grants to states versus direct payments). Economic policy differences avoid the really serious issues, such as Should property rights or profits be limited and the economy redesigned? When a mass movement outside the two-party system emerges, the parties first try to fragment it or absorb its message to weaken its threat to their position. If that fails, they cooperate to use government authority to repress the challengers.[42]

Although each person makes a party choice, across the polity, specific social groups regularly support one party or another. Jews and Catholics more than Protestants, nonwhites more than whites, urban more than rural residents, self-identified liberals more than conservatives, and working class more than upper middle class or the rich have supported the Democratic Party, and since the 1980s, women more than men have supported it.[43] For example, the odds are about 7 in 10 that a white Protestant man who resides in a small town or rural area, calls himself conservative, and is in the middle or upper class will identify with the Republican Party.

Party support is patterned because people develop shared interests, understandings, and beliefs, and they favor a party with policies that correspond to their interests. People develop common understandings and interests from a shared social location, and candidates or parties create and target policies that correspond to these interests. Before the 1970s, children tended to adopt the partisan identity of their parents, but since then, Americans have become less partisan and fluctuate more with the larger political climate.[44] Since the mid-1990s, overall American partisan self-identity shifted from the Democratic Party toward the Republican

Party and Independent positions. For example in 1970, about 44 percent of voters said they were strong or plain Democrats. This dropped by 8 percent by the mid-1990s, while those calling themselves Republicans grew by 5 percent. The social backgrounds of Republicans also changed. In the 1970s, more women than men were Republicans, but after the mid-1980s, more women than men identified with the Democratic Party. Republicans attracted whites and middle or upper middle class people more than racial minorities or working class people. Since the 1980s, the racial gap and class gap have grown.

National survey data from the 1990s show 30–40 percent of Americans saw no difference between the political parties, and 39–45 percent felt, "People like me don't have much say about what government does."[45] Partisan support can be consistent with seeing no difference between parties and political alienation if a few very interested and highly ideological activists emphasize party differences, if people vote based on emotional-symbolic appeals or loyalties disconnected from government policies, and if people see no alternative but act pragmatically to choose what helps them from available options.

SOCIAL DIFFERENCES IN VOTING—PARTISANSHIP AND PARTICIPATION

Political sociologists debate how social divisions or cleavages affect voting, choice of party, and other political involvement. Below we examine the three major cleavages—class, race, and gender.

Class Politics

Class Voting and Class Politics

Class voting and class politics are major concerns in political sociology.[46] **Class voting is the strength of a relationship between an individual's social class and his/her choice of a party or candidate.** For example, do working class people select candidate X, while capitalists select candidate Y? **Class politics is how class identity or substantive class interests affect a person's orientation toward politics.** It is the salience of class for politics, including nonelectoral politics. Class politics modifies the class-vote linkage and explains why a social class goes with a vote choice. For example, if candidates and parties are disconnected to class interests and voters lack a class identity, then social class will be unimportant for politics. Likewise, classes engage in dissimilar forms of political activity. Instead of a single bipolar continuum, from full engagement to total withdrawal, class participation involves a collection of strategies that classes can use to advance their interests. For example, a wealthy person might donate $50,000 to a political party to advance his/her class interests, as class politics but not class voting. Class voting is one expression of class politics; and the same act, casting a vote, may have different effects in different contexts.[47]

An awareness and identification with one's social class can affect political behavior and voting. People who strongly identify with a social class in a context where the parties offer clear class-linked policies will vote for the party that represents their class. Research suggests that few Americans were class conscious in the 1960s–1980s or saw their class interest closely aligned with a political party.[48]

Historical Studies   Across the industrializing world, during the late nineteenth and early twentieth centuries, a rapidly growing industrial working class frequently clashed with the class of factory owners, investors, and financiers. Until the twentieth century, working class males could vote in only a few nations. As the franchise spread, it followed a similar pattern from the top of the stratification system downward. First, wealthy majority-group males could vote, and lastly, low-income people, females, and racial-ethnic minorities got the vote. In the nineteenth century, moderate reformers read Karl Marx's predictions about a working class revolution, witnessed violent clashes based on class at home and abroad, and saw socialist egalitarian ideas spreading rapidly among industrial workers. The reformers blended lofty democratic ideals with a desire to defuse worker radicalism and urged expanding the franchise beyond wealthy property owners. They reasoned that once they could vote, workers would express their demands (e.g., for improved working conditions, schools for their children) using the ballot box instead of clashes at street barricades. Elections could channel energy and anger into peaceful political contests and protect the social order from violent overthrow. **The democratic class struggle thesis says intense conflict between capitalists (e.g., business owners, bankers, large investors) and workers was converted into a peaceful electoral competition.**[49]

Looking at the transition of the United States to an industrial society from the 1870s to 1940s, scholars tried to explain "American Exceptionalism," or why America failed to produce a militant working class movement aligned with a leftist party as occurred in Western Europe. They asked why, "American worker's class consciousness is by and large independent of their other political concerns and activities . . . . A large and persistent barrier appears to separate American worker's class consciousness from their other political orientations and activities" (Brooks 1994, 186).

One group in the *New Political History* school offered an ethnocultual explanation. They examined voting records and said that social class was irrelevant in America because in a nation of diverse immigrants, people voted based on their ethnic background and religion. Political parties were "political churches" organized around ethnicity and religion not social class.[50] By contrast, those of the *New Labor History* school conducted qualitative, case studies of specific communities. They discovered many ideologically aware, politically mobilized workers and held that American workers were as class-conscious and militant as the Western Europeans. To them, class was more than a shared income-level or occupation; it was an awareness of shared interests that emerged out of a process of struggle. The urban working class drew on republican (i.e., locally based participation) artisan traditions to defend individual rights and assert independence, creating a distinct form of class consciousness. Workers expressed their common class interests in demonstrations, parades, strikes, or riots, but only rarely by voting.[51] Owner-capitalists also mobilized against workers, forming groups outside of electoral politics.[52]

The findings of the two schools are not contradictory. New labor researchers used in-depth case studies about specific local communities, instead of the statistical analysis of voting records across many locales. Grassroots workplace politics can operate differently from electoral politics. People were organized as workers at the factory and acted collectively to advance common demands, but they voted as ethnic groups at home. American political institutions, until the New Deal, reinforced the separation. "From the 1870s to the 1930s, class sentiments were widespread among American workers, but before the 1930s, the structure of political power in American society . . . made it harder to mobilize class sentiments in the political arena than the workplace" (Oestreicher 1988, 1269).

The structure of American political institutions made electoral mobilization along social class lines difficult. Workers organized in small factories, made specific demands, and engaged in collective activities that grew into larger movements. Occasionally they shared community-ethnic ties (e.g., the Irish worked in one factory and lived in one neighborhood) that were mobilized to support the class-based demands. Electoral mobilization by class failed because both parties were connected to the business community and were unresponsive to worker-initiated demands, especially after the municipal reform movement (see Chapter 4). Also, American's decentralized political institutions required workers to organize across large geographic units (e.g., an entire city, state, or region) and activate thousands of political helpers to gain electoral control or build a new party. In addition, many workers were recent immigrants who did not share a language or could not vote. In cities, machine politicians often satisfied immediate local demands, making a separate worker's party unnecessary. When workers elected a local politician, the power of the business community prevented proworker politicians from delivering on promises, leading to their defeat in the next election. Overt government repression also weakened attempts to form a strong worker's party.

Classic Era Studies   American voters realigned along class lines during the New Deal era and "in every American election since 1936 . . . the proportion voting Democratic increases sharply as one moves down the occupational or income ladder" (Lipset 1960, 303). During the 1950s and 1960s, nonclass factors (e.g., region, religion) moderated class voting as political parties sought voters beyond one class. In 1963, Robert Alford developed a measure of class voting.[53] **The Alford Index is a rough measure of class voting that puts all voters into two classes— blue-collar/manual and white-collar/non-manual—and all votes for two political parties—prolabor and probusiness—then calculates how much voters cast ballots for the party of their class.** Early studies found class voting and class differences on specific policy issues.[54]

Political sociologists also looked at the impact of a person moving up or down in the class hierarchy. They hypothesized that people moving up would become conservative as they conformed to their new, higher-class position, and people moving down would resent losing their social position and become radicalized. Yet few studies backed the hypothesis; instead, they found that class origin had less influence when an older person entered a new class and high inflow into a class made it politically heterogeneous. High rates of social mobility weaken class politics because when people often and easily move into or out of a class, they are less attached to a class. The results suggested that a mix of class origin, class destination, and situational conditions shape political behavior.[55]

Political sociologists also tested the status inconsistency thesis, or consistency across occupational prestige, income, education, and so forth. **The status inconsistency thesis states that status-consistent people experience less social stress, are politically moderate, and support the party of their class, but people with inconsistent statuses experience great stress, which encourages political extremism and support for parties of other social classes.** After a great amount of empirical research, the results were inconclusive, and political sociologists dropped the status inconsistency thesis.[56]

Most classic era political sociologists accepted a mass society view that said an industrial society fosters upward mobility and nonclass allegiances, but rapid social and technological change weakens community ties and fosters political alienation among the working class. In short, nonvoting by workers was an unfortunate but practical cost of social stability. By contrast, highly educated, informed, middle- and high-income people who embraced core cultural values upheld social stability. Many critics rejected the mass society view and its elitist implications. They saw it as justifying the political exclusion of the poor, working class, and lower-middle class.[57] To them, upper or upper-middle class, especially high-income white Protestants (i.e., WASPs) who are insulated from the rest of society and "have their own separate consciousness and understandings" (Hamilton 1972, 507) were a threat to democracy. These economically conservative people could turn antidemocratic to defend their privileges and social–economic power, while the working class supported democratic values and moderate economic policies.[58]

Contemporary Research   Political sociologists are divided over the role of social class in American politics. Some embrace the **declining significance hypothesis that says that class voting was a product of the Age of Industrial Capitalism and is irrelevant in a postindustrial society.**[59] While class voting grew with the New Deal, it has since declined with the rise of a postindustrial or information society. By the 1970s, class divisions weakened, and class is now a minor factor. Other political sociologists embrace the **trendless fluctuation hypothesis that says social class remains a continuing basis of major societal conflict.**[60] They say that the form and organization of classes have changed, but class remains society's most fundamental division. It quietly waits in the background for conditions to change. Once conditions change, people will quickly recognize class interests and mobilize as classes. Political institutions suppress and divert social tensions away from class divisions, so few people align as classes and class conflict remains at low levels. The evidence and arguments for the two hypotheses center on three issues: (1) different definitions of class and politics, (2) how they see nonvoting, (3) and the relevance of culture. Next we consider each.

Declining significance studies focus on elections and view society as having many overlapping classes arrayed along a continuum. *Class* is defined as a mixture of income level, occupational prestige, and other SES factors (e.g., race, education, income). Trendless fluctuation studies define social class as a few qualitative categories based on control over the means of production.[61] In this view, a tiny but powerful upper class of large investors, business owners, and top managers who receive profits, rent, and investments are at the peak. Ninety-five percent of the population works for businesses, nonprofit organizations, or government. They can be divided into four classes: (1) managers and supervisors who obey, work closely with, and assist the owners; (2) technical experts and celebrities who have privileges because of specialized education or skills; (3) ordinary workers employed in factories, stores, and offices or in transportation and construction; and (4) self-employed small business owners or farmers who only hire family members or a few helpers. Studies that use a gradational view find little evidence of class voting or class politics, but those using a categorical definition find it to be significant.[62] Trendless fluctuation studies see U.S. political parties as muting electoral class cleavages. Parties encourage nonclass divisions and shift class issues into nonelectoral forms, local issues (e.g., workplace safety, neighborhood environment), or cultural divisions (e.g., rights regarding race, sex, religion). Indeed, "one of the main hallmarks of the new politics of culture in contemporary America is the decreasing relevance of the electoral arena in the resolution of political conflicts."[63]

The two hypotheses also differ on the issue of nonvoting. According to the trendless fluctuation school, nonvoting is a political choice to reject both political parties. As Burnham (1984, 134) argued, "the 'real' class struggle, the point at which class polarization is most salient, is not found in the contests between Democrats and Republicans in the active electorate, but between the active electorate as a whole and the nonvoting half of the adult population . . . . " Studies that focus on voters alone find little evidence for class voting, but those that consider nonvoting by class find evidence of strong and persistent class voting.[64]

A third issue concerns nonclass-based, cultural divisions. Declining significance studies suggest that cultural divisions, such as race, gender, sexuality, lifestyle, or postmaterialist values, have displaced class as the major societal cleavage.[65] For example, political institutions intensify racial divisions and encourage people to see one another as members of different races, instead of members of opposing classes. Racial identity and consciousness push class aside. As Huckfeldt and Kohfeld (1989, 22–23) observed, "The politics of class has declined in American politics as the politics of race became ascendant. While partisan differences between whites and blacks have grown more extreme in the postwar period, partisan differences between the white working class and the white middle class have been nearly extinguished . . . higher levels of partisan differentiation by race generally produce lower levels of partisan differentiation by class among whites." Without racial harmony or class solidarity, racial divisions dominate politics and racial ideologies inhibit class-based politics. We examine racial divisions in politics below.

Social Class and Channels of Participation

Social class is associated with voting and political involvement beyond voting (e.g., making donations, working for a campaign), and political participation rises as people move up the class hierarchy. Rosenstone and Hansen (1993, 238) observed, "no matter what form citizen participation takes, the pattern of class inequality is unbroken. Inequalities are not dispersed, they are cumulative." Studies based on surveys or voting statistics include about 80–85 percent of the population but miss extremes of the class system. The poor (about 15 percent of the population) rarely vote and avoid surveys, while for the very rich (the top 1–2 percent), voting is less relevant than campaign donations, shaping the public agenda, lobbying government officials, or being candidates. Among voters, people with higher SES tend to be involved in other activities (e.g., campaign volunteers). A tiny percentage of individuals and most large companies regularly donate money. As one observer noted, "Money is not coming from ordinary Americans . . . American elections are paid for, overwhelmingly by economically interested industries and a small handful of individuals" (Wayne 1996).

Less than 10 percent of the population donates money in an election. The odds of making a donation and its size grow directly with a person's income. For example, under 6 percent of people donated money to a candidate in 2000. Donations varied by income—1.5 percent of people with family incomes under $25,000 donated to over 20 percent of people with incomes over $105,000.[66] Among the wealthiest families, about half donated money (see Table 5.4).[67]

Beyond elections, people exert political influence over elected officials, affect how the government operates and implements policy, and shape the thinking of other citizens. We next turn to the impact of class beyond voting.

TABLE 5.4	Campaign Donations by Family Income Level					
Family Income Level	**Percent Who Donated Money**	**(N)**	**Amount Donated Among Those Giving Money**			
			Under $100	**$100–$499**	**Over $500**	**N**
Under $10,000	0.7%	(149)	100%	0%	0%	(1)
$10,000–$19,999	3.5%	(200)	66.7%	33.3%	0%	(6)
$20,000–$29,999	6.0%	(199)	70%	20%	10%	(10)
$30,000–$39,999	5.6%	(198)	60%	30%	10%	(10)
$40,000–$59,999	7.0%	(257)	45.5%	45.5%	9.1%	(11)
$60,000–$75,000	7.5%	(107)	62.5%	37.5%	0%	(8)
Over $75,000	16.0%	(156)	25%	45.8%	29.2%	(24)
Total	6.5%	(1266)	48.6%	37.1%	14.3%	(70)

Source: Calculated from data in the 1996 General Social Survey (NORC).

PACs and Participation by the Upper Class   The American upper class is a collectivity with about 2 million people who are tied together by intermarriage, elite private schooling, similar residence, and shared leisure activities. Overlapping networks of family ties, business ownership, and participation on the boards of directors of banks and corporations foster class cohesion. If you only look at individuals, you may miss the social class acting as a unit. "By focusing on individuals, the class itself gets lost" (Zeitlin and Ratcliff 1988, 88). Upper class political participation includes individual actions (e.g., voting, donations), informal socializing (e.g., at private clubs, campaign dinners), serving in government office (e.g., most cabinet officials are upper class), and financing and leading key organizations (e.g., policy institutes, corporations, political action committees).[68] The upper class is a distinct social community that votes by using its wealth in addition to casting ballots. Its members hold top posts in corporations and control vast organizational resources. They employ public relations and mass media experts to advocate and widely disseminate their views.

According to the old wealth liberalism thesis, established wealthy of the upper class support politically liberal policies and candidates more than the "new rich." This is because people who inherit great wealth and have been part of the upper class for generations learn elite responsibility or feel guilt about their vast wealth holdings. With a secure social position and sheltered wealth, they do not demand public policies to give them an edge in the aggressive, competitive struggle to move up the class hierarchy. Burris (2000) examined the thesis and discovered that among the richest 400 Americans who donated over $100,000 to politicians, the old rich support conservatives more than the new rich do. He surmised that new rich were less conservative because many rose from small business ownership or grew up in middle class surroundings; they have economically diverse family, friends, and neighbors. By contrast, the old rich operate within narrow social networks and have little contact with the nonrich.

Channels of participation used by the upper class vary over time. Today, money is a primary means of participating in elections and determining policy. In U.S. elections, individual contributors provide about one-half of the money, Political Action Committees (PACs) provide a third, and the remainder comes from the candidates themselves.[69] The money goes for consultants, pollsters, voice coaches, make-up artists, speechwriters, promotional literature, broadcast advertising, an army of helpers, and travel expenses. The United States and many nations established rules to govern campaign spending (see World View 5.2), but in most cases, they ended the worst abuses while the money and influence only reappear later in new forms that get around the new laws or rules.

Candidates and parties in the United States spend large sums of money on elections. For example, they spent $570 million in the 1999–2000 election for the House of Representatives alone—about 1.3 million dollars per seat, and 26 percent over the 1997–1998 election. In the Senate, where one-third of the 100 seats are up every 2 years, spending is even greater—$435 million was spent or about $13 million per seat and a 51 percent increase over the 1997–1998 election.[70] Billionaire Michael Bloomberg won the 2001 New York City mayoral election by

WORLD VIEW 5.2   Globalization and Declining Voter Turnout

Alexandra Moss (2003) argued that globalization may be a cause of declining voter participation across Western Europe. More specifically, globalization may contribute to decreased levels of civic engagement (i.e., people becoming disconnected from society), and decreased civic engagement reduces voter turnout. Some feel that European attachments may be growing more toward their local communities or the European Union (EU) while their attachments to their specific nation-states may be weakening. Countering this idea are low voter turnout rates for EU elections. In contrast to national elections, EU turnout rates are very low at around 20–30 percent, while they remain well above the 50 percent level for national elections. Of course one factor that keeps European voting rates high is that many European nations have compulsory voting laws, automatic voter registration, and elections on holidays or weekends. Europeans tend to be proud of their high voter turnout rates. Yet it remains to be seen whether the forces of globalization that tend to emphasize individual consumption and use media or products with nonlocal origins will weaken social bonds and contribute to voter disinterest.

spending nearly $79 million of his personal wealth—about $93 for every vote he received. His losing opponent spent $16.5 million. Much of the money went for television advertisements; Bloomberg ran three times more advertisements than his opponent.[71]

Political Action Committees (PACs) are a legal way for large organizations and individuals to make campaign donations on which systematic records are kept. Before the 1970s, the Tillman Act (1907) and the Federal Corrupt Practices Act (1925) governed campaign donations and outlawed direct corporate contributions, but they were full of exceptions and loopholes. Election law changes in response to the Watergate scandal and other political corruption in the 1970s lead to the creation of PACs. "The 1972 reelection effort of President Richard Nixon included practices bordering on extortion, in which corporations and their executives were, in essence, 'shaken down,' for cash donations. Up to $30 million was legally and illegally contributed by the business sector . . ."(Sabato 1984, 5). The Policy Planning Network, specifically the Committee for Economic Development, comprised of top corporate executives, initiated new campaign finance laws.[72] Besides quieting public outcry and blocking demands for very strict limits, the new laws clarified the legal environment and institutionalized "business involvement in campaign finance" by tightening campaign finance disclosure and producing systematic public records.[73] Under the new rules, corporations could not directly give money to candidates but had to form a corporate PAC and register it with the Federal Election Commission. Company funds can operate the PAC (e.g., pay for staff, office space, phone, supplies), and the PAC can solicit donations from management employees and stockholders. A corporate PAC could contribute up to $5,000 per candidate to an unlimited number of candidates.[74]

Once PACs were formed, executives pressured their employees to donate to PACs, and the fines for violating the rules were small. Larger firms, ones that face government regulation, and firms in less competitive industries, are most

"I may be awhile. I'm soliciting funds for my
reëlection campaign."

likely to form PACs.[75] Labor unions and independent membership organizations (e.g., National Rifle Association, Sierra Club), ideological groups, and business trade associations (e.g., realtors, trucking companies) have PACs. The number of PACs grew until the mid-1980s then leveled off. About 8 percent of the PACs were formed by labor unions, 44 percent by corporations, and the remainder by independent organizations. About 44 percent of PACs are inactive, and 60 percent of major corporations have a PAC.[76] Between 1972 and 2000, PAC contributions for Congressional elections grew from $8.5 to $245.5 million.

Leading trade PACs include the American Medical Association, National Rifle Association, and National Association of Home Builders. The banking, insurance, pharmaceutical, and automobile dealer industries are influential.[77] PACs also assist politicians with public relations. For example, in 1995 public relations consultants advised Republicans who wanted to cut Medicare spending but who feared a political backlash by the elderly to tell the public they sought to "preserve, protect and improve" Medicare.[78]

Compared to voting, we know far less about the political behavior of big business.[79] Studies on PACs reject the pluralist model that businesses operate in politics independently without coordination.[80] Clawson and Neustadt (1989) tested elite, statist, and power-structure models by examining PAC donations to U.S. Congressional candidates. According to the elite model, individual companies pursue their direct, short-term interests, and donations follow business divisions (e.g., size, region, industry, domestic versus multinational). The statist model holds that politically active firms are ones with specific links to government (e.g., defense industry, regulated industry, or government supplier). The power-structure model holds that there is an inner circle of the upper class that develops a classwide perspective and exerts united political influence through corporations.[81] The authors found support for both the power structure and the statist models. Other studies reinforce this picture. A study of taxes paid by large corporations supported the power structure model.[82] A study found that firms with criminal records and that were defense contractors were more politically active than others.[83] Research on specific policy areas (e.g., health care) or international trade found that firms coordinate their political activity.[84] PAC activities are supplemented by lobbying, and most corporations with PACs also have a lobbying office in Washington.[85] Qualitative studies bolster the statistical studies to show that PACs act in a coordinated manner; and corporations resolve their interfirm disputes informally before entering the political arena.[86] "Corporations favored one candidate over another by at least a 2 to 1 margin in 93 percent of all races" (Su, Neustadt and Clawson 1995:23). For example, leaders of a business PACs held monthly meetings, and the chief executive officer of a major corporation (PepsiCo), who also headed the leading big business organization (Business Roundtable), urged corporations to support identified "probusiness" candidates.[87] It appears, there is a "remarkable unity among corporate committees" (Eismeier and Pollock 1988, 34). Corporations coordinate and target their donations to support specific probusiness candidates.[88] Corporate agreement may not be class coordination but donations suggest that the inner circle capitalists are more politically conservative than networked corporate PACs.[89]

The research into PAC donations cannot show whether the upper class shapes election outcomes or controls policy, but they indicate coordinated classwide action and targeted PAC donations.[90] For example, in the 10 closest races for the House of Representatives in 1996, the winning candidate outspent the loser by $371,000, and "Campaign donations from corporations or their officers were crucial . . . ."[91] PACs also buy influence to shape the public agenda and gain access to politicians after elections. For example, the 75 large corporations and individuals, who each gave $250,000 donations in 1996, were known as "season ticket holders." One top executive whose corporation gave $500,000 to the Republican Party said, "There is no question—if you give a lot of money, you will get a lot of access . . . . All you have to do is send a check" (Van Natta and Fritsch 1997). Senate leader Trent Lott defended unlimited soft money donations from big corporations, calling them the "the American Way" (Seelye 1997). Senator Lott played a major role in killing a campaign finance reform law, then presided over a fundraising dinner at which executives and lobbyists paid $100,000 a plate to meet with him.[92]

While regulated PAC donations have grown rapidly, the quantities of unregulated soft money donations exploded. In the 2000 election they were twice as large as 4 years earlier.[93] **Soft money is campaign donations outside the limits and regulations of the Federal Election Campaign Act, since it is not officially for a specific candidate but promotes ideological or business interests**. For example, in the year when Congress debated tobacco legislation, four of the eight largest soft money donors were tobacco companies.[94] Often interest groups outside an election district make very large donations. This suggests a nationwide plan to purchase political influence. For example, of $200,000 one candidate raised, only $1,000 came from inside his district.[95] According to the Federal Election Commission in the 2000 Presidential election,[96] "The largest percentage increases for both parties continue

**"Some of it is soft and some of it is hard, but
the main thing is that all of it is money."**

to be in nonfederal, or 'soft money' . . . . Republicans raised $244.4 million, an increase of 73% over the same period in 1995–1996, the last presidential cycle, while Democrats raised $243 million, a 99% increase . . . . [Soft money is] 35% of Republican Party financial activity . . . and 47% of Democratic Party fundraising."

PAC contributions are associated with voting by members of Congress, but making a precise connection is difficult to document because members cast votes on many issues, PACs focus more on shaping the details within laws, and the two parties may agree on issues.[97] It is clear that, "one constant indicated by all research approaches is that the rewards of political action are enormous, especially for those businesses which are the most active" (Boies 1989, 831). Many PACs seek narrow benefits for one company or industry. Ninety percent of corporate PAC officials report they won a tax loophole for their firm and note that votes in Congress are less important than making minor changes in the language of a law to create hidden benefits.[98] For example Federal Express spent 1.2 million dollars in lobbying, made four corporate jets available to Congressmen for flights, and donated $600,000 to campaigns so they could change legislation to exempt their firm from labor relations and noise control laws.[99] In addition to PAC money, members of Congress can accept unlimited donations without reporting the donors for tax-exempt research and education organizations. About one-half of the members of Congress have such organizations (see Case in Point 5.3). Influence from donations, and even outright vote buying, also occurs in local or state government.[100]

Beyond making donations and lobbying, resource-rich organizations engage in **astroturf lobbying which occurs when political advocates try to look**

| CASE IN POINT 5.3 | An Alternative Way to Donate to Politicians |

The tax-exempt organization of Senator Jesse Helms, the Helms Center, is based at Wingate College, a small private college in North Carolina. In 1996, the Center had assets of $6.2 million and took in $1.3 million in donations, but it does not release the names of donors. Nonetheless, some donors are known, and well-known PAC contributors can get around the $5,000 limit on legal donations by contributing to the Center. Philip Morris, Inc. gave $200,000 in one year, and the Center received $750,000 from R.J. Reynolds. Since Mr. Helms became the head of the Senate Foreign Relations committee, donations to the center from foreign governments rose, such as $100,000 from the Kuwait government. Despite all donations, the Center only spent $350,000 in 1996. Its major activities are to sponsor a free enterprise conference for high school youth, to bring two political speakers to Wingate College each year, and to provide jobs for Mr. Helm's friends and associates. Most importantly, the Center gives donors a way to show their appreciation for the Senator's work and to ensure access to his busy schedule (see Baker 1998).

like a grass roots organization of ordinary, concerned citizens, but in reality, they are a front for an industry group or private firm that pays for the organization.[101] A group can stimulate grassroots activity or create a nonprofit front organization without revealing its financial sources. The practice began in the 1980s, and now some public relations firms specialize in such grassroots lobbying. Creating the ". . . semblance of citizen's movements, on demand, has also become a big business" and was an $800 million industry by the mid-1990s (Mitchell 1998, A14). The goal of astroturf lobbying is to convince the public and politicians that broad support exists, because they are often suspicious of explicit appeals by wealthy, self-interested industry groups. For example, the tobacco industry organized prosmoking groups, while the railroad and trucking industries have astroturf groups to limit safety regulations. In addition to astroturf lobbying, large firms can politically mobilize people in other ways. For example, Senator Robert Dole proposed a law that required banks to withhold federal taxes on interest earnings, as occurs with payroll earnings, to reduce tax underreporting and improve government efficiency. The banking industry organized an opposition campaign in newspaper advertisements and placed inserts in 80 million customers' monthly account statements. The political action of the banking industry worked—22 million people contacted their Congressional representatives, and the proposed law was withdrawn.[102]

Beyond defending or advocating their own positions, wealthy people and resource-rich organizations can go on the offensive to attack opponents by sponsoring news reports, journalistic investigations, or buying negative advertising. For example, one multimillionaire gave $1.8 million to a conservative magazine specifically "to obtain information about the activities of Mr. Clinton and his wife Hilary, during their years in Arkansas."[103] Another gave $100,000 to a private consulting firm that specializes in last minute negative advertising in political campaigns. Consulting firms can avoid donation limits and not reveal the

CLOSER LOOK 5.2   **Legal Actions Designed to Dampen Citizen Participation**

A tiny percentage of the public is politically involved beyond elections (e.g., voting, campaigning, donations). Sometimes called "gladiatorial" participants, a few highly motivated people assert their views in conventional politics by writing letters to officials, testifying at public hearings, circulating petitions, and the like. They may complain about a failure to enforce laws and regulations, criticize excessive costs or unusual expenses, or highlight irregular and biased procedures.

Strategic Lawsuits Against Public Participation (SLAPP) occur "when aggrieved citizens speak out to any branch of government or the electorate, behavior protected by the U.S. Constitution, publicly asserting that some condition is offensive" (Canan et al. 1993, 350). The response is a civil lawsuit against the nongovernmental person or organization for publicly complaining or contacting a government agency. The purpose of the lawsuit is to shift the complaint out of the public political arena and into a court setting where legal procedures and court/attorneys fees are involved. This derails the dispute and switches combat from political to judicial rules,

favoring organizations or individuals with greater resources.

Most SLAPP targets are public interest groups, civic organizations, or individual citizens while most SLAPP filers are business owners or industry groups. A filer cannot take someone to court for public speech, so suits redefine the offense claiming a defense of economic or occupational interest. For example, a citizen opposes rezoning rural land for a shopping center and begins a petition drive. The shopping center developer may file a lawsuit against the citizen claiming defamation and loss of business asking for $100,000 in damages. Although most (about 70 percent) SLAPPS are lost, they have a chilling effect on citizens who consider complaining, and they create fear and anxiety about public participation. Three principles are illustrated by SLAPPS: (1) the venue of a battle over political interests shifts between public and legal arenas, (2) different organizations have or can use various resources (e.g., publicity, legal costs) in different venues, and (3) political actors who have more resources may threaten legal action or use intimidation as a strategy in political disputes.

Sources: Canan et al. 1993, Cobb and Ross 1997b, Pring and Canan 1996, and Zipper 1999.

names of donors.[104] Another offensive technique is SLAPP, Strategic Lawsuits Against Public Participation (see Closer look 5.2).

If wealthy people and large corporations have great political influence, why do they complain loudly about interference by big government?[105] In part, this is a legacy of American industrial development. In other nations, class-consciousness capitalists battled feudal aristocrats for control of the state then built a strong state to defend and assist them. Without an entrenched aristocracy to overthrow and in a large country with an open frontier, American capitalists have preferred a weak distributive state. Also, capitalists fear state authority as an alternative to market-based, private authority. As citizens won a voice in government, state authority over business grew in response to citizen demands for consumer product safety, workplace protections, or corporate accountability. Capitalists resisted such popular democratic demands as limits on their autonomy. Lastly, America's business community is politically divided over the distribution of state favors. Each business leader loudly opposes state actions that favor his/her competitors but at the same time quietly seeks favorable government treatment for her/his own business interests. Nonetheless, powerful industries often get what they want (Case in Point 5.4).

Racial Politics and Participation

The United States is a multiracial/ethnic society in which race is a pivotal cleavage, but until the 1960s, racial minorities were largely excluded from national electoral politics. Researchers have just started to look beyond the white-black division to examine Latino, Asian, and other racial minorities and interminority relations.[106] Racial-ethnic categories are the outcomes of social–political processes, including state actions. Race-ethnic group categories and boundaries are created or reinforced through voting rules, immigration policies, judicial rulings, social programs, and census classifications. Such actions classify and treat peoples of diverse backgrounds, self-identities, or experiences as if they were essential, homogenous categories.[107] Yet, the racial-ethnic categories are fluid and arbitrary. People come to highlight certain physical or social features by using racial-ethnic categories, but the specific array of categories they use and how the categories get assigned varies widely by historical period and country. Once the state adopts a set of racial categories, they are solidified. For example, the United States treated people of African ancestry as three-fifths of a person for

---

CASE IN POINT 5.4   **Some Channels of Political Participation Yield Big Results**

In 1997, in what was one of the biggest corporate welfare giveaways that went little noticed by the American public, the federal government gave the broadcast industry free use of public airwaves worth an estimated $7 to $15 billion. "Broadcast television is the lone industry, FCC officials say, that Congress has said does not have to pay for the use of previously used space on the nation's airways, which are public property" (Wayne 1997a). The Congressional action is explained by several factors. First, the broadcast industry has powerful lobbies that spent over $4 million lobbying in the first 6 months of 1996 alone. The lobbying can get personal. The head of the industry's main trade association, the National Association of Broadcasters, with a $35 million budget, was the college roommate of Senate Majority Leader Trent Lott. Senator Lott took a lead role in pushing the giveaway. Second,

television broadcasters can influence how voters see their elected officials, so politicians are wary to cross the media interests. In addition, during the past decade, television interests and the corporations that own them gave $9 million in campaign contributions, $6 million in PAC money, and $3 million in soft money. In 1995–1996 alone, the industry gave $3.5 million to both political parties. Perhaps you have heard of some names in the broadcast industry: Walt Disney, owner of Capital Cities/ABC; General Electric, owner of NBC; News Corporation, owner of FOX; and Westinghouse, owner of CBS. The broadcast industry has come out strongly against giving candidates for public office free advertising time. The free time is a campaign reform proposal to increase electoral competition and reduce candidate dependence on privately donated money (see Wayne 1997a).

Source: Wayne, Leslie (1997a), "Broadcast Lobby's Formula: Airtime + Money = Influence." *New York Times*, May 5, 1997.

representation in Congress, said American Indians could not be taxed, and said people who migrated from certain Asian nations could not become citizens or own land. Racial categories can be a source of pride, self-identity, and solidarity for collective political action, or they can be used by outsiders to divide, exploit, or condemn people. State actions reify the categories (i.e., treat them as real and fixed), whether or not they correspond to an individual's self-identity or personal experience. Once created, the categories can reinforce group boundaries, alter a person's self-definition, and influence the conflicts and alliances that develop among groups.[108]

Blacks

Despite gaining new legal rights in the 1960s, turnout rates for blacks are lower than for whites. Race is not the cause, "the evidence seems clear that it is not being black per se but the socioeconomic conditions that usually accompany being black that lead to lower participation" (Verba and Nie 1972, 157). There are two types of political alienation: trust in government and efficacy. *Efficacy* refers to "people's perception of their ability to influence government" (Gamson 1968, 42); a person with high efficacy feels empowered to influence government. *Trust* is whether a person believes that government operates for his/her benefit (versus ignoring or working against him/her). Trust and efficacy can be cross-classified to create a four-fold typology of types.[109] In the 1960s, few blacks trusted a white-run government that had denied them rights for decades, and distrustful blacks who lacked efficacy rarely participated. Yet many highly distrustful blacks felt efficacy because of group solidarity as members of a self-conscious, active racial community, and they actively participated in politics[110] (see Chart 5.4).

Black political participation is higher than expected based on levels of education and income because of two factors: membership in a black church or having a high racial group consciousness. The black church has been a major source of political organization and collective action; religiously involved African Americans tend to feel closer to other blacks and express a need to work together.[111] Likewise,

---

c h a r t   5 . 4

TYPOLOGY OF BLACK POLITICAL PARTICIPATION

Level of Trust	Level of Efficacy	
	Low	**High**
High	Powerless	Full integration
Low	Full alienation	Distrustful

Sources: Adapted from Shingles (1981) and Miller et al. (1981).

blacks who feel greater racial solidarity, live in racially homogenous areas, and have strong racial pride, have high political participation rates.[112] The election of black politicians also increases black political participation, but many whites resist supporting black candidates.[113] The election of a black mayor raises trust in government, political information, and efficacy among African Americans—it reduces alienation and increases engagement in politics.[114]

Black and white political alienation may differ, but a new political administration or policies affect alienation for both races.[115] Political activism or alienation can be a self-reinforcing cycle, increasing or depressing participation. For example, blacks elect black officeholders, policy is changed, and black feelings of efficacy and empowerment rise.[116] Alternatively, alienation contributes to an inability to elect black officials, which intensifies preexisting feelings of alienation and fuels a further withdrawal from politics. It also appears that segregation in urban areas depresses political and civic participation, while racial heterogeneity has the opposite effect.[117]

Latinos

The U.S. Latino population is growing rapidly and will soon exceed the size of the black population. The Latino population is very diverse; it varies by heritage or origin (e.g., Mexican, Puerto Rican, Cuban) and length of residence. This diversity weakens group identity and political collective action. Latinos are also divided by language and citizenship; about 60 percent of Latinos are citizens; thus, nearly 40 percent are formally excluded from the polity.[118] Their Spanish language and length of U.S. residency creates political divisions among Latinos.[119] Their religious beliefs also affect Latino politics. Most African Americans belong to Protestant dominations that support political involvement. Most Latinos are Roman Catholics, and only a few Catholic groups actively work to organize Latinos. Although religious communities can promote solidarity, racial-ethnic factors overlap with religious traditions to affect political activism.[120]

Latinos embrace American cultural ideals, yet "Latinos, regardless of national origin, have more non-voters as a share of the adult population than does any other major racial or ethnic group . . . " (DeSipio 1996, 30).[121] Low education levels, a lack of citizenship, uncertain language facility, and frequent residence changes all contribute to low voter turnout. Participation rates vary among Latino groups, and the local social context affects participation.[122] For example, Chicago's Latinos have low internal political efficacy (personal power, competence) and high external efficacy (the government is responsive), but low voting rates. The overwhelming power of one political party and a strong political machine in the city may explain the situation.[123] Cuban Americans in South Florida vote at higher rates than blacks and non-Latino whites. High Cuban American incomes combine with strong ethnic-ideological solidarity to facilitate high turnout.[124] Latinos are highly interested in local issues, tend to respond if activated by Latino groups, and shift their party support.[125] Specific features (e.g., citizenship, education, language) that explain low Latino participation are likely to weaken with time and assimilation.

Asians

Little research has been conducted on the rapidly growing Asian-American population. The Asian-American population has many languages and cultures which weakens its capacity to act politically in a unified, collective way. Like Latinos, many Asians are recent immigrants, and about 57 percent are not citizens.[126] Asian Americans are the most socially and economically diverse minority group. Large numbers have low education and income, but many others have high levels of education and income. Income and education have a weaker impact in increasing voting among Asian Americans. Asian groups vary in citizenship and voting—Filipinos have the highest citizenship rate and Asian Indians the lowest; Japanese regularly vote, while persons of Chinese, Vietnamese and Korean ancestry rarely vote.[127]

High rates of assimilation and intermarriage with the white-Anglo population weakens a distinct Asian identity or collective presence. Some Asian Americans have created ethnic organizations, but most serve a single Asian group (e.g., Chinese, Korean, or Japanese), and pan-Asian solidarity is weak.[128] Asians donate to political campaigns at lower rates than white-Anglos or blacks and tend to support candidates of the same ancestry. In many ways, Asian patterns parallel those for Latinos in that English-language skills, citizenship status, immigration generation, and length of residence affect Asian political participation.[129]

Patterns by Group

Political participation and partisanship vary by racial-ethnic group (see Table 5.5). White-Anglos tend to donate money, vote, and support the Republican Party. African Americans support the Democratic Party and are highly interested in politics, but few donate money or volunteer, and many feel alienated. Asians are least likely to follow politics, vote, or support a political party, but they have low alienation and show high confidence in the government. Despite low turnout and limited interest, Latinos volunteer and support the Democratic Party. American Indians are most alienated group with little trust in government or party attachment.

The Gender Gap

A gap implies that something is missing. The gender gaps in income, schooling, or job promotions imply that women are behind or unequal to men. **The gender gap in electoral politics and policy preferences refers to women voting and holding policy positions that differ from men in a way that favors a distinct "women's position."** First noticed in 1980, women's organizations highlighted the gap to get political parties to be responsive to women's concerns.[130] It appeared for four reasons: (1) political pollsters first began to separate survey poll results by gender, (2) debate over the Equal Rights Amendment (a constitutional amendment to insure gender equality), (3) abortion rights became a hot political issue, and (4) conservative politicians advocated traditional family values to reassert traditional gender roles.

TABLE 5.5	Percentages of Political Participation, Efficacy, and Partisanship by Ethnic Group (1990s)								
Ethnic Heritage	Interested in Politics	Gives Money	Volunteered	Voted	Feels Alienated	Lacks Trust	Partisanship		
							Democrat	Moderate	Republican
European	42%	9%	6%	74%	71%	21%	30%	35%	35%
African	46	2	2	65	79	20	67	27	6
Asian	26	4	4	38	68	10	26	54	20
Latino	36	4	7	45	72	21	46	37	17
American Indian	8	4	4	60	83	26	34	43	23
Total	42	8	6	69	73	21	35	35	30

Source: Calculated from General Social Survey, 1990–1998. Main or first ethnicity was coded into five categories (rounded to whole percentages).
Interested in Politics = Very or fairly interested in political events.
Volunteer = Volunteered or participated in an electoral campaign (e.g., rally, button).
Alienated = Agrees that elected officials don't care about the average person.
No trust = Has hardly any confidence in Congress.
Partisanship = Democrat/Republican Strongly favors or identifies with the Democratic/Republican Party;
Moderate/Independent or only leans towards a party. Other and no opinion omitted.

Publicity over the gender gap raised sensitivity to women's concerns in close elections and encouraged symbolic appointments of women to visible public posts. As Kenski (1988, 57) noted, "the gender gap does exist and appears in voter turnout, party identification, presidential evaluation, presidential elections, and congressional elections."

Voting Differences

After women won the right to vote in 1920, male politicians were apprehensive that women and men would vote differently. Until the 1960s, they often voted the same. Women were less interested in politics and voted less than men, and married women usually followed their husband's voting behavior. This was true in many countries. "In all societies for which we have data, sex is related to political activity, men are more active than women" (Verba, Nie, and Kim 1978, 234). Yet lower education levels and detachment from the paid labor force may explain women's low participation rates.[131] Women's voting rates grew in the 1960s. By 1980, it exceeded that of men.[132] In addition, politicians and others noticed the dissimilarity in how men and women voted. Women, who had leaned toward the Republican Party, shifted to the Democratic Party. There are four explanations for the gender gap.

Socialized to Nurture Girls are socialized to value nurturing, cooperation, and traditional moral behavior more than boys. The greater value women place on caring for other people and on the needs of children and the elderly leads them to support politicians who favor expanded social programs and "nurturing" public policies.[133]

Men Became Republicans   Women changed little, but many men moved to the Republican Party.[134] "Women in virtually every segment of the white electorate . . . are more Democratic because men of almost every type moved to the GOP" (Kaufmann and Petrocik 1999, 870). In the 1960s and early 1970s, a majority of men and women identified with the Democratic Party and supported social programs for the poor, disabled, elderly, and children. During the 1980s, men became more individualistic and attracted to a Republican Party message of toughness, traditional patriarchal families, military preparedness, tax cuts, and conservative social values. Single mothers and women who worked full time outside the home felt left out, and they retained a Democratic Party affiliation, changing less than men.[135] Democratic leaders sought electoral support from working women by promoting women's issues (e.g., improved child care, improved health care, gun control, safe schools), programs to care for the less fortunate, and clean environment regulations.

Workforce Participation and Independence   With high divorce rates and a later age of marriage, women increasingly live independently of men. As their schooling and paid work increased, women gained the experience, self-confidence, and financial freedom to think independently about political issues and develop their own ideas about voting. Also, divorced or single mothers often have low incomes and may depend on social services, so their interests are to preserve a welfare state.[136]

Feminist Ideals   Many younger and college-educated women embraced the political ideals and goals of the women's movement. In elections, they support candidates and parties that reflect feminist messages and back public policies that advance feminist-oriented ideals.[137]

While each explanation is part of the picture, Manza and Brooks (1998, 1261) argued that "rising labor force participation among women provides the best way of understanding the gender gap to date" (see Figure 5.1). Support for this idea is found in the fact that working women were more likely to vote for Bill Clinton, the opposite of men (see Table 5.6). Despite stereotypes, women are not affected by emotional appeals or images any more than men are. Women tend to favor female candidates, especially ones who are identified as feminist, an effect strongest in nonpartisan races. Thus, gender and partisan identity compete to influence voting.[138]

Policy Issue Differences

Voting differences are "a function of distinctive male versus female issue preferences" (Chaney et al. 1998, 333). Men and women differ on many policy issues, such as economic development, foreign policy, environment, social programs, and criminal justice, and this creates a voting gap.[139] They differ significantly on

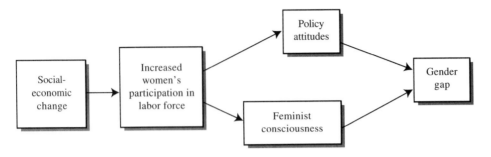

Figure 5.1
A model of the gender gap in U.S. voting.
Source: Manza and Brooks (1999, 153)

TABLE 5.6	Percentage of Voters Who Voted for Bill Clinton in 1992		
	Men	**Women**	**Gender Gap**
Working Full or Part-time?			
Yes	38	52	+14
No	52	50	−2
Among Those Who Worked: Hours Worked Per Week			
40 or more	36	53	+17
21–39 hours	41	52	+11
Under 20 hours	52	46	−6
Education Level			
Graduate degree	44	64	+20
College degree	35	50	+15
High school diploma	36	49	+13
Does Respondent Call Self A Feminist?			
Yes	64	72	+8
No	38	48	+10
Does Respondent Follow News on Women's Concerns?			
Follow	46	62	+16
Does not follow	38	38	0
How Important Are Women's Issues?			
Important	50	51	+1
Not important	31	44	+13

Source: Calculated from General Social Survey, 1993–1996.

TABLE 5.7	Women's Support of Policy Issues (1972–2002)		

Among those with an opinion, the percentage of women over men.

Year	Favor Gun Control Law	Oppose Death Penalty	Say Too Little Spent for Health Care
1972	+19.8	+13.8	na
1973	+12.7	+13.1	−1.9
1974	+18.1	+7.5	−3.2
1975	+15.1	+12.8	−0.6
1976	+15.0	+11.6	−1.6
1977	+15.6	+10.7	+3.6
1978	na	+9.3	+1.4
1980	+12.8	+12.5	+7.1
1982	+9.0	+7.7	+0.8
1983	na	+12.1	+0.8
1984	+15.8	+9.4	+6.3
1985	+13.3	+5.7	+6.6
1986	na	+12.6	+9.5
1987	+14.6	+5.5	+6.3
1988	+15.2	+8.9	+4.0
1989	+16.7	+9.5	+5.1
1990	+12.5	+4.4	+6.0
1991	+13.1	+7.2	+10.0
1993	+15.1	+9.3	+10.3
1994	+14.8	+6.0	+7.4
1996	+13.9	+10.4	+10.3
1998	+10.8	+9.6	+11.8
2000	+16.6	+11.8	+6.5
2002	+9.0	+12.7	+13.2

na = Not asked.

Source: Calculated from General Social Survey, 1972–2002.

social welfare and environmental issues, and women show greater concern about health risks[140] (see Table 5.7).

The political difference by gender has been summarized as "economic man – social woman."[141] Male socialization emphasizes rugged individualism; short-term rational calculations; and competitive, market-based solutions; while women focus on the community; long-term consequences; and compassionate, coopera-tive, and egalitarian solutions. The gendered value orientations affect choices about issues or candidates.

In the United States, the gender gap shows women favoring and voting in a left-liberal direction, while in Western Europe, women are more right-conservative.[142] In Australia, Britain, and the United States, education, marital status, and labor force participation produce a gender gap, but ideology is critical in the United States. "As a group, women are significantly more likely to be on the left in their views on political issues; this is the major favor explaining their different electoral choices" (Studlar et al. 1998, 795). The American gender gap is strongest among white-Anglo women and is less pronounced among racial-ethnic minorities.[143]

Activist Differences

Politically active women sharpened the 'gender gap.' Women activists and campaign contributors in both political parties tend to be more liberal than their male counterparts, especially on foreign policy and women's issues.[144] "Much of the exaggeration of gender differences, we believe, is caused by the fact that our evidence is derived from political and cultural elites . . . " (Shapiro and Conover 1997, 522). Indeed, women who feel closest to feminism (about 20 percent of adult American women) account for much of the gender gap on policy issues.[145] These women have been resocialized to a coherent set of values and mobilized through consciousness-raising by the women's movement. Although "feminist issues were only weakly related to the vote among both men and women," the women's movement altered the issue agenda (Miller 1988, 268).

Gender is not only about women, and how women differ politically. Over time, political tension over gender has grown, especially among people under age 30. For example, Carolyn Lewis (1999) divided women into three groups based on their answers to attitude questions: traditional, moderate, and feminist. She found that traditional women had less education and were older. Feminists were younger and most educated, and moderates were in between. Traditional women wanted to limit abortion and felt that a belief in God was essential, but all the women valued prayer, felt pride in women's accomplishments, and were angry about the mistreatment of women. Moderate and feminist women both voted for female candidates who were vocal on feminist issues, such as sexual harassment and child care.

In sum, a gender gap appeared in the 1980s and "the 1990s might be characterized as an era of gender wars rather than the gender gap" (Andersen 1997, 32). Gender politics is more than voting, it includes a range of social, political, and economic relations.[146] International comparisons show that women's political participation is highest where women have greater socioeconomic equality and have had the right to vote for longer, where left-liberal political parties hold power and cultural-religious attitudes accept gender equality, and where the political system has strong parties with multimember electoral districts. Despite intense political debate over gender, Americans have been slow to implement gender equality in government. The United States has one of the lowest rates of women holding major positions in national and state legislatures (e.g., the U.S. Congress) among advanced nations.[147]

A REALIGNMENT IN THE 1970S–1980S

You learned about critical elections and electoral realignments earlier. Many political sociologists believe there was a political realignment in the 1970s–1980s without a clearcut "critical election." The social base of support for political parties shifted, ideological polarization grew, and third-party movements appeared. Some believe 1964 marked the realignment, and that it was based on a racial division, but others see it occurring in the 1980s based on an ideological division.[148]

A Race-based Realignment?

After the 1960s, large numbers of new African American voters joined the polity and backed the Democratic Party. Some ask whether this contributed to weakened white support for the Democratic Party. Blacks occupy an economic role similar to working-class whites, but these whites are sensitive to the racial competition and are less willing to cooperate with blacks in the same political coalition.[149] As blacks aligned with the Democrats, the Republican Party shifted its policy positions to encourage white Southerners to defect from the Democratic Party.[150] Thus, partisan competition grew from racial division.

Edsall and Edsall (1991) hold that a realignment based on race and taxes ended the New Deal regime. Republican partisan rhetoric connected race and taxes to two other controversial issues, a "rights revolution" and guaranteed group-based representation. In the 1960s, social programs for low-income people and racial minorities grew under the War on Poverty and civil rights legislation. An unanticipated outcome was deeper racial divisions. Whites who had been sympathetic to civil rights ideals withdrew support as they experienced economic distress in the 1970s. Conservative rhetoric blamed poor blacks for their poverty and told whites that their high taxes went to undeserving blacks who were lazy, promiscuous, used illegal drugs, and so forth. Social conservatives opposed groups mobilized after the civil rights movement who sought equal treatment in the "rights revolution." Non-black racial minorities, gays, women, and the disabled now sought new rights.

Leaders in the Democratic Party had shifted from economic liberalism (i.e., workplace protection and programs for the working class and poor), to social liberalism and legal protections for racial minorities and many disadvantaged groups. Traditional Democratic supporters among unionized second- or third-generation, European-heritage, working class Northerners and lower- to middle-income Southern white Protestants, grew wary. They had backed the Democratic Party since the mid-1930s, because it advanced policies to help the working class and poor. In the 1940s and early 1950s, when 40 percent of the U.S. labor force was unionized, union members were central in the New Deal coalition. Most were politically active and most voted Democratic. By the 1990s, union membership declined to about 10 percent of the labor force. As racial issues grew divisive, traditional support weakened. Southern whites turned from the Democratic Party as black political power grew.[151] By the 1980s, even white liberals began to waver in their support for affirmative action.[152]

In the New Deal regime, the core partisan division was economic. Democrats favored an activist government that offered social welfare programs, business regulation, and income equalization. Republicans opposed programs for the poor and taxes on the rich and favored free market business autonomy. By the late 1960s, public issues had become "race coded." Nonreligious, upper-middle income white professionals increasingly backed the Democratic Party, while self-employed people became more solidly Republican.[153] This created a cultural gap, and traditional Democrats—white, less educated, socially traditional, strongly Christian, and populist—felt disaffected.

Taxes imply redistribution. The government takes money from high income people to use it for programs for the public good and public spending for all people. Republicans had always opposed taxes on supporters (e.g., upper-income people, small and large business owners, landlords). They now added a racially coded message: hard-working, middle-income [white] people paid high taxes that went to lazy, drug-taking, promiscuous, immoral [black] people. The race-coded message said that whites worked and paid taxes while blacks lived off of government programs, and it shaped how whites interpreted events. Ideological messages do not have to fit all the facts to change thinking, especially among people already upset and confused. In the 1970s, lower- and middle-income whites felt economic distress but did not know why.

During the 1970s, the United States experienced a severe recession. After steady annual growth in real personal income from 1950 to 1970, the incomes of most working- and middle-class people stagnated until the mid-1990s. The inflation-adjusted incomes of most Americans did not change between 1972 and 1992, and blue-collar factory workers experienced high unemployment and declining wages. Family incomes only kept up because people worked more hours or sent more family members into the paid labor force. However, upper-income people (the top 10–20 percent) saw their incomes grow from the 1970s to 1990s. The income stagnation and growing inequality from the 1970s to 1990s had several causes, but many people experienced it as rising uncertainty and a squeeze in living standards. Simultaneously, taxes rose to pay for the Vietnam War, the massive savings and loan bailout, Social Security and Medicare benefit increases, and social programs (e.g., education, student loans, urban renewal, welfare), and to replace corporate income taxes that had been reduced, shifting the tax burden to individuals.

The Republican Party blended economic conservatism with right-wing populism (i.e., big government is bad and local "little" people need more power) and social conservatism (i.e., defend traditional cultural–religious values). The message was that pro-big government, liberal Democrats caused social problems (e.g., drug use, unwed mothers, crime). As Clement and Myles (1994, 100) astutely observed, "the repertoire of protest and resistance in North American political culture continues to bear the imprint of this populist past."

The Republican Party messages connected visible social problems to the Democrats and offered a simple explanation for complex and difficult-to-see social and economic forces (e.g., urban decay, technological change, structural employment shifts, globalization). Many anxious voters accepted the mix of racial stereotypes, populist resentment, and religious morality. As Rae (1992, 641) observed, "By skillful exploitation of the deep cultural cleavages within modern American society the Republicans thus built a durable presidential coalition composed of their traditional, white Protestant, upper-middle-class business base; middle and working class (formerly Democratic) Catholic voters; white southerners; and fundamentalist and evangelical Protestants."

The Democratic Party was ill prepared. In the 1960s, it was associated with inflation, social unrest, and an unpopular war. The party lost in 1968 and by a greater margin in 1972. The 1974 Watergate scandal and resignation of Richard Nixon hurt the Republican Party. Although Democrats benefited from Republican misfortune, their New Deal coalition was dissolving. They held onto power through gerrymandering, pork barrel spending (i.e., public works to gain votes in a politician's district), and facing weak Republican challengers.

Demographic changes also hurt the Democratic Party base. In the 1970s, many middle-income whites left large cities for suburbs that had a tradition of voting Republican. Low-income racial minorities remained behind in decaying ghettos. Republican-backed policies created an "underclass" by cutting social programs, urban housing, and mass transportation, while giving tax breaks and federal aid for suburban growth and for corporations that "deindustrialized" and abandoned the cities.[154] Republican politicians demonized the urban underclass as being full of immoral and lazy "welfare cheaters," promiscuous unwed mothers, drug addicts, and violent criminals. The underclass symbolically linked race with declining traditional social values (i.e., a lack of self-reliance, moral character, and diligence). Republican Party supporters became increasing white and more middle or working class.[155]

CONCLUSION

In this chapter, we have seen that the ideal model of a full participatory democracy with equal participation and voice by all citizens does not match the reality of American politics. Voting rates in the United States are among the lowest in the advanced industrial world largely due to specific features of U.S. political institutions. There is an electoral bias that favors higher income people, reinforces their participation in other ways, and has politicians attentive to their needs. The bias and other factors create policy pressures that favor high-income people and large firms over others in society.

Class politics includes voting based on class and conditions that link social class to political actions. Classes differ by levels and channels of participation, and these vary across time. The historical record suggests

that in certain periods, social cohesion and the intensity of political participation can rise or fall. Such fluctuation directly affects participation by class, gender, and race, and it shapes public policy.

During the last 40 years blacks moved into the Democratic Party. At the same time, whites who had supported the Democratic Party moved toward the Republican Party for noneconomic, cultural issues. A gender gap developed as women's political activity grew and women favored different policy positions than men. As more women participated in the paid workforce, they embraced gender equality and moved toward the Democratic Party. Simultaneously, men moved toward the Republican Party.

Large percentages of voters see little difference between the parties, which depresses voting rates. Some researchers argue that a re-alignment occurred in the 1970s and the bases of support for the two major parties that had been stable since the mid-1930s shifted. Whites in the Southern states and middle-income whites abandoned the Democratic Party for the Republican Party, while racial minorities, ideological liberals, feminists, and previously excluded groups moved into the Democratic Party.

In Chapter 6 we will look at unconventional politics, from disorganized riots to organized social or political movements. We will see how people join together and act collectively in struggles for power as they try to influence the direction of state and society.

KEY TERMS

Alford Index

Astroturf Lobbying

Class Politics

Class Voting

Communal Political Participation

Conventional Politics

Declining Significance Hypothesis

Democratic Class Struggle Thesis

Gender Gap

Gerrymandering

Instrumental Political Participation

Particularistic Political Contact

Piven and Cloward Turnout Proposition

Political Action Committees (PACs)

Rational Choice Theory of Voter Turnout

Rational Ignorance

Resource Theory of Voter Turnout

Soft Money

Status Inconsistency Thesis

Symbolic Political Participation

Trendless Fluctuation Hypothesis

REVIEW QUESTIONS

1. What does the standard definition of political participation used in political science omit? What are the consequences of such omissions?

2. Explain the differences between instrumental, symbolic, and communal forms of political participation.

3. Contrast the electoral and nonelectoral forms of participation.

4. What factors discourage people from participating in politics?

5. Describe each of the five models of participation. What does each say increases or decreases participation?

6. How can it be that only about one-fourth of the population selects the U.S. President in a democracy? Explain how a minority of the population can control elections.

7. Contrast individual versus nonindividual factors affecting voter turnout. Which is more important and why?

8. In what ways does the design of the U.S. electoral system serve to reinforce the power and social position of wealthy or upper-income people?

9. How does class voting differ from class politics? How important is social class

for voting and other forms of political participation?

10. How important is race in whether people participate in electoral politics and how they vote? What differences exist among racial minority groups?

11. Explain the gender gap and how women's and men's political behaviors differ.

12. What is a political realignment and how does it affect the direction of politics?

RECOMMENDED READINGS

Clawson, Dan, Alan Neustadt, and Mark Weller. 1998. *Dollars and Votes: How Business Campaign Contributions Subvert Democracy.* Philadelphia: Temple University Press.

Lee, David J. and Bryan S. Turner (eds.). 1996. *Conflicts About Class: Debating Inequality in Late Industrialism.* New York: Longman.

Manza, Jeff and Clem Brooks. 1999. *Social Cleavages and Political Change.* New York: Oxford University Press.

Palast, Greg. 2003. *The Best Democracy Money Can Buy.* New York: Plume, Penguin.

Peschek, Joseph. 1987. *Policy Planning Organizations, Elite Agendas and America's Rightward Turn.* Philadelphia: Temple University Press.

Piven, Frances Fox and Richard A. Cloward. 2000. *Why Americans Still Don't Vote: And Why Politicians Want It That Way.* Boston: Beacon.

Rosenstone, Steven J. and John Mark Hansen. 1993. *Mobilization, Participation and Democracy in America.* New York: Macmillan.

ENDNOTES

1. DeLuca (1995, 1) names leading political scientists Bernard Berelson and Samuel Huntington.
2. Ginsberg and Weissberg (1978) and Hill and Hinton-Anderson (1995).
3. See related examples in Eliasoph (1998, 193).
4. The civic virtue model is also called a mass society view of nonparticipation and is discussed further in Chapter 1. Cassel (1999) calls this having a participatory attitude.
5. The SES or resource model is described in Brady et al. (1995). Also see Leighley and Nagler (1992), Rosenstone (1982), Verba and Nie (1972), Verba, Nie, Kim (1978), and Verba, Scholzman, and Brady (1993). Rational choice models are also discussed below.
6. Rosenstone and Hansen (1993) discuss rational ignorance.
7. Berman (1997), Ginsberg and Weissberg (1978), Gray and Caul (2000), Jackson (1997), Rosenstone and Hansen (1993), Wielhouwer and Lockerbie (1994), and Zaller (1992) discuss the mobilization thesis. As Verba, Nie, and Kim (1978, 81) observed, "parties and voluntary associations have an independent effect on citizen participation rates—independent that is of the resources and motivation associated with the citizens' socioeconomic level."

Browning et al. (1984) argue for a mobilization approach for black and Latino participation in city-level politics and Wilcox and Singleman (2001) for New Christian Right mobilization.

8. Depoliticization is discussed by Avey (1989), DeLuca (1995), Piven and Cloward (1988), and Zipp (1985).
9. The importance of group solidarity for political action is discussed in Delaney et al. (1988), Radcliff (2001), and Radcliff and Davis (2000) on unions. Also see Calhoun-Brown (1996), Leifer (1981), Shaw, del la Garza, and Lee (2000), and Tate (1991) on the impact of racial identity.
10. See Rosenstone and Hansen (1993). Also see Putnam (1995) on social capital.
11. For social capital or network explanations of political participation/nonparticipation and view see Cassel (1999), Huckfeldt, et al. (1993, 1995), Huckfeldt and Sprague (1995), Mackuen and Brown (1987), Pomper and Sernekos (1991), and Weatherford (1982). At the interpersonal level, people who are married and living with a spouse who votes are more likely to vote, and vice versa (Straits 1990).
12. See Knack (1992). Jackson (1995) notes that education is strongly associated with voter turnout because it

increases knowledge in politics, civic virtue, and a person's ability to deal with voter registration procedures. Also see Weakliem and Heath (1994) on limitations of simple rational choice thinking.

13. For comparisons of voter turnout rates across nations, also see Burnstein (1971) and Powell (1986). Therborn (1977) provides a useful overview of the expansion of the franchise in different nations.

14. On changes in voter turnout rates over time in the United States see Cavanaugh (1981), Hout and Knoke (1975), Kleppner and Baker (1980), Kleppner (1982), Piven and Cloward (1988), Rosenstone and Hansen (1993), and Rusk (1970).

15. See Ragsdale and Rusk (1993) for a related discussion of major causes.

16. See Bartle (1998) on atheoretical lists and Ragsdale and Rusk (1993).

17. See Verba, Nie, Kim (1978); Verba, Schlozman, Brady and Nie (1993); Wolfinger and Rosenstone (1980) on the impact of SES on voting.

18. Disagreements over the decline of class voting are widely debated (see Brooks and Manza 1997a, 1997b, 1997c; Clark and Lipset 1996; Dalton et al. 1984; Hill and Leighley 1996, Hout et al. 1995; Lee and Turner 1996; Leighley and Nagler 1992; Manza et al. 1995; Manza and Brooks 1996; Nadeau and Stanley 1993; Owens and Wade 1988; Pakulski and Waters 1996; Weakliem 1993, 1997; Weakliem and Heath 1994; Zipp et al. 1982).

19. See Rosenstone (1982) for the impact of unemployment and poverty on nonvoting.

20. See Abramson and Aldrich (1982), Boyd (1981), Delli Carpini and Keeter (1996), Hughes and Conway (1997), Ragsdale and Rusk (1993), and Somin (1998) on ignorance and attitudes. House and Mason (1975), and Southwell (1986, 1987, 1995) emphasize alienation. A rational choice approach is presented in Aldrich (1993), Filer et al. (1993), Jackman (1987, 1993), Jackson (1997), Suzuki and Chappell (1996), and Weakliem and Heath (1994). Also see Oliver and Wolfinger (1999) on jury duty.

21. See Kaempfer and Lowenberg (1993), Rosenstone et al. (1984), and note 5 above. In a study of 22 nations, Jackman and Miller (1995, 484) conclude, "levels of voter turnout are a function of institutional and election procedures." Zipp (1985) argues that the lack of real choice causes people to not vote.

22. For more on how a divided government tends to lower turnout rates and helps account for lower turnout rates in the United States see Franklin and Hirczy (1998).

23. As Rosenstone and Hansen (1993, 184) noted, "changes in the electoral calendar that removed gubernatorial elections from presidential years are one part of the explanation of the decline in voter turnout since 1960." Also see Jackman and Miller (1995, 483) on the impact of voter fatigue on turnout in the United States.

24. See Rosenstone and Hansen (1993, 187).

25. The lack of party competition depressing voter turnout is discussed in Croteau (1995), Crepaz (1990), Ferguson and Rogers (1986), Piven and Cloward (1988), Southwell (1996), Winders (1999), Zipp and Smith (1982). Also see Abramson and Aldrich (1995) on the impact of the American system on depressing third parties.

26. Four conditions might account for a noncompetitive election: (1) a district has a high level of consensus or agreement among most people; (2) many people in a district feel ignored and do not vote, but a small, active segment votes; (3) challenger candidates cannot mount a serious campaign and are locked out; (4) one party has a very powerful organization and controls the public offices.

27. See Tom DeLay's "Chef d'oeuve," *The Economist,* October 18, 2003.

28. For a recent discussion of gerrymandering see Rush (1994).

29. For more on the impact of voter registration rules on voter turnout see Fenster (1994), Highton (1997), Kleppner and Baker (1980), Knack and White (1998), Nagler (1991), Oliver (1996), Oliver and Wolfinger (1999), Piven and Cloward (1988), Powell (1986), Quigley (1995), Teixeira (1987, 1992), and Wolfinger and Rosenstone (1980).

30. See Firebaugh and Chen (1995).

31. McDonald and Popkin (2001).

32. See Delaney et al. (1988), Squire et al. (1987), Tate (1991, 1994), Timpone (1998), Wolfinger and Rosenstone (1980). Also see note 16 above.

33. Stoker and Jennings (1995) discuss the impact of marriage. See Kaufman (1999) on the negative impact of associationism (joining voluntary associations) on voter turnout in nineteenth-century America.

34. Teixeira (1987) discusses the impact of a decline in newspaper reading. Ansolabehere et al. (1994) argue that negative advertising depresses turnout by about 5 percent, but Finkel and Geer (1998) disagree. For a broader comparative study of efficacy see Hayes and Bean (1993).

35. Paxton (1999) examines this thesis.

36. The decline in door-to-door campaigning and the rise of media-based political party campaigning are discussed by Ginsberg (1984). Also see Gerber and Green (2000a, 2000b), Oliver (1996), and Wielhouer and Lockerbie (1994). Clawson, Neustadtl and Scott (1992, 7) observe, "Money has always been a critically important factor in campaigns, but the shift to expensive technology has made it the dominant factor. Today money is the key to victory and substitutes for everything else."

37. See Radcliff (1992).

38. The lack of party identification difference between voters and nonvoters is found in Piven and Cloward (1988), Teixeira (1987), and Wolfinger and Rosenstone (1980). Erikson (1995) rejects Radcliff's (1994) statement that turnout favors Democrats and shows that voter turnout by state makes no difference in which party wins presidential elections.

39. On the different policy views of voters versus nonvoters see Bennett and Resnick (1990), Kleppner (1982), and Quigley (1995). Also see Pacek and Radcliff (1995) for cross-national data.

40. Data from the 2002 General Social Survey show that about 18 percent of people with family incomes under $20,000 say they contacted an elected representative about an issue in the past 5 years, compared to over 48 percent of those with family incomes in excess of $110,000.

41. See Piven and Cloward (1988, 2000). Radcliff (1992) also provides a relevant discussion.

42. See Rosenstone et al. (1984) on third-party politics in America.

43. For example see Hamilton (1972), Knoke (1972b, 1974b), Lipset (1960), and Wright (1976). Knoke (1974a) noted that those who attend religious services tend to conform to the party choice of others of the religion (e.g., Catholics support the Democrats).

44. See Beck and Jennings (1991) on family influence and the decline of partisanship in the post-1965 period. Sears and Funk (1999) and Sears and Valentino (1997) found that partisan allegiance ideology and social attitudes persist with small changes across an adult's lifetime. Broad shifts in political climate or dramatic political events can cause a modest change.

45. Calculated from National Election Survey data from 1996, 1998, and 2000.

46. On the difference between class politics and class voting also see Hout et al. (1995), Rempel (1998), and Wright (2000).

47. See Eliasoph (1998), Southwell (1996), and Winders (1999).

48. For a discussion of class consciousness and politics see Guest (1974), Mann (1973), and Weakliem (1993).

49. For more on the democratic class struggle see Alford (1963), Korpi (1983), and Lipset (1960). Also see Hout et al. (1995) and Manza et al. (1995).

50. A good example of the New Political History and ethnocultural voting is Kleppner (1982). Also see Formisano (1994) for an overview and criticism of this label.

51. A listing of studies of local political activism by the New Labor Historians can be found in Oestreicher (1988). For more on class consciousness see Katznelson (1986), Mann (1973), and Orr and McNall (1991).

52. See Haydu (1999b) and Isaac (2002) on nineteenth-century owner-capitalist political mobilization.

53. For more on the Alford Index see Alford (1963), Korpi (1972), and Hout et al. (1995).

54. Lipset (1960) remains the classic in this tradition.

55. Early work of social mobility and politics can be found in Lipset and Bendix (1959) and Lipset and Zeterberg (1964). See Jackman (1972), Lopreato et al. (1976), Segal and Knoke (1968, 1972). Blee (1985) discussed mobility and politics among women. See De Graaf et al. (1995) on mobility and politics in Britain, the Netherlands, Germany and the United States.

56. The idea of status inconsistency and politics was outlined in Lenski (1966, 1967). Rush (1967) suggested that inconsistency produces status politics projection of a person's anxieties onto scapegoats and right-wing extremism. Others found mixed or contradictory evidence for it. See Blocker and Riedesel (1978), Eitzen (1972), Hamilton (1972), Hamilton and Wright (1986), Hartman (1974), Jackson and Curtis (1972), Kelly and Chambliss (1966), Knoke (1972a, 1972b), Olsen and Tully (1972), Salopek and Vanderpool (1976), Segal (1969), Whitt (1983), Wilson (1979), Wright (1976), and Zimmermann (1978).

57. See Wright (1976) and Hamilton and Wright (1986).

58. See Hamilton: (1972, 523).

59. Emphasis on a decline in social class can be found in Clark and Lipset (1996), Crepaz (1990), Dalton et al. (1984), Dalton (1996), Inglehart (1984), Inglehart and Abramson (1999), and Inglehart and Baker (2000).

60. Emphasis on the continued significance of social class can be found in Brooks and Manza (1997b, 1997c), Hill and Leighley (1996), Hout et al. (1995), Manza et al. (1995), and Manza and Brooks (1996). Brym et al. (1989) and Nakhaie (1992) analyze Canadian class voting and find that leftist voting occurs with mobilization, i.e., when a viable left party is an electoral alternative. On Canada also see Clement and Myles (1994), Langford (1996), and Nakhaie (1992).

61. See also Manza and Brooks (1999, 65–68) for a multicategory class scheme with voting data.

62. For discussion on definitions of class and their impact on class voting see Crompton (1993), Hout, et al. (1995), Langford (1996), Nakhaie (1992), Weakliem and Heath (1994), Wright (1985, 1991), Zipp et al. (1982).

63. From Rae (1992, 644).

64. Combining class voting with nonvoters is discussed as total class voting in Hout et al. (1995) and Manza and Brooks (1999). Also see Zipp (1985). Using a two-stage model of nonvoting—not registering to vote and not voting among the registered—Timpone (1998) found that each stage was associated with different factors, and some (e.g., race and gender) had opposite effects in each stage. Education, income, membership in nonchurch groups, home ownership, political efficacy, and strength of party identification effected registering (but not voting). Candidate differences, marital status, and race affected turnout but not registering to vote. This suggests looking at each stage of the process.

65. See on cultural divisions other than class as central voting cleavages Dalton et al. (1984), Dalton (1996), Inglehart (1984), and Rae (1992).

66. Computed from the 2000 National Election Survey.

67. Allen and Broyles (1989) analyzed political contributions of very wealthy families for the 1972 elections and found that one-half donated, with donations more likely from those deeply involved in corporate governance, oil companies, or in industries with government regulation.

68. The financing of policy institutes by wealthy individuals, corporations and foundations created by wealthy families is discussed in Akard (1992), Allen and Broyles (1991),

Anker et al. (1987), Burris (1987, 1991, 1992b), Clawson and Clawson (1987), Domhoff (1978, 1996), Jenkins and Schumate (1985), Mintz and Schwartz (1985) and Useem (1983, 1984, 1987). See Domhoff (1974) on upper class clubs.

69. The sources of money for campaigns can be found in the *Statistical Abstract of U.S.* (various years).

70. Federal Elections Commission, Press Release May 15, 2001 "FEC Reports on Congressional Financial Activity for 2000" http://www.fec.gov/press/051501congfinact/ 051501congfinact.html downloaded December 5, 2001.

71. See Michael Cooper, "At $92.60 a Vote, Bloomberg Shatters Election Record," *New York Times*, December 4, 2001.

72. The history of early campaign finance laws and events of the 1970s are reviewed in Clawson, Neustadtl, and Scott (1992, 10–11). Also see Clawson, Neustadt, and Weller (1998); Eismeier and Pollock (1986, 1988); Koenig (1987); and Sabato (1984, 1996), for a general discussion.

73. See Andres (1985, 215).

74. For discussion of election finance law changes and the operation of PACs see Eismeier and Pollock (1988, 2–3, 15–18), Clawson, Neustadtl and Scott (1992, 28–52), Matasar (1986, 7–22), and Sabato (1984, 3–10). See Berke (1987) on pressure on managers and small fines for violations.

75. The types of firms likely to make PAC contributions are documented in Andres (1985). Also see Grier, Munger, and Roberts (1994), Mizruchi (1992) and Mizruchi and Koenig (1988, 1991).

76. For more on PAC patterns see Burris (1987), Matasar (1986), and Sabato (1984).

77. See Sabato (1984, 18–25).

78. See Jacobs (1998, 113).

79. Clawson and Neustadtl (1989, 749)

80. Research that rejected pluralism include studies that found negative evidence for, "The contention that business is politically divided [that is] is central to pluralism . . . " (Clawson, Neustadt, and Bearden 1986, 797). Some studies include Akard (1992), Boies (1989), Clawson, Neustadt and Bearden (1986), Domhoff (1996) and Jacobs (1988).

81. On the interconnected web or inner circle of capitalists see Domhoff (1996) and Useem (1983, 1984).

82. See (Jacobs 1988).

83. For example see Boies (1989). Also see Grier, Munger, and Roberts (1994).

84. This is discussed in Dreiling (2000), Jacobs (1998), and Mintz (1995).

85. See (Sabato 1984, 124).

86. From Mizruchi (1989, 1990a, 1990b) and Mizruchi and Koenig (1988, 1991). Also see Clawson, et al. (1992, 1998), Burris (1991, 1987), Neustadt (1990), Neustadt and Clawson (1988), Neustadt et al. (1991), Su et al. (1993, 1995).

87. See Clawson, Neustadtl and Bearden (1986, 810)

88. Clawson, Neustadt and Bearden (1986) and Mizruchi (1990a, 1990b).

89. Burris (1991). Also see Burris (1992a) and Burris and Salt (1990). Clawson et al. (1992, 1998) disagree.

90. Romer and Snyder (1994) found that ties exist between particular PACs and particular Congressional committees and donations change as committee composition changes, suggesting careful targeting.

91. From Lewis, Neil A. "Corporate Gifts Aided G.O.P. in Close Races," *New York Times*, January 10, 1997.

92. Abramson, Jill. "Menu at G.O.P. Feast: Soft Money Galore," *New York Times*, November 5, 1997.

93. Clymer, Adam. "Parties 'Soft Money' Donations Continue To Soar, Report Says," *New York Times*, June 6, 2000.

94. See Van Natta and Fritsch (1997).

95. From Clawson, Neustadtl and Scott (1992, 9).

96. Federal Election Commission "Party Fundraising Escalates," January 12, 2001 Press Release. http://fecweb1.fec.gov/press/011201partyfunds.htm downloaded December 4, 2001.

97. See discussion in Sabato (1984, 133–36). Moore and Chachere (1995) found a relationship between PAC contributions and voting in the U.S. Senate.

98. See Clawson, Neustadtl, and Scott (1992, 95) for a discussion of winning loopholes and (1992, 118) for the importance of minor changes in the language of laws. Also see Brooks, Cameron, and Carter (1998) who argue that PAC contributions by agricultural interests influenced Congressional voting.

99. See Lewis, Neil A. "This Mr. Smith Gets His Way with the Power Brokers in Washington," *New York Times*, October 12, 1996.

100. For examples see Cushman, John H. Jr. "Corporate Gifts Open Door to Governor's Inner Sanctum," *New York Times*, May 17, 1997; "Little local difficulties," *Economist*, April 11, 1998, p. 21; and Sack, Kevin. "Fighting a Local Tradition: Vote Buying," *New York Times*, March 23, 1997.

101. Astroturf lobbying is discussed in Mitchell (1998), Sanchez (1996), Savage (1995) and Zipper (1999). Also see "When a Grass-Roots Drive Actually Isn't," *New York Times*, March 26, 1995.

102. From Rosenstone and Hansen (1993, 110).

103. Lewis, Neil A. "Almost $2 Million Spent in Magazine's Anti-Clinton Project, but on What?" *New York Times*, April 15, 1998.

104. See Wayne (1997a, 1997b).

105. This issue is extensively discussed by Vogel (1978, 1983, 1996).

106. For an example see Abelmann and Lie (1995) and Chang (2001).

107. For discussions of census and race see Kertzer and Arel (2002), Nobles (2000), and Rodriquez (2002).

108. See Nagel (1994, 1995) on the construction of ethnicity.

109. See Guterbock and London (1983) and Shingles (1981).

110. See Danigelis (1977, 1978), Olsen (1970), Orum (1966), Tate (1994), and Verba, Scholzman and Brady (1993).

111. For more on the role of black churches see Calhoun-Brown (1996), Cassel (1999), Ellison (1991), Henry (1990), Huckfeldt, Plutzer, and Sprague (1993), and Wilcox and Gomez (1990). We will return to this later in a discussion of the civil rights movement.

112. The importance of community and racial solidarity for black participation is discussed in Bledsoe et al. (1995), Calhoun-Brown (1996), Ellison (1991), Hackey (1992), Huckfeldt and Kohfeld (1989), London and Hearn (1977), Miller, et al. (1981), and Wilcox and Gomez (1990). Leifer (1981) provides a general theory of ethnic mobilization that emphasizes the importance of leadership to organize people along ethnic lines.

113. See Terkildsen (1993). Sigleman and Sigleman (1995) suggest that white voters are not uniformly negative but they evaluate candidates based on ideology and trust conservative candidates more. Gay (2001, 2002) found that whites are less likely to contact a congressional representative who is black, while increases in African American activity is modest. Santoro (1995) found that strong local civil rights organizations and having black elected officials significantly increased the size and scope of Affirmative Action programs.

114. From Bobo and Gilliam (1990). Radcliff and Saiz (1995) note that high black turnout at the state level is associated with conservative, anti-black policies and suggest this may be a backlash against black activism.

115. For a discussion of differences in political alienation by blacks and whites see Herring, House, and Mero (1991).

116. For more on political participation among African Americans see Bobo and Gilliam (1990), Meier and England (1984), Verba and Nie (1972, 157–160). Also see Browning et al. (1984) on city-level politics and Timpone (1995) on voter registration drives. Cohen and Dawson (1993) note that African Americans living in isolated, low-income neighborhoods have lower political participation than other blacks.

117. Oliver (1999, 2001). Also see Kinder and Medelberg (1995) on the impact of white isolation from blacks on white policy positions.

118. Citizenship information is from U.S. Bureau of Census (1998), Table 4.

119. Newton (2000) found that Latinos who voted for Proposition 187 in California did so for cultural-identity reasons (English speaking, long-time U.S. residence) rather than out of economic threat. Also see "Hispanic Voters Hard to Profile, Poll Finds," *New York Times,* October 4, 2002.

120. For a discussion of Latino participation in politics see Arvizu and Garcia (1996), Chavez (1992), de la Garza et al. (1992), DeSipio (1996), Hero (1992), Hwang and Murdock (1991), Longoria et al. (1990), and Welch et al. (1975).

121. de la Garza, Falcon and Garcia (1996) discuss shared values between the white-Anglos and Mexican Americans.

122. See DeSipio (1996, 87–118), Hero (1992, 58–64), and Hritzuk and Park (2000).

123. Michelson (2000) provides a detailed study of Chicago Latinos and argues that voting may be more symbolic than instrumental in the context.

124. See Stowers (1990) on Cuban political participation. Arvizu and Garcia (1996) note that among eligible Latino voters, Cuban participation is very high, reflecting the welcoming of Cubans to the United States and their high socio-economic status.

125. See DeSipio (1996) and Shaw, de la Garza, and Lee (2000).

126. See U.S. Census (1998), Table 4.

127. See Lien, Collet, Wong, and Ramakrishnan (2001) and Nakanishi (2001).

128. For a discussion of political participation by Asian Americans see Fugita and O'Brien (1991) and Lien (1998).

129. See studies cited in Lien, Collet, Wong, and Ramakrishnan (2001) and Lien (2001).

130. See Howell and Day (2000), Mueller-Eckhardt (1991) and Mueller et al. (1988) for an overview of the gender gap. Bonk (1988), and Mueller (1987) discuss the role of organized feminism in highlighting the gender gap.

131. "Among those women who are both educated and employed, the sex gap in psychological involvement in politics is minimal" (Verba, Nie, and Kim 1978, 267).

132. Kaufmann and Petrocik (1999) argue that partisanship and policy differences began earlier, in the mid-1960s.

133. Trevor (1999) argues that gender socialization is a central factor. With regard to environmental issues, Blocker and Eckberg (1989, 1997) find that female socialization to nurture is not a central factor.

134. Norrander (1997) and Kaufmann and Petrocik (1999).

135. See Kaufmann and Petrocik (1999) and Wirls (1986).

136. See Blee (1985), Manza and Brooks (1998, 1261) and Somma (1992).

137. On feminist ideals see Bonk (1988), Conover (1988), Conover and Shaprio (1993), and Cook and Wilcox (1991).

138. See discussion in Plutzer and Zipp (1996), Shapiro and Convor (1997), and Schlozman et al. (1995).

139. On gender policy differences see Andersen (1997), Blocker and Eckberg (1989, 1997), Bord and O'Connor (1997), Chaney et al. (1998), Conover and Shapiro (1993), Dolan (1998), Hurwitz and Smithey (1998), Kaufmann and Petrocik (1999), Miller (1988), Scholzman et al. (1995), Shapiro and Mahajan (1986), and Solomon et al. (1989).

140. See Kaufmann and Petrocik (1999) on welfare issues and Bord and O'Connor (1997) and Solomon et al. (1989) on health risks and envrionmental concerns.

141. See Gidengil (1995).

142. The finding for Western Europe where women are more right-conservative is long-standing and may be affected by religiousity (see Lipset 1960). Also see Norris (1988) and Studlar and McAllister (1998).

143. See Lien (1998) and Welch and Sigelman (1989, 1992, 1993).

144. For more on gender differences see Costantini (1990), Rapoport et al. (1990), Scholzman et al. (1995), and Wilcox et al. (1993).

145. See Conover (1988, 1003) and Cook and Wilcox (1991).

146. See Orloff (1993). Marshall (1998) argues that even in 1895, voter gender differences were not uniformly male or female, but reflected a complex of class and ethnic factors. Also see Clement and Myles (1994) on the role of gender.

147. See Kenworthy and Malami (1999) and Studlar, McAllister, and Hayes (1998).

148. Huckfeldt and Kohfeld (1989) and Carmines and Stimson (1984) argue that race is central, while Abramowitz (1994) and Abramowitz and Saunders (1998) see it occurring later based on ideological polarization more tied to economic issues. Also see Sabato (1989) on whether the 1980 election was a realignment.

149. See Huckfeldt and Kohfeld (1989, 91).

150. For an elaboration see Huckfeldt and Kohfeld (1989, 123–129). Abramowitz and Saunders suggest that white males and Southerners became ideologically polarized and changed (1998). Carmines (1994) and Carmines and Stimson (1982, 1984) argue that race became the primary basis for ideological polarization and partisan division by 1972. Haynes and Jacobs (1994, 98–99) note that Republicans can be politically hurt by their macroeconomic policies but stress that noneconomic issues harm Democrats. Kiecot and Nelsen (1991) note that region interacted with religion to affect party and political belief.

151. See Giles and Hertz (1994) for a study of partisanship in Louisiana.

152. See Gilens, Sniderman, and Kuklinski (1998) on white liberal nonsupport of affirmative action policy. Manza and Brooks (1997) argue that the religious cleavage declined somewhat between the 1950s and 1990s, but Catholics did not change party affiliation. Instead, socially liberal Protestants left the Republican Party.

153. See Manza and Brooks (1999) on voting data for the self-employed and professionals.

154. See Heying (1997).

155. From Bolce and De Maio (1993). Also see Gilens (1994) on white views of blacks and welfare.

PROTEST AND MOVEMENTS

INTRODUCTION

Have you ever participated in a demonstration or protest? Have you seen protesters at a march or carrying signs? In Chapter 5, we looked at political involvement/participation through institutional channels. Now we go beyond established channels to examine a range of activities, from disorganized riots to organized movements, or what McAdam, Tarrow, and Tilly (1996) called "contentious politics." In these struggles for power, people try to shape the direction of state and society. Sometimes state officials view protesters as domestic enemies, while protesters feel they must go beyond conventional forms of participation to be politically effective. ■

Unconventional Politics

Political sociologists study many forms of collective behavior and protest (i.e., crowds, riots, movements, rebellions). At one extreme are disorderly mobs that protest a grievance in the streets, such as the antiglobalization rioters in Seattle in 1999 opposing the World Trade Organization. At the other end are polished, movement organizations (e.g., the Sierra Club) that blur into standard lobbying as they try to shift the political agenda. Research into unconventional politics expanded after the 1960s but little synthesis resulted. McAdam, Tarrow, and Tilly (1996, 18) noted, "More than most areas of research, the study of contentious politics suffers from malaise." Challengers to power holders may intensify from a movement to a full-scale revolution (see Summary 6.1).

The very boundaries of unconventional politics are in dispute. The nineteenth century French writers Gustave LeBon (1841–1931) and Gabriel Tarde (1843–1904) saw crowds and mobs as social pathologies governed by a distinct, irrational mentality and imitation.[1] By the 1930s, Hebert Blumer's model of collective behavior connected crowds to both social and personal disorganization. Through the classic era, collective behavior researchers considered fads, crowds, mobs, riots, and rebellions to be a single type of activity (i.e., an ill-organized, formless collection of people who expressed symbolic meanings). They used contagion theories that emphasized how crowd or movement participants ceased to think normally and their self-control broke down. At the same time, structural, functional, and modernization theorists pointed to rapid social change and system strain as generating political crises and disruptive collective behavior.[2] They saw collective protests as expressing individual deprivation or alienation exacerbated by societal strain. These explanations dissolved with an explosion of new studies beginning in the 1970s.

The boundary between conventional and unconventional politics, including social movements, has blurred since the 1970s. Some political sociologists see the emergence of a social movement society and discuss new social movements that subsume cultural change and new self-identities. Protesters and movements are borrowing tactics from conventional politics (e.g., press releases, lobbying, lawsuits); simultaneously, institutionalized political organizations are borrowing tactics from protesters and movements to create hybrid social movements/interest group organizations.[3] Others see protest movements and established interest groups that affect public opinion blending, and political parties absorbing most forms of protest.[4] Still others vehemently distinguish among them.[5] They argue that the study of truly radical politics disappears when scholars fail to distinguish conventional politics from movements.[6]

Social–political movements that engage in contentious politics vary greatly by size and resources, area of emphasis (e.g., environment, racial equality,

SUMMARY 6.1   Movements and Revolutions

Demarcating a social–political movement from a revolution may seem straightforward at first. A revolution is a broad and decisive form of political conflict that seeks the overthrow of the state and dramatic change or replacement of the social–economic system. A social movement is limited, unconventional protest that challenges the power structure and tries to change policy or influence beliefs and values. Yet the line between them is not always clear. Jack Goldstone (1998) argued that they are best viewed as two points along a continuum of political activity rather than as qualitatively different phenomena.

People overuse the word *revolution* for dramatic effect. We hear of a banking revolution, the Industrial Revolution, the green revolution, a fashion revolution, various technological revolutions, and so forth. Macro-level political or societal revolutions, such as the American, Chinese, French, Iranian, Mexican, or Russian revolutions, are well-known and extensively studied. Political sociologists explain the causes, dynamics, and consequences of revolutions. Revolutions are central ideas in most theories of society; they both show extreme cases of collective social–political behavior and swiftly reveal the fundamental features of a social–economic–political order. Revolutions are an infrequent, extreme, collective political event. They differ from other political events by having very intense conflict, involving a wide scope of disruption, affecting most of the population, and producing drastic change in social–political relations. A transformation or complete reorganization of society is frequently the goal if not always the result of a revolution. Here are some widely used definitions of revolution:

- "the sudden and violent overthrow of an established political order" (Friedrich 1966, 5)

- "a special kind of social change, one that involves the intrusion of violence into civil social relations . . ." (Johnson 1966, 1)
- "the forcible overthrow of a government followed by the reconsolidation of authority by new groups, ruling through new political (and sometimes social) institutions . . ." (Goldstone 1991, 37)
- "a rapid fundamental and violent change in the domestic values and myths of a society, and in its political institutions, social structure, leadership, government activity and policies" (Huntington 1968, 264)
- "attempts by subordinate groups to transform the social foundations of political power" (Kimmel 1990, 6)
- "rapid, basic transformations of a society's state and class structure; they are accompanied and in part carried through by class based revolts from below" (Skocpol 1979, 4)
- "an extralegal takeover of the central state apparatus which destroys the economic and political power of the dominant social group of the old regime" (Trimberger 1978, 12)
- "a rapid, forcible, durable shift in collective control over a state that includes a passage through openly contested sovereignty" (McAdam, Tarrow, and Tilly 1996, 24)
- "a social movement in which the participants are organized to alter drastically or replace totally the existing social, economic, and political institutions" (DeFronzo 1991, 8)

In summary, a revolution is the rapid, forcible overthrow of a ruling class and taking control of the state, usually with violence, to alter fundamental power relations in a society and transform its major social, political, and economic institutions.

economic equality, business regulation), goals (e.g., reformist, revolutionary, conservative), membership (e.g. students, farmers), and tactics (e.g., petitions, boycotts, marches). Some are global, such as movements for women's rights or for a clean environment, and others are local, such actions as stopping the opening of a new shopping center or expanding a highway. In sum, contentious or unconventional politics includes a broad range of political activities. Its exact boundaries are ill-defined, but they extend from mild protest actions that only modestly stretch the limits of conventional politics to very violent upheavals that transform entire societies. Each political sociological model views contentious politics differently.

Political Sociological Models

Pluralists assume that under normal conditions, conventional channels of participation and routine democratic politics offer all citizens access to the polity. People can form political parties or interest groups and express their desires in an orderly manner, and peaceful movements are merely a type of interest group. Disorder and disruptive unrest—protests, violent riots, or armed struggle—are unnecessary and illegitimate, and they threaten stable democratic institutions. For pluralists, the causes of political unrest are rapid social–economic change that institutions cannot adjust to quickly enough, channels of democratic participation that fail to operate properly, or marginal and poorly socialized people who do not fully embrace democratic norms and values. For pluralists, state officials and public leaders should not tolerate violent unrest, because it violates the basic "rules of the game" of democracy. In contrast to those using violence, legitimate movements that employ moderate tactics will be more politically effective.

Advocates of an *elite model* divide protest movements into two categories. The first type includes disorganized attempts by the masses to challenge elite power. These are doomed to fail but can consume state resources until they are suppressed. Also, elites may use them for their own purposes. The other type includes actions by counterelites to dislodge and replace the existing power elite. Elite theorists study the formation of elite alliances and coalitions, the rise of counterelites outside established institutions, and elite manipulation of disorganized mass unrest for their own purposes. For example, elites seeking to gain power may encourage mass unrest and then use the disruption to expand their power base (e.g., win supporters, threaten greater unrest) or press for a political objective (e.g., enact a new policy, increase law enforcement, cut a government program).

In the *statist model*, the movements involve a variety of interest groups. This model focuses on the processes by which movements become formal, bureaucratic, and institutionalized. It emphasizes that to succeed and achieve goals, a movement must create a leadership structure, use existing networks, gather resources including professional expertise, and form alliances with other organizations. It also emphasizes how the success or failure of movements and legal/policy arrangements in one historical period can shape the opportunities or limit the developments of movements later in time.

Political sociologists who use a *power-structure model* say that protest movements and unrest can express genuine opposition to the ruling class. They differentiate among various forms of unrest. Some forms threaten the heart of the social–economic system, other forms affect it indirectly, and still others are irrelevant or counterproductive. For example, serious unrest over demands for much stricter environmental controls can threaten profits and cripple the economy; on the other hand, violence that emerges in a wild Mari Gras festival or because a sports team lost does not threaten the social–economic order. The state's response also varies by the seriousness of the unrest and by how much the unrest threatens the powerful class of a society. The state may diffuse or redirect unrest, offer symbolic redress, co-opt the challengers, or vigorously repress the challengers.

Those who apply a *structuralist model* see the capitalist economy as unstable with ongoing contradictions that generate the conditions for social unrest. The contradictions foster coalitions or alliances among classes or class segments that are critical to the development of massive unrest. They emphasize how specific mixes of economic and political conditions can create opportunities for unrest and affect the likely outcome of unrest.

The *class-struggle model* includes a wide range of unrest, from disorganized rioting to revolutionary movements, as political struggles. Political sociologists who use this model to analyze the timing and conditions that initiate unrest, its varying intensities, its stages of development, and the conditions associated with its success or failure. They note that struggles in one area (e.g., for racial equality in voting) can spread to other areas (e.g., gender equality in the workplace), and expand into a major protest. They see the beliefs, ideas, and social relations that arise among protesters as critical for success and recognize that violent tactics might be an effective strategy. As Giugni (1999, xvii) argued ". . . in contrast to the pluralist's claim that moderation in politics is more effective than disruption, the use of force or disruptive tactics by social movements improves their chances of reaching their goals" (see Chart 6.1 for overview).

PROTEST AS POLITICS

Throughout human history, people near the bottom of society have engaged in urban riots, peasant uprisings, slave revolts, mutinies, mass strikes, and insurrections to express their grievances, acquire power, or advance their political views. This was especially true when people lacked access to democratic channels to participate in conventional politics. When people could not vote, felt ignored or betrayed by officials, or felt that officials were opposing their vital concerns, they sometimes used mass protest. An early example is the Whiskey Rebellion (see Case in Point 6.1). A more recent example is the 1992 Los Angeles race riots, the most deadly race riots in U.S. history.

Until the late 1960s, few political sociologists saw disruptive social unrest as being a form of serious political expression. To them, unrest that lacked articulate leaders to make specific demands, a coherent ideology, or a stable organization, and it was irrational, emotional, and apolitical. Since they thought it was

chart 6.1

POLITICAL–SOCIOLOGICAL MODELS OF PROTEST MOVEMENTS

Model	What Are Protest Movements?	What Causes Unrest and Protest?
Pluralist	Under normal conditions, they are just another interest group. Serious protest is unnecessary unless normal democratic channels fail.	They are caused by rapid social change that strains the social system or marginalized people who are not fully socialized to democratic norms.
Elitist	They are often real challenges to rule by the established elite.	They are caused by the masses rising up, or by counterelites who want to dislodge and replace the existing ruling elite.
Statist	They represent a variety of interest groups that are still early in the process of formation and are moving toward becoming a bureaucratic organization.	They are caused by diverse interests in a society when some attempt to assert their interests or to deny interests asserted by their opponents.
Power-Structure	Some are serious challenges by lower classes to the established ruling class, but others are merely expressive-symbolic outbursts.	The serious forms of unrest are caused when the lower classes organize together or form alliances and then rise up.
Structuralist	They represent coalitions or alliances among classes or class segments.	They arise from deep contradictions and strains of the capitalist system.
Class-Struggle	They are one of the many forms of political struggle for power in a class society.	They are caused when some try to acquire power or repel others, and they change form or tactics based on the responses of allies and opponents.

nonpolitical and believed that America had a well-functioning democracy, many also ignored politically disenfranchised people whose demands were outside the conventional political channels. As a result, they failed to anticipate and were ill equipped to explain the origin, expansion, size, or intensity of six years of nationwide protest, urban riots, demonstrations, and unrest in the 1960s.

In response to unrest in the 1960s, officials and researchers quickly launched commissions and academic studies to examine the violence, marches, riots, and racialism by large numbers of college students and African Americans. As they began to study urban riots, civil rights activism, and antiwar protest, political sociologists first relied on prevailing explanations of collective behavior. The traditional model of collective behavior, social breakdown theory, said that social strain creates a disruptive psychological condition that leads to social unrest or protest movements. Thus, weakened social norms and social disorganization

CASE IN POINT 6.1   The Whiskey Rebellion

The Whiskey Rebellion of 1794 is a famous case of unconventional politics and vigorous protest in early American history. The Whiskey Rebellion in western Pennsylvania was a populist uprising against Alexander Hamilton's Whiskey Excise Tax. The whiskey tax hit western Pennsylvania grain farmers hard because for them, whiskey was a crop and a currency in addition to being produced for personal consumption. The participants in the uprising organized local political groups, refused to register stills, terrorized tax collectors, ambushed a postal carrier, and held a two-day siege on a local official's house. In a gun battle, two protesters were killed. Eventually 5,000 rebels marched through the city of Pittsburgh after first threatening to burn it down. Later, the President of the United States sent in 15,000 army troops to quell the disturbance. The rebellion ended, but 32 men were arrested and tried for treason; only 2 were convicted. This rebellion is similar to other forms of mass mobilized rural resistance that opposed state-building efforts elsewhere. Some local elites participated in the rebellion, but unlike others who remained uninvolved, the involved elites were less connected into networks of patronage and more dependent on local resources.

Sources: Connor (1992) and Gould (1996).

create distress and discontent, and the marginal, detached, or alienated members of society who feel distress engage in extreme behavior or unrest. The researchers expected to find that the 1960s rioters and protesters were marginal members of society. They also used relative deprivation theory from psychology. It held that a minority that feels itself to be deprived of social status or resources, compared to the majority group, may grow frustrated and resentful. After a trigger event, they convert their frustration into violence against property or persons of the majority group. Researchers expected to find that 1960s rioters and protesters were people with the weak internal self control and feelings of personal deprivation. Since they believed that the unrest was fundamentally irrational, as people went on a wild, uncontrolled rampage, researchers expected to find a geographic pattern of rioting that followed a simple contagion model. In general, they expected to find that the student protesters and urban rioters would be uninformed, authoritarian, insecure, and detached social isolates.

As dozens of research findings poured in, nearly all contradicted the traditional theories. The traditional breakdown explanations received almost no support.[7] Instead of finding social disorganization and a breakdown of social norms, the studies documented serious racial separation, widespread mistreatment, and deep anger among protesters. For example, when researchers asked whether urban rioting was a form of protest or criminal behavior, people who had ignored or denied conditions of injustice were the main ones who called it crime and not protest.[8] Instead of being disturbed, irrational troublemakers, protesters were objecting to very poor living conditions and felt mistreated and ignored. Other studies documented that the media had indeed ignored the poor conditions and mistreatment, so few in the public were aware of it.[9] A summary of 50 empirical studies that used the relative deprivation theory to explain riot participation found only 4 studies that supported it.[10] Clark McPhail (1971, 1064) noted, "[T]here is considerable reason for rejecting the sociological and popular cliché that absolute or relative deprivation, and the ensuing frustration or discontent or despair is the root cause of rebellion." Instead of frustrated individuals, protesters saw and responded to events politically.[11] As Doug McAdam (1982, 12) observed, "Perhaps the most glaring weakness . . . is the assertion that movement participants are distinguished from the average citizen by some abnormal psychological profile." Instead of simple personal gain or contagion, the targets of rioting and of vandalism clearly had political symbolism.[12] Instead of marginal members of society, political activists and protesters were more socially integrated, better educated, less authoritarian, and more morally and politically aware than their apathetic or uninvolved counterparts.[13] As summarized by Eisinger (1974, 598, 599), "By all standard indicators of socioeconomic status, protesters are better off than non-protesters . . . black protesters not only resemble the socioeconomic norm of the black community, but they are also drawn disproportionately from its more integrated, stable element." If some black rioters were marginal or isolated, it was because the white community had actively marginalized and isolated them in racially separate ghettos.

Later studies confirmed that the 1960s urban riots took place in cities that had greater racial segregation, more severe racial economic inequality, more intense interracial job competition, and where riots had occurred previously.[14] After years of research, McPhail and Wohlstein (1983, 595) observed, "while we know far more today than 15 years ago about behaviors within gatherings, demonstrations and riots, much of what we know is that traditional characterizations are inaccurate and traditional explanations no longer suffice." By the 1970s, political sociologists recognized that the unruly protests were a form of political expression. They moved beyond abstract macro-level theories of societal strain and micro-level observations of small-group processes in riots and crowds.[15] They increasingly saw protest as a complex bargaining process and struggle for power in which protest leaders appealed to multiple constituencies in a political context.[16] As Herbert Blumer (1978, 51) remarked," One does not understand collective protest by merely studying the protesting group, by trying to find out what kinds of people compose it and their views, their motives, and their actions. One must identify the other groups acting in the arena (echelons of authority, agents of authority, interest groups and the general public) and observe what they do."

The traditional view of collective behavior, unrest, and protest faced serious criticism.[17] It assumed that the participants were marginal, abnormal, or isolated individuals; it saw protest as due to individual psychological difficulties and not as a collective political phenomenon; it treated protest as a mechanical reaction to a trigger event, not as an intentional endeavor of politically activated people; it focused on the immediate situation of unrest and did not examine the entire background or the larger political context of protest; and it failed to include the reactions and responses of authorities and others as a part of the process. As political sociologists expanded the study of protest and unconventional politics, they looked at large-scale, organized collective action—the movement.

MOVEMENTS AND COUNTERMOVEMENTS

Before 1800, movements were rare. They are a form of political action that emerged with the rise of the nation-state. During state formation processes, people adopted new collective political activities (e.g., petition drives, strikes, public speeches, mass meetings, marches) that replaced traditional forms of popular protest (e.g. peasant uprisings). Compared to traditional forms, the movement was less physically violent, focused more directly on the state, was organized as a sustained collective campaign, and employed modular actions (i.e., it used flexible protest tactics that different people could adopt for use in a variety of settings).[18] The movement form spread from Britain to Western Europe and North America then diffused around the world.[19] See Chart 6.2 on some major movements.

Movements are important because they can alter power relations, force policy change, and produce broad cultural, political, and institutional change. They are intimately linked to the state, as Craig Jenkins (1995, 17) observed, "movements

---

chart 6.2

EXAMPLES OF MOVEMENTS IN THE LATE TWENTIETH-CENTURY UNITED STATES

Advocate Greater Rights for Excluded Groups

Racial-Ethnic Minority: American Indian, antiapartheid, black power, Chicano rights, civil rights, farm workers, Puerto Rico liberation movements

Gender: Equal rights, men's liberation, pro-choice, reproductive rights, women's rights movements

Low Income: Homeless, poor people's rights, tenant's rights, welfare rights movements

Sexual Minority: Gay-lesbian-bisexual-transgender movement

Advocate an Ideological Position or a Public Issue

Conservative Social Issues: Anti-ERA, antiabortion, antipornography, antibussing, antiimmigrant, Moral Majority, white separation/supremacy movements

Liberal: Antinuclear power, consumer rights, children's rights, free speech, prolabor, student rights movements

International Issues: Antiwar, draft resistance, peace, sanctuary movements

Other Moral Issues: Anti-drunk driving, antismoking, animal rights, environmental protection, handgun control movements

constitute a claim for political representation [and] . . . modern states entail some system of representing social interests vis-à-vis the state." Movements introduce dynamic energy into politics that other political institutions or parties absorb, and they have been at the forefront of fights to expand democratic rights.[20] Postpluralist theories see them as explaining how new issues advance onto the political agenda.[21]

Political sociologists offer multiple definitions of movements. The study of movements is an unusual area because it "straddles a divide that ordinarily separates one kind of social analysis from another . . . causal and purposive explanation," as Charles Tilly (1978, 6) remarked. A *causal explanation* emphasizes external forces that act upon and cause a behavior; a *purposive explanation* emphasizes people's internal choices and decisions about their interests or grievances. The internal and external duality is evident in many definitions (see Closer Look 6.1).

Charles Tilly (1999) objected to definitions of movements as "solidaristic, coherent groups" with "a continuous, self-contained life history." He argued that people form a movement in processes of organized interactions with others around them. He offered an analogy. Just as a soccer team in a match only acts *as a team* through its interactions with another team and in the context of the athletic event, a collection of people only acts *as a movement* when they interact with

---

CLOSER LOOK 6.1   Definitions of a Social–Political Movement

1. A movement is a *"collectivity acting with some degree of organization* and continuity outside of institutional channels for the purpose of promoting or resisting change in the group, society, or world order of which it is a part" (McAdam and Snow 1997, xviii).

2. A movement is *"a set of opinions and beliefs* in a population which represents preferences for changing some elements of the social structure and/or reward distribution of a society" (McCarthy and Zald 1977, 1217–1218).

3. A movement is a "sustained *series of interactions* between power holders and persons successfully claiming to speak on behalf of a constituency . . . [and] those people who make publicly visible demands for changes in the distribution or exercise of power, and back those demands with public demonstrations of support" (Tilly 1984, 306).

4. Movements are "collective *challenges to existing arrangements* of power and distribution by people with common purposes and solidarity, in sustained interaction with elites, opponents, and authorities" (Meyer and Tarrow 1998, 4).

5. Movements are *"networks of interaction"* that may not necessarily include formal organizations. Movement participants have a "sense of collective belonging" that "prevails on links of solidarity" and there is "the presence of a vision of the world and of a collective identity" (Della Porta 1999, 16–19).

6. Movements are a type of "cognitive praxis" (i.e., created *ways of seeing, thinking, communicating,* and acting) (see Eyerman and Jamison 1991) that can "make power visible" (Melucci 1997).

Note: Emphasis added in above quotes.

others in a political setting. Giugni (1998a) shared Tilly's concerns and warned against reducing movements to their organizations or their members (e.g., the feminist movement is the National Organization of Women). It is also inaccurate to limit a movement's history only to when it engages in visible, public activities (e.g., protest marches in the street, petition drives), because movements may be dormant or hidden.

In sum, social movements have the following shared features:[22]

- a network or group of people who act collectively within or beyond formal organizations
- a set of shared beliefs, ideas, and symbols that is created and maintained by the group
- a feeling of solidarity, belonging, or common identity among the people involved
- a challenging, action-oriented stance that often breaks with convention, generating conflict, sustained confrontations or interactions with other groups or institutions across time
- a goal that requires a major change in social–political conditions and challenges to the status quo

Thus, **a movement is a network of interacting people with a set of shared beliefs and a common identity that acts collectively over a sustained period of time in relation to others to achieve a change-oriented goal.** In addition to the specific sphere (e.g., political, economic, social, religious, education) in which they operate, movements can be classified by their goals.

Political sociologists classify movements in many ways, such as by their goals, ideology, constituency, tactics, relationship to the state, impact. Often classifications reflect a specific theory or historical period. Roberts and Kloss (1974, 7) reminded us that, "it is the political context that largely determines not only concept definition but the consequences of word use as well." Chart 6.3 contains a list of movement classifications. It is not a mutually exclusive listing; often one author's classification uses a term that is similar to a different term used by another author (e.g., transformative and revolutionary). Rather than debate the merits of each system or invent yet another one, we can describe a movement using terminology from any system.

As they examined movements, political sociologists developed the concept of a countermovement.[23] A **countermovement is a movement that develops in direct response to and in opposition to another movement.** It is a reaction to another, initial movement; the movement and countermovement are a single unit—an interacting dyad. As Meyer and Staggenborg (1996, 1632) noted, "Movements thus create their own opposition, which sometimes takes the countermovement form. Once a countermovement is mobilized, movement and countermovement react to one another." The goal of a countermovement is to resist what the other movement advocates. A countermovement is not government action to suppress a movement, or opposition to a profession's program or teachings (e.g., sex education, teaching of evolution). Most recent countermovements

c h a r t   6 . 3

TYPES OF MOVEMENTS

Classified by Type of Change

Transformative   seeks to transform or totally change the entire social structure or major parts of it.

Reformative   tries to reform or slightly alter social structure or a part of it.

Redemptive   wants to change individuals totally and believes social problems will be solved when individuals undergo a dramatic personal change.

Alternative   wants to significantly change or remove character defects of individuals.

Classified by Degree or Direction of Political Change

Reform   seeks modest improvements in certain areas of society without real change in its basic structure.

Radical   seeks dramatic change in a significant area of society and will disrupt/alter parts of its basic structure.

Revolutionary   tries to dramatically change the basic structure and completely upset the entire system of power in a society.

Reactionary   wants a return to conditions the way they were at a time in the past.

Classified by Function

Norm-oriented   wants to change the rules/laws by which society operates.

Value-oriented   wants to change societal values or what people hold to be most important.

Classified by Political Connection

Political   affects relations of power, inequality, injustice, oppression, or political issues.

Nonpolitical   seeks to achieve personal salvation, individual growth or improvement, spiritual renewal, or create a separate utopia.

Classified by Traditional Right-Left Ideology

Right-wing   tries to preserve existing inequalities and limit the power of groups at or near the bottom of society.

Conservative   wants to maintain conditions as they are and prevent significant or rapid change.

Left-wing   seeks to increase the power of people or groups at or near the bottom of society.

Classified by Social Class vs. Other Basis

Class   tries to achieve a specific benefit or goal of an economically defined group.

Status   wants to enhance or maintain the social position/status/prestige of a group.

Expressive   expresses group feelings without achieving a specific, concrete purpose.

Classified by Claims Relative to Other Groups

Competitive	claims resources that are also claimed by other groups who are defined as rivals or competitors.
Reactive	reasserts and defends claims when another group challenges or violates them.
Proactive	asserts group claims on an area that is new, extends its claims/rights.

Classified by Oppositional vs. Broad Support

Consensus	seeks to affirm a vague ideal and has very broad support with little or no opposition.
Conflict	confronts organized opposition as it tries to alter power relations, changes basic policies, or alters social structure.

Classified as Industrial vs. Post-industrial Cleavage

Old	organized around social class, traditional inequalities, and the ideologies and issues of an industrial society.
New	not organized around the materialism of industrial society but instead around postindustrial cultural issues of identity or life; promotes creation and expression of new postmaterialist social identities.

Other

Revitalization	is a deliberate effort by a group to create a more satisfying culture, often by recovering key features of a past type of community or set of social relations as a method of renewal. Often it is based on religious beliefs or a desire to expel impure or foreign elements.

Sources: Buechler (1995); DeFronzo (1991, 8–9); Fitzgerald and Rodgers (2000); Gusfield (1963, 20–24); Johnson, Laraña, and Gusfield (1994); Melucci (1994); Schwartz and Paul (1992); Tilly (1978, 144–148); Wallace (1956); Wilson (1973, 22–29); and Wood and Jackson (1982, 6–12).

in the United States are on the ideological right (e.g., antibusing, stop ERA [Equal Rights Amendment], or anti-abortion), but all are not conservative. We will return to countermovements later.

We can organize political–sociological studies of movements into three approaches: resource mobilization, political process, and constructionism (and a subtype of it called new social movements).[24] Each has developed branches; they overlap and borrow ideas from one another, and no unified synthesis has yet emerged.

THREE APPROACHES TO THE STUDY OF MOVEMENTS

Resource Mobilization Approach

The resource mobilization (RM) approach was developed in the 1970s. It was soon adopted by most political sociologists as they abandoned traditional theories. RM was a paradigm shift. It offered different assumptions, new concepts, stimulating questions, and transformed the study of movements.[25] As McAdam, McCarthy, and Zald (1996, xi) noted, "it would be hard to convey to an outsider just how much the study of social movements has changed . . . ." RM's central premise is simple: People always have grievances, movements arise when the aggrieved mobilize the resources needed to express demands in a visible collective manner. It emphasizes ". . . organizational variables in deliberate efforts to mobilize resources in accounting for the growth, development, success, and decline of social movements."[26]

We can trace the origins of RM to two late 1960s studies. Michael Lipsky (1968) analyzed how leaders of civil rights protest movements directed actions toward diverse groups. In response to limits on their effectiveness, the leaders simultaneously bargained with officials for gains, kept followers happy, and attracted third-party support. They also worked with the mass media that filtered or selectively allowed only some information through to the public and attracted outside supporters (e.g., Northern white liberals with resources [money, status, influence, votes]). Protest leaders depend on followers, yet the followers both helped and limited leaders. For example, some followers were unwilling or unable to engage in certain protest actions. They lacked money or time, or they feared retaliation (e.g., losing jobs or apartments) or physical violence. On the other hand, when the threat of violence was real, protest leaders used the media to communicate the threat of violence. This helped protesters gain support from reference publics, especially when the media showed nonthreatening, innocent people (e.g., young children, the elderly) taking chances to acquire a shared symbolic-moral goal. A scarcity of organizational resources (e.g., skilled professionals such as lawyers, financial resources, secretarial help, and nonprofessionals to devote time and energy) limited the leaders.

Thus, protest movement leaders face a dilemma. What they must do to maintain the protest organization and cohesion among followers can go against winning outside, third-party support. Leaders need cohesion, discipline and loyalty in the protest organization, because it is a source of strength when bargaining with officials. This suggests a strategy of one strong leader within a single disciplined protest organization, but sometimes a movement adopts a divided leadership strategy. You may have heard of the "good cop, bad cop" prisoner interrogation method. It works like this — two police officers (cops) ask the prisoner questions. To the prisoner, one cop is angry, irrational, and offensive; the other is moderate, rational, and considerate. The "good cop" protects the prisoner from the worst actions of the "bad cop" and wins the prisoner's trust. Behind the scenes, both cops cooperate against the prisoner. A radical and a moderate protest leader might do the same with state officials.

As protest leaders bargain with state officials for real benefits, they must also renew intangible, symbolic rewards for followers and excite them to maintain solidarity and loyalty. If the leaders fail to do this, the followers might become apathetic. So even if protesters cannot win concrete, material rewards, protest actions may give them psychological gratification and increase solidarity. Sometimes militant or radical leaders arise who use angry rhetoric and refuse to compromise. The radical rhetoric can increase group cohesion, but it rarely wins real results and may frighten away third-party supporters. Lipsky argued that protest leaders adopt diverse strategies to deal with multiple groups. They can tell outsiders (e.g., officials and third-party supporters) one thing but may tell followers something different, or make vague public statements but specify what the statements really mean to followers. A "natural" role conflict for leaders reinforces a situation in which leaders say more than he or she actually does. In addition, the leaders who are best at making exciting public speeches at rallies and providing "vision" often lack the skills needed to complete the routine administrative tasks of running an organization.

Lipsky's analysis gave the RM approach three ideas: (1) protest movement leaders need to build and maintain stable organizations for followers, (2) they need to rationally decide among various bargaining strategies as they deal with multiple constituencies, and (3) movement success depends on acquiring or maintaining sufficient resources (e.g., followers, media access, third-party supporters, organizational resources).

Another landmark study for the RM approach was Marcur Olson's *Logic of Collection Action* (1965). Building on economic theory, he developed a rational choice model of collective behavior. Olson noted that a wholly self-interested, rational individual would not contribute to or join an organization (e.g., a protest movement or labor union) to gain collective benefits if he/she could share in benefits (i.e., higher pay, improved conditions) without incurring the costs of being a member. Many collective organizations seek public or group benefits for a category of people and not just the active participants. From the viewpoint of the larger group, it is logical to support the organization because most people get benefits, but from the viewpoint of a single individual, it is not rational, in pure self-interested terms, to support the organization. If each individual follows her/his own immediate self-interest, collective organizations will fail, and ultimately all individuals will be worse off.

Olson's argument is simple, powerful, and has far-reaching implications. For example, an environmental advocacy organization asks Joe for a donation and to volunteer some time. Joe sincerely wants a cleaner environment, but he makes a cool, self-interested, rational calculation. If he contributes, the organization will go on to clean up the environment. If he does not contribute, other people will contribute, and organization will still work for a cleaner environment. He can be a "free rider" and enjoy the benefits of a clean environment without paying. Olson showed that if only one person fails to contribute, it makes no difference. However, if each person follows his/her self interest and does the same thing, the organization or movement will collapse. This means that collective organizations are doomed to fail with two exceptions. One exception is that the organization delivers *selective incentives* that go only to contributing participants. For example, members alone get a T-shirt or coffee mug or newsletter. The other exception is that the organization delivers *collective nonmaterial benefits* to members such as feelings of moral idealism, commitment to ideological values, a set of friends or a network of like-minded people, and a sense of belonging or group solidarity.

Political sociologists elaborated the RM approach based on criticisms of traditional collective behavior theory, and refined it as they studied the protests that swept across the United States, Western Europe, and Japan in the 1960s. A few authors developed the outline of the RM approach in a short three-year period.[27] They share a set of core assumptions and concepts, and see movements as extending the dynamics of conventional politics, not as abreactions.[28] For a comparison of traditional and RM approaches see Chart 6.4.

To better understand RM, we can look at its positions on five issue areas: (1) individual motivation, (2) the mobilization process, (3) resources, (4) movement organization, and (5) movement outcomes.

Five Major Issues in RM

Individual Motivation   RM theorists reject the traditional approach's overemphasis on irrationality and individual psychology to explain unrest and protest

---

chart 6.4

TRADITIONAL AND RESOURCE MOBILIZATION APPROACHES TO THE STUDY OF MOVEMENTS

	Traditional Approach	Resource Mobilization Approach
Movements are extensions of:	Other unusual collective behaviors (cults, fads, mobs, religious sects).	Conventional politics and political bargaining for power.
Movement grievances or discontents are:	The products of structural strain (e.g., rapid social change, breakdown in norms).	Constant and ever-present for many people, but they do not always recognize or are not always able to act upon them.
What activates movements and protests?	Built up emotional frustrations, discontent, and unmet expectations.	The combination of a movement entrepreneur, an infusion of resources, and a favorable political environment.
Key Question	Who participates in movements?	What makes movements likely to succeed?
Participants are:	People driven by pent-up emotion, irrational fears, or uncontained anger.	Rational but disaffected people who try to use a variety of effective tactics.
Movement success is due to:	A large movement social base, goals that do not contradict broad societal norms, and skilled leaders who can compromise.	The presence of enough resources (i.e., money, expertise, followers, allies) for a movement organization and favorable political conditions (i.e., divided elites, weak opponents, allies in government, protests by other related movements).

Sources: Buechle (1999), Jenkins and Perrow (1977), McAdam (1982), McCarthy and Zald (1977).

movements. They adopt a rational choice model of psychological motivation.[29] RM assumes that individuals are self-interested and rational when they participate in protest or join a movement. Individuals make strategic decisions and calculate long- and short-term costs and benefits. They make informed (albeit imperfect) choices about how to best advance their material, symbolic, or value-based interests. In other words, people form or join movements to advance their individual self-interest, and movements pursue specific goals designed to meet the collective interests of members.[30] RM recognizes the involvement of three types of people in a movement: adherents, constituents, and potential beneficiaries.[31] *Adherents* support movement goals, *constituents* provide resources to a movement, and *potential beneficiaries* gain when a movement attains its goals. These types may overlap and be the same people, or they can be different. For example, conscience adherents and conscience constituents advance a movement's cause, but they do not benefit from it. Thus, a person's rational pursuit of self-interest is not restricted to seeking direct benefits for herself or himself. A person can have an interest in assisting others who will be potential beneficiaries. For example, some males support the goal of women's equality and contribute time or money to its achievement but do not receive benefits themselves. They do so for moral, ideological, or other reasons, and they may receive inner satisfaction from giving support. Others outside the movement are divided into *bystander publics*, who are neither adherents nor opponents, and *opponents*, who disagree with a movement's goals and work against the movement.

Mobilization Processes   Critical questions for RM include: How are people mobilized? What transforms separate individuals into an integrated social–political unit willing to engage in coordinated collective behavior? Mobilization is a process by which a group acquires, accumulates, and organizes resources (e.g., followers, ideology, money, weapons, votes, alliances, organization).[32] Mobilization occurs in several mutually reinforcing ways: through people's existing social contacts or networks; through organizational resource of preexisting social institutions; and through highly energetic, visionary leaders. RM says that adherents are a major resource. As Klandermans and Oegema (1987, 520) remarked, "the motivation to participate is a function of the perceived costs and benefits of participation." The costs of joining decline and benefits rise if a person knows someone already in a movement. A "micro-mobilization" process occurs in which new adherents have friends already in a movement and interpersonal social networks are a major recruitment pathway. Also, a movement's organizational structure can facilitate or inhibit recruitment. Studies found that people joined the animal rights, antihunger, antinuclear, civil rights, farm labor, and women's movement through interpersonal networks.[33] Micro-level interpersonal networks facilitated recruitment in many times and places—to protests in nineteenth century France or prodemocracy movements in Eastern Europe and China in the late 1980s (see World View 6.1).[34]

The role of interpersonal networks on movement recruitment is illustrated in studies of very different movements. Snow, Zurcher, and Eckland-Olson

WORLD VIEW 6.1   **Worker Movements in Nineteenth Century France**

France was a center of several large-scale worker political uprisings during the nineteenth century. Although we often speak of *the* French Revolution, France had a series of revolutions. The Revolution of 1789 ended the long-established monarchy and was the peak of the revolutionary movements from 1787 to 1799. Yet there were also revolutions in 1830 and 1848, and the Paris Commune uprising of 1871. France saw the rise and fall of Napoleon, and the restoration and fall of the monarchy several times. Politics swung between collective uprisings by peasants and workers on one side, and wealthy aristocrats connected to the monarch and attempts by rising capitalists who fought to defend/restore their privileges on the other. The conflict was a result of "The process of statemaking affected French people's interests, and therefore stimulated popular collective action, when organization and political opportunity permitted . . ." (Tilly 1986, 396).

The Paris Commune was an insurrection by workers against the French government from March to May 1871. The Commune spread beyond Paris to other major cities, and during it, workers took charge of running the city and put into practice many of the ideals of socialism and communism. The Commune was defeated in a bloody battle in which 20,000 workers were killed (compared to about 750 government troops). After their defeat, another 38,000 workers were arrested. Despite the defeat, radical political ideas continued to circulate, and workers periodically engaged in protest. In the 1890s, French workers formed a nationwide labor organization that supported the principle of a general strike (i.e., all the workers in the entire nation would go on strike simultaneously for political and economic demands).

Karl Marx studied French politics. The 1871 Commune greatly influenced his thinking about the revolutionary potential of workers. Many political sociologists (Aminzade 1981, 1984, 1993; Hanagan 1980; Sewell 1980; Tilly 1986) studied French workers to understand how divergent groups in the working class joined and mobilized into a political movement. Not unlike the situation in many nations, French workers were sharply divided by trade/craft and held different political views (e.g., anarchist, socialist, republican).

The studies revealed that preexisting social ties among people and social networks were a critical factor in creating a movement. The networks and social solidarity arose through persistence of preexisting traditional communities, local working-class neighborhoods, or around labor exchange centers. For example, Roger Gould (1991, 1993) looked at participation in the Paris Commune and found that neighborhood social networks among workers were an important predictor of participation in urban uprisings. Preexisting social ties among neighbors helped to create a sense of solidarity that later became the basis for taking political action as a movement. During the period of politicized protest, workers overcame their divisions by trade or skill level because of their local informal social ties with friends, family, and neighbors.

Christopher Ansell (1997) looked at French workers in the 1880s and 1890s and found the workers divided by trade, skill level, and political beliefs. Like Gould, he found that social networks were important for building a political movement, but this time it was a network that grew up around local labor halls/lodging centers called *bourses du travail*. Skilled workers traveled from town to town and stayed at these centers that began to appear across France after 1886. In addition to providing lodging for workers of trades, the centers had libraries, offered classes, and were a meeting place for labor unions. They helped workers find jobs and assisted with travel funds.

In addition to social networks that bound people together, worker political mobilization required having ideas, symbols, and language that could enable workers to interpret their condition and around which they could rally (Sewell 1980). Common symbols could bring together workers with diverse backgrounds and interests. Ansell (1997, 384) noted that, "Symbols are not all equally powerful in their mobilizing potential nor is the same symbol equally powerful at all times. The symbol must provide a concrete way for its audience to perceive an abstract concept." In his study, Ansell (1997) found that the symbol of a general strike became a unifying force for the French workers. It was a dominant symbol that linked together many other ideas and condensed meaning in a way that evoked emotion, spoke to the needs and desires of many different people, and anchored people's common experiences. Workers rallied around this symbol and broke free of their competing loyalties to craft, locale, or party to join together as a united force.

(1980) examined recruitment into two Eastern religious sects in the United States—Nichiren Shoushu Buddhist movement and Hare Krishna—and found that Nichiren Shoushu used networks, but the Hare Krishna did not. They concluded that a movement's organizational structure can either encourage or diminish using interpersonal networks for recruitment. A closed organization that demands isolation and exclusive commitment to a communal life is less likely to use interpersonal networks than one with an open organizational structure and an engaged, nonexclusive focus. Klandermans and Oegema (1987) studied recruitment into the Dutch peace movement. They found that structural (i.e., interpersonal network) and cognitive (i.e., ideological commitment) factors affected recruitment. People who were committed to the movement's goals and had close friends or associates as participants were most likely to join.[35] McAdam and Paulsen (1993) looked at the 1964 Mississippi Freedom Summer Project. It was a campaign to bring hundreds of white, Northern college students to the South to register black voters and assist in struggles for racial equality. It was a high-risk activity; early in the summer prosegregationist whites and local law enforcement personnel kidnapped and killed three participants. The researchers found that successful recruitment fit four conditions: (1) someone had approached them in a specific recruitment attempt, (2) there was a clear link between a person's self-identity and the movement's goals, (3) social ties existed to others who were already involved in the movement, (4) and family and friends expressed little opposition.[36]

Beyond micro-mobilization processes, RM focuses on social movement organization (SMO) leaders and activists in mobilization. They see a role for the risk-taking, innovative entrepreneur who combines skills, time, and motivational vision.[37] **Movement entrepreneurs are individuals who seek to build and lead a movement organization by taking risks and investing a lot of time and energy.** Early RM theorists proposed that professionals external to an SMO acted as movement entrepreneurs, recruited, and organized people into an SMO.

Later studies discovered that entrepreneurs often differed from movement professionals. Movement entrepreneurs possess informal motivational skills and are indigenous to it; they initiate a movement. Movement professionals have formal organizational skills and arrive later; they help to maintain an established SMO.[38]

Early RM studies focused on rational cost-benefit calculations and structural–organizational factors. Over time, social identity and cultural factors from a constructionist approach (discussed later in this chapter), were added.

Resources   Resources are critical in RM theory. In addition to adherents (i.e., movement members/followers), a movement needs both tangible (e.g., money, office facilities, office supplies) and intangible (e.g., skills, media attention, legitimacy) assets. In general, movement success depends on the availability and quantity of discretionary resources. Despite the centrality of resources, Craig Jenkins (1983a, 533) noted, "little agreement exists on the types of resources that are significant." Indeed, Cress and Snow (1996, 1090) argued, "The resource concept is surprisingly slippery and vague given its ubiquity in the social movement literature . . . . The resource concept thus remains nearly as ambiguous as it did when it was introduced more than twenty years ago." In addition to needing a *quantity* of resources, movements need *diverse types* of resources: human, material, organizational, informational, financial, political, ideological, and moral. This raises the question of whether having sufficient amounts of particular types of resources is a critical factor at specific stages in movement development.[39]

The resources can be internal (self-generated) or external (from outsiders). A key question is: Does receiving external resources impose limits on movement activities?[40] "The most distinctive contribution of resource mobilization theory" according to Craig Jenkins (1993a, 533), "has been to emphasize the significance of outside contributions and the cooptation of institutional resources by contemporary social movements." External resources can be important, especially for movements of poor people, but they are not always overriding. Studies of the civil rights movement found that independent, indigenous local resources played a major role in movement growth.[41]

Two theses explain why SMOs that depend on external resources feel pressures to moderate or tame their political actions (i.e., employ noninflammatory rhetoric, use peaceful and nondisruptive tactics, maintain low visibility).[42] **The social control thesis states that external contributions to or elite patronage of radical movements places limits on movement actions and forces the movement to become more moderate.** This is because external elite groups try to control a movement, and their desire for control is an equal, if not more important motive for making contributions, than is any sympathy they have with movement goals. **The resource dependency thesis states that movement deradicalization associated with receiving external funds is an unintended consequence of an SMO becoming more bureaucratic and professional.** This thesis says that bureaucratic forces, not political control, channel SMO energies and resources in ways that moderate the tactics, goals, and rhetoric of a radical movement.[43] For example, establishment benefactors, such as major foundations, require regular meetings, standard accounting practices, a regularly employed staff, and a permanent office address.[44] However, some nonelite benefactors may encourage SMOs to be vocal and to engage in unruly actions to secure demands.

Organization   The RM approach borrows heavily from organizational sociology, and it treats the social movement organization (SMO) as a type of formal organization. **A SMO is a complex, formal organization that identifies its goals with those of a social movement.** Extending the SMO idea, RM approach also examines a social movement industry (SMI) and social movement sector.[45] An SMI parallels the concept of industry in economics; it includes all the SMOs that have goals aligned with a movement. Many movements have multiple SMOs (see the White Separatist movement discussed later in this chapter). A social movement sector consists of all the SMIs in a society—the area of the polity that involves movements. There are few studies of the social movement sector. It appears that in the United States it grew in size from the 1960s to the 1980s and competition among SMOs intensified for funding, members, and space on the public agenda, so they became specialized and turned to routine tactics.[46]

The concepts—SMO, SMI, and movement sector—suggest that they share the constraints that affect all formal organizations (e.g., need to maintain an organization, relation with competing SMOs). A formal organizational structure and professional staff confer both advantages and limitations. For example, SMOs that have a formal, bureaucratic structure with a professional, paid staff are more likely to survive and can more easily form coalitions. Yet many are more oriented toward maintaining the organization itself than advancing the movement's goals, and they are less likely to adopt radical, direct-action political tactics.[47]

Organizational sociology provided RM with many concepts and propositions and it included the implicit assumption that all SMOs adopt a similar bureaucratic form and that the form has a similar impact on all SMOs. Yet many SMOs try to limit centralization, restrict their size, reduce differences within the internal organizational hierarchy, and maintain democratic decision-making.[48] Formality and professionalism in an SMO can either inhibit or facilitate volunteer activism; it depends on other conditions.[49] For example, SMOs may adopt a specific legal form as a nonprofit entity for tax purposes, but the form can restrict its activities and create a dependency relationship. The dependency is less a function of the legal status than due to the type of external benefactors on which the SMO depends.[50] Nonetheless, a formal, professional SMO tends to be moderate. Jenkins and Eckert (1986, 827) found that, "Insofar as professional SMOs promote symbols of reform without substance, they may work against the development of powerful indigenous challenges."

Outcomes   A fundamental premise of RM is that the SMOs with more re-sources will be more successful. Yet specifying the meaning of "success" is difficult. One limitation of organizational concepts is that the standard goals of a business, such as selling more products or making higher profits, do not easily translate into achieving political goals. Also, a common measure of success is organizational survival, but the survival of an SMO that achieves few of its movement goals does not indicate its political success. An alternative measure of "success" could be to mobilize people or create a sense of solidarity among adherents. As Giugni (1999, xv) remarked, "the study of the consequences of social movements is one of the most neglected topics in the literature."

Movement success does not have a single, simple meaning. We need to consider five issues when defining the success of a movement.

1. We cannot just compare the explicit goals expressed by movement leaders against political outcomes, because movements are often heterogeneous with multiple, evolving goals. In addition, movement participants can hold diverse subjective meanings of movement goals and objectives that are not in the public statements of leaders. For example, all environmental movement adherents want a cleaner environment, but to some, this means widespread recycling and cleaner air and water, while to others it means eliminating genetically engineered foods, plastics, internal combustion engines, deforestation, and nuclear power.

2. If we focus exclusively on a movement's explicit intentions, we may overlook its many unintended positive and negative consequences. Charles Tilly (1999, 268) reminded us that, "Movements also leave political by-products that lie outside their programs and sometimes even contradict them: new police personnel and practices; the generation of rival movements and organizations; alterations in laws of assembly and association, and publication; co-optation of activists. . . ." Beyond narrow policy outcomes, movements can bring about broad collective benefits (e.g., improved conditions for the uninvolved population), increase solidarity or create new identities among mobilized people, and open up new forms of consciousness. A large-scale movement often triggers unintended consequences beyond its initial goals. We need to consider all outcomes on social groups and on the broader culture, as well as the durability over time.[50a]

3. While many reform movements try to alter the direction of a public policy, in some cases success occurs by altering the policymaking process itself. A comparison of two movements, illustrates the difference.[51] The nuclear freeze movement grew into one of the largest movements in U.S. history in the 1980s. An estimated 2,000 local freeze organizations existed across the country, polls showed 70 percent public support, referenda in support of it passed in 9 of 10 large states, and a profreeze demonstration attracted 750,000 in New York City in 1982. Within three years, Rochon and Mazmanian (1993, 83) observed, "the freeze movement rapidly collapsed . . . . Despite the massive support gained in the Cold War chill of the early 1970s, the freeze movement

soon melted without a trace." The movement lobbied Congress for its public goal—enacting a specific resolution. After bitter haggling over wording, Congress passed a vague resolution that had no effect on international diplomacy. Having achieved its public goal but incompletely, the movement collapsed. At about the same time, another protest movement arose over the handling and disposal of hazardous waste and toxic materials. Initially, movement activists tried to alter public policy, but they shifted to demand public involvement in the policy process. They wanted to "enable continuing intervention by movement activists in the myriad local siting, health, safety, and land use issues that constantly arise in the toxics area" according to Rochon and Mazmanian (1993, 84). Instead of new legislation, they sought formal involvement in implementing law. This brought movement activists into decentralized, democratic decisionmaking at all levels of government across the country. Using legal tactics, local publicity, and scientific information to block projects, the movement established new dispute resolution mechanisms in environmental agencies that included input from environmentalists.

4. Reform-oriented and radical SMOs may require different measures of success. Radical movement organizations differ in their internal structure, ideology, tactics, methods of communication, and measures of success. Radical SMOs, such as the Industrial Workers of the World (IWW) in the 1910s and the Student Nonviolent Coordinating Committee (SNCC) of the 1960s, did not have long-term organizational survival and failed to create new public policy. Yet they were highly successful in shifting the boundaries of thought, expanding public discourse, and widening the range of political action. They interjected new ideas that broke through the dominant hegemony. For a radical movement, this may be the best measure of its success.[52] Likewise, success may be in a movement's legacy that persists in institutions and public beliefs for a century after the SMO itself has disappeared. By opening up some political options and closing down others, a movement creates "path dependency." It sets a trajectory for future conditions. For example, the populist movement of late nineteenth century America advocated laws, rules, and regulations on business activities that altered the evolution of the modern corporation.

5. A movement's outcomes are not solely under its control. Outcomes depend on the concurrence of other events and the responses of other groups. For example, a movement may win new public pension benefits for the elderly. Yet securing the benefits could be due to the outbreak of war that occurred after the movement lost its effectiveness. Amenta and Young (1999b, 23) said methodologically, "researchers must ascertain what might have happened in its absence," be aware of better or worse alternatives, and evaluate the impact of a movement on the alternative adopted. In addition, movement outcomes may involve cooptation (i.e., a redirection of movement goals or resources to a different purpose). A different group might take a movement's symbols, members, or resources for its own purposes. For example, a local labor union

invests in helping the homeless to win positive publicity and more employment for its members instead of to reduce homelessness. Cooptation may allow a movement to expand rapidly and gain resources but at the cost of distorting or shifting the direction of its goals.

Example Movements

Next we look at four movements in the United States that make the RM ideas more concrete: white separatist, handgun control, anti-drunk driving, and the homeless. These movements are summarized in Chart 6.5. The first two (handgun control and anti-drunk driving) are highly visible, organized at the national level, comprised of middle-class adherents, and seek specific policy remedies. Both organize the victims of violent acts and adopt a strong moral stance. Although they are not as large or long-standing as some other movements (e.g., antiabortion, animal rights, environmental, women's, or the gay-lesbian movements), they illustrate features of a consensus movement. The other two conflict movements (white separatist and homeless) are not well known, less visible, fragmented into many local organizations, and have low-income or working class adherents. The white separatists want to reorganize the entire society, while homeless activists seek local improvements for beneficiaries. As Dobratz and Shanks-Meilie (1997, 2) observed in their study of white separatists, "little social scientific writing on the current movement exists. . . ." There are also few studies on the homeless movement, because it operates locally and does not have middle class adherents.[53]

Handgun Control Movement   The United States has few rules regarding gun ownership and high levels of gun-related violence. At the same time, a large majority of the public supports legal limitations on handguns. About one-fourth of U.S. men and 15 percent of women own pistols, but 71% of men and 86% of women favor gun control laws.[54] A national movement to expand legal controls over handguns began in 1974 with the founding of Handgun Control Incorporated (HCI). HCI has about 400,000 members who pay $15 in annual dues; it maintains a small office and a political action committee. In the 1970s, a coalition of religious and nonprofit groups formed a second organization, the National Coalition to Ban Handguns.[55] Handgun control is a consensus movement but faces intense resistance from a powerful countermovement whose adherents are ideologically committed. Consensus movements rarely rely on their members alone for resources, do not intensely engage followers, and cannot mobilize fully because of the free rider problem. The movement's broad public support limits its strategic repertoire, and it cannot antagonize the powerful institutions or groups on which it depends.

The leading countermovement organization to the handgun control movement is the National Rifle Association (NRA). The NRA was founded in 1871. For many years, it held moderate positions and was oriented toward marksmanship. In 1934 the National Firearms Act was introduced in the U.S. Congress to regulate machine gun sales and to require the registration of all handguns. The law was not enacted, but the NRA mobilized adherents to oppose the law's handgun provisions. It remained moderate "until the late 1970s," as Carter (1997, 67) explained "when it was expanded and solidified to the point where it was deemed that virtually all gun control regulations should be resisted." In 1977, the NRA shifted to a rigid anti-gun control stance. It became a major political force, opposing gun control legislation at the local and national levels. Gun control is visible in public debates and support rapidly expands in immediate response to nationally publicized shooting incidents. It is a hot issue in many election campaigns, but intense, well-organized NRA opposition has prevented the gun control movement from achieving most of its goals.

Anti-Drunk Driving Movement   Political sociologists have studied the cultural and political dimensions of alcohol drinking in the United States, where it is viewed as an ongoing social–moral problem requiring state controls. The anti-drunk driving movement is part of a larger, long-standing, antialcoholism movement.[56] SMOs focusing on drunk drivers appeared in the 1980s. This was not prompted by an increase in fatalities caused by drunk drivers. Rather, it was an individualist message consistent with a political shift to a retributionist orientation and a heightened use of victims rights rhetoric (see Chapter 9).[57]

Two anti-drunk driving SMOs developed—Remove Intoxicated Drivers (RID) and Mothers Against Drunk Drivers (MADD). MADD grew rapidly from 36 local groups in 1981 to 400 by 1986. The movement reached all but one state, and McCarthy and Wolfson (1996, 1073–1074) observed, "Local cadres established an outpost in almost every large community in the United States." It received significant national publicity and endorsements from politicians and celebrities. MADD adopted a federation organizational structure. In it, local chapters are "franchised" and must follow the mission and procedures of the national organization. MADD has been more successful than RID because it builds on its national visibility, makes greater use of leaders visiting local chapters, and has more structured organizational involvement to support its activism. By contrast, the smaller and the less visible RID adopted a grassroots, bottom-up organizational structure and receives little national publicity.

Anti-drunk driving is a consensus movement. It seeks broad public support, is not organized around serious structural social conflict, encounters no almost opposition, and is endorsed by official institutions. Like most consensus movements, it does not produce mass mobilization. Paradoxically, it is a movement with many resources but little mobilization. This is because according to Schwartz and Paul (1992, 211) "institutional support and constituent support are fundamentally different processes and require very different tools of analysis."

White Separatist Movement   Since the end of the U.S. Civil War in 1865, a movement that rejects the war's outcome and favors reasserting white's prewar power and influence has reappeared many times. Over the years, the movement grew or shrank in size, but its core base of adherents and major beliefs changed little. Today it is decentralized and fragmented into many small SMOs. The White Separatist Movement wants to reorganize American society along racial lines separating whites from others with whites dominating over others.[58] Its adherents oppose multiculturalism, racial integration, racial equality, and most civil rights legislation. The movements mobilized against the 1960s civil rights movement and formed countermovement SMOs. Some members have aligned themselves with specific Christian religious beliefs or neofascist movements. Since the movement opposes major public policies and legislation, engages in sporadic acts of violence, and has many adherents who are outside society's mainstream, the White Separatist movement is subject to government surveillance and derision in the mass media.

Homeless Movement   In the 1980s, the large numbers of homeless people in U.S. cities became a visible social issue. Shortly thereafter, a movement arose to advocate for improving conditions for people living on streets, in cars, and in public parks. Many cities have local SMOs for the homeless. They demand more shelters, greater public respect with less police harassment, and improved health and social services. A national SMO, the National Coalition for the Homeless, is a loose confederation of local SMOs with a small group of activists that presses for national-level action. At its peak, it assembled 250,000 homeless people and supporters in Washington DC in 1989.[59]

SMOs for the homeless face a major obstacle in obtaining resources, because the primary adherents and beneficiaries are indigent. The SMOs engage in short-lived, local protest campaigns, but their viability is tenuous because of both a scarcity of resources and their position as a conflict movement that targets a powerful opposition—city governments and the local business community. Major resources for homeless movement SMOs include moral support, basic supplies, office space, informational support, and volunteers. Most resources originate from outside the SMO or its direct beneficiaries. In their study of 15 SMOs, Cress and Snow (1996, 1105) found that "the bulk of resources acquired by 14 of 15 SMOs came from nonconstituent facilitative organizations." Homeless SMOs have effectively obtained tangible benefits for homeless people by using disruptive tactics, especially in situations where there is an irresponsible city government but some key local allies.

Political Process Approach

Political sociologists developed the *political process* (PP) approach more to extend than to reject the resource mobilization approach. PP focuses on the processes of collective action in a political struggle rather than on movement resources or the organizational structure of SMOs. While RM explains success/failure by looking to a movement's ability to attract resources, build organizations, and expand its base of supporters, PP adds the impact of the larger political environment to the explanation. PP explores how social or political structures facilitate or inhibit a

FOUR ILLUSTRATIVE MOVEMENTS

	White Separatist	Homeless
SMOs	*Core*: Aryan Nation, Ku Klux Klan, National Association for the Advancement of White People, White Aryan Resistance, and White Youth Alliance *Nazi Wing*: American Nazi Party, National Socialist Party of America, and White Aryan Legion *Skinhead Wing*: American Front, Chicago Area Skinheads, Hammerskins, and White American Skinheads *Christian Identity Wing*: Christian Defense League, Church of the Creator, Silent Brotherhood,and U.S. Christian Posse Association	Many local organizations, such as Boston Union of the Homeless, Detroit Union of the Homeless, Heads Up!, Homeless People United
Adherents	Predominately white working-class Protestants in small towns, geographically concentrated in the Southeast, Midwest, and Northwest	Homeless people and sympathetic middle class bystanders
Goals	Separate the races and increase the power of whites relative to other races	Achieve better material conditions, rights, and respect for homeless people
Resources	Financial donations from benefactors, volunteers	Social service and religious groups, charities, and volunteers
Tactics	Cross-burnings, rallies, marches, newsletters, physical assaults, religious meetings, rock music concerts, tax resistance, and Web sites	Marches, sit-ins, tent cities, lobbying, newsletters, legal incorporation as a charity
Counter-movement SMOs	Anti-Defamation League of B'nai B'rith, Center for Democratic Renewal, Klanwatch Project, and the Southern Poverty Law Center	None
Government Officials	See the movement as a threat and seek to control, suppress, or eliminate it through law enforcement and legal actions	Varies; sometimes support, generally indifference or hostility
Media Role	View the movement with hostility and emphasize the stereotype of a violent, unruly, uneducated mob	Varies, sympathetic or divisionary reports

Continued on page 254

c h a r t   6 . 5
CONTINUED

	Hand-Gun Control	Anti-Drunk Driving
SMOs	Handgun Control Inc., Coalition to Stop Gun Violence, Violence Policy Center	MADD (Mothers Against Drunk Driving), Remove Intoxicated Drivers (RID)
Adherents	Urban dwellers, political liberals, women, and health professionals	Middle-income educated women in suburbs and small towns
Goals	Reduce violence due to handgun ownership and use by enacting laws and strict regulations	Reduce traffic deaths and accidents due to alcohol use by enacting laws and providing education
Resources	Membership from mass mailings, endorsements from celebrities and professionals	Local chapters linked to a national organization office
Tactics	Legislative lobbying, letter-writing campaigns	Public Service Announcements, local talk shows, victim assistance
Counter-movement SMOs	Citizens Committee for the Right to Keep and Bear Arms, Gun Owners of America, National Rifle Association (NRA)	None (but there is some liquor-industry and tavern-owner resistance)
Government Officials	Divided support and opposition	Strong support
Media Role	Largely ignores the movement; some positive support	No opposition; generally supportive

Sources: On the hand gun movement see Carter (1997). On the anti-drunk driver movement see Gusfield (1981, 1996), McCarthy (1994), McCarthy and Wolfson (1996), Reinarman (1988), Weed (1989, 1990, 1991), and Wolfson (1995). On the white separatist movement see Barkun (1996), Blee (2002), and Dobratz and Shanks-Meile (1997). On the homeless movement see Cress (1997), Cress and Snow (1996, 2000), Wagner and Cohen (1991).

movement's ability to pursue power through collective action. Distinctions between the two approaches are subtle. For example, for RM social networks are a system of contacts that is an important resource to facilitate recruitment or activism in a movement. PP networks are a web of social relationships in which people have mutual understandings and shared experiences. This web is critical to the process of converting mutual understandings of those involved in a movement's activity into feelings of solidarity with other movement adherents.[60]

The PP approach holds that SMOs need meso-level mobilization (i.e., a community-level commitment) in addition to micro-mobilization processes of individual recruitment.[61] Community-based, face-to-face interaction and a shared identity become a basis for building challenger groups. Groups who staged eighteenth century French rebellions or twenty-first century American groups that blocked hazardous waste both used local social institutions (e.g., neighborhoods organizations, service clubs, churches) to foster communal ties. In contrast, the RM approach cannot easily explain some types of local protests (e.g., against a plant closing, against high property taxes), because it does not emphasize embedded community ties and a web of interpersonal relationships.

Critics say RM errs by trying to create a single theory that can explain all movements, from conventional political movements that are more like interest groups to radical protest movements or mass insurgency.[62] Thus, it best explains SMOs such as the Sierra Club, Common Cause, NAACP, NOW, or the ACLU that became bureaucratic and focus on lobbying officials, contacting the media, preparing reports, and soliciting funds. Critics also believe that RM relies too much on economic analogies. For example, it sees movement adherents as consumers and movement leaders as managers who sell a product (e.g., ideas, goals) in the political marketplace. As SMO competition intensifies, SMO managers direct their efforts to raise more funding and satisfy "customers." This makes the RM approach better suited for consensus movements and less appropriate for radical challenger-protest movements.

The PP approach recognizes movements that originate outside the polity and only enter it after many years of struggle by using unconventional political tactics. As they initially begin to form outside the polity, long-standing social attachments and common beliefs are critical for movement survival. The movements emerge within an organizational environment and develop a resource base in a dynamic, interactive process with multiple actors. A movement's growth, vitality, and success depend on strategic choices made by movement participants and leaders. Because elite actions can damage or facilitate a movement, PP includes elite, state, or police responses to a movement as part of the explanation of a movement's success or failure.[63] Government repression and unfavorable political conditions may increase the chances that a movement will demobilize and withdraw from collective action or its efforts backfire (see World View 6.2).[64] Likewise, one movement's actions can spill over to affect another movement, with movements sharing adherents, ideas, tactics, or identities.[65] Movements may develop one of several organizational forms to deal with collective action concerns; the forms are templates or scripts for action that become part of an organizational repertoire that movements adopt under different situations or share with others.[66]

The RM approach emphasizes structural factors internal to a movement.[67] By contrast, the PP approach looks at the broader political conditions that surround a movement.[68] Doug McAdam (1982) initiated the political process approach in his study of the struggle of U.S. blacks for equality between the 1930s and 1970s. He saw the movement as a long, continuous process rooted in the constant interplay between environmental conditions and movement factors.

Over time the study of movements shifted from looking at individual participants and crowd situations, to examining the structure of an SMO and its ability to obtain resources, to looking at the whole political environment in which a movement emerges, develops, and operates.

WORLD VIEW 6.2   Iran's Revolution and Patterns of Protest

The 1979 Iranian Revolution transformed the country from a secular-modernizing path to a fundamentalist Islamic theocratic state under Ayatollah (i.e., spiritual leader) Ruholla Khomeini. Iran has a complex history. In the early 1950s, it was led by a popular left-leaning government that had plans to nationalize the oil industry. In 1953, the government forced the hereditary monarch Mohammad Reza Pahlavi, the shah (emperor), who had led a right-wing regime during the 1940s out of the country. The Shah had come from a long line of royalty that could be traced back to the 1500s of ancient Persia (the name of Iran until 1934). Shortly thereafter, to protect Western oil interests and to counter left-wing politics in the region, the United States and British intelligence agencies (the CIA and MI5 respectively) sponsored a coup/military operation that overthrew the elected government and brought the Shah back into power.

The Shah was an absolute dictator who was friendly to Western interests. He curbed some traditional elites to help small farmers and pursued policies for rapid westernization and economic growth. He also ruled with a cruel internal secret police force (SAVAK) and spent billions of dollars buying Western military weapons. After 26 years in power, a religious-nationalist revolution forced him to flee in 1979. In November 1979, revolutionary militants stormed the U.S. Embassy in Tehran and took 70 Americans captive. This triggered a 444-day hostage crisis for Jimmy Carter's presidency and helped bring President Ronald Reagan to power. The Reagan administration quickly ended the hostage crisis through secret negotiations that involved some illegal activities. Shortly after the end of the hostage crisis, the eight-year Iran-Iraq war (1980–1988) began. In the war, Iraq had 375,000 casualties and 60,000 were taken prisoner. Iran's losses are estimated at over 1 million killed or maimed. At the end of the war, conditions remained almost unchanged

from their prewar status. Iraq won the war militarily but without a real victory. Just two years later, Iraq invaded Kuwait to trigger the 1991 Persian Gulf War. This contributed to events that ultimately led to the 2003 U.S. invasion of Iraq.

Political sociologists have studied the political dynamics of the Iranian 1979 revolution. The Shah's land reform program was a push for industrialization but it caused an agricultural decline and a large-scale migration to urban areas where many ex-farmers relied on menial jobs. The jobs disappeared during oil gluts in the early 1970s creating massive urban unemployment (Amjad 1993). The industrialization policies contributed to the growth of secular urban professionals, but the Shah suppressed their demands for democracy. The policies also offended traditional religious leaders, who spread a fundamentalist religious ideology among recently arrived urban workers. The Shah's policies also offended small-scale traditional merchants who supported political change but did not favor a fundamentalist religious ideology. The theocratic state was the outcome of clashes among competing factions after the revolution (Parsa 1995).

Prior to the revolution the Iranian state was powerful and used brutal repression, but state repression can have unintended effects on protest. Rasler (1996) noted that its short-term (one week) effect was to reduce levels of protest, but it had a long-term (six week) positive impact of diffusing protest geographically. The repression had the unintended effect of expanding micro-mobilization (i.e., individuals joining of the protest movement) for many reasons, including its harsh measures against some opponents (i.e., secular, university-based) while sparing a few others (e.g., social networks around local markets, mosques). She argues (1996, 149) that a resource mobilization approach fails to adequately incorporate the "tactical moves and countermoves among contending parties. . . ." The intergroup dynamics among several groups in a rapidly changing conflict situation can produce unanticipated results (e.g., repression ends up accelerating protest) that do not follow from the levels of the state's or protester's resources alone.

Kurzman (1996) noted that the Iranian Revolution is an example of a mismatch between the structural conditions for revolution (e.g., political power, organizational capacity, resources) and the subjective perceptions of the population. In 1978 shortly before the revolution, the Iranian state and the Shah's forces were very powerful and the population was fearful. Quickly, in a cycle of rapidly rising protest and intensifying government repression, a large section of the population (e.g., urban secular intellectuals, merchants, workers) overcame their fear and shifted their support to the protesting opposition. This mass shift in favor of the revolutionaries arose from a belief that the government could not crush them, and it became self-fulfilling. Thus, a massive change in people's perceptions and beliefs about protest can alter the political opportunity structure in ways that affect the outcome of protest movements.

Three Key Concepts

Three concepts are central in a PP explanation: (1) organizational readiness, (2) insurgent consciousness or "cognitive liberation," and (3) political opportunity structure.

Organizational Readiness   The first concept is closest to the RM approach. **Organizational readiness includes the organizational resources of potential movement members.** Readiness may develop over a long period. It is the accumulation of resources within a favorable political environment that improves a group's bargaining position. Preexisting, indigenous organizations can be important for readiness. For example, the black church was critical for the development of the U.S. civil rights movement. McAdam (1982, 43–48) saw existing organizations as offering the movement four resources:

1. Members—People who already belong to an organization and have a web of associations and interactions out of which a new movement can grow.
2. Solidarity Incentives—The "free rider" problem can be overcome by "appropriating" the solidarity incentives that people have formed with an existing organization.
3. Communication Network—An existing infrastructure of contact and information sharing speeds and spreads news.
4. Leaders—Individuals who developed skills, knowledge, reputation, and recognition in one organizational setting can transfer those resources to a new, emerging movement.

Cognitive Liberation   A second concept injects a subjective-symbolic dimension and adds emotions, beliefs, and ideas to the objective structural resources and political conditions. Insurgent consciousness, also called **cognitive liberation, is a transformation in the beliefs of an aggrieved population such that people collectively come to redefine existing relations and see a potential to significantly restructure political, economic, or social relations.** A successful movement, especially by people near the bottom of society who are engaging in protest, requires a shift in understandings and what people believe to be possible. People must collectively come to share a new vision and attach new meanings to events. Bert Klandermans (1991, 8) noted that "grievance interpretation" is a critical process; multiple possible interpretations of people and events are possible, and the "interpretations of reality rather than reality itself guide political actions." Speaking of the civil rights movement, Aldon Morris (1999, 523) observed, "The existence of favorable conditions does not guarantee that collective action will materialize. Agency is required for such action to occur. People must develop an oppositional consciousness that provides them with a critique of the status quo and reasons to believe that acting collectively will lead to change."

Political Opportunity Structure   Later researchers elaborated on the third concept central in the PP approach. **Political opportunity structures are shifts in the political environment that affect the relative balance of power between elite and challenger groups and provide openings during the course of events that allow challenger groups to advance.** Political Opportunity Structures (POS) include elite cleavages, shifts in political institutions, and new opportunities to form coalitions among protest groups. For example, Piven and Cloward (1992, 321) used POS when they observed that lower class protest movements "tend to emerge at junctures when larger societal changes generate political volatility and realignment and new political possibilities [and] disruptive protest itself makes an important contribution to elite fragmentation and electoral dealignment." They discussed two related ideas, a "crisis situation" that alters an event's meaning and significance, and a "triggering event" that is of little significance in isolation, but that can profoundly accelerate or dampen a movement under particular conditions.

The POS varies across time and space. For example, Elisabeth Clemens (1997, 67–81) observed that opportunities to improve women's working conditions in the early twentieth century United States varied widely by geographic region. She argued that the U.S. federal structure constituted a distinctive political opportunity structure—political conditions in each state affected movement success, plus movement success or failure in a nearby state also affected opportunities. In studies of the women's suffrage movement, civil rights movement, farm worker unrest, and protest by the unemployed in the United States, the appearance of an "opening" or opportunity at a specific point in time proved critical.[69]

Later researchers added the idea of tactical innovation (i.e., that movements develop new tactics and draw upon a repertoire of tactics from other movements or countermovements.[70] **Tactical innovation is part of the interactive process between movements and authorities or countermovements in which**

a movement invents new tactics because old ones are no longer effective. As part of the protest process, a SMO creates, borrows, and modifies political tactics to express its demands. Political authorities, other powerful organizations, or countermovements may be caught off guard at first, but they adapt and try to render the new tactic ineffective. In response, the SMO innovates and uses a new tactic. Jeffrey Broadbent (1998, 360) noted that, "tactics mirror the structured weakness of the political opportunity structure," so tactics and the POS are contingent and fit together.

For example, an SMO invents the tactic of a sit-in. At first, it is highly effective. Yet, over time, its surprise impact fades and opponents neutralize its effect. The SMO then shifts to other tactics (e.g., the economic boycott). Shifts into the legal arena and litigation can be forms of tactical innovation.[71] This illustrates how the political process of a movement is dynamic and interactive. A variation on tactical innovation is venue shifting. **Venue shifting occurs when an SMO or its opponents change the level of government or geographic location for activities to better advance goals or defend a position.** An SMO may use a tactic in one setting (e.g., a clinic) and then shift to another (e.g., shopping malls) or apply a tactic at one level of government (local) and then shift to another (e.g. national) in a gamelike interaction with opposing forces or authorities.[72]

The PP approach also recognizes that different dynamics may govern different stages of a movement—its emergence, development, and decline. A factor may be present at each stage but may operate differently depending on the stage. For example, organizational readiness may become the capacity to develop and sustain an organization while avoiding problems such as oligarchization. Insurgent consciousness may become an ability to attribute problems to external forces. The political opportunity structure may involve changes in the environment that are in part created by the emergence of the SMO (see Figure 6.1 for a model of the PP approach).

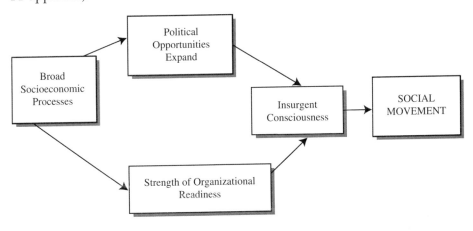

Figure 6.1
Political process model of movement emergence.
Source: Figure 3.1 in McAdam (1982, 51).

Refining the Concept of Political Opportunity Structure

Sidney Tarrow (1994, 85–86) argued that POS is a central concept that "helps us to understand why movements sometimes gain surprising, but temporary leverage against elites or authorities and then quickly lose it despite their best efforts [and] how mobilization spreads from people with deep grievances and strong resources to those in very different circumstances." Yet political sociologists also have criticized the concept's looseness and lack of specificity. As McAdam (1996, 24) remarked, "the widespread adoption and general seductiveness of the concept carries with it its own dangers." Gamson and Meyer (1996, 273) went further to say POS is "in danger of becoming a sponge that soaks up virtually every aspect of the social movement environment. . . . It threatens to become an all-encompassing fudge factory for all the conditions and circumstances that form the context for collective action."

If we can trace the POS idea back to Eisinger (1973) who referred to "open" versus "closed" city government structures and Tilly (1978) who discussed the role of repressive or nonrepressive national governments, we see that the POS includes state structure and actions. A state that has an open structure will allow public access and be nonrepressive; it offers more opportunities for movements than a state with a "closed structure" that blocks access and responds with repression.[73] State strength and capacity also affect the POS. Stronger states offer fewer opportunities than weaker states. Electoral conditions are also part of the POS. Highly competitive elections and periods of electoral realignments provide more opportunities. The structure of the dominant class and of movement allies can affect the POS significantly. Multiple or divided elites, and strong allies offer greater opportunities. A multiorganizational field of many SMOs tends to offer more opportunities.[74] Researchers have not exhausted looking into how aspects of the POS affect various types of movements or specific movement activities.[75] An illustration of the importance of POS is provided in Kriesi and Wisler's (1999) study of direct democracy (i.e., public referendums). They argued that a weak state institutional structure (i.e., less state capacity) and divided political elites were critical features of the POS in the United States and Switzerland. In both situations, the POS allowed the referendum to spread.[76]

The POS operates along two dimensions: state versus nonstate sector and stable versus transient factors. Stable factors are structural and fixed over time. Transient factors appear for only a short time (see Chart 6.6). Features of the state include the following: the state structure has open vs. closed access, critical elections with open competition versus closed elections, a competitive vs. noncompetitive party system, the degree of repression, and the presence of foreign threat. Opportunities are greatest under open state structure, critical elections with intense competition, the competitive party system, low repression, and no foreign threat. They are also greater with a divided elite power structure, many allies and related SMOs, weak countermovements, a diverse mass media, a strong civic culture, and international supporters.

In addition to the state/nonstate and stable/transient dimensions, Koopmans and Statham (1999a, 1999b) argued that POSs operate at two levels: institutional

---

c h a r t   6 . 6

CONDITIONS THAT EXPAND THE POLITICAL OPPORTUNITY STRUCTURE AND ARE FAVORABLE FOR CHALLENGER MOVEMENTS

State Sector	Stable Factors	Transient Factors
State access/structure	Open, federal/multivenue	Newly created
Elections	Open	Critical/contested/realigning
Party system	Competitive multiparty	Divided parties
Repression	Low level, declining	Contested from below
Foreign affairs	No major threat	Outside distraction

Nonstate Sector	Stable Factors	Transient Factors
Power structure	Disorganized structure	Internal elite conflicts
Many allies/SMOs	Active, share support/ideas	Active, share support/ideas
Countermovements	Present and active, but weak	Weakened, declining
Mass media	Decentralized, pluralistic, autonomous	Open phase of attention cycle
Civic culture	Strong, public spaces exist	Increased openness
International sphere	Allies provide indirect support	Allies provide direct support

Sources: Amenta and Zylan (1991), Diani (1996), Gamson and Meyer (1996), Kerbo and Shaffer (1992), Kischelt (1986), Koopmans and Statham (1999a, 1999b), Kriesi et al. (1997), Kriesi and Wisler (1999), Maney (2001), McAdam (1996), Meyer and Staggenborg (1996), Rucht (1996), and Tarrow (1994).

and discourse. Both are necessary for a movement to have a major impact. At the level of discourse, a media opportunity structure is important.[77] Mass movements rely on the media to communicate with followers and potential supporters, to counter their opponents, and to make their ideas known to government officials and the larger public. The media can ignore, silence, marginalize, or trivialize a movement, its ideas and actions; or it can be sympathetic and present the point-of-view of movement activists. Greater opportunities exist when the mass media are diverse and pluralistic organizationally, have divided ownership and weak coordination, are not under direct state control with imposed uniformity, and are highly autonomous with professional journalists who have strong norms of independence and diversity.

Amenta and associates expanded the POS concept with the idea of "political mediation" to explore the interaction between the POS and SMO resources. They illustrated the concept in studies of the Townsend Movement (see Case in Point 6.2).[78] In the political mediation model, mobilized resources and specific opportunities in the environment interact to allow resource mobilization that would not occur in the absence of the political opportunities. Thus, movements are most successful where/when a favorable POS combines with abundant resources.

CASE IN POINT 6.2   **Townsend Movement Success and Political Mediation**

Dr. Francis Townsend, a physician concerned about many destitute elderly people, launched a movement in 1934 in California that quickly spread nationally. It grew to 3,000 local clubs (with 150 members each) in 1935 and 7,000 clubs (with 300 members each) in 1936. Townsend advocated a national pension plan with immediate, adequate pensions for all citizens over the age of 60 that would be funded by a "pay-as-you-go" sales tax. Instead of his plan, the U.S. Congress passed the Old Age Assistance and Old Age Insurance provisions of the Social Security Act. Social Security was mixed assistance for the poor and insurance that paid low pensions based on prior wage levels. It did not cover all people and was funded by payroll taxes. Although it was less generous, the Social Security Act undercut the Townsend Plan, and by 1950, the movement was dead. In a narrow sense, the movement failed because its specific plan was not adopted.

Yet by forcing a national assistance plan for the elderly, it delivered "collective benefits" and improved the condition of a large section of the population. The Townsend movement had greater success in geographic areas with structural opportunities (i.e., where voting laws and political party structures were more open) and under favorable political conditions (e.g., larger public service bureaucracies, liberal Democratic Party was stronger). The movement shows that a simple resource mobilization approach is inadequate. It compares movement goals to outcomes and expects mobilized movement resources to produce success. This case suggests expanding the RM model to incorporate all movement consequences and recognizing how political opportunities *mediate* the relationship between a movement's resources and its impact, i.e., opportunities shape how and whether a movement can use resources effectively.

Sources: Amenta, Cattruthers, and Zylan (1992), Amenta and Zylan (1991), and Quadagno (1988).

The International Dimension

Political sociologists are just starting to examine seriously the international dimension of movements. Jenkins and Schock (1992, 180) noted that few theories of movements have examined the international dimension, and "Their strength has been in accounting for collective action in terms of the mobilization of specific groups and the changing structure of political opportunities." Consideration of the international dimension of movements involves three issues: (1) diffusion across borders, (2) factors within one nation, and (3) global social movements.[79]

The first issue is how a movement in one nation can have effects that cross national borders. This includes coordinating movement actions across multiple national settings and the mutual influence of movements in different nations on one another. Most studies focused on a single SMO or single movement, while a few considered linkages among several movements in a single nation. But very few considered multiple movements across different nations. This issue involves two processes: (1) transnational advocacy networks and (2) diffusion. Transnational advocacy networks develop when separate SMOs in several nations share similar goals and establish links to one another by exchanging individuals, tactics, and information. Thus, the networks connect the separate national SMOs. For example,

Keck and Sikkink (1998, 230) observed, "The idea of 'violence against women' as a global issue did not initially exist. Instead activists campaigned independently around different practices: against rape and domestic battery in the United States and Europe, female genital mutilation in Africa, female sexual slavery in Europe and Asia, dowry death in India, and torture and rape of political prisoners in Latin America." The network to combat violence against women emerged in the late 1980s and 1990s through a series of international meetings that brought together women's groups from diverse nations. Interactions among national women's organizations, the United Nations, major charities, and academic institutions helped build a global network around a common goal. A second process is international diffusion. Movement activists in one nation learn of the activities of SMOs in other nations through international media and personal contact. Researchers observed a pattern in which movements arise at the same time in several nations without explicit coordination. In addition, ideas, tactics, organizational forms, and even movement activists diffuse across national borders. For example, many nations have indigenous people, sometimes called Fourth World or First Nation people (e.g., Yanomami of Brazil; Shuar and Quichuas in Ecuador; Maori of New Zealand; aboriginals of Australia; Native Americans, Inuit, and native Hawaiians in the United States; Ainu of Japan). The United Nations notes there are 300 million indigenous people in more than 70 countries. The indigenous people in one nation have begun to have contact with, learn ideas about political organization, and share their demands for human rights with groups in other nations. Yet systematic explanations and theorizing of these patterns have barely begun.[80]

A second issue is the impact of international forces on movements in one nation. As McAdam (1996, 34) observed, "movement scholars have, to date, grossly undervalued the impact of *global* political and economic processes in structuring the *domestic* possibilities for successful collective action" [emphasis in original]. The specific national context is a well-recognized and important part of the POS. Kitschelt (1986, 84) compared the antinuclear movement in Sweden, France, West Germany, and the United States and found that different domestic political opportunities in each nation shaped movement success. Kriesi et al. (1997, 64) compared movements in the Netherlands, Germany, France, and Switzerland and concluded that, "the most relevant level of the POS is the national one."[81]

Political sociologists recognize that the political institutions of a nation-state are central to the POS but are less certain about how international conditions or pressures affect the POS and influence domestic movements. For example, international pressures may facilitate a division among domestic elites, weaken a supporting ally, diminish a nation's repression, or encourage the opening of state access. Doug McAdam (1998) and John Skrentny (1998) argued that international criticism and pressures over racial segregation and discrimination in the 1950s and 1960s helped shift the POS in the United States and create an opening for the civil rights movement. In the context of Cold War international competition, racial practices in the U.S. tarnished its professed image of promoting equality and democracy.

A third issue is the rise of global social movements (GSM). O'Brien et al. (2000, 12) noted, "A global social movement is one which operates in a global, as well as local, national and international space." Some movement organizations are global (e.g., Amnesty International, Green Peace) while others are nationally based but have a global scope (e.g., women, labor, environment). Globalization processes in the 1990s brought about a growth of multinational corporations, multinational economic coordinating organizations, and international agencies. It also increased the interaction between GSMs and transnational organizations. Thus, a global elite organization, such as the World Bank, repeatedly counters GSMs from the women's movement, such as Development Alternatives with Women for a New Era. As O'Brien et al. (2000, 224) observed, "one can discern the emergence of a distinct section of the GSM community with the inclination and the ability to engage MEI's [multi-lateral economic institution] on an ongoing basis." Globalization raises questions about the practice of only looking at movements, their constituencies, movement goals, and the forces that shape them within national borders. Just as the rise of the nation-state in the late eighteenth and early nineteenth centuries changed politics and gave rise to the movement as a new form of political expression, the early twenty-first century globalization may force changes in how we think about movements and political dissent. For example, Bleiker (2000, 2) argued, "Dissent has become a significant transnational phenomenon . . . *transversal* phenomenon—a political practice that not only transgresses national boundaries, but also questions the spatial logic through which these boundaries have come to constitute and frame the conduct of international relations" [emphasis in original].

Cycles of Protest and Abeyance

The levels of protest and degree of movement activism are uneven across time. Movements emerge and expand in clusters; that is, many appear in a short time period. **A cycle of protest is when protest follows a pattern of expansion and decline; unrest and protest begin, spread, peak, and fade.** In a short time, the number of SMOs, level of activity, pace of tactical innovation, intensity of conflict, geographic scope, areas of society involved, new political ideas offered, and number of people in movements all expand very rapidly. A political "opening" occurs at the peak allowing a major, broad-based redirection of politics, but it only lasts for a few years then fades.[82] The observation of waves of activity reinforces the idea that there are several SMOs in one movement, and that different movements with similar goals have a mutually reinforcing positive effect upon one another.

Sidney Tarrow (1988, 1991, 1994) studied the waves or cycles of protest. He argued that transient openings in the POS explain the cyclical expansion of protest and movements. Although protest and movements grow because new ideas and tactics diffuse, an opening in the POS explains the timing and pattern of protest cycles. Other factors that build a broad wave of protest include: new popular expectations about what movements can accomplish, increased flows of resources due to a greater density of SMOs, the creation of many experienced movement activists, the sharing of information among various movements, and expanded legitimacy for new forms of political activity.[83] The cyclical pattern suggests that a protest movement can persist across decades or over centuries under varied political conditions. After a period of expansion and success, it may face hostility or indifference, but instead of dying out or disappearing entirely the movement may shrink in size and temporarily submerge. During these quiet periods, the movement can preserve its core ideals with a few resources. In a sense, it is waiting until conditions change and new political opportunities improve. It may adopt a hibernation strategy or abeyance structure during these times. **Abeyance refers to a period of time when a social movement ceases but does not disappear.** For example, the movement for women's equality in the United States has persevered for over a century. For periods of a decade or longer, it declined and ceased to be a mass movement. Yet it survived through periods of public hostility, such as the 1950s, with a small number of alienated, marginalized, and isolated but committed adherents. During abeyance, the movement became more centralized and less inclusive. It preserved a distinct set of values and beliefs, held onto a skeletal activist network, sustained its goals and tactics, and maintained a collective identity. The movement reactivated, with some modification, during a resurgence phase at another time. Abeyance enables a movement to continue and reappear, but often the movement pays in terms of lost adherents, the stagnation or a reversal of movement goals, and missed opportunities.[84]

The abeyance process offers us three insights. First, it encourages us to adopt a long-term view of movements. Movements can rise and expand to prominence, then fall and shrink to near invisibility, only to rise again and assume slightly different forms. Second, abeyance highlights the dynamic interaction that develops between a movement and the larger political environment. It shows that a movement can continue under an unfavorable POS. Lastly, abeyance focuses our attention on the cultural dimension. It highlights how movements can transform the identities of individual people. A person's involvement in a movement can profoundly alter his or her entire outlook, core values, and sense of self. Many people who become active in movements undergo a significant inner change. In addition to offering a set of beliefs, interpretations and values, movements can shape how adherents understand themselves and their place in the world. This continues after protest peaks. For example, several visible leaders of 1960s leftist protest movements renounced their views and embraced conservative politics in the 1980s. Despite intense media attention on the few outspoken leaders, many thousands of 1960s movement participants had a different experience. Studies have documented that movement involvement had an impact that lasted throughout the lifetime of participants.[85] Later in life, 1960s activists differed from others. They remained more politically active, were less conventional and conformist (i.e., less likely to marry, had lower incomes), and maintained values consistent with their earlier political activity. Summarizing 20 years of research, Doug McAdam (1999, 122) observed, "They have continued not only to voice the political values they espoused in the 1960s but to act on those values as well." In follow up research he found that 1960s activists maintained many values and life-course changes, but the impact weakened with the cohorts that followed them. Thus, movement involvement can produce a self-transformation and facilitate the construction of a new self-identity among followers. After the movement fades, few adherents change back, forget their experience, and completely rejoin society's mainstream.

Researchers who adopted the RM and PP approaches emphasized the structural side of movements. They did not ignore beliefs, movement culture, or self-identity, but these factors were never central in their analyses. The constructionist approach puts cultural issues at the center of its analysis. We examine it next.

Constructionist Approach

The constructionist approach (CA) on movements is part of the broader constructionist theory that appeared in the 1980s as a synthesis of trends in social psychology and social problem theory.[86] Both constructionists and the new social movement approach (to be discussed later in this chapter), view movements as being simultaneously political and cultural phenomena and emphasize symbols, ideas, culture, media, subjectivity, emotion, and self-identity.

The CA argued that unfavorable objective conditions can continue indefinitely until or unless people interpret/reinterpret the conditions as being unacceptable. People only accept the necessity of protest and join a movement after they develop certain understandings of conditions. Since understandings and meanings develop by interacting with others and by using interpretative frames, the interactions/frames determine whether grievances emerge. The RM approach says conditions create grievances that are constant, and grievances trigger protest when organization and resources become available.[87] By contrast, the CA says social conditions are open to multiple interpretations, and they only become a source of grievances if, and when, people come to assign certain meanings to them.

Political sociologists who use the CA criticize the RM and PP approaches for giving insufficient weight to the ideological dimension.[88] Klandermans (1992, 77) noted that the RM and PP approaches "did not take into account mediating process through which people attribute meaning to events and interpret situations." People do not experience conditions of the social world in a direct, unmediated manner; instead, they rely on cultural beliefs, interpretative frames, and idea systems. CA theorists also question the rational choice assumptions about individual motivation used by the RM and PP approaches. Instead of a mechanical, straightforward, and rational process of decision-making, the CA views individuals as structurally located in a web of social relations, organizational settings, and cultural contexts that profoundly shape their perceptions and values as well as their ability to act on the perceptions and values. The relations in which a person is enmeshed and the symbolic-ideational contexts that she/he regularly experiences shape the perceptions and values. The relations/contexts are in motion and are constantly shaping and reshaping individual perceptions and emotional responsiveness.[89]

The CA holds that a movement's ability to alter perceptions of reality is often critical to its success. It is similar to, but goes beyond the idea of insurgent consciousness. Changing people's understandings of conditions and what they believe to be possible can be just as important as altering the objective, material conditions of society. Snow and Benford (1992, 136) argued that a movement must engage ". . . in the production and maintenance of meaning for constituents, antagonists, and bystanders or observers." For CA, a major task of movements is to change how people see the world and to transform individual identities. New ideas, identities, and symbols, not just new policy achievements, can change political discourse and events for generations to come. Aldon Morris (1992, 369) remarked, "In the past, RM analysts developed a framework that brought the structural side of social movement activity into clear focus. The social-psychological-cultural aspect . . . was either underdeveloped or thought to be analytically non-problematic. But it makes little sense to deny the importance of culture, ideology, symbols, media framing, collective identities, and meaning construction in the origins and outcomes of collective action."

It is easy to overstate the cultural-subjective vs. structural-objective divide between CA and other approaches. The CA views objective and subjective dimensions as mutually reinforcing one another. It does not believe that symbolic-subjective change alone is enough. "One may win the battle of words while practices remain unchanged or even change for the worse," observed William Gamson (1998, 65). Objective conditions affect perceptions and vice versa. Doug McAdam (1994, 39) said, "It is extremely hard to separate these objective shifts in political opportunities from the subjective processes of social construction and collective attribution . . . The causal importance of expanding political opportunities, then is, inseparable from the collective definitional process by which the meaning of these shifts is assigned and disseminated." The CA uses several concepts to explain movements: movement frames, oppositional cultures, and movement identities. We will examine each next.

Movement Frames

The movement frame is the single most influential idea in the CA.[90] Movements and other collective actors can advance a frame or schemata of interpretation. Erving Goffman (1974, 21) noted that a frame "allows its user to locate, perceive, identify and label a seemingly infinite number of concrete occurrences." A frame is a type of cognitive tool or resource.[91] Frames "are ways of organizing thinking about political issues. One should ask not whether they are true or false . . . but about their usefulness in increasing understanding and their economy and inclusiveness in providing a coherent explanation of a diverse set of facts," according to William Gamson (1992a, 71). **A movement frame is a cognitive scheme that a movement creates and disseminates; it organizes thinking, interprets events, and guides action.** A frame has embedded assumptions, beliefs, and values. It offers a definition of the situation that organizes how a person comes to understand, makes sense of, and interprets events. It does this by highlighting and accentuating certain features of events, while downplaying others.

In this way, it directs a person to draw inferences and connect one situation to others or to past events. Frames can alter the form and direction of interpretations, affect perceptions, and shape the discourse of officials, followers, opponents, supporters, and bystander publics.

Movements are not the only providers of frames. Many groups, organizations, and institutions provide frames, so there are media frames, government agency frames, corporate frames, and so forth. Major institutions, such as schools, mass media outlets, government agencies, corporate public relations departments, have special departments to construct, refine, maintain, and apply frames.[92] These frames usually support the hegemonic or dominant version of social reality, and they tend to reinforce an elite perspective on events. People use the frames to render ambiguous situations or events meaningful and expect authoritative sources to engage in framing. Frames help people make sense of the world by answering these questions: What happened? Is it important? What does it mean? For example, hours after the September 11, 2001 World Trade Center attack, top U.S. government officials had to frame the event for the public. The initial media frame was that it was an airplane accident. This was quickly dropped as events unfolded. The issue became, should officials frame it as the horrible act of a handful of solitary terrorists and unlikely to reoccur, or should they frame it as the first salvo in a far-reaching, full-scale global war by a menacing, formidable, concealed enemy seeking to destroy Western civilization? The event's meaning was unclear and few facts were available. The interpretation they picked would shape public perceptions of the event and limit or facilitate their future actions.

Frames help to make the rapid, chaotic flow of events meaningful. They organize experience and simplify the world. Movement frames are similar to a scientific paradigm—they organize knowledge, provide questions, resist change, and point to the future.[93] Movement frames also mobilize potential adherents. A frame is more than an ensemble of individual attitudes, beliefs, and perceptions; it is a system of overlapping affective, cognitive, and discursive elements that has been actively created by interaction and negotiation. The verb *framing* indicates that constructing meaning is a task and dynamic process. It involves contestation, reflection, and effort (see Summary 6.2).

Master Frames and Aligning Processes A master frame is a generic, broad frame that subsumes specific collective active frames of a movement by being less restrictive and more comprehensive. Master frames bring movements together. They are broad in scope, inclusive, flexible and have cultural resonance (discussed later in this chapter). Collective action master frames build on preexisting themes in the larger culture. For example, in the contemporary United States, they may include a rights theme, a personal choice theme, a pluralism theme, and a descent into immoral behavior theme. The antiabortion movement frames itself as a moral crusade to save unborn children, its "abortion-is-murder" theme fits within a larger theme of combating the spread of antimoral, selfish behavior, a weakening of the traditional family, and declining respect for sacred beliefs. The pro-choice movement frames itself as the defender of women rights-equality. Its frame fits within larger themes of opposing the imposition of unwanted

SUMMARY 6.2	Three Types of Movement Framing

- *Diagnostic framing* specifies the issue, concern or problem; it identifies the adversary or enemy; and often it indicates where the boundary between good and evil lies.
- *Prognostic framing* specifies the solution to the problem and explains what needs to be done. It answers the question, how should we proceed? It also explains why alternative solutions or explanations are inadequate.
- *Motivational framing* specifies why action is necessary. It explains the seriousness of the issue or problem and clarifies the urgency of a response. Motivational framing provides movement adherents and potential supporters with a way to express their motives. It urges people's involvement by outlining the severity of the issues as well as the efficacy and propriety of taking action as a movement.

It tells people what is really at stake and why the movement's cause is a just one.

EXAMPLE

Opponents to capital punishment say the issue is that the government kills innocent people and acts cruelly. They believe people who favor capital punishment do so out of blind revenge, ignorance, sadism, or crude bloodlust (diagnostic). They propose abolishing capital punishment, ensuring fairer and better legal proceedings, and providing humane and effective substitutes, such as life imprisonment without parole (prognostic). They say that the death penalty is ineffective, immoral, inhumane, and allows for irreversible mistakes. It may be killing innocent people and not reducing crime. Moreover, it erodes basic feelings of humanity by spreading the acceptance of uncivilized and brutal acts (motivational).

government or traditional religious authority on an individual; upholding women as fully autonomous individuals; and defending a person's ability to make his/her own health, moral, and lifestyle decisions (see Case in Point 6.3).

Master frames develop during cycles of protest. Movements that emerge early in a cycle provide an ideational anchor for later movements and help to build a master frame. The master frame unifies multiple movements in a cycle. It gives them a shared focus and constrains them. During a cycle of protest, opponents and countermovements offer competing master frames. As competing frames emerge, they can weaken the anchoring of the master frame and challenge it.[94] Movement tactics affect the actual conditions or environment and anchor the master frame. Early studies explained cycles of protest as being based on changes in the POS, but a master frame also helps to explain the clustering of movements. As Swart (1995, 469) observed, "movement actors utilize the master frames generated by prior movements because they represent successful and culturally potential ideational themes . . . master frames require a certain amount of recontextualization in order to resonate with the particulars of any movement that might adopt them."

Frame alignment is linking a movement's frame to an individual's interpretative framework. It is how one person's understanding of the world converges with that of the movement. Alignment operates through four processes:

1. *Bridging* is linking two or more ideologically congruent but disconnected frames.

CASE IN POINT 6.3   **Example of Cultural Themes in a Movement Frame**

The white separatist movement offers an example of a frame that has persisted for generations and unites a number of SMOs. The frame has six themes:

1. **White racism**—A belief that races are natural divisions, that physical traits of races are connected to specific cultural features and intelligence, and that the white race is superior to all others. Includes a strong desire to reverse or destroy laws, programs, and ideas that were promoted by the 1960s civil rights movement.

2. **White separatism**—A desire to separate the races, limit nonwhite population growth, and end interracial marriage. Whites should leave behind racially integrated society to maintain a pure racial stock and promote a distinct white culture.

3. **Anti-Semitism**—Hostility towards Jews combined with a belief that Jews control the banking industry, the mass media, and the federal government.

4. **Isolationism**—Strongly opposes nonwhite immigration to the United States and is suspicious of most international organizations, cooperation, and agreements.

5. **Christianity**—Specific interpretations of Protestant Christian beliefs that privilege Anglo-Saxon, German, and Scandinavian peoples and espouse a "divine right" for whites to dominate all other peoples of the world.

6. **Populism**—Hostility toward the national/central government and instead favors local authority held by "ordinary" people (i.e., those with little formal education or experience beyond the local area).

2. *Amplification* is clarifying and intensifying a frame by illustrating how it bears on a specific issue and has real effects on an individual.

3. *Extension* is stretching the boundaries of a primary frame so that it encompasses points of view, people, issues, or events that are adjacent to or incidental to its core goals.

4. *Transformation* is modifying a frame by jettisoning old ideas and beliefs and incorporating and nurturing new ones to reframe in ways that can garner support, secure commitment, or respond to new situations.

Frames vary in potency; some have a more powerful impact than others. Three factors influence frame potency.

1. *Empirical credibility* is the degree to which a frame appears to be true and consistent with documentary evidence that supports (or at least does not contradict) its main claims.

2. *Narrative fidelity* is whether a frame resonates with a society's major cultural values and themes (i.e., as found in national legends, myths, folktales, and stories).

3. *Experiential commensurability* is whether a frame matches the everyday experiences of people's lives and fits with their first-hand experiences.

Movement leaders try to formulate and articulate their frame in ways that attach it to highly respected, dominant cultural beliefs and values to establish *frame resonance.* In part, it is a rhetorical strategy by the movement as "Effective rhetoric draws familiar elements from a common repertoire and uses them in new combinations or with innovative interpretations," noted Williams (1995, 140).

Movements in the United States try to attach their frame to ideological symbols in American civil religion and dominant cultural discourse, or the "public good." There are three types of the public good—convent, contract, or stewardship. Convent is of Christian origin and implies a duty-bound relationship with God and the common good to transcend, supreme authority. Contract comes from the idea of a legal contract that builds on citizenship incorporation. For example, once a person is a citizen, they have rights and duties. Stewardship also has Christian roots and environmental ties; it suggests harmony with nature and careful management for future generations.[95] As Williams (1995, 126) argued, "By talking about the public good in a particular way, movements simultaneously legitimate their involvement and solutions, while casting aspersions on their opponents' position. The rhetorical struggle is part of all public politics; a vision of the public good is a valuable tool in this process." If a frame has narrative fidelity or cultural resonance, it can spread quickly and many attract people. The frame can be repeated over and again, until it becomes part of a body of shared cultural knowledge. In contrast, a frame that lacks narrative fidelity is likely to falter or fade immediately. Success depends largely on whether a frame connects to the stories, myths, tales (e.g., George Washington and the cherry tree) and themes of a culture. Framing is "an act of cultural appropriation." For example, Martin Luther King, Jr. borrowed ideas of nonviolence from Gandhi and made it an ideological cornerstone for the civil rights movement.[96] Nonetheless, competing frames may build on the same cultural theme.

Equal opportunity is a core theme in U.S. culture; that is, each individual, regardless of background, should have a fair chance to succeed and advancement should be based on individual effort not family connections or inherited wealth. It is related to other values, such as self-reliance, hard work, and diligence. For example, supporters framed affirmative action with the equal opportunity theme. They argue that majority group individuals used their gender or race to advance in ways that minorities could not. Affirmative action would equalize opportunities, ensure that minorities had an equal chance to advance, and create a level playing field. Later, affirmative action opponents introduced the counter frame of reverse discrimination and also used the cultural theme of equal opportunity. They connected the idea of reverse discrimination to [skin] color blindness and opposition to government programs that created "differential group privileges" (i.e., provided a class of people with benefits that are denied to other people).[97] The reverse discrimination frame had a double power to invalidate—the symbolic-laden term "discrimination" was inverted and the same equal opportunity theme that had justified affirmative action was employed. As Gamson (1998, 75) observed, "The essence of frame contests is competition about what evidence is seen as relevant and what gets ignored." In the framing contest between affirmative action and reverse discrimination, the reverse discrimination frame downplays privileges originating in the private sphere and elevates a core conservative value—the private market. In effect, it treats all market outcomes as legitimate, while it denigrates state actions to advance equality as being illegitimate.

Another example comes from Haydu's (1999a, 1999b) study of a nineteenth century employer's movement against unions. He asked, why the movement selected a frame that portrayed unions as anti-American, violent, and interfering with managerial rights. He found that parts of this frame were consistent with similar frames that employers had already developed and applied in other political arenas. They engaged in *frame correspondence*; that is, they coordinated the frame of one political area with framing activities in other areas to make them mutually reinforcing.

Frame Conflict   Frames are used in political struggles and can themselves be sites of struggle. Some frame conflicts are internal to a movement. Movements are not monolithic or entirely homogenous, so internal differences can develop. For example, Benford (1993a) studied the nuclear disarmament movement and identified disputes over diagnostic framing, prognostic framing, and frame fidelity. One faction's diagnostic frame focused on the atomic bomb, another's on political events that might cause war. One's prognostic frame urged civil disobedience, and another's urged taking legal action. A dispute arose over how to treat the symbol of the American flag, highlighting different attachments to core cultural values. He (1993b, 208) also found that framing attempts do not always have desired results but may immobilize or divide people instead. These *framing hazards* develop when urgency, efficacy, and propriety in motivational framing become unbalanced (i.e., people feel overwhelmed by the problem or adherents get so over-involved that they initiate individual actions beyond acceptable movement boundaries).

Framing is part of the combative interaction between a movement and countermovement. For example, McCaffrey and Keys (2000) studied symbolic combat between the pro-choice and antiabortion movements and noted three framing strategies:[98] (1) *polarization-vilification* combines exaggerating the "us versus them" or black/white dichotomy with rhetorical actions that label a person's opponents as being corrupt, insincere, or malevolent; (2) *frame debunking* attacks and undermines an opponent's frame; and (3) *frame saving* wards off attacks on one's own frame or counters debunking actions. Framing combat highlights the symbolic-ideation dimension of struggle. Framing as Della Porta (1999, 69) noted, is an "interactive process: movements, parties, media, government, and state apparatuses (including the police) engage in . . . a process of reality construction." Frames are a joint production of movement activists, antagonists, and others in a contentious, evolving process. Movement organizers construct an initial frame, but nonmovement members or movement opponents can undermine it, and a frame can shift with the stages in a cycle of protest.[99] In her study of radical movements in Europe, Della Porta (1999) observed that political discourse was polarized into law-and-order (authoritarian, prorepression) and civil rights (defense of democratic rights) coalitions. Each side presented its position as a battle of good versus evil. The law-and-order coalition evoked a frame (e.g., state of siege, terrorism, civil war, criminal gangs) to justify military involvement and repression. The civil rights coalition evoked a counterframe (e.g., freedom, democracy, constitutional rights, police brutality). After a series of encounters, a compromise evolved that was pragmatic depolarization. The law-and-order coalition broadened the forms of political expression it would permit while the civil rights coalition excluded and stigmatized the most violent forms of radical protest. As a result, the state permitted new forms of democratic participation (e.g., loud demonstrations, marches, sit-ins) that went beyond conventional, formalistic participation (e.g., parades, speeches, voting) but excluded other violent forms of protest (e.g., bombings, kidnappings, arson). At the peak of intense turmoil, the boundaries of political expression and democratic participation became issues in the forefront. They overshadowed the specific grievances being protested. The outcome was to shift the frames and expand the boundaries of legitimate democratic participation.

Movements create, sustain and extend the boundaries of a frame.[100] Snow and Benford (1988, 5) remarked, "Movements themselves are engaging in meaning-work . . . in the struggle over the production of ideas and meanings." Frames that resonate with the dominant cultural beliefs are more potent and spread quickly, but aligning a frame with dominant cultural beliefs can inhibit its radicalism.[101] This makes controlling a frame a critical issue. Competing SMOs might try to steal elements from another's frame. This has two implications. The frame may disperse and become part of a broad cultural shift that attracts many adherents. Alternatively, competitors may deplete the frame's unique strengths and undercut it as a distinct, coherent vision for social change.[102]

The media and movements mutually influence one another in frame conflict. Movements provide the media with compelling symbols and ideas, newsworthy activity, and dramatic, colorful people or events. As Klandermans (1992, 88) observed, "Social movement organizations have a profound impact on media discourse; they frame issues, define grievances, and stage collection action to attract the attention of the mass media." At the same time, media can assist or harm movements in how they disseminate messages or images about the movement, its actions, and its frame. The media can amplify, transmit, distort, or block a movement's frames, or can create a new framing of a movement and its issues. For example, Wisler and Giugni (1999) studied the effect of mass media on the policing of protest movements by looking at the media frame used to discuss protest and the amount of media coverage. They found that when the media framed a protest as being a civil rights issue and gave it extensive coverage, antimovement policing was mild and pacifying. By contrast, when the media framed the protest as a law-and-order issue and ignored it, the police adopted a repressive response. The idea of frames is extensively used and an entire vocabulary has developed to discuss aspects of it (see Summary 6.3).

The injustice frame is a special type that helps people who have little power to redefine a situation or condition as being morally unfair and unjust.[103] It facilitates transforming personal and collective grievances into demands for a remedy. The **injustice frame is part of a broad collective action frame that excites**

SUMMARY 6.3 Framing Vocabulary

collective action frame—A frame that organizes and packages meaning for people by focusing attention, embellishing injustice, and assigning blame so that people will recognize and accept the remedy of acting collectively to address a grievance.

competitive framing—A dynamic, interaction process between a movement and a countermovement; each advances its frame and debunks the opponent's.

diagnostic framing—The process of explaining what is the core problem or situation; it identifies targets and sources of concern and focuses attention on them.

frame alignment—The process of linking an individual's interpretation and understanding of events to a movement's frame, so that the beliefs, values, and goals of the individual and of the movement are made congruent, and both interpret events similarly.

frame bridging—The process of connecting two or more movements; an idea or belief created by one movement or countermovement is borrowed and used to advance the goals of another movement.

frame correspondence—A movement synchronizes, coordinates, or shares frames (or major parts of frames) across multiple settings, so that a frame developed for one setting is reused in another.

frame debunking—The process of attacking and discrediting an opponent's frame by highlighting contradictions, questioning moral standing, or offering opposing evidence.

frame extension—The process of adding complementary items or issues to a frame, usually to a master frame, to provide new interpretations and solutions.

frame preservation—Strategies movements use to maintain an existing frame in the face of repeated contradictory evidence or events, often by redefining issues and using highly ambiguous language.

frame reconstruction—The process of generating a new frame within the same tradition as a previous one.

frame repertoire—The range of potentially acceptable frames that are available at a given time for a movement to use.

frame saving—A defensive action movement undertaken to restore creditability to one's frame that opponents have attacked or debunked.

frame transformation—Putting forth a radically new frame with new values.

framing hazards—Immobilization or other mobilization difficulties that can occur when the elements in a motivational frame are not balanced.

injustice frame—Part of a collective action frame that excites moral indignation or righteous anger toward a concrete target and demands action because a sense of justice has been transgressed.

master frame—A flexible and inclusive interpretative system of ideas through which different movements in a cycle of protest can assign blame, motivate adherents, and direct action.

motivational framing—The process of a movement providing arguments, appeals, and reasons for people so that they become involved and engage in movement actions.

prognostic framing—The process of explaining what needs to be done in order to rectify the situation as it has been diagnosed.

strategic framing—A movement's decisions to develop and articulate a frame in particular ways and use it in various settings so that it will bring the movement maximum benefit.

Sources: Babb (1996), Benford (1993b), Benford and Snow (2000), Clemens (1998), Cress and Snow (2000), Gamson (1992a, 1992b), Haydu (1999a, 1999b), Klandermans and Goslinga (1996), McCaffrey and Keys (2000), Snow and Benford (1988, 1992), Snow et al. (1986), Tarrow (1992), and Zald (1996).

moral indignation and anger in adherents toward a specific target and stimulates them to demand action because the target violated a standard of moral justice. An important feature of this frame is that it connects a cognitive sense of injustice with both an emotional response and concrete targets and objects that are seen as causing the injustice. It is closely related to oppositional consciousness and subcultures, a topic that we will examine next.

Oppositional Consciousness and Subcultures

A critical task for a protest movement by subjugated people is to awaken, arouse, and motivate people about their condition. Movement framing can help people in a subordinate, oppressed position to break through the dominant hegemony, recognize their oppression, and work collectively to end it. Yet, a frame cannot persist at the level of abstract ideas alone; it needs a concrete social foundation in people's daily lives and experiences.[104] People outside the power structure can desire significant social action and mobilize to achieve it, but first they need "cognitive liberation" to break through the dominant hegemony of ideas, beliefs, and values. Hegemonic consciousness, as Aldon Morris (1992, 363) observed, "always presents itself as a set of values and beliefs that serve the general welfare . . . [It] is always sustained by public institutions that are meant to attend to the general welfare: the government, schools, media, and a host of lesser institutions . . . . In contrast, oppositional consciousness is that set of insurgent ideas and beliefs constructed and developed by an opposed group for the purpose of guiding its struggle to undermine, reform, or overthrow a system of domination."

A critical ideological task for a radical protest movement is to construct an oppositional way of thinking, or an oppositional consciousness.[105] **Oppositional consciousness is an entire outlook or worldview that a subordinate group can develop, it stands outside of, and in opposition to, the dominant way of thinking and seeing events that reflects and reinforces a society's power structure.** It is broader than a frame; it is a new way to understand, perceive, and feel about a range of issues, events, and life experiences. An oppositional consciousness encourages identification with the group, adopting the injustices that have been or are being committed against the group as a person's own, taking a stand against and opposing the injustices, and embracing a shared interest with others to fight the injustices. The adherent who has an oppositional consciousness identifies a specific dominant group as causing or benefiting from the injustices, sees that group's actions as forming a system of oppression, and consolidates her/his beliefs and feelings into an intense moral condemnation.

An oppositional consciousness is reactive. It opposes more than it creates or defends, and it is narrow in scope. It is the consciousness of one part of society that rejects and opposes parts of the hegemonic belief system and power structure. Hegemonic consciousness is the outlook of the ruling/dominant classes or those at the top of the power structure. As such, it encompasses the entire society and all its issues, and it restrains and represses the ideas, beliefs, and behaviors that threaten its position of dominance.[106] It does not repress all subordinate groups equally but grants some privileges or compensations relative to others. As Aldon Morris (1992, 364) argued, "oppositional consciousness is usually fashioned to confront a particular enemy and advance a limited set of interests. Rarely does a dominant group's overall ruling position come under attack." In addition, oppositional consciousness may exist as an incomplete patchwork of ideas. It may rise and fall, expand and contract in different periods of history. It can "lie dormant within the institutions, life-styles, and culture of oppressed groups."[107] An oppositional consciousness is a *system* of beliefs, ideas, emotions, and perceptions. Ideas and beliefs can only be sustained through social practices and in a social environment that supports, nourishes, and reinforces them, such as a distinct subculture formed by a movement.

A movement subculture includes the social practices, values and traditions that sustain a set of symbols, rituals, institutions, and social relations consistent with its frame. It supports a web of friendships, moral beliefs, and neighborhood or communal solidarity. Over time, movement members embrace frame values, amplify the frame, and connect the frame to other cultural institutions and beliefs. A movement subculture links agency to structure, personal identity to political practice, and organization to action. Thus, an oppositional subculture sustains an oppositional consciousness. The subculture protects, nurtures, and enables a distinct worldview to persist, specifically an oppositional consciousness. It is rarely wholly unique but shares elements of the dominant culture and worldview. Morris and Braine (2001, 26) observed, "Oppositional culture contains the frameworks of oppositional ideas and worldviews that permeate the large cultures [and] . . . partially developed critiques of the status quo as well as knowledge of isolated acts or prior episodes of organized collective action."

An oppositional subculture is a set of social practices, beliefs, traditions, symbols, and patterns separate from the larger dominant culture that sustain an oppositional or counterhegemonic consciousness. For example, in the late nineteenth century, an American labor–political organization called the Knights of Labor built and sustained an organizational framework for a working-class subculture. Through picnics, parades, reading rooms, musicals, dances, labor newspapers, cigar boxes, flags, drinking mugs, rituals, badges, singing clubs, and so forth, the Knights elaborated and spread their political program and set of beliefs (i.e., a distinct movement frame). The Knights created and sustained an oppositional subculture in dozens of working communities. The subculture gave people a new way to see and interpret events, a political program and plan of action, and a set of communal activities that encouraged building a social life with others who shared the same views and beliefs.[108] Likewise, the women's movement created and sustained not only a belief system, movement frame, political program, and SMOs, but a distinct feminist subculture. The movement spawned a subculture in opposition to the larger patriarchal culture. As Gelb and Hart (1999, 155) observed, "a women's culture has been advanced through bookstores, art galleries, publishing companies, and cooperatives."

Movement Identity

We looked at the long-term biographic impact of movement activism earlier. One branch of the CA moves beyond the cultural–ideological level to the social–psychological level. It focuses on the concept of self and identity—collective, group, and individual identity. A movement can create collective identities (e.g., we are environmental activists) and link them to individual identities (e.g., I am an environmentalist). The two types of identity are distinct but related. They are joined in processes of social group identification.[109] It is the relationship between a sense of "we-ness" and "one-ness." Both collective and individual identities are socially constructed.

A critical movement task is to alter the self-identity of its adherents. This occurs in several ways.[110] First, a person's self concept changes structurally as he/she adopts a new identity as an activist (e.g., feminist, civil rights advocate, conservationist). This transformation of self is a permanent shift in how a person defines herself/himself. Second, at any given time, people possess multiple identities. Some are more central to the core of self than others. A movement can push the movement identity from the periphery and toward the core of a person's self. Lastly, people's multiple identities vary in salience; they are rank ordered, and some are able to "trump" or override others. Active participation can shift a person's movement identity upward, so it overtakes other identities.

The processes of identity transformation or reconstruction involve what Snow and McAdam (1999) called identity convergence; it is a coalescence of a movement and an individual. It is similar to the frame alignment process, but operates at the micro-level of a person's inner self. The movement's collective identity converges with an individual's personal identity, so that involvement in the movement becomes central to the person's self-conception. Thus far, we have considered three widely used approaches to the study of movements (see Chart 6.7). We will examine next a subtype of CA called new social movements.

New Social Movements

The new social movement (NSM) approach fits within a broad constructionist theory and shares its emphasis on culture, meaning, and identity. It differs in three respects: (1) it relies on a macro-historical theory of social change not found in CA, (2) it concentrates on personal identity formation/self-realization, and (3) it is largely concerned with middle-class cultural movements and not traditional political movements.[111] New social movements tend to be grassroots, antibureaucratic and antihierarchical, post-modern, and identity-oriented. They are less concerned with challenging the state or changing national policy than with changing the person and his/her immediate situation. The NSM approach rejects old right-left ideologies based on class and economic distribution issues. Instead, it is concerned with lifestyle, identity, self-expression, and opening up cultural "space." NSMs try to change a specific sphere of life, not remake the entire society. They take the feminist phase, "the personal is the political" and turn it into a call to dissolve the boundary between politics and one's personal lifestyle. They blend politics with personal life choices. Thus, one's actions and choices about how to live are reframed as political actions. For example, an

chart 6.7

CENTRAL CONCEPTS OF THE THREE MAJOR APPROACHES TO MOVEMENTS

Resource Mobilization Approach

Movement entrepreneurs

Movement professionalization

Social capital and networks

Social movement industry

Social movement organization (SMO)

Political Process Approach

Abeyance

Cognitive liberation

Cycles of protest or reform

Organizational readiness

Political mediation

Political opportunity structures (POS)

Constructionist Approach

Collective identity construction

Movement frames (frame alignment, master frames, etc.)

Oppositional consciousness

Oppositional subculture

individual's decision to not have children is seem simultaneously as a personal life choice and as a political act.

Most NSMs have appeared since the 1980s. They differentiate themselves from the goals, tactics, and methods of old movements and SMOs by working outside both conventional political channels and the channels typically used by social movements. NSMs see themselves as the products of a postindustrial information society or postcapitalist world. Johnson, Laraña, and Gusfield (1994, 21, 23) noted, "'Old movements coalesced around shared grievances and perceptions of injustice . . . New Social Movements display a paradoxical relationship between identity and grievances." NSMs merge collective grievances with personal identity (i.e., how one interacts with others in everyday life). While the goal of a few NSMs is to reorganize society in their image, most focus on a few narrow issues and only seek to create social-political space to allow individuals to engage in an activity, lifestyle, or cultural practice. A wide range of movements can be classified as "new" (e.g., women's, gay-lesbian, environmental movements). Many lifestyle choice movements (e.g., alternative medicine, anti-smoking, home schooling) and movements seeking rights for ascribed status segments of society (e.g., disabled, race-ethnic, aged) can be considered NSMs. Movements that focus on a person's religious beliefs (e.g., New Age, Christian identity) and noneconomic ideologies (e.g., animal rights) also fit into the NSM category. To some degree, the anti-drunk driving, antihandgun, and White Separatist movements discussed earlier could be classified as NSMs.

Although NSMs appear new, they have a great deal in common with many historically old movements. They are similar to older movements such as antislavery, protemperance, and movements that created religious utopian communities.[112] Whether NSMs really differ from other movements and warrant a separate approach has yet to be answered. Interest in NSM is strongest in Western Europe where traditional right-left ideological divisions had been strongest and permeated most movement frames. The NSMs are also of greatest interest among theorists who argue that there will be a fundamental shift to a post-materialist, post-industrial society in which new cultural divisions are paramount.[113]

CONCLUSION

In this chapter, we examined political action beyond conventional channels. We looked at unrest, protest, and political–social movements, a major form of political expression that arose concurrent with the nation-state. Political sociologists have devoted a great deal of attention to collective behavior by challenging groups. After a break with the explanations of the classic era that saw protest, unrest, and movements as irrational, emotional outbursts, political sociologists developed new explanations that understood protest and movements as a form of political behavior.

Since the 1970s, political sociologists developed three approaches to study movements: resource mobilization, political process, and constructionist. Each approach contains a rich array of concepts and explanations, and each has been applied in many studies of movements. Political sociologists who developed later approaches identified weaknesses in previous approaches but also elaborated upon and built on the earlier approaches.

In chapter 7 we examine the role of ideas, beliefs, and symbols in politics, including the role of political ideology. Political beliefs and values have a major impact on a person's choices about political involvement and the direction of her or his political efforts. Decisions to completely withdrawal from politics or become an active member of a movement, and whether political involvement will be in a right-wing, left-wing or other direction, are shaped by how a person sees and understands political issues.

KEY TERMS

Abeyance	Cycle of Protest	Master Frame
Cognitive Liberation	Frame Alignment	Mobilization
Countermovement	Injustice Frame	Movement

Movement Entrepreneur	Political Opportunity	Social Control Thesis
Movement Frame	Structure (POS)	Social Movement
Oppositional Consciousness	Resource Dependency	Organization (SMO)
Oppositional Subculture	Thesis	Tactical Innovation
Organizational Readiness	Revolution	Venue Shifting

REVIEW QUESTIONS

1. What distinguishes conventional from unconventional politics?

2. Outline the traditional theory of collective behavior. Why did this view change in the 1960s–1970s?

3. What are the major tenets of the resource mobilization approach to social movements?

4. What are the major tenets of the political process approach to social movements? What is the idea of a political opportunity structure and why is it important in the approach?

5. How do the political process and resource mobilization approaches agree and how do they differ?

6. What is the importance and relevance of looking at the international dimension of movements?

7. What explains a cycle of protest? How does abeyance fit into the cycle?

8. What are the major tenets of the constructionist approach to social movements?

9. What is a master frame of a movement? How do movement frames come into conflict?

10. What factors are necessary for a movement's frame to be powerful and successful?

11. Explain the relevance of creating an oppositional consciousness and a movement subculture.

12. Why are new social movements called "new?" How does the new social movement approach differ from a political process or a constructionist approach?

RECOMMENDED READINGS

Della Porta, D. and Mario Diani. 1999. *Social Movements: An Introduction.* Malden, MA: Blackwell.

Gamson, William A. 1990. *Strategy of Social Protest, 2nd ed.* Belmont, CA: Wadsworth

Laraña, E., H. Johnson, and J. Gusfield (eds). 1994. *New Social Movements from Ideology to Identity.* Philadelphia: Temple University Press.

McAdam, Doug. 1982. *Political Process and the Development of Black Insurgency, 1930–1970.* Chicago: University of Chicago Press.

McAdam, Doug, John McCarthy, and Mayer Zald (eds). 1996. *Comparative Perspectives on Social Movements.* New York: Cambridge University Press.

Morris, Aldon and Carol McClung (eds). 1992. *Frontiers in Social Movement Theory.* New Haven, CT: Yale University Press.

Olson, Marcur. 1965. *Logic of Collective Action.* Cambridge, MA: Harvard University Press.

Tarrow, Sidney. 1994. *Power in Movement.* New York: Cambridge University Press.

ENDNOTES

1. LeBon (1895) and Tarde (1890).

2. A review/summary can be found in Jenkins and Schock (1992). Also see Stryker, Owens and White (2000).

3. See Giugni and Passy (1998) and Tarrow (1998b). Also see Clemens (1997) on the borrowing of organizational forms between movements and more traditional interest groups.

4. Burstein (1998a, 1998b, 1999) and Hanagan (1998) forcefully argue this. Wilson (1974, 10) observed that, "the borderline between a political party and a social movement is a hard one to draw empirically."

5. See Della Porta (1999) and Piven and Cloward (1992) who argue this point strongly.

6. Fitzgerald and Rodgers (2000) and Szasz (1992) make arguments against blurring based on radical U.S. movements.

7. For a cogent discussion of the breakdown model see Useem (1980) who applies it to later antibusing protest.

8. On defining protest see Jeffries, Turner, and Morris (1971) and Turner (1969).

9. Johnson, Sears, and McConahay (1971) discuss press coverage.

10. From McPhail (1971, 1063). Also see Miller, Bolce, and Halligan (1977) and Orum (1972, 1974). A comprehensive review of critiques can be found in Jenkins and Schock (1992).

11. For discussion of socialization see Isaac, Mutran, and Stryker (1980). Also see Geschwender (1968) on relative deprivation theory.

12. See Beck and Aldrich (1972) and Stark et al. (1974).

13. For studies on the backgrounds of black activists, leftist radicals, student antiwar protesters, and black rioters see Cryns and Finn (1973); Granberg and Corrigan (1972); Hall, Rodeghier, and Useem (1986); Paige (1971); Portes (1971); and Ransford (1968). Also see Schuman (1972) on differences between college antiwar protesters and antiwar opinion within the general public. Pultzer (1987) supports this in his study of radicalism in 1976.

14. Olzak, Shanahan, and McEneaney (1996) provide a comprehensive review.

15. See Blumer (1978) and McPhail and Wohlstein (1983).

16. Lipsky (1968).

17. For a summary of criticisms see McAdam (1982), Jenkins (1983a), and Jenkins and Schock (1992).

18. Tarrow (1993, 76–77) compares traditional versus modern forms of protest and discusses modular forms of protest.

19. Giugni (1998a, xiii–xiv) and Tilly (1999, 256).

20. Giugni (1998a) discusses the consequences and implications of movements. Also see Hanagan (1998) who argues that movements benefit from absorption into parties because they acquire access to routine politics.

21. For a discussion of postpluralist theories and movements see Jenkins (1995) and McFarland (1998).

22. For a list of movement features see Della Porta and Diani (1999, 11–20), Diani (1992), McAdam and Snow (1997).

23. Early discussions of countermovements can be found in Lo (1982a), McCarthy and Zald (1977, 20), and Mottl (1980). Also see the discussion in Meyer and Staggenborg (1996).

24. For an outline of these three approaches see Buechler (1999) and Diani (1992).

25. Buechler (1993) and Jenkins and Schock (1992) both call it a paradigm shift.

26. Quote is from Stryker, Owens, and White (2000, 2–3). Also see Minkoff (1999b) on long term survival of two SMO's.

27. See Gamson (1975), Jenkins and Perrow (1977), McCarthy and Zald (1977), Piven and Cloward (1977), and Zald and Meyer (1978).

28. See Morris and Herring (1987).

29. See Ferrer (1992) and Stryker, Owens, and White (2000) for discussion. Tilly (1978) lays out rational actor or rational choice assumptions. Also see Zafirovski (1999b) for a general discussion of public choice and political sociology.

30. This is discussed in Ferree (1992) and Fireman and Gamson (1979).

31. The types are explained in McCarthy and Zald (1977, 1987). Also see Jenkins (1983a, 534–536), and Ennis and Schrever (1987) on types of movement supporters.

32. On the idea of mobilization see Tilly (1978, 7).

33. The importance of networks for member recruitment is studied in Barkan and Cohn (1993), Barkan, Cohen, and Whitaker (1995), Cable (1992), Cable, Walsh, and Warland (1988), Hirsch (1986), Jasper and Poulsen (1995), Jenkins (1982, 1985), McAdam (1982), McAdam and Paulsen (1993), Mueller (1994), Opp and Gern (1993), and Staggenborg (1991). Also see McCarthy (1996) and Tilly

(1978, 62–64) for a theoretical discussion of networks in recruitment and Marwell, Oliver, and Prahl (1988) for a mathematical simulation model of a critical mass in networks.

34. See Ansell (1997) and Gould (1991, 1993) on France, Pfaff (1996) and Pfaff and Yang (2001) on Germany, and Zuo and Benford (1995) on China. Also see Robnett (1996) on the distinct role of African American women in micromobilization in the U.S. civil rights movement.

35. Opp and Gern (1993) found a similar pattern in German democratization movements of 1989. Oegema and Klandermans (1994) found that preexisting preparedness, features of mobilization, and individual factors all had a role in failed recruitment or movement members who quit.

36. Also see Wiltfang and McAdam (1991) on predictors of risk involvement in the Sanctuary Movement.

37. See discussion of movement entrepreneurs in Jenkins (1983a) and Staggenborg (1988). See Santaro and McGuire (1997) on insider activists.

38. Staggenborg (1988) argues that movement entrepreneurs and SMO professionals are different. Also see Buechler (2000, 36). Pichardo (1988) noted that Morris (1981, 1984) and others found indigenous sources of leadership.

39. See Oliver and Marwell (1992) on types of resources. In a study of California farm workers, Ganz (2000) argued that a non-traditional resource, being resourceful which includes the new uses of information, thinking innovatively, and developing new strategies, can compensate for limited traditional resources.

40. From Cress and Snow (1996, 1998).

41. Civil rights movements studies are by McAdam (1982) and Morris (1981, 1984, 1993).

42. For a discussion of the social control thesis see Jenkins and Eckert (1986). Haines (1984) argues that outside funding for moderate civil rights SMOs grew in response to radical unrest.

43. Also see Cress (1997) and Cress and Snow (1998, 2000).

44. See Jenkins and Eckert (1986) for elaboration regarding the black movement.

45. See McCarthy and Zald (1977).

46. Evertt (1992) discusses the social movement sector and changes in it over time. See Oliver and Marwell (1992) on the development of different resources and movement technologies.

47. For discussion and examples from the women's movement see Staggenborg (1988).

48. See Jenkins (1983a, 542) and Staggenborg (1988, 1994) for discussion.

49. For a discussion of different effects of professionalism see Kleidman (1994).

50. Cress (1997) discusses legal incorporation and its effect of homeless SMOs.

50a. Andrews (1997, 2001) found long term outcomes to the 1960s civil rights movement in Southern states. Counties where the civil rights movement had been most active, more blacks voted and ran for political office and anti-poverty programs to help low-income blacks were larger. Also see Colby (1985).

51. From Rochon and Mazmanian (1993) and Ennis and Schreuer (1987) on the freeze movement.

52. See Fitzgerald and Rodgers (2000) on differences between radical and reform movements.

53. Cress and Snow (1996, 1091; 2000, 1095) and Wagner and Cohen (1991, 545) made this point.

54. Calculated from the 2000 General Social Survey by the author.

55. The primary source on the antigun movement is Carter (1997).

56. See Gusfield (1981, 1996). Also see Blocker (1989, 130–161) on the relationship between long-standing American Temperance Movement and recent actions to limit alcohol use or abuse.

57. Reinarman (1988) discusses the impact of the larger political climate and New Right.

58. The White Separatist movement is discussed in Barkun (1996), Blee (2002), and Dobratz and Shanks-Meile (1997).

59. On the homeless movement see Cress (1997), Cress and Snow (1996, 1998, 2000), and Wagner and Cohen (1991).

60. Also see Fireman and Gamson (1979), Klandermans (2002), and Klandermans and Oegema (1987).

61. See Lo (1992) for a discussion of meso-mobilization and the importance of community.

62. Critics include Fitzgerald and Rodgers (2000), Lo (1992), and Piven and Cloward (1992).

63. Marx (1979) and Tilly (1978) discuss the elite responses to movements. On the impact of policing see Della Porta (1996, 1999), Della Porta and Reiter (1998), and Wisler and Giugni (1999). McCarthy and McPhail (1998) use the term public order management to discuss the mutual interaction between policing/social control and movement actions.

64. See Morris and Herring (1987, 170). See Loveman (1998) on the rise of human rights organizations in three Latin American nations despite high levels of political repression. Olzak and Olvier (1998) found that state repression in the United States and South Africa reduced short-term protest but increased long-term conflict.

65. The idea of movement spillover is explained by Meyer and Whittier (1994).

66. Clemens (1993; 1997, 45–53) discusses the development of organizational forms and repertoires. Tarrow (1993) discusses the emergence of a new repertoire of activity around the French Revolution.

67. Clemens (1993), Gamson (1990), and Staggenborg (1988, 1989, 1994).

68. On environmental effects see Amenta and Zylan (1991), Goldstone (1980), Kriesi et al. (1997), and Tarrow (1988, 1992, 1994, 1996).

69. See McCammon, Campbell, Granberg, and Mowery (2001) on the idea of a gendered opportunity structure, in which changes in gender relationships alter the views of institutional leaders about proper gender roles, thereby opening new opportunities. See Jenkins (1985) on farm workers, Kerbo and Shaffer (1992) on the unemployed, and McAdam (1982) on civil rights.

70. McAdam (1983) describes the concept of tactical innovation. Also see Colby (1985) on innovations by a white countermovement in southern states.

71. Litigation and legal processes as part of social movement activity are discussed in Burstein (1991a, 1991b), Handler (1978), McCann (1998), and Meranto (1998). Barnes and Connolly (1999) discuss how judicial climate can close the POS.

72. Meyer and Staggenborg (1996) discuss shifting venues. Also see McAdam (1998) on shifting national contexts.

73. Jenkins and Schock (1992) suggested a U curve relationship between POS and collective action. Movement activity is greatest in extremely closed, repressive and extremely open, nonrepressive situations. This is because high repression and closure can spark massive unrest, although repression can also block movement success.

74. Klandermans (1992) discusses the importance of multiple SMOs.

75. See McAdam (1996) and McAdam and Snow (1997). Gotham (1999) argued that political opportunities can shift ideas in the political culture.

76. Also see Banaszak (1998) who compared the referendum in the United States and Switzerland on women's suffrage.

77. A discussion of media opportunity structures can be found in Sampedro (1997). Also see Diani (1997) who provided a typology of successful framing strategies that vary by the POS.

78. See Amenta and Zylan (1991); Amenta, Cattruthers, and Zylan (1992a); Amenta and Young (1999a).

79. This three-part division is similar to that offered by Giugni (1998b).

80. See Koopmans (1993), Oliver and Meyer (1998), and Watanabe (2000) on "protest waves" or "cycles of protest" at the same time in different nations. Discussions of the diffusion of movement ideas, tactics, etc. can be found in McAdam and Rucht (1993) and Reimann (2001).

81. Rucht (1996) is an example of this type of study. Also see Koopmans and Statham (1999a, 1999b).

82. For a full discussion with examples from the 1968 wave of protest in France see Tarrow (1991, 1998b). Mueller (1999) noted that the protest cycle in Tarrow does not fit that of declining Lenist regimes, as in East Germany.

83. These factors are suggested by Minkoff (1997b). She argues that the rapid growth in new SMOs creates organizational density that promotes the cycle of protest.

Also see Minkoff (1997a) on how movements create social capital.

84. See Taylor (1989) on the concept movement abeyance and movement abeyance structures, with specific references to the women's movement. Sawyers and Meyer (1999) discuss costs or missed opportunities of abeyance. Also see Freeman (1975) on the early women's movement, Staggenborg (1998) on maintaining a movement in abeyance, and Edward and Marullo (1995) who outline specific features associated with the survival of movement organizations in an era of general movement decline.

85. See Fendrich and Lavoy (1988); Hirsch (1990); Marwell, Aiken, and Demerath (1987); McAdam (1989, 1999); and Sherkat and Blocker (1994, 1997). Also see Whittier (1997) on generational processes.

86. See Zald (1996) for a useful summary of the history of social movement theory.

87. This criticism is outlined in greater detail in Snow et al. (1986) and in Benford (1993b, 197)

88. See Williams (1995) for this criticism. Suh (2001) attempts to combine POS with framing in the Constructionist Approach.

89. Ferree (1992) provides a critique of rational choice and presents an alternative.

90. This discussion draws on Benford and Snow (2000), Gamson (1992a, 1996, 1998), McAdam (1994), Snow et al. (1986), and Snow and Benford (1992, 2000).

91. See Williams (1995, 125).

92. Noakes (2000) offers an analysis of official frames.

93. Babb (1996) discusses similarities between movement frames and scientific paradigms.

94. From Snow and Benford (1992).

95. Williams (1995, 130–138) outlines the ideal types of the public good.

96. See McAdam (1994, 37–38).

97. This discussion builds on Gamson (1998).

98. Also see Zald (1996) on the concept of competitive framing and Meyer and Staggenborg (1998) on countermovements.

99. For a discussion using the antinuclear movement see Adair (1996). Also see Kubal (1998) on shifting frames in the environmental movement.

100. See Snow et al. (1986).

101. For a discussion of how the dominant culture can "de-radicalize" a frame see Tarrow (1992).

102. See Tarrow (1992).

103. Gamson (1992b) elaborates on the concept of an injustice frame. Also see Klandermans (1992, 85).

104. See Gamson (1992a), Goodwyn (1976), Klandermans (1984), Klandermans and Oegema (1987), and McAdam (1982).

105. The definition of oppositional consciousness is from Mansbridge (2001, 4–5)

106. This discussion draws heavily on Morris (1992, 363).

107. Quote is from Morris (1992, 370). Van Dyke (1998) found subculture was important in explaining patterns of American college protest in the 1960s.

108. This builds on the analysis of Neuman (1988b). Also see Voss (1996).

109. From Klandermans and deWeerd (2000). Also see Hobson and Lindholm (1997) on Sweden. Polletta and Jasper (2001) and Taylor and Whitter (1992) discuss collective identity.

110. See Kiecolt (2000, 112–115).

111. On the new social movement see Buechler (1995), Johnson et al. (1994), Melucci (1994), and Pichardo (1997). Also see Bernstein (1997) on how new movements use strategic displays of identity at different times for different purposes. On identity issues see Hunt, Benford, and Snow (1994). Gamson (1995) discusses the specifics of disrupting old identities and creating new self-identity as part of the processes of a new social movement.

112. See Calhoun (1993b) for a discussion of how new movements have much in common with old ones.

113. See Dalton (1996), Betz (1990), Inglehart (1984), Inglehart and Abramson (1999), Inglehart and Baker (2000), Inglehart and Klingemann (1979).

POLITICAL IDEAS AND BELIEFS

CHAPTER OUTLINE

INTRODUCTION

Do you think that democracy is the best type of government? Do you believe that the media distorts information? Where did your ideas, beliefs, and knowledge come from? Most likely, you learned them in school; read about them in books, newspapers or magazines; saw them on television or in the movies; or heard them from friends, teachers, parents, coworkers, or neighbors. In the last two chapters, we considered conventional and unconventional forms of participation, but we did not probe into sources of the ideas, opinions, or beliefs that people use when they participate. We now look at beliefs, symbols, and political thinking. We examine how people evaluate issues and make decisions, look at political thinking, and explore the relationship between ideas and politics. ∎

Ideas about Politics and Political Ideas

Politics involves more than factual information and rational decisions; it includes symbols, myths, emotions, and feelings of moral outrage. Volatile emotional issues, such as racial inequality, terrorist attacks, and unjust authority, are political. Most political issues "are essentially distributive, and those that are moralistic . . . [are ones] that place uncompromising evaluations in the forefront, and appeal primarily to the emotional well-springs of communal loyalties."[1] For example, many people have strong attachments to their national flag; they display it with honor, glorify it in songs, and respect it in public ceremonies. It is just a piece of colored cloth, but its symbolic meaning is powerful. Political symbols take many forms—buildings or monuments (e.g., the White House and Statue of Liberty in the United States), music (e.g., national anthems), words (e.g., justice, freedom), colors (e.g., red, white, and blue), social groups (e.g., family farmers), organizations (e.g., the Red Cross) (see World View 7.1). Political symbols can evoke strong emotions that profoundly shape how people evaluate issues and make decisions.

Some people think about politics in a systematic, well-organized manner using coherent ideas that logically build on carefully selected core assumptions and values, but most of us rely on a loose collection of semi-organized and somewhat contradictory ideas. Whether you rely on clichés from television sitcoms and jumbled thoughts, or carefully build on theories from weighty books, ideas guide your political actions. Every day, we are bombarded by hundreds of messages trying to shape our opinions and beliefs. Some try to convince us to buy a product, while others tell us that one policy is better than another. Some are honest attempts to inform, but others are deceptive. The attempts to persuade, both honest and deceptive, can influence what we hold to be true, how we think, and how we evaluate public issues.

Persuasive messages do not encounter a blank slate; they interact with our preexisting beliefs and knowledge. For example, my neighbor and I watched a television commercial by a politician running for state supreme court judge. It was an attempt to persuade. The candidate said she would be "tough on crime," promised to "lock up" violent criminals, and claimed that her opponent was unconcerned and would let criminals go free to terrorize peaceful citizens. My neighbor and I evaluated the message using our preexisting knowledge and beliefs. My neighbor believed our community was not very safe. From newspaper headlines, television news, television shows and movies, and listening to her friends, she "knew" that criminals hurt innocent people, crime is out of control, and criminals rarely served long sentences. Based on her knowledge and beliefs, she formed a positive opinion of the candidate. I saw the commercial differently. I was familiar with the candidate's opponent and neither was "soft on crime."

WORLD VIEW 7.1

Symbolic Closure, Memory, and Healing: Reconciliation in South Africa

History sometimes offers us extraordinary events in which abstract concepts, such as truth and justice, become concrete and real. One such event was the Truth and Reconciliation Commission. It showed a way to resolve violent conflicts, promote reconciling differences, and rebuild together rather than focus on punishment, revenge, and divisiveness. The South African government created the Truth and Reconciliation Commission (TRC) with the Promotion of National Unity and Reconciliation Act in 1995 to deal with incidents under apartheid.

South Africa's political history is long and complex, but until 1994, its regime was based on apartheid (i.e., an extensive system of legal racial segregation and subjugation of the black African majority population by whites) that depended on violence and widespread human rights abuses. When the native African people finally gained control of the government, the question was how to resolve the decades of mistreatment and abuse. The TRC was the outcome of a negotiated settlement to end struggles for control of South Africa; it was a war that neither side won. During the negotiations, the white regime's military and security chiefs wanted blanket amnesty, while African rebelling forces demanded swift trials. A compromise was reached under the leadership of President Nelson Mandela.

Many people feared the end of apartheid would trigger an outbreak of general civil war with a revenge-based bloodbath. This did not happen. In a dramatic and historic process, the new native-African-led government sought a peaceful resolution. The process was not without some ups and downs, but it was founded on the idea that a stable peace meant more than ending the violence. It was based on a desire to build peace around the ideals of reconciliation and coexistence. Chaired by Archbishop Desmond Tutu,

the TRC investigated human rights violations, made it possible to understand why people participated in grotesque actions, and sought to prevent a reoccurrence of the violence in the future. The TRC used restitutive, rather than a retributive justice, and the process was open and public, with the national and international public and media invited to join in the process.

The TRC had three parts, the Human Rights Violations Committee (HRV), the Reparation and Rehabilitation Committee (R&R), and an autonomous Amnesty Committee. The R&R Committee developed a policy for reparations and rehabilitation for victims and survivors based on what was revealed in the HRV hearings. The TRC legally compelled people to attend hearings and give evidence. If a subpoena was refused, people faced legal penalties, including fines and jail terms. A key provision was that the Amnesty Committee could grant amnesty if an individual made full disclosure of all relevant facts relating to acts of violence. Both the white military forces and the black African rebel forces were eligible for amnesty for acts of political violence committed between March 1960 and May 1994. Anyone receiving amnesty was immune to prosecution in South Africa's civil or criminal courts. Some people applied for amnesty but did not receive it, and they faced criminal and civil charges. The Truth and Reconciliation Commission linked amnesty to truth telling, exchanging a possibility of amnesty for unimpeded truth.

The TRC did not please all South African citizens. Many survivors of torture, rape, and abduction, or the loved ones of people who were tortured and murdered wanted to see the perpetrators harshly punished, and the flood of retold gruesome events was often challenged.

In the end, the truth that came out of over two years (1995–1998) of TRC hearings was justice. It is not a kind of justice where "justice equals

Continued on page 288

Continued from page 287

punishment" but one where "justice means uncovering what really happened." This kind of justice could not work in an ordinary adversarial system, and it required the opportunity for amnesty. It was also a kind of justice that allowed the victims and survivors to tell their painful stories and reveal the reality of their experience to the public. The TRC was centered on an ideal of restorative justice, as opposed to retribution. It was built on the ideas of victim reparation and offender rehabilitation. The TRC was the beginning of a long healing process. The process included memorials and symbolic ceremonies to recognize and respect the past but not to dwell on it and to focus instead on the enormous task of moving all sides forward to a peaceful future.

Sources: Rotberg and Thompson (2000), Shea (2000), Waldmeir (1998), Klandermans, Roefs, and Olivier (2001), and Wilson et al. (2001).

Moreover, state government supreme court judges interpret the constitutionality of laws, and they have little to do with local crime policy. The candidate on the television was manipulating emotions (e.g., fear of crime), stretching the truth (e.g., her opponent cares little), and misleading voters by saying that only she can solve the problem. From official government crime reports, I knew the crime rate in our area has been steadily declining. Our neighborhood is safer today than anytime in the past decade. I also knew that studies indicate that the length of jail sentences has little impact on the crime rate, and mass media images of criminals are filled with misleading stereotypes. Based on my knowledge and beliefs, I formed a negative opinion of the same candidate from the same commercial.

A critical first step in understanding the impact of symbols, beliefs, and ideas on politics is to be alert to their influence. As Zaller (1992, 4–5) warned, ". . . politically inattentive persons will often be unaware of the implications of persuasive communications they encounter, and so often end up 'mistakenly' accepting them." Recognizing political issues triggers a politicization process. "Politicization is the creation of a state of mind about what is personal or private and what is subject to open discussion and public authority" (Edelman 1977, 120). **Politicization moves issues, symbols, ideas, or moral principles from the unconscious background, or an individual's personal experience, and places them on the public agenda.** For example, the September 11, 2001 terrorist attack on New York's World Trade Center towers triggered politicization; it shifted the private–public boundary. Many people felt an intense emotional shock from the attack, and it immediately rose to the number one national public issue. Privately held symbols, beliefs, and feelings (e.g., pride in one's nation, fear of foreigners, sense of injustice, religious belief) flooded into the public arena. Sociologist C. Wright Mills called an awareness of politicization (i.e., seeing connections between private, personal feelings and public issues) part of the sociological imagination.

c h a r t   7 . 1

SUMMARY OF POLITICAL–SOCIOLOGICAL MODELS OF SYMBOLIC POLITICS

Model	Symbolic Aspect of Politics
Pluralist	It is an expression of basic societal values and is reflected in public opinion.
Elite	It is manipulated by elites to gain and hold onto power and is an aspect of ideology that distorts clear thinking among the masses.
Statist	It is an expression of basic societal values but also can be a restraint on the autonomy of state managers who often are guided by independent scientific-professional thinking.
Power-Structure	The capitalist class controls the means of idea and symbol production; it uses symbols and ideas to advance its class interests and hold onto power.
Structuralist	It is a built-in part of the fundamental structures that legitimate and reproduce domination by the capitalist class, and it is woven into the fabric of daily activities so it is difficult to notice.
Class-Struggle	It is an area of conflict as opposing classes and groups try to advance their ideas, agendas, and interests in symbolic as well as material forms.

Models of Political Sociology

The models of political sociology differ over the role of symbols in politics (see Chart 7.1). For *pluralists* basic values are shared throughout society. In a democratic polity, public opinion shapes voting and other forms of political behavior. Individuals can freely obtain information and discuss ideas without restrictions and then form opinions. The symbolism and the mass media educate the public, organize public opinion, and express diverse public views. By contrast, the *elite model* views symbols and ideas as vital in how political, business, religious, and media elites hold onto power. Elites create, manipulate, and control the ideas and symbols to rule over the masses. The mass media disseminate selective information, mold public opinion in particular directions, and censor oppositional ideas. The *statist model* follows much of the pluralist view, but instead of treating public opinion as the primary source of ideas, treats it as limiting how autonomous state managers can act. Independent professionals, knowledge workers, and experts inside or outside of government are major source ideas for public policies and government actions. State managers develop ideas in organized professions (i.e., science or law), and borrow from other countries or other levels of government. They refine the ideas and insert them into government organizations, hire and train staff to apply them, and develop bureaucratic procedures to implement them. The ideas become part of the institutional structure that shapes current and subsequent policies. Adherents of the *power-structure model* agree with the elite model and hold that, "Public opinion has little or no influence on presidential actions or congressional legislation except as a constraint in times of unpopular wars or domestic social upheaval" (Domhoff 1998, 171). They argue that cultural-symbolic messages are molded by patterns of wealth ownership and the profit principle. The social class that owns great wealth and runs major banks and corporations also owns the production and distribution of ideas. These capitalist class members and their allies ensure that new ideas do not threaten their position of dominance. In the *structuralist model*, society is understood to be an integrated ensemble of economic, political, and ideological structures. Ideological structures legitimate and reproduce conditions of domination. They operate in many spheres (e.g., family, religion, school, art) spreading symbols, values, patterns of thought, and ways of behaving that support the other structures. Instead of an active ruling class that directly manipulates or controls ideas, they believe that ideological assumptions, ideas, attitudes, and beliefs are built into the fabric of institutions, social relationships, and culture. The culture industry disseminates symbols, values, and images that reinforce the political and economic system, and this makes conscious manipulation unnecessary. The culture of consumerism, market forces, profit pressures, and consumer taste operate to select and reinforce a system of values and beliefs. Political sociologists who use the *class-struggle model* place struggles over ideas, agendas, and symbols at the center of politics. As in the structuralist model, built-in assumptions and cultural beliefs are treated as extremely powerful political forces. Battles for people's hearts and minds are inseparable from battles for power and dominance. Unlike the structuralist model, the system of ideas and values is seen as being unstable and porous. It is subject to breaches, and people can resist the dominant way of thinking. The advocates of opposing ideas, beliefs, and values confront and battle one another in various cultural sites, including the mass media and schools.

SYMBOLIC POLITICS AND IDEOLOGY

We will consider two sides of symbolic politics: the politics of symbols and the symbolic aspect of politics. **The politics of symbols refers to the creation, elaboration, and use of symbols for political purposes.** For example, a politician says hardworking people who spent years building up a family business (symbol 1) cannot pass the family business onto their children (symbol 2) because of high inheritance taxes by greedy big government (symbol 3). In reality, the politician wants to cut taxes for very wealthy people. The politician failed to say that the first $1 million of inheritance is already tax free and the tax cut only goes to the richest 1 percent of the population, most of whom are worth well over $10 million. The politician manipulates symbols to win popular support for a proposal that would otherwise be unpopular. The **symbols of politics are a subset of all cultural symbols that stands for specific political values, institutions, or ideas.** Symbols are everywhere—logos for brands such as Nike or signs of religious belief such as the Christian cross or Jewish Star of David. Some symbols carry significant political meaning. For example, the Statue of Liberty signifies the values of individual freedom and liberty, especially for people who lack freedom and liberty. Symbols can become targets; New York's World Trade Center was a symbol of American-controlled global capitalist power and the Pentagon is a symbol of America's military power.

The Politics of Symbols Is Real Politics

Symbols are very influential in politics. In his classic book, *The Symbolic Uses of Politics,* Murray Edelman (1964, 40) argued, "This is not to suggest that signs or symbols in themselves have any magical force as narcotics. They are, rather, the only means by which groups not in a position to analyze a complex situation rationally adjust themselves to it. . . ." In other words, symbols simplify complex political issues for people. We tend to experience the world through symbols. They operate like a script or a lens to implicitly organize ideas, values, and experiences. The "packaging role" of symbols makes it more difficult to recognize them.[2] The intense and broad conflict sparked by some public issues, such as abortion in the United States, is because of their moral–political symbolism.[3]

Cultural myths have many common features with political symbols. Every nation has myths about its origin and critical historic events. For example, the "log cabin myth" is widespread in the United States. In it, most American presidents have come from humble origins, some having grown up in lowly, rustic log cabins; and anyone who has sufficient drive and ability can rise to become president. The myth reinforces egalitarian democratic values and negates the image that a small, rich elite rules America. It is a myth because it is false; "Most of the Presidents were born to families at or very near the top of the American social and economic order."[4] Myths often have some truth in them but are misleading. They simplify reality and convey implicit messages, and they can persist despite negative evidence because people rely on them as scripts, or simplified stories, to make sense of a confusing world.

Symbols of Politics: Heroes, Rituals, Public Celebrations, and Ceremonies

During a trip to Budapest, Hungary in 1998, I visited an outdoor sculpture garden outside the city. It was more of a graveyard for discarded public statutes and monuments from the communist era. I saw physical representations of political symbols, such as the hammer and sickle, and people who were no longer revered, such as statutes of Marx and Lenin. A swift, dramatic change in the political regime relegated these once prominent, proud symbols to an abandoned weed-filled outpost located miles from the city.

Political symbols are not the oddity of a failed regime. Hungary's swift regime change only made it easier to see the symbols of political heroes, rituals, celebrations, and ceremonies. The heroes, rituals, monuments, historical exhibits, celebrations, and ceremonies of a nation both foster a sense of belonging or feeling of collective membership, and they tell a story of events that reinforces a particular interpretation with in-built values. Most public ceremonies, monuments or historical exhibits provide a widely accepted version of events, values, and beliefs. Yet, creating public symbols is never politically neutral; it always includes some points of view and excludes others. "Commemorative activity is by definition social and political, for it involves the coordination of individual and group memories whose results may appear consensual when they are, in fact, the product of processes of intense contest, struggle, and, in some instances, annihilation."[5] Political symbols are representations of values. They are, "one strategy by which groups attempt to gain or maintain power" as Gusfield and Michalowicz (1984, 424) observed.

Disputes over interpretations of official events or monuments reveal tension about the underlying values and power relations in symbolic politics. For example, in the United States disputes arose when gay people asked to march in an official St. Patrick's Day parade, when officials declared a national holiday for the slain civil rights leader Martin Luther King, Jr., when the Vietnam War memorial in Washington was unveiled, and when the plane that dropped the first atomic bomb at Hiroshima was placed on exhibit at the Smithsonian museum.[6] In each case, a disagreement erupted over which values and interpretation of events would be elevated in a public ritual, celebration, holiday, or commemoration. Barthel (1996) says that a similar process occurs when certain sites are designated as "historic" and to be preserved but others are not, when particular persons are honored by a monument, or when certain events are featured in public museums. They simultaneously legitimate and privilege one particular interpretation of a place, person, or event. For example, the Vietnam War memorial in Washington, DC has become a sacred site. People go there to engage in rituals honoring those who died. Yet some people objected to it because it was not sufficiently masculine and did not glorify war heroes in a traditional patriotic fashion. Because of the political controversy over the memorial, the government built a traditional statute of three soldiers with a flag near the Vietnam memorial.[7]

When creating an exhibit, museum curators select some aspects for emphasis and omit others to produce a story with symbolic messages. For example, through its construction and presentation, a museum exhibit might express the implicit message that, brave young soldiers fought valiantly to defend and protect our sacred homeland. A story is created by what is selected, emphasized, or omitted. It rarely is a false story, but it is one particular version of what happened. Other versions are "silenced" by being absent from an official, public setting. In highlighting certain people, actions, or events, exhibits implicitly promote certain values or beliefs over others.[8] Few people who visit a museum exhibit, view a public monument, or participate in a public ritual are conscious of the implicit symbolic messages or realize that they are being given one selective interpretation to the exclusion of others. It takes a lot of time, cultural knowledge, and cognitive energy to "read" or decode symbolic messages that appear in an exhibit.

Public memory is manifest in museums, monuments, holidays, and public celebrations.[9] **Public memory is a system of understandings, beliefs, and** interpretations about past events and individuals that gives people a feeling of collective identity, meaning, and purpose. Other vehicles of public memory include school textbooks, popular historical novels or biographies, and film or television recreations of historical events. By disseminating one interpretation of historical figures or events, public memory expresses political–cultural values or beliefs in a concrete form. Thus, the first act of new Iraq government in 2003 was to eliminate the old holidays.[10]

Public memory changes over time. For example, American heroes, such as George Washington or Abraham Lincoln, did not always occupy their current esteemed position in the public memory. Historians, novelists, journalists, curators, and political advocates constructed and disseminated specific memories about them. Likewise, an esteemed public memory of President John F. Kennedy and Martin Luther King, Jr., only appeared after they had been assassinated, and it differed significantly from their public image when they were alive. Public memory creation is an ongoing process. For example, the recreated historical theme park of colonial Williamsburg, Virginia lacked black slaves for decades, and a central dimension of daily colonial life was erased. Slowly, after pressure from the civil rights movement, the voices and presence of black people were added to the recreation of colonial America.[11]

The public memories can be carefully crafted.[12] Political processes shape the creation of public memory, or the official version of the past, by emphasizing some parts of the history and obscuring or suppressing other parts. Opposing political advocates may attempt to gain control over public memory creation to advance their own values and version of events. Some politically organized but marginal groups (e.g., American Indians, Latinos, Japanese Americans sent to concentration camps) have created their own museums, monuments, holidays, or celebrations to preserve memories and offer alternative interpretations to the dominant public memory.

Public festivals and rituals usually convey implicit political messages. For example, spectator sporting events combine a display of talent and competition with the renewal of the social bonds of in-group solidarity. We can "read" the Olympics as a symbolic festival that channels national struggles over status, prestige, and power into a regulated, nonlethal, nonmilitary format. For a brief period in the sporting realm, international competition assumes the form of contests of physical skill and athletic achievements by representative individuals and teams. Olympic medals symbolize a nation's vigor and strength, bringing it global honor and prestige. Once media coverage brought a larger audience, colorful pageantry increased, and the Olympics increasingly became a forum for the celebration of nationalism. Many national governments sustain and regulate sports, sometimes with cabinet-level sports agencies, because political leaders believe that sports reinforce the values of self-discipline and skill development and elevate constructive competition while building group solidarity.[13] Political symbols also enter sports in ritual observances (e.g., playing the national anthem) or become visible with protest, as when two American athletes gave the black power salute at the 1968 Mexico City Olympics.[14] The symbolic messages in rituals can be double-edged and may permit multiple readings. In addition to promoting the official values and ideas, opponents may try to capture them and use them against government authorities.[15] In sum, symbolic politics is real politics. The symbolic dimension of politics extends deep into a spiritual or transcendent level. We will see this next with civil religion.

Civil Religion and Political Witches

For most of human history, the supreme political leader in a country also held a unique, high religious position with sacred responsibilities and powers. This is evidenced by Roman emperor worship cults, the Chinese mandate of heaven, the European divine right of kings, and the Japanese emperor's role in Shinto religion. The top elected political official is rarely assigned a sacred religious role in today's democracies, but something of a sacred dimension still exists. Many people are in awe of those who hold concentrated power, and power itself acquires a sacred religious aura.

Religion and politics frequently mix, even in nations with a constitutional mandate to separate church and state. Thus, European settlers brought to the United States customs, traditions, and legal–moral principles rooted in Judeo-Christian religious beliefs, practices, or teachings where they became embedded in mainstream American culture.[16] Christian beliefs, principles, and values permeate the secular national culture. For example, government offices close on Christian religious holidays, public officials and witnesses in a court of law must swear on the Christian holy book, public streets and buildings are decorated on major Christian holidays, and many laws originate in Christian moral doctrine. References to the Judeo-Christian god appear on money and in the official Pledge of Allegiance.

The forms and intensity of religious influence in politics vary over time. For example, American public schools once mandated that children recite Christian (specifically Protestant) prayers. Legal disputes continue over government actions that endorse specific religious beliefs, and the culture would look different if all its religious elements vanished, or if all religious faiths were treated equally. Political movements such as the American Revolution, proslavery and antislavery movements, populism ideals in the 1890s, Prohibition in the 1920s, and civil rights in the 1960s all justified their causes by referring to Christian religious ideals.[17] Even in the twenty first century we see that a local town council wants a Christian cross in a public park, or a judge posts the Ten Commandments in his courtroom.

Civil Religion

Like most nations, the United States has a civil religion. **Civil religion is a transcendent faith in the nation that celebrates and sanctifies a nation's way of life by giving official rituals, holidays, symbols, and monuments a spiritual meaning and connecting them to something larger, treating them with reverence and assigning them a quasi-religious moral meaning.** Civil religion is embedded in the scripts or narratives of films, fiction, and public memory. It presents exemplary people (e.g., heroes, villains), familiar plots or legends (e.g., small town boy wins success through hard work), and venerates core values (e.g., freedom from tyranny).[18] America's civil religion includes faith that it is a unique nation that has a sacred purpose. "American civil religion mythologizes and legitimizes the American polity by conveying to the political process a progressive, teleological, foreordained, transcendent purpose."[19]

Major themes of America's civil religion are individual choice and personal achievement. Heroic myths emphasize unrestricted individual choice and praise rugged individuals and entrepreneurs. Businesses, schools, and government agencies promote individualism. It is reinforced in sports, the media, political speeches, and advertising. Yet an emphasis on individual free choice can obscure structured inequality, and it discourages discussing systematic political and economic power, so that "avoidance may itself become culturally legitimate."[20]

Symbolic politics and civil religion also explain the fierce emotional and legal controversy that periodically erupts over the issue of flag desecration. A national flag is emblematic of the nation and has deep roots in nationalism. Civil religion symbolically transforms a secular object, a flag, into a sacred icon. Citizens show the same reference toward the national flag that religious believers display toward holy religious objects.[21] If a citizen fails to honor and venerate the flag, it is a "sacrilege" and implies he/she is politically disloyal and morally impure.

Manifestations of civil religion abound in the judicial system. For example, judges wear religiouslike robes and treat the Constitution as a sacred text that has been passed down from revered ancient, hallowed wise men—the founding fathers. Public schools teach civil religion through daily rituals (e.g., patriotic music, Pledge of Allegiance, holidays), in formal curriculum, and extracurricular activities.[22] Many holiday celebrations are modeled on Christian worship rituals, and even the word, *holiday,* originated with "holy day." Civil religion is compatible with an official separation of church and state because the nation itself is being worshiped.[23] U.S. presidents regularly espouse principles of civil religion. Observers noted a major source of President Ronald Reagan's remarkable popularity came from his skills in articulating the themes of civil religion to the American public.[24]

Civil religion also shapes how people think about political issues, protest, and legal decisions.[25] The sociologist Louis Wirth (1936, xiv–xv) saw it as limiting political thinking when he said, "frank and objective inquiry into the most sacred and cherished institutions and beliefs is more or less seriously restricted in every country in the world. . . . That there is an area of 'dangerous thought' in every society is, therefore, scarcely debatable. While we recognize that what is dangerous to think about may differ from country to country and from epoch to epoch, on the whole *the subjects marked with the danger signal are those which the society or the controlling element in it believe to be so vital and hence so sacred that they will not tolerate their profanation by discussion.* But what is not easily recognized is the fact that thought, even in the absence of official censorship, is disturbing, and, under certain conditions, dangerous and subversive (emphasis added)."

Thus, a serious, neutral investigation into core values, beliefs, and assumptions can be dangerous because debating sacred ideas is taboo and challenging them is heretical.

The theorist Emile Durkheim theorized that every society ". . . has a set of shared beliefs, values and symbols that express the highest aspirations of the collectivity . . ." but he failed to specify whose beliefs, values, and symbols they would be.[26] In the twentieth century, white small business owners, clergy, and self-employed professionals who resided in villages, small towns, and smaller cities supplied the core beliefs and symbols of America's civil religion.[27]

Some observers think that "culture wars" and the mobilization of particular religious groups in the United States during the 1980s (discussed later in this chapter) was a battle over civil religion. As the principles, symbols, and themes of traditional civil religion became less relevant, or ceased to offer moral cohesion, opposing groups fought to interject their own beliefs and control its direction.[28] Civil religion not only provides cultural–political "saints" or patriotic heroes; it also helps to create their opposite—enemies who embody cultural/political evil, the political witches.

Political Witches

Traditionally, a witch is an ugly, elderly woman with supernatural powers who performs such evil acts as black magic, sinister satanic rituals, and religious heresy. Witches appear in children's Halloween costumes, fables and folktales, Shakespeare's plays, and Hollywood horror movies. In the late Middle Ages in Europe and in colonial America, "sane," reasonable people, church officials, and government leaders hunted down, tortured, and killed innocent people because they believed that these people were witches. Witches are also relevant to contemporary political processes. A witch is someone who does not believe in the dominant religion, embraces evil, and creates misfortune for others. Witch crazes and witch hunts are a form of mass hysteria that also clarify social boundaries and reaffirm the moral order. Witch hunts strengthen social solidarity by forcefully defining deviance in settings where the social order is weakened. They bring together anxious, uncertain, threatened, or insecure people and offer them stability, certainty, and security by identifying the source of anxiety and unease. As it clarifies and validates the line between right and wrong, a witch hunt also promotes a sense of unity and membership in a righteous, moral community.[29]

A political witch is a heretic to civil religion who advocates ideas, beliefs, and values that threaten the nation. **Political witch hunts are mass movements, often state supported, that clarify and affirm the boundaries of acceptable political ideas and values while building solidarity around the civil religion.** The anticommunist crusade of Senator Joseph McCarthy in the early 1950s is America's best-known political witch hunt, although witch hunts are found in many countries.[30] Political leaders evoke civil religious symbols during political witch hunts to consolidate their hold on power and advance their own political goals.[31] Civil religion provides positive symbols and rites that give political life a sacred meaning; political witch hunts offer a set of parallel negative symbols and rites. "Through such activities as the purge, trial, investigation, accusation, arrest and imprisonment, society creates its own enemies to ritually reaffirm the very sacred national purposes, which subversives are supposedly undermining. . . . Political witch hunts are the ritual mechanisms that transform individuals, organizations or cultural artifacts from things of this world into actors within a mythical universe."[32] In a process similar to political witch hunts, political leaders may use domestic or foreign threats to impose "compulsory patriotism" (i.e., the forced glorification of political symbols with punishment for nonconformists) and intensify control over the population (see Case in Point 7.1). Next we will turn to ideologies, which are secular or nonreligious belief systems that also shape political thought and action.

 CASE IN POINT 7.1   **Compulsory Patriotism after the September 11 Terrorist Attack?**

In addition to outrage, a broad-based outpouring of American patriotism followed the September 11, 2001 attack on the New York World Trade Center. Hidden under the landslide of public support, a few voices questioned the military response and the imposition of certain domestic security measures. A few asked the taboo question, Could a deficiency in the United States or in government policy have contributed to or provoked this kind of attack? Despite a national list of enemies and dissenters, the firing of a few professors and journalists, and curbs on the media, no political witch hunt developed. Yet intense pressure to display patriotism grew. In Wisconsin, the state legislature passed a law in August 2001 mandating the display of a national flag in all classrooms, and either daily playing the national anthem or reciting the Pledge of Allegiance by all public school students. Previously, saying the Pledge of Allegiance was a widespread voluntary practice in most schools. Shortly after the September 11 attack, members of the school board in the city where I live implemented the new law by playing an instrumental version of an anthem over loudspeakers in all schools each day. They wanted to respect the beliefs of students who felt uncomfortable about the religious clause in the Pledge and the

violence mentioned in the anthem. They immediately ignited a national outrage. Headlines across the country announced (incorrectly), "School Board Bans Pledge." After a very heated, overflow public meeting, local conservative activists led by an ex-Congressman initiated a petition drive to recall all the "unpatriotic" school board members who voted to play the anthem instead of requiring each student and teacher to sing the anthem or recite the pledge publicly. School board members held that imposing patriotism violated fundamental American political principles, and they felt that a person's true love of country must be voluntary and originate as a sincere inner commitment. By contrast, the conservative activists demanded compulsory patriotism (i.e., requiring students to outwardly display their patriotism). Defenders of the school board said that it seemed to be a gross contradiction in a nation founded on defending individual rights and freedom from government impositions to reduce patriotism to coerced conformity in a public setting as required by the new government edict. The recall attempt failed to gain enough signatures, but the incident highlights the issue of compulsory patriotism, the significance of intense emotions in politics, and the role of political symbols.

"Flagless in a patriotic zone?"

IDEOLOGY

Ideology is a core concept in political sociology. **Ideology refers to an interconnected set of assumptions, beliefs, values, and ideas that guides how people think about and evaluate issues.** Yet the term has multiple meanings and those who embrace opposing ideologies often fight over definitions. As David McLellan (1986, 1) noted, "Ideology is the most elusive concept in the whole of social science. For it asks about the basis and validity of our most fundamental ideas. As such, it is an essentially contested concept . . .." In the next sections, we review the development of the concept, examine types of ideology, and consider major ideologies.

A Brief History of the Concept

The term, *ideology,* first appeared in the early 1800s. It described Enlightenment thinkers who favored a rational system of ideas and beliefs, or an *ideo-ology* (i.e., a science of ideas), and hoped it could replace the feudal-era emphasis on total obedience to traditional and religious authorities without analysis or rational debate. The French ruler Emperor Napoleon I gave ideology a negative connotation and favored "knowledge of the human heart" over it. Definitions of ideology have been embroiled in theoretical debates and political conflicts for over two centuries.[33]

Two major nineteenth century social theorists, Karl Marx and Emile Durkheim, shaped the concept's early development. Karl Marx advanced a materialist theory in which the society's dynamics ultimately originated with its "base"; that is, its material conditions and production of goods and services. He included ideology as part of the "superstructure," which also included religion, morality, law, education, customs, language, and ideas. The superstructure rests on the base that supports and determines it. Marx outlined his thinking on ide-

CLOSER LOOK 7.1   **Marx's Theory of Ideology**

- Ideas develop out of material conditions and real human relationships. They do not appear on their own, but arise from people's everyday actions and life experiences. Although ideas originate in material conditions, they can have an independent effect of influencing subsequent behavior and material conditions. As Marx and Engles (1947 [1846], 13–16) stated, "The production of ideas, of conceptions, of consciousness, is at first interwoven with the material activity and the material intercourse of men, the language of real life. Conceiving, thinking . . . appears as the direct efflux of their material behavior. . . . Life is not determined by consciousness, but consciousness by life."

- Ideas are integral to how one social class comes to politically dominate and economically exploit other classes. The ruling ideas, or ideas that people learn and accept as "official," are the ruling class's ideas. The ruling class controls both the means of material and idea production that it uses to maintain power. According to Marx and Engles (1947 [1846], 39), "The ideas of the ruling class are in every epoch the ruling ideas: i.e., the class, which is the

ruling material force of society, is at the same time its ruling intellectual force . . . generally speaking, the ideas of those who lack the means of mental production are subject to it. . . ."

- Ideas that reinforce political domination appear to be natural and universal. This "naturalizing" makes ruling class ideas very seductive. They do not appear to come from or only defend the interests of one social class; they appear to apply to everyone. One way the ruling class rules is "to represent its interest as the common interest of all members of society . . . it will put its ideas in the form of universality, and represent them as the only rational, universally valid ones." (Marx and Engles 1947 [1846], 41).

- People in classes beneath the ruling class can be misled and develop false ideas about their situation. They embrace ruling class ideas instead of ones that best reflect their own true class situation. Such a false consciousness restricts their ability to see their true situation and to act in their collective self-interest. They can overcome this limitation through political struggle (see Eagleton 1991, 70–90 and McLelland 1986).

ology in *The German Ideology* (Marx and Engles 1947 [1846]), which can be summarized into four key points (see Closer Look 7.1).

Although Emile Durkheim rarely used the term, he argued that science differs from and is opposed to ideology that is a type of distorted thinking. Unlike ideology, science can overcome distortion and get to the truth. Durkheim argued that each society has an idea or value system that acts as a "social cement" to integrate people around shared beliefs and create a collectivity. People assign a sacred (civil religion) value to the social cement (i.e., ideas, beliefs, and values about their unity) and create a feeling that they are part of a larger purpose.[34] In the Durkheimian tradition, "Ideology creates . . . models of moral order that can be visualized. . . ."[35] An ideology and morality (i.e., what is right and wrong) are mutually reinforcing. Just as people create and engage in rituals to signify morality, they create political rituals and social institutions to reflect, represent, and generate enthusiasm for the tenets of ideology. An ideology only continues if social resources (e.g., people, organizations) sustain it. Interestingly, over the course of the nineteenth century, the definition of ideology reversed from meaning a rational, scientific critique of illusionary thinking to meaning distorted and antiscientific ideas.

Early in the twentieth century, three European theorists refined the concept of ideology—the Hungarian Georg Lukacs (1885–1971), the Italian Antonio Gramsci (1891–1937), and the German Karl Mannheim (1893–1947). Lukacs studied how material conditions give rise to an ideology and create false consciousness. For Lukacs, thought is rooted in a person's specific social location, and science alone cannot overcome false thinking. Distorted thinking is having a partial, superficial, or incomplete view that arises from living in a specific social location under specific historical conditions. Thus, a limited perspective creates false thinking. He felt the only way to break through it is to learn to see beyond one's particular social position and adopt the standpoint of all parts of society across human history.[36]

Karl Mannheim also explored the connections between one's social position and his/her mode of thinking, or worldview. Like Lukacs, Mannheim saw distorted thought as originating in a person's particular position in society. To move beyond it, he offered relationalism. **Relationism is a special type of non ideological thinking that intellectuals can achieve from their unique social positions by openly accepting people from all sectors of society, looking at events from multiple points of view, and developing special methods for analyzing ideas.**[37]

We encountered Antonio Gramsci's idea of hegemony in Chapter 1. Gramsci broadened and deepened the concept of ideology, replacing it with hegemony. To him, ideology was a set of distorted ideas and values that rulers impose upon a people. Hegemony also includes what rulers do, purposely or not, to win the consent of the ruled. It has cultural, political, legal, and economic dimensions and includes procedures, such elections, and symbols, such as singing the national anthem, to win loyalty from the ruled. It extends to diverse institutions, organizations, and activities (e.g., Boy Scouts, commercial television) that build and support the structure power and domination.[38]

The Frankfurt School, a group of German intellectuals associated with the Institute for Social Research, founded in Germany in 1923, refined thinking about ideology. Many in the Frankfurt School left for the United States during the 1930s as Hitler rose to power.[39] They used Marx's ideas but rejected orthodox Marxism and integrated thinking from Mannheim, Gramsci, and Sigmund Freud. They rejected Durkheim's great faith in science but used his notion that ideology can be a kind of social cement. They held that ideology profoundly shapes social relations because it is inside culture, language, art, music, and personality development. They advanced, "theories of the capitalism, of the structure of the state, and the rise of instrumental reason; analysis of developments in science, technology and technique, of the culture industry and mass culture, of family structure and individual development, and of the susceptibility of people to ideology. . . ."[40] The Frankfurt School held that a near-invisible dominant ideology permeated all cultural institutions, and few people could escape it. It reinforced capitalist economic relations and the structure of political power, shaping all modes of thought, daily habits, and the very sense of a person's "self."[41]

Although they differed from the Frankfurt School, three late twentieth century French theorists, Louis Althusser, Michel Foucault, and Pierre Bourdieu, extended the discussion on ideology. Compared to earlier theorists, they saw ideology as being deeper, more concealed, and more pervasive.

Louis Althusser (1918–1990) was a leading structuralist theorist in the class-analysis framework of political sociology and contributed the concept of the Ideological State Apparatus. **The Ideological State Apparatus is a set of major institutions (e.g., schools, churches, families, media, sports, and political parties) that operates as a loosely connected system, in conjunction with politics and the economy, to shape people, their identities, and their consciousness so they will conform to the needs of capitalism**. Althusser "reoriented the study of ideology by emphasizing that ideology have, first of all, a material existence" and that "ideologies exist in apparatuses forming part of the State. . . ."[42] Althusser argued that ideology is more than ideas; it has a material form and penetrates and configures social institutions, daily habits, and routine activities. Beyond the mind alone, it molds a way of life.[43]

Michel's Foucault's (1926–1984) writings focused on discourse and the relationship between power and knowledge. He saw the organizational form of institutions, modes of thought and speech, and types of knowledge as containing power relations. Similar to Gramsci's concept of hegemony and Althusser's idea that ideology takes a material form, Foucault said that power operates in the very forms of people's discussions, the patterns of their daily activities, and the categories they think in when classifying other people or social relations (e.g., male/female, different races). He sought to dissolve distinctions among thought, discussion, and physical activity. He argued that we can only do what we discuss, and we only discuss what we can think. Thus, our way of thinking places limits on our actions. Ideology is how power relations operate through our thoughts, discussions, and daily actions.[44]

Pierre Bourdieu (1930–2002) wrote widely on culture and argued that symbolic forms (i.e., language, ideas, myths, cultural knowledge) are central to maintaining relations of inequality and power. Symbolic forms allow power relations to be disguised or hidden, so the relations appear to be taken for granted, inevitable, or natural. Symbols both integrate the parts of society together and serve as a basis for domination. Rulers and others apply physical violence (i.e., the use of physical force to compel people to act in certain ways) to enforce and sustain power. They can also apply symbolic violence. **Symbolic violence is the use of language, morality, rules, ideas, and other symbolic forms to compel people and sustain power relations**. Thus, elites define proper forms of speaking, upright moral behavior, and rules of polite conduct. People rarely recognize that symbolic violence is part of a system of domination, but accept it as legitimate. Its physical traces appear in the form of school records, job promotion rules, or books of etiquette. Symbolic violence leaves scars that are as real as physical violence,

CLOSER LOOK 7.2   **Contributions of Therborn to the Discussion of Ideology**

The Swedish thinker, Göran Therborn (1980) offered ideas on ideology that can be condensed into six major points:

- Ideology plays a critical role in organizing, maintaining, and altering the power relations in a society.
- Ideology is an ongoing, evolving process; it is never static.
- Ideology has multiple forms; its ideas can be true or false, tightly integrated, or loose and fragmented. It can be both the common sense of ordinary people and the idea system of intellectuals.

- Ideology offers people a mental framework and gives meaning to people's lives by telling them what exists now, what is good and bad, and what is possible in the future.
- Ideology and daily actions and practices are interdependent. Material conditions create ideas, and ideas take on a material manifestation and affect events. Ideology is more than just ideas.
- Multiple ideologies are in contention at any given time; ideologies exist in a field with competing and opposing ideologies that have varying degrees of significance and vitality.

but they are emotional, psychic, and mental.[45] Other European thinkers, such as Göran Therborn, also advanced discussions of ideology (see Closer Look 7.2).

We can summarize two centuries of European debate on ideology in six principles.

1. *Sociology of Knowledge Principle.* Ideas and beliefs arise from the material reality of social–economic life. People develop beliefs and ideas based on experiences they have in their location in society and their daily life situations. Such ideas can "feed back" and influence actions and material conditions.
2. *Unequal Distribution Principle.* Ideas and beliefs are unevenly distributed among individuals, groups, or organizations. Different sectors of society hold beliefs that differ in content and degree of coherence.
3. *Deception Principle.* Ideas and beliefs have the potential to obscure, mask, or hide the past or present. They can also disclose, reveal or make apparent what was previously unknown. Many people have inaccurate ideas and make erroneous decisions, but this can be overcome through political action.
4. *Material Form Principle.* Ideology is not just a collection of ideas and beliefs in people's minds; it also has a material form in daily activities, language, institutions, laws, and so forth.
5. *Power Principle.* The exercise of power, dominance, and governance depends on a system of ideas and beliefs. Power and ideology are interdependent; all power relations have an ideological dimension.
6. *Political Struggle Principle.* Many societies have multiple, competing ideologies; the creation, dissemination, and rise to dominance of an ideology is the result of contested, ongoing struggle.[46]

American Views of Ideology

Political sociologists agree that ideology is essential for examining people's thinking, the use of power, and political rule. The Europeans saw ideology as having a deep and broad influence, but Americans adopted a very different approach. A large group of American political sociologists said ideology was a threat in other countries but inconsequential in the United States. They held that their ideas were nonideological, rational, scientific, pragmatic, and realistic, but that those of opponents were tainted by ideology. The proposition that a person's point of view is "not itself ideological has been alive and well since the Second World War and living mainly in America."[47]

Next we consider four approaches that American political sociologists used to examine ideology: the end of ideology thesis, closed thinking, constrained beliefs, and self-labeling.

According to the *end of ideology thesis*, ideologies are contentious, destructive idea systems rooted in the clashes of opposing social classes during early industrial capitalism. Once a society evolves beyond an early industrial form to become highly rational-scientific and post-industrial, the social structure will no longer have class conflict, making ideology obsolete. Others similarly argue that a set of postmaterialist values have arisen since the 1970s in advanced industrial nations that have replaced the old materialistic ideologies based on opposing social classes.[48]

In the *closed thinking approach*, ideology is a rigid, non rational, and closed way of thinking. It is thought control based on deception and distortion that antidemocratic revolutionary leaders, especially of communist and fascist movements, have used to seize power and build a totalitarian state. In open democratic societies, by contrast, ideology is nearly absent. Universal suffrage, pluralism, civil liberties, and free speech undermine ideology so it only surfaces in fringe, extremist movements. Thus, ideology is a characteristic of totalitarian dictatorships.[49]

The *constrained belief approach* began with Philip Converse's (1964) classic study of political belief. Many quantitative social researchers built on his definition of ideology—a coherent set of individual beliefs, values, and attitudes that people use to cognitively organize ideas and guide their evaluation of candidates and policy. The set of attitudes are a less sophisticated version of the formal ideologies (see next section in this chapter) that intellectuals and politicians use. Studies that used survey questions to measure ideology found that about 5 percent of Americans were highly ideological (i.e., their thinking and attitudes were organized around a set of consistent and stable core principles). This ideological minority tended to be highly educated with an intense interest in politics, such as political party activists. The vast majority of Americans did not think ideologically but were flexible and varied their political thinking over time. Still others were highly apathetic with logically inconsistent views that fluctuated erratically.[50]

The *self-label approach* asks people to name their ideologies. Thus, saying, "I am a liberal" or "I am conservative" is a significant symbolic act that people use to anchor their interpretation of political events. Gerson (1996, 2) noted, "... Americans, perhaps more than any other people, object to political labels with a curious ferocity. . . . This does not obviate the use of labels; actually, it makes them more important because they are less self-evident." One weakness of this approach is that the public appears to be confused about ideology and many (about 40 percent) use ideological labels incorrectly.[51] They will call conservative politicians or policies liberal and vice versa. It is because few people learn ideological systems in school, they are not part of popular discourse, the media and politicians use ideological labels inconsistently, political parties are not highly ideological, and many people are not attentive to political issues.[52] Plus, many ideological stands are issue-specific and only weakly connected to other issues.[53]

A person's income level is a better predictor of her/his position on key policies than is an ideological self label (see Table 7.1). For example, about 10 percent of high-income people want to equalize incomes versus nearly one-third of low-income people, and about 55 percent of high-income people want the government to do less versus 22 percent of the low-income group. The differences by ideological self-label are small. Strong conservative identification ranges from 14 to 24 percent for the two extreme income groups.

Self-labeling is a public statement and is only weakly associated with taking specific policy positions.[54] More significantly, conservatives and liberals appear to adopt ideological self-labels for different reasons.[55] Nonetheless, people can use ideological labels loosely in a symbolic or heuristic way.[56] For example, a person uses a label to sort through media statements and candidates to support in an election.

Studies found both increased liberalism and growing conservatism in the United States—both an ideological convergence and a growing polarization.[57] During the 1980s and 1990s, fewer Americans adopted a liberal label, but people increasingly embraced liberal stands on some issues (e.g., accepting women working outside the home, equal rights for racial minorities) and conservative stands on others (e.g., approving capital punishment, favoring welfare cuts). More liberal thinking on racial issues also may have had a major electoral impact.[58]

Few people use all-encompassing and internally consistent ideologies. As Jennifer Hochschild (1981, 236–237) argued, "a simple liberal-conservative dimension does not provide a pattern for belief systems once we move beyond well-socialized elites . . . [we should] stop trying to place all issues and all people along a single liberal-conservative dimension." Instead of operating along a single continuum, individual ideology (i.e., attitudes and values that guide thinking) may be issue-specific. Thus, there is a crime ideology, a race ideology, a welfare ideology, a gender ideology, and so forth with the linkages among the domains either loose or tightly locked together for individuals.

European and American theorists diverge in their views of ideology, but the views are compatible if we see them as being focused on different levels of reality. Americans tend to focus on explicit surface-level individual attitudes, while Europeans emphasize core beliefs and values that are embedded in cultural institutions and language. The Americans require ideology to be visible and easily measured,

TABLE 7.1	Survey Results on Income Level and Ideology

Percentage of Americans at Various Income Levels Who Say:

Family Income Level	Should Government Equalize Incomes?*			Should the Government Do More or Less?**		
	Yes	Maybe	No	More	Ok	Less
Under $10,000	50.0	39.8	10.2	37.2	44.2	18.6
$10–19,900	31.3	55.4	13.4	23.9	47.7	28.4
$20–29,900	28.6	52.9	18.5	35.9	38.5	25.6
$30–39,900	31.7	50.0	18.3	31.4	47.1	21.6
$40–49,900	28.4	50.0	21.6	20.5	54.8	24.7
$50–59,900	26.1	59.4	14.5	19.4	59.7	20.9
$60–74,900	23.9	53.7	22.4	16.4	53.7	29.9
$75–89,900	19.4	54.8	25.8	21.0	46.8	32.3
$90,000+	20.2	47.6	32.3	17.1	46.3	36.6
All Income Groups	29.1	51.2	18.9	25.4	47.8	26.8

Percentage of Americans at Various Income Levels Who Self-Identify Ideologically As***

Family Income Level	Liberal	Lean Toward:		Lean Toward:	Conservative
		Liberal	Moderate	Conservative	
Under $10,000	17.7	11.3	32.3	19.4	19.4
$10–19,900	14.0	7.6	45.9	12.8	19.8
$20–29,900	14.9	14.9	40.5	11.3	18.5
$30–39,900	16.9	10.8	38.5	14.2	19.6
$40–49,900	11.3	15.7	40.0	14.8	18.3
$50–59,900	11.5	18.6	38.1	14.2	17.7
$60–74,900	16.8	12.6	37.9	17.9	14.7
$75–89,900	8.8	14.3	40.7	18.7	17.6
$90,000+	14.5	11.0	30.1	22.5	22.0
All Income Groups	14.3	12.6	38.2	16.0	18.9

*Survey Question: "Do you think the government should do something to equalize incomes between the rich and poor (1), or government should not concern itself (7). Answer Categories Shown: YES = 1 and 2, Maybe = 3, 4 and 5, NO = 6 and 7.

**Survey Question: "Do you think the government is doing too many things or could do more? Where do more = 1 Doing too much = 5. Answer Categories Shown: More = 1, OK = 2, 3, 4, Too Much = 5.

***Survey Question: "Would you call yourself an extremely liberal, liberal, leaning toward liberal, moderate, leaning toward conservative, conservative, or extremely conservative?" Answer Categories Shown: Extreme Liberal combined with Liberal, and Extreme Conservative combined with Conservative.

Sources: Computed from the 2002 General Social Survey, a random sample of roughly 1,800 adult Americans, with the family income levels collapsed into major groups. No answer, refused to answer and don't know responses have been excluded from the table.

**"You'll be happy to know, Father, he's not a Liberal,
Moderate or Conservative. Jason's a nothing."**

while the Europeans say that an ideology can shape and limit a person's thoughts, values, and beliefs, even if he/she cannot express ideas in the form of explicit ideological opinions. Americans rely on survey research, while European use historical and cultural studies to show that the organization of social institutions limits consciousness and restricts what people can think about and discuss.

Ideology and Public Opinion

Because many classic era political sociologists believed that the United States was ideology free and because U.S. universities emphasize quantitative survey methodology, public opinion is studied more than ideology in America. Polling and survey research organizations extensively monitor public opinion for political elites, government agencies, electoral campaign organizations, corporate marketing departments, and the mass media.

What is public opinion? For most people, it is what polling yields, but public opinion existed long before survey research and opinion polls appeared in the mid-twentieth century. The idea of "the public" grew from Enlightenment-era ideals about democracy and was preceded by ideas about "the people," such as "the crowd" (emotional mob in one place) or "the mass" (many isolated individuals). The *public* is a self-aware collection of people who discuss social and political issues, and who develop and share views on the major issues. Mustafa Emirbayer and Mimi Sheller (1999, 156) ". . . define publics as open-ended flows of communication that enable socially distant interlocutors to bridge social-network positions, formulate collective orientations, and generate psychical 'working alliances' in pursuit of influence over issues of common concern."

The French Enlightenment philosopher Jean-Jacques Rousseau (1712–1778) advanced the idea of public opinion. He felt the state should reflect the "general

SUMMARY 7.1	Six Definitions of Public Opinion

1. The simple sum of many separate individual opinions or answers (most widely used definition).
2. What the majority actually believes, its social norms, and what most people express in public.
3. The clash of opposing interests; a mix of ideas crystallized and communicated by interest groups.

4. Ideas on key issues as formulated and expressed by political leaders and mass media journalists.
5. A rhetorical fiction or imaginary creation; a convenient label for "what people think."
6. The views expressed by publics (i.e., concerned citizens who interact and express ideas about issues).

Source: Adapted from Glynn et al. (1999, 17–26).

will," or what people want when they think of the entire community. Opinion includes an individual's ideas and general beliefs held across the society. Thus, **public opinion means the individual and collective thinking about current issues affecting society that self-aware people discuss in their exchanges**. (For other definitions of public opinion see Summary 7.1.)

The technology used to measure public opinion has altered its meaning. Early modes for expressing opinion included strikes, parades, riots or demonstrations, debates in coffee houses or taverns, town meetings, soap box speeches, books and magazine articles, newspaper articles and letters to the editor, and burning the effigy of a person, as well as elections, referenda, and petitions. For example, nineteenth century American and British people expressed disapproval by hanging banners along streets, loudly banging on pots and pans, or by illumination (i.e., all residents of a street placing candles in windows). People can express opinions by refusing to pay taxes, appearing at a public hearing, or writing graffiti. Polling technology has overshadowed the various ways a public can express opinions.[59]

Critics believe something is lost when public opinion is reduced to poll results.[60] They say polls take the "public" out of public opinion and substitute isolated individuals. Polls convert a specific behavior (e.g., checking a questionnaire box) into an attitude (i.e., one's inner thoughts and beliefs) in a way that eliminates the interpersonal interaction of ordinary social contexts. Polling constrains the range of open personal expression into a set of narrow, limited responses (e.g., agree or disagree with an issue) and transforms popular demands into "objects of persuasion" that can be monitored, managed, and manipulated by governmental and bureaucratic elites for their own purposes.[61]

Polling technology creates a specific form of "public opinion." Most opinion polling reshapes what people accept as "public thinking" in ways that force it to conform to the parameters of elite political discourse. Thus, when the mass media offer poll results as scientifically-measured public thought, what they present is very limited.[62]

As the nation-state developed, public officials created systems of surveillance, rational administration, and control over a nation's people and territory. Officials wanted to know about conditions in their nation and introduced the population census, government census, and opinion measurement.[63] As techniques of opinion measurement advanced, government and corporate leaders increasingly sought to monitor the desires of citizens, employees, and workers. A major goal was to detect early signs of what could develop into discontent or unrest.

The Context of Opinion Formation

Opinion polling relies on an implicit model of autonomous individuals forming and holding opinions in isolation. It is often misleading because people typically develop, express, and change opinions in dynamic social contexts that include the views of others. Both an intimate environment of friends or family and the broader public mood affect a person's views. The broad mood and the cultural forces emphasized by European theorists can influence the individual attitudes studied by the Americans. Individual and collective opinions are interrelated. Next we examine three context-based processes that affect opinion: (1) pluralistic ignorance, (2) false consensus, and (3) the spiral of silence.

Pluralistic ignorance is when people falsely believe that the majority holds an opinion, when it is actually held by a minority.[64] It is a special case of inaccurately perceiving other people's thinking. For example, you personally believe that abortion is wrong in all situations except to save the life of the mother or in the case of rape or incest. You rarely discuss the issue, but based on fragments of conversations and others' silence, you believe that people around you feel abortion is acceptable under any situation. But you are wrong, and they agree with you. Misperceiving majority opinion occurs when a person believes that his/her own opinion is socially unacceptable, and assumes that others hold an opposite opinion. The belief that one is in the minority stimulates an idea that most others differ.

False consensus occurs when a person believes that his/her opinion is natural or normal, and that those who disagree hold deviant opinions. It is the opposite of pluralistic ignorance. A person's confidence that her/his view is normal and correct promotes a belief that only a few people hold different views. For example, prolife activists who feel secure that their antiabortion beliefs are right and normal see pro-choice believers as a tiny, extreme, radical minority. They become indignant and feel that stubborn, misguided thinking prevents others from agreeing with them because they are so certain that their view is true. False consensus develops because most people limit their personal interactions to a narrow social world of like-minded people.[65]

The spiral of silence is when extensive media attention leads people to believe that an opinion is widely held, and those who agree with the opinion are emboldened to speak out, the undecided or apathetic go along with it, and those who disagree keep silent. The misperception of an overwhelming majority opinion encourages people in the minority to self-censor. Silence by people who disagree further reinforces a perception of consent around the majority opinion and the absence of dissent.[66] A well-documented example of the spiral of silence in the United States occurred during the 1991 Persian Gulf War. Pervasive one-sided mass media coverage created a powerful impression of great popular support for the war. In reality, many Americans were ambivalent or opposed to the war. Heavy media viewers were most likely to believe that most people supported the war, while dissidents felt uncomfortable expressing their opposition in the face of apparent overwhelming support.[67] Thus, the extensive, one-sided media coverage facilitated self-censorship and a spiral of silence.

The three processes work together as a self-reinforcing cycle. People who believe they hold a majority view become vocal and openly express their opinions (false consensus). This leads people who think differently to feel that they are a minority (pluralist ignorance). As the mass media cover the vocal people, it reinforces the impression of a consensus, and people who believe they are in the minority tend to self-censor (spiral of silence). These processes create a strong pressure to conform to an apparent majority, with the media and political leaders shaping what people believe to be the majority view. In this way, the "mood of the country" affects individual opinion.

Political Knowledge and Opinion

People develop their ideas and opinions based on information. Yet both well-informed citizens and those with false beliefs or inaccurate information participate in politics. This is not a problem if only a few people hold false beliefs and lack information, or if the false beliefs are irrelevant to major public issues. However, if many people are misinformed or hold false beliefs about key public issues, it seriously threatens democracy. Larry Bartels (1996, 195) noted, "One of the most striking contributions to political science of half a century of survey research has been to document how poorly ordinary citizens approximate a classical idea of informed democratic citizenship." Yet researchers have done "little to investigate empirically the electoral consequences of voter ignorance." Studies suggest that a large percentage of adult Americans hold false or inaccurate beliefs about social conditions that have a direct bearing on major public issues. The misperceptions are not random, but tend to favor people with social privileges and economic power so that as Delli Carpini and Keeter (1996, 100) noted, ". . . misinformation disproportionately benefits those with economic and political power." For example, most white Americans seriously misestimate the size of racial minorities in the population.[68] They also greatly overestimate socioeconomic equality and underestimate levels of racial discrimination compared to careful studies and what African Americans regularly report.[69] This means many whites form opinions about race-related public programs, such as affirmative action, based on an inaccurate view of the relevant social conditions.

Holding an erroneous belief is not the same as being ignorant.[70] A mistaken belief can have multiple origins, including childhood experiences, schooling, selective perceptions, one's immediate social environment, and mass media images. For example, the mass media show black people in negative situations (e.g., receiving welfare, criminals) much more than is the actual case.[71] A mistaken belief can influence voting and opinions about public issues. For example, a centerpiece of President Ronald Reagan's policy agenda greatly cut spending for programs to aid the poor, the schools, and the environment. After several years of budget cutting, about one-fourth of the American public believed exactly the opposite had occurred (i.e., that spending grew in those areas).[72]

People may lack the information required for informed, responsible political decisions, but possess irrelevant information. For example, in the 1992 presidential election, nearly 90 percent of the population could identify the name of the President's dog or knew about a remark that a candidate made criticizing a fictional television character, but fewer than 20 percent could identify a candidate's position on central campaign issues, such as the environment or use of the death penalty. More people can name the actors who play television judges and provide light entrainment than can name the real judges who sit on the U.S. Supreme Court.[73] For example, in 1986, then Vice President George H. W. Bush had won two national elections and had served in the second highest national elective office for six years. Yet only one in four Americans were able to identify him or knew what office he held.[74] The question is, Why do people lack political knowledge and how do they make political decisions without it?

Why People Lack Political Knowledge   People pay attention and seek out information if they see an issue as being relevant to their immediate concerns, but they dissociate from it when they cannot see its effect on them.[75] People tend to limit their attentiveness to political information.[76] When they fail to see how a political issue is relevant to their everyday concerns, they do not bother to acquire knowledge about it. People see issues as irrelevant for several reasons. For example, people may say that the president's support for strong environmental legislation is irrelevant because they feel that voters have no influence in selecting the president, the president is powerless to affect the environment, they do not care about the environment, or they cannot link political actions to their daily lives. The last reason—an inability to make connections—is critical. For example, someone may not see how an environmental law relates to their child getting sick because they do not see connections between a general law and their specific child. There are several reasons why it is difficult to see the linkages (see Summary 7.2).

Powerful interests can contribute to the erroneous information or ignorance. For example, companies that pollute can divert public attention and confuse people who favor stronger environmental regulations by forming an advocacy group named Clean Environment Now that actually weakens environmental laws through its lobbying efforts.

How People Decide Without Political Knowledge   Well-informed, highly attentive people who connect politics to their daily lives tend to hold stable and consistent opinions.[77] Apathetic, uninformed people who cannot make connections tend to hold erratic, contradictory opinions and are easily swayed by mass media interpretations of events.[78] They are most susceptible to biased messages and manipulative persuasion. In addition, "resistance to persuasion depends very heavily on the availability of countervailing communications, either in the form of opposing information or of cueing messages from oppositional elites . . . ."[79]

| SUMMARY 7.2 | **Why People Cannot See the Links between Politics and Their Daily Lives** |

- The issue involves complicated technical information.
- Long delays come between political acts and visible results in people's lives.
- Politicians deal with many issues, weakening linkages between one politician and one issue.
- Policy budgets, bureaucratic agencies, and administrative regulations obscure the connections.

- Opposing politicians, special interest groups, or officials in other government agencies delay or block the passage of a law or implementation of a policy.
- Politicians or interest groups may purposefully obfuscate the connections.

| SUMMARY 7.3 | **How People Place New Political Information in a Context** |

- *Predispositions* are "stable, individual-level traits that regulate the acceptance or non-acceptance of political communications the person receives" (Zaller 1992, 22).
- A *schema* is a loose set of connected ideas or organized knowledge about a person, object, or concept that people use when making judgments (Knight and Erikson 1997).

- *Heuristics* are shortcuts such as symbols or respected leaders. "Citizens often compensate for their limited information about politics by taking advantage of judgmental heuristics." Sniderman, Brody, and Tetlock (1991, 19) quoted in Delli Carpini and Keeter (1996, 51).

People interpret messages based on personal experiences.[80] They place new information in a context of what they already know and believe using predispositions, schema, or heuristics (see Summary 7.3).

People develop opinions based on issue relevance, background knowledge, self-identity, predispositions, past experiences, and media messages. They tend to resist information that contradicts their preexisting beliefs, values, and knowledge but accept what is consistent with it.[81] Putting the population on a continuum, about 30 percent are uninformed, see politics as irrelevant, lack strong predispositions, hold erratic and contradictory views, and are swayed easily by persuasive messages. At the opposite end, about 30 percent are highly informed, hold clear predispositions, connect public issues to their personal lives, hold stable and consistent views, and are not easily swayed by persuasive messages. This leaves about 40 percent in the middle with modest information. Schooling, more than income, affects political awareness, as does getting news from newspapers or magazines rather than from television.[82] Studies suggest that well-educated, older males who regularly read newspapers are more informed about a range of issues.

Although levels of education in the population have risen over time, Delli Carpini and Keeter (1996, 199) noted, "it is clear that during the past forty years, a substantial decline in overall political engagement among the public has occurred." Does this matter? If everyone was well-informed, support for some issues (e.g., abortion, racial justice, social programs) would shift to a less conservative direction because the disadvantaged tend to be the least informed. Limited knowledge and an inability to see connections can compound the other political weaknesses of the disadvantaged.[83]

Opinion as Ideology

Well-informed people with stable opinions are more ideological,[84] but ideology is confused with attitudes. As Clyde Wilcox (1997, 3) noted, "there is no consensus on just how attitudes relate to other concepts, such as values, beliefs, opinions, habits, and identifications . . . the meaning of these terms . . . remain[s] imprecise, primarily because these are words from our ordinary language and therefore carry many meanings." Most people apply a loose set of vague ideas, but the consequences of this are unclear. "Even scholars who study public opinion and elections have not been able to identify the exact influence of ideology on electoral politics"[85] There are several types of ideology.

Types of Ideology

Confusion over ideology arises from its many meanings. One author identified 16 different meanings.[86] Most political sociologists accept the six principles from European theorists presented earlier in this chapter, but ideologies also vary along two dimensions: degree of formality and evaluation. **A formal ideology is an explicit, coherent, highly consistent, and formal system of thought**. Professional thinkers or intellectuals (e.g., writers, journalists, party leaders, professors) develop and elaborate on them in speeches and writings (e.g., books, magazine articles, party platforms). **An informal ideology is an ongoing, implicit set of general ideas and predispositions that are integrated into most people's daily existence.** The second dimension evaluates ideology as being neutral or negative. Combining the two dimensions creates four types of ideology (see Chart 7.2): programmatic (formal and neutral), interpretative (informal and neutral), tyrannical (formal and negative), or deceitful (informal and negative).

Major Formal Ideologies

Politicians and intellectuals often draw on formal ideologies. Next we review ideal types, or pure models, of eight formal ideologies relevant to contemporary politics in the United States.[87]

Traditional Conservatism

Traditional conservatives may appear to be reactionary (i.e., they react against change and seek a return to the past), but their core principle is to conserve and

chart 7.2

FOUR MEANINGS OF IDEOLOGY

	Formal and Visible	Informal and Hidden
Neutral	Programmatic	Interpretative
Negative	Tyrannical	Deceitful

preserve the positive values, qualities, and virtues of the past. They fear rapid change or the violent overthrow of established authority, as in the French Revolution. They value duty, honor, and etiquette. Conservatives try to preserve tradition, hierarchy, refined taste, and moral authority. They see all parts of society as fitting together into an organic whole with each person having a fixed, proper place. They advocate strong respect for religious authority, patriarchy, and the traditional family (i.e., heterosexual, monogamous with dependent spouse, children). Since they assume that humans are imperfect with "original sin," they feel that people need strong authority and well-established values to rein in moral weaknesses and wicked, sinful impulses.

Traditional conservatives defend inequalities of wealth and income. They also defend inheritance from past generations because the transfer of status and wealth to offspring and preservation of wealth differences upholds the social–legal order. They favor a powerful state that can defend the nation, maintain order, and protect domestic economic interests, often with a mercantilist policy. They distrust highly unstable, chaotic free markets.

Traditional conservatives often defend monarchy and the aristocracy. Even today, many are suspicious of popular, participatory democracy, and excessive equality. Since moral uprightness and talent are scarce, they distrust the mass of ordinary people and prefer the judgment of people with high social standing who will uphold aristocratic responsibility. They believe that rule by a few responsible, talented, and worthy people represents the accumulated wisdom of the past. Traditional conservative values are reflected in the system of judicial appointments—a process in which a leader appoints a few respected "wise" people to positions of great authority from which they are not easily removed. Traditional conservatives accept limits on the rights of ordinary citizens, including the use of government secrecy, wiretaps and media censorship, as necessary to protect and preserve a strong, righteous nation.

Classical Liberalism

Classical liberalism sprung from the rising entrepreneurial and merchant classes of early capitalism that opposed the traditional landed aristocrats, absolute monarchs, and a rigid feudal system. It began as oppositional, revolutionary thinking that sought to liberate or free a rising capitalist class from the shackles of feudalism. Liberty and freedom remain its core values. Classical liberals emphasize individualism and utilitarianism in which each individual has natural rights at birth. They hold that each individual best knows her/his own interests, and success should depend on personal merit or achievement, not family heritage or tradition. They support the "rule of law" (i.e., applying the same law to all individuals equally and fairly) and protecting individual rights with legal procedures and written contracts. Their ideas fill the speeches and writings of leaders from the American and French revolutions.

In the economic realm, classical liberals defend private property ownership and making profits, but they differ from traditional conservatives by embracing dynamic competition in open markets. Classical liberals emphasize opportunity and advancement based on hard work, talent, innovation, and risk taking in the marketplace, with large rewards going to those who succeed. Some embrace a simplistic version of Darwin's evolutionary theory in which claims about a natural law, vigorous competition, and survival of the fittest justify wealth accumulation by a few winners and have little regard for the many losers. Classical liberals uphold the republican ideal of self-rule in which ordinary citizens govern themselves with little outside political authority as well as the democratic ideal of active, equal citizen participation in public decisions. Classical liberals also defend open, free expression and believe people should have great freedom to think, say, and act so long as no one is harmed.

Libertarian Conservatism

Libertarians seek to extend radically the individualism in classical liberalism. They intensely oppose the traditional conservative principle of persevering the past which both confines basic human freedoms and dampens dynamic economic change. Libertarians oppose almost all government, religious, or other limits on personal decisions and strongly favor individual free choice—no laws against taking drugs, engaging in unconventional sexual activities, and so forth. To them, each individual knows what is best and should be free to pursue his/her desires.

Libertarians embrace free market capitalism and limited government involvement in the economy. They prefer self-help, voluntarism, or private enterprise solutions to government programs. Some want to expand the market and private ownership to public services such as roads, the postal system, the water supply, and so forth. Libertarians also believe that individuals should be able to accumulate wealth without limits. Libertarians favor open democratic participation and oppose limits on individual political action or expression, with only a bare minimum of legal protection to prevent excessive direct harm to another person against her/his will or the exploitation of children. They stop just short of anarchism. While anarchists seek to abolish all state authority and propose a world without governments, only small, voluntary self-rule groups, libertarians accept the necessity of a state, but believe that government should be strictly limited to what is minimally essential to maintain individual freedom and property (e.g., provide national defense, prevent attacks of one person on another, and print money).

Communism and Socialism

Communism and socialism are related ideologies that fall under the broad label, Marxism. Marxism includes a philosophy of human nature; a theory of history, society, and economics; and a political program. In Karl Marx's theory of history, primitive communism existed in the distant past and a new version will come in the distant future. Human history contained slave, feudal, and capitalist societies. Communist society would only historically arise after a society passed through an advanced stage of capitalism and moved beyond the transitional stage of socialism. It would be plentiful, humane, free, and democratic with peaceful international relations. The communist label is confusing, because some elites adopted parts of the ideology and mixed it with their own ideas and methods of rule not found in Marxism (e.g., ex-Soviet Union, Cuba, China, North Korea). Because movements and elites stole the term, communism has been associated with harsh dictatorships in militaristic nations with undeveloped capitalism.

Socialist ideology was developed from Marxist theory as a reaction against the great economic inequality and human misery produced by rapid industrialization and unregulated early capitalism. Unlike reform liberals (discussion to follow in this chapter), Socialists do not want to fix capitalism; they want to replace it because capitalism, with its markets and private property, generates massive human misery; destroys human freedom, true democracy, and international peace; and prevents the creation of a humane world with social–political equality. Socialists oppose aristocratic tradition and want to build a new society organized around egalitarian principles. They believe that competitive individualism and market-oriented solutions only increase inequality, destroy communities, undermine humane social relations, and generate human misery. They oppose all forms of inequality such as that based on race, gender, or other social backgrounds. Unlike the classical liberals and libertarians, they see individual freedom in the market and personal liberty from tradition as insufficient; true freedom and happiness require ending inequality and economic deprivation.

Marxist economic theory states that capitalism is fundamentally a system based on one class advancing by exploiting other people, and this exploitation is the source of social and political injustice. Capitalism is not all bad; it also breaks down traditional feudal restrictions on people, encourages rapid technological progress, and vastly increases material wealth. Socialists want first to tame capitalism, then dismantle and replace it with a new economic system. In a market system, owners are motivated to gain profits and accumulate private wealth instead of serve human needs, and owners, not workers, decide how to produce goods and services. By contrast, in a socialist "command economy," democratic and scientific plans can determine the production of goods and delivery of services in ways that will best address the actual needs of all people equally. It will occur under collective management with worker control.

Communists and Socialists advocate participatory democracy and political equality, but believe that political democracy without economic equality is incomplete and distorted. Political and economic democracy are both needed.

Eventually in future communism, the state will no longer be necessary and will wither away, but how to reach it is an issue. Democratic socialist parties, active in Scandinavia and Western Europe, advocate a deliberate, slow, peaceful transition toward socialism through electoral politics. Their goal is to use democratic political means to gain control over the state, then to work to contain capitalism, promote social equality, improve living conditions, and move slowly toward the public ownership of the economy. They favor a strong state with high income and wealth taxes, an end to wealth inheritance, intense business regulation, strong worker and consumer rights, laws against racial and gender discrimination, and an extensive social welfare state. Revolutionary communists oppose the democratic socialists and argue for a violent revolution with a rapid consolidation of power and the elimination of dangerous capitalist enemies. Revolutionary communists believe that only a small group of dedicated followers and a highly disciplined vanguard party can carry out the task. They say that free expression and participatory democracy must wait until after the revolutionary struggle is complete and threats from anticommunist enemies end.

Reform Liberalism

Reform liberalism (also called progressive or social democratic liberalism) differs from classical liberalism. Like socialism, it began in the nineteenth century in response to the growing inequality and misery that rapid industrialization and unregulated capitalism created. Reform liberalism blends a deep commitment to political democracy with fostering a humane, tame version of capitalism. It borrowed ideas from humanism, based in Christian teachings, and from ideals in socialism. Reform liberals feared that untamed capitalism would foster radicalism and violent rebellions that would destroy both capitalism and democracy. They presented a moderate response against both unrestricted, raw capitalism (e.g., libertarianism) and radical anticapitalism (i.e., communism) and provided the ideological foundation for reform policies during the Progressive Era (1910s), the New Deal Era (1930s), and the Great Society Era (1960s). Reform liberals want to preserve the warmth and security of a traditional, caring community and to end oppressive authority and arbitrary power by a small traditional elite. They defend individual rights and market capitalism but question excessive competition and individualism that produce self-destructive behavior, unlimited greed, and selfishness.

Reform liberals advocate a moderate version of the democratic socialist welfare state. They defend private property and capitalist markets but believe that the government must subordinate both to a larger public good. Since an uncontrolled market generates extremes in wealth, income, and power, a democratic government must take wealth from the rich and redistribute it. Reform liberals believe that the state should ensure a minimal standard of living (e.g., food, shelter, education) and decent quality of life (e.g., healthcare, schools, parks, museums) for all people based on the principle of humane social justice. They advocate political equality, full participation, and democracy in which all people have an equal voice. They extend the idea of equal protection beyond fair treatment under the law to protecting everyone's social and economic dignity. Reform liberals will limit some individual rights to protect people who may be weak, infirm, aged, and less competitive. They also embrace maternal or nurturing values, and want a strong state that provides the moral responsibility to end abuse and protect the health and well-being of all people.

Fascism

People sometimes confuse Fascism with Communism, but Fascism is an extreme right-wing ideology and a mirror opposite of the extreme left-wing ideology, Communism. They advocate opposing goals and are intense enemies. Both are nondemocratic with a willingness to use violence to overturn current society. Fascists arose in the early twentieth century in opposition to the communists. They share some traditional conservative values and are patriarchal, elitist, and assume that a natural inequality exists among people. Yet they believe only select aspects of the past are worth preserving and favor technological progress that requires a break with the past to create a new, superior society. Fascists are anti-intellectual and admire physical stamina, skill, and strength. Fascists believe that certain people, races, and religious groups are naturally superior to others. Natural leaders with physical ability, ideological purity, and moral strength have a right and duty to rule over inferior people. Fascists revere the church, the nation, the state, and the family; they scorn physical weakness, racial impurity, and immorality.

   Fascists defend private property and capitalism but are willing to subordinate private property, profits, and the market to the national interest. Fascists will control or redirect capitalism for political goals. In Germany, fascism, or the Nazi party, was national socialist and borrowed socialist symbols and slogans in its quest for power. Fascists are strongly nationalist and favor a powerful central government and military to advance the national interest. They will subordinate individuals for the good and glory of the nation. Individual legal rights and free expression are not valued because they may interfere with leaders who are building a strong, unified, and proud nation.

Populism

Populism is a partial or incomplete ideology often found in combination with other more complete ideologies. Populism is widespread in the United States.[88] It appeared in several political movements and third political parties in U.S. history and in the speeches of politicians. Populists oppose elites, centralized authority, and educated experts; they favor decentralized self-rule by ordinary people with practical experience, common sense, and local roots. There are right-wing and left-wing versions of populism. Right-wing populists borrow ideas from fascism, libertarianism, or classical liberalism. They emphasize local control, traditional morality, preserving unequal racial-gender relations, and protections for small business owners and farmers. They oppose immigration, big government, taxes, and foreign ideas. Left-wing populists borrow from communism, socialism, or reform liberalism. They emphasize social equality and decentralized economic as

SUMMARY 7.4   Social Bases of Ideologies

Traditional Conservatism—Members of the socially dominant racial group (i.e., whites), deeply religious people, "old money," people strongly attached to patriarchy and nationalism, residents of rural areas and small towns.

Classical Liberalism—Business owners, top corporate executives, and wealthy investors.

Libertarian Conservatism—Similar to classical liberalism but younger and educated people, business owners, technical experts in competitive or technologically innovative areas, and cosmopolitan urban residents.

Reform Liberalism—Lower income people; racial or religious minorities; highly educated professionals (e.g., teachers, lawyers, doctors), especially those working in the nonprofit or public sector

employment; government employees; and urban residents.

Socialism-Communism—Nonreligious people, lower-income people, unionized blue-collar workers, unemployed people, racial-ethnic minorities, and highly educated professionals working in the public or nonprofit sector.

Fascism—Similar to traditional conservatism but younger people and those who believe they experienced a decline in social respect or authority.

Populism, Right-Wing—Less educated people, small business owners, and residents of rural areas and small towns.

Populism, Left-wing—Blue-collar and lower white-collar workers, racial-ethnic minorities, small business owners, underemployed people, some highly educated professionals, and urban residents.

well as political power. Left-wing populists advocate greater racial-ethnic and gender equality, community control, and environmental protection. They oppose large multinational corporations and banks, most technical experts, and remote wealthy elites.

Different social groups tend to support different ideologies among those listed above (see Summary 7.4).

Left-Right Continuum

Political sociologists and others often use a left-right ideological continuum. By the early twenty-first century, its usefulness declined as new issues and political movements appeared. Communists and socialists are on the far left, while social democrats and reform liberals are slightly left of center. Fascists and libertarians are to the extreme right, while conservatives and classical liberals are slightly right of center. Left-wing values are egalitarian and humanitarian with strong support for equal citizen participation, government intervention in the market, and protections for the disadvantaged (e.g., women, children, racial minorities, elderly, disabled). Right-wing values uphold private property and traditional authority, defend inequality, and accept limited political participation. Government limits on private market forces or restrictions on people who have wealth and power are opposed.

| CLOSER LOOK 7.3 | **The Political Consequences of Individualism and Self-Help Thinking** |

Individualism is a core ideological theme deeply embedded in mainstream U.S. culture. It originated with classical liberal ideological assumptions but continues to shape people's everyday understandings of many issues. The widespread use of a therapeutic language and large medical–psychological and self-help industries are ideological-based individual solutions in America that operate to dampen collective political action. As Cloud (1998, 160) argues, "The therapeutic discourse of healing, emotional support, identity constitution and maintenance, spiritual growth, and personal identity has been a natural ally of liberalism and capitalism. The therapeutic is rooted in liberalism's assumption about how change happens and how problems are solved." The worldview fostered in a therapeutic model focuses on making individual adjustments to restore personal happiness and order. It "dislocates social and political conflicts onto individuals or families, privatizes both the experience of oppression and possible modes of resistance to it, and translates political questions into psychological issues to be resolved through personal, psychological change" (Cloud 1998, xviii–xix). Self help, personal growth, and individual responsibility become alternatives to engaging in organized political action. It is a way of thinking that disengages people from politics and substitutes personal change for collective political action. In short, the message is "change oneself" rather than act together to change society. It is a way of thinking and seeing the world that directs frustration and anger toward pursuing private, individual actions of coping, adapting, and adjusting to conditions, and away from engaging in collective public confrontation to affect societal change.

Informal Ideology

Few people use formal ideologies. Most think politically using a loose system of values, beliefs, and ideas. Such an informal ideology is consistent with the European view that ideology resides in the assumptions, values, and beliefs that are embedded in language, culture, and daily practices.[89] As a part of culture, an informal ideology offers people resources or strategies for use in politics. It facilitates the adoption of certain courses of action and makes it easier to understand certain ideas rather than others. The informal ideology may not be very visible, and most people see it as common sense, the way things are, or natural. Just as fish do not recognize the water in which they swim, people embrace the assumptions, themes, or values of an informal ideology without awareness. A central theme in the informal ideology that most Americans use is individualism (see Closer Look 7.3).

An informal ideology can blend with broad cultural beliefs, national values, and symbolic politics making it difficult to see. It becomes more visible in periods of rapid change or when opposing groups clash over it. This happened in the United States in the 1980s in the form of widely debated culture wars that were intense disputes over cultural issues.

Culture Wars

Most observers agree that symbolic discourse and ideological debate shifted sharply in the 1980s in the United States. You read about the realignment thesis in Chapter 4. It explains the shift as due to a white backlash against black gains and Republican Party activism around it. Next we examine another explanation, culture wars and the New Christian Right (NCR).

The New Christian Right

Mixing religious symbols with political messages to achieve political objectives is neither new nor unique. Around the world, leaders and political movements often have used religious beliefs in their efforts to advance, resist, redirect, or reverse social change. Many twentieth century movements in the United States from Prohibition in the 1910s, to civil rights in the 1960s, and antiabortion in the 1980s, have used religious themes and symbols.[90]

A national political movement based on forms of conservative Christianity rose in the U.S. in the late 1970s. Led by figures from religious television programs, such as Jim Baker, Jerry Farwell, and Pat Robertson, it attracted right-wing political activists, such as Phyllis Schafley, Paul Weyrich, and Richard Viguerie, and conservative intellectuals, such as William Bennett, Robert Bork, and Lynn Cheney.[91] The movement operated through many political organizations (e.g., National Christian Action Coalition, Eagle Forum, Religious Roundtable, Christian Coalition, Christian Voice, Concerned Women for America, the Moral Majority, and the 700 Club).[92] The movement's goal was to mobilize politically conservative Christians and promote a set of traditional conservative social and cultural values.[93] Activists sought to advance their values in government, schools, and the media, and see their vision of American culture rise to a position of pre-eminence.[94]

The New Christian Right (NCR) is a countermovement.[95] **A countermovement primarily opposes the goals of social change advocated by another social–political movement.** The NCR countered the Anti-Vietnam War, Youth, Women's, and New Left movements of the late 1960s. Except for the women's movement, the others had largely disappeared before the New Christian Right arose, but it sought to eradicate their impact from U.S. culture and its institutions. The NCR had a long list of policy objectives—reinstate Christian prayer in public schools, outlaw abortion, end laws protecting homosexuals, stigmatize unwed teen mothers, restore patriarchy, eliminate public broadcasting, curtail nonreligious programs for the poor, encourage gun ownership, expand use of the death penalty, and impose strong legal penalties for immorality (e.g., illegal drug use, profanity in song lyrics, pornography).

The goal of the New Christian Right was to restore an imagined past under the banner of "family values." This came from a conviction that the nation had abandoned such values which caused a moral collapse and a weakening of the United States as an international power. The NCR sought to end social ills by restoring the social–moral order of a "Golden Age"—when children daily recited Christian prayers in public schools, Christian religious symbols festooned public buildings, premarital sex and unwed pregnancies were unknown, abortions and homosexual acts were strictly taboo, divorce was rare, and women obeyed husbands and devoted their lives to raising children.[96]

The New Christian Right emerged from past groups that had organized around anticommunism, fundamentalist Christianity (the Bible is the literal truth) and traditional social values. Some movement leaders had been involved in conservative politics in the 1960s or associated with prosegregationist presidential candidate George Wallace.[97] NCR leaders were similar to right-wing activists of the 1950s and 1960s (i.e., well-educated, ideologically conservative Republican Party members).[98] The NCR included a diverse array of conservative Christian groups (fundamentalist, Pentecostal, evangelicals and charismatics), but each had separate religious organizations, theological doctrines, and sets of leaders.[99]

The new movement emerged from efforts by Republican party leaders to expand their political base by cooperating with evangelical Protestant Christian leaders, such as Billy Graham. In the late 1970s, a small group of Republican Party activists, led by Jesse Helms, Newt Gingrich, Patrick Buchanan and others, began a concerted effort to mobilize and organize previously inactive conservatives around religious themes.[100] They merged economic ideas from classical liberal and libertarian ideology with a religious social agenda (see Summary 7.5).

The primary enemy the NCR identified was "secular humanism;" not a movement or an organization.[101] **Secular humanism was created by the New Christian Right to represent the growing influence of highly educated, left-liberal, non religious humanists.** NCR leaders believed that secular humanism had displaced a sacred worldview based on God-given principles from sacred religious texts with a worldview based in science, philosophy, literature, and the arts. Secular humanists substituted secular critical thinking, rational debate, the scientific method, and tolerance for diversity for obedience to religious authority. It opposed imposing moral and religious views on people and was politically aligned with reform liberals, feminists, and defenders of gay and lesbian rights.[102]

New Christian Right leaders linked Christian moral–spiritual values to specific political and economic policies. For example, they held that government welfare programs caused dysfunctional families, immoral behavior, and chronic dependency because they were derived from atheistic values and communist-socialist ideas. Such programs undermined individual responsibility and religious-based morality. Even conservative intellectuals who resisted the movement's extreme stands embraced its premise that cultural and moral decay was the primary source of American social problems. Their conservatism was a mixture of faith in capitalism and ideas drawn from elements in the Protestant religious doctrine. "American conservative ideology captures the libertarian emphasis on material progress and individual success. . . . At the same time, it adopts the traditionalist concern with social stability and spiritual values. . . ."[103]

The New Christian Right took themes from mainstream U.S. culture, but many of its objectives have been advocated by right-wing parties and quasi-fascist movements in Europe, East Asia, and Latin America throughout the

SUMMARY 7.5   Issues on the New Christian Right Agenda

- **Schooling**—Favors prayer in public schools, textbook censorship, and tuition tax credit/vouchers for private and religious schools. Opposes sex education and bilingual education.
- **Homosexuality**—Opposes gay rights, domestic partner agreements or benefits, legal same-sex marriage, and antidiscrimination protections for homosexuals. Some also oppose HIV-AIDS health funding.
- **Gender Equality**—Opposes abortion rights, the Equal Rights Amendment, gender equality in sports or the workplace, and programs associated with feminist ideas (e.g., battered women's shelters).
- **Family Relations**—Opposes day care programs and legal rights for children. Favors tax breaks for stay-at-home moms, greater restrictions on obtaining a divorce, and required marriage for unwed mothers.
- **Free Speech/Media**—Opposes pornography and the "fairness doctrine." Favors government censorship of film, popular music, and television programs.
- **Race Relations**—Opposes busing for racial equality, affirmative action programs, and open housing laws.

- **Foreign Affairs**—Favors a large, strong military and opposes nonmilitary foreign aid programs. Hostile toward communist and Islamic nations but strongly supportive of Israel.
- **Federal Government**—Seeks abolition of the National Endowment for the Arts, National Endowment for the Humanities, Public Broadcasting Corporation, U.S. Department of Education, Medicare, and the Internal Revenue Service. Favors public funding for religious-based social services.
- **Crime**—Supports capital punishment and mandatory, long prison terms. Favors punishment over rehabilitation (unless religious-based) for law offenders and limiting the legal rights of law violators.
- **Immigration**—Favors greatly restricted immigration, English-only legislation, the deportation of illegal immigrants, monitoring legal aliens, and loyalty tests for persons not born in the United States.
- **Other**—Opposes laws on gun control. Favors displays of Christian religious symbols or teachings in public places (e.g., courthouses, public parks).

Sources: Compiled from Barsamian (1995), Bruce (1988, 1998), Himmelstein (1983), Hunter (1991), Jorstad (1987, 6–8), Mendoza (1995), Moen (1989, 10–26, 86–88), Nakagawa (1995), and Wilcox (1992).

twentieth century. These movements share the goals of restoring firm male authority in a traditional family, strengthening religious and moral authority, cutting government aid for the poor, promoting racial–cultural purity, blocking the entry of foreigners, censoring deviant artistic or political ideas restricting expressions of sexuality, and building a strong military.[104]

The NCR movement grew in three phases.[105] In the expansion phase from 1978 to 1984, activists created many organizations, gained high-profile media attention, and appeared on the national political agenda. The movement successfully got 29 bills favoring school prayer introduced in the U.S. Congress and five NCR members elected to the U.S. Senate.[106] However, leaders made public relations blunders and generated intense opposition as they pushed moral issues in Congress. In this period, the NCR backed President Ronald Reagan (president from 1980 to 1988), but

**"The specials marked with asterisks are
recommended by the Christian right."**

he only gave the movement limited concrete support.[107] The movement retrenched in the next phase, from 1985 to 1986, as many NCR organizations folded and membership numbers stagnated or fell. Media attention, and with it movement influence, dissolved. The movement's moral rigidity and brashness, as well as its stated refusal to compromise, contributed to its decline. In addition, NCR leaders had aligned with unpopular causes, such as white South African rule and harsh anticommunist foreign dictators.[108] As white apartheid rule fell and the Cold War ended, they looked increasingly out of touch with events. The last phase, which has occurred since the Moral Majority disbanded in 1989, saw a regrouping of the movement into a loose network of organizations active in local politics and as a faction within the Republican Party. A small number of restructured organizations emerged that are more attentive to membership needs and that seek a theologically broader range of public support.[109] The new political strategy has been to soften and repackage movement goals into less extreme forms that can bring mainstream support into its political campaigns. The NCR also intensified its political organizing at the local level (e.g., city councils, school boards, state legislatures).

Explanations of the New Christian Right

Political sociologists who studied the appearance, growth, and impact of the NCR noted that its symbolic targets (e.g., school prayer, abortion court rulings) actually occurred 17 and 6 years respectively before the movement appeared on the scene in 1979.[110] This suggests that the movement's origins lie deeper than the self-professed claims made by its leaders. We next review three explanations for the rise of the New Christian Right—the status decline, culture war, and culturally embattled theses.

Status Decline Thesis

The status decline thesis states that people who feel threatened by social—economic decline act politically to restore their position of high social status. People who believe their position of social–cultural dominance has declined try to restore a situation (real or imagined) in which they stood proud and had the respect of others.[111] Joseph Gusfield (1963) outlined the thesis in *Symbolic Crusade,* a classic study on the Prohibition movement. He argued that small town, middle-class Protestants reacted to the growing social–economic influence from waves of new immigrants, many of whom were Catholic or Jewish. The immigrant groups brought new social values, different lifestyles and tolerated drinking of alcoholic beverages. As their numbers grew and some became economically successful, old-line, established Protestants who frowned on drinking alcohol and rowdy behavior felt their authority to set the community's moral standards slip. Excessive drinking had long existed, but the established middle-class Protestants now publicized it as a major moral problem. To the old social elite, drinking symbolized an invasion of unrestrained behavior and alien values. They mounted a campaign to demonize drinking alcohol and outlawed it in 1920. By making drinking alcohol illegal, they sought to restore their position of authority in the social–moral hierarchy of society. While the Prohibition movement was a fight over the morality of drinking on the surface, in reality it was a high-status group struggling to regain social and political power over lower-status challengers.

According to the status decline thesis, political clashes reflect underlying anxieties, not what people say nor their economic interests. Applied to the Red Scare under Joseph McCarthy, the thesis emphasized that supporters were drawn by anxiety over being displaced in a new social environment, not by a fear of communism.[112] Applied to the New Christian Right, it suggests that devout Christians and economic conservatives felt their social position was under attack. The response was religious, in part because fundamentalist beliefs offer clear, authoritative moral rules for bewildered, insecure people.[113] Studies suggest that compared to others, fundamentalist Christians are less likely to value and pursue advanced schooling, more likely to hold punitive attitudes and support using physical punishment to discipline children, and more likely to strongly support capital punishment.[114] They are also less tolerant of social, political and other diversity and less supportive of civil liberties.[115]

In the status decline thesis, rural, less-educated people who adhered to a traditional religious morality felt displaced by nonreligious, well-educated experts in urban centers who promoted social diversity, the expression of new unconventional ideas, and advanced schooling. Social–political authority and laws that relied on secular thinking or scientific studies had displaced the social position and status of rural, religiously oriented people. The NCR is also populist and pits ordinary local people against central government with its educated experts.[116] America's decentralized political institutions, weak political parties, and openness to local electoral pressure facilitated the rise of the NCR.[117] After years of research, few studies support the status decline explanation for rise of the NCR.[118]

The Culture Wars Thesis

The **cultural war thesis** holds that a new, deep cultural division emerged in the United States over the issue of secularization. Symbolic-moral issues have displaced older divisions of social class and status concerns to become the primary basis of politics and voting. The thesis paints a picture of a clash of opposing religious and cultural worldviews instead of racial, status, or class divisions. Its main exponent, James Hunter (1991), said that the New Christian Right was more than the political mobilization of a previously inactive social group over its declining status. The NCR signaled a deep rift in U.S. society and attracted people from all religious traditions who held a nonsecular worldview. A cleavage developed between people holding opposing core values and beliefs: traditionalists who believed that the social order must be rooted in established religious-moral principles, and secularists and liberal religious believers who welcomed nonreligious morality and scientific reasoning. A new religious division of fundamentalism versus others replaced old divisions (e.g., Protestant, Catholic, Jew). The fundamentalists supported a NCR agenda while mainstream Protestants and others remained neutral. The culture war was over controlling the basic values that would guide American culture. There is little solid research to support the cultural war thesis.[119] While NCR activists have become a major faction within the Republican Party, only a small percentage of the public endorses the NCR's worldview or political program. The movement produced political cleavage over the issue of abortion rights. It is a symbolic division pitting traditional gender roles rooted in religious morality against a commitment to gender equality and secular individual rights.[120]

Culturally Embattled Thesis

The **culturally embattled thesis says that people organize politically to protect their lifeworld and defend their cultural beliefs from external encroachment.** Thus, political elites who organized the NCR attempted to preserve a specific subculture. **A lifeworld is a system of understanding rooted in a set of values and beliefs that gives people a sense of moral order, outlines major categories of life, and assigns moral value to them.** A person's lifeworld identifies the types of people, the events, and the actions a person encounters, and assigns moral meaning to them (i.e., right and good or wrong and evil). It provides a secure sense of social place. Some people seek out and want to live in a subculture among others who share a distinct lifeworld. This surrounds them with a supportive community of like-minded people. When they encounter a powerful alternative moral order that contradicts the core principles of their lifeworld, they become anxious, frustrated, and confused. If they sense that the alternative moral order is expanding and penetrating into most spheres of life and will soon overwhelm their lifeworld, they mobilize to defend their moral–social order from encroachment.[121]

The culturally embattled and status decline arguments are similar. The former emphasizes socialization, social identity, and a cultural environment; it holds that people act to preserve a meaning system that gives order to their daily lives and actively defend it from an alien incursion. The latter emphasizes social status and position; it says that people who held high social status will try to restore their past position of dominance. "As opposed to status discontent explanations . . . moral reform movements are an outgrowth of socialization processes and an expression of cultural values . . . [they are] explainable in terms of learning experiences and particular cultural environments."[122] While the status decline thesis received limited support, more studies back the culturally embattled thesis.[123] It appears that the New Christian Right movement represents a cultural minority organized in a religiously-based subculture; it only gained visiblity after its members became defensively politically mobilized.[124]

Compared to the general U.S. population, NCR supporters tend to reside in the South or Midwest and be rural or suburban, less educated, and white. Fifteen to 20 percent of the population support NCR ideas but few are active participants.[125] The tax status of organized religious groups prevents them from being directly involved in electoral politics, but many circumvent this by providing information, such as voting guides. Using reliance on voting guides as a measure, nearly 20 percent of Americans show some support for the NCR.[126]

New Christian Right followers and others with little schooling or a deeply religious self-identity, often see social issues and events in simplistic moral terms (i.e., a battle of good versus evil). By contrast, secular social scientists and policy experts tend to employ abstract concepts, such as social inequality, group conflict, and globalization.[127] The abstract secularism in the mass media, schools, and other institutions alienated strongly religious people who had limited education, and they found that the NCR leaders "spoke their language" of moral decay and eroding traditional religious values. In the United States, religious identification has a bigger impact on political party identity than all noneconomic divisions except race. Since the 1980s, New Deal partisan alignments based on social class have weakened and new alignments based on religious-oriented ideological–cultural beliefs have strengthened.[128]

The culturally embattled thesis focuses on the motivations of NCR followers but ignores other factors, such as the role of elite leaders, organizational conditions, and external resources used to mobilize followers. The NCR leaders came from a different social base than its followers, and they were critical in forming the movement. Indeed, "observers seem to find two distinct groups within the movement: a small elite of well-educated, mostly professional, middle class activists and a large, constantly changing mass membership of marginally educated, lower- and working-class followers."[129] The NCR movement strength was limited to a few geographic areas, grew with help from Republican Party political activists, and depended on infusions of external organizational and financial resources.[130]

Legacies of the New Christian Right

Several factors explain why the NCR did not achieve its goal of transforming society by imposing a strict conservative Christian moral order and classical liberal economic policies. First, it lacked religious cohesion and unity and was a coalition of diverse religious groups, each with a separate organization and theology.[131] For example, who is a conservative Christian? Should it be based on self-identification, a belief in theological doctrine, or membership in a religious denomination? Less than one-half of persons who identify themselves as fundamentalists attend a fundamentalist church or believe in fundamentalist religious doctrine, and only about one-third of people who both attend fundamentalist services and believe in the doctrine call themselves fundamentalists.[132] Second, conservative Christians tend to be apolitical, and many do not embrace NCR economic policies. Plus, the movement could not reach beyond Protestants.[133] A third reason was the movement's inability to expand beyond a limited base of Southern and Midwestern whites. Many African Americans endorse conservative religious principles, but the NCR has attracted little black support because of its economic conservatism, racial segregation in its subculture, and lingering racism among Southern white supporters.[134] Also, while the NCR's extreme rhetoric of moral absolutes and a rigid adherence to principles may have mobilized followers, it alienated moderate mainstream Americans. In fact, the NCR's influence in the Republican Party may have pushed liberal Protestants out and toward the Democratic Party.[135] The NCR attracted limited electoral support and several of its organizations (e.g., the Moral Majority) generated more negative than positive opinion in the electorate.[136] Clyde Wilcox (1994, 244) observed, "In 1985, [Reverend Jerry] Farwell ranked in most surveys as one of the most unpopular men in America. . . ."

The NCR's primary legacy has been to polarize ideological self-labels. Between the 1970s and 1990s, the percentage of Americans calling themselves "conservative" rose from about 37 to 47 percent. While some people may have become more conservative in their beliefs, the evidence does not suggest a major shift. Despite changes in self-labeling, public support for many liberal policy positions increased.[137] Thus, self-labels may indicate less of a real shift in attitudes than the increased visibility of polarizing symbols. Divisive debates over major cultural symbols (e.g., what is the family) may have heightened the symbolic differences, and the ideological labels have reoriented around the symbols. As Miller and Hoffmann (1999, 741) concluded, "Thus, the key change over time is not in actual attitudes, but in self-categorizing behavior."

A second NCR legacy was to widen existing divisions over cultural or moral issues. "The politicization of moral issues may be one of the most important and enduring political developments of the 1990s . . . . Approximately two-thirds of voters perceived a difference between the parties' position on moral issues."[138] As the NCR fought to gain control over cultural symbols, it magnified divisions over social–moral issues and sharpened social boundaries. The symbols became more visible and their moral meanings more salient. In the contest to control symbols, a gap grew between group members who attached one meaning to the symbols and everyone else, crystallizing attitudes. As the NCR sharpened the divide between people, politicians and political parties did not remain passive bystanders. Some actively encouraged the polarization or aligned with specific groups and symbols as a way to win potential voters.[139] As new issues advanced onto the public agenda, people aligned into opposing cultural camps.

A third NCR legacy was to accelerate the detachment of the political parties from the New Deal alignment. It helped replace New Deal economic issues with social–moral ones (e.g., racial equality, abortion, crime, gay rights, stem cell research). As the public agenda changed, the NCR became a major faction within the Republican Party with veto power.[140] The NCR "cannot determine the Republican presidential candidate, and any candidate too closely tied to the movement would probably lose. But the Republicans would have difficulty nominating a candidate they directly oppose."[141]

A decade after its decline, the NCR repackaged its message to appeal to a broader audience. For example, support for school prayer and a religious-oriented curriculum became "school choice," tuition tax credits, and vouchers. NCR leaders became more politically sophisticated and concealed their religious agenda from public view to better advance political goals.[142] The movement played a role in the election of George W. Bush in 2002, and NCR leaders took major positions in his administration (see Case in Point 7.2). Many people in leading cultural institutions (e.g., television producers, teachers, school administrators, textbook publishers) try to avoid offending the vocal NCR movement.[143]

CASE IN POINT 7.2   The Enduring Influence of the New Christian Right

The influence of the New Christian Right's ideological agenda continues 20 years after its creation, shaping both domestic and international issues. Domestically, the movement pressures state government and local school boards to remove the teaching of evolution from school curriculum and to prohibit "gay tolerance" clubs organized by students. A major national-level success for the movement has been its involvement in convincing the U.S. federal government to give public money to private religious organizations and having them deliver pubic social programs (e.g., homeless shelters, drug treatment programs). A second success has been to have the federal government intensely promote sexual abstinence program in schools while virtually excluding other birth control and sexual health information, although there is no evidence of the effectiveness of the program. As data from the Allan Guttmacher Institute suggest, the United States has the highest rates of both births and abortions among women under 20 years old, and has more limits on disseminating birth control information to teens than other advanced nations. At the international level, the New Christian Right successfully pressured the federal government to oppose United Nation's programs on sex education, family planning, and protecting the rights of children.

Sources: "U.N. Forum Stalls on Sex Education and Abortion Rights," New York Times, May 10, 2002. "School Board Seeks Curb on Gay Tolerance Clubs," New York Times, February 12, 2000. "To Outlaw Gay Group, District May Ban Clubs," New York Times, February 10, 2000. "Abstinence Program Advances," New York Times, April 25, 2002. "Bush Plans to Let Religious Groups Get Building Aid," New York Times, January 23, 2003. "Senate Passes Version of Religion Initiative," New York Times, April 10, 2003. "Abstinence Is Focus of U.S. Sex Education," New York Times, December 15, 1999. "Critics Say Government Deleted Sexual Material From Web Sites to Push Abstinence," New York Times, November 26, 2002. On the George W. Bush activities to promote abstinence see: http://www.whitehouse.gov/news/releases/2002/02/welfare-book-06.html. On the Allan Guttmacher Institute see http://www.agi-usa.org/.

CONCLUSION

In this chapter, we examined the role of ideas, symbols, beliefs, and knowledge in politics. The symbolic dimension of politics includes how the people of a nation see their heroes, celebrations and monuments, the civil religion they worship, and the political witches they fear. We also examined the concept of ideology. We reviewed the historical development of the concept and its treatment by American researchers. European theorists increasingly defined ideology as being a fundamental part of a national culture integrated into power relations. American researchers either denied the presence of ideology or treated it as an attitude cluster, and linked it to processes of public opinion formation. These views are compatible if ideology operates at two levels: a deep level of cultural institutions and a surface level of individual attitudes. In addition to examining informal ideology, we reviewed seven formal ideologies that influence contemporary politics. Lastly, we looked at the rise of the New Christian Right. In Chapter 8, we will turn to schools and the mass media as major institutions that transmit symbols, beliefs, and ideas.

KEY TERMS

Civil Religion	Informal Ideology	Public Opinion
Culturally Embattled Thesis	Lifeworld	Relationalism
Culture War Thesis	Pluralistic Ignorance	Secular Humanism
False Consensus	Political Witch Hunts	Spiral of Silence
Formal Ideology	Politicization	Status Decline Thesis
Ideological State Apparatus	Politics of Symbols	Symbolic Violence
Ideology	Public Memory	Symbols of Politics

REVIEW QUESTIONS

1. What does it mean to say that symbolic politics is real politics? In what ways can symbols affect politics?

2. Give two examples of political myth or public memory in the United States. Explain the political messages people receive from each.

3. How does civil religion shape politics? Give examples of two major themes in America's civil religion. Explain their significance in contemporary politics.

4. What positive functions to strengthen society result from political witches?

5. Explain the six principles that arose from a century of European debate over the meaning of political ideology.

6. How does European tradition to the study of ideology differ from the late twentieth century American empirical approach? Identify the four approaches used by American researchers to study ideology.

7. What is the relationship between ideology and public opinion? How do they differ? How are they alike?

8. How does social context affect public opinion? Specifically, how do pluralistic ignorance, false consensus, and the spiral of silence alter public opinion? What do they imply about public opinion in a democracy?

9. How well informed are Americans about public affairs? How do people with little information or who are poorly informed about politics make political decisions?

10. Take one formal ideology on the left side and one on the right side of the left-right continuum and explain their major themes, principles, and differences.

11. What is the New Christian Right? When did it begin? What does it stand for? What kinds of people are its followers? Explain how its beliefs fit with formal ideologies of the political "right."

12. Why did the New Christian Right weaken by the late 1980s? What is its political legacy?

RECOMMENDED READINGS

Bellah, Robert N. 1992. *Broken Covenant: American Civil Religion in a Time of Trial, 2nd ed.* Chicago: University of Chicago Press.

Bruce, Steve, 1998. *Conservative Protestant Politics.* New York: Oxford University Press.

Delli Carpini, Michael X. and Scott Keeter. 1996. *What Americans Know About Politics and Why It Matters.* New Haven: Yale University Press.

Edelman, Murray. 1964. *The Symbolic Uses of Politics.* Urbana, IL: University of Illinois Press.

Glynn, Carroll J., Susan Herbst, Garrett O'Keefe, and Robert Shapiro. 1999. *Public Opinion.* Boulder CO: Westview.

Hunter, James Davison. 1991. *Culture Wars: The Struggle to Define America.* New York: Basic Books.

Lewis, Justin. 2001. *Constructing Public Opinion.* New York: Columbia University Press.

Zaller, John R. 1992. *The Nature and Origins of Mass Opinion.* New York: Cambridge University Press.

ENDNOTES

1. Quote is from Schwartz (1981, 66).

2. See Kertzer (1998, 7) for discussion.

3. For more on the politics of abortion see Adams (1997), Luker (1984), and Scott and Schuman (1988).

4. Quote is from Pressen (1984, 170).

5. Quote is from Gillis (1994, 5).

6. For a discussion of the Vietnam Memorial, see Bodnar (1994) and Wagner-Pacifici and Schwartz (1991). On the Enola Gray—the plane that dropped the bomb on Hiroshima—see Dower (1995), Little (1997), and Thelen (1995). On the St. Patrick's Day Parade and gay people in New York see Finkelstein (1999) and on Boston see "The scornin' o' the pink," *The Economist*, June 24, 1995, p. 26

and Greenhouse (1995). On the Martin Luther King, Jr. holiday, see Alozie (1995) and Goldberg (1999).

7. From Wagner-Pacifici and Schwartz (1991). Also see Schwartz and Bayma (1998) on the politics of recognition.

8. See Barhel (1996) and Schwartz (1996b) for discussion.

9. As Bodnar (1994, 75) noted, "Public memory emerges from the intersection of official and vernacular cultural expressions . . . [it] is a system of beliefs and views that is produced from a political discussion that involves the fundamental issues related to the entire existence of a society. . . ." Also see Barthel (1996) and Halbwachs (1992).

10. "Interim Leaders Support by U.S. Meet in Baghdad: In First Step, Council's Member's Abolish Hussein's Holidays," *New York Times*, July 14, 2003.

11. See the study on Williamsburg by Gable and Handler (1996) and Handler and Gable (1997). Rosenzweig and Thelen (1998) provide a discussion of public history.

12. See Schwartz (1987, 1991a, 1991b, 1996a, 1996b, 1997, 1998) on the constructed memory of George Washington and Abraham Lincoln. Also see Fine (1996) on President Harding.

13. See Gusfield and Michaelowicz (1984) on sports and symbols.

14. See Welch (2000) on the Olympics incident (pp. 3–4) and the anthem at sporting events (p. 41).

15. See Pfaff and Yang (2001) for elaboration and examples from China and Eastern Europe.

16. For a discussion of church–state relations in the United States and political issues see Demerath (1998), Demerath and Williams (1984), and Williams and Demerath (1991).

17. See Brauer (1976), Billings (1990), Hammond (1989), Thomas (1989), and Williams and Alexander (1994) on the relationship between politics and religion in American history.

18. For a discussion of civil religion see Anthony and Robbins (1982), Bellah (1967, 1970, 1992, 1998), Hammond (1976, 1989), Mathisen (1989), Thomas and Filippen (1992), Wimberly (1979), Wimberly and Christenson (1980, 1982), and Wuthnow (1987, 177–184). Demerath (1998) argues that civil religion in the United States is strong but not unique.

19. Quote is from Merelman (1989, 487).

20. Quote is from Merelman (1989, 491).

21. See Welch and Bryan (1996, 1998) and Welch (2000) on the flag.

22. See Hammond (1989) on the constitution and Gamoran (1990) on schooling. Also see Hibbing and Theiss-Morse (1996) and Merelman (1996) on civics education.

23. Williams and Demerath (1991) discuss civil religion and the separation doctrine. They find church and state separation means state separation from nonmainstream religious beliefs but not the religious beliefs of the majority.

24. From Adams (1987).

25. See White (1985).

26. Quote from Hughey (1983, 170).

27. For a discussion of the social basis of American civil religion see Hughey (1983).

28. See Demerath and Williams (1985).

29. For more on witch hunts see a classic study by Erikson (1966) on American Puritans and Currie (1968) on Europe.

30. Political witch hunts are discussed in Bergesen (1977, 1984).

31. See Goodin (1981).

32. Quote is from Bergesen (1977, 221, 223).

33. See Eagleton (1991, 63–70) and McLellan (1986, 3–7) on the development of ideology as a concept. Wolf (1999, 30–47) summarizes the concept in the context of related ideas in the late nineteenth and early twentieth centuries.

34. See Durkheim (1965 [1915]) and Thompson (1986, 30–34) and McLellan (1986, 36–38). For a general discussion of Durkheim see Lukes (1973).

35. Quote is from Wuthnow (1987, 156).

36. On Lukacs see Eagleton (1991, 93–107) and McLellan (1986, 25–29).

37. On Mannheim see Eagleton (1991, 107–110) and McLellan (1986, 40–49).

38. On Gramsci see Femia (1981), Joll (1977), Sasson (1987), and Simon (1982). Also see Billings (1990) on the use of religion as an oppositional ideology. The relationship between political domination and hegemony is discussed in Cheal (1979), Salamini (1974), and Sallach (1974).

39. The intellectuals include Theodor Adorno (1903–1969), Walter Benjamin (1892–1940), Erich Fromm (1900–1980), Max Horkheimer (1895–1973), Leo Lowenthal (1900–1993), and Herbert Marcuse (1898–1979).

40. Quote is from Held (1980, 38).

41. On the Frankfurt School and critical theory see Bottomore (1984), Connerton (1980), Held (1980), Jay (1973), and Wiggershaus (1994).

42. Quote from MacDonnel (1986, 27).

43. A discussion of Althusser can be found in Benton (1984) and McCarney (1980).

44. Additional information that discusses Foucault's work can be found in Cousins (1984), Dumm (1996), Sheridan (1980), and Smart (1985).

45. On Bourdieu and symbolic violence see Fowler (1997), Swartz (1997, especially pp. 82–93), and Thompson (1984, 42–72).

46. Wuthnow (1987, 149–161) discusses the idea of multiple contesting or competing ideologies.

47. Quote is from McLellan (1986, 5).

48. Postmaterialist values and ideas are discussed in Betz (1990), Brooks and Manza (1994), Dalton (1996), Dalton et al. (1984), Duch and Rusk (1993), Inglehart (1984), Inglehart and Abramson (1999), Inglehart and Baker (2000), Inglehart and Klingemann (1979), and Marks (1997).

49. McLellan (1986, 50–56) discusses American views of ideology.

50. For an application of this approach see the analysis by Stimson (1975) the 1972 Presidential election.

51. See Knight and Erikson (1997).

52. Smith (1997) describes confusion over ideological labels.

53. See Zaller (1992, 270).

54. See Conover (1984), Conover and Feldman (1981, 1984) on the relationship between subjective self-identity and policy positions. Conover and Feldman (1984) discuss the use of interpretative schemes.

55. See Neuman (1986).

56. Roemer (1994) argued that heuristic use of party is highly rational when people are uncertain. Also see Huckfeldt et al. (1999) who argue that partisan and ideological self-labels are critical heuristic devices that enable people to make sense of politics, especially those for whom these are accessible (i.e., easily retrieved from memory).

57. See Chafetz and Ebaugh (1983), Davis (1980, 1992), Evans (2003), Herring (1989), and Phelan et al. (1995). Brint (1984) argues for a liberalizing trend due to occupational and educational changes.

58. Brooks (2000) argues that liberalized racial attitudes caused a smaller margin for Republican Party presidential victories in the 1980s and Democratic Party presidential victories in the 1990s.

59. For a discussion of the "invention" of public opinion see Zaret (1996) and Justin Lewis (1999).

60. See Ginsberg (1986, 62–83) and Justin Lewis (2001).

61. Ginsberg (1986, 83) discusses public opinion as social control.

62. Justin Lewis (2001) argues that American mass media present public opinion by overemphasizing central-right views.

63. On the history of government statistics see Desrosières (1998), Kertzer and Arel (2002), and Porter (1995). Also see Alonso and Starr (1987) on recent U.S. examples. Government studies of domestic morale in World War II and enemy propaganda in World War I stimulated public opinion polling.

64. On pluralistic ignorance see Glynn et al. (1999, 187–188), Kuran (1995, 76–81), and Shamir and Shamir (1997).

65. See Glynn et al. (1999, 192–198). Two studies by Huckfeldt et al. (1995, 1998) suggest that people depend heavily on micro-social environments and that the opinion processes create distortion.

66. Also see Eveland, McLeod, and Singorielli (1995); Glynn, Hayes, and Shanahan (1997); Katz and Baldassare (1992, 1994); Lin and Salwen (1997); and Noelle-Neumann (1984) on the spiral of silence.

67. Also see Altheide (1995, 179–212), Delli Carpini and Keeter (1996, 99–101), Iyengar et al. (1994), Pan and Kosicki (1994), and Iyengar and Simon (1993) on misperceptions about the Persian Gulf War and media effects. Eveland, McLeod, and Signorielli (1995) found that perceived public war support significantly predicted whether an individual supported the war.

68. See Nadeau et al. (1993). Delli Carpini and Keeter (1996, 81) note that 8 percent of the population was correct.

69. See Feagin (1991), Gilens (1999), Kluegal (1990), Kluegal and Smith (1982, 1983), Sears et al. (1997), Sniderman et al. (1984), and Sniderman and Hagen (1985).

70. On the difference between ignorance and mistaken belief see Kuklinski, Quirk, and Schwieder (1998).

71. See Gilens (1999).

72. See Delli Carpini (1996, 264).

73. See Delli Carpini (1996, 101).

74. See Zaller (1992, 16).

75. From Gamson (1992b, 127).

76. See Zaller (1992) on attentiveness and opinion formation.

77. As Delli Carpini and Keeter (1996, 236) remarked, "Better informed citizens hold more opinions, have more stable opinions, that are resistance to irrelevant or biased information . . . and have opinions that are more internally consistent with one another and with the basic ideological alignments that define American politics."

78. See Bartels (1993) and Delli Carpini (1996, 230–237), and the discussion of media in Chapter 7.

79. Quote is from Zaller (1992, 267).

80. For a study of media and other information on opinion formation see the study by Gamson (1992b).

81. See Zaller (1992).

82. See Delli Carpini and Keeter (1996). Bartels (1996) argues informed voters may create up to a 10 percent change in voting, and incumbent candidates greatly benefit.

83. See Delli Carpini and Keeter (1996, 238–267).

84. From Delli Carpini and Keeter (1996, 238).

85. Quote is from Knight and Erikson (1997, 91).

86. From Eagleton (1991, 1–2). See Heywood (1998, 6) for a list of 10 definitions. Also see Williams and Demerath (1991, 426, footnote 3) on contrasting meanings of ideology.

87. On formal ideologies see Dolbeare and Dolbeare (1976), Heywood (1998), Hoover (1987), and Sargent (1987).

88. See LaClau (1977). Also see Wasserman (1979) on George Wallace's campaign for president as a recent case of right-wing populism.

89. Szalay and Kelly (1982) suggest that informal ideology organizes beliefs, and they argue that standard survey attitude questions cannot measure ideological belief systems and cultural perceptions.

90. See Himmelstein (1983) and Oldfield (1996) on religion in political movements.

91. See Oldfield (1996, 100) on the New Right and the New Christian Right.

92. Also see Moen (1992, 66).

93. See Bruce (1988, 67–68) on networks. As Wilcox (1994, 249) noted, "The secular New Right and the Republican party lent resources to help form Christian Right groups in order to facilitate the political conversion of white, evangelical Christians to Republican politics."

94. Quote is from Bruce (1988, 41).

95. For a discussion of the concept of countermovement see Lo (1982a) and Mottl (1980).

96. See Levitas (1986a, 1986b) on New Right utopias. See Hammond (1994) on the family values issue in voting.

97. From Bruce (1988, 57–59). Martin (1996) provides a useful historical overview.

98. See Wilcox (1987, 1992). As Wilcox (1992) says, "Supporters of the fundamentalist Right of the 1980s were similar in many ways to the Christian Right of the 1950s."

99. See Oldfield (1996, 21–23) and Wilcox (1992).

100. Oldfield (1996, 116) notes that Republicans courted the New Christian Right and vice versa. Also see Brennan (1995), Bromley and Shupe (1984), Green and Guth (1991), and Green et al. (1996).

101. See Diamond (1995).

102. For a discussion of the secular humanism and the New Christian Right see Bruce (1988, 76–80, 189), Heinz (1983), Jorstad (1987, 27–39), Moen (1989, 90), and Wilcox (1992).

103. Quote is from Himmelstein (1983, 23).

104. See Beatty and Walter (1988), David (1986), Payne (1980), and Seidel (1986) on New Christian Right positions.

105. Moen (1992, 1994) discusses the phases of the New Christian Right. Also see Rozell and Wilcox (1996). Hopson and Smith (1999) discuss the growth of the movement in political discourse.

106. See Moen (1989, 56, 96) on political success in Washington, and Hertzke (1988) on New Right lobbying.

107. See Moen (1990).

108. New Christian Right foreign policy in the mid-1980s is illustrated by Jerry Farwell's support of the dictator Ferdinand Marcos in the Philippines and the apartheid regime of South Africa (Jorstad 1987, 158–160).

109. Rozell et al. (1998) note that the movement was able to overcome some internal religious divisions in the 1990s.

110. See Moen (1989, 13).

111. Also see Lipset and Raab (1978). Wood and Hughes (1984) offer a useful review of the thesis.

112. See Bell (1955), Lipset and Raab (1978), Lo (1982a), Wasserman (1990), and Zurcher and Kirkpatrick (1976) for discussions of right-wing groups and the status decline thesis. Also see Rogin (1967) on Joseph McCarthy.

113. Kiddie (1998) provides a general review of fundamentalism.

114. On fundamentalism and education see Darnell and Sherkat (1997) and Sherkat and Darnell (1999). Grasmick and Morgan (1992) and Grasmick and Davenport (1992) discuss the fundamentalist support for physical punishment and the death penalty. Ellison and Sherkat (1993) and Ellison et al. (1996) discuss the greater use of corporal punishment to discipline children by conservative Protestants.

115. See Wilcox and Jelen (1990). Belsey (1986) discusses civil liberties. Beatty and Walter (1984) examine levels of political intolerance among specific religious denominations.

116. See Hertzke (1991) and Oldfield (1996, 51–53). Also see Williams and Alexander (1994) on populism and religion.

117. See Bruce (1988, 69). Keddie (1998, 717) also observes that decentralized American political institutions facilitate the rise of fundamentalist politics. Also see Bruce (1998, 164–175).

118. On the status decline thesis and the New Christian Right see Moen (1988), and Simpson (1983).

119. On the culture war thesis see Bolce and DeMaio (1999), Davis and Robinson (1996), Demerath and Yang (1997), DiMaggio et al. (1997), Evans (1997), Green et al. (1995), and Miller and Hoffman (1999). Downey (2000) subsumes it with cultural pluralism and finds weak support, with a tri-modal distribution.

120. On the abortion cleavage see Adams (1997), Fried (1988), Hout (1999), Lo (1982a), and Luker (1984).

121. For discussion see Calhoun-Brown (1997), Harper and Leicht (1984), Page and Clelland (1978), and Wilcox (1992). Also see Hunter (1983; 1991) on how the New Christian Right presents an entire symbolic universe.

122. Quote is from Wood and Hughes (1984, 89, 96).

123. See Bruce (1988), Green (1993), Harper and Leicht (1984), Oldfield (1996), Simpson (1983), and Wilcox (1992).

124. See Jelen (1992) and Wald et al. (1988), and Wilcox et al. (1999) on the importance of a religious community for politics.

125. Woodberry and Smith (1998).

126. See Regnerus et al. (1999). Also see Miller (1985).

127. From Regnerus et al. (1999).

128. See Layman (1997), Layman and Carmines (1997), and Levine and Carmines (1997). See Manza and Brooks (1997) on religion in American politics. Kiecolt and Nelsen (1991) emphasize the interaction of religion, region, and party.

129. Quote is from Lienesch (1982, 413).

130. Green et al. (1993) present a model that shows that demand (motivations by followers), supply of activism (elite organizers), and strategic choice (conditions of organization) each contributed equally to the rise of the movement. They note that 92 percent of the movement's political activity occurred within the Republican Party. Also see Sigelman et al. (1987) on Moral Majority support.

131. Woodberry and Smith (1998) provide an overview of the different types of conservative Christian religions in America. Also see Beatty and Walter (1988) and Wilcox, Rozell and Gunn (1996) on coalitions in the New Christian Right.

132. The figures are from Wilcox (1992, 58).

133. Bruce (1994, 1995), Guth (1983), Jelen and Wilcox (1992), and Rozell et al. (1998) discuss internal divisions. Appleby (1997) and Jelen (1997, 67) emphasize the inability to attract conservative Roman Catholics. Elifson and Hadaway (1985) examine those who supported school prayer. Johnson et al. (1986) discuss merging conservative economic ideology with social conservatism. Also see Gerteis (1998) on divisions in the right.

134. For a discussion of race in the New Christian Right see Berlet and Quigley (1995), Bruce (1988, 176), Calhoun-Brown (1997), Emerson et al. (1999), Green et al. (1997), Nakagawa (1995), Quigley (1995), Wadsworth (1997), and Wilcox (1992, 1994).

135. Manza and Brooks (1999, 95–126).

136. See Fowler and Hertzke (1995) and Wilcox (1992).

137. From Knight and Erikson (1997).

138. Quote is from Abramowitz (1997, 225).

139. The polarization is discussed in Evans (2003), Lyman (1997), and Miller and Hoffmann (1999).

140. See Hallum (1991) and Rozell and Wilcox (1996).

141. Quote is from Woodberry and Smith (1998, 48).

142. See Jorstad (1987, 65–68), Moen (1992), and Wilcox (1994).

143. From Bruce (1988, 125).

CULTURAL INSTITUTIONS AND TOLERANCE

INTRODUCTION

You have probably spent much of your life in school settings, and when you were not in school, you probably devoted a lot of time to media (such as television, videos, movies, and recorded music). How did the schooling and the media shape your views and understanding of political concerns? In Chapter 7, we looked at the roles of symbols and ideas in politics. Yet the symbolic dimension of politics and ideology develop and persist in a larger institutional context. Few of us create entirely new ways of thinking or invent unique value systems; instead, the ideas and beliefs that mold our thinking come from the cultural institutions around us. ■

Cultural Institutions

Some cultural institutions (e.g., family, religious group, school) engage in primary socialization while others (e.g., mass media, museums, stores, workplace) are involved in secondary socialization. Institutions create, maintain, preserve, and extend the material and nonmaterial culture. They are of interest to political sociologists because they originate and reinforce a society's assumptions, values, and beliefs; they provide the "social cement" that holds a society together and shapes what people value or scorn. Cultural institutions are not static; they are always changing and are often a site of conflict among competing social–political interests.

One priority of members of the New Christian Right (NCR) that you read about in Chapter 7 was to gain influence over public schools and the mass media. This was based on their belief that schools and media disseminated ideas and values that they opposed.[1] At the same time, NCR opponents on the political left criticized schools and the mass media for spreading conservative values and believed, "The sphere of education has been one of the most successful areas in which the Right has been ascendant."[2] Both sides agreed that, "If culture is a system of ideas, then the institutions which specialize in the transmission of this system—institutions such as schools and the media—are crucially important."[3] In this chapter, we examine two cultural institutions, schools and the mass media, and consider a closely related topic—the democratic values of tolerance.

Models of Political Sociology

Each model of political sociology has a view on schooling and the media (see Chart 8.1). For *pluralists*, schools are an integrative and meritocratic institution. They provide youth with the knowledge and skills needed in modern society. Since access is open and is based on achievement, schools ensure that individuals can advance based on their talents, motivation, and accomplishments. In addition to imparting vocational skills, schools socialize youth to essential norms, beliefs, and values, including fairness, democratic participation, and tolerance for others. Pluralists also see the mass media as important because they supply diverse ideas and information that citizens use for making decisions about public issues. Access to the media is open and used by diverse interest groups to communicate their views to the public.

According to the *elite model,* schools and the media are clearly stratified. There is one schooling track for elites and another for the masses. In the elite track, separate schools (usually private) prepare the children of the elites for future positions in the elite. Since talent is limited, the elites also recruit a few talented nonelites who are also in this track to replenish their ranks. Elite schooling enhances social capital (discussed later in this chapter), and encourages socializing with other future elites. It also imparts the skills, values, and attitudes needed to rule. By contrast, schools in the mass track sort and select the children of the masses to prepare them for lower and middle ranks of the occupational structure. They impart vocationally oriented, technical skills (e.g., engineering,

c h a r t   8 . 1

SUMMARY OF POLITICAL–SOCIOLOGICAL MODELS OF SCHOOLING AND MEDIA

Schooling

Model	What Content Is Taught?	Who Controls Schools?
Pluralist	Democratic values and job skills	Parents, teachers, citizens, and interest groups
Elite	Two parts: (1) obedience and job skills or leadership and (2) high culture	Top leaders in business, government, religion, etc.
Statist	Neutral information and nationalist beliefs and values	Autonomous professionals in government and education
Power-structure	Procapitalist beliefs and values and allegiance to the existing social–political order	Capitalists (wealthy investors and top corporate executives) and their allies
Structuralist	Procapitalist beliefs and values and allegiance to the existing social–political order	Autonomous professionals in government and education
Class-struggle	Mixed; contradictory and shifting values, beliefs, and skills, depending on who has power	A shifting balance among educators, politically mobilized groups, and powerful interests

Mass Media

Model	Media Messages		Form of Media Control	
	Consistency of Messages	Impact on Political Thinking	Uniformity of Control	Directness of Control
Pluralist	Contradictory	Minor impact	Fragmented	Direct
Elite	Consistent	Major impact	Uniform	Direct
Statist	Semiconsistent	Minor impact	Fragmented	Indirect
Power-structure	Consistent	Major impact	Uniform	Direct and indirect
Structuralist	Mostly consistent	Major impact	Uniform	Indirect
Class-struggle	Mixed, contradictory	Varying impact	Mixed	Direct and indirect

accounting) instead of a broad-based leadership education. Mass schooling also socializes youth to the values of conformity and obedience that prepares them for positions in the lower levels in authority hierarchies.

Elites own and control the mass media. They use it to provide the masses with entertainment, information, and perspectives that reinforce dependency. Elites use all types of media because it is available and helps them to understand the masses, but they also have specialized elite media outlets (e.g., magazines, cable channels) that provide them with information, entertainment, and perspectives on events needed for ruling society.

The *statist model* emphasizes the autonomy of educational and media institutions. It holds that the organization of schooling and media (e.g., centralized vs. decentralized, private vs. public) is important to their operation. Likewise, the inertia from past decisions creates an institutional framework that constrains schools and the mass media. Within the institutional framework, professional educators and media specialists influence the content and direction of schooling or media.

Political sociologists who use a *power-structure model* largely agree with the elite model on schooling and the mass media, but they argue that members of the ruling class, not elites, are in control. They say that the capitalist class controls fundamental educational policy. For example, wealthy capitalists and top corporate officials are on the boards of trustees or regents of public and private universities where they set the basic policies for educational administrators and faculty. The capitalist class also owns the mass media and operates the media in ways that simultaneously generate profits and ensure capitalist class survival. Small differences among the various media owners and advertisers create an impression of diversity, but the media owners and advertisers agree on the core issue of protecting their position of power in society.

According to the *structuralist model,* schools and the media are major transmitters of the dominant ideology. Schools disseminate a procapitalist worldview, not because individual classroom teachers or administrators consciously want to, but because it is built into the fabric of schooling and how schools fit with other institutions (e.g., business, government, religion). Procapitalist ideological assumptions and values are infused into the curriculum and official knowledge and skills. For example, if schools did not teach students the types of attitudes and skills wanted by business owners and powerful elites, the students would be unprepared to succeed in business after they graduated, and the schools would be called failures. This model also sees procapitalist constraints on the mass media. Private ownership compels media producers to follow market logic and create a steam of "products" (e.g., entertainment, symbols, ideas, cultural messages) that can both satisfy consumers and generate profits for owners. The dependence on sales and advertising revenue constrains media. Advertisers manipulate consumer desires and bombard consumers with implicit procapitalist messages.

Adherents of the *class-struggle model* view schools and the media as sites of cultural conflicts and power struggles. They only rarely produce or transmit messages that will upset the social–political order. Conflicts can develop for three reasons. First, factions within the dominant class compete and fight with one another through cultural institutions. The disagreements sometimes spill over into larger society or create other disagreements. Second, schooling and the media are not under total control. Autonomous or hostile groups can sometimes capture areas of schooling or some secondary media outlets. Third, schools and the mainstream media present contradictory messages. Noncapitalist themes may be embedded a procapitalist lesson or media story. These factors foster ongoing struggles over messages, values, and ideas in schools and the media. In some historical periods, political openings have allowed competing forces to develop and spread oppositional messages, putting schools or the media at the center of conflict.

THE MEANING AND PURPOSE OF SCHOOLING

Every nation-state provides its population with formal education. In advanced industrial nations, virtually everyone attends school for twelve or more years during the formative stages of their lives. Schools help realize ideals such as social justice, democracy, and equality, and they are embroiled in racial-ethnic, religious, class, and gender divisions. Politics has long shaped schooling. As Steven Brint (1998, 19–20) noted, "Institutions of schooling have always been stamped by the ideas and ideals of particular groups and organizations . . . [and] change when new class or organizational interests gain power." Politics operates both at the micro level of day-to-day activities among students and teachers in classrooms and at the macro level of how schools fit into the larger society. Politics affect the primary, secondary, and tertiary levels of schooling but in different ways. For example, the politics of kindergartens differ from those of institutions preparing physicians. Schools provide knowledge and skills; socialize students to moral, political, and economic values; and select people for future occupations.

You are probably aware of schooling's visible goal of imparting skills and knowledge, but as Brint (1998, 101) observed, "the transmission of school knowledge is a less important activity of schooling than the other two major purposes, socialization and social selection." As a socialization institution, schools convey core beliefs, attitudes, and outlooks. As a social selection institution, schooling reinforces the class-stratification system. Beyond family background, schools have their biggest impact on whether parents successfully transfer their social–economic position to their offspring. This is because schools impart important social, cognitive, and cultural resources that influence a person's ability to rise (or fall) in the stratification system.

Schooling and Nation-Building

Schools played a critical role in nation-building; they standardized national language, built the population's capacity to carry out economic and military tasks, socialized the populace to common values, instilled a patriotic-nationalist vision, and reinforced loyalty to the nation-state over competing institutions.[4] As public schooling expanded, the state displaced other ways of disseminating skills and values. Early in the nineteenth century, many nations replaced their patchwork of voluntary and private schools with public school systems.[5] For example, adult literacy rose in the U.S., and by 1850, only 9 percent of U.S. adults were illiterate, compared to rates of 10 to 40 percent in Western Europe.[6] Mass literacy is a cornerstone of democratic citizenship that opens a flood of political opinions, ideas, and information.

The dispersal of a nationalist ideology, weakening of traditionalism, and growth of the working class, more than industrialism alone, spurred the expansion of public schooling.[7] "The task of public schooling" Andy Green (1990, 59) said, "was not so much to develop new skills for the industrial sector as to inculcate habits of conformity, discipline, and morality that would counter the widespread problems of social disorder and encourage acceptance of the values of competitive capitalism." As public schooling reorganized and controlled most organized learning in society, it also gave the state more influence over people's private lives.

Public schooling is education for the "national interest," but *the national interest is not a neutral or objective idea*. It is shaped by different social classes and cultural groups, and ultimately those with the greatest power define the national interest (see World View 8.1).[8] Opposing political groups fought to control both the form and direction of school expansion, and competition among elite groups has been a central dynamic in school expansion.[9] The specific conditions of state formation, including alliances and struggles among groups, shaped how schools socialized people to become citizens with lessons in civic or moral education.[10]

Economists have a theory of education and society called the human capital thesis. The **human capital thesis holds that schooling stimulates economic growth by creating a more productive workforce.** The thesis suggests that a major rationale for a state to develop and offer schooling is to strengthen the national economy. However, studies found that the positive impact of higher education on economic growth in advanced nations was small.[11] The effect of schooling on economic growth depends on a nation's economic and technological levels and on specific types of schooling offered and chosen. Besides being a "production good" (i.e., an investment that will produce future economic returns), schooling can be a "consumption good" (i.e., something people acquire for pleasure or social status). It contributes to economic growth when the supply of people with specific labor skills matches the economy's labor force needs.[12] Time lags and cultural–political factors can create a mismatch between types and amounts of schooling people acquire and demands of the economy. When the economic demand is low, schooling also serves a warehousing function by removing surplus young people from the labor force to lower unemployment and minimize political disruption.[13]

An imbalance can develop between a strong public demand for more schooling—due to a cultural emphasis on achievement and a desire for upward occupational mobility—and the limited supply of highly desirable jobs. In the United States this imbalance contributed to the rise of a stratified system of post-high school, or tertiary-level, schooling. Instead of directly telling many students they have no chance for upward mobility, high-school students are rechanneled in realistic directions,[14] which may cause students to become discouraged or readjust their expectations. Cultural values and patterns of state formation explain the emphasis on equal educational opportunity in the United States. Compared to other nations, the decentralized U.S. system pro-

Political Symbols and Banning Headscarves in France

In France, Christian students have long worn crosses and Jewish students the skullcap. After 15 years of debate, beginning in September 2004, France will ban the wearing of all religious symbols in public schools to protect the national interest. The issue reached the highest levels of political debate after dozens of Muslim girls were expelled from school for refusing to remove their headscarves, or the hijab. France has a Muslim population of five million, the largest in Europe. It also has a strong secular tradition that goes back to the French Revolution, and a government commission now wants the ban on religious symbols to strengthen the tradition of public secularism in law.

Muslim, Jewish, and Christian leaders in France condemned the ban on wearing religious signs, such as headscarves or crucifixes. Muslim women have long worn the hijab, and they wear it for many reasons—to appear righteous and spiritually pure, to fend off leering men and sexual harassment, to reduce costs as they use it as an inexpensive wardrobe, to conceal their social class (which Western clothes emphasize), to hide their gray hair (among older women), or to appease their fathers and husbands.

The fundamental issue is the position of Muslims in French society. Must they conform to the social norms and customs of the majority, or can they retain significant aspects of their culture and religious tradition? At a time when leaders of the European Union are debating whether the Union will retain its Christian character when it accepts Turkey as a member, the headscarf issue has a broader significance.

France differs from the rest of Europe, although similar disputes have developed in Germany and have been resolved with each state government setting its own policy. Britain, Denmark, and Greece allow teachers and pupils to wear headscarves. Belgium and the Netherlands leave it up to individual schools. Italy and Spain are silent and permit it. Only Turkey, where the vast majority are Muslims, bans women from wearing the hijab in schools and public places. It is part of Turkey's strict secular policy.

As Shore (2004) observed, "Symbols are like magic mirrors: people see in them what they want to see. A Confederate flag to some is a symbol of southern pride. To others it's a mark of oppression. . . . Symbols remind us of our unique experience with the larger issue they represent, and they reflect many of our deepest longings and fears. This could not be more true of the hijab, the Muslim headscarf and veil currently causing so much furor in France. . . . Ethnic French look upon the hijab and see 9/11."

Sources: Shore, Zachary 2004. "Fanatically Secular, France Places Scarves under Siege." *American Institute for Contemporary German Studies Advisor,* John Hopkins University, January 9, 2004. http://www.aicgs.org/c/shorec.shtml. Also see *The Economist,* "Veil of Tears," January 15, 2004; "Scarf Wars," December 11, 2003; and "All over an Inch of Flesh" and "To Ban or Not to Ban," October 23, 2003.

duces great local variation in the educational curriculum, teaching approaches, and the amount learned.[15] Some other nations, such as Sweden, have a more uniform, egalitarian, and standardized school system that sets high expectations for all students. By contrast, the U.S. school system is very diverse with local variations and many routes or branches that tend to reflect and reinforce social and economic inequalities.[16]

Political–cultural forces that shaped the historical expansion of schooling have a continuing effect. Before 1800, schooling was largely private and reserved for elites. Early in U.S. history, white citizens acquired fairly equal and open access to public schools. The United States created a large system of free public elementary education with the "common school" in the 1830s, which was built on three ideas: (1) schools were open to the children of all classes, (2) public funds paid for schools, and (3) schools were secular or nonreligious. These ideas reflected the cultural values and political ideals of an egalitarian, settler nation of small farmers, craftspeople, and shopkeepers with great ethnic diversity and with many recent immigrants.

The common school reflected a political ideal to create educated mass of citizens who could participate in democracy and unite to build the young nation. Nonetheless, the common schools were controversial. Opponents objected because the schools were an intrusion into parental rights, imposed taxes, and were "godless." Another radical idea—coeducation or mixing girls and boys—soon spread. In 1837, Massachusetts was the first state to offer public schooling with co-education. Teaching also changed. It slowly moved from an ad hoc arrangement to a recognized profession, and the school year lengthened. Throughout the nineteenth and early twentieth centuries, controversy repeatedly erupted over the state's authority to educate children and collect taxes for that purpose. A compromise was to decentralize. Schooling decisions were made by locally elected school boards or state governments, not by a centralized, national education agency as is the case in most other countries.

At first, the common schools provided only primary-level education and taught basic skills, but state governments slowly added more advanced education. By the late 1800s, most states had established public high schools and colleges. At that time, only a tiny percentage of the population attended. In 1870, less than three percent of American school-aged children enrolled in high schools.[17] Officials created the middle or junior high school in 1910 and the twelve year, 6-3-3 system. Over the years, the proportion of youth going on to higher schooling grew and the mandated age for compulsory education rose. Since the 1870s, the percentage of the age-relevant population attending school has been higher in the United States than in any other country.[18]

From the 1910s to the 1930s, mass secondary schooling spread through the public comprehensive high school. As with the common school, all students attended a single type of high school without formal stratification among schools. The comprehensive high school was also controversial and triggered heated political battles.[19] As Richard Robinson (1986, 541) summarized the battles, "the business classes did try to limit and stratify education. They fought compulsory schooling because such laws restricted the use of child labor. They wanted separate programs of vocational education to prepare working class children for manual and clerical labor to subsidize their own job training costs. They wanted to restrict . . . [courses] so that working class students only learned subjects with direct job relevance . . . [and] to restrict academic high schools to the small middle classes."

In Europe, a dual-track system of secondary schools was established with vocational education for youth from the working class and academic schools for youth from the business and professional classes. In the United States, a political coalition of working class voters and educational professionals defeated business-led proposals to create dual-track high schools. The U.S. outcome was affected by its decentralized political institutions, broad-based parties, and the importance of electoral politics in deciding school issues.[20] Because they served all parts of society, the comprehensive high schools did not promote the creation of separate organizations along class lines and legitimated the ideals of individual merit and inequality (discussed later in this chapter).[21]

Since the late 1960s, a majority of U.S. high school graduates have begun some tertiary-level schooling. Higher education systems differ widely among nations, reflecting the politics and history of each.[22] Tertiary-level schooling imparts academic knowledge and job skills, instructs in cultural knowledge and modes of reasoning, and selects people for future occupations. Perhaps its most important core function is social selection. Much of the selection occurs at entry points—some are "selected out" by not continuing, while others are "selected in" going to different types of schooling. It continues by completion rates, academic majors, and job placement. Debates over access (e.g., Affirmative Action, student financial aid) center on this social selection function.

Schooling at the tertiary-level is more highly stratified than at the primary or secondary levels. At each level of schooling, some do not continue. In the United States, about 30 percent of students never finish high school.[23] Nearly one-half of high school graduates who begin work on a four-year college degree never finish it. Of the U.S. adult population, 25 percent have a four-year degree or more advanced education; among younger adults aged 25 to 34, this figure is 29 percent. About two-thirds of students go to public institutions and one-third attend private institutions, with large differences in the prestige, programs, quality, and cost of schooling. A strong relationship exists between a student's socioeconomic background and the type of schooling he/she pursues. Students from low-income and working-class families tend to attend two-year community colleges or technical schools; those from middle-class families tend to go to less competitive private four-year colleges or public universities, and those from upper-income families attend private Ivy League or selective liberal arts colleges. Most of the elite universities use "legacy preferences," which is a preference for admitting the children of alumni. For example, the odds of an applicant to Harvard University getting admitted is about four times better than other applicants if her/his parents are Harvard graduates. At Notre Dame University, the children of alumni make up about one-fourth of the entering class. Many political leaders, including President George W. Bush and Vice President Dick Cheney, had their entry into higher schooling made easier because their parents were alumni.[24]

Teritary-level schooling has three additional specialized functions: (1) to create new knowledge, (2) to preserve and refine cultural heritage and artistic capacity, and (3) to provide public service. Thus, research universities are responsible for creating new knowledge (i.e., scientific discoveries, new philosophies) and preserving cultural heritage (i.e., art museums, historical studies, literary criticism). Higher education institutions also provide government agencies, community groups, and others free advice and consultation services.

The political dynamics of how the stratified U.S. tertiary-level system grew are complex, but community colleges illustrate the process. Today, over one-third of high school graduates who continue their schooling attend a two-year community or vocational-technical college; 96 percent of these are public institutions. This was not always the case. Once most community colleges were private and offered a nonvocational, liberal arts program.[25] Shortly after World War II many new students began to pursue higher educations. Community college officials realized that they could not compete with established four-year colleges. Rather than face defeat, they experienced "anticipatory subordination" and redirected their focus to specialize in vocational training that would avoid directly competing with four-year colleges. They realigned community college offerings to address local businesses needs by producing students that had job-relevant or vocational training that prepared them for immediate entry into skilled blue-collar and nonmanagerial white-collar jobs. High school counselors tend to "cool out" or encourage students from blue-collar families who wanted to continue schooling by directing them to community colleges. **Cooling out is the process of adjusting and lowering students' expectations to accept less prestigious schooling and lower status jobs than they wanted as a realistic alternative.**[26]

By recasting themselves as vocational-training institutions, community colleges closed the gap between high student aspirations and a limited number of openings for the most desirable jobs. In exchange for abandoning their dreams of attending a prestigious four-year college and attaining a high-status job, students were offered short-range upward mobility and job security in a lower-level occupation at a lower salary for less cost or less time in school. Government officials supported the recasting as a low-cost way to satisfy voter demands for expanded tertiary education while also increasing the supply of trained entry-level workers to help local businesses. Business leaders did not directly request a public vocational training system; rather, community college leaders took the initiative and responded to the "structural power of the business community" based on its position of hiring graduates. It was an example of the power of the business community and the structural dependence of schools. In the words of Brint and Karabel (1989, 217), "The business community was able to "profoundly influence the behavior of other institutions—including institutions of higher education—without having to do anything at all."

School Knowledge, Socialization, and Social Selection

School knowledge is the subset of all skills, information, and beliefs that is in the curriculum and which schools identify, organize, and legitimate. These particular skills, types of knowledge, and forms of understanding become "official" knowledge. A person may learn a great deal outside of school, but school knowledge has a privileged status.[27] Thus, knowing about Shakespeare or physics is important, but knowing the names and favorite foods of the members of a pop music group is not. School knowledge changes over time. For example, until the 1870s, most U.S. high schools taught Greek and Latin and few taught math or science. Educators and others debate what schools should teach.

In the decentralized United States, state officials mandate that public schools teach about certain subjects but forbid teaching about others (see Case in Point 8.1). School knowledge is often a political compromise, but most nations agree on many aspects of it. Despite differences, such as requiring instruction about religion, housekeeping, or farming, primary-level school knowledge is similar worldwide.[28]

Socialization and Building Cultural and Social Capital

In addition to the formal, explicit curriculum, schools also advance an unwritten or hidden curriculum. **The hidden curriculum is implicit instruction that instills compliance to formal authority, adherence to bureaucratic procedures, and the structured pursuit of competitive individual rewards.**[29] It includes school culture or the "habitus" of school (i.e., a set of categories of perception and habits of behavior used for understanding).[30] Schools appear to engage in a neutral, objective process of selecting people based on individual merit and achievement. In reality, they advance school knowledge and values in a hidden curriculum that tends to reflect the norms, values, and outlooks of the upper-middle and upper class.

Students coming from different cultural backgrounds or low-income families tend to be less familiar or comfortable with the culture, official knowledge, and hidden curriculum of schooling. As a result, they are less likely to succeed in school or complete a degree. Nonconformists are labeled as personal failures by schools, and once labeled as such, the student's success beyond school is limited.

CASE IN POINT 8.1   **Textbook Selection and Control over Schooling**

Heated political debate develops in state government education committees that set curriculum standards and select a list of textbooks that primary and secondary teachers can use. For example, a group of ardent conservatives who were elected to the education committee of Kansas eliminated the theory of evolution from the official state science curriculum, making it an option for local school districts. Because of the economics of publishing, active textbook committees in two populous states, Texas and California, greatly influence the production of school textbooks for the national market. Especially in Texas, right-wing political activists tried to block textbooks that focused on social conflict, involved clarifying values, or presented any negative images of the United States. Conflict over textbooks by social conservatives caused the Texas legislature to limit the board of education's power over textbooks in 1995 (see Lyman 1998). Some observers feel that this means state governments are a tool for cultural hegemony and allow conservative activists to censor ideas and control school knowledge. A study of the Texas board fails to support this claim and found that "issues that are commonly associated with cultural politics are treated as forms of public input and disassociated from professional interests and decision making . . . they are not a major part of the enterprise of formulating school knowledge" (Wong 1991, 16). The board prioritizes narrow technical or instrumental issues over substantive content concerns. Thus, they pay more attention to whether a textbook has end-of-chapter questions than to the substantive knowledge asked for in the questions.

Murray Edelman (1977, 39, 53) described the process: "Dominant categories of speech and of thought define the economically successful and politically powerful as meritorious, and the unsuccessful and politically deviant as mentally or morally inadequate. . . . Schoolteachers and counselors also usually perceive merit in terms of conformity to middle-class opinion and norms." By labeling students who resist social conformity or do not master official knowledge as failures, schools affirm and legitimate inequalities among students that often originate in family background.

Schooling can also shape a person's political beliefs and attitudes. Highly educated people tend to be more politically aware, active, and tolerant (discussed later in this chapter), but they are also less egalitarian. This is because schooling promotes a belief in equal opportunity and individual achievement that puts the responsibility and blame for failure on the individual.[31] For example, many leftist political radicals are well-educated but do not have high-income, high-status jobs. Observers speculated that these "overeducated" persons succeeded in school but failed to reap corresponding social and financial rewards, so they redirected their resentment over a lack of personal success toward the established social–political order and adopted radical leftist beliefs. However, studies have found little support for this overeducated radical thesis. Instead, it appears that the strong emphasis on competitive individual achievement in schooling encourages overeducated people to self-blame (e.g., have low self-esteem or depression) or to redirect their energies to areas outside their careers (e.g., they value leisure activities or family more than their occupation).[32] Schools also create cultural and social capital (see Closer Look 8.1).

Social Selection and Credentialism

Schools both facilitate individual social mobility and reproduce a system of inequality. They select who will advance to positions of status and power in society and who will remain behind. By obscuring the impact of different family backgrounds and a class bias in school knowledge, unsuccessful students are labeled as failures. At the same time, schooling offers successful students (i.e., those who mastered school knowledge, methods of reasoning, and modes of behavior) valuable credentials.[33] Credentials are formal, visible indicators of success in school in the form of credits, certificates, and diplomas. They certify that a person possesses the privileged, legitimized knowledge that schools disseminate and that are critical in the process of social class formation. This is because they regulate who gets access to valued occupations and positions of authority.[34] Contrary to popular belief, only a few occupations directly require the skills taught in schools, and school grades are not closely connected to later success on the job.[35] Most people learn job-relevant skills at the workplace. Employers largely use grades and credentials to screen applicants; the credentials tell employers who acquired the dominant social norms, values, and status culture.[36] **Credentialism is the idea that organizations and employers substitute the possession of credentials for the work of evaluating an individual's skills or abilities, and that people with credentials have a valuable social resource.**

CLOSER LOOK 8.1   Cultural and Social Capital

CULTURAL AND SOCIAL CAPITAL

Beyond promoting school knowledge and conformity to school behaviors, schooling also builds and rewards students for possessing cultural and social capital. **Cultural capital is symbolic wealth in the form of refined aesthetic and intellectual taste that is positively valued in high status groups of a society.** Cultural capital may include knowing a foreign language, appreciating works in art galleries, enjoying classical music, and understanding serious poetry or literature. For example, an American student with substantial cultural capital can speak French, play the violin, loves to view statutes of Michelangelo, and reads the Brontes or Jane Austin for fun. Schooling promotes cultural capital and rewards the students who acquire it because it reflects the values of high status, elite culture (See DiMaggio 1982 and Karen 1991a). A child's awareness of and interest in cultural capital often begins in the family. High status families will send their children to schools that strongly nurture and reinforce it. This is because possessing cultural capital will ease the child's entry into private, elite colleges and facilitate the young person's advancement into a top-level management career in major banks and corporations (See Cookson and Persell 1985, Levine 1980, and Useem and Karabel 1986). As they inculcate admiration and respect for the elite taste, schools simultaneously devalue the cultural forms and taste of society's powerless groups. They tend to stigmatize or penalize students who embrace the cultural values or practices of the low-income or powerless (e.g., black street culture, barrio culture, rap or hip hop, billiards, working on cars, watching professional wrestling and drag races), compared to the students who aspire to or imitate elite culture. As Bourdieu and Passeron (1990) argued, official knowledge and cultural taste in formal schooling are rooted in the position of power of social classes and elites, and that knowledge or taste is not intrinsically superior to that of workers or lower income people. Formal schooling implicitly acknowledges status hierarchies and validates elite cultural habits and tastes.

Schools also provide students with social capital. **Social capital is a resource in the form of interpersonal contacts, acquaintances, and connections that a person can draw upon.** In ordinary parlance, it is networking or who you know. Schools are settings in which people establish social ties, make friends, and find marriage partners. Some parents select schools based on social capital considerations. For example, private elite boarding schools for secondary education developed around 1900 in the United States to help maintain the upper class, and one of their most important functions was to enhance intra-class social capital. The social capital students acquire at private boarding schools can be more significant than academic grades or cultural capital for upper class entry (Burt 1999, Karen 1991a, Portes 1998, Putnam 1995, and Zweigenhaft 1993).

Credentials signal that a person knows how to follow rules, adhere to certain behavioral norms, obey authority, and use generally accepted modes of expression and reasoning. They also provide the students who have conformed to school requirements with improved access to a lifetime of social and financial rewards in the occupational structure.

Sociologists developed three theories to explain the relationship between public schooling and social inequality—correspondence, resistance, and semi-autonomy. We will examine these theories next.

Three Theories of Schooling

A correspondence theory of schooling says that schools have a middle-class bias that works against students from disadvantaged socioeconomic backgrounds and selects students to enter future positions in a manner that parallels the student's family class background.[37] According to the theory, behind a veil of neutrality, schools promote the values and outlook of the upper middle class. They prepare students from middle-class families with the social skills, modes of reasoning, and outlook to become managers, supervisors, and professionals. Schools socialize students from working-class families differently by instilling obedience and complacency and imparting limited skills that prepare them to take low-level jobs. Thus, schooling reproduces the system of social classes and the power structure.[38] In a more general, cultural version of the theory, Bourdieu and Passeron (1990) argued that schools maintain the social structure by reproducing class culture.

Later theorists argued that schools do not stream students into future social class positions; but rather that schools are a battleground. **The resistance theory holds that acts of student rebellion, resistance to school authority, and dropping out of school are expressions of struggle among social classes or other groups (e.g., ethnic, religious) over the content of education and power in society.** Students, and some teachers, resist or convert educational practice for subversive goals. Resistance theorists interpreted the attitudes and traits of rebellious or disadvantaged students as indicators of social–political struggle.[39]

Others recognized that much of student resistance is apolitical, self-destructive, and individualistic. In addition, little empirical research supports the thesis that schools socialize working-class students to be rule-dependent and obedient and middle class students to be more independent.[40] **The semi-autonomy theory holds that most conflicts about schooling occur outside the classroom as many competing stakeholders (e.g., students, parents, faculty, administrators, public officials, employers of graduates) fight to dictate the direction of education, and schools have partial autonomy from dominant class forces of society.** For example, classroom teachers find themselves in a contradictory position. Very few teachers come from the elite or dominant class, yet they have learned the game and mastered dominant forms of thinking, knowledge, and behavior. They know that mastering and adapting to the dominant culture will improve the odds that a student can move upward in the occupational structure. At the same time, many teachers do not wholly embrace the rules, views, and values of the dominant culture. Many recognize that rigidly imposing the dominant culture and acting as agents of social control can destroy students' vitality and alienate them. Some teachers are attracted to alternative values (e.g., humanism, equality, idealism, participatory democracy) and try to balance them against dominant values (e.g., efficiency, consumerism, competition). Thus, students, teachers, and others engage in constant debate, struggle, and negotiation with one another over the content and operation of schooling. They also debate and struggle with external groups who try to impose their own beliefs onto schools. Martin Carnoy (1989, 9) expressed this idea, "The education system is not simply an instrument of business or of other dominant groups to shape youth . . . into some conception held by these groups of what social roles these youth should fill. Schooling is a product of the conflict between the dominant and the dominated."

Political Struggles and School Reform Movements

We next look at schooling conflicts in the United States at each level of schooling.

Disputes in higher education frequently involve wider ideological conflicts because many intellectuals in contemporary society find employment in colleges and universities. Ideally, the principles of academic freedom and tenure protect college faculty, allowing them to freely investigate, debate, and make public statements on any topic. Professors have greater freedom of speech than people in most other occupations, but U.S. history shows that "college and university governing boards were highly sensitive to local and regional distributions of economic and political power."[41] In certain periods, thousands of teachers and professors were harassed or fired for not conforming politically or for taking unpopular stands. During the 1890s, after World War I, and during the McCarthy Red Scare era, government officials and others targeted college faculty for defending, expressing, or writing "radical" views and expelled large numbers from U.S. universities.[42]

For example, in the McCarthy Red Scare era of the 1950s, politicians and advocacy groups attacked educators for spreading "subversive ideas." By 1950, 36 states required that all public teachers sign loyalty oaths. In New York City alone, officials dismissed 300 teachers for political reasons. Harassment took other forms and spread. Soon faculty were fired at the University of California, University of Washington, University of Vermont, Ohio State University, Wayne State University, and Rutgers University among others. Officials put the names of dismissed or suspect teachers on black lists to block them from getting other jobs. Some black lists continued in use until the early 1960s. In many states, self-appointed patriotic groups also reviewed high school and college textbooks to ensure that they did not contain any so-called subversive ideas.[43]

The Red Scare ended long ago, but similar episodes in U.S. history and in other countries reveal an important point about the relationship between political power and schooling. Ideally, a college or school is a place in society where people can gather to develop, disseminate, and openly express a wide range of opinions, beliefs, and ideas. If a powerful group feels that unacceptable ideas are being expressed and feels threatened, it tries to limit the flow of ideas and free expression, often making teachers or students the targets of suppression.

More recently, U.S. colleges and universities felt a different kind of outside pressure. During 1980s, some corporate leaders and members of the policy planning network believed that college faculty had acquired an antibusiness bias during protest era of the 1960s–1970s and that graduating students did not sufficiently endorse America's class and power structure. To instill more procapitalist beliefs and values in students, they pressured colleges to establish new academic programs, created new research centers, or funded endowed chairs (i.e., independently funded faculty positions) for faculty members who would endorse free enterprise, promote entrepreneurship, and advocate "American values." Their goal was to foster a more business-friendly curriculum, align university research better with direct business needs, and ensure that business-friendly university administrators were appointed to leadership posts. Also, public funding for colleges and universities was reduced and dependence on private sector funds grew. At the high school level, they provided new probusiness course materials and promoted the addition of courses in economics. This probusiness education campaign had lightened by the mid-1990s. By that time, ties to the business community were stronger, endowed chairs and research centers were operating, and universities had become responsive to the interests of the business community.[44] As Press and Washburn (2000, 46) remarked, "universities themselves are beginning to look and behave more like for-profit companies."

Since the 1980s, other trends in U.S. tertiary schooling underwent significant change. At least since the 1950s, a student's family or class background had been having a weakening impact on whether he/she attended college. Higher education had rapidly expanded in the 1970s. New social groups, especially women and blacks, gained access to higher education because they won recognition as officially recognized social categories.[45] The historical trend for greater access stopped, then reversed in the mid-1980s. At that time, politicians advanced new agendas and public support for funding higher education waned. As a result, tuition levels increased and public financial support declined. As a consequence, a student's family and class background has become an increasingly important predictor of college attendance since the 1990s. This has been "a marked retreat in public commitment to advanced educational opportunity."[46]

Political pressures are also evident in the governing boards that oversee colleges or universities. Public and private colleges or universities have a board of trustees or board of regents that is similar to the Board of Directors of a private corporation. Board members are appointed and most are corporate executives, major campaign contributors to top-level politicians, or ex-politicians. Occasionally, a governing board will impose its political values over the objections of the faculty. A board might mandate that all students take a specific course or test, or it might eliminate an academic major. For example, in New York state, board members criticized a public university for holding a conference on sexuality, and it also imposed a new required curriculum for all students. In California, conservatives on the board led opposition to affirmative action programs in public universities.[47] In sum, the larger political environment can influence tertiary-level schooling. Next we look at political movements that have shaped K–12 public schooling in the United States.

Three School Reform Movements

Schooling in the United States at the K–12 level is frequently criticized, and large-scale movements periodically arise to improve or reform it in some way. Three major reform movements in the twentieth century are, the progressive (1900s to 1910s), the equity (1960s to early 1970s), and the excellence (mid-1980s to late 1990s). Each was linked to a larger political agenda and politically mobilized groups seeking to change the direction of public schooling.[48] The reforms hinged on a tension between promoting equality and protecting and preserving social economic privileges.

The Progressive School Reform Movement   The Progressive School Reform movement was part of the larger Progressive political movement that advocated limiting concentrated corporate wealth, reducing industrial disputes and class conflict, helping the immigrant poor, expanding popular democracy, and reforming government by increasing the numbers of trained professionals in bureaucratic and legal administrations. The reformers believed public schools should prepare future citizens who would be active, informed participants in democracy. They opposed authoritarian school discipline and rote memorization, and instead advocated a humane, problem-solving and critical-thinking approach to learning. "Progressive education was an attempt . . . to develop a school experience that would benefit the whole child's intellectual, social, artistic and moral development."[49] Reformers also sought to professionalize teaching, giving more highly trained teachers greater autonomy. They encouraged teachers to establish creative environments in which each student could fully develop her/his total personality; in these settings all students would come together and each could develop to his/her greatest potential. Many Progressive educational ideas remain as a part of teacher training today, such as educating the whole person, maximizing student potential, and emphasizing critical thinking and self-expression.

The Equity School Reform Movement   The Equity School Reform movement of the 1960s was aligned with the civil rights and related movements. Sometimes called "new progressive," it sought to expand the opportunities for all children, promote racial integration of schools, increase local community control, provide an inclusive curriculum that recognized the achievements of all people, and expand affirmative action in hiring and promotion. It also advocated accepting and "mainstreaming" students with learning or physical disabilities and expanding bilingual education. Equity reformers wanted teachers to make schooling more relevant for disadvantaged students, encourage active learning, and be flexible so they could reach out to all students. They also encouraged recognizing student rights and giving students choices. Yet they inflamed white racial hostility, demonstrating how schools are central to racial politics.[50] A legacy of this movement is the ideal of multiculturalism in the form of prodiversity attitudes and academic materials that represent people of all ethnic and racial heritages.

The Excellence School Reform Movement   The Excellence School Reform movement began in the mid-1980s and continues today. It was a backlash against the Equality movement which Excellence reformers blamed, along with teacher's unions and school officials, for a decline in student achievement despite rising school costs. The reformers observed that standardized test scores had fallen, fewer students enrolled in rigorous science or foreign language courses, and barely literate students were graduating from high schools.[51] They saw this as threatening to U.S. international economic competitiveness. Instead of advocating the principle of the common school (i.e., equal public schools that accepted everyone), the reformers instead advocated the principles of economic efficiency and high academic standards. They sought to punish public schools that could not get pupils up to new, higher academic standards by reducing financial support. The Excellence reformers had great faith in market mechanisms. They believed that if schools were required to compete for students, their quality would improve. The reform advocates did not accept the idea that educators were autonomous professionals, such as physicians, nurses, engineers or lawyers, but instead labeled the educators as self-serving.[52] The reformers held that teachers, education experts, and schools needed to become more accountable to the business community and to parents. The reformers felt that "altering the governance of schooling, whether via open-catchment policies, magnet schools, charter schools, or vouchers, would empower parents and make schools more responsive to their wishes."[53] In addition, these reformers attracted followers from the New Christian Right who felt alienated from public schools and saw Excellence reforms as a way to get public schools to teach their religious-oriented values.[54] A major federal education bill signed by President Bush in December 2001 that mandated annual nationwide testing was one of the Excellence movement's proposals. See Chart 8.2 for Excellence movement proposals.

Critics of the Excellence reforms see them as "a drift toward privatization"[55] that will destroy the goal of providing quality public schooling for all youth of various abilities, races, and socioeconomic backgrounds. Critics say that primary

---

c h a r t   8 . 2

PROPOSALS OF THE EXCELLENCE EDUCATIONAL REFORM MOVEMENT

- Strengthen the curriculum and go back to basics by adding requirements, limiting student choice, offering a narrow range of subjects, and cutting bilingual education. A strong curriculum includes traditional Western literature; American history; and more mathematics, science, and economics. (The teaching of economics in high schools greatly expanded in the early 1980s due to corporate political mobilization discussed in Chapter 5 as part of business-sponsored programs to educate the public about free enterprise capitalism).
- Institute a review process that is external to the classroom teacher and school, and give business and political elites the ability to hold teachers and schools accountable. This includes formal student assessment with regular standardized tests, graduation tests, and tests for teachers to make it visible to outsiders that schools are reaching the standards and to reduce the influence of local teachers.
- Introduce business personnel policies into schools with merit pay plans, easier teacher dismissal, reduced teacher autonomy, and multiple levels of teachers. Also, hire more people who have "real work" business experience instead of traditional teacher training.
- Expand the differences among schools, apply market competition to schools, and create high quality programs at certain schools. Give parents a choice of schools with tax funded vouchers that can be used for any school, including private and religious schools.

outcomes of the reforms will be to dramatically increase the differences among public schools and to expand private schooling. School choice or voucher programs will allow more-educated and higher-income parents to abandon weaker public schools that also serve children from disadvantaged family backgrounds (i.e., lower income, racial minorities), and those schools will decline further. At the same time, private and suburban public schools that have been most responsive to vocal, higher-income parents will flourish.[56] Some Excellence reform proposals have been implemented. Early research suggests that low-income and racial minority parents possess less information to make informed choices about schools compared to white, higher-income parents.[57] In the areas where school choice programs exist, white parents have used their freedom of choice to avoid schools that enroll higher percentages of racial minority students. They did this even when the schools did not differ by level of student safety, academic quality, or other school characteristics.[58]

Politics and School Reform

The debates over school reform reflect contending ideological and political values and beliefs about the role of schooling.[59] Various "politically creative interest groups construct coalitions, adapt to the broader cultural environment, and tailor meanings of school to further their own interests" (Davies 1999, 1). They use school reform to advance their ideological goals, protect their socioeconomic position, or gain access to lower cost labor for their businesses. For example, Excellence reform leaders have aligned with ideological conservatives whose primary values are individual freedom, market-based solutions, and efficiency.[60] Political activists outside of education back the movement, such as conservative multimillionaire businessmen who gave money to promote voucher programs in California, Michigan, and Wisconsin.[61] After voters rejected the referendums on vouchers in 2000, Excellence reform leaders shifted tactics. They targeted politicians directly and renamed the voucher programs to distract critics in the public.[62] Supporters of voucher-based schooling include a mix of deeply committed classical liberal or libertarian ideological believers, parents who reject integration by race and class, some religious conservatives, and upper-income class parents who want to insure that their offspring get a competitive advantage over others.

As Katznelson and Weir (1985, 213) observed, debate over school reform "masks key changes in the relationship between schooling and social space in the postwar years—changes that challenge common schooling and the capacity of democratic politics to shape public education." The debate ignores two major factors that profoundly shaped public schooling: residential segregation by race and class, and intense parental desire to provide their children with competitive advantages for upward social mobility.

The Excellence reform movement is a product of late twentieth century political and economic forces. In the 1950s and earlier, public schools were sharply segregated by race and class. They also taught local values and beliefs. This changed as a result of the government actions during the 1960s to equalize public schooling.[63] Despite the changes, an achievement gap remained between students of different income levels and racial backgrounds. A major reason this gap existed was because racial polarization increased in cities and the suburbs grew greatly in the 1960s–1970s with a massive middle-class "white flight" to the suburbs. Since school funding and attendance were residentially based, past inequalities were recreated and new forms introduced. Two types of public schools developed based on class and race: (1) high-quality suburban schools for middle and upper middle class children, and (2) low-quality inner-city and remote rural schools largely for the poor and racial minority children. Court-imposed desegregation programs had a limited impact. Most public schools remain racially segregated due to residential separation by race and class, and many actually resegregated in the 1990s.[64]

School inequalities are fueled by parental financial and social status concerns that are realized through political actions. Suburban homeowners want to protect the property values of their houses, which is the biggest source of middle class wealth. House values are closely correlated to the quality of a local school district. By defending "their schools," suburbanites are also preserving a financial investment. Upper middle class parents want to transfer their social position on to their children. They believe this is best achieved by schools that reinforce middle-class norms and values. Recall that schooling's impact on socialization and social selection is larger than its ability to provide academic skills and knowledge. For this reason, increased differentiation among schools will result in larger disparities in socialization and social selection. With current trends, secondary-level schooling may become more like tertiary-level schooling (i.e., hierarchical and very stratified with a tight relationship between family social background and school quality).[65] As financially advantaged parents send their offspring to the schools that best socialize and prepare students for future success, students from disadvantaged families will go to weaker schools and find it increasingly difficult to compete or advance. A likely outcome is greater social closure. **Social closure is a general stratification process whereby the people currently occupying higher social or economic positions engage in actions to restrict the upward movement of or greater competition from people in lower positions.** Katznelson and Weir (1985, xiii) concluded that the Excellence reforms will probably move public K–12 schooling in the U.S. "toward a more segmented curricula and toward education that is sharply segregated by the class position of parents."

After years of schooling, people continue to learn, develop beliefs, and acquire ideas and information from other sources, and the mass media are perhaps the most important source. Next we see how the media shape views of many events, including politics, and how they provide information needed by effective, active citizens.

MASS MEDIA FORMS AND FUNCTIONS

The mass media are not a part of the state in most democratic nations, yet they are integral to the polity and politics. They are called the "mass" media because they communicate to the entire population and are accessible by everyone, in contrast to media restricted to certain people or to one organization or social strata. The media come in print (e.g., books, magazines, newspapers), broadcast (e.g., television, radio), recorded (e.g., video, movies, CDs DVDs), and electronic (e.g., Internet) formats and have multiple functions (see Chart 8.3).

The mass media are part of a larger culture industry that includes "news, sports, film, TV comedy and drama, entertainment 'parks,' tourists excursions, and footage of distant wars and conflicts."[66] It extends to sports events, concerts, museums, theatres, fairs, art galleries, and performing arts centers. Its public or noncommercial sector (e.g., public libraries, museums) is a tiny and declining part of the whole. Increasingly, the media embrace private corporate sponsors, making the public sector more of an adjunct to the market-based private sector.

Very few people control mass media production facilities, resources, and technologies. They create symbol-laden media products (i.e., visual, audio, text) that are mass distributed and consumed by the public. The products carry explicit and implicit symbolic messages. Media producers can design specific ideas or meanings into messages or include them unintentionally; the meanings can be weighty and profound, or trivial and banal; a media product may carry a single simple message or multiple complex and conflicting ideas. Huge financial resources and organizational coordination are required to spread media messages across a large country and beyond national borders to reach most people and to repeat similar messages across multiple media formats. These are critical structural features necessary to reach and influence the mass public.

Political sociologists want to understand the creation, distribution, and impact of the symbolic content in media messages because they can have significant political effects, even if unintended. As Page and Shapiro (1992, 376) noted, "We believe that the American public may be regularly exposed to certain kinds of misleading or biased information and interpretations that affect preferences concerning a wide range of foreign and domestic policies. This pattern is very likely the result from normal market forces, together with government control of certain types of information; from the nation-state system and the loyalties and

chart 8.3

MAJOR FUNCTIONS OF THE MASS MEDIA

Entertain—Amuse, generate pleasure, divert attention, and stimulate interest

Socialize—Spread values, beliefs, and norms into the culture

Inform—Disseminate facts, opinions, and information

Persuade—Encourage people to obey officials, vote for candidates, or purchase products

Legitimate—Promote mass acceptance of authorities, ideas, and institutions

Produce—Create symbolic products, profits for firms, and jobs in the media industry

interests it generates; from our predominately capitalist economy; and from the disproportionate resources with which business and other organized interests produce and disseminate political information."

How the Mass Media Affect People

Political sociologists explain mass media influence on public attitudes using several models. The earliest idea was a simple *hypodermic needle model*. In it, media consumers are passive observers who are "injected" with political messages; the more they see a message, the greater its impact. Later researchers found little support for this model and developed the resonance and competition models.[67] In the *resonance model* (or cultural interpretation model), people possess varying levels of receptiveness to the media. They select which media to consume, are differentially attentive to it, and interpret messages in an interpretative process shaped by their backgrounds and beliefs. The messages interact with a person's background, and different people viewing the same message can take away different understandings. A person's preexisting disposition (i.e., values, attitudes, beliefs) filters media messages and shapes his/her interpretation.[68] Although a person receives a large volume of diverse messages in multiple media formats (e.g., talk shows, advertisements, news programs, sitcoms), he or she only recalls and is strongly influenced by those that fit predispositions. Messages that are consistent with many other messages also have a bigger impact. Thus, the impact of one specific message may be small, but the cumulative effect of numerous direct and indirect messages can be very large.[69] In the *competition model*, the media messages are contradictory and interdependent. This is especially the case for "attack ads" (i.e., media messages designed to neutralize an opponent's ad) and messages designed to attract media exposure. Media messages can refer to, build on, neutralize, or displace other media messages.

Putting the models together, we see that media messages can provide new information, draw attention to an issue, shape evaluation, and "prime" the audience (priming effects are discussed later in this chapter) but are strongest when they are personally relevant, repeated, and congruent with other messages. Also, messages have their greatest impact on the least informed and most politically disinterested people.[70] Iyengar and Kinder (1987, 60) argued that, "The power of television news to set the public agenda depends partly on which public we have in mind. . . . The more removed the viewer is from the world of public affairs, the stronger the agenda-setting power of television news." Message impact is greatest for people who only hear one side of an issue or who rely on a single source. For example, research on the knowledge about issues surrounding the 2003 Iraq war found that Americans who primarily relied on news from the Fox television network had far more misconceptions about it than other people, and their misconceptions closely fit the President's Iraq war policy.[71] In general, exposure to a variety of opposing messages encourages people to reflect on what they hear and form an independent opinion.

The mass media affect the elites differently than the masses. Elites tend to believe that the issues receiving media attention will shape public views and public opinion conforms to media presentations. For elites, the media is a window to mass opinion. Although it may be inaccurate, they believe the media's impact on others is far stronger than on themselves.[72] Elites also tend to over-read transitory, unformed mass opinion by projecting their more ideological thinking onto it.[73]

Media format (e.g., film, television, newspaper) shapes its use and impact. For example, learning about politics via television news differs from learning about it via newspapers. Television news is more simplistic, entertaining, and emotionally engaging. People who rely on it tend to be less informed than those who read newspapers or newsmagazines.[74] Also, people with fewer cognitive reasoning skills prefer television news, since newspapers can be difficult for a person with limited schooling.[75] A well-educated person has the information processing skills required to process complex written ideas, infrequently used words, and long sentences, so she/he learns fastest from the printed news. By contrast, a less-educated person acquires knowledge more efficiently via television.[76] In this way, mass media formats accentuate the preexisting political knowledge gap among people (see Table 8.1 and Table 8.2).

The television format creates a feeling of authenticity and is more trusted by most people than written news.[77] It enables media-savvy performers and politicians to connect emotionally with viewers/voters in a way that hides the degree to which their presentation has been preplanned, scripted, acted, and staged.

TABLE 8.1   Frequency of Media Use for News by Americans

Level of Schooling	Newspaper (%)		TV News (%)		Radio News (%)*	
	Never	Daily	Never	Daily	Never	Daily
Less than high school	41.1	29.4	30.0	41.1	56.2	21.9
High school diploma	30.4	30.4	29.3	24.9	44.3	27.5
Post high school schooling	25.5	31.4	25.0	27.2	31.4	29.0
4-year college degree	20.4	35.1	26.4	27.6	34.3	30.5
Advanced degree	10.9	51.4	20.8	32.8	23.9	43.7

*From 1998 National Election Survey data.

TABLE 8.2   Changes in Newspaper Readership by Level of Schooling, 1996 to 2002

Percentage of Americans Who Say They Do Not Read a Daily Newspaper

Level of Schooling	1996	2002	Change over six years
Less than High School	35	35	No change
High School Diploma	27	25	2 percent more readers
Post High School Schooling	25	20	5 percent more readers
4-Year College Degree	19	18	1 percent more readers
Advanced Degree	16	18	2 percent fewer readers

Source: Compiled from the 1996 and the 2002 National Election Survey. Percentages have been rounded to whole numbers.

"Let's run through this once more—and, remember, you choke up at
Paragraph Three and brush away the tear at Paragraph Five."

Although it generates trust and accentuates spontaneous emotional engagement
between the viewer and the televised person, the television format also discourages analytic discussion and detached, careful, and deliberative reflection on
ideas. As P. K. Manning (1996, 266–267) remarked, "Television, like cinema and
theatre, frames conduct powerfully because it obviates the technological, physical
and social mechanisms that produce it . . . television mimics conversation. . . . It
presents the opportunity for pseudo-interaction between a mass anonymous audience and televised figures . . . [creating a] sense of immediacy, intimacy, and
shared emotive expression . . ." (see Summary 8.1).[78]

Because the process of producing media images is unseen, it is possible that
images are manipulated. Many politicians create polished images or stage
events to increase their television appeal. For example in 2001, lobbyists for
large corporations urged their wealthy members to "dress down" (i.e., take off
coats and ties and wear working-class clothing) while attending a Republican
Party rally in Washington D.C., and they even distributed hard hats. The rally
was to demonstrate support for a tax cut that would primarily benefit higher-
income people. The change of clothing was intended to create a (mis)impres-
sion of working-class support for television viewers. In the summer of 2002,
White House media people rearranged President Bush's platform at Mount
Rushmore, so television viewers would see his profile perfectly aligned with
the mountain's carved Presidents. In a 2003 speech at a factory, White House
image-makers manipulated the televised image to match the speech's message
by covering over boxes that said "Made in China" and adding empty boxes that
said "Made in U.S.A."[79]

SUMMARY 8.1

The Characteristics and Effects of Television Presentations

1. **Episodic Presentations**—The flow of stories is a series of disconnected episodes, and "episodic understanding leads to fragmentary understanding" (Cook 1998, 112). It also creates feelings of futility, blaming individuals, and evasion of government responsibility.

2. **Oversimplification**—Understanding events requires a knowledge base, but television assumes little prior knowledge, so it turns complex issues into simple battles of good versus evil or strong versus weak. When presenting more than one side of an issue, it shows the two views as polar opposites, accentuating differences and skipping subtleties. "News tends to emphasize conflict, dissension, and battle; out of a journalistic convention that there are two sides to any story" (Schudson 1995, 9).

3. **A Focus on Individuals and Visuals**—Television is successful when it personalizes and makes the story "real" for viewers, and it shows them visual images. It focuses on "who did it" and shows particular people or victims of events. It rarely presents abstract ideas or events that are not visible or that lack concrete, easily identifiable villains or victims.

4. **Accent on the Dramatic**—Dramatic events (e.g., life and death, violence, moral outrage) attract viewer attention and can be highlighted with visuals, sound, positioning, and "breathless" commentary that is full of superlatives and intense adjectives. Television reinforces the values of speed, excitement,

and action over other values, such as slow deliberation, quiet reflection, or careful consideration.

5. **Present Focus Without Context**—Television presents stories as here and now or in the very recent past. Only rarely does it refer to the origins that many current events or issues have in the distant past or their connection with many other distant events and issues. This creates a television reality that has no memory of the past and cannot see interconnections among social problems or public events. The "preoccupation with a constant present tense, and with what's new rather than what's constant, denies news attention to preexisting social problems and discourages solutions" (Cook 1998, 112).

6. **Unspoken Selection**—Television cannot show and explain everything it covers, so it selectively presents events and issues, including some and omitting others. This process creates an interpretation or frame for events, one that is invisible and not discussed. Viewers receive a selective picture and particular interpretation, but it appears to be a complete, objective picture of reality. Viewers often believe that what television presents is most important and what it omits is not. "We need to be aware of the role such media play in editing and distorting the information we receive when visual imagery on TV can give the impression that what is being seen is what is most significant . . ." (Altheide 1995, 175).

Sources: See Iyengar (1996) and Schudson (1995, 10).

Changes in the Mass Media

The media industry experienced dramatic technological, commercial, and political changes in the past decade. The technological changes are most noticeable due to tremendous advances in speed and decreased cost of computers and communication equipment, the diffusion of satellites and cable, portable phones, video and CDs, and an explosive expansion of the Internet. Yet the commercial changes are just as dramatic. Smaller, specialized media firms have been consolidated into a few, much larger firms.[80] In recent years government regulation over the media companies has loosened, allowing firms to grow bigger and gain greater dominance in local media markets.[81] This can shape public information. A study found that the way newspapers reported on changes in government regulation depended on their ownership—newspapers that were owned by big media corporations reported more favorably on the weakening of government regulation over the media.[82]

Many media firms are small parts of large conglomerates (i.e., firms that produce products in diverse and unrelated industries). For example, the electronics firm Sony also makes films and owns a music label, and the industrial giant Westinghouse owns CBS television and a radio network. Media firms produce and distribute material in multiple media formats (e.g., publishing, film, television, cable, music, telecommunications) and integrate content material across the formats. For example, one company produces a film, publishes a book about the film, distributes videos of the film, and sells a music CD of the film soundtrack. Also, a growing integration among media formats blurs the distinction between kinds of media content, such as entertainment and news.[83] "Hard news" reporting on television blurs into fictional stories, causing the boundaries that had separated fact from fictional entertainment and promotional advertising to dissolve. Thus, news events supply stories for entertainment (e.g., TV drama, movies) then become a part of an advertising campaign.[84] A related trend is the rise of entertainment firms that integrate mass media into the larger culture industry. For example, Disney owns a television network; produces movies, music, and cartoons; sells related toys and clothing; manages theme parks; and builds planned resorts and residential communities. One company manages and sells a total entertainment experience. A last trend is for media firms to become increasingly global and distribute media products worldwide. Major firms, such as Time-Warner, Inc. and Disney once generated all their income in the United States. They now generate about one-third of it outside the United States and expect the non-U.S. share to exceed 50 percent by 2010.[85] U.S. firms dominate world media, but few foreign firms, except the Australian Rupert Murdock's Fox, penetrated the U.S. market. Since 1990, U.S. films accounted for over half of box-office sales for films in Japan and the European Union.[86] Yet few Americans watch films produced in Japan or Europe.

Except for candidate advertising during an election, the media has a minor impact on voting. Yet in terms of power, ideology, and hegemony, the changes taking place in the mass media and larger cultural industry have dramatic and vast political consequences. We now turn to the topic of mass media and politics.

Mass Media and Politics

Mass Media and Voting

The mass media have limited effects on voting because of selective attention and prior attitudes, and because people mix media information with other sources, such as interpersonal social contacts, when they vote.[87] Nonetheless, candidates and issue advocates use political advertising to influence voters. Political advertising enlarges the gap between well-informed, active voters and others. Political activists learn from and follow the ads, but others "tune out" and gain little information. Also, the rapid growth in so-called "attack ads" ". . . makes voters disenchanted with the business of politics as usual."[88] A heavy exposure to attack ads reduces efficacy (i.e., a person's feeling that he/she has an impact on politics) and increases the odds that a person will not vote. This demobilization effect is greatest among peripheral voters (i.e., those who already have low levels of interest in politics and weak ties to political parties.[89] The mass media offers candidates or political groups the opportunity to promote ideas to a wider audience. For example, the well-known right to life issue did not arise spontaneously from individuals; it was created, elaborated, and promoted in the media by political activists.[90] The media may have a larger long-term, cumulative impact on how people understand and think about issues.

Liberal Bias in the Media

The frequently heard charge of a liberal bias in the media implies that journalists, editors, and producers manipulate media messages to alter the public's thinking. It originated with conservative politicians and advocacy groups. In reality, there is very little evidence that media stories have a liberal bias. Nonetheless, the charges succeeded in making media employees more cautious about how they report the news. Studies document that the personal views of individuals working in the media industry tend to be slightly more liberal on social issues but more conservative on economic issues than the public at large. Any bias is limited because professional journalists rely on factual information, experts, and explicit knowledge. Michael Schudson (1995, 70) summarized, "Reporters are progressive in their implicit, conscious, but not often worked-out political views. . . ." The personal views of journalists are less significant for what appears in the media than are the organizational, economic, cultural, and other pressures that set "news values," establish the requirements of an interesting story, create demands for meeting deadlines, and allow the media company to stay in business.[91]

More significantly, politics and the mass media are interdependent. According to Timothy Cook (1998, 13), "we cannot make simple interpretations of political effects on the news or of the media's effects on politics. The two are so intertwined. . . ." U.S. government gives the mass media subsidies and tax breaks, and it uses the media to communicate with its citizens.[92] Politicians depend on media to help them cajole and captivate the public.[93] Simultaneously, the spectacle of politics and actions of politicians provide the media with a great deal of material, "politics is show business and show business is politics."[94]

Censorship

Censorship is the exclusion of or restriction on what the media reports or shows, or the forced inclusion of messages intended to alter audience views. Official, government-mandated media censorship is pervasive in totalitarian regimes but rare in open democracies. Calls by advocacy groups to impose government limits on the sexual or violent content in films or music lyrics have been largely unsuccessful.[95] During wartime, the public accepts censorship. For example, after the September 11, 2001 terrorist attack on the World Trade Center towers, many in the public did not oppose media censorship that later expanded to present viewpoints that supported White House policy goals.[96] During the 2003 U.S. invasion of Iraq, television executives talked of a "Fox Effect," referring to highly opinionated, pro-American coverage that was strongly supportive of the war and that attracted large viewing audiences to the Fox News Network.[97]

Few people are aware that the U.S. government has censored the media in the absence of a foreign threat or war. For example, between 1998 and 2000, television networks submitted the scripts of major television shows (such as *ER, Touched by an Angel,* or *Beverly Hills 90210*) to a government antidrug office before airing them. "Thought police" in a government office scrutinized scripts to eliminate messages that could make taking illicit drugs appear positive and inserted hidden antidrug messages that reinforced the government's War on Drugs. For example they changed scenes to show popular characters turning down marijuana or a character's life being ruined by cocaine. Script writers and producers of the television programs were not aware that the media's corporate executives had worked out a secret deal to allow government censorship so that they could avoid paying for antidrug advertisements that had been mandated by the U.S. Congress.[98]

Corporate executives can engage in direct censorship. For example, in 2003 television networks banned "Not in Our Name" messages paid for by a group opposed to the pending U.S. invasion of Iraq. Likewise, MTV refused ads by antiwar groups but regularly ran military recruitment advertising.[99] In 2004 CBS executives refused to air a $2 million paid 30-second advertisement during the Superbowl game by the advocacy group "MoveOn" that criticized the Bush administration on the federal deficit. Interestingly, the Bush administration had backed a policy allowing CBS to expand its control over local television markets just six months earlier.[100]

A democracy requires more than an absence of media censorship to thrive; it requires active debate and discussion on a wide range of views.[101] Most media censorship is more subtle and is imposed indirectly by media corporations. As Michael Schudson (1995, 170) observed, "The media in the United States in the 1990s, as in the 1960s, are more completely controlled by private corporations than are the media in any other industrialized country in the world." **Corporate**

censorship is action by the owners, managers, or editors of media organizations to delete ideas and remove stories from mass distribution that they believe can harm their corporate financial or political interests. The interests
extend to the banks that loan money to media companies, investors who own
media stocks, and firms that advertise in the media. Most censorship is invisible
and takes place quietly within the media corporate bureaucracy. For example,
producers and editors who do not want to risk their careers and have their rep-
utations harmed by creating media stories that might offend media owners or
sponsors will self-censor. Other more direct forms of corporate censorship occur
as well (see Case in Point 8.2).

The Media as Social Critic

The opposite of censorship is the media's role as social critic, exposing wrongdoing and criticizing major social, political, or economic leaders or institutions.
Many professional journalists, producers, and writers in democratic societies
feel that they have a responsibility to raise tough questions and present opposing points of view. Partial autonomy from state control and competition among
media firms creates a loyal opposition role for the mass media. It also defuses
criticism that the media are under government control. Nonetheless, this independence is partial and varies widely by period, format, and topic. It operates
within "bounded pluralism" (discussed later in this chapter). The criticism is
usually in the format of a morality story that is popular with mass audiences
since many people understand public issues in moral terms.[102] In television programs or film, it follows a set story line that first reveals a wrong then rectifies
the wrong and restores moral order (see Chart 8.4).

Social issues become concrete by showing a few "bad guys," or an isolated
flaw, never an endemic feature of the social–political order. Solutions are provided by the lone hero, or a few such courageous people, but never by a broad-
based political movement demanding radical change. This format of exposing
wrongs and staying within a restricted problem-solution format offers tame criticism that does not threaten the established power structure.

Agenda Setting and Public Policy

Agenda Setting   The mass media significantly shape the public agenda and influence the opinions that people develop and the importance they attach to an issue.[103] People believe that the issues receiving news attention are salient for the
community as a whole. The speed with which media messages affect the public
varies by media formats: Television is the fastest, followed by newspapers, then
news magazines.[104] "By attending to some problems and ignoring others, television news shapes the American public's political priorities."[105] Moreover, the impact of media-generated perceptions (e.g., the economy is doing well) on voters
can be larger than changes in the actual conditions.[106] The media also have an **attention cycle in which an issue rapidly rises from obscurity to prominence,
dominates the media for a short time, and then fades from public attention.**[107]
In this cycle, the issue pushes out other stories for a limited period before fading

CASE IN POINT 8.2   **Examples of Corporate Censorship**

1. The largest target of consumer boycotts, General Electric, was not mentioned in NBC's *Today Show* program on consumer boycotts because General Electric is the corporate owner of the NBC television network (Gamson et al. 1992, 379).

2. A comedy about corporate ownership and mass media domination was removed in a replay of *Saturday Night Live* because the television executives of NBC and its owner, General Electric, objected (*Nation* 1998).

3. The Fox Network dropped a television drama based on a book about the sexual harassment charges against Supreme Court Justice Clarence Thomas because the owner of Fox, Rupert Murdoch objected to it. Murdoch, who owns media outlets around the world, is a member of the Cato Institute (a leading conservative think tank), a major Republican Party donator, and a personal friend of Justice Thomas (Solomon 1998). "Mr. Murdoch has a history of supporting conservative politicians as well as curtailing projects that might affect the financial health of his company" (Fabrikant 1998).

4. The editor of the largest newspaper in Mississippi and part of the Gannett corporation newspaper chain was fired after reporting a mysterious car crash involving the state's governor. The crash occurred mid-day after the governor had lunch with a woman who was not his wife. The governor was close to important national leaders in the Republican Party. One observer called it an effort to move the state's biggest newspaper to the right, toward traditional conservatism, as part of a movement occurring across the South (Peterson 1997).

5. The Public Broadcasting Service (PBS) refused to air an independently produced program about workplace discrimination because some of its funding came from labor unions. Yet PBS airs programs such as *Wall Street Week, Adam Smith's Money World* and *Nightly Business Report* that are funded by corporations. It also aired a flattering documentary on the *New York Times* newspaper produced by a relative of the paper's owner and funded by the paper (Jackson 1998).

6. The ABC news program *20/20* dropped a report on health and safety problems at Disney properties. Although on the record officials claimed that Disney Corporation's ownership of ABC did not influence the decision, off the record executives admitted there had been pressure from Disney (Carter 1998).

7. Based on pressure from a major advertiser, Proctor and Gamble, in 2001 CBS canceled reruns of episodes of the program *Family Law* that dealt with controversial issues (such as interfaith marriage, the death penalty, and handgun ownership). America's largest consumer product firm monitors every TV program it sponsors and refuses to advertise on programs it believes might offend some potential customers (Carter 2001).

8. In early Spring 2004, Disney Corporation, owner of Miramax Films, tried to block the release of a documentary film highly critical of the George W. Bush administration, *Fahrenheit 9/11* by Michael Moore. Disney's contract with Miramax says it can block films that have a NC-17 rating or that are way over budget; neither was the case here. It is not clear whether Disney's action was due to pressure from political conservatives or economic fears about the treatment of Disney-owned properties in Florida, where George W. Bush's brother is the Republican governor.

The film won the Palme d'Or award at the Cannes Film Festival and after its independent release in June 2004 it went on to break box office records. Even after its release, two Midwestern theatre chains, Fridley (34 theatres in Iowa and Nebraska) and the GKG chain (268 theatres in Illinois and Michigan), refused to book it in their theatres because the chain owners objected to Mr. Moore's political message.

c h a r t   8 . 4

FORMULA FOR A MORALITY STORY OF MEDIA-BASED SOCIAL CRITICISM

1. Expose the bag guys—corrupt government officials, a foreign enemy, a powerful immoral person who has illicit desires or is motivated by excessive greed.

2. Connect the bad guys to a serious social problem, such as an environmental catastrophe, health problem, national threat, or violence to a defenseless person.

3. Present a hero or heroine—the lone individual motivated by higher principles, a victim seeking justice, a true patriot, or an avenging vigilante.

4. Show how a hero or heroine can overcome difficult obstacles, defeat the bad guys, and save the day.

and disappearing. A major reason for this cycle is that media outlets have a limited *carrying capacity*; that is, they have a limited number of pages or hours of broadcast that restricts the amount and length of attention given to an issue. Putting an issue on the public agenda requires extensive coordination and careful timing to avoid saturating the audience.[108] Public opinion shifts to follow what people believe is the dominant opinion, and they believe that the issues or opinions presented by the media are the major ones of a community.[109] It is not a benign effect, as Diana Mutz and Joe Soss (1997) observed, "By influencing the perceptual environment in which policy debates transpire, media coverage may have important effects on the balance of power among contending policy factions. . . ."

Priming   The mass media has the powerful capacity to prime. **Priming is how the mass media shape the standards people use when judging politicians, policies, or issues by calling attention to some matters as opposed to others.** When people evaluate a candidate, politician, issue, or government action, they employ specific standards and focus on certain aspects (e.g., a politician's

CLOSER LOOK 8.2   The Race Card and Media Priming

Mendelberg (2001) analyzed a famous media message distributed by George H. W. Bush's 1988 presidential campaign on television and in flyers. The "Willie Horton" advertisement told the story of an imprisoned black man who, while released on a short-term furlough, committed brutal and vicious crimes against a white couple. Explicitly, the message criticized the anticrime stands of Bush's electoral opponent as being weak. Yet it contained a powerful implicit message expressed through the visual image of Mr. Horton, who never used the name Willie himself, that showed him looking menacing. The message was designed by Bush's campaign officials to prime the audience by activating their existing racial resentments and stereotypes of black men as violent criminals who preyed on innocent whites. This ad used racial priming, which implicitly induced white voters to think based on deeply felt racial fears without explicitly calling direct attention to Mr. Horton's race or that of his victims. Few people recognized the hidden racial message at first, and an explicit charge of racism in the message was not fully recognized until three years later, after President Bush vetoed civil rights legislation. Mendelberg found that the priming was highly effective in triggering racial feelings among white voters and linking the feelings to their choice of candidate. She argued that priming works most powerfully when it remains implicit, and is not directly stated. It is highly successful in large part because the media consumers are themselves not consciously aware of it. In fact, once the implicit priming message becomes explicit and recognized, its power quickly fades. Thus, priming operates to shape a media viewer's feelings and evaluations so long as it remains beyond conscious, overt thinking. Priming triggers resentment and feelings that people do not comfortably express overtly, and it tends to activate specific resentments. Thus, racial priming will trigger a person's hidden racial resentments and feelings, but the triggered feelings do not spill over to nonracial issues. Mendelberg noted that a similar process appears to be operating for gay rights in the United States and for immigration issues in Germany and Austria.

judicial appointments, position on abortion, or personal moral conduct). Given the hundreds of details and issues, public attention is selective. Through priming, the media organizes and filters information (i.e., it includes some and excludes other details), offering implicit standards that people deploy as they evaluate an event, policy, or politician.[110] Priming also works by including subtle, almost hidden messages that trigger predispositions (see Closer Look 8.2).

Elites, movements, and media organizations interact and work together to control the agenda and priming.[111]

Media and Public Policies   Media messages can shape public thinking about issues and how target groups are portrayed. Three common target groups for government programs are deviants (e.g., drug users, criminals, flag burners), dependents (e.g., children, disabled, elderly), and the protected (e.g., veterans, farmers, small business owners, scientists). Others (e.g., the wealthy, large labor unions) are rarely target groups. Media messages inform both the target groups and the public about the program's goals. They also teach lessons about legitimate and illegitimate government assistance and whether or not participation

CLOSER LOOK 8.3 — Why American's Hate Welfare: Politics of Race and the Media

Americans do not really hate welfare. Americans are willing to provide financial assistance to poor people. What they dislike is rewarding the undeserving poor. They mistakenly believe most welfare benefits go to poor black people, and they hold a stereotype that blacks are immoral and not committed to the work ethic. Hence, they are undeserving. So welfare becomes a code word for race. Much opposition to welfare is based on mistaken information about welfare combined with racial stereotypes. The negative stereotypes of black people are centuries old and apply only to a tiny percentage of African Americans, but they remain alive and popular today because of the mass media. The mass media repeatedly present a highly distorted picture of poverty. Print and broadcast media images from the 1960s onward tend to portray most poor as black people, and associate black people with the least deserving groups among the poor. Americans are neither mean-spirited nor highly racist, but they have embraced serious misrepresentations and misperceptions that are reinforced in media reports.

Sources: Clawson and Trice 2000, Gilens 1995, 1996a, 1996b, 1999, Iyengar and Kinder 1987.

by the targeted is welcomed.[112] Next we examine five policy areas where media messages have significant effects: poverty, crime, labor relations, health care, and foreign policy.

1. Poverty and Welfare. Television with its visual images and packaged stories is a major source of information for the public, yet it distorts welfare, the conditions of poverty, and the characteristics of poor people. Reports emphasize poverty as a threat (e.g., illegal drugs, violent crime, gun-carrying gang members), poverty as suffering (e.g., hunger, homelessness, lack of health care), welfare programs as wasteful, and most poor people as racial minorities. Rarely do viewers see the overall income distribution showing how low wages contribute to poverty or the less visible, structural causes of poverty. Some highly relevant facts are almost never shown, for example, that most of the poor do not live in urban neighborhoods and that most poor people are not racial minorities but whites. In addition, the poor in the United States are rarely compared with the poor of other nations that have few poverty problems due to different government policies. The print media repeats distorted images and negative stereotypes.[113] As a result, many Americans are misinformed, not uninformed, about welfare; they are confident about their misinformation.[114]

Racial beliefs and prejudices play a large role in how people absorb television messages. Whites who watch television stories about poverty show little sympathy for blacks and tend to blame individual blacks more than white poverty victims (see Closer Look 8.3).[115] Over the last 30 years, whites increasingly blame blacks for poverty and oppose government aid programs. Thus, Schuman and Krysan (1999, 853) found that "white beliefs about the causes of black advantage have not been set in stone . . . they have changed dramatically, evidently in response to events happening in the country, or at least 'happening' as portrayed by the media. . . ."

The media distort poverty and welfare in three ways: (1) *They lower the priority the public gives to poverty policy.* A focus on stereotypes and visual images disconnects symptoms from causes; it makes poverty appear inevitable. Iyengar (1991, 101) argued that media presentations . . . "indirectly reduced public support for social welfare programs and increased public approval of leaders committed to slashing such programs." (2) *They reduce public sympathy for poor people.* Media reports promote "blaming the victim" by presenting specific episodes of poverty that show poverty as an issue for specific individuals, not as a societywide concern. (3) *They encourage equating race with poverty.* The media reinforce a link between being poor and membership in a racial group, particularly African Americans. According to Entman (1995, 150),"The concepts 'black person' and 'poverty' are so thoroughly intertwined in television news that the white public's perceptions and feelings about poverty appear difficult to disentangle from their thinking about African Americans. . . ."

The reinforcement of negative racial stereotypes and hostility about welfare illustrates race coding. **Race coding occurs when the media or political actors present issues or events in a manner that reinforces negative racial stereotypes without explicitly mentioning race.** Racial coding attaches preexisting negative racial attitudes and emotions to specific events or situations.[116] It occurs through repeated associations that show visual images of one race with exaggerated negative images of problems or dangers (e.g., violence, promiscuity, drug use). Gilliam and Iyengar (2000, 572) explained that the ". . . local news programming 'racializes' political discourse by making policy opinions increasingly intertwined with questions of race [and] . . . racial appeals—explicit or coded are now common in political campaigns."

2. Crime. Crime is a major news item. Crime, especially violent crime, constituted over one-half of local television news coverage in the late 1990s. What television shows "is not an accurate reflection of the real world of crime."[117] The media emphasize violent street crime, while in reality, most crime is nonviolent. The media emphasize older victims and successful police action much more than occurs in reality. Stories that emphasize a language of victims, crime targets, and perpetrators produce a climate of fear.[118]

In addition, media images of crime reinforce "the frame of reference offered by a government bureaucracy or other authority with respect to crime problems" and it can "only infrequently be called into question. . . ."[119] For example, for illegal drug stories journalists have relied very heavily on official sources, only citing law enforcement officials and conservative politicians. Officials in health care or rehabilitation, academic experts, and liberal politicians were rarely cited as sources. So the media presented views of conservative politicians and law enforcement officials as the only legitimate ones.[120] Studies

SUMMARY 8.2   News and Social Control

Communication media contribute to social control in several ways

- Market research on media usage (e.g., which programs are viewed, songs listened to, products purchased) allows firms to detect, track, and monitor consumer behaviors (Altheide 1995).
- Television's "episodic framing is a powerful form of social control" (Iyengar 1991, 140) that promotes a particularistic definition of problems. It deflects structural or government responsibility and gives a fragmented picture that blames individuals.

In addition, the media contribute to official definitions of the situation and disseminate social messages about deviance and punishment. In this way, the media help to define what is appropriate behavior and the standards of "normalcy" in society. Normalcy and justice become intertwined.

- Media displays of crime and deviance and its containment by police and the criminal

justice system provide lessons on boundaries of normative behavior and the consequences of violating laws and norms.
- Videotapes and transcripts of suspects and court proceedings released by police to convict wrongdoers puts the "public eye" on offenders, reinforces the social control role of officials, and teaches the public how the state administers justice.
- "Gonzo justice" is the use of extraordinary means to spotlight deviance and punish people through public stigma and humiliation (e.g, when a judge orders an offender to wear a sign or lose weight). "Gonzo justice is not synonymous with the news media, but the extraordinary measures . . . fit comfortably with news media formats, while the moral-myth statements virtually ensure an interested audience. An agents' view of social order is enhanced through mass-mediated formats designed to promote circulation and TV ratings" (Altheide 1995, 108).

show that short-term increases in public concern about drug crime follow greater media attention, not an actual increase in the incidence of crime.[121] In general, the media also perform a social control function (see Summary 8.2).

The media racially codes crime and television reports highlight a crime suspect's race when the person is nonwhite and the crime is violent.[122] Media reports of crime are episodic (i.e., separate individual incidents). This ". . . not only diverted attention from societal responsibility, but also attracted attention to individual responsibility."[123] Such an individualistic focus obscures how societywide racial division and prejudice contribute to criminal behavior. White viewers tend to be more hostile toward and favor harsher punishments for criminals when news programs portray a crime suspect to be black as opposed to white.[124]

3. Health Care. Popular support for national public health insurance shifted dramatically during a 1994 debate over new public policy. Following elite prompts, the media framed the public debate in terms of "cost versus equal access." During the debate, people who were less aware of the health care issue shifted their views the most. Their concern for equality declined because media reports emphasized the cost considerations. As Kock (1998, 211) observed, "Through rhetoric, political elites attempt to draw attention to particular features of a policy proposal—while drawing attention away from others. . . ." Thus, the media's framing of the national insurance issue significantly altered how the public saw the policy choices.[125]

4. Labor Relations. Media bias can occur through the selective use of sources and by how the story is framed. In one example, the media framed a proposed law designed to protect the rights of workers, increase employee protections, and equalize pay entirely as a "labor issue." The media cited business sources that opposed the law as if they represented the general public, and the law was presented as "prolabor" and "antibusiness." The media repeated business claims that the law would increase union power without questioning it. The media could have framed the story differently, such as, from the point of view of the people the law was designed to help—the workers. In that frame, the law's goal was to defend workers from corporate power, and it was needed because worker's wages had declined as business profits rose. By presenting business's position as representing the general interest and presenting labor's position as representing a specialized, narrow interest, the media created a distorted picture.[126] A bias was introduced through the presentation of sources, the selection of materials, and the emphasis on certain news items. Without a critical inquiry and access to alternative information sources, media viewers would be unaware that they were getting a one-sided picture of an issue.

5. Foreign Policy. The media influences foreign affairs in three ways. First, the media project a nation's ideas, values, and beliefs beyond its borders. By promoting and extending the reach of a nation's beliefs and culture, the media supplements its national foreign aid, military intervention, and other tools of foreign policy. Second, the media distribute internally information about the world beyond national borders, shaping public beliefs and opinions. Lastly, the media inform the public about the government's foreign policy actions.

The U.S. media substantially extend the influence of American culture beyond U.S. borders. People in over 100 countries avidly consume American-made films, news, music, and television programs that disseminate U.S. cultural views, economic beliefs, and political values. Thus, when people in Hong Kong watch MTV or viewers in Italy see American soap operas, they also encounter embedded symbolic messages about U.S. culture.[127]

People around the world consume U.S. media, but very few Americans see foreign media. The information Americans use to form opinions, develop beliefs, and judge foreign policy depends almost entirely on American-dominated media. This is not limited to news programs. For example, the *National Geographic* magazine presents a particular view of the outside world and reinforces beliefs with its selection of photographs. By showing smiling foreigners in colorful clothing who want to copy American-style consumerism, the magazine resolves American anxieties about a strange, dangerous outside world. This dangerous, alien, unknown world is tamed with the message that, despite poverty and periodic unrest, everyone loves America. By including and omitting specific visual images, negative consequences of U.S. military and commercial interests disappear.[128]

Many U.S. media reports about foreign political or military events are unbalanced. In addition to creating a spiral of silence, or stifling dissent, one-sided media coverage can change public opinion about political leaders, trust in government, and patriotic feelings.[129] Media distortion of foreign events extends beyond military actions. For example, in the 1980s the communist government in Poland, killed one priest and Latin American paramilitary groups friendly to the U.S. government killed a priest. The Polish killing received 137 to 193 times more press coverage.[130] By amplifying certain events while burying others, the flow of images and information that is available can profoundly shape how people understand the world.

Hegemony and Cultural Politics

Most effects of the mass media arise less from overt acts of censorship and conscious manipulation than from the capitalist marketplace and the structural constraints of corporate media ownership. As Thomas Cook (1998, 168) argued, "Contemporary news organizations are primarily oriented toward their audiences, not as citizens, but as consumers. The most prominent audiences for news are advertisers." Schiller (1989, 43) observed that profitability is the primary goal and, "If a creative product, no matter what its inherent quality, cannot be viewed as a potential money maker, salable in a large enough market, its production is problematic at best . . . the commercial imperative prevails." The pressure for profits affects the types of media messages disseminated, "Whatever their particular ideology, those groups and forces that can muster the most substantial financial, institutional, educational and organizational resources . . . are the ones best able to promote their ideas in the marketplace."[131]

Technological change, ownership consolidation, and an intensified profit-orientation over the past decade created greater pressures to cut costs and attract viewers. The mass media adopt a corporate point of view because "Most of the mass media organizations are themselves part of large business corporations, with corporate interests of their own and reasons to be concerned about corporate advertisers. . ."[132] (see Summary 8.3).

About a dozen large corporations own most of the mass media including most newspapers, TV and radio stations, film studios, and publishing firms. A primary motivation of media executives and owners (stockholders) is to increase revenues, profits, and market share. Specific companies also exercise overt, direct influence as corporate censorship (discussed previously in this chapter) or buy advocacy advertising to express views on a public issue. For example, Mobil Corporation mounted a high profile advertising campaign in the late 1970s on energy issues, the environment, and government regulation.[133] This is rare. The editorial and artistic portion of the media has some independence from profit-oriented or the business side of the culture industry.

SUMMARY 8.3

Three Trends in U.S. Television News During the Past Decade

- News has become less international, more parochial, and locally oriented, with the average number of minutes devoted to foreign coverage dropping by half since 1990.
- News covers fewer serious current events about politicians and government activity, and has more "soft news" that is not keyed to a specific time, and more practical information (e.g., consumer finances, improving health, personal lifestyle).
- More news stories cover celebrity gossip or are "water cooler stories" about popular events with drama that many people follow and can gossip about with fellow workers. (See "Stop Press," *Economist*, July 4, 1998, pp. 17–19.)

Yet ultimately, media products that do not generate profits disappear. This is the most powerful form of media control.

By responding to market demands, the production of media products is affected. Because more viewers/readers mean more advertising and other revenue, media firms compete to produce increasingly colorful products with dramatic excitement and captivating images to attract more viewers/readers. Competitive demands for a "hot" story reduce journalistic time for background research and fact checking, creating more sensational, superficial media products.

Although media firms seek the largest number of consumers, they also earn high profits by creating products that appeal to the views and tastes of specialized markets of upper-income viewers and offering them to advertisers. Ginsberg (1986, 137, 148) observed, "particularly in the political realm, the print and broadcast media and the publishing industry are most responsive to the tastes and views of the more 'upscale' segments of the potential audience. The preferences of these audience segments have a profound effect on the content and orientation of the press, of radio and television programming, and of books, especially in the areas of news and public affairs. . . . the marketplace of ideas is dominated by the views of elite strata. The more exposed they are to the market, the more likely it will be that ordinary people will see the world through the eyes of the upper classes." Market pressures alone contribute to unbalanced reports on public issues. The concerns of lower income people tend to be underpresented, while the values and views of those with higher incomes or wealth dominate.

A Corporate Voice   In a media-saturated society where the media are owned by private, for-profit firms, media values merge with commercial values. Cultural symbols and forms of creative expression become products to be owned and sold for a profit. Cultural worth is subordinated to market value. For example, good art is defined by how much money it can bring, while bad art is what no one will buy. This renders pure aesthetic judgment nearly irrelevant.

Public expression depends on the ability to purchase media space (e.g., television time, billboards) and the "right" of free expression is limited to those who do not interfere with the rights of others to generate profits.

The ownership structure and market pressure produce a corporate media voice. **The corporate voice is a set of assumptions and values embedded into symbolic expression that protects and justifies the place of the private corporation in society.** The assumptions and values of the corporate voice are so pervasive that they are unquestioned. Schiller (1989, 44) remarked, "As the cultural industries occupy pivotal positions of social, political, and even economic power . . . their symbolic outputs, however entertaining, diverting, aesthetic, or informative are essentially elements of corporate expression. . . . The corporate voice now constitutes the national symbolic environment." The voice seems natural and synonymous with core social values; it promotes the inviolability of private property, sanctity of profits, and protection of copyrights.

The corporate voice is not an automatic defense of all corporations; the media industry can discipline individual firms. In fact, through its consumer protection policing role, the media can amplify attacks on a specific firm and intensify consumer awareness. For example, in August 2000 Firestone Tire was forced to recall tires after defects caused accidents and killed people. At first, the executives worked with government officials to investigate and quietly resolve the safety issue, but intense publicity forced the firm to undertake an expensive recall. Media policing concentrates on a few high-profile consumer cases that involve major brands, but ignores many other consumer concerns because of audience attention overload, insufficient drama, and too few affected consumers. Criticism that temporarily focuses on one firm or product tends to build reassurance and legitimate the general corporate system with the message: There may be a few bad apples and a rare mistake or unsafe product might occasionally slip through, but the government, industry officials, and the media will detect and resolve the problems, and the overall business system is fundamentally sound. The mass media rarely present one, unified view on issues; criticism is evident, yet its range and type is limited, an issue we next examine.

Bounded Pluralism   Bounded pluralism is a characteristic of U.S. mass media. **Bounded pluralism is an apparent plurality of viewpoints or perspectives in the media, but in fact, the viewpoints stay within a set of unseen boundaries that are rarely breached.** Despite a diversity of media messages, the media are limited and homogenize culture by emphasizing enduring values.[134] The messages pull media consumers toward a conventional, middle position. For example, heavy television viewers are more likely to conform to "mainstream" or moderate values than are light viewers. Heavy viewers show less diversity of opinion on public issues and less divergence in political self-designation.[135] Studies find that "those who watch a great deal of television tend to exhibit higher levels of mainstream and stereotypical thinking. . . ."[136]

The media encourage homogenization but also reinforce certain forms of differentiation through uneven consumer access to and use of different media outlets. Subgroups in the population (e.g., by race, age, gender) may use specific media outlets (e.g., television channels on cable, films, magazines) and develop distinct understandings of the same event or story. For example, in 1991 the Los Angeles police seriously beat a black man named Rodney King. Someone video-taped the event, and it was widely disseminated on television. Various broadcast programs and newspapers presented contrasting stories of the event. People from diverse social backgrounds used different media outlets and developed very different interpretations of the event's meaning.[137] The mass media do not create a uniform view of events, but a person's social background and position interact with differential media use to create that individual's view.

Diversity does not mean that all the media outlets are equal, that all parts of society have equal media access, or that the diversity is limitless. The mass media are highly stratified. A few media outlets overwhelm and penetrate the entire culture, while other minor outlets occupy tiny, isolated niches. Dominant outlets with a broad impact present a narrow range of views, and emphasize mainstream or establishment views. They organize public thinking about major issues, set the public agenda, and fix boundaries of debate. In the United States, news media organize issues and provide political information in ways that are similar to political parties in some other countries.[138] Yet, unlike political parties, they are privately owned for-profit businesses, closed and nonelected, and their political role is not subject to careful public discussion.

Leaders of established organizations with substantial resources (e.g., corporations, colleges, the government) have great media access while those outside the mainstream (extremists, protesters) have limited access. To gain access, opposition groups must engage in extreme acts that provide visual drama (e.g., protests, riots). Yet the acts may backfire and generate negative public opinion because of the media's focus on the disruptive tactics instead of on the group's political message.[139]

The media do not cover all political events equally. By selecting certain issues or events for emphasis, while downplaying or ignoring others, the flow of media messages raises or lowers the visibility of issues, creates an informed or ignorant public, and permits or stifles protest. As one observer noted, "if newspapers and television reporters or editors decide to overlook protest tactics, protest organizations will not succeed. Like the tree falling unheard in the forest, there is no protest unless protest is perceived and projected."[140] A comparison of all potential issues and events with those receiving media attention found persistent media bias. One study found that newspapers only reported on about one-third of all political events not led by politicians. They mostly covered business sponsored events, protests with overt conflict, and larger events. A more liberal newspaper covered social movement events more than a moderate-conservative newspaper.[141] Another study of demonstrations in Washington, D.C. by McCarthy et al. (1996, 487) found that "the picture of Washington demonstrations portrayed in the mass media differ dramatically from that generated by permit records." The media covered larger demonstrations, flamboyant or violent actions, and demonstrations at the peak of an attention cycle. Coverage also substantially varied by media outlet.[142]

Journalists and the media industry tend to rely on experts and people in positions of authority to be the credible, authoritative news sources. Yet this practice sets boundaries on reporting and reinforces mainstream views.[143] People with official expertise, social influence, political power, or money have great access to the media, and the media disseminates their views that subsequently set the boundaries of mainstream discourse. Because their views are given prominence by the media, they acquire greater legitimacy. As Michael Schudson (1995, 19) observed, "When the media offer the public an item of news, they confer upon it public legitimacy." Just as schools teach "school knowledge," the media present "public knowledge" or the official version of news, and their version of events becomes the one against which all views are judged to be true or false.

Media-Constructed Reality   A major source of the media's political influence resides in its capacity to structure symbolic messages, manage images, set agendas, and frame stories. In this way, the media creates a sense of reality and reinforces certain values, beliefs, and understandings. For example, American media fortify views on democracy, justice, property rights, and citizenship; they buttress beliefs about social inequality, political power, and the national interest; and they uphold ideas about desirable public policy, social change, and legitimate authority.[144] Most journalists and others in the media industry argue that they personally are independent, honest, and objective, but this is not at issue. As Chomsky (1989, 12) argued, "What is at issue is not the honesty of opinions expressed or the integrity of those who seek facts but rather the choice of topics and highlighting of issues, the range of opinions presented, the unquestioned premises that guide reporting and commentary, and the general framework imposed for the presentation of a certain view of the world."

Journalists say they report facts not fiction, yet staying within convention, not fiction, is at issue.[145] Media conventions place messages into the world of media consumers, but the unrecognized conventions also embed perspectives within media messages and fix the limits of public discussion.[146] The media construct a sense of reality and legitimate national culture within bounded pluralism. Built-in assumptions, more than the explicit messages, shape how people see the world. The public treats media news representations as objective facts.[147] However, the news is shaped by specific historical and cultural institutions; it is not a timeless entity that reflects objective reality or neutral facts. For example, the role and form of newspapers and what people considered to be news varies over time. It differed in the 1890s, 1930s, and 1990s.[148] The people who create media reports operate within financial limitations, organizational rules, and professional norms that shape what becomes news. These form a framework that silences some perspectives while it accentuates others.

Media *objectivity* is not media *neutrality*. Media objectivity means that one's personal view is not expressed and reports are not unbalanced; neutrality means that no point of view, type of values, or set of beliefs is favored. As Iyengar and Kinder (1987, 132) observed, "That television news is politically objective does not mean that television news is politically neutral. If the politics of television news are difficult to see, it is partly because they are so familiar and comfortable." Media objectivity and diversity—no personal point of view or balance of different views—can exist without political neutrality, because media messages contain an implicit point of view and set of values. Mass media messages operating within the context of dominant cultural values and official sources also reinforce certain values and ideas, but the public only sees objectivity. For example, few in the U.S. public notice that its media glorify democracy, celebrate capitalism, uphold individualism, and condemn demagogues, bureaucracy, and corruption because they internalized those values. By failing to present alternatives and being silent on larger issues, the media implicitly limits debate and shields established institutions from critical examination.[149]

The media build a sense of reality through a continual flow of symbolic messages with mutually supporting values and implicit beliefs. For example, if people repeatedly see television news reports, newspaper stories, television entertainment programs, and films that portray almost all criminals as African Americans, they accept it as real. A few explicit messages to the contrary, especially if presented in isolated educational formats, will not erase the message or its sense of reality for most people.

Media and schooling shape political values. A central value, tolerance for political dissent and nonmainstream views, is essential for effective democratic politics. We turn to it in the next section.

Political Tolerance

Tolerance for opposing points of view is a core democratic value. Schools officially promote it, it fosters a free and open mass media, and it is furthered by an open media. Tolerance means that the majority will respect minority points of view, tolerate dissent, and allow disagreeable, even offensive, ideas to be expressed. The principle of tolerance is embodied in protections of freedom of speech, press and assembly, and the right to due process in the U.S. Constitution. It gives legal protection to people with different beliefs and prevents the majority from forcing one viewpoint onto all people and treating legitimate dissent as subversion.[150]

Political sociologists study tolerance by looking at four things: (1) individual characteristics associated with support for tolerance, (2) the relationship between racial attitudes and tolerance, (3) social contexts that promote tolerance, and (4) historical trends in tolerance and conditions that trigger historical periods of great intolerance.

Individual-Level Tolerance

Early researchers looked at the social psychology of tolerance, or "hearts and minds" tolerance, to learn why certain individuals hold intolerant attitudes.[151] They blamed a distinctive "authoritarian personality" that came from child-rearing practices. Authoritarian people are deeply hostile toward outsiders, readily use force and physical punishment, and hold an absolutist orientation. They cannot accept ambiguity and favor strong, powerful leaders. Today, the authoritarian personality explanation is rarely used, but researchers recognize that personality factors can have a role in some situations.[152] Beginning with Samuel Stouffer's (1955) classic study, *Communism, Conformity and Civil Liberties,* researchers found that intolerance is strongly correlated with a person's age, low education level, and rural residence. Belonging to certain Protestant fundamentalist religious denominations and attending services frequently is also associated with intolerance.[153] Tolerance is associated with high levels of political knowledge, strong self-esteem, psychological flexibility, and residing in an urban-cosmopolitan setting.[154] A person's racial heritage and subjective social class also influence tolerance.[155]

Despite formal legal protections, public support is weak for the rights of racial, ethnic or language minorities, people with various sexual orientations, physically or mentally disabled people, and those with dreaded diseases such as AIDS, to be free of discrimination in housing, employment, schooling and public accommodations. Legal protections for tolerance or expanding civil liberties do poorly in referendum votes. As Gamble (1997, 261) observed, "Citizens in the political majority have repeatedly used direct democracy to put the rights of political minorities to a popular vote . . . anti-civil rights initiatives have an extraordinary record of success: voters have approved three-quarters of these . . . ."[156] A small percentage of the public is strongly committed to social–political tolerance, and when basic rights are put up to a vote, it often polarizes the majority against minorities. This reveals a *paradox of democracy: The vast majority may not vote to defend rights which weaken democracy's foundation, while elites will sometimes defend tolerance and the basic rights needed for democracy to function.*[157]

Schooling and Tolerance

Researchers have repeatedly documented a positive relationship between amount of schooling and level of tolerance: As people attain more schooling, they show increased tolerance toward political deviants and non conformists. Despite a consistent pattern, researchers disagree about its cause. As Bobo and Licari (1989, 290) remarked, "The reasons why education is related to tolerance need to be pursued more directly." Political sociologists use three explanations: the cognitive development and flexibility, socialization, and ideological refinement models.

The Cognitive Development and Flexibility Model   One explanation is that schooling increases a person's cognitive skills, cultural knowledge, and cognitive flexibility, and these increase tolerance. Schooling exposes people to new ideas and acquaints them with diverse situations or people, opening them up to accept diversity. It builds a broader frame of reference and improves their ability to think in abstract and complex ways. As people acquire critical reasoning abilities and see multiple viewpoints, they think more flexibly and accept greater ambiguity. Factual information and higher-level reasoning also increase a person's commitment to democratic values.[158] This implies that tolerance grows over time as the population's level of schooling rises. Yet the impact of schooling may be limited. When highly educated but intolerant people are presented with new information that contradicts their current beliefs, they adhere to a fixed position and do not change.[159] In general, noncognitive people who usually respond with their immediate emotions tend to be less tolerant than those who adopt the highly cognitive and semidetached learning style that schooling encourages.[160]

The Socialization Model   Critics of the cognitive development model argue that what schools teach is a key factor. Schooling will be associated with tolerance only if the curriculum promotes tolerance. In courses of study or cultural–political settings that ignore tolerance, schooling is unrelated to tolerance.[161] In addition, other forms of socialization, such as the mass media or political leaders, can influence support for tolerance.[162] Marcus et al. (1995, 152) noted, "Opinion leaders and political elites bear a special responsibility when they articulate how democratic principles ought to be applied." The socialization model implies that if the school curriculum fails to teach and promote tolerant values, or if antitolerant political groups gain control over the curriculum, the positive impact of schooling on political tolerance would vanish.

The Ideological Refinement Model   This explanation holds that schools only teach people how to act in sophisticated ways and present a pleasant, tolerant exterior face in public (i.e., to speak a language of tolerance and display civility on the surface). Schools cannot instill a deep commitment to tolerance, they can only provide the verbal skills and vocabulary that enable people to defend and justify their self-interests without giving crude and intolerant or socially inappropriate reasons.[163] Schools teach privileged groups how to defend their high social and economic position by using sophisticated arguments that are clothed with an appearance of tolerance. Some studies indirectly support the ideological refinement model. Americans strongly support the ideals of tolerance when the ideals are phrased in very general terms, but this support nearly disappears when issues are phrased in terms of specific and realistic situations. This suggests that the tolerance is held at a superficial level. Kuklinski et al. (1991, 14) summarized, "If one finding has persisted throughout 30 years of research on political tolerance, it is that many Americans endorse civil liberties in the abstract but reject them in concrete applications." Support for tolerance greatly weakens in concrete situations, and it declines even more when people are asked to tolerate a group that they fear.[164] When people are asked to tolerate target groups who they fear or strongly dislike, the relationship between schooling and tolerance almost vanishes.[165]

In sum, tolerating diverse people, positions, and ideas is a cornerstone of an effective democracy. Support for the ideals of tolerance is broad but only at the surface level. People are most tolerant when it matters least—when they are comfortable and unthreatened. When it really matters—in concrete situations close to home and in confrontations with noxious groups—support for tolerance nearly evaporates. This may be a reason why shortly after the September 11 terrorist attack, when many Americans were very fearful, there were many incidents of violence, harassment, or discrimination against innocent people who appeared to be Muslims or from Arabic countries. Racially prejudiced people and people who are attracted to right-wing extremist ideologies show greater intolerance than would be expected for their age, level of schooling, and psychological and similar individual factors. Next we examine intolerance and hostility toward racial-ethnic minorities.

Bigotry, Right-Wing Ideology, and Political Tolerance

Political tolerance is associated with other forms of tolerance. Politically tolerant people also tend to be more tolerant of diverse lifestyles, racial-ethnic heritages, or even music. You may wonder why a politically intolerant person also would be more intolerant of heavy metal, Gospel, or rap music than a tolerant person, all other things being equal. The common element is a dislike of "otherness" and a desire to set exclusive boundaries. Intolerance appears to flow from a general discomfort with what appears to be strange, different, or dissimilar.[166]

People of all ideological positions do not support democratic civil liberties equally. People who label themselves as ideological conservatives and support right-wing views are less tolerant and less supportive of basic civil liberties. This may be because they overstate the threat coming from the political left, and this increases their intolerance.[167] Despite little threat, they appear willing to restrict rights when they confront opposing ideas.[168]

Negative attitudes toward racial minorities are also associated with intolerance and ideological conservatism. Ideological conservatives appear to embrace values and reasoning that are unsympathetic towards racial minorities.[169] Since the U.S. federal government began to promote racial equality in the 1960s, researchers have asked whether white resistance to it came from racism or from a conservative antipathy towards government intervention.[170]

Symbolic Racism

Traditional racial prejudice, a belief in the in-born inferiority of some races, has declined in the United States since the 1960s. Today, it is socially inappropriate to express crude, overtly racist views openly in public. Many whites conform to the norms of racial tolerance in public but continue to defend racial inequality. **Symbolic racism is an indirect racism that occurs when whites deny their racial prejudice but refuse to treat the people of different racial groups equally and oppose attempts to equalize conditions across races**. Instead of opposing racial equality from a belief in race-based biological inferiority, they oppose it because they believe in stable cultural-behavioral differences by race (i.e., a particular race lacks a work ethic, motivation, morals, etc.) or because they have an ideological opposition to government programs that "interfere" in "natural" conditions. In both symbolic racism and political tolerance, people seek to exclude or deny rights to an outsider group. As with a surface commitment to abstract tolerance, a symbolic racist expresses a surface commitment to abstract racial equality but will oppose specific, concrete actions to reduce racial inequality. Although symbolic racists justify their opposition on cultural or ideological grounds, the outcome is the same as for a traditional racist.[171] People who make symbolic racist claims tend to score high on measures of traditional racial prejudice.[172] Some research suggests that they may be expressing their deep-seated desires to maintain social inequality and dominance (see Closer Look 8.3).

Social Contexts That Encourage or Discourage Tolerance

Studies on tolerance shifted from a focus on individual attitudes to exploring how a person's social setting encourages or discourages tolerance. Thus, people who live in urban environments tend to be more tolerant.[173] Settings also influence perceived political freedom (i.e., the freedom that people believe they have).[174] If people believe they are in an intolerant setting, they act accordingly and self censor. Thus, despite formal legal rights, a large percentage of Americans feel that they cannot act in a free, open way, and they believe that formal rights of free speech do not apply to them. As Gibson (1992, 341) found, "significant numbers of Americans perceive that the government would *not* allow them to express their opposition to government policy through convention and unconventional political activity." For example, one-third of people are afraid to write a letter to an elected representative who expresses an opinion that they disagree with. Gibson (1992, 343) concluded that, "perceived governmental constrains on freedom and self-censorship are surprisingly high." Intolerant people feel least able to express political ideas, while highly tolerant people self-censor the least.

Exposure to social diversity appears to be a critical factor that promotes greater tolerance and allows the open expression of opposing points of view. Gibson (1992, 344) found that, "Political homogeneity generates and reinforces a close-mindedness that is not conducive to political tolerance." Social settings in which people hold diverse opinions and express them tend to encourage open debate and discussion. By contrast, social settings in which everyone agrees and conformity reigns tend to encourage self-censorship.

So far, we looked at how schooling, social groups, ideologies, and community settings affect political tolerance; next, we look at historical periods when the national mood shifted and affected tolerance.

Trends in Tolerance and Intolerance Triggers

Researchers found that a period's "political climate" interacts with tolerance.[175] This has much in common with moral panics (see Chapter 12) that foster a sense of fear and enable certain groups to advance their views in the public agenda. Increased fear of an enemy, a deviant group, or people of a

Intolerance and a Desire to Dominate Other People

In the 1990s, a group of social psychologists developed a theory that goes beyond the literature on tolerance and symbolic racism to offer a micro-level foundation for political intolerance and oppression. According to the social dominance theory, all people vary in their degree of a personality trait called social dominance orientation (SDO). Some people have strong feelings of dominance, prefer hierarchy, and want to exclude outside groups. People in high status positions of authority tend to have higher SDO. This is because of a combination of self-selection and recruitment characteristics and the context around high status positions reinforces a SDO worldview. Social dominance theory has two assumptions: (1) societies tend to create arbitrarily-set systems of social hierarchy (i.e., based on social categories such as race, ethnicity), and (2) most forms of group conflict (i.e., racism, ethnocentricism, nationalism) are manifestations of "the same basic human predisposition to form group-based hierarchies" (Sidanius and Pratto 1999, 38). Thus, SDO is a psychological product of group dominance cultures (Pratto et al. 2000, 374).

SDO is linked to feelings of group competition and seeing intergroup relations in zero-sum terms (Jackson and Esses, 2000; Esses, et al. 2001). Several studies found that the well-documented relationship between political conservatism, prejudice, and a desire to exclude others (i.e., racism, ethnocentrisms, and xenophobia) is spurious. Both political conservatism and racial prejudice can be explained by SDO (Sidanius, Pratto, Bobo 1996; Sidanius and Pratto 1999, 97).

Social dominance orientation is a worldview that locates all groups in an inegalitarian, hierarchical order. "It expresses general support for the domination of certain socially constructed groups over other(s)" including those of race, sex, nationality, ethnicity, religion, class, region, caste, and so forth (Sidanius and Pratto 1999, 61). Sidanius and Pratto (1999) identify 45 studies in eleven nations that examined SDO.

SDO is found among people in all group-dominance societies (i.e., societies with social inequality). Although it primarily operates at the social psychological level, it is linked to macro-level politics through "legitimating myths." A legitimating myth is a mixture of "attitudes, values, beliefs, stereotypes, and ideologies that provide moral and intellectual justification for the social practices that distribute social value . . ." (Sidanius and Pratto 1999, 45). The myths provide people with socially acceptable justifications to maintain, defend or increase social inequality. Thus, people with high SDO will support hierarchy-reinforcing policy choices, not so much because of policy content, but because the justifications for the policy positions are appealing to them. For example, Pratto and Lemieux (2001) divided people into high and low SDO. They found that high-SDO people supported nationalistic arguments and policies to maintain dominance over new immigrants, while low-SDO people favored policies to include immigrants. When they framed the situation as immigrants being a national threat, low-SDO people found the policy unappealing, but high-SDO people embraced it. When they framed the immigration policy as promoting equality, it was unappealing to high-SDO people but endorsed by low-SDO people. Thus, people's support for immigration policy appeared to be based less on the substantive issue of immigration than on whether the rationale behind the policy was that it would either reinforce or reduce social inequality and majority group dominance.

| CASE IN POINT 8.3 | **Appeal for Tolerance Draws Wrath of College Crowd** |

At the 2001 winter commencement at the California State University–Sacramento, the keynote speaker was Ms. Janis Heaphy, the publisher of the nationally recognized, award-winning newspaper, the *Sacramento Bee*. When Heaphy urged citizens to safeguard free speech rights; oppose unlawful detainment; and uphold lawful, fair trials, the crowd of 10,000 erupted into loud booing, heckling, and shouting that forced her off the stage after five minutes. She was unable to finish her nine-minute speech. In the speech, Heaphy did not question President Bush's war on terrorism or the build up of domestic security, and she praised the call to patriotism. It was when she asked whether American values for tolerance might be harmed in an unquestioned drive for security at any cost, that the crowd, which consisted of mostly parents and friends of graduating students and the graduating college seniors, exploded in an uproar. Apparently, the crowd did not want to hear about American values of tolerance or defending basic U.S. Constitutional rights. After the World Trade Center terrorist attack, which occurred three months earlier, they displayed a lingering mob mentality and blind emotional response that eclipsed any reasoned commitment to defending core democratic values.

Source: Egan, Timothy. "In Sacramento, a Publisher's Questions Draw the Wrath of the Crowd." *New York Times*, December 21, 2001.

different race, religion, or ideology can erode support for tolerance. Historical examples in the United States include the Salem witch trials, nineteenth century nativist movements, "anti-Red" campaigns in 1918–1920, imprisoning Japanese Americans in 1941–1945, and the 1950s "McCarthy" period. During such periods, the public's commitment to civil liberties and to protect the feared group quickly evaporated and defending the social–political order became a higher priority than maintaining fundamental civil liberties. Individuals who did not bend to mass conformity and who continued to defend basic democratic values and constitutional rights found themselves under attack (see Case in Point 8.3). This illustrates how individual beliefs and values always operate in a broader institutional context and political climate.

CONCLUSION

In this chapter we explored ideas and symbols in politics by focusing on two cultural institutions: schools and the mass media. We saw that schooling serves three functions: (1) disseminating official or school knowledge, (2) socializing youth, and (3) social selection. Political conflicts affect these functions. Political struggles periodically appeared over the role of schooling, including major reform movements that extend to the present. Educational reforms are affected more by ideological battles outside of schools than by features in schools.

We also looked at the mass media as part of the culture industry and saw its political influence, including its effects on the political agenda and impacts on several policy areas, and we looked at the impact of race coding and bounded pluralism on public discourse. We saw how tolerance is at the foundation of a democracy and reviewed explanations for tolerance. While people express general support for tolerance in the abstract, their support almost evaporates when it really matters (i.e., applying tolerance to specific situations and to groups they fear).

In Chapter 9, we explore social control. In addition to government rules, regulations, and acts of repression that operate to control the population, we will examine the role of law and legal institutions that legitimate and uphold peace in the social–political order.

KEY TERMS

Attention Cycle

Bounded Pluralism

Censorship

Cooling Out

Corporate Censorship

Corporate Voice

Correspondence Theory
   of Schooling

Credentialism

Cultural Capital

Hidden Curriculum

Human Capital Thesis
   of Schooling

Priming

Race Coding

Resistance Theory
   of Schooling

School Knowledge

Semi-Autonomy Theory
   of Schooling

Social Capital

Social Closure

Symbolic Racism

REVIEW QUESTIONS

1. How does schooling contribute to nation-building? In what ways did the common school in the United States contribute to national development and reflect national ideals?

2. In what ways do the social and political purposes of secondary and tertiary schooling differ? How does each contribute to individuals building social and cultural capital?

3. Compare the reproduction and resistance theories of schooling and how each fits with the models of political sociology.

4. Outline the three major American secondary school reform movements of the twentieth century, including the

major goals and supporters of each. How does each reflect political forces beyond schooling?

5. What is the resonance model of mass media? How does it compare with the competition model? What types of people are most influenced by political media messages and why?

6. How does media format, specifically television, influence the types of media messages and their affect on people? What are the political consequences of these effects?

7. What is liberal bias in the media? Why does it occur? How does it operate? How is this related to the media's role as a social, critical, or consumer advocate?

8. What are the major forms of censorship of the American mass media today? What is included or excluded from the mass media, with what effect, and why?

9. Take two of the contemporary American public policy areas discussed in this chapter and explain how the mass media affects political discussion and policy debate.

10. How can the mass media have great diversity, yet also be highly controlled?

What are the primary forms of control over the mass media, how do they operate and what are their political effects?

11. What is the significance of political tolerance for democratic politics? What people tend to be most or least tolerant?

12. What causes tolerance to weaken and vanish or to strengthen?

RECOMMENDED READINGS

Apple, Michael W. 1992. *Official Knowledge.* Boston: Routledge.

Gilens, Martin. 1999. *Why Americans Hate Welfare.* Chicago: University of Chicago Press.

Lewis, Justin. 2001. *Constructing Public Opinion: How Political Elites Do What They Like and Why We Appear to Go Along With It.* New York: Columbia University Press.

Lutz, Catherine A. and Jane Collins. 1993. *Reading National Geographic.* Chicago: University of Chicago Press.

Katznelson, Ira and Margaret Weir. 1985. *Schooling for All.* Berkeley: University of California Press.

Rampton, Sheldon and John Stauber. 2003. *Weapons of Mass Deception: The Uses of Propaganda in Bush's War on Iraq.* New York: Penguin Books.

Schudson, Michael. 1995. *The Power of News.* Cambridge, MA: Harvard University Press.

ENDNOTES

1. See Heinz (1983) on the importance of schools in the New Christian Right.

2. Quote is from Apple (1989, 38).

3. Quote is from Merelman (1989, 476).

4. Hibbing and Theiss-Morse (1996) and Merelman (1996).

5. See Green (1990, 3–20). On the international expansion of schooling, see Benavot et al. (1991), Kamens, Meyer, and Benavot (1996), Meyer, Ramirez, and Soysal (1992), Meyer, Kamens and Benavot (1992), and Ramirez and Boli (1987).

6. From Green (1990, 24–25).

7. For discussion see Green (1990, 47). Meyer et al. (1979) discusses in the U.S. situation.

8. From Green (1990, 79).

9. Archer (1979) discusses school expansion and competition. Also see Katznelson and Weir (1985, 28–33). See Ralph and Rubinson (1980) on U.S. schooling and immigration.

10. Hahn (1999) discusses citizenship education. Also see Gamoran (1990) on civil religion and U.S. schools.

11. See Dronkers (1993), Walters and Rubinson (1983), and Walters and O'Connell (1990).

12. Meyer et al. (1979) provide a major statement on this point.

13. See Walters (1984).

14. From Brint and Karabel (1989, 11).

15. Stevenson and Baker (1991) discuss how centralized and decentralized control affect the curriculum.

16. See Green (1990, 315).

17. This is discussed by Katznelson and Weir (1985, 57).

18. See Rubinson (1986), especially Table 1 on page 522.

19. Hogan (1985) and Wrigley (1982) discuss Chicago schooling conflicts between World War I and World War II.

20. See Rubinson (1986).

21. Rubinson (1986, 544) compares the American with the European pattern.

22. On national systems of higher education, see Clark (1983, 1984). On the history of American higher education see Barrow (1990), Geiger (1988, 1993), Kerr (1991), and Noble (1977).

23. See Greene and Forster (2003).

24. See "The Cure of Nepotism," *The Economist,* January 10, 2004.

25. See history and politics of community colleges in Brint and Karabel (1989) and Dougherty (1994).

26. Clark (1970) offers a classic statement on "cooling out."

27. On school knowledge, see Apple (1979, 1992), and Apple and Weis (1983).

28. See Meyer et al. (1992).

29. See Apple (1979) and Bergenhenegouwen (1987).

30. The concept of habitus is from Pierre Bourdieu; also see Hannerz (1992).

31. On individualism see Bobo (1991); Kluegal and Smith (1986); and Phelan, Link, Stueve, and Moore (1995). The emphasis on individualism is associated with the spread of psychology (see Frank, Meyer, and Miyahara 1995).

32. See study by Burris (1983) on the overeducated.

33. Hannerz (1992, 114–118) discusses how culturally valued knowledge is packaged. Also see Edelman (1977).

34. See Wright (1985) on the relationship between credentials and social class. Robinson (1986) discusses how credentials affect social mobility prospects.

35. Collins (1979) outlines the argument in his classic work on credentials.

36. See Bills (1988).

37. For a classic outline of correspondence theory, see Bowles and Gintis (1976).

38. See Fuller (1983), Fuller and Rubinson (1992), Rubinson (1986), and Walters and O'Connell (1988).

39. Davies (1995) provides a good review of recent models of schooling.

40. For discussion see Bills (1983) and Rubinson (1986).

41. See Barrow (1990, 35).

42. Bannister (1987), Baritz (1960), Barrow (1990), and Ross (1991), Schwendinger and Schwendinger (1974), and Silva and Slaughter (1980) discuss the suppression of dissent in U.S. higher education.

43. See Caute (1978), Goldstein (1978), Lader (1979), Schultz and Schultz (1988), and Schrecker (1986).

44. For a discussion of responsiveness to business in the past, see notes 8 and 9 above and Barrow (1990). Some sources on trends toward corporate alignment include Rhoades and Slaughter (1991, 1997), Silva and Slaughter (1984) and Slaughter (1988, 1990). On downsizing in the 1990s, see Gumport (1993) and Slaughter and Silva (1983, 1985). Examples of politically conservative attacks on university faculty toward the end of the 1990s include D'Souza (1991), Kimball (1990) and Sykes (1988).

45. See Karen (1991b) on changing access to higher education.

46. Quote is from Lucas (1996, 530).

47. The examples come from Fuentes (1998) and Arenson (2000).

48. See Berube (1994) on the three movements. Brint (1998, 275–290) and Katz (1971, 105–146) also discuss school reform movements.

49. Quote is from Berube (1994, 14).

50. A good example is Longshore (1982).

51. Brint (1998, 127–128 and 279–280) reviews some of the criticisms.

52. As Katznelson and Weir (1985, 213) observed, "The . . . issues of schooling for all are today less about schooling on its own terms than about fundamental, perhaps intractable, features of the American regime."

53. Quote is from Davies (1999, 9).

54. Sikkink (1999) found that conservative religious Protestants are alienated, but among the Protestant groups, lower class people are most alienated.

55. Quote is from Berube (1994, 93).

56. See Green (1990, 315) and Levin (1999). Witte (2000) offers an analysis of a school voucher experiment.

57. Schneider et al. (1997, 1998) examine the social characteristics of parents making choices among schools.

58. Saporito (2003) and Saporito and Lareau (1999) examine race and actual school choices.

59. Feinberg (1989) argues that foundations, government agencies, and private groups complaining about declining education and urging excellence are ideological attacks on equity that do not draw on observation of actual schools but infer from statistical trends or rely on romanticized and idealized "timeless ideals."

60. Kahne (1996, 92–118) reviews the debate on school choice.

61. See "V-Day for Vouchers," *The Economist,* July 15, 2000.

62. See "School Vouchers: A Rose by Other Name?," *New York Times,* December 20, 2000.

63. See Katz (1971) and Levine (1999).

64. See Orfield and Eaton (1996) and Rivkin (1994). Also see Orfield and Yun (1999) and Orfield (2001).

65. Astin (1992) makes this argument.

66. Quote is from Schiller (1989, 34).

67. For a critique of this model, see Ansolabehere et al. (1995) and Becker and Kosicki (1995).

68. See Ansolabehere et al. (1995), Becker and Kosicki. (1995), Neuman et al. (1992), and Neuman (2001).

69. On how media messages can override personal experience see Iyengar and Kinder (1987, 52–53).

70. On agenda setting's impact on television among less educated people see Ginsberg (1986, 146), Iyengar and Kinder (1987, 58–60), and Weaver (1996). Hill (1985) notes that attentive viewers of more dramatic news are most affected by television agenda setting. Also see Mutz and Martin (2001) on diversity of views in media.

71. See Steven Kill et al. "Misperceptions, the Media, and the Iraq War." Program on International Policy Attitudes, University of Maryland, October 2, 2003.

72. For discussion, see Becker and Kosicki (1995, 53–56).

73. Neuman (1986, 22) discusses this idea and related research.

74. Neuman et al. (1992, 97–99) discusses results on the effect of television and cites related research.

75. See Neuman (1982) on processing TV and Neuman et al. (1992, 106–108) on TV and cognitive ability.

76. See Iyengar (1990a) and Kleinnijenhuis (1991).

77. See Mendelberg (2001, 150).

78. See Denton and Holloway (1995) and Meyrowitz (1995) on television creating attachments to politicians. Hibbing and Theiss-Moore (1998) document the more powerful emotional impact of broadcast media.

79. See "Something Borrowed, Something Blue," *Washington Post*, March 9, 2001, Page A16. Also see Rampton and Stauber (2003) on media manipulation during the 2002–2003 Iraq invasion. "Keepers of Bush Image Lift Stagecraft to New Heights," *New York Times*, May 16, 2003.

80. On corporate mergers in the media industry see Powell (1987) and McChesney (1997).

81. See "Media Companies Succeed in Easing Ownership Limits," *New York Times*, April 16, 2001.

82. The study is reported in Gilens and Hertzman (2000).

83. Blurring lines between entertainment and news is discussed by Schudson (1995, 171).

84. See Altheide (1995) and Schudson (1995) on the blurring of entertainment, news, and advertising.

85. See Held et al. (1999, 346–360), McChesney (1997) and Smith (1980) on global media expansion.

86. See Held et al. (1999, 355–356).

87. See Mondak (1995) and Weaver (1996). Also see Huckfeldt et al. (1995, 1998) on how opinion is formed in social networks of interaction.

88. Quote is from Ansolabehere et al. (1995, 26).

89. On how negative television ads demobilize voters see Ansolabehere et al. (1995) and Ansolabehere and Iyengar (1995). Wattenberg and Brians (1999) question demobilization effects.

90. See Ginsberg (1986, 111–113) for a discussion of media and "right to life" politics.

91. On liberal bias in the media see Domke et al. (1999), Erbe (1998), Evarts and Stempel (1974), Hart and Rendall (1998), Shaffer et al. (1982), Plutzer, Maney, and O'Connor (1998), and Watts et al. (1999). Also see Bielby and Bielby (1994) on organizational pressures that shape prime time television programming.

92. See Cook (1998, 38–59).

93. Halberstam (1979) discusses the making/breaking of politicians by media organizations.

94. From Lazere (1987, 10).

95. For a discussion of the politics of censoring music lyrics see Binder (1993).

96. See Jim Rutenberg and Bill Carter, "Network Coverage a Target of Fire From Conservatives," *New York Times*, November 7, 2001, and Allesandra Stanley, "Opponents of War Are Scare on Television." *New York Times*, November 9, 2001.

97. See "Cable's War Coverage Suggests a New 'Fox Effect' on Television Journalism," *New York Times*, August 16, 2003. For discussion of how Rupert Murdoch's right-wing political news influence in his media empire see David Kirkpatrick, "Mr. Murdoch's War," *New York Times*, April 7, 2003 and Ken Auletta, "Vox Fox," *The New Yorker* 79, no. 13 (May 26, 2003), pp. 58–73.

98. Marc Lacey and Bill Carter, "In a Deal with TV Networks, Drug Office is Reviewing Scripts," *New York Times*, January 14, 2000, and Don Van Natta, Jr., "Drug Office Will End Scrunity of TV Scripts," *New York Times*, January 20, 2000, and Gary Fields and Ted Boehm, "War on Drugs Enlists Hollywood To Bolster Impact," *Wall Street Journal*, July 12, 2002.

99. See Nat Ives, "On the Issue of Iraq, Advocacy Ads Meet with Rejection from TV Networks," *New York Times*, March 13, 2003.

100. This is recounted in John Nichols, "Bush helps CBS, CBS helps Bush," *The Nation*, January 22, 2004.

101. See Schudson (1995, 169) for why ending censorship does not create democracy.

102. For a discussion on moralizing, see Neuman et al. (1992, 72–74).

103. For more on agenda setting by the media see Gamson and Modigliani (1989), Gamson et al. (1992), Schudson (1995), and Weaver (1996).

104. Wanta and Hu (1994) report that television can affect the public agenda in one to four weeks, newspapers in three to five weeks, and magazines in eight to eleven weeks.

105. From Iyengar and Kinder (1987, 33).

106. For an example in the 1992 Presidential election see Heatherington (1996).

107. McCarthy, McPhail and Smith (1996, 481) define the attention cycle.

108. On media attention cycles and agenda setting see Hilgartner and Bosk (1988). Also, see Gamson (1989) on "framing" in the news.

109. Several studies suggest this. Mutz and Soss (1997) argue that this media effect, more than actually changing public opinion to favor a policy, is important.

110. See Iyengar and Kinder (1987, 63–65).

111. On how media affect agenda setting, see Gamson and Wolfsfeld (1993), and Kleinnijenhuis and Rietberg (1995).

112. See Schneider and Ingram (1993, 1995) on target groups.

113. See Entman (1995) and Gilens (1996a, 1996b). Also, see Hansenfeld and Rafferty (1989) on American attitudes about social welfare programs and Heaven and Furnham (1988) on the racial and economic attitudes.

114. Kuklinski, Quirk, and Schwieder (1998).

115. See Entman (1995, 152–153), Iyengar (1990b) and Iyengar and Kinder (1987). Iyengar and Kinder (1987, 38–40) found that white Americans evaluated the unemployment issue depending on whether the person shown on television was black or white, with whites

showing little sympathy for and more likely to blame a black victim.

116. For a discussion of race coding by the media, see Gilens (1996b). Also see Feagin (1991) on the consequences for the lives of middle-class and upper-class African Americans.

117. Quote is from Gilliam and Iyengar (2000, 562).

118. On the media creation of fear, see Altheide (1997), Altheide and Michalowski (1999), Chiricos, Eschholz, and Gertz (1997), Chiricos, Padgett, and Gertz (2000), Heath and Gilbert (1996) and Williams and Dickinson (1993).

119. Quote is from Sacco (1995, 146).

120. See the content analysis study by Welch and Fenwick (1997). Welch, Weber, and Edwards (2000) also found a heavy reliance by the media on official sources and interpretations for corrections policy.

121. See the research of Beckett (1994, 1995, and 1997).

122. See Gilliam and Iyengar (2000). Also see Chiricos, Hogan and Gertz (1997).

123. Quote is from Iyengar (1991: 41–42).

124. See Dixon and Linz (2000), Gilliam and Iyengar (2000), and Hurwitz and Peffley (1997) on racial stereotypes and crime and its contribution to white punitive attitudes toward blacks accused of crime.

125. In addition to Kock (1998), see Mintz (1995) on health policy debate.

126. For the study of this legislation and media coverage see Knight and O'Connor (1995).

127. See Wheeler (1997: 188–189).

128. For a discussion of *National Geographic,* see Lutz and Collins (1993).

129. A discussion of some effects during the Persian Gulf War can be found in Iyengar and Simon (1993), McLeod et al. (1994), Pan and Kosicki (1994), Parker (1995), Steele (1995).

130. From Herman and Chomsky (1988). For this and other examples see Wheeler (1998, 187).

131. Quote is from Ginsberg (1986, 131).

132. Quote is from Danielian and Page (1994, 1077).

133. For examples, see Schudson (1995, 183).

134. See Cook (1998, 81, 88) and Gans (1979).

135. For a study of the mainstream effect see Gerbner et al. (1984, 1987).

136. Quote is from Neuman et al. (1992, 9).

137. Jacobs (1996) discusses how people using different media outlets construct divergent meanings. Also see Manning (1996), Solomon (1993), and Vseem (1997) on media coverage and the cultural politics of the Rodney King event.

138. See Cook (1998, 83) and Schudson (1995, 31) on U.S. mass media being similar to political parties elsewhere.

139. On media access, see Danielian and Page (1994), Gamson and Wolfseld (1993), and Giltin (1980).

140. From Lipsky (1968, 1151) cited in McCarthy et. al. (1996).

141. The study of two newspapers can be found in Oliver and Myers (1999).

142. See McCarthy et al. (1996) and Smith, McCarthy, McPhail, and Augustyn (2001).

143. For further discussion on the reliance on authorities, see Cook (1998, 91–95) and Schudson (1995, 11). See also Steele (1995) on its relation to media coverage of the Persian Gulf War.

144. See Gamson and Modigliani (1989), Gamson et al. (1992), Gamson, and Wolsfeld (1993).

145. See Schudson (1995, 55).

146. The study of institutional processes in prime time television programming by Bielby and Bielby (1994) suggests greater homogeneity and less diversity in the cultural product of a television series.

147. On "making news" through organizational procedures that become "facts" see Tuchman (1973, 1978, 1980).

148. On newspapers, see Schudson (1978, 1995, 39–71).

149. For a discussion, see Iyengar and Kinder (1987, 132–133).

150. Gibson and Bingham (1982) and Gibson (1989) provide useful discussions of political tolerance.

151. The terms "hearts and minds" tolerance and a criticism of it comes from Weissberg (1998).

152. Schuman, Bobo, and Krysan (1992) argue that less-educated people appear to have an authoritarian personality but it depends on how it is measured, especially among the less educated.

153. See Beatty and Walter (1984) on religion and political intolerance.

154. See Abrahamson and Carter (1986), Altemeyer, (1988), Delli-Carpini and Keeter (1996, 220–223), Jelen and Wilcox (1990). Nunn et al. (1978) and Wilson (1985, 1986, 1991, 1995, 1996). Also see Marcus, Pierson, and Sullivan (1980), Tuch (1987) and Wald et al. (1996) on the positive urban effect.

155. See Sullivan et. al. (1982, 125).

156. Frey and Goette (1998) observe, the anti-tolerance findings found by Gamble (1997) hold for the United States but not other countries such as Switzerland.

157. See McClosky and Brill (1983).

158. See Nunn et al. (1978).

159. See Marcus et al. (1995, 204).

160. See Marcus et al. (1995, 174–175). Kuklinski et al. (1991) found that cognitive deliberation to civil liberties does not raise political tolerance. Chong (1992) also discusses people deliberating civil liberties questions.

161. For empirical support and discussion, see Weil (1982, 1985).

162. See Marcus et al. (1995, 152, 225).

163. See Jackman (1978), and Jackman and Muha (1984) on schooling and ideological sophistication.

164. See Marcus (1995, 37–38).

165. See Sullivan et al. (1979) and (Marcus 1995, 43) on schooling and tolerance toward disliked or feared groups.

McCutcheon (1985) argues there are four sets of tolerance views: general tolerance, general intolerance, anti-right intolerance, and anti-left intolerance.

166. Bryson (1996) discusses musical tastes and relations between cultural boundaries and political tolerance. Also, see Oliver and Mendelberg (2000) on how out-group hostility explains white's negative racial attitudes.

167. See Marcus et al. (1995, 155–156).

168. This discussion is based on Sullivan et al. (1982) and McClosky and Brill (1983).

169. See McClosky and Brill (1983) and Apostle et al. (1983).

170. See Kuklinski and Parent (1981) and Margolis and Haque (1981).

171. For a review of changes in American racial attitudes and the symbolic racism literature, see Bobo (1983), Huddy and Sears (1995), Kluegal (1990), Kluegal and Smith (1982, 1983, 1986), Mendelberg (2001), Sears et al. (1979, 1981, 1988), Schuman, Steeh, and Bobo (1985), Smith (1981a, 1981b), Schuman and Bobo (1988), Sniderman, et al. (1985, 1986, 1991), and Young (1985). Also, see Weir (1994) on the related idea of "defensive localism."

172. See Sears (1988) and Williams et al. (1999) on contemporary or symbolic racism and traditional racism.

173. Abrahamson and Carter (1986) and Wilson (1985, 1991, 1992, 1995, 1996).

174. Also, see Wood and Hughes (1984).

175. Nunn, et al. (1978).

LAW, CRIME, AND CONTROL

INTRODUCTION

Have you or a friend ever been stopped or questioned by a police officer? Have you ever attended a court session or legal hearing? If so, you had direct experience with the topic of this chapter—law, crime, control, and justice. We examined the symbolic-ideological dimension of politics in Chapter 7. Now we turn to law and its enforcement (i.e., police, courts, prisons), because they are major parts of the state. One issue we will look at is the expansion in the U.S. imprisonment rate since the late 1970s. For 50 years, between 1929 and 1980, the imprisonment rate changed very little and remained in a narrow band from 93 to 137 per 100,000 persons. After 1980 it climbed steadily until, by 1999, it was 468 per 100,000.[1] Today, the United States has the second highest imprisonment rate in the world, after Russia.[2] Moreover, as Schlosser (1998, 52) noted, "Crimes that in other countries would usually lead to community service, fines, or drug treatment—or would not be considered crimes at all—in the United States now lead to a prison term." This dramatic change in crime policy has had no real effect on criminal behavior, but it has weakened political legitimacy and increased deprivation among the poor and especially among racial minorities.[3]

Law and law enforcement are inherently political. David Kairys (1982b, 17) argued that, "Law is simply politics by other means." Expanding, elaborating, and enforcing laws are part of nation-state development as Anthony Giddens (1987, 151) noted, "The expansion of sovereignty was partly achieved through the centralization of methods of law enforcement. . . ." Power struggles developed over enacting and enforcing law, defining certain acts to be criminal, and limiting undesirable behavior and ideas. Laws and official social control brought hardship for people lacking power and benefits for those with power as they expanded or restricted freedoms and rights.

The sociologist Emile Durkheim argued that a central classification of society is between normal-legal and deviant-criminal. All societies generate normative boundaries. Crime is violating or social control is upholding the boundaries. Thus, "public rituals of punishment and exclusion . . . is a means by which healthy societies reinforce their normative boundaries."[4] Political sociologists see the political processes of specific settings affecting the intensity and forms of social control.[5] They look at the impact of politics on the moral order of a society and examine state actions to control the populations residing within its borders. ■

The Nation-State, Law, and Justice

In every society, people create norms, rules, and standards of behavior as well as informal and formal systems of control that reinforce obedience to these norms. A chief function of the state is to identify, pronounce, and enforce rules of proper conduct in the form of laws. Laws existed before the nation-state, but the nation-state greatly expanded and transformed legal institutions. As governing elites extended their political control over the people and property, they clarified standards of conduct and formalized authority. Anthony Giddens (1987, 98–99) observed, "The promulgation of abstract codes of law, which apply to the whole population of a state, is . . . connected to the notion of sovereignty . . . [T]he expansion of codified law . . . is then part and parcel of a generalized apparatus of power." In the process of consolidating power, state leaders established systems of law, justice, and punishment. Past political participation affected how the systems of law and control developed.[6] Where the state-society boundary was weak or blurred, as in the United States, lawsuits became integral to creating public policy and laws closely conformed to public opinion.[7] Surveillance, or the state's systematic monitoring of people, has been a growing dimension of law and social control.

Our current ideas about law, legal rights, an independent judiciary, and professional policing grew with the ascent of the nation-state. The nation-state defines behavior as legal or illegal, imposes punishments and penalties on law violators, and evokes the ideals of justice, fairness, and impartiality to legitimate its actions. Abbott (1988, 185) remarked that "Legal work is legitimate because its procedures allow cultural values of fairness, justice, and order to be realized." The contemporary legal system evolved in five overlapping historical processes (see Chart 9.1)

Political sociologists see the state and politics as fundamental to understanding law, crime, and control, but many criminal justice specialists ignore the state. "Criminologists and legal scholars," Richard Quinney (1974, 21) complained, "generally neglect the state as a focus of inquiry." They fail to acknowledge the impact of political processes.[8] Next we examine how the political sociology models explain law, crime, and social control.

Models of Political Sociology and the Law, Crime, and Control

For *pluralists*, law reflects the societal consensus on basic values, traditions, and beliefs. Legal institutions and law are neutral regarding ideological disputes and partisan concerns.[9] A mix of electoral politics and interest group bargaining shape what is enacted into law but within basic societal values. The abortion debate in the United States illustrates how divergent groups with competing moral and religious views seek laws that reflect their moral views. Pluralists see the intense disagreement over the abortion issue as an exception to the prevailing consensus. Yet, even on this contentious issue, most people remain committed to basic values, are willing to compromise, and obey the law.

The widely shared norms, values, and beliefs in the law make it essential for the general social good; crime is a nonpolitical, antisocial act. Controlling crime

---

c h a r t   9 . 1

DEVELOPMENT OF THE NATION-STATE AND LEGAL INSTITUTIONS

1. The state became the sole definer of law, and it displaced other institutions and forms of law.

2. As the state expanded to affect more areas of the population's social, political, and economic lives, it expanded the scope, reach, and inclusiveness of the law.

3. The state increasingly had its laws written, organized them into a distinct body of knowledge, and applied them with specialized institutions and officials.

4. The state enforced laws by threatening or directing organized violence against law violators.

5. State officials and intellectuals elaborated complex systems of ideas, ideologies, and symbols to legitimate the law, law enforcement, and application of punishments.

is a neutral, technical issue of how to protect law-abiding citizens and efficiently maintain the social order. Surveillance is an accepted aspect of law enforcement. Political repression is absent from a democratic society with a few, very rare exceptions when weak political institutions permit the temporary abuse of authority for personal gain.[10]

In the *elite model*, law and legal institutions are tools elites deploy to defend their power from competing elites and challenges by the masses. Political, business, mass media, religious, and other elites shape what becomes law, and their primary interest is protecting their power and privileges. For example, elites in the political parties press for election laws that make it very difficult to organize challenger parties. In the United States, bipartisan (i.e., two-party) committees set the number of signatures necessary to get on a ballot, the percentage of votes needed for public campaign funds, and rules for campaign contributions to protect the two major parties and create barriers to third-party challengers. Elite theorists argue that crime and law enforcement differ by the elite and mass. Ordinary crimes, usually by the masses, involve one citizen harming another (e.g., rape, robbery). White collar or corporate crimes involve business elites acting against other elites or against the public. Crimes of repression are when political elites aggressively suppress other elites or the masses to defend or expand their power. Also, government and business elites try to enhance their power by expanding state surveillance to monitor and control citizens.

According to the *statist model*, law, legal institutions, and legal reasoning are enmeshed in formal organizations, professionalism, and state policymaking. Legal institutions provide independent modes of knowledge and rule creation that developed into systems of formal, rational decision-making. Independent, expert professionals apply abstract rules to specific cases and strive to be neutral (i.e., beyond partisanship or ideology). The law and legal institutions can be resources and can operate like a filter, facilitating some state actions but inhibiting others. In the absence of an existing legal principle or process, undertaking a new policy can be difficult and time-consuming. Well-developed principles and processes facilitate the quick enactment of new laws or policies, but past precedent may restrict their form. The statist model is similar to the pluralist model on crime, control, surveillance, and repression, but it differs on state surveillance. In the statist model, state officials expand surveillance and control based on an organizational interest in making state administration and planning more effective and efficient.

Political sociologists who use a *power-structure model* argue that the law and legal institutions reflect ruling class interests and have a built-in class bias. The legal order is an instrument "employed by the ruling class for their own benefit."[11] It defends and reinforces dominant class power. The people who write, enforce, and interpret laws are members of, or socialize with and work for, the dominant class; they share, articulate, and advance its outlook, interests, and values. Appeals to abstract symbols like justice, obtuse legal language, and esoteric legal processes are ways to hide the law's dominant class bias. The legal system reinforces class power in many ways and obscures seeing the reality of social-economic power relations. For example, the law specifies how a buyer and seller should make a legal contract; it treats each as an equal, rational, and fully informed party who voluntarily enters into an agreement. The law ignores inequalities among the parties. For example, one party faces racial discrimination, has few alternatives, and has less money. Because the inequalities are ignored or unspoken in law, the contract will favor the party with wealth and power. Thus, by ignoring power and wealth inequalities, the law reinforces dominant class power. Richard Quinney (1974, 18) outlined this view, "The legal system provides the mechanism for the forceful and violent control of the rest of the population. In the course of battle, the agents of law (police, prosecutors, judges, and so on) serve as the military force for the protection of domestic order . . . and serve the needs of the ruling class. The rates of crime . . . are an indication of the extent to which the ruling class, through its machinery or criminal law, must coerce the rest of the population. . . ." In the model, levels of official control, surveillance, or overt repression vary by historical period. When the ruling class is unchallenged and its power is secure, it uses mild forms of control; but when it feels threatened, it mobilizes the coercive institutions (e.g., police, military, courts, prisons) to increase surveillance and repression.

Those who use a *structuralist model* say the needs of capitalism mold the law to serve economic (i.e., accumulation) and legitimation functions. The law maintains capitalist workplace relations, provides a foundation for private property, and facilitates business transactions, contracts, and market exchange. As Hunt (1993, 21) argued, "Law . . . operates both as a form of coercive domination and of ideological domination. . . . Legal coercion operates at a number of different levels. . . . First and foremost, coercion is applied to protect and reinforce the property relations of capitalist society." In addition, law and legal institutions are a part of dominant class hegemony; they deflect criticism and opposition to state power by appearing to be neutral "rules of the game" and above the interests of any one class. "The 'function' of the legal system," according to Michael Burawoy (1978, 51), "is to define a set of formal rules which regulates and preserves capitalist relations. But in order to do this its operation must appear legitimate. The law must define and enforce fair rules . . . appear to emerge from its own logic and not in response to particular interest groups." For example, a law says that people cannot sleep on a public park bench, and police will arrest and punish law violators. The law's formality and its application to all violators give an appearance of neutrality, but in practice, 95 percent of law violators come from one social class. The law does not apply to the conditions or activities of other classes. Thus, the law's formal neutrality obscures its true class nature.

There is some flexibility and relative autonomy in the law, yet its fundamental form and content remain within capitalist boundaries.[12] The legal order *as a whole* reinforces capitalism and dominant class power *most of the time*. Legal ideas do not perfectly reflect class interests. Inconsistencies in the legal order mean that in specific historic circumstances, the legal order can contradict dominant class interests. Sumner (1979, 277) argued that, "Legal discourse represents an historically constituted unity of politics and ideology and therefore stands for something much wider than itself." Legal autonomy allows the state to discipline particular capitalists to uphold the entire system of capitalism. Social control, surveillance, and repression of the subordinate classes are ongoing state functions that vary in form and intensity with the specific needs of capitalism and strength of the dominant class.

For the *class-struggle model*, law and legal institutions are arenas in which opposing classes and groups struggle for power. Protracted political and ideological struggles determine the legal order's direction. "Losers" face state coercive power and may find their behavior criminalized, or defined as illegal, while the "winners" are protected by the law.[13] Since the dominant class wins most struggles, the law largely reflects its interests. Yet an oppositional group occasionally wins and can direct part of the legal order against the dominant class for a while. Legal institutions contain contradictions that reflect a mix of economic power, religious belief, customs, and philosophy. Struggles interject new contractions into law and contending groups can exploit the contradictions during struggles. Spitzer (1983, 117) observed, "The concrete struggles, disputes, and agreements that are transformed into law leave their imprint on both the form of legal institutions and the content of legal ideas." Winners of political–ideological struggles win power to define crime. Thus, if they win prohibitionists define the selling and drinking of alcohol to be a crime and alcohol makers and drinkers are criminals. If they lose, drinkers are not criminals. State surveillance is a means by which winners of state power attempt to exercise their control over others, but it can also cause struggle. Chart 9.2 offers an overview of the positions of the political–sociological models on law, social control, and surveillance.

LAW AND LEGAL INSTITUTIONS

Sociology developed with a keen awareness of legal institutions and law. Karl Marx, Max Weber, and Emile Durkheim all studied the law. Marx and Weber received academic degrees in law, Weber spent seven years practicing it, and Durkheim wrote about law throughout his career. For each, law was a central institution for politics and social organization.[14]

What Is Law?

Law has multiple meanings. It can be a natural process (e.g., the law of gravity), rules enforced by threat (e.g., the law of the West or the law of the jungle), a formal rule enforced by a state official (e.g., police), or common, widely accepted practices arising over time (e.g., a legal document must be signed in black ink to be legally valid) but not written or enacted by a legislature. Great atrocities (e.g., Hitler ordering mass killings of Jews, Saddam Hussein killing Kurds) may violate international law but not the written laws of the nation in which they occur.

c h a r t   9 . 2

POLITICAL SOCIOLOGICAL MODELS ON LAW, CRIME CONTROL, AND SURVEILLANCE

Model	Law	Crime Control and Surveillance
Pluralist	Law reflects the widely shared norms, values, and beliefs of a society.	Controlling crime is a neutral, technical issue of protecting citizens and maintaining social order; surveillance is a vital part of law enforcement.
Elitist	Law is a tool that elites use to defend their power and privileges from competing elites and to keep the masses in their place.	Crime control varies greatly by type of crime (elite vs. mass). Elites use surveillance to enhance their ability to monitor and control the citizen masses.
Statist	Laws are formal-rational rules used by neutral, independent professionals that both facilitate and limit state actions.	State surveillance and control arise from an organizational interest by state officials to effectively administer the social order.
Power-Structure	Law has a class bias, and it defends and reinforces dominant class power.	Control is mild and surveillance minimal when the class is secure; control grows coercive and surveillance expands when it is threatened.
Structuralist	Law supports capitalist class hegemony, it appears neutral but protects class interests; it also sustains capitalist economic relations.	Surveillance and crime control are ongoing state functions that vary with the specific needs of capitalism and the strength of the dominant class.
Class-Struggle	Law is an arena of conflict. It contains contradictions that opposing groups exploit; struggles can introduce new contradictions.	The winners of contests for political–ideological power define crime and how to control it with surveillance and other means.

There is also divine law and church law. Here we are concerned with law of the contemporary nation-state.[15]

U.S. laws build on a framework of late seventeenth- and eighteenth-century British law. British law, in turn, grew from a mixture of Roman, canon (Catholic Church), feudal (lord and master relations), royal (pronouncements of a king), merchant (Roman law used by business), and natural (from seventeenth century philosophy) law.[16] Most English-speaking countries use a common law system derived from medieval England.[17] Common law builds on custom and precedent in court decisions. Its name came from being "common," or widely shared, rather than purely local.

Law and Customs

Law can reinforce, contradict, or introduce customs and norms. Major social-economic change can stimulate new laws and overturn past customs. A classic example occurred during the breakdown of feudal relations in Western Europe. Under feudalism, the peasants and serfs who lived on a manor had traditional rights to hunt and gather firewood on the lord's property. As feudal relations collapsed and capitalism spread, state officials rewrote laws to reflect emerging ideas about private property. In the new laws, manor property was defined as the landowner's individual private property. The peasants ceased to be dependents tied to the manor community. Peasants gained legal rights as free individuals and could leave the manor to find work elsewhere, but they lost their customary rights to hunt or gather firewood on manor land. The law reflected emerging capitalist relations and redefined a centuries-old custom as illegal behavior—what the peasants had done for generations became poaching or theft.[18] Law often codifies changes in social-economic relations (see Closer Look 9.1).

Law has both coercive and educational dimensions. Its coercive dimension is evident when a law compels conformity, sometimes contradicting local norms. For example, a local norm may say 14 is a proper age for marriage, but a law says that marriage partners must be at least 18. The law's educational dimension raises the awareness about and consolidates popular support around a new norm by giving it legitimacy. After years of being forced by law to wait until 18, people may accept 18, and not 14, as the normal marriage age.[19]

Many laws originate in custom and tradition, but all parts of a society may not share the same custom. Power and state centralization often determine whether a specific custom is converted into a national law. Also, customs and laws change at different rates. Customs can change in response to new conditions, but written laws remain in force. How law is applied or enforced may allow certain "illegal" customs to continue. Officials might enforce laws in a "reasonable" way by ignoring some law violations that are common practice or by not enforcing some laws that are "on the books," so people may be unaware that a law formally prohibits a custom (see the Living Law vs. Black Law section later in this chapter).

Types of Law

Civil law has two meanings. One meaning contrasts it with common law. In common law, legal principles are based on separate, decentralized judicial decisions applied to specific cases. In civil law, legal principles are based on core ideals established by centralized state authority. After the Roman Empire collapsed, canon law of the medieval church retained many legal principles and ideas from Rome. Over time, state officials in continental Europe revised many of the canon laws into civil law principles. The most famous is the Code Napoléon. The legal code developed under Napoléon Bonaparte has been modeled or copied by over 70 nations and remained almost unchanged for 150 years in France. After four years of debate, it was published in 1804 and was a simplified, uniform set of laws that consolidated and replaced over 14,000 decrees

CLOSER LOOK 9.1   The State, Property Law, and Power

Property refers to both physical objects (e.g., car, house, land) and social relationships (e.g., an owner's ability to use a car, house, and land in ways that other people cannot). Property law specifies social relationships that arise from ownership because what a person does with property affects others (e.g., if I drive my car recklessly, if my house is a fire hazard, if I dig a deep hole that causes my neighbor's house to collapse). Property laws assign powers based on relationships to the property. Such laws assign power over things to the owner and power over other people. For example, owning a car gives me power to take apart my car's engine, or power over a thing. It also gives me power over other people if I decide to lease the car to someone else and determine how much they must pay me to use it and tell them they cannot use it on the weekend. Likewise, I have the power to sell my house, or power over a thing. Property-based power over other people is easiest to see in an employment relationship. If I own a business, in the role of employer, I have the power to hire or fire workers, tell them when and how to work, and what they may say or wear in the workplace. I decide whether they get any benefits and whether their pay is higher than the legal minimum. If a worker accomplishes little during the working day, I am obligated to pay the agreed upon wage for the time the worker was under my control. If a worker accomplishes a great deal and creates vast wealth, I can pay

the same amount and keep the remainder for myself. My property rights do not give me the power to beat a worker if I am dissatisfied with his/her work, but I do have the power to send the worker home after part of a day's work with only partial pay.

Property-based power has three features. First, the state enforces it through law. Second, it limits owner obligations. For example, when I hire a worker, unless explicitly stated, I do not have to provide the worker with shelter, food, or clothing. Once this was the expected, but now I only need to pay wages. If I sell my property to another, I sell the power relationships attached to it to the new owner. Third, the state's legal order permits, encourages, and enforces certain power relations and not others. The rights and power that adhere to property ownership are not inexorable and inevitable, but changed over time and vary by political system.

Today I can sell a product for a price I decide. At other times or places, I might not be allowed to sell a product below a certain price, I could beat a slow worker, or I might be required to pay a worker an entire year's salary whether or not she/he showed up or did any work. Thus, property rights are a political outcome, but most people act as if the rights and associated powers are natural or inevitable. When people treat the outcome of political processes as being natural and inevitable, they rarely challenge or try to change them.

enacted by France's revolutionary government. The Code abolished feudal privileges, upheld property rights, ensured the equality of all citizens under the law, protected freedom of religion, required separation of the church and the state, identified males as the head of the family, and limited the grounds for divorce. Civil law influenced the development of legal systems in much of the non-English-speaking world. A second meaning of civil law contrasts it with criminal law. Civil law governs relationships among individuals or private business transactions, while criminal law deals with offenses against the state or against laws to protect the general public order.

There are many types of law beyond the common/civil law distinction. Substantive law specifies a person's rights and what is prohibited. Procedural law specifies the proper process for filing charges or what constitutes legitimate evidence in a court. Public law specifies the duties of government officials. And private law specifies the proper form of wills, marriages, and adoptions. Specialized areas have their own laws (e.g., constitutional law, tax law, patent law, environmental law, family law, civil rights law, antitrust law, banking law, consumer law, marine law, and real estate law).[20] In addition, administrative rules are similar to formal law.

Likewise, laws are of unequal importance. Most involve a minor adjustment to the current system, but a few mark historical turning points and reshape the state-society relationship.[21] For example, antitrust law, which first developed in the United States in 1890 and is now used in some form throughout the world, redefined state–business relations to promote market competition among businesses and prohibit private monopolies.

Law and Legitimacy

Law also legitimates state actions and puts limits on the discretion of state officials. Historically, a rising class of merchants and capitalists challenged the absolute authority of kings as being arbitrary and capricious. In the turmoil, as capitalism displaced feudalism, laws were enacted to impose order over chaotic economic, political, and social behavior and gradually created a stable, predictable framework. Decrees by kings and religious officials became systematic and codified, evolving into the "rule of law." The rule of law meant a state official could not do whatever he/she wanted, but was constrained to operate within established legal rules and procedures. Also, legal rules slowly changed to be consistent with other laws. Codified laws in writing seemed to separate the laws from the people occupying state positions, which helped to legitimate state action.[22]

To say that legal processes *legitimated* state actions means that the public accepts state actions as being moral or just *because they conform to the law*. Without written laws, actions such as confiscating property or income as a tax or fine, placing a person in prison, or closing a business would be seen as unacceptable, immoral, and unjust. The significance of legal legitimation is illustrated when military dictators who have absolute authority feel they must create laws to justify their brutal actions. Often they go to the time and expense of creating laws and holding trials, rather than simply sending enemies to the firing squad immediately because they seek a cloak of legal legitimacy.

The rule of law rests on two fallacies: normative and consensus model. **The normative fallacy states that law contains within it an ideal model of what social-economic-political relations should be and confuses that model with actual conditions.** The law itself fails to reveal the sources of its ideal model or to acknowledge the gap between the model and reality. The law's model contains assumptions about social roles (e.g., mother, sister, professor, or thief) and the expected behavior of people in these roles. For example, family law assumes that a marriage is the outcome of two rational, independent, and mature people who develop strong, loving relations. The couple intends to live together, stay married, accept sexual fidelity, and have and raise offspring. In reality, many people stumble into marital relations in a complex, confused way based on mixed motives. **The consensus model fallacy states that law assumes that all members of society agree on certain fundamental beliefs, values, and ideas.** This assumption is also found in pluralist and functional social theories.

Law and the Legal Order

The law is part of a broader idea—the legal order.[23] The **legal order refers to social-economic-political relations governed by state rules and the process that creates and enforces the rules.** It includes law (i.e., procedures, written rules, legal ideas, principles); legal institutions and organizations; the social-political-economic order supported by legal institutions; and people whose job is to create, administer, enforce, and/or oversee law. The legal order, "performs a myriad of functions; it resolves disputes, creates official norms, educates people in certain value sets, provides employment for a professional class, etc."[24] Most of those in the legal order (e.g., police, judges, legislators, legal bureaucrats, prison officials) are state employees, but others (e.g., lawyers, litigants, law school professors) are formally outside of the state. The legal order, Chambliss and Seidman (1982, 180) observed, "is a living institution, created by people occupying position in a social structure. It does not, however, arise automatically from 'social needs.' It reflects the fundamental contradictions and conflicts of the time."

Laws tend to address surface problems or symptoms rather than resolve deeply rooted structural causes. As a result, the legal order is filled with short-term, partial resolutions to fundamental social, political, and economic divisions. For example, in the United States, open housing laws, equal employment laws, and hate crime laws all address surface manifestations of deeply rooted racial inequality. The root causes continue to generate conflicts that result in new court cases and statutes. Over time, this results in a patchwork of partially overlapping, conflicting statutes and legal decisions. Gaps in this patchwork create openings in the legal order that make it indeterminate; that is, not fixed or wholly predicable. The gaps also create opportunities for new legal interpretations, and opposing political interests may exploit the gaps to interject their ideas and values into the legal order.[25]

Societal contradictions can find expression in the legal order's patchwork, and political conflicts can persist within it. New laws may be the result of conflicts rooted in structural changes (e.g., long-term increases in social diversity or economic inequality) or in public opinion triggered by an event (e.g., a sensational shooting, an advocacy group's protest).[26] Yet a new law may only reproduce the conflict as new legal categories within the legal order.[27] Once inside the legal order, a law affects other laws and social relations. Likewise, the winner of a legal–political conflict may try to codify their advantages and mode of thinking into judicial decisions or statutes that will influence subsequent legal interpretations. This occurs because, as Clark and Dear (1984, 104) noted, "Laws are formalized outcomes of the political process, but once enacted, they become the rules and standards by which individuals and classes have to act." But the law may be contested repeatedly. For example, the winning side in a conflict over deep-seated racial tensions may get ideas and principles written into new civil rights laws. In this way, the racial tensions are absorbed into the legal order. The tensions remain, but they have been reconstituted into a legal form. The process may have modified and converted the tension into legal categories, but the tension was not totally resolved.

Law and Ideology

The legal order is a repository of ideological thinking. As Colin Sumner (1979, 7) noted, "Laws are not just functional instruments, they are displays of ideology." Ideology is introduced in three ways: (1) law mystifies it or hides its full reality, (2) it contains embedded value assumptions, and (3) it falsely presents itself as being neutral (see Summary 9.1).[28]

SUMMARY 9.1	Three Mechanisms by Which Ideology Enters the Legal Order

MYSTIFICATION

The legal order obscures, hides, and makes it difficult to see and understand events and processes. According to Steven Spitzer (1983, 114), "Part of the significance of law in class societies resides in its ability to mystify social life." Legal language hides and adds an aura of mystery to social, moral, and political ideas and values after they have entered the legal order (Fitzpatrick 1980). "Certainly, legalese mystifies the law and makes laypersons incapable of dealing with it" (Chambliss and Seidman 1982, 131). By creating "a fog" around ideas, issues, and values, the legal order removes them from public debate and insulates them from direct challenge. There may be open debate when passing legislation, but once inside the legal order, disputes are constrained by a specialized language, set of categories, and mode of reasoning. Anyone entering legal proceedings with values that differ from the legal order will be frustrated and feel blocked by its implicit rules, language, and method of argument. The implicit rules and meanings of terms in the legal order are difficult for a layperson to decode or "read," however, this is no accident (Sumner 1979, 62–67, 225–229). Chambliss and Seidman (1982, 133) charged that, "A principal consequence of the obscurity . . . [is that] lawyers become indispensable, and that inevitably enhances the power and control of those who have the money to pay for lawyers."

EMBEDDED VALUES

The legal order contains embedded assumptions, values, and beliefs in its language and mode of reasoning. It relies on an implicit social theory that buttresses the rights, powers, and interests of certain groups or social classes, and it carries forward the moral values and ideas of past eras (Sumner 1979, 273). Hunt (1993, 25) argued that, "Law is ideological in that it conveys or transmits a complex set of attitudes, values and theories about aspects of society . . . ones that reinforce and legitimize the existing social order . . . [R]ules of law affirm the social and economic relations that exist in capitalist society." The legal order transforms people's ordinary social practices and relations by reconstructing them within a legal worldview. As the legal order converts ordinary practices and relations into legal forms and categories, it inserts assumptions and values. For example, contract law contains a model of society comprised of free individuals, and a legal contract appears to be a voluntary agreement between equal, autonomous individuals. In reality, a contract is usually an agreement that people with opposing interests and unequal power negotiate (Sumner 1979, 265). The legal order removes important social features of the relationship (e.g., a past friendship or intimate relations) from consideration as it converts them into legal terms. In this way legal language truncates social relations and strips away their critical aspects, substituting its own legal viewpoint (Chambliss and Seidman 1982, 119–136).

FALSE NEUTRALITY

The legal order presents itself as being neutral and objective with fair procedures, an appearance that fosters its legitimacy. As Farrell and Holmes (1991, 530) observed, there is an "unquestioned American commitment to the premise of equality before the law." Public acceptance of it is the myth of legality, **"The myth of legality is the belief that judicial decisions are based on autonomous legal principles . . . [it] holds that cases are decided by the application of legal rules formulated and applied through a politically and philosophically neutral process of legal reasoning"** (Scheb and Lyons 2000, 929). Scheb and Lyons (2000) observed that over one in four Americans accept the myth; those who accept it tend to be well-educated political moderates. Accepting the myth is strongly associated with holding positive views of the Supreme Court. It is a myth because in actuality, the legal order is not neutral and it does not treat all parties equally. The legal order indirectly advances certain interests and values. The values often originate in "natural law" (i.e., a philosophical principle) as if they were neutral, but they come from particular social and economic interests. Some political sociologists believe, like Hunt (1993, 18), that "The distinctive feature then of legal systems . . . [is] that they embody the material interests of the ruling class in a universal form, and thus present law and the embodiment of the interests of the community as a whole . . . law comes to be seen as the embodiment of universal notions of 'justice' and 'right'." A claim of being neutral is a powerful defense against challenges to the values that are embedded within the legal order (Kidder 1983, 204). This includes stereotypes used in court proceedings (Farrell and Holmes 1991).

As illustrated in the park bench example discussed earlier in this chapter, laws appear neutral and applicable to all people (i.e., no one can sleep on a park bench), but in practice, only certain categories of people are affected (i.e., destitute people without homes). By censoring the relevant social context, the legal order depoliticizes public issues and transforms potentially contested political issues into neutral-appearing legal categories and principles. This illusion of neutrality masks how the legal order actually operates to favor certain groups or classes. Tigar and Levy (1977, 279) argued that, "Laws lock into words, expressed as commands, the rights or duties which a particular group will use its power to protect or enforce, and provide predictable modes of settling disputes. . . ." A party in a dispute may demand that a law be enforced or taken to the courts. While it appears to be a demand to enforce an objective standard or hold a hearing before a neutral arbitrator, in reality it shifts the dispute to a setting that favors the party. For example, a landlord in a tenant-landlord dispute may take the issue to court. If landlord interests have been previously embedded in the housing law, taking it to court will introduce a landlord advantage. This explains why corporate persons (e.g., businesses, schools, churches) win most legal disputes with individuals. Also, as a corporate person's size and power increases, the chances that it will win a legal contest also grow.[29]

The legal order has a dual nature; it is both a system of instrumental-administrative procedures and a set of symbolic-ideological justifications. The two sides can complement and contradict one another. The procedural side efficiently processes tasks but cannot self-justify. It needs a moral anchoring beyond itself (i.e., ideological justification about abstract ideals like truth or justice). If the procedural side is detached from the substantive side, legal outcomes can appear to be unjust. For example, an honest, innocent person gets caught up in technical procedures and is sentenced to a prison term (i.e., a young mother who accidentally caused the death of her child), or the evildoer (e.g., a hardened murderer) goes free on a technicality. The disjunction between the two sides introduces openings for contradictions and public opposition in the legal order.[30]

Legal Reasoning

The legal order has a form of language and mode of reasoning that differs from other professional fields and from common sense. The outcomes of judicial hearings, legal decisions, or arguments by a legal authority can differ from outcomes produced by applying common sense or scientific reasoning. Legal arguments use a classification system of legal categories and specify how categories of people fit with categories of intention or action.[31] Legal classifications (e.g., spouse, juvenile, murder, injury) have specific legal meanings and may vary by area of law. Thus, a person legally can be a spouse with regard to tax law but not inheritance or immigration law.[32]

When legal specialists make a formal argument, they convert ordinary, commonsense facts into legal categories and apply abstract legal rules or principles. The legal principles specify the proper relations that should operate among the categories and yield a normative outcome (i.e., this is a good or proper result). The legal order has the capacity to insert normative outcomes (i.e., what is desirable) into decisions without explicitly acknowledging the normative values.[33] Legal reasoning allows a person to infer from facts (e.g., this is a husband) to normative statements (e.g., he ought to do X) without having to explicitly evoke a moral value (e.g., it is morally good for all husbands to do X). Like an ideology, legal reasoning fuses cognitive and evaluative elements together and blurs value judgments with factual statements. This enables law to conceal its implicit moral or political values.

Specialized legal language is not more precise than ordinary language. Indeed, legal phases are often long-winded, repetitive, and obscure. Instead, legal language invokes, in a kind of a code, specialized meanings that are understood by legal insiders. This creates a barrier between insiders and outsiders. Instead of fixed precision, legal phrases provide legal authorities with the discretion to decide the exact meaning of a legal phase in a specific situation.[34] Legal reasoning permits the reconstruction of complex social situations into simplistic legal terms, converting them into either/or legal terms (i.e., win/lose, innocent/guilty).[35] By transforming ordinary events into the formal categories governed by abstract legal rules, the events take on a universal appearance. Legal arguments "flatten the normative diversity of the social world" and present a single, authoritative interpretation of events that overrules all other interpretations.[36] This is how the legal order, backed by state authority, redefines the boundaries of acceptable or unacceptable, legitimate or illegitimate, criminal or legal, and natural or unnatural.[37] The legal order is guided by ongoing interpretations and applications of principles, not by a rigid, fixed adherence to the intentions of legislators or the words in monolithic legal texts. As with any written text, the readers of legal texts employ interpretative strategies to construct meaning. Law schools and judicial decisions establish and teach rules of acceptable textual interpretation, limiting the range of possible text readings. Legal language and modes of reasoning have vague terms, contradictory statements, and loose principles. This looseness introduces an elasticity that allows the legal order to be responsive to new conditions or to shifts in public opinion. It is a source of the legal order's partial autonomy.

The accepted textual interpretations of law tend to be conservative for three reasons.[38] First, legal reasoning is not self-reflexive in the course of its application. Debate about the legal order itself is out of bounds during a legal proceeding. Legal reasoning thus insulates, or prevents the existing law from being called into question. It only allows limited interpretations of vague legal texts.[39] Second, **legal reasoning looks to past rulings and judgments and relies on precedent, called stare decisis, which appears to be narrow.** Yet, Kairys (1982b, 15) noted that it "in fact provides and serves to disguise enormous discretion." The state decision principle assumes wise forefathers discovered something of great value, and we must continue to revere it without serious question. Perhaps many forefathers were unscientific, poorly informed, prejudiced, and just trying to preserve their own privileges by excluding others. When modes of reasoning other than precedent (e.g., scientific) are applied in a legal proceeding, the results are mixed. If judges and officials rely on scientific experts alone, then any democratic values embedded in law are undermined or the proceedings are opened to wider political pressures.[40] Third, the legal order contains an abstract model of social relations with assumptions from one particular model of society. Often, this is a model based on consensus and functional integration that tends to privilege the values of social stability, continuity, and consistency.[41]

The Relative Autonomy of Legal Institutions

The legal order is indeterminate and has partial independence from external power relations, conflicts, and prevailing ideologies; that is, it does not automatically yield fixed outcomes. While this reinforces an appearance of neutrality, it

SUMMARY 9.2   **Three Sources of the Legal Order's Autonomy**

- The role of arbitrator in the social conflicts among various groups and an appearance of being an independent, neutral party that is "above politics."
- A reliance on ambiguous precedent, vague interpretive principles, and a mode of reasoning full of abstraction, technical jargon, and obtuse language that creates flexibility and indeterminacy.
- Legal professionalism, self-regulated schooling, and the partial insulation of judicial posts from politics permits the legal order to be semidetached from immediate, direct political pressure.

Sources: See Balbus (1977) and Thompson (1975, 262) for discussions of the relative autonomy of legal institutions.

is a *partial autonomy* that cannot violate the fundamentals of the political-economic order (see Summary 9.2).

The partial autonomy is double-edged. On one hand, the legal order does not automatically follow powerful economic interests and can adjust to diverse values or uphold competing norms and traditions. Legal professionals can make semi-independent judgments free from a rigid adherence to statutes or the desires of powerful groups. On the other hand, the legal order can be unresponsive to public opinion or democratic pressures and can impose state power.[42] Thus, it is both independent from blind obedience to powerful interests and from the popular demands of democratic citizens.

Living Law vs. Black Law

Law as written in the books, called "black law," for the color of ink, differs from living law or law-in-practice. Living law involves questions of which laws are enforced and how?[43] Bureaucratic organizations that enforce laws transform written law into ongoing operations in ways that reflect their own interests to sustain the organization. It matches organizational needs to have legitimate sense of purpose, show effectiveness, match work levels to the amount of resources provided, and continue to employ staff. Organizations try to accomplish visible tasks that have positive symbolic value without running too far afoul of people or organizations that have economic or political power.[44]

The legal order's semiautonomy gives it room to adjust living law to internal considerations, or the prejudices of judges, ideological assumptions in past judicial decisions, and values embedded in legal categories. Other internal considerations include political beliefs, ideology, and interests that politicians insert into statutes; organizational or procedural rules favoring certain groups and interests; law enforcement priorities; and a judge's choice to use legal theories with political beliefs and viewpoints. External and internal forces often get intertwined. For example, a judge is elected or appointed by

SUMMARY 9.3   **The Legal Order and Conflict Resolution**

- When conflicts move into the courts, they are "legalized" (i.e., converted into the language, categories, and reasoning of the legal order). This legitimates legal procedures as the appropriate (i.e., peaceful, fair, just, neutral) way to settle conflicts and extends the legal order's reach beyond the state itself.
- The legal order diffuses conflict and displaces serious, violent confrontations by offering challengers symbolic victories.

It channels conflicts that might threaten state legitimacy (e.g., major racial unrest) into the courts, grants official recognition of claims, and can create new legal rights (e.g., civil rights law).
- The legal order reinforces the social acceptance of the fairness of the overall court system by "advertising" the state as being responsive to society and interested in achieving the abstract principle of justice.

a politician based on the priorities that she/he is expected to advance once in office.

Dispute settlement is an important legal function. Disputes involve a range of human and business relations (e.g., husband/wife, neighbors, one business versus another, employer/employee, stockholder/company, student/teacher). Most disputes are settled outside a formal judicial setting (i.e., arbitrators negotiate out-of-court settlements), but even these tend to be modeled on legal modes of reasoning and rules of fairness. In this way, the legal order extends beyond the state (e.g., police, courts, judges) to affect broader social and economic relations. The judicial system also has a significant role in conflict resolution (see Summary 9.3).[45]

The State, the Courts, and the Legal Profession

Lawyers

The law depends on specially trained people.[46] The preparation and role of lawyers varies greatly by country. For example, Great Britain distinguishes barristers, or lawyers who appear in court, from solicitors, or lawyers who do other legal paperwork. In Japan other specialists do most of the work American lawyers perform (e.g., prepare contracts or write wills).[47] The U.S. legal profession is a highly stratified group with professional schools, self-governing organizations, and codes of ethics. Some lawyers earn very high incomes and serve the elite, while others earn little and serve the poor. The government also imposes regulations (e.g., barring some people from becoming a lawyer). The legal profession has a monopoly on legal services. This "was the result of deliberate strategy to capture and control the marketplace for legal services," according to Kidder (1983, 216). In the late nineteenth century, lawyers consciously created the appearance of being apolitical, technical experts.[48] By the mid-twentieth century, they had reduced competition from related professions and consolidated their hold over the legal order.[49]

To become a lawyer in the United States today requires three years of specialized training in law schools beyond a bachelor's degree. As Kennedy (1982, 40) remarked, "Law schools are intensely political places." In addition conveying a body of knowledge, a mode of reasoning, legal procedures, and norms of professional conduct, law schools teach an attitude toward economy and society.[50] Many law school entrants undergo an ideological transformation, from being social justice idealists to pragmatists willing to advance elite interests; they abandon their ideals advancing social justice and focus on building a career in the "real world" of legal practice.[51] They learn that for a practical career, most opportunities and rewards go to lawyers who represent wealthy individuals and corporations.

While few lawyers specialize in public service or public interest law (e.g., defending the poor, fighting for a clean environment), the legal profession has long provided legal services to the poor as part of its code of ethics through **pro bono, or free legal work**.[52] Yet this is more of the ideal than a reality. In the United States only about one in three poor people who need a lawyer can get one. In recent years, major law firms reduced pro bono work to expand their lawyers' profit-generating work. For example, pro bono work by the 50,000 lawyers working in major U.S. law firms dropped from 56 hours per lawyer per year in 1992 to 36 hours in 1999. In this same period, politicians cut public legal services to assist the poor and restricted the kinds of cases that public service lawyers could accept.[53] The ideal is that everyone has equal access to legal services. The reality is that those who can afford to pay high legal fees get the best legal services, while the rest get low quality or no legal services at all.[54]

The Judiciary

Courts and judges are central in the legal order. "Too often the judiciary is ignored in analysis of the state in capitalist democracies," observed McCammon (1994, 1040). In court, citizens demand rights, seek liberty from state control, resolve conflicts, and find their conduct under publicly scrutiny. The judiciary is a diverse, multilayered system that operates at the local, state, and federal levels with a varying scope of authority and jurisdiction. The judiciary sets legal order's fundamental parameters. Judicial authority is aristocratic; judges are an insular, high status group. They appeal to tradition or higher principles and make pronouncements "above" mass, popular opinion.

Politics influences the judiciary in many ways. One is social background, as Vago (1991, 67) remarked, "Judges come from the middle or upper classes and have a history of party identification if not activism." They are "among the staunchest supporters of the myth of legal reasoning."[55] State-government judges are appointed or elected. In the United States, federal judges are presidential appointments, affirmed by the Senate, and serve for life. Also political-ideological factors, patterns of judicial retirement and resignation, and presidential elections influence judges.[56] The judiciary is also influenced by political–ideological movements among academics, legal scholars, and politicians. The U.S. judiciary has been affected by two such movements since the late 1970s, Neoclassical and Law and Economics. The Neoclassical Legal movement sought to reduce the use of ethical, sociological, and humanistic-economic criteria within the legal order, end indeterminate sentences with discretion by judges and corrections officials, and increase punishment over rehabilitation for offenders. Its goal was to treat all individuals as formally equal without regard to substantive inequalities among them. The Sentencing Reform Act of 1984 that encouraged deterrence, imprisonment, and determinate or fixed-length sentences was its primary achievement.[57] **Determinate sentencing specifies a fixed, rigid minimum penalty for a crime (e.g., 5 years in prison with no parole) and prohibits alternation of it by judges or corrections officials. Indeterminate sentencing gives a very broad range of penalties for a crime (e.g., probation to 5 years) and allows judges and corrections officials to adjust a sentence significantly based on an offender's social and criminal background, the specific circumstances of a crime, and changes in the offender's behavior and attitude.** The "Law and Economics" movement sought to overturn many business regulations enacted in the Progressive, New Deal, or Great Society eras, and to replace them with a laissez-faire approach based on neoliberal economic theory (discussed further in Chapter 10).[58] Its leaders "argue that efficiency provides a neutral, objective standard for judicial decision-making."[59] During the 1980s, several of the movement's leaders assumed posts at top law schools, in regulatory agencies, or in federal courts.

Supreme Court

The highest court is simultaneously a legal and a political institution. The Court rules on significant legal issues that have advanced up through a system of lower courts and on major constitutional disputes such as the division of powers within the state. It interprets how issues fit within the Constitution. The Court's decisions have major ramifications for the rest of the legal order. Three models explain decisions of the U.S. Supreme Court (see Summary 9.4).

A pure legal model, in which the Court only uses neutral reasoning and precedent, is the least accurate. Studies suggest that, "support for this most fundamental of all legal decisions [*Stare Decisis*] remains extremely low."[60] Beyond their official rulings, Supreme Court justices can advance a political agenda through their discretion in selecting which cases to hear, by answering legal questions not raised by the parties before them, and by disregarding issues that the parties want to argue.[61] The Court is influenced by the political views of the president, who appoints justices, by senators, who must approve Court appointees, and by an awareness that other government agencies must implement its decisions and that the U.S. Congress can overturn Court decisions.[62] Court decisions tend to reflect changes in public opinion and the ideological orientation

SUMMARY 9.4	Three Models That Explain U.S. Supreme Court Decision-Making

- A **pure legal model** holds that Supreme Court decisions are governed by abstract reasoning in an autonomous, neutral legal system. Justices decide based on stare decisis (i.e., legal precedent) and apply neutral legal principles insulated from external political pressures and the personal views of individual judges. The model flows from the myth of legality and "those who adhere to the myth of legality expect Supreme Court justices to transcend ordinary political pressures to render decisions in an atmosphere of detachment and objectivity" (Scheb and Lyons 2000, 931).
- The **attitudinal model** holds that justices are insulated from external pressures but confronted with ambiguous legal principles and a myriad of contradictory precedents. This frees justices to apply their personal ideological views in rulings. They hide personal beliefs in obtuse legal language and bolster them with selected precedents.
- A **public mood model** holds that Supreme Court decisions generally reflect mass public opinion. Perhaps after a time lag, and more on some issues than on others, the Court is responsive to electoral politics and shifts in public mood. In addition, there is feedback because Supreme Court decisions have the effect of shifting public attention to major issues, rearranging political influence, and altering the rules of political conflicts.

Sources: Attitude model—Mishler and Sheehan (1996) and Segal and Spaeth (1993). Public mood model—Canon (1992) and Flemming, Bohte, and Wood (1997).

of the president and Congress. In periods of electoral realignment, the Court lags behind the public and tends to legitimate groups with more social– economic power.[63] Since 1981, the Court has become more politicized. It reflects public opinion less and has instead leaned toward a conservative ideology, most likely because of political factors in the appointment process.[64] For example, opinion poll data show strong public support for environmental protection but the Court has upheld few environmental cases. Nonetheless, the public continues to support the Court strongly.[65]

Court decisions can reverberate throughout the economy, society, and politics. They set forth legal principles that are largely accepted as irreversible. Court rulings define private property, alter how the market economy operates, set the basis for marriage, and establish new employer–employee rights.[66] For example, rulings on labor law cases have shaped the legal rights of workers by putting limits on labor militancy and upholding employer authority.[67] This is how the legal order establishes the parameters of labor–management power struggles and the boundaries of state power.

CRIME AND COERCIVE STATE POWER

Among major forms of nation-state power, is coercive power. **Coercive state power is the control and application of organized violence, backed by formal authority, to cajole, compel, or coerce the population to obey laws and con-**

form to the established political–economic order. Specialized agencies enforce obedience to law, monitor behavior, intercede in personal affairs, apprehend law violators, and incarcerate or impose punishments on the disobedient. In the United States, about 660,000 state and local, and 74,000 federal law enforcement officers (e.g., police, sheriffs, marshals) carry weapons and make arrests. They are backed by 200,000 civilian police personnel, over a 1 million staff in the judiciary and corrections, and ultimately by the National Guard and military.[68] Armed officers who use violence, handcuffs, or prison cells are the physical reality of the concept of coercive power.

Law enforcement officials compel conformity to the law, and most people display compliance and give at least an appearance of obedience. People engage in behavioral strategies to satisfy their desires while appearing to obey the law.[69] Actual law enforcement is shaped by resource limitations, organizational effectiveness, and political priorities. Law enforcement officers rarely threaten physical violence, but their ability to enforce law ultimately rests on the state's monopoly over organized violence. If they are unable to exercise legal authority over a territory (e.g., an inner city neighborhood, a remote rural area), the state has lost de facto sovereignty over that area.

Crime is not easy to define. Not all law violations are crimes, and crime takes many forms. Crime is a violation of criminal law (i.e., laws to uphold the social–political order, and prevent harm to others and their property), and its violation is associated with a penalty. Both individuals and organizations can break the law. Individuals may violate law by failing to purchase a license for a dog, driving too fast, not paying taxes, paying someone for sexual relations, or sleeping drunk on a park bench. A corporation may violate law by hiring illegal aliens, failing to pay the minimum wage, dumping toxic wastes, bribing a factory inspector, or conspiring with competitors to fix prices.

Crimes are committed for many reasons. Some crime is not due to immoral or evil behavior per se but to correcting a moral wrong that is outside the state's legal processes. People may live by moral codes older than the state's written laws, and these can exist beside written laws. Sometimes the moral codes and their enforcement are consistent with written, official law; when they are not, people may commit self-help crime. **Self-help crime occurs when a person, family, or friends try to remedy an injury or loss to property, person, or honor by going outside of the legal order.** An example of self-help crime is retaliatory homicide—a killing in retaliation for what people view as an injustice in their local cultural context. Self-help crime occurs when one man cheats another to win a game of cards and the cheated man beats up the winner, or when an older sister goes after the people who attacked her younger sister with a knife, causing serious injury. The cheated man and the older sister feel that what they did is fair and that they are restoring moral justice, but the state's legal order defines their actions as crime.[70]

Street Crime

Crime comes in many forms—white-collar, corporate, political, hate, tax, organized, victimless, and so forth. The media, the public, and law enforcement

focus on street crime (i.e., illegal acts of interpersonal violence or property theft or destruction committed by individuals). Yet, nonstreet crimes actually cause more total financial loss and personal injury.[71] The assumptions behind street crime are that we all understand and agree on what is morally right and wrong, we know what is legal and illegal, and we try to obey the law. Reality does not match these assumptions. In reality, people agree only on vague moral principles, are often unsure of exactly what is illegal, and violate some laws sometimes. If they know the law, they may decide whether to obey it or not, but often they do not know the law.[72]

Street crime is explained using four factors:

1. Structural—Socioeconomic conditions and forces such as racism or unemployment as the cause of crime.
2. Subcultural—Crime is caused by a community's or group's values that differ from the mainstream.
3. Rational—Crime is based on a cost/benefit calculation of opportunities for gain versus punishment for getting caught.
4. Volition or individual pathology—Crime occurs when people are willing to use any method for personal gain, have evil motives, or lack personal morality.

In the United States, volition is the most popular explanation, followed by rational decision then subcultural factors. Americans rarely embrace a structural explanation because it could require reexamining inequalities of wealth and power and contradict deeply held cultural beliefs.

Political sociologists are less interested in explaining the causes of crime than in examining the processes by which the state criminalizes actions and people. They ask, Why does the state classify some acts as illegal, and how does it respond to people it classifies as actual or potential lawbreakers? They recognize that crime is "a condensation symbol expressing a variety of public anxieties about seemingly intractable structural problems."[73]

Public (Mis)Perceptions of Crime

In an ideal democracy, public policy would reflect the desires of most citizens and all citizens would be well informed. Yet many people are misinformed about crime. Most people believe that crime rates are constantly rising, violent crime is increasing the fastest, a tiny part of the population commits most crimes, most offenders are repeaters, and most offenders on parole are repeat offends.[74] The media, inflammatory politicians, and self-serving public agencies amplify these misperceptions. Some are repeated so frequently that people believe them to be inevitable. Messner and Rosenfeld (1994, 4) noted, "The pervasive fear of crime observed in the United States is not an inevitable feature of modern, industrial societies. On the contrary, it is a distinctly American phenomenon." Fear and misperception affect processes of law enforcement as well (see Case in Point 9.1).

During the 1980s, many U.S. politicians and much of the public shifted their thinking about crime and reversed a 200-year trend of crime policy. Instead of rehabilitation, they demanded far harsher punishments for criminals and felt a need for "... imposing more controls, increasing disincentives, and, if necessary, segregating the dangerous sector of the population" (Garland

---

 CASE IN POINT 9.1   **Misperceptions about Crime**

An illustration of misperceptions about crime is in the policy area of immigration. For over a century, many in the U.S. public saw a link between immigration and crime. For example, a 1996 survey found that one-third of respondents believed that immigrants increased crime (calculated by the author from the National Opinion Research Center's General Social Survey, 1996). Such perceptions have fueled demands for stricter immigration controls and were reflected in the 1996 Illegal Immigration Report and Immigrant Responsibility Act. The 1996 federal law greatly increased the budget and enforcement staff of the Immigration and Naturalization Service. Yet much of the public outcry was based on misperceptions. After they adjusted arrest and imprisonment rates for the age and sex of immigrants, researchers found that immigrants are actually less likely to commit crimes than the general U.S. population. At the same time, differential treatment of immigrants by the criminal justice system increases the odds of their conviction and imprisonment over that of U.S. citizens. The increased immigration control measures and hasher policy may have been based on unacknowledged racial and anti-immigrant beliefs, alarmist political rhetoric, and a misunderstanding of the facts.

Source: Hagan and Palloni (1999).

2001, 102). Nonetheless, Kevin Smith (1997, 363) noted that these, "politically popular options for dealing with violent crime are by and large not achieving their policy objectives." Studies find little evidence that harsh punishment deters criminal behavior and reduces crime. In fact, they may have the opposite effect.[75] Moreover, "Disregarding evidence that crime does not readily respond to severe sentences, or new police powers, or a greater use of imprisonment, legislatures have readily adopted a punitive 'law and order stance'" (Garland 2001, 132). It appears that popular emotions, politics, and cultural beliefs about crime—more than any objective, factual analysis—has shaped public beliefs and crime control policies. Crime policy became highly politicized, and ". . . since the 1970s, a quite different set of criminological ideas has begun to emerge to influence government policy" (Garland 2001, 15). In the new thinking, crime is not caused by individual deprivation or societal problems; rather, crime arises from insufficiently stringent state control over unruly parts of the population. A complementary idea is the need for harsher punishment. These punitive views are not shared equally by all parts of society, and there is a persistent gender division toward crime that parallels the electoral gender gap.[76]

CONTROL AND SURVEILLANCE

Sociologists have long discussed and elaborated on the concept of social control. It refers to internal self-regulation in society, often through informal social means, and is distinguished from coercive control, or an imposed control that is associated with threat.[77] A state can use both kinds of control, but it mostly uses coercive control through various informal and formal mechanisms to uphold laws, maintain order, and oversee the population. Political sociologists focus on the state's formal mechanisms and monitoring of the population. This includes state officials watching people, imposing fines, putting people in prison, or taking an offender's life.

The legal order and state control system are shaped by other social institutions and cultural values that can have distant historical origins. For example, the rapid expansion into the frontier lands of the United States during the nineteenth century with a weak state spawned a vigilante form of crime control. Vigilantism occurs when private citizens "take the law into their own hands" or administer justice outside a formal state-sanctioned legal structure. This was common in parts of the American Wild West and the South until 1900. Little and Sheffield (1983, 804) noted, "Usually led by men of wealth, property and influence, vigilante movements tended to uphold those with the greatest stake in the status quo." Vigilantism cultivates certain values toward policing, law enforcement, and crime control—great responsiveness to popular desires, vague moral standards, and few limits on the methods of enforcement.[78] Eventually, a formal state-organized policing system developed in urban areas and spread in the twentieth century.

Policing

The police are state actors devoted to routine behavior control and "internal pacification." Most police operate at the local level to maintain social order and enforce laws. Historically, their purpose has varied from forcing religious observance, to enforcing residency requirements, to overseeing labor-management conflicts.[79] "One important difference among police systems," Bayley (1975, 361) noted, "is the extent to which police tasks include an active role in political life as opposed to preoccupation primarily with prevention of crime and maintenance of public order." In the mid-nineteenth century, local governments of most industrial cities created police forces. Next we examine how political sociologists see police at the local, state, and national levels.

Local Police

The modern local police can be traced to a mixture of private night watchmen and constables in London in 1829. The number of local police officers rapidly grew at the end of the nineteenth century, especially in cities. Between 1860 and 1915, the number of police officers relative to the size of the population doubled in the United States. For example, the Chicago police force grew from about 500 officers, or 1 per every 1,000 citizens in 1880, to over 4,500, or 1 per every 528 citizens in 1915. Police growth in this period was caused by a series of violent strikes and ethnic conflicts due to the rapid inflow of immigrants, not by rising crime rates.[80] In the era prior to labor laws, strikers were labeled as criminals and the police defended factory owner interests.[81] The police also regulated the recent immigrants' lifestyles and leisure activities that traditional elites saw as objectionable or immoral (e.g., drinking, gambling). During the twentieth century, the racial composition of a city, the city tax revenue, and local politics influenced the growth in police force size more than changes in crime rates.[82] In short, political demands and available resources produced police growth more than crime rates. For example, in 1980, Proposition 13 forced large local tax cuts in California. Many cities reduced spending on parks and recreation, but spending on the police rose; local politics not crime determined whether or not spending on police grew.[83]

Today, a typical local police officer averages about one arrest per week and devotes most of his/her time to regulating, supervising, watching, and socializing other people.[84] Police officers rarely use violence, and the nature of police work varies greatly by neighborhood and the area's level of local conflict, crime, and social class. Most people assume that police use violence defensively, in response to violent people they encounter. However, political factors better explain levels of police violence. In the United States, police use of violence is highest in locales with greater racial inequality and a rising black population, and lower in cities with black mayors. Police use of violence is higher where racial groups compete economically and fight for political influence.[85] Jacobs and O'Brien (1998, 860) concluded, "police use of lethal force varies with the degree of inequality between races, the presence of blacks, and local political arrangements that increase black control over the behavior of law enforcement."

State Police

State police forces were established in the late nineteenth century to contain strikes and industrial disputes. They worked with state militias to quell social unrest, but the state militia were "federalized" into the National Guard with the Dick Act (1903) and placed under the federal government.[86] Today's state police forces are mini-armies that exceed 2,500 officers in six states.[87] A state's politics and traditions better than its population or crime rate predict the size of a state police force. For example, Delaware has more state police officers than Wisconsin (561 versus 495), but Wisconsin's population is seven times greater. Vermont, which has the lowest violent crime rate, has four times more state police officers per 10,000 people than does Florida, which has the highest violent crime rate.[88]

Federal Police

Many countries have national police forces. The U.S. federal government created a secret service in 1865, but its first real federal police force began in 1908 with the Bureau of Investigation in the Department of Justice. In 1924, the president appointed J. Edgar Hoover (1895–1972) as director of what he renamed the Federal Bureau of Investigation (FBI). Hoover was repeatedly reappointed until his death. Today the FBI has over 7,000 special agents and is responsible for investigating federal crimes; coordinating local crime control; and overseeing internal security matters, including espionage, terrorism, treason, and sedition. Until the Homeland Security Department began operation in January, 2003 and consolidated parts of 22 agencies, federal policing was scattered across many agencies (e.g., Immigration, Border Patrol, Customs, Drug Enforcement Administration).

Symbolic Meaning of the Police

Policing has instrumental and symbolic dimensions; that is, the police accomplish tasks and convey symbolic messages. Most discussions focus on the instrumental dimension and on how police operations can be fairer and more efficient, but the police are also a cultural category with rituals and symbols (e.g., ceremonies of booking offenders, uniforms, cars, handcuffs). The core symbolic meaning of police is guardianship. The police appear as a force of order, good, and authority and defenders against an "other" that represents aggression, violence, and disorder. As Ian Loader (1997, 8) observed, ". . . the idea of policing brings to mind (and stomach) sensations of order, authority and protection; it makes possible for people to believe that a powerful force for good stands between them and an anarchic word, that the state is willing to defend its citizens."

The state defends the social order and protects "good citizens" from threats to person or property through policing. A "police voice" is presented in the media and in public documents. It is an official authoritative representation of crime events, including images and a vocabulary to classify, judge, and condemn certain behaviors. Dramatic media portrayals of the police (e.g., in novels, television, film) and the iconography of police work (e.g., fingerprinting, riot shields, helicopters) communicate the symbolic message that police will oversee and contain dangerous, risky, uncertain, and fragile areas of social reality. By defining and containing the chaotic, unsafe areas of social reality, the promise of policing is protection, security, and comfort for the citizenry.[89]

Militarization of the Police

Traditionally the police are separate from the military. The police operate under local supervision, work alone or in small units, maintain community order, follow the law, and interact closely with ordinary citizens. They have minimal weapons that they only use in extreme situations. The military are under national control, organized into large units, protect national resources or borders by combating foreign aggressors, and use sophisticated weapons and intense violence. Democratic nations do not direct military force against their own civilians, except in unusual situations of large-scale unrest or civil war.

During the 1980s War on Drugs in the United States, police and military cooperation increased as did the use of deadly weapons and military tactics by police. **The militarization of police refers to a transfer of military surveillance and weapons technology; military combat and operational tactics; and military language, training, and orientation to local police forces and increased police–military cooperation in ways that blur internal and external security functions.** In a political climate of near hysteria over uncontrollable violent crime, politicians called for drastic measures. Simultaneously, the military needed to justify its sophisticated technology and make itself useful with the end of the Cold War and the "menace of communism." These factors combined to spur militarization. Also, the War on Drugs called for military involvement to intercept drugs crossing U.S. borders or into other countries. After the 2001 World Trade Center attack, police militarization accelerated.

Militarization has symbolic-ideological and practical-instrumental dimensions. Symbolically, police borrow a way of talking and thinking about crime from the military. Kraska (1999, 209) noted, "Metaphors play a powerful role in the construction of reality: they shape discursive practices, clarify values and understanding, and guide problem solving processes. Military crime and drug problems through militaristic metaphors . . . result in thoughts and actions which correspond to the military/war paradigm." Instrumentally, local police get military-based technology, training, and organizational forms.[90] By 1995, 89 percent of U.S. police departments serving communities of 50,000 or more had paramilitary units; this was double the percentage in 1980. Calls for using paramilitary units grew tenfold from 1980 to 1995.[91] Special Weapons and Tactics (SWAT) teams have been normalized into mainstay policing as high-status, elite units with militaristic cultures and a preoccupation with danger.[92] SWAT teams in battle-dress uniforms use equipment designed for military combat and military-style communications. They promote a military culture and encourage local police to see some citizens as hostile enemies in military terms. Yet SWAT team use is unrelated to reduced crime.[93] Some political sociologists see police militarization as a dangerous trend that may represent a "historical shift in the nature of the state" toward a "garrison state" or form of police state.[94]

Crime Control

Crime control is more than policing; it involves assumptions about the causes of crime, criminal law and enforcement practices, and responses to law violation. The models of political sociology see crime control differently. Because pluralists see crime as based on rational decisions rooted in individual preferences with a calculation of costs (i.e., odds of getting caught and severity of punishment) versus benefits (i.e., achieving a criminal goal of theft or sustaining injury). Controlling crime requires law enforcement resources and police efficiency that can alter a criminal's decision-making equation and raise the "cost" of criminal activity.[95] The other political sociology models hold that power-holders shape what gets defined as criminal behavior and modes of crime control, and that law enforcement is largely directed to contain actions or people that threaten the social-economic hierarchy or power holders. Modes of crime control depend on alternatives to prison and the ideology of politically activated groups. Crime policy depends on political forces that shape the criminalization processes and systems of law enforcement and control.

Capital Punishment

Only two advanced democracies, the United States and Japan, impose the death penalty for nonwartime crimes. In 2001, over 3,700 prisoners in the United States were under a death sentence and 98 were executed. Japan had 44 prisoners under a death sentence and 3 were executed. Since 1976, when the Supreme Court legalized capital punishment after a 10 year hiatus, the United States executed 687 persons.[96] Virtually all of Africa, Asia, and Eastern Europe use capital punishment, but it is nonexistent in Western Europe and Scandinavia. In the Americas, only six former British Caribbean colonies[97] and three other nations (Chile, Cuba, and Guatemala) endorse capital punishment.[98] In the decentralized U.S. system, state governments carry out most executions. Since 1976, 38 of the 50 U.S. states and the federal government accepted capital punishment. Ten states carry out 83 percent of the executions and 8 of these 10 were Confederate States during the Civil War. Public support for the death penalty in the United States has grown rapidly since 1980, and currently about 70 percent of U.S. citizens support it. Despite this broad support, "Those most likely to support the death penalty are white males with less than a college degree . . . [and] political conservatives who identify with the Republican party and reside outside of urban areas."[99] Most people's reasons for supporting the death penalty are nonrational (i.e., their political and cultural–moral beliefs) (see Closer Look 9.2).[100]

Death penalty opponents object on moral-human rights grounds and cite legal flaws, high costs, racial bias, and the execution of innocent people. They note that 80 percent of the 682 defendants charged with capital offenses from

CLOSER LOOK 9.2   **Why Do Many Americans Support the Death Penalty?**

Local context is a powerful predictor of American attitudes toward the death penalty. Support is higher in areas with high local homicide rates, but homicide is itself caused by a breakdown of community. More than objective conditions, people's political values and ideological beliefs are critical. Baumer, Messner, and Rosenfeld (2003, 868) found that, "the results are consistent with suggestions that conservative politicians exploit concerns about crime in a manner that effectively increases support for punitive policies, even among those who do not hold a conservative ideology themselves . . . independent of levels of violence, the political context in which social problems are framed has an important influence on public sentiment about capital punishment . . . such as exposure to political initiatives or media coverage of crime and punishment, or indirectly through collective socialization processes whereby some elements of conservative ideology (e.g., support for capital punishment), but not others, become contagious and spread throughout the community. . . . [Also] we found that % black exhibits a significant positive effect on support for the death penalty. . . ." In short, a more conservative political climate increases public support for the

death penalty support, and among whites, so does a having large number of black people living in an area. In addition to local context factors, death penalty support is encouraged by a normative acceptance of certain beliefs or attitudes. When pressed, Americans now offer beliefs in vengeance rather than retribution as a justification. Haas (1994, 133) explained the difference between these beliefs, "Vengeance is . . . an unmeasured infliction of punishment on the offender . . . aimed at satisfying the victim's and society's desire for retaliation, and it is not limited by considerations of desert, proportionality, fairness or equality. Retribution . . . is a measured infliction of punishment that is imposed by the courts and based on careful consideration of the severity of the offense and the offender's blameworthiness and deservedness. It is rooted in the . . . belief that a civilized society must set moral limits on the amount of punishment. . . ." In an analysis U.S. Supreme Court decisions Haas (1994, 146) found that, like the American public, the Court's justification for applying the death penalty changed over time, and by the 1990s, it "embraced vengeance—not retribution—as the primary social justification for imposing the punishment of death."

1995–2000 were racial minorities. A 1987 U.S. Supreme Court decision (*McCleskey v. Kemp*) ruled that claims of a racial bias in death penalty cases were not sufficient to demonstrate unconstitutional discrimination. Justice Lewis Powell stated, "If we accepted McCleskey's claim that racial bias has impermissibly tainted the capital sentencing decision, we could soon be faced with similar claims as to other types of penalty." Academic research has documented a clear racial bias in use of the penalty, but in 2001, the U.S. Justice Department claimed there is no such bias.[101]

The United States is one of a handful of nations in the world to execute offenders for crimes they committed before reaching adulthood (18 years old) and offenders who suffer from mental illness or mental retardation. Since 1990, seven nations have legally executed prisoners who were under 18 years old at the time of the crime. They include the Democratic Republic of Congo, Iran, Nigeria, Pakistan, Saudi Arabia, the United States, and Yemen. The greatest number of nonadult offenders (15) was in the United States. A recent study found that many juveniles charged as adults in the United States do not understand legal matters, and their level of understanding is similar to that of a mentally ill adult who would be declared incompetent to stand trial.[102] In Texas alone, 25 people were on death row for crimes committed prior to adulthood, and 23 of those 25 people are non-White.[103]

The death penalty is not applied carefully in the United States. Courts invalidated most (68 percent) of death penalty sentences because the convictions contained serious legal flaws. Also, convicted people have been found to be innocent. Of people executed in the United States since 1900, 26 were later found to be innocent.[104] This happens because police and prosecutors are anxious to get convictions in murder cases. In over 300 cases, it was later learned that police and prosecutors had concealed evidence or presented false evidence to get a conviction. Most people convicted of murder get court-appointed defense lawyers, many who are often seriously underpaid or professionally incompetent.[105]

The opposition to capital punishment is substantial. The leading organization of lawyers in the United States—the American Bar Association—called for a moratorium on executions in 1997. In 1999 the National Council of Catholic Bishops called for ending capital punishment, and most religious groups question it.[106] The international trend is clear: In 1965, 11 nations stopped using the death penalty; by 1999, 105 had stopped. "The most glaring exception to the emerging international consensus on the death penalty is the United States. As other Western democracies have condemned and abandoned it, America has defended it with increasing vigor."[107]

Prisons

Incarceration is a less severe form of crime control. Here too, recent U.S. experience differs from other advanced countries and its own past. After remaining nearly constant from 1925 to 1973, U.S. incarceration rates quadrupled; and nearly 12 percent of the male population has been found guilty of a felony.[108] In testimony before the U.S. Commissioner on Civil Rights, Marc Mauer (2003, 2) noted, "the U.S. rate of incarceration of 702 inmates per 100,000 populations represented not only a record high, but situates this nation as the world leader in its use of imprisonment . . . the U.S. now locks up its citizens at a rate 5–8 times that of the industrialized nations to which we are most similar, Canada and western Europe." Rates of incarceration per 100,000 in other countries are as follows: Canada 116, Spain 125, England and Wales 139, Germany 91, France 85, and Sweden 73. Mauer continued (2003, 6–7), "There is little evidence to indicate that changes in crime have been the driving force in expanding the prison population . . . the unprecedented prison population increase of recent years is explained not by crime rates but by changes in sentencing and drug policy." Beckett and Sasson (2000, 9) observed, "In some countries, persons guilty of public intoxication or drug possession are largely ignored or diverted into treatment programs. In the United States, they are more likely to be arrested and incarcerated." In the past 30 years, violent crime rates, especially for murder, and overall property crime rates declined, only drug crimes grew. The dramatic shift in public attitudes in the 1980s, new statutes, changed law enforcement practices, and new sentencing policies have caused imprisonment rates to rise by almost 400 percent.

Public attitudes in the United States became much more punishment-oriented or punitive. For example, support for the death penalty rose from 38 percent in 1965 to 71 percent in 1999. Flanagan (1996b, 82) found that "public support for rehabilitation as the superordinate goal of prisons declined precipitously during the past quarter century." Today, only about 10 percent of prisoners with histories of substance abuse get drug treatment in U.S. prisons.[109] Political conservatives oppose drug rehabilitation, and among conservatives, opposition is associated with anti-welfare state attitudes, punitive beliefs on crime, and anti-black racial prejudice among whites.[110] U.S. prison officials have increasingly lowered food quality, reduced exercise opportunities, and cut television privileges to maximize the punishment impact of prison. In sum, "the United States is not content with depriving criminals of their freedom . . . it also seems bent on doing all it can to make their lives more miserable."[111]

Since the 1970s, the crime control framework in the U.S. shifted away from penal welfarism to a retributivist model. **In a penal welfarism model, crime is seen as caused by individual deficiencies, and the focus is on rehabilitating offenders and preparing them for a return to society.** Criminal justice specialists develop individualized correction programs to treat specific offenders. **In a retributivist model, crime is understood to be a "normal" societal condition, and the focus is on managing its level; instead of rehabilitating, reintegrating, or assisting offenders; they are segregated, excluded, and punished.** In the U.S., the retributivist model works a preventive partnership with the profit-making private sector and a sovereign state strategy of intensified authoritative control and expressive forms of punishment. Garland (2001, 3, 102) explained this process, "The last three decades have seen an accelerating movement away from the assumptions that shaped crime control and criminal justice for most of the twentieth century. The central agencies of the modern criminal justice state have undergone quite radical shifts in their working practices and organizational missions. . . . Instead of idealism and humanity, penal policy discussions increasingly evoked cynicism about rehabilitative treatment, a distrust of penological experts, and a new righteousness about the importance and efficacy of punishment." For example, in a three-year period in the early 1980s, antidrug funds going to federal government agencies to provide education, treatment, and rehabilitation dropped from 53 percent to 11 percent, while funds going to law enforcement agencies (the FBI, Drug Enforcement Administration, and Department of Defense) increased by 89 percent.[112] People were being arrested and sent to prison with much longer sentences for actions that previously were not considered to be serious.

The upsurge in imprisonment affects different sections of the population differently. Low-income racial minorities are most likely to be arrested and imprisoned. This is not a simple function of their violating laws more often than middle and upper income whites. Illegal drug use (e.g., marijuana, cocaine) by high-school youth varies little by race.[113] During the 1980s, penalties were increased for laws that low-income minorities tended to violate, their likelihood of being detected and caught by police increased, and judges required more prison time. Arrest rates became more racially unbalanced. For example, in 1980 police arrested white and black youths for drug offenses at the same rate. Ten years later, blacks arrest rates were five times higher than white arrest rates.[114] States with higher percentages of racial minorities have higher drug arrest rates.[115] After the changes in sentencing in the 1980s, blacks received sentences that were 49 percent longer than whites received for similar crimes.[116] The U.S. prison population is darkening; the percentage of white state and federal prisoners dropped from 59 percent in 1974 to 21 percent in 1999.[117] By the 1990s, 1 in 4 young (20–29 year old), African American males was in jail, prison, or on probation or parole.[118]

Imprisonment has destroyed the lives of millions, but other individuals, communities, and companies have gained from high imprisonment rates and have developed a vested economic interest in having more people imprisoned for longer periods. State-government prison and correction spending grew nearly tenfold from 1980 to 1999, while the total number of people employed in corrections increased from 1.27 million in 1980 to 2.2 million in 1999.[119] Prison building has been a kind of economic development for depressed communities. It creates business for construction companies, jobs as correctional personnel, demand for the companies that supply certain products (prison beds, prison food), and benefits for the new for-profit prison companies. The amounts of money involved are huge. Soap alone costs $100,000 a year for the New York City jail system. The prison telephone market generates $1 billion per year for phone companies, since prisoners must call their families collect and use the phone company that the prison system selects.[120] In addition, 1,310 industries now operate in the U.S. prison system, generating $1.6 billion in sales as prisoners make shoes, gloves, false teeth, parts for Boeing aircraft, and logos for Lexus autos, and do telemarketing.[121] Prisoners receive 25 cents to $1.15 per hour for labor that companies pay the prison officials $5 to $7 per hour for.[122] More than calls to reinstate chain gangs have created reminders of prison systems of the distant past (see Case in Point 9.2).

Increased imprisonment and new policies elevated private, for-profit prisons. In 1985, fewer than 1,000 prisoners were in private prisons. By 1999, they housed 138,000 prisoners.[123] Eighty percent of prisoners in private prisons are in correctional facilities owned by just two companies.[124] Some question the morality and ethics of delegating coercive state authority that deprives citizens of liberty to for-profit companies.[125] Private prison advocates offer an ideological defense of minimum-sized government, although their claims of government cost savings are not always valid.[126]

Expanded incarceration has created a criminal justice–industrial system or **prison-industrial complex, which is a mutually reinforcing set of powerful bureaucratic, economic, and political interests that depend on continued high incarceration rates for their success.** The complex lobbies for more prisons irrespective of whether imprisonment improves public safety, reduces crime, or

| CASE IN POINT 9.2 | Convict Labor and Social Control of Blacks in the Post-Civil War South |

Sometimes history presents us with haunting parallels to current conditions. One instance is the relationship between the dramatic shift in corrections policy in the contemporary United States. After the American Civil War, a big problem for the whites who ran local and state government in the post-Reconstruction South was how to control the large numbers of black ex-slaves. In some states, ex-slaves made up as much as 50 percent of the population. In the chaos and disruption of the period, many roamed the countryside destitute and impoverished, facing frequent arrests for vagrancy or petty theft. Others became tenant farmers or sharecroppers who did not always obey white landowners or pay their debts. Local governments were very poor and needed a low-cost way to control this "dangerous population." At the same time, white business and landowners sought low-cost labor to replace slaves. The contract convict labor system "solved" these overlapping concerns. It allowed local law enforcement officials to arrest, briefly imprison, then contract out, or lease, convicted blacks to work for whites. Blacks could get sentences of hard labor for "crimes" of vagrancy, spitting,

swearing, or trespassing. New laws imposed 3- to 10-year sentences for stealing a few chickens or something worth 10 dollars. In several Southern states, the prisoner population grew by as much as 300 percent in a few years, and blacks made up as much as 95 percent of the Southern prison population. Convict labor became an important revenue source for state and local governments. Black and white convicts were separated and treated differently. The conditions for black convict laborers were similar to those of slavery, with slave job classifications and whippings for disobedience. Most female convicts worked as household domestics or field hands. Male convicts worked in the fields, built railroads, and worked in mines and construction. For about 30 years, the convict lease system solved labor shortage and discipline problems for Southern whites. In conjunction with lynching, it reimposed white authority and supremacy over blacks. "The convict lease system was an economic substitute for slavery, but also a political replacement, insofar as it helped to redefine the boundaries of the South on the basis of color" (Adamson 1983, 567).

Sources: Adamson (1983), Myers and Massey (1991), and Myers (1990). Clarke (1998), Crozine, Creech, and Crozine (1983), Crozine, Huff-Crozine, and Creech (1988). Tolnay, Beck and Massey (1989, 1992) argue that lynching is associated with both black-white economic competition and black threats to white political power. Massey and Myers (1989) found no relation among lynching, incarceration, and legal executions in Georgia in this period.

renders justice.[127] Increased prison spending has reduced spending for social services and higher education.[128] Dyer (2000, 6) argues that cuts in social programs and welfare to pay to prisons may ultimately increase incarceration, "Because much of the funding for corrections is now coming at the expense of social programs that have been shown to deter people from criminal behavior . . . the more prisoners whose incarceration we pay for through this diversion of funds, the more future prisoners we create."

Why Did U.S. Crime Policy Change?

Political sociologists developed three explanations for the shift toward punitive attitudes and prison growth: (1) labor market, (2) moral panic, and (3) political institutions. Next we consider each.[129]

Labor Market Model

The labor market model uses a structuralist political sociology model. Its 1939 original form, **the Rushe-Kirchheimer thesis says that a relationship exists between the demand for labor and changes in incarceration rates, such that an excess of unemployed workers who may be disruptive and sufficient state financial capacity produce increased imprisonment rates.**[130] The state removes and incarcerates a portion of the surplus working class population to contain a potentially disruptive, nonproductive segment of society. This also diverts public attention from economic issues and imposes discipline on the working class through state-backed intimidation.

Results on the Rushe-Kirchheimer thesis have been mixed.[131] Refined research found that specific labor market conditions matter and deindustrialized areas with economic distress had higher arrest rates.[132] High unemployment has a strong effect on rising property crime rates, and in competitive labor markets is associated with imprisonment rates.[133] Also, a demographic increase in young people and growing economic inequality were linked to imprisonment rates and police expansion.[134] Young people are less integrated into the labor force, more likely to be unemployed, and likely to cause social disruption. Inequality may be associated because official control agencies often protect the wealthy. According to Jacobs and Helms (1997, 1367), "If the police are weakened, the affluent are much more likely to be victimized . . . the police act as a buffer to contain street crime and other threats to the public order within the least affluent areas [and] . . . elites should reap substantial benefits from police departments that are strong enough to protect them from underclass violence." Other studies found unemployment associated with substitutes for imprisonment, such as welfare programs and changes in crime laws.[135] Other empirical support comes from findings that state-level imprisonment rates from 1880 to 1920 changed primarily due to the availability of state resources.[136] Prisoner populations grew slower where politics blocked prison construction and where substitutes to prison (e.g., rehabilitation programs, parole, community service) were available. When political forces blocked substitutes to prison, then prison became the main resource available to state officials trying to control a potentially disruptive population. Rates of imprisonment increase after an election and with the success by the Republican Party.[137] Thus, "incarceration is intrinsically political . . . incarceration is one method the modern state uses to manage latent political conflict created by economic cleavages . . . conservative shifts in the political climate are likely to produce punitive reactions to crime."[138] Consistent with the structuralist model, conscious elite actions are not required.[139] In a cross-national study of imprisonment, Sutton (2004, 183) found that, "strong unions and social democratic parties exert political influence in support of a range of ameliorative social policies, including less punitive response to crime." He concluded that political institutional factors that also shaped economic conditions, more than economic conditions alone, determine imprisonment rates. In sum, as the U.S. economy deindustrialized during the 1970s, imprisonment grew to control the surplus working class population because a coalition of elites promoted punitive attitudes and blocked more humane rehabilitation-oriented alternatives.

Moral Panic Model

The moral panic model combines the elite model with constructionist theory to emphasize the War on Drugs and a politicization of street crime.[140] Moral panics are responses to a belief in a "boundary crisis" in the social-moral order that is not triggered by objective conditions but by new public perceptions (also see Chapter 12).[141] Beckett and Sasson (2000, 4–5) argue that, ". . . conservative politicians, together with the mass media and activists in the victims rights movement, have kept the issue of crime at the top of the nation's political agenda. Focusing on the most sensational and violent crimes, these actors have promoting policies aimed at 'getting tough' and 'cracking down.' As a result, the criminal justice system has become more punitive, and its scope and expense are now unparalleled. . . ."

Conservative elites who fought against the values of the civil rights movement and 1960s youth culture felt a boundary crisis. They mobilized politically to amplify fears of a social breakdown and to push "law and order" to the top of the political agenda as part of their broader political mobilization around conservative goals.[142] Rural whites, religious fundamentalists, and strong Republicans were receptive to the law-and-order message, but the message was not enough alone.[143] The Safe Streets and Crime Control Act (1968) signaled a push to shift criminal justice. By 1980, Republican Party strategists advocated ending the "welfare state" (i.e., cutting programs and services to poor blacks) and replacing it with a "security state" (i.e., control black street crime). About the same time, poor blacks began to consume cocaine differently (i.e., crack), creating a link between taking drugs and street crime. This allowed conservative elites to shift their law-and-order efforts into a moral crusade that demonized drug users.

By the mid-1980s, elites in government, law enforcement, the media, and business had joined the anti-drug war.[144] Leaders in both political parties found that drug war rhetoric attracted voters, law enforcement elites discovered that it increased staff and budgets, media elites found that sensationalizing violent drug crime had entertainment value, which attracted viewers and brought in advertising revenue. Ferrell (1999, 406) observed, "Working within organizational imperatives of efficiency and routinization, media institutions regularly rely on data selectively provided by policing and court agencies . . . [and] highlight the public issues chosen by criminal justice institutions . . . ." Business elites found that dramatizing crime helped to sell security services, equipment, background checks, and real estate. A few local elites resisted politicizing crime and the moral panic in their local areas because they felt it would divide the community by race, weaken the image of a community, and raise taxes for law enforcement.[145] Even in these areas, national publicity about crime, drugs, and violence dominated local news.[146]

With street crime at the top of the agenda, public attention to other issues declined. Scheingold (1991, 173) noted, "To politicize crime is, in short, to divert attention from structural reforms, which are costly and divisive, to volition response, which are much less costly and encourage society to close its ranks against deviants." The "race coded" moral panic diverted attention from other government actions (e.g., aiding corporate deindustrialization, cutting most social programs, weakening labor and environmental laws, reducing health and consumer safety regulations, giving tax cuts to the wealthy). "Street crime," Scheingold (1995, 165) observed, "offers a way to channel public anger and anxiety away from amorphous social and economic threats and toward criminals. . . ."

Political Institutions Model

This explanation blends the statist and class-struggle models with new institutional theory.[147] It emphasizes how political institutions interacted with changing cultural–ideological values and political struggles in the 1980s. In the U.S. institutional context, officials or judges who regularly deviate from popular opinion find their careers blocked and politicians imposing directives on them. Because officials have little insulation from changing public opinion, mobilized political–ideological groups that are able to shape volatile public opinion can have a very large impact on public policy. As Savelsberg (1994, 939) argued, "Public opinion as measured by opinion polls, media presentations, and knowledge in the political and academic sectors underwent radical changes. The search for socio-structural causes of crime was declared irrelevant by politicians and prominent scholars. Punitive attitudes peaked, and punishment increased. . ." (see World View 9.1).

The three models are complementary and emphasize political factors. In the absence of progressive alternatives, electoral politics, the media, and ideological struggles triggered a moral panic that directed public fears against a vulnerable low-income, minority population.[148] Imprisonment grew to stigmatize and contain an economically marginal, surplus population expanded by deindustrialization. American cultural forces also had a role (see World View 9.2). As Sutton (2000, 379) noted, "police functions in the United States are organized locally, policy-making authority is dispersed among the states, and judges and prosecutors must constantly renew the approval of voters—structured conditions that create a chronic vulnerability to moral panics."

Surveillance

As the nation-state developed and consolidated control over the territory and population it claimed, officials created surveillance and monitoring systems.[149] The systems had three objectives:

1. To monitor national political boundaries to prevent the unwanted incursion of potential enemies and ideas or the departure of valued national resources;

WORLD VIEW 9.1   German vs. U.S. Responses to Crime

A comparison of crime policy in the United States and Germany by Savelsberg (1994) shows the role of political institutions. The nations have similar crime patterns, and the crime rates changed in both after 1970. However, incarceration rates remained stable in Germany, but they exploded in the United States. He explains this outcome by differences in four areas: (1) public opinion, (2) opinion's effect on policy, (3) electoral systems and bureaucracy, and (4) academic research.

PUBLIC OPINION

In Germany, public beliefs about crime remained stable (i.e., law offenders continued to be viewed as victims who need rehabilitation and reintegration into society). In the 1980s in the United States, public opinion shifted to blame criminal behavior on an intentional individual decision instead of on social context. Crime victims were not the source of growing putative attitudes in the United States. In fact, crime victims have less harsh attitudes toward offenders than others because the main victims (African Americans, women, inner city residents) favor rehabilitation. Those with low levels of victimization (middle-class suburban white males) are very putative because crime-related opinions developed with a conservative political movement. In an analysis of political speeches, Savelsberg (1994) found that U.S. elites reversed the causal logic linking crime to ghettos. In the 1960s and 1970s, they said ghetto conditions caused crime, so improving ghetto conditions would reduce crime. In the 1980s, they said crime caused ghetto conditions, so fighting crime and imprisoning people would improve ghetto conditions. The public failed to notice this reversal or logical incongruity. Thus, a powerful ideological movement in the United States caused public attitudes regarding crime to change.

OPINION'S EFFECT ON POLICY

Germany is a corporatist state in which the major sectors of society (e.g., the professions, students, farmers, industry groups, unions, religions, etc.) are highly organized. Each sector combines the shared, collective interests of individuals and families, and the government formally accepts input from each. Also, German news media are organized around the corporatist sectors and most are nonprofit. Expressing opinions through corporatist organizations encourages careful, deliberative policy discussion and negotiation among sector leaders for the common good. The United States is a decentralized, fragmented state with strong competitive-individualist values. Individuals, classes, and interest groups form temporary coalitions to express their self-interests. Most of the U.S. mass media are privately owned and respond to market demands by sensationalizing issues to attract a large audience. In the United States, opinion polling is an obsession. The media and politicians monitor, try to influence, and respond to public opinion, so shifts in public opinion have a rapid and dramatic impact on the direction of policy.

ELECTORAL SYSTEMS AND BUREAUCRACY

Germany has "bureaucratic universalism." It is a parliamentary system of strict party discipline in which candidates depend on the party and elected party members obey the party. Citizens vote for a party more than an individual candidate, so the party controls politicians. This insulates politicians from short-term shifts in public opinion. It also insulates the executive branch because the leader of the dominant party heads the executive branch. Also, a large and permanent bureaucracy, not political appointees, makes most of the administrative decisions in government. With little personnel turnover, a cadre of highly specialized, well-trained, permanent professional civil servants insulated

Continued on page 426

Continued from page 425

from shifting public opinion make policy. German judges rise within the judicial system in a highly professional, competitive civil service system. They advance solely based on specialized knowledge and respect by professional peers. By contrast, the United States has "universalistic personalism." Elected officials have weak ties to political parties, which are little more than loose coalitions formed for elections. Candidates create personal connections to electoral constituencies and supporters rather than rely on a large, powerful political party organization. This makes them very sensitive to contributors, voters, and public opinion. The executive branch and government bureaucracy also follow public opinion because top bureaucratic officials are politically appointed and easily replaced, making them dependent on the president, powerful lobbyists, and public opinion. Judges are politically appointed or elected. Their advancement depends as much as on political favors, ideology, or partisanship as on their professional competence.

ACADEMIC AND POLICY RESEARCH

German universities are detached from society. Faculty members are highly respected and have great autonomy, insulating them from public opinion and politicians. Research funds and the curriculum are not tied to public opinion or politicians. The U.S. tradition of pragmatism and public influence over research funds lets business, the government, or local elites set research priorities. Politically defined goals strongly influence the allocation of research funds, especially in the social sciences, and political groups influence the school curriculum. Funding follows popular issues more than going to less popular issues on which new knowledge is needed. In the United States, applied knowledge on criminal justice is tied to popular opinion and views of politicians. (Also see Savelsberg, King, and Cleveland, 2002).

| WORLD VIEW 9.2 | Canada, So Similar Yet So Very Different from the United States |

Canada is very much like the United States in more ways than having a similar land area. Both were originally British colonies and were settled by a massive influx of European immigrants in the nineteenth century who spread into a vast wilderness, often encountering native people and engaging in bloody conflicts with them. Both are high-income, advanced capitalist democracies with federal systems in which about 75 percent of the multiracial population resides in urban areas. English is the dominant language in both countries, and both legal systems are based on British common law. The dominant religion in both is overwhelmingly Christian and predominately Protestant. The nations have been allies in World War I, World War II, and the 1991 Persian Gulf War. Both imprisoned innocent Japanese settlers during World War II and cooperated closely on the anticommunist side during the Cold War.

In other ways the two nations are very different, especially on crime and many social issues. Canada did not fight a revolution, but peacefully separated from Britain. It adopted a parliamentary, multiparty system of government. Canada did not have a Civil War, but the issue of Quebec separation remains. Runaway slaves and draft resisters opposed to the Vietnam War escaped from the United States into Canada. Unlike the United States, Canada has strict gun control laws, universal health insurance, medical marijuana, and legalized same-sex marriages. Canada does not have the death penalty, yet "the United States has had a much higher rate of reported violent crime than Canada. The homicide rate was three times higher in the United States than it was in Canada, while the American rate for aggravated assault was double the Canadian rate.

For robbery, the rate was 65% higher in the United States" (Statistics Canada 2001). Attitude survey data also show that Canadians are far more accepting of immigrants than Americans. Thus, Canada looks a lot like the United States except on issues of crime control and social-welfare programs, where it looks more like Western Europe. Deep racial-economic divisions in the United States rooted in three centuries of slavery, the Civil War, and the racially segregated South may account for some of the differences.

Source: "Statistics Canada," *The Daily*, Tuesday, December 18, 2001.

2. To survey the nation's physical-economic-social landscape to account for the resources that could be mobilized for national modernizing or military goals;
3. To track the size and location of the population—citizens and noncitizens within the borders—and monitor to their actions and expression of ideas.

Over time, new modes of surveillance arose, including border police, a population census, physical surveys of the national territory, secret police agencies, official media censors, and systems of passports and other official identity documents. One type of surveillance collects, codes, and stores information on people and organizations for general planning purposes or to offer public services (e.g., official statistics). A second type monitors and oversees the activities of less powerful people.[150]

The form and intensity of surveillance varies by nation and historical era. The legacy of past forms of rule and cultural values, a nation's internal divisions/conflicts, and the level of threat felt by state officials explains the variation. The United States developed various forms of surveillance. Until the Homeland Security Department was created, the intelligence apparatus was spread across many agencies (see Chart 9.3) and private organizations.

Passports and Immigration Control

Nation-states want to monitor and control the population within and crossing their borders. To facilitate this, most instituted official identification systems that record key cultural markers (e.g., age, sex, race, legal status) and issued identity cards. In the United States, officials have yet to create a single identity card and

chart 9.3

DOMESTIC SURVEILLANCE AND INTELLIGENCE FUNCTIONS

In the contemporary United States, national surveillance, or intelligence functions, had been dispersed among many federal government agencies. Many of these have now been consolidated into the Homeland Security Department (indicated by *).

Executive Branch Departments

Department of Agriculture
> Animal and Plant Health Inspection Service*
> Forest Service
> National Agricultural Statistics Service
> Plum Island Animal Disease Center*

Department of Commerce
> Bureau of Economic Analysis
> Critical Infrastructure Assurance*
> National Oceanic and Atmospheric Administration
> U.S. Census Bureau

Department of Defense
> National Biological Weapons Defense Analysis Center*
> National Communications System*
> Defense Security Service
> Defense Technology Security Administration
> National Intelligence Agency

Department of Energy
> Energy Security and Assurance Program*
> Environmental Measurements Laboratory*
> National Infrastructure Simulation and Analysis Center*
> National Nuclear Security Administration
> Nuclear Incident Response Team*
> Office of Intelligence
> Lawrence Livermore National Laboratory*

Department of the Interior
> Bureau of Indian Affairs
> Bureau of Land Management
> U.S. Geological Survey
> Minerals Management Service

Department of Health
> Centers for Disease Control

Department of Justice
> Border Patrol*
> Bureau of Prisons
> Domestic Emergency Support Teams*
> Immigration and Naturalization Service*

Federal Bureau of Investigation (FBI)
> National Infrastructure Protection Center*

National Drug Intelligence Center
Office of Domestic Preparedness*
U.S. Marshall's Service
U.S. Parole Commission

Department of the State
> Bureau of Consular Affairs (passports)

Department of Transportation
> Coast Guard*
> Transportation Security Administration*

Department of the Treasury
> Customs Service*
> Federal Law Enforcement Training Center*
> Office of Intelligence Support
> United States Secret Service*

Department of Labor
> Bureau of Labor Statistics

Independent Agencies
> General Services Administration
> > Federal Computer Incident Response Center*
> > Federal Protective Service*
>
> Central Intelligence Agency (CIA)
> Federal Emergency Management Agency (FEMA)*
> National Security Agency
> Selective Service Administration
> United States Postal Service
> > Office of the Inspector General

---

instead use a patchwork of overlapping documents, such as a driver's license, Social Security number, visa, and passport. The passport emerged as an official document to facilitate state control over the movement of people within and across territorial borders. As Torpey (2000, 6) argued, "the right to authorize and regulate movement has been intrinsic to the very construction of states . . . [and is part of] the need for states to identify unambiguously who belongs and who does not." The state identified and scrutinized documents to track the movement of people as it "embraced" (i.e., claimed, surrounded, and managed) people and resources. Historically, the national-level government constructed official identities for or categories of people to replace local papers, such as birth registers or church records. This included physical branding in some nations, colonial New England, and Southern states in the 19th century. State officials would like to deploy new identification technologies (e.g., fingerprints, DNA, or retina scans along with electronic databases) to replace identification documents.[151] Officials use state identification systems to determine which people can legitimately claim state benefits (e.g., physical protection, social programs) and who should be watched for political or security reasons (i.e., criminals, aliens, terrorists).[152] Officials divide the population into categories, such as "ours and safe" versus "alien and potentially dangerous." In addition to determining who is entitled to state benefits and protections, they want to track who can be called for military service and the size of the labor market.

State control over border crossings also exists in immigration policy. Early in United States history, immigration was a state government concern. The federal government did not issue passports certifying national citizenship until 1856.[153] The Immigration Act of 1891 shifted control over immigration to the Department of the Treasury in the federal government and established federal border inspection stations.[154] In 1903, the federal government expanded immigration authority to a Bureau of Immigration and placed it in the Department of Commerce and Labor, and it became the Bureau of Immigration and Naturalization with the Naturalization Act of 1906.

Open, unregulated immigration into the United States ended after World War I. Conservative elites gained power and restricted free expression during wartime and imposed strict controls and political exclusion after the war. Responding to fears that a flood of racially inferior people wanted to immigrate, officials required immigrants to take literacy tests in 1917 and increased restrictions through the 1920s. Asian immigration was blocked, and the rules against hostile aliens, temporarily enacted during World War I, became permanent. In 1924, a border police was established to patrol the Mexican border. Soon police checks, health inspections, and financial requirements were added. Immigrants were to apply at U.S. embassies in foreign countries, in a system of remote border control.[155]

For the next 40 years, U.S. immigration law changed little, although the immigration service was moved to the Justice Department in 1940 when foreign aliens became a national security issue rather than labor and employment issue. In 1965 after the shift in attitudes stimulated by the civil rights movement, the United States abolished racial quotas and replaced them with an international waiting list. The number of immigrants was frozen until 1990. At that time, the total number of new entrants grew, but new rules redefined "desirable" entrants as people with family ties, financial wealth, or scare job skills. A 1996 immigration law expanded surveillance over entrants, toughened border enforcement, reduced opportunities for political or humanitarian asylum seekers, made it easier to deport long-term resident immigrants, and ended some immigrants' due process rights. Major high-technology corporations successfully lobbied Congress to increase the number of educated foreign workers allowed to enter to reduce their shortage of skilled technical labor and reduce their wage costs. After the 2001 World Trade Center attack, control over immigration and borders tightened. In 2003, the immigration service was transferred from the Justice Department to the new Department of Homeland Security. Thus, U.S. immigration policy shifted over time to reflect a desire for population growth, racial exclusion, business demands for labor, and national security fears.

Domestic Political Surveillance

The division between domestic and foreign intelligence/surveillance is hotly debated. Foreign intelligence for national security is widely accepted, but domestic intelligence is not. U.S. domestic surveillance has a long history of covert spying, mail interception, tapping telephone lines, using informers, and secret entry into private homes and offices. Before the 1940s, it was largely at the local level and often was backed by vigilante groups.

The public accepted domestic surveillance as legitimate to fight serious criminals and combat subversion (i.e., people engaging in sedition and treason, trying to overthrow the government, working for an unfriendly foreign power, or engaging in espionage). Subversion is a controversial and fluid term. At times, government officials expanded it to include a wide range of legal, peaceful citizen demands for new rights, minority demands for equal treatment under the law, the expression of unconventional or controversial ideas, and workers demands to organize labor unions.

After World War II, new security organizations were established to fight the Cold War. They were to defend national security by countering domestic and foreign communist threats. In the 1950s, this expanded to defend a particular view of the American way of life. The U.S. Congress created an un-American Activities Committee to investigate subversion and dissent. Some politicians attributed the lack of any evidence that directly linked domestic dissent to a foreign nation to the great skill and cunning of their adversaries. Their fears of communism were so intense that they believed that anyone who disagreed with them was disloyal or contaminated with foreign-inspired ideas. They ordered security agencies to spy on U.S. citizens based on very weak evidence.[156]

In the 1960s, widespread domestic political protest developed with large public demonstrations. Racial minorities organized to demand voting rights and an end to racial segregation, others opposed the foreign policy of a war in Southeast Asia, and students protested on other policies such as police brutality and school dress codes. A few small, ultra-radical groups engaged in violent acts, such as bombings, bank robberies, and kidnappings.

The state surveillance apparatus created in the 1950s to fight the Cold War was still in place. Over time, the FBI had blurred the functions of crime control, antisubversion, and fighting communism under the highly power and conservative leader, J. Edgar Hoover.[157] Officials expanded the Cold War surveillance apparatus and redirected it against the domestic political protesters. For example, officials engaged in illegal burglaries to plant secret listening devices in the homes of family and friends of protest leaders. Military agents secretly posed as college students to observe college professors. Under J. Edgar Hoover, the FBI activities expanded well beyond past limits and treated any nonconservative viewpoint with suspicion. It drew up a list of thousands of people to place in "detention" or concentration camps if necessary, including the civil rights leader Martin Luther King, Jr. and monitored the speeches and research of academics, including many sociologists.[158] It secretly observed and compiled information on legal organizations favoring a wide range of issues, including international peace, gay rights, civil rights, women's rights, tenant's rights, legalization of marijuana, and improved treatment for prisoners.[159] The FBI organized efforts by local, state, and federal law enforcement agencies to spy on hundreds of thousands of citizens and began to create a "totalitarian police-state" scale of domestic spying operations in the United States.[160]

A range of government agencies were drawn into the expanding domestic surveillance. According to Donnor (1980, 287), "By the late 1960s the intelligence units of the armed forces had become, next to the FBI, the most important single component of domestic intelligence." Private companies and voluntary associations contributed surveillance data to security agencies. Even the Internal Revenue Service monitored tax filing of people who voiced dissent with White House policies. During the 1973 Senate confirmation hearings of L. Patrick Gray III as FBI director, the bureau argued that Congress had authorized its domestic surveillance responsibility. Donner (1980, 69) reports ". . . the Bureau had insisted that it wore two separate and quite different hats: a general investigative hat for probing violations of law and, far more important, an internal security hat."

The rapid expansion of domestic surveillance came to a dramatic, sudden halt in the mid-1970s. Within a year of Mr. Gray's 1973 confirmation hearings, Congress put restrictions on domestic surveillance. After J. Edgar Hoover, the extremely powerful FBI director for four decades died in 1973, and the Watergate crisis that forced President Nixon to resign from office in 1974, there were extensive public revelations about abuses of power and widespread illegal activity by surveillance agencies. Under a cloak of national security, elected officials had been directing illegal actions against their political opponents and sometimes members of Congress. Evidence was uncovered documenting that government agencies had illegally targeted people who opposed the policies of White House officials, including political candidates and peaceful citizens, and planned to expand the scope of illegal actions (see Case in Point 9.3). As lawsuits, revelations of wrongdoing, and public scrutiny grew, state and local police disbanded political investigations of questionable legality and quickly destroyed their "red squad" records.[161]

Investigations and Congressional hearings on the abuse prompted intelligence agency reforms and a partial dismantling of the domestic surveillance apparatus. Public sympathy favored the individuals and groups that had been the targets of domestic surveillance. In 1976, President Ford banned the CIA from engaging in domestic intelligence, and the FBI closed many questionable investigations.[162] The Intelligence Surveillance Act (1978) also limited foreign surveillance.[163] In a few years, the issue of domestic surveillance abuse had vanished from the public agenda.[164] In the 1980s, the Soviet Union was once again an "evil empire," but it soon collapsed and was no threat.

By 1990, state officials quietly revived domestic surveillance but directed it against new enemies—drug users and dealers. For example, in 1993 the FBI broke into buildings secretly to install hidden listening or video devices 300 times—a 600 percent increase over 1983.[165] In 1994 a new law required telephone companies to install equipment that would make secret listening easier.

CASE IN POINT 9.3   **The Huston Plan for Expanded Domestic Surveillance**

During the Watergate investigations in late 1973, the public learned about the Nixon administration's development and intention to implement the Huston Plan to expand surveillance of and intelligence gathering on domestic enemies. The origins of the plan went back nearly two decades and were justified by national security. The plan called for consolidating domestic intelligence gathering activities that had been dispersed among many government agencies (Federal Bureau of Investigation, National Security Agency, Central Intelligence Agency) and placing them under direct White House control. Surveillance was to expand against targeted persons who opposed the war in Vietnam, groups opposed to nuclear weapons, civil rights activists, liberal-left academics and journalists, and other anti-establishment types. The plan authorized many clearly illegal actions, such as wiretaps, opening mail, break-ins, undercover spies, and the electronic monitoring of law-abiding citizens who disagreed with White House policy. Until it was uncovered as part of the Watergate affair, the White House and top security officials had intended to keep the Huston Plan secret from the public and most of the federal government, including members of Congress. After the panic over the World Trade Center terrorist attack, the passage of the Homeland Security Act and plans to centralize intelligence/surveillance activities 30 years later has accomplished what the Huston Plan could not.

Sources: Donnor (1980, 263–268), Goldstein (1978, 485–486), Morgan (1980, 49), and Theoharis (1978, 13–39).

In 1996, FBI agents secretly listened to 1.3 million telephone conversations; only 15 percent had illegal content. Following government priorities, they pursued antidrug and antiterrorism activities, but ignored violations of antitrust, civil rights, or anticorruption laws. Today, domestic surveillance is rapidly expanding in the wake of the September 11, 2001 terrorist attack with the so-called Patriot Act (2001) and the Homeland Security Department. Forms of surveillance not seen in 40 years are being revived, such as monitoring library books checked out, and are historically unprecedented except in wartime or during the red scare periods.[166]

Surveillance, Power, and Control

Surveillance is fundamentally about power and control. A monitoring agent (e.g., an organization or person) accumulates, documents, and organizes information on others. The information becomes a resource available only to the monitoring agent, giving him/her power over the person being monitored. The monitoring agent can manipulate, compare, and classify observed details and can use the information to take actions against the monitored person. Officials can compare monitored speech and behavior against an abstract standard of "proper" speech and behavior. The monitoring agent, not the person monitored, sets the standard and decides whether there is enough conformity to it.

Surveillance by the state or other organizations, in itself, increases conformity and reduces freedom. A monitored person who is aware of surveillance tends to self-monitor and give an appearance of being in conformity. Few monitored people have a choice but to accept surveillance. For example, a manager installs an electronic system to monitor employees, a storeowner mounts surveillance cameras to watch customers, or police and private security officers watch public spaces. The employee, customer, or person in a public space has no choice but to be scrutinized. Surveillance by the managers, owners, and security officers enhances their power over others.

Surveillance Society and Official Control

The idea of surveillance conjures up the image of the omnipresent Big Brother who constantly watches everyone that George Orwell described in his novel *1984*, written in 1949, about a terrifying totalitarian society. In the novel, a totalitarian state maintains power and exercises total thought control through widespread surveillance and intimidation. The novel's frightening implications made it a classic. The level of surveillance most people experience today is approaching the levels that Orwell feared, yet most people passively accept it. In fact, early twenty-first century voyeur television has perversely turned the fear of omnipresent watching into a form of popular entertainment.

Social, political, and technological changes of the last 30 years have created a surveillance society in many advanced industrial nations. **A surveillance society is one in which people in positions of bureaucratic authority regularly and systematically monitor numerous aspects of the lives of the population to exercise control over them.** In such a society, if you refuse to be watched, your existence is limited. You could not work for employers who monitor employees, shop in stores with security cameras and undercover security personnel, or go to public places watched by cameras or police. Like a character in the novel *1984*, you would be banished from most of today's urban life. William Staples (1997, 30) said, "the generalized surveillance of all of us . . . [suggests] we are witnesses to the emergence of a new regime of discipline and social control." Most of the public accepts expanded video monitoring, despite a loss of privacy and the low accuracy of camera monitoring.[167] Listening devices, Internet message monitoring, and metal detectors generate little public opposition because of a combination of fear, a blind faith in technological solutions, and a belief that mainstream or "normal" people have nothing to fear.[168] Also, today's decentralized, overlapping, and semiprivate surveillance systems, instead of the single, centralized surveillance government system described in *1984*, reduces concern. Many nonmainstream people feel very uncomfortable. Surveillance systems target and scrutinize the less powerful, marginalized members of society—people who do not conform to average behavior and beliefs of the broad middle class.[169] Some people feel that normalizing observation has begun to blur the line between daily living and being in a penal institution, where officials can constantly monitor prisoners.[170] A curious aspect of a surveillance society is that the "citizens-prisoners" accept and even desire monitoring by others. Instead of fighting the loss of their privacy and personal freedom, many people actually embrace it. This comes from a strange mix of a great fear of harm by criminals and terrorists, combined with a great trust in powerful organizations and with a bit of vanity over getting attention from others. However, surveillance increases state capacity in ways that can erode the foundations of a democratic society.[171] Steven Vago (1991, 164) observed, "The government has shown a strong tendency to closely watch the activities of persons who threaten it. . . . There is a thin line between government control of dissent and the creation of a police state."

Much of the recently expanded surveillance is beyond state direction. Private policing and security have grown rapidly since 1970. In 1970 the United States had about 1.4 public police or security officers for each private security worker.[172] By 1999, more people worked in private security than in public security and corrections (e.g., police officers, sheriffs, detectives, jailers).[173] Estimates suggest that the private security industry is twice the size of the public sector.[174] In most large cities, people encounter private security officials at home if they live in a multi-unit building, at the workplace, when they use public transit or shop, and when they attend a sporting event or go to a hospital. In the affluent suburbs, private security guards protect exclusive clubs and entire gated neighborhoods. Shearing and Stenning (1983, 493) noted, "What is new about modern private security is its pervasiveness and extent to which its activities have expanded into public, rather than purely private places." Private security and policing were common early in nation-state development. They were replaced because public police were cost-efficient for wide geographic areas, permitted state coordination, and had political legitimacy. According to Spitzer and Scull (1977, 23), "When functions once delegated to private police were turned over to the state, the dominant class could ideologically separate enforcement of 'constitutional authority' from its own [narrow class interests] . . . it was far easier to claim that the social order was preserved by the 'rule of law and not men'." By the twentieth century, maintaining the social order was a 'public commodity' or state function, but private policing continues to offer benefits to business interests. Private security borrows public police symbolism (e.g., uniform, badges) and authority at no cost, it facilitates private sanctions or remedies at lower cost, and involves less publicity than court action. It is also highly flexible and can be quickly expanded or contracted based on the needs of a business.[175] Many stores detain suspected shoplifters in a private jail without legal safeguards such as police, lawyers, or legal trial. For example, Macy's department stores in New York use chain-link holding cells. Store employees body search, photograph, handcuff, and interrogate suspected shoplifters. Nearly all of the 12,000 shoplifters caught at Macy's in 2002 signed confessions and paid "fines" of up to five times the value of what they were suspected of taking. Only about one-half were sent to the police.[176]

Private security differs from public security in three ways: (1) it is tailored to the needs of a business client or employer, not the public; (2) it is integrated into the business's ongoing operations and organizational structure; (3) it relies on private authority and sanctions that are rarely integrated with the public police. Despite rhetoric about private security being a "junior partner" to the public police, this rarely occurs. Private security monitors vast expanses of public working and living space, with a priority on defending the employer's interests and private property, not on protecting public safety.[177] In some ways, private security is a throwback to the medieval situation. In the medieval era, territory had some highly secure compounds that were under local, nondemocratic authority; between the compounds were large expanses of less safe areas. Today some people live in walled, gated neighborhoods, shop in malls where private security forces patrol and closely watch, and work in well-guarded private office towers. They travel between these secure compounds in their locked vehicles, fearful of encountering strangers. Growing private surveillance signals a blurring of the line between state and private functions, as corporate interests increasingly appropriate aspects of state sovereignty. This implicit transfer of state functions to private businesses may undermine the state's rational-legal legitimation as being democratic in the long term.[178]

CONCLUSION

We examined the development and structure of the legal order, the control of crime, including imprisonment, and surveillance. In the closing years of the twentieth century, surveillance and imprisonment significantly expanded. Private involvement in social control and surveillance also increased. Three models—labor market, moral panic, and political institutions—explain the growth in imprisonment and shifts in crime control policy. Several themes run through the topics. First, the ability to control which actions will be labeled as legal or illegal is an important political resource. Second, law and legal order often appear to be apolitical, but they are often profoundly political in their application. Third, specific political events and ideological movements can shape the legal order and criminal justice system. Lastly, social groups and state officials can use the legal order to advance their interests.

In Chapter 10, we turn from street crime and state control over the general population to examine the laws, rules, and regulations that affect the business community.

KEY TERMS

Black Law	Determinate Sentencing	Militarization of the Police
Coercive State Power	Indeterminate Sentencing	Myth of Legality
Consensus Model Fallacy	Legal Order	Normative Fallacy

Penal Welfarism Model

Prison-Industrial Complex

Pro Bono

Retributivist Model

Rushe-Kirchheimer Thesis

Self-Help Crime

Stare Decisis

Surveillance Society

REVIEW QUESTIONS

1. How did law and legal institutions grow out of the historical development of the modern nation-state? In what ways did changes in legal rights reflect newly emerging economic relations?

2. Contrast how pluralists and class-struggle theorists understand the operation of law in society.

3. What does it mean to say that legal processes legitimate state actions? What is the relationship between the legal order and legitimacy and between law and the political stability of society?

4. How can the "winner" of a legal–political conflict codify advantages into the legal order? How might this affect subsequent law and legal interpretations?

5. What does it mean to say that the law or legal order is ideological? In what ways it is ideological?

6. How does legal reasoning operate and what is the role of a specialized legal language with legal categories? Why might the outcome of a legal decision differ from common sense?

7. What are the sources and limits of the autonomy of the legal order?

8. What three models explain Supreme Court actions? What relation do they have to the political sociology models?

9. What is the militarization of the police? Why did it occur? How does it relate to the concept of coercive state power?

10. What explains the rise in U.S. imprisonment rates since the mid-1970s? Why did American people become more punitive?

11. What is a prison-industrial complex? What is its relation to the two crime models (penal welfarism, retributivist)?

12. What is the source of a surveillance society and its likely consequences? Explain the general relationship between surveillance and political power.

RECOMMENDED READINGS

Balbus, Isaac D. 1977. *The Dialectics of Legal Repression*. New Brunswick, NJ: Transaction Books.

Beckett, Katherine. 1997. *Making Crime Pay: Law and Order in Contemporary American Politics*. New York: Oxford University Press.

Chambliss, William J. 1999. *Power, Politics and Crime*. Boulder CO: Westview.

Garland, David. 2001. *The Culture of Control: Crime and the Social Order in Contemporary Society*. Chicago: University of Chicago Press.

Staples, William G. 1997. *The Culture of Surveillance: Discipline and Social Control in the United States*. New York: St. Martin's Press.

Wolfe, Alan. 1973. *The Seamy Side of Democracy*. New York: David McKay.

ENDNOTES

1. See *Sourcebook of Criminal Justice Statistics* online at http://www.albany.edu/sourcebook/, Section 6.

2. See http://www.lindesmith.org/library/sentence/behndbrs.html#figure1

3. Pettit and Western (2004) and Savelsberg (1994) provide a summary of the change in U.S. policy and its consequences.

4. Quote is from Sutton (2000, 354).

5. Sutton (2000, 355) argued that, "punishment practices and the institutional forces they express, are the outcomes of historically contingent political projects."

6. Somers (1993) provides a detailed discussion of law and citizenship development by comparing France and England and two regions in England in the eighteenth century.

7. Boyle (2000) presents a comparative analysis of legal systems by the degree of state-society interpenetration.

8. Also see Beckett and Sasson (2000) and Wonders and Solop (1993) who make the same point.

9. See Vago (1991, 17) for a quick review of the pluralist view of law.

10. For the pluralist view see Chambliss and Seidman (1982, 33–37, 140–142), Chambliss (1993a, 6–7), and Kidder (1983).

11. Quote is from Chambliss and Seidman (1982, 36).

12. For a discussion of the relative autonomy issue see Spitzer (1983, 107).

13. More on the role of custom and ruling class benefits from law is outlined in Chambliss (1975).

14. See Scheppele (1994, 384–385).

15. For a discussion of types of law see Kidder (1983).

16. See Tigar and Levy (1977, 8–10).

17. This includes the United States, except the state of Louisiana, which has a civil law system from French control.

18. For a summary of E. P. Thompson's study on the Black Act, see Chambliss and Seidman (1982, 178–180).

19. Gramsci argued for law's educative function. See Cain (1983) and Chambliss and Seidman (1982, 65–80).

20. For a discussion of meanings and types of law see Vago (1991, 9–11).

21. See Chambliss (1993a).

22. Chambliss and Seidman (1982, 57–60) discuss the rule of law.

23. See Chambliss and Seidman (1982, 3–6).

24. From Chambliss and Seidman (1982, 76).

25. See Chambliss (1993a).

26. See Galliher (1980) for a discussion of structural factors and triggering events.

27. For a discussion see Jessop (1982, 84–90).

28. In a slightly different formulation, Chambliss and Seidman (1982, 61) argued that ideology "rests upon three pillars: an autonomous legal system, universalistic rules and legalistic reasoning." Also see Foster (1990) on the rise of apolitical legal practice in the United States and Seron and Munger (1996) for an overview of law and ideology.

29. Hagan (1982) found sharp differences between corporate persons and individuals in the legal system.

30. See Sumner (1983) for a discussion of the disjuncture between formal, procedural law and substantive law.

31. The role of legal classification and categories is discussed by Corrigan and Sayer (1981, 40–41).

32. Dibble and Pekowsky (1973, 519) discuss the use of legal categories in legal forms of reasoning.

33. This argument and the relation between ideological and legal reasoning is from Dibble and Pekowsky (1973).

34. For a discussion of legal language see Chambliss and Seidman (1982, 119–133).

35. See Kessler (1993) for a discussion of legal reasoning.

36. See Scheppele (1994, 396–397).

37. Kessler (1993) argues for this distinction creation process in legal language and reasoning.

38. Dibble and Pekowsky (1973, 546) argued that, "Legal culture is tilted in the conservative direction, entirely apart from the ties which lawyers or judges have with the ruling classes and ruling institutions in their society."

39. See Stryker (1990b, 131, fn 8) for elaboration.

40. For a discussion of scientific and legal forms of reasoning in legal-regulatory settings see Stryker (1994).

41. See Chambliss and Seidman (1982). Also see Quinney (1977).

42. See Sugarman (1983) for a discussion.

43. On the concept of "living law" see Kidder (1983, 12–33), Miller (1976, 30), and Nieberg (1969, 64).

44. For a discussion of organizational needs in law enforcement see Chambliss and Seidman (1982).

45. This discussion builds on Sarat and Grossman (1975, 1215–1216).

46. See discussion in Scheppele (1994) on legal pragmatism and Seron and Munger (1996) on the legal profession.

47. Kidder (1983, 214–215) provides a brief overview.

48. See Foster (1990) for a detailed discussion of the move to be above politics in the legal profession.

49. Halliday, Powell, and Granfors (1993) describe two patterns of development of state bar associations.

50. See Kennedy (1982, 42–45) on legal education.

51. On law student views, see Erlanger, Cahill, Epp, and Haines (1996) and Granfield and Koenig (1992, 1996).

52. Castelnuovo (1979) says public interest law is an attempt to use legal concepts and procedures to oppose dominant class interests, to defend people at the bottom of society, and to advance the public interest.

53. See Kidder (1983, 233–236) and "Legal Firms Cutting Back on Free Services for Poor," *New York Times,* August 17, 2000.

54. See Liptak, Adam. "County Says It's Too Poor to Defend the Poor," *New York Times,* April 15, 2003.

55. See Kairys (1982a, 3).

56. See Barrow and Zuk (1990) for a study of U.S. federal judge turnover patterns, 1900–1987.

57. See Savelsberg (1992) on sentencing guidelines; Garland (2001) on neoclassical ideology and the legal order.

58. Farber (1987) summarizes the law and economics movement. Also see Scheppele (1994). For a general discussion of neoliberalism see Campbell (2001).

59. From Mensch (1982, 36).

60. See Segal and Spaeth (1996, 987).

61. The agenda-setting role of the Court is discussed in McGuire and Palmer (1995, 1996) and Perry (1991).

62. On public mood influence on the Court see Flemming and Wood (1997), Flemming, Bohte, and Wood (1997), Link (1995), and Stimson, MacKuen, and Erikson (1995). Segal and Spaeth (1993, 1996) and Segal, Epstein and Cameron (1995) provide support for an attitudinal model. Also see Segal and Spaeth (1996). On Senate lobbying see Caldeira and Wright (1998). On Congress overturning decisions see Meernik and Ignagni (1997). Also see Epstein, Hoekstra, Segal and Spaeth (1998) on the effects from the political environment that change voting by justices on the Supreme Court.

63. Ideological shifts in the Supreme Court's interpretations of statutes and the legitimizing role of the court are discussed in Funston (1975) and Lasser (1985). Also see Kairys (1982a, 5) who argued that, "the law is a major vehicle for the maintenance of existing social and power relations."

64. Mishler and Sheehan (1993) provide an analysis of Supreme Court decisions.

65. See Mondak and Smithey (1997) for a review of public support for the Court and for a mathematical model of it.

66. On property relations see Campbell and Lindberg (1990). On the market see Dobbin and Dowd (2000) and Roy (1997). On labor see Forbath (1991), McCammon (1990, 1993, 1994), Orren (1994, 1995), and Tomlins (1985).

67. McCammon (1993, 1994) forcefully makes this point.

68. For statistical information see Statistical Abstract of the United States, 1999, Section 5, and the Sourcebook of Criminal Justice Statistics (November 2000).

69. Edelman (1992) provides a description of organizational compliance to civil rights law.

70. See Black (1984). Also see Kubrin and Weitzer (2003) on retaliatory homicide. Gould (1999, 2000) discusses related violence (feuds and revenge) as rational behavior.

71. On types of crime and the relative costs in terms of money and lives see Chasin (1997) and Reiman (1990).

72. From Chambliss and Seidman (1982, 265–267).

73. Quote is from Scheingold (1991, 7). Also see Cohen (1996) on crime and politics.

74. See Flanagan (1996a), LaFree (1999), and Roberts and Stalans (2000, 26–33).

75. Kevin Smith (1997, 363).

76. Beckett (1995) discusses crime policy differences by gender.

77. Janowitz (1978, 27–52) offers a detailed discussion of social control.

78. Little and Sheffield (1983) provide a discussion of early vigilantism in the United States and England. Also see Culberson (1990).

79. Bayley (1975) provides a review of the early development of policing in Europe. Also see Steedman (1984) on early British policing.

80. See Harring (1983, 34).

81. From Harring (1983, 143).

82. See Chamlin (1990) and Liska, Lawrence, and Benson (1981).

83. An analysis of spending priority changes due to Proposition 13 can be found in Saltzstein (1986).

84. From Harring (1983, 16).

85. Jacobs and O'Brein (1998) and Jacobs and Wood (1999) provide a detailed analysis of this issue.

86. See Karson (1958, 33–75) and Perlman and Taft (1935). State police forces were created in most states between 1901 and 1910 primarily to contain labor unrest. See Adams (1966) and Faulkner (1931, 64–65) for a discussion of police. Ekrich (1974, 206–207) discusses the Dick Act and federalization of the militia.

87. The six states are California, Massachusetts, New Jersey, Pennsylvania, New York, and Texas.

88. Data calculated from the *Sourcebook of Criminal Justice Statistics*.

89. See Loader (1997).

90. See Haggerty and Ericson (1999), Kraska and Kappeler (1997), and Simon (1999).

91. See Kraska and Kappeler (1997).

92. From Kraska and Kappeler (1997) and Kraska and Paulsen (1997). Also see Simon (1999) on SWAT.

93. See "The Sultans of SWAT," *The Economist*, October 2, 1999, pp. 28–29.

94. From Kraska (1999, 213). Garrison state is discussed in Chapter 12.

95. See Liska (1987) for a detailed explanation of the rational-economic or pluralist view. Also see Garland (2001) on the rational choice model of crime control.

96. Japan executed 28 persons since 1993, when capital punishment resumed in that country. Also see Radelet and Borg (2000).

97. The countries are the Bahamas, Barbados, Belize, Grenada, Guyana, and Jamaica.

98. See Hood (1990) and Sarat (1998).

99. Quote is from Longmire (1996, 106).

100. For an excellent summary and overview on the death penalty in the United States see Radelet and Borg (2000).

101. On racial bias in the application of the death penalty see Ekland-Olson (1988) on Texas, Russell (1994) on Georgia, and Vito and Keil (2000) on Kentucky.

102. See "MacArthur Study of Competence To Stand Trial," Research Network on Adolescent Development and Juvenile Justice, http://www.mac-adoldev-juvjustice.org/ (Downloaded July 27, 2003).

103. *Juveniles on Death Row*, http://sun.soci.niu.edu/~critcrim/ dp/faq/juvlist.html (Downloaded January 9, 2001).

104. See http://justice.policy.net/jpreport/section2.html and "The Death Penalty: One in Seven Wasn't Guilty," *The Economist*, November 28, 1998.

105. Berlow (1999) argues that prosecutors concealed or used false evidence in 381 homicide convictions, and that larger percentages of defense lawyers are incompetent or have been disbarred.

106. See Nieburh, Bustav. "Catholic Bishops Seek End to Death Penalty," *New York Times*, April 3, 1999.

107. "The Cruel and Even More Unusual Punishment," *The Economist*, May 15, 1999, pp. 95–97.

108. See "A Stigma That Never Fades," *The Economist*, August 10, 2002, pp. 25–27.

109. See Schlosser (1998, 54).

110. Timberlake, Rasinski, and Lock (2001) report on U.S. attitudes for the 1984–1998 period.

111. See "Prisons in America," *The Economist*, March 15, 1997, p. 33.
112. Calculated from information provided in Beckett and Sasson (2000, 64). Funds were taken from fighting white-collar crime and put into the drug war, and white-collar crime enforcement shifted (Poveda 1992).
113. See Chambliss (1999, 75) and Meier (1992, 43) for statistics on high school drug use by race.
114. See Miller (1996, 84–85) for changing arrest rates.
115. See Meier (1992, especially pp. 56–58).
116. From Miller (1996, 65).
117. From Miller (1996, 55, 84) and *Sourcebook on Criminal Justice Statistics 1999*, Table 6.5.
118. See Messner and Rosenfeld (1994, 5) and Miller (1996, 7).
119. See *Sourcebook of Criminal Justice Statistics*, page 25.
120. See Dyer (2000, 14).
121. From Dyer (2000, 19).
122. From Dyer (2000, 233).
123. See Chambliss (1999, 33) and *Sourcebook of Criminal Justice Statistics 1999*, Table 1:82.
124. The two are Wackenhut Corrections Corporation and Corrections Corporation of America (from *Sourcebook of Criminal Justice Statistics 1999*, Table 1:82).
125. From Shichor (1995, 50–57).
126. See Shichor (1995, 74).
127. Discussion of a prison-industrial complex can be found in Chambliss (1999), Lilly and Knepper (1993), Miller (1996, 228–233), Shichor (1995, 238–240), and Schlosser (1998).
128. For a discussion of corrections and higher education spending see Chambliss (1999, 125–128).
129. See Liska (1997) on models of social control. He argues for comparing crime control and social welfare.
130. For the initial thesis see Rusche and Kirchheimer (1939).
131. See Barlow and Barlow (1995), Barlow, Barlow and Chiricos (1993), Inverarity and McCarthy (1988) and Michalowski and Carlson (2000). See Jacobs and Helms (1996) and Lessan (1991) and Liska (1987, 80–81) for reviews of past studies.
132. See Petras and Davenport (1991) on urban deindustrialization.
133. See Grant and Martinez (1997) on property crime. Also see Colvin (1990) and Inverarity and McCarthy (1988). Crutchfield (1989) argues that crime rates also vary by labor market segment in a similar manner.
134. See Cappell and Sykes (1991) and Jacobs and Helms (1996, 1997).
135. Colvin (1990), Lessan (1991), Fording (1997, 2001), and Sutton (2000) discuss welfare. Barlow and Barlow (1995) discuss new crime control strategies. Also see Beckett and Western (2001) and Michalowski and Carlson (2000).
136. See Sutton (1987).
137. See Jacobs and Helms (1996, 1997).
138. Quote is from Jacobs and Helms (1996, 352, 353).
139. See Jacobs and Helms (1997, 1384–1385).
140. On moral panic see Beckett (1994, 1997), Beckett and Sasson (2000), Chambliss (1994, 1999), Merlo and Benekos (2000), and Scheingold (1991, 1995). See Chapter 3 on constructionism. Also see Roundtree et al. (1996) on crime fear.
141. Liska (1987) discusses the relationship between boundary crisis and crime policy.
142. Kennedy (1997) sees parallels between the 1970s conservative mobilization and ones in the 1820s and 1890s.
143. An analysis of law and order support in this period can be found in Bennett and Tuchfarber (1975).
144. See Beckett (1997) for details.
145. See Scheingold (1991, 62–64) on the first two of these.
146. The "comparatively safe" argument is outlined in Liska and Baccaglini (1990).
147. New institutionalism is discussed in Chapter 3.
148. This is the argument of Chambliss (1994) and Reiman (1990).
149. From Dandeker (1990).
150. Giddens (1987, 14) discusses the two types.
151. See Torpey (2000, 15–20).
152. From Torpey (2000, 71).
153. See Torpey (2000, 94–95).
154. From Torpey (2000, 100–102).
155. Taken from Torpey (2000, 120).
156. See Donner (1980, 1990).
157. Donnor (1980, 90–95).
158. See Keen (1999).
159. From Donnor (1980, 150–164).
160. See Donnor (1990) and Theoharis (1978).
161. See Donnor (1990).
162. See Goldstein (1978, 540).
163. See Morgan (1980, 8).
164. Also see Theoharis (1978).
165. See Burnham (1997) on the FBI in recent years.
166. See Hentoff. "Eyeing What You Read," *Village Voice*, February 14, 2002) and Foerstel (1991). CRS Report for Congress. Doyle, Charles, "Libraries and the USA Patriot Act," February 26, 2003, http://www.ala.org/Content/NavigationMenu/Our_Association/Offices/ALA_Washington/Issues2/Civil_Liberties,_Intellectual_Freedom,_Privacy/The_USA_Patriot_Act_and_Libraries/CRS215Libraries Analysis (Downloaded July 28, 2003).
167. See Williams and Johnson (2000) on cameras watching public spaces. Davies and Thasen (2000) found high error rates for persons viewing surveillance videotapes.
168. On lack of concern see Shaw, Shaprio, Lock, and Jacobs (1998).
169. For a critique of surveillance and its impact on minorities see Fiske (1998).
170. Staples (1997, 35–37) discusses this in detail.
171. See Gross (1974) on the issue of "friendly fascism."
172. See Shearing and Stennig (1983) and Shearing and Stennig (1987).
173. From U.S. Bureau of Labor Statistics data.
174. From "Welcome to the new world of private security," *The Economist*, April 19, 1997, pp. 21–26. Also see Nalla and Newman (1991).
175. See Spitzer and Scull (1977).
176. See Elliott, Andrea, "In Stores, Private Handcuffs for Sticky Fingers," *New York Times*, June 17, 2003.
177. See Shearing and Stenning (1983, 503).
178. From Spitzer (1979).

THE POLITICS OF BUSINESS POLICY

INTRODUCTION

Do you pay taxes and feel corporations pay their fair share? Have you wondered whether the food you eat and water you drink is safe, and do you expect government agencies ensure their safety? Are medications you take effective and advertised honestly? Have you ever paid a very high price for something because the business selling it had no competitors? These are just a few aspects of business policy. Whether you own a business, are employed by a business, or are simply a consumer, business regulations affect your daily life. In this chapter, we consider the state-economy relationship and focus on three areas of it:

(1) the state provides a platform on which private enterprise and the "free market" operate; (2) the state extracts resources from the private economy, usually in the form of taxes, and directly or indirectly distributes public resources to business; and (3) the state has a system of regulations that limit how business operates, encouraging certain business activities but prohibiting others. ■

Historical Background

Feudal society was centered on agriculture. Most of the people were serfs or peasants who worked for a small landowning elite. Economic activity was restricted and prearranged rules and traditions controlled the exchanges of goods, labor, or service. The market sector was tiny and was limited to the towns where artisans, craftspeople, handcraftsmen, and traders brought products to shops or market fairs to sell for a profit. Most businesses had an individual owner with family members, plus a few hired helpers or apprentices at most. Rarely did a workshop or elementary factory employ more than two dozen people. As capitalism expanded, the workshops grew into small factories, traders grew into trading/shipping companies, and one-person shops grew into large stores. Business organizations advanced from single owner-operators with a few helpers to companies employing hundreds of workers. By the late nineteenth century, as industrialization accelerated and spread, the modern corporation appeared and became the leading business organization. Its owners relied on bankers, investors, and shareholders for capital or funds and hired a large staff of managers, supervisors, accountants, and other white-collar employees to assist in operating complex business operations. By end of the twentieth century, corporations had become huge bureaucracies employing tens or hundreds of thousands of people with branch offices around the globe. Many produce a range of products and services, engage in advanced research, and operate massive marketing systems. An ascent to massive size also occurred in banking and finance. In this context, we consider this chapter's chief focus, the contemporary state-economy relationship.

State and Economy

The state-economy relationship has been a central concern for political sociology from the beginning. It operates on multiple levels—looking at the compatibility between capitalism and democracy, seeing how large companies secure special favors from government, and examining whether consumers benefit from laws against fraudulent advertising. Capitalism, the type of economic/social system of today's advanced countries, emerged with rise of the nation-state. Capitalism and the nation-state have been interdependent from the earliest stages of their development.

Advanced economies are highly complex and there are multiple forms of capitalism. In fact, comparative capitalism is a growing subfield of inquiry.[1] In all advanced nations, the business community is comprised of numerous large and small private organizations, as well as individual owner-operators. The state depends on the business community to produce and distribute goods and services, generate national wealth, provide employment and a standard of living for the population, and create material resources that it uses. About 90 percent of the working population works for someone else; only a small percentage own a business. Most owners have very small-scale businesses with fewer than a dozen employees. A tiny percentage of all business owners directly or indirectly own the large corporations that employ most people and produce most goods and services.

This points to the central predicament of capitalism and the democratic state: Very few people are capitalists (i.e., own a business), but together they hold great economic power and control the economy. At the same time, the vast majority of people are not capitalists, but together they hold political power and control the state's direction. So long as the owners and nonowners have common interests and see major issues alike, there is no problem. However, if owners and nonowners develop fundamentally opposing interests on critical issues, then owners' economic power can clash with the nonowners' democratic political power. For example, if owners pay very low wages to earn huge profits, abolish all restrictions over them, and demand no business taxes, their workers may rebel. If the nonowners demand very high wages and benefits that eat up all profits, take control of all business decisions, and impose very high business taxes, most capitalists will either shut their businesses or sell out and leave the country.

A central issue in political sociology, and a main focus of this chapter, is how does a society resolve the tension between democratic state and capitalist economy? In democratic–capitalist societies, the state depends on the private market economy, or the means of production, owned and controlled by a relative handful of people. Yet a democratic state tries to be responsive to the demands of the vast majority of people who are nonowners.

Political sociologists are interested in both state actions to control business and in the business community's political efforts to influence those actions, or what Gabriel Kolko (1963) called political capitalism. **Political capitalism is when business interests use political outlets to attain stability, predictability, and security in their economic, social, or political environment.**[2] Business owners may press for government actions to help them overcome specific business barriers so they can make higher profits. As Harland Prechel (2000, 10) noted often, "big business mobilized politically to refine state business policy." Political capitalism operates on three levels: (1) business leaders must translate their goals into specific policies, (2) they need to agree on which specific policies to advance politically, and (3) they must exercise influence over areas of the state to ensure policy implementation.[3]

Models of Political Sociology

Pluralists view the state and economy as loosely interconnected, with voters and interest group competition shaping business policies. Business is just one of many interest groups. Perhaps it is a little more influential than most and more focused on economic concerns. Pluralists emphasize divisions within the business community and its lack of unity. Since the state is a neutral organization that ultimately reflects desires of voters and interest group pressure, business policy can be strongly pro- or antibusiness and can favor specific businesses or other economic interests (e.g., workers, farmers, consumers). If most voters believe that businesses are too powerful or abusive, they can demand stricter rules and controls. When the economy is not working well, voters can demand that government improve conditions. If voters believe businesses are benign and fair, they may allow business interests to pressure government or lobby politicians for their particular interests.

In the *elite model* view, the state and the economy are two major, but not exclusive, sources of elite power. Business policy reflects the alliances, compromises, or conflicts among competing elites. Business elites are powerful, but they must work with other elites. Often, one set of business elites uses the state to gain advantages over others. If the masses become upset with business, elites can manipulate images and rhetoric to offer symbolic responses that have little real effect except to placate the discontent without harming powerful elites.

Those who use the *statist model* see the state and economy as distinct organizational arenas. Business policy primarily reflects the state's organizational structure and arrangements. State managers have the autonomy to press demands onto the business community that it might oppose. Organizational forces (e.g., demands for bureaucratic expansion, state capacity, intergovernment cooperation or cooperation), the legacy of past policy decisions, and professional and technical experts combine to shape business policies, although specific narrow business interests might form cooperative arrangements with specific state agencies. In general, the mass of ordinary citizens have little influence over business policy. If they become upset over high unemployment, abusive business practices, or severe economic dislocations, their collective voting power might press state officials to take action.

Political sociologists who use a *power-structure model* see a capitalist class in control of the economy and wielding great influence over the state. Capitalists actively initiate and use business policy for their own purposes. Organized segments of the class shape the form and direction of specific policies. Ordinary citizens are left out of business policy discussions unless they join in massive protest movements and press anticapitalist measures, but even then any policies adopted can be switched back once the protest dissipates and capitalist control returns.

In the *structuralist model,* state and economy are highly interdependent and the vital core of society. Business policy has two roles, to legitimate or maintain peaceful acceptance among noncapitalists and to help maintain basic capitalist accumulation processes. Business policy is a central state steering mechanism that helps keep capitalism operating smoothly. State managers, organized capitalist groups, and ordinary citizens all have only limited influence over business policy. Most business policy is based on signals from the economy (e.g., rising unemployment, declining profits) and advice from professional and technical experts who want a healthy capitalism. Despite rare, short-term lapses due to an upsurge of public protests, selfish business pressures, or insufficient knowledge by the technical experts, business policy generally reinforces the expansion of capitalism.

According to the *class-struggle model,* business policy is a site within the state where various capitalist class segments compete. Business policy is often a source of new conflicts over which opposing business or non-business groups try to advance their interests. Establishing a new state agency or business policy rarely reflects unified capitalist dominance or the autonomy of state officials; rather, policies are the outcome of struggles in specific historical periods as business or other interests struggle for control. As Harland Prechel (2000, 152) argued, "The key issue to understanding capital-state relations is not whether class segments are united or divided, but rather the historical conditions under which the capitalist class is more or less unified or divided. Similarly, the key issue is not whether states are autonomous from the capitalist class or class segments but rather the historical conditions under which they become more or less autonomous." Because business policy has a large effect on the business community, it is an area over which fierce struggles are waged (see Chart 10.1 for a summary).

c h a r t   1 0 . 1

POLITICAL–SOCIOLOGICAL MODELS AND BUSINESS POLICY

Political–Sociological Model	State-Economy Relationship	State Influence	What Determines Business Policy Direction?	Role of Nonbusiness Groups
Pluralist	Very loose	Divided, weak, and neutral	Voters, public opinion, competing interest groups	Very powerful
Elitist	Very loose	Unified, powerful, and neutral	Competing political and business elites	Absent
Statist	Close	Divided, powerful, and largely neutral	State managers and organizational constraints	Weak
Power-Structure	Close	Semidivided, powerful, and has clearprocapitalist bias	Organized capitalists	Absent
Structuralist	Extremely close	Unified, powerful, and strongly defends capitalism	Technical experts	Very weak
Class-Struggle	Moderately close	Divided, moderately powerful, and has procapitalist bias	Outcome of conflict among capitalist class segments and other mobilized groups	Varies; generally weak

A PLATFORM FOR A MARKET ECONOMY

The state provides a basic platform that enables the capitalist economic system to operate. The business community relies on this indirect support system. The state ensures territorial defense, personal safety and property protection, and general social stability; it creates and maintains a legal and monetary system (i.e., prints money, oversees banks, affects money supply); and it sustains a nation's hard (e.g., transportation network, communication system, energy supply) and soft (e.g., language, cultural values, family system) infrastructures.

The state's role in sustaining capitalism is at the center of opposing views of state-economy relationship. One view is a "neoliberal" position shared by most neo-classical economists. It describes the state-economy relationship by positing the ideal of a "natural market" governed by an "invisible hand." In the private marketplace, individual buyers and sellers engage in numerous individual exchanges and transactions. Business managers or owners rationally try to maximize gains in a context of supply and demand, market efficiency, and technological innovation. Together these factors contribute to business development and produce national wealth. The state is a distinct sphere with separate logic from that of the market, and it is outside the "natural" processes of business development and private economic activity. Its role is minimal; it offers a bare platform to allow the market to operate (i.e., provide national defense, print money, uphold a legal system, and so forth). State intervention into market relations creates "unnatural" disturbances and disrupts efficient, pure market operations. The only justifications for state intervention are a few exceptional areas of market failure (i.e., where the market cannot work).

The alternative, economic sociology view challenges the neoclassical ideal and sees the natural market as a misleading myth.[4] Economic sociologists say markets are fundamentally social-political institutions that require state support. Markets, by necessity, depend on the state, and the idea of a free market is very problematic. Neil Fligstein (1990, 8) argued, "It is one thing to say you are in favor of free markets, and quite another to define what a free market is. That definition has shifted over time. . . . Laws regarding incorporation, antitrust, and the regulation of industries are important aspects of state definitions." The notion that the state *intervenes* into some preexisting, natural market is historically inaccurate and illogical, as William Roy (1997, 12) observed, "Even the freest of markets requires specific government actions and policies to enforce contracts, punish cheaters, regulate money and ensure stability. There is no such thing as nonintervention." In a neoliberal view, state and market are separate, distinct entities; in reality, they always have been intertwined parts of a single process. Indeed, "markets and other forms of economic governance are intimately linked to an ancillary set of other institutions, including the state."[5] Thus, markets are state creations, and state-building is part of market development.[6] States constitute markets and make them possible. Dobbin and Dowd (2000, 633) argued, ". . . key characteristics of markets (e.g., strategies, optimality, interests) are not purely 'natural,' as some economists are wont to argue, but are in part socially produced. Both public policy and structural power [in the business community] contribute to the variance in markets." Framing the issue as state versus market creates a misleading and false dichotomy. Peter Evans (1995, 10) acutely observed, "Sterile debates about 'how much' states intervene have to be replaced with arguments about different kinds of involvement and their effects. . . . The appropriate question is not 'how much' but 'what kind'."

The state not only makes a system of market capitalism possible, but economic sociologists say state actions and political forces have profoundly affected the direction, shape, and structure of business enterprise development. So-called natural market forces, efficiency, or technological change are often less significant than political forces in explaining the development of the form, size, and composition of the business corporation. The corporation appeared in the nineteenth century as a newly created, legalized form of private property. Four factors distinguish it from a single-proprietor type of business enterprise: (1) it is immortal and can be perpetuated indefinitely; (2) it has a tremendous capacity to obtain outside financing; (3) it offers its owners limited liability and protects them from great personal financial risk, and (4) it has an ability to expand in size, function, and geographic reach almost without limit. As you will see in this chapter, political forces (e.g., tax policy, business regulation, and laws) had a large role in creating the type of large corporations that now operate and their economic power.

Industrial Policy and Political Economy Systems

Political sociologists do not believe that there is a single model of capitalist state-economy relations. Especially after the demise of "command" style economies in communist regimes, they recognize that political forces, conflicts, state institutions, and national dynamics have produced alternative ways to organize a capitalist political economy under specific historical conditions. As Dobbin (1994, 2) remarked, "modern capitalist economies and the policies that support them are organized in quite different ways and show no compelling signs of convergence." For simplicity, two major ideal types of advanced capitalism can be distinguished: (1) a market-dominant, liberal or neoliberal state model, and (2) a coordinated-market, nonliberal, corporatist or developmental state model. These two models constitute two entire systems of how individual corporations make decisions, how interfirm relations within the business community operate, how labor relations are conducted, and how social programs are designed and delivered.[7] In liberal-market capitalism (LMC), business executives make individual decisions primarily from information in market mechanisms (e.g., competitor behavior, price changes, shifting market shares, or stock market indicators) while in coordinated-market capitalism (CMC), executives use many nonmarket mechanisms that are embedded in political and other institutions, such as industry associations, trade unions, public-private negotiations, and partnerships with other businesses or social groups.[8] In short, corporate strategy and business behavior operate differently depending upon the state-economy model in which it operates. Hall and Gingerich (2001, 4) noted that the two models form, "an underlying continuum, running between market and strategic coordination." Among advanced nations, Australia, Britain, Canada, Ireland, New Zealand, and the United States are as classified as LMC, while Austria, Belgium, Netherlands, Denmark, Finland, Germany, Japan, Norway, Sweden, and Switzerland have CMC. Other advanced nations, such as, France, Spain, and Italy, are mixed.[9]

In the LMC model, the state intervenes into markets; however, "the strong state of liberalism . . . is fundamentally different from the strong state of non-liberalism, in that the former serves to liberate markets and contracts from social constraints and collective obligations while the latter tries to do the opposite," according to Streeck (2001, 7). Under LMC, even strong states encourage market forces, while in CMC, the state offers alternatives to the market. The two models are distinguished by their *type of state-economy relationship* more than *the amount of state intervention*. CMC nations have developed a distinct approach in opposition to a LMC model because of its instability and problems, rather than as a positive alternative model.[10]

Compared to CMC nations, those with LMC tend to have lower tax levels, less government planning and business direction, weaker state capacities, meager social benefit programs, and fewer laws to support organized labor. Most English-speaking countries moved toward a LMC model over the past decade. This convergence was caused less by a natural tendency than as part of a self-conscious political program.[11] Since 1980s an intense version of the LMC model, sometimes labeled market fundamentalism, grew in the United States and other English-speaking nations, specifically Australia, Great Britain, New Zealand (see World View 10.1). Campbell and Pedersen (2001, 1) noted that it has, "market deregulation, state decentralization, and reduced state intervention" and was "a shift away from Keynesian economic ideas, which emphasized political management of aggregate demand, to a more conservative discourse based on monetarist, supply-side, and rational expectation theories."

LMC nations that adopt strong neoliberal policies reject industrial planning or an industrial policy. Hooks (1990b, 125) noted that, "Industrial planning refers to a state's deliberate effort to determine the production and distribution activity of specific economic sectors, and these efforts frequently require interventions and negotiations with individual firms." With an industrial policy, the state plans, coordinates, and develops programs to advance a nation's general economic expansion, technological advances, balanced economic sectors, worker retraining, regional-geographic distribution, and international trade. The United States lacks a national industrial policy, but the state aids business in other ways, including a policy of increased government spending during economic downturns, which was named after the economist John Maynard Keynes (1883–1946). In the 1980s, the United States shifted toward an intense form of LMC or neoliberalism. To understand why and how this occurred and its implications, we need to review the major events that led up to it.

WORLD VIEW 10.1   New Zealand's Neoliberal Transformation

In the late 1970s and early 1980s, several small countries, such as Chile and New Zealand, reorganized their state-economic relations and experimented with a sharp turn to a free market approach. The leading British political theorist, John Gray (1998, 39) remarked, "The neo-liberal experiment in New Zealand is the most ambitious attempt at constructing the free market as a social institution to be implemented [it is] . . . the most far-reaching transformation of a hitherto interventionist state we have yet to witness." In the 1950s, New Zealand had been the world's 3rd richest country per capita, but it dropped to around 20th place by the mid-1980s after oil prices rapidly rose and preferential access for farm produce into Britain ended. Economic stagnation, inflation, and instability followed. Then from 1984 to 1990, with a new regime, the government reversed course and adopted a neoliberal model based on a lean government with an emphasis on free markets. Many existing business and social policies were dismantled, and government controls over rents, prices, interest rates, and wages were eliminated. State enterprises were sold to private investors, business and agricultural subsidies were abolished, and tariffs were greatly reduced. Taxes and social programs were sharply cut, labor laws were revised to encourage individual contracts instead of collective bargaining by unions, and public schooling was decentralized and private fees for it encouraged. For a while, the restructured economy grew and new foreign investment poured in, but it has since stagnated. Economic inequality increased and social cohesion declined. By 2002 some neoliberal "reforms" have been reversed, but New Zealanders still may be more accepting of neoliberal experimentation in their state-economy relationship.

Sources: "Can the Kiwi economy fly?," *The Economist,* November 30, 2000; Gray (1998), McAllister and Vowles (1994), Roper (1991), Silva (1993), and Wilkes (1991).

America's Post-World War II Economy

The hard infrastructure (e.g., roads, bridges, harbors, railways, electrical systems, health care system) and industrial capacity of the United States emerged from World War II in very good condition, while the war destroyed the infrastructure and industrial capacity of competing industrial nations. During World War II (1941–1945) and the Korean War (1950–1953), the United States expanded its industrial capacity and invested heavily in infrastructure for national defense. In the following two decades, U.S. multinational firms expanded overseas aided by a foreign/military policy that encouraged and protected U.S. investments in countries of geo-political-military importance. To gain better access to low-cost raw materials that could supplement abundant U.S. natural resources, U.S. firms also entered ex-colonies in Asia, Africa and the Middle East and expanded into Latin America. At the same time, the state subsidized growth in the aerospace, petrolchemical and other defense-related industries. The infusion of state investment accelerated growth in some geographic areas, such as California and the Sun Belt (e.g., Texas, Arizona), while the Snow Belt in the Midwest and Northeast fell behind.[12] These conditions created a vibrant industrial economy in which most skilled blue-collar and white-collar workers could reach a middle class lifestyle with rising real (i.e., post-inflation) incomes.

By the early-1970s, the economy entered a period of volatile instability. The costly and unpopular war in Vietnam (1965–1970) deeply divided the country politically and created high inflation. At the same time, civil rights and other protest movements won social programs, housing benefits, and urban renewal, often reinforcing racial divisions and the out-migration of whites from major cities.[13] During the 1970s, new consumer and environmental movements demanded corporate responsibility, clean air and water, safer consumer products, better working conditions, and employment fairness that added to corporation costs. On top of this, international competition intensified and world oil prices increased as the oil exporting countries organized and demanded much higher profits.

The profits of major U.S. firms stagnated and declined. Companies held back on wage increases, wages did not keep pace with inflation, so real wages fell for most people. To achieve the same purchasing power, more women entered the paid labor force and people worked more hours. U.S. industry also began to lose out in international markets. Simply put, after years with little serious international competition, many firms had grown soft and fat. They failed to improve worker skill levels or reinvest profits into upgrading technology or production processes. The industrial system that had produced 30 years of success only worked until the conditions that allowed it to operate changed (e.g., international competitors, changes in technology). Through the late 1970s, the economy suffered from stagflation. **Stagflation describes an unusual economic situation in the 1970s that combined stagnant economic growth, high unemployment rates, and high inflation.** Political and corporate leaders and academics debated whether to shift from the existing LMC model to industrial policy. Economic problems grew worse in 1981–1982, as the United States suffered its worst economic downturn since the 1930s.

One set of political leaders, borrowing ideas from countries that had adopted a nonliberal CMC model, proposed a U.S. industrial policy. Under it, the federal government would actively direct private business and would strongly encourage private investments in targeted areas as it had during World War II, only this time the goal was to improve productivity, profits, and global competitiveness. Two versions of the industrial policy were offered. One would reindustrialize and update existing industries; the other would abandon old "sunset" industries in favor of a shift to promote newly emerging high-tech industries. Both involved government coordinated planning with business subsidies, loan guarantees, tax incentives, government procurements, research and development funding, infrastructure development, worker retraining assistance, international trade policies, and business regulations.[14]

A set of political leaders opposed to industrial policy emerged subsequent to meetings by conservative economists and executives sponsored by the Heritage Foundation. In a series of academic reports, conferences, press releases, and lobbying activities, they attacked industrial policy and offered an alternative vision. By 1983 the economy began to recover. With divisions inside organized labor and strong business community opposition to it, most political leaders turned against industrial policy. By 1984 it had disappeared from the public agenda.

The alternative strategy to industrial policy was to strengthen and deepen the LMC model. This neoliberal vision gained momentum as politically active corporate executives, bankers, advocacy groups, and some academic experts urged reinventing the economy around an intensified LMC model.[15] In simple terms, they blamed the nation's economic problems on "big government," and their solution was to reduce taxes, especially on the wealthy and on business, deregulate or rollback environmental and safety regulations, accelerate international trade, increase worker productivity by holding down wages and unions, and expand free-market probusiness policies.

From the late 1980s and through the late 1990s, U.S. corporations recovered profitability and international competitiveness through a more flexible approach. They introduced flexible labor practices and reduced labor costs by relocating production facilities from older U.S. cities to low-wage regions in the U.S. (e.g., Southern right to work or antiunion states or rural or small town areas with low taxes and nonunion workers) or to third-world countries. They hired professional consultants to bust labor unions using new legal procedures, they relied more on subcontractors and temporary workers, and they introduced labor-saving technology to reduce the number of high-wage jobs by using automation. They increased flexible production. Flexible production differs from old-style manufacturing by keeping close track of costs through new accounting, recordkeeping and planning systems; by using new technology to speed the work pace; and by adding computer-assisted design and computer-controlled production process. They also increased flexible investment, which shifted investment from manufacturing products to a mix of goods and services. In search of profits, firms moved into financial, information, real estate, and service industries that were not locked into a single location and could take advantage of emerging information and communication technologies. Investments moved to eliminate barriers of space, time, or currency, and corporations opened in new locations around the globe.[16]

A new system of "flexible accumulation" emerged from the various ideas and techniques. Flexible accumulation encourages using contingent workers who receive lower pay, few fringe benefits, and little job protection. They are contingent, unlike the old, full-time, permanent workforce. A firm only employs them for a limited time for specific tasks then jettisons them. Some estimates suggest as much as 30 percent of new jobs created in the U.S. were contingent.[17] Contingent workers were not a temporary response to a short-term downturn in the business cycle as in the past. Now they were a new way to organize a workforce. By the 1990s, executives increased corporate restructuring and downsizing by eliminating large numbers of middle management, white-collar workers.[18] Wall Street investors greeted the announcements of downsizing or large white-collar layoffs favorably because it made the corporations "lean and mean," nimble, fast, and flexible. Corporations increased profitability in a fast changing economy by shedding the old 1940s–1960s industrial model, called Fordism.

Fordism had a large, fixed, blue-collar workforce (often unionized), large-scale factories located in cities, firms that stayed in one community for decades, and mass production product lines that changed only a little from year to year. Under Fordism, many corporate executives accepted paying high wages and offering most workers a rising standard of living as a necessary cost of doing business. It bought "labor peace," among what was then a heavily unionized labor force, and helped blue- and white-collar workers to be consumers who could buy products. By the 1980s when union membership declined, production moved across international borders, and new export markets opened up, this was less important. With increased global mobility, Third World workers easily underbid less-skilled American workers, and selling in global markets meant consumers could be anywhere. At the same time, the American working family could maintain their standard of living, even if their wages had stagnated, by working longer and buying products produced in overseas, low-income nations. As productivity and profits grew, the upper 20 percent of income earners gained most, and the income-wealth gaps between the rich and others grew larger.

Corporate power and economic concentration (i.e., a smaller number of large corporations control a very big percentage of their industry) grew. Changes in antitrust and corporate tax laws make it easier for U.S. corporations to restructure, buy up other companies, or merge. There have been four large-scale corporate merger waves in the U.S.—the late 1890s, the late 1920s, the 1960s, and the 1980s. Each time, the state facilitated the corporate restructuring. As Stearns and Allan (1996, 714) noted, "While many specific characteristics of mergers vary across merger waves, each wave has been preceded by the state providing merger promoters with legal freedom to execute mergers." Legal-political changes encouraged the 1980s corporate merger wave. Bowman (1996, 170–171) observed that, "antitrust decisions of the Supreme Court under Chief Justices Warren Burger and William Rehnquist, and the enforcement policies . . . under Presidents Ronald Reagan and George Bush, significantly revised antitrust law and policy to enable firms to compete more effectively in the global marketplace . . . the scope and scale of this movement has been truly remarkable by any previous measure."

Intensified neoliberal principles spread to other areas of state policy.[19] As Henig et al. (2003, 37–38) noted, "One of the most significant developments in recent theory and research on public policy has been the elaboration of a broad theory of privatization that incorporates empirical claims, into a normative case for increased reliance on market forces as a means of achieving public ends. . . . Notions that seemed provocative but quaint . . . four decades ago now occupy center stage. This development has dramatically changed the terms of the debate." A state-centered industrial policy for the United States failed in a LMC institutional structure accompanied by a strong neoliberal ideological climate that was hostile toward government. What developed in its absence was an ad hoc mixture of tax and corporate subsidy policies, military procurements, and business policies; a patchwork "corporate welfare" system.

Politics of Taxes and Distribution

Politics of Taxes

Taxes are intensely political. During his 1988 presidential campaign, candidate George H. W. Bush made a famous promise, "Read my lips, no new taxes." Going back on that pledge shortly after the election wrecked his political career. Twelve years later, another Texas oil executive, his son George W. Bush, pushed through the largest tax reduction in U.S. history. Tax rebellions in the eighteenth century contributed to the French Revolution, and grassroots tax revolts to freeze property taxes that began in California in the 1970s quickly spread across the United States (see Case in Point 10.1). John Campbell (1993, 163) remarked, "the study behind taxation and pubic finances . . . is one of the best starting points for an investigation of society, and particularly of political life."

Taxation involves the state applying its legal authority and coercive power to extract resources from individuals and organizations in state-controlled territory. All states have demanded taxes, tributes, fees, tolls, tariffs, duties, and dues from citizen/subjects for centuries. Taxes pay for operating the state administration

---

 CASE IN POINT 10.1   Tax Revolts

Periodically, people rise up collectively against taxes. This has happened in many countries over the centuries. In the United States in 1978, California voters overwhelming passed Proposition 13 that froze or lowered property taxes across the state. Similar antitax movements quickly followed in other states. Although the rhetoric of the California antitax movement emphasized the heavy tax burden on middle-class homeowners, subsequent studies found that the primary beneficiaries of the tax reductions were business owners and wealthy or upper-middle class homeowners. The populist, antielitist, and antibusiness tax revolt message was first carried by a lower-middle class base without a political party or business involvement. However, a small-business owner who was active in the Republican Party soon assumed leadership and redirected the movement's agenda to attract support from wealthy homeowners and business owners. Renters, who tend to be low-income people, were left out but disproportionately felt the reductions in

local public services that resulted. About 15 years after Proposition 13, two Pacific Coast states had referendums for imposing new taxes. Oregon was to introduce a sales tax and Washington State an income tax. In both states, opposition to the new taxes largely came from middle-aged people who had high levels of political cynicism about government and who believed that government was filled with inefficiency and waste. Younger, educated people and government employees tended to accept the new taxes. The tax revolts suggest that political symbolism may be just as important as the level of an increase in taxes in generating political opposition. Antitax movements appear to mix populist-libertarian, antigovernment symbolism with some real resentment over taxes. The primary beneficiaries of most tax revolts are high-income people and business owners, but the political symbolism and resentment it inflames tends to attract a broad political base of people who typically receive relatively few benefits once the tax reductions are implemented.

Sources: Bowler and Donovan (1995), Lo (1990), Sears and Citrin (1982), Steel and Lovrich (1998).

and carrying out state programs and activities. National tax systems began in Europe in the fourteenth century with feudal dues. As Braithwaite and Drahos (2000, 89) observed, "The most important driving force behind the evolution of national tax systems was war . . . European rulers did not develop tax policy as part of some overall plan of economic development. Rather, tax policy was driven by the exigencies of military conflict or its possibility."

Taxes come in many forms. Some are very direct and visible (e.g., sales tax, real estate or property tax, inheritance tax, income tax), others are indirect and hidden (e.g., excise tax, value-added tax, alcohol and cigarette taxes, tariffs on imported products). Individuals, families, and organizations pay taxes. Most businesses pay taxes on their net income or profits, and employers may pay payroll taxes to employ workers (e.g., social security, unemployment insurance, workmen's compensation). Some taxes blur into quasi-tax sources of government revenue with labels like user fees or tariffs. For example, I recently purchased a car and paid the following for it: a tariff (i.e., a tax on imported goods), a sales tax, an excise tax on the tires, an automobile license fee, an automobile title fee, and a vehicle registration fee. To drive, I pay for roads through income taxes, gasoline taxes, and a local property tax. If I use a toll road, I also pay a toll—a narrowly targeted form of taxation. Taxes have been placed on almost every imaginable good, service, or activity. Goods, services, or activities that are taxed in one nation or level of government might not be taxed in another, or they may be taxed using very different methods.

Tax Burdens

Public discourse is filled with complaints about the burden of high taxes. For example, a Texas medical doctor complained about high taxes and backed President George Bush's 2001 tax cut. He felt he deserved the promised $12,000 reduction in taxes on his $290,000 annual income. He said his family is just treading water to meet expenses and could not afford luxuries. Even living in the low-tax state of Texas (ranked 47th nationally) his family had to reduce the hours of the full-time nanny who looks after their children, now must clean their private swimming pool themselves, and could no longer take week-long skiing vacations. To reduce costs they thought of moving, but could not find a house selling for under $1 million in their neighborhood.[20] The same tax cut gave $300 to low-income workers. Of all the total tax reductions, 70 percent went to businesses, not individuals.[21]

Much of the complaining over taxes is based on the ideal of paying no taxes, but it frequently expresses political conflict. After all, "tax struggles are among the oldest forms of class struggle," noted Campbell (1993, 168). Once we get beyond slogans that "taxes are too high" and the obfuscation over tax issues, we can see the real political dynamics of taxation. As a percentage of the national economy, taxes have grown in all advanced industrial nations from an average of about 29 percent in the 1960s to over 40 percent now. The tax burden, as a percentage of the economy, varies from 27.1 percent in Japan to 54.2 percent in Sweden and comes from different kinds of taxes. Thus, the United States gets about

40 percent of its tax revenue as income taxes. France, Greece, and the Netherlands get about 17 percent, 13 percent, and 15 percent respectively from income taxes. By contrast, Denmark depends on income taxes for 51 percent of its tax revenue. Some nations rely more on taxing workers and employers through payroll taxes, while others rely on indirect forms of consumption or direct sales taxes (see Table 10.1).

The United States has a very complex tax system. Most of the complexity is due to special provisions in the system to benefit particular activities or groups and to use taxation to achieve political objectives indirectly. A highly complex tax system increases public perceptions of unfairness, makes evading taxes easier, and raises the total cost of collecting taxes (see Summary 10.1). A nation's tax policy reflects its cultural beliefs, political conflicts, and ideals. The first income tax was enacted by Great Britain in 1799, France followed in 1909. The United States enacted its first national income tax in 1913, after amending the Constitution because an income tax enacted in 1895 was declared unconstitutional.

TABLE 10.1 2001 Total Tax Revenue as a Percentage of the Gross Domestic Product (GDP)

Country	Percent of GDP	Tax Source (% of all taxes)					
		Income	Corporation	Payroll	Property	Goods & Services	Consumption (Sales)
Australia	31.5	43.3	15.2	6.6	9.5	25.5	8.5
Austria	43.7	22.5	4.8	40.3	1.3	27.9	18.7
Canada	35.8	38.5	10.0	15.8	10.4	24.7	14.0
Denmark	48.8	51.6	5.6	3.9	3.6	33.2	19.6
France	45.3	17.4	5.9	39.5	7.3	26.6	17.5
Germany	37.9	25.0	4.4	40.4	2.4	27.4	17.9
Greece	37.8	13.3	6.4	32.3	3.8	41.0	22.6
Ireland	31.1	30.9	10.7	13.8	5.2	38.7	22.2
Italy	42.7	25.0	7.0	29.5	4.8	27.4	14.2
Japan	27.1	18.8	13.3	38.4	10.5	18.8	8.9
Netherlands	41.4	15.2	10.6	39.9	4.9	27.7	16.9
New Zealand	35.1	41.8	10.9	0.9	5.7	36.0	26.0
Norway	40.3	27.3	9.7	23.3	2.4	37.2	21.3
Poland	34.1	22.0	7.5	33.1	3.0	34.4	20.3
Spain	35.2	20.8	7.3	35.2	6.0	29.4	16.6
Sweden	54.2	35.0	5.7	33.5	8.3	18.2	13.6
Switzerland	35.7	31.8	6.0	6.0	35.7	8.3	10.0
United Kingdom	37.4	27.5	11.0	11.0	17.6	10.7	18.1
United States	29.3	40.5	9.0	23.7	10.6	16.6	7.6

Source: Column 1, Organization for Economic Cooperation and Development, *Basic Structural Statistics, Main Economic Indicators*, May 2003. Other Columns, OECD *Tax and the Economy, A Comparative Assessment of OECD Countries*, No 6 (2001).

SUMMARY 10.1   Tax Complaints and Issues

1. **Fairness**—People are more accepting of taxes if they believe that taxes are fairly imposed. Fairness means that two people or organizations in an identical financial or social situation pay the same amount. People are likely to object when they suspect that others in the same situation are paying substantially less in taxes.

2. **Types of Taxes**—People are more accepting of taxes if they accept the basic principles (e.g., moral, economic, social) that dictate imposing taxes on certain activities/groups/objects and not on others to encourage or discourage behavior. People are more likely to object when they disagree with the principles or feel that taxation is contradictory, arbitrary, or without clear principles.

3. **Transparent and Efficient Collection**—People are more accepting of taxes if they can clearly see the basis for computing taxes and that taxes are collected quickly and efficiently. People are more likely to object when they cannot easily see how taxes are computed or when the system of calculating and paying taxes is very inefficient.

4. **Indirect versus Direct Taxes**—People are more accepting of indirect taxes (i.e., taxes that are unseen and are built into costs) rather than direct taxes (i.e., taxes that are very visible). People are more likely to object to visible taxes, especially if they are forced to pay a specific amount directly.

5. **Official versus Effective Tax Rates**—People are more accepting of taxes if the official tax rates match what people actually pay. People are more likely to object when certain categories of people or organizations in specific situations get exemptions, breaks, or loopholes so that their actual amount paid is much more or less than official rates.

6. **Simplicity**—People are more accepting of taxes if they are simple and collected all at one time. People are more likely to object when there are many different types of taxes paid to many units for various purposes at different times, and the process of calculating taxes is complicated.

7. **Equity Progressive/Regressive**—People tend to be more accepting of taxes if they believe that the burden is proportionate to their ability to pay. Since, high income people have a greater ability to pay, even if they pay a higher percentage in taxes, their ability to obtain life's necessities and have a high standard of living is less affected than someone who has a low income. In most nations income taxes are *progressive* (i.e., low-income people are exempt, and the rate of tax increases as a person's income level rises). *Regressive taxes* tax people at lower income levels at higher rates.

8. **Benefits from Tax Revenue**—People are more accepting of taxes when they have a clear idea of the purpose of the tax revenue, and especially if they can see benefits from the taxes. People will object the loudest to taxes when they see little or no positive outcome of the taxes connected to their daily lives and activities, or when the benefits largely accrue to people or organizations or are for activities to which the taxpayers object. Theda Skocpol (1995b, 8) argued that, "Especially since the 1980s, conservatives have proclaimed that Americans invariability hate taxes. But history shows that middle-class Americans have been quite willing to pay taxes when they were sure that these monies would go for worthy purposes from which they along with other citizens would benefit."

Braithwaite and Drahos (2000, 94) noted, "Tax policy and law remained in the U.S. and elsewhere deeply rooted in national life and culture. The endless differences in the ways that states treated income and capital for tax purposes, the kinds of taxes they imposed, the thousands of exemptions and qualifications they allowed to the basic principles of tax law reflect their different interest group politics, as well as their perception of how equality and justice were achieved through the tax system."

Determinates of Taxation

In addition to paying for the cost of waging war, "the geopolitical and fiscal crisis, as well as economic conditions, create pressure on political elites to raise taxes," concluded Campbell (1993, 168). Taxes are often imposed on one part of society to provide benefits to another, and "there are few areas in which the redistributive interests of social classes come into sharper conflict than tax policy."[22] The degree to which individual taxes are progressive (i.e., upper-income people pay a higher percentage in taxes than low-income people) varies widely by country. Taxes in the United States are among the least progressive.[23] Income, inheritance, luxury goods (e.g., yachts, furs), capital gains, and wealth taxes tend to be progressive, while consumption taxes (e.g., sales tax, cigarettes, gasoline, etc.) tend to be regressive (i.e., lower-income people pay more). This is because low-income people must use their entire incomes for consumption, while the wealthy can save or invest most of theirs. For example, two people each pay $50 in sales tax. Yet the tax is 14 percent of the poor person's weekly earnings of $350 and 1 percent of the rich person's $4,500 weekly earnings. The "equal" $50 tax is 14 times more of a burden on the poor person based on ability to pay. Flat tax proposals to simplify income taxes would have a similar regressive effect.

Since 1980, total taxes coming from corporate income declined in the United States. The official tax rates changed somewhat, but the real reason has been changes in technical tax rules and accounting systems. The political party in power influences corporate tax collection, and Democratic Party administrations collect more in business taxes.[24] Corporate tax law changes, specifically the Tax Reform Act of 1986 and the Revenue Act of 1987, gave corporations new ways to restructure mergers, acquisitions, and create divisions as subsidiaries without paying taxes. The tax law changes accelerated corporate mergers and encouraged corporations to adopt a subsidiary form of organization.[25]

The progressiveness of individual income tax depends on three factors: (1) the income level at which taxation begins, (2) the number of income brackets in the tax code, and (3) the tax rate in each bracket. It is also being affected by the sources of income included as taxable and tax "adjustment factors" (e.g., marital status, age, number of children, physical disability). In the United States, the current income tax system has five brackets with the rates beginning at 15 percent for a single person in the lowest income bracket and peaking at 39.5 percent for the highest bracket. Internationally, rates for a single person in the bottom bracket vary from under 1 percent in Switzerland to 25 percent in Sweden and 26 percent in Ireland. The rate for the top bracket varies from 11.5 percent in

Switzerland to over 50 percent in France, Germany, and the Netherlands. The number of brackets varies from one, or a flat tax, in Sweden to ten brackets in Switzerland.[26]

The official tax system may be progressive, but the effective tax rates (i.e., what people actually pay after all taxes, deductions, etc. are included) may not. The marginal effective tax rate (i.e., the actual amount paid on additional earnings over a certain level) is often regressive. For example, a low-income married couple in the United States who have two children and earn two-thirds of an average factory worker's salary pays 40 percent of each additional dollar earned in taxes. In other countries, this rate may be higher, as in Australia where it's 80 percent, or lower, as in Japan where it's 18 percent.

State governments in the United States vary widely in government size, state budgets, and taxing plans. Revenue collected per state resident varies from $2,608 in Florida to $5,526 in Delaware, and the number of state government employees per 10,000 residents varies from 104 in Illinois to 448 in Hawaii.[27] Seven of the 50 states have no income tax. Among those with a state income tax, the top tax bracket ranges from 2.8 percent in Pennsylvania to 11 percent in Montana. Six states have a flat income tax, while others have up to 10 income brackets. The 45 states that have a sales tax (not including city or local sales taxes) range from 2.9 percent in Colorado to 7.75 percent in California. Only five states apply the sales tax to food (Illinois, Louisiana, Missouri, Tennessee, and Virginia) while others exempt certain items (e.g., clothing, prescription drugs). Every state taxes gasoline with rates from 7.5 cents per gallon in Georgia to 30 cents in Rhode Island. So-called "sin" taxes vary widely. The beer tax ranges from 2 cents per gallon in West Virginia to $1.07 in Alaska. For wine, it ranges from 11 cents per gallon in Louisiana to $2.25 in Florida. Cigarette taxes have risen in recent years. As of July 2003, state cigarette taxes ranged from 3 cents per pack in Kentucky to $2.05 in New Jersey.[28] After New York City raised its city cigarette tax from 8 cents to $1.50 per pack in 2003, the total cost for a pack of cigarettes rose to $7.00 in New York City. The same pack costs about $2.00 in Kentucky. Many state and local governments have a property tax, usually on real estate or sometimes automobiles or other property. For example, my brother-in-law moved from Colorado to Wisconsin. The value of his house was the same, but his property taxes were twice as much because of higher property tax rates in Wisconsin. A comparison of all state and local taxes (including income, property, general sales, alcoholic beverage, motor fuels, public utilities, tobacco, inheritance, etc.) among the 50 U.S. states shows a range from 8.4 percent in Tennessee to just over 12.8 percent in Maine of the average state resident's income.[29]

Every state has a corporate income tax and these rates range from 4 percent in Kansas to 9.99 percent in Pennsylvania. Thirty-one states charge a flat rate for all corporations. The average effective corporate tax rate has dropped from 9.0 percent in 1980 to 5.9 percent in 2001. About one-fourth of the decline was due to tax cuts, the remainder was due to adding tax loopholes and shelters. Without the existence of tax shelters, in 2001 corporations and banks would have paid state governments 35 percent more. Some states lost as much as 50 percent of what they could have ordinarily collected because of such tax shelters (see the Tax Avoidance section later in this chapter).[30]

The numerous types and levels of taxation illustrate two points. First, in a federal system, each unit of government is a site where contests over taxes and other issues occur. Second, individuals and businesses may benefit or alter their behavior (e.g., where they live, what they purchase) based on tax considerations. State governments set taxes for specific purposes (e.g., to attract businesses or retirees, to reduce smoking or drinking) and in response to political pressure from certain groups (e.g., businesses or wealthy people who threaten to leave unless taxes are lowered).

Tax Avoidance

Since taxes were first collected, some people and businesses have tried to avoid paying them. While outright lying or cheating is clearly illegal, many legal ways exist to avoid paying taxes. In 2002, the U.S. Internal Revenue Service (IRS) reported that 152,000 people filed bogus tax returns, claiming to owe no taxes or to be owed a refund, and 1,500 businesses stopped collecting taxes for employees or claimed they did not have to pay income taxes.[31] While anyone can try to avoid taxes, high income people and corporations have the most legal opportunities to avoid taxes. For example, corporate executives who use a corporate jet for personal travel pay very little. A first-class ticket from New York to Paris may cost $6,000 to $14,700 in a private luxury jet. If you are a top executive and use a corporate jet for your personal vacation, you only pay $486 in fees. The actual value of the trip is not counted as being income, and "The practice of using company planes for personal travel is widespread."[32]

Inheritance preserves intergenerational wealth and societywide economic inequality, so taxing inheritance is a highly progressive form of taxation. Most nations have an inheritance tax; the U.S. began its tax in 1916. Yet recently U.S. politicians railed against the injustice of inheritance taxes, which they called "death taxes." As one Congressman claimed, "The death tax is one of the most unfair taxes because it taxes farmers, ranchers and small business owners twice and sometimes three times. They spend their whole lives paying taxes, and then the federal government taxes the value of whatever is left at the time of death."[33] Despite the heated rhetoric about hurting small business owners and family farmers, under 2 percent of the population, primarily the very rich, pay the federal inheritance tax. Over 90 percent of it is paid by the nation's richest 5 percent. This is largely because the first $1 million of inheritance is tax free. Under 10 percent of taxed inheritances were on a family business or farms, most of them were on stock and real estate investments.[34] President George Bush's 2001 tax cut law included a phased-in abolition of the federal government's inheritance tax.

Banks and corporations have more tax avoidance options. In general, tax avoidance is greatest among the largest corporations and in the more politically organized sectors of the business community (e.g., industries with a few large corporations).[35] Some businesses avoid state government taxes by creating a "paper" corporation in another state that has lower taxes and transferring their nonphysical assets (e.g., copyrights, trademarks, patents, loans) to the paper corporation. The paper corporation can be a one-person office, but it might earn many millions in corporate income. Another tactic is to shift business income to an offshore tax haven to avoid paying national-level taxes.[36] For example, one of the world's largest media corporations, Rupert Murdoch's News Corporation and its subsidiaries paid $238 million in corporate taxes worldwide over a four year period ending in 1999. In the three countries in which News Corporation primarily operates (Australia, the United States, and Britain) official corporate tax rates are 36 percent, 35 percent, and 30 percent respectively, but News Corporation's effective tax rate was about 6 percent. For comparison, Disney, another world media empire, paid 31 percent of its income in taxes. From 1988 to 1999 the News Corporation made $2.1 billion in profits in Britain but paid no taxes. The company has a complex structure with 800 subsidiaries and funnels much of its income to 60 of them that are located in tax havens such as the Cayman Islands, Bermuda, the Netherlands Antilles, or the British Virgin Islands.[37]

Leading investment and accounting firms help major corporations avoid taxes. For example, tax advisors at Merrill Lynch helped the Allied Signal Corporation avoid $180 million in U.S. taxes. Allied Signal transferred its taxable income to a foreign partner company and brought the money back into the United States tax-free. For their advice, Merrill Lynch received its cut of $25 million. Some such tax shelters are illegal, but the odds of getting caught and the penalties are small. One financial advisor estimated the odds of getting caught were less than 1 in 50, especially after staff reductions at the Internal Revenue Service. He said for a possible $100 million in tax savings, it was worth the risk.[38] Some corporations transfer money to foreign paper partners in small countries with special tax treaties, like Barbados, Bermuda, or Luxembourg, converting taxable incomes into tax deductible expenses. Others legally incorporate in a tax haven country but keep their physical headquarters in the United States.[39] When some in Congress tried to outlaw this practice in 2002, they had to withdraw the proposal due to intense corporate political pressure.[40]

Weakening the government's tax-collection capacity aids tax avoidance, because it is easier to avoid taxes when tax collection agencies cannot enforce the tax laws or investigate tax fraud. In 1998 a number of politicians attacked the IRS for being "overzealous" in collecting taxes from their wealthy business supporters; they cut the IRS budget and directed it to focus less on enforcement and more on assisting taxpayers.[41] As a result, tax audits and enforcement efforts declined by more than one-half.[42] Tax enforcement shifted from large corporations to individuals, and among individuals, from the wealthy to the working poor. For example, audits of people who earned over $100,000 dropped from 1 in 33 to 1 in 150.[43] When the head of the IRS retired at the end of 2002, he said tax evasion was fast growing among the wealthy. For example, the IRS identified 82,100 people who had illegal offshore bank accounts to hide income in 2001. Yet it could only pursue 17,000 of them because of a lack of law enforcement resources.[44] Many state governments also reduced tax enforcement activities which, "primarily benefit cheats in the highest incomes, especially investors in partnerships," three-quarters of whom are in the richest two percent of the population.[45] As the effective tax rate on corporations and the wealthy dropped by about one-third over the past decade, the effective tax rate paid by others has risen.

Tax Consequences

Special tax reductions can encourage behaviors (e.g., businesses will invest in an area; people will save for retirement, buy a house, preserve farmland, or donate to a charity) or discourage behaviors (e.g., smoking, drinking, wasting energy). Tax effects may be intended or unintended (e.g., the marriage penalty in the U.S. income tax code discourages marriage, property tax systems encourage urban sprawl). Tax expenditure is an area of tax policy intended to advance an objective (e.g., encourage oil exploration, help low-income people). **Tax expenditures are a form of hidden spending by the government through tax breaks, tax reductions, etc. for specific purposes.** Instead of collecting taxes and then spending the tax money for a specific purpose, the government exempts particular activities from taxation. Two types of tax expenditure are revenue loss (i.e., reduced tax liabilities via a refund, exception, deduction) and incentives (i.e., targeted subsidies or transfers).

Tax expenditures use the tax code to distribute benefits. For example, instead of giving parents a $400 check to help with child-rearing expenses, they get a $400 tax refund. This is not government spending; it is manipulating the tax system to achieve the same purpose. Yet this method does not deliver the benefit to all parents; very low-income parents who owe little or no income tax are excluded. Likewise, when the government does not tax a corporation's employee pension funds, a company pays less in taxes and its employees indirectly benefit. Instead, the government could have collected taxes and given all citizens higher social security or public pension payments. Tax expenditures reduce direct government spending, hide state benefits from public view, and allow benefits to be targeted to the most affluent citizens. They circumvent the delivery of public benefits to all citizens.[46]

To generate the same total tax revenue, lowering a rate or adding exemptions to one type of tax (e.g., income) usually shifts the tax burden to other taxes (e.g., sales). This alters the share of the tax burden various social groups must pay. For example, reducing income tax rates and increasing the sales tax rates helps high-income people and shifts the tax burden toward lower- and middle-income people. Tax politics often centers on shifting the tax burden among different groups. An organized group might lobby or direct campaign contributions to convince legislators to grant it a specific tax exemption and shift the tax burden onto unorganized and unaware taxpayers.

Many parts of the U.S. "welfare state" (i.e., social programs) are hidden within the tax code, especially parts that disproportionately benefit middle and high income people. One of the largest is the home mortgage deduction. It originated in 1913 as part of the first income tax. Originally the goal was to help high-income people and keep tax collections on interest payments simple. Over time, promoting private homeownership became its major justification.[47] During the 1930s and 1940s, low- and middle-income people gained access to home loans and long-term mortgages. Today, about 67 percent of Americans own a home. Home ownership rates are over 60 percent in Australia, Canada, Ireland, Japan, Norway, Spain, and Italy, but are lower in Austria (58%), Germany (41%), and Switzerland (31%).[48] Most people borrow money to buy a house. "The proportion of owner-occupied dwellings that are mortgaged differs widely between countries, standing at just over 60% in England and the United States, just over 50% in Canada and New Zealand, and only 38% in Australia."[49] Countries with high rates of home-ownership tend to have less generous social welfare programs to equalize incomes.[50] In addition to income level, home ownership (versus renting) in the U.S. greatly varies by race, age, and urban location. For example, 71 percent of whites, 46 percent of African Americans, and 45 percent of Latinos own homes; 40 percent of people under age 35 own homes, while 80 percent of people aged 50 or older own homes; and in New York City and San Francisco, 30–35 percent of people own homes compared to over 80 percent of people in many suburbs and small towns. The United States and many countries offer a tax reduction on part of the cost of borrowing money for a house (see Table 10.2).

Here's how it works. I go to a bank and borrow $200,000 at 6 percent for 30 years. Each month I pay the bank $1,200. Over the 30-year period, I will pay back the entire $200,000 plus $241,677 in interest. After 30 years, the house I bought for $200,000 will probably be worth more than $200,000 due to inflation. Odds are it will be valued at $400,000. The best part is that of the $441,677 I paid to the bank over 30 years, the federal government helped out with $241,677 by giving me tax deductions. It is like getting $241,677 free of income tax. If I paid $1,200

TABLE 10.2	Housing Tax Rules in Several Advanced Nations			
	Local Property Tax	Capital Gains Tax	National Tax Break on Mortgage Interest	National Tax Break on Property Tax
Australia	Yes	No	No	No
Canada	Yes	No	No	No
France	Yes	No	Credit	No
Germany	Yes	No	No	No
Italy	Yes	Yes	Deduction	No
Japan	Yes	No	No	No
Sweden	No	Yes	Deduction	No
United Kingdom	No	No	Deduction	No
United States	Yes	Yes	Deduction	Deduction

Source: McDonald, John, "Tax Treatment of Residences: An International Comparison," *Illinois Real Estate Newsletter*, 1994, pp. 8–10, http://www.business.uiuc.edu/orer/V8-1-3.pdf.

per month in rent for an apartment for 30 years and did not buy a house, I would get no tax break. Also, it only works if I owe the federal government enough in taxes. Low-income people cannot get the full benefit. If I sell the house before the 30-year mortgage is up, I get extra tax help. In the first year, I pay $2,456 toward the amount I borrowed, or the principal, and $11,933 in interest. Each year, the amount going toward the principal grows and the interest share declines. Since the tax deduction is for interest payments, the tax break is biggest in the early years. Again, this system works best if I have a large income and owe a lot in taxes. If I'm wealthy enough to buy a nice, expensive second vacation home and borrow money to buy it, the federal government gives me the same tax break on it as well. Some tax code benefits are designed for low-income people, but they tend to work rather differently (see Case in Point 10.2).

Distributing Resources

Corporate Welfare and Business Subsidies

The state relies on private businesses for tax revenue, employment, and social stability. Beyond taxes, the state has few alternative sources of revenue, so it encourages business activity indirectly (e.g., schooling that provides a well-trained labor force; transportation infrastructure, such as airports or roads, to move goods and people) and directly (e.g., entrepreneurial development programs, incubator low-rent buildings, grants or low-interest loans to business) to increase revenue. In the public's perception and media images, welfare in the United States is seen as a transfer of payments from the government to poor

---

 CASE IN POINT 10.2   **The Low-Income Beneficiaries of the Earned Income Tax Credit Program Are Not Trusted**

Sometimes the target of intensified enforcement of tax law takes a curious turn based on what appear to be political interests. The Earned Income Tax Credit (EITC), which began in 1975, gives a tax credit or reduction to very low-income families with children; however, it does not reach the poorest people or those without children. The amount a family with four children received under the program was $1,976 in 2001. Enforcement actions intensified in 1999, and in 2003, the Bush administration announced a tightening of the EITC rules that required the four million working poor who receive EITC to provide extensive documentation. Charging widespread cheating, the administration hired 650 additional IRS workers to go after potential EITC cheaters. Already 1 in 64 ETIC beneficiaries faces a tax audit compared to 1 in 400 owners of investor partnerships, which are primarily used by wealthy people. The estimated total amount in taxes avoided or not paid by the EITC program is about one-fifth of the amount for investor partnerships. No additional IRS workers will be checking on possible tax cheating by investor partnerships, which are owned by people who are far more likely to vote for and make campaign contributions to President George W. Bush than is anyone who collects EITC.

Sources: Walsh, Mary Williams. "IRS Tightening Rules for Low-Income Tax Credit," *New York Times*, April 25, 2003. Johnston, David Clay. "Reducing Audits of the Wealthy, IRS Turns Eye on Working Poor," *New York Times*, December 15, 1999. Also see Howard (1997, Chapter 7).

individuals, especially to "undeserving" mothers and their children. Yet the U.S. federal government spends roughly \$170–\$200 billion per year on corporate welfare—over four times more than it spends on welfare for the poor.[51] **Corporate welfare is a system of tax breaks, subsidies, special incentives, allowances, and other monetary and nonmonetary transfers of state resources to private corporations, largely based on political influence and for particularistic gain.** Corporate welfare is a sought-after "state intervention" that distributes public resources to specific business firms or to an industry.

The images of individual welfare are of an undeserved "handout" of taxpayer money. By contrast, corporate welfare is depicted as promoting jobs and economic growth, whether or not it really does. This fundamental dualism occurs for two reasons. First, corporations are shown to provide jobs, pay taxes, and create social benefits, while low-income individuals are stigmatized and depicted as being lazy and immoral. In the media, many groups (e.g., an environmental group fighting for clean air, homeless people seeking better shelters) are labeled as "special interests," while the business community is implicitly treated as acting in society's interest. Olson and Chaplin (1998) noted that holding an ideological belief in a natural, self-regulating market reinforces welfare dualism and contributes to corporate welfare's invisibility. State aid to individuals is outside the market, so it appears unnatural or harmful in a neoliberal context. Corporations are part of the market, so aiding them reinforces "natural" economic processes and appears beneficial. Second, corporate welfare comes as tax credits, accounting rule changes, loans at below market interest rates, tax-exempt bonds, and low-cost use of public resources, such as water, acreage, and minerals. Because it is not a separate budget item, it is very difficult to see or estimate corporate welfare accurately (see Chart 10.2).

Both corporate welfare and industrial policy are forms of state intervention into the market. They differ in that corporate welfare is a mix of ad hoc

chart 10.2

THE WELFARE DUALISM

Question	Corporate Welfare	Individual Welfare
How is welfare seen?	Incentives for the industrious	Handouts to the undeserving
What is the result of welfare?	Benefits for society, job creation, and community development	Drains society; is a work disincentive
What is the long-term result?	Generates income and improvements	A tax burden; creates dependency
How are recipients viewed?	Productive; works in society's interest	Unproductive; a selfish special interest

Source: Adapted from Olson and Champlin (1998).

benefits scattered across policy areas and is largely hidden. Individual firms, trade associations, or industries initiate and negotiate specific benefits using their political influence. By contrast, industrial policy is an explicit, planned, and integrated government program. Visible planning officials, executive branch bureaucracies, and business leaders together initiate and negotiate industrial policy. It is designed to strengthen the national economy or achieve broad national goals (e.g., increase international competitiveness, reduce unemployment, speed technological innovation). The justifications for corporate welfare benefits are often the same as for industrial policy, but the distribution of corporate welfare benefits depends on political influence because it is less transparent.[52] "Governments are often under pressure (from members of the business community) to use the corporate tax system to support specific industries or business even if this may lead to more complexity and less transparency, equity, or neutrality . . ." (OECD 2001, 26). The idea of transparency applies to the activities of government or other organizations. **Transparency is the principle that calculations, procedures, or deliberations should be set up so that anyone can easily observe them and follow the steps to a clear outcome.** A lack of transparency weakens legitimacy and makes secret special deals, corruption, and fraud easier.

Why did the U.S. adopt corporate welfare instead of industrial policy? The answer is fourfold. First, the dominant ideological beliefs reject direct state controls on corporations and "telling them what to do," except perhaps during the emergency of an all-out, defensive war. Second, institutionally the state is fragmented and decentralized with weak capacity. Policy authority is dispersed among many agencies with overlapping mandates, and an independent judiciary vetoes policy initiatives that depart from past practice. Moreover, individual officials face little party discipline and have substantial deal-making influence. Third, the business community is politically divided. Except during crisis periods, most corporations and industry groups seek particularistic benefits, i.e., benefits that accrue to a specific firm or industry. Thus, patron-client relationships develop to obtain what are called "distributive" government benefits. Lastly, political parties, labor unions, and political movements did not organize around and demand industrial policy. Without strong political pressure from outside the business community for an industrial policy and with disagreements over economic policy goals, corporate welfare filled the policy vacuum.

Since the 1970s, efforts to foster a favorable business climate shifted from the federal to the state level of government under a policy of new federalism. State governments offered tax breaks and incentive packages to attract businesses or prevent them from leaving. States often cut their welfare programs for individuals as they expanded their corporate welfare incentive programs. Many got into bidding wars with one another, each tendering more alluring benefits (e.g., free land, a tax holiday, government-paid worker training, new roads, new water and sewer lines) to attract corporate relocation. For example, Whirlpool built a factory in Oklahoma and hired 1,100 people. The company gets 4.5 cents from the state government for each dollar paid in wages for a 10-year period.[53] Studies show that a state's labor situation (i.e., favors nonunion states), social programs (i.e., favors states with low benefit levels), fiscal capacities (i.e., favors states with more resources), and electoral context (i.e., favors conservative and probusiness states) are what has attracted new industry during the past 20 years. The incentive programs attracted few new businesses. It is unclear whether the cost, in terms of foregone tax revenue and shifting tax burdens, exceeded the overall economic benefit a state received; in fact, many of the businesses would have located in the same states for reasons other than the government incentive programs.[54]

"Pork Barrel" Politics

The state distributes economic benefits both programmatically and tactically. Programmatic distribution, such as a tax reduction for the wealthy or a health-care program for the poor, affects overall levels of economic inequality. Tactical distribution ignores overall inequality, and instead targets benefits to particular industries or geographic locations.[55] Examples include tariffs to protect an industry or locating a public construction project in a specific voting district. Tactical distribution directs public money to boost a local economy, attract voters, or reward potential/past supporters. The governments of most nations distribute spending and public works projects (e.g., new roads, bridges, dams, parks, schools) to satisfy the interests and needs of officials and politicians. With tactical distribution, improved public service delivery, additional jobs and business profits, and community prestige are not distributed based on the needs of all citizens. Often they are unnecessary or overpriced. Tactical distribution rewards narrow, specific interests for their past support or political donations. Much of this is called "pork barrel" politics. The term comes from the post-Civil War era and originated with a practice of distributing salt pork from a barrel to slaves on a Southern plantation. The slaves had to compete to get their share of the reward. **Pork barrel politics is the tactical allocation of government benefits by a politician who uses his/her government position to direct benefits in ways that are inefficient or wasteful from the standpoint of an entire polity, are targeted at specific geographic areas or favor particular groups, and are designed to reward past or encourage future political support.**

Classic pork barrel politics is when a politician arranges (through political deals with other politicians, exchanging votes, inserting special items into a law, pressuring a government agency) to have a public project (e.g., a new highway or building) located in her/his district. The politician takes credit for taking care of local constituents, impresses voters, or rewards campaign contributors. In addition to public works projects, "pork" includes farm programs, military bases, buying government supplies, and even academic research funds.[56] For example, the U.S. Congress funds new highways and approved $215 billion in 1998—a 40 percent increase over previous levels. The committee in charge received 2,000 special requests from Congressmen and accepted 1,000 of them, covering 80 percent of districts.[57] In another case, the U.S.

Army Corps of Engineers leased lakefront land rent-free for 50 years to a private developer in 2003 so that he could build a golf course, marina, and housing. By coincidence, the developer is a lobbyist and a major fundraiser with close ties to the U.S. senator who helped with the deal. The Corps reports that such deals are not that unusual and that it has 1,300 other rent-free leases.[58]

While there is a great deal of pork, as Hird (1991, 430) remarked, "considerable confusion exists over the definition of pork." He distinguished *programmatic pork*—a broad program, inefficient from a national perspective, but intended to show voters visible benefits—from *allocative pork*—funding targeted to a specific district at the expense of more deserving ones. Pork can be used to influence swing voters or to maintain a core of supporters.[59] It operates at all levels of government, and politicians use pork distribution to discipline or reward party members or to seek party leadership positions.[60] Corporate welfare can be pork barrel when politicians target benefits (e.g., subsidies, tax breaks, construction projects, purchase contracts) to businesses in a geographic area or to a specific industry or firm. Typically, broad-based revenues pay for pork, but its benefits are concentrated narrowly in a geographic area or for a specific group. It produces inefficient, unfair, or wasteful allocation, denies benefits to more deserving others, and forces people outside the rewarded area to pay for benefits that are limited to a targeted group. Pork is difficult to control because the beneficiaries receive high and concentrated rewards, while the costs per person are low and diffused widely over many unorganized nonbeneficiaries.

Agricultural Sector

Until the end of the nineteenth century, the United States economy was largely agricultural. For example, in 1900 over 40 percent of the U.S. population lived on farms. The U.S. Department of Agriculture (USDA) was established during the transition to an industrial-dominated economy. A farm boom in the first decade of the twentieth century was followed by a 20-year agricultural depression, covering most of 1920s and 1930s. Under the New Deal, the USDA grew to account for 16 percent of federal spending from 1933 to 1939, and farmers were a critical part of the early New Deal electoral coalition.[61] Agricultural politics were split between agribusiness—the large-scale commercial farmers who organized into the American Farm Bureau Federation and aligned with the USDA extension service—and small-scale family and tenant or sharecropper farmers. During the New Deal, officials had two broad policy choices—to build a system of rural social programs to help impoverished tenants and sharecroppers and to institute land-use controls to empower them, or to impose limits to control overproduction while facilitating efficiency through technological modernization and offering successful farmers subsidies. The first option would upset the rural power structure, the second option would help larger farmers the most. The production limit and subsidy program won out.[62]

World War II was a boom time for agriculture. It increased demand and reduced the surplus labor pool on farms. In 1930, 25 percent of the U.S. population lived on farms; by 1950 this number had dropped to 15.2 percent. Total land in agricultural production changed little and average farm size grew from 157 to 216 acres. The farm population continued to drop and was only 1.5 percent by 1990, while the average farm size grew to nearly 500 acres. Although the farm population was tiny and shrinking, it retained economic, political, and ideological power. Farmers feed the nation and are a major source of exports. Farm-state legislators hold over one-half of U.S. Senate seats. Farmers are critical to the electoral college in presidential elections, and the family farm is a sacred icon of U.S. culture.

Each year the federal government gives agricultural businesses and farm or ranch owners about $20 billion in subsidies. The 1996 Freedom to Farm Act was intended to reduce subsidies and eliminate them by 2002. Instead, farm subsidy payments tripled from 1996 to 1999. "The subsidies have helped the biggest producers and processing in an increasingly industrialized agricultural system dominated by fewer and fewer corporations. A handful of companies now control an overwhelming share of the nation's beef, poultry, and pork production."[63] Subsidies protect apples, lentils, chickpeas, onions, ginseng, and milk, among other products. In 2002, North Dakota saw a 68 percent increase in federal farm payments to $678 million, or just over $1,000 for every state resident. In New York State, the average dairy farmer gets $15,200, and apple farmers get $12,925 per year in federal payments.[64]

According to a 2003 survey, "Public attitudes on agricultural subsidies are very much at odds with U.S. policies . . . a strong majority favors subsidies for small farmers [but] . . . a majority opposes subsidies for large farming businesses—the primary recipient of subsidies" (Kull et al., 2004, 3). Seventy-seven percent favor help for small farmers, but 65 percent oppose giving aid to large farming businesses. Despite "family farm" rhetoric, large farmers and agribusinesses get most of the farm subsidies. For example, one Texas farmer received $1.38 million in direct payments during the 1990s. After the Freedom to Farm Act, his payments grew from $164,621 in 1996 to $741,839 in 1999. This enabled him to expand his cropland from 700 acres to 8,000 acres in just five years. As he said, "We're successful primarily because of government help." Large agricultural operators use the federal subsidy payments to get larger by buying out their smaller neighbors.[65] Farm subsidies are not just paying for growing crops. The government also pays subsidies for irrigation water supplies and grazing land. For example, ranchers who graze cattle on public land pay $1.43 per animal per month, while the cost on unsubsidized private land is $11 per animal per month.[66] The subsidies violate free market rules by guaranteeing minimum prices and imposing no limits on maximum prices or profits. Ironically, some of the same people who fiercely oppose government handouts and defend free-market principles accept the government subsidies and are building personal fortunes with them.

THE REGULATORY STATE

Business regulation is an essential state activity that maintains the economy's operation and limits the market's self-destructive tendencies. Marc Eisner (1993, 203) stated, "The history of regulation is the history of state-economy relations and institutional change." Harris and Milkis (1996, viii) noted, "the study of regulation sheds light on the defining elements of contemporary American politics." Braithwaite and Drahos (2000, 9–10) argued that, "Modernity cannot be comprehended without understanding regulation . . . there are few projects more central to the social sciences than the study of regulation." No advanced democracy has unregulated markets without government oversight. In CMC nations, regulations are publicly negotiated in state-business mediation processes, built into industrial policy, and incorporated into business practices. In LMC nations, regulatory laws set forth general principles that fix the outer limits of acceptable business conduct. Specialized agencies administer and enforce the regulations, and businesses operate without interference unless they violate the regulations. "Regulation provides a means whereby the public interest, as defined or interpreted by legislative bodies, commissions, agencies, and courts can be invoked to subject corporate decisions to the standards of social responsibility. Typically, regulation consists of establishing rules and procedures that prohibit certain forms of behavior" according to Bowman (1996, 138).

A range of agencies and programs, laws, and activities at the international, national, and subnational levels administer business policy. The United States places much of its business policy in specialized regulatory agencies that have rule-making, rule monitoring, and rule enforcement duties, combining administrative, policing, and judicial functions. The regulations may focus on one industry (e.g., trucking, airlines), govern market competition (e.g., antitrust), or protect consumers, workers, investors, or the environment from abuse. Compared to an industrial policy, regulation is a loose, weak method of controlling business activity. James Q. Wilson (1974, 153) said the reason for regulation is, "that the American government is not powerful enough to impose radical solution for the problems of business behavior (by nationalizing firms or sectors); but neither is it powerful enough to ignore demands for political solutions. . . . The result in piecemeal regulation made possible by either quiet bargaining on behalf of benefited interests or populistic appeals on behalf of larger publics."

Business regulation is at the critical intersection of political and economic power. In the United States, it began about 120 years ago and is filled with contradictory and overlapping mandates, laws, and rules that are located in a diverse array of offices in the executive, legislative, judicial, and administrative or independent agency branches. Some regulations arose from protest movement demands; others originated at the request of specific industries. Popular demands for regulation are often expressed in terms of moral outrage over unjust, unfair, or unreasonable practices, illustrating how regulation has both symbolic and instrumental sides.

Business regulation expanded in three major spurts or waves—in the Progressive Era (1910–1915), the New Deal Era (1933–1939), and the Great Society Era (1964–1968). In each period, business regulation rose to the top of the public agenda, new laws were enacted, and new agencies established. For example, the Progressive Era spawned the Federal Trade Commission (FTC) and Federal Reserve Board, the New Deal Era saw the creation of the National Labor

Relations Board (NLRB) and the Securities and Exchange Commission (SEC), and during the Great Society Era, the Consumer Protection Agency, the Occupational Health and Safety Administration (OSHA), and the Environment Protection Agency (EPA) were created. After each expansion period, there was relative quiet and many regulations were slowly relaxed through judicial decisions, presidential or Congressional limits, or direct business pressure. For example, after Progressive Era expansion the Supreme Court overturned more than 130 regulatory laws and rules.[67]

The state has altered the form, shape, and size of the business corporation through regulation. For example, antitrust laws were enacted after a national upsurge in populist protest of farmers, labor unions, and small business owners. Antitrust statutes and rulings outlawed an early form of business organization—the trust. In it many separate business firms joined together to operate in a coordinated way; they adjusted production and prices to maximum profits for trust members. The trust operated like a cartel. **A cartel is a system of limited competition in which all or most firms of an industry collectively adjust production, set prices, and allocate resources to maximize industry profits and stability.** Cartels are illegal in the United States but legal in several other advanced industrial nations that have specific protective legislation. A successful cartel usually requires a coordinating agency, standards or rules, and an enforcement mechanism that keeps members working together. U.S. antitrust law also had antimonopoly provisions. **A monopoly is the absence of economic competition in an industry because a single firm controls all production and prices and receives all the (usually very high) profits.** The aim of the antimonopoly provisions was to increase market competition and limit increases in company size.

Thus, regulations have forced corporations to grow in certain ways.[68] Antitrust laws indirectly legitimated the modern corporation and fixed limits on its behavior. Since the trust was illegal, firms created holding companies (i.e., one company legally owns several others) or merged (i.e., one firms buys or absorbs other firms to create a larger firm). Over time, larger and more complex corporations developed that relied on stock markets and banks for funding. Becoming a monopoly was illegal, so corporations expanded and increased market share until only a few large firms remained, creating oligopolies. **An oligopoly is an industry market situation in which a small number of large firms control an entire, or nearly the entire, industry.**

Some in the business community have opposed all regulation, but many others favor self-regulation to state regulation. Self-regulation can occur alongside of and work with government regulation. Self-regulation often occurs through voluntary trade associations and business groups that are industry specific or general (e.g., National Association of Manufacturers, Chamber of Commerce). They have public relations, lobbying, and standard-setting functions. For example, a trade association or the Better Business Bureau might try to end abusive business practices, similar to an agency like the Federal Trade Commission or the Consumer Protection Agency. Yet, because they are private, voluntary associations, they have meager monitoring capacity and enforcement powers. In addition, they rarely directly oppose the more powerful members of a trade association or the business community.

The specific mix of state versus self-regulation has varied across time. In the 1920s and in the early 1930s under the National Recovery Administration, the United States experimented with extensive self-regulation, similar to a cartel or corporatist arrangement. The experiment ended because of insufficient business cooperation, numerous anticompetitive practices, and antitrust law violations.[69] Although official self-regulation ended, business organizations continued to coordinate industry interests and present standards, issues, and practices to regulatory agencies.

There are many types of business regulation. Regulations try to stimulate market competition, standardize industry practices, mediate conflicts among the firms in an industry or between business and labor, prevent the sale of unsanitary food or ineffective medicine, prohibit hazardous and unhealthy workplaces, or block misleading or insufficient information about stocks and bonds (see Closer Look 10.1). Political sociologists often distinguish social regulation (e.g., consumer protection, occupational safety and health) from economic regulation (e.g., insider trading restrictions, antitrust, banking rules). The former protect the health of workers or consumers but tend to decrease business profits. The latter tend to stabilize business relations in an industry or in the overall economy.

 CLOSER LOOK 10.1   The Devil Is in the Regulatory Details

Government agencies charged with regulating business activities take broad and vague mandates in statutes (e.g., improve safety, increase competition, reduce pollution) and convert them into very specific, highly detailed rules and regulations to administer and enforce on the business firms. They have discretionary decision-making in how specific rules are written and decide how to administer and enforce them. Most business regulation occurs out of the public eye, and regulators try to balance their legal mandate with accommodating other needs.

Ever since Upton Sinclair's *The Jungle* showed the horrific conditions of the meatpacking industry in 1906, food safety has been a regulatory issue. For example, the United States Department of Agriculture (USDA) has a regulatory role to

protect consumers by ensuring food safety. You may occasionally hear new reports of people becoming sick or dying form spoiled or contaminated food or a food product being recalled over health concerns. Inspection guidelines changed in 1998, and the number of recalls grew from 44 then to 118 a year in 2002. For example 20 million pounds of hot dogs and deli meats were recalled in January 2000 after being linked to 14 deaths and 97 illnesses. In July 2002 there was the second-largest recall of meat in the national history. Sometimes the food is sold to restaurants or to schools, companies, hospitals, or airline food services. Yet about half of the recalls are never made public, and the names of stores that sell contaminated food is a legally protected trade secret. For example, during a three-year period in the late 1990s,

Continued on page 472

Continued from page 471

the USDA had 61 unpublicized recalls, 31 for very serious problems, known as Class 1 recall. Even state government health officials do not always learn about food recalls. When 10,000 pounds of ground beef sold in Indiana, Michigan, Ohio, and Florida was recalled for having ground glass in it, the Indiana Department of Health was never informed, and neither the USDA nor the company would reveal which stores carried the tainted product. Why are many serious recalls kept secret? The USDA wants to protect the public but not damage the reputation or harm the food companies, and companies legally challenge the USDA if it does not protect them. Thus, when USDA found unacceptably high levels of bacterial contamination at a meat company that supplies 45 percent of the ground beef to school lunch programs and to WalMart chain stores, the company went to court and charged that the USDA was causing "irreparable harm" and lacked the authority to regulate all contamination, and stated that the bacteria in question, salmonella, is usually destroyed in cooking. The Centers for Disease Control and Prevention estimates that there are 1 million cases of illness and 556 deaths related to salmonella poisoning each year in the United

States. In the end, the court ruled that the plant could continue to sell the meat because "meat from the plant had not caused any outbreaks of food poisoning and that if the company was shut down, it would go out of business." Beyond the issue of inspecting meat products are other concerns, such as the widespread use of growth hormones in cattle, that may prevent U.S. beef from being imported into Western Europe.

Food safety regulation is not the only area where administrative details clash with other priorities. Each year dozens of people die in the roughly 12,000 abandoned mines in the United States; 78 were killed between 2000 and 2002. A government program to clean the mines was created in 1977, and it has an adequate budget. In fact, over $1.5 billion is in a fund for mine clean up. But in 2002 only $174 million will be spent, compared to the $350 million coming in through taxes on mines and interest on the accumulated surplus. Why? Few people demand mine clean up, and they are unorganized and do not have a political voice. By not spending the money, the government keeps mine taxes low and can apply the accumulated savings to help cover spending in other areas of the federal budget.

Sources: "Europeans Threaten Ban on U.S. Beef Imports," *New York Times,* April 22, 1999; "Meat Recalls Often Going Unreported," *Wisconsin State Journal,* March 14, 1999; "New U.S. Standards for Meat are Snarled in Court Fight," *New York Times,* December 4, 1999; "Judge Gives Meat Plant a Reprieve from Closing" *New York Times,* December 11, 1999; "Meat-recall Information Kept Hidden: Privacy Rules, Poor Communication Have Left Consumers in the Dark," *Denver Post,* August 4, 2002; "19 Million Pounds of Meat Recalled after 19 Fall Ill," *New York Times,* July 19, 2002; "Lack of Oversight and Will Put Meat Consumers at Risk," *Philadelphia Inquirer,* June 5, 2003; "Death Toll Rises but Money in Mine Fund Goes Unspent: Critics Blame Budget-balancing Gimmicks," *New York Times,* September 26, 2001. Also see Maney and Plutzer (1996) on the lack of media bias in reports on food safety issues.

Capture Theory and Iron Triangles

In explaining business regulation, few political sociologists accept a naive public interest theory of regulation. It suggests that voters demand action against offensive business behaviors; the government responds by enacting new regulatory law in the public interest and creating an enforcement agency; and the agency enforces regulations as intended. Instead, most endorse some version of capture theory. **Capture theory states that business regulatory agencies begin by actively enforcing rules in the public interest, but as the political conditions that gave rise to business regulation change, agencies slowly align with the business interests they are supposed to regulate and business influence**

grows until agencies defend the regulated business's interests instead of the public interest. Marver Bernstein (1955) presented a classic life cycle version of capture theory to explain independent regulatory commissions. He argued that at birth, new commissions are energetic and have many interested external supporters. During their middle years, the external supporters dissipate and lose interest, while officials, now charged with administering detailed regulations, adjust to the practical realities of waning public concern, limited resources, and intense industry pressure. With time, officials compromise and yield to industry pressure. In old age, commissions have been "captured" and identify with and protect the regulated industries. Thus, the independent regulatory commission evolved from being a part of the government to enforce rules on industry in the public interest to being a place within government that protects a regulated industry. Theodore Lowi (1979) offered an "interest-group liberalism" version of capture theory that included other government policies. He argued that in a democracy, the public forwards its concerns to the government, and the government expands in response to specific demands by delegating authority to fragmented administrative agencies. Powerful interest groups (e.g., a regulated industry) that are directly affected by a policy will cluster about the administering agency and exert concentrated political pressure on it. Facing strong external pressure and having few allies inside government, the agency tries to minimize vocal complaints by moving toward powerful private interests in little-seen routine negotiations. Eventually, most regulatory agencies end up protecting resource-rich, well-organized interest groups. This is because of decentralized power, vague statutes, limited resources, distracted politicians, and an agency's desire to be democratically open to vocal interest groups, which in this case happen to be those of the regulated industry.

Some political sociologists criticized and refined capture theory. For example, Berry (1984, 526) argued that, "capture theory presents an overly simplistic and thus inaccurate representation of regulatory politics." It treats capture as an inherent aspect of all regulation, and it does not specify the exact mechanisms that cause capture. Others criticized capture theory for being discrete (i.e., all or nothing) and not treating capture as a matter of degree and for not treating different types of regulation, industries, or agencies differently.[70] The theory is also criticized for not adjusting for the origins of regulation (i.e., whether protest groups or a regulated industry initiated the regulation). Political sociologists refined capture theory in four areas: (1) the internal operation of regulatory agencies, (2) an agency's external environment, (3) agency autonomy from other areas of the state, and (4) the dynamics of regulatory policy.

Regulatory laws often delegate discretion to an agency. The ways an agency transforms authorizing law into specific rules and uses its discretion can affect regulation, including the degree and form of capture. Laws can be broad and agency resources very limited. As the agency staff try to convent vague legal mandates into concrete rules and procedures, often beyond public view, they tend to bend to pressures from regulated firms, especially ones that have the resources to mount legal or technical challenges to specific rules.[71] As Peter Yeager (1991, 34, 35) observed, "it is in the less visible, technically oriented implementation stage at which a new law's impacts are finally determined. . . . Officials present policy determinates as rational formulations, neutrally (non-politically) reached through a process based on technical expertise, particularly legal and scientific knowledge beyond the ken of most citizens." A related issue is the application of scientific-technical knowledge and use of outside experts. Expanded scientific-technical requirements can greatly influence agency operations and decision-making processes. For example, the infusion of economic models and criteria altered antitrust decision-making.[72] Eisner (1993, 132) noted that, "the imposition of economic analysis seemed . . . to entail a subversion of the politically defined goals." Scientific-technical knowledge may limit agency political-legal authority, but it does not always depoliticize agency decisions.[73] Science can be used for or against specific regulatory actions as it removes issues from political-legal authority. "Science need not function to depoliticize state action and suppress class conflict," instead internal struggles arise, and scientists with incompatible views may not remain in government positions.[74]

A second refinement of capture theory looks at the composition of regulated businesses and others in the agency's external environment and the distribution of costs and benefits among them. How an agency enforces regulations can depend on the cost/benefit structure of those involved.[75] The numbers and size of regulated firms, others affected by regulation, professional communities (e.g., economists, lawyers), other areas of government, organized lobbies and interest groups, and business trade associations that supply technical information all can influence the form and extent of "capture."[76] James Q. Wilson examined the pattern among groups that pay the costs of regulation and that benefit from regulation. Depending on the concentration or diffusion of costs and benefits, he identified several outcomes, with one—client—being close to traditional capture theory (see Chart 10.3).

A third refinement of capture theory incorporates other areas of the state. U.S. regulatory agencies operate with the executive branch, the judiciary, Congress, other regulatory agencies, and other levels of government. Each can pressure a regulatory agency, and a regulated industry or its opponents can influence other parts of the state to support or block agency actions. For example, the routine failure to allocate adequate agency funds may be a political decision to reduce business regulation without causing public outrage. As Eisner (1991, 45, 117) remarked, "Congress supports and protects the FTC so long as it remains in a state of relative inactivity. As agency activism increases, the coalition of corporate interests increases in size, as does the pressure to place restraints on the FTC . . . Congress has rewarded the FTC for mediocrity, penalized it for fulfilling its mandate."

A last refinement includes the political dynamics of regulatory origin and policy implementation. Regulation operates in a changing environment that includes the regulated industry, proregulation advocacy groups, and other parts of the state. An agency can deliver symbolic responses to one group (e.g., the public) and different responses to others (e.g., the regulated). For example, Burk (1985, 1024) studied the Securities and Exchange Commission, to see

c h a r t   1 0 . 3

FOUR OUTCOMES OF BUSINESS REGULATORY POLITICS

	Costs of Regulation	
Benefits of Regulation	**Concentrated**	**Dispersed**
Concentrated	Interest Group	Client
Dispersed	Entrepreneurial	Majoritarian

Costs and Benefits

Concentrated Costs—A few businesses pay high costs. Examples: Heavily polluting steel mills must buy expensive new antipollution cleaners; dangerous coal mines must install expensive safety equipment.

Dispersed Costs—Almost all businesses must pay and costs are low. Examples: All workplaces must install warning signs for job safety; all firms advertising must be certain their claims are honest.

Concentrated Benefits—Only a few groups or sectors of society see improvements. Example: Only firms in the trucking industry see reduced costs.

Dispersed Benefits—Nearly everyone gains from the change. Examples: Electric energy rates are lowered; air quality is improved.

Types of Politics

Interest Group—A small number of opposing groups form a close relationship with the regulatory agency and battle each other for influence over it.

Entrepreneurial—An interest organization mobilizes those who benefit and has influence over the agency.

Client—A small number of powerful business groups form a close relationship with the regulatory agency and have great, unchallenged influence over it.

Majoritarian—Elected officials or autonomous state managers mobilize public opinion among those who benefit and press for regulation.

Source: Adapted from Wilson (1980).

whether the public at-large, government officials, or the regulated industry pressed for the new regulation. He concluded, "No single, simple theory has been found which solves all these problems." Instead, regulation arose from a dynamic crafting in specific historical situations to symbolically meet public demands, address certain concerns of the regulated industry, and fulfill instrumental needs of state officials (i.e., for electoral support, political authority, effective administration). Others found that businesses reacted to new regulations by first accommodating them, then, when political conditions changed and allowed it, business quickly attacked and undermined the regulations.[77] Studies show that the types and levels of regulation have varied based on the presidential administration. This suggests that partisan pressures and lobbying influence regulatory agencies.[78] A mutually adaptive adjustment model emphasizes the dynamic roles of multiple actors—regulatory agency officials, the regulated industry, interest groups opposed to the regulated industry, and politicians.[79] For a summary of regulatory models see Chart 10.4.

Studies examined the violators of business regulatory laws to explain why they broke the law and found that the main reason firms did so was to make higher profits.[80] This suggests that firms see government regulations as simply another barrier to making profits. They are likely to violate regulations if the risk of getting caught or the penalties are low. Combined with other studies, we see that firms may use political capitalism to capture an agency or influence politicians to weaken regulations that limit their profits. If their political actions to capture an agency do not work, businesses may try to improve their profit prospects by violating the regulations and trying not to get caught.

chart 10.4

MODELS OF BUSINESS REGULATORY AGENCIES

Model	Time Period	
	Agency Creation	Subsequent History
Naive Public Interest	Public opposes specific business behaviors and regulations enacted in public interest	Agency continues to operate in original public interest
Cooptation	Public opposes specific business behaviors and regulation enacted in public interest	Over time, agency shifts to allow regulated industry to ignore agency actions because of limited resources, changing staff, and lack of countervailing pressures
Client-Based	Regulated interests join to initiate regulation in their self-interest	Regulated industry determines agency actions
State-Autonomy	Politicians and state officials initiate regulation	Regulatory officials and technical experts determine agency actions
Mutually Adaptive Adjustment	Public interest groups, regulated or other business, or elected politicians initiate regulation	Regulated interests, agency officials, elected politicians, and opposing regulatory agency negotiate

Sources: Chatov (1978), Eisner and Meier (1990), Moe (1985), and Wood and Anderson (1993).

Iron Triangles

In his farewell address, President Ronald Reagan warned of "iron triangles," by which he meant members of Congress, the mass media, and special interest groups. He believed that they had thwarted his objectives and impeded his attempts to improve government.[81] **An iron triangle refers to a stable but narrow network, alliance, or coalition of public and private sector interests that cooperate to control an area of public policy.** The private sector interests in a triangle jointly defend and advance their economic or ideological objectives around a specific policy area. Iron triangles tend to form in areas where a government agency distributes resources or advantages that can help specific firms or business sectors. Triangles tend to be found around business regulations because the regulations can profoundly affect business operations and profits. Firms try to affect regulations individually and through trade associations, lobbying groups, or industry political action committees.

Traditionally, a "triangle" is a three-part, semi-insulated alliance of a Congressional subcommittee, a government agency, and a set of private interests. It develops a durable, distinct viewpoint and mutually beneficial arrangements that are insulated from public pressure. The triangle contradicts the pluralist idea of a division of government powers, a neutral state, and a plurality of competing interest groups and describes policy areas in the United States and other countries.[82] The iron triangle metaphor is colorful and useful, as long as we do not treat the "iron" as being too solid, accept that a "triangle" can have more than three sides, and recognize that its coordination and stability vary over time. McCool (1998, 558) criticized the term and argued for replacing it with, "a coalition of policy-influencing and policy-making entities that work together via one or more identifiable strategies in response to conflict or potential conflict over policy." He (1998, 565) said, "Rather than asking whether a certain policy area is controlled by an iron triangle, or an issue network, or some other form of subsystem, it may be more instructive to assess the level of conflict. . . ."[83] Conflict intensifies when opposing interests are of equal power and issues are zero-sum (i.e., one side only gains if the other side loses).

Regulatory Regimes

The business regulation "policy domain" (see World View 10.2) shifted direction several times, and the shifts can be understood using the concept of "regulatory regime."[84] Eisner (1993, 1) called a regulatory regime, "a historically specific configuration of policies and institutions which structures the relationship between social interests, the state, and economic actors . . . [each is] a unique synthesis of interests, political-economic ideas, and administrative reform doctrines." A new regime emerges when new laws, rules, or objectives are instituted in multiple regulatory areas and coordinated with new agencies, organizations, and procedures. **A regulatory regime is a constellation of mutually reinforcing ideas, institutions, and policies that orient multiple areas of business regulation around a few core principles, endorses a particular business-government**

WORLD VIEW 10.2   Comparing Policy Domains

Each political issue, debate, policy, and struggle is not separate and isolated; rather, they operate in clusters called policy domains. Burstein (1991, 328) defined a policy domain as, "a component of the political system that is organized around substantive issues," while Knoke et al. (1996, 9) called it, "a complex organization in which collectively binding decisions are made, implemented, and evaluated with regard to specific topics." Others use terms such as issue domains, subsystems, or policy areas. **A policy domain is a semiporous topic area around which are clustered an interacting, interrelated set of policies (i.e., laws, regulations, programs), organizations (e.g., government agencies, political party factions, movement organizations, think tanks), and political actors (e.g., lobbyists, interest groups, activists).** While a few actors and organizations join or leave a policy domain, a core of them tends to specialize around a topic and remain stable across time. Examples of policy domains include business regulation, energy, health, labor, environment, or transportation, and they can operate across levels of government (e.g., local, regional, national, international). Rarely are policy domains perfect matches to specific government agencies. For example, health policy is found in a government health agency, but spills into labor, education, insurance, social security, veterans, women's, and other agencies. In some nations, two policy domains may be relatively insulated from one another (e.g., labor versus social programs in Germany), while in other nations the two may be closely aligned (e.g., business regulation and taxation in the U.S.). Because each domain is semiautonomous, the domain's political organizations and actors are usually more powerful in shaping policy than are general sociopolitical forces/conditions that operate across all domains.

In the late 1970s, several advanced nations faced an economic condition called stagflation—declining corporate profits, technological dislocations, and rapid inflation due to huge oil price increases. The national governments of Germany, Japan, and the United States, each controlled by a conservative political party, acted in the 1980s to adjust to the globalizing economy in different ways. In the United States, business taxes were cut, welfare programs sharply reduced, rules protecting labor unions weakened, and military spending rose. In Japan, government-owned industries were privatized, economically depressed areas received government aid, and worker retaining programs were created. In Germany, welfare programs were maintained as worker education and retaining programs were vastly expanded. The diverse responses to similar problems reveal how political institutional settings can affect the policy in a domain.

David Knoke and associates (1996) argued that the process and outcomes in the labor policy domain in Germany, Japan, and the United States in the early 1980s varied by the nation's institutional structure. In these three nations they found, "the boundary between state and society blurred. . . . [and] Substantial interpenetrations between state and civil society [developed]" (1996, 122), but state-society intersection operated differently in each country. In Germany, corporatist organizations resulted in compromises between labor and business "peak" organizations working with government that did not develop into open conflict. Germany had a history of powerful unions, strong labor laws, and well-established union–business negotiation arrangements. In Japan, a set of business, labor, and government organizations forged a cooperative program. While a small group of leftist unions fought for traditional union protections, the government created programs of business assistance and gave organized labor special help and benefits. This reflected a strong central government and the relatively weak position of labor unions that had accommodated to big business interests by the 1960s. In the United States, the issues and actors where highly polarized. Organized labor with minority group allies fought to preserve social safety-net protections and government regulation of the workplace, while business pushed for pure free market-based policies. This reflected America's fragmented, decentralized political institutions and a history of rancorous labor-business conflict. The authors summarized the web of interactions in the labor policy domain in Germany as being collaborative, in Japan as coordinated, and in U.S. as contentious.

relationship, and remains in place for a period of years. The regulatory regime concept highlights the connections among: (1) parts within a single area of business regulation (e.g., different kinds of pollution or contamination, such as air, water, soil, or toxic waste, and their testing, timelines, and quality standards), (2) links from one area to other regulatory areas (e.g., workplace safety, environment, consumer protection, antitrust, energy), and (3) qualitative shifts that occur over time in overall tone and direction of regulation (e.g., justifications for it, general goals or objectives, methods of enforcement).

Four business regulatory regimes have appeared in U.S. history (see Chart 10.5). The Progressive Era regime tried to end abuses by extremely powerful corporations or banks that were undermining basic market functions. It used independent regulatory commissions staffed by professionals, usually lawyers. In the New Deal Era, the focus was on restoring economic confidence and stability by creating quasicorporatist mediation arrangements among the involved parties under government oversight. During the Great Society Era, the focus was on protecting the health and safety of consumers and workers and on halting environmental damage. The government demanded that businesses meet specific health, safety, or environmental standards that were backed by scientific data and agency experts. We will examine the Reagan Revolution (1980–1988) in more detail later, but it emphasized deregulation—removing past regulations, cutting back on agencies, and reorienting regulations to enhance corporate profits. Each new regulatory regime did not entirely displace the previous ones; rather, it pushed aside the past regimes, modified the parts of the regulation system, and moved the entire regulation system in a new direction. The regulatory regime is a useful but limited concept. It cannot explain why regime change occurs; it treats business regulation in isolation from broader changes in other policy domains or in the entire state-economy relationship, and it cannot explain why a regulatory regime adopts a specific direction and rejects alternative paths.

Rise and Fall of Business Regulation

Together, the ideas of a regulatory regime, waves of regulatory expansion, and the dynamic modification version of capture theory sensitize us to the historical–political context in which business regulation operates. We can now examine the surge of regulations in the 1970s and the subsequent deregulation reaction in the early 1980s.

chart 10.5

MAJOR BUSINESS REGULATORY REGIMES IN TWENTIETH CENTURY AMERICA

Regulatory Regime	Historical Period	Type of Regulations	Origin Condition	Primary Objective	Innovation
Market	Progressive Era (1905–1915)	Antitrust, food and drugs, banking, railroads	Development of large corporations	Recreate market conditions through administration	Independent commissions
Association	New Deal Era (1934–1939)	Agriculture, transportation, financial, labor relations	Great Depression	Restore economic stability to banking-finance, industry, and agriculture	Quasipublic interest associations, mediation
Societal	Great Society (1968–1976)	Consumer and environmental protection, worker safety	Post-materialist values	Prevent hazards to health and environment	Mandates, timetables, limits on agency discretion
Efficiency	Reagan Revolution (1980–1988)	Deregulation	1970s stagflation	Eliminate barriers that interfere with large corporations	Centralized authority with ideological appointees

Sources: Eisner (1993, 1–9); Harris and Milkis (1996).

Between 1968 and 1975 major protest movements demanded civil rights for African Americans and other marginalized groups, large-scale antiwar and student movements grew, and the 1974 Watergate scandal resulted in President Richard Nixon's resignation. In this context, public concerns over big business power and widespread dishonesty by federal officials intensified. For example, 31.4 percent of Americans said they had a "great deal" of confidence in big business in 1973. This was 2.7 times more than those with "hardly any" confidence. Three years later, more people said they had "hardly any" than a "great deal" of confidence in business. In 1973, 29.9 percent had a "great deal" of confidence in the federal government, which was 1.5 times more than those saying they had "hardly any." By 1975, only 13.7 percent said they had a "great deal" of confidence, while 30.3 percent now said they had "hardly any" confidence in the government.[85] Opinion polls showed widespread public backing for business regulation and fears that reduced regulation might harm the public. Support for consumer and environmental protection were exceptionally high (80–89 percent). The percentage who believed businesses were making excessive profits grew from 26 percent in 1971, to 45 percent in 1975 and 51 percent in 1979. The percentage of who felt that big business had too much concentrated power grew from 66 to 79 percent in the same period. Many people favored breaking up big businesses into smaller firms. Support for this proposal rose to over one-half the public by 1979.[86] The 1970s regulatory regime emerged in this political–historical context with three distinguishing features: (1) the scope of regulation, (2) regulatory objectives, and (3) regulatory policy administration.

Regulatory Scope   Social regulations already existed for food or health safety, but advocacy groups for consumer safety and the environment pushed to greatly expand its scope to improve the quality of the environment, workplace safety, and the health and safety of mass consumer products. For example, they wanted to raise drinking water standards, create safeguards that would prevent oil spills, require that new cars be safer, end the sales of toys that injured children, and have factories install safety shields on dangerous machines (see Chart 10.6). The new regulations cut across all industries. Unlike previous regulations that helped certain industries or firms, new regulations often did not benefit a single firm, but improved conditions for all consumers or the public.

Regulatory Objectives   New regulation was also part of a broader "push for participatory democracy."[87] Many activists who joined citizen lobby groups and worked for new social regulations ". . . did not want simply to discipline business, but wanted to alter fundamentally the way business decisions were made; the point of participatory democracy was to involve people directly in decisions that affected the quality of their lives . . ." according to Harris and Milkis (1996, 80). Consumer protection and environmentalism challenged the basic premises of capitalism; they placed improving the quality of life for all people above businesses making profits.[88] Before 1970, federal environmental protection barely existed.[89] Environmental regulation was particularly threatening, because more than past business regulation, it questioned both how capitalism operated and its fundamental morality as well.

Regulatory Policy Administration   The new administration of regulation differed from the past in two ways: it was specific with limited agency discretion, and it encouraged citizen participation. These features were motivated by criticisms of the failures of past regulation and an awareness of capture theory. Advocates saw that some past social regulatory laws (e.g., the Water Pollution Control Law of 1948) had turned into pork barrel programs to distribute federal funds, and they sought to prevent this from occurring again. Many of the new regulations had explicit standards and timelines, relied on scientific expertise, and assumed that engineering solutions to problems could be developed under regulatory pressure. Sometimes, this was not realistic. As Eisner (1993, 147) pointed out, "The courts have expanded the EPA's duties without simultaneously expanding its resource base, and they have promoted the creation of stringent standards without careful consideration of the underlying scientific assumption or the technological or economic data." The regulations also "imposed significant costs that were of uncertain magnitude,

chart 10.6
NEW BUSINESS REGULATIONS ENACTED 1969–1977

Year	New Law Enacted	Target Beneficiary
1969	Mine Safety and Health	Workplace
1969	National Environmental Policy	Environment
1970	Poison Prevention Packaging	Consumer
1970	Clear Air Amendment	Environment
1970	Cigarette Advertising	Consumer
1970	Railroad Safety	Workplace/Consumer
1970	Tire Safety	Consumer
1970	Water Quality Improvement	Environment
1970	Occupational Safety and Health	Workplace
1972	Consumer Product Safety	Consumer
1972	Bumper Standards	Consumer
1972	Ocean Dumping	Environment
1972	Pesticide Regulation	Environment
1972	Federal Water Pollution Control	Environment
1972	Noise Pollution and Control	Environment
1973	Safe Drinking Water	Environment
1974	Hazardous Materials Transportation	Workplace/Environment
1974	Clear Air Amendments	Environment
1974	Federal Trade Commission Authorization	Consumer
1974	Safe Drinking Water	Environment
1974	Seat Belt and School Bus	Consumer
1974	Magnuson-Moss Warranty Improvement	Consumer
1974	Energy Policy and Conservation	Environment
1974	Coal Leasing	Environment
1976	Hart-Scott-Rodino Anti-Trust Amendments	Consumer
1976	Federal Rail Safety	Workplace
1976	Toxic Substances Control	Environment
1976	School Bus Safety	Consumer
1976	Medical Devices Safety	Consumer
1976	Clear Water Act Extension	Environment
1976	Safe Drinking Water Extension	Environment
1976	Surface Minding Control and Reclamation	Environment
1976	Saccharin Study and Labeling	Consumer

New Regulatory Agency Created

Consumer Product Safety Commission	1972
Environmental Protection Agency	1970
Nuclear Regulatory Commission	1975
National Highway Safety Administration	1970
Occupational Health and Safety Commission	1973
Mine Safety and Health Administration	1973
Office of Surface Mining	1977

Source: Harris and Milkis (1996, 82, 93).

timing, and competitive effects."[90] For example, new regulations might demand that businesses meet certain standards on a timeline, although the current technology was inadequate for business to reach the standards.

A second change was to give citizen public interest advocacy groups a voice in the regulatory implementation process. Some new regulations included complex procedures that allowed for significant public input and review. They opened up the regulatory process to advocacy groups. The groups could compel an agency to meet the requirements outlined in regulatory statutes. Nonbusiness groups were empowered, and channels of access opened up outside the established business power structure. A premise of the new regulation was the inflammatory idea that ordinary citizens, not corporate executives or state officials, knew what was best for consumers, the workplace, and the environment. Ultimately, this is what established power elites most feared.

Corporations in other advanced nations faced similar new regulations, but U.S. corporate executives reacted to them very differently from executives in CMC nations. Vogel (1981, 158) noted that unlike the United States, "issues of corporate social performance have not produced much tension between business and government elites in Western Europe and Japan . . . the overall volume and severity of environmental, consumer, and occupational health and safety standards in Western Europe and Japan are not sufficiently different from those affecting business managers in the United States to account for the uniqueness of the latter's political response." He argued that ironically the most pro-capitalist state (the United States) had experienced the most virulent anti-regulation business reaction. He attributed this less to economic than to political–ideological factors. One factor was that U.S. business elites traditionally took an adversarial, antistate stance rooted in their neoliberal ideological beliefs. For example, business opposed environmental regulations less because of their compliance costs than because they represented the state impinging on an executive's sacrosanct private authority to run his/her business.[91] A second factor was that the United States lacked the mediating institutions of CMC nations that fostered smooth business–government relations. A last factor was that U.S. corporate elites were central in the larger political countermovement against social reforms of the 1960s–1970s.[92]

Deregulation Wave of the 1980s

In a swift, dramatic reversal, a new president and officials rolled back the business regulations that had been enacted just a few years earlier with tremendous public backing.[93] A strict neoliberal mode of thinking swept through national policy discourse offering a rationale for massive deregulation. **Deregulation was a set of political–ideological justifications and policy actions with the objective of rescinding, ceasing to enforce, or eliminating business regulations to release market forces.** Numerous regulations were eliminated under the rhetorical banner of "regulatory relief" that was presented as a miracle cure—it would revive the economy, lower unemployment, and reduce inflation by improving the profitability and international competitiveness.

The deregulator's critique of past business regulation was that when a regulatory agency set transportation routes, fixed rates or charges, and established service quality and safety standards, and so forth it interfered with pure market forces. For example, by controlling price changes, limiting the entry of new competitors, and approving business practices, a regulatory agency would distribute business activity and profits differently than what would occur under pure, "natural" market conditions without any state involvement. The deregulators argued that a pure market would always maximize efficiency, lower consumer prices while improving service and quality, and ensure a fair distribution of business profits. For them, almost all business regulation was anticompetitive and wasteful because it deviated from the pure market. They acknowledged that a pure market might create some short-term instability or harm certain noncompetitive businesses, but they believed it would produce the greatest economic growth, efficiency, and productivity, and it would be most beneficial to society as a whole and be in the public interest.

By the end of the 1970s, conservative politicians and corporate elites had pushed the business regulation issue to the top of the public agenda, framing it as over- or excessive regulation. A politically mobilized business community allied with a group of legal scholars and economists set out to overturn 70 years of U.S. business regulation. For example, the Business Roundtable, first organized in 1973 to represent the CEOs of America's 200 largest corporations, became an active supporter of deregulation. "By 1980, the Roundtable had acquired a unique reputation as both a powerful business lobby capable of building broad-based coalitions and a bipartisan political organization. . . . Its presence represents more than a temporary resurgence of corporate political activity to meet a crisis. Corporate America has become politicized and has shown no signs of returning to business as usual."[94] As Harland Prechel (2000, 271) argued, in each new phase of political capitalism, business policy ". . . was the outcome of class-based political pressures that originated outside the state." In the 1980s phase, he summarized, "Corporate political behavior produced massive tax breaks for industrial corporations, relaxed antitrust enforcement, and created the conditions for massive industrial consolidation."[95] The deregulators sought to reorganize the entire business regulation system to enable large U.S. corporations to become more profitable.[96]

In each of the past regulatory regime shifts, politicians enacted laws and created new government agencies. Deregulation differed. Politicians changed agency personnel, overhauled administrative procedures, and adjusted technical rules to curtail regulation. It was a quicker and less visible regime shift that locked out opponents to it.

Shortly after President Ronald Reagan assumed office in 1981, he appointed his Vice President, George H. W. Bush, to lead the Task Force on Regulatory Relief. The Heritage Foundation assisted by providing the task force with a report outlining how to dismantle regulations and reorganize agencies. The method was to sharply cut agency budgets, redraw organizational charts, remove proregulation staff, relocate authority to state-level governments, and block nonbusiness access to the agencies. As Harris and Milkis (1996, 10) noted, "If deregulation in the 1980s was rooted in politics and ideology, it was because the regulatory programs of the 1970s successfully imbedded the concept of participatory democracy in regulatory institutions."

Deregulators went beyond weakening the existing regulatory regime to proactively replace it with an alternative regulatory system that was backed by a new state-economy philosophy and supporting institutions. The past principle guiding federal business regulation had been to tame or control private business behavior for public social–political goals. The new principle was to eliminate all government-based barriers that might inhibit higher corporate profits. The "public interest" in regulation was redefined to mean highly profitable corporations based on a neoliberal model of economic growth.

A new executive branch agency staffed by political appointees, the Office of Information and Regulatory Affairs (OIRA), was given the task of reviewing all business regulations. It gave business lobbyists an "off-the-record opportunity to argue issues they had lost at the agency level."[97] For example, the first director of the newly created OIRA, James Miller, conducted 36 private meetings over noise regulations, 32 of them were with trade groups, corporate executives, or business lobbyists. Shortly after the meetings, he issued orders delaying or rescinding numerous regulations. Mr. Miller, well-known in academic and government circles for his conservative views, had served on the Task Force on Regulatory Relief, and was appointed to head the Federal Trade Commission in 1982.[98] He carried out the mislabeled Federal Trade Commission Improvement Act of 1980 that "restricted the agency's authority and further reduced its autonomy" (Eisner 1991, 178).

A 1978 change in the Civil Service Law had expanded the presidential power to make political appointments. The incoming Reagan administration took advantage of the legal change to make three times more political appointments than past administrations. Most of those appointed had little prior public administrative experience but had been partisan activists in political campaigns. The personnel changes politicized the regulatory bureaucracy. Much of existing regulatory staff was replaced, and loyal political appointees were placed in critical positions of authority. As deregulation spread across economic areas, it produced some economic benefits but at the cost of greater instability, consolidation, bankruptcies, and corporate malfeasance. For example, airline deregulation lowered ticket prices, changed routing, and allowed new industry entrants, but it increased airline bankruptcies lowered in-flight service quality and reduced flights to small cities. Trucking deregulation lowered costs and altered long-distance driving rules, but it increased industry consolidation. Energy deregulation allowed consolidation and directly contributed to the 2001 Enron collapse and scandal.[99] Financial industry deregulation most directly affected the Savings and Loan sector (see Case in Point 10.3).

Harris and Milkis (1996, 97) remarked, "The policy program initiated by the Reagan administration raised regulatory relief to a status unprecedented in our recent political history." Personnel changes and budget reductions hit most regulatory agencies. For example, Mark Fowler, a conservative attorney who had worked for media corporations, was appointed to head the Federal Communications Commission. One of his first acts was to eliminate requirements that broadcasters devote time for social purposes because he favored pure, market-based solutions. The budget and staff of the Environmental Protection Agency (EPA) were cut by nearly 25 percent between 1981 and 1982. By 1982, the number of enforcement cases declined by one-third.[100] Within one year of a new director talking office, the EPA's Office of Enforcement was abolished and the number of cases sent to the Justice Department for law violations dropped from 198 to 31.[101] Many EPA officials and staff were forced out, and new proindustry officials were appointed. At the Antitrust Division, the staff was reduced from 352 attorneys in Washington, DC and 122 in field offices in 1980 to 166 and 95 respectively by 1986. Adjusted for inflation, the Federal Trade Commission's budget declined by 50 percent between 1981 and 1985.[102]

The deregulators reinterpreted the previous 100 years of antitrust doctrines, legal judgments, and statutes in a way that redirected antitrust enforcement efforts away from policing the predatory actions by corporations that expanded

CASE IN POINT 10.3   **What Has Deregulation Wrought?**
The Savings and Loan Case

The savings and loan industry (S&L) was established during the New Deal Era to provide a new type of financial institution that would offer mortgages to modest-income homeowners because few banks would. Until the late 1970s, the industry prospered and grew under a strict regulatory system. In 1976, S&Ls provided roughly two-thirds of all mortgages in the United States. Things then quickly changed. By 1979 they provided 37 percent of residential mortgage money and only 16.4 percent in 1980. During the late 1970s, a combination of high inflation and intense competition for savings after other regulations created new types of financial accounts for individuals caused large numbers of people to withdraw their S&L deposits to invest in other accounts (e.g., money market accounts) that paid much higher interest rates. The S&L industry was left with almost no money to lend and a bare trickle of income from the fixed-rate, low-interest 30-year mortgages made over the previous decades. During the massive deregulation wave of the early 1980s, the S&L's problems were blamed on outmoded business regulations and rules that limited competition among various kinds of financial institutions. While some in the S&L industry lobbied for deregulation, Glasberg and Skidmore (1998a, 111) argued, "deregulation legislation does not appear to have been pursued by the industry in order to facilitate looting of the thrift institutions. . . . Nor does it appear to have been the state's agenda to facilitate such behavior." It was part of a broader reorganization of state-economy relations. With deregulation, interest rate rules were relaxed, operating regulations eliminated, barriers to investment dropped, and government audits of the few remaining regulations also cut back. During the 1980s S&Ls could engage in high-risk, speculative investments and use questionable bookkeeping to make large profits. Existing S&Ls changed their practices and new investors entered the industry. Under deregulation, S&L financial practices were "let loose," making it possible for fraud to become standard operating procedure because deregulation greatly expanded the opportunities for fraud at very low risk. Calavita and Pontell (1991) argue that deregulation facilitated making "collective embezzlement" the standard operating procedure of the industry. By the late 1980s, many of the high-risk investments failed, S&Ls began going bankrupt, and instances of fraud by individual S&L executives came to light. In 1988 the news was filled with reports of widespread fraud in the S&L industry. When President George H. W. Bush took office in Janaury 1989, he announced a plan to bail out the industry and investigate crimes. Congress passed the Financial Institutions Reform, Recovery and Enforcement Act of 1989 (FIRREA) authorizing $75 million each year for three years to prosecute financial fraud; it ended up costing nearly double that amount. In the end, the price taxpayers will be paying for the bailout over a 40-year period is about $400–500 billion, amounting to several thousand dollars per taxpayer per year. The media carried stories of individual fraud and greed and a few individuals went to jail, but the underlying political and organizational causes were rarely mentioned. With some help from lobbying and campaign contributions by industry members, the primary beneficiaries of the bailout ended up being the larger financial institutions.

Sources: Calavita and Pontell (1991, 1994); Calavita, Pontell, and Tillman (1997); Glasberg and Skidmore (1997a, 1997b, 1998a, 1998b), Skidmore and Glasberg (1996), Zey (1998).

their power and created monopolylike conditions. Instead, they defined aggressive business practices and increased corporate size as being beneficial for global competition. They jettisoned the century-old core antitrust tenet that treated large corporations as a powerful social–political force that the federal government should watch and control. The eight years of rolling back regulation under the Reagan administrations was followed by four years of quiet pragmatism under George H. W. Bush and moderation by the Clinton administration. The neoliberal shift to reduce regulations remained the primary direction, and it was again intensified after 2001 (see Case in Point 10.4).

CASE IN POINT 10.4   Diets and Deception

Protecting consumers from false and deceptive advertising has been an objective of business regulation for nearly a century. False advertising can be detrimental for any product, but may be more serious for health-care products. The U.S. Food and Drug Administration (FDA) in the Department of Health and Human Services began as the Bureau of Chemistry in the U.S. Department of Agriculture in 1862. It became the Food and Drug Administration in 1930 and was transferred from the Department of Agriculture in 1953. The FDA regulates products that account for over 25 percent of consumer spending, including food, food and nutritional supplements, medical diagnostic devices, prescription and over-the-counter drugs, biological products, and cosmetics. Yet regulations are subject to political processes, and changes in regulatory laws or their administration can have widespread consequences.

U.S. regulations governing health supplements were changed by the Dietary Supplement Health and Education Act (DSHEA) of 1994, which deregulated the marketing and sales of herbal products, loosened controls on advertising claims, and removed the need to report adverse effects. Under DSHEA, a company is responsible for determining the safety of what it manufactures and ensuring that its claims about it are true. In short, dietary supplements do not need FDA approval. The company does not have to provide evidence of its safety or effectiveness before selling the product. This means that widely advertised products like Cellasene can claim to be "a safe, natural, clinically studied herbal supplement"

that melts away unnecessary cellulite, or lumpy fat deposits, when in reality, such claims are unproven. The only studies on it were conducted by the company and lack scientific credibility. The product contains four times the recommended dose of iodine which may cause tremors, weight loss, insomnia, and menstrual irregularity. Another widely used herbal supplement, ephedra, is derived from the Chinese plant ma huang. It has been used for years in China as a cold remedy. Chemically, it is a powerful amphetaminelike compound that is now sold for weight loss. In a dispute, company officials have refused to give government regulators data from their studies of it. Again, the studies fail to meet high scientific standards. Since herbal supplements are a multi-billion dollar industry, it is little wonder that firms manufacturing and marketing ephedra products use the DSHEA to shield them from government regulation, even though ephedra caused some 100 deaths.

Although the manufacture of prescription drugs remains regulated, regulations on marketing them were relaxed with the 1997 Food and Drug Administration Modernization Act. The pharmaceutical industry spends $30 billion per year on research and $19 billion on promotion, yet consumer advertising grew by 150 percent between 1997 and 2001 after the law relaxed regulations. Advertising drugs can greatly increase sales, even though physicians must write prescriptions for them, and the ads are often misleading. Between 1997 and 2002, the FDA issued 88 disciplinary letters to pharmaceutical firms for violating rules governing false or misleading advertising.

Sources: "Caveat Emptor," *The Economist,* August 28, 1999; "Investigators Find Repeated Deception in Ads for Drugs," *New York Times,* December 4, 2002; "Expert Panel Finds Flaws in Diet Pill Safety Study," *New York Times,* July 23, 2003.

State Projects and Structural Constraints

The Reagan administration advanced deregulation, but it started before his administration and extended beyond it[103] (see Case in Point 10.5). As Yeager (1991, 312) noted, "The nation had never seen anything quite like the Reagan administration's blunt assault on social regulation . . . in most fundamental respects, the Reagan agenda was not novel. . . ." Deregulation was more than a goal of the Reagan administration, and it was more than a regulatory regime.

We can place deregulation in the broader context of a LMC model of state-economy relations. Glasberg and Skidmore (1997b) suggested seeing deregulation as a "state project," a very abstract idea they borrowed from Jessop (1990). **A state project refers to a loosely bound ensemble of theories and beliefs, organizations and individuals, and specific state units that are coordinated and united around a common vision or theme; this unity is not permanent but is the result of various internal and external political struggles.** A state project is a logic or master-frame that guides how officials and state agencies carry out specific tasks by giving them a common purpose and direction.[104] The concept of state project helps us contrast one regulatory regime with the others and with other state activities, put regulation in historical context, and relate all policy regimes to broader political struggles. It has a social dimension (i.e., networks of people who interact with one another), an ideational dimension (i.e., a set of mutually reinforcing assumptions, beliefs, explanations, and expectations), and an organizational-operational dimension (i.e., committees, bureaus, task forces, agencies).

At the level of ideas, the deregulation project drew on a complex combination of libertarian ideology, neoclassical economic theory, conservative political beliefs, and neoliberal values. It explained conditions, justified actions, and gave people a vision of a possible future. On a social level, elected politicians, political party activists, movement organizations, government and corporate officials, and intellectuals joined together to elaborate, promote, and implement deregulation. They developed new judicial interpretations, trained students in a new way of thinking, enacted new laws, wrote and decided specific policies, and so forth. On the organizational-implementation level, the project required mechanisms (i.e., a movement, organizations, policies) to put it into practice. Once installed or in place, it selected some and rejected other state activities (i.e., people, laws, government programs, political organizations). It also encompassed numerous policy areas and all levels and branches of government.

The core principle of the deregulation project is that business regulation must never infringe on capitalist accumulation, productivity, and profitability. The only acceptable ideological–political justifications are ones that reinforce the tenets of private property and the market.[105] This goes beyond business-state cooperation to imply that state agencies must be subordinated to business interests. The deregulation project extends beyond business regulation; it is interdependent with the structural constraints of the state-economy relationship and buttresses those constraints.[106] Business regulation and deregulation do not stop

CASE IN POINT 10.5   Has the Deregulation Revolution Returned?

Ronald Reagan's first administration (1981–1984) is famous for its early deregulation push, particularly in the areas of consumer protection, worker health and safety, environmental protection, and antitrust law. Despite a slight regulatory expansion during the Clinton administration years, what remained was a much smaller regulatory system with more probusiness rules. Roughly 20 years later, the George W. Bush administration placed deregulation on the top of the agenda. "Not since the Reagan administration's wholesale reversals of regulatory policies have the scales tipped so abruptly. . . . Just as during the so-called Reagan Revolution, the deregulatory agenda is largely a reflection of a pro-business agenda" (New York Times, May 23, 2001). In December 2002, the White House released a list of 300 health, safety, consumer, and environmental regulations to be eliminated after more than 1,700 private business groups or allies had made requests. For example, Boeing wanted to reduce the amount of fresh air required in airline cabins, the Heritage Foundation wants to allow health benefits to be listed on wine bottles, and so forth.

The sweep of deregulation targeted at environmental protection goes beyond the well-publicized decision not to honor the international Kyoto Protocol. Within four months of a new administration, a video by a lobbying group advocating drilling for oil in the Alaskan wilderness appeared on an official Interior Department Web site, and a mining lobbyist was appointed to the Interior Department's second highest post. Within two years, a fellowship to study the environment was eliminated; a top EPA official quit, citing attempts to gut the Clean Air Act; a lobbyist for a major chemical corporation was appointed to head the EPA; rules on arsenic in drinking water were relaxed; EPA rules were revised to exempt energy firms from the Clean Air Act and allow building on land contaminated with toxic waste; previously protected wilderness areas were opened to recreational snowmobiling; and wetland protection rules were loosened. Some commitment to deregulation is attributed a general libertarian or neoliberal ideology, but according to Andrew Austin (2002, 75), "The force behind Bush's policies is the antienvironmental countermovement." The think tanks in the Policy Planning Network sponsored the antienvironmental countermovement. The countermovement is a coalition of corporate leaders and neoliberal ideological enthusiasts that sponsors critiques of proenvironmental scientific evidence, prepares policy reports, lobbies politicians, seeks appointments to government posts, sponsors "astroturf" groups, and conducts a public relations campaign. Central to the public relations campaign is "greenwashing." Greenwashing uses three arguments: (1) most additives and pollutants are really quite harmless, (2) voluntary self-regulation by corporations best ensures public safety, and (3) lax consumer behavior is the major cause of environmental problems.

Sources: "Bush Is Putting Team in Place for Full-Bore Assault on Regulation," *New York Times,* May 23, 2001; "Video Inspires New Dispute over Alaska Refuge Drilling," *New York Times,* April 12, 2002; "White House Ends Environmental Fellowship," *New York Times,* April 14, 2002; "Bush Picks Industry Insiders to Fill Environmental Posts," *New York Times,* May 12, 2002; "Top EPA Official Quits, Criticizing Bush's Policies," *New York Times,* March 1, 2002; "EPA Says It Will Change Rules Governing Industrial Pollution," *New York Times,* November 23, 2002; "White House Identifies Regulation That May Change," *New York Times,* December 20, 2002; "Approval of Snowmobiles Contradicts Park Service Study," *New York Times,* January 31, 2003; "Changes in Defining Wetland Anger Critics of Army Corps," *New York Times,* February 11, 2003; "EPA Relaxes Restrictions on Sales of Contaminated Land," *New York Times,* September 3, 2003. Also see McCright and Dunlap (2003) on the antienvironmental countermovement.

at the boundaries of the state but are interwoven into broader actions by institutional investors, capitalists in other nations, and international financial agencies. For example, if a regulatory policy seriously threatens a firm or industry, the firm's value in the stock market will drop. This is an added regulatory sanction, yet the threat of a serious stock market disruption also intimidates regulatory officials and elected politicians and prevents them from pursuing actions that might alarm private investors and capitalists. For example, Baumgartner and Jones (1991, 1051) studied nuclear power regulation and argued that, "the decisions by investors, reflected in stock and bond markets, influence (and are influenced by) the dynamics of the policy process . . . [this suggests treating the] stock market as a primary venue for political action." We cannot isolate the structural constraints of capitalism to produce corporate profits and mollify investors from state regulation-deregulation actions.

The structural constraints uphold capitalist relations and maintain the state-economy relationship. This does not stop individual firms or entire industries from trying to circumvent the law or engineer specific decisions for their narrow benefit.[107] The structure of political institutions and their openness to lobbying and private campaign contributions can shape business regulations. For example, Calavita, Tillman, and Pontell (1997, 34–35) argued, "while the state has a structural interest in economic stability and therefore in containing collective embezzlement, instrumental influences on state actors can—and periodically do—neutralize that structural interest and derail the regulatory agenda . . . the saving and loan industry and its individual members were able to shield themselves temporarily through effective lobbying of key members of Congress and other officials."[108]

Structural constraints operate at the third dimension of power; they are the overall set of political choices and the range of viable alternatives that operate within invisible and rarely questioned boundaries. For example, the EPA sought to control pollution at a copper smelting plant in Tacoma, Washington that was creating the highest arsenic levels in the United States. The EPA presented the community with a choice, either continue dangerous exposure levels that will result in more cancer deaths among local children, or close the plant at the cost of 650 jobs. "In the lack of national policy options (lack of a national industrial policy, little subsidized research and development in environmental controls, few relocation and dislocation policies), this was the only choice offered to the citizenry. Government's view of the pollution problem is thus constrained by the traditional political economic limits on its role in economic relations."[109] Charles Noble (1986), in his analysis of OSHA, noted that people had blamed the law itself, how the law was administered, and the Reagan administration's deregulation efforts for a failure to implement the Occupational Health and Safety Act. The actual blame, he argued, was outside all of these. It was in the structural constraints of a system of state-economy relations and participation-activism, or lack of it, among affected people.

Business Regulation, State Expansion, and Autonomy

The discussions of corporate welfare, pork barrel politics, and business regulation imply that an increase in the state size does not always expand state autonomy. Prechel argued (2000, 172) that the reverse often occurs, and a "decline in state autonomy occurs as it becomes more involved in economic activity." This happens because, "rather than providing a basis of state autonomy, once established, state structures provide capitalists with a legitimate political-legal apparatus within which to pursue their interests politically."[110] Thus, private business interests often adapt to expanded legal-political authority and use the state apparatus to advance their own interests. This includes expanded presidential power, as Salamon and Siegfried (1977, 1030) noted, "Far from expanding presidential power per se, the expansion of administrative rule making really contributes to the influence of the private subsystem of actors who alone have the resources to retain Washington legal counsels and research staffs." Thus, state growth creates new avenues for business influence, and it is the larger, wealthier corporations that possess the greatest capacity to take advantage of those avenues.[111]

We should not confuse state prominence with state autonomy. Such confusion arises when people see the public and private sector in simple, zero-sum terms; that is, as one advances the other automatically declines, and they equate greater state size and visibility with state independence.[112] Instead, "The extension of the state's authority may reduce its autonomy because new organizational structures provide class and subclass segments with legitimate mechanism within which to exercise political power" such that "over the long run, this process produces a state that is more prominent, but less autonomous from the economy and capitalist class."[113] In the context of U.S. political capitalism, state size and visibility can grow simultaneous with the business community adapting the enlarged state apparatus and authority to its own private objectives.

CONCLUSION

In this chapter we have looked at the state-economy relationship. You have seen how different models of the relationship shape the patterns of business, and how political capitalism in the United States is manifest in tax policy and business regulatory policy. You saw that instead of an explicit industrial policy, the United States created a less-visible system of corporate welfare. You also saw how business regulation developed over time and examined the deregulation state project that has arisen in response to it. In Chapter 11 we will look at social policy, and the rise of what is called the "welfare state" in advanced societies.

KEY TERMS

Capture Theory	Monopoly	Regulatory Regime
Cartel	Oligopoly	Stagflation
Corporate Welfare	Policy Domain	State Project
Deregulation	Political Capitalism	Tax Expenditures
Iron Triangle	Pork Barrel Politics	Transparency

REVIEW QUESTIONS

1. What is the central predicament of democracy and capitalism? Use examples from tax policy and business regulation to illustrate how this predicament has been resolved in the United States.

2. Why is state intervention a misleading way to characterize the relationship between state and economy? Why is the issue not the presence or degree of intervention, but its specific form?

3. Why is the U.S. system of business–government relations based on corporate welfare and not industrial policy?

4. What would a "fair" tax system look like, and what specific features make it fair?

5. How do the consequences of taxation or avoiding taxation affect business and individual actions?

6. Who gets most agricultural subsidies and why?

7. In what ways is pork barrel politics similar to or different from corporate welfare?

8. How are the capture theory of business regulation and iron triangles interrelated?

9. What features of the 1970s regulation regime distinguished it from others and made it more threatening to business interests?

10. In what ways is deregulation similar to or different from previous waves of business regulation?

11. What are similarities and differences among a policy domain, a regulatory regime, and a state project?

12. How can the size and visibility of the state increase, but its autonomy decrease?

RECOMMENDED READINGS

Braithwaite, John and Peter Drahos. 2000. *Global Business Regulation.* New York: Cambridge University Press.

Eisner, Marc Allen. 1993. *Regulatory Politics in Transition.* Baltimore: John Hopkins University Press.

Fligstein, Neil. 1990. *The Transformation of Corporate Control.* Cambridge, MA: Harvard University Press.

Howard, Christopher. 1997. *The Hidden Welfare State: Tax Expenditures and Social Policy in the United States.* Princeton, NJ: Princeton University Press.

Prechel, Harland. 2000. *Big Business and the State: Historical Transitions and Corporate Transformation, 1880s–1990s.* Albany, NY: SUNY Press.

Roy, William. 1997. *Socializing Capital: The Rise of Large Industrial Corporation in America.* Princeton, NJ: Princeton University Press.

Endnotes

1. This is also called the "varieties of capitalism" discussion. For examples see Hall and Gingerich (2001), Hall and Soskice (2001), Soskice (1999), and Streeck (2001).
2. See Kolko (1963, 3).
3. From Prechel (2000, 277).
4. See Berk (1994), Campbell, et al. (1991), Dobbin (1994), Dobbin and Dowd (2000), Fligstein (1990), Jacoby (1997), Lie (1993, 1997), Powell and DiMaggio (1991), Roy (1997). For an overview see Swedberg (1997).
5. Campbell and Lindberg, (1990, 637).
6. See Neil Fligstein (1996, 657) on markets and state-building. Also see O'Riain (2000).
7. For discussion of these types see Hall and Soskice (2001) and Huber and Stephens (2000). O'Riain (2000) suggests a four-part typology, adding state-socialist and "developmental" newly industrialized states.
8. Soskice (1999) elaborated on the LMC and CMC distinction.
9. See Hall and Soskice (2001).
10. See Streeck (2001) for discussion, specifically of the German and Japanese cases.
11. See Cronin (2000) on the issue of convergence between the United States and the United Kingdom.
12. See Hooks and Bloomquist (1992) and Hooks (1994) on the regional impact of defense spending.
13. See Quadagno (1994) and Wilson (1996).
14. See Shoch (1994) for a discussion of industrial policy.
15. See Useem (1984) on corporate mobilization.
16. For discussions of the increased corporate mobility with information and service sector changes, and its global effects on social relations and urban formations see Sassen (1998, 2000, 2001).
17. For elaboration see B. Rubin (1995, 310) and B. Rubin (1996).
18. See DiPrete (1993, especially page 92).
19. Arkard (1995) argued that 1980s–1990s neoliberalism is not a radical departure from the 1960s.
20. See Yardley, Jim. "Well-off but Still Pressed, Doctor Could Use Tax Cut," *New York Times,* April 7, 2001.
21. See Rosenbaum, David. "Pack of G.O.P. Tax Cuts is Approved by House Panel," *New York Times,* October 13, 2001.
22. See Campbell (1993, 169).
23. For a comparison see Alesina, Glaeser, and Sacerdote (2001, 193).
24. See Quinn and Shapiro (1991a, 1991b) for a study of U.S. corporate taxes 1955 to 1987.
25. In a series of papers, Zey and Swenson (1998, 1999, 2001) document this change. Also see Prechel and Boies (1998).
26. From OECD (2001).
27. From *Statistical Abstract of the United States* (2001) for 2000. Alaska is excluded because of its revenue sources.
28. Federation of Tax Administrators, http://www.taxadmin. org/fta/rate/tax_stru.html (Downloaded July 30, 2003).
29. This excludes Alaska, which gets about six percent of its state revenue from oil sources.
30. See "Corporate Tax Sheltering and the Impact on State Corporate Income Tax Revenue Collections," report of the Multi-state Tax Commission, Washington D.C., July 15, 2003.
31. Johnston, David Clay. "U.S. Discloses That Use of Tax Evasion Plans is Extensive," *New York Times,* May 22, 2002.
32. Johnston, David Clay and Geraldine Fabrikant. "Cheap Seats in Private Jets for Executive on Vacation," *New York Times,* September 12, 2002.
33. *News from Congressman Pete Sessions,* 5th District Texas, June 5, 2002, http://www.house.gov/sessions/press/6-05-02-permanent-DeathTaxRepeal.html.
34. Stevenson, Richard. "The Long Arm of Small Business," *New York Times,* June 12, 1997.
35. See Salamon and Siegfried (1977).
36. From Multi-state Tax Commission (2003).
37. See "Rupert laid bare," *The Economist,* March 18, 1999.
38. "Shame Shelters for Business Flourish as Scrutiny Fades," *New York Times,* December 19, 2000. "Reducing Audits of the Wealthy, I.R.S. Turns Eye on Working Poor," *New York Times,* December 15, 1999.
39. Johnston, David Clay. "Tax Treaties with Small Nations Turn into a New Shield for Profits," *New York Times,* April 16 2002. McIntyre, Robert S. "Putting Profits over Patriotism," *The American Prospect,* March 25, 2002.
40. McIntyre, Robert S. "The Tax Cheaters Lobby," *American Prospect,* November 18, 2002.
41. Johnston, David Clay. "A Smaller I.R.S. Gives Up on Billions in Back Taxes," *New York Times,* April 13, 2001.
42. Johnston, David Clay. "Income-Tax Enforcement is Broadly Declining, New U.S. Data Indicate," *New York Times,* April 8, 2001.
43. Johnston, David Clay. "Reducing Audits of the Wealthy, I.R.S. Turns Eye on Working Poor," *New York Times,* December 15, 1999; "Cuts in Tax Enforcement Cost the States Billions," *New York Times,* April 12, 2001; and "Tax Inquiries Fall as Cheating Increases," *New York Times,* April 14, 2003.
44. Johnston, David Clay. "Departing Chief Says the I.R.S. Is Its Losing War on Tax Cheats," *New York Times,* November 5, 2002.
45. Johnston, David Clay. "Cuts in Tax Enforcement Costs the States Billions," *New York Times,* April 12, 2002.
46. See Howard (1997, 31).
47. See Howard (1997, 51–55).
48. Data are from International Union of Tenants, http://www. iut.nu/facts_fig.htm (Downloaded August 1, 2003).
49. From Webster, Simon. "Comparing International Housing Markets," *Financial Services Review, 56,* November 2000, http://www.acca.co.uk/publications/fsr/56/20347.
50. From Conley and Gifford (2003).
51. Olson and Champlin (1998) discuss corporate welfare and compare it to individual welfare in the U.S.
52. Of course, political influence also can shape the details of industrial policy.
53. See "Taxes Help Foot the Payrolls As States Vie for Employers," *New York Times,* August 11, 1998.
54. For studies on state economic development see Grant (1995, 1996), Grant and Hutchinson (1996), Grant and Wallace (1994) and Green, Fleischmann, and Kwong (1996).
55. See Dixit and Londregan (1996) for discussion of this distinction.

56. On the trend for pork barrel allocations of government funds for academic research see Savage (1999).

57. From "Hey Big Spenders," *The Economist,* March 28, 1998.

58. "How to Lease Federal Lands and Not Pay Rent," *New York Times,* March 13, 2003.

59. See Dixit and Londregan (1996).

60. See Shepsle and Weingast (1981) and Stein and Bickers (1994) on conditions favoring the use of pork barrel rewards. Joel Thompson (1986) discusses the partisan use of pork barrel rewards in state government.

61. See Hooks (1991b:70) on development of the USDA.

62. On agricultural policy development see Gilbert and Howe (1991), Hooks (1990a), Kirkendall (1975), McConnell (1969), and Skocpol and Finegold (1982).

63. Quote from Weiner, Tim. "Congress Agrees to $7.1 Billion in Farm Aid," *New York Times,* April 14, 2000. For additional information see "Agriculture Secretary vs. Sacred Cow," *New York Times,* December 11, 2001.

64. See "'Freedom to Farm' Law Becomes Freedom to Add Subsidies," *New York Times,* June 6, 2002.

65. From "Far From Dead, Subsidies Fuel Big Farms," *New York Times,* May 14, 2001.

66. See "Subsidised Cow Chow," *The Economist,* March 9, 2002.

67. From Eisner (1993:12).

68. For an elaboration of this argument see Dobbin and Dowd (2000), Fligstein (1990) and Roy (1997). Also see Storper and Salais (1997) on rejecting state intervention models and on how business executives make decisions.

69. See Neuman (1988a) for an elaboration of the corporatist experiment in the United States.

70. See Berry (1984) and Freudenburg and Gramling (1994.)

71. This idea builds on Yeager (1987, 1991). Also see Eisner (1993), Freudenburg and Gramling (1994), and Lynxwiler, Shover, and Clelland (1983) on agency discretion.

72. Eisner and Meier (1990) and Eisner (1991) discuss the role of economists in antitrust agencies.

73. On the role of scientific-technical knowledge and expertise in business regulation see Eisner (1993, 13–17), Stryker (1989, 1990a,1990b), and Yeager (1991).

74. This quote is from Stryker (1990a, 691) who discusses the general issue of science and regulation.

75. See Berry (1979, 1984) on agency autonomy and external groups, specifically with regard to utility regulation.

76. Nadel (1971) observed that regulatory agencies respond to organized, attentive business clients.

77. Szasz (1984, 1986) found little evidence that OSHA regulations imposed unacceptably high economic costs on industry, and industry responses were politically, not economically, based. Calavita (1983) found that OSHA's actions were largely symbolic.

78. See Moe (1982) and Wood and Anderson (1993) on the influence of the presidential party.

79. For an elaboration and discussion of the mutually adaptive adjustment model see Moe (1985).

80. Simpson and Piquero (2002) found that executives who violate business regulations make rational calculations to do so and are more likely to do so if a firm is having economic problems and the illegal act will produce significant

gains. Simpson (1986, 1987) also found that antitrust violations are related to a profit squeeze.

81. From Peterson (1990–1991).

82. Other terms for a triangle are subgovernments, power triads, issue communities, or advocacy coalitions. Also see Knoke et al. (1996). Kerbo and McKinstry (1995) and Colignon and Usui (2001, 2003) on iron triangles in Japan.

83. Others who question the iron triangle metaphor include Gais, Peterson, and Walker (1984) and Peterson (1990–1991).

84. Eisner (1993, 1–9) and Harris and Milkis (1996, 25–30) developed the concept of regulatory regime.

85. Calculated by the author from General Social Survey Data (various years).

86. See Eisner (1993, 173–174).

87. See Harris and Milkis (1996, 10).

88. This idea was elaborated in Harris and Milkis (1996, 65). See also Kraft (2000) on the environmental movement.

89. See Yeager (1991, 63–83) for a history of water quality and pollution laws.

90. Quote is from Eisner (1993, 121–122).

91. See Szasz (1984, 1986).

92. Also see Prechel (2003) who emphasizes the role of corporate political mobilization and PAC contributions.

93. As Eisner (1993, 176) noted, "Although there is little to suggest that regulatory reform and deregulation had a significant impact on inflation, there is no question that presidents repeatedly presented their initiatives in this light."

94. Quote is from Bowman (1996, 147, 148).

95. Quote is from Prechel (2000, 257).

96. See Prechel (2000, 232–233).

97. Quote is from Harris and Milkis (1996, 105).

98. See Harris and Milkis (1996, 113).

99. See Prechel (2003, 328–331), "Enron, Preaching Deregulation, Worked the Statehouse Circuit," *New York Times,* February 9, 2002.

100. From Eisner (1993, 151).

101. See Yeager (1991, 318).

102. From Eisner (1991, 190).

103. See Noble (1986), Eisner (1991), and Yeager (1991).

104. For a similar idea of state projects and racial formation see Omi and Winant (1994) for the area of racial relations.

105. See Yeager (1991, 40).

106. This idea comes from Lo (1998) and Noble (1986).

107. See "Enron, Preaching Deregulation, Worked the Statehouse Circuit," *New York Times,* February 9, 2002. Also see Kitschelt (2000) on the patterns of linkages between citizens and politicians, such as those in the United States, which he called clientalism, that might increase this type of activity.

108. Also see Calavita, Pontell, and Tillman (1997).

109. See Yeager (1991, 326).

110. Quote is from Prechel (2000, 274).

111. This point is made by many, but see Yeager (1987) for a regulatory example.

112. O'Riain (2000) calls this an older neoliberal paradigm of thinking.

113. Quote is from Prechel (2000, 155, 156).

SOCIAL PROGRAMS AND POLICIES

INTRODUCTION

What kind of health care coverage do you have? Is it adequate? If you were the parent of a critically ill child, could you take off from work for two weeks to care for the child without losing pay or your job? When you or your parents are elderly, how will you pay for daily living expenses over what may be 20 years of retirement? If you lost your job and could not find a new one within six months, how would you pay for living expenses in the interim? Every day people face questions such as these, and many look to the state for help. The state in all advanced nations directly or indirectly offers social programs designed to help people meet the ups and downs of daily living and improve their well-being.

In Chapter 10 you learned about the state-economy relationship and saw that different nations organize the state-economy relationship differently. Through its business policies and other programs, the state provides a foundation for the economy and delivers benefits to the business community (i.e., owners in a capitalist society). In this chapter we turn to the state-society relationship. We will examine how the state provides for the everyday needs of most ordinary people. This chapter focuses on social programs and the welfare state.

The term *welfare state* is widely misunderstood, but it is a type of state-society relationship that developed across all advanced capitalist societies during the twentieth century. As Amy Gutmann (1988a, 3) observed, "Every modern industrial state is a welfare state." Americans have particular trouble understanding the welfare state. Dawley (1991) noted that it appears as a contradiction between individualism and the responsibility to look after the needs of others. The welfare state is at the center of debates over how to distribute societal resources, life chances, and quality of life. It "has come to play a crucial—perhaps dominant—role in the study of stratification" (i.e., the study of social-economic inequality).[1] The welfare state and social stratification mutually shape one another; you cannot really understand one without the other. The welfare state structures the form and degree of social, economic and political inequality, and it is itself shaped by the class relations and patterns of inequality in a society. As Gösta Esping-Andersen (1990, 23) explained, "The welfare state is not just a mechanism that intervenes in, and possibly corrects, the structure of inequality; it is, in its own right, a system of stratification." Welfare states have a large impact on the basic quality of life. For example, infant mortality rates are much lower in nations that have stronger, more extensive welfare state programs.[2] ∎

UNDERSTANDING THE WELFARE STATE

The term welfare state is associated with a set of public social insurance measures developed in Great Britain and based on a report by William Beveridge (1879–1963) in which he contrasted an open, democratic, humane advanced industrial society (i.e., Britain) with a totalitarian, inhuman industrial state (i.e., Nazi Germany). In one, the state unified and provided for the well-being of its people. In the other, the state set some groups against others and waged war against other nations. In this context, we can identify three early sources of the welfare state.

One source is Chancellor Otto von Bismarck (1815–1898) who led Germany for roughly 30 years. In 1862 Bismarck became the prime minister of Prussia, one of the weakest kingdoms of Europe. Nine years later, after three successful wars, he led a powerful, unified German Empire. Bismarck tried to ban a nascent Social Democratic political party, but it continued to grow and mobilize workers in an era filled with industrial conflict and mass unemployment. To defeat the rising influence of socialists and social democrats, Bismarck enacted social legislation (e.g., accident insurance, pensions, socialized medicine) that would woo the workers away from egalitarian socialist ideas. Thus, one origin of the welfare state is preemptive, antisocialist action initiated by a traditional patriarchal regime.[3]

A second source of the welfare state arose from specific proposals by various European and Scandinavian left-wing parties (e.g., Socialist, Communist, People's, Social Democratic, Reform Liberal) early in the twentieth century. They fought for equal opportunities, a more equitable distribution of wealth, social programs to protect workers who became injured or unemployed, health care for all, housing assistance, and a minimal standard of living for the elderly and disadvantaged. The idea gained clarity and support in the trauma of the 1930s Great Depression. Social Democratic governments in Denmark, France, Norway, and Sweden advanced it in the 1930s. Yet as Myles (1989, 17) noted, "It was only in the context of the economic boom following World War II that the welfare state emerged in a form that represented a radical break with the past." In Great Britain, a moderate alliance formed between the Labour and Liberal parties to enact public pension, health, and unemployment insurance laws between 1908 and 1911. Later, after World War II, the British Labor Party created a comprehensive system of social programs based on the Beveridge report to improve the quality of life for all citizens. After the long and difficult war, it was a kind of moral compact between the British state and its war-weary people. "Major reforms of British social policy were planned during World War II and were quickly put into place after the war."[4]

A third source of the welfare state is found in the United States, which still lacks a true European-style welfare state.[5] The United States created a highly fragmented patchwork system comprised of voluntary charity programs, local government assistance, employer-provided help, and targeted federal benefit programs that together offered uneven coverage. For example, the federal government had a pension program to care for Civil War veterans and their widows.[6] It expanded, until by the end of the nineteenth century, it covered two-thirds of native-born white males outside the South and consumed 41 percent of all federal revenue.[7] Unlike the broad-based European programs for the industrial working class and the poor, this large program was tied to Republican Party patronage and was not targeted to help the needy. Orloff (1993b, 137) summarized, "In ethnic terms, the post-Civil War pension system . . . helped native-born whites and early immigrants; in class terms it assisted the middle class and upper strata of the working class most." In the Progressive Era, scattered state-government programs for job injury (workmen's compensation) and widows laid the foundation for a federal welfare state that had minimum wage, poverty aid, and disability programs in the 1930s.[8]

These three divergent origins—preemptive action by conservative governments to block leftist gains, highly egalitarian social programs advocated by politically mobilized social democratic or labor parties, and a patchwork of partial programs to help specific groups—provided the groundwork for the contemporary welfare state.

Confusion over the Welfare State

The welfare state idea confuses many Americans because of a historical change in the meaning of the word *welfare*. To many, *welfare* means poverty-reduction programs, but these are just a small part of the welfare state. Especially after political clashes in the 1970s and 1980s, welfare became a volatile political symbol, obscuring its original meaning.[9] Webster's unabridged dictionary defines *welfare* as, "the state of being or doing well; the condition of health, prosperity and happiness and well-being," and the Oxford English Dictionary adds, "thriving or successful progress in life, prosperity." The political philosopher Michael Walzer (1988, 16) argued, "The welfare state was imagined as a systematic form of mutual assistance, replacing the unsystematic and unreliable forms that had existed before." Polarized political debate in the United States displaced the idea that welfare means collectively helping people and caring for each other. In most people's minds, the original meaning has been superseded, and welfare is an unpopular, wasteful government program that spreads dependency. This shift reflects the success of right-wing advocates who opposed the idea that the state, rather than the private market alone, should ensure public well-being.

A second reason for the confusion is the rugged individualism and populist aversion to centralized political authority in American culture. In the neoliberal ideological thinking that pervades much of current public discourse, the state is an unnatural, greedy force, in contrast to a "natural" market and civil society. Such allusions cloud out alternative images of a state—the protector of national sovereignty, a beneficent servant of the people's will, the provider of services to people in need, the upholder of justice and defender of basic rights, and a guarantor of economic prosperity for all. Understanding the "welfare state" requires restoring the idea of well-being to the term welfare and reexamining the state's role and the meaning of citizenship. Ultimately, the issue of a welfare state hinges on the question, How should a democratic state distribute the privately generated wealth of capitalism?

Recall the concept of citizenship developed by T. H. Marshall discussed in Chapter 2. For Marshall, the welfare state is part of a long-term historical expansion of citizenship. With the dissolution of feudalism, the state extended civil rights by abolishing slavery and serfdom, creating "free persons." Later, people won political rights, particularly the right to vote, to express dissident ideas, and to hold public office. After civil and legal rights, came political rights, and finally the last stage was an extension of social rights.[10] Social rights make the other rights effective. By guaranteeing everyone a basic, minimal level of economic security, people could exercise political-civil rights such as liberty, the right to vote, freedom of conscience, and so forth.[11] Moon (1988) termed this Hegel's dilemma: Capitalism only grows if people have basic political rights, but capitalism generates inequalities of wealth and power that undermine those very political rights. To permit capitalist expansion and ensure an effective political democracy simultaneously, the state must provide basic social rights and shield people from capitalism's harmful consequences.

A third reason for confusion is that the United States has an unusual form of the welfare state. It was created piecemeal over decades in fragmented forms with large parts of it still hidden from view. Although its major advance was the enactment of Social Security in the 1930s Depression, its roots go back much earlier. The American welfare state has partial, overlapping, and contradictory goals, and it is administered at many levels under frequently changing tiles, rules, mandates and levels of funding. Even researchers with special training find it difficult to keep track of all its parts. We need to look at the welfare state's historical growth and the breath of its actions.

The ideology present in most discussions of the welfare state also can create confusion. An ideology mixes factual statements with emotional appeals, value assumptions, and popular misconceptions. This distortion fuels confusion. For example, many people criticize welfare state programs as being wasteful, corrupt, inefficient or ineffective. A careful analysis reveals that most of the programs are operating just fine with regard to their original program goals. What is happening is that a person has ideological beliefs and values opposed to the program's goals. Because critics are reluctant to admit that they oppose the goals on purely ideological grounds, they instead use the more acceptable and simplistic criticism of government waste.[12] Thus, someone angry over welfare fraud—meaning fraud in public benefit programs for poor people—does not criticize other more, wasteful, corrupt, or less efficient public benefit programs because ideologically they accept their goals. Confusing values of effectiveness or efficiency with a program's goals only spreads misunderstanding and avoids an honest debate over the role of the state.

A last source of confusion is that welfare state programs try to satisfy a large array of other, sometimes unrelated, political, social, economic, or ideological goals. Moreover, the mixture of goals embedded in a social program in one country may contradict those of a program with the same name in a different country. For example, a welfare state provides a "social wage" or income maintenance (i.e., state-provided income support through unemployment insurance) and similar programs as a percentage of the average person's income. As Alexander Hicks (1999, 8–9) observed, "programs bearing the label 'income maintenance' . . . address the problem of income insecurity in ways that may concurrently advance goals as far-ranging as status differentiation, class fragmentation, clientelistic dependence, curtailment of market distortions, self-reliance, human capital investment, recommodification, decommodification, social and economic rights, redistribution; and worker, partisan, or citizen solidarity." You will encounter the ideas of recommodification and decommodification later in this chapter.

Defining the Welfare State

The welfare state's original purpose was to buffer working class people from the uncertainties and havoc of working for early, chaotic industrialism and to protect the most vulnerable members of society (i.e., the very poor, infirm, elderly, or disabled). Harold Wilensky (1975, 1) offered the following widely used but contested definition: "government-protected minimum standards of income, nutrition, health, housing, and education, assured to every citizen as a political right, not as charity." Others broadened the definition to include notions of justice, equality, and caring. The general notion of well-being is central to the welfare state, and it goes beyond providing minimal material living standards. **The welfare state means a state responsibility to ensure the well-being, health, happiness, and prosperity of all its citizens**. This means more than spending for specific public programs, although researchers typically measure the welfare state's size using government budget categories. The welfare state also includes laws, legal rights, public standards, regulations, and methods of delivering benefits or services. Sociologists, political scientists, economists, and historians as well as people in social work, health care, or gerontology study the welfare state. Each field uses its own perspective, terminology, and disciplinary orientation.

The idea of a "well-being" or welfare state is broad. Jane Lewis (2002, 348) remarked, "Defining the goal of welfare states in terms of well-being rather than work and wages means that policies must address the distribution of time." Having time away from work for leisure, family, and friends is important for well-being. As part of its welfare state, France adopted the 35-hour work week in 2000 for employers of 20 or more people, and most advanced nations mandate a minimum amount of vacation for all employees (see Table 11.1). The United States differs from other nations and is far more obsessed with work. For example, a typical full-time employee in the United States puts in 1,952 hours per year; this is more than in any other advanced nation. In Canada and United Kingdom it is 1,735 hours, a little higher than the 1,550 hours found in Germany or Sweden. Even "work crazy" Japan is at 1,890 hours. The United States is closer to countries like China, Thailand, and Bangladesh where workers put in 2,280 hours. More striking, however, is that over the past 20 years total hours worked declined in other nations but increased in the United States, by 30 hours since 1983. Why? It is due to a combination of cultural values, consumerism, no vacation policy, and the U.S. welfare-state. While Americans tend to ask for more money, Western Europeans bargain for time off.[13]

Welfare states ensure collective well-being by providing citizens with "social goods." Whether the welfare state provides for a basic need through cash transfer or a public service is less critical than recognizing *how* it provides social goods. Two well-recognized social goods are health care and a retirement pension. A social good is what people define as being essential for a humane quality of life, minimal human decency, or a complete member of society. Sometimes called basic needs, social goods are tied to a society's values and beliefs and include security about maintaining a level of life's necessities (e.g., food, shelter, clothing), health, and key opportunities (e.g., ability to travel locally or to obtain an education). It is "social" in that it is a shared responsibility with the larger community or society at large. Social goods depend on national living standards and can change over time. Beyond the basics, many other public services, such as assistance to the disabled, low-cost childcare, and public cultural-leisure facilities (e.g., public parks, public radio and television, libraries, or public museums) are social goods.

Charles Noble (1997, 7) argued that, "welfare states exist to protect the public from unregulated market forces. That is, their rationale and to a significant

TABLE 11.1	**Minimum Paid Vacation Mandated for Full-Time Workers with One Year of Service for Select Nations**
Country	**Mandated Vacation Benefit for Workers**
Australia	No national law, but 4 weeks is standard
Belgium	20 days, premium pay
Canada	At least 2 weeks, determined by provincial law
Czech Republic	4 weeks
France	5 weeks
Germany	4 weeks
Ireland	4 weeks
Italy	Mandated vacation; length determined by employment contract
Japan	10 days paid time off (includes other leave time)
Netherlands	4 weeks
Poland	18 working days
Spain	30 calendar days
Sweden	5 weeks
United Kingdom	No national law, but is implementing European Union directive that requires four weeks of annual leave
United States	No national requirement

Source: Keller, William L., Timothy J. Darby, and American Bar Association. International Labor Law Committee. *International Labor and Employment Laws.* 2 vols. Washington, DC: Bureau of National Affairs, 1997, 2002 Supplements.

Average Paid Vacation Time in the United States by Type of Employer

Employer	**Vacation Time**
Medium and large private establishments	9.6 days (1997)
State and local governments	12.6 days (1998)
Small private establishments	8.1 days (1996)

Source: U. S. Bureau of Labor Statistics, Employee Benefits Survey and http://www.ilr.cornell.edu/library/research/QuestionOfTheMonth/default.html.

degree their principal effect." Two traditional welfare state goals are to provide minimal economic security and to promote social-economic equality.[14] Four additional goals ensure a broad sense of well-being among people: (1) a comfortable, safe living environment with personal security (i.e., no child abuse, fear of assault, spousal abuse);[15] (2) humane care for people needing assistance, especially young children, the infirm or disabled, and frail elderly;[16] (3) personal dignity and autonomy, with alternative life choices, also called agency;[17] and (4) inclusion, solidarity, cohesion, and feelings of community.[18] These six goals include the full scope of well-being and go beyond those of a traditional welfare state (see Summary 11.1).

| SUMMARY 11.1 | Six Broadly Defined Goals of the Welfare State |

Goal 1. Ensure that all people have basic economic security for survival—Assure a minimal level of income continuation when unemployed, injured, disabled, or retired and a basic level of food, housing, health care, transportation, and education. *Example programs*: unemployment insurance, disability insurance, health care, pension, public/social housing or housing subsidies, and public transportation.

Goal 2. Promote social-economic equality and inclusion—Assure that no social group is excluded from full economic-social participation in society due to poverty status, race-ethnicity, gender, physical-cognitive ability, sexuality, etc. *Example programs*: minimum wage laws, access rights for the disabled, schooling for students with special needs, fair housing laws, and antidiscrimination and hate-crime laws.

Goal 3. Create a safe and humane living environment with personal safety— Guarantee all people physical protection from exploitation or abuse. *Example programs*: antichild abuse, battered women's shelters, spousal abuse protection, antisexual slavery and child exploitation laws, and sexual harassment protection.

Goal 4: Provide humane care for people in need of assistance—Provide humane care and assistance to all persons in need, especially young children, the disabled, and the elderly. *Example programs*: paternity and maternity leave programs, child-care centers, elder-care facilities, and in-home care assistance.

Goal 5. Ensure personal dignity and autonomy—Enable all people to develop and express alternative life choices and live a dignified, secure life with the choices. *Example programs*: Aids for disabled people, family assistance, programs that support individual parenting and alternative lifestyles.

Goal 6. Build cohesion and quality of life among families and the local communities—Strengthen social bonds, cohesion, and deep emotional relations by supporting family, collective leisure, and cultural enjoyment. *Example programs*: Child-care assistance; limits on work hours; mandatory paid vacations; free public libraries, concerts, museums; public parks, recreation centers, and playgrounds; public meeting facilities for clubs, neighborhood organizations, and interest associations.

Sources: Brush (2002), Goodin et al. (1999), Korpi (2000), Quadagno (2000), Schneider (1982).

The welfare state's boundaries can extend beyond the state or public sector, and the private sector also can provide social goods. For example, in one nation a social good, such as health care, is provided as a public service directly distributed to all people as a right of citizenship and paid for with general taxes. In another nation, the same social good is delivered through private, profit-making firms and allocated on the basis of ability to pay. Each welfare state may deliver the same social good differently. Traditionally, a welfare state meant the state alone provided economic security and promoted equality. Yet in some nations the market or other nonmarket providers (e.g., a charity or religious group, or a mutual support/solidarity organization) provides social goods with state aid or encouragement. The provider, state or nonstate, critically changes the character of a welfare state (see Chart 11.1).

chart   11.1

ALTERNATIVE PROVIDERS OF SOCIAL GOODS

Provider	Basis for Provision	Examples
State	Citizenship or legal rights	Public schooling, public food and shelter for destitute homeless, public pension (Social Security)
Market	Private purchase or private job benefit	A working couple sends a child to a private daycare center, an employee gets health insurance as a job benefit
Family	Emotional attachment	Parents provide free housing for their unemployed 35-year-old son, a daughter cares for her bedridden 85-year-old mother
Charity or religious group	Belief and religious faith	A church supports a youth recreation center, United Way sponsors a big brother/big sister program
Mutual support	Communal solidarity	A social movement supports a rape crisis center; eight neighbors form a babysitting cooperative, a labor union donates time to helping clean up a disaster area.

Political sociologists ask three questions about the welfare state: (1) What is its origin and the cause of its expansion? (2) What are its various forms and why does a form develop? (3) What are its social–political consequences? Most attention has gone to the first question, and the last two have only become issues since 1990. Because the welfare state is central to the state-society relationship of advanced societies, its origin and expansion have been major concerns in the political sociological models you have read about in throughout this book.[19]

MODELS OF POLITICAL SOCIOLOGY AND THE WELFARE STATE

Pluralists offer three explanations of welfare state origin and expansion—(1) industrialization-modernization, (2) national cultural values, and (3) interest-group pressure. The first explanation, also called "logic of industrialism," holds that industrialization, and specifically its demographic-technological dimension, is the primary cause of the welfare state's appearance and expansion.[20] In traditional, preindustrial society, care of the sick, the elderly, the unemployed, orphans, the disabled, etc., fell to the extended family, the clan, a local religious congregation, or the village. With sometimes meager resources and expertise, these groups maintained a sense of community in small homogenous rural settings with little geographic mobility and dense social relationships. As traditional-agrarian societies declined, the social support system of extended families and traditional assistance also broke down. Industrialization-modernization brought about a wage-earning labor force, urbanization, geographic mobility, more divorce, secularization, increased life expectancy, and complex organizations. It also created new social needs, such as survival during unemployment and elder care. With greater societal wealth, organizational capacity, and secular, rational-scientific knowledge, modern industrial society had the resources to address the new social needs. Since industrialism caused the welfare state, the explanation predicts a convergence among industrial societies to create similar welfare states, and it assigns a very minor role to political parties or institutions.

In the cultural values explanation, a society's deep-rooted cultural values are expressed in its public programs.[21] Differences among countries, in terms of rates of economic growth, levels of interpersonal violence, provision of social benefits, political institutions, and so forth reflect a country's dominant social–cultural values. Each nation's welfare state is unique because it reflects national religious–cultural values. Thus, a frontier pattern of settlement, the absence of a feudal heritage, and the small independent farmers in the United States gave rise to the populist-democratic values of individualism, self-sufficiency, voluntarism, and distrust of government. This explains why the United States is the smallest, weakest, and most fragmented welfare state among the advanced nations.

An interest-group explanation views state programs as a response to the diverse demands of voters and politically organized groups.[22] Interest groups form around any social cleavage (e.g., class, race, age, gender, region, religion) and once mobilized, they form coalitions with others to seek benefits from the state for their group. Benefits, or public programs, result from competition by politicians for votes and interest group lobbying. Organized interests apply pressure and supply selective information to affect specific government agencies, and a policy network of interest groups develops around a government agency to protect or pressure for change in programs. Thus, once created, welfare state programs continue to reflect interest group demands. In the political-business cycle version, welfare state expansion is tied to changes in the business cycle.[23] Politicians increase social benefits in periods of economic downturn when unemployment rises and voters demand more help. The interest group argument suggests little coordination in the overall mix of welfare state programs, and that the mix of social programs reflects the power of any combination of specific interest groups and mobilized voters, including privileged groups.

In the *elite model*, political entrepreneurs and elite coalitions create social programs to satisfy specific sectors of the masses and to build a client base. Elites created welfare state programs to win mass support. Also, elites of public and private organizations that deliver social programs seek to protect and perpetuate the programs.[24]

Political sociologists who use a *statist model* see the state adding social programs only after it develops sufficient administrative capacity to do so.[25] Administrative capacity includes the resources of a bureaucracy, administrative personnel, organizational structure, and so forth that enable the state to translate popular demands into specific programs. The organizational structure, constitutional form, and political coalitions within the state set parameters for welfare state growth and offer periodic openings to add new programs or change existing ones. For example, a highly fragmented, decentralized state offers many "veto points" for opponents to block social welfare initiatives, so it will have a small welfare state. By contrast, a highly centralized state can adopt social programs more readily.[26] State managers and professional experts do not always wait for interest group demands but may initiate new programs and attract interest groups to form around them. Thus, the state, as an institution, is an active, independent force in welfare state growth. A legacy of preexisting laws, policies and programs can limit social programs or push them to grow in particular directions. As Huber, Ragin, and Stephens (1993, 722) summarized, "legacies work in several ways: they promote growing expenditures, they provide organizational models and institutional set-ups for new programs, and, among those groups privileged by existing programs, they create resistance to egalitarian reform." An important type of legacy is the policy feedback (see Closer Look 11.1 and Figure 11.1).

CLOSER LOOK 11.1   Policy Feedback

Political sociologists developed the idea of policy feedback to explain how, "As politics creates policies, policies remake politics" (Skocpol 1992a, 58). The policies in a specific area (e.g., business policy, social policy, transportation or labor policy) are not only the result of current political forces, alliances, and contests. New policy directions are affected by both the policy legacy (e.g., past legal precedents, bureaucracies, procedures, ideological justifications) and policy feedback. **Feedback occurs when a policy created at one point in time influences the creation of state institutional structures and builds the political capability of groups around the structures, and the structures and capabilities, in turn, affect subsequent policy** (see Figure 11.1). Orloff (1988, 25) noted, once enacted, "social policies in turn reshape the organization of the state itself and the goals and alliances of social groups involved in ongoing political struggle." Feedback can be positive or negative. Earlier policy can build certain institutional pathways and strengthen certain groups that facilitate one type of later policy while simultaneously creating institutional barriers and weakening opposing groups. In addition, Skocpol (1992a, 59) argued that, "[P]ositive or negative policy feedbacks can also 'spill over'

from one policy to influence the fate of another policy proposal that seems analogous in the eyes of relevant officials and groups." For example, an early policy of pension benefits for U.S. Civil War combat veterans established a Bureau of Pensions in the federal government and helped to organize veterans. It facilitated the programs expansion to the widows of veterans and noncombat veterans. Yet the program grew huge and was associated with patronage politics, so these features drew criticism and limited establishing a broad public pension system. Another example is the program of tax deductions for mortgage payments. The program did not establish a powerful government housing agency and added to tax collection complexity. It aided real estate and banking interests and helped middle-income people who organized defend or urge an expansion of the tax deductions for privately financed and purchased housing. A weak state agency and the lack of a politically organized constituency hindered an alternative housing policy, such as publicly provided or cooperative housing or using government reserves to finance housing. By contrast, in Singapore, extensive public housing and financial support was central in its welfare state and most of the nation's population lives in good quality, public housing.

Figure 11.1
Policy feedback.
Source: Adapted from Skocpol (1992a, 58).

A well-studied example of policy legacy is the U.S. Social Security program. The program reinforced race and gender inequality because the initial Social Security programs excluded occupations that were predominately black or female. Benefits were based on number of years worked and wages, so excluded groups and low-income groups received low or no benefits. Preexisting programs, such as Veterans Benefits, Workmen's Compensation and Mother's Aid had been targeted for whites alone and excluded the South due to its preindustrial, racially segregated labor relations.[27] We will examine the impact of race and gender on the welfare state later in this chapter.

A *power-structure model* holds that politically organized, far-sighted capitalists pressed for welfare state programs.[28] Politically astute capitalists designed and promoted social programs to short-circuit more radical alternatives and to defuse social unrest. Expanding social programs was more efficient than sending in troops to quell mass demonstration, riots, and burning cities. Corporate, monopoly sector capitalists recognized that by offering a limited welfare state to quiet unrest and encourage acceptance of the status quo, they could hold onto power in the long-run. As Domhoff (1996, 118–119) argued, the Social Security Act, "was shaped by rival segments of the ruling class within the context of pressure of major social disruption . . . [and] the richest and most powerful corporate empire of the early twentieth century . . . played a major role in shaping old age pension and unemployment insurance."[29]

The *structuralist model* is similar to the logic of the industrialism model.[30] Structuralists hold that the welfare state was initiated to sustain capitalism. The capitalist state needs to promote economic growth (i.e., an accumulation function) and maintain social peace (i.e., a legitimation function). The welfare state supports and serves the accumulation function by reinforcing the competitiveness of labor markets. It is widely acknowledged that, "the general function of welfare policy in early nineteenth century Britain and North America was to mobilize an unwilling population to enter a nascent industrial labor force" by breaking down existing attitudes and work habits.[31] When the state demeans poor people and provides them with minimal social benefits, they are forced to accept low wages and work under terms dictated by capitalists. Employed workers who have social benefits attached to their jobs can be intimated into staying with it when the alternative is destitution. Social programs also socialize, or spread across society, the costs of reproducing, or continuing, the working class as a whole. This lowers the direct costs for capitalists. For example, public schools give young people the skills, attitudes, and beliefs that capitalists want in workers. Public pensions, unemployment insurance, and so forth absolve owners from providing for workers who are too old or sick to continue working. Public health and sanitation prevent outbreaks of disease that might reduce labor productivity.

The welfare state's legitimation function is to encourage beliefs and behaviors consistent with the continuation of capitalism. A welfare state shows workers that raw capitalist market forces have been "tamed" or civilized by abolishing child labor, providing retirement benefits, stopping horrific industrial accidents, and keeping the starving masses off the streets. In this way, it undercuts drives to organize a radical working class movement that might seek to overthrow capitalism. Over time, the advanced capitalist economic system is intergrated with a welfare state. Claus Offe (1984, 188) argued that the welfare state is an irreversible development of capitalism, and "the 'dismantling' of the welfare state would result in widespread conflict and forms of anomie and 'criminal' behavior. . . ." Without the welfare state, advanced capitalism would require new kinds of legitimation (i.e., ideologies, beliefs) or would have to use more repressive, authoritarian polices of social control.

The *class-struggle model* (also called the social-democratic or power resources model) has a well-developed explanation for the welfare state. Since the 1980s, most political sociologists embraced some version of it.[32] It holds that conflicts among opposing social classes in specific social-historical settings explain the timing, size, and form of the welfare state. The largest, most comprehensive, and most egalitarian forms of the welfare state are found in nations with a strong, politicized labor movement and social democratic or labor parties that regularly won elections. As Huber and Stephens (2001a, 3) summarized, "the balance of class power is the primary determinant of variation through time and across countries in welfare state effort."[33] The welfare state is a concession that a politically organized working class won in alliance with others (especially small business owners and farmers). A social disruption or social control version the explanation applied to the United States says that without a social democratic party, the government welfare programs expanded to respond to lower class protest.[34] Officials expanded welfare benefits for specific social groups to temporarily "buy" peace when threatened by massive unrest and rioting. Once order was restored and the groups became quiet and demobilized, welfare benefits were reduced or eliminated. Some suggest that unrest alone cannot create pressure for social programs, but it must occur in conjunction with prior public debates over inequality, in a context of competitive elections, or as part of a larger social–political movement.[35] In short, public awareness, close elections, and political movements, plus unrest cause welfare state expansion.

Evaluation of the Explanations

As Myles and Quadagno (2002) observed, political scientists, historians, and others studied the welfare state for decades, but only recently have they tested competing explanations with detailed historical accounts and statistical, cross-national comparisons. Reflecting on his own study, Hicks (1999, 180) offered a summary that applies to 30 years of research findings, "no single perspective emerges preeminent. Instead, factors associated with every perspective play consequential roles in determining social spending."[36] Next, we look at empirical support for each.

Pluralist Model

Early studies supported the logic of industrialism explanation, but it was seriously questioned by subsequent evidence. Jill Quadagno (1988, 3) remarked, "Empirically, the logic of industrialism perspective fared well in the cross-national studies based on data for the 1940s to 1960s, but when the research became more longitudinal and incorporated broader time spans, the argument floundered." Early studies looked at data from one point in time, but the explanation was about origins and development over time. Contrary to the theory's predictions, the most highly industrialized nations, or states in the United States, did not create the earliest social programs or the largest welfare states.[37] Different levels of industrial development fail to explain the differences in welfare state size, although having a minimal level of economic development may be a precondition to begin building a welfare state.[38] Another difficulty was that the early studies measured a welfare state by total government social spending. They did not disaggregate spending into specific areas, consider particular populations covered by benefits, or the acquisition of legal social rights.[39] The model failed to explain why some nations failed to cover certain sectors of the population or provide specific types of programs. Lastly, tests of the convergence thesis across nations failed, and political factors more than the level of economic development appeared to explain welfare state growth.[40]

The interest group explanation also did not fare well. As Pampel and Williamson (1989, 43) noted, "Empirical support for interest group theory is only just emerging . . . quantitative studies are few." One problem was the argument that social programs grew in response to interest group demands. Logically, if there are no social programs, then no interest groups wanted them. Yet many competing interest groups have demanded programs. There is also a danger of circular reasoning—the creation or growth of a program was called evidence for a group's demand, and demand also is a cause of the program's creation and growth. Also, simply because an interest group demands a program does not mean that it is the cause of its creation or expansion. A political group or elite may initiate a program for others, as in the case of the antiworking class Bismarck who created programs that were for the working class. Another criticism is that systematic inequalities in resources, wealth, organizational power, and access to the political process by interest groups are not fully recognized. Likewise, the state is treated as neutral mechanism that merely mirrors the outcome of interest group demands, with state itself having no impact of its own.

The cultural values explanation has been criticized for failing to link specific beliefs and values to specific programs. As Theda Skocpol (1992a, 16) remarked, "proponents of this approach have so far failed to pinpoint exactly how cultural values, intellectual traditions, and ideological outlook have concretely influenced processes of political conflict and policy debate." The key causal factor, cultural values, is loose and undefined; it includes virtually every theme or event in a nation's history. This explanation is also in danger of circular reasoning—welfare states appeared, expanded, and took a particular form in a nation because it fit a nation's values. If a welfare state did not appear, then it must not have fit with the nation's values. Features of the welfare state become both an indicator of cultural values (i.e., the cause) and evidence of the kinds of programs people wanted (i.e., the result). In addition, it assumed a consensus around common cultural values, ignoring the complexity, contradictions, and diversity of values in a nation. After examining cultural values toward social welfare among both elites and populace in the United States, Great Britain, and Canada, Ann Orloff (1993b, 57) concluded, "cultural values cannot alone explain the specifics of policy preferences or ultimate policy outcomes. . . ." The values may be a secondary factor that operates in conjunction with other contextual factors, but they cannot explain the timing, scope, or details of welfare states.

The *elite model's* explanation of the welfare state is not highly developed; nevertheless, the example of Bismarck and similar elite-initiated early programs suggests that political elites may play a role. Others argue that once in place, elite groups defend welfare state programs to protect them, but the statist model makes the same observation and includes the impact of an existing policy system as well as direct and indirect beneficiaries.

The explanation of the *statist model* has received substantial support, specifically its idea of a conditioning effect of state structure and of policy legacy. The explanation has been criticized for accepting an unlimited range of nonclass interest groups and assigning autonomous state managers too large of a role. Its recognition of political learning by state managers and reformist intellectuals is a strength.[41] The learning takes place at different levels of government or outside of government, and it sets parameters within which state managers are restricted. Officials can develop only details within the parameters.[42] However, if powerful political groups are unhappy with welfare state programs, they can force the state to replace specific officials and technical experts.[43] Thus, the institutional structure of the state may constrain, more than directly cause, welfare state development.

The explanation offered by the *power-structure model* is criticized for not recognizing historical variation in the power of capitalists and internal capitalist divisions. While a few capitalists are farsighted and back welfare programs, the state has autonomy from direct capitalist control. Also, it largely ignores the role of culture or ideology and assumes that capitalists are highly aware, knowledgeable, and cohesive.

The *structuralist model* explanation is criticized for being functionalist and teleological.[44] Everything the state does ends up maintaining or protecting capitalism, and the needs of capitalism seem to automatically cause the rise of a welfare state. Another criticism by Pampel and Williamson (1989, 33) of studies using this model is that "they devote little attention to explaining the diversity among similar capitalist nations."

The *class-struggle model*, or a power-resources explanation, suggests that the working class (and their allies) use the welfare state to improve their quality of life, income, and political positions relative to the capitalist class (and their allies). Workers use democratic political rights (e.g., voting, political parties) and their right to form or join labor unions to redistribute and equalize resources (i.e., wealth, income, health care, etc.). In simple terms, the more powerful the working class, the bigger the welfare state and the more powerful the capitalist class, the smaller the welfare state. Misra (2002, 21) argued, "While both pluralist and statist theories have made important contributions to theories of the welfare state, class theories have been among the most successful at predicting the formation of welfare states, welfare state spending, and welfare state effects." Indeed, class struggle/power resources is the dominant explanation of welfare state growth, with a statist model being the only real contender.[45] Consistent with the model, the level of social unrest or rioting was closely correlated with welfare expansion in the United States.[46] Support also comes from empirical studies of welfare state expansion in Western Europe.[47] It appears that worker political strength and consciousness had the greatest causal impact on the form and size of a welfare state. Welfare states are strongest and most redistributive where workers are heavily unionized, politically organized behind socialist ideals, and form winning electoral alliances. By contrast, welfare states are weakest and least redistributive where workers are not highly unionized, are politically weak and disorganized, and socialist or labor political party alternatives are absent or rejected in elections. These findings also fit well with the democratic class struggle thesis (discussed earlier in Chapter 6). While social democratic political resources are the primary force in welfare state expansion, it is likely that they do so only within the constraints of political institutions.[48]

The class-struggle or power-resources explanation illustrates a contradictory process. Social democratic parties rely on an alliance of workers and other social groups (e.g., small business owners, farmers, professionals) for numerical voting power. To win allies, they must offer concessions to a coalition of nonworker supporters. They also raise worker's living standards, so workers are more like the middle class. At the same time, they also cannot cause serious harm to capitalism, or they will increase unemployment (harming workers) and frighten away voters (who increasingly have a middle-class orientation).[49] These factors, plus the high cost of an extensive welfare state public support system puts pressures on Social Democratic parties to abandon strong income equalizing measures. In short, a combination of successfully raising worker's living standards, attracting an alliance of nonworkers at the polls, and the capitalist economic system tend to rein in or deradicalize the socialist-oriented welfare state.

WELFARE STATE EXPANSION

Whether measured as total social spending, percentage of the population covered, or range of programs, by any measure, all advanced capitalist democracies expanded their welfare states in the post World War II period, at least through the mid-1980s (see Table 11.2). The expansion was uneven across countries and faster in some years than others, but expansion is undeniable. In the early 1950s, most advanced nations devoted about 10 percent of their economies to traditional welfare-state programs; by 1990 they devoted an average of about 20 percent.[50]

Early, simple explanations of welfare state expansion assumed a single cause for both the origin and the subsequent expansion of welfare states, a single pathway to expansion, one process in operation for the entire history of industrial capitalist democracy, and one type of welfare state (indicated by government spending for social programs).[51] Political sociologists now recognize the complexity—the initial origin and later expansion of welfare states can have different causes, alternative developmental pathways exist, the pathways or processes in a nation can shift across historical periods, and welfare states can assume several alternative forms.[52]

TABLE 11.2 State Social Program Expenditures* 1980–1998 for Selected Countries					
	State Social Program Spending as a Percentage of Gross Domestic Product (GDP)				
Country	1980	1985	1990	1995	1998
Australia	11.32	13.50	14.36	17.79	17.81
Austria	23.33	25.13	25.00	27.88	26.80
Canada	13.26	16.97	18.25	19.23	18.03
Denmark	29.06	27.87	29.32	32.41	29.81
France	21.14	26.62	26.45	28.98	28.82
Germany	20.28	20.98	20.29	26.70	27.29
Greece	11.48	17.89	21.64	21.15	22.73
Ireland	16.92	22.04	19.02	19.61	15.77
Italy	18.42	21.27	23.87	23.75	25.07
Japan	10.12	10.96	10.80	13.47	14.66
Netherlands	27.26	27.43	27.92	25.92	23.90
Norway	18.55	19.68	26.00	27.62	26.97
Poland	–	–	16.19	24.74	22.83
Spain	15.78	18.03	19.29	20.94	19.71
Sweden	29.00	30.18	31.02	33.03	30.98
Switzerland	15.17	16.25	19.80	26.20	28.28
United Kingdom	18.19	21.27	21.62	25.84	24.70
United States	13.13	12.87	13.36	15.41	14.59

Note: Included expenditures by state: old age cash benefits, disability cash benefits, occupational injury and disease, sickness benefits, services for the elderly and disabled people, survivors, family cash benefits, family services, active labor market programs, unemployment, health, housing benefits, other contingencies.

Source: OECD Social Expenditures Database 2001.

As political sociologists looked at the historical development of welfare states, it became clear that Germany under Bismarck was an innovator and the United States was a laggard. Around 1900, the percentage of the labor force entitled to state social benefits for job injuries ranged from a high of 71 percent in Germany to 39 percent in Britain and about 15 percent in Austria, Denmark, Norway, and Switzerland.[53] Alexander Hicks (1999) identified three pathways of welfare state expansion. In pre-1920 Western Europe, a paternalistic-conservative elite in Austria and Germany initiated and expanded the welfare state; in Denmark, Italy, Sweden, and Great Britain, labor parties allied with other political parties and pushed for social programs; and in Belgium and the Netherlands, a powerful Catholic party with a strong patriarchal state urged welfare state expansion. At the onset of the 1930s Great Depression the percentage of workers who could get unemployment benefits was 58 percent in the United Kingdom; 44 percent in Germany; 34 percent in Austria; and about 20 percent in Belgium, Denmark, Italy, and Switzerland.[54] By 1930, 12 European nations had adopted the core program areas of a welfare state.[55] Except where fascist dictatorships rose (i.e., Italy, Germany, Japan, and Spain), most advanced nations saw left-leaning or socialist parties gain power during the 1930s, often extending into the 1940s wartime and immediate postwar period (see Chart 11.2).[56]

During the 1930s, in the 1940s war period, and in the immediate post-war reconstruction phase, welfare states developed along one of three pathways: (1) a social democratic pathway clearest in Scandinavia but also present in Australia and New Zealand, (2) a centralist market-oriented pathway in Canada and the United States, and (3) a Catholic party pathway in Belgium, the Netherlands, France, and Austria, and in Italy in the postwar era. Hicks (1999, 95–96) stated, "the historical record for 1931 to 1940 shows that the entry of social democratic parties into government, rare earlier, was a major impetus to that decade's income security reforms. The same holds for the 1941 to 1950 period . . . where social democratic (and kindred) parties are lacking, most remaining adoptions have direct explanations in the activities of extremely strong secular-centrist parties or of Catholic parties." Hicks noted that by 1950, most advanced nations, with the exceptions of Canada, Denmark, Germany, Switzerland, and the United States, had adopted the five core welfare state programs (i.e., public pension, work injury, health care, unemployment, family aid), and by the mid-1950s almost all had the programs.

The mid-1950s to the mid-1980s was the welfare state's Golden Age. Spending for social programs, measured as a percentage of Gross National Product, nearly doubled in all advanced industrial nations. In the mid-1980s, social program spending stopped growing, and even declined slightly in some nations. Some argued that the welfare state grew in size in the 1970s due to the effects of deindustrialization (i.e., manufacturing factories closing or relocating).[57] They note that nations with employment disruptions had greater welfare state expansion, particularly in relevant programs (e.g., unemployment insurance, job training).[58] Political factors remained important, but changes in the global econ-

> ## chart 11.2
> ## YEAR SOCIAL WELFARE PROGRAM ADOPTED IN SELECTED NATIONS

Country	Workmen's Compensation	Old Age Insurance	Health Care	Unemployment Insurance	Family Allowance
Austria	1887	1906	1888	1920	1948
Australia	1902	1908	1944	1944	1941
Canada	1908*	1927	1971	1940	1944
Denmark	1894	1892	1892	1907	1952
France	1898	1910	1930	1905	1932
Germany	1884	1889	1883	1927	1954
Greece	1914	1934	1922	1945	1958
Ireland	1897	1908	1911	1911	1944
Italy	1898	1912	1928	1919	1937
Netherlands	1901	1913	1930	1916	1939
Norway	1895	1936	1909	1906	1946
Spain	1932	1919	1932	1919	1938
Sweden	1901	1913	1891	1934	1947
Switzerland	1901	1946	1891	1924	1960
United Kingdom	1897	1908	1911	1911	1945
United States	1910*	1935	None	1935	None

* State or local level.

Sources: Schneider (1982) and Hicks (1999, 35, 51).

omy and how nations fit into it also influenced the timing and form of welfare state expansion.[59]

Studies of the welfare state's Golden Age show that partisan politics powerfully shaped welfare state development, with left parties encouraging expansion.[60] Nonetheless, welfare states are embedded in state institutional settings and constrained by the overall state-economy relationship. Certain constitutional systems (i.e., centralized executive branch, strong disciplined parties, parliamentary system, and proportionate representation) that minimize veto points and a CMC state-economy pattern produced faster and broader welfare state expansion.[61]

Policy legacy played a role in welfare state expansion. Welfare states have an influence on the societies in which they operate. They alter the political culture, citizenship rights, interest group composition, and state organizational structure.[62] As King (1987, 851) noted, "The persistence of the welfare state generates societal support for its institutions and policies." Beyond the ideological dimensions and direct beneficiaries, support also grew among those who deliver social programs (e.g., state workers, physicians, teachers, social workers).

WELFARE STATE REGIMES

In a major study, Gösta Esping-Andersen (1990) reoriented the study of welfare states. Rejecting the assumption that there was a single welfare state, he examined social programs and policies across advanced nations and found several distinct approaches to the welfare state, or ideal type welfare state regimes. Others have since modified his three-type model in minor ways, but his central idea of welfare state regimes is now widely accepted. **A welfare state regime is a mutually reinforcing configuration of welfare state goals, policies, and institutions that has a distinct logic of organization, integration with society, and historical origin.** A welfare state regime essentially is able to, "bunch particular values together with particular programs and policies. Different sorts of welfare regimes pursue different policies, and they do so for different reasons. Each fixates narrowly on its own reasons. . . . [They] represent different ways of organizing not only . . . social welfare policy, but also the productive sector of the capitalist economy."[63] Thus, no single welfare state emerged in advanced capitalist societies; rather, nations developed one of a few alternatives based on combinations of historical–political forces. The welfare state regimes are tied to how labor markets are organized. Regimes influence the cost of hiring workers, the capacity of workers to strike, costs of training workers, willingness of workers to invest in acquiring new skills, and ability of firms to engage in wage-cutting competition.[64] A regime is also integrated into the national system of social stratification-inequality; it simultaneously is shaped by that system and helps to recreate or change the system of inequality.

Esping-Andersen's three regime types have been modified to three major plus two minor regime types. The *Liberal-Market Regime* (LMR) is based on classical or neoclassical theories of political economy. It asserts that the market is a superior means of allocating resources to any alternative, and state intervention only distorts "natural" market relations. Its core value is liberty (i.e., freedom from state interference to pursue private interests in the marketplace), and its implicit goal is to strengthen the market and encourage reliance on it. In this regime, public assistance is a **means-tested program in which a person must pass a test of needs before receiving a service or benefit and only those with the greatest need receive the benefits.** Under means testing, only the most destitute receive benefits. All others must enter the market as workers, who sell their labor to others for wages, or as business owners. Anyone who does not enter market relations is socially stigmatized and punished. Goodin et al. (1999) noted, "The primary policy task in liberal welfare policy lies in separating out those unwilling to work from those genuinely unable to do so. One strategy—favored in the 1832 revisions of the English Poor Law, and arguably still practiced in many places today—is to make the condition of welfare beneficiaries so wretched that only those genuinely in need of them would be remotely tempted to apply for such benefits." The primary threat in such a regime is dependency—people become dependent on public handouts instead of their own efforts. The LMR weakens the bargaining position of workers who have few alternatives to the labor market, and it strengthens the position of employers. LMR welfare states are found in nations with LMC state-economy relations that are partially open to international trade (mostly English-speaking nations—Canada, Ireland, United Kingdom, United States).[65] A LMR reinforces stratification along existing market-generated lines of economic inequality. One minor regime type, Wage Earner Regime (found in Australia and New Zealand) is similar to the LMR.[66]

The Christian Democratic Regime (CDR) is based on a compulsory insurance model.[67] It originated with Bismarck's early conservative reforms and is found in countries with strong Catholic or Christian Democratic political parties. Its primary value is community. It offers people safety, security, and certainty through cooperative mutual assistance, and most people see the state as a provider of economic security. The major threat to it is selfish individualism— people refusing to cooperate or help others. The CDR is found in nations with corporatist state structures, CMC state-economy relations, and an economy open to international trade.[68] Most social programs have public or private sector employees contribute, and they receive benefit levels proportionate to the size of their contributions. The CDR is not highly redistributive, and it solidifies divisions among people based on their level of earnings, since social programs treat people differently based on their income, skill and social status, or political organization. Yet the CDR also has family-reinforcing features. It stratifies society based on a mix of market-generated inequality and collective organization (e.g., civil servants, skilled unionized workers). Austria, Belgium, France, Germany, and Italy follow this regime, and to and a lesser degree the Netherlands and Switzerland.[69] East Asian regimes (e.g., Japan, Singapore) share many features of the CDR.[70]

The Social Democratic Regime (SDR) emphasizes social citizenship as a right and the equal worth of all citizens. Since its primary value is equality, it gives all people equal benefits irrespective of earnings or contributions. **It has universal social programs in which benefits are a right of citizenship and all people are entitled to public services and benefits, regardless of their income level**. The SDR equalizes economic and social conditions among all people, with materialistic greed being its primary threat. This regime is also found in nations with corporatist governments. Nonetheless, "It should also be emphasized that social democrats are, first and foremost democrats. As such, they would be unwilling to implement [social policies] . . . without the full support of a democratic majority."[71] The SDR challenges the market; it offers people an alternative to submitting to market forces. For example, people can get very close to their regular income when they are sick, unemployed, absent for paternal leave or educational leave, or as a retirement pension. The SDR guarantees all people equal "middle class" living standards and reduces class differences. The SDR is primarily found in Scandinavian nations (see Chart 11.3).

chart 11.3

CLASSIFICATION OF WELFARE STATE REGIMES

Social Democratic

Denmark

Finland

Norway

Sweden

Christian Democratic

Austria

Belgium

France

Germany

Italy

Netherlands*

Switzerland

Liberal-Market

Canada

Ireland

United Kingdom

United States

Wage-Earner

Australia

New Zealand

East Asian

Japan

---

*Esping-Andersen and Goodin classify the Netherlands as Social Democratic; Hicks, Huber and Stephens, and Moller et al. classify it as Christian Democratic. Some studies classify Wage-Earner regimes as Liberal-Market.

Sources: Esping-Andersen (1990, Table 3.3) and modified by Goodin et al. (1999, Table 4.6), Hicks (1999, Table 4.2), Huber and Stephens (2001a, Table 4.1), Moller et al. (2003), and White and Goodman (1998).

Stier et al. (2001, 1733–1734) summarized the regimes stating, "Each of the welfare models represents a distinct relationship between the state and the market. The liberal regime is based on the predominance of the market. . . . In the social democratic regime, . . . the state is fully responsible for assuring the welfare of its citizens irrespective of market forces. . . . The conservative regime represents a third model in which the state, the market, and other institutions—mainly the family and the church—share responsibility for citizens' welfare" (see Chart 11.4).

Esping-Andersen (1990) used the concept of decommodification to explain the alternative logics in each welfare state regime. He noted that in feudal society most individuals were outside a market economy. With the rise of capitalism, most people's survival depended on selling their labor power (i.e. time, skills, effort) in a labor market in exchange for money wages. As market relations spread and market exchange dominated people's social–economic relationships, most physical objects, services, and people's labor increasingly were

c h a r t   1 1 . 4

FEATURES OF MAJOR WELFARE STATE REGIMES

	Type of Welfare State Regime		
	Liberal-Market	**Christian-Democratic**	**Social-Democratic**
Political-economic theory	Neoclassical liberalism	Conservative, Christian-Catholic social theory	Socialist
Core value	Liberty	Community	Equality
Social program entitlement based on	Dire need	Contributions and place in society	Right of citizenship
State-economy relationship	Liberal market	Coordinated market	Coordinated market
Openness to world trade	Low–Medium	Medium–High	High
Decommodification	Low	Moderate	High
Corporatist system	Low	Medium–High	High
Primary responsibility system	Individual responsibility	Modified collective responsibility	Collective responsibility
Main task	Separate out deserving poor (truly needy) from undeserving loafers	Provide all groups with security and stability and encourage cooperation	Redistribute income and expand social and economic equality
Main threat	Dependency	Selfish individualism	Greed
Example nation	United States	Germany	Sweden

Sources: Van Voorhis (2002), with modifications based on Aspalter (2001), Goodin et al. (1999), Hicks and Kenworthy (1998), and Huber and Stephens (2001a).

turned into commodities. This is the process of commodification in capitalism. A commodity is something that can be bought or sold in exchange for something else. You may have heard the phrase, "everything has a price." The primary "something else" is the medium of exchange, or money. Decommodification is an attempt to block or reverse the commodification process. As Esping-Andersen (1990, 21–22) remarked, "Decommodification occurs when a service is rendered as a matter of right, and when a person can maintain a livelihood without reliance on the market." **Decommodification provides an alternative to the**

market and makes it possible to live (i.e., obtain all survival needs) without depending on the market. It lets a person opt out of selling his/her labor power in the market and lets her/him live beyond the tyranny of market forces. It strengthens the position of workers and weakens that of employers. Decommodification represents the polar opposite of the neoliberal principles on which the LMR is based. With decommodification, the market is not the sole provider of social goods. Instead, the state (and to a lesser degree other nonstate providers) offer a way to circumvent the market. By contrast, the LMR encourages people to depend on the private capitalist market for all their needs. It subordinates most of people's social needs to the dictates of the capitalist market.

The idea of welfare state regimes clarified thinking about what welfare states do. Since there are several regime types, each having a distinct logic, welfare states do different things! It also clarified thinking about the historical development of welfare states—regimes developed along different historical pathways and reflect different power relations and social conflicts. As Hicks (1999, 120–121) remarked, the welfare state regimes "are historical residues of shifting and conflicting projects, not single or decisively overriding ones. . . . Their different political contexts reflect more than one political project or era." Different forms of the state organization and political party groupings, different levels of worker mobilization and left party strength, and different systems of business strength and organization combined to shape specific welfare state regime outcomes.[72]

Poverty Reduction

A major goal of most welfare states is to promote equality and reduce poverty, but only a few studies looked at this across advanced industrial societies.[73] Given the diversity of welfare states and the many ways to reduce poverty (e.g., target programs for the poor or offer universal social programs, provide benefits from general taxes or make them contributory and deliver benefits based on past earnings), political sociologists have only started to explore the relationship between welfare states and poverty reduction.[74] Poverty is complex. There are many definitions of poverty, but most studies examine relative poverty (i.e., not absolute needs for bare physical survival). A common measure is a certain percentage (e.g., 50 percent) below the average income (i.e., median or midpoint) level of a society. The United States created its official poverty line in the 1960s, but social scientists agree that a percentage of the average (i.e., median) income level is more accurate. **The poverty line was the arbitrary dollar amount created in the 1960s for the bureaucratic purpose of estimating the size of the poor population**. It was to be a temporary estimate. The line was based on a preexisting study of the U.S. Department of Agriculture on the amount a family would need to spend on food to meet their minimal nutritional needs. To estimate minimal living costs, officials multiplied minimal food costs by three, because in the 1950s most poor people devoted roughly one-third of their incomes to buying food.[75] Nonetheless, it has become a permanent fixture for the delivery of a range of social programs in the U.S. It has not been updated for 45 years, except for inflation increases and adjustments for the number of family members. Many recommendations have been made to recalculate the poverty line, but all become embroiled in political controversies because more people would be classified as poor than by the current poverty line.

The United States has many antipoverty programs. Some well-known ones provide child care services (e.g., Head Start), free lunches in schools, food stamps, and AFDC (discussed later in this chapter). Poor people are eligible for health care through **Medicaid, a federal government means-tested medical insurance program for the poor,** and **general assistance a program provided in about one-half of the United States that delivers small amounts of short-term direct income assistance for very poor people who cannot receive benefits from federal government aid programs for the poor**. Other benefit programs do not require poverty status and only indirectly reduce poverty. These include the public pension part of Social Security, **unemployment insurance (a social program that provides limited income assistance for a period of time to people who were previously employed and met other criteria)** and **Medicare (a U.S. federal government medical insurance program for the elderly that is not means tested)**. Some are federal-government programs, some are state-government or local programs, and many are partnerships requiring contributions by several levels of government.

Inequality is related to, but it differs from, poverty. Inequality refers to the size of gap between the poor and nonpoor. Low inequality is when the nonpoor are modestly better off than the poor, and people are at a similar level to one another. High inequality is when the nonpoor vary widely, with some far richer than both the poor and many other nonpoor. Economists measure inequality by a statistic, the Gini coefficient. In addition to overall poverty, poverty varies among parts of the population (e.g., among the elderly, single mothers, children). The most common way to evaluate poverty reduction is to compare the poverty rate before social programs with the rate after their implementation. Various nations differ in how effective their welfare states are in reducing poverty (see Table 11.3). Comparing the three welfare state regimes, the SDR reduces both poverty levels and inequality the most, and the LMR does so the least.[76] In related welfare state areas, such as employment security (i.e., protected while unemployed and help with being able to get another job),[77] health care coverage,[78] and old-age pensions,[79] the relative rankings of the welfare state regimes (SDR as most effective to LMR as least effective) is not very different.

The ranking is a generalization, and there is variation. For example, poverty varies by its extent (i.e., percentage of the population that is poor), its depth (i.e., the distance between the average wage and the poor), its duration (i.e., the length of time that people stay poor), and its reoccurrence (i.e., the ability of the poor to stay out of poverty and not fall back into it).[80] Goodin et al. (1999, 167) found that the SDR, "not only reduces poverty more than the other two regimes, but reduces it even more over five years and ten years than over a single year," the CDR was moderately successful in reducing poverty, and "Liberal Welfare Regimes, in contrast, are strikingly bad at combating poverty in every respect."

| | | % Total | % Poor | % Single | | Overall |
Country	Regime Type	Population in Poverty	after Social Programs	Mothers in Poverty	% Children in Poverty	Inequality Rank
Australia	L-M*	23.2	12.9	44.6	15.9	5
Canada	L-M	23.4	11.7	40.4	16.5	3
Denmark	S-D	26.9	7.5	6.5	5.9	10
France	C-D	21.6	7.5	21.4	10.3	7
Germany	C-D	22.0	7.6	24.0	7.4	9
Ireland	L-M	na	10.1	16.9	14.7	4
Italy	C-D	18.4	6.5	16.1	13.1	6
Netherlands	C-D	22.8	6.7	10.9	7.3	11
Norway	S-D	12.4	4.0	16.9	4.5	12
Spain	C-D	28.2	10.4	n/a	n/a	n/a
Sweden	S-D	34.1	6.7	4.6	5.0	13
Switzerland	C-D	10.6	9.1	20.2	7.1	8
United Kingdom	L-M	29.2	14.6	35.2	20.9	2
United States	L-M	26.7	19.1	57.7	25.3	1

TABLE 11.3 Impact of Welfare Benefits on Reducing Poverty in Selected Nations

Note: Poverty = 50 percent below median income. Columns 1–2 for early 1990s, Columns 3–4 for late 1980s. Inequality rank includes overall income inequality (Gini coefficient). Social programs include all social benefits and tax effects. L-M = Liberal Market, C-D = Christian Democratic, S-D = Social Democratic.

Sources: First two columns, Kerbo and Gonzalez (2003, 186), except Ireland, Norway, and Switzerland. Ireland and last two columns, Korpi (2000). Also Moller et al. (2003) for Norway and Switzerland in first two columns.

Korpi and Palme (1998) identified the **"paradox of redistribution"—the greater the extent to which benefits are targeted to the poor and only the poor, instead of creating general social equality, the less overall reduction in poverty**. They (1998, 663) noted that, "while support for targeting has decreased among social scientists, it has increased among policy makers in Western countries. . . . [because] If the goal of social policy is limited to the reduction in poverty, then universal programs that also benefit the nonpoor are a waste of resources." Yet nontargeted programs that are not means-tested may reduce poverty more effectively. Moller et al. (2003, 44) found that, "One of the most effective antipoverty policy instruments is child and family allowances." Overall, Moller et al. (2004, 45), concluded "the welfare state itself and the balance of political power are central determinates of poverty reduction."

GENDER AND THE WELFARE STATE

The welfare state is not gender neutral. Gender has been a central, if unrecognized, issue in all welfare states since their founding. As recently as 1993, "little of the mainstream comparative research on the welfare state has considered gender relations," but over the last decade it moved to the center of social policy debates.[81] Ann Shola Orloff (1996, 51) summarized, "Gender relations, embodied

in the sexual division of labor, compulsory heterosexuality, discourses and ideologies of citizenship, motherhood, masculinity and femininity, and the like, profoundly shape the character of welfare states." Gender not only shaped the
character of welfare states, but social programs diminish or reinforce the level and
specific forms of societal gender inequality. They affect parenting, intra-family
relations, and expressions of sexuality. In addition, women, through the
women's movement, political parties, or state agencies, have had a significant
role in pushing welfare state programs in a more woman-friendly direction.[82]

The very design of a welfare state contains assumptions about gender relations, family patterns, economic conditions, and how people allocate their time
and effort in daily life among paid work; caring for children; engaging in recreation; obtaining health care; maintaining a household by cooking, cleaning, and
laundry, and so forth. Traditional gender ideology assumes a model of "separate
spheres." In it, adult males and females each maintain distinct areas of life. The
male sphere is paid employment and public life, while the female sphere is domestic household work and private life in and around a home and/or children.
This arrangement is expressed as the **male/breadwinner (and female/caregiver)
mode** (M-B). **It assumes that all adults are in a stable marital relationship with
one wage-earning worker, the male, and a female who provides all domestic
chores and caregiving (i.e., child rearing, elder care, illness care) as unpaid labor**.

Social changes, such as rising female labor force participation and educational
attainment, shifts in divorce and marital patterns, longer life expectancy among the
elderly, and births out of wedlock, that have swept across the advanced world over
the past 50 years dislocated M-B assumptions that may not have held for a large
section of the population in the past in any case. Female labor force participation
rates have risen rapidly in advanced industrial nations since 1960. By 1999, over
50 percent of women worked outside the home in every advanced nation, except
for Italy and Spain, and over 40 percent of mothers with preschool-aged children
worked outside the home, except in Japan.[83] Interestingly, higher rates of female labor force participation is both a cause and a result of social program expansion.
This is because working women demand expanded public social services to replace activities they used to do as unpaid labor, and women make up a majority of
the people employed in delivering social programs.[84]

New gender relationships and family patterns altered welfare state expectations. Some people long for a return to the M-B model. Others try to reconfigure
social policies to better support full autonomy and economic independence for
women and to acknowledge the legitimacy of caregiving. In a traditional social-
welfare system with M-B assumptions, the focus was on helping working males
within a context of traditional heterosexual, patriarchal family relations. It assumed that all able-bodied adult males who could find employment and worked
full-time would earn a "family-wage" (i.e., enough to provide for self, spouse, and
offspring with an adequate standard of living). Social programs were designed
around the male's participation in the labor force, with unemployment benefits,
health care, work injury/disability protection, and pension benefits. Adult females
were expected to be married and perform all care work and domestic tasks as unpaid labor; they were to rely on the husband as their source of income and for

social benefits. Women's paid employment outside the home was deemed to be unnecessary and undesirable. Young, single women were supposed to be waiting for marriage and living with their family of origin. Older and widowed women received benefits associated with a deceased husband's employment, supplemented by aid from their adult children or extended family. Thus, the traditional welfare state covered working males of all ages, both single and married and adult males who could not work due to work injury or a severe disability. Yet it ignored divorced or never-married adult females with or without children. The traditional system was centered on providing the male-breadwinner worker-citizen with income/employment protection, and it assumed traditional gender roles with a social stigma suppressing both divorce and childbirth out of wedlock. As Jane Lewis (2001, 152) remarked, "the male breadwinner model worked at the level of prescription. Policy makers treated it as an 'ought' in terms of relationship between males and females. . . ." Thus, traditional ideas about proper gender relations, female dependency, and family law, a package sometimes called "familism," were built into social welfare system design.[85] Today, different welfare states provide working women and mothers with a range of benefits. Some countries provide extra job protection, maternity benefits, and public child care (e.g., Belgium, Denmark, France, Sweden), while others have little parental leave and public child care (e.g., Australia, United Kingdom, United States). For example, since the mid-1990s, the United States has offered 12 weeks of unpaid maternity leave for only about one-half of the labor force. Compared to other countries, this looks rather meager (see World View 11.1, Chart 11.5).

WORLD VIEW 11.1   **Does the United States Have a Family Unfriendly Welfare State?**

Not only is the United States the only advanced nation lacking a universal health care program, but by almost any measure, it also has the least poverty-reducing and least family-friendly welfare state. U.S. poverty programs are less effective at reducing the percentage of people living in poverty than are the programs in other advanced nations. The U.S. rate of poverty reduction is 28 percent, while in other advanced nations it is 50–80 percent. The United States also has the highest percentage of single mothers and children living in poverty. About 22.4 percent of U.S. children live in poverty—a higher rate than in 22 other nations—and over half of all single mothers live in poverty. The United States introduced its first national unpaid maternity leave in 1993. It is shorter (three months) than that of other nations and ex-

cludes nearly half the workforce because it only applies to larger employers. By contrast, France introduced a paid maternity leave policy 80 years earlier and offers up to 3 years of leave. Leave policies vary in other European nations and Japan, but the United States is way behind most of the world (see Chart 11.5). Parents in the United States can deduct some child-care costs from taxes. In France, parents with children receive free child-care to low-income families and at low cost for other families. This is more generous than Germany, but less generous than most Nordic countries. While the child-care is widely available in Europe, reaching up to 80 percent of children, only 14 percent of U.S. children are in publicly subsidized child-care.

Sources: Christopher (2002a), Henneck (2003), Kerbo and Gonzalez (2003, 186), Korpi (2000), United Nations Children's Fund (2000).

The three major welfare state regimes differ on gender equality, child rearing, and female labor force participation (see Table 11.4). In the LMR, men are freed of child-care duties and can enter the labor market for income. Women are also pulled into the labor market by LMR, but they are expected to work full-time. They receive relatively good monetary rewards relative to being unpaid at home caring for children. The LMR leaves child care to be supplied by the private market and paid for by the parents. Among the three welfare state regimes, the LMR has the largest gender wage gap. This is because many mothers must withdrawal from the workforce temporarily when their children are very young and suffer employment-related costs (e.g., lower pay, loss of seniority, loss of job benefits). In a sense, a LMR forces parents or mothers to bear almost all child rearing costs without state assistance, and it penalizes mothers who leave the labor force temporarily to care for their children.

The CDR protects the family but without directly reducing gender inequality. Family policies under a CDR tend to support a modified M-B model and

---

chart 1 1 . 5

NATIONS THAT OFFER WOMEN 14 OR MORE WEEKS OF MATERNITY LEAVE

Algeria	Democratic Republic of the Congo	Norway
Australia	Denmark	Panama
Austria	Djibouti	Poland
Azerbaijan	Estonia	Portugal
Belarus	Finland	Romania
Belgium	France	Russian Federation
Benin	Gabon	Senegal
Brazil	Germany	Seychelles
Bulgaria	Greece	Slovenia
Burkina Faso	Guinea	Somalia
Cameroon	Hungary	Spain
Canada	Ireland	Sweden
Central African Republic	Italy	Togo
Chile	Japan	Ukraine
Comoros	Luxembourg	United Kingdom
Congo	Madagascar	Venezuela
Costa Rica	Mali	Vietnam
Côte d'Ivoire	Mauritania	
Croatia	Mongolia	
Cuba	Netherlands	
Cyprus	New Zealand	
Czech Republic	Niger	

Note: The United States offers 12 weeks of unpaid leave and only for about one-half of the workforce.
Source: International Labor Organization. *Maternity Protection at Work* Report V(1), Table 1, 1999.

TABLE 11.4	Alternative Gender Models of the Welfare State, Selected Nations			
Country	Gender Model	More Males Than Females in Paid Labor Force (%)*	More Males Than Mothers Working (%)**	Negative Attitude Regarding Women Working (%)***
Australia	Market	34	47	34
Austria	General family	30	42	34
Canada	Market	23	28	21
Denmark	Dual career	9	8	n/a
France	General family	26	33	n/a
Germany	General family	32	53	38
Ireland	General family	55	60	36
Italy	General family	46	43	34
Japan	Market	36	n/a	39
Netherlands	General family	43	58	27
Norway	Dual career	17	16	24
Sweden	Dual career	6	7	18
Switzerland	Market	30	n/a	n/a
United Kingdom	Market	25	47	27
United States	Market	23	34	28

*Percentage of persons aged 25–54 in the labor force in 1983–1990.
**Mothers with a least one preschool-aged child, around 1990.
***Attitude for persons aged 25–54 in 1994.
Source: Korpi (2000).

compensate mothers for the time they invest in child care. It pushes men into the labor market, but lets women work part-time and leave a job to raise children without suffering major financial penalties. This slightly reduces the gender gap. A CDR offers financial support for child rearing at home instead of in public child care. It does not give women equal labor market access, but encourages them to work only part time.

The SDR promotes gender equality in the labor market by providing full benefits for part-time work. State subsidized child care encourages both men and women to enter the workforce equally. Gender equality is higher than in the other regimes. The state not only shoulders most child rearing costs, but also makes it easy for women to combine paid work with parenting without additional costs. The SDR provides funds and direct services for child care. Female labor force participation is high, due to the expansive welfare state programs often staffed by women.[86]

Three issues relevant to a gender-sensitive welfare state are access to work, recognition of care work, and the ability to form an autonomous household.[87] The work-access issue takes three forms: (1) unimpeded opportunities for full-time equal employment, (2) an absence of penalties for part-time work or an interrupted work career, and (3) full acknowledgment of women's unpaid domestic labor. These issues are reflected in each regime's gender effects. As Julia O'Connor (1993, 508) noted, most social policies "fail to take seriously the problem of combining paid and unpaid work." Care work (i.e., providing nurturing, emotional attention, and assistance to others, especially children, disabled, and elderly) is frequently overlooked. "Care work crosses the boundaries between informal and formal, public and private, paid and unpaid work . . ." observed Jane Lewis (2002, 345). Care work has been part of a traditional female gender role, and paid occupations specialized in providing care work are overwhelmingly staffed by women (e.g., nurses, daycare workers). Care work tends to be decommodified labor because it puts a higher value on nurturing and sustaining emotional bonds than on maximizing income. A gender-based parallel to the economic idea of decommodification is detachment from a traditional patriarchal family. The state would support women-based autonomous households that do not depend on males to be the household head or a wage earner. Often this is (mis)categorized as single motherhood. Single motherhood rates have risen among most Western nations, and single women have very high poverty rates. A major reason for high poverty rates is that fathers do not contribute to child support. For example, in the United States only 57 percent of divorced and 34 percent of separated or never-married mothers get the payments from fathers awarded to them by the courts.[88] Examining the impact of welfare state programs on poverty rates among single women, Christopher et al. (2002) found that every nation's welfare state system reduces single women's poverty, but there is great variation among nations. It was very limited in Australia, Canada, France, Germany, and the United States, but effective in the Netherlands and Sweden.

If we contrast the M-B model with alternative ideal household arrangements that combine paid employment and providing domestic tasks, several alternative arrangements are evident. The male and female can be in paid employment full time, part time, or not at all. Domestic tasks can be provided full time, part time by either the male or the female as a supplement, or by the state or others beyond a household. Looking at the full picture, the M-B model is just one of six possible household arrangements (see Chart 11.6). Its opposite is the autonomous woman household without a male partner. The M-B model can be modified by adding part-time female employment and varying male or other support for domestic tasks. Two versions of the dual-career arrangement shift the division between paid employment and providing domestic tasks. Each of the six arrangements combines paid work with domestic tasks.

Walter Korpi (2000) looked at alternative household arrangements and asked: Does a welfare state support full-time female participation in the labor force or unpaid female domestic work? Does it enable both parents to combine paid labor with parenting? He examined only two of the six household arrangements outlined in Chart 11.6—M-B and full-time dual career. If a welfare state strongly supported the M-B pattern, it would encourage in-home child rearing and provide cash allowances for families that raise children, offer tax breaks for children and an unemployed mother, or support limited daycare only for older

	Paid Employment		Caregiving and Domestic Tasks		
Household Arrangement	Male	Female	Male	Female	Other*
Male breadwinner	Full-time	None	None	Full-time	None
Male primary earner 1	Full-time	Part-time	None	Primary	Supplement
Male primary earner 2	Full-time	Part-time	Supplement	Part-time	Supplement
Dual career	Full-time	Full-time	Supplement	Supplement	Primary
Full partnership	Part-time	Part-time	Part-time	Part-time	None
Autonomous woman	Absent	Full- or part-time	Absent	Primary or supplement	Supplement or primary

chart 11.6

ALTERNATIVE HOUSEHOLD ARRANGEMENTS

*Other includes services provided by kin, the state, or the voluntary sector or purchased in the market.
Sources: Crompton (2001), Lewis (2001), and Pfau-Effinger (1999).

preschool children. If a welfare state strongly supported a dual-career arrangement, it would offer free public child care for young children (e.g., under age 2), pay full maternity leave and paternity leave, and provide public services to care for the frail elderly. When Korpi (2000) examined whether contemporary welfare states supported the M-B, the dual-career, or neither arrangement, he found substantial variation but a correspondence between household arrangements and the three welfare state regimes. Nations with the CDR best supported the M-B household, SDR best supported dual-career households, and LMR supported neither (i.e., offered little or no support for child care or families). Thus, the welfare state regimes not only reflect alternative state-economy relations, but also reinforce different household arrangements with implications for gender relations. Within a regime type, specific political forces of a nation can have a large effect on its family policies (see Case in Point 11.1).

Do "materialist" ideas and values produce a more gender-sensitive welfare state?[89] **A maternal welfare state is one in which government social programs and benefits are based on protecting and providing a minimal level of income to women, especially married or widowed women with children.** For example, Koven and Michel (1990) found that women and children received fewer benefits in welfare states where women were directly involved in shaping the welfare state (e.g., Great Britain, United States) than where they were largely excluded (e.g., France, Germany). They attribute the difference to more centralized

CASE IN POINT 11.1   **Failed Universal Public Child Care in the United States**

Free, public high-quality, child care is a dual-career family's dream, and it is available in Western European welfare states. In the late 1960s, support for a universal public child-care system grew in the United States. In 1967, eight daycare bills were introduced into Congress. They were not successful, but they demonstrated interest in the idea. In 1971, the same year the U.S. Congress passed the Equal Rights Amendment to the U.S. Constitution (later defeated because not enough states ratified it), it also passed the Comprehensive Child Development Act to establish public, universally available child care, but President Richard Nixon vetoed it. Instead, tax credits for private child care were enacted, and the Head Start program for disadvantaged preschoolers was continued. Thus, what continued was the bifurcated system of means-tested public services for the stigmatized poor and tax breaks that encouraged middle-class parents to purchase private services in the market.

Why did the universal child-care proposal fail? It became a heated political controversy that ignited divisions over gender roles, family, and race. By 1970 nearly 20 percent of U.S. preschool-aged children were in child care, although many were in the Head Start program for poor families. As women's entry into the paid labor force grew and studies showed that child care had no detrimental impact on child development, middle-class families sought it for their children. Opinion polls showed that a majority of men and women supported federally funded child care. The proposal for universal child care drew broad support from the National Organization

for Women, Conference of Mayors, League of Women Voters, and National Council of Negro Women, among others, and a coalition of union and civil rights activists joined to back the law. Civil rights leaders hoped that universal child care would stop the attempts in Southern states to block black people's access to Head Start programs. The law had bipartisan support, Democrat Walter Mondale and Republican Jacob Javits cosponsored the bill in the U.S. Senate. Yet details of the bill were linked to 1960s antipoverty and civil rights legislation. An ideological backlash had been growing against Great Society social programs and the child care bill attracted an oppositional coalition of conservative Southerners and right-wing Republicans. Conservative aides in the White House, such as Patrick Buchanan and John Ashbrook, warned that the law was government social engineering and family control, and right-wing ideological leaders drew parallels to child care in Nazi Germany and the Soviet Union. The child care law helped the New Right join its opposition to state intervention with defending a traditional patriarchal family. The defeat of the law was an early symbolic victory for the emerging countermovement. Although the women's movement had not led the move for a child care law, the New Right framed it as an attack on the traditional American family. The coalition of the child care law's supporters were unable to mobilize middle-class parents behind the law, and it fragmented. As Quadagno (1994, 153) argued, "day care legislation divided rather than united its potential supporters."

Source: Morgan (2001) and Quadagno (1994, Chapter 6).

states in France and Germany. Historical studies on the United States suggest that women actively helped to establish many early social programs. Some argue that women introduced maternal-humanizing values, and these values shaped and expanded the welfare state. Yet maternal values can be double-edged. They define women as being first and foremost mothers and emphasize that women need special protections based on traditional gender stereotypes (e.g., weak, frail, emotional). Based on maternalist values, social benefits are extended to women not because women are capable, equal citizens, but because of their childbearing function and "natural weaknesses" as females. Recall that France and Germany have a CDR (i.e., regimes led by conservative elites who expanded the welfare state top-down based on a religious and pro-traditional family ideology). This explains their high level of benefits for women and children. Women and families also get higher benefits where women have been active in social democratic political movements and labor unions (i.e., SDRs).[90] Lastly, in LMR gender equality has been linked to women entering the market as workers, and protection from commodification was framed in terms of maternal values and preserving traditional gender roles.

Social welfare benefits targeted to women and children may be instituted either out of maternal values and a desire to preserve traditional gender and family relations from the market, or alternatively to advance antimarket decommodification and promote egalitarian relations. This explains why gender-egalitarian attitudes do not correlate with welfare states that provide more benefits for women and children.[91] Such benefits (e.g., child care, family aid, maternity leave) can indicate a protection of traditional gender relations or the promotion of gender equality.

AMERICAN EXCEPTIONALISM?

Political sociologists often asked why the welfare state in the United States is so unusual. The reason is what is called American exceptionalism. As Amenta, Bonastia, and Caren (2001, 213) observed, "Comparative scholars want to know why American social insurance programs were relatively late in coming and patchy in character as compared to those of Western Europe, why the United States spends less on social policy . . . historical scholars ask why the United States developed the mix of policies that it did, focusing often on the 1930s and 1960s, when gains were made. Other scholars address differences in social policy across U.S. states, which vary widely on programs. . . ." You will see that the LMR welfare state of the United States is exceptional compared to others largely because it is obscured from view, it is intensely market-reinforcing, and it tends to fortify existing social and economic inequalities.

The U.S. Case in Comparative Context

The U.S. welfare state is different from all others. Looking at the three main welfare state regimes, what emerges is that the U.S. welfare state very closely fits the model of a LMR. This largely explains its low level of social spending, its reliance on market-based solutions, the use of targeted and mean-tested programs, and its limited family support. LMRs have the highest levels of income inequality, the highest child poverty rates with the fewest benefits for families or working mothers, the least funding for public job training or the unemployed, and the smallest poverty reduction. This is because they decommodify the least (i.e., they do the least to soften the harsher side of market capitalism). Except for the absence of a universal public health care system, the U.S. welfare state does not look markedly different from other LMRs. This redirects the question from focusing on expectionalism to asking, Why did the United States embrace a LMR instead of the alternative regimes, and why did it embrace it so vigorously?

LMRs develop where worker movements, unions, and left parties are weak or have been defeated, where confessional or religious-oriented parties do not exist or did not align with conservative elites, and where the state-economy relations are configured as LMC, not along corporatist or CMC lines. The institutional structures, power relations, and political struggles in a specific nation produce such a combination of conditions. The U.S. political culture and its ideological climate are antistatist, its political institutions are highly decentralized, and its Constitutional form (e.g., federalism, independent judiciary, weak parties, non-parliamentary system) offers powerful economic interests greater access to the state.[92] In addition, we need to consider the entire configuration of other public programs and policies as part of the explanation. As Amenta, Bonastia, and Caren (2001, 216) argued, "Works that address a wider view of social policy have altered the standard images of and stories about American social policy. . . ."

The U.S. Case in Historical Context

Political sociologists, historians, and others examined early the U.S. welfare state, but until recently, few placed it in the context of other welfare states.[93] Today, we recognize that the U.S. welfare state has a LMR, but this is only part of the story. Like other LMR welfare states, many U.S. programs are means-tested and contributory (i.e., individuals pay specific taxes that are tied to program benefits). The United States has a patched-together assortment of social programs—some are direct transfers (e.g., money is provided directly, such as Social Security), some are public services (e.g., health care is provided, Health Start childcare), and others are in-kind benefits (e.g., public housing, food stamps). Specific benefit programs often reflect a particular combination of political interests. For example, the **food stamp program, which is vouchers given to poor people by the U.S. federal government that can only be used to purchase food items,** was designed to satisfy farm demands to increase agricultural product consumption, ideological conservative demands to impose controls on poor people's behavior, health advocates desires to improve nutrition among the poor and children, and liberal-reformers' attempts to raise the benefit levels of poor people. As Orloff (1993a, 12) remarked, "modern welfare programs embody the interests and demands of conflicting groups."

The U.S. welfare state prior to its major expansion in 1935 has varied and complex origins. Studies documented how disaster relief, Civil War veteran pensions, mother's pensions, women's clubs, and state or local government programs shaped specific features of the welfare state (see Closer Look 11.2).[94] Such studies shed light on many early efforts that started social programs and that affected subsequent welfare state development.

CLOSER LOOK 11.2   Natural Disaster Relief and the American Welfare State

One contributor to the growth of the American welfare state was disaster relief. When tragedies appear to be caused by a natural disaster or an act of God, the federal government has long offered assistance. Thus, aid is seen as legitimate if a person is homeless due to a natural disaster. The circumstance's cause, whether or not it is within a person's control, is a critical factor. In fact, federal funds for the needy who are classified as disaster victims have expanded at the same time that aid for people whose situation was attributed to laziness or moral failure was cut. In the moral division between the deserving versus the undeserving poor, disaster victims are placed among the deserving poor, even if they are able-bodied and in middle-income circumstances. This suggests reexamining the category of a disaster.

During the Great Depression of the 1930s, conservatives who opposed providing government help for the millions of starving and unemployed argued that unemployment, economic depression, and drought were not natural disasters. The advocates of federal aid said they were and successfully urged adherence to tradition. Since 1794, the government provided aid to the blameless victims of sudden catastrophes. As Landis (1999) noted, ""Disaster relief became the template for the welfare state because people, engaged in practical politics and legal work, settled upon it as the most promising avenue for securing funding for relief of economic distress. In a legal and political system in which precedent plays a key legitimating role, reciting the history of past relief was a common practice in justifying policies in the present."

What makes something a disaster? A critical factor is the ability to have a group's need publicly presented and accepted as being caused by forces beyond their control. For example, the governor of Massachusetts in 1995 sought to have much of the state declared a disaster area and sought disaster aid in unemployment benefits, food stamps, interest free loans, and housing assistance for fishermen unable to work because of a sharp decline in available fish. Yet others noted that the fishermen had over-fished and depleted the area, so it was a problem of their own making. A "disaster" causally links a situation to a more distant event to which responsibility can be assigned, and it involves a mass of people, not a single person. The line between nature-caused (e.g., weather-related, earthquake, fire) and human-caused is not always clear-cut. People who decide to build in a flood plain or an unsuitable beach area, then suffer flood or hurricane damage, may claim they suffered from a natural disaster but could have chosen a safe location and not have suffered financial loss. Likewise, some events beyond a person's control (e.g., factories relocate to another country, losing housing due to fire and not having private insurance) may force thousands of people into poverty. Yet if the cause is presented as isolated to specific individuals, the event is less likely to be considered a disaster. It is therefore illegitimate as a basis for government aid. The way that many journalistic accounts try to humanize and personalize poverty by telling individual stories and not linking them to larger structural factors that affect many people, may paradoxically contribute to the public not accepting the situation of the poor as a legitimate reason to receive government aid.

Sources: Landis (1999). Also see Handler and Hasenfeld (1991).

A welfare state first emerged in the United States between 1900 and World War II. As Orloff (1993b, 7) remarked, "In Britain, Canada, and the United States, as across Europe and in Australia and New Zealand, a number of social policy reforms, including old age pensions, worker's compensation, mother's pensions, and health and employment insurance, were proposed and enacted in the years between the turn of the century and World War II." Helping impoverished people was one objective of the just-emerging welfare state, and even then, it reflected LMR principles. Early efforts targeted the deserving poor who could not be helped by private charity and removed children and the elderly from poor relief or the poorhouses. From the beginning, a critical distinction was made between the deserving and undeserving poor. **The deserving poor (also called worthy poor) are adults who are not able-bodied and are incapable of working for a reason that is beyond their control (e.g., poor health, elderly). They would be willing to work in the paid labor force if they were capable. The undeserving poor are adults who are able-bodied and capable of working, but who voluntarily decide not to work in the paid labor force.** A deserving poor person would accept the lowest paying and most demeaning job in the labor market.

Until the late 1800s, "outdoor relief" was used in which a person continued to live in his/her own dwelling and received some public payments. To better monitor people, it was replaced by "indoor relief" (i.e., public institutions for the poor or poorhouses). **A poorhouse was an institution to house and feed the destitute poor and designed to keep them off the streets and reform them; sometimes it also served as a hospital or workhouse** in which work was required. Fear of being sent to the poorhouse stimulated the development of public pensions.[95] Later, in the mid-twentieth century, outdoor relief returned.[96] Before a person could receive government aid, she/he had to exhaust all family help. A person gave up his/her citizenship rights by receiving public aid.

Early poor relief programs were irregular and unevenly distributed minimal aid that was arbitrarily administered at the local level. They were replaced by citizenship-based, uniformly distributed, and professionally administered national welfare state programs. Early in the twentieth century, many urban areas had **settlement houses—a Progressive Era method of providing welfare from a house located in a poor immigrant neighborhood from which middle-class reformers gave counseling, direct material help, legal and medical aid, and cultural assimilation.** In the 1920s, prior to federal legislation, 21 states had instituted a form of pensions, but almost all were administered by county-level governments and counties could decide to opt out. "All were means-tested, required long periods of state and county residence and citizenship, and included a number of behavioral standards"[97] The programs provided minimal survival needs, avoided interferring with market forces, and, in Southern states, did not upset a system of racial segregation and white domination. Often coalitions of reformers, labor union activists, and voluntary association members pressed to establish these rudimentary, local social programs (see Case in Point 11.2).

CASE IN POINT 11.2   **Fraternal Order of the Eagles and the American Welfare State**

The Fraternal Order of Eagles was a voluntary association of white, predominately native-born working class men founded by trade unionists in Seattle in 1898. It grew in membership to reach 500,000 in 1924 and primarily operated outside of the Southern states. The membership included small business owners, skilled craft workers, and unskilled industrial workers and opened to accept women members in 1929. Like similar voluntary mutual-benefit organizations before the 1930s, it provided sickness and death benefits to members who were often not covered by any public or employer benefit program. From first years of the twentieth century through the onset of the 1930s Great Depression, the Eagles carried out campaigns in which they advocated for mother's pensions, the eight-hour workday, worker's injury insurance, and old-age pensions. They often formed local coalitions with labor organizations that lobbied state-level governments to establish social programs. In the 1920s, they faced an uphill battle. This was an era in which old-age public pensions were attacked by opponents as being "un-American" or were declared unconstitutional by some state courts. In the few states where the Eagles, in a coalition with others, were successful, benefit programs had a local county option (i.e., a county-level government determined specific benefit levels and could opt out or not participate in the program). Benefit levels were extremely low and few people were covered. When the Great Depression occurred, governments disbanded even these inadequate public programs because of insufficient funds to continue them. The significance of groups like the Eagles is that they were one of several decentralized, voluntary organizations that, along with other early reformers, helped to lay the institutional foundations for what eventually developed into an American welfare state.

Sources: Orloff (1993b, 53–54) and Quadagno (1988, 67–70).

Shadow Welfare State

The U.S. welfare state combines public programs with a private system of welfare capitalism. Many public social programs are called **entitlements, or programs in which certain individuals are entitled by law to benefits.** Many entitlement benefits depend on past contributions (e.g., Social Security) while others are means-tested (e.g., Medicaid). In addition, the U.S. welfare state builds on an extensive system of private entitlements. A person's location in private market relations, not legal citizenship rights, entitles her/him to social benefits. This feature distinguishes America's welfare state from others. As Hacker (2002, 8) remarked, "private benefits although nominally situated in the private sector, have become an essential adjunct to public social programs in the United States. They are systematically intertwined with public policy." The private benefits are part of **welfare capitalism, a system of social benefits for employees provided by the employer.** It forms a hidden or "shadow" welfare state that operates beside or beneath the visible, public one. The line between the public and shadow welfare state "is not a rigid barrier. Most of these supposedly private programs are heavily subsidized with public monies."[98]

How did the private shadow welfare state get started? In the late 1800s, welfare capitalism emerged from paternalistic attempts by employers to reform and

Americanize recent immigrants. It was a strongly antiunion movement led by employers who voluntarily offered workers recreation facilities, profit sharing, insurance plans, pensions, and paid vacations. Such benefits humanized the work environment, lessened workplace tensions, uplifted morale, and attracted quality employees. Private benefits were a form of extra worker compensation integrated into an employer's personnel policies and political strategies. The private benefits rewarded workers, promoted loyalty, fended off unions, and structured career advancement paths within a firm. Employers often initiated benefit programs after a violent strike to instill loyalty and realign workers with the firm instead of with fellow workers.[99] During the 1920s, large corporations promoted welfare capitalism as part of their efforts to repel unionization.[100] Yet, even at its peak, "Comprehensive welfare capitalism—including financial benefits, career jobs, company unions, and supervisor training programs—was limited to an elite group of companies employing at most a fifth of the industrial labor force."[101] In addition, labor unions were creating mutual benefit plans for members and a large private insurance industry arose in the United States.[102] In the 1930s Great Depression, most firms abandoned welfare capitalism, and it nearly disappeared. Most importantly, welfare capitalism represented what Jacoby (1997, 4) called, "the belief that industrial unrest and other problems could be best alleviated by this distinctively American approach: private, not governmental; managerial, not laborist." From the beginning, employers dictated the rules, set benefit levels, and managed the program, seeing it as an extension of attempts to discipline their workforce. As Quadagno (1988, 85) observed, "Employers also had wide latitude in interpreting misconduct rules which contains numerous grounds for revoking pension rights."

After the 1935 Wagner Act (also called the National Labor Relations Act), the welfare capitalism system took two tracks. Along one track, employers rewarded their white-collar managerial and sometimes skilled nonunion workers with benefit packages that included profit sharing and fringe benefits unrelated to seniority. Along a second track, unionized workers negotiated benefits that were tied to seniority. The private benefit system developed partly in reaction to and partly as an extension of expanding public social programs and benefits.[103] As the visible and contested public side of the welfare state grew in the post-New Deal era, "The federal government has simultaneously simulated the expansion of private-sector social welfare programs in the form of employee benefits."[104]

As early as 1926, the federal government had exempted from taxes employer contributions to pension plans and benefits.[105] This simultaneously lowered employer taxes and improved worker benefits. Yet few employers responded to this encouragement. When the 1935 Social Security Act was passed, few employers offered private pensions. Only five percent of employees were covered by pensions and their benefits were meager. Social Security provided a minimal public pension for the huge mass of low- and middle-wage workers. Many employers acted to reward their high-income, white-collar employees by creating integrated private pensions in which they added private benefits on top of Social Security levels. It was a low-cost way to give managerial and technical employees higher benefits. Thus, Social Security had an unexpected effect of stimulating supplemental private pensions.[106] As Social Security expanded, private pensions also grew, both in terms of the percentage of workers covered and the benefit levels. For example, in 1940, about 55 percent of the working population was covered by Social Security; today it is about 95 percent. In 1940, about 15 percent of the workforce had a private pension; today it is about 47 percent.[107]

During World War II, nearly one-third of the private-sector U.S. labor force was unionized. Due to the war, strikes were forbidden and wages were frozen. Fringe benefits were excluded from the wage freeze. Employers could offer, and unions eventually sought, private benefits as a substitute for wage increases. A law on excess profits contained a benefit equalization section that said if employers provided benefits, they had to offer them to at least 70 percent of employees and could not exclude the nonmanagement workers. Intended to reduce workplace tensions during the war, it indirectly encouraged private benefit expansion. Since corporate income taxes were very high during wartime, employers saw nontaxed pension contributions as financially attractive.[108] Essentially, they could pay taxes that went into a publicly controlled benefit system, or save on taxes by putting the same money into private pension benefits. The private benefits could strengthen employee discipline and commitment to a particular firm.

Labor unrest greatly increased in the immediate postwar period. There were more work stoppages between 1946 and 1953 than anytime between 1934 and 2004. A Congress dominated by conservative Republicans passed the 1947 Taft Hartley Act. It was intended to roll back gains labor won in the New Deal, weaken unions, and put an end to the labor unrest. The law eliminated the union's right to a "closed shop," imposed penalties for unauthorized strikes, and banned union control over most fringe benefit funds. Employers wanted to continue to dictate fringe benefits and remove benefits from union-management negotiations, but the National Labor Relations Board overruled them. At first, many employers refused to obey, and over half of all work stoppages from 1949 to 1950 were over the issue of fringe benefits. The eventual agreement was that employers did not have to offer private benefits, but they did have to negotiate them with labor unions. Although at first unions had viewed private benefits as a cheap substitute for wages, they grew to accept them after a combination of higher taxes on wages, a recognition that public benefits would not grow, and a defeat of their political demands for a bigger voice in workplace decisions.[109] It is important to note that the labor-management system in the United States differs significantly from systems in other advanced nations, even those with a LMR welfare state and an LMC state-economy relationship, and it contributed to enlarging the private benefit system. For example, union membership rates (also called union density) are 39 to 113 percent lower in the United States than in other LMR nations.[110] The United States combines weak union ties to political parties, a unregulated labor market, and decentralized labor-management bargaining to create a hyper-market model. Bruce Western (1997, 195) observed,

"The model was perfected in the United States, where cutthroat competition among workers and unbridled employer resistance to unions defeated labor organizations through the postwar period."

The private and public sides of America's welfare state differ in several ways (see Chart 11.7). The private side is largely hidden. Even welfare state analysts tend to ignore it, or assume that it is residual (i.e., what is left over after public benefits). The private side is hard to see because it is buried in hundreds of regulations, tax breaks, and so forth that encourage private benefits, and it slowly grew, piecemeal over time decentralized in individual firms. America's decentralized political institutions spawned a fragmented public welfare state, and it also encouraged a parallel, fragmented private side. Public assistance for private benefits is often buried in technical details, riders to legislation, administrative hearings, or courts away from contentious and open public forums. Although attempts to expand public social programs have faced political barriers and vocal opposition, private benefits did not. Private benefit expansion is a good example of how a second dimension of power operates.

The distribution of private benefits differs from public social programs and encourages different political coalitions. Hacker (2002, 179) argued that the shadow welfare state grew because, "such policies are more likely to gain the support of political actors otherwise opposed to government action in social policy . . . private social benefits are generally less visible and less costly, at least at the onset, . . . [and] fragmentation that poses significant barriers to the passage of major public programs provides multiple points of access through which these more modest policies can enter. . . ." Often, the exact same organizational and political forces that vigorously opposed offering inclusive, visible, public benefits would encourage an expansion of exclusive, hidden private benefits.[111] Over time the large private benefit system became an impediment to expanding public social programs. Both public and private social benefits

---

chart 1 1 . 7

COMPARING PRIVATE AND PUBLIC SOCIAL BENEFITS

	Public	**Private**
Visibility	Visible	Invisible
Enacted in Time	Clustered	Scattered
Conflict Level	High	Low
Intermediaries	Limited role	Major role
Mandatory	Compulsory	Voluntary
Distribution	Progressive	Regressive
Character	Universal entitlement	Exclusive discretionary reward

Sources: Hacker (2002, 35, 40–47). Also see Stevens (1988) and Howard (1997).

have policy feedbacks, but the role of intermediaries (e.g., private insurance companies, benefit providers) is far greater in providing private benefits. They are important allies in political coalitions that defend private benefits. Being hidden protects private benefits. They are also protected by being interwoven with public benefits and political–institutional structures (e.g., iron triangles) with powerful corporate interests. Hacker (2002, 57) noted that, "more so than many direct-spending programs, these approaches create resourceful and mobilized vested interests." These are just some of the results of the private, shadow welfare state system (see Chart 11.8).

c h a r t   1 1 . 8

CONSEQUENCES OF THE SHADOW U.S. WELFARE STATE

1. It narrows the scope of public debate over social programs and shifts issues to the private sector for unilateral employer determination or into processes of private labor-management negotiation.

2. It shifts the public benefit reliance from being a universal state provision to the private sector, and within the private sector, to highly differentiated provisions by specific employers.

3. It shifts public allegiance and commitment around benefits from the democratic state to the market-based solutions and a specific employer.

4. It shifts the basis for claiming benefits from being a universal and public citizenship right to being a private, contingent patron-client reward.

5. It reduces pressure to expand and improve public benefit levels by offering private sector alternatives.

6. It depoliticizes labor union demands for greater control and structural change by shifting their focus to winning concrete social benefits for members not available from the state.

7. It creates a closely tied, interdependent relationship of mutual influence between public and private social benefits.

8. It reinforces social–economic inequality by creating a stratified, two-track system that provides low-level public benefits to some and high-level private benefits to others.

9. It helps sustain a political coalition among private sector intermediary benefit providers, private employers, and middle- and upper-middle class beneficiaries to oppose expanding inclusive public benefits for lower-income people.

10. It weakens national cohesion or solidarity and increases social distance, offering an inclusive quality of life with relative comfort and security to certain social sectors that overlay with other societal divisions, such as race.

Sources: Stevens (1988). Also see Howard (1997) and Jacoby (1997).

Laws and tax breaks encouraged expanding the private benefit system, which provides benefits for only some people, as a substitute for expanding the public welfare state programs, which provides benefits for virtually every citizen. While public social programs have modest redistributive or even progressive effects, private benefits programs are highly regressive (i.e., they benefit higher-income people rather than lower-income people). Many public programs are directed at helping the poor and vulnerable. By contrast, most private benefits are designed to help only high-income people. For example, among the lower 20 percent of income earners, 15.7 percent have pensions and 23.7 percent have health insurance. These percentages steadily increase with income. Among upper-middle income people, 72.1 percent receive private pensions and 68.8 percent have health insurance.[112] Access to other private benefits, such as mortgage tax deductions, also grows with family income. For example, a family earning $15,000 or less gets an average tax break from private employer-paid health insurance of $71 per year. A family earning over $100,000 gets a tax benefit of $2,357 per year. About 150 million Americans have employer-based private health insurance. Public programs cover another 70 million. This leaves about 41 million people without health insurance coverage. Yet the United States spends far more than nations that cover 100 percent of their populations with a national health plan. Generous social welfare states, such as Sweden or France, cover their entire populations but spend one-third less (as a percent of GDP) than the United States. Other LMR nations (e.g., Canada, New Zealand, United Kingdom) also provide universal health care and spend less than the United States.[113] The U.S. welfare state has both less equity and less efficiency.

Many politicians criticize public social programs for being unresponsive to the public and "growing out of control," yet the little-noticed private benefit programs have grown much faster. The trend in recent years by federal government has been to further privatize responsibility for retirement and health care, and to shift financial risk from employers to individuals. Beginning in the 1970s, new legislation expanded private retirement plans (e.g., tax deferred individual retirement accounts [IRA], 401k, and similar plans). This improved retirement benefits without creating a new public program, raising taxes, or adding to employer costs. It also created a new market and profit stream for stock brokers and investment firms, and it reduced public pressure to raise benefit levels. As with most private benefit programs, most people using this program are among the top 20 percent of income earners.[114] For example, under 10 percent of people earning under $30,000 have an IRA and less than 20 percent own a 401k account. Participation rates steadily grow with income and more than double for higher income groups.[115]

The large shadow welfare state makes the United States very different from other LMR nations. For comparison, in SDR countries, private benefit programs represent about 4 percent of the total national social spending. In CDR nations, they represent about 9 percent of all social spending. In LMR countries excluding the United States, they are about 13 percent of the total social spending. In the United States, they are nearly 34 percent of social spending (see Table 11.5).[116]

	Public and Private Social Welfare Expenditures as a Percentage of the Gross Domestic Product in Selected Nations in 1995		
TABLE 11.5			
Country	Total Public Social Spending with Education Excluded (%)	Public Spending Plus Tax Expenditures and Private Benefits (%)*	Total Social Spending From Private Expenditures (%)
Australia	20.3	21.6	13.9
Canada	20.8	21.2	16.5
Denmark	37.6	24.4	3.3
Germany	30.4	27.7	6.5
Ireland	21.8	18.7	8
Italy	26.5	22.3	6.3
Netherlands	30.1	25	15.2
Sweden	36.4	27	5.9
United Kingdom	25.9	26	15
United States	17.1	24.5	33.9

*Taxable part of public expenditures and duplication removed.
Source: Hacker (2002, 338).

What makes the United States distinctive is not its level of social spending, but how it distributes benefits. Looking at the U.S. welfare state shows total social spending differs little from spending in other countries (see center column of Table 11.5). While the United States spends less than any other advanced nation for public benefits, it is the undisputed leader in private benefits. Benefits in most nations are overwhelmingly public and are distributed as a basic right to all citizens. In the United States, a very large share is hidden and private, and benefits are distributed depending on a person's position in the labor market.

Race and the American Welfare State

Racial politics has had a large role in shaping U.S. social policies.[117] From the earliest stages, the United States essentially had a white-only welfare state, and this only changed in the 1960s. Even after the welfare state expanded in 1935, African American, American Indian, Asian American, and Latino people were either excluded outright, or incorporated in ways that kept them in a subordinate position. During its first 30 years, the U.S. welfare state essentially reproduced and reinforced a system of racial inequality.

The leading U.S. welfare state program, Social Security, contained built-in features in its design and implementation to exclude or devalue nonwhites, particularly African Americans. The 1935 Social Security Act included provisions for old age pensions, unemployment insurance, Aid to Dependent Children (later Aid to Families with Dependent Children, or AFDC), and old age assistance. **AFDC was a federal government program that started in the New Deal Era and continued until 1996 that provided limited income and other**

help to poor women with children. The latter two programs were means-tested. Although lower-income people should benefit from means-tested programs, local administrators were charged with separating the deserving from the undeserving poor.[118] Loosely written rules and local-level discretion allowed them to distribute benefits unequally by race. Quadagno (1994, 9) argued that "means-tested programs of the American welfare state had less to do with maintaining class divisions than with maintaining racial segregation." Farm and domestic workers, overwhelmingly African American, were excluded from the first two Social Security programs until the mid-1950s. Then African Americans were only slowly included in the welfare state.[119] Even after they were included, their more frequent periods of unemployment, lower wages, and shorter life expectancies, meant blacks as a group received fewer Social Security benefits than did whites.[120]

In the early years of Social Security, public old age assistance was under local control. Especially in the Southern states, it was at the county government level. In a Jim Crow era when blacks were not allowed to vote, the local white power structure used federal social programs to reinforce the sharecropping system and provide planters with a supply of low-cost, docile, immobile black laborers. At landlord request, the aid offices closed when planters had a greater demand for labor, and black people in need received lower assistance payments than whites. For example, in Louisiana in 1937, "when black labor was in heavy demand, the governor arbitrarily ordered that the payment to black recipients be 'cut in half,' while payments for white recipients remained the same."[121]

The most controversial social program of the welfare state was Aid to Children, later AFDC. As Stephanie Moller (2002, 467) remarked, "Understanding the racial inequalities of AFDC is imperative because it was the largest and longest antipoverty program serving single-mother families in the United States. The program spanned six decades and became the foundation for 1996 welfare reforms. . . ." In the early years, the Aid to Children program assistance went to white widows. For example in 1939, 86 percent of the AFDC caseload consisted of white children, and nearly one-half lived with their widowed mothers. This was an era when unmarried or divorced mothers were rare or ostracized. By the 1960s, only seven percent of assistance went to the children of widows and 44 percent were black.[122] Several methods were used to exclude blacks. For example, the program had an "unsuitable home" provision, a carry-over from pre-Social Security pensions, it excluded aid to children found in homes where they were not cared for or that lacked "good Protestant upbringing." Eventually this rule was applied to unmarried women who lived with a man. In some Southern states, 95 percent of the children living in "unsuitable homes" were black.[123]

Racial discrimination did not end with World War II and other social trends affected the programs. Between 1948 and 1953, the number of widowed mothers in the Aid to Dependent Children program dropped by 25 percent, while the number of mothers who were unwed or abandoned grew by 28 percent, and the number of divorced women increased by 9 percent. During this period, the number of black children on AFDC grew from 14 percent in 1937 to 31 percent in 1950 and to 48 percent in 1961. These changes stimulated state governments to enact a wave of stringent restrictions in the 1950s. By 1959, 20 states made it mandatory for a poor woman to accept work if a place could be found for her children. This contradicted the original intent of the AFDC which had been to keep mothers at home so they could care for children. Reese (2001) found that higher eligibility restrictions and work requirements were most frequent in states with large black populations and where landowners needed cheap agricultural labor. This was as early version of **workfare, or programs that provide income and benefits for the poor contingent upon the poor person receiving work-related training, looking for paid employment, or staying employed in a very low-wage or part-time situation,** that eventually became the basis for the major 1996 welfare reform. Thus, three factors shaped modifications in this leading social program in the 1950s: (1) defending the racial status quo, (2) supplying landowners with low-cost labor, and (3) enforcing traditional patriarchal values. Even after African Americans were equally covered, following reforms due to the 1960s Civil Rights laws, states that had more single black than single white mothers continued to give black mothers lower benefits than whites.[124]

Racial differences can be found in most other New Deal social programs. Federal Housing Administration (FHA) permitted red-lining, restrictive covenants, and encouraged lending practices for mortgages that protected segregated white neighborhoods from black inclusion and largely excluded black people. Public housing projects selected tenants on the basis of race.[125] The labor legislation preserved employment segregation because unions (especially the craft-based American Federation of Labor) were allowed to continue to exclude black workers.

Thus, the major welfare state expansion in the New Deal perpetuated a two-tier, racially-segregated system of social benefits and reinforced existing racial segregation in housing and employment. Only in the Great Society era of the 1960s did a racially based dual welfare state system change with the **War on Poverty—a collection of new programs or the expansion of social programs for low-income people that were initiated under the Lyndon Johnson administration (1964–1968).** Quadagno (1994, 31) noted the change, "While the New Deal had excluded African Americans, the War on Poverty would favor them. While the New Deal had conspired with southern elites to deny political and social rights to African Americans, the War on Poverty would integrate them into local politics, local job markets, and local housing markets." Once the mainly white welfare state was extended to cover nonwhites, public opposition to the U.S. welfare state greatly increased. Quadagno (1994, 196) observed, "opposition to government intervention is not the central element in public antagonism to social programs. . . . It was not until the antipoverty programs became linked to the pursuit of civil rights that support waned."[126]

The history of the U.S. welfare state—from its early pre-New Deal origins, through a long period of racial exclusion, to the growth of a large shadow side—illustrates the low priority assigned to one of the welfare state goals listed earlier in this chapter—further national solidarity, cohesion, and feelings of community. Little in the U.S. welfare state is universal and for all citizens; instead, most programs target benefits to particular social groups. Instead of an inclusive approach to incorporate all citizens and treating everyone alike, the U.S. welfare state embraces an exclusionary approach in which each sector of society is treated differently. The outcome is an increase, not a decrease, in social division and inequality. For example, in a period of national unity shortly after World War II, a major welfare state program offered free college education, low interest loans for housing, free medical care, and preference in hiring. The GI bill offered generous welfare state benefits, but it was only for military veterans. It did not include most women, most racial minorities, males who were too young or old to be in the military, recent immigrants, and men with physical or mental disabilities or unconventional religious beliefs. The GI bill expanded the welfare state along the lines of a SDR, but unlike the SDR welfare states of Western Europe, it did not cover all citizens. As Mink (1990, 113) observed, "The GI Bill for example . . . reached a potential 78 percent of the civilian male population over the age of 17 after World War II; 'Rosie the Riveter' had no comparative avenue to higher education. . . ."

The American welfare state conforms to market principles differentially based an individual's situation with regard to other social inequalities and political strength. Politically organized sectors of the population and people in privileged economic situations are most likely to be shielded from the market's harsh side effects and receive first-class social benefits. At the same time, people in disadvantaged positions face the full brunt of raw market forces and get meager benefits, often with stipulations attached. In short, there is one welfare state for the poor, single women, racial minorities, and the lower class, and another welfare state for the white middle- and upper-middle classes. Charles Noble (1997, 155) observed, "It has also made economic sense for the more affluent middle classes to choose private market solutions over public goods and universal access to state-run programs . . . better situated, and more affluent, the middle classes have had a very different relationship with market capitalism than workers have."

While part of American exceptionalism comes from its LMR welfare state, it is distinct from other LMRs in three mutually reinforcing ways: (1) it is more intensely market reinforcing and procommodification, (2) it has a large shadow private benefit side that maintains and intensifies inequality, and (3) it has perpetuated racial and other inequalities. Such distinctiveness is due to the structure of political institutions (e.g., decentralized, fragmented, divided powers; electoral and party systems), the alignments and outcomes of past political struggles, and specific cultural–historical features (e.g., having been a slave society, being continental in size, immigrant settled). The structure of the American welfare state itself has consequences for political alliances in a policy feedback process. "The structure of the welfare state itself both divided potential supporters and encouraged people who might be expected to benefit from public provision to ally themselves with the same corporate elites and upper- and upper-middle

" I should like to propose a bonanza for the rich."

class voters who had traditionally opposed economic [reform] liberalism," according to Noble (1997, 116).

Recent trends in several nations to reduce welfare state benefits, privatize benefits that are now public, and further **devolution, or turning national-level programs over to state or local-level governments,** all indicate a rejection of the welfare state ideal that says the state has a responsibility to unify people and provide for the well-being of all citizens equally.[127] Devolution exacerbates differences among local areas in levels of social benefit provision.[128] One last factor that distinguishes social policies in the U.S. is the tenor of debate and discourse around the welfare state. Quadagno (1998, 113) argued, "American exceptionalism has been explained in terms of structural variables such as the strength of organized labor or the nature of the state. Yet, the U.S. appears to be on the verge of becoming a welfare-state leader in undoing the core programs of the New Deal. . . . Understanding this paradigm shift requires a departure from analysis solely on the socio-economic and political-institutional features of the welfare state. It also requires a sustained analysis of the discursive structures that have sustained it."

WELFARE STATE DISCOURSE

The discourse and symbols around the welfare state influence what people accept to be true, possible, or desirable for it. White and Goodman (1998, 17) observed that, "welfare needs to be examined in terms of political discourses as much as, if not more than, in terms of a set of policies." A welfare state is more than a collection of social programs, benefits, laws, agencies, and so forth; it is also a set of assumptions, ways of talking, and ideas. How people think about the welfare state affects what becomes social policy, and once established, social policies and programs, feed back to affect discussions and attitudes. Orloff

(1993b, 79, 89) put it as follows, "The ideological orientations of political actors do have an impact on the sorts of policy initiatives they suggest. . . . Ideological perspectives and cultural frameworks to some extent limit the 'universe of policy discourse,' but this is influenced as well by the specific features of existing policies and administrative organizations." Thus, discourse about social programs is important to understand the origin, expansion, modification, and contraction of welfare states.[129]

Welfare states have a policy feedback to affect social divisions, electoral politics, and public attitudes.[130] For example, social policies can encourage people to act and think either in cooperative, mutually supportive ways or as antagonistic, competitive individuals. An early study by Coughlin (1979, 13) found, "where social welfare institutions are most developed . . . the collectivist components of mass ideology predominate. Conversely, where institutional development lags, individualism and collectivism are either equally balanced (as in Canada) or individualism is dominant (as in the United States)." People in different nations accept varying degrees of general inequality, even if they agree that certain jobs should get higher pay than others.[131] Attitudes toward economic issues and economic inequality vary by welfare state regime as well as by country.[132] People living in SDR countries tend to support many public social programs and favor a highly egalitarian income distribution, and those in CDR countries also support many programs but accept more income inequality, while those in LMR countries oppose many social programs and find very unequal income distributions to be acceptable.[133]

Discourse has played a large role in shaping social programs in the United States. The symbolism and rhetoric around welfare in particular have been a political battlefield. Beyond race coding the antipoverty programs, and heaping scorn on welfare recipients, factual information about poverty and welfare has been highly politicized and manipulated for ideological purposes. Alice O'Connor (2001, 17) argued that the relevance of poverty facts has less to do with rational discussion or careful presentations than with, "the power to determine the terms of debate—to contest, gain, and ultimately to exercise ideological hegemony over the boundaries of political discourse." Because the terms of debate set boundaries between what is politically privileged and what will be hopeless, political elites and policy experts struggle to control the basic assumptions about programs and to set the terms of debate.

Debates over antipoverty policy in the United States illustrate this process. By the mid-1960s, War on Poverty politicians embraced a theory that most in the academic community had found flawed, the culture of poverty thesis. **The culture of poverty thesis states that the primary cause of poverty is a unique set of cultural beliefs and values held by poor people and transmitted across generations**. Within public policy circles, the terms of debate shifted from asking, Are poor people different from the nonpoor? to How are the poor different? Poor black people who lived in segregated urban areas were assumed to suffer from a "pathology."[134] O'Connor (2001, 241) noted, "research on the 'causes and consequences' of poverty concentrated on the characteristics of poor people."

Studies on poverty reduction were limited to finding efficient ways to deliver social benefits to the poor and policymakers pushed the structural theory of poverty out of the debate. **The structural theory of poverty states that the root causes of poverty do not lie in individual behavior, personal characteristics, or the culture of poor people but are in systematic discrimination, provision of inadequate schooling, insufficient or very low-paying jobs, and general conditions in the economy.** Despite its faults, the War on Poverty improved the quality of life for most people in poverty. The War on Poverty cut the overall percentage of people living below the poverty line almost in half; it raised the living allowance for a family of four from $388 to $577 per month; it reduced the number of poor people living in housing without indoor plumbing from 20 percent to 11 percent; and it cut the percentage of poor who had never been to a physician from 20 percent to 8 percent. "Medicaid and Medicare brought first-time medical care to a substantial number of the nation's poor. . . . Infant mortality rates dropped significantly, particularly among blacks and the poor, life expectancy increased; and the gap between black and white life expectancy narrowed."[135] Nonetheless, conservative critics charged that the War on Poverty had been a complete failure, and they set out to dismantle it.

In the 1980s the terms of debate again shifted in what Quadagno (1999) called the "third transition" in the history of the U.S. welfare state.[136] Politicians and antiwelfare critics continued to prop up the **welfare queen image—a mythological woman created by conservative politicians to attack welfare programs; she is African American, unwed, refuses to work, purposely had many children by different men to increase her welfare benefits, and lives a luxurious life by manipulating government programs for the poor.** However, the economists and conservatives that joined around 1980 to push for neoliberal business policies (discussed earlier in Chapter 10) also developed an attack on social policies.[137] They argued that social programs had harmed economic growth and development, although studies contradict this view.[138] To sell their ideas to a broad audience, the conservative advocates affiliated with policy think tanks offered a simple, accessible explanation for poverty. The poverty issue was not about people who were poor, but it was about the evil of welfare dependency. New assumptions emerged—welfare programs "never worked" and the biggest problems of poor people were caused by dependency (i.e., preferring government aid over working) and family structure (i.e., unmarried mothers).

Dependency became the central symbol of welfare.[139] In the new discourse frame, the poverty "problem" was a person's reliance on public assistance, and "success" was a person moving off of public antipoverty assistance to any wage labor, no matter how poorly paying, dangerous, or unstable. The antiwelfare campaign did not turn Americans against helping the poor; rather, it reframed welfare issue from how to assist poor people to how to end dependency. Combined with populist derisions of "big government," the campaign positioned dependency as the polar opposite of virtuous individualism (i.e., self-sufficiency, personal responsibility, being a wage laborer), and it was "as much an argument about what is wrong with America as an argument about welfare policy."[140] People no longer saw welfare as a social program that helped the poor survive and that had been won after decades of political struggles by low-income people and workers. In the new frame, welfare was a dreadful, elite-designed program imposed onto the poor that both wasted taxpayer money and fostered dependency. Race-coding implied that welfare was especially imposed on helpless, uninformed African Americans. In the new discourse, welfare programs created dependency, and dependency caused poor people's pathologies—illegal drug use, violence, crime, teen pregnancy, single motherhood, and unemployment. End welfare, according to the frame, and poor people's pathologies will largely vanish. Although such claims had no scientific support, the mass media and many politicians embraced and disseminated the **welfare dependency thesis which states that receiving government social benefits creates an addictivelike dependence to continue receiving the benefits and destroys a person's self-esteem, motivation to work, and self-sufficiency**. The public relations campaign to advance the dependency thesis was highly effective, and soon the public accepted it as being true. As O'Connor (2000, 556) observed, "Ever since the publication of Charles Murray's *Losing Ground* (1984), investigating the relationship between policy and poverty has never been the same."

The frame of the new welfare discourse was reflected in the 1996 Personal Responsibility and Work Opportunity Reconciliation Act and its new anti-poverty program, Temporary Assistance for Needy Families (TANF). As O'Connor (2001, 286) noted, "All of the experts agreed that the legislation was a triumph of politics over scientific knowledge." The law reflected a coming together of bipartisan opposition to spending public money, state-level government's desire for more control over poverty programs, and an ideological tone to "get tough" on the poor (similar to "getting tough" on crime with punitive policies).[141] Information was manipulated up to and after the 1996 "end welfare as we know it" law. For example, reports of poor women crossing state lines in search of higher welfare benefits were actually politically fabricated and intended to inflame people.[142]

A study of media reports during the two years leading up to the 1996 welfare reform law found that public officials offered a uniform, stereotypical picture of the poor. They portrayed welfare recipients as being incompetent, childlike, and bewildered by the world of work. Instead of using the image of a scheming "welfare queen," they used a picture of extreme ineptitude due to personal defects and a need for strong moral, paternalistic guidance to achieve self-sufficiency.[143] Post-TANF media reports widely praised welfare reform as being a huge success. The primary basis for the claim of success was that welfare caseloads had declined. This extremely narrow focus reflected how the mass media and elite discourse had already reframed the welfare issue.[144] In the new frame, the new program was not judged by whether it reduced poverty rates, whether people in the program ceased being poor, whether poor people's quality of life had improved, or whether economic inequality lessened. By all these criteria, welfare reform failed.[145] Even the measures of caseload reduction used to tout its success had complications; nonetheless, the media loudly declared success. Other results of TANF, such as a sharp drop in welfare recipients who enrolled in postsecondary education, went unnoticed.[146] By narrowing the standard of program success, the antiwelfare advocates gained a reputation as successful policy innovators.[147]

The U.S. experience with 1980s–1990s welfare reform is not an isolated case. In the same period, other U.S. social programs were reduced, and welfare state expansion stopped in other nations. At first, political sociologists explained welfare state retrenchment by simply reversing explanations of welfare-state expansion. The pluralist/logic of industrialization argument was rephrased into a widely repeated neoliberal one about the impact of globalization and the forces of international economic competition. It said the greatly increased mobility of financial investment and production across international borders since the early 1980s meant that nations had to compete to offer a favorable business climate. Since a nation with a large social welfare state had high social program costs, more taxes, and many business regulations, corporations found it less attractive for investing. Thus, in the "race to the bottom" nations had begun to rescind or roll back welfare states and create a promarket, friendly business environment. A class-struggle/power resources argument held that leftist parties and unions have become weak and more "mainstream." Welfare retrenchment was due to their losing political power. Others saw retrenchment as creating a deep divide between private and public sector workers, or insiders protected in the welfare state versus outsiders not covered (e.g., recent immigrants, the very poor). However, the dynamics of retrenchment looked different from those of expansion.[148]

The neoliberal, globalization explanation is widely used to interpret welfare state retrenchment, but few studies support it.[149] Instead, different welfare state regimes appear to respond to globalization and changing their welfare state in very different ways. Hicks (1999, 217), argued, "anti-welfarist effects (pro-retrenchment effects) emerge for exclusionary state structures . . . significant pro-welfarist effects (anti-retrenchment effects) emerge for social democracy, social democratic governments apparently appropriating the role of welfare-state guardian. . . ." The form and degree of welfare state retrenchment varies by the state's political structure, leftist political capacity, and the ideological climate. The greatest retrenchment occurred in nations with a fragmented-exclusionary state structure, disorganized unions and left political parties, and where the ideological right dominates policy discourse. It is more limited where there is a centralized and parliamentary form of state, strong unionization, left parties remain vibrant, and the ideological discourse is varied. As Hicks (1999) argued, nations with a strong political left and a well-institutionalized inclusive-universalistic welfare state, particularly those with a corporatist structure, have retrenched slower and their retrenchment has been more moderate (see Chart 11.9).

chart   11.9

PATTERNS OF WELFARE STATE RETRENCHMENT

| | Welfare State Retrenchment | |
Left Political Strength	Late (Post 1982)	Early (Pre 1982)
Strong	Austria, Belgium, Finland, France, Germany, Netherlands, Norway, Switzerland, Sweden	Australia
Weak	Japan, New Zealand, United Kingdom	Canada, Denmark, Ireland, Italy, United States.

Source: Hicks (1999, 235)

Others emphasized the role of ideology in retrenchment. Huber and Stephens (2001a, 2001b) found two major reasons for welfare state reductions: (1) cuts due to rising unemployment and (2) ideologically driven cuts. They note (2001b, 125) that, "There are only a few cases of large-scale ideologically-driven cuts. The most dramatic were by Thatcher in Britain, the National (conservative) government in New Zealand, and the Reagan administration in the United States."[150] Thus, the dominance of neoliberal ideas in public discourse plays an independent role, particularly in a few LMR nations, in justifying and shaping how welfare states are being cut. In these cases, decommodification effects of the welfare state are being overturned and aggressive recommodification is the order of the day.[151]

CONCLUSION

In this chapter we have examined the basis for social policies and the welfare state in particular. You have seen the major goals of the welfare state idea, and its historical origins. You have also seen how alternative political sociology models explain welfare state expansion. A major development in the study of welfare states was recognizing alternative welfare state regimes. This helped clarify the alternative paths to welfare state development and the diverse outcomes associated with welfare states. We also saw that welfare states are gendered institutions. Not only do different welfare states affect gender inequality and family relations, but also they support alternative household relations. Turning to the United States, you saw how its welfare state has certain distinct features. In particular, it is a far more intense version of the Liberal Market welfare-state regime, it has a large private side, and it has a history of reinforcing racial inequality. Lastly, you learned that discourse, or how people discuss social policy, can have an important independent role.

KEY TERMS

Aid to Families with Dependent Children (AFDC)

Culture of Poverty Thesis

Decommodification

Deserving Poor

Devolution

Entitlement

Food Stamp Program

General Assistance

Male-Breadwinner Model

Maternal Welfare State

Means-Tested Program

Medicaid

Medicare

Paradox of Redistribution

Policy Feedback

Poorhouse

Poverty Line

Settlement House

Structural Theory of Poverty

Undeserving Poor

Unemployment Insurance

Universal Social Programs

War on Poverty

Welfare Capitalism

Welfare Dependency Thesis

Welfare Queen

Welfare State

Welfare State Regime

Workfare

REVIEW QUESTIONS

1. What is the welfare state and what are its goals? What makes it so confusing?

2. What explanations provided by two of the political sociological theories receive the greatest support in accounting for the welfare state's expansion?

3. Contrast the principles of each welfare state regime and the key points in the pathways to their development.

4. How do poverty reduction and inequality reduction differ? Which welfare state is best at doing each?

5. What alternative household types do each of the three welfare state regimes support? How?

6. Why is a maternalist approach to welfare states double-edged?

7. What is the "shadow welfare state" in the United States? Why and how did it develop? How does it differ from the public welfare state in the United States?

8. What is the relationship between the American welfare state and racial equality?

9. In discussions of welfare state retrenchment, what are the major issues, and what factor seems to be strongest in how the United States and Great Britain responded?

10. Esping-Andersen stated that "the welfare state is a system of social stratification." What specific features of the American welfare state made it a system of stratification?

11. The most controversial antipoverty program in the United States has been AFDC. It was abolished in 1996. What made the program controversial and what was the logic behind the new welfare reform?

12. Explain the concept of decommodification, and contrast it with the idea of recommodification. How do specific social programs advance one or the other?

RECOMMENDED READINGS

Esping-Andersen, Gösta. 1990. *The Three Worlds of Welfare Capitalism.* Princeton, NJ: Princeton University Press.

Hacker, Jacob S. 2002. *The Divided Welfare State.* New York: Cambridge University Press.

Huber, Evelyne and John D. Stephens. 2001. *Development and Crisis of the Welfare State: Parties and Politics in Global Markets.* Chicago: University of Chicago Press.

Marmor, Theodore R., Jerry L. Mashaw, and Philip L. Harvey. 1990. *America's Misunderstood Welfare State.* New York: Basic Books.

Quadagno, Jill. 1988. *The Transformation of Old Age Security: Class and Politics in the American Welfare State.* Chicago: University of Chicago Press.

Skocpol, Theda. 1995. *Social Policy in the United States.* Princeton, NJ: Princeton University Press.

ENDNOTES

1. Quote is from Pampel and Williams on (1989, 1). See also Esping-Andersen (1990, 3).
2. For studies that document this see Conley and Springer (2001) and Lewis Michael (1999).
3. For an additional discussion of Bismarck's reforms and a comparison with Great Britain see Dickinson (1986) and Rimlinger (1971). A great deal of early social welfare expansion, even in countries that later had strong social democratic pressures or socialist parties, was because of strong conservative preemptive Christian Democratic parties according to Esping-Andersen and Van Kersgergen (1992).
4. See Amenta and Skocpol (1988, 98–88) for a summary of the history of this.
5. This is not to imply that the voluntary and local initiatives were limited to the United States. See Koven and Michel (1990) on women's nonnational government contributions, and Jane Lewis (1994) in Britain. Amenta, Clemens, Olsen, Parikh and Skocpol (1987), Orloff (1988), Skocpol, Abend-Wein, Howard, and Lehmann (1993) illustrate the importance of local-level programs.
6. On the veterans program see Skocpol (1992a, 1993, 1997).
7. See Nelson (1990, 128) on population coverage and Skocpol (1992a, 128) on budget statistics.
8. Amenta and Skocpol (1988), Skocpol and Amenta (1986), Skocpol and Finegold (1982), Skocpol and Ikenberry (1983).
9. See Cammisa (1998) on the rhethoric and symbolism of welfare, and Smith (1987) for survey data on changing connotations.
10. For the T. H. Marshall source see Myles (1989).
11. From Moon (1988, 43).
12. See Marmor et al. (1990, 237–238).
13. Data for the year 1995 or close to it from the OECD, *Labor Force Statistics, Appendix* and ILO, *Key Indicators of the Labour Market* (2002).
14. This is argued by Schneider (1982) but is expressed by many others. These two fit three of the four purposes of a welfare state offered by Marmor, Mashaw and Harvey (1990).
15. Quadagno (1987, 117) and Gordon (1990) discuss the overlap between social welfare and social control. Also see Brush (2002) and Shaver (2002).
16. This is a major concern of many feminist theorists. See Crompton (2001) and McDaniel (2002).
17. Orloff (1996), O'Connor (1993), Huber and Stephens (2001a), and Korpi (2000) discuss this specifically with regard to gender. Brush (2002) describes this in terms of body rights and personhood.
18. Social capital is used here, but mobilization is also mentioned by Shalev (1983). Also see Goodin et al. (1999). Quadagno (2000) argues that racial-ethnic group inclusion should be an explicit welfare state goal. Davies (1997) contrasts the European principle of the welfare state as government-led social inclusion and U.S. conservative principle of voluntary self-help and mutual aid without government involvement.
19. For related reviews of the theories see Amenta and Carruthers (1988), Ashford (1986), Esping-Andersen (1990), Hicks (1999), Huber and Stephens (2001a). Korpi (1989), Misra (2002), Myles and Quadagno (2002), Orloff (1988, 1993b), Pampel and Williamson (1989), Quadagno (1987, 1988), and Skocpol (1992b).
20. Examples of the logic of industrialism model include Cutright (1965), Jackman (1975), Pampel and Williamson (1989), Wilensky (1975), and Wilensky and Lebeaux (1958). A good summary can be found in Myles and Quadagno (2002). Misra (2002, 25) and Korpi (1989, 311) offer summaries of the theory.
21. For examples see Ashford (1986) and Rimlinger (1971). Skocpol (1992b) gives examples from American historians. Also see Almond and Verba (1963) on the concept of political culture.
22. For interest groups see Grønbjerg (1977) and Janowitz (1976). Finegold (1988) and Hansen (1987) use a version of it for agricultural policy. Pampel and Williamsom (1989) are sympathetic to this model.
23. Myles (1989, 29) describes the political business cycle argument. Most studies found limited evidence for it, although Schultz (1995) found support for it operating in Great Britain with regard to transfer payments.
24. Paul Pierson (1994, 1996, 2001) makes this argument for why social-welfare programs are not cut back.

25. Orloff (1993a, 1993b), Skocpol (1992), and Orloff and Skocpol (1984). Also see Amenta and Skocpol (1988).

26. On this point see Huber and Stephens (2001a); Huber, Ragin and Stephens (1993); and Noble (1997). Noble (1997, 16) argued that business's political power is greatest with decentralized government.

27. See Quadagno (1987, 1988). Also see Bane (1988) on feminization of poverty and social policy in the U.S. and Meyer (1996) on gender inequality in U.S. Social Security benefits.

28. Representatives of this perspective include Berkowitz and McQuaid (1980), Domhoff (1990, 1996, 1998), Ferguson (1995), Gordon (1994), Kolko (1963), Levine (1988), Quadagno (1988), Weinstein (1968). Also see Manza (1993, 2000a).

29. Also see Orloff and Parker (1990) and Skocpol and Amenta (1985) who summarize the power structure position and criticize it, but see Griffin, Wallace and Rubin (1986) and Swenson (1997).

30. O'Connor (1973) offers a well-recognized example of structuralism. Less known are Clark and Dear (1984). Jessop (1982, 1990) provides an overview of neomarxist theories of the state, and his work on Poulantzas (Jessop 1985) is a useful overview of another major theorist.

31. From Myles (1989, 15).

32. See Esping-Andersen and van Kersbergen (1992). Quadagno (1987, 115) who said, "A substantial body of evidence supports the social democratic view." For example, see Korpi (1983, 1989) and Shalev (1983).

33. On differences in the power and organization of the working class in different countries and an explanation of the timing and form of social insurance programs see Dickinson (1986).

34. This argument was made in Piven and Cloward (1971, 1977) also see Quadagno (1987, 117) and Rosenthal (1983).

35. See Kerbo and Shaffer (1992) and Valocchi (1990).

36. Huber, Ragin, and Stephens (1993, 738) also remarked, "Our results confirm key findings from all three of the principles explanations of welfare state expansion. . . ."

37. See Amenta (1998), Amenta and Carruthers (1988) on states in the U.S. Other studies with negative evidence for the theory can be found in Orloff (1993b) and Quadagno (1987).

38. See Hicks (1999) Appendix to Chapter 1 for a detailed explanation of the precondition argument.

39. Esping-Andersen (1990, 19–21) and Myles (1989, 63–66)

40. For example see Björn (1979), Hage and Hanneman (1980), Montanari (2001), and Williamson and Weiss (1979).

41. From Amenta et al. (1987).

42. From Valocchi (1989).

43. See Stryker (1990a).

44. Korpi (1989) makes this criticism.

45. Myles and Quadagno (2002).

46. See Fording (1997, 2000), Isaac and Kelly (1981), Hicks and Swank (1983), Jenkins and Brents (1989), Kerbo and Shaffer (1986, 1992), Piven and Cloward (1977). Schram and Turbett (1983).

47. For a review of studies see Esping-Andersen and van Kersberger (1992). Examples of supportive studies include Furniss and Tilton (1977); Huber, Ragin and Stephens (1993); Korpi (1983, 1989); Hicks (1999); Hicks and Misra (1993); and Hicks and Swank (1984, 1992).

48. Hicks (1999, 181) argues this perspective.

49. See Przeworski (1985).

50. See Hicks (1999, 153–155).

51. Huber, Ragin, and Stephens (1993) and Huber and Stephens (2001a) outline this critique. Also see Therborn (1987) who outlines similar criticisms.

52. King (1987) notes that origin and expansion may have different causes.

53. See Mares (2003).

54. From Mares (2003).

55. From King (1987) the four areas are job accident insurance, health insurance, public pension, and unemployment insurance. The twelve nations include Austria, Germany, Belgium, Denmark, Finland, France, Italy, the Netherlands, Norway, Sweden, Switzerland, and the United Kingdom.

56. Hicks (1999).

57. Iversen and Cusack (2000). Also see Moller et al. (2003).

58. Iversen and Cusack (2000) argue that in liberal-market economies (e.g., the United States), employment losses in the traditional sectors shifted to expanding private service employment, requiring less welfare state growth.

59. Usui (1993, 1994) discussed international and world-system effects.

60. From Huber and Stephens (2001a).

61. Hicks (1999); Hicks and Swank (1992); Huber, Ragin, and Stephens (1993); and Huber and Stephens (2001a).

62. King (1987) and Pierson (1996).

63. Quote is from Goodin et al. (1999, 5).

64. For a discussion of labor market effects see Pierson (2000, 794).

65. See Huber and Stephens (2001a, 102–103) on the role of international trade openness.

66. The wage-earner regime has high minimum wage laws and means-tested welfare programs. It tries to force everyone into the paid labor market, with welfare programs for only the poorest. While health care is offered, most other protections are the individual wage-earner's responsibility. For a semicorporatist element of government negotiating with unions see Aspalter (2001), Castles and Mitchell (1991).

67. Esping-Andersen called this conservative but based on Hicks (1999) and Huber and Stephens (2001a), it would be better labeled as Christian Democratic.

68. See Hicks and Kenworthy (1998).

69. The Netherlands is classified as Social Democratic by Esping-Andersen (1990) but seems to better fit Christian Democratic based on Hicks (1999), Huber and Stephens (2001a), and Van Voorhis (2002).

70. See White and Goodman (1998) on East Asian welfare states.

71. Quote is from Goodin et al. (1999, 48).

72. See Hicks (1999) and Hicks and Kenworthy (1998). Mares (2001) discusses the historical impact of different business organization forms in Germany and France. Also see discussions in Pierson (2001) and Huber and Stephens (2001a).

73. Bradley et al. (2003) make this point strongly.

74. Korpi and Palme (1998) lay out the problem in this way.
75. For a explanation of its establishment see O'Connor (2001, 184).
76. Brady et al. (2003), Goodin et al. (1999), Huber and Stephens (2001a), Kenworthy (1999), Korpi and Palme (1998), and Moller et al. (2003).
77. See DiPrete and McManus (2000), Goodin, et al. (1999), and McManus and DiPrete (2000). These findings suggest that Liberal-Market regimes have a short-term positive impact because people can quickly switch to a new job, but overall Social Democratic or Christian Democratic regimes provide more buffering.
78. Korpi (1989) provides a comparative study of health care protection.
79. On pensions see Gran (1997), Myles (1989), and Ragin (1994). Also see Huber and Stephens (2001a, 108–110) and Korpi and Palme (1998) for additional support.
80. See Goodin, et al. (1999).
81. Quote is from Orloff (1993a, 304). See Thistle (2002) for a useful, complementary summary. Also see Gainsbury (1996).
82. Koven and Michel (1990), Orloff (1988), Skocpol (1992a), Skocpol, Abend-Wein, Howard, Lehmann (1993), and Wilkinson (1999). Although she focuses on a specific British case, Jane Lewis (1994) discusses maternalism and women's involvement in welfare state development. Also see Myles and Quadagno (2002).
83. See OECD statistics.
84. See Huber and Stephens (2001b).
85. On familism see Orloff (1993).
86. See Gornick and Jacobs (1998); Gornick, Myers, and Ross (1998); Huber and Stephens (2001b); and Stier et al. (2001, 1733–1734).
87. Orloff (1993a) argues for work access and an ability to form an autonomous household. See Jane Lewis (2001, 2002) and McDaniel (2002) on care work. Thistle (2002) also discusses care work and argues that instead of a new gender regime, a void was left after the old regime collapsed.
88. See Christopher et al. (2002, 223). Also see Christopher (2002a, 2002b).
89. This draws heavily on Wilkinson (1999). Also see Jane Lewis (1994).
90. On women in labor movements and effects on public pensions see Hill and Tigges (1995).
91. For survey results see Kunzler et al. (1999).
92. Noble (1997, 27) argued, "decentralized institutions and electoral systems that have favored two-party systems have frustrated the efforts by private and public actors who have wanted to build more comprehensive welfare states." Combined with winner-take all, single-representative elections and early, white male enfranchisement it weakened the working class capacity to form class-based political action.
93. See Amenta, Bonastia, and Caren (2001, 222).
94. Amenta, Bonastia, and Caren (2001); Skocpol and Amenta (1986); and Skocpol and Ikenberry (1983) provide overviews. See Clemens (1997); Skocpol, Abend-Wein, Howard, and Lehmann (1993); and Wilkinson (1999) on the role of women's groups and organizations. Especially see Skocpol (1992a, 1993) on the significance of Civil War veterans' pensions.
95. Orloff (1993b, 7–8).
96. Sutton (1991) describes how asylums were often used as a form of indoor relief in the United States.
97. Orloff (1993b, 18).
98. Quote is from Howard (1997, 31).
99. From Quadagno (1988, 90).
100. See Griffin, Wallace and Rubin (1986) for an extensive discussion of employer activity against unions.
101. Quote is from Jacobs (1997, 20). See Dobbin (1992) on differences in types of firms that offered benefits.
102. Dobbin (1992, 1428–1429) provides detailed information on the insurance industry's role.
103. This point is strongly made in Dobbin (1992).
104. Quote is from Stevens (1988, 125).
105. Stevens (1988, 128–129).
106. See especially Dobbin (1992, 1434) on this argument.
107. From Hacker (2002: 78–79).
108. Stevens (1988, 130). Dobbin (1993, 1437) argued that the effects of a wage freeze and tax law changes came too late during World War II to explain the large early expansion of private pensions.
109. From Stevens (1988, 134–142).
110. See Western (1997, 53–65, 89). Statistics calculated from Table 6.1.
111. From Howard (1997).
112. These statistics and those that immediately follow come from Hacker (2002, 37, 39).
113. From Hacker (2002, 184–185).
114. See Hacker (2002, 157).
115. These statistics come from tables in Hacker (2002, 169).
116. See Hacker (2002, 19).
117. Also see Brown (1999) and Lieberman (1998). Manza (2000b) provides a good overview. Amenta, Bonastia, and Caren (2001) also provide an overview on race and the American welfare state.
118. This is explained in Misra (2002, 30).
119. See Lieberman (1998).
120. From Quadagno (1994).
121. From Quadagno (1988, 134).
122. Berkowitz (1991, 101–102) and Soule and Zylan (1997).
123. On unsuitable homes see Soule and Zylan (1997). Berkowitz (1991, 102) cites the case of Louisiana.
124. See details in Moller (2002).
125. For more on housing see Gotham (2002), Hirsch (1998), and Quadagno (1994).
126. This is analyzed in detail in Gilens (1995, 1996a, 1996b, 1999).
127. A nice summary of this idea can be found in Zald (1985).
128. For example historical studies by Amenta (1996), Amenta and Poulsen (1996), Amenta and Zylan (1991), Amenta et al. (1987), Amenta, Cattruthers, and Zylan (1992) show differences in program provision.
129. Davies (1997, 40) and Schmidt (2002) argue that discourse matters can have a causal influence on welfare reform, altering perceptions of interests and overcoming institutional obstacles.

130. See Pierson (1994) on policy feedback.

131. See Kelley and Evans (1993). Bell and Robinson (1978) compare the United States and England.

132. From Andress and Heien (2001).

133. See Arts and Gelissen (2001), Kosonen (1987), and Svallfors (1997) for details of the study.

134. O'Connor (2001, 197–200) provides a discussion of shifting policy discussions.

135. From Noble (1997, 98–99).

136. The first was the New Deal of the 1930s and the second was the Great Society of the 1960s.

137. Katznelson (1981b, 324–325) argued that a shift within the economics profession was the cause of rethinking social policy-state linkages, and via think tanks, it had a very large effect on U.S. policy discourse. Noble (1997, 107) noted that by the mid-1970s, a broad business coalition "had formed to lobby against government regulation, labor-law reform, and social spending, and for tax cuts targeted on business."

138. Studies by Midgley (2001) and Midgley and Tang (2001) directly question this within the United States.

139. Schram (1995) talks about this shift. Also see Ehrenreich (1987) and Piven (1998, 2001).

140. Quote is from Piven (1998, 31).

141. Beckett and Western (2001) found a relationship between poverty and imprisonment rates between 1975 and 1995, suggesting that getting tough on the poor and "getting tough" on crime are closely related.

142. See Schram, Nitz, and Kreuger (1998) on the creation of the welfare migration problem.

143. From Lens (2002).

144. From Schram and Soss (2001).

145. One evaluation of the program is summarized in Corcoran et al. (2000). Also see Curran and Abrams (2000), Mink (2001), and Verber (2001).

146. For documentation and discussion see Mazzeo, Rab, and Eachus (2003).

147. From Schram and Soss (2001).

148. Pierson (1996) made this argument clearly. Also see Clayton and Pontusson (1998).

149. Iversen (2001), Iversen and Cusack (2000), Hicks (1999), Huber and Stephens (2001b), Moller et al. (2003), Montanari (2001), Stephens, Huber, and Ray (1999), and Swank (2001, 2002).

150. Also see a similar argument in King and Wood (1999).

151. Pierson (2001) argues welfare state regimes restructured differently by cutting costs and reconfiguring programs. Korpi (2003) makes a slightly different argument but does not appear to disagree. Clayton and Pontusson (1998) showed how the restructuring increased economic inequality. King and Wood (1999) discuss the relationship between recent neoliberal ideological movements and restructuring LMR with LMC.

CONCLUSION

INTRODUCTION

This last chapter offers comments on the direction of political sociology and on issues raised throughout the book. The roots of political sociology lie in the nineteenth century conflicts over industrialization, consolidating the nation-state, and spreading democracy. The field expanded during the twentieth century to examine the causes of dictatorship and democracy, the nature of citizenship and law, the impact of several institutional forms of the state on politics, conventional and unconventional political participation, symbolic and cultural politics, state-economy relations, and the rise of a welfare state. Political sociologists used four key concepts—power, state, hegemony, and struggle—and several models of the state and politics as they strived to understand and explain the dynamics of political power. ■

ISSUES IN POLITICAL SOCIOLOGY

This chapter has three sections. In the first section, we look at five issues that stretch across two or more topic chapters and continue to be of relevance. The issues include how moral panics can rise up and alter the political landscape, how ordinary people asserted their views through the courts, whether a dealignment of the U.S. political system has occurred, where the military fits into politics and society, and what kinds of crimes a state can commit. In the next section, we briefly consider three broad themes confronting political sociology in the twenty-first century: globalization, inclusion, and integrity. In the last section, we reexamine the models of political sociology that you have been reading about since Chapter 3.

Cultural Politics and Moral Panics

Political sociologists often stand aloof when a new issue or problem first appears on the public agenda and quickly captures public attention. Hesitant to accept it at face value immediately or to join the rush of popular excitement, a political sociologist looks into the deeper causes and consequences of the issue, and compares public reactions to it with the actual conditions. This is because he or she is aware that social problems and issues are socially constructed and spread by identifiable social–political processes.[1] You encountered similar ideas in Chapter 7 when we considered the importance of symbols and ideas in politics and in Chapter 8 when we saw that cultural institutions have a political role. To spread and mobilize public interest in a new social problem or issue, government officials and the leaders of major institutions will label an event or condition as an urgent crisis that requires sacrifices, and "the belief in a crisis relaxes resistance to government interferences with civil liberties and bolsters support for executive actions, including discouragement or suppression of criticism. . . ."[2]

When societal reactions quickly swell dramatically out of proportion to actual conditions and take a moral tone, political sociologists see it as a moral panic.[3] **A moral panic occurs when many people rapidly start to see a number of evildoers posing a serious and growing threat to society, and they demand greater social control or punishment to reaffirm the moral order**. Moral panics occurred in many countries and at many points in history. They include many actors—the media, the public, lawmakers and politicians, and political groups. During the panic, claims-makers greatly exaggerate a real problem, and public anxiety over it spreads rapidly.[4] According to Goode and Ben Yehuda (1994, 31), "The moral panic, then, is characterized by the feeling, held by a substantial number of the members of a given society, that evildoers pose a threat to society and to the moral order as a result of their behavior and, therefore, 'something should be done' about them and their behavior."

A moral panic requires trigger events; a cooperative and willing mass media; a receptive public climate; and opinion leaders or officials who define the moral problem, identify the targeted evildoers, and offer solutions. Political sociologists cannot predict when a moral panic will erupt, its specific target, or when it will fade. A scapegoat or "folk devil" is identified that the public comes to see as the primary source of evil. The public projects its fears onto the scapegoat. A moral panic focuses public attention on a specific "evil" that becomes a symbolic moral threat to the social order—casting evil spells, stealing and abusing children, pilfering national security secrets, hijacking cars or planes, and so forth. The panic follows a cycle: first public anxiety is heightened and key targets, evildoers, sinful behavior, and the like are identified. Next, officials provide a solution that offers a unity of purpose, discharges public unease, and assures the public that their leaders are eradicating the evil and reinstating public order. The panic ends by leaders maintaining, restoring, or altering the boundaries and hierarchy of the social–moral order.

Resolving a moral panic will trigger state actions to persecute and punish targeted groups that have little power.[5] A resolution elevates the people who are not labeled as evildoers, affirms the social order, and renews moral boundaries. Edelman (1988, 12) observed, "Problems come into discourse and therefore into existence as reinforcements of ideologies. . . . They signify who is virtuous and useful and who is dangerous or inadequate, which actions will be rewarded and which penalized." There are several types of moral panics (see Chart 12.1). Some political advocacy groups now consciously incorporate moral panics into their media strategies to manipulate political symbols, advance their political goals, and shape the public agenda.[6]

c h a r t   1 2 . 1

FOUR TYPES OF MORAL PANICS BASED ON THE CLAIMS-MAKERS

Type of Panic	Description
Interest group	An interest group or the mass media independently identifies a "folk devil" and labels the source of social anxiety.
Elite-created	Public officials consciously create a panic to repress dissent, divert attention, or assert greater social control.
Grassroots	Genuine public concern over a change in conditions is greatly magnified in the media to generate escalating attention and frenzied excitement (see Hunt 1997).
Foreign-initiated	A foreign enemy is a threat or causes some harm but triggers a larger, much longer lasting, and far more intense response than would ordinarily occur (see Ungar 1990).

As a moral panic advances a worldview and restores the moral order, it also raises the social or material position of certain people and institutions. In a mutually reinforcing process, the panic justifies giving social status, political authority, and material resources to the defenders of the moral–political order; and the defenders use the heightened status, authority, and resources to further strengthen their moral views. Moral panics often become institutionalized. They leave behind a memory, a vision of reality, and a moral language; they also leave behind new official policies, laws, and bureaucracies. These secondary or derivative results take on their own logic. Individuals advance in careers, professions create new experts, and large organizations establish specialized agencies devoted to the problem identified by the panic. Leaders of the panic present themselves as experts on the problem and elaborate on the targeted evil. This creates a basis for their authority and continued existence.[7]

As a moral panic spreads and polarizes public discussion, anyone who questions it, or who remains totally disengaged, may find they are no longer trusted. A refusal to join in the frenzy arouses a suspicion of befriending the evildoers. As the moral panic becomes overwhelming, even its leaders may no longer be able to control or stop it. Public officials may go along out of self-defense or use it as a vehicle for personal advancement. A self-interested, calculating person may assume leadership of a widespread moral outrage as a strategy to acquire more political power or wealth. Moral panics are primarily about power—the power to define public problems, to set the public agenda, to specify moral boundaries, and to assert moral authority, as well as the power to denigrate, demonize, and stigmatize categories of people or behaviors.

Example of a Moral Panic

Moral panics are reoccurring processes found in most societies. One developed in the United States during the 1980s and 1990s. The public was bombarded with stories of illegal drugs destroying the lives, devastating urban neighborhoods, breeding crime and violence, promoting illicit sex and disease, and spreading moral decay. Political leaders, law enforcement officials, and leaders of major institutions mounted a massive War on Drugs. They allocated billions of dollars to fight the war and enlisted tens of thousands of police officers, teachers, social workers, religious and community leaders as soldiers in the battle. All levels of government enacted new laws with harsh penalties. Schools, churches, and community centers joined to disseminate antidrug messages. By the late 1990s, people in many occupations faced mandatory drug tests and prisons were overflowing with antidrug law offenders.[8] While drug use had increased some, the level of increase and its timing did not match the massive outcry. Political, social, and media elites had greatly exaggerated and misrepresented conditions with dramatic claims about street crime and illegal drugs ravaging the nation, converting a legitimate concern into a national moral panic.[9]

Symbolic politics may have created the War on Drugs, but its results have been more than symbolic. The moral panic created an imbalance between the actual danger of illicit drug abuse and the enduring consequences on people's lives and the tone of politics. Harsh new laws remain in force, millions of people are in prison, billions of dollars are gone, and huge social control bureaucracies employing thousands continue to operate.

Political sociologists draw two lessons about second dimensional power and symbolic politics from America's War on Drugs of the 1980s. First, it is misleading to focus exclusively on the official reasons for a public policy and ignore the political interests involved and the symbolic dimension. The official rhetoric implies that the government operates in a pure administrative or technical environment of rational decisions, inputs, outputs, and efficiency. This rational-legal justification is only a small part of the entire picture and ignores symbolic politics.

Second, officials may continue to promote and fund ineffective programs that consistently fail to yield intended results because the programs are symbolic successes and deliver real organizational benefits. This is especially true when a targeted evildoer group of a moral panic has little power and pays the costs of programs.[10] The ineffective programs continue because they benefit powerful social groups and deliver symbolic rewards. On the other hand, highly effective programs that produce intended material results may be eliminated, not for any actual deficiencies, but due to a shift in the symbolic political environment, a realignment of political coalitions, or vocal opposition groups.[11] For example, officials cut highly effective drug rehabilitation programs at the same time they were expanding punishment policies that were documented as being ineffective or counterproductive. Because public programs express cultural messages, their expansion or elimination may depend on the cultural symbolism and moral rhetoric, not on their actual effectiveness. For example, the DARE program (see Case in Point 12.1) combines several powerful symbols: people of the community (symbol: local voluntary participation) worked with the schools and the police (symbol: guardians of social–moral order) to combat illegal drug use (symbol: a moral–social evil) and protect young children (symbol: innocent victims). The symbolic message is that parents, police, and school officials can save children from drugs if they work together locally. The program's symbolic power as a crusade against the moral evil of drugs protected it despite it being a failure.

Politics Via the Courts

You have seen (in Chapters 4 and 5) that citizens can express their political demands and desires in conventional politics through the electoral channel (e.g., voting, working for a campaign, donating money) or the nonelectoral channel (e.g., lobbying, forming policy planning think tanks, political action committees). Powerful organizations, well-organized and financed interest groups, and wealthy individuals usually have greater access to the nonelectoral channel, although ordinary citizens can mobilize into protest movements and use unconventional politics (Chapter 6). Ordinary citizens also express demands via another nonelectoral means within conventional politics—through the legal order.

CASE IN POINT 12.1   The Politics of DARE

I often see bumper stickers about the DARE (Drug Abuse Resistance Education) program on cars in my college's parking lot or as I drive in my community. DARE is a voluntary antidrug program operated in 3,000 communities in all 50 states that has reached 20 million students at a cost of over $700 million per year. A nonprofit organization operates the program, but it receives federal, state, and local funds. In the program, trained police officers make presentations to school children to warn them against taking illicit street drugs and teach them to resist peer pressure. Research has repeatedly documented that DARE is ineffective in reducing youth drug use. Yet the program remains popular with politicians, community leaders, school officials, police officers, and parents. This is irrational if the program's only purpose is what it explicitly claims—eliminating drug use among youth.

Organizationally DARE helps local officials and businesses, federal politicians, law enforcement agencies, and the schools connect with others and put forth a united front in the War on Drugs. Beyond generating feelings of mutual support and involvement, DARE is a vehicle for expressing visible opposition to illicit drug use. DARE gives political and organizational interests a visible symbolic outlet for demonstrating that they care and are doing something about a serious menace in their community. By facilitating a public display of moral virtue, the program enables people to join others in a crusade to combat a well-publicized evil. This powerful force maintains the program. Attempts to end it, such as in Salt Lake City, are very controversial and have resulted in charges of being "soft on crime."

Sources: Beckett (1994); Chambliss (1994); Janofsky (2000); and Wysong, Aniskiewicz, and Wright (1994).

Recall that in the 19th century, politics in the United States was based on a system of courts and parties (see Chapter 4), and the legal order has a degree of autonomy from society and the rest of the state (see Chapter 9). Sometimes ordinary people can express views through the courts that cannot be expressed easily otherwise. This occurs in several ways, and the courts are a site where opposing political interests sometimes clash.

Jury trials in the Anglo-American legal tradition provide ordinary citizens with democratic access to the legal order. Three examples of citizens using the legal order to oppose powerful interests are jury nullification, punitive jury awards, and class action lawsuits. **Jury nullification is the principle that citizen juries have a right to reject a law on moral grounds and vote to acquit defendants despite a law violation**. It appears in controversial cases when the public wants to show opposition to an unpopular law. For example, shortly before the Civil War Northern juries regularly refused to convict abolitionists who violated the 1850 Fugitive Slave Law, during the Vietnam War juries refused to convict draft evaders, in the 1990s some all-black juries refused to convict young black men of drug charges. Numerous jury acquittals may cause the government to back down from enforcing a specific law.[12]

Punitive damage awards are when a citizen jury rules for a person injured by the products or actions of a corporation and imposes a very large monetary award to punish the offending corporation. Ordinary working- and middle-class people tend to serve on juries and will grant sizable awards when a wealthy, powerful organization shows blatant disregard for and causes injury to ordinary citizens. Examples of punitive damages may include a child who is attacked in an unsafe building because a landlord did not obey basic safety regulations, a hospital that makes careless mistakes and causes a patient to become seriously disabled, or an employer who fails to install a safety feature on a machine that causes a worker's death. The jurors may impose multi-million dollar penalties to force the wealthy landlord, hospital, or employer to be more careful. More significantly, the penalties are a way to redress an imbalance in power and resources and send a symbolic message to powerful, wealthy interests that they should be more careful and respectful toward ordinary citizens.

Class action lawsuits occur when a large group of people are harmed by another party, usually a large corporation, and many of the injured parties join in a civil lawsuit to vindicate the rights of and gain benefits for the entire class of injured people. For example, employees have filed class action lawsuits against employers who discriminate against them, consumers have filed suits against firms (e.g., tobacco companies, airlines) for knowingly selling harmful products or fixing prices, and shareholders have filed suits against the managements of a company for making poor decisions. For large corporations, the lawsuits are difficult to win and expensive to lose. As soon as a judge approves a class action, the companies tend to settle without going to a jury because they fear that juries will favor the ordinary, less powerful plaintiff.

Some government officials, the defenders of large companies, and the very wealthy oppose citizens using the legal order to redress injuries. They want to limit the use of criminal cases decided by peers, jury nullification, large punitive awards, and class action lawsuits. For example, jury nullification hinges on judicial instructions to jurors. If a judge fails to inform juries of this right, the judge can create an ideological shield for unpopular state actions. This occurred in many Vietnam War protest trials when judges who supported the government's war policy failed to inform juries about all aspects of the law. The well-publicized "tort reform" movement is a conservative countermovement intended to restrict jury behavior and tip the balance of power in favor of corporate interests. **Tort reform is change in the legal order that will restrict large punitive damage awards and class action lawsuits against large corporations.** As a result of tort reform, the percentage of federal civil trials going before juries in the United States between 1962 and 2000 dropped from 5.4 percent to 1.4 percent, and judges are overturning jury penalties at twice the rate they did a few years ago.[13] Most likely to be overturned are jury-imposed penalties for violations of consumer protection and workplace safety laws that try to protect ordinary citizens from injury and keep large, financially powerful organizations in check. The state of Texas has led tort reform by limiting the size of damage awards. For example, when a small town jury awarded $250,000 to a father whose daughter was beheaded by an improperly medicated psychiatric patient, the Texas Supreme Court overruled the jury and gave the father nothing. When a jury imposed a $42 million penalty on an oil company that grossly violated safety standards resulting in an explosion that killed a worker, the Texas Court reduced the penalty to \$200,000. Lobbying and campaign contributions from the business community, including large billboards attacking "runaway juries" have resulted in 30 states instituting limits on the size of punitive jury awards between 1995 and 1999.[14] A leader of tort reform and limits on class action lawsuits, George W. Bush, advocated similar federal changes less than a month after he became President in 2001 and Congress cooperated.[15] As president, Bush has drawn heavily on members of the Federalist Society, a private club/organization of highly conservative lawyers that strongly opposes these and similar uses of the legal order by ordinary citizens.[16]

Dealignment

You read about the idea of a political realignment in Chapters 4, 5, and 7. Some political sociologists see a "dealignment" instead of a realignment.[17] **A dealignment is a breakdown of past alignments with a failure to create a strong, stable new coalition indicated by an exhaustion of alternatives followed by a mass withdraw from politics.**[18] As Ferguson and Rogers (1986, 29) observed, "If anything, the 1984 election gave evidence of further electoral dealignment, with voting defined ever less sharply along partisan lines and a continued decline in the capacity of conventional politics to organize and integrate electoral demand." In essence, realignment means that voting, policy, and public opinion align but along a different cleavage, while dealignment suggests that the linkage among them weakens.

Some voters may have realigned in the 1970s, but their support for the Republican Party was suppressed by a liberal shift in public opinion to accept racial equality and expanded rights for women and gays. Liberal social attitudes diffused to weaken voter support for Republicans in what otherwise might have been a major electoral realignment.[19] The dealignment argument is that the 1980s saw less of a realignment among the ordinary voters than a dramatic national policy shift due to a realignment among "political investors."

The concept of political investors helps to integrate voting patterns and policy changes of the 1980s–1990s, models of political sociology (see Chapter 3), and privileged access via campaign donations and Political Action Committees (PACs) (Chapter 5). **Political investors are politically active business and financial interests, capitalists, and ideological elites who provide major political institutions with support and give the policy agenda its basic direction.** The Policy Planning Network (PPN) and PAC are two visible mechanisms used by political investors when they make investments. In a dealignment argument, many ordinary citizens became disengaged from politics and shifted in response to a realignment among political investors. "More specifically, realignments occur when cumulative long-run changes in industrial structures (commonly interacting with a variety of short-run factors, notably steep economic downturns) polarize the business community, thus bringing together new and powerful blocks of investors with durable interests. . . . The real market for political parties is defined by major 'investors'—groups of business

"Do your owners treat you well? Mine are very kind."

firms, industrial sectors, or, in some (rare) cases, groups of voters" (Ferguson and Rogers 1986, 22–23, 45).

This process rejects a fundamental pluralist assumption that public policy will reflect changes in public opinion and voting. "For many issues . . . public policy seems unrelated to public opinion or even opposed to it" (Burstein 1981, 294). Policy and parties shifted in response to political investors, not ordinary voters. This redirection depressed voter interest and detached voters from their traditional party affiliations. *Thus, new voting patterns did not cause a change in public policies, instead voting patterns shifted in response to new policies that were imposed from above by political investors.*[20]

Two questions regarding the models of political sociology are: (1) Are capitalists unified or fragmented? and (2) Why does capitalist political unity develop?[21] The answers are that during key political junctures, a crisis develops and intraclass political divisions among the capitalists subside. This allows the class to unify and act as a cohesive political unit. In certain periods of U.S. history, such as the 1910s and 1930s, American business owners and leading investors grew cohesive and mobilized politically.[22] Such a critical political juncture occurred in the late 1970s and the early 1980s. Political sociologists largely agree that" . . . North American corporate leaders have a clear vision of their class interests and since the seventies have articulated these interests in an especially forceful way" (Clement and Myles 1994, 114). During the 1980s, class politics intensified and the capitalist class united around an ideological effort to redirect American politics.[23] Something similar occurred in Great Britain. The underlying cause was a transition to a new stage of corporate organization and global capitalism.[24] As capitalists politically mobilized, most other classes remained fragmented and demobilized. Class voting declined and social divisions within other classes (by race and cultural values) grew (see Chapter 5 on class voting). Many ordinary citizens became disenchanted and withdrew from electoral politics.

The old political investor coalition broke apart before the formation of a new regime. The New Deal regime was an electoral alignment, a set of policies, and a coalition of political investors. Large banks, multinational firms, and organized labor were the primary political investors in the New Deal coalition.[25] The coalition broke down in the 1970s for several reasons. In the 1970s the United States suffered high inflation and its deepest recession since the 1930s. The recession stalled blue-collar wages and hurt corporate profits, productivity, and economic growth for nearly a decade. Federal officials imposed wage and price controls for the first time since World War II, but U.S. multinational corporations were facing intense international competition, and the U.S. share of the world gross national product (GNP) and of world trade dropped steadily. This crisis triggered a restructuring of the international financial system for the first time since the late 1940s. Yet, these efforts did not bring a quick return to profitable economic growth. In addition, the 1968 Democratic Party convention in Chicago was a turning point—many antiwar delegates were excluded and beaten by the police. Reforms in party rules opened it to diverse new groups who pushed it ideologically leftward. In 1972, they nominated an outsider candidate, George McGovern who promised anticorporate policies. This frightened many business leaders who saw McGovern and the Democrats as mounting a radical attack on the very foundations of capitalism.

In the mid-1970s, the capitalist class mobilized politically and advanced an ideology that attacked business regulations enacted during the 1960s. As Campbell (2001, 169) noted, "during the 1970s, conservative think tanks such as the Heritage Foundation, the American Enterprise Institute, and the Manhattan Institute pioneered aggressive approaches to distilling academic knowledge into simple forms and disseminating them to the government through brief position papers and to the public through popular books, journal articles, radio and television appearances, and op-ed newspaper pieces." They promoted a neoliberal philosophy that said markets develop naturally, the pursuit of individual self-interest creates a healthy economy, and government intervention hurts market efficiency. This highlights the role of ideas for policy and state building as "elite and other actors deliberately package and frame policy ideas in order to convince each other as well as the general public that certain policy proposals constitute plausible and acceptable solutions to pressing problems" (Campbell 2001, 162).

Corporate leaders and private foundations mounted a vigorous public relations offensive with new think tanks, books and magazines, and television series designed to shift the attitudes of opinion leaders (e.g., newspaper editors, teachers, mayors). "They also launched major efforts to influence public opinions and the attitudes of other elites. Many firms sponsored studies by academics and consultants. . . . they launched a broad campaign to influence the media" (Ferguson and Rogers 1986, 86). The corporate public relations campaign fueled popular anger and redirected it away from big business and toward big government by arguing that government regulations, corporate taxes, and taxes on the rich hurt American firms in international competition and blocked investments needed for economic growth. As Page and Shapiro (1992, 374–375) summarized, "A strong public relations offensive against social and regulatory programs was conducted by experts and publicists (and politicians) financed by conservative corporate interests . . . the sheer volume of misleading rhetoric in the 1970s and early 1980s was great . . . and helped win public support for the deep tax cuts of 1981, which proved to be a bonanza for corporations and the wealthy. . . ." The campaign to shift the national policy paradigm using public relations techniques worked. "This mobilization paid dramatic dividends. The only period when business unified around a strategy of aggressive ideological conservatism . . . is also the only period when conservatives made significant advances, including both the election of 1980 and the policy triumphs of 1981" (Clawson, Neustadtl, Scott 1992, 146). By the late 1980s, the capitalist class unity began to weaken, but by that time federal policy had shifted and the New Deal coalition had broken apart[26] (see Summary 12.1).

The alternative explanations (e.g., race-based realignment, rise of New Christian Right, dealignment) for a reorientation of American politics in the 1980s are not contradictory. At a critical historical juncture, three interrelated events coincided. Republican Party activists merged the symbols of race, welfare, and taxes

---

SUMMARY 12.1	**The Impact of the Dealignment-Realignment Movement**

1. Public confidence and trust in government, partisanship, and electoral participation declined. Political sociologists debated the cause of declining public trust, but they agreed that levels of political alienation and withdrawal from electoral politics were much higher (see Lipset and Schneider 1987, Nye 1997).

2. New political movements appeared. One set promoted populist, religious, and conservative "backlash" movements against themes of the 1960s. Another set promoted a continuation of 1960s themes, including advancing women's equality, expanding minority rights, and environmental protection.

3. Federal New Deal-style redistributive programs and business regulations were dismantled and taxes on business and high-income people were sharply reduced from previous levels. Federal policy became more socially conservative and probusiness than expected based on public opinion or voting patterns alone (See Lo and Schwartz 1998).

4. During the 1990s partisan bickering intensified and political stalemates became more frequent. The power of special interests grew and specific parts of the business community received exemptions from regulations, tax breaks or subsidies, or special benefits.

to break up the New Deal coalition and win over Southern whites. Corporate leaders mobilized and invested heavily in electoral campaigns and ideological organizations that used new public relations techniques to push their message. A group of political elites organized culturally embattled conservative Christians into a political movement. During decade of the 1980s, a conservative social ideology was wed to neoliberal economic policy and the symbolic use of race, religion, and region to reorient politics. Before these three processes weakened, they had reversed many 1960s-era policies, polarized cultural debate, and moved the national political agenda ideologically rightward. Early in the twenty-first century, tax and economic policies now greatly favor large corporations and investors over workers, consumers, or lower income people. Conservative Christian religious-oriented morality has gained a strong presence in public schools, the media, and government offices. Opposition to some forms of gender/racial equality is now legitimate in public discourse. The antidrug moral panic of the 1980s that was part of the process of shifting in the entire political framework has been overtaken by an ongoing anti-Islamic War on Terrorism.

Military State and Society

Most discussions of the modern state build on Max Weber's thesis that the state upholds a ". . . monopoly of the legitimate use of physical force in the enforcement of its order" (1978, 54). In previous chapters, you have seen the importance of war-making for nation-state development (Chapter 2), the rise of a welfare-warfare state within U.S. political institutional development (Chapter 4), the militarization of domestic policing (Chapter 9), and the military as an aspect of corporate welfare business policy and as part of an "iron triangle" (Chapter 10). The military is an important institution and aspect of the state. Now we will focus on how the military relates to the larger economy and society.

The citizen-soldier idea was a major feature in the spread of democracy and was critical in the American and French revolutions. It was manifest in mass citizen armies that opened the officer corps to all social classes and groups. Civilians "civilized" the military and intergrated it with the rest of society, and military service attached citizens directly to the state. In the United States, military service has been a criterion for generous welfare-state benefits (see Chapter 11). Conscription, or the military draft, brought all sectors of society into the military, although the children of upper-income people often avoided service. An all-volunteer military, as the United States adopted in 1973, is part of a historical decline in the mass armed force since 1945. An all-volunteer military raises issues for democracy. First, it separates the military from the rest of society, fostering a military organization, culture, and set of values that are distinct from civilian society. Second, it makes recruitment into both the officer corps and enlisted service personnel less broadly representative of the entire society. There is less a danger that the officer corps will stage a military coup than that they will become ideologically separated, a source of political division, and a distinct pressure group within the state. Over the years, the U.S. military has remade itself and remained open to new social and technological trends. It has actively recruited and promoted racial minorities and women and has used technical training and education benefits to attract new recruits from the working class. These trends, plus a large citizen militia (i.e., national guard) and reserve armed forces, has enabled it to retain the citizen-solider tradition.[27]

Political sociologists have examined the political power of the military. Harold Lasswell (1902–1978) developed the idea of a "garrison" state in the 1940s in response to the spread of fascist regimes, the Soviet Union's totalitarianism, and World War II.[28] **A garrison state is when military leaders dominate the state, and the state and society are reorganized around the primary objective of being prepared for continual warfare**. Lasswell argued that the military would grow and expand to overpower civilian areas of the state because of technological advances in weaponry and persistent international tensions. The "specialists on violence" would develop managerial and technological skills and be placed in positions of power and be in control of society. They would redirect society around the goal of constant readiness for war, militarizing all social institutions and dissolving the distinction between civilian and military spheres. Although Lasswell's idea was dropped, in the 1950s, C. Wright Mills included the military in his description of the power elite (see Chapter 3).

Echoing concerns outlined by C. Wright Mills in the *Power Elite,* President Dwight D. Eisenhower in his 1961 farewell address warned against the influence of a "military industrial complex" (MIC).[29] He feared that the intimate relationship between large corporations and the Department of Defense forged during World War II and intensified in the Cold War era would drain tax funds and distort U.S. economic and military priorities. Large defense industry firms had become financially dependent on securing lucrative military contracts, and they hired many ex-military officials to be corporate executives or consultants. At the same time, business needs shaped plans for new weapons development and the location of military bases. **The military industrial complex is a network of people, military organizations, and defense industry suppliers that developed a shared interest**.

The MIC originated in World War II and its immediate aftermath. The war had sidetracked New Deal social–economic reform programs, and its "mobilization not only had a decisive impact on the outcome of the war, it transformed the U.S. economy" according to Gregory Hooks (1991b, 2). During the war, civilian goods production plummeted, and the federal government provided investment funds, technical direction, and a market for military goods. Defense spending grew from 40 percent to over 90 percent of all federal spending between 1940 and 1945. During the immediate post-war years, government-owned factories and facilities provided a windfall to the defense firms that purchased $5.7 billion worth of surplus property (e.g., factories, warehouses, raw materials, trucks, port facilities) from the government for $1.2 billion.[30] For example, the federal government wanted the steel industry to expand to meet wartime needs, but the industry refused to invest in new plants and equipment saying it would not be profitable. The government altered tax laws to help, built 29 new open-hearth furnaces and 17 electric furnaces, and provided more than two-thirds of new investment funds during wartime. After the war, the steel industry acquired the property at a huge discount. During wartime, the steel industry made record profits, and studies subsequently showed that it would have been able to expand without government help.[31]

World War II left a legacy of an enlarged government and military-defense establishment, a closer business-government relationship, and a stronger industrial defense sector in the economy. The post-war transfer of government resources boosted the big business sector. As of June 1946, 70 percent of all surplus property was sold to the 250 largest U.S. corporations.[32] The business-government ties grew closer during the Korean War, and firms supplying the war effort were likely to grow into corporate giants during the last half of the twentieth century.[33]

World War II had reoriented state goals around building industrial expansion and military defense (see Case in Point 12.2). Shortly after the war, at a critical juncture in the late 1940s, an alliance of conservatives, anti-New Deal Republicans, and Southern Democrats, gained political influence in Congress. They defeated a proposal for expanded post-war state economic planning to achieve full employment with expanded social-labor benefits. Instead, they dismantled existing state economic planning capacity or transferred it to the Pentagon.[34] For example, they removed references to "full employment" from the 1946 Employment Act and replaced them with affirmations to "free enterprise." They replaced New Deal egalitarian priorities for the state to assist workers, consumers, the elderly, and others with new goals of assisting the business community. This was part of a business-led campaign that continued into the 1950s. It pit an American Way of Life organized around free-enterprise, church, and private business leadership against the evils of godless communism, labor unions, and collectivist economic ideas.[35]

The MIC continues into the present via three routes: (1) government defense purchases and investments, (2) the circulation of personnel between the military and defense-industry corporations, and (3) indirect foreign policy reinforcement. In the first 20 years of the Cold War, defense spending remained at roughly 10 percent of the GNP.[36] During this era the aluminum, aircraft, steel, electronics, communications, chemical, oil, and energy industries grew under Pentagon-directed plans, investments, and purchases. These industries are in the monopoly sector of the economy (i.e., large-size, limited competition, high profits, capital intensive, heavily unionized labor). Not surprisingly, concentration among the largest industrial firms rapidly grew in this era.[37] When the Cold War ended in 1989 many people expected a large "peace dividend" from reductions in military expenditures. Between 1978 and 1986, military spending had increased and was at a peacetime peak. Military expenditures declined only slightly, and the promised peace dividend never materialized. As Markusen (1998, 145) noted, "A plethora of organizations—corporations, trade associations, trade unions, local and state governments—have organized to defend federal military receipts in the 1990s." The political forces surrounding the defense industry maintained a large system of defense contracting, often producing weapons or equipment that the U.S. military said it did not want or need. After

CASE IN POINT 12.2 | **The Pentagon and the Pattern of U.S. Industrial Expansion**

The rise of the warfare state after World War II meant, "The shift from defense to national security blurred the difference between times of peace and times of war and put pressure on the U.S. state to manage society more intensively at all times" (Hooks 1990b, 366). During the Cold War era (1949–1989), the U.S. military establishment (i.e., the Pentagon) had significant autonomy within the federal government, and it was the biggest sector of federal spending. For example, between 1950 and 1970, spending for military areas never fell below 40 percent of total federal spending, and it exceeded half of federal spending in many years. Military bases provided local jobs and purchased local services across the United States, providing an important economic boost to local communities. In addition to the military's size and its relative freedom from the rest of government and society, its spending and purchases had a significant impact on the pattern of American industrial expansion. Unlike some other advanced nations, the United States never has had a peacetime *industrial policy,* in which the central government directs how key sectors of private industry will invest and expand their production, but the Pentagon created a de facto industrial policy in the name of "national security," especially in high-tech and energy industries. During the 1950s and 1960s, the U.S. military and related departments employed as many as 30 percent of all U.S. scientists and engineers. Military support for research and development, its significant purchasing power, and its involvement in production planning affected key industries, including the aircraft, communications, and computers industries. The military affected many other areas as well. National defense was part of the rationale for the construction of the huge interstate highway system, and it affected educational curriculum from elementary through graduate school.

Source: See Hooks (1990b, 1991b).

the Cold War ended, military contractors remained profitable and sought additional government funds for research and exporting weapons overseas. For example, the federal government provided about 80 percent of the research and development funds in the aerospace industry spending. In 1995, the Aerospace Industries Association won over $7 billion in government subsidies to increase its exports to other nations.[38]

Whether it is closing an unneeded military base or keeping an unwanted weapon in production, political pressures to protect jobs, provide local economic development, and maintain corporate profits have overridden the attempts by military planners to create a more efficient, effective national defense. For example, the military has questioned the $200 million B-1 bomber since it began production in 1988. The plane was vulnerable to attack, a 1991 study found it could not fly in snow, and recurrent engine problems prevented its use in the 1991 Persian Gulf War. When the Pentagon tried to phase it out in 2001, Congressional representatives, corporate interests, and communities fearing a loss of local jobs lobbied to continue it. Ironically, the same politicians who most strongly defend retaining very expensive and noneffective weapons or military facilities soley to benefit local constituents also claim to favor cutting "wasteful" government spending, lowering taxes, and building a strong, effective national defense.[39]

C. Wright Mills saw the military industrial complex primarily in terms of an interchange of elite personnel. This still occurs. For example, five of eight members on the board of directors of Alliant Techsystems, an aerospace and defense firm, are retired military officers or government officials. This is not unique to the defense contractors. Ex-ambassadors sit on the boards of firms from countries where they served, and regulatory agency officials sit on the boards of firms in the industries they regulated. A 2003 study found that 38 ex-military generals or admirals, 82 ex-members of the U.S. Congress, 32 ex-members of the cabinet, 25 ex-state governors, and four ex-vice presidents sit on the boards of directors of the nation's leading corporations.[40]

U.S. foreign policy also reinforced and expanded the MIC. Major foreign policy objectives in the Cold War Era (1949–1989) were to contain communism, prevent its expansion into new geographic areas, and suppress leftist political unrest and movements. As part of the containment policy, the U.S. built a global network of military bases and strengthened its allies, both economically and militarily. Foreign policy and defense officials believed that allies with stable governments, strong military forces, and vibrant capitalist economies that promised rising living standards would ultimately defeat communism.

The Cold War foreign policy objective simultaneously helped the U.S. business community in general and the defense industry sector of it in particular. To strengthen the market economies of allied nations (sometimes called the "free world"), U.S. officials encouraged and protected the investments and loans from U.S. banks and corporations and from U.S-dominated international agencies (e.g., World Bank, International Monetary Fund). Allied governments and firms were expected or required to purchase U.S. goods. At the same time, rules on importing goods from allied nations into the United States were relaxed. In addition, the U.S. strengthened the military capability of allies by signing defense treaties, locating U.S. military bases in allied nations, providing allies with military training, and selling allies weapons that were made by United States companies.

U.S. firms benefited from the foreign policy in several ways. When U.S. banks and corporations invested in allied nations, they got higher profit rates than were available domestically. When allies bought military weapons, the sales and profits of the U.S. defense firms rose. Under trade policies, allies bought technologically sophisticated and high-profit items from the United States. In exchange, U.S. firms imported raw materials or labor-intensive, low-technology, and low-profit items from allies.[41] Military expenditures stimulated U.S. economic growth in the 1947–1976 period, and military spending within the United States also appears to have influenced domestic voting patterns.[42] Thus, for at least 50 years, the MIC has been integrated into the U.S. economy and many federal policies.

Advanced nations vary in their commitment to build and maintain military forces. The state uses the military to project power outside its borders or to quell civil war. Among advanced nations today, the United States spends more per citizen and allocates a greater percentage of its economy to military spending than any other nation (see Table 12.1). This is lower than nations that engaged in ongoing, permanent, domestic or international military conflicts. The top 10 nations

TABLE 12.1 Military Expenditures by Advanced Nations in (2000 or the Closest Year Available)		
Country	Military Spending as Percentage of GDP	Military Spending per Capita
Austria	0.8	$183.25
Australia	2.0	$475.78
Belgium	1.4	$299.43
Canada	1.1	$246.39
Czech Republic	2.1	$116.04
Denmark	1.4	$460.00
Finland	2.0	$347.25
France	2.57	$778.03
Germany	1.38	$466.06
Greece	4.91	$574.90
Hungary	1.75	$107.20
Ireland	0.9	$180.27
Italy	1.64	$349.99
Japan	1.0	$321.12
Korea (South)	2.8	$264.88
Netherlands	1.5	$404.54
New Zealand	1.2	$131.93
Norway	2.13	$687.94
Poland	1.71	$90.61
Portugal	2.2	$127.53
Spain	1.15	$214.59
Sweden	2.1	$495.13
Switzerland	1.0	$348.95
United Kingdom	2.32	$530.30
United States	3.2	$986.20

Sources: http://www.nationmaster.com/ and CIA Factbook, 2002.

in the percentage of GDP devoted to military spending are North Korea, Angola, Eritrea, Saudi Arabia, Ethiopia, Oman, Qatar, Israel, Jordan, and Maldives.

In several nations, military elites have played a modernizing role. In nations such as Brazil, Egypt, Japan and Turkey, the military was a highly disciplined and educated force separate from traditional elites. Military leaders seized control of the state and "modernized" the state (i.e., introduced reforms to limit industrialization, instituted land reform, curtailed the power of religious leaders). They sought to create a modern, secular society (see World View 12.1).

In sum, the military is more than simply a means to maintain order or defend territorial borders; it has had several significant roles in shaping the modern nation-state. At times, the military has been a way to expand democracy, at times

WORLD VIEW 12.1   The Military and Revolutions from Above

In several nations such as Brazil, Egypt, Japan, Peru, and Turkey, military elites allied with a group of top state officials to overthrow the government in a brief civil war and abolish the power of the old aristocracy to pursue a national program of industrialization and modernization (i.e., Western models of rational, secular organization). Ellen Kay Trimberger (1978) analyzed these revolutions and identified the following five features:

1. They were initiated by top military leaders and some top state officials of the old regime.
2. Mass participation was limited, and military leaders opposed mass uprisings when they broke out.
3. The extra-legal takeover of the state did not involve large-scale violence, executions, or emigration.
4. The new leaders began pragmatic, incremental, and methodological changes not driven by ideology.
5. The changes of the new government destroyed the old aristocracy's economic and political base.

These "revolutions from above" were carried out by the military leadership and parts of the upper bureaucracy that were not too closely allied with the old upper class. Thus,

they were situations in which the state developed autonomy from the dominant class of society. The goal of the military officials was to strengthen their nation, either in response to a foreign threat or to end a position of relative weakness. They undertook revolutionary actions in a context of other nations that were more advanced or had moved rapidly ahead of their nation. In short, they saw their own nation as weak and had a vision of how to strengthen and modernize it, but they felt blocked from implementing changes to strengthen the nation because of the deep-rooted power of an old aristocracy or upper class.

While the military leaders opposed the old upper class, they also did not want to involve the masses of peasants or urban workers in a self-conscious, organized movement. Rather than mobilize or develop a social base of support among the downtrodden masses, the revolutionary leaders forged compromises with segments of the old upper class after they had achieved power. For example, in both the revolutions of Meiji, Japan (1868) and Ataturk, Turkey (1923), the military elite that initiated a revolution was somewhat autonomous from the old established economic elite, had become politicized around the goal of nation-building, felt blocked by an entrenched old upper class, and faced an international situation with uncertainties.

it acted alone to change the direction of the state, and at times state officials or others used it to advance their own objectives, but its significance cannot be denied.

Crimes of the State

Beyond using the military, state officials have many alternative mechanisms for maintaining order, cultivating support, harming opponents, or suppressing popular dissent. They can provide positive incentives by allocating public jobs and giving promotions in a patronage system (see Chapter 4) or targeting benefits or social services (e.g., access to jobs or housing, bonus payments) based on various criteria, including loyalty and conformity (see Chapters 10 and 11). They can punish or harm opponents or disfavored groups by mounting a witch hunt (Chapter 6) against them, targeting restrictions on access to rewards or services (e.g., not improving roads, reducing public services like garbage pick up), or using petty harassment (e.g., frequent police stops, Internal Revenue Service tax audits). These "state social control" activities (see Chapter 9) can blur into active attempts to gain power, punish opponents, or suppress popular expression that cross the line of legality.[43]

State officials can use their positions of authority to criminalize expressions of dissent, protest, or challenges to their power. **Political crimes are peaceful, legitimate protest actions or challenges to state authority that state officials have made illegal to limit dissent**. State officials legally control or limit dissenters, protesters, or challengers by criminalizing the opposition, often by enacting new laws or applying vague existing laws.[44] In addition to creating new specific laws, officials often use conventional laws against political challengers. Austin Turk (1982, 40–41) argued that, "Conventional crime laws have been used politically wherever subjects have struggled against the terms of their subjection— economic, racial, or political. . . . Additionally, in a gray area between conventional crime laws and explicit political crime laws, specialized bodies of law have been created defining accepted 'etiquettes' of labor relations, race relations, and conventional politics." Laws against political crime are usually vague and are applied and interpreted in a looser manner than are conventional laws.[45]

State authorities sometimes label political opponents as "criminal" and not "political" in order to delegitimatize opponents. They also claim the opposition is rooted in individual abnormalities (e.g., maladjusted childhood, mentally unstable, low intellect, poor moral judgment) instead of being based on legitimate political reasons. The officials imply that accepting established political authority is normal, and only abnormal fanatics would challenge them. By using their authoritative position to influence the social boundaries of right and wrong or acceptable and unacceptable, state officials have an advantage that their opponents lack.

Most people see crime as an illegal act by an individual person, group (e.g., gang, mafia), or organization (e.g., company), but the state itself can also commit crime. **State-organized crime involves official government policy that violates its own laws, the laws of other nations, or international law**. Ross (1998, 332) listed state-organized crime including, "cover ups, disinformation, unaccountability, corruption, violation of domestic and/or international law . . . [and actions] perceived by the majority of the population as illegal and socially harmful." It is not the lone corrupt public official who embezzles funds, accepts a bribe, or plots an illegal act for personal gain; rather, it is a conscious, systematic policy of illegal acts to defend, protect, or advance the power and position of a group of state officials, a public agency, or the state as an institution by causing financial, social, personal, or symbolic harm or a loss of power for a social group, an organization, or other elites.

State-organized crimes can be directed against the state's own citizens or people in other countries. Actions committed beyond a state's borders usually encounter less domestic opposition because officials claim they are advancing the national interest. Such actions include covert (i.e., secret) illegal acts to achieve a specific objective (e.g., assassinate a leader as a method of weakening

chart 12.2

TYPES OF DOMESTIC STATE-ORGANIZED CRIME

- Officials illegally limit political participation, deny legal rights, or refuse to deliver required services to a targeted group. For example, in the 1960s, Southern officials prohibited African Americans from serving on juries and made it impossible for them to vote.

- Officials illegally target other state officials or political elites for harm. For example, Republican Party officials in President Richard Nixon's administration hired people to burglarize the Watergate offices of the Democratic Party during Nixon's reelection campaign.

- Officials order law enforcement agencies to illegally monitor, intimidate, or harass citizens who are engaged in legal, peaceful dissent or protest. For example, officials order police to stop members of environmental protest groups to check for driving violations or drug possession and to search their homes, listen to their phones, and read their mail.

- Officials illegally use their positions to advance their collective self-interests. For example, elected state officials have government employees illegally work for their reelection and misuse state resources (e.g., government cars, office equipment, postage) for their reelection campaigns.

- Officials provide financial or other support, including passive acceptance, to nongovernment groups that engage in illegal acts. For example, officials who oppose abortion knowingly allow an antiabortion group to block entrances, vandalize, and beat up people entering an abortion clinic.

a foreign country, supply weapons to a group that will overthrow a government). For example, seventeenth century England encouraged piracy and smuggling to accomplish its political-military goals. From the 1950s to 1970s the U.S. Central Intelligence Agency (CIA) organized and sponsored assassinations and coups against elected governments in Iran, Guatemala, Chile, and elsewhere as part of a policy to block proleftist and anticapitalist forces.[46] In the 1980s, the Reagan administration supported the "contras" who tried to overthrow the elected government of Nicaragua, and illegally provided weapons to Iran in exchange for U.S. hostages. State-organized domestic crimes are complicated, because the state is the primary institution that labels acts as criminal and enforces law. This makes it easier to keep illegal actions secret or to lie about illegal activities (see Chart 12.2).

THREE CONTINUING CHALLENGES

Globalization

Globalization is a hotly contested term and an idea that is still evolving. It may well be the single most important social-political-economic process taking place at the onset of the twenty-first century. We will not get into the complications of trying to offer a definitive definition, but we need to expand on our working notion of it from Chapter 2. There we defined it as, "the rapid growth of internationally connected economic, social and cultural relations spurred by new communication, transportation, and shifts in the world economy." David Held et al. (1999) identified four dimensions of the globalization process that fill in or build the core idea of interconnections around the world.

- The first dimension is *extensiveness.* This means various networks are widening their spans of reach around the globe. The networks can be political, military, commercial, social, cultural, religious, humanitarian, and so forth. They are increasingly spread to cross national borders and appear in many different distant nations.
- A second dimension is greater *interconnectedness.* This implies layers on top of the extensive network. It refers to increasing the degree of connections in terms of number and diversity of links that bind together a network. Instead of a single thread or linkage, they are numerous, overlapping, and of multiple types (e.g., personal, financial, cultural).
- The third dimension is an increased *velocity* of global flows. Velocity has to do with speed. Global velocity simply means greater speed (and less time) crossing national borders and going to many distant nations.
- The last dimension is *disparate impact.* This one is a little different than the other dimensions. Unlike the others, it refers to the result or consequence of the others in combination. Global impact means that the choices, alternatives, power relations, and so forth in one particular geographic location are increasingly likely to be affected by, and to affect, the choices, alternatives, and power relations elsewhere. The elsewhere can be across national borders and in distant nations.

In summary, globalization is an historical process of growing interconnections formed around the world in terms of extensiveness, velocity, and impact. The span of cross-border networks, the density and diversity of linkages, the rate of change and speed of flows across distances, and the mutual effects that events and conditions in different locations have on one another have all rapidly grown in the past two decades. In short, the world is becoming smaller. It is increasingly difficult to ignore events, people, money, ideas, power relations, conflicts, and so forth beyond national borders. Globalization is so contentious and confusing because it is still in-process and can go in alternative directions. Opposing interests that seek to push it back or move it toward certain directions are actively using symbols and language to persuade others to support their positions.

A major idea you have learned in this book is that the nation-state arose during the transition from feudalism to capitalism. By the middle of the twentieth century, the nation-state grew to become the premier institution that organized people, power, resources, and territory around the world. The nation-state has two sides. Its political-institutional form is the state, and its cultural-people side is the nation. Many issues discussed in this book regarding power, hegemony, and struggle centered on the state and occurred within a single nation.

Yet political events within a nation are connected to global and international processes and the position of a nation in the world economy. We did not explore the linkages between a nation's position in the world system and national political dynamics in detail, but we cannot ignore them.[47] One example can illustrate the connection. Schwartzman (1998, 159) observed, "In the last several decades, the world has experienced a democratic revival. In 1974, only 39 countries (25% of the world's independent nations) were democratic. By 1996, 66% were using elections to choose their top leaders. Dismantling totalitarian regimes and replacing them with democratic ones are momentous societal transformations." Political sociologists asked, What caused the transitions to democracy? Were they internal to a nation or were they global, world-system factors? Korzeniewicz and Awbrey (1992) suggested that position in the world economy or world system was crucial. They divided 90 nations into three categories based on world system theory: (1) core (i.e., advanced, highly-industrialized, rich nations), (2) semi-periphery (i.e., medium-income, industrializing nations that are tied to core nations), and (3) periphery (i.e., low income nations with low levels of industrialization, that often only supply raw materials or agricultural products). Next, they looked at whether the level of democracy was high, medium or low in each of three time periods—1970, 1980, and 1990. They discovered that almost all the "transitions to democracy" occurred in nations that were in the same position in the world economy, and most moved from a low to a medium level of democracy (see Table 12.2). Results such as these suggest that a nation's position in the world economy is very important for understanding major domestic political events.

Debate continues over when exactly globalization began and its direction, but observers increasingly agree that we are witnessing a historic transition similar in magnitude to the dissolution of feudalism and the rise of industrialism-capitalism that occurred 300–400 years ago. You may recall that the transition process triggered numerous other significant changes, including the rise of the nation-state and the spread of democracy. If observers are correct, and what we now call globalization is the start of a similar type of transition, we can anticipate that it will bring about profound changes in the forms of the state, organization of peoples-cultures-territories, and fundamental modes of exercising power and being politically involved.

Globalization is having, and it will continue to have, many effects on the social, political, and economic conditions in specific countries. It can raise or lower the relative power that groups and organizations have within a society, and it can diffuse political forms, such as democratization. It can also introduce cultural–political ideas from one society into others. As discussed earlier in the book, globalization may also affect politics as transnational organizations and collectivities assume a larger role (e.g., transnational corporations and banks, international institutions like the World Bank or World Trade Organization, social protest movements).

At the same time that globalization signals a larger impact on local life from the outside or external forces, it also signals that local events take on wider ram-

| TABLE 12.2 | World Economic Position and Type of Regime from 1970 to 1990 |

Degree of Democracy by Decade	Position in World Economy			Total
	Periphery	Semiperiphery	Core	
1970				
Low	35	25	2	62
Medium	2	2	–	4
High	2	5	17	24
Total	39	32	19	90
1980				
Low	34	22	2	58
Medium	3	7	–	10
High	2	3	17	22
Total	39	32	19	90
1990				
Low	32	5	2	39
Medium	5	21	–	26
High	2	6	17	25
Total	39	32	19	90

Source: Korzeniewicz and Awbrey (1992).

ifications. In short, globalization is a two-way street, often summarized in the phase "global-local." Globalization mean that distant events will have a larger impact than in the past, and that local events may have a broader effect as well. Globalization simultaneously creates new opportunities and unexpected threats, new bridges and higher barriers. As new political opportunities and bridges across political divides emerge and new threats and barriers to political mobilization and organization appear, the focus of political sociology will change from its previous almost exclusive focus on the nation-state.

It is premature to declare the demise of the nation-state. However, its place in politics will undoubtedly change with globalization. Exactly how, when, and by what means are the real questions. Since the nation-state has shaped "everything political" for well over a century, and because it defined how societies are organized, as the role of the nation-state changes everything political will also change. As Robinson (2001, 190) stated, "globalization poses a challenge to theoretical work on the state." Recall that the entire framework of political sociology in the classic era was replaced by a tidal wave of new theories, concepts, and issues in the 1970s–1980s. The shift in the field of political sociology to address globalization fully will be larger. Peter

Evans (1997, 64) has warned that the danger of globalization is less that the nation-state will disappear than that "meaner, more repressive ways of organizing the state's role will be accepted." It also raises the question of how the people and leaders of different nations will respond to changing conditions wrought by globalization (see Case in Point 12.3).

There are competing ideas regarding how to think about the international context and globalization. For example, the world culture or world society approach outlined by John Meyer et al. (1997) or Ronald Inglehart (1984) holds that nation-state development will be shaped by worldwide cultural processes.[48] Meyer and associates argued that many features of the contemporary nation-state derive from models elsewhere in the world that spread through communication and organizational linkages among nation-states. Inglehart sees rising material conditions leading to a major, worldwide shift in basic cultural values. In these theories, international pressure on nation-states does not originate in a conflict-filled world economic-political system[49] or from warfare and economic-political competition among nation-states;[50] rather, it is due to mutual modeling. Likewise, states do not create their form and functions internally, but borrow extensively from one another. For example, once a few key nations adopt a particular innovation (e.g., human rights), it tends to spread quickly until most nations have adopted some form of it. These external pressures can coincide with domestic internal pressures to create particular political forms or actions in a nation-state.

You may feel that a world-scale transition as huge as globalization that will last over a century is so much bigger than you are that there is little you can do about it, so you might disregard it. Do not be fooled. It is highly likely that globalization will have many effects on your daily life, and on the lives of your family members, your friends, neighbors, coworkers, and children. Globalization will change how politics operates—power, state, hegemony, and struggle—during your lifetime. Whether it comes in the form of war, terrorism, cultural fusion, foreign competition, financial markets, intercultural communication, immigration, or international travel, evidence of globalization is everywhere, and the meaning of national borders and being a citizen is in question.

Inclusion

Inclusion means, "bringing people, groups, ideas, or behaviors into the polity." The larger theme of inclusion goes beyond bringing something into the polity; it is to cross a boundary or border. As Michèle Lamont and Virág Molnár (2002, 167) noted, "In recent years, the idea of 'boundaries' has come to play a key role in important new lines of scholarship across the social sciences." The boundaries can be physical-territorial, political, cultural, social, and so forth. They are the foundation of creating and sustaining inequalities or differences of class, race-ethnicity, gender, religion, nationality, and sexuality. A broader way to see inclusion (and its counterpart, exclusion) involves not only thinking of crossing boundaries, but also seeing how boundaries are created, maintained, contested, or dissolved. Thus, the issue of inclusion is more than crossing over, or going

CASE IN POINT 12.3   Global Leadership, but in What Direction?

Early in the twenty-first century, the United States is undisputedly the richest and most powerful nation in the world. With the forces of globalization and an increasing interdependence in the world, we can examine how this nation is balancing its own interest as a nation-state with its position relative to the rest of the global community.

From the 1980s until 2000, the United States was far behind in paying its dues to the United Nations and not at the top of the list, in either absolute or relative terms, of international aid donors. Although the United States remains below all other nations in the percent of national income going to foreign aid, because of its very high income and enormous size, it is now the leader in absolute foreign aid spending.

On several other international issues, the United States has actively promoted its own narrow national interests, or fought to protect its sovereignty, corporate interests, or the values of powerful groups in the United States, rather than seeing itself as a member of the world community.

1. The United States has blocked sex education and family planning, and pressured the United Nations to adopt abstinence, even though abstinence programs are not as effective in stopping the spread of sexually transmitted diseases, such as HIV.

2. Officials from 150 governments laid groundwork at the World Health Organization for a new global treaty to control tobacco use and stamp out adolescent smoking. The treaty was blocked by the United States in 2001 on the grounds it would harm the "free speech" for American tobacco companies.

3. The United States refused to sign the 1997 international ban on the use of antipersonnel landmines that kill or maim 15,000 to 20,000 people each year, mostly civilians. The only nations other than the United States outside the treaty are Russia, China, Iran, Libya, North Korea, Burma, Syria, and Cuba.

4. In 2002, the United States renounced its obligation to work with the International Criminal Court. It would be the world's first human rights court and provide legal protection against human rights abuses, war crimes, and genocide. Over 60 nations, including most U.S. allies (e.g., Canada and members of the European Union) had signed. The George W. Bush administration took the unusual step of unsigning the international treaty that had been signed by President Clinton in 2000.

5. In 2001, the United States announced it was backing out of the 1997 Kyoto Accord, a treaty that it had previously signed with 54 other nations. The agreement was designed to limit emissions by industrial nations of greenhouse gases, which most scientists believe cause global warming.

6. In November 1989, 190 nations ratified and adopted the Convention on the Rights of the Child. Only two nations, the United States and Somalia, have not ratified it yet. The treaty addressed the human rights of children and set minimum standards for the protection of their rights, including opposition to child soldiers. As recently as April 25, 2003, the United State restated its opposition, largely in defense of parental rights and punishments, including the death penalty, for acts committed while a person was under 18.

Sources: "After U.S. Objects, World Fails to Agree to Curb Smoking Ads," *New York Times* November 29, 2001. "U.S. Renounces Obligations to International Court," *New York Times,* May 6, 2002. "The Court the U.S. Doesn't Want," *New York Review of Books* 45, (no. 18). (November 19, 1998), pp. 45–46. "Oh, and Somalia too," *Economist,* May 4, 2002. Also see "Convention on the Rights of the Child," http://www.unicef.org/crc/crc.html. For April 25, 2003 statement see http://www.humanrights-usa.net/statements/0425Child.html. Human Rights Watch on Landmines http://www.hrw.org/campaigns/mines/1999/.

inside or outside a boundary; it is an issue of social divisions, differences, hierarchies, and inequalities.

We use various types of borders and boundaries to organize the categories of our lives and our relations with other people. For example, social boundaries separate our lives into home, work, or school; they separate private and personal life from public life, work from play, male from female, and so forth. We use boundaries as tools in interpersonal and group relations. People struggle over social-cultural-political boundaries to define "us" and "them" and who we are. In a sense, inclusion, exclusion, and boundaries become central to issues of identity. They go to the heart of questions such as Who am I? Who are you? Are we the same or different?

Once constructed, boundaries help to define us; they help us create community and define people as belonging to distinct nations, races, cultures, and so forth. Boundaries can be used to include some but exclude others by making lateral (i.e., difference in degree or type but essentially equal) or hierarchical (i.e., ones of rank or inequality in power, wealth, opportunity, life chances) distinctions. As discussed earlier in the book, inclusion and exclusion are central to many political processes and are at the heart of many political struggles.

Recall that a critical event in the rise of the nation-state was for the state to reinforce its territorial borders and to highlight the differences among nations. As the nation-state created boundaries, it excluded or defined as different the people, cultures, ideas, language, religion, and institutions of other nations—they were foreign or alien. Simultaneously, the nation-state built internal unity; it homogenized the culture and population on the inside. The state standardized official school knowledge and language, and it built transportation, commercial, communication, and similar systems within a nation. The state brought together the people of a nation. Thus, boundaries and borders help to define commonality and to create an identity. When a person says, "I am an American," "I am a Canadian," "I am Swiss," "I am a Brazilian," or "I am Japanese," she/he is, in part, affirming an identity based on inclusion within national cultural–political boundaries. The historical-political organization of the globe into separate nations created borders/boundaries; and the new boundaries sparked the parallel processes of inclusion and exclusion.

Some issues of the inclusion-exclusion processes include the permeability of borders, crossing borders, and being on the frontier between two borders. These issues become more concrete when we see the issue of inclusion in cases for a person living on both sides of a border, such as a border between two racial groups (biracial), two genders (bisexual), two cultures (bicultural), or two nation-states (dual citizenship). In terms of the nation-state, the issue becomes one of being included as a citizen of one nation or culture alone, or being at the intersection or the border between nations and sharing the identities of more than one. As Wilson and Donnon (1998, 13) remarked, "Citizenship, state nationalism, and various other social ties draw border people away from the border, inward to the center of power and culture within the state." Thus, pressures exist to be included on one side of a border alone and to not transgress or straddle it. Yet full inclusion on one side often means exclusion from the other side.

Most political sociologists discuss events and issues within a nation-state. Sometimes they consider relations among several nation-states. However, as the nation-state changes with globalization, the boundaries are shifting. The boundaries that once separated states (e.g., political institutions, power relations) or nations (e.g., peoples, cultures) are changing, both around the globe and inside nation-states. Some boundaries are dissolving, some are being newly created, and the forms of boundaries are changing. As social-political-cultural boundaries change, so do processes of inclusion and exclusion. Since inclusion-exclusion and borders are major political dynamics, as they undergo change, the study of their politics must also change.

Inclusion is a broad idea that touches on many issues throughout the book. For example, you can ask whether you, or any group in society, is included or excluded from being a full citizen, having a say or vote in decisions, receiving social welfare benefits, and so forth. Many political institutions, power relations, and organizations (e.g., movements, political parties) are built around including some certain types of people, behaviors, organizations, or ideas, but keeping out or excluding others. Creating, maintaining, and violating various boundaries (e.g., legal, moral, political, economic) that delineate who is to be included or excluded can be a major source of political conflict.

Boundaries that mark inclusion-exclusion are essential in the process of maintaining most forms of inequality and domination. The boundary may be visible (e.g., gender, race, national origin) or invisible (e.g., subtle prejudice based on religious or political belief), and it may be informal or formal (e.g., established in law). Some people believe that the boundaries are necessary, just, and fair, and therefore should be defended and preserved. Others may see the same boundaries as unjust and believe they should be dismantled. Once people develop strong beliefs that the boundaries, and their inclusion or exclusion are just or unjust, they organize politically to be true to and realize their beliefs. The shifting and changing of borders may bring new opportunities, stimulate creativity, and increase excitement for many people, but it also increases fear, anger, and anxiety for others.

Integrity

Like globalization and inclusion, integrity is an idea that has a lot of baggage. It has three parts or dimensions. The first is incorruptibility; this implies being firm and not changing or wavering in adherence to a code—especially a moral, ideological, or artistic code. It means to hold true to core beliefs and values and to uphold their principles or standards. A second dimension is unimpairment. This implies being without a fault or weakness and maintaining unbroken and unblemished continuity. Lastly, integrity implies completeness. It is the quality of being undivided in devotion to an entire set of principles. In short, **integrity is when a person is fully honest and true to himself/herself and to his/her colleagues, friends, and family, nation, and belief system**. People or organizations without integrity tend to lie, cheat, deceive, manipulate, and/or misinform.

Political integrity is more evident in the area of political symbols, beliefs, words, and ideas. A theme throughout this book has been the importance of beliefs and ideas to political events, processes, and struggles. Beliefs and ideas are central in hegemony and to both the second and third dimensions of power. For example, what gets on the agenda and what people believe to be possible has an enormous political impact. People battle over beliefs, ideas, symbols, and words at school; in the courtroom; in the media; in political speeches; and elsewhere. You have seen how symbols, ideas, and words are used or manipulated to generate national pride, spread moral panic, create a sense of fear, justify a political action, and redirect public policy.

A high degree of political integrity (i.e., incorruptible, unimpaired, and complete) would be the opposite of corruption in government, manipulated media images, hidden political maneuvers, backroom deals and special privileges, and distortion of the truth (see World View 12.2). A loss of integrity also implies a loss of legitimacy for politicians or political institutions. It signals the breakdown of communication and trust. When a political regime or system loses integrity, and can no longer be true to itself and to others, it can quickly fall. This may be a reason for the rapid fall of the communist systems in the ex-Soviet Union and Central Europe. It is also why maintaining at least the appearance of integrity is so important, even when integrity itself has been lost. Politicians will tell lies, the mass media present distorted images, a company release misinformation—all to create an illusion of integrity.

Political sociology asks, how does a person, organization, or nation build, spread, maintain, or destroy integrity. Maintaining integrity helps to maintain power, while an absence of integrity creates cynicism and may lead to a reliance on coercion. Globalization and inclusion also have implications for integrity.

WORLD VIEW 12.2   Which Countries Are Corrupt?

An absence of bribes and similar corruption in commercial and social life is a critical indicator of a truly open and free society. Transparency International, the world's leading nongovernmental organization that fights corruption, ranked 133 countries in 2003 on a carefully developed corruption index. The organization defines corruption as an abuse of public office for private gain. The composite index is made up of information from 17 polls of the perceptions of well-informed business people, academics, and country analysts as to how much corruption is occurring among public officials and politicians. A high corruption ranking indicates a country where the following is more frequent: parents bribe underpaid teachers to obtain schooling for their children, patients bribe nurses to receive basic medical supplies, or government officials demand bribes before providing most public services. In these countries, corrupt officials also steal vast amounts of public funds. The index focuses on the corruption by public officials, and it does not measure people making secret payments to finance political campaigns, banks that engage in money laundering, or multinational companies that pay secretly to obtain favorable access to a country. The United States did not even make it into the 15 cleanest countries, but it ranked 18th because of bid rigging, kickbacks for government purchases, and bribes paid to government officials.

13 Least Corrupt Countries (in order from least corrupt)

Rank*	Country	2003 score**
1	Finland	9.7
2	Iceland	9.6
3	Denmark	9.5
3	New Zealand	9.5
5	Singapore	9.4
6	Sweden	9.3
7	Netherlands	8.9
8	Australia	8.8
8	Norway	8.8
8	Switzerland	8.8
11	Canada	8.7
11	Luxembourg	8.7
11	United Kingdom	8.7

12 Most Corrupt Countries (from most corrupt)

Rank*	Country	2003 score**
133	Bangladesh	1.3
132	Nigeria	1.4
131	Haiti	1.5
129	Myanmar	1.6
129	Paraguay	1.6
124	Angola	1.8
124	Azerbaijan	1.8
124	Cameroon	1.8
124	Georgia	1.8
124	Tajikistan	1.8
122	Indonesia	1.9
122	Kenya	1.9

*Countries with tied rank are in alphabetical order.
**Highest possible score for least corrupt = 10; Lowest
possible score = 1.

Source: http://www.transparency.org/cpi/2003/ cpi2003.html#cpi (downloaded July 10, 2004).

Globalization means both challenges to and opportunities for the politics of integrity. It can be a challenge because honesty and commitment to principles can be rooted locally and have a very narrow focus. Globalization may introduce outside, foreign, beliefs, ideas, and ways of seeing events that are disruptive to or upset established views. When a locally-based system of integrity is disrupted from the outside, it may be seen as a threat and may trigger a defensive response to include insiders and exclude outsiders. The rise of ethnic-racial conflicts in the world illustrates this process as does a deepening commitment by some to rigid and politicized versions of religious beliefs.[51] Globalization also presents opportunities for bridging cultural divides and expressing forms of integrity that are highly inclusive across a much broader span of humanity. Worldwide humanitarian organizations and movements for human rights, social justice, gender equality, the environment, democracy, and the like illustrate this process.[52] Global-inclusion processes are the foundation of transnational nongovernment organizations (NGOs). The inclusion of cultures and people from different nations can also stimulate highly creative and dynamic cultural interchange.

The challenges to and defenses of integrity can take the form of institutional manipulation and popular dissent or protest. This suggests greater attention to what Bleiker (2000) called "trans-territorial dissent practices" or forms of dissent that flow across national borders. Instead of focusing on political struggles and dissent exclusively in terms of organizations, processes, beliefs systems, or events inside national boundaries or between states, he urges a shift to look at practices and actions that cross spatial boundaries. The "connections, resistances, and identity formations" to which he refers include music from different countries, forms of street protest that other groups mimic or borrow across borders, internet Web sites and underground magazines that are used by people in many nations, the international outrage against gender-based abuse (Asian sexual trafficking of women and girls, African genital mutilation practices, the Taliban's treatment of women), sharing political symbols (e.g., goddess of democracy modeled on the U.S. Statute of Liberty built in Tiananmen Square by Chinese students protesting for democracy), and the global the worldwide televising of the breaking apart of the Berlin Wall.

The principle of integrity appears to have a place in what may be an emerging global-level polity. Basic political rights, such as fair elections or freedom of the press are increasingly becoming forms of global-level political integrity (see World View 12.3). Ideas, tactics, organizational forms, and so forth flow more easily across international borders. For example, the ideas of Mohandas Gandhi that were developed first in South Africa and used to end colonial rule in India, were borrowed by the American civil rights movement and then copied from Americans by black South Africans to end the apartheid regime. A global polity does not mean the end of national polity, just as national polity does not mean the end of local community politics (except in totalitarian states). An overlay of multiple levels raises the question: Which levels are more important at different times? Political integrity involves many rights: human rights and the protection of rights such as freedom of speech, freedom of the press, and the right to form parties, as well as social-economic rights.[53]

Traditionally, citizenship meant a tie to the nation-state, but this too may be changing. Just as inclusion within the state is giving way to other forms of inclusion, substantive, participatory citizenship is forming around political units

WORLD VIEW 12.3   **Actual Press Freedom around the World**

The amount of freedom of press around the world tells us much about the actual level of functioning democratic freedoms. In October 2002, the independent, international non-government organization, Reporters Sans Frontières (Reporters Without Borders) published the first worldwide press freedom index. The index was created by asking journalists, researchers, and legal experts 50 questions about a wide range of press freedom violations (e.g., murders or arrests of journalists, censorship, pressure, state monopolies, punishment of press law offences, media regulation). The index provided a portrait of the situation between September 2001 and October 2002. It does not take into account all of the human rights violations, only those that directly affect press freedom, including threats to the free flow of information via the Internet. Reliable information was available on 139 countries. In the lowest-ranked countries, press freedom or independent newspapers do not exist and the government tightly controls the media, banning or greatly limiting foreign media. The United States was not even in the top 10; its low ranking (17th) was due to the arrest and imprisonment of journalists, usually when they refused to reveal their sources in court. Also, since the

September 11, 2001 World Trade Center attack, several U.S. journalists have been arrested for crossing security lines at official buildings. The 12 highest-ranked countries (in order from the most to least free) are: Finland, Iceland, Norway, Netherlands, Canada, Ireland, Germany, Portugal, Sweden, Denmark, France, and Australia and Belgium (tied). The 12 lowest-ranked countries (in order from least to most free) are: North Korea, China, Burma, Turkmenistan, Bhutan, Cuba, Laos, Eritrea, Vietnam, Iraq, Libya, and Tunisia. How widespread is misinformation about current events is in the United States? One report by the Program on International Policy Attitudes at the University of Maryland showed that nearly one-third of Americans believed that the United States had found weapons of mass destruction in Iraq after the 1993 invasion, one-third believed that Iraq helped the al-Qaida terrorists support the September 11 attack, and over one-half believed that some of the September 11 attackers were Iraqi. All of these beliefs are false. Apparently many people's knowledge or beliefs about current events are based less on a close, unbiased study of news reports than on an intense emotional response to events that shapes what they believe to be factually true.

Sources: http://www.rsf.fr/article.php3?id_article=4116 (downloaded January 4, 2003) and "How Americans Link Iraq and September 11," *The New York Times,* March 2, 2003.

other than the nation-state. You can simultaneously be a citizen of your neighborhood, city, nation, and the world. Citizenship at each level involves a sense of membership or identity and a collection of rights and responsibilities.

MODELS OF POLITICAL SOCIOLOGY

You first learned about the three major frameworks and several models of political sociology in Chapter 3, and about theoretical developments beyond the major frameworks. You saw how the models approached a variety of questions and issues in Chapters 4 through 11. As mentioned in Chapter 3, the frameworks and models tend to concentrate on different areas or levels of political life, and each model has its strengths and weaknesses. In short, no single model is perfect, but the models, plus related theories, help political sociologists to analyze and inquire into political concerns and processes. In addition to providing assumptions, concepts, hypotheses, and directions for inquiry, the models also help political sociologists synthesize diverse findings and formulate more complete, comprehensive explanations. Because the models are linked to larger social theories and to political–moral values, you can assess them and discover which one(s) are most helpful in expanding and deepening your own understanding.

Political sociologists continue to use all the models to some degree, but some have won wider acceptance because they provide a large, fertile set of concepts and hypotheses, are applicable to many significant questions, and suggest explanations that are consistent with a growing body of empirical evidence. Twenty to 30 years ago, many political sociologists found the pluralist, elite, and structuralist models to be most valuable. Today this is less the case, and the statist, power-structure, and class-struggle models are more widely endorsed. Many political sociologists try to combine the strengths of different models and integrate them with recent developments from the constructionist, rational choice, and new institutionalism theoretical approaches. While you may want a single, final answer telling which model is correct, there is no such answer because knowledge is not static and political sociologists continue to explore new issues and develop new ideas.

CONCLUSION

Political sociology emerged to explain nineteenth century unrest over industrialization, the consolidation of the nation-state, and spread of democracy, especially as class conflicts swept across Europe. During the twentieth century, it acquired a greater coherence and expanded to examine other issues. As political sociology moves into the twenty-first century, it will continue to explore power, state, hegemony, and struggle, but it will also examine issues of globalization, inclusion-exclusion, and integrity. The three issues are interrelated, and each offers possibilities in the future for developing positive opportunities and posing new political threats.

Recall that political sociology is as much a perspective (i.e., way of looking at issues and asking questions) as a fixed body of knowledge or set of theories. A theme of this book is that many intractable societal problems that

appear to be inevitable or unsolvable can be traced to deeply held cultural beliefs and entrenched political conflicts. Thus, the very political institutions and cultural beliefs that people most prize often contribute to the problems that they find to be most intractable. For example, American's deeply held value of competitive individualism and material success have exacerbate many social problems, such as crime, and have thwarted finding solutions to them. Messner and Rosenfeld (1994, 9) observed, "a concern with citizenship and with the performance of political roles for the furtherance of the collective good is conspicuously absent from the American Dream." An issue for the future is whether concerns over citizenship and the political pursuit of the collective good will be part of the dreams each individual has for his/her future.

KEY TERMS

Class Action Lawsuits

Dealignment

Garrison State

Globalization*

Inclusion*

Integrity

Jury Nullification

Military Industrial Complex

Moral Panic

Political Crime

Political Investors

Punitive Damage Awards

State-Organized Crime

Tort Reform

appeared in previous chapters

REVIEW QUESTIONS

1. What makes the 1980s–1990s U.S. War on Drugs a moral panic? What are its social–political causes and consequences as a moral panic?

2. Compare class action lawsuits and punitive jury awards. What sectors of society back the tort reform? Why?

3. How does a realignment differ from a dealignment? Are the two always in conflict with one another?

4. Why did the military-industrial complex (MIC) develop, and what have its effects been on politics and the economy?

5. If the state is the source of all laws and law enforcement, how can the state commit a crime?

6. Globalization will generate many new challenges, and it will also create opportunities. Discuss a challenge and an opportunity that you have seen or expect to see as a result of globalization.

7. What experience have you had with lateral or hierarchal borders or boundaries? Which ones have you been included within and which ones have you been excluded from?

8. Describe what political integrity means to you, and relate it to the idea of being a global citizen.

RECOMMENDED READINGS

Bleiker, Roland. 2000. *Popular Dissent, Human Agency, and Global Politics.* New York: Cambridge University Press.

Boli, John and George Thomas (eds). 1999. *Constructing World Culture.* Stanford, CA: Stanford University Press.

Ferguson, Thomas. 1995. *Golden Rule: The Investment Theory of Party Competition and the Logic of Money-Driven Political Systems.* Chicago: University of Chicago Press.

Held, David, Anthony McGrew, David Goldblatt, and Jonathan Perraton. 1999. *Global Transformations.* Stanford, CA: Stanford University Press.

Hooks, Gregory. 1991. *Forging the Military-Industrial Complex: World War II's "Battle of the Potomac."* Urbana, IL: University of Illinois Press.

O'Brien, Robert, Anne Goetz, Jan Scholte, Marc Williams. 2000. *Contesting Global Governance: Multilateral Economic Institutions and Global Social Movements.* New York: Cambridge University Press.

Thompson, Kenneth. 1998. *Moral Panics.* New York: Routledge.

Wallerstein, Immanuel. 1991. *Geopolitics and Geoculture.* New York: Cambridge University Press.

ENDNOTES

1. On social problem theory see summary in Neuman (1998). Also see Gusfield (1967).
2. Quote is from Edelman (1977, 48).
3. See Barnes and Crawford (1999), Goode and Ben Yehuda (1994), and Thompson (1998).
4. Ungar (1990) describes U.S. moral panic of the Cold War Era.
5. Schneider and Ingram (1993) provide a typology of targeted groups in a constructionist perspective.
6. Discussed in McRobbie and Thornton (1995).
7. As Edelman (1988, 17) argued the problem or crisis of a moral panic is accompanied by new typologies and ways of organizing thinking that are adopted in popular discussion, news records, and academic discussion. Also see Altheide and Johnson (1980) and Edelman (1988, 85–89) on how new ways of organizing information are incorporated into bureaucratic organizations.
8. Statistics on the Drug War see Chambliss (1994) and Beckett (1997).
9. See Beckett (1994, 1995, 1997). Also, see Brownstein (1991).
10. As Schneider and Ingram (1993, 337–338) argued ". . . groups will often receive burdens even when it is illogical from the perspective of policy effectiveness. The highly predictable popularity of tough criminal justice statutes . . . are vivid illustrations of the political attractiveness of punishment directed at powerless, negatively viewed groups."
11. Schneider and Ingram (1993) discuss target groups. Schneider and Ingram (1995) is relevant. It is a response to a comment by Robert Lieberman, is informative, and agrees with much of Lieberman's institutional perspective.
12. Barkan (1983) discusses jury nullification.
13. See "Juries, Their Powers under Seige, Find Their Role Being Eroded," *New York Times,* March 2, 2001.
14. See "Some Plaintiffs Losing Out in Texas' War on Lawsuits," *New York Times,* June 7, 1999.
15. See "The 2000 Campaign: Campaign Notebook: A Wistful Bush Reflects on Hearth and Home," *New York Times,* January 28, 2000; "The Litigation Machine," *Business Week,* January 29, 2001; Pear, Robert. "Class Action Bill Favorable to Business Passes House," *New York Times,* March 14, 2002; Oppel, Richard. "House Expected to Pass Bill to Rewrite Rules on Class-Action Lawsuits," *New York Times,* June 12, 2003.

16. See "A Hostile Takeover," *The American Prospect* (Spring 2003) by Martin Garbus and "A Conservative Legal Group Thrives in Bush's Washington" *New York Times* (April 18, 2001) by Neil Lewis. Also see Heinz, Southworth and Park (2003) on a national network of activist ideologically conservative lawyers.
17. See Ferguson and Rogers (1981, 1986), and Ferguson (1995). Some political scientists define dealignment to mean a breakdown in party loyalty and partisanship and emphasize changes in the class structure to a post-industrial society with post-materialist values among other factors. For example see Dalton, *et al.* (1984) and Beck (1984).
18. This dealignment thesis differs from that of political scientists who see dealignment as weakening party loyalty based on a failure to transfer partisanship from parent to child, changes in class structure, or post-materialist values. Also see Gerteis (1998).
19. This argument is most forcefully demonstrated by Brooks (2000).
20. Hill and Hinton-Anderson (1995) argue that public opinion and policy mutually affect one another, with the elites shaping policy that then shapes opinion. Burstein (1998b, 2003) agrees, but he strongly defends the pluralist position that public opinion shapes most public policy.
21. For an example see Mizruchi (1992).
22. For discussion of class unity in specific historical eras see Roy (1981, 1991). For examples of the debate over political organization and action by the capitalist class in the New Deal era see Allen and Broyles (1991), Domhoff (1990, Chapter 4), Levine (1988), Manza (1993), Skocpol (1980), Finegold and Skocpol (1995), Skocpol and Amenta (1985), and Swenson (1997).
23. See Akard (1992), Broyles (1993), Burris and Salt (1990), Clawson et al. (1992, 1998), Ferguson and Rogers (1986), Manley (1994), Su, Neustadt and Clawson (1995), and Useem (1983, 1984). Some argue that the primary division was different regionally based factions of the capitalist class (Sale 1975, Jenkins and Shumate 1985), and others document coordination among government leaders and major capitalists to resolve the international crisis (see Sklar 1980).
24. For discussion see Useem (1984) and May, McHugh, and Taylor (1998). Also see Scott (1991, 1996).

25. Webber and Domhoff (1996) challenge this argument of Ferguson (1995) and argue that no major business group aligned with the Democratic Party in the New Deal Era and only smaller businesses, New York City businesses, Jews, and southerners supported the Democrats. Also see Jenkins and Brents (1989) on rival blocks of capitalists during the New Deal.

26. See Akard (1992), Clawson et al. (1996), Clawson and Su (1990), and Su et al. (1993).

27. Janowitz (1975, 1976).

28. For discussion see Stanley (1996).

29. For a discussion and the impact of the MIC see Ansell (1996), Gibbs (1996), and Melman (1970, 1985).

30. From Hooks (1991b, 156).

31. See Prechel (1990) and (2000, 79–80, 157–159) for details on the steel industry.

32. From Hooks (1991b, 158).

33. For details see Hooks and Luchansky (1996) and Luchansky and Hooks (1996).

34. From Hooks (1991b, 205).

35. See Fones-Wolf (1994) and Robin (2001).

36. See Hooks (1991b, 238).

37. On the contrast between the monopoly and competitive sectors of the economy see Averiff (1968), Hodson (1978, 1983) and O'Connor (1973).

38. Gholz and Sapolsky (1999–2000) and Markusen (1998).

39. Dao, James. "Much-Maligned B-1 Bomber Proves Hard to Kill," *New York Times,* August 1, 2001.

40. "The Suits Inside Battledress," *Economist,* April 19, 2003, p. 52–53.

41. See Waddell (1999).

42. See Griffin, Devine, and Wallace (1982) and Mintz and Hicks (1984).

43. See Giddens (1987, 172) on internal pacification and Migdal (1988, 22) on state social control. One aspect of state social control is managing the label "terrorism." The state identifies and defines terrorism, a term with a very loose, unstable, and vague meaning that "depends in the final analysis on control of the labeling process" (Chadwick 1997, 338). On terrorism also see Crenshaw (1992), Gibbs (1989), Johnson (2001), Kumamoto (1991), Kuzma (2000), Miller (1988), Oliverio (1997), and Turk (2004).

44. See Turk (1982, 34).

45. From Turk (1982, 54–67).

46. See Chambliss (1993b, 306–308).

47. See Jenkins and Schock (1992) and Schwartzman (1998) for reviews and discussions of this linkage. A good example can be found in Skocpol's (1979) work on revolutions.

48. For more on this approach see Boli and Thomas (1997, 1999); Kamens, Meyer, and Benavot (1996), Meyer, Ramirez, and Soysal (1992), Meyer (2000), Thomas and Meyer (1984).

49. For examples see Chase-Dunn (1989), Evans, et al. (1985), and Wallerstein (1976).

50. For examples see Mann (1988), Tilly (1975), and Skocpol (1979).

51. Esping-Andersen (1999), Pettigrew (1998), and Wimmer (2002) on the European case.

52. O'Brien, Goetz, Scholte, and Williams (2000) provide examples of this process. Also see Dryzek and others (2002) on the international growth of environmentalism.

53. See Fraser (1994) on human rights.

GLOSSARY

(Chapter in which term appears.)

A

abeyance A period of time when a social movement ceases but does not disappear. (6)

absolutist state A hybrid or transitional form of the state that laid the foundation for the modern nation-state. The nobility or feudal aristocracy continued to rule, but elements of a modern nation-state started to appear and the nation had not yet developed. (2)

adaptable pattern A pattern of state bureaucracy in which the government hires independent professionals who move back and forth between the private and public sector, and top positions are held by political appointees instead of permanent government staff, who are often held in low regard. (4)

affirmative action A set of policies, programs, and procedures designed to improve the employment and educational opportunities for minority group members and women. (4)

agenda-setting Control over what are seriously considered issues. Alternative options or issues that exist are prevented from entering the formal decision-making process or are assigned a very low priority. (1)

Aid to Families with Dependent Children (AFDC) A U.S. federal government program that started in the New Deal Era and continued until 1996 that provided limited income and other help to poor women with children. (11)

Alford Index A rough measure of class voting that puts all voters into two classes—blue-collar/manual and white-collar/non-manual—and all votes for two political parties—prolabor and probusiness—then calculates how much voters cast ballots for the party of their class. (5)

astroturf lobbying Political advocates try to look like a grass roots organization of ordinary, concerned citizens, but in reality, they are a front for an industry group or private firm that pays for the organization. (5)

attention cycle The rapid rise of an issue from obscurity to prominence in the media, and dominates the media for a period of time, then fades from public attention. (8)

B

black law Law as it is written in books (versus law applied in practice). (9)

bounded pluralism An apparent plurality of viewpoints or perspectives in the media, but in fact, the viewpoints stay within a set of unseen boundaries that are rarely breached. (8)

C

capture theory The idea that business regulatory agencies begin by actively enforcing rules in the public interest, but as the political conditions that gave rise to business regulation change, agencies slowly align with the business interests they are supposed to regulate and business influence grows until agencies defend the regulated business's interests instead of the public interest. (10)

cartel A system of limited competition in which all or most firms of an industry collectively adjust production, set prices, and allocate resources to maximize industry profits and stability. (10)

censorship The exclusion of or restriction on what the media reports or shows, or the forced inclusion of messages intended to alter audience views. (8)

circulation of elites Over time, various conditions trigger the rise or fall of different social groups into elite positions. (3)

citizenship The tie or relationship between an individual and the state. (2)

civil citizenship rights Rights attached to being a full member of society and receiving equal treatment regardless of factors such as race or ethnicity, gender, age, disability, sexual orientation, marital status, or income level. (2)

civil religion A transcendent faith in the nation that celebrates and sanctifies a nation's way of life by giving official rituals, holidays, symbols, and monuments a spiritual meaning and connecting them to something larger, treating them with reverence and assigning them a quasi-religious moral meaning. (7)

civil society The "space" in society beyond the state occupied by voluntary, semi-autonomous, citizen-based groups. (2)

class action lawsuits When a large group of people are harmed by another party, usually a large corporation, and many of the injured parties join in a civil lawsuit to vindicate the rights of and gain benefits for the entire class of injured people. (12)

class politics How class identity or substantive class interests affect a person's orientation toward politics. (5)

class voting The strength of a relationship between an individual's social class and his/her choice of a party or candidate. (5)

coercion The use or threat to use force (e.g., physical injury to oneself or loved ones, imprisonment, confiscation of property) to compel compliance. (1)

coercive state power The control and application of organized violence, backed by formal authority, to cajole, compel, or coerce the population to obey laws and conform to the established political–economic order. (9)

cognitive liberation A transformation in the beliefs of an aggrieved population such that people collectively come to redefine existing relations and see a potential to significantly restructure political, economic, or social relations. (6)

communal political participation A person or organization participates by displaying her/his membership in the polity (or a subgroup within it). (5)

consensus model fallacy An ideal legal model of society that assumes that all members of society agree on certain fundamental beliefs, values, and ideas. (9)

conventional politics Legal, open influence to affect government agencies, elected officials, or other citizens about recognized political issues. (5)

cooling out The process of adjusting and lowering student expectations to accept less prestigious schooling and lower status jobs than they wanted and accepting it as a realistic alternative. (8)

coordinated pattern A pattern of state bureaucracy in which the government hires people specially trained to be government officials, people stay with public service for an entire career, and bureaucrats who worked their way up hold top positions and are highly respected. (4)

corporate censorship Action by the owners, managers, or editors of media organizations to delete and remove stories from mass distribution that they believe can harm their corporate financial or political interests. (8)

corporate liberal thesis A group of farsighted, class-conscious capitalists became politically organized and had a direct, active role in introducing liberal reforms during periods of social–political crisis. (3)

corporate voice A set of assumptions and values embedded into symbolic expression that protects and justifies the central place of the private corporation in society. (8)

corporate welfare A system of tax breaks, subsidies, special incentives, allowances, and other monetary and nonmonetary transfers of state resources to private corporations, largely based on political influence and for particularistic gain. (10)

corporatism A state–society relationship in which society is divided into pillars or sectors that are recognized by the state. (2)

correspondence theory of schooling Schools have a middle-class bias that works against students from disadvantaged socioeconomic backgrounds and selects students to enter future positions in a manner that parallels the student's family class background. (8)

countermovement A movement that develops in direct response to and in opposition to another movement. (6)

credentialism The idea that organizations and employers substitute the possession of credentials for the work of evaluating an individual's skills or abilities, and that people with credentials have a valuable social resource. (8)

critical elections Unusual elections in which many blocks of voters change party affiliation, voter turnout is very high, parties are more ideologically polarized, and voting shifts from past patterns. (4)

culturally embattled thesis People organize politically to protect their lifeworld and defend their cultural beliefs from external encroachment. (7)

cultural capital Symbolic wealth in the form of refined aesthetic and intellectual taste that is positively valued in high status groups of a society. (8)

cultural nationalism Nationalism that defends and strengthens the cultural identity and institutions of a nation. (2)

culture of poverty thesis A theory stating that the primary cause of poverty is a unique set of cultural beliefs and values held by poor people and transmitted across generations. (11)

culture war thesis A deep cultural division emerged over secularization in which symbolic-moral issues displaced older divisions of social class and status concerns to become the primary basis of politics and voting in the U.S. (6)

cycle of protest When protest follows a pattern of expansion and decline; unrest and protest begin, spread, peak, and fade. (6)

D

dealignment A breakdown of past alignments with a failure to create a strong, stable new coalition indicated by an exhaustion of alternatives followed by a mass withdraw from politics. (12)

declining significance hypothesis Class voting was a product of the Age of Industrial Capitalism and is irrelevant in a postindustrial society. (5)

decommodification Provides an alternative to the market and makes it possible to live (i.e., obtain all survival needs) without depending on the market. (11).

deliberative democracy Decision-making based on a conversation among rational, open-minded equals who gather to discuss, present arguments, and listen to various positions before they vote to make a collective decision. (2)

demand overload When each interest group or individual person vigorously participates and expresses a separate interest and chaos is created because the government cannot respond to all the disparate demands. (3)

democracy A type of collective decision-making, or a process, by which people reach decisions together that will apply to all. (2)

democratic class struggle thesis Intense conflict between capitalists (e.g., business owners, bankers, large investors) and workers was converted into a peaceful electoral competition. (5)

democratic elitism A theory that says rule by multiple, competing elites, while the mass of ordinary people have limited participation, is inevitable, if not desirable. (2)

democratic society A society with a lively civil society in which people organize themselves into groups outside of government control based on their shared interests or beliefs (e.g., churches, labor unions, clubs) and democratic processes prevail throughout all institutions and collective social activities. (2)

deregulation A set of political–ideological justifications and policy actions with the objective of rescinding, ceasing to enforce, or eliminating business regulations to release market forces. (10)

deserving poor Adults who are not able-bodied and are incapable of working for a reason that is beyond their control (e.g., poor health, elderly). They would be willing to work in the paid labor force if they were capable (also called worthy poor). (11)

determinate sentencing Specifying a fixed, rigid minimum penalty for a crime (e.g., 5 years in prison with no parole) for a crime and prohibiting alternation of it by judges or corrections officials. (9)

developmental state thesis A high capacity, relatively autonomous state can coordinate and direct private industrial expansion to build an internationally competitive economy. (2)

devolution The process of turning national-level programs over to state or local-level governments. (11)

distributive state A state in which the government controls vast resources that it gives to favored individuals and businesses. It also gives them tax waivers and the right to collect tolls and taxes foreign goods to protect local industry. (4)

E

economic nationalism Nationalism that defends and strengthens the economic position of one nation relative to other nations. (2)

elite-managerial model A model in the managerial framework that sees society as divided into powerful elites and powerless masses, with the elite in control of politics. (3)

encouragement Government and nongovernment programs that target parts of the population and provide incentives to facilitate their participation in the polity. (4)

entitlement Federal programs in which certain individuals are entitled by law to benefits. (11)

exclusion Denying full integration into the polity (e.g., not letting people or groups vote, speak, or express views or denying use of public services). (4)

F

false consensus When a person believes that his/her opinion is natural or normal, and that those who disagree hold deviant opinions. (7)

federalism A system that divides the nation-state's political authority between the central national government and other localized levels of government. (4)

first dimension of power Observable conflict among competing interests. (1)

food stamp program A type of in-kind assistance in which vouchers are given to poor people by the U.S. federal government can only be used to purchase food items. (11)

formal citizenship The official, legal definition of a citizen in political–legal theory. (2)

formal ideology An explicit, coherent, highly consistent, and formal system of thought with a mix of assumptions, values, and beliefs. (7)

frame alignment Linking a movement's frame to an individual's interpretative framework. (6)

G

gender gap In electoral politics and policy preferences it refers to women voting and holding policy positions that differ from men in a way that favors a distinct "women's position." (5)

general assistance A program provided in about one-half of the states in the United States that delivers small amounts of short-term direct income assistance for very poor people who cannot receive benefits from federal government aid programs for the poor. (11)

gerrymandering The practice of drawing election district boundaries in a way that favors one political party or another. (5)

globalization The rapid growth of internationally connected economic, social, and cultural relations spurred by new communication, transportation technology, and shifts in the world economy. (2)

H

hate crime laws Laws designed to provide legal protection from hostile acts based solely on a person's race, gender, religion, or sexual orientation. (4)

hegemony Moral and ideational leadership of society attained with the consent of major social groups. (1)

hidden curriculum Implicit instruction that instills compliance to formal authority, adherence to bureaucratic procedures, and the structured pursuit of individual rewards. (8)

human capital thesis of schooling Schooling stimulates economic growth by creating a more productive workforce. (8)

I

ideological state apparatus A set of major institutions (e.g., schools, churches, families, media, sports, and political parties) that operates as a loosely connected system, in conjunction with politics and the economy, to shape people, their identities, and their consciousness so they will conform to the needs of capitalism. (7)

ideology An interconnected set of assumptions, beliefs, values, and ideas that guides how people think about and evaluate issues. (7)

inclusion Bringing people, groups, ideas, or behaviors into the polity. (4) (12)

indeterminate sentencing Giving a very broad range of penalties for a crime (e.g., probation to 5 years) and allowing judges and corrections officials to adjust a sentence significantly based on an offender's social and criminal background, the specific circumstances of a crime, and changes in the offender's behavior and attitude. (9)

informal ideology An ongoing, implicit set of general ideas, beliefs, values, and predispositions that are integrated into most people's daily existence. (7)

injustice frame Part of a broad collective action frame that excites moral indignation and anger in adherents toward a specific target and stimulates them to demand action because the target violated a standard of moral justice. (6)

inner circle A subset of capitalists in a network of interlocking positions among top corporate and bank boards of directors who (1) occupy positions on several different boards of directors, (2) have a family background in or marry into old upper-class wealth, and (3) interact socially with one another. (3)

institution A coherent system or framework of people, organizations, and ideas that operate together in a patterned, or rule-governed, manner across time. (4)

instrumental political participation A person or organization deliberately tries to affect politics to accomplish a specific goal. (5)

integrity When a person is fully honest and true to himself/herself and to his/her colleagues, friends, family, nation, and belief system. (12)

iron triangle A stable but narrow network, alliance, or coalition of public and private sector interests that cooperate to control an area of public policy. (10)

J

jury nullification The principle that citizen juries have a right to reject a law on moral grounds and vote to acquit defendants despite a law violation. (12)

L

legal order Social-economic-political relations governed by state rules and the process that creates and enforces the rules. (9)

lifeworld A system of understanding rooted in a set of values and beliefs that gives people a sense of moral order, outlines major categories of life, and assigns moral value to them. (7)

lynching An extra-legal act, usually by a vigilante mob, with the tacit consent of local law enforcement officials, in which a person is tracked down and publicly killed. (4)

M

male/breadwinner model A model of family-household relations that assumes all adults are in a stable marital relationship with one wage-earning worker, the male, and a female who provides all domestic chores and caregiving (i.e., child rearing, elder care, illness care) as unpaid labor. (11)

master frame A generic, broad frame that subsumes multiple specific collective action frames of a movement by being less restrictive and more comprehensive. (6)

Maternal Welfare State A model of government social programs and benefits based on protecting and providing a minimal level of income to women, especially married or widowed women with children. (11)

means-tested program An eligibility requirement in social programs in which a person must pass a test of needs before receiving a service or benefit and only those with the greatest need receive the benefits. (11)

Medicaid A U.S. federal government means-tested medical insurance program for the poor. (11)

Medicare A U.S. federal government medical insurance program for the elderly that is not means tested. (11)

militarization of the police A transfer of military surveillance and weapons technology; military combat and operational tactics; and military language, training, and orientation to local police forces and increased police–military cooperation in ways that blur internal and external security functions. (9)

military industrial complex A network of people, military organizations, and defense suppliers that developed a shared interest and work to defend that interest. (12)

mobilization A process by which a group acquires, accumulates, and organizes resources (e.g., followers, ideology, money, weapons, votes, alliances, organization). (6)

monopoly The absence of economic competition in an industry because a single firm controls all production and prices and receives all the (usually very high) profits. (10)

moral panic A situation that occurs when many people rapidly start to see a number of evildoers posing a serious and growing threat to society, and they demand greater social control or punishment to reaffirm the moral order. (12)

movement A network of interacting people with a set of shared beliefs and a common identity that acts collectively over a sustained period of time in relation to others to achieve a change-oriented goal. (6)

movement entrepreneurs Individuals who seek to build and lead a movement organization by taking risks and investing a lot of time and energy. (6)

movement frame A cognitive scheme that a movement creates and disseminates that organizes thinking, interprets events, and guides action. (6)

myth of legality A belief that judicial decisions are based on autonomous legal principles and that cases are decided by the application of legal rules formulated and applied through a politically and philosophically neutral process of legal reasoning. (9)

N

nation A collection of people with a common culture, and by implication, a common territory. (2)

nation-state A joining of political organization (the sovereign state) with a distinct cultural community (the nation or people). (2)

nationalism A mode of discourse, a movement, and an emotional sentiment about the nation. (2)

non decisions Situations that occur when a policy alternative is not formulated, people do not mobilize, or candidates do not advance because of the overwhelming odds of failure. (1)

normative fallacy Law contains within it an ideal model of what social-economic-political relations should be and confuses that model with actual conditions. (9)

O

oligopoly An industry market situation in which a small number of large firms control an entire, or nearly the entire, industry. (10)

oppositional consciousness An entire outlook or worldview that a subordinate group can develop that stands outside of, and in opposition to, the dominant way to think and see events and that reinforces a society's power structure. (6)

oppositional subculture A set of social practices, beliefs, traditions, symbols, and patterns separate from the larger dominant culture that sustains an oppositional or counterhegemonic consciousness. (6)

organizational readiness The organizational resources of potential movement members. (6)

P

paradox of redistribution The greater the extent to which social benefits are targeted to the poor and only the poor, instead of creating general social equality, the less overall reduction in poverty. (11)

participatory citizenship The idea that authentic citizenship requires that all citizens participate and be engaged in political and civil life; citizenship is more than a set of rights passively attached to people. (2)

participatory democracy Active, equal participation by all people in nonpolitical institutions (e.g., civic organizations, workplace, churches) has a powerful educational function that fosters, and may be a critical precondition for, a genuine political democracy. (2)

particularistic political contact When a person contacts a government official or office to obtain a particular material benefit for herself/himself or his/her family or business. (5)

party system An arrangement of political party competition that has a level of voter activity, key issues, major social divisions, and patterns of party behavior. (4)

penal wefarism model A model of control that sees crime as caused by individual deficiencies and focuses on rehabilitating offenders and preparing them for a return to society. (9)

Piven and Cloward turnout proposition The American voting system operates in a way that silences citizens who desire a more activist government and who advocate left liberal social policies. (5)

plural elites A view that each sector of society, such as business, government, mass media, labor, or religion, has its own separate elite, and that the elites are of nearly equal importance and compete with one another. (3)

pluralism A framework in political sociology that understands politics primarily in terms of many competing interest groups, concentrates on the first dimension of power, and views the state as a neutral mechanism that balances and responds to citizen demands (3).

pluralistic ignorance When people falsely believe that the majority holds an opinion, when it is actually held by a minority. (7)

policy domain A semiporous topic area around which are clustered an interacting, interrelated set of policies (i.e., laws, regulations, programs), organizations (e.g., government agencies, political party factions, movement organizations, think tanks), and political actors (e.g., lobbyists, interest groups, activists). (10)

policy feedback When a policy created at one point in time influences the creation of state institutional structures and builds the political capability of groups around the structures, and the structures and capabilities, in turn, affect subsequent policy. (11)

policy legacy A body of preexisting law, past policy actions, procedures and rules, or bureaucratic agencies and staff that influence subsequent action. (3)

Policy Planning Network (PPN) A collection of overlapping think tanks, private foundations, advocacy groups, and individuals that supply ideas, arguments, justifications, and models for public policy on contemporary issues. (4)

Political Action Committee (PAC) A legal way for organizations and individuals to make campaign donations in the U.S. on which systematic records are kept. (5)

political capitalism A situation in which business interests use political outlets to attain stability, predictability, and security in their economic, social, or political environment. (10)

political citizenship rights A citizen's rights to participate in governance or rule, including the right to vote, to run for public office, to form a political party, to circulate petitions, and to recall elected officials. (2)

political crimes Peaceful, legitimate protest actions or challenges to state authority that state officials have made illegal to limit dissent. (12)

political formula A myth that the elites create and disseminate to justify their rule. (3)

political investors Politically active business and financial interests, capitalists, and ideological elites who provide major political institutions with support and give the policy agenda its basic direction. (12)

political machine A disciplined organization of party followers that reached down to the ward or neighborhood level and responded to specific neighborhood or family needs in exchange for loyalty at election time. (4)

political nationalism Nationalism that defends national interests and strengthens institutions of national sovereignty, including the military. (2)

political opportunity structures (POS) Shifts in the political environment that affect the relative balance of power between elite and challenger groups and provide openings during the course of events that allow challenger groups to advance. (6)

political patronage A way to fill government posts in which party loyalists receive government jobs as a reward for political support. (4)

political regime An interwoven mode of governance that includes a party system, relations among levels of government, the central policy divisions, and organizational structure of national government. (4)

political sociology The study of power and relationships between society and politics. (1)

political witch hunts Mass movements, often state supported, that clarify and affirm the boundaries of acceptable political ideas and values while building solidarity around the civil religion. (7)

politicization Moving issues, symbols, ideas, or moral principles from the unconscious background, or an individual's personal experience, and placing them on the public agenda. (7)

politics of symbols The creation, elaboration, and use of symbols for political purposes. (7)

polity The institutions, organizations, people, processes, rules, and symbols that operate together (loosely or tightly) as the politics of a specific nation-state. (4)

polyarchy Rule by many; it refers to contemporary representative democratic institutions that have elected officials, universal suffrage, fair elections, free speech, and so forth. (2)

poorhouse Early institutions to house and feed the destitute poor, designed to keep them off the streets and reform them; sometimes it also served as a hospital or workhouses in which work was required, also called "indoor relief." (11)

pork barrel politics The tactical allocation of government benefits by a politician who uses his/her government position to direct benefits in ways that are inefficient or wasteful from the standpoint of an entire polity, are targeted at specific geographic areas or favor particular groups, and are designed to reward past or encourage future political support. (10)

poverty line The arbitrary dollar amount created in the 1960s for the bureaucratic purpose of estimating the size of the poor population. (11)

power A *relationship* between two or more people (or groups); it is a *capacity* or ability to influence others; it *can be possessed, accumulated, or held*; and it is *unequal* in that one person or group has more than the other. (1)

power elite A tightly interconnected, overlapping single network of elites who have shared interests and rule society. (3)

priming How the mass media shape the standards people use when judging politicians, policies, or issues by calling attention to some matters as opposed to others. (8)

prison-industrial complex A mutually reinforcing set of powerful bureaucratic, economic, and political interests that depend on continued high incarceration rates for their success. (9)

privileged access When some people or groups have significant advantages compared to others in selecting candidates, having a voice in elections, placing issues on the public agenda, or influencing policymaking (4).

pro bono Part of a legal code of ethics saying that lawyers should do free legal work for low income people. (9)

public memory A system of understandings, beliefs, and interpretations about past events and individuals that gives people a feeling of collective identity, meaning, and purpose. (7)

public opinion The individual and collective thinking about current issues affecting society that self-aware people discuss in their exchanges. (7)

punitive damage awards When a citizen jury rules for a person injured by the products or actions of a corporation and imposes a very large monetary award to punish the offending corporation. (12)

R

race coding The media or political actors present issues or events in a manner that reinforces negative racial stereotypes without explicitly mentioning race. (8)

rational choice theory of voter turnout Individuals make instrumental decisions about whether to invest time and effort into voting, and they vote if or when they believe it is likely to make a difference for their immediate personal situation. (5)

rational ignorance People rationally decide not to invest the time and effort into following and participating in politics if they expect it to have little impact. (5)

realignment theory Periods of regime stability are punctuated by transition periods, during which

several areas of a regime, particularly the party system, the voting patterns of social groups, national policies, and the organizational form of the national government, experience rapid, significant change. (4)

regulatory regime A constellation of mutually reinforcing ideas, institutions, and policies that orient multiple areas of business regulation around a few core principles, endorses a particular business-government relationship, and remains in place for a period of years. (10)

relationism A special type of nonideological thinking that intellectuals can achieve from their unique social positions by openly accepting people from all sectors of society, looking at events from multiple points of view, and developing special methods for analyzing ideas. (7)

relative autonomy of the state The state has room to maneuver independent of social group or class demands, but it cannot violate the basic tenets of capitalism or oppose the long-term interests of the capitalist class. (3)

removal of direct barriers An inclusion mechanism that ends blockages to a group's entrance to the polity and expands access for a group that is not fully included in the polity.

repression The use of organized violence to maintain social order. (4)

resistance theory of schooling Acts of student rebellion, resistance to school authority, and dropping out of school are expressions of struggle among social classes or other groups (e.g., ethnic, religious) over the content of education and power in society. (8)

resource dependency thesis Movement deradicalization associated with receiving external funds is an unintended consequence of an SMO becoming more bureaucratic and professional. (6)

resource theory of voter turnout Individuals who have more social and economic resources (e.g., money, time, civic skills) are more likely to vote. (5)

retributivist model A model of crime control in which crime is understood to be a "normal" societal condition, and the focus is on managing its level; instead of rehabilitating, reintegrating, or assisting offenders, they are segregated, excluded, and punished. (9)

revolution The rapid, forcible overthrow of a ruling class and taking control of the state, usually with violence, to alter fundamental power relations in a society and transform its major social, political, and economic institutions. (6)

Rushe-Kirchheimer thesis A relationship exists between the demand for labor and changes in incarceration rates, such that an excess of unemployed workers who may be disruptive and sufficient state financial capacity produce increased imprisonment rates. (9)

S

school knowledge A subset of all knowledge; the skills, information, and beliefs that schools put into the curriculum, deem to be important, and legitimate as official. (8)

second dimension of power Barely visible processes that limit or shape the operation of the first dimension of power. (1)

secular humanism A label created by the New Christian Right for the growing influence in society of highly educated, left-liberal, nonreligious humanists. (7)

self-help crime Crimes committed when a person, family, or friends try to remedy an injury or loss to property, person, or honor by going outside the legal order. (8)

semi-autonomy theory of schooling Most conflicts about schooling occur outside the classroom as many competing stakeholders (e.g., students, parents, faculty, administrators, public officials, employers of graduates) fight to dictate the direction of education, and schools have partial autonomy from dominant class forces of society. (8)

settlement house A Progressive Era method of providing welfare from a house located in a poor immigrant neighborhood from which middle-class reformers gave counseling, direct material help, legal and medical aid, and cultural assimilation. (11)

social capital A resource in the form of interpersonal contacts, acquaintances, and connections that a person can draw upon. (8)

social closure A general stratification process whereby the people currently occupying higher social or economic positions engage in actions to restrict the upward movement or greater competition from people in lower positions. (8)

social control thesis The idea that external contributions to or elite patronage of radical movements places limits on movement actions and forces the movement to become more moderate. (6)

social-economic citizenship rights A citizen's rights to a minimal standard of living (e.g., a right not to starve or freeze to death), including the right to safe working conditions, a healthy environment, decent housing, medical care, schooling, maternity leave and child care, and a pension. (2)

social movement organization (SMO) A complex, formal organization that identifies its goals with those of a social movement. (6)

soft money Campaign donations outside the limits and regulations of the Federal Election Campaign Act, since it is not officially for a specific candidate but promotes ideological, interest group, or business interests. (5)

sovereignty Unquestioned state authority to rule over a specific territory. (2)

spiral of silence Extensive media attention leads people to believe that an opinion is widely held, and those who agree with the opinion are emboldened to speak out, the undecided or apathetic go along with it, and those who disagree keep silent. (7)

spoils system A system in which the winning political party distributes jobs and favors (i.e., the spoils) to its followers and loyalists. (4)

state All the government, or the public sector, plus much of what immediately surrounds it, connects it to society, and holds it together. (1)

state autonomy State independence from external or nonstate interests. (3)

state capacity The state's ability to effectively mobilize resources to carry out tasks. (3)

state project A loosely bound ensemble of theories and beliefs, organizations and individuals, and specific state units that are coordinated and united around a common vision or theme; this unity is not permanent but is the result of various internal and external political struggles. (10)

statist-managerial model A model in the managerial framework that views the state as an institution that has its own interests. (3)

status decline thesis People who feel threatened by social–economic decline act politically to restore their position of high social status. (7)

status inconsistency thesis Status-consistent people experience less social stress, are politically moderate, and support the party of their class, but people with inconsistent statuses experience great stress, which encourages political extremism and support for parties of other social classes. (5)

steering mechanism (state as) The state distills and advances general capitalist class interests and stands apart from the narrow, short-term, conflicting, and incomplete interests that individual capitalists express. (3)

stagflation A term to describe an unusual economic situation in the 1970s that combined stagnant economic growth, high unemployment rates, and high inflation. (10)

stare decisis Legal reasoning that looks to past rulings and judgments, and relies on precedent. (9)

state-organized crime Official government policy that violates its own laws, the laws of other nations, or international law. (12)

structural dependence thesis The state depends on a healthy private economy for its resources and this requires the state to uphold capitalism. (3)

structural selectivity State agencies create coherent policies or programs based on rationality, law, and science that are more than simply reflections of immediate political pressures in society. (3)

structural theory of poverty The root causes of poverty do not lie in individual behavior, personal characteristics, or the culture of poor people but are in systematic discrimination, provision of inadequate schooling, insufficient or very low-paying jobs, and general conditions in the economy. (11)

struggle The peaceful and nonpeaceful actions by a group or coalition of people to expand or defend their position of power that meets with opposition from others. (1)

substantive citizenship The actual practices, conditions, and experiences of various citizens in specific situations. (2)

surveillance society A society in which people in positions of bureaucratic authority regularly and systematically monitor numerous aspects of the lives of the population to exercise control over them. (9)

symbolic political participation A person or organization visibly affirms (or rejects) political ideas or processes in an attempt to influence the actions or thinking of others. (5)

symbolic racism An indirect racism that occurs when whites deny their racial prejudice but refuse to treat the people of different racial groups equally and oppose attempts to equalize conditions across races. (8)

symbolic violence The use of language, morality, rules, ideas, and other symbolic forms to compel people and sustain power relations. (7)

symbols of politics A subset of all cultural symbols that stands for specific political values, institutions, or ideas. (7)

system of courts and parties A nineteenth century American political situation in which courts and political parties had greater significant influence than today, while the national government and administrative bureaucracy was small and weak. (4)

T

tactical innovation Part of the interactive process between movements and authorities or countermovements in which a movement invents new tactics because old ones are no longer effective. (6)

tax expenditures A form of hidden spending by the government through tax breaks, tax reductions, etc. for specific purposes. (10)

think tank An organization (usually nonprofit, nongovernment) in which one or more researchers, writers, journalists, or others develop, refine, elaborate, and publicized ideas about policy issues. (4)

third dimension of power Invisible influence and domination that is built into patterns of thought, terms and categories of language, and the very way that activities are organized. (1)

tort reform A conservative political movement that seeks change in the legal order in a way that will restrict large punitive damage awards and class action lawsuits against large corporations. (12)

totalitarian state A nondemocratic state with a controlled and very restricted civil society, limited public expression, and little or no real popular participation in selecting leaders. (2)

transparency The principle that calculations, procedures, or deliberations should be set up so that anyone can easily observe them and follow the steps to a clear outcome. (10)

trendless fluctuation hypothesis Social class remains a continuing basis of major societal conflict. (5)

tyranny of the majority A situation in which government facilitates or permits the majority's (or a powerful vocal minority's) religious, ideological, or cultural beliefs to be imposed on all people and suppresses minority dissent. (2)

U

undeserving poor Poor adults who are "able-bodied" and capable of working, but who voluntarily decide not to participate in the paid labor force. (11)

unemployment insurance A social program that provides limited income assistance for a period of time to people who were previously employed and met other criteria. (11)

universal social programs A social program in which benefits are a right of citizenship and all people are entitled to public services and benefits, regardless of their income level. (11)

urban growth coalition A cooperative political arrangement between the local business community and city officials to promote private economic expansion. (4)

V

venue shifting When an SMO or its opponents change the level of government or geographic location for activities to better advance goals or defend a position. (6)

W

War on Poverty A collection of new programs or the expansion of social programs for low-income people that were initiated under the Lyndon Johnson administration (1964–1968). (11)

welfare capitalism A system of social benefits for employees provided by the employer. (11)

welfare dependency thesis A theory that receiving government social benefits creates an addictivelike dependence to continue receiving the benefits and destroys a person's self-esteem, motivation to work, and self-sufficiency. (11)

welfare queen The image of a mythological woman created by conservative politicians to attack welfare programs. She is African American, unwed, refuses to work, purposely had many children by different men to increase her welfare benefits, and lives a luxurious life by manipulating government programs for the poor. (11)

welfare state A state responsibility to ensure the well-being, health, happiness, and prosperity of all its citizens. (11)

welfare state regime A mutually reinforcing configuration of welfare state goals, policies, and institutions that has a distinct logic of organization, integration with society, and historical origin. (11)

workfare A broad term for programs that provide income and benefits for the poor contingent upon the poor person receiving work-related training, looking for paid employment, or staying employed in a very low-wage or part-time situation. (11)

BIBLIOGRAPHY

A

Abbott, Andrew. 1988. *The System of Professions: An Essay on the Division of Expert Labor.* Chicago: University of Chicago Press.

Abelmann, Nancy and John Lie. 1995. *Blue Dreams: Korean Americans and the Los Angeles Riots.* Cambridge, MA: Harvard University Press.

Abrahamson, Mark and Valerie J. Carter. 1986. "Tolerance, Urbanism and Region." *American Sociological Review* 51, pp. 287–294.

Abramowitz, Alan I. 1994. "Issue Evolution Reconsidered: Racial Attitudes and Partisanship in the U.S. Electorate." *American Journal of Political Science* 38, pp. 1–24.

Abramowitz, Alan I. 1997. The Cultural Divide in American Politics: Moral Issues and Presidential Voting. In *Understanding Public Opinion,* ed. B. Norrander and C. Wilcox, pp. 211–226. Washington, DC: Congressional Quarterly.

Abramowitz, Alan I. and Kyle Saunders. 1998. "Ideological Realignment in the U.S. Electorate." *Journal of Politics* 60, pp. 634–653.

Abrams, P. 1988. "Notes on the Difficulty of Studying the State." *Journal of Historical Sociology* 1, pp. 58–89.

Abramson, Paul R. and John Aldrich. 1982. "The Decline in Electoral Participation in America." *American Political Science Review* 76, pp. 502–521.

Abramson, Paul R. and John Aldrich. 1995. "Third-Party and Independent Candidates in American Politics: Wallace, Anderson and Perot." *Political Science Quarterly* 110, pp. 349–368.

Adair, Stephen. 1996. "Overcoming a Collective Action Frame in the Remaking of an Antinuclear Opposition." *Sociological Forum* 11, pp. 347–375.

Adams, David S. 1987. "Ronald Reagan's Revival: Voluntarism as a Theme in Reagan's Civil Religion." *Sociological Analysis* 48, pp. 17–29.

Adams, Graham. 1966. *Age of Industrial Violence, 1910–1915.* New York: Columbia University Press.

Adams, Greg D. 1997. "Abortion: Evidence of an Issue Evolution." *American Journal of Political Science* 41, pp. 718–737.

Adams, Julia. 1999. "Culture in Rational Choice Theories of State Formation." In *State/Culture: State Formation after the Cultural Turn,* ed. G. Steinmetz, pp. 98–122. Ithaca, NY: Cornell University Press.

Adamson, Christopher R. 1983. "Punishment After Slavery: Southern State Penal Systems, 1865–1890." *Social Problems* 30, pp. 556–569.

Adorno, Theodor W., Else Frenkel-Brunswick, Daniel Levinson, and R. Nevitt Stanford. 1950. *The Authoritarian Personality.* New York: Harper.

Akard, Patrick J. 1992. "Corporate Mobilization and Political Power: The Transformation of U.S. Economic Policy in the 1970s." *American Sociological Review* 57, pp. 597–615.

Akard, Patrick J. 1995. "The Return of the Market?: Reflections on the Real 'Conservative Tradition' in U.S. Policy Discourse." *Sociological Inquiry* 65, pp. 286–308.

Albrow, Martin. 1997. *The Global Age: State and Society Beyond Modernity.* Stanford, CA: Stanford University Press.

Aldrich, John H. 1993. "Rational Choice and Turnout." *American Journal of Political Science* 37, pp. 246–278.

Alesina, Alberto, Edward Glaeser, and Bruce Sacerdote. 2001. "Why Doesn't the United States Have a European-style Welfare State?" *Brookings Papers on Economic Activity* 2, pp. 187–277.

Alford, Robert R. 1963. *Party and Society.* Chicago: Rand McNally.

Alford, Robert R. and Eugene Lee. 1968. "Voting Turnout in American Cities." *American Political Science Review* 62, pp. 796–813.

Alford, Robert R. and Roger Friedland. 1975. "Political Participation and Public Policy." *Annual Review of Sociology* 1, pp. 429–479.

Alford, Robert R. and Roger Friedland. 1985. *Powers of Theory: Capitalism, the State and Democracy.* New York: Cambridge University Press.

Allen, Michael Patrick. 1991. "Capitalist Response to State Intervention: Theories of the State and Political Finance in the New Deal." *American Sociological Review* 56, pp. 679–689.

Allen, Michael Patrick. 1992. "Elite Social Movement Organizations and the State: The Rise of the Conservative Policy-Planning Network." *Research in Politics and Society* 4, pp. 87–109.

Allen, Michael Patrick and Philip Broyles. 1989. "Class Hegemony and Political Finance: Presidential Campaign Contributions of Wealthy Capitalist Families." *American Sociological Review* 54, pp. 275–287.

Allen, Michael Patrick and Philip Broyles. 1991. "Campaign Finance Reforms and the Presidential Campaign Contributions of Wealthy Capitalist Families." *Social Science Quarterly* 72, pp. 738–750.

Almond, Gabriel A. 1983. "Corporatism, Pluralism, and Professional Memory." *World Politics* 35, pp. 245–260.

Almond, Gabriel A., Eric Nordlinger, Theodore Lowi, and Sergio Fabbrini S. 1988. "The Return of the State." *American Political Science Review* 82, pp. 853–901.

Almond, Gabriel and Sidney Verba. 1963. *The Civic Culture: Political Attitudes and Democracy in Five Nations.* Princeton, NJ: Princeton University Press.

Alonso, William and Paul Starr (eds.). 1987. *The Politics of Numbers.* New York: Russell Sage Foundation.

Alozie, Nicholas. 1995. "Political Tolerance Hypotheses and White Opposition to a Martin Luther King Holiday in Arizona." *Social Science Journal* 32, pp. 1–16.

Alpert, Irvine and Ann Markusen. 1980. "Think Tanks and Capitalist Policy." In *Power Structure Research*, ed. G. W. Domhoff, pp. 173–197. Beverly Hills, CA: Sage.

Altemeyer, Bob. 1988. *Enemies of Freedom: Understanding Right Wing Authoritarianism.* San Francisco: Jossey Bass.

Altheide, David L. 1995. *Ecology of Communication: Cultural Formats of Control.* New York: Aldine de Gruyter.

Altheide, David L. 1997. "The News Media, the Problem Frame, and the Production of Fear." *Sociological Quarterly* 38, pp. 647–668.

Altheide, David L. and John M. Johnson. 1980. *Bureaucratic Propaganda.* Boston: Allyn and Bacon.

Altheide, David L. and Sam Michalowski R. 1999. "Fear in the News: A Discourse of Control." *Sociological Quarterly,* 40, pp. 475–503.

Amenta, Edwin. 1998. *Bold Relief: Institutional Politics and the Origins of Modern American Social Policy.* Princeton, NJ: Princeton University Press.

Amenta, Edwin and Bruce Carruthers. 1988. "The Formative Years of U.S. Social Spending Policies." *American Sociological Review* 53, pp. 661–678.

Amenta, Edwin and Drew Halfmann. 2000. "Wage Wars: Institutional Politics, WPA Wages, and the Struggle for U.S. Social Policy." *American Sociological Review* 65, pp. 506–528.

Amenta, Edwin and Jane D. Poulsen. 1996. "Social Politics in Context: The Institutional Politics Theory and Social Spending at the End of the New Deal." *Social Forces.* 75, pp. 33–61.

Amenta, Edwin and Theda Skocpol. 1988. "Redefining the New Deal." In *The Politics of Social Policy in the United States,* ed. A. Weir, O. Orloff, and T. Skocpol, pp. 81–122. Princeton, NJ: Princeton University Press.

Amenta, Edwin and Michael Young. 1999a. "Democratic States and Social Movements: Theoretical Arguments and Hypotheses." *Social Problems* 46, pp. 153–168.

Amenta, Edwin and Michael Young. 1999b. "Making an Impact: Conceptual and Methodological Implications of the Collective Goods Criterion." In *How Social Movements Matter,* ed. M. Giugni, D. McAdam, and C. Tilly, pp. 22–41. Minneapolis, MN: University of Minnesota Press.

Amenta, Edwin and Yvonne Zylan. 1991. "It Happened Here: Political Opportunity, the New Institutionalism and the Townsend Movement." *American Sociological Review* 56, pp. 250–265.

Amenta, Edwin, Chris Bonastia, and Neal Caren. 2001. "U.S. Foreign Policy in Comparative and Historical Perspective." *Annual Review of Sociology* 27, pp. 213–234.

Amenta, Edwin, Bruce Cattruthers, and Yvonne Zylan. 1992. "A Hero for the Aged? The Townsend Movement, The Political Mediation Model, and U.S. Old Age Policy, 1934–1950." *American Journal of Sociology* 98, pp. 308–339.

Amenta, Edwin, Elisabeth Clemens, Jefren Olsen, Sunita Parikh, and Theda Skocpol. 1987. "The Political Origins of Unemployment Insurance in Five American States." *Studies in American Political Development* 2, pp. 137–182.

Amenta, Edwin, Kathleen Dunleavy, and Mary Bernstein. 1994. "Stolen Thunder? Huey Long's 'Share Our Wealth,' Political Mediation, and the Second New Deal." *American Sociological Review* 59, pp. 678–702.

Aminzade, Ronald. 1981. *Class, Politics, and Early Industrial Capitalism: A Study of Mid-nineteenth Century Toulouse, France.* Albany, NY: State University of New York Press.

Aminzade, Ronald. 1984. "Capitalist Industrialization and Patterns of Industrial Protest: A Comparative Urban Study of Nineteenth-century France." *American Sociological Review* 49, pp. 437–453.

Aminzade, Ronald. 1993. *Ballots and Barricades: Class Formation and Republican Politics in France, 1840–1871.* Princeton, NJ: Princeton University Press.

Amjad, Mohammad. 1993. "Rural Migrants, Islam and Revolution in Iran." *Research in Social Movements, Conflicts and Change* 16, pp. 35–50.

Amsden, Alice H. 1989. *Asia's Next Giant.* New York: Oxford University Press.

Anbinder, Tyler. 1992. *Nativism and Slavery.* New York: Oxford University Press.

Andersen, Kristi. 1979. *The Creation of a Democratic Majority, 1928–1936.* Chicago: University of Chicago Press.

Andersen, Kristi. 1997. "Gender and Political Opinion." In *Understanding Public Opinion,* ed. B. Norrander and C. Wilcox, pp. 19–36. Washington, DC: Congressional Quarterly Press.

Anderson, Benedict. 1991. *Imagined Communities: Reflections on the Origin and Spread of Nationalism.* New York: Verso.

Anderson, Margo and Stephen E. Fienberg. 1999. *Who Counts?: The Politics of Census-taking in Contemporary America.* New York: Russell Sage Foundation.

Anderson, Perry. 1974. *Lineages of the Absolutist State.* London: New Left Books.

Andres, Gary. 1985. "Business Involvement in Campaign Finance: Factors Influencing the Decision to Form a Corporate PAC." *PS* 18, pp. 213–220.

Andress, Hans-Jurgen and Thorsten Heien. 2001. "Four Worlds of Welfare State Attitudes? A Comparison of Germany, Norway, and the United States." *European Sociological Review* 17, pp. 337–356.

Andrews, Kenneth T. 1997. "The Impacts of Social Movements on the Political Process: The Civil Rights Movement and Black Political Electoral Politics in Mississippi." *American Sociological Review* 62, pp. 800–819.

Andrews, Kenneth T. 2001. "Social Movements and Policy Implementation: The Mississippi Civil Rights Movement and the War on Poverty, 1965 to 1971." *American Sociological Review* 66, pp. 71–95.

Anker, Laura, Peter Seybold, and Michael Schwartz. 1987. "The Ties that Bind Business and Government." In *The Business Elite as a Ruling Class.* ed. M. Schwartz, pp. 97–122. New York: Holmes Meier.

Ansell, Amy. 1996. "Business Mobilization and the New Right." In *Business and the State in International Relations,* ed. R. Cox, pp. 57–78. Boulder, CO: Westview.

Ansell, Christopher K. 1997. "Symbolic Networks: The Realignment of the French Working Class, 1887–1894." *American Journal of Sociology* 103, pp. 359–390.

Ansell, Christopher K. and Arthur L. Burris. 1997. "Bosses and the City Unite! Labor Politics and Political Machine Consolidation, 1870–1910." *Studies in American Political Development* 11, pp. 1–43.

Ansolabehere, Stephen and Shanto Iyengar. 1995. *Going Negative: How Attack Ads Shrink and Polarize the Electorate.* New York: Free Press.

Ansolabehere, Stephen, Shanto Iyengar, Adam Simon, and Nicholas Valentino. 1994. "Does Attack Advertising Demobilize the Electorate?" *American Political Science Review* 88, pp. 829–838.

Ansolabehere, Stephen, Shanto Iyengar, and Adam Simon. 1995. "Evolving Perspectives on the Effects of Campaign Communication." *Research in Political Sociology* 7, pp. 13–32.

Anthony, Dick and Thomas Robbins. 1982. "Spiritual Innovation and the Crisis of American Civil Religion." *Daedalus* 111, pp. 215–234.

Apostle, Richard, Charles Glock, Thomas Piazza, and Marijean Suelzle. 1983. *The Anatomy of Racial Attitudes.* Berkeley, CA: University of California Press.

Apple, Michael W. 1979. *Ideology and Curriculum.* Boston: Routledge and Kegan Paul.

Apple, Michael W. 1989. "The Politics of Common Sense: Schooling, Populism and the New Right." In *Critical Pedagogy, the State, and Cultural Struggle,* ed. H. Giroux and Peter McLaren, pp. 32–49. Albany, NY: SUNY Press.

Apple, Michael W. 1992. *Official Knowledge.* Boston: Routledge.

Apple, Michael W. and Lois Weis. 1983. "Ideology and Practice in Schooling." In *Ideology and Practice in Schooling,* ed. M. Apple and L. Weis, pp. 3–33. Philadelphia: Temple University Press.

Appleby, R. Scott. 1997. "Catholics and the Christian Right: An Uneasy Alliance." In *Sojourners in the Wilderness,* ed. C. Smidt and J. Penning, pp. 93–113. Lanham, MD: Rowman & Littlefield.

Apter, David. 1965. *The Politics of Modernization.* Chicago: University of Chicago Press.

Arblaster, Anthony. 1994. *Democracy,* 2nd ed. Minneapolis: University of Minnesota Press.

Archer, Margaret Scotford. 1979. *Social Origins of Educational Systems.* Beverly Hills, CA: Sage.

Arendt, Hannah. 1958. *The Origins of Totalitarianism,* 2nd ed. New York: Meridian.

Arenson, Karen W. 2000. "SUNY Fight Over Curriculum Mirrors Larger National Debate." *New York Times,* June 6, 2000.

Armstrong, John. 1982. *Nations before Nationalism.* Chapel Hill, NC: University of North Carolina Press.

Arts, Wil and John Gelissen. 2001. "Welfare States, Solidarity and Justice Principles: Does the Type Really Matter?" *Acta Sociologica* 44, pp. 283–299.

Arvizu, John R. and Chris F. Garcia. 1996. "Latino Voting Participation: Explaining and Differentiating Latino Voter Turnout." *Hispanic Journal of Behavioral Science* 18, pp. 104–128.

Ashford, Douglas E. 1986. *The Emergence of Welfare States.* London: Basil Blackwell.

Aspalter, Christian. 2001. "Different Worlds of Welfare Capitalism." Australian National University Graduate Program in Public Policy, Discussion Paper No. 80.

Astin, Alexander. 1992. "Educational 'Choice': Its Appeal May be Illusory." *Sociology of Education* 65, pp. 255–260.

Austin, Andrew. 2002. "Advancing Accumulation and Managing its Discontents: The U.S. Anti-environmental Countermovement." *Sociological Spectrum* 22, pp. 71–105.

Averitt, Robert T. 1968. *The Dual Economy: The Dynamics of American Industry Structure.* New York: Norton.

Avey, Michael J. 1989. *The Demobilization of American Voters: A Comprehensive Theory of Voter Turnout.* Westport, CN: Greenwood Press.

B

Babb, Sarah. 1996. "A True American System of Finance: Frame Resonance in the U.S. Labor Movement, 1866 to 1886." *American Sociological Review* 61, pp. 1033–1052.

Bachrach, Peter and Morton S. Baratz. 1963. "Decision and Nondecisions: An Analytic Framework." *American Political Science Review* 57, pp. 633–634.

Badie, Bertrand and Pierre Birnbaum. 1983. *The Sociology of the State,* trans. Arthur Goldhammer. Chicago: University of Chicago Press.

Baker, Jean H. 1983. *Affairs of Party: The Political Culture of Northern Democrats in the Mid-Nineteenth Century.* Ithaca, NY: Cornell University Press.

Baker, Russ. 1998. "Jesse Helm's Honeypot." *Nation* 267, no. 3 (July 20, 1998), pp. 22–24.

Balbus, Isaac D. 1977. *The Dialectics of Legal Repression.* New Brunswick, NJ: Transaction Books.

Balibar, Etienne. 1996. "The Nation Form: History and Ideology." In *Becoming National,* ed. G. Eley and R. Suny, pp. 132–149. New York: Oxford University Press.

Balkan, Sheila, Ronald J. Berger, and Janet Schmidt. 1980. *Crime and Deviance in America: A Critical Approach.* Belmont, CA: Wadsworth.

Balough, Brian. 1991. "Reorganizing the Organizational Synthesis: Federal-Professional Relations in Modern America." *Studies in American Political Development* 5, pp. 119–172.

Banaszak, Lee Ann. 1998. "Use of the Initiative Process by Women Suffrage Movements." In *Social Movements and American Political Institutions,* ed. A. Costain and A. McFarland, pp. 99–114. Lanham, MD: Rowman and Littlefield.

Bane, Mary Jo. 1988. "Politics and Polices of the Feminization of Poverty." In *The Politics of Social Policy in the United States,* ed. M. Weir, A. S. Orloff, and T. Skocpol, pp. 381–396. Princeton, NJ: Princeton University Press.

Bannister, Robert C. 1987. *Sociology and Scientism: The American Question for Objectivity, 1880–1940.* Chapel Hill, NC: University of North Carolina Press.

Barbalet, J. M. 1988. *Citizenship: Rights, Struggle, and Class Inequality.* Minneapolis: University of Minnesota Press.

Barhel, Diane. 1996. "Getting in Touch with History: The Role of Historical Preservation in Shaping Collective Memories." *Qualitative Sociology* 19, pp. 345–364.

Baritz, Loren. 1960. *The Servants of Power: A History of the Use of Social Science in American Industry.* Middletown, CT: Wesleyan University Press.

Barkan, Steven E. 1983. "Jury Nullification in Political Trials." *Social Problems* 31, pp. 28–44.

Barkan, Steven E. and Steven F. Cohn. 1993. "Commitment Across the Miles: Ideological and Microstructural Sources of Membership Support in a National Anti-hunger Organization." *Social Problems* 40, pp. 362–373.

Barkan, Steven E., Steven Cohen, and William Whitaker. 1995. "Beyond Recruitment: Predictors of Differential Participation in a National Antihunger Organization." *Sociological Forum* 10, pp. 113–134.

Barkey, Karen and Sunita Parikh. 1991. "Comparative Perspectives on the State." *Annual Review of Sociology* 17, pp. 523–549.

Barkun, Michael. 1996. *Religion and the Racist Right: The Origins of the Christian Identity Movement,* rev. ed. Chapel Hill, NC: University of North Carolina Press.

Barlow, David E. and Melissa Hickman Barlow. 1995. "Federal Criminal Justice Legislation and the Post-World War II Social Structure of Accumulation in the United States." *Crime, Law and Social Change* 22, pp. 239–267.

Barlow, David E., Melissa Hickman Barlow, and Theodore G. Chiricos. 1993. "Long Economic Cycles and the Criminal Justice System in the U.S." *Crime, Law and Social Change* 19, pp. 143–169.

Barnes, Donna A. 1987. "Organization and Radical Protest: An Antithesis?" *Sociological Quarterly* 28, pp. 575–594.

Barnes, Donna A. and Catherine Connolly. 1999. "Repression, the Judicial System, and Political Opportunities for Civil Rights Advocacy During Reconstruction." *Sociological Quarterly* 40, pp. 327–345.

Barnes, Ronald and Charles Crawford. 1999. "School Shootings, the Media, and Public Fear: Ingredients for a Moral Panic." *Crime, Law, and Social Change* 32, pp. 147–168.

Barrow, Clyde W. 1990. *Universities and the Capitalist State: Corporate Liberalism and the Reconstruction of American Higher Education, 1894–1928.* Madison, WI: University of Wisconsin Press.

Barrow, Clyde W. 1993. *Critical Theories of the State.* Madison, WI: University of Wisconsin Press.

Barrow, Deborah J. and Gary Zuk. 1990. "An Institutional Analysis of Turnover in the Lower Federal Courts, 1900–1987." *Journal of Politics* 52, pp. 457–476.

Barsamian, David. 1995. "The Right-Wing Attack on Public Broadcasting." In *Eyes Right,* ed. C. Berlet, pp. 159–165. Boston: South End Press.

Bartels, Larry M. 1993. "Messages Received." *American Political Science Review* 87, pp. 267–286.

Bartels, Larry M. 1996. "Uninformed Voters: Information Effects in Presidential Elections." *American Political Science Review* 40, pp. 194–230.

Barth, Frederick. 1969. *Ethnic Groups and Boundaries: The Social Organization of Cultural Differences.* Boston: Little, Brown.

Barthel, Diane. 1996. "Getting in Touch with History." *Qualitative Sociology* 19, pp. 345–364.

Bartle, John. 1998. "Left-Right Position Matters, But Does Social Class? Causal Models of the 1992 British General Election." *British Journal of Political Science* 28, pp. 501–529.

Barzel, Yoram. 2002. *A Theory of the State: Economic Rights, Legal Rights, and the Scope of the State.* New York: Cambridge University Press.

Basham, Patrick. 2002. "The Illiberal Reality of European-style Campaign Reform." *CATO Institute.* (March 13, 2002), http://www.cato.org/dailys/03-13-02.html

Bates, Robert, Rui de Figueiredo, and Barry Weingast. 1998. "The Politics of Interpretation: Rationality, Culture and Transition." *Politics and Society* 26, pp. 221–256 and 26, pp. 603–642.

Baumer, Eric P., Steven F. Messner, and Richard Rosenfeld. 2003. "Explaining Spatial Variation in Support for Capital Punishment: A Multilevel Analysis." *American Journal of Sociology* 108, pp. 844–875.

Baumgartner, Frank R. and Bryan D. Jones. 1991. "Agency Dynamics and Policy Subsystems." *Journal of Politics* 53, pp. 1044–1074.

Bayley, David H. 1975. "The Police and Political Development in Europe." In *The Formation of Nation States in Western Europe*. ed. C. Tilly, pp. 328–379. Princeton, NJ: Princeton University Press.

Beatty, Kathleen Murphy and B. Oliver Walter. 1984. "Religious Preference and Practice: Reevaluating Their Impact on Political Tolerance" *The Public Opinion Quarterly* 48, pp. 318–329.

Beatty, Kathleen Murphy and B. Oliver Walter. 1988. "Fundamentalism, Evangelicals and Politics." *American Politics Quarterly* 16, pp. 43–59.

Beck, E. M. and Stewart E. Tolnay. 1990. "The Killing Fields of the Deep South: The Market for Cotton and the Lynching of Blacks, 1882–1930." *American Sociological Review* 55, pp. 526–539.

Beck, Gerald. 1991. "Corporate Liberalism Reconsidered: A Review Essay." *Journal of Policy History* 3, pp. 70–84.

Beck, Paul Allen and M. Kent Jennings. 1991. "Family Traditions, Political Periods and the Development of Political Orientations." *Journal of Politics* 53, pp. 742–763.

Beck, Paul Allen. 1984. "The Dealignment Era in America." In *Electoral Change in Advanced Industrial Democracies: Realignment or Dealignment?*, ed. R. Dalton, S. Flanagan and P. Beck, pp. 240–266. Princeton, NJ: Princeton University Press.

Beck, Richard and Howard E. Aldrich. 1972. "Patterns of Vandalism during Civil Disorders as an Indicator of Selection of Targets." *American Sociological Review* 37, pp. 533–547.

Becker, Gary S. 1976. *The Economic Approach to Human Behavior*. Chicago: University of Chicago Press.

Becker, Gary S. 1981. *A Treatise on the Family*. Cambridge, MA: Harvard University Press.

Becker, Gary S. 1996. *Accounting for Tastes*. Cambridge MA: Harvard University Press.

Becker, Gary S. and William M. Landes. 1974. *Essays in the Economics of Crime and Punishment*. New York: Columbia University Press.

Becker, Howard and William C. Rau. 1992. "Sociology in the 1990s." *Society* 30, pp. 70–74.

Becker, Lee and Gerald M. Kosicki. 1995. "Understanding the Message-Producer/Message-Receiver Transaction." *Research in Political Sociology* 7, pp. 33–62.

Beckett, Katherine. 1994. "Setting the Public Agenda: 'Street Crime' and Drug Use in American Politics." *Social Problems* 41, pp. 425–448.

Beckett, Katherine. 1995. "Media Depictions of Drug Abuse: The Impact of Official Sources." *Research In Political Sociology* 7, pp. 161–182.

Beckett, Katherine. 1997. *Making Crime Pay: Law and Order in Contemporary American Politics*. New York: Oxford University Press.

Beckett, Katherine and Theodore Sasson. 2000. *The Politics of Injustice: Crime and Punishment in America*. Thousand Oaks, CA: Pine Forge Press.

Beckett, Katherine and Bruce Western. 2001. "Governing Social Marginality: Welfare, Incarceration, and the Transformation of State Policy." *Punishment and Society* 3, pp. 43–59.

Bell, Daniel, ed. 1955. *The Radical Right*. Garden City, New York: Doubleday.

Bell, Daniel. 1960. *End of Ideology*. Glencoe, IL: Free Press.

Bell, Daniel. 1964. *The New American Right*. Garden City, NY: Doubleday.

Bell, Wendell and Robert V. Robinson. 1978. "An Index of Evaluated Equality." *Comparative Social Research* 1, pp. 235–270.

Bellah, Robert N. 1967. "Civil Religion in America." *Daedalus* 96, pp. 1–21.

Bellah, Robert N. 1970. *Beyond Belief: Essays on Religion in a Post-Traditional World*. New York: Harper and Row.

Bellah, Robert N. 1992. *Broken Covenant: American Civil Religion in a Time of Trial*, 2nd ed. Chicago: University of Chicago Press.

Bellah, Robert N. 1998. "Religion and the Legitimation of the American Republic." *Society* 35, pp. 193–201.

Bellent, Russ and Chip Berlet. 1992. *Coors Connection: How Coors Family Philanthropy Undermines Democratic Pluralism*, 2nd ed. Boston: South End Press.

Belluck, Pam. 1998. "Gay Church Sues TV Station for Rejecting an Infomercial." *New York Times*, October 28, 1998.

Belsey, Andrew 1986. "The New Right, Social Order and Civil Liberties." In *The Ideology of the New Right*, ed. R. Levitas, pp. 167–197. New York: Polity Press.

Benavot, Aaron, Yun-Kyung Cha, David Kamens, John W. Meyer, and Suk-Ying Wong. 1991. "Knowledge for the Masses: World Models and National Curricula, 1920–1986." *American Sociological Review* 56, pp. 85–100.

Bendix, Reinhard. 1964. *Nation-Building and Citizenship*. New York: John Wiley.

Bendix, Reinhard. 1968. *State and Society: A Reader for Comparative Political Sociology*. Boston: Little Brown.

Bendix, Reinhard and Seymour Martin Lipset. 1957. "Political Sociology." *Current Sociology* 6, pp. 79–99.

Benford, Robert D. 1993a. "Frame Disputes within the Nuclear Disarmament Movement." *Social Forces* 71, pp. 677–701.

Benford, Robert D. 1993b. " 'You Could be the Hundredth Monkey': Collective Action Frames and Vocabularies of Motive within the Nuclear Disarmament Movement." *Sociological Quarterly* 34, pp. 195–216.

Benford, Robert D. and David A. Snow. 2000. "Framing Processes and Social Movements: An Overview and Assessment." *Annual Review of Sociology* 26, pp. 611–639.

Bennett, Stephan E. and David Resnick. 1990. "The Implications of Non-voting in the United States." *American Journal of Political Science* 34, pp. 771–802.

Bennett, Stephen E. and Alfred Tuchfarber. 1975. "The Social Structural Sources of Cleavage on Law and Order." *American Journal of Political Science* 19, pp. 419–438.

Bensel, Richard Franklin. 1984. *Sectionalism and American Political Development, 1880–1980*. Madison, WI: University of Wisconsin Press.

Benton, Ted. 1984. *The Rise and Fall of Structural Marxism: Althusser and His Influence*. New York: St. Martins.

Berelson, Bernard, Paul Lazarfeld, and William McPhee. 1954. *Voting*. Chicago: University of Chicago Press.

Berezin, Mabel. 1991. "The Organization of Political Ideology: Culture, State, and Theater in Fascist Italy." *American Sociological Review* 56, pp. 639–652.

Berezin, Mabel. 1994. "Cultural Form and Political Meaning." *American Journal of Sociology* 99, pp. 1237–1286.

Bergenhenegouwen, G. 1987. "Hidden Curriculum in the University." *Higher Education* 16, pp. 535–543.

Bergesen, Albert J. 1977. "Political Witch Hunts." *American Sociological Review* 42, pp. 220–233.

Bergesen, Albert J. 1984. *The Sacred and the Subversive: Political Witch Hunts as National Rituals*. Storrs, CT: Society for Scientific Study of Religion.

Berk, Gerald. 1994. *Alternative Tracks: The Constitution of American Industrial Order, 1865–1917*. Baltimore: John Hopkins University Press.

Berke, Richard L. 1987. "Election Unit Studies Funds and Business." *New York Times*, December 7, 1987.

Berkowitz, Edward D. 1991. *America's Welfare State: From Roosevelt to Reagan*. Baltimore: John Hopkins University Press.

Berkowitz, Edward D. and Kim McQuaid. 1980. *Creating the Welfare State*. New York: Praeger.

Berlet, Chip and Margaret Quigley. 1995. "Theocracy and White Supremacy." In *Eyes Right*, ed C. Berlet, pp. 15–43. Boston: South End Press.

Berlow, Alan. 1999. "The Wrong Man." *Atlantic Monthly* 284 (November), pp. 66–91.

Berman, Sheri. 1997. "Civil Society and Political Institutionalization." *American Behavioral Scientist* 40, pp. 562–574.

Bernstein, Marver H. 1955. *Regulating Business by Independent Commission*. Princeton, NJ: Princeton University Press.

Bernstein, Mary. 1997. "Celebration and Suppression: The Strategic Uses of Identity by the Lesbian and Gay Movement." *American Journal of Sociology* 103, pp. 531–565.

Berry, William D. 1979. "Utility Regulation in the States: Policy Effects of Professionalism and Salience to the Customer." *American Journal of Political Science* 23, pp. 263–277.

Berry, William D. 1984. "An Alternative to the Capture Theory of Regulation: The Case of State Public Utility Commissions." *American Journal of Political Science* 28, pp. 524–558.

Bertz, Hans Georg. 1990. "Value Change and Postmaterialist Politics: The Case of West Germany." *Comparative Political Studies* 23, pp. 239–256.

Berube, Maurice. 1994. *American School Reform: Progressive, Equity and Excellence Movements, 1883–1993*. Westport, CT: Praeger.

Best, Joel, ed. 1989. *Images of Issues: Typifying Contemporary Social Problems*. New York City, NY: Aldine de Gruyter.

Best, Joel. 1993. "But Seriously Folks." In *Reconsidering Social Constructionism*, ed. J. Holstein and G. Miller, pp. 129–149. New York City, NY: Aldine de Gruyter.

Betz, Hans-Georg. 1990. "Value Change and Postmaterialist Politics." *Comparative Political Studies* 23, pp. 239–257.

Bielby, William T. and Denise D. Bielby. 1994. "All Hits Are Flukes': Institutionalized Decision Making and the Rhetoric of Network Prime Time Development." *American Journal of Sociology* 99, pp. 1287–1313.

Biersteker, Thomas J. and Cynthia Weber. 1996. "The Social Construction of State Sovereignty." In *State Sovereignty as Social Construct*, eds. T. Biersteker and C. Weber, pp. 1–21. New York: Cambridge University Press.

Billings, Dwight B. 1990. "Religion as Opposition: A Gramscian Analysis." *American Journal of Sociology* 96, pp. 1–31.

Billington, Ray Allen. 1964. *The Protestant Crusade, 1800–1960*. Chicago: Quadrangle.

Bills, David B. 1983. "Social Reproduction and the Bowles-Gintis Thesis of a Correspondence Between School and Work Settings." *Research in Sociology of Education and Socialization*. 4, pp. 185–210.

Bills, David B. 1988. "Credentials and Capacities: Employer's Perceptions of the Acquisition of Skills." *Sociological Quarterly* 29, pp. 439–450.

Binder, Amy. 1993. "Constructing Racial Rhetoric: Media Depictions of Harm in Heavy Metal and Rap Music." *American Sociological Review* 58, pp. 753–768.

Birch, Anthony H. 1993. *The Concepts and Theories of Modern Democracy*. New York: Routledge.

Birnbaum, Pierre. 1982. "The State versus Corporatism." *Politics and Society* 11, pp. 477–501.

Björn, Lars. 1979. "Labor Parties, Economic Growth and the Redistribution of Income in Five Capitalist Democracies." *Comparative Social Research* 2, pp. 93–128.

Black, Donald. 1984. "Crime as Social Control." In *Toward a General Theory of Social Control*, Vol. 2, ed. D. Black, pp. 1–28. New York: Academic Press.

Blau, Peter M. 1997. "On Limitations of Rational Choice Theory for Sociology." *American Sociologist* 28, pp. 16–21.

Bledsoe, Timothy, Susan Welch, Lee Singelman, and Michael Combs. 1995. "Residential Context and Racial Solidarity among African Americans." *American Journal of Political Science* 39, pp. 434–458.

Blee, Kathleen M. 1985. "Mobility and Political Orientation: An Analysis of Sex Differences." *Sociological Perspectives* 28, pp. 385–400.

Blee, Kathleen M. 2002. *Inside Organized Racism: Women in the Hate Movement*. Berkeley, CA: University of California Press.

Bleiker, Ronald. 2000. *Popular Dissent, Human Agency, and Global Politics*. New York: Cambridge University Press.

Block, Fred. 1977a. "The Ruling Class Does Note Rule: Notes on the Marxist Theory of the State." *Socialist Revolution* 33, pp. 6–28.

Block, Fred. 1977b. "Beyond Corporate Liberalism." *Social Problems* 24, pp. 352–361.

Block, Fred. 1981. "The Fiscal Crisis of the Capitalist State." *Annual Review of Sociology* 7, pp. 1–27.

Block, Fred. 1987. *Revising State Theory: Essays in Politics and Postindustrialism.* Philadelphia: Temple University Press.

Blocker, Jack S., Jr. 1989. *American Temperance Movements: Cycles of Reform.* Boston: Twayne.

Blocker, T. Jean and Douglas Lee Eckberg. 1989. "Environmental Issues as Women's Issues." *Social Science Quarterly* 70, pp. 586–593.

Blocker, T. Jean and Douglas Lee Eckberg. 1997. "Gender and Environmentalism: Results from the 1993 General Social Survey." *Social Science Quarterly* 78, pp. 841–858.

Blocker, T. Jean and Paul Riedesel. 1978. "The Nonconsequences of Objective and Subjective Status Inconsistency: Requiem for a Moribund Concept." *Sociological Quarterly* 19, pp. 332–339.

Blumer, Herbert. 1978. "Social Unrest and Collective Protest." *Studies in Symbolic Interactionism* 1, pp. 1–54.

Bobo, Lawrence. 1983. Whites' Opposition to School Busing: Symbolic Racism or Realistic Group Conflict? *Journal of Personality and Social Psychology* 45, pp. 1196–1210.

Bobo, Lawrence. 1991. "Social Responsibility, Individualism, and Redistributive Policies." *Sociological Forum* 6, pp. 71–92.

Bobo, Lawrence and Franklin D. Gilliam, Jr. 1990. "Race, Sociopolitical Participation and Black Empowerment." *American Political Science Review* 84, pp. 377–393.

Bobo, Lawrence and Frederic Licari. 1989. "Education and Political Tolerance." *Public Opinion Quarterly* 53, pp. 285–308.

Bocock, Robert. 1986. *Hegemony.* New York: Travistock.

Bodnar, John. 1994. "Public Memory in an American City: Commemoration in Cleveland." In *Commemorations: The Politics of National Identity,* ed. J. Gillis, pp. 74–89. Princeton, NJ: Princeton University Press.

Boies, John L. 1989. "Money, Business and the State: Material Interests, Fortune 500 Corporations and the Size of Political Action Committees." *American Sociological Review* 54, pp. 821–832.

Bolce, Louis and Gerald de Maio. 1993. "The 1992 Republican 'Tent:' No Blacks Walked In." *Political Science Quarterly* 108, pp. 255–271.

Bolce, Louis and Gerald de Maio. 1999. "Religious Outlook, Culture War Politics, and Antipathy toward Christian Fundamentalists." *Public Opinion Quarterly* 63, pp. 29–61.

Boli, John and George M. Thomas. 1997. "World Culture in the World Polity: A Century of International Non-Governmental Organization." *American Sociological Review* 62, pp. 171–190.

Boli, John and George M. Thomas, eds. 1999. *Constructing World Culture.* Stanford, CA: Stanford University Press.

Bollen, Kenneth A. 1991. "Political Democracy: Conceptual and Measurement Traps." In *On Measuring Democracy: Its Consequence and Concomitants,* ed. A. Inkeles, pp. 3–20. New Brunswick, NJ: Transaction Books.

Bollen, Kenneth A. and Robert W. Jackman. 1985. "Political Democracy and the Size Distribution of Income." *American Sociological Review* 50, pp. 438–457.

Bonk, Kathy. 1988. "The Selling of the 'Gender Gap': The Role of Organized Feminism." In *The Politics of Gender Gap: The Social Construction of Political Influence,* ed. C. M. Mueller, pp. 82–101. Newbury Park, CA: Sage.

Bord, Richard and Robert E. O'Connor. 1997. "The Gender Gap in Environmental Attitudes: The Case of Perceived Vulnerability to Risk." *Social Science Quarterly* 78, pp. 830–840.

Bottomore, Tom B. 1983. *A Dictionary of Marxist Thought.* Cambridge, MA: Harvard University Press.

Bottomore, Tom B. 1984. *The Frankfurt School.* New York: Travistock.

Bourdieu, Pierre and Jean-Claude Passeron. 1990. *Reproduction in Education,* 2nd ed. Thousand Oaks, CA: Sage.

Bowler, Shaun and Todd Donovan. 1995. "Popular Responsiveness to Taxation." *Political Research Quarterly* 48, pp. 79–99.

Bowles, Samuel and Herbert Gintis. 1976. *Schooling in Capitalist America: Educational Reform and the Contradictions of Economic Life.* New York: Basic Books.

Bowles, Samuel and Herbert Gintis. 1986. *Democracy and Capitalism.* New York: Basic Books.

Bowman, Scott R. 1996. *The Modern Corporation and American Political Thought.* University Park, PA: Pennsylvania State University Press.

Boyd, Richard. 1981. "Decline of U.S. Voter Turnout." *American Politics Quarterly* 9, pp. 123–159.

Boyle, Elizabeth Heger. 2000. "Is Law the Rule? Using Political Frames to Explain Cross-National Variation in Legal Activity." *Social Forces* 78, pp. 1195–1226.

Bradley, David, Evelyne Huber, Stephanie Moller, François Nielsen, and John D. Stephens. 2003. "Distribution and Redistribution in Postindustrial Democracies." *World Politics* 55, pp. 193–228.

Brady, David W. 1981. "Critical Elections, Congressional Parties and Clusters of Policy Changes." *British Journal of Political Science* 8, pp. 79–99.

Brady, David W. and Phillip Althroff. 1974. "Party Voting in the U.S. House of Representatives, 1890–1910: Elements of a Responsible Party System." *Journal of Politics* 36, pp. 753–775.

Brady, Henry, Sidney Verba, and Kay Lehman Scholzman. 1995. "Beyond SES: A Resource Model of Political Participation." *American Political Science Review* 89, pp. 271–294.

Braithwaite, John and Peter Drahos. 2000. *Global Business Regulation.* New York: Cambridge University Press.

Brand, Donald R. 1983. "Corporatism, the NRA, and the Oil Industry." *Political Science Quarterly* 98, pp. 99–118.

Brass, Paul R. 1994. "Elite Competition and Nation-Formation." In *Nationalism.,* ed. J. Hutchinson and A. D. Smith, pp. 83–89. New York: Oxford University Press.

Brauer, Jerald, ed. 1976. *Religion and the American Revolution.* Philadelphia: Fortress Press.

Brennan, Mary C. 1995. *Turning Right in the Sixties: The Conservative Capture of the GOP*. Chapel Hill, NC: University of North Carolina Press.

Breuilly, John. 1994. "The Sources of Nationalist Ideology." In *Nationalism*, ed. J. Hutchinson and A. D. Smith, pp. 103–113. New York: Oxford University Press.

Bridges, Amy. 1992. "Winning the West to Municipal Reform." *Urban Affairs Quarterly* 27, pp. 494–518.

Bridges, Amy. 1994. "Creating Cultures of Reform." *Studies in American Political Development* 8, pp. 1–23.

Bridges, Amy and Richard Kronick. 1999. "Writing the Rules to Win the Game: The Middle-Class Regimes of Municipal Reformers." *Urban Affairs Review* 34, pp. 691–706.

Bright, Charles C. 1984. "The State in the United States during the Nineteenth Century." In *Statemaking and Social Movements*, eds. C. Bright and S. Harding, pp. 121–158. Ann Arbor, MI: University of Michigan Press.

Brint, Steven. 1984. "New Class and Cumulative Trend Explanations of Liberal Political Attitudes Among Professionals." *American Journal of Sociology* 90, pp. 30–71.

Brint, Steven. 1998. *Schools and Societies.* Thousand Oaks, CA: Pine Forge Press.

Brint, Steven and Jerome Karabel. 1989. *The Diverted Dream: Community Colleges and the Promise of Educational Opportunity in America, 1900–1985*. New York: Oxford University Press.

Brinton, Mary C. and Victor Nee, eds. 1998. *The New Institutionalism in Sociology*. New York: Russell Sage Foundation.

Broadbent, Jeffrey. 1988. "State as Process: The Effect of Party and Class on Citizen Participation in Japanese Local Government." *Social Problems* 35, pp. 131–144.

Broadbent, Jeffrey. 1998. *Environmental Politics in Japan: Networks of Power and Protest*. New York: Cambridge University Press.

Brogan, Joseph V. 1996. "A Mirror of Enlightenment: The Rational Choice Debate." *The Review of Politics*, 58, pp. 793–806.

Bromley, David G. and Anson Shupe. 1984. *New Christian Politics*. Macon, GA: Mercer University Press.

Brooke, James. 1998. "Friends and Strangers Mourn Gay Student in Wyoming." *New York Times*, October 17, 1998.

Brooke, James. 1999a. "Rocky Mountain States Resisting Move to Broaden Hate-Crime Laws." *New York Times*, February 5, 1999.

Brooke, James. 1999b. "Gay Murder Trial Ends with Guilty Plea." *New York Times*, April 6, 1999.

Brooks, Clem. 1994. "Class Consciousness and Politics in Comparative Perspective." *Social Science Research* 23, pp. 167–195.

Brooks, Clem. 2000. "Civil Rights Liberalism and the Suppression of a Republican Political Realignment in the United States, 1971 to 1996." *American Sociological Review* 65, pp. 483–505.

Brooks, Clem and Jeff Manza. 1994. "Do Changing Values Explain the New Politics? A Critical Assessment of the Postmaterialist Thesis." *Sociological Quarterly* 35, pp. 541–571.

Brooks, Clem and Jeff Manza. 1997a. "The Social and Ideological Bases of Middle-Class Political Realignment in the United States, 1972–1992." *American Sociological Review* 62, pp. 191–209.

Brooks, Clem and Jeff Manza. 1997b. "Class Politics and Political Change in the United States, 1952–1992." *Social Forces* 76, pp. 379–408.

Brooks, Clem and Jeff Manza. 1997c. "Social Cleavages and Political Alignments in U.S. Elections." *American Sociological Review* 62, pp. 937–946.

Brooks, Jonathan, A. Colin Cameron, and Colin Carter. 1998. "Political Economics Act Committee Contributions and U.S. Congressional Voting on Sugar Legislation." *American Journal of Agricultural Economics* 80, pp. 441–455.

Brown, David. 1994. *The State and Ethnic Politics of South-East Asia*. New York: Routledge.

Brown, E. Richard. 1979. *Rockefeller Medicine Men: Medicine and Capitalism in America*. Berkeley, CA: University of California Press.

Brown, Michael K. 1999. *Race, Money, and the American Welfare State*. Ithaca, NY: Cornell University Press.

Browning, Rufus P., Dale R. Marshall, and David Tabb. 1984. *Protest Is Not Enough*. Berkeley, CA: University of California Press.

Brownstein, Henry H. 1991. "The Media and the Construction of Random Drug Violence." *Social Justice* 18, pp. 85–103.

Broyles, Philip A. 1993. "The Corporate Elite Goes To Washington: Presidential Campaign Contributions of Corporate Officers." *Social Science Research* 22, pp. 72–91.

Bruce, Steve. 1988. *The Rise and Fall of the New Christian Right: Conservative Protestant Politics in America, 1978–1988*. New York: Oxford University Press.

Bruce, Steve. 1994. "The Inevitable Failure of the New Christian Right." *Sociological Analysis* 55, pp. 229–242.

Bruce, Steve. 1995. *The Rapture of Politics: The Christian Right as the United States Approaches the Year 2000*. New Brunswick, NJ: Transaction Publishers.

Bruce, Steve. 1998. *Conservative Protestant Politics*. New York: Oxford University Press.

Brundage, W. Fitzhugh. 1993. *Lynching in the New South: Georgia and Virginia, 1880–1930*. Urbana, IL: University of Illinois Press.

Brush, Lisa D. 2002. "Changing the Subject: Gender and Welfare Regime Studies." *Social Politics* 9, pp. 161–186.

Brustein, William. 1991. "The 'Red Menace' and the Rise of Italian Fascism." *American Sociological Review* 56, pp. 652–664.

Brustein, William. 1996. *The Logic of Evil: The Social Origins of the Nazi Party, 1925–1933*. New Haven, CT: Yale University Press.

Brym, Robert J., Michael W. Gillespie, and Rhonda L. Lenton. 1989. "Class Power, Class Mobilization and Class Voting: The Canadian Case." *Canadian Journal of Sociology* 14, pp. 25–44.

Bryson, Bethany. 1996. " 'Anything but Heavy Metal': Symbolic Exclusion and Musical Dislikes." *American Sociological Review* 61, pp. 884–899.

Buechler, Steven M. 1993. "Beyond Resource Mobilization? Emerging Trends in Social Movement Theory." *Sociological Quarterly* 34, pp. 217–236.

Buechler, Steven M. 1995. "New Social Movement Theories." *Sociological Quarterly* 36, pp. 441–464.

Buechler, Steven M. 2000. *Social Movements in Advanced Capitalism: The Political Economy and Cultural Construction of Social Activism.* New York: Oxford University Press.

Buenker, John D. 1978. *Urban Liberalism and Progressive Reform.* New York: Norton.

Burawoy, Michael. 1978. "Contemporary Currents in Marxist Theory." *American Sociologist* 13, pp. 50–64.

Burch, Peter H. 1980. *Elites in American History*, vol. 3, *The New Deal to the Carter Administration.* New York: Holmes and Meier.

Burk, James. 1985. "The Origins of Federal Securities Regulation: A Case Study in the Social Control of Finance." *Social Forces* 63, pp. 1010–1029.

Burnham, David. 1997. "The F.B.I." *Nation* 265, Issue 5 (August 11, 1997).

Burnham, James. 1943 [1970]. *The Machivalleians: Defenders of Freedom.* Chicago: Gateway.

Burnham, Walter Dean. 1967. "Party Systems and Political Process." In *The American Party Systems: Stages of Political Development*, eds. W. N. Chambers and Walter Dean Burnham, pp. 277–307. New York: Norton.

Burnham, Walter Dean. 1970. *Critical Elections and the Mainsprings of American Politics.* New York: Norton.

Burnham, Walter Dean. 1984. "The Appearance and Disappearance of the American Voter." In T. Ferguson and J. Rogers, eds. *The Political Economy*, pp. 112–139. Armonk, NY: M. E. Sharpe.

Burris, Val and James Salt. 1990. "The Politics of Capitalist Class Segments: A Test of Corporate Liberalism Theory." *Social Problems* 37, pp. 341–359.

Burris, Val. 1983. "The Social and Political Consequences of Overeducation." *American Sociological Review* 48, pp. 454–467.

Burris, Val. 1987. "Business Partisanship of American Business: A Study of Corporate Political Action Committees." *American Sociological Review* 52, pp. 732–744.

Burris, Val. 1991. "Interlocks and the Political Behavior of Corporations and Corporate Elites." *Social Science Quarterly* 72, pp. 537–551.

Burris, Val. 1992a. "PACs, Interlocks and Regional Differences in Corporate Conservatism: Comment." *American Journal of Sociology* 97, pp. 1451–1455.

Burris, Val. 1992b. "Elite Policy-Planning Networks in the United States." *Research in Politics and Society* 4, pp. 113–134.

Burris, Val. 2000. "The Myth of Old Money Liberalism: The Politics of the Forbes 400 Richest Americans." *Social Problems* 47, pp. 360–378.

Burstein, Paul. 1971. "Social Structure and Individual Political Participation in Five Countries." *American Journal of Sociology* 77, pp. 1087–1110.

Burstein, Paul. 1981. "The Sociology of Democratic Politics and Government." *Annual Review of Sociology* 7, pp. 291–319.

Burstein, Paul. 1991a. "Policy Domains: Organization, Culture and Policy Outcomes." *Annual Review of Sociology* 17, pp. 327–350.

Burstein, Paul. 1991b. " 'Reverse Discrimination' Cases in the Federal Courts: Legal Mobilization By a Countermovement." *The Sociological Quarterly* 32, pp. 511–528.

Burstein, Paul. 1991c. "Legal Mobilization as a Social Movement Tactic: The Struggle for Equal Employment Opportunity. *American Journal of Sociology* 96, pp. 1201–1225.

Burstein, Paul. 1998a. "Interest Organizations, Political Parties, and the Study of Democratic Politics." In *Social Movements and American Political Institutions*, eds. A. Costain and A. McFarland, pp. 39–56. Lanham, MD: Rowman and Littlefield.

Burstein, Paul. 1998b. "Bringing the Public Back In: Should Sociologists Consider the Impact of Public Opinion on Public Policy?" *Social Forces* 77, pp. 27–62.

Burstein, Paul. 1999. "Social Movements and Public Policy." In *How Social Movements Matter*, eds. M. Giugni, D. McAdam, and C. Tilly, pp. 3–21. Minneapolis: University of Minnesota Press.

Burstein, Paul. 2003. "The Impact of Public Opinion on Public Policy: A Review and an Agenda." *Political Research Quarterly* 56, pp. 29–40.

Burt, Ronald S. 1999. "The Social Capital of Opinion Leaders." *Annals of the American Academy of Political & Social Science*, 566, pp. 37–55.

Butcher, Kristen F. and Anne M. Piehl. 1998. "Cross-City Evidence on the Relationship between Crime Immigration and Crime." *Journal of Policy Analysis and Management* 17, pp. 457–493.

Butterfield, Fox. 1997. "Many Black Men Barred from Voting, Study Shows." *New York Times*, January 30, 1997.

C

Cable, Sherry. 1992. "Women's Social Movement Involvement: The Role of Structural Availability in Recruitment and Participation Processes." *Sociological Quarterly* 33, pp. 35–50.

Cable, Sherry, Edward Walsh, and Rex Warland. 1988. "Differential Paths to Political Activism: Comparisons of Four Mobilization Processes after the Three Mile Island Accident." *Social Forces* 66, pp. 951–969.

Cain, Maureen. 1983. "Gramsci, The State, and the Place of Law." In *Legality, Ideology and the State*, ed. D. Sugarman, pp. 95–117. New York: Academic Press.

Calavita, Kitty. 1983. "The Demise of the Occupational Safety and Health Administration: A Case Study in Symbolic Action." *Social Problems* 30, pp. 437–448.

Calavita, Kitty and Henry N. Pontell. 1991. "Other's People's Money Revisited: Collective Embezzlement in the Savings and Loan and Insurance Industries." *Social Problems* 38, pp. 94–112.

Calavita, Kitty and Henry N. Pontell. 1994. "The State and White-collar Crime: Saving the Savings and Loans." *Law and Society Review* 28, pp. 297–324.

Calavita, Kitty, Henry N. Pontell, and Robert H. Tillman. 1997a. *Big Money Crime: Fraud and Politics in the Savings and Loan Crisis.* Berkeley, CA: University of California Press.

Calavita, Kitty, Henry N. Pontell, and Robert Tillman. 1997b. "The Savings and Loan Debacle, Financial Crime, and the State." *Annual Review of Sociology* 23, pp. 19–38.

Caldeira, Gregory A. and John R. Wright. 1998. "Lobbying for Justice: Organized Interests, Supreme Court Nominations, and the United States Senate." *American Journal of Political Science* 42, pp. 499–523.

Calhoun, Craig. 1992. "Sociology, Other Disciplines, and the Project of a General Understanding of Social Life." In *Sociology and Its Publics,* eds. T. C. Haliday and M. Janowitz, pp. 137–196. Chicago: University of Chicago Press.

Calhoun, Craig. 1993a. "Nationalism and Ethnicity." *Annual Review of Sociology* 19, pp. 211–239.

Calhoun, Craig. 1993b. "New Social Movements of the Early Nineteenth Century." *Social Science History* 17, pp. 385–427.

Calhoun, Craig. 1994. "Nationalism and Civil Society." In Social Theory and the Politics of Identity, ed. C. Calhoun, pp. 304–336. Cambridge, MA: Blackwell.

Calhoun, Craig. 1997. *Nationalism.* Minneapolis: University of Minnesota Press.

Calhoun-Brown, Allison. 1996. "African American Churches and Political Mobilization: The Psychological Impact of Organizational Resources." *Journal of Politics* 58, pp. 935–953.

Calhoun-Brown, Allison. 1997. "Still Seeing in Black and White: Racial Challenges for the Christian Right." In *Sojourners in the Wilderness,* eds. C. Smidt and J. Penning, pp. 115–137. Lanham, MD: Rowman & Littlefield.

Callahan, David. 1998. "State Think Tanks on the Move." *The Nation* 267 (October 12), pp. 15–20.

Callahan, David. 1999a. The Think Tank as Flack. *The Washington Monthly* 31 (November), pp. 21–24.

Callahan, David. 1999b. $1 Billion for Conservative Ideas. *The Nation* 268 (April 26), pp. 21–23.

Cammisa, Anne Marie. 1998. *From Rhetoric to Reform: Welfare Policy in American Politics.* Boulder, CO: Westview.

Camobreco, John F. 1998. "Preferences, Fiscal Policies, and the Initiative Process." *Journal of Politics* 60, pp. 819–829.

Campbell, Angus, Donald Stokes, Philip E. Converse, and Warren E. Miller. 1960. *The American Voter.* New York: Wiley.

Campbell, John L. 1993. "The State and Fiscal Sociology." *Annual Review of Sociology* 19, pp. 163–185.

Campbell, John, L. 1997. "Recent Trends in Institutional Political Economy." *International Journal of Sociology and Social Policy* 17, pp. 15–56.

Campbell, John L. 1998. "Institutional Analysis and the Role of Ideas in Political Economy." *Theory and Society* 27, pp. 377–409.

Campbell, John L. 2001. "Institutional Analysis and the Role of Ideas in Political Economy." In *Rise of Neoliberalism and Institutional Analysis,* ed. J. Campbell and O. Pedersen, pp. 59–190. Princeton, NJ: Princeton University Press.

Campbell, John L. and Leon Lindberg. 1990. "Property Rights and the Organization of Economic Activity by the State." *American Sociological Review* 55, pp. 634–647.

Campbell, John L. and Ove K. Pedersen. 2001. "Introduction: The Rise of Neoliberalism and Institutional Analysis." In *The Rise of Neoliberalism and Institutional Analysis,* eds. J. L. Campbell and O. Pedersen, pp. 1–23. Princeton, NJ: Princeton University Press.

Campbell, John L., J. Rogers Hollingsworth, and Leon Lindberg, eds. 1991. *Governance of the American Economy.* New York: Cambridge University Press.

Canan, Penelope, Michael Hennessy, and George Pring. 1993. "The Chilling Effect of SLAPPS: Legal Risk and Attitudes Toward Political Involvement." *Research in Political Sociology* 6, pp. 347–369.

Canon, Bradley C. 1992. "The Supreme Court as a Cheerleader in Politico-Moral Disputes." *Journal of Politics* 54, pp. 637–653.

Caporaso, James, ed. 1989. *The Elusive State: International and Comparative Perspectives.* Newbury Park, CA: Sage.

Cappell, Charles L. and Thomas M. Guterbock. 1992. "Visible Colleges: The Social and Conceptual Structure of Sociology Specialties." *American Sociological Review* 57, pp. 266–273.

Cappell, Charles L. and Gersham Sykes. 1991. "Prison Population Growth Prison Commitments, Crime, and Unemployment." *Journal of Quantitative Criminology* 7, pp. 155–199.

Carmines, Edward G. 1994. "Political Issues, Party Alignments, Spatial Models and the Post-New Deal Party System." In *New Perspectives on American Politics,* eds. L. Dodd and C. Jillson, pp. 77–97. Washington, DC: Congressional Quarterly Press.

Carmines, Edward G. and James A. Stimson. 1982. "Racial Issues and the Structure of Mass Belief Systems." *Journal of Politics* 44, pp. 2–20.

Carmines, Edward G. and James A. Stimson. 1984. "The Dynamics of Issue Evolution in the United States." In *Electoral Change in Advanced Industrial Democracies,* eds. R. Dalton, S. Flanagan, and P. A. Beck, pp. 134–153. Princeton, NJ: Princeton University Press.

Carnoy, Martin. 1989. "Education, State and Culture in American Society" In *Critical Pedagogy, the State, and Cultural Struggle,* eds. H. Giroux and P. McLaren, pp. 3–23. Albany, NY: State University of New York Press.

Carter, Bill. 1998. "ABC Shelves Report on Parent Disney." *New York Times,* October 15, 1998.

Carter, Bill. 2001. "CBS Drops Reruns as Big Advertiser Pulls Commercials." *New York Times,* August 17, 2001.

Carter, Greg Lee. 1997. *The Gun Control Movement.* New York: Twayne Publishers.

Cassel, Carol A. 1999. "Voluntary Associations, Churches, and Social Participation Theories of Turnout." *Social Science Quarterly* 80, pp. 504–517.

Castelnuovo, Shirley. 1979. "Public Interest Law: Crisis of Legitimacy or Quest for Legal Order Autonomy." *Research in Law and Society* 2, pp. 231–249.

Castles, Francis and D. Mitchell. 1991. "Three Worlds of Welfare Capitalism or Four?" Luxembourg Income Study, Working Paper 63.

Caute, David. 1978. *The Great Fear.* New York: Simon and Schuster.

Cauthen, Nancy K. and Edwin Amenta. 1996. "Not for Widows Only: Institutional Politics and the Formative Years of Aid to Dependent Children." *American Sociological Review* 61, pp. 427–448.

Cavanaugh, Thomas. E. 1981. "Changes in American Voter Turnout, 1964–1976." *Political Science Quarterly* 96, pp. 53–65.

Chadwick, Elizabeth. 1997. "Terrorism and the Law: Historical Contexts, Contemporary Dilemmas, and the End(s) of Democracy." *Crime, Law and Social Change* 26, pp. 329–350.

Chafetz, Janet Saltzman and Helen Rose Fuch Ebaugh. 1983. "Growing Conservatism in the United States." *Sociological Perspectives* 26, pp. 275–298.

Chai, Sun-Ki and Michael Hechter. 1998. "The Theory of the State and Social Order." In *Problem of Solidarity: Theories and Models*, eds. P. Doreian and T. J. Fararo, pp. 61–112. New York: Routledge.

Chambers, William Nisbet. 1967. "Party Development and the American Mainstream." In *The American Party Systems: Stages of Political Development*, eds. W. N. Chambers and W. D. Burnham, pp. 3–32. New York: Oxford University Press.

Chambliss, William J. 1975. "Toward a Political Economy of Crime." *Theory and Society* 2, pp. 149–170.

Chambliss, William J. 1993a. "On Lawmaking." In *Making Law: The State, the Law and Structural Contradictions*, eds. W. Chambliss and M. Zatz, pp. 3–25. Bloomington, IN: Indiana University Press.

Chambliss, William J. 1993b. "State-organized Crime." In *Making Law: The State, the Law and Structural Contradictions*, eds. W. Chambliss and M. Zatz, pp. 290–314. Bloomington, IN: Indiana University Press.

Chambliss, William J. 1994. "Policing the Ghetto Underclass: The Politics of Law and Law Enforcement." *Social Problems* 41, pp. 177–194.

Chambliss, William J. 1999. *Power, Politics and Crime.* Boulder, CO: Westview.

Chambliss, William J. and Robert Seidman. 1982. *Law, Order and Power*, 2nd ed. Reading, MA: Addison-Wesley.

Chamlin, Mitchell B. 1990. "Determinants of Police Expenditures in Chicago, 1904–1958." *Sociological Quarterly* 31, pp. 484–485.

Chaney, Carole Kennedy, Michael Alvarez, and Jonathon Nagler. 1998. "Explaining the Gender Gap in U.S. Presidential Elections, 1980–1992." *Political Research Quarterly* 51, pp. 311–340.

Chang, Gorden H, ed. 2001. *Asian Americans and Politics: Perspectives, Experiences, Prospects.* Stanford, CA: Stanford University Press.

Chase-Dunn, Christopher. 1989. *Global Formation.* Cambridge, MA: Blackwell.

Chasin, Barbara H. 1997. *Inequality and Violence in the United States.* Atlantic Highlands, NJ: Humanities Press.

Chatov, Robert. 1978. "Government Regulation: Process and Substantive Impacts." *Research in Corporate Social Performance and Policy* 1, pp. 223–254.

Chavez, Linda. 1992. "Hispanics, Affirmative Action and Voting." *Annals of the American Academy of Political and Social Science* 523, pp. 75–88.

Cheal, David J. 1979. "Hegemony, Ideology and Contradictory Consciousness." *Sociological Quarterly* 20, pp. 109–117.

Chiricos, Ted, Sarah Eschholz, and Marc Gertz. 1997. "Crime News and Fear of Crime: Toward an Identification of Audience Effects." *Social Problems* 44, pp. 342–357.

Chiricos, Ted, Michael Hogan, and Marc Gertz. 1997. "Racial Composition and Fear of Crime." *Criminology* 35, pp. 107–131.

Chiricos, Ted, Kathy Padgett, and Marc Gertz. 2000. "Fear, TV News, and the Reality of Crime." *Criminology* 38, pp. 755–785.

Chomsky, Noam. 1989. *Necessary Illusions: Thought Control in Democratic Societies.* Boston: South End Press.

Chong, Dennis. 1993. "How People Think, Reason, and Feel about Rights and Liberties." *American Journal of Political Science* 37, pp. 867–899.

Christensen, Søren, Peter Karnøe, Jesper Strandgaard Pederson, and Frank Dobbin. 1997. "Actors and Institutions." *American Behavioral Scientist* 40, pp. 392–396.

Christopher, Karen. 2002a. "Family-Friendly Europe." *The American Prospect* (April 8, 2002), pp. 59–61.

Christopher, Karen. 2002b. "Welfare State Regimes and Mothers' Poverty." *Social Politics* 9, pp. 60–86.

Christopher, Karen, Paula England, Timothy Smeeding, and Katherine Phillips. 2002. "The Gender Gap in Poverty in Modern Nations." *Sociological Perspectives* 45, pp. 219–242.

Chua, Beng Huat. 1995. *Communitarian Ideology and Democracy in Singapore.* New York: Routledge.

Chua, Beng Huat. 1997. *Political Legitimacy and Housing: Stakeholding in Singapore.* New York: Routledge.

Clark, Burton R. 1970. "The Cooling Out Function in Higher Education." *American Journal of Sociology* 65, pp. 569–576.

Clark, Burton R. 1983. *The Higher Education System: Academic Organization in Cross-national Perspective.* Berkeley, CA: University of California Press.

Clark, Burton R. 1984. *Perspectives on Higher Education: Eight Disciplinary and Comparative Views.* Berkeley, CA: University of California Press.

Clark, Gordon L. and Michael Dear. 1984. *State Apparatus: Structures and Language of Legitimacy.* Boston: Allen and Unwin.

Clark, Terry Nichols and Seymour Martin Lipset. 1996. "As Social Classes Dying." In *Conflicts About Class: Debating Inequality in Late Industrialism*, eds. D. Lee and B. Turner, pp. 42–48. New York: Longman.

Clarke, James W. 1998. "Without Fear or Shame: Lynching, Capital Punishment, and the Subculture of Violence in the American South." *British Journal of Political Science* 28, pp. 269–289.

Clawson, Dan and Mary Ann Clawson. 1987. "Reagan or Business? Foundations of the New-Conservatism." In *The Structure of Power in America*, ed. by M. Schwartz, pp. 201–217. New York: Holmes and Meier.

Clawson, Dan and Alan Neustadtl. 1989. "Interlocks, PACs, and Corporate Conservatism." *American Journal of Sociology* 94, pp. 749–773.

Clawson, Dan and Tie-ting Su. 1990. "Was 1980 Special? A Comparison of 1980 and 1986 Corporate PAC Contributions." *Sociological Quarterly* 31, pp. 371–388.

Clawson, Dan, Alan Neustadtl, and James Bearden. 1986. "The Logic of Business Unity: Corporate Contributions to the 1980 Congressional Elections." *American Sociological Review* 51, pp. 797–811.

Clawson, Dan, Alan Neustadtl, and Denise Scott. 1992. *Money Talks: Corporate PACS and Political Influence.* New York: Basic Books.

Clawson, Dan, Alan Neustadtl, and Mark Weller. 1998. *Dollars and Votes: How Business Campaign Contributions Subvert Democracy.* Philadelphia: Temple University Press.

Clawson, Dan, Tie-ting Su, and Alan Neustadtl. 1996. "Shift Happens: Corporations and the Struggle over American Politics, 1976–1986." *Social Science Quarterly* 77, pp. 928–931.

Clawson, Rosalee A. and Rakuya Trice. 2000. "Poverty as We Know It: Media Portrayals of the Poor." *Public Opinion Quarterly* 64, pp. 53–64.

Clayton, Richard and Jonas Pontusson. 1998. "Welfare-State Retrenchment Revisited." *World Politics* 51, pp. 67–98.

Clemens, Elisabeth S. 1993. "Organizational Repertoires and Institutional Change: Women's Groups and the Transformation of U.S. Politics, 1890–1920." *American Journal of Sociology* 98, pp. 755–798.

Clemens, Elisabeth S. 1997. *The People's Lobby: Organizational Innovation and the Rise of Interest Group Politics in the United States, 1890–1925.* Chicago: University of Chicago Press.

Clemens, Elisabeth S. 1998. "To Move Mountains: Collective Action and the Possibility of Institutional Change." In *From Contention to Democracy*, eds. M. Giugni, D. McAdam, & C. Tilly, pp. 109–123. Lanham, MD: Rowman and Littlefield.

Clemens, Elisabeth S. and James Cook. 1999. "Politics and Institutionalism: Explaining Durability and Change." *Annual Review of Sociology* 25, pp. 441–466.

Clement, Wallace and John Myles. 1994. *Relations of Ruling: Class and Gender in Postindustrial Societies.* Montreal: McGill-Queens University Press.

Cloud, Dana L. 1998. *Control and Consolation in American Culture and Politics: Rhetoric of Therapy.* Thousand Oaks, CA: Sage.

Clubb, Jerome M., William H. Flanigan, and Nancy H. Zingale. 1980. *Partisan Realignment: Voters, Parties, and Government in American History.* Beverly Hills, CA: Sage.

Clymer, Adam. "College Students Not Drawn to Voting or Politics, Poll Shows." *New York Times*, January 12, 2000.

Cobb, Roger W. and Charles D. Elder. 1983. *Participation in American Politics: The Dynamics of Agenda-Building.* Baltimore: John Hopkins University Press.

Cobb, Roger W. and Marc Ross. 1997a. "Agenda Setting and the Denial of Access: Key Concepts." In *Cultural Strategies of Agenda Denial*, eds. R. Cobb and M. Ross, pp. 3–24. Lawrence, KS: University of Kansas Press.

Cobb, Roger W. and Marc Ross. 1997b. "Denying Agenda Access: Strategic Considerations." In *Cultural Strategies of Agenda Denial*, eds. R. Cobb and M. Ross, pp. 25–45. Lawrence, KS: University of Kansas Press.

Cobban, Alfred. 1994. "The Rise of the Nation-State System." In *Nationalism*, eds. J. Hutchinson and A. D. Smith, pp. 245–250. New York: Oxford University Press.

Cohen, Cathy and Michael Dawson. 1993. "Neighborhood Poverty and African American Politics." *American Political Science Review* 87, pp. 286–302.

Cohen, Joshua. 1988. "Deliberation and Democratic Legitimacy." In *The Good Polity*, eds. A. Hamlin and P. Pettit. New York: Basil Blackwell.

Cohen, Joshua. 1998. "Democracy and Liberty." In *Deliberative Democracy*, ed. J. Elster, pp. 185–231. New York: Cambridge University Press.

Cohen, Joshua and Joel Rogers. 1992. "Secondary Associations and Democratic Governance." *Politics and Society* 20, pp. 392–472.

Cohen, Miriam and Michael Hanagan. 1996. "Politics, Industrialization and Citizenship." In *Citizenship, Identity and Social History*, ed. C. Tilly, pp. 91–130. New York: Cambridge University Press.

Cohen, Robin. 1997. *Global Diasporas: An Introduction.* Seattle: University of Washington Press.

Cohen, Stanley. 1996. "Crime and Politics: Spot the Difference." *British Journal of Sociology* 47, pp. 1–21.

Colby, David C. 1985. "Black Power, White Resistance, and Public Policy: Political Power and Poverty Program Grants in Mississippi." *The Journal of Politics* 47, pp. 579–595.

Coleman, James S. 1990. *Foundations of Social Theory.* Cambridge, MA: Harvard University Press.

Colignon, Richard A. 1997. *Power Plays: Critical Events in the Institutionalization of the Tennessee Valley Authority.* Albany, NY: State University of New York Press.

Colignon, Richard A. and Chikako Usui. 2001. "The Resilience of Japan's Iron Triangle." *Asian Survey* 41, pp. 865–895.

Colignon, Richard A. and Chikako Usui. 2003. *Amakudari: The Hidden Fabric of Japan's Economy.* Ithaca, NY: Cornell University Press.

Collier, Ruth Berina and David Collier. 1979. "Inducement versus Constraints: Disaggregating 'Corporatism'." *American Political Science Review* 73, pp. 967–986.

Collins, Randall. 1968. "A Comparative Approach to Political Sociology." In *State and Society: A Reader in Comparative Political Sociology*, ed. R. Bendix, pp. 42–67. Boston: Little Brown.

Collins, Randall. 1979. *The Credential Society: An Historical Sociology of Education and Stratification.* New York: Academic Press.

Colvin, Mark. 1990. "Labor Markets, Industrial Monopolization, Welfare and Imprisonment: Evidence from a Cross-Section of U.S. Counties." *Sociological Quarterly* 31, pp. 441–458.

Conley, Dalton and Brian Gifford. 2003. "Home Ownership, Social Insurance, and the Welfare State," http://home.nyu.edu/~dc66/pdf/res_home_welfare.pdf, (downloaded August 1, 2003).

Conley, Dalton and Kristen Springer. 2001. "Welfare State and Infant Mortality." *American Journal of Sociology* 107, pp. 768–807.

Connell, R. W. 1990. "The State, Gender and Sexual Politics." *Theory and Society* 19, pp. 507–544.

Connerton, Paul. 1980. *The Tragedy of Enlightenment: An Essay on the Frankfurt School.* New York: Cambridge University Press.

Connor, George E. 1992. "The Politics of Insurrection: A Comparative Analysis of the Shays', Whiskey, and Fries' Rebellions." *Social Science Journal* 29, pp. 259–282.

Conover, Pamela Johnston. 1984. "The Influence of Group Identification on Political Perceptions and Evaluations." *Journal of Politics* 46, pp. 760–785.

Conover, Pamela Johnston. 1988. "Feminists and the Gender Gap." *Journal of Politics* 50, pp. 985–1010.

Conover, Pamela Johnston and Stanley Feldman. 1981. "The Origins and Meaning of Liberal/Conservative Self Identifications." *American Journal of Political Science* 25, pp. 617–645.

Conover, Pamela Johnston and Stanley Feldman. 1984. "How People Organize the Political World: A Schematic Model." *American Journal of Political Science* 28, pp. 95–126.

Conover, Pamela Johnston and Virginia Shapiro. 1993. "Gender, Feminist Consciousness and War." *American Political Science Review* 37, pp. 1079–1099.

Converse, Phillip E. 1964. "The Nature of Belief Systems in Mass Publics." In *Ideology and Its Discontent,* ed. David E. Apter, pp. 206–261. New York: Free Press.

Cook, Elizabeth and Clyde Wilcox. 1991. "Feminism and the Gender Gap: A Second Look." *Journal of Politics* 53, pp. 1111–1122.

Cook, Thomas E. 1998. *Governing With the News: The News Media as a Political Institution.* Chicago: University of Chicago Press.

Cookson, Peter W. and Caroline Hodges Persell. 1985. *Preparing for Power: America's Elite Boarding Schools.* New York: Basic Books.

Cooper, Jerry M. 1977. "The Army as Strikebreaker: The Railroad Strikes of 1877 and 1894." *Labor History* 18, pp. 179–196.

Coppedge, Michael and Wolfgang H. Reinicke. 1991. "Measuring Polyarchy." In *On Measuring Democracy: Its Consequence and Concomitant,* ed. A. Inkeles, pp. 47–68. New Brunswick, NJ: Transaction Books.

Corcoran, Mary, Sandra Danziger, Ariel Kalil, and Kristin Seefeldt. 2000. "How Welfare Reform Is Affecting Women's Work." *Annual Review of Sociology* 26, pp. 241–269.

Corrigan, Philip and Derek Sayer. 1981. "How the Law Rules: Variations on Some Themes in Karl Marx." In *Law, State and Society,* eds. B. Fryer, A. Hunt, D. McBarnet, and B. Moorhouse, pp. 21–52. London: Croom Helm.

Corzine, Jay, James Creech, and Lin Huff-Corzine. 1983. "Black Concentration and Lynchings in the South." *Social Forces* 61, pp. 774–796.

Corzine, Jay, Lin Huff-Corzine, and James C. Creech. 1988. "The Tenant Labor Market and Lynching in the South: A Test of the Split Labor Market Theory." *Sociological Inquiry* 58, pp. 261–278.

Coser, Lewis R. 1956. *The Functions of Social Conflict.* New York: Free Press.

Coser, Lewis R. 1967. *Continuities in the Study of Social Conflict.* New York: Free Press.

Costantini, Edmond. 1990. "Political Women and Political Ambition: Closing the Gender Gap." *American Political Science Review* 34, pp. 741–770.

Coughlin, Richard M. 1979. "Social Policy and Ideology." *Comparative Social Research* 2, pp. 3–40.

Cousins, Mark. 1984. *Michel Foucault.* New York: St. Martins.

Cousins, Mark and Athar Hussian. 1984. *Michel Foucault.* New York: St. Martins.

Cox, Andrew. 1981. "Corporatism as Reductionism." *Government and Opposition* 16, pp. 78–95.

Crane, Diana and Henry Small. 1992. "American Sociology Since the Seventies." In *Sociology and Its Publics,* ed. T. Haliday and M. Janowitz, pp. 197–235. Chicago: University of Chicago Press.

Creech, James C., Jay Crozine, and Lin Huff-Corzine. 1989. "Testing Theory and Lynching." *Social Forces* 67, pp. 631–633.

Crenshaw, Edward M. 1995. "Democracy and Demographic Inheritance: The Influence of Modernity and Proto-Modernity on Political and Civil Rights, 1965 to 1980." *American Sociological Review* 60, pp. 702–718.

Crenshaw, Martha. 1992. "Current Research on Terrorism: The Academic Perspective." *Studies in Conflict and Terrorism* 15, pp. 1–11.

Crenson, Matthew. 1971. *The Unpolitics of Air Pollution.* Baltimore: John Hopkins University Press.

Crepaz, Markus M. L. 1990. "The Impact of Party Polarization and Postmaterialism on Voter Turnout: A Comparative Study of 16 Industrial Democracies." *European Journal of Political Research* 18, pp. 183–205.

Cress, Daniel M. 1997. "Nonprofit Incorporation among Movements of the Poor: Pathways and Consequences for Homeless Social Movement Organizations." *Sociological Quarterly* 38, pp. 343–360.

Cress, Daniel M. and David A. Snow. 1996. "Mobilization at the Margins: Resources, Benefactors, and the Viability of Homeless Social Movement Organizations?" *American Sociological Review,* 61, pp. 1089–1109.

Cress, Daniel M. and David A. Snow. 1998. "Mobilizing at the Margins." In *Social Movement and American Political Institutions,* eds. A. Costain and A. McFarland, pp. 73–98. Lanham, MD: Rowman and Littlefield.

Cress, Daniel M. and David A. Snow. 2000. "The Outcomes of Homeless Mobilization: The Influence of Organization, Disruption, Political Mediation, and Framing." *American Journal of Sociology* 105, pp. 1063–1104.

Crompton, Rosemary. 1993. *Class and Stratification: An Introduction to Current Debates.* New York: Polity.

Crompton, Rosemary. 2001. "Gender Restructuring, Employment, and Caring." *Social Politics* 8, pp. 266–291.

Cronin, James E. 2000. "Convergence by Conviction: Politics and Economics in the Emergence of the 'Anglo-American Model.' " *Journal of Social History* 33, pp. 781–804.

Croteau, David. 1995. *Politics and the Class Divide.* Philadelphia: Temple University Press.

Crotty, William J. 1977. *Political Reform and the American Experiment.* New York: Harper & Row.

Crozier, Michel J., Samuel P. Huntington, and Joji Watanuki. 1975. *The Crisis of Democracy.* New York: New York University Press.

Crutchfield, Robert D. 1989. "Labor Stratification and Violent Crime." *Social Forces* 68, pp. 489–512.

Cryns, Arthur and Jeremy D. Finn. 1973. "A Multivariate Analysis of Some Attitudinal and Ideological Correlates of Student Activism." *Sociology of Education* 46, pp. 127–142.

Cuff, Robert D. 1973. *The War Industries Board.* Baltimore: John Hopkins Press.

Culberson, William C. 1990. *Vigilantism.* Westport, CT: Greenwood Press.

Curran, Laura and Laura Abrams. 2000. "Making Men into Dads: Fatherhood, the State, and Welfare Reform." *Gender and Society* 14, pp. 662–678.

Currie, Elliott. 1968. "Crimes without Criminals: Witchcraft and Its Control in Renaissance Europe." *Law and Society Review* 3, pp. 7–32.

Cutright, Phillips. 1963. "National Political Development: Measurement and Analysis." *American Sociological Review* 28, pp. 253–264.

Cutright, Phillips. 1965. "Political Structure, Economic Development and National Social Security Programs." *American Journal of Sociology* 70, pp. 537–550.

D

Dahl, Robert A. 1961. *Who governs? Democracy and power in an American city.* New Haven, CT: Yale University Press.

Dahl, Robert A. 1971. *Polyarchy: Participation and Opposition.* New Haven, CT: Yale University Press.

Dahl, Robert A. 1982. *Dilemmas of Pluralist Democracy: Autonomy versus Control.* New Haven, CT: Yale University Press.

Dahl, Robert A. 1998. *On Democracy.* New Haven, CT: Yale University Press.

Dahrendorf, Ralf. 1994. "The Changing Quality of Citizenship." In *The Condition of Citizenship*, ed. B. van Steenbergen, pp. 10–19. Thousand Oaks, CA: Sage.

Dalton, Russell J. 1996. *Citizen Politics: Public Opinion and Political Parties in Advanced Industrial Democracies*, 2nd ed. Chatham, NJ: Chatham House.

Dalton, Russell J., Paul A. Beck, and Scott Flanagan. 1984. "Electoral Change in Advanced Industrial Democracies." In *Electoral Change in Advanced Industrial Democracies*, eds. R. Dalton, S. Flanagan, and P. Beck, pp. 3–22. Princeton, NJ: Princeton University Press.

Dandeker, Christopher. 1990. *Surveillance, Power, and Modernity.* New York: St. Martin's Press.

Danielian, Lucig H. and Benjamin Page. 1994. "The Heavenly Chorus: Interest Group Voices on TV News." *American Journal of Political Science*, 38, pp. 1056–1079.

Daniels, Roger. 1964. *The Politics of Prejudice.* Berkeley, CA: University of California Press.

Daniels, Roger. 1971. *Concentration Camps USA: Japanese Americans and World War II.* New York: Holt, Rinehart and Winston.

Daniels, Roger. 1988. *Asian American: Chinese and Japanese in the United States Since 1850.* Seattle: University of Washington Press.

Daniels, Roger. 1989. *Concentration Camps: North America*, rev. ed. Malabar, FL: Robert Krieger Publishing.

Danigelis, Nicholas. 1977. "A Theory of Black Political Participation in the United States." *Social Forces* 56, pp. 31–47.

Danigelis, Nicholas. 1978. "Black Political Participation in the United States: Some Recent Evidence." *American Sociological Review* 43, pp. 756–771.

D'Antonio, William. 1992. "Sociology's Educational Foundations: Facing the Challenge of Ambivalence." *Sociological Focus* 25, pp. 111–120.

Darnell, Alfred and Darren E. Sherkat. 1997. "The Impact of Protestant Fundamentalism on Educational Attainment." *American Sociological Review* 62, pp. 306–315.

David, Miriam. 1986. "Moral and Maternal: The Family in the Right." In *The Ideology of the New Right*, ed. R. Levitas, pp. 135–166. New York: Polity Press.

Davies, Graham and Sonya Thasen. 2000. "Closed-Circuit Television: How Effective an Identification Aid?" *British Journal of Psychology* 91, pp. 411–427.

Davies, Scott. 1995. "Leaps of Faith: Shifting Current in Critical Sociology of Education." *American Journal of Sociology* 100, pp. 1448–1478.

Davies, Scott. 1999. "From Moral Duty to Cultural Rights: A Case Study of Political Framing in Education." *Sociology of Education* 72, pp. 1–21.

Davies, Stephen. 1997. "Two Concepts of Welfare: Voluntarism and Incorporatism." In *The Welfare State*, eds. E. Paul, F. Miller, and J. Paul, pp. 39–68. New York: Cambridge University Press.

Davis, James A. 1980. "Conservative Weather in a Liberalizing Climate: Change in Selected NORC General Social Survey Items, 1972–78." *Social Forces* 58, pp. 1129–1156.

Davis, James A. 1992. "Changeable Weather in a Cooling Climate Atop the Liberal Plateau: Conversion and Replacement in Forty-Two General Social Survey Items, 1972–1989." *Public Opinion Quarterly* 56, pp. 261–306.

Davis, Nancy J. and Robert V. Robinson. 1996. "Are the Rumors of War Exaggerated? Religious Orthodoxy and Moral Progressivism in America." *American Journal of Sociology* 102, pp. 756–787.

Dawley, Alan. 1991. *Struggles for Justice: Social Responsibility and the Liberal State.* Cambridge, MA: Harvard University Press.

De Graaf, Nan Dirk, Paul Nieuwbeerta, and Anthony Heath. 1995. "Class Mobility and Political Preferences: Individual and Contextual Effects." *American Journal of Sociology* 100, pp. 997–1027.

De la Garza, Rodolfo, Angelo Falcon, and F. Chris Garcia. 1996. "Will the Real Americans Please Stand Up: Anglo and Mexican-American Support of Core American Political Values." *American Journal of Political Science* 40, pp. 335–351.

De la Garza, Rodolfo, Louis DeSipio, F. Chris Garcia, John Garcia, and Angelo Falcon. 1992. *Latino Voices: Mexican, Puerto Rican, and Cuban Perspectives on American Politics.* Boulder, CO: Westview.

DeFronzo, James. 1991. *Revolutions and Revolutionary Movements.* Boulder, CO: Westview.

Delaney, John Thomas, Marick F. Masters, and Susan Schwochau. 1988. "Unionism and Voter Turnout." *Journal of Labor Research* 9, pp. 221–236.

Della Porta, Donatella. 1996. "Social Movements and the State." In *Comparative Perspectives on Social Movements*, eds. Doug McAdam, John McCarthy, and Mayer Zald, pp. 62–92. New York: Cambridge University Press.

Della Porta, Donatella. 1999. "Protest, Protesters, and Protest Policing: Public Discourses in Italy and Germany from the 1960s to the 1980s." In *How Social Movements Matter*, eds. M. Giugni, D. McAdam, and C. Tilly, pp. 66–96. Minneapolis: University of Minnesota Press.

Della Porta, Donatella and Mario Diani. 1999. *Social Movements: An Introduction.* New York: Basil Blackwell.

Della Porta, Donnatella and Herbert Reiter, eds. 1998. *Policing Protest: The Control of Mass Demonstrations in Western Democracies.* Minneapolis: University of Minnesota Press.

Delli Carpini, Michael X. and Scott Keeter. 1996. *What Americans Know About Politics and Why It Matters.* New Haven, CT: Yale University Press.

DeLuca, Tom. 1995. *The Two Faces of Political Apathy.* Philadelphia: Temple University Press.

Demerath, N.J. III. 1998. "Excepting Exceptionalism: American Religion in Comparative Relief." *Annals of the American Academy of Political and Social Science* 558, pp. 28–39.

Demerath, N. J. III and Rhys Williams. 1984. "A Mythical Past and Uncertain Future." *Society* 21, no. 4, pp. 3–10.

Demerath, N. J. III and Rhys Williams. 1985. "Civil Religion in an Uncivil Society." *Annals of the American Academy of Political and Social Science* 480, pp. 154–166.

Demerath, N. J. III and Yonghe Yang. 1997. "What American Culture War?" In *Culture Wars in American Politics*, ed. R. H. Williams, pp. 17–38. New York: Aldine.

Denham, Andrew. 1996. *Think Tanks of the Right.* Brookfield, VT: Dartmouth Publishing.

Denton, Robert E. and Rachel L. Holloway. 1995. "Presidential Communication as Mediated Conversation: Interpersonal talk as Presidential Discourse." *Research in Political Sociology* 7, pp. 91–116.

Denzin, Norman. 1990. "The Long Good-bye: Farewell to Rational Choice Theory." *Rationality and Society*, 2, pp. 504–508.

DeSipio, Louis. 1996. *Counting the Latino Vote: Latinos in the New Electorate.* Charlottesville, VA: University of Virginia Press.

Desrosières. 1998. *The Politics of Large Numbers: A History of Statistical Reasoning.* Cambridge, MA: Harvard University Press.

Destler, Chester McArthur. 1946. *American Radicalism, 1865–1901: Essays and Documents.* New London, CT: Connecticut College.

Deutsch, Karl W. 1966. *Nationalism and Social Communication: An Inquiry into the Foundations of Nationality.* Cambridge, MA: MIT Press.

Diamat, Alfred. 1981. "Bureaucracy and Public Policy in Neocorporatist Settings." *Comparative Politics* 14, pp. 101–124.

Diamond, Sara. 1995. "The Christian Right Seeks Domination." In *Eyes Right*, ed. C. Berlet, pp. 44–49. Boston: South End Press.

Diani, Mario. 1992. "The Concept of Social Movement." *Sociological Review* 40, pp. 1–25.

Diani, Mario. 1996. "Linking Mobilization Frames and Political Opportunities: Insights from Regional Populism in Italy." *American Sociological Review* 61, pp. 1053–1069.

Diani, Mario. 1997. "Social Movements and Social Capital: A Network Perspective on Movement Outcomes." *Mobilization* 2, pp. 129–147.

Dibble, Vernon K. and Berton Pekowsky. 1973. "What Is and What Ought to Be: A Comparison of Certain Characteristics of the Ideological and Legal Styles of Thought." *American Journal of Sociology* 79, pp. 511–549.

Dickinson, James. 1986. "Spiking Socialist Guns: The Introduction of Social Insurance in Germany and Britain." *Comparative Social Research* 9, pp. 69–108.

DiGaetano, Alan. 1988. "The Rise and Development of Urban Political Machines." *Urban Affairs Quarterly* 24, pp. 243–267.

DiMaggio, Paul J. 1982. "Cultural Capital and School Success: The Impact of Status Culture Participation on the Grades of U.S. High School Students." *American Sociological Review* 47, pp. 189–201.

DiMaggio, Paul J. and Walter W. Powell. 1991. "Introduction." In *The New Institutionalism in Organizational Analysis*, eds. W. Powell and P. DiMaggio, pp. 1–40. Chicago: University of Chicago Press.

DiMaggio, Paul J., John Evans, and Bethany Bryson. 1997. "Have American Social Attitudes Become More Polarized?" In *Culture Wars in American Politics*, ed. R. Williams, pp. 63–100. New York: Aldine.

DiPrete, Thomas A. 1993. "Industrial Restructuring and the Mobility Response of American Workers in the 1980s." *American Sociological Review* 58, pp. 74–96.

DiPrete, Thomas A. and Patricia McManus. 2000. "Family Change, Employment Transitions, and Welfare State." *American Sociological Review* 65, pp. 343–370.

DiTomasso, Nancy K. 1980. "Class Politics and Public Bureaucracy." In *Classes, Class Conflict and the State*, ed. M. Zeitlin, pp. 135–152. Cambridge, MA: Winthrop.

Dixit, Avinash and John Londregan. 1996. "The Determinates of Success of Special Interests in Redistributive Politics." *Journal of Politics* 58, pp. 1132–1155.

Dixon, Travis L. and Daniel Linz. 2000. "Race and Misrepresentation of Victimization on Local Television News." *Communication Research* 27, pp. 547–574.

Dobbin, Frank R. 1992. "The Origins of Private Social Insurance: Public Policy and Fringe Benefits in America, 1920–1950." *American Journal of Sociology* 97, pp. 1416–1450.

Dobbin, Frank R. 1993. "The Social Construction of the Great Depression." *Theory and Society* 22, pp. 1–56.

Dobbin, Frank R. 1994. *Forging Industrial Policy: The United States, Britain, and France in the Railway Era.* New York: Cambridge University Press.

Dobbin, Frank R. and Timothy Dowd. 2000. "The Market That Antitrust Build." *American Sociological Review* 65, pp. 631–658.

Dobratz, Betty A. and Stephanie L. Shanks-Meile. 1997. *White Power, White Pride!* New York: Twayne Publishers.

Dolan, Kathleen. 1998. "Voting for Women in the Year of the Woman." *American Journal of Political Science* 42, pp. 272–293.

Dolbeare, Kenneth M. and Patricia Dolbeare. 1976. *American Ideologies: The Competing Political Beliefs of the 1970s,* 3rd ed. Chicago: Rand McNally.

Dolny, Michael. 1998. "What's in a Label? Right-wing Think Tanks are Often Quoted, Rarely Labeled." *EXTRA!* May/June 1998.

Dolny, Michael. 2000. "Think Tanks: The Rich Get Richer." *Extra!* May/June 2000.

Domhoff, G. William. 1967. *Who Rules America?* Englewood Cliffs, NJ: Prentice Hall.

Domhoff, G. William. 1970. *The Higher Circles.* New York: Random House.

Domhoff, G. William. 1974. *The Bohemian Grove and Other Retreats.* New York: Harper and Row.

Domhoff, G. William. 1975a. "Analyzing Power Structures." *Insurgent Sociologist* 5, pp. 4–5.

Domhoff, G. William. 1975b. "Social Clubs, Policy-Planning Groups, and Corporations." *Insurgent Sociologist* 5, pp. 173–184.

Domhoff, G. William. 1976. "I am Not an Instrumentalist." *Kapitalistate* 4–5, pp. 221–224.

Domhoff, G. William. 1978. *The Powers That Be.* New York: Vintage.

Domhoff, G. William. 1980. *Power Structure Research.* Beverly Hills, CA: Sage.

Domhoff, G. William. 1983. *Who Rules America Now? A View of the '80s.* Englewood Cliffs, NJ: Prentice Hall.

Domhoff, G. William. 1990. *The Power Elite and the State: How Policy is Made in America.* New York: Aldine de Gruyter.

Domhoff, G. William. 1996. *State Autonomy or Class Dominance: Case Studies on Policy Making in America.* New York: Aldine de Gruyter.

Domhoff, G. William. 1998. *Who Rules America? Power and Politics in the Year 2000,* 3rd ed. Mountain View, CA: Mayfield.

Domke, David, Mark Watts, and Dhavan V. Shah. 1999. "The Politics of Conservative Elites and the 'Liberal Media' Argument." *Journal of Communication* 49, pp. 35–58.

Donner, Frank J. 1980. *The Age of Surveillance: The Aims and Methods of America's Political Intelligence System.* New York: Vintage.

Donnor, Frank J. 1990. *Protectors of Privilege: Red Squads and Police Repression in Urban America.* Berkeley, CA: University of California Press.

Dougherty, Kevin J. 1994. *The Contradictory College: The Conflicting Origins, Impacts and Futures of Community Colleges.* Albany, NY: State University of New York Press.

Dowd, Timothy J. and Frank Dobbin. 1997. "The Embedded Actor and the Invention of Natural Economic Law." *American Behavioral Scientist* 40, pp. 478–489.

Dower, John W. 1995. "Hiroshima, Nagasaki and the Politics of Memory." *Technology Review* 98, pp. 48–52.

Downey, Dennis J. 2000. "Situating Social Attitudes: Toward Cultural Pluralism Between Cultural Wars and Contemporary Racism." *Social Problems* 47, pp. 90–111.

Downs, Anthony. 1957. *An Economic Theory of Democracy.* New York: Harper.

Dreiling, Michael. 2000. "The Class Embeddedness of Corporation Political Action in Defense of NAFTA." *Social Problems* 47, pp. 21–48.

Drinkard, James. 1995. "In D.C., More than Ever Money Buys Access." *Capital Times* (Madison, WI), April 25, 1995.

Drinnon, Richard. 1987. *Keeper of Concentration Camps: Dillon S. Meyer and American Racism.* Berkeley, CA: University of California Press.

Dronkers, Jaap. 1993. "Educational Expansion and Economic Output in a European Industrial Nation During 1960–1980: The Netherlands." *International Perspectives on Education and Society* 3, pp. 33–52.

Dryzek, John S. 1996a. "Political Inclusion and the Dynamics of Democratization." *American Political Science Review* 90, pp. 475–487.

Dryzek, John S. 1996b. *Democracy in Capitalist Times.* New York: Oxford University Press.

Dryzek, John S., Christian Hunold, David Schlosberg, David Downes, and Hans Christian Hernes. 2002. "Environmental Transformation of the State: The U.S.A., Norway, Germany and the U.K." *Political Studies* 50, pp. 659–682.

D'Souza, Dinesh. 1991. *Illiberal Education: The Politics and Race and Sex on Campus.* New York: Vintage.

Duara, Prasenjit. 1996. "Historicizing National Identity or Who Imagines What and When." In *Becoming National,* eds. G. Eley and R. Suny, pp. 151–177. New York: Oxford University Press.

Duch, Raymond M. and Jerrold Rusk. 1993. "Postmaterialism and the Economic Condition." *American Journal of Political Science* 37, pp. 747–780.

Dumm, Thomas L. 1996. *Michel Foucault and the Politics of Freedom.* Thousand Oaks, CA: Sage.

Dunn, Marvin. 1980. "The Family Office: Coordinating Mechanisms of the Ruling Class." In *Power Structure Research,* ed. G. Domhoff, pp. 7–16. Beverly Hills, CA: Sage.

Durkheim, Emile 1915 [1965]. *The Elementary Forms of the Religious Life.* New York: Free Press.

Dye, Thomas D. 1986. *Who's Running America? Institutional Leadership in the United States.* Englewood Cliffs, NJ: Prentice Hall.

Dye, Thomas D. and L. Harmon Zeigler. 1970. *The Irony of Democracy.* Belmont, CA: Wadsworth.

Dyer, Joel. 2000. *The Perpetual Prisoner Machine.* Boulder, CO: Westview.

E

Eagleton, Terry. 1991. *Ideology: An Introduction.* New York: Verso.

Easterbrook, Gregg. 1986. "Ideas Move Nations." *Atlantic Monthly* 257 (January), pp. 66–80.

Easton, David. 1981. "The Political System Besieged by the State." *Political Theory* 9, pp. 303–325.

Economist. 1998a. "Democracy in Texas: The Frontier Spirit." (May 16, 1998).

Economist. 1998b. "How Far Can You Trust the People." (August 15, 1998).

Edelman, Lauren B. 1992. "Legal Ambiguity and Symbolic Structures: Organizational Mediation of Civil Rights Law." *American Journal of Sociology* 97, pp. 1531–1577.

Edelman, Murray. 1964. *The Symbolic Uses of Politics.* Urbana, IL: University of Illinois Press.

Edelman, Murray. 1977. *Political Language: Words that Succeed and Policies That Fail.* New York: Academic Press.

Edelman, Murray. 1988. *Constructing the Political Spectacle.* Chicago: University of Chicago Press.

Edsall, Thomas B. and Mary D. Edsall. 1991. *Chain Reaction: The Impact of Race, Rights and Taxes on American Politics.* New York: Norton.

Edwards, Bob and Sam Marullo. 1995. "Organizational Mortality in a Declining Social Movement: The Demise of Peace Movement Organizations in the End of the Cold War." *American Sociological Review* 60, pp. 908–927.

Edwards, Michael. 2001. "Introduction and Overview." In *Global Citizen Action*, eds. M. Edwards and J. Gaventa, pp. 1–14, Lynne Rienner Publishers.

Ehrenreich, Barbara. 1987. "The New Right Attack on Social Welfare." In *The Mean Season: The Attack on the Welfare State*, eds. F. Piven, R. Cloward, B. Ehrenreich, and F. Block, pp. 161–195. New York: Pantheon.

Eisinger, Peter K. 1973. "The Conditions of Protest Behavior in American Cities." *American Political Science Review* 67, pp. 11–28.

Eisinger, Peter K. 1974. "Racial Differences in Protest Participation." *American Political Science Review* 68, pp. 592–606.

Eismeier, Theodore J. and Philip H. Pollock III. 1986. "Politics and Markets: Corporate Money in American National Elections." *British Journal of Political Science* 16, pp. 287–310.

Eismeier, Theodore J. and Philip H. Pollock III. 1988. *Business, Money and the Rise of Corporate PACs in American Elections.* New York: Quorum Books.

Eisner, Marc Allen and Kenneth Meier. 1990. "Presidential Control versus Bureaucratic Power: Explaining the Reagan Revolution in Antitrust." *American Journal of Political Science* 34, pp. 269–287.

Eisner, Marc Allen. 1991. *Antitrust and the Triumph of Economics.* Chapel Hill, NC: North Carolina University Press.

Eisner, Marc Allen. 1993. *Regulatory Politics in Transition.* Baltimore: John Hopkins University Press.

Eitzen, Stanley. 1972. Status Consistency and Consistency of Political Beliefs." *Public Opinion Quarterly* 36, pp. 541–548.

Ekland-Olson, Sheldon. 1988. "Structured Discretion, Racial Bias, and the Death Penalty: The First Decade after Furman in Texas." *Social Science Quarterly* 69, pp. 853–873.

Ekrich, Arthur A. Jr. 1974. *Progressivism in America.* New York: New Viewpoints.

Eley, Geoff and Ronald Grigor Suny. 1996. "Introduction: The Movement of Social History to the Work of Cultural Representation." In *Becoming National*, eds. G. Eley and R. Suny, pp. 3–37. New York: Oxford University Press.

Eliasoph, Nina. 1998. *Avoiding Politics: How Americans Produce Apathy in Everyday Life.* New York: Cambridge University Press.

Elifson, Kirk and C. Kirk Hadaway. 1985. "Prayer in Public Schools: When Church and State Collide." *Public Opinion Quarterly* 49, pp. 317–329.

Ellison, Christopher G. 1991. "Identification and Separation: Religious Involvement and Racial Orientations Among Black Americans." *Sociological Quarterly* 32, pp. 477–494.

Ellison, Christopher G. and Darren E. Sherkat. 1993. "Conservative Protestantism and Support for Corporal Punishment." *American Sociological Review* 58, pp. 131–144.

Ellison, Christopher G., John Bartkowski, and Michelle Segal. 1996. "Conservative Protestantism and the Parental Use of Corporal Punishment." *Social Forces* 74, pp. 1003–1028.

Elster, Jon. 1986. *Rational Choice.* Oxford UK: Blackwell.

Elster, Jon. 1998. "Introduction." In *Deliberative Democracy*, ed. J. Elster, pp. 1–18. New York: Cambridge University Press.

Emerson, Michael, Christian Smith, and David Sikkink. 1999. "Equal in Christ, But Not in This World: White Conservative Protestant Explanation of Black-White Inequality." *Social Problems* 46, pp. 398–417.

Emirbayer, Mustafa and Mimi Sheller. 1999. "Publics in History." *Theory and Society* 28, pp. 145–197.

Ennis, James G. 1992. "The Social Organization of Sociological Knowledge: Modeling the Intersection of Specialties." *American Sociological Review* 57, pp. 259–265.

Ennis, James G. and Richard Schreuer. 1987. "Mobilizing Weak Support for Social Movements: The Role of Grievance, Efficacy and Cost." *Social Forces* 66, pp. 390–409.

Entman, Robert M. 1995. "Television, Democratic Theory, and the Visual Construction of Poverty." *Research in Political Sociology* 7, pp. 139–160.

Epstein, Lee, Valerie Hoekstra, Jeffrey Segal, and Harold Spaeth. 1998. "Do Political Preferences Change? A Longitudinal Study of U.S. Supreme Court Justices." *Journal of Politics* 60, pp. 801–818.

Erbe, Bonnie. 1998. " 'Liberal Media' Bias is a Myth That Gives the Right a Target." *The Capital Times* (Madison, WI), June 24, 1998, p. 11A.

Erikson, Kai T. 1966. *Wayward Puritans; A Study In The Sociology Of Deviance*. New York: Wiley.

Erikson, Robert S. 1995. "State Turnout and Presidential Voting." *American Politics Quarterly* 23, pp. 387–397.

Erlanger, Howard, Mia Cahill, Charles Epp, and Kathleen Haines. 1996. "Law Student Idealism and Job Choice: Some New Data on an Old Question." *Law and Society Review* 30, pp. 851–864.

Esping-Andersen, Gösta. 1990. *The Three Worlds of Welfare Capitalism*. Princeton, NJ: Princeton University Press.

Esping-Andersen, Gösta 1999. "Politics without Class: Postindustrial Cleavages in Europe." In *Continuity and Change in Contemporary Capitalism*, eds. H. Kitschelt, P. Lange, G. Marks, and J. Stephens, pp. 293–316. New York: Cambridge University Press.

Esping-Andersen, Gösta and Kees van Kersbergen. 1992. "Contemporary Research on Social Democracy." *Annual Review of Sociology* 18, pp. 187–208.

Esses, Victoria, John Dovidio, Lynne Jackson, and Tamara Armstrong. 2001. "The Immigration Dilemma: The Role of Perceived Group Competition, Ethnic Prejudice, and National Identity." *Journal of Social Issues* 57, pp. 389–412.

Etzioni, Amitai. 1993. "Power as a Societal Force." In *Power in Modern Societies*, eds. M. Olson and M. Marger, pp. 18–28. Boulder, CO: Westview.

Evans, John. 1997. "Worldviews of Social Groups as the Source of Moral Value Attitudes: Implications of the Culture Wars Thesis." *Sociological Forum* 12, pp. 371–399.

Evans, John. 2003. "Have American's Attitudes Become More Polarized? An Update." *Social Science Quarterly* 84, pp. 71–90.

Evans, Peter, Dietrich Rueschemeyer, and Theda Skocpol, eds. *Bringing the State Back In*. New York: Russell Sage Foundation.

Evans, Peter, Dietrich Rueschemeyer, and Evelyne Huber Stephens. 1985. *States versus Markets in the World System*, Beverly Hills, CA: Sage.

Evans, Peter. 1995. *Embedded Autonomy: States and Industrial Transformation*. Princeton, NJ: Princeton University Press.

Evans, Peter. 1997. "The Eclipse of the State? Reflections of Stateness in an Era of Globalization." *World Politics* 50, pp. 62–87.

Evarts, Dru and Guido Stempel. 1974. "Coverage of the 1972 Campaign by TV, News Magazines and Major Newspapers." *Journalism Quarterly* 51, pp. 645–648.

Eveland, Jr. William, Douglas McLeod, and Nancy Singorielli. 1995. "Actual and Perceived U.S. Public Opinion: The Spiral of Silence during the Persian Gulf War." *International Journal of Public Opinion Research* 7, pp. 91–109.

Everett, Kevin Djo. 1992. "Professionalization and Protest: Changes in the Social Movement Sector, 1961–1983." *Social Forces* 70, pp. 957–976.

Eyerman, Ron and Andrew Jamison. 1991. *Social Movements: A Cognitive Approach*. University Park, PA: Pennsylvania State University Press.

F

Fabrikant, Geraldine. 1998. "Fox Drops Drama Based on Charge Against Justice Thomas." *New York Times*, September 14, 1998.

Falk, Richard. 1994. "The Making of Global Citizenship." In *The Condition of Citizenship*, ed., B. van Steenbergen, pp. 127–140. Thousand Oaks, CA: Sage.

Faludi, Susan. 1991. *Backlash: The Undeclared War Against American Women*. New York: Crown Publishers.

Farber, Daniel A. 1987. "The 'Law and Economics' Movement." *Research in Social Problems and Public Policy* 4, pp. 21–37.

Farrell, Ronald and Malcolm D. Holmes. 1991. "The Social and Cognitive Structure of Legal Decision-Making." *Sociological Quarterly* 32, pp. 529–542.

Faulkner, Harold U. 1931. *The Quest for Social Justice, 1898–1914*. New York: Macmillan.

Faulkner, Harold U. 1951. *From Versailles to the New Deal: A Chronicle of the Harding-Coolidge-Hoover Era*. New Haven, CT: Yale University Press.

Faulks, Keith. 2000. *Political Sociology: A Critical Introduction*. New York: New York University Press.

Feagin, Joe R. 1991. "The Continuing Significance of Race: Antiblack Discrimination in Public Places." *American Sociological Review* 56, pp. 101–116.

Feinberg, Walter. 1989. "Fixing the Schools: The Ideological Turn." In *Critical Pedagogy, the State, and Cultural Struggle*, eds. H. Giroux and P. McLaren, pp. 69–91. Albany, NY: State University of New York Press.

Femia, Joseph V. 1981. *Gramsci's Political Thought: Hegemony, Consciousness, and the Revolutionary Process*. Oxford, UK: Clarendon Press.

Fendrich, James Max and Kenneth L. Lovoy. 1988. "Back to the Future: Adult Political Behavior of Former Student Activists." *American Sociological Review* 53, pp. 780–784.

Fenster, Mark J. 1994. "The Impact of Allowing Day of Registration Voting on Turnout in U.S. Elections from 1960 to 1992." *American Politics Quarterly* 22, pp. 74–88.

Ferguson, Thomas. 1995. *Golden Rule: The Investment Theory of Party Competition and the Logic of Money-Driven Political Systems*. Chicago: University of Chicago Press.

Ferguson, Thomas and Joel Rogers. 1981. "The Reagan Victory: Corporate Coalitions in the 1980 Campaign." In *The Hidden Election*, eds. T. Ferguson and J. Rogers, pp. 3–64. New York: Panethon.

Ferguson, Thomas and Joel Rogers. 1986. *Right Turn: The Decline of the Democrats and the Future of American Politics*. New York: Wang and Hill.

Ferree, Myra Marx. 1992. "Rational Choice Theory and Resource Mobilization." In *Frontiers in Social Movement Theory*, eds. A. Morris and C. Mueller, pp. 29–52. New Haven, CT: Yale University Press.

Ferree, Myra Marx, William Gamson, Jurgen Gerhards, and Dieter Rucht. 2002. "Four Models of the Public Sphere in Modern Democracy." *Theory and Society* 31, pp. 289–324.

Ferrell, Jeff. 1999. "Cultural Criminology." *Annual Review of Sociology* 25, pp. 395–418.

Filer, John E., Lawrence Kenny, and Rebecca Morton. 1993. "Redistribution, Income, and Voting." *American Journal of Political Science* 37, pp. 63–87.

Fine, Gary Alan. 1996. "Reputational Entrepreneurs and the Memory of Incompetence: Melting Supporters, Partisan Warriors and Images of President Harding." *American Journal of Sociology* 101, pp. 1159–1193.

Finegold, Kenneth. 1988. "Agriculture and the Politics of U.S. Social Provision." In *The Politics of Social Policy in the United States,* eds. M. Weir, A. Shula Orloff and T. Skocpol, pp. 199–234. Princeton, NJ: Princeton University Press.

Finegold, Kenneth and Theda Skocpol. 1995. *State and Party in America's New Deal.* Madison, WI: University of Wisconsin Press.

Finkel, Steven E. and Edward N. Muller. 1998. "Rational Choice and the Dynamics of Collective Political Action: Evaluating Alternative Models with Panel Data." *American Political Science Review.* 92, pp. 37–50.

Finkel, Steven E. and John G. Geer. 1998. "A Spot Check: Casting Doubt on the Demobilizing Effect of Attack Advertising." *American Journal of Political Science* 42, pp. 573–595.

Finkelstein, Katherine. 1999. "Bronx Is Joining Controversy Over St. Patrick's Day Parade." *New York Times,* March 14, 1999.

Firebaugh, Glenn and Kevin Chen. 1995. "Vote Turnout of Nineteenth Amendment Women: The Enduring Effect of Disenfranchisement." *American Journal of Sociology* 100, pp. 972–996.

Fireman, Bruce and William A. Gamson. 1979. "Utilitarian Logic in the Resource Mobilization Perspective." In *The Dynamics of Social Movements,* eds. M. Zald and J. McCarthy, pp. 8–45. Cambridge, MA: Winthrop.

Fishkin, James S. 1996. "The Televised Deliberative Poll: An Experiment in Democracy." *The Annals of the American Academy of Political and Social Science.* 546, pp. 132–140.

Fiske, John. 1993. *Power Plays, Power Works.* New York: Verso.

Fiske, John. 1998. "Surveilling the City: Whiteness, the Black Man, and Democratic Totalitarianism." *Theory, Culture and Society* 15, pp. 67–88.

Fitzgerald, Kathleen J. and Diane Rodgers. 2000. "Radical Social Movement Organizations: A Theoretical Model." *Sociological Quarterly* 41, pp. 573–593.

Fitzpatrick, Peter. 1980. "Law, Modernization and Mystification." *Research in Law and Society* 3, pp. 161–178.

Flanagan, Timothy J. 1996a. "Public Opinion on Crime and Justice." In *Americans View Crime and Justice: A National Public Opinion Survey,* eds. T. Flanagan and D. Longmire, pp. 1–15. Thousand Oaks, CA: Sage.

Flanagan, Timothy J. 1996b. "Reform or Punish: Americans Views of the Correctional System." In *Americans View Crime and Justice: A National Public Opinion Survey,* eds. T. Flanagan and D. Longmire, pp. 75–92. Thousand Oaks, CA: Sage.

Flemming, Roy B. and B. Dan Wood. 1997. "The Public and the Supreme Court: Individual Justice Responsiveness to American Policy Moods." *American Journal of Political Science* 41, pp. 468–498.

Flemming, Roy B., John Bohte, and B. Dan Wood. 1997. "One Voice Among Many: The Supreme Court's Influence on Attentiveness to Issues in the United States, 1947–92." *American Journal of Political Science* 41, pp. 1224–1250.

Fleurbaey, Marc. 1993. "An Egalitarian Democratic Private Ownership Economy." *Politics and Society* 21, pp. 215–233.

Flexner, Eleanor. 1968. *A Century of Struggle: The Women's Rights Movement in the United States.* New York: Atheneum.

Fligstein, Neil. 1987. "The Intraorganizational Power Structure: Rise of Finance Personnel to Top Leadership in Large Corporations, 1919–1979." *American Sociological Review* 52, pp. 44–58.

Fligstein, Neil. 1990. *The Transformation of Corporate Control.* Cambridge, MA: Harvard University Press.

Fligstein, Neil. 1996. "Markets as Politics: A Political-Cultural Approach to Market Institutions." *American Sociological Review* 61, pp. 656–673.

Fligstein, Neil. 1997. "Social Skill and Institutional Theory." *American Behavioral Scientist* 40, pp. 397–405.

Flyvbjerg, Bent. 1998. *Rationality and Power: Democracy in Practice.* Chicago: University of Chicago Press.

Foerstel, Herbert N. 1991. *Surveillance in the Stacks: The FBI's Library Awareness Program.* Westport, CT: Greenwood Press.

Fones-Wolf, Elizabeth A. 1994. *Selling Free Enterprise: The Business Assault on Labor and Liberalism, 1945–1960.* Urbana, IL: University of Illinois Press.

Forbath, William E. 1991. *Law and the Shaping of the American Labor Movement.* Cambridge, MA: Harvard University Press.

Fording, Richard C. 1997. "The Conditional Effect of Violence as a Political Tactic." *American Journal of Political Science* 41, pp. 1–29.

Fording, Richard C. 2001. "The Political Response to Black Insurgency." *American Political Science Review* 95, pp. 115–130.

Formisano, Ronald. 1994. "The Invention of the Ethnocultural Interpretation." *American Historical Review* 99, pp. 453–477.

Formisano, Ronald. 1999. "The 'Party Period' Revisited." *Journal of American History* 86, pp. 93–121.

Foster, James Carl. 1990. *The Ideology of Apolitical Politics: Elite Lawyers' Response to the Legitimation Crisis of American Capitalism, 1870–1920.* New York: Garland Press.

Fowler, Bridget. 1997. *Pierre Bourdieu and Cultural Theory.* Thousand Oaks, CA: Sage.

Fowler, Robert Booth and Allen D. Hertzke. 1995. *Religion and Politics in America: Faith, Culture, and Strategic Choices.* Boulder, CO: Westview Press.

Frank, David John, John W. Meyer, and David Miyahara. 1995. "The Individualist Polity and the Prevalence of Professionalized Psychology: A Cross-national Study." *American Sociological Review* 60, pp. 360–377.

Franklin, Marg N. and Wolfgang Hirczy. 1998. "Separated Powers, Divided Government, and Turnout in U.S. Presidential Elections." *American Journal of Political Science* 42, pp. 316–326.

Fraser, Elvis. 1994. "Reconciling Conceptual and Measurement Problems in the Comparative Study of Human Rights." *International Journal of Contemporary Sociology* 35, pp. 1–18.

Fraser, Nancy and Linda Gordon. 1994. "Civil Citizenship against Social Citizenship." In *The Condition of Citizenship*, ed. B. van Steenbergen, pp. 90–107. Thousand Oaks, CA: Sage.

Freeman, Jo. 1975. *The Politics of Women's Liberation.* New York: McKay.

Freudenburg, William R. and Robert Gramling. 1994. "Bureaucratic Slippage and Failures of Agency Vigilance: The Case of the Environmental Studies Program." *Social Problems* 41, pp. 214–239.

Frey, Bruno S. and Lorenz Goette. 1998. "Does the Popular Vote Destroy Civil Rights?" *American Journal of Political Science* 42, pp. 1343–1348.

Fried, Amy. 1988. "Abortion Politics as Symbolic Politics: An Investigation into Belief Systems." *Social Science Quarterly* 69, pp. 137–154.

Friedland, Roger and Robert R. Alford. 1991. "Bringing Society Back In: Symbols, Practices, and Institutional Contradictions." In *The New Institutionalism in Organizational Analysis.* eds. W. Powell and P. DiMaggio, pp. 204–231. Chicago: University of Chicago Press.

Friedman, Jeffrey. 1996. "Nationalism in Theory and Reality." *Critical Review* 10, pp. 155–168.

Friedman, Milton. 1963. *Capitalism and Freedom.* Chicago: University of Chicago Press.

Friedrich, Carl J. ed. 1966. *Revolution.* New York: Atherton.

Fuentes, Annette. 1998. "Trustees of the Right's Agenda." *The Nation* (October 5, 1998), pp. 19–20.

Fugita, Stephen S. and David J. O'Brien. 1991. *Japanese American Ethnicity: The Persistence of Community.* Seattle: University of Washington Press.

Fuller, Bruce. 1983. "Youth Job Structure and School Enrollment, 1890–1920." *Sociology of Education* 56, pp. 145–156.

Fuller, Bruce and Richard Rubinson. 1992. "Does the State Expand Schooling? Review of the Evidence." In *The Political Construction of Education,* eds. B. Fuller and R. Rubinson, pp. 1–28. New York: Praeger.

Funston, David. 1975. "The Supreme Court and Critical Elections." *American Political Science Review* 69, pp. 795–811.

Furness, Norman and Timothy Tilton. 1977. *The Case for the Welfare State.* Bloomington, IN: Indiana University Press.

Fusfeld, Daniel R. 1984. "Government and the Suppression of Radical Labor, 1877–1918." In *Statemaking and Social Movements,* eds. C. Bright and S. Harding, pp. 344–377. Ann Arbor, MI: University of Michigan Press.

G

Gable, Eric and Richard Handler. 1996. "After Authenticity at an American Heritage Site." *American Anthropologist* 98, pp. 568–578.

Gais, Thomas L., Mark Peterson, and Jack Walker. 1984. "Interest Groups, Iron Triangles, and Representative Institution in American National Government." *British Journal of Political Science* 14, pp. 161–185.

Galliher, John F. 1980. "The Study of the Social Origins of Criminal Law: An Inventory of Research Findings." *Research in Law and Society* 3, pp. 301–319.

Gamble, Barbara S. 1997. "Putting Civil Rights to a Popular Vote." *American Journal of Political Science* 41, pp. 245–269.

Gamoran, Adam. 1990. "Civil Religion in American Schools." *Sociological Analysis* 51, pp. 235–256.

Gamson, Joshua. 1995. "Must Identity Movements Self-destruct? A Queer Dilemma." *Social Problems* 42, pp. 390–407.

Gamson, William A. 1968. *Power and Discontent.* Homewood, IL: Dorsey.

Gamson, William A. 1975. *The Strategy of Social Protest.* Homewood, IL: Dorsey Press.

Gamson, William A. 1989. "News as Framing." *American Behavioral Scientist* 33, pp. 157–161.

Gamson, William A. 1990. *Strategy of Social Protest,* 2nd ed. Belmont, CA: Wadsworth.

Gamson, William A. 1992a. "The Social Psychology of Collective Action." In *Frontiers in Social Movement Theory,* eds. A. Morris and C. M. Mueller, pp. 53–76. New Haven, CT: Yale University Press.

Gamson, William A. 1992b. *Talking Politics.* New York: Cambridge University Press.

Gamson, William A. 1996. "Framing Political Opportunity." In *Comparative Perspectives on Social Movements,* eds. D. McAdam, J. McCarthy, and M. Zald, pp. 291–311. New York: Cambridge University Press.

Gamson, William A. 1998. "Social Movements and Cultural Change." *From Contention to Democracy,* eds. M. Giugni, D. McAdam, and C. Tilly, pp. 57–77. Lanham, MD: Rowman and Littlefield.

Gamson, William A. and David S. Meyer. 1996. "Framing Political Opportunity." In *Comparative Perspectives on Social Movements,* eds. D. McAdam, J. McCarthy and M. Zald, pp. 275–290. New York: Cambridge University Press.

Gamson, William A. and Andre Modigliani. 1989. "Media Discourse and Public Opinion on Nuclear Power: A Constructionist Approach." *American Journal of Sociology* 95, pp. 1–37.

Gamson, William A. and Gadi Wolfseld. 1993. "Movements and Media as Interacting Systems." *Annals of the American Academy of Political and Social Science* 528, pp. 114–125.

Gamson, William A., David Croteau, William Hoynes, and Theodore Sasson. 1992. "Media Images and the Social Construction of Reality." *Annual Review of Sociology* 18, pp. 373–393.

Gans, Herbert. 1979. *Deciding What's News: A Study of CBS Evening News, NBC Nightly News, and Newsweek.* New York: Vintage.

Ganz, Marshall. 2000. "Resources and Resourcefulness: Strategic Capacity in the Unionization of California Agriculture, 1959–1966." *American Journal of Sociology* 105, pp. 1003–1162.

Garland, David. 2001. *The Culture of Control: Crime and the Social Order in Contemporary Society.* Chicago: University of Chicago Press.

Garon, Sheldon. 1997. *Molding Japanese Minds: The State in Everyday Life.* Princeton, NJ: Princeton University Press.

Gastil, Raymond Duncan. 1991. "The Comparative Survey of Freedom: Experiences and Suggestions." In *On Measuring Democracy,* ed. by A. Inkeles, pp. 21–46. New Brunswick, NJ: Transaction Books.

Gaventa, John. 1980. *Power and Powerlessness.* Urbana, IL: University of Illinois Press.

Gay, Claudine. 2001. "The Effect of Black Congressional Representation on Political Participation." *American Political Science Review* 95, pp. 589–617.

Gay, Claudine. 2002. "Spirals of Trust? The Effect of Descriptive Representation on the Relationship Between Citizens and Their Government." *American Journal of Political Science* 46, pp. 717–732.

Geiger, Roger L. 1988. "Public and Private Sector in Higher Education: A Comparison on International Patterns." *Higher Education* 17, pp. 699–711.

Geiger, Roger L. 1993. *Research and Relevant Knowledge: American Research Universities Since World War II.* New York: Oxford University Press.

Gelb, Joyce and Vivien Hart. 1999. "Feminist Politics in a Hostile Environment." In *How Social Movements Matter,* eds. M. Giugni, D. McAdam, and C. Tilly, pp. 149–181. Minneapolis: University of Minnesota Press.

Gellner, Ernest. 1983. *Nations and Nationalism.* Ithaca, NY: Cornell University Press.

Gellner, Ernest. 1987. *Culture, Identity and Politics.* New York: Cambridge University Press.

Gerber, Alan S. and Donald P. Green. 2000a. "The Effects of Canvassing, Telephone Calls, and Direct Mail on Voter Turnout: A Field Experiment." *American Political Science Review* 94, pp. 653–663.

Gerber, Alan S. and Donald P. Green. 2000b. "The Effects of Nonpartisan Get-Out-the-Vote Drive." *Journal of Politics* 62, pp. 846–857.

Gerbner, George, Larry Gross, Michael Morgan, and Nancy Signorielli. 1984. "Political Correlates of Television Viewing." *Public Opinion Quarterly* 48, pp. 283–300.

Gerbner, George, Larry Gross, Michael Morgan, and Nancy Signorielli. 1987. "Charting the Mainstream: Television's Contribution to Political Orientations." In *American Media and Mass Culture,* ed. D. Lazere, pp. 441–464. Berkeley, CA: University of California Press.

Gerson, Mark. 1996. *The Neoconservative Vision: From the Cold War to Culture Wars.* Lanham, MD: Madison Books.

Gerteis, Joseph. 1998. "Political Alignment and the American Middle Class, 1974–1994." *Sociological Forum* 13, pp. 639–669.

Geschwender, James A. 1968. "Explorations in the Theory of Social Movements and Revolutions." *Social Forces* 42, pp. 127–135.

Gholz, Eugene and Harvey Sapolsky. 1999–2000. "Restructuring the U.S. Defense Industry." *International Security* 24, pp. 5–51.

Gibbs, David. 1996. "The Military Industrial Complex, Sectoral Conflict, and the Study of U.S. Foreign Policy." *Business and the State in International Relations* ed. R. Cox, pp. 41–56. Boulder, CO: Westview.

Gibbs, Jack P. 1989. "Conceptualization of Terrorism." *American Sociological Review* 54, pp. 329–340.

Gibson, James L. 1989. "Understandings of Justice: Institutional Legitimacy, Procedural Justice, and Political Tolerance." *Law and Society Review* 23, pp. 469–496.

Gibson, James L. 1992. "The Political Consequences of Intolerance: Cultural Conformity and Political Freedom." *American Political Science Review* 86, pp. 338–356.

Gibson, James L. and Richard D. Bingham. 1982. "On the Conceptualization and Measurement of Political Tolerance." *American Political Science Review* 76, pp. 603–620.

Giddens, Anthony. 1982. *Profiles and Critiques in Social Theory.* Berkeley, CA: University of California Press.

Giddens, Anthony. 1987. *The Nation State and Violence.* Berkeley, CA: University of California Press.

Gidengil, Elisabeth. 1995. "Economic Man-Social Woman? The Case of the Gender Gap in Support for the Canada-United States Free Trade Agreement." *Comparative Political Studies* 28, pp. 384–408.

Gilbert, Jess and Carolyn Howe. 1991. "Beyond 'State vs. Society': Theories of the State and New Deal Agricultural Policies." *American Sociological Review* 56, pp. 204–220.

Gilens, Martin. 1995. "Racial Attitudes and Opposition to Welfare." *Journal of Politics* 57, pp. 994–1014.

Gilens, Martin. 1996a. "Race and Poverty in America: Public Perceptions and the American News Media." *Public Opinion Quarterly* 60, pp. 515–541.

Gilens, Martin. 1996b. "Race Coding and White Opposition to Welfare." *American Political Science Review* 90, pp. 593–604.

Gilens, Martin. 1999. *Why Americans Hate Welfare: Race, Media and the Politics of Antipoverty Policy.* Chicago: University of Chicago Press.

Gilens, Martin and Craig Hertzman. 2000. "Corporate Ownership and News Bias." *Journal of Politics* 62, pp. 369–386.

Gilens, Martin, Paul Sniderman, and James Kuklinski. 1998. "Affirmative Action and the Politics of Realignment." *British Journal of Political Science* 28, pp. 159–183.

Giles, Michael and Kaenan Hertz. 1994. "Racial Threat and Partisan Identification." *American Political Science Review* 88, pp. 317–326.

Gilliam, Franklin, Jr. and Shanto Iyengar. 2000. "Prime Suspects: The Influence of Local Television News on the Viewing Public." *American Journal of Political Science.* 44, pp. 560–573.

Gillis, John R. 1994. "Memory and identity: The History of a Relationship." In *Commemorations: The Politics of National Identity,* ed. J. Gillis, pp. 3–24. Princeton, NJ: Princeton University Press.

Gimpel, James. 1993. "Reform Resistance and Reform Adopting Machines: The Electoral Foundation of Urban Politics: 1910–1930." *Political Research Quarterly* 46, pp. 371–382.

Ginsberg, Benjamin. 1972. "Critical Elections and the Substance of Party Conflict: 1844–1968." *Midwest Journal of Political Science* 16, pp. 603–625.

Ginsberg, Benjamin. 1984. "Money and Power: The New Political Economy of American Elections." In *The Political Economy,* eds. T. Ferguson and J. Rogers, pp. 163–179. Armonk, NY: M.E. Sharpe.

Ginsberg, Benjamin. 1986. *The Captive Public: How Mass Opinion Promotes State Power.* New York: Basic Books.

Ginsberg, Benjamin and Robert Weissberg. 1978. "Elections and the Mobilization of Popular Support." *American Journal of Political Science* 22, pp. 31–55.

Gitelman, Howard M. 1984. "Management's Crisis of Confidence and the Origin of the National Industrial Conference Board, 1914–1916." *Business History Review* 58, pp. 153–177.

Gitlin, Todd. 1980. *The Whole World Is Watching: Mass Media in the Making of the New Left.* Berkeley, CA: University of California Press.

Giugni, Marco. 1998a. "Social Movements and Change." In *From Contention to Democracy,* eds. M. Giugni, D. McAdam, and C. Tilly, pp. xi–xxvi. Lanham, MD: Rowman and Littlefield.

Giugni, Marco. 1998b. "The Other Side of the Coin: Explaining Cross-national Similarities Between Movements." *Mobilization* 3, pp. 89–105.

Giugni, Marco. 1999. "How Movements Matter." In *How Social Movements Matter,* eds. M. Giugni, D. McAdam, and C. Tilly, pp. xiii–xxxiii. Minneapolis: University of Minnesota Press.

Giugni, Marco and Florence Passy. 1998. "Contentious Politics in Complex Societies." In *From Contention to Democracy,* eds. M. Giugni, D. McAdam, and C. Tilly, pp. 81–107. Lanham, MD: Rowman and Littlefield.

Glasberg, Davita Silfen and Dan Skidmore. 1997a. *Corporate Welfare Policy and the Welfare State: Bank Deregulation and the Savings and Loan Bailout.* New York: Aldine de Gruyter.

Glasberg, Davita Silfen and Dan Skidmore. 1997b. "The Dialectics of State Economic Intervention: Bank Deregulation and the Savings and Loan Bailout." *Sociological Quarterly* 38, pp. 67–93.

Glasberg, Davita Silfen and Dan Skidmore. 1998a. "The Role of the State in the Criminogenesis of Corporate Crime: A Case Study of the Savings and Loan Crisis." *Social Science Quarterly* 79, pp. 110–128.

Glasberg, Davita Silfen and Dan Skidmore. 1998b. "The Dialectics of White-Collar Crime." *American Journal of Economics and Sociology* 57, pp. 423–449.

Glenn, Evelyn. 2000. "Citizenship and Inequality: Historical and Global Perspectives." *Social Problems* 47, pp. 1–20.

Gluck, Carol. 1985. *Japan's Modern Myths: Ideology in the Late Meiji Period.* Princeton, NJ: Princeton University Press.

Glynn, Carroll J., Andrew Hayes, and James Shanahan. 1997. "Perceived Support for One's Opinion and Willingness to Speak Out: A Meta-Analysis of Survey Studies on the 'Spiral of Silence'." *Public Opinion Quarterly* 61, pp. 452–463.

Glynn, Carroll J., Susan Herbst, Garrett O'Keefe, and Robert Shapiro. 1999. *Public Opinion.* Boulder, CO: Westview.

Goldberg, Carey. 1999. "Contrarian New Hampshire To Honor Dr. King, at Last," *New York Times,* May 26, 1999.

Goldfield, Michael. 1989. "Worker Insurgency, Radical Organization and New Deal Labor Legislation." *American Political Science Review* 83, pp. 1257–1282.

Goldstein, Robert Justin. 1978. *Political Repression in Modern America: 1870 to the Present.* New York: Schenkman.

Goldstone, Jack A. 1980. "The Weakness of Organization: A New Look at Gamson's The Strategy of Social Protest." *American Journal of Sociology* 85, pp. 1017–1042.

Goldstone, Jack A. 1991. "An Analytic Framework." In *Revolutions of the Late Twentieth Century,* eds. J. Goldstone, T. Gurr, and F. Moshiri, pp. 37–51. Boulder, CO: Westview.

Goldstone, Jack A. 1998. "Social Movements or Revolutions? On the Evolution and Outcomes of Collective Action." In *From Contention To Democracy,* eds. M. Giugni, D. McAdam, and C. Tilly. pp. 125–145. Lanham, MD: Rowman & Littlefield.

Goode, Erich and Nachman Ben Yehuda. 1994. *Moral Panics: The Social Construction of Deviance.* Cambridge, MA: Blackwell.

Goodin, Robert E. 1981. "Civil Religion and Political Witch Hunts." *Comparative Politics* 14, pp. 1–15.

Goodin, Robert E., Bruce Headey, Ruud Muffels, and Henk-Jan Dirven. 1999. *The Real Worlds of Welfare Capitalism.* New York: Cambridge University Press.

Goodwyn, Lawrence. 1976. *Democratic Promise: The Populist Movement in America.* New York: Oxford University Press.

Gordon, Colin. ed. 1980. *Power/Knowledge: Selected Interviews and Other Writings 1972–1977 by Michel Foucault.* New York: Pantheon.

Gordon, Colin. 1994. *New Deals: Business, Labor, and Politics in America, 1920–1935.* New York: Cambridge University Press.

Gordon, David. 1968. "Immigrants and Urban Government Form in American Cities, 1944–60." *American Journal of Sociology* 74, pp. 158–171.

Gordon, Linda. 1990. "Family Violence, Feminism and Social Control." In *Women, the State and Welfare,* ed. L. Gordon, pp. 178–198. Madison, WI: University of Wisconsin Press.

Gornick, Janet and Jerry Jacobs. 1998. "Gender, the Welfare States, and Public Employment." *American Sociological Review* 63, pp. 688–710.

Gornick, Janet C., Marcia Meyers, and Katherin Ross. 1998. "Public Policies and the Employment of Mothers: A Cross-national Study." *Social Science Quarterly* 79, pp. 35–54.

Gotham, Kevin Fox. 1999. "Political Opportunity, Community Identity, and the Emergence of a Local Anti-expressway Movement." *Social Problems* 46, pp. 332–354.

Gotham, Kevin Fox. 2002. *Race, Real Estate, and Uneven Development.* Albany, NY: State University of New York Press.

Gould, Frank. 1983. "The Growth in Public Expenditures: Theory and Evidence from Six Advanced Democracies." In *Why Governments Grow,* ed. C. L. Taylor, pp. 217–239. Newbury Park, CA: Sage.

Gould, Roger V. 1991. "Multiple Networks and Mobilization in the Paris Commune, 1871." *American Sociological Review* 56, pp. 716–729.

Gould, Roger V. 1993. "Trade Cohesion, Class Unity and Urban Insurrection: Artisanal Activism in the Paris Commune." *American Journal of Sociology* 98, pp. 721–754.

Gould, Roger V. 1996. "Patron-client Ties, State Centralization, and the Whiskey Rebellion." *American Journal of Sociology* 102, pp. 400–429.

Gould, Roger V. 1999. "Collective Violence and Group Solidarity: Evidence from a Feuding Society." *American Sociological Review* 64, pp. 356–380.

Gould, Roger V. 2000. "Revenge as Sanction and Solidarity Display: An Analysis of Vendettas in Nineteenth Century Corsica." *American Sociological Review* 65, pp. 682–704.

Graber, Doris. 1984. *Mass Media and American Politics.* Washington, DC: Congressional Quarterly Press.

Gran, Brian. 1997. "Three Worlds of Old-Age Decommodification?" *Journal of Aging Studies* 11, pp. 63–79.

Granberg, Donald and Gail Corrigan. 1972. "Authoritarianism, Dogmatism and Orientations Toward the Vietnam War." *Sociometry* 35, pp. 468–476.

Granfield, Robert and Thomas Koenig. 1992. "The Fate of Elite Idealism: Accommodation and Ideological Work at Harvard Law School." *Social Problems* 39, pp. 315–331.

Granfield, Robert and Thomas Koenig. 1996. "Learning Collective Eminence: Harvard Law School and the Social Production of Elite Lawyers." *Sociological Quarterly* 33, pp. 503–520.

Grant, Don Sherman II. 1995. "The Political Economy of Business Failure Across the American States, 1970–1985." *American Sociological Review* 60, pp. 851–873.

Grant, Don Sherman II. 1996. "The Political Economy of New Business Formation across the American States, 1970–1985." *Social Science Quarterly* 77, pp. 28–42.

Grant, Don Sherman II and Richard Hutchinson. 1996. "Global Smokestack Chasing: A Comparison of the State-level Determinants of Foreign and Domestic Manufacturing Investment." *Social-Problems* 43, pp. 21–38.

Grant, Don Sherman II and Ramiro Martinez, Jr. 1997. "Crime and the Restructuring of the U.S. Economy: A Reconsideration of the Class Linkages." *Social Forces* 75, pp. 769–798.

Grant, Don Sherman II and Michael Wallace. 1994. "The Political Economy of Manufacturing Growth and Decline across the American States, 1970–1985." *Social Forces* 73, pp. 33–63.

Grasmick, Howard G., Elizabeth Davenport, and Mitchell Chamlin. 1992. "Protestant Fundamentalism and the Retributive Doctrine of Punishment." *Criminology* 30, pp. 21–45.

Grasmick, Howard G., Carolyn S. Morgan, and Mary Baldwin. 1992. "Support for Corporal Punishment in the Schools." *Social Science Quarterly* 73, pp. 177–187.

Grattet, Ryken, Valerie Jenness, and Theodore Curry. 1998. "The Homogenization and Differentiation of Hate Crime Law in the United States, 1978 to 1995." *American Sociological Review* 63, pp. 286–307.

Gray, John. 1998. *False Dawn: The Delusions of Global Capitalism.* New York: New Press.

Gray, Mark and Miki Caul. 2000. "Declining Voter Turnout in Advanced Industrial Democracies, 1950 to 1997." *Comparative Political Studies* 31, pp. 1091–1122.

Green, Andy. 1990. *Education and State Formation: The Rise of Education Systems in England, France and the USA.* New York: St. Martins.

Green, Donald and Ian Shapiro. 1994. *Pathologies of Rational Choice Theory.* New Haven, CT: Yale University Press.

Green, Gary P., Arnold Fleischmann, and Tsz Man Kwong. 1996. "The Effectiveness of Local Economic Development Policies in the 1980s." *Social Science Quarterly* 77, pp. 609–625.

Green, John C. 1993. "Pat Robertson and the Latest Crusade: Religious Resources and the 1988 Presidential Campaign." *Social Science Quarterly* 74, pp. 157–168.

Green, John C. 1995. "The Christian Right and the 1994 Elections: An Overview." In *God at the Grass Roots: the Christian Right in the 1994 Elections,* eds. M. Rozell and C. Wilcox, pp. 1–18. Lanham, MD: Rowman and Littlefield.

Green, John C. and James L. Guth. 1991. "The Bible and the Ballot Box: The Shape of Things to Come." In *The Bible and the Ballot Box,* eds. J. Guth and J. Green, pp. 207–225. Boulder, CO: Westview.

Green, John C., James L. Guth, and Kevin Hill. 1993. "Faith and Election: The Christian Right in Congressional Campaigns, 1978–1988." *Journal of Politics* 55, pp. 80–91.

Green, John C., James L. Guth, Lyman A. Kellstedt, and Corwin E. Smidt. 1996. *Religion and the Culture Wars: Dispatches from the Front.* Lanham, MD: Rowman and Littlefield.

Green, John C., Corwin E. Smidt, Lyman A. Kellstedt, and James L. Guth. 1997. "Bring in the Sheaves: The Christian Right and White Protestants, 1976–1996." In *Sojourners in the Wilderness,* eds. C. Smidt and J. Penning, pp. 75–91. Lanham, MD: Rowman and Littlefield.

Greenberg, David F, ed. 1993. *Crime and Capitalism: Readings in Marxist Criminology.* 2nd ed. Philadelphia: Temple University Press.

Greene, Jay and Greg Forster. 2003. "Public High School Graduate and College Readiness Rates in the United States." *Education Working Paper,* No. 3. New York: Manhattan Institute.

Greenfeld, Liah. 1992. *Nationalism: Five Roads to Modernity.* Cambridge, MA: Harvard University Press.

Greenfeld, Liah. 1996. "The Modern Religion?" *Critical Review* 10, pp. 169–191.

Greenhouse, Linda. 1995. "Gay Group and Parade Backers Battle." *New York Times,* April 25, 1995.

Grier, Kevin B., Michael Munger, and Brian Roberts. 1994. "The Determinates of Industrial Political Action, 1978–1986." *American Political Science Review* 88, pp. 911–926.

Griffin, Larry J., Joel Devine, and Michael Wallace. 1982. "Monopoly Capital, Organized Labor, and Military Expenditures in the United States, 1949–1976." *American Journal of Sociology* 88, pp. S113–153.

Griffin, Larry J., Michael Wallace, and Beth Rubin. 1986. "Capitalist Resistance to the Organization of Labor before the New Deal: Why? How? Success?" *American Sociological Review* 51, pp. 147–167.

Grønbjerg, Kirsten A. 1977. *Mass Society and the Extension of Welfare, 1960–1970.* Chicago: University of Chicago Press.

Gross, Bertram. 1974. "Friendly Fascism: A Model for America." In *Criminal Justice in America,* ed. R. Quinney, pp. 414–428. Boston: Little, Brown.

Guest, Avery. 1974. "Class Consciousness and American Political Attitudes." *Social Forces* 52, pp. 496–509.

Gumport, Patricia J. 1993. "The Contested Terrain of Academic Program Reduction." *Journal of Higher Education* 64, pp. 283–311.

Gusfield, Joseph R. 1963. *Symbolic Crusade: Status Political and the American Temperance Movement.* Urbana, IL: University of Illinois Press.

Gusfield, Joseph R. 1967. "Moral Passage: The Symbolic Process in Public Designations of Deviance." *Social Problems* 15, pp. 175–188.

Gusfield, Joseph R. 1981. *The Culture of Public Problems.* Chicago: University of Chicago Press.

Gusfield, Joseph R. 1996. *Contested Meanings: The Construction of Alcohol Problems.* Madison, WI: University of Wisconsin Press.

Gusfield, Joseph R. and Jerzy Michalowicz. 1984. "Secular Symbolism: Studies of Ritual, Ceremony and the Symbolic Order in Modern Life." *Annual Review of Sociology* 10, pp. 417–435.

Guterbock, Thomas and Bruce London. 1983. "Race, Political Orientation and Participation: An Empirical Test of Four Competing Theories." *American Sociological Review* 48, pp. 439–453.

Guth, James L. 1983. "The New Christian Right." In *The New Christian Right: Mobilization and Legitimation,* eds. R. Liebman and R. Wuthnow, pp. 31–45. New York: Aldine.

Gutmann, Amy. 1988a. "Introduction." In *Democracy and the Welfare State,* ed. A. Gutmann, pp. 3–12. Princeton, NJ: Princeton University Press.

Gutmann, Amy. 1988b. "Distributing Public Education in a Democracy." In *Democracy and the Welfare State,* ed. A. Gutmann, pp. 107–130. Princeton, NJ: Princeton University Press.

H

Haas, Kenneth C. 1994. "The Triumph of Vengeance Over Retribution: The United States Supreme Court and the Death Penalty." *Crime, Law and Social Change* 21, pp. 127–154.

Habermas, Jürgen. 1994. "Citizenship and National Identity." In *The Condition of Citizenship,* ed. B. van Steenbergen, pp. 36–48. Thousand Oaks, CA: Sage.

Hacker, Jacob S. 2002. *The Divided Welfare State.* New York: Cambridge University Press.

Hackey, Robert B. 1992. "Competing Explanations of Voter Turnout among American Blacks." *Social Science Quarterly* 73, pp. 71–89.

Hagan, Everett E. 1962. *On the Theory of Social Change.* Homewood, IL: Dorsey.

Hagan, John. 1982. "The Corporate Advantage: A Study of the Involvement of Corporate and Individual Victims in a Criminal Justice System." *Social Forces* 60, pp. 993–1022.

Hagan, John and Alberto Palloni. 1999. "Sociological Criminology and the Mythology of Hispanic Immigration and Crime." *Social Problems* 46, pp. 617–632.

Hage, Jerald and Robert A. Hanneman. 1980. "The Growth of the Welfare State in Britain, France, Germany, and Italy." *Comparative Social Research* 3, pp. 45–70.

Haggerty, Kevin D. and Richard V. Ericson. 1999. "The Militarization of Policing in the Information Age." *Journal of Political and Military Sociology* 27, pp. 233–255.

Hahn, Carole L. 1999. "Citizenship Education: An Empirical Study of Policy, Practices and Outcomes." *Oxford Review of Education* 25, pp. 231–251.

Haines, Herbert H. 1984. "Black Radicalization and the Funding of Civil Rights, 1957–1970." *Social Problems* 32, pp. 31–43.

Halberstam, David. 1979. *The Powers That Be.* New York: Dell.

Halbwachs, Maurice. 1992. *On Collective Memory.* Chicago: University of Chicago Press, trans. Lewis Coser.

Hale, Edward Everett. 1886. *Man without a Country and Other Tales.* Boston: Roberts Brothers.

Halkides, Mihalis. 1995. "How Not to Study Terrorism." *Peace-Review* 7, pp. 253–260.

Hall, John A. 1995. "Nationalisms, Classified and Explained." In *Notions of Nationalism,* ed. S. Periwal, pp. 8–33. New York: Central European Press.

Hall, John A. and G. John Ikenberry. 1989. *The State.* Minneapolis: University of Minnesota Press.

Hall, Peter A. 1981. "Political Sociology." *Current Perspectives on Social Theory* 2, pp. 15–20.

Hall, Peter A. and Daniel Gingerich. 2001. "Varieties of Capitalism and Institutional Complementarities in the Macroeconomy." Varieties of Capitalism Workshop Paper, Center for European Studies, University of North Carolina, (November 3–4, 2001).

Hall, Peter A. and David Soskice, eds. 2001. *Varieties of Capitalism: The Institutional Foundations of Comparative Advantage.* New York: Oxford University Press.

Hall, Peter A. and Rosemary Taylor. 1996. "Political Science and the Three New Institutionalisms." *Political Studies,* 44, pp. 936–957.

Hall, Robert, Mark Rodeghier, and Bert Useem. 1986. "Effects of Education on Attitude to Protest." *American Sociological Review* 51, pp. 564–573.

Halliday, Terrence, Michael Powell, and Mark Granfors. 1993. "After Minimalism: Transformations of State Bar Associations from Market Dependence to State Reliance, 1918 to 1950." *American Sociological Review* 58, pp. 515–535.

Hallum, Anne M. 1991. "From Candidates to Agenda Setters: Protestant Leaders and the 1988 Presidential Campaign." In *The Bible and the Ballot Box,* eds. J. Guth and J. Green, pp. 31–41. Boulder, CO: Westview.

Hamilton, Gary G. and John R. Sutton. 1989. "The Problem of Control in the Weak State: Domination in the United States, 1880–1920." *Theory and Society* 18, pp. 1–46.

Hamilton, Richard F. 1972. *Class and Politics in the United States.* New York: John Wiley.

Hamilton, Richard F. and James D. Wright. 1986. *The State of the Masses.* New York: Aldine.

Hammond, Philip. 1976. "The Sociology of American Civil Religion: A Bibliographic Essay." *Sociological Analysis* 37, pp. 169–182.

Hammond, Philip. 1989. "Constitutional Faith, Legitimating Myth, Civil Religion." *Law and Social Inquiry* 14, pp. 377–391.

Hammond, Philip. 1994. "Religion and Family Values in Presidential Voting." *Sociology of Religion* 55, pp. 277–290.

Hanagan, Michael. 1980. *The Logic of Solidarity: Artisans and Industrial Workers in Three French Towns, 1871–1914.* Urbana, IL: University of Illinois Press.

Hanagan, Michael. 1997. "Citizenship, Claims-making and the Right to Work: Britain, 1884–1911." *Theory and Society* 26, pp. 449–474.

Hanagan, Michael. 1998. "Social Movements: Incorporation, Disengagement, and Opportunities—A Long View." In *From Contention to Democracy,* eds. M. Giugni, D. McAdam, and C. Tilly, pp. 3–30. Lanham, MD: Rowman & Littlefield.

Handler, Joel F. 1978. *Social Movements and the Legal System.* New York: Academic Press.

Handler, Joel F. and Yeheskel Hasenfeld. 1991. *The Moral Construction of Poverty.* Newbury Park, CA: Sage.

Handler, Richard and Eric Gable. 1997. *The New History in an Old Museum: Creating the Past at Colonial Williamsburg.* Durham, NC: Duke University Press.

Haney, Lynne A. 2000. "Feminist State Theory: Applications to Jurisprudence, Criminology, and the Welfare State." *Annual Review of Sociology* 26, pp. 641–666.

Hannerz, Ulf. 1992. *Cultural Complexity: Studies in the Social Organization of Meaning.* New York: Columbia University Press.

Hansen, John Mark. 1987. "Choosing Sides: The Creation of an Agricultural Policy Network in Congress, 1919–1932." *Studies in American Political Development* 2, pp. 183–230.

Hansenfeld, Yeheskel and Jane A. Rafferty. 1989. "The Determinants of Public Attitudes Toward the Welfare State." *Social Forces* 67, pp. 1027–1048.

Harding, Susan. 1984. "Reconstructing Order Through Action: Jim Crow and the Southern Civil Rights Movements." In *Statemaking and Social Movements,* eds. C. Bright and S. Harding, pp. 378–402. Ann Arbor, MI: University of Michigan Press.

Harper, Charles L. and Kevin Leicht. 1984. "Explaining the New Religious Right: Status Politics and Beyond." *New Christian Politics,* eds. D. Bromley and A. Shupe, pp. 101–110. Macon, GA: Mercer University Press.

Harring, Sidney L. 1983. *Policing a Class Society: The Experience of American Cities, 1865–1915.* New Brunswick, NJ: Rutgers University Press.

Harris, Richard and Sidney Milkis. 1996. *The Politics of Regulatory Change: A Tale of Two Agencies,* 2nd ed. New York: Oxford University Press.

Hart, Peter and Steve Rendall. "Meet the Myth-makers: Right-Wing Media Groups Provide Ammo for 'Liberal Media' Claims." *EXTRA!* (July/August 1998).

Hartman, Moshe. 1974. "On the Definition of Status Inconsistency." *American Journal of Sociology* 80, pp. 706–721.

Hattam, Victoria C. 1992. "Institutions and Political Change: Working Class in England and the United States, 1820–1896." *Politics and Society* 20, pp. 133–136.

Hawley, Ellis. 1974a. "Herbert Hoover, the Commerce Secretariat and the Vision of an 'Associative State,' 1921–1928." *Journal of American History* 61, pp. 120–139.

Hawley, Ellis. 1974b. "Herbert Hoover and American Corporatism, 1929–1933." In *The Hoover Presidency,* eds. M. Fairsold and G. Mazuzan, pp. 101–133. Albany, NY: State University of New York Press.

Haydu, Jeffrey. 1999a. "Counter Action Frames: Employer Repertoires and the Union Menace in the Late Nineteenth Century." *Social Problems* 46, pp. 313–331.

Haydu, Jeffrey. 1999b. "Two Logics of Class Formation? Collective Identities among Proprietary Employers, 1880–1900." *Politics and Society* 27, pp. 507–527.

Hayes, Bernadette C. and Clive S. Bean. 1993. "Political Efficacy: A Comparative Study of the United States, West Germany and Australia." *European Journal of Political Research* 23, pp. 261–280.

Haynes, Stephen E. and David Jacobs. 1994. "Macroeconomics, Economic Stratification, and Partisanship: A Longitudinal Analysis of Contingent Shifts in Political Identification." *American Journal of Sociology* 100, pp. 70–103.

Hays, Samuel. 1998. "The Politics of Reform in Municipal Government." In *The Politics of Urban America: A Reader,* 2nd ed., eds. D. Judd and P. Kantor, pp. 126–145. Needham Heights, MA: Allyn and Bacon.

Hearn, Frank. 1984. "State Autonomy and Corporatism." *Contemporary Crises* 8, pp. 125–145.

Heater, Derek. 1999. *What is Citizenship?* Malden, MA: Polity Press-Blackwell.

Heath, Linda and Kevin Gilbert. 1996. "Mass Media and Fear of Crime." *American Behavioral Scientist* 36, pp. 1441–1463.

Heatherington, Marc J. 1996. "The Media's Role in Forming Voter's National Economic Evaluations in 1992." *American Journal of Political Science* 40, pp. 372–395.

Heaven, Patrick C. L. and Adrian Furnham. 1988. "Race Prejudice and Economic Beliefs." *The Journal of Social Psychology.* 127, pp. 483–489.

Hector, Michael and Satoshi Kanazawa. 1997. "Sociological Rational Choice Theory." *Annual Review of Sociology* 23, pp. 191–214.

Hefner, Robert W., ed. 2001. *The Politics of Multiculturalism: Pluralism and Citizenship in Malaysia, Singapore, and Indonesia.* Honolulu: University of Hawaii Press.

Heinz, Donald. 1983. "The Struggle to Define America." In *The New Christian Right: Mobilization and Legitimation,* eds. R. Liebman and R. Wuthnow, pp. 133–148. New York: Aldine.

Heinz, John P., Ann Southworth, and Anthony Paik. 2003. "Lawyers for Conservative Causes: Clients, Ideology, and Social Distance." *Law and Society Review* 37, pp. 5–50.

Heisler, Barbara Schmitter. 1991. "A Comparative Perspective on the Underclass: Questions of Urban Poverty, Race and Citizenship." *Theory and Society* 20, pp. 455–483.

Held, David. 1980. *Introduction to Critical Theory: Horkheimer to Habermas.* Berkeley, CA: University of California Press.

Held, David. 1987. *Models of Democracy.* Cambridge, UK: Polity Press.

Held, David. 1989. *Political Theory and the Modern State: Essays on State, Power and Democracy.* Stanford, CA: Stanford University Press.

Held, David. 1995. *Democracy and the Global Order: From the Modern State to Cosmopolitan Governance.* Stanford, CA: Stanford University Press.

Held, David, Anthony McGrew, David Goldblatt, and Jonathan Perraton. 1999. *Global Transformations: Politics, Economics and Culture.* Stanford, CA: Stanford University Press.

Henig, Jeffrey R., Thomas Holyoke, Natalie Lacireno-Paquet, and Michele Moser. 2003. "Privatization, Politics, and Urban Services: The Political Behavior of Charter Schools." *Journal of Urban Affairs* 25, pp. 37–54.

Henneck, Rachel. 2003. *"Family Policy in the U.S., Japan, Germany, Italy, and France." Briefing Paper, Council on Contemporary Families* (May 2003), http://www.contemporaryfamilies.org/Int'l%20Family%20Policy.htm (downloaded September 1, 2003).

Henry, Charles P. 1990. *Culture and African American Politics.* Bloomington, IN: Indiana University Press.

Herman, Edward S. and Noam Chomsky. 1988. *Manufacturing Consent: The Political Economy of the Mass Media.* New York: Pantheon.

Hero, Rodney. 1992. *Latinos and the U.S. Political System.* Philadelphia: Temple University Press.

Herring, Cedric. 1989. "Convergence, Polarization, or What?: Racially Based Changes in Attitudes and Outlooks, 1964–1984." *Sociological Quarterly* 30, pp. 267–281.

Herring, Cedric, James House, and Richard Mero. 1991. "Racially Based Changes in Political Alienation in America." *Social Science Quarterly* 72, pp. 123–134.

Hertzke, Allen D. 1988. *Representing God in Washington: The Role of Religious Lobbies in the American Polity.* Knoxville, TN: University of Tennessee Press.

Hertzke, Allen D. 1991. "Harvest of Discontent: Religion and Populism in the 1988 Presidential Campaign." In *The Bible and the Ballot Box,* eds. J. Guth and J. Green, pp. 3–27. Boulder, CO: Westview.

Heying, Charles H. 1997. "Civic Elites and Corporate Delocalization." *American Behavioral Scientist* 40, pp. 657–668.

Heywood, Andrew. 1998. *Political Ideologies: An Introduction,* 2nd ed. New York: Worth Publishers.

Hibbing, John R. and Elizabeth Theiss-Morse. 1996. "Civics Is Not Enough: Teaching Barbarics in K–12." *PS: Political Science and Politics* 29, pp. 57–62.

Hibbing, John R. and Elizabeth Theiss-Morse. 1998. "The Media's Role in Public Negativity Toward Congress: Distinguishing Between Emotional Reactions and Cognitive Evaluations." *American Journal of Political Science* 42, pp. 475–498.

Hibbing, John R. and Elizabeth Theiss-Morse. 2001. "Process Preferences and American Politics: What People Want Government to Be." *American Political Science Review* 95, pp. 145–153.

Hicks, Alexander M. 1988. "Social Democratic Corporatism and Economic Growth." *The Journal of Politics* 50, pp. 677–704.

Hicks, Alexander M. 1995. "Is Political Sociology Informed By Political Science?" *Social Forces* 73, pp. 1219–1229.

Hicks, Alexander M. 1999. *Social Democracy and Welfare Capitalism.* Ithaca, NY: Cornell University Press.

Hicks, Alexander M. and Lane Kenworthy. 1998. "Cooperation and Political Economic Performance in Affluent Democratic Capitalism." *American Journal of Sociology* 103, pp. 1631–1672.

Hicks, Alexander M. and Joya Misra. 1993. "Political Resources and the Growth of Welfare in Affluent Capitalist Democracies, 1960–1982." *American Journal of Sociology* 99, pp. 668–710.

Hicks, Alexander M. and Duane H. Swank. 1983. "Civil Disorder, Relief Mobilization, and AFDC Caseloads: A Reexamination of the Piven and Cloward Thesis." *American Journal of Political Science* 27, pp. 695–716.

Hicks, Alexander M. and Duane H. Swank. 1984. "On the Political Economy of Welfare Expansion." *Comparative Political Studies* 17, pp. 81–118.

Hicks, Alexander M. and Duane H. Swank. 1992. "Politics, Institutions, and Welfare Spending in Industrialized Democracies, 1960–82." *The American Political Science Review* 86, pp. 658–674.

Hicks, Alexander M., Joya Misra, and Tang Nah Ng. 1995. "The Programmatic Emergence of the Social Security State." *American Sociological Review* 60, pp. 329–349.

Hicks, John D. 1961. *Rehearsal for Disaster: The Boom and Collapse of 1919–1920.* Gainesville, FL: University of Florida Press.

Higher Education Research Institute. 2002. The American Freshman: National Norms for Fall 2001. Executive Summary, http://www.gseis.ucla.edu/heri/heri.html.

Highton, Benjamin. 1997. "Easy Registration and Voter Turnout." *Journal of Politics* 59, pp. 565–575.

Higley, Stephen Richard. 1995. *Privilege, Power, and Place: The Geography of the American Upper Class.* Lanham, MD: Rowman and Littlefield.

Hilgartner, Stephen and Charles L. Bosk. 1988. "The Rise and Fall of Social Problems: A Public Arenas Model." *American Journal of Sociology* 94, pp. 53–78.

Hill, Dana Carol and Lean Tigges. 1995. "Gendering the Welfare State." *Gender and Society* 9, pp. 99–119.

Hill, David B. 1985. "Viewer Characteristics and Agenda Setting By Television News." *Public Opinion Quarterly* 49, pp. 340–350.

Hill, Kim Quaile and Angela Hinton-Anderson. 1995. "Pathways of Representation: A Causal Analysis of Public Opinion-Policy Linkages." *American Journal of Political Science* 39, pp. 924–935.

Hill, Kim Quaile and Jan Leighley. 1996. "Political Parties and Class Mobilization in Contemporary United States Elections." *American Journal of Political Science* 40, pp. 787–804.

Himmelstein, Jerome L. 1983. "The New Right." In *The New Christian Right: Mobilization and Legitimation,* eds. R. Liebman and R. Wuthnow, pp. 13–30. New York: Aldine.

Hindess, Barry. 1993. "Citizenship in the Modern West." In *Citizenship and Social Theory,* ed. B. Turner, pp. 19–35. Newbury Park, CA: Sage.

Hird, John A. 1991. "The Political Economy of Pork: Project Selection at the U.S. Army Corps of Engineers." *American Political Science Review* 85, pp. 429–456.

Hirsch, Arnold R. 1998. *Making the Second Ghetto: Race and Housing in Chicago, 1940–1960.* Chicago: University of Chicago Press.

Hirsch, Eric L. 1986. "The Creation of Political Solidarity in Social Movement Organizations." *Sociological Quarterly* 27, pp. 373–388.

Hirsch, Eric L. 1990. "Sacrifice for the Cause: Group Processes, Recruitment, and Commitment in a Student Social Movement." *American Sociological Review* 55, pp. 243–254.

Hobsbawm, Eric. 1983. "The Context, Performance and Meaning of Ritual: The British Monarchy and the Invention of Tradition, 1820–1917." In *The Invention of Tradition,* eds. E. Hobsbawn and T. Ranger, pp. 101–164. New York: Cambridge University Press.

Hobson, Barbara and Marika Lindholm. 1997. "Collective Identities, Women's Power Resources, and the Making of Welfare States." *Theory and Society* 26, pp. 475–508.

Hochschild, Jennifer. 1981. *What's Fair? American Beliefs About Distributive Justice.* Cambridge, MA: Harvard University Press.

Hochschild, Jennifer. 1999. "Affirmative Action as Culture War." In *The Cultural Territories of Race,* ed. M. Lamont, pp. 343–370. Princeton, NJ: Princeton University Press.

Hodson, Randy. 1978. "Labor in Monopoly, Competitive and State Sectors of Production." *Politics and Society* 8, pp. 429–480.

Hodson, Randy. 1983. *Workers' Earnings and Corporate Economic Structure.* New York: Academic Press.

Hogan, David J. 1985. *Class and Reform: School and Society in Chicago, 1880–1930.* Philadelphia: University of Pennsylvania Press.

Holston, James and Arjun Appadurai. 1999. "Introduction: Cities and Citizenship." In *Cities and Citizenship,* ed. J. Holston, pp. 1–20. Durham, NC: Duke University Press.

Hood, Roger. 1990. *The Death Penalty: A World-wide Perspective.* New York: Oxford University Press.

Hooks, Gregory. 1990a. "From an Autonomous to a Captured State Agency: The Decline of the New Deal in Agriculture." *American Sociological Review* 55, pp. 29–43.

Hooks, Gregory. 1990b. "The Rise of the Pentagon and U.S. State Building: The Defense Program as Industrial Policy." *American Journal of Sociology* 96, pp. 358–404.

Hooks, Gregory. 1991a. "The Variable Autonomy of the State: A Comment on Steel and the State." *American Sociological Review* 56, pp. 690–693.

Hooks, Gregory. 1991b. *Forging the Military-industrial Complex: World War II's "Battle of the Potomac."* Urbana, IL: University of Illinois Press.

Hooks, Gregory. 1993. "The Weakness of Strong Theories: The U.S. State's Dominance of the World War II Investment Process." *American Sociological Review* 58, pp. 37–53.

Hooks, Gregory. 1994. "Regional Processes in the Hegemonic Nation: Political, Economic, and Military Influences on the Use of Geographic Space." *American Sociological Review* 59, pp. 746–772.

Hooks, Gregory and Leonard E. Bloomquist. 1992. "The Legacy of World War II for Regional Growth and Decline: The Cumulative Effects of Wartime Investments on U.S. Manufacturing, 1947–1972." *Social Forces* 71, pp. 303–337.

Hooks, Gregory and William Luchansky. 1996. "Warmaking and the Accommodation of Leading Firms: Defense Procurement and Corporate Growth, 1939–1959." *Political Power and Social Theory* 10, pp. 3–37.

Hoover, Kenneth. 1987. *Ideology and Political Life.* Monterey, CA: Brooks/Cole.

Hopcroft, Rosemary L. 1998. "The Importance of the Local: Rural Institutions and Economic Change in Preindustrial England." In *The New Institutionalism in Sociology,* eds. M. Brinton and V. Nee, pp. 277–304. New York: Russell Sage Foundation.

Hopson, Ronald E. and Donald R. Smith. 1999. "Changing Fortunes: An Analysis of Christian Right Ascendance within American Political Discourse." *Journal for the Scientific Study of Religion* 38, pp. 1–13.

Horowitz, Irving Louis. 1993. *The Decomposition of Sociology.* New York: Oxford University Press.

House, James and William Mason. 1975. "Political Alienation in America, 1952–1968." *American Sociological Review* 40, pp. 123–147.

Hout, Michael. 1999. "Abortion Politics in the United States, 1972–1994: From Single Issue to Ideology." *Gender Issues* 17, pp. 3–34.

Hout, Michael and David Knoke. 1975. "Change in Voting Turnout, 1952–1972." *Public Opinion Quarterly* 44, pp. 18–21.

Hout, Michael, Clem Brooks, and Jeff Manza. 1995. "The Democratic Class Struggle in the United States, 1948–1992." *American Sociological Review* 60, pp. 805–828.

Howard, Christopher. 1997. *The Hidden Welfare State: Tax Expenditures and Social Policy in the United States.* Princeton, NJ: Princeton University Press.

Howard, Michael. 1994. "War and Nations." In *Nationalism,* eds. J. Hutchinson and A. D. Smith, pp. 254–257. New York: Oxford University Press.

Howell, Susan E. and Christine L. Day. 2000. "Complexities of the Gender Gap." *Journal of Politics* 62, pp. 858–874.

Hritzuk, Natasha and David Park. 2000. "The Question of Latino Participation: From SES to a Social Structural Explanation." *Social Science Quarterly* 81, pp. 151–166.

Huber, Evelyne and John D. Stephens. 2000. "Partisan Government, Women's Employment, and the Social Democratic Service State." *American Sociological Review* 65, pp. 323–342.

Huber, Evelyne and John D. Stephens. 2001a. *Development and Crisis of the Welfare State.* Chicago: University of Chicago Press.

Huber, Evelyne and John D. Stephens. 2001b. "Welfare State and Production Regimes in the Era of Retrenchment." In *New Politics of the Welfare State,* ed. P. Pierson, pp. 108–145. New York: Oxford University Press.

Huber, Evelyne, Charles Ragin, and John D. Stephens. 1993. "Social Democracy, Christian Democracy, Constitutional Structure and the Welfare State." *American Journal of Sociology* 99, pp. 711–749.

Huckfeldt, Robert and Carol Weitzel Kohfeld. 1989. *Race and the Decline of Class in American Politics.* Urbana, IL: University of Illinois Press.

Huckfeldt, Robert and John Sprague. 1995. *Citizens, Politics and Social Communication.* New York: Cambridge University Press.

Huckfeldt, Robert, Paul A. Beck, and Russell L. Dalton. 1998. "Ambiguity, Distorted Messages, and Nested Environmental Effects on Political Communication." *Journal of Politics* 60, pp. 996–1030.

Huckfeldt, Robert, Eric Plutzer, and John Sprague. 1993. "Alternative Contexts of Political Behavior: Churches, Neighborhoods and Individuals." *Journal of Politics* 55, pp. 365–381.

Huckfeldt, Robert, Paul A. Beck, Russell J. Dalton, and Jeffrey Levine. 1995. "Political Environments, Cohesive Social Groups and the Communication of Public Opinion." *American Journal of Political Science* 39, pp. 1025–1054.

Huckfeldt, Robert, Jeffrey Levine, William Morgan, and John Sprague. 1999. "Accessibility and the Political Utility of Partisan and Ideological Orientations." *American Journal of Political Science* 43, pp. 888–911.

Huddy, Leonie and David O. Sears. 1995. "Opposition to Bilingual Education: Prejudice or the Defense of Realistic Interests?" *Social Psychology Quarterly* 58, pp. 133–143.

Hughes, John E. and M. Margaret Conway. 1997. "Public Opinion and Political Participation." In *Understanding Public Opinion,* eds. B. Norrander and C. Wilcox, pp. 191–226. Washington, DC: Congressional Quarterly Press.

Hughey, Michael W. 1983. *Civil Religion and Moral Order.* Westport, CT: Greenwood Press.

Hunt, Alan. 1993. *Explorations in Law and Society: Toward a Constitutive Theory of Law.* New York: Routledge.

Hunt, Arnold. 1997. " 'Moral panic' and moral language in the media." *British Journal of Sociology* 48, pp. 629–648.

Hunt, Scott A., Robert D. Benford, and David Snow. 1994. "Identity Fields." In *New Social Movements from Ideology to Identity,* eds. E. Laraña, H. Johnson, and J. Gusfield, pp. 185–208. Philadelphia: Temple University Press.

Hunter, Floyd. 1953. *Community Power Structure.* Chapel Hill, NC: University of North Carolina Press.

Hunter, James Davison. 1983. "The Liberal Reaction." In *The New Christian Right: Mobilization and Legitimation,* eds. R. Liebman and R. Wuthnow, pp. 150–166. New York: Aldine.

Hunter, James Davison. 1991. *Culture Wars: The Struggle to Define America.* New York: Basic Books.

Huntington, Samuel P. 1968. *Political Order in Changing Societies.* New Haven, CT: Yale University Press.

Huntington, Samuel P. 1991. *The Third Wave: Democratization in the Late Twentieth Century.* Norman, OK: University of Oklahoma Press.

Huntington, Samuel P. 1992. "Clash of Civilizations." *Foreign Affairs* 72, pp. 22–49.

Hurwitz, Jon and Mark Peffley. 1997. "Public Perceptions of Race and Crime: The Role of Racial Stereotypes." *American Journal of Political Science* 41, pp. 375–401.

Hurwitz, Jon and Shannon Smithey. 1998. "Gender Differences on Crime and Punishment." *Political Research Quarterly* 51, pp. 89–115.

Hutchinson, John and Anthony Smith. 1994. "Introduction." In *Nationalism,* eds. J. Hutchinson and A. D. Smith, pp. 3–13. New York: Oxford University Press.

Hwang, Sean-Shong and Steve H. Murdock. 1991. "Ethnic Enclosure or Ethnic Competition: Ethnic Identification Among Hispanics in Texas." *Sociological Quarterly* 32, pp. 469–476.

I

Ikegami, Eiko. 1996. "Citizenship and National Identity in Early Meiji Japan, 1868–1889: A Comparative Assessment." In *Citizenship, Identity and Social History,* ed. C. Tilly, pp. 185–211. New York: Cambridge University Press.

Ikenberry, John and Theda Skocpol. 1987. "Expanding Social Benefits: The Role of Social Security." *Political Science Quarterly* 102, pp. 389–416.

Immergut, Ellen M. 1998. "The Theoretical Core of the New Institutionalism." *Politics-and-Society* 26, pp. 5–34.

Inglehart, Ronald. 1984. "The Changing Structure of Political Cleavages in Western Society." In *Electoral Change in Advanced Industrial Democracies,* eds. R. Dalton, S. Flanagan, and P. A. Beck, pp. 25–69. Princeton, NJ: Princeton University Press.

Inglehart, Ronald and Paul R. Abramson. 1999. "Measuring Postmaterialism." *American Political Science Review* 93, pp. 665–678.

Inglehart, Ronald and Wayne E. Baker. 2000. "Modernization, Cultural Change, and the Persistence of Traditional Values." *American Sociological Review* 65, pp. 19–52.

Inglehart, Ronald and Hans Klingemann. 1979. "Ideological Conceptualization and Value Priorities." In *Political Action: Mass Participation in 5 Western Democracies,* eds. S. Barnes and M. Kaase, pp. 203–303. Beverly Hill, CA: Sage.

Inkeles, Alex and David H. Smith. 1974. *Becoming Modern: Individual Change in Six Developing Countries.* Cambridge, MA: Harvard University Press.

Inverarity, James M. and David McCarthy. 1988. "Punishment and Social Structure Revisited: Unemployment and Imprisonment in the United States, 1948–1984." *Sociological Quarterly* 29, pp. 263–280.

Inverarity, James M. 1976. "Populism and Lynching in Louisiana, 1889–1896: A Test of Erikson's Theory of the Relationship between Boundary Crisis and Repressive Justice." *American Sociological Review* 41, pp. 262–280.

Ireland, Doug. 1998. "Homophobia Kills." *Nation* 267, no. 14, p. 7.

Isaac, Larry. 2002. "To Counter 'The Very Devil'" and More: The Making of Independent Capitalist Militia in the Gilded Age." *American Journal of Sociology* 108, pp. 406–439.

Isaac, Larry and William R. Kelly. 1981. "Racial Insurgency, the State and Welfare Expansion." *American Journal of Sociology* 86, pp. 1348–1386.

Isaac, Larry, Elizabeth Mutran, and Sheldon Stryker. 1980. "Political Protest Orientations Among Black and White Adults." *American Sociological Review* 45, pp. 191–213.

Iversen, Torben. 2001. "The Dynamics of Welfare State Expansion." In *The New Politics of the Welfare State,* ed. P. Pierson, pp. 45–79. New York: Oxford University Press.

Iversen, Torben and Thomas R. Cusack. 2000. "The Causes of Welfare State Expansion." *World Politics* 52, pp. 313–349.

Iyengar, Shanto. 1990a. "The Accessibility Bias in Politics: Television News and Public Opinion." *International Journal of Public Opinion Research* 2, pp. 1–15.

Iyengar, Shanto. 1990b. "Framing Responsibility for Political Issues." *Political Behavior* 12, pp. 19–40.

Iyengar, Shanto. 1991. *Is Anyone Responsible? How Television Frames Political Issues.* Chicago: University of Chicago Press.

Iyengar, Shanto. 1996. "Framing Responsibility for Political Issues." *Annals of the American Academy of Political and Social Science* 546, pp. 59–71.

Iyengar, Shanto and Donald R. Kinder. 1987. *News That Matters: Television and American Opinion.* Chicago: University of Chicago Press.

Iyengar, Shanto and Adam Simon. 1993. "News Coverage of the Gulf Crisis and Public Opinion." *Communication Research* 20, pp. 365–384.

J

Jackman, Mary R. 1972. "Social Mobility and Attitude Toward the Political System." *Social Forces* 50, pp. 462–472.

Jackman, Mary R. 1978. "General and Applied Tolerance: Does Education Increase Commitment to Racial Integration." *American Journal of Political Science* 22, pp. 302–324.

Jackman, Mary R. and Michael Muha. 1984. "Education and Intergroup Attitudes: Moral Enlightenment, Superficial Democratic Commitment or Ideological Refinement." *American Sociological Review* 49, pp. 751–769.

Jackman, Robert W. 1975. *Politics and Social Equality: A Comparative Analysis.* New York: Wiley.

Jackman, Robert W. 1987. "Political Institutions and Voter Turnout in the Industrial Democracies." *American Political Science Review* 81, pp. 405–423.

Jackman, Robert W. 1993. "Rationality and Political Participation." *American Journal of Political Science* 37, pp. 279–290.

Jackman, Robert W. and Ross A. Miller. 1995. "Voter Turnout in Industrial Democracies during the 1980s." *Comparative Political Studies* 27, pp. 467–492.

Jackson, Elton and Richard Curtis. 1972. "Effects of Vertical Mobility and Status Inconsistency: A Body of Negative Evidence." *American Sociological Review* 37, pp. 701–713.

Jackson, Janine. "Film Rejection Highlights PBS Bias." *EXTRA!* (January/February 1998).

Jackson, Lynne M. and Victoria Esses. 2000. "Effects of Perceived Economic Competition on People's Willingness to Help Empower Immigrants." *Group Processes and Intergroup Relations* 3, pp. 419–435.

Jackson, Robert A. 1995. "Clarifying the Relationship between Education and Turnout." *American Politics Quarterly* 23, pp. 279–300.

Jackson, Robert A. 1997. "The mobilization of U.S. State Electorates in the 1988 and 1990 Elections." *Journal of Politics* 59, pp. 520–537.

Jacobs, Andrew. 1999. "Gay Couples are Divided by '96 Immigration Laws." *New York Times,* March 23, 1999.

Jacobs, David C. 1988. "Corporate Economic Power and the State: A Longitudinal Assessment of Two Explanations." *American Journal of Sociology* 93, pp. 852–881.

Jacobs, David C. 1998. "Labor and Social Legislation in the United States: Business Obstructionism and Accommodation." *Labor Studies Journal* 23, pp. 52–74.

Jacobs, David C. 1999. *Business Lobbies and the Power Structure in America.* Westport, CT: Quorum Books.

Jacobs, David C. and Ronald E. Helms. 1996. "Toward a Political Model of Incarceration." *American Journal of Sociology* 102, pp. 323–357.

Jacobs, David C. and Ronald E. Helms. 1997. "Testing Coercive Explanations for Order: The Determinants of Law Enforcement Strength." *Social Forces* 75, pp. 1361–1392.

Jacobs, David C. and Robert M. O'Brien. 1998. "The Determinates of Deadly Force: A Structural Analysis of Police Violence." *American Journal of Sociology* 103, pp. 837–862.

Jacobs, David C. and Katherine Wood. 1999. "Interracial conflict and interracial homicide." *American Journal of Sociology* 105, pp. 157–190.

Jacobs, Ronald N. 1996. "Civil Society and Crisis: Culture, Discourse, and the Rodney King Beating." *American Journal of Sociology* 101, pp. 1238–1272.

Jacoby, Sanford M. 1997. *Modern Manors: Welfare Capitalism Since the New Deal.* Princeton, NJ: Princeton University Press.

James, David R. 1988. "The Transformation of the Southern Racial State: Class and Rate Determinates of Local-state Structures." *American Sociological Review* 53, pp. 191–208.

Janofsky, Michael. 2000. "Antidrug Program's End Stirs up Salt Lake City." *New York Times* (September 16, 2000).

Janoski, Thomas and Alexander Hicks. 1994. *The Comparative Political Economy of the Welfare State.* New York: Cambridge University Press.

Janoski, Thomas. 1990. "Conflicting Approaches to Citizenship Rights." *Comparative Social Research* 12, pp. 209–238.

Janowitz, Morris. 1968. "Political Sociology." *International Encyclopedia of Social Science* 12, pp. 298–307.

Janowitz, Morris. 1976. *Social Control of the Welfare State.* Chicago: University of Chicago Press.

Janowitz, Morris. 1978. *The Last Half-century: Societal Change and Politics in America.* Chicago: University of Chicago Press.

Jasper, James M. and James D. Poulsen. 1995. "Recruiting Strangers and Friends: Moral Shocks and Social Networks in Animal Rights and Anti-nuclear Protests." *Social Problems* 42, pp. 493–512.

Jay, Martin. 1973. *The Dialectical Imagination: A History of the Frankfurt School and the Institute of Social Research, 1923–1950.* Boston: Little, Brown.

Jelen, Ted. 1992. "Political Christianity: A Contextual Analysis." *American Journal of Political Science* 36, pp. 692–714.

Jelen, Ted. 1997. "Religion and Public Opinion in the 1990s." In *Understanding Public Opinion,* eds. B. Norrander and C. Wilcox, pp. 55–68. Washington, DC: Congressional Quarterly Press.

Jelen, Ted and Clyde Wilcox. 1990. "Denominational Preference and the Dimensions of Political Tolerance." *Sociological-Analysis* 51, pp. 69–81.

Jelen, Ted and Clyde Wilcox. 1992. "The Effects of Religious Self-Identification on Support for the New Christian Right." *Social Science Journal* 29, pp. 199–211.

Jenkins, J. Craig. 1982. "The Transformation of a Constituency Into a Movement." In *The Social Movements of the 1960s and 1970s,* ed. J. Freeman, pp. 52–70. New York: Longman.

Jenkins, J. Craig. 1983. "Resource Mobilization Theory and the Study of Social Movements." *Annual Review of Sociology* 9, pp. 527–553.

Jenkins, J. Craig. 1985. *The Politics of Insurgency: The Farm Worker Movement of the 1960s.* New York: Columbia University Press.

Jenkins, J. Craig. 1995. "Social Movements, Political Representation, and the State." In *The Politics of Social Protest,* eds. C. J. Jenkins and B. Klandermas, pp. 14–38. Minneapolis: University of Minnesota Press.

Jenkins, J. Craig and Barbara G. Brents. 1989. "Social Protest, Hegemonic Competition, and Social Reform: A Political Struggle Interpretation of the Origins of the American Welfare State." *American Sociological Review* 54, pp. 891–909.

Jenkins, J. Craig and Craig Eckert. 1986. "Channeling Black Insurgency: Elite Patronage and Professional Social Movement Organization in the Development of the Black Movement." *American Sociological Review* 51, pp. 812–829.

Jenkins, J. Craig and Charles Perrow. 1977. "Insurgency of the Powerless: Farm Worker Movements, 1946–1972." *American Sociological Review* 42, pp. 249–268.

Jenkins, J. Craig and Kurt Schock. 1992. "Global Structures and Political Processes in the Study of Domestic Political Conflict." *Annual Review of Sociology* 18, pp. 161–185.

Jenkins, J. Craig and Teri Schumate. 1985. "Cowboy Capitalists and the Rise of the 'New Right': An Analysis." *Social Problems* 33, pp. 130–145.

Jenness, Valerie. 1995. "Social movement growth, domain expansion, and framing processes: The Gay/Lesbian Movement and Violence Against Gays and Lesbians as a Social Problem." *Social Problems* 42, pp. 145–170.

Jenness, Valerie and Ryken Grattet. 2001. *Making Hate a Crime: From Social Movement Concept to Law Enforcement Practice.* New York: Russell Sage Foundation.

Jessop, Bob. 1982. *The Capitalist State: Marxist Theories and Methods.* New York: New York University Press.

Jessop, Bob. 1985. *Nicos Poulantzas: Marxist Theory and Political Strategy.* New York: St. Martins.

Jessop, Bob. 1990. *State Theory: Putting the Capitalist State in its Place.* University Park, PA: Pennsylvania University Press.

Johnson, Chalmers. 1966. *Revolutionary Change.* Boston: Little Brown.

Johnson, Chalmers. 1982. *M.I.T.I. and the Japanese Miracles: The Growth of Industrial Policy, 1925–1975.* Stanford, CA: Stanford University Press.

Johnson, Chalmers. 1997. "Soft Totalitarianism in China." *NPQ: New Perspectives Quarterly* 14, pp. 18–21.

Johnson, Gene and Beth Mintz, eds. 1988. *Networks of Power: Organization Actors at the National, Corporate and Community Levels.* New York: Aldine.

Johnson, Hank, Enrique Laraña, and Joseph Gusfield. 1994. "Identities, Grievances, and New Social Movements." In *New Social Movements from Ideology to Identity,* eds. E. Laraña, H. Johnson, and J. Gusfield, pp. 3–35. Philadelphia: Temple University Press.

Johnson, James. 1996. "How Not to Criticize Rational Choice Theory." *Philosophy of the Social Sciences* 26, pp. 77–92.

Johnson, Larry C. 2001. "The Future of Terrorism." *American Behavioral Scientist* 44, pp. 894–913.

Johnson, Paula, David O. Sears, and John McConahay. 1971. "American Sociology and Black Americans Black Invisibility, the Press, and the Los Angeles Riot." *American Journal of Sociology* 76, pp. 698–721.

Johnson, Stephen, Joseph Tamney, and Sandy Halebsky. 1986. "Christianity, Social Traditionalism and Economics Conservatism." *Sociological Focus* 19, pp. 299–314.

Joll, James. 1977. *Antonio Gramsci.* New York: Penguin.

Jorstad, Erling. 1987. *The New Christian Right, 1981–1988: Prospects for a Post-Reagan Debate.* Lewiston, NY: Edwin Mellen Press.

K

Kaempfer, William H. and Anton D. Lowenberg. 1993. "A Threshold Model of Electoral Policy and Voter Turnout." *Rationality and Society* 5, pp. 107–126.

Kahne, Joseph. 1996. *Reframing Educational Policy: Democracy, Community and Individual.* New York: Teachers College, Columbia University.

Kairys, David. 1982a. "Introduction." In *The Politics of Law: A Progressive Critique,* ed. D. Kairys, pp. 1–8. New York: Pantheon.

Kairys, David. 1982b. "Legal Reasoning." In *The Politics of Law: A Progressive Critique,* ed. D. Kairys, pp. 11–17. New York: Pantheon.

Kalberg, Stephen. 1993. "Cultural Foundations of Modern Citizenship." In *Citizenship and Social Theory,* ed. B. Turner, pp. 91–114. Newbury Park, CA: Sage.

Kamens, David, John W. Meyer, and Aaron Benavot. 1996. "Worldwide Patterns in Academic Secondary Education Curricula." *Comparative Education Review* 40, pp. 116–138.

Kaplan, Fred. 1998. "Conservatives Plant a Seed in NYC." *Boston Sunday Globe,* February 22, 1998.

Karen, David. 1991a. "'Achievement' and 'Ascription' in Admission to an Elite College: A Political Organizational Analysis." *Sociological Forum* 6, pp. 349–380.

Karen, David. 1991b. "The Politics of Class, Race, and Gender: Access to Higher Education in the United States, 1960–1986." *American Journal of Education* 99, pp. 208–237.

Karson, Marc. 1958. *American Labor Unions and Politics, 1900–1918.* Carbondale, IL: Southern Illinois University Press.

Kashiwazaki, Chikako. 1998a. "Citizenship, State Membership and Nationhood: Association or Disassociation?" *Research in Political Sociology* 8, pp. 81–102.

Kashiwazaki, Chikako. 1998b. "*Jus Sanguinis* in Japan: The Origins of Citizenship in Comparative Perspective." *International Journal of Comparative Sociology* 39, pp. 278–300.

Katz, Cheryl and Mark Baldassare. 1992. "Using the L Word in Public: A Test of the Spiral of Silence in Conservative Orange County California." *Public Opinion Quarterly* 56, pp. 232–235.

Katz, Cheryl and Mark Baldassare. 1994. "Popularity in a Freefall: Measuring a Spiral of Silence at the End of the Bush Presidency." *International Journal of Public Opinion Research* 6, pp. 1–2.

Katz, Michael B. 1971. *Class, Bureaucracy and Schools: The Illusion of Educational Change in America.* New York: Praeger.

Katznelson, Ira. 1981a. *City Trenches: Urban Politics and the Patterning of Class in the United States.* Chicago: University of Chicago Press.

Katznelson, Ira. 1981b. "A Radical Departure Social Welfare and the Election." In *The Hidden Election,* eds. T. Ferguson and J. Rogers, pp. 313–338. New York: Pantheon.

Katznelson, Ira. 1986. "Working Class Formation: Constructing Cases and Comparisons." In *Working Class Formation: 19th Century Patterns in Western Europe and the United States,* eds. I. Katznelson and A. Zolberg, pp. 3–44. Princeton, NJ: Princeton University Press.

Katznelson, Ira and Bruce Pietrykowski. 1991. "Rebuilding the American State: Evidence from the 1940s." *Studies in American Political Development* 5, pp. 301–339.

Katznelson, Ira and Margaret Weir. 1985. *Schooling for All: Class, Race and the Decline of the Democratic Ideal.* Berkeley, CA: University of California Press.

Kaufman, Jason. 1999. "Three Views of Associationism in 19th Century America: An Empirical Examination." *American Journal of Sociology* 104, pp. 1296–1345.

Kaufman, Karen M. and John R. Petrocik. 1999. "The Changing Politics of American Men: Understanding Sources of the Gender Gap." *American Journal of Political Science* 43, pp. 864–887.

Keck, Margaret E. and Kathryn Sikkink. 1998. "Transnational Advocacy Networks in the Movement Society." In *The Social Movement Society,* eds. D. Meyer and S. Tarrow, pp. 217–238. Lanham, MD: Rowman & Littlefield.

Keddie, Nikki R. 1998. "The New Religious Politics: Where, When, and Why Do Fundamentalisms Appear?" *Comparative Studies in Society and History* 40, pp. 696–723.

Keen, Michael Forrest. 1999. *Stalking the Sociological Imagination.* Westport, CT: Greenwood.

Keller, Suzanne. 1963. [1991] *Beyond the Ruling Class: Strategic Elites in Modern Society.* New Brunswick, NJ: Transaction Publishers.

Keller, Morton. 1977. *Affairs of State: Public Life in Late Nineteenth Century America.* Cambridge, MA: Harvard University Press.

Keller, Morton. 1990. *Regulating a New Economy: Public Policy and Economic Change in America, 1900–1933.* Cambridge, MA: Harvard University Press.

Kelly, Dennis and William Chambliss. 1966. "Status Consistency and Political Attitudes." *American Sociological Review* 31, pp. 375–381.

Kelly, Jonathan and M. D. Evans. 1993. "The Legitimation of Inequality." *American Journal of Sociology* 99, pp. 75–125.

Kennedy, Devereaux. 1997. "Crime waves, culture wars and societal transformation." *Crime, Law and Social Change* 26, pp. 101–124.

Kennedy, Duncan. 1982. "Legal Education as Training for Hierarchy." In *The Politics of Law: A Progressive Critique*, ed. D. Kairys, pp. 40–61. New York: Pantheon.

Kenski, Henry C. 1988. "The Gender Factor in a Changing Electorate." In *The Politics of Gender Gap: The Social Construction of Political Influence*, ed. C. M. Mueller, pp. 38–60. Newbury Park, CA: Sage.

Kenworthy, Lane. 1999. "Do Social-welfare Policies Reduce Poverty? A Cross-National Assessment." *Social Forces* 77, pp. 1119–1139.

Kenworthy, Lane and Melissa Malami. 1999. "Gender Inequality in Political Representation: A Worldwide Comparative Analysis." *Social Forces* 78, pp. 235–269.

Kerber, Linda K. 1997. "The Meanings of Citizenship." *Dissent* 44, no. 3, pp. 33–37.

Kerbo, Harold R. and L. Richard Della Fave. 1979. "The Empirical Side of the Power Elite Debate: An Assessment and Critique of Research." *Sociological Quarterly* 20, pp. 5–22.

Kerbo, Harold R. and Juan Gonzalez. 2003. "Class and Non-class Voting in Comparative Perspective." *Research in Political Sociology* 14, pp. 175–196.

Kerbo, Harold R. and John A. McKinstry. 1995. *Who Rules Japan? The Inner Circles of Economic Power*. Westport, CT: Praeger.

Kerbo, Harold R. and Richard Shaffer. 1986. "Unemployment and Protest in the United States, 1890–1940: A Methodological Critique and Research Note." *Social Forces* 64, pp. 1046–1056.

Kerbo, Harold R. and Richard Shaffer. 1992. "Lower Class Insurgency and the Political Process: The Response of the U.S. Unemployed, 1890–1940." *Social Problems* 39, pp. 139–154.

Kerr, Clark. 1991. *The Great Transformation of Higher Education, 1960–1980*. Albany, NY: State University of New York Press.

Kertzer, David I. 1998. *Ritual, Politics and Power*. New Haven, CT: Yale University Press.

Kertzer, David I. and Dominique Arel. 2002. "Census, Identity Formation and the Struggle for Political Power." In *Census and Identity*, eds. D. Kertzer and D. Arel, pp. 1–42. New York: Cambridge University Press.

Kessler, Mark. 1993. "Legal Discourse and Political Intolerance: The Ideology of Clear and Present Danger." *Law and Society Review* 27, pp. 559–597.

Key, V. O. 1955. "A Theory of Critical Elections." *Journal of Politics* 17, pp. 3–18.

Kidder, Robert L. 1983. *Connecting Law and Society*. Englewood Cliffs, NJ: Prentice Hall.

Kiecolt, K. Jill. 2000. "Self-Change in Social Movements." in *Self, Identity, and Social Movements*, eds. S. Sheldon, T. Owens, and R. White, pp. 110–131. Minneapolis, MN: University of Minnesota Press.

Kiecolt, K. Jill and Hart M. Nelson. 1991. "Evangelicals and Party Realignment, 1976–1988." *Social Science Quarterly* 72, pp. 552–569.

Kimball, Roger. 1990. *Tenured Radicals: How Politics Has Corrupted Our Higher Education*. New York: Vintage.

Kimmel, Michael S. 1990. *Revolution: A Sociological Interpretation*. Philadelphia: Temple University Press.

Kinder, Donald and Tali Mendelberg. 1995. "Cracks in American Apartheid: The Political Impact of Prejudice among Desegregated Whites." *Journal of Politics* 57, pp. 402–424.

King, Desmond S. 1987. "The State and the Social Structures of Welfare in Advanced Industrial Societies." *Theory and Society* 16, pp. 841–868.

King, Desmond S. and Stewart Wood. 1999. "The Political Economy of Neoliberalism." In *Continuities and Change in Contemporary Capitalism*, eds. H. Kitschelt, P. Lang, G. Marks, and J. Stephens, pp. 371–397. New York: Cambridge University Press.

Kirkendall, Richard S. 1975. "The New Deal and Agriculture." In *The New Deal: The National Level*, Vol. 1. Edited by J. Braeman, R. Bremner and D. Brody, pp. 83–109. Columbus, OH: Ohio State University Press.

Kiser, Edgar. 1996. "The Revival of Narrative in Historical Sociology: What Rational Choice Theory Can Contribute." *Politics and Society* 24, pp. 249–271.

Kitschelt, Herbert B. 1986. "Political Opportunity Structures and the Political Protest: Anti-nuclear Movements in Four Democracies." *British Journal of Political Science* 16, no. 5, pp. 7–85.

Kitschelt, Herbert B. 2000. "Linkages Between Citizens and Politicians in Democratic Politics." *Comparative Political Studies* 33, pp. 845–879.

Klandermans, Bert. 1984. "Mobilization and Participation: Social-psychological Expansions of Resource Mobilization Theory." *American Sociological Review* 49, pp. 583–600.

Klandermans, Bert. 1991. "The Peace Movement and Social Movement Theory." *International Social Movement Research* 3, pp. 1–39.

Klandermans, Bert. 1992. "The Social Construction of Protest and Multiorganizational Fields." In *Frontiers in Social Movement Theory*, eds. A. Morris and C. M. Mueller, pp. 77–103. New Haven, CT: Yale University Press.

Klandermans, Bert. 2002. "How Group Identification Helps to Overcome the Dilemma of Collective Action." *American Behavioral Scientist* 45, pp. 887–900.

Klandermans, Bert and Sjoerd Goslinga. 1996. "Media Discourse, Movement Publicity, and the Generation of Collective Action Frames." In *Comparative Perspectives on Social Movements*, eds. D. McAdam, J. McCarthy, and M. Zald, pp. 312–337. New York: Cambridge University Press.

Klandermans, Bert and Dirk Oegema. 1987. "Potentials, Networks, Motivations, and Barriers: Steps towards Participation in Social Movements." *American Sociological Review* 52, pp. 519–531.

Klandermans, Bert and Marga deWeerd. 2000. "Group Identification and Political Protest." In *Self, Identity, and Social Movements*, ed. S., Stryler, T. Owens and R. White, pp. 68–90. Minneapolis, MN: University of Minnesota Press.

Klandermans, Bert, Marlene Roefs, and Johan Olivier. 2001. "Grievance Formation in a Country in Transition: South Africa, 1994–1998." *Social Psychology Quarterly* 64, pp. 41–54.

Kleidman, Robert. 1994. "Volunteer Activism and Professionalism in Social Movement Organizations." *Social Problems* 41, pp. 257–276.

Klein, Ethel. 1984. *Gender Politics.* Cambridge, MA: Harvard University Press.

Kleinnijenhuis, Jan. 1991. "Newspaper Complexity and the Knowledge Gap." *European Journal of Communication* 6, pp. 499–522.

Kleinnijenhuis, Jan and Ewald M. Rietberg. 1995. "Parties, Media, the Public and the Economy: Patterns of Societal Agenda-setting." *European Journal of Political Research* 28, pp. 95–118.

Kleppner, Paul. 1979. *The Third Electoral System, 1853–1892: Parties, Voters, and Political Cultures.* Chapel Hill, NC: University of North Carolina Press.

Kleppner, Paul. 1982. *Who Voted? The Dynamics of Electoral Turnout, 1870–1980.* New York: Praeger.

Kleppner, Paul. 1987. *Continuity and Change in Electoral Politics, 1893–1928.* Westport, CT: Greenwood Press.

Kleppner, Paul and Stephen C. Baker. 1980. "The Impact of Voter Registration Requirement on Electoral Turnout, 1900–1916." *Journal of Political and Military Sociology* 8, pp. 205–226.

Kluegel, James R. 1990. "Trends in White's Explanation of the Black-white Gap in Socioeconomic Status, 1977–1989." *American Sociological Review* 55, pp. 512–525.

Kluegel, James R. and Eliot R. Smith. 1982. "White's Beliefs About Black's Opportunity." *American Sociological Review* 47, pp. 518–531.

Kluegel, James R. and Eliot R. Smith. 1983. "Affirmative Action Attitudes: Effects of Self-Interest, Racial Affect and Stratification Beliefs on Whites' Attitudes." *Social Forces* 61, pp. 797–824.

Kluegel, James R. and Eliot R. Smith. 1986. *Beliefs About Inequality: Americans' Views of What Is and What Ought to Be.* New York: Aldine.

Knack, Stephen. 1992. "Civic Norms, Social Sanctions, and Voter Turnout." *Rationality and Society* 4, pp. 133–156.

Knack, Stephen and James White. 1998. "Did States' Motor Voter Programs Help the Democrats?" *American Politics Quarterly* 26, pp. 344–366.

Knight, Graham and Julia O'Connor. 1995. "Social Democracy Meets the Press: Media Coverage of Industrial Relations Legislation." *Research in Political Sociology* 7, pp. 183–206.

Knight, Kathleen and Robert Erikson. 1997. "Ideology in the 1990s." In *Understanding Public Opinion,* eds. B. Norrander and C. Wilcox, pp. 91–110. Washington, DC: Congressional Quarterly Press.

Knoke, David. 1972a. "Community and Consistency: The Ethnic Factor in Status Inconsistency." *Social Forces* 51, pp. 23–33.

Knoke, David. 1972b. "A Causal Model for the Political Party Preferences of American Men." *American Sociological Review* 37, pp. 679–689.

Knoke, David. 1974a. "Religious Involvement and Political Behavior." *Sociological Quarterly* 15, pp. 51–65.

Knoke, David. 1974b. "A Causal Synthesis of Sociological and Psychological Models of American Voting Behavior." *Social Forces* 53, pp. 92–101.

Knoke, David. 1982. "The Spread of Municipal Reform: Temporal, Spatial, and Social Dynamics." *American Journal of Sociology* 87, pp. 1314–1339.

Knoke, David, Franz Pappi, Jeffrey Broadbent, and Yutaka Tsujinaka. 1996. *Comparing Policy Networks: Labor Politics in the U.S., Germany and Japan.* New York: Cambridge University Press.

Kock, Jeffrey W. 1998. "Political Rhetoric and Political Persuasion: The Changing Structure of Citizens Preferences on Health Insurance During Policy Debate." *Public Opinion Quarterly* 62, pp. 209–229.

Koenig, Tom. 1987. "Business Support for Disclosure of Corporate Campaign Contributions: An Instructive Paradox." ed., M. Schwartz, *The Business Elite as a Ruling Class,* pp. 82–96. New York: Holmes and Meier.

Kohl, Jürgen. 1983. "The Functional Structure of Public Expenditures: Long-term Changes." In *Why Governments Grow,* ed. C. L. Taylor, pp. 201–216. Newbury Park, CA: Sage.

Kolko, Gabriel. 1963. *Triumph of Conservatism: A Reinterpretation of American History, 1900–1915.* Chicago: Quadrangle.

Koopmans, Ruud. 1993. "The Dynamics of Protest Waves: West Germany, 1965 to 1989." *American Sociological Review* 58, pp. 637–658.

Koopmans, Ruud and Paul Statham. 1999a. "Ethnic and Civic Conceptions of Nationhood and the Differential Success of the Extreme Right in Germany and Italy." In *How Social Movements Matter,* eds. M. Giugni, D. McAdam, and C. Tilly, pp. 225–251. Minneapolis: University of Minnesota Press.

Koopmans, Ruud and Paul Statham. 1999b. "Political Claims Analysis: Integrating Protest Event and Political Discourse Approaches." *Mobilization* 4, pp. 40–51.

Kornhauser, William. 1959. *The Politics of Mass Society.* New York: Free Press.

Korpi, Walter 1972. "Some Problems in the Measurement of Class Voting." *American Journal of Sociology* 78, pp. 627–642.

Korpi, Walter. 1978. *The Working Class and Welfare Capitalism.* New York: Routledge and Kegan Paul.

Korpi, Walter. 1983. *The Democratic Class Struggle.* New York: Routledge.

Korpi, Walter. 1989. "Power, Politics and State Autonomy in the Development of Social Citizenship." *American Sociological Review* 54, pp. 309–328.

Korpi, Walter. 2000. "Faces of Inequality: Gender, Class, and Patterns of Inequalities in Different Types of Welfare States." *Social Politics* 7, pp. 127–191.

Korpi, Walter. 2003. "Welfare-state Regress in Western Europe." *Annual Review of Sociology* 29, pp. 589–609.

Korpi, Walter and Joakim Palme. 1998. "The Paradox of Redistribution and Strategies of Equality." *American Sociological Review* 63, pp. 661–687.

Korpi, Walter and Michael Shalev. 1980. "Strikes, Power and Politics in the Western Nations, 1900–1976." *Political Power and Social Theory* 1, pp. 301–334.

Korzeniewicz, Roberto and Kimberley Awbrey. 1992. "Democratic Transitions and the Semiperiphery of the World System." *Sociological Forum* 7, pp. 609–640.

Kosonen, Pekka. 1987. "From Collectively to Individualism in the Welfare State?" *Acta Sociologica* 30, pp. 281–293.

Kourvetaris, George A. and Betty Dobratz. 1982. "Political Power and Conventional Political Participation." *Annual Review of Sociology* 8, pp. 289–317.

Kousser, J. Morgan 1974. *The Shaping of Southern Politics: Suffrage Restriction and the Establishment of the One-party South.* New Haven, CT: Yale University Press.

Koven, Seth and Sonya Michel. 1990. "Womanly Duties." *American Historical Review* 95, pp. 1076–1108.

Kraditor, Aileen S. 1981. *The Ideas of the Woman Suffrage Movement, 1890–1920.* New York: Norton.

Kraft, Michael E. 2000. "U.S. Environmental Policy and Politics: From the 1960s to the 1990s." *Journal of Policy History* 12, pp. 17–42.

Kraska, Peter B. 1999. "Militarizing Criminal Justice: Exploring the Possibilities." *Journal of Political and Military Sociology* 27, pp. 205–215.

Kraska, Peter B. and Victor Kappeler. 1997. "Militarizing American Police: The Rise and Normalization of Paramilitary Units." *Social Problems* 44, pp. 1–18.

Kraska, Peter B. and Derek Paulsen. 1997. "Grounded Research into U.S. Paramilitary Policing: Forging the Iron Fist inside the Velvet Glove." *Policing and Society* 7, pp. 253–270.

Krasner, Stephen D. 1978. *Defending the National Interest: Raw Materials Investments and U.S.Foreign Policy.* Princeton, NJ: Princeton University Press.

Krasner, Stephen D. 1984. "Approaches to the State: Alternative Conceptions and Historical Dynamics." *Comparative Politics,* 16, pp. 223–246.

Kriesi, Hanspeter and Dominique Wisler. 1999. "The Impact of Social Movements on Political Institutions." *How Social Movements Matter,* eds. M. Giugni, D. McAdam, and C. Tilly, pp. 42–65. Minneapolis: University of Minnesota Press.

Kriesi, Hanspeter, Ruud Koopmans, Jan Duyvendak, and Marco Giugni. 1997. "New Social Movements and Political Opportunities in Western Europe." In *Social Movements,* eds. D. McAdam and D. Snow, pp. 52–65. Los Angles: Roxbury.

Kristof, Nicholas D. and Sheryl Wudunn. 1994. *China Wakes: The Struggle for the Soul of a Rising Power.* New York: Times Books.

Kubal, Timothy J. 1998. "The Presentation of Political Self: Cultural Resonance and the Construction of Collective Action Frames." *Sociological Quarterly* 39, pp. 539–554.

Kubrin, Charis and Ronald Weitzer. 2003. "Retaliatory Homicide." *Social Problems* 59, pp. 157–180.

Kuklinski, James, Ellen Riggle, Victor Ottati, Norbert Schwarz, and Robert Wyer. 1991. "The Cognitive and Affective Bases of Political Tolerance Judgments." *American Journal of Political Science* 35, pp. 1–27.

Kuklinski, James, Paul Quirk, and David Schwieder. 1998. "Just the Facts, Ma'am: Political Facts and Public Opinion." *Annals of the American Academy of Political and Social Science* 560, pp. 143–154.

Kull, Steven, Clay Ramsay, Stefan Subias, and Evan Lewis. 2004. "Americans on Globalization, Trade and Farm Subsidies." *The Program on International Policy Attitudes-Knowledge Networks Poll,* Center on Policy Attitudes, University of Maryland (January 22, 2004).

Kumamoto, Robert. 1991." Diplomacy from Below: International Terrorism and American Foreign Relations, 1945–1962." *Terrorism* 14, pp. 31–48.

Kunzler, Jan, Hans-Joachim Schulze, and Suus van Hekken. 1999. "Welfare States and Normative Orientations toward Women's Employment." *Comparative Social Research* 18, pp. 197–225.

Kuran, Timur. 1995. *Private Truths: Public Lies: The Social Consequences of Preference Falsification.* Cambridge, MA: Harvard University Press.

Kurzman, Charles. 1996. "Structural Opportunity and Perceived Opportunity in Social-movement Theory: The Iranian Revolution of 1979." *American Sociological Review* 61, pp. 153–170.

Kuttner, Robert. 2002. "Philanthropy and Movements." *American Prospect* 13 (July 15), pp. 2–3.

Kuzma, Lynn M. 2000. "Trends: Terrorism in the United States." *Public Opinion Quarterly* 64, pp. 90–105.

L

LaClau, Ernesto. 1977. *Politics and Ideology in Marxist Theory.* Atlantic Highlands, NJ: Humanities Press.

Lader, Lawrence. 1979. *Power on the Left: American Radical Movements.* New York: Norton.

LaFree, Gary. 1999. "Declining Violent Crime Rates in the 1990s." *Annual Review of Sociology* 25, pp. 145–168.

Lamont, Michèle and Virág Molnár. 2002. "The Study of Boundaries in the Social Sciences." *Annual Review of Sociology* 28, pp. 167–195.

Landis, Michele. 1999. "Fate, Responsibility, and "Natural" Disaster Relief: Narrating the American Welfare State." *Law and Society Review* 33, pp. 257–318.

Lane, Robert E. 1962. *Political Ideology.* New York: Free Press.

Langford, Tom. 1996. "The Politics of the Canadian New Middle Class: Public/Private Sector Cleavage in the 1980s." *Canadian Journal of Sociology* 2, pp. 153–183.

Laqueur, Walter, ed. 1976. *Fascism: A Reader's Guide.* Berkeley, CA: University of California Press.

Lasser, William. 1985. "The Supreme Court in Periods of Critical Realignment." *Journal of Politics* 47, pp. 1174–1187.

Layman, Geoffrey C. 1997. "Religion and Political Behavior in the United States: The Impact of Beliefs, Attitudes and Commitment from 1980 to 1994." *Public Opinion Quarterly* 61, pp. 288–316.

Layman, Geoffrey C. and Edward Carmines. 1997. "Cultural Conflict in American Politics: Religious Traditionalism, Postmaterialism, and U.S." *Journal of Politics* 59, pp. 751–778.

Lazere, Donald. 1987. "Introduction: Entertainment as Social Control." In *American Media and Mass Culture: Left Perspectives*, ed. D. Lazere, pp. 1–26. Berkeley, CA: University of California Press.

LeBon, Gustave. 1895. *The Crowd: A Study of the Popular Mind.* London: Ernest Benn.

Lee, David J. and Bryan S. Turner, eds. 1996. *Conflicts About Class: Debating Inequality in Late Industrialism.* New York: Longman.

Lehmbruch, Gerhard. 1979. "Liberal Corporatism and Party Government." In *Trends in Corporatism Intermediation,* eds. P. Schmitter and G. Lehmbruch, pp. 147–183. Beverly Hills, CA: Sage.

Leicht, Kevin, T. Jenkins, and J. Craig. 1998. "Political Resources and Direct State Intervention: The Adoption of Public Venture Capital Programs in the American States, 1974–1990." *Social Forces* 76, pp. 1323–1345.

Leifer, Eric M. 1981. "Competing Models of Political Mobilization: The Role of Ethnic Ties." *American Journal of Sociology* 87, pp. 23–47.

Leighley, Jan and Jonathan Nagler. 1992. "Socioeconomic Class Bias in Turnout, 1964–1988: The Voters Remain the Same." *American Political Science Review* 86, pp. 725–736.

Lens, Vicki. 2002. "Public Voices and Public Policy: Changing the Societal Discourse on 'Welfare'." *Journal of Sociology and Social Welfare* 29, pp. 137–154.

Lenski, Gerhard E. 1966. *Power and Privilege.* New York: McGraw-Hill.

Lenski, Gerhard E. 1967. "Status Inconsistency and the Vote, a Four Nation Test." *American Sociological Review* 32, pp. 298–301.

Lentner, Howard H. 1984. "The Concept of the State: A Response to Stephen Krasner." *Comparative Politics* 16, pp. 367–377.

Lerner, Robert, Althea K. Nagai, and Stanley Rothman. 1996. *American Elites.* New Haven, CT: Yale University Press.

Lessan, Gloria. 1991. "Macro-economic Determinants of Penal Policy: Estimating the Unemployment and Inflation Influences on Imprisonment Rates in the United States, 1948–1985." *Crime, Law and Social Change* 16, pp. 177–198.

Levin, Henry. 1999. "The Public-Private Nexus in Education." *American Behavioral Scientist* 43, pp. 124–138.

Levine, Jeffrey and Edward Carmines. 1997. "The Rise of Ideology in the Post-New Deal Party System, 1972–1992." *American Politics Quarterly* 25, pp. 19–35.

Levine, Rhonda F. 1988. *Class Struggle and the New Deal: Industrial Labor, Industrial Capital, and the State.* Lawrence, KS: University of Kansas Press.

Levine, Steven B. 1980. "The Rise of American Boarding Schools and the Development of a National Upper Class." *Social Problems* 28, pp. 73–92.

Levitas, Ruth. 1986a. "Competition and Compliance: The Utopias of the New Right." In *The Ideology of the New Right,* ed. R. Levitas, pp. 80–106. New York: Polity Press.

Levitas, Ruth. 1986b. "Introduction: Ideology and the New Right." In *The Ideology of the New Right,* ed. R. Levitas, pp. 1–24. New York: Polity Press.

Lewin, Tamar. 1998. "Crime Costs Many Black Men the Vote, Study Says." *New York Times,* October 21, 1998.

Lewis, Carolyn V. 1999. "Are Women Voting for Women? Feminist and Traditional Values in the Female Electorate." *Women and Politics* 20, pp. 1–28.

Lewis, Jane. 1994. "Gender, the Family and Women's Agency in Building of 'Welfare States:' The British Case." *Social History* 19, pp. 37–55.

Lewis, Jane. 2001. "The Decline of the Male Breadwinner Role." *Social Politics* 8, pp. 152–169.

Lewis, Jane. 2002. "Gender and Welfare State Change." *European Societies* 4, pp. 331–357.

Lewis, Justin. 1999. "The Opinion Poll as a Cultural Form." *International Journal of Cultural Studies* 2, pp. 199–221.

Lewis, Justin. 2001. *Constructing Public Opinion: How Political Elites Do What They Like and Why We Appear to Go Along With It.* New York: Columbia University Press.

Lewis, Michael. 1999. "A Path Analysis of the Effect of Welfare on Infant Mortality." *Journal of Sociology and Social Welfare* 26, pp. 125–136.

Lichtman, Allan J. 1976. "Critical Election Theory and the Reality of American Presidential Politics, 1916–1940." *American Historical Review* 81, pp. 317–348.

Lichtman, Allan J. 1983. "Political Realignment and 'Ethnocultural' Voting in Late Nineteenth Century America." *Journal of Social History* 16, pp. 55–82.

Lie, John. 1993. "Visualizing the Invisible Hand: The Social Origins of 'Market Society' in England, 1550–1750." *Politics and Society* 21, pp. 275–305.

Lie, John. 1997. "Sociology of Markets." *Annual Review of Sociology* 23, pp. 341–360.

Lieberman, Robert C. 1998. *Shifting the Color Line: Race and the American Welfare State.* Cambridge, MA.: Harvard University Press.

Lien, Pie-te. 1998. "Does the Gender Gap in Political Attitudes and Behavior Vary Across Racial Groups?" *Political Research Quarterly* 51, pp. 869–894.

Lien, Pie-te. 2001. "Voting Participation: Race, Gender and the Comparative Status of Asian American Women." In *Asian Americans and Politics,* ed. G. Chang, pp. 173–229. Stanford, CA: Stanford University Press.

Lien, Pie-te, Christian Collet, Janelle Wong, and S. K. Ramakrishnan. 2001. "Asian Pacific-American Public Opinion and Political Participation." *PS* 34, pp. 625–630.

Lienesch, Michael. 1982. "Right-Wing Religion: Christian Conservatism as a Political Movement." *Political Science Quarterly* 97, pp. 403–425.

Lijphart, Arend. 1997. "Unequal Participation: Democracy's Unsolved Dilemma." *American Political Science Review* 91, pp. 1–15.

Lilly, J. Robert and Paul Knepper. 1993. "The Corrections-commercial Complex." *Crime and Delinquency* 39, pp. 150–166.

Lin, Carolyn and Michael Salwen. 1997. "Predicting the Spiral of Silence on a Controversial Public Issue." *Howard Journal of Communication* 8, pp. 129–141.

Link, Michael W. 1995. "Tracking Public Mood in the Supreme Court." *Political Research Quarterly* 48, pp. 61–78.

Lipset, Seymour Martin. 1959a. "Political Sociology." In *Sociology Today*, eds. R. Merton, L. Bloom, and L. Cottrell, pp. 81–114. New York: Basic.

Lipset, Seymour Martin. 1959b. "Some Social Requisites of Democracy." *American Sociological Review* 53, pp. 71–85.

Lipset, Seymour Martin. 1960. *Political Man: The Social Bases of Politics.* New York: Doubleday.

Lipset, Seymour Martin. 1963. First New Nation. New York: Basic Books.

Lipset, Seymour Martin. 1994. "The Social Requisites of Democracy Revisited." *American Sociological Review* 59, pp. 1–22.

Lipset, Seymour Martin and Rheinhard Bendix. 1959. *Social Mobility in Industrial Society.* Berkeley, CA: University of California Press.

Lipset, Seymour Martin and Earl Raab. 1978. *The Politics of Unreason,* 2nd ed. Chicago: University of Chicago Press.

Lipset, Seymour Martin and William Schneider. 1987. "The Confidence Gap During the Reagan Years, 1981–1987." *Political Science Quarterly* 102, pp. 1–23.

Lipset, Seymour Martin and Hans Zetterberg. 1964. "A Theory of Social Mobility." In *Sociological Theory*, ed. L. Coser and B. Rosenberg, pp. 437–462. New York: Macmillan.

Lipset, Seymour Martin, Martin Trow, and James Coleman. 1956. *Union Democracy.*

Lipsky, Michael. 1968. "Protest as a Political Resource." *American Political Science Review* 62, pp. 1144–1158.

Liska, Allen E. 1987. "A Critical Examination of Macro Perspectives on Crime Control." *Annual Review of Sociology* 13, pp. 67–88.

Liska, Allen E. 1997. "Modeling the Relationships Between Macro Forms of Social Control." *Annual Review of Sociology* 23, pp. 39–61.

Liska, Allen. E. and William Baccaglini. 1990. "Feeling Safe by Comparison: Crime in the Newspapers." *Social Problems* 37, pp. 360–374.

Liska, Allen E., Joseph Lawrence, and Michael Benson. 1981. "Perspectives on the Legal Order: The Capacity for Social Control." *American Journal of Sociology* 87, pp. 413–426.

Little, Craig B. and Christopher Sheffield. 1983. "Frontiers and Criminal Justice: English Private Prosecution Societies and American Vigilantism in the Eighteenth and Nineteenth Centuries." *American Sociological Review* 48, pp. 796–808.

Little, Monroe. 1997. "Remembering Hiroshima: Cultural Politics, World War II and American Consciousness." *Western Journal of Black Studies* 21, pp. 34–42.

Lloyd, David and Paul Thomas. 1998. *Culture and the State.* New York: Routledge.

Lo, Clarence Y. 1982a. "Countermovements and Conservative Movements in the Contemporary U.S." *Annual Review of Sociology* 8, pp. 107–134.

Lo, Clarence Y. 1982b. "Theories of the State and Business Opposition to Increased Military Spending." *Social Problems* 29, pp. 424–438.

Lo, Clarence Y. 1990. *Small Property Versus Big Government.* Berkeley, CA: University of California Press.

Lo, Clarence Y. 1992. "Communities of Challengers in Social Movement Theory." In *Frontiers in Social Movement Theory*, eds. D. Morris and M. Mueller, pp. 224–248. New Haven, CT: Yale University Press.

Lo, Clarence Y. and Michael Schwartz, eds. 1998. *Social Policy and the Conservative Agenda.* New York: Blackwell.

Loader, Ian. 1997. "Policing and the Social: Questions of Symbolic Power." *British Journal of Sociology,* 48, pp. 1–18.

Loewenberg, Samuel. 2002. "The Brussels Hustle: American Lobbyists Struggle in the EU," http://www.jrn.columbia.edu/studentwork/reutersjournal/2002/loewenberg.asp.

Logan, John and Harvey Molotch. 1987. *Urban Fortunes.* Berkeley, CA: University of California Press.

Logan, John, Rachel Bridges Whaley, and Kyle Crowdes. 1997. "The Character and Consequences of Growth Regimes: An Assessment of 20 Years of Research." *Urban Affairs Review* 32, pp. 608–630.

London, Bruce and John Hearn. 1977. "The Ethnic Community Theory of Black Social and Political Participation: Additional Support." *Social Science Quarterly* 57, pp. 883–891.

Longmire, Dennis. 1996. "American's Attitudes About the Ultimate Weapon." In *Americans View Crime and Justice: A National Public Opinion Survey*, eds. Timothy Flanagan and Dennis Longmire, pp. 93–108. Thousand Oaks, CA: Sage.

Longoria, Thomas, Jr., Robert D. Wrinkle, and Jerry L. Polinard. 1990. "Mexican American Voter Registration and Turnout: Another Look." *Social Science Quarterly* 71, pp. 356–361.

Longshore, Douglas. 1982. "Race Composition and White Hostility: A Research Note on the Problem of Control in Desegregated Schools." *Social Forces* 61, pp. 73–78.

Lopreato, Joseph, Frank Bean, and Sally Cook Lopreato. 1976. "Occupational Mobility and Political Behavior: Some Unresolved Issues." *Journal of Political and Military Sociology* 4, pp. 1–15.

Loveman, Mara. 1998. "High-risk Collective Action: Defending Human Rights in Chile, Uruguay, and Argentina." *American Journal of Sociology* 104, pp. 477–525.

Lowi, Theodore J. 1979. *The End of Liberalism,* 2nd ed. New York: Norton.

Lucas, Samuel R. 1996. "Selective Attrition in a Newly Hostile Regime: The Case of the 1980 Sophomores." *Social Forces* 75, pp. 511–534.

Luchansky, Bill and Gregory Hooks. 1996. "Corporate Beneficiaries of the Mid-Century Wars: Respecifying Models of Corporate Growth, 1939–1959." *Social Science Quarterly* 77, pp. 301–313.

Luker, Kristin. 1984. *Abortion and the Politics of Motherhood.* Berkeley, CA: University of California Press.

Lukes, Steven. 1973. *Emile Durkheim: His Life and Work.* New York: Penguin.

Lukes, Steven. 1974. *Power: A Radical View.* London: Macmillan.

Lustig, R. Jeffrey. 1982. *Corporate Liberalism: The Origins of Modern American Political Theory, 1890–1920.* Berkeley, CA: University of California Press.

Lutz, Catherine A. and Jane L. Collins. 1993. *Reading National Geographic.* Chicago: University of Chicago Press.

Lyman, Geoffrey C. 1997. "Religion and Political Behavior in the United States: The Impact of Beliefs, Affiliations and Commitment from 1980–1994." *Public Opinion Quarterly* 61, pp. 288–316.

Lyman, Rick. 1998. "Best Little Election Year Brawl in Texas is for Control over Schools," *New York Times,* October 12, 1998.

Lynxwiler, John, Neal Shover, and Donald Clelland. 1983. "The Organization and Impact of Inspector Discretion in a Regulatory Bureaucracy." *Social Problems* 30, pp. 425–436.

M

MacDonnel, Diane. 1986. *Theories of Discourse: An Introduction.* New York: Basil Blackwell.

MacKuen, Michael and Courtney Brown. 1987. "Political Context and Attitude Change." *American Political Science Review* 81, pp. 471–490.

Madrid, Arturo. 1990. "Official English: A False Policy Issue." *Annals of the American Academy of Political and Social Science* 508, pp. 62–66.

Maier, Charles. 1984. "Preconditions for Corporatism." In *Order and Conflict in Contemporary Capitalism,* ed. J. Goldthorpe, pp. 60–80. New York: Oxford University Press.

Malloy, James M. 1977. "Authoritarianism and Corporatism in Latin America: The Modal Pattern." In *Authoritarianism and Corporatism in Latin America,* ed. J. Malloy, pp. 3–21. Pittsburgh: University of Pittsburgh Press.

Maney, Ardith and Eric Plutzer. 1996. "Scientific Information, Elite Attitudes, and the Public Debate Over Food Safety." *Policy Studies Journal* 24, pp. 42–56.

Maney, Gregory M. 2001. "Transnational Structures and Protest: Linking Theories and Assessing Evidence." *Mobilization* 6, pp. 83–100.

Manley, John F. 1994. "The Significance of Class in American History and Politics." In *New Perspectives on American Politics,* eds. L. Dodd and C. Jillson, pp. 15–46. Washington, DC: Congressional Quarterly Press.

Mann, Michael. 1973. *Consciousness and Action Among the Western Working Class.* New York: Macmillan.

Mann, Michael. 1987. "Ruling Class Strategies and Citizenship." *Sociology* 21, pp. 339–354.

Mann, Michael. 1988. *States, War and Capitalism: Studies in Political Sociology.* Cambridge, MA: Basil Blackwell.

Mann, Michael. 1995. "A Political Theory of Nationalism and Its Excesses." In *Notions of Nationalism,* ed. S. Periwal, pp. 44–64. New York: Central European Press.

Mannheim, Karl. 1936. *Ideology and Utopia.* New York: Harvest Books.

Manning, P. K. 1996. "Dramaturgy, Politics and the Axial Media Event." *Sociological Quarterly* 37, pp. 261–279.

Mansbridge, Jane. 2001. "The Making of Oppositional Consciousness." In *Oppositional Consciousness: The Subjective Roots of Social Protest,* eds. J. Mansbridge and A. Morris, pp. 1–19. Chicago: University of Chicago Press.

Manza, Jeff. 1993. "Four Theories of Political Change and the Origins of New Deal Labor Registration." *Research in Political Sociology* 6, pp. 71–116.

Manza, Jeff. 2000a. "Political Sociological Models of the U.S. New Deal." *Annual Review of Sociology* 26, pp. 297–322.

Manza, Jeff. 2000b. "Race and the Underdevelopment of the American Welfare State." *Theory and Society* 29, pp. 819–832.

Manza, Jeff and Clem Brooks. 1996. "Does Class Analysis Still Have Anything to Contribute to the Study of Politics?" *Theory and Society* 25, pp. 717–724.

Manza, Jeff and Clem Brooks. 1997. "The Religious Factor in U.S. Presidential Elections, 1960–1992." *American Journal of Sociology* 103, pp. 38–81.

Manza, Jeff and Clem Brooks. 1998. "Gender Gap in U.S. Presidential Elections: When? Why? Implications?" *American Journal of Sociology* 103, pp. 1235–1266.

Manza, Jeff and Clem Brooks. 1999. *Social Cleavages and Political Change.* New York: Oxford University Press.

Manza, Jeff, Michael Hout, and Clem Brooks. 1995. "Class Voting in Capitalist Democracies Since World War II" *Annual Review of Sociology* 21, pp. 137–162.

March, James G. and Johan P. Olsen. 1989. *Rediscovering Institutions.* New York: Free Press.

March, James G. and Johan P. Olsen. 1995. *Democratic Governance.* New York: Free Press.

Marcus, George E., James Pierson, and John L. Sullivan. 1980. "Rural-urban differences in tolerance: Confounding Problems of Conceptualization and Measurement." *Rural Sociology* 45, pp. 731–737.

Marcus, George E., John L. Sullivan, Elizabeth Theiss-Morse, and Sandra Wood. 1995. *With Malice Toward Some: How People Make Civil Liberties Judgments.* New York: Cambridge University Press.

Mares, Isabela. 2001. "Firms and the Welfare State." In *Varieties of Capitalism.* eds. by P. Hall and D. Soskice, pp. 184–212. New York: Oxford University Press.

Mares, Isabela. 2003. *The Politics of Social Risk: Business and Welfare State Development.* New York: Cambridge University Press.

Margolis, Diane Rothbard. 1989. "Considering Women's Experience." *Theory and Society* 18, pp. 387–416.

Margolis, Michael and Khondaker Haque. 1981. "Applied Tolerance or Fear of Government? An Alternative

Interpretation of Jackman's Findings." *American Journal of Political Science* 25, pp. 241–255.

Markoff, John. 1996. *Waves of Democracy.* Thousand Oaks, CA: Pine Forge Press.

Marks, Gary N. 1997. "The Formation of Materialist and Postmaterialist Values." *Social Science Research* 26, pp. 52–69.

Markusen, Ann. 1998. "America's Military Industrial Makeover." In *Social Policy and the Conservative Agenda,* eds. C. Lo and M. Schwartz, pp. 142–150. Malden, MA: Blackwell.

Marmor, Theodore, Jerry Mashaw, and Philip Harvey. 1990. *America's Misunderstood Welfare State.* Basic Books.

Marshall, Susan E. 1986. "In Defense of Separate Spheres: Class and Politics in the Antisuffrage Movement." *Social Forces* 65, pp. 327–351.

Marshall, Susan E. 1998. "The Gender Gap in Voting Behavior: Evidence From a Referendum on Women Suffrage." *Research in Political Sociology* 8, pp. 189–208.

Marshall, T. H. 1950. *Citizenship and Social Class and Other Essays.* Cambridge, UK: Cambridge University Press.

Martin, Ross M. 1983. "Pluralism and the New Corporatism." *Political Studies* 31, pp. 86–102.

Martin, William. 1996. *With God on Our Side: The Rise of the Religious Right in America.* New York: Broadway Books.

Marwell, Gerald, Michael T. Aiken, and N. Jay Demerath III. 1987. "The Persistence of Political Attitudes among 1960s Civil Rights Activists." *Public Opinion Quarterly* 51, pp. 359–375.

Marwell, Gerald, Pamela Oliver, and Ralph Prahl. 1988. "Social Networks and Collective Action: A Theory of the Critical Mass III." *American Journal of Sociology* 94, pp. 502–534.

Marx, Anthony W. 1998. *Making Race and Nation: A Comparison of the United States, South Africa and Brazil.* New York: Cambridge University Press.

Marx, Gary T. 1979. "External Efforts to Damage or Facilitate Social Movements." In *The Dynamics of Social Movements,* eds. M. Zald and J. McCarthy, pp. 94–125. Cambridge, MA: Winthrop.

Marx, Karl. 1859 [1970]. *A Contribution to the Critique of Political Economy.* [translated by S. W. Ryazanskaya, edited by Maurice Dobb]. New York: International Publishers.

Marx, Karl and Frederick Engles. 1947 [1886]. *The German Ideology.* New York: International Publishers.

Massey, James L. and Martha A. Myers. 1989. "Patterns of Repressive Social Control in Post-reconstruction Georgia, 1932–1935." *Social Forces* 68, pp. 458–488.

Massey, Rachel Ida. 1994. "Impediments to Collective Action in a Small Community." *Politics and Society* 22, pp. 421–434.

Matasar, Ann B. 1986. *Corporate PACs and Federal Campaign Financing Laws: Use or Abuse of Power.* New York: Quorum Books.

Mathisen, James. 1989. "Twenty Years After Bellah: Whatever Happened to American Civil Religion?" *Sociological Analysis* 50, pp. 129–146.

Mauer, Marc. 2003. "Comparative International Rates of Incarceration." Testimony presented to U.S. Commissioner on Civil Rights. *The Sentencing Project* (June 20, 2003).

Mauzy, Diane K. and R. S. Milne. 2002. *Singapore Politics under the People's Action Party.* New York: Routledge.

May, Timothy, John McHugh, and Tom Taylor. 1998. "Business Representation in the UK Since 1979: The Case of Trade Associations." *Political Studies* 76, pp. 260–275.

Mayntz, Renate. 1975. "Legitimacy and the Directive Capacity of the Political System." In *Stress and Contradiction in Modern Capitalism,* eds. L. Lindberg, R. Alford, C. Crouch, and C. Offe, pp. 261–274. Lexington, MA: Lexington Books.

Mazzeo, Christopher, Sarah Rab, and Susan Eachus. 2003. "Work-first or Work-only." *Annals of the American Academy of Political and Social Science* 586, pp. 144–171.

McAdam, Doug. 1982. *Political Process and the Development of Black Insurgency, 1930–1970.* Chicago: University of Chicago Press.

McAdam, Doug. 1983. "Tactical Innovation and the Pace of Insurgency." *American Sociological Review* 48, pp. 735–753.

McAdam, Doug. 1989. "The Biographical Consequences of Activism." *American Sociological Review,* 54 pp. 744–760.

McAdam, Doug. 1994. "Culture and Social Movements." In *New Social Movements from Ideology to Identity,* eds. E. Laraña, H. Johnson, and J. Gusfield, pp. 36–57. Philadelphia: Temple University Press.

McAdam, Doug. 1996. "Conceptual Origins, Current Problems, and Future Directions." In *Comparative Perspectives on Social Movements,* eds. D. McAdam, J. McCarthy, and M. Zald, pp. 23–40. New York: Cambridge University Press.

McAdam, Doug. 1998. "On the International Origins of Domestic Political Opportunities." In *Social Movements and American Political Institutions,* eds. A. Costain and A. McFarland, pp. 251–266. Lanham, MD: Rowman and Littlefield.

McAdam, Doug. 1999. "The Biographical Impact of Activism." In *How Social Movements Matter,* eds. M. Giugni, D. McAdam, and C. Tilly. pp. 119–148. Minneapolis: University of Minnesota Press.

McAdam, Doug and Ronnelle Paulsen. 1993. "Specifying the Relationship between Social Ties and Activism." *American Journal of Sociology* 99, pp. 640–668.

McAdam, Doug and Dieter Rucht. 1993. "The Cross-national Diffusion of Movement Ideas." *Annals of American Academy of Political and Social Science* 528, pp. 56–74.

McAdam, Doug and David Snow. 1997. "Social Movements: Conceptual and Theoretical Issues." In *Social Movements: Readings on Their Emergence, Mobilization and Dynamics,* eds. D. McAdam and D. Snow, pp. xviii–xxvi. Los Angeles: Roxbury.

McAdam, Doug, John McCarthy, and Mayer Zald. 1996. "Preface." In *Comparative Perspectives on Social Movements,* eds. D. McAdam, J. McCarthy and M. Zald, pp. xi–xiv. New York: Cambridge University Press.

McAdam, Doug, Sidney Tarrow, and Charles Tilly. 1996. "To Map Contentious Politics." *Mobilization.* 1, pp. 17–34.

McAllister, Ian and Jack Vowles. 1994. "The Rise of New Politics and Market Liberalism in Australia and New Zealand." *British Journal of Political Science* 24, pp. 381–402.

McCaffrey, Dawn and Jennifer Keys. 2000. "Competitive Framing Processes in the Abortion Debate: Polarization-vilification, Frame Saving, and Frame Debunking." *Sociological Quarterly* 41, pp. 41–61.

McCammon, Holly J. 1990. "Legal Limits to Labor Militancy: U.S. Labor Law and the Right to Strike Since the New Deal." *Social Problems.* 37, pp. 206–229.

McCammon, Holly J. 1993. "From Repressive Intervention to Integrative Prevention: The U.S. State's Legal Management of Labor Militancy, 1881–1978." *Social Forces* 71, pp. 569–602.

McCammon, Holly J. 1994. "Disorganizing and Reorganizing Conflict: Outcomes of the State's Legal Regulation of the Strike Since the Wagner Act." *Social Forces* 72, pp. 1011–1150.

McCammon, Holly J., Karen Campbell, Ellen Granberg, and Christine Mowery. 2001. "How Movements Win: Gendered Opportunity Structures and U.S. Women's Suffrage Movements, 1866–1919." *American Sociological Review* 66, pp. 49–70.

McCann, Michael W. 1998. "Social Movements and the Mobilization of Law."*In Social Movements and American Political Institutions,* eds. A. Costain and A. McFarland, pp. 201–215. Lanham, MD: Rowman and Littlefield.

McCarney, Joe. 1980. *The Real World of Ideology.* Atlantic Highlands, NJ: Humanities Press.

McCarthy, John D. 1994. "Activists, Authorities, and Media Framing of Drunk Driving." In *New Social Movements from Ideology to Identity,* eds. E. Laraña, H. Johnson, and J. Gusfield, pp. 133–167. Philadelphia: Temple University Press.

McCarthy, John D. 1996. "Constraints and Opportunities in Adopting, Adapting, and Inventing." In *Comparative Perspectives on Social Movements,* eds. D. McAdam, J. McCarthy, and M. Zald, pp. 141–151. New York: Cambridge University Press.

McCarthy, John D. and Clark McPhail. 1998. "The Institutionalization of Protest in the United States." In *The Social Movement Society,* eds. D. Meyer and S. Tarrow, pp. 83–110. Lanham, MD: Roman and Littlefield.

McCarthy, John D. and Jackie Smith. 1996. "Assessing Media, Electoral, and Government Agendas." In *Comparative Perspectives on Social Movements,* eds. D. McAdam, J. McCarthy, and M. Zald, pp. 291–311. New York: Cambridge University Press.

McCarthy, John D. and Mark Wolfson. 1996. "Resource Mobilization by Local Social Movement Organizations: Agency, Strategy, and Organization, the Movement Against Drinking and Driving." *American Sociological Review* 61, pp. 1070–1088.

McCarthy, John D. and Mayer Zald. 1987. "Resource Mobilization and Social Movements." In *Social Movements in An Organizational Society.* eds. M. Zald and J. McCarthy, pp. 15–42. New Brunswick, NJ: Transaction.

McCarthy, John D. and Mayer N. Zald. 1977. "Resource Mobilization and Social Movements: A Partial Theory." *American Journal of Sociology* 82, pp. 1212–1241.

McCarthy, John D., Clark McPhail, and Jackie Smith. 1996. "Images of Protest: Dimensions of Selection Bias in Media Coverage of Washington Demonstrations, 1982–1991." *American Sociological Review* 61, pp. 478–499.

McCelland, David C. 1961. *The Achieving Society.* New York: Free Press.

McChesney, Robert W. "The Global Media Giants." *EXTRA!* (November/December 1997).

McClosky, Herbert and Alida Brill. 1983. *Dimensions of Tolerance.* New York: Russell Sage.

McConnell, Grant. 1969. *The Decline of Agrarian Democracy.* New York: Atheneum.

McCool, Daniel. 1998. "The Subsystem Family of Concepts: A Critique and Proposal." *Political Research Quarterly* 51, pp. 551–570.

McCormick, Richard L. 1981a. *From Realignment to Reform: Political Change in New York State, 1893–1910.* Ithaca, NY: Cornell University Press.

McCormick, Richard L. 1981b. "The Discovery That Business Corrupts Politics: A Reappraisal of the Origins of Progressivism." *American Historical Review* 86, pp. 247–274.

McCormick, Richard L. 1986. *The Party Period and Public Policy: American Politics from the Age of Jackson to the Progressive Era.* New York: Oxford University Press.

McCormick, Richard L. 1997. *Public Life in Industrial America, 1877–1917,* revised and expanded. Washington, DC: American Historical Association.

McCright, Aaron and Riley Dunlap. 2003. "Defeating Kyoto." *Social Problems* 50, pp. 348–373.

McCutcheon, Allen L. 1985. "A Latent Class Analysis of Tolerance for Nonconformity." *Public Opinion Quarterly* 49, pp. 474–488.

McDaniel, Susan A. 2002. "Women's Changing Relations to the State and Citizenship: Caring and Intergenerational Relations in Globalizing Western Democracies." *The Canadian Review of Sociology and Anthropology* 39, pp. 125–150.

McDonagh, Eileen Lorenzi. 1992a. "Representative Democracy and State-building in the Progressive Era." *American Political Science Review* 86, pp. 938–950.

McDonagh, Eileen Lorenzi. 1992b. "Electoral Bases of Policy Innovation in the Progressive Era." *Journal of Policy History* 4, pp. 162–187.

McDonald, Michael P. and Samuel Popkin. 2001. "The Myth of the Vanishing Voter." *American Political Science Review* 95, pp. 963–974.

McFarland, Andrew S. 1991. "Interest Groups and Political Time: Cycles in America." *British Journal of Political Science* 21, pp. 257–284.

McFarland, Andrew S. 1998. "Social Movements and Theories of American Politics." In *Social Movements and American Political Institutions,* eds. A. Costain and A. McFarland, pp. 7–19. Lanham, MD: Rowman and Littlefield.

McGann, James G. and R. Kent, Weaver, eds. 2000. *Think Tanks and Civil Societies: Catalysts for Ideas and Action.* Transaction Publishers.

McGerr, Michael E. 1986. *The Decline of Popular Politics: The American North, 1865–1928.* New York: Oxford University Press.

McGlen, Nancy E. and Karen O'Connor. 1983. *Women's Rights: the Struggle For Equality in the Nineteenth and Twentieth Century.* New York: Praeger.

McGuire, Kevin T. and Barbara Palmer. 1995. "Issue Fluidity on the U.S. Supreme Court." *American Political Science Review* 89, pp. 691–702.

McGuire, Kevin T. and Barbara Palmer. 1996. "Issues, Agendas, and Decision-making on the Supreme Court." *American Political Science Review* 90, pp. 853–865.

McLelland, David. 1986. *Ideology.* Milton Keynes, England: Open University Press.

McLeod, Douglas M., William Eveland, and Nancy Signorielli. 1994. "Conflict and Public Opinion: Rallying Effects of the Persian Gulf War." *Journalism Quarterly* 71, pp. 20–31.

McManus, Patricia and Thomas Diprete. 2000. "Market, Family, and State Sources of Income Instability in Germany and the United States." *Social Science Research* 29, pp. 405–440.

McPhail, Clark and Ronald Wohlstein. 1983. "Individual and Collective Behaviors within Gatherings, Demonstrations, and Riots." *Annual Review of Sociology* 9, pp. 579–600.

McPhail, Clark. 1971. "A Civil Disorder Participation: A Critical Examination of Recent Research." *American Sociological Review* 36, pp. 1058–1073.

McRobbie, Angela and Sarah Thornton. 1995. "Rethinking 'Moral Panic' for Multi-Mediated Social Worlds." *British Journal of Sociology* 46, pp. 559–574.

Meernik, James and Joseph Ignagni. 1997. "Judicial Review and Coordinate Construction of the Constitution." *American Journal of Political Science* 41, pp. 447–467.

Meier, Kenneth J. 1992. "The Politics of Drug Abuse: Laws, Implementation, and Consequences." *Western Political Quarterly* 45, pp. 41–69.

Meier, Kenneth J. and Robert E. England. 1984. "Black Representation and Educational Policy: Are They Related?" *American Political Science Review* 78, pp. 392–403.

Meisel, James H., ed. 1965. *Pareto and Mosca.* Engelwood Cliffs, NJ: Prentice-Hall.

Melman, Seymour. 1970. *Pentagon Capitalism.* New York: McGraw Hill.

Melman, Seymour. 1985. *Permanent War Economy,* rev. ed. New York: Simon Schuster.

Melucci, Alberto. 1994. "A Strange Kind of Newness." In *New Social Movements from Ideology to Identity,* eds. E. Laraña, H. Johnson, and J. Gusfield, pp. 101–130. Philadelphia: Temple University Press.

Melucci, Alberto. 1997. "The Symbolic Challenge of Contemporary Movements." In *Social Movements: Perspectives and Issues,* eds. S. Buecher and F. Cylke, pp. 259–294. Mountain View, CA: Mayfield.

Mendelberg, Tali. 2001. *The Race Card.* Princeton, NJ: Princeton University Press.

Mendoza, David C. 1995. "Culture Wars and Freedom of Expression." In *Eyes Right,* ed. C. Berlet, pp. 155–158. Boston: South End Press.

Mensch, Elizabeth. 1982. "The History of Mainstream Legal Thought." In *The Politics of Law: A Progressive Critique,* ed. David Kairys, pp. 18–29. New York: Pantheon.

Meranto, Oneida. 1998. "Litigation as Rebellion." In *Social Movements and American Political Institutions,* eds. A. Costain and A. McFarland, pp. 216–232. Lanham, MD: Rowman and Littlefield.

Merelman, Richard M. 1989. "On Culture and Politics in America: A Perspective from Structural Anthropology." *British Journal of Political Science* 19, pp. 465–493.

Merelman, Richard M. 1996. "Symbols as Substance in National Civics Standards." *PS: Political Science and Politics.* 29:53–57.

Merlo, Alida V. and Peter J. Benekos. 2000. *What's Wrong with the Criminal Justice System: Ideology, Politics and Media.* Cincinnati, OH: Anderson Publishing.

Messner, Steven F. and Richard Rosenfeld. 1994. *Crime and the American Dream.* Belmonth, CA: Wadsworth.

Meyer, David S. and Suzanne Staggenborg. 1996. "Movements, Countermovements, and the Structure of Political Opportunity." *American Journal of Sociology* 101, pp. 1628–1660.

Meyer, David S. and Suzanne Staggenborg. 1998. "Countermovement Dynamics in Federal Systems: A Comparison of Abortion Politics in Canada and the United States." *Research in Political Sociology* 8, pp. 209–240.

Meyer, David S. and Sidney Tarrow. 1998. "A Movement Society: Contentious Politics for a New Century." In *The Social Movement Society,* eds. D. Meyer and S. Tarrow, pp. 1–28. Lanham, NJ: Rowman and Littlefield.

Meyer, David S. and Nancy Whittier. 1994. "Social Movement Spillover." *Social Problems* 41, pp. 277–298.

Meyer, John. 1999. "The Changing Cultural Context of the Nation State: A World Society Perspective." In *State/Culture: State Formation after the Cultural Turn,* ed. by G. Steinmetz, pp. 123–143. Ithaca, NY: Cornell University Press.

Meyer, John W. 2000. "Globalization: Sources and Effects on National States and Societies." *International Sociology* 15, pp. 233–248.

Meyer, John W., David H. Kamens, and Aaron Benavot. 1992. *School Knowledge for the Masses.* London: Falmer.

Meyer, John W., Francisco Ramirez, and Yasmin N. Soysal. 1992. "World Expansion of Mass Education, 1870–1980." *Sociology of Education* 65, pp. 128–149.

Meyer, John, John Boli, George Thomas, and Francisco Ramirez. 1997. "World Society and the Nation State." *American Journal of Sociology* 103, pp. 144–181.

Meyer, John W., David Tyack, Joane Nagel, and Audri Gorden. 1979. "Public Education as National Building in America, 1870–1930." *American Journal of Sociology* 85, pp. 591–613.

Meyer, Madonna Harrington. 1996. "Making Claims as Workers or Wives: The Distribution of Social Security Benefits." *American Sociological Review* 61, pp. 478–499.

Meyrowitz, Joshua. 1995. "New Sense of Politics: How Television Changes Political Drama." *Research in Political Sociology* 7, pp. 117–138.

Michalowski, Raymond and Susan Carlson. 2000. "Crime, Punishment, and Social Structures of Accumulation." *Journal of Contemporary Criminal Justice* 16, pp. 272–292.

Michelson, Melissa. 2000. "Political Efficacy and Electoral Participation of Chicago Latinos." *Social Science Quarterly* 81, pp. 136–150.

Midgley, James. 2001. "The United States: Welfare, Work and Development." *International Journal of Social Welfare* 10, pp. 284–293.

Midgley, James and Kwong-leung Tang. 2001. "Social Policy, Economic Growth and Developmental Welfare." *International Journal of Social Welfare* 10, pp. 244–252.

Migdal, Joel S. 1988. *Strong Societies and Weak States: State-society Relations and State Capabilities in the Third World.* Princeton, NJ: Princeton University Press.

Miliband, Ralph. 1969. *The State in Capitalist Society.* New York: Basic.

Miliband, Ralph. 1977. *Marxism and Politics.* New York: Oxford University Press.

Miliband, Ralph. 1982. *Class Power and State Power.* London: Verso.

Mill, John Stuart. 1859 [1956]. *On liberty.* Edited by Currin V. Shields. New York: Liberal Arts Press.

Mill, John Stuart. 1869. *The subjection of women.* New York: D. Appleton and Company.

Miller, Abraham H., Louis H. Bolce, and Mark Halligan. 1977. "The J-Curve Theory and the Black Urban Riots: An Empirical Test of Progressive Relative Deprivation Theory." *American Political Science Review.* 71, pp. 964–982.

Miller, Alan and John Hoffman. 1999. "The Growing Divisiveness: Culture Wars or War of Words?" *Social Forces* 78, pp. 721–752.

Miller, Arthur. 1976. *The Modern Corporate State: Private Government and the American Constitution.* Westport, CT: Greenwood Press.

Miller, Arthur. 1988. "Gender and the Vote: 1984." In *The Politics of Gender Gap: The Social Construction of Political Influence,* ed. by C. M. Mueller, pp. 258–282. Newbury Park, CA: Sage.

Miller, Arthur, Patricia Gurin, Gerald Gurin, and Oksana Malanchuk. 1981. "Group Consciousness and Political Participation." *American Journal of Political Science* 25, pp. 494–511.

Miller, Jerome G. 1996. *Search and Destroy: African American Males in the Criminal Justice System.* New York. Cambridge University Press.

Miller, Reuben. 1988. "The Literature of Terrorism." *Terrorism* 11, pp. 63–87.

Miller, Wesley. 1985. "The New Christian Right and Fundamentalist Discontent: The Politics of Lifestyle Concern Revisited." *Sociological Focus* 18, pp. 325–336.

Mills, C. Wright. 1956. *The Power Elite.* New York: Oxford University Press.

Mink, Gwendolyn. 1990. "The Lady and the Tramp: Gender, Race and the Origins of the American Welfare State." In *Women, the State and Welfare,* ed Linda Gordon, pp. 92–122. Madison, WI: University of Wisconsin Press.

Mink, Gwendolyn. 2001. "Violating Women: Rights Abuses in the Welfare Police State." *Annals of the American Academy of Political and Social Science* 577, pp. 79–93.

Minkoff, Debra C. 1997a. "Producing Social Capital: National Social Movements and Civil Society." *American Behavioral Scientist,* 40, pp. 606–619.

Minkoff, Debra C. 1997b. "The Sequencing of Social Movements." *American Sociological Review* 62, pp. 779–799.

Minkoff, Debra C. 1999. "Bending with the Wind: Strategic Change and Adaptation by Women's and Racial Minority Organizations." *American Journal of Sociology* 104, pp. 1666–1703.

Mintz, Alex and Alexander Hicks. 1984. "Military Keynesianism in the United States, 1949–1976: Disaggregating Military Expenditures and Their Determination." *American Journal of Sociology,* 90, pp. 411–417.

Mintz, Beth. 1995. "Business Participation in Health Care Policy Reform: Factors Contributing to Collective Action." *Social Problems* 42, pp. 408–428.

Mintz, Beth and Michael Schwartz. 1981. "The Structure of Intercorporate Unity in American Business." *Social Problems* 29, pp. 87–103.

Mintz, Beth and Michael Schwartz. 1985. *The Power Structure of American Business.* Chicago: University of Chicago Press.

Mintz, Beth and Michael Schwartz. 1986. "Capital Flows and the Process of Financial Hegemony." *Theory and Society* 15, pp. 77–102.

Mishler, William and Reginald Sheehan. 1993. "The Supreme Court as a Countermajoritarian Institution: The Impact of Public Opinion on Supreme Court Decisions." *American Political Science Review* 87, pp. 87–101.

Mishler, William and Reginald Sheehan. 1996. "Public Opinion, the Attitudinal Model, and Supreme Court Decision Making." *Journal of Politics* 58, pp. 169–200.

Misra, Joya. 2002. "Class, Race and Gender in Theorizing Welfare States." *Research in Political Sociology* 11, pp. 19–52.

Mitchell, Alison. 1998. "A New Form of Lobbying Puts Public Face on Private Interest." *New York Times,* September 30, 1998.

Mitchell, Alison. 2000. "Bush Draws Campaign Theme from More Than 'the Heart.'" *New York Times,* June 12, 2000.

Mitchell, Timothy. 1990. "Everyday Metaphors of Power." *Theory and Society* 19, pp. 545–577.

Mitchell, Timothy. 1991. "Limits of the State: Beyond Statist Approaches and Their Critics." *American Political Science Review* 85, pp. 77–96.

Mitchell, Timothy. 1999. "Society, Economy and the State Effect." In *State/Culture: State Formation after the Cultural Turn,* ed. G. Steinmetz, pp. 76–97. Ithaca, NY: Cornell University Press.

Mizruchi, Mark S. 1982. *The American Corporate Network: 1904–1974.* Beverly Hills: Sage.

Mizruchi, Mark S. 1989. "Similarity of Political Behavior Among Large American Corporations." *American Journal of Sociology* 95, pp. 401–424.

Mizruchi, Mark S. 1990a. "Determinates of Political Opposition Among Large American Corporations." *Social Forces* 68, pp. 1065–1088.

Mizruchi, Mark S. 1990b. "Similarity of Ideology and Party Preference Among Large American Corporations." *Sociological Forum* 5, pp. 213–240.

Mizruchi, Mark S. 1992. *The Structure of Corporate Political Action, Interfirm Relations and Their Consequences.* Cambridge, MA: Harvard University Press.

Mizruchi, Mark S. and Thomas Koenig. 1986. "Economic Sources of Corporate Political Consensus: An Examination of Interindustry Relations." *American Sociological Review* 51, pp. 482–491.

Mizruchi, Mark S. and Thomas Koenig. 1988. "Economic Concentration and Corporate Political Behavior: A Cross-industry Comparison." *Social Science Research* 17, pp. 287–305.

Mizruchi, Mark S. and Thomas Koenig. 1991. "Size, Concentration and Corporate Networks: Determinants of Business Collective Action." *Social Science Quarterly* 72, pp. 299–313.

Mizruchi, Mark S. and Linda Brewster Stearns. 1988. "A Longitudinal Study of the Formation of Interlocking Directorates." *Administrative Science Quarterly* 33, pp. 194–210.

Moe, Terry M. 1982. "Regulatory Performance and Presidential Administration." *American Journal of Political Science* 26, pp. 197–224.

Moe, Terry M. 1985. "Control and Feedback in Economic Regulation: The Case of the NLRB." *American Political Science Review* 79, pp. 1094–1116.

Moen, Matthew C. 1988. "Status Politics and the Political Agenda of the Christian Right." *Sociological Quarterly* 29, pp. 429–438.

Moen, Matthew C. 1989. *The Christian Right and Congress.* Tuscaloosa, AL: University of Alabama Press.

Moen, Matthew C. 1990. "Ronald Reagan and the Social Issues: Rhetorical Support for the Christian Right." *Social Science Journal* 27, pp. 199–207.

Moen, Matthew C. 1992. *The Transformation of the Christian Right.* Tuscaloosa, AL: University of Alabama Press.

Moen, Matthew C. 1994. "From Revolution to Evolution: The Changing Nature of the Christian Right." *Sociology of Religion* 55, pp. 345–357.

Mollenkopf, John H. 1983. *The Contested City.* Princeton, NJ: Princeton University Press.

Moller, Stephanie. 2002. "Supporting Poor Single Mothers: Gender and Race in the U.S. Welfare State." *Gender and Society* 16, pp. 465–484.

Moller, Stephanie, David Bradley, Evelyne Huber, Francois Nielsen, and John D. Stephens. 2003. "Determinates of Relative Poverty in Advanced Capitalist Nations." *American Sociological Review* 68, pp. 22–51.

Mondak, Jeffrey J. 1995. "Media Exposure and Political Discussion in U.S. Elections." *Journal of Politics* 57, pp. 62–85.

Mondak, Jeffrey J. and Shannon I. Smithey. 1997. "The Dynamics of Public Support for the Supreme Court: 1972–1994." *Journal of Politics* 59, pp. 1114–1142.

Montanari, Ingalill. 2001. "Modernization, Globalization and the Welfare State: A Comparative Analysis of Old And New Convergence of Social Insurance Since 1930." *British Journal of Sociology* 52, pp. 469–494.

Moon, J. Donald. 1988. "The Moral Basis of the Democratic State." In *Democracy and the Welfare State,* ed. Amy Gutmann, pp. 27–52. Princeton, NJ: Princeton University Press.

Moore, Barrington, Jr. 1966. *Social Origins of Dictatorship and Democracy.* Boston: Beacon.

Moore, William J. and Denise R. Chachere. 1995. "The Political Influence of Unions and Corporations on COPE Votes in the U.S. Senate, 1979–1988." *Journal of Labor Research* 16, pp. 203–222.

Moran, Richard. 1996. "Bringing Rational Choice Theory Back to Reality." *Journal of Criminal Law and Criminology* 86, pp. 1147–1160.

Morgan, Kimberly. 2001. "A Child of the Sixties: The Great Society, the New Right, and the Politics of Federal Child Care." *Journal of Policy History* 13, pp. 215–250.

Morgan, Richard E. 1980. *Domestic Intelligence: Monitoring Dissent in America.* Austin, TX: University of Texas Press.

Morris, Aldon D. 1981. "Black Southern Sit-in Movement: Analysis of Internal Organization." *American Sociological Review* 46, pp. 744–767.

Morris, Aldon D. 1984. *The Origins of the Civil Rights Movement.* New York: Free Press.

Morris, Aldon D. 1992. "Political Consciousness and Collective Action." In *Frontiers in Social Movement Theory,* eds. A. Morris and C. M. Mueller, pp. 351–373. New Haven, CT: Yale University Press.

Morris, Aldon D. 1993. "Birmingham Confrontation Reconsidered: An Analysis of the Dynamics and Tactics of Mobilization." *American Sociological Review* 58, pp. 621–636.

Morris, Aldon D. 1999. "A Retrospective on the Civil Rights Movement: Political and Intellectual Landmarks." *Annual Review of Sociology* 25, pp. 517–539.

Morris, Aldon D. and Naomi Braine. 2001. "Social Movements and Oppositional Consciousness." In *Oppositional Consciousness,* eds. J. Mansbridge and A. Morris, pp. 20–37. Chicago: University of Chicago Press.

Morris, Aldon D. and Cedric Herring. 1987. "Theory and Research in Social Movements: A Critical Review." *Annual Review of Political Science* 2, pp. 137–198.

Mosca, Gaetano. 1939. *The Ruling Class: Elementa di Scienzia Politica.* [translated by Hannah D. Kahn, edited by Arthur Livingston]. New York: McGraw-Hill.

Moss, Alexandra H. 2003. "The Globalization of Indifference." *The Harvard Political Review–World* (12/07/03), http://www.hpronline.org/news/2001/06/01/bworldb/The-Globalization.Of.Indifference-83258.shtml.

Mosse, George L., ed. 1966. *Nazi Culture.* New York: Grosset and Dunlap.

Mosse, George L., ed. 1979. *International Fascism: New Thoughts and New Approaches.* Beverly Hills, CA: Sage.

Mottl, Tahi L. 1980. "The Analysis of Countermovements." *Social Problems* 27, pp. 620–635.

Mouffe, Chantal. 1979. "Hegemony and Ideology in Gramsci." *Research in Political Economy* 2, pp. 1–31.

Mueller, Carol McClurg. 1987. "Collective Consciousness, Identity Formation and the Rise of Women in Public Office in the United States.". In *The Women's Movement of the United States and Western Europe,* Eds. M. F. Katzenstein and C. M. Mueller, pp. 89–108. Philadelphia: Temple University Press.

Mueller, Carol McClurg, ed. 1988. *The Politics of the Gender Gap: The Social Construction of Political Influence.* Newbury Park, CA: Sage.

Mueller, Carol McClurg. 1994. "Conflict Networks and the Origins of Women's Liberation." In *New Social Movements from Ideology to Identity,* ed. E. Laraña, H. Johnson, and J. Gusfield, pp. 234–265. Philadelphia: Temple University Press.

Mueller, Carol McClurg. 1999. "Claim 'Radicalization?' The 1989 Protest Cycle in the GDR." *Social Problems* 46, pp. 528–547.

Mueller-Eckhardt, Carol. 1991. "The Gender Gap and Women's Political Influence." *Annals of the American Academy of Political and Social Science* 515, pp. 23–37.

Muller, Edward N. 1995. "Economic Determinates of Democracy." *American Sociological Review* 60, pp. 966–982.

Multi-state Tax Commission. 2003. "Corporate Tax Sheltering and the Impact on State Corporate Income Tax Revenue Collections." Report of July 15, 2003, http://www.mtc.gov/TaxShelterRpt.pdf (downloaded July 30, 2003).

Murray, Charles. 1984. *Losing ground: American social policy, 1950–1980.* New York: Basic Books.

Murray, Geoffrey and Audrey Perera. 1996. *Singapore: The Global City State.* New York: St. Martins.

Murray, Robert K. 1955. *Red Scare: A Study of National Hysteria, 1919–1920.* Minneapolis: University of Minnesota Press.

Murray, Robert K. 1973. *The Politics of Normalcy: Government Theory and Practice in the Harding-Coolidge Era.* New York: Norton.

Mutz, Diana C. and Joe Soss. 1997. "Reading Public Opinion: The Influence of News Coverage on Perceptions of Public Sentiment." *Public Opinion Quarterly* 61, pp. 431–451.

Mutz, Diana C. and Paul Martin. 2001. "Facilitating Communication Across Lines of Political Difference." *American Political Science Review* 95, pp. 97–114.

Myers, Martha A. 1990. "Economic Threat and Racial Disparities in Incarceration: The Case of Postbelleum Georgia." *Criminology* 28, pp. 627–650.

Myers, Martha A. and James L. Massey. 1991. "Race, Labor and Punishment in Postbellum Georgia." *Social Problems* 38, pp. 267–283.

Myles, John F. 1979. "Differences in the Canadian and American Class Vote: Fact or Pseudofact?" *American Journal of Sociology* 84, pp. 1232–1237.

Myles, John F. 1989. *Old Age in the Welfare State: The Political Economy of Public Pensions,* rev. ed. Lawrence, KS: University of Kansas Press.

Myles, John and Jill Quadagno. 2002. "Political Theories of the Welfare State." *Social Service Review* 76, pp. 34–57.

N

Nadeau, Richard and Harold W. Stanley. 1993. "Class Polarization in Partisanship among Native Southern Whites, 1952–1990." *American Journal of Political Science* 37, pp. 900–919.

Nadeau, Richard, Richard Miemi, and Jeffrey Levine. 1993. "Innumeracy about Minority Population." *Public Opinion Quarterly* 57, pp. 332–347.

Nadel, Mark V. 1971. *The Politics of Consumer Protection.* Indianapolis: Bobbs Merrill.

Nagel, Joane. 1994. "Constructing Ethnicity: Creating and Recreating Ethnic Identity and Culture." *Social Problems* 41, pp. 152–176.

Nagel, Joane. 1995. "American Indian Ethnic Revival." *American Sociological Review* 60, pp. 947–965.

Nagler, Jonathan. 1991. "The Effect of Registration Laws and Education on U.S. Voter Turnout." *American Political Science Review* 85, pp. 1393–1405.

Nakagawa, Scot. 1995. "Race, Religion and the Right." In *Eyes Right,* ed. C. Berlet, pp. 279–288. Boston: South End Press.

Nakanishi, Don T. 2001. "Beyond Electoral Politics." In *Asian Americans and Politics,* ed. G. Chang, pp. 102–129. Stanford, CA: Stanford University Press.

Nakhaie, M. Reza. 1992. "Class and Voting Consistency in Canada: Analyses Bearing on the Mobilization Thesis." *Canadian Journal of Sociology, Cahiers Canadiens de Sociologie* 17, pp. 275–299.

Nalla, Mahesh K. and Graeme R. Newman. 1991. "Public versus Private Control: A Reassessment." *Journal of Criminal Justice* 19, pp. 537–547.

Nardulli, Peter F. 1995. "The Concept of a Critical Realignment, Electoral Behavior, and Political Change." *American Political Science Review* 89, pp. 10–22.

Nash, Kate. 2000. *Contemporary Political Sociology: Globalization, Politics and Power.* Malden, MA: Basil Blackwell.

Nation. "Saturday Night Censored," July 13, 1998.

Nee, Victor. 1998. "Sources of the New Institutionalism." In *The New Institutionalism in Sociology,* eds. M. Brinton and V. Nee, pp. 1–16. New York: Russell Sage Foundation.

Nee, Victor and Paul Ingram. 1998. "Embeddedness and Beyond: Institutions, Exchange and Social Structure." In *The New Institutionalism in Sociology,* eds. M. Brinton and V. Nee, pp. 19–45. New York: Russell Sage Foundation.

Nelson, Barbara. 1990. "The Origins of the Two-Channel Welfare State: Workmen's Compensation and Mother's Aid." In *Women, the State and Welfare,* ed. L. Gordon, pp. 123–151. Madison, WI: University of Wisconsin Press.

Nettl, J. P. 1968. "The State as a Conceptual Variable." *World Politics* 20, pp. 559–592.

Neuman, W. Lawrence. 1982. "Why Reform Fails: The Rise and Fall of Antimonopoly Reform in the United States, 1875–1975." PhD dissertation, University of Wisconsin-Madison.

Neuman, W. Lawrence. 1988a. "A Corporatist Experiment in Antitrust Regulation: The Federal Trade Commission's Trade Practice Conferences." *National Journal of Sociology* 2, pp. 33–68.

Neuman, W. Lawrence. 1988b. "Questions Of Working Class Formation In Late 19th Century America." Paper presented at the Midwest Sociological Society, Minneapolis, MN.

Neuman, W. Lawrence. 1998. "Negotiated Meanings and State Transformation: The Trust Issue in the Progressive Era." *Social Problems* 45, pp. 315–335.

Neuman, W. Lawrence. 2001. "Fear of the Alien Other: Cultural Anxiety and Opinions About Japan." *Sociological Inquiry* 71, pp. 335–356.

Neuman, W. Lawrence and Ronald J. Berger. 1988. "Competing Perspectives on Cross-national Crime: An Evaluation of Theory and Evidence." *Sociological Quarterly* 29, pp. 281–313.

Neuman, W. Russell. 1982. "Television and American Culture: The Mass Medium and the Pluralist Audience." *Public Opinion Quarterly* 46, pp. 471–487.

Neuman, W. Russell. 1986. *The Paradox of Mass Politics: Knowledge and Opinion in the American Electorate.* Cambridge: Harvard University Press.

Neuman, W. Russell, Marion R. Just, and Ann N. Crigler. 1992. *Common Knowledge: News and the Construction of Political Meaning.* Chicago: University of Chicago Press.

Neumann, Franz. 1944. *Behemoth: The Structure and Practice of National Socialism, 1933–1944.* New York: Oxford University Press.

Neustadtl, Alan. 1990. "Interest Group PACmanship: An Analysis of Campaign Contributions, Issue Visibility and Legislative Impact." *Social Forces* 69, pp. 549–564.

Neustadtl, Alan and Dan Clawson. 1988. "Corporate Political Groupings: Does Ideology Unify Business Political Behavior?" *American Sociological Review* 53, pp. 172–190.

Neustadtl, Alan, Denise Scott, and Dan Clawson. 1991. "Class Struggle in Campaign Finance? Political Action Committee Contributions in the 1984 Elections." *Sociological Forum* 6, pp. 219–239.

Newton, Lina Y. 2000. "Why Some Latinos Supported Proposition 187: Testing Economic Threat and Cultural Identity Hypotheses." *Social Science Quarterly* 81, pp. 180–193.

Nieberg, H. L. 1969. *Political Violence.* New York: St. Martins Press.

Noakes, John A. 2000. "Official Frames In Social Movement Theory: The FBI, HUAC, and the Communist Threat in Hollywood." *Sociological Quarterly* 41, pp. 657–680.

Noble, Charles. 1986. *Liberalism at Work: The Rise and Fall of OSHA.* Philadelphia: Temple University Press.

Noble, Charles. 1997. *Welfare as We Knew It: A Political History of the American Welfare State: A Political History of the American Welfare State.* New York: Oxford University Press.

Noble, David F. 1977. *America by Design: Technology and the Rise of Corporate Capitalism.* New York: Alfred Knopf.

Nobles, Melissa. 2000. *Shades of Citizenship: Race and the Census in Modern Politics.* Stanford, CA: Stanford University Press.

Noelle-Neumann, Elizabeth. 1984. *Spiral of Silence.* Chicago: University of Chicago Press.

Nordlinger, Eric. 1981. *On the Autonomy of the Democratic State.* Cambridge, MA: Harvard University Press.

Norrander, Barbara. 1997. "The Independence Gap and the Gender Gap." *Public Opinion Quarterly* 61, pp. 464–476.

Norris, Pippa. 1988. "The Gender Gap: A Cross-National Trend?" In *The Politics of Gender Gap: The Social Construction of Political Influence,* ed. C. M. Mueller, pp. 217–234. Newbury Park, CA: Sage.

North, Douglas C. 1998. "Economic Performances through Time." In *The New Institutionalism in Sociology,* eds. M. Brinton and V. Nee, pp. 247–257. New York: Russell Sage Foundation.

Nozick, Robert. 1974. *State, Anarchy and Utopia.* New York. Basic Books.

Nozick, Robert. 1995. *The Nature of Rationality.* Princeton, NJ: Princeton University Press.

Nunn, Clyde Z., Harry Crockett Jr., and William J. Allen Jr. 1978. *Tolerance for Nonconformity.* San Francisco: Jossey Bass.

Nye, Joseph S., Jr. 1997. "Introduction: The Decline of Confidence in Government." In *Why People Don't Trust Government,* eds. J. Nye, P. Zelikow, and D. King, pp. 1–18. Cambridge, MA: Harvard University Press.

O

O'Brien, Robert, Anne Goetz, Jan Scholte, and Marc Williams. 2000. *Contesting Global Governance: Multilateral Economic Institutions and Global Social Movements.* New York: Cambridge University Press.

O'Connor, Alice. 2000. "Poverty Research and Policy for the Post-welfare Era." *Annual Review of Sociology* 26, pp. 547–562.

O'Connor, Alice. 2001. *Poverty Knowledge: Social Science, Social Policy, and the Poor in 20th Century America.* Princeton, NJ: Princeton University Press.

O'Connor, Julia S. 1993. "Gender, Class, and Citizenship in the Comparative Analysis of Welfare Regimes." *British Journal of Sociology* 44, pp. 501–518.

O'Connor, James. 1973. *The Fiscal Crisis of the State.* New York: St. Martins.

O'Connor, James. 1984. *Accumulation Crisis.* New York: Basil Blackwell.

O'Connor, James. 1987. *The Meaning of Crisis.* New York: Basil Blackwell.

O'Riain, Seán. 2000. "States and Markets In An Era of Globalization." *Annual Review of Sociology* 26, pp. 187–213.

OECD (Organisation for Economic Co-operation and Development). 2001. *Tax and the Economy: A Comparative Assessment of OECD Countries No. 6.* Paris: OECD.

Oegema, Dirk and Bert Klandermans. 1994. "Why Social Movement Sympathizers Don't Participate: Erosion and Non-conversion of Support." *American Sociological Review* 59, pp. 703–722.

Oestreicher, Richard. 1988. "Urban Working Class Political Behavior and Theories of American Electoral Politics, 1870–1940." *Journal of American History* 74, pp. 1257–1286.

Offe, Claus. 1972a. "Political Authority and Class Structures—An Analysis of Late Capitalist Societies." *International Journal of Sociology* 2, pp. 73–108.

Offe, Claus. 1972b. "Advanced Capitalism and the Welfare State." *Politics and Society* 2, pp. 479–488.

Offe, Claus. 1973. "The Abolition of Market Control and the Problem of Legitimacy, Parts I and II." *Kapitalistate* 1–2: 08–116; 73–76.

Offe, Claus. 1974. "Structural Problems of the Capitalist State." *German Political Studies* 1, pp. 31–59.

Offe, Claus. 1976. "Political Authority and Class Structures." In *Critical Sociology,* ed. P. Connerton, pp. 388–421. Baltimore: Penguin.

Offe, Claus. 1984. *Contradictions of the Welfare State.* Cambridge, MA: MIT Press.

Ojito, Mirta. 1997. "Bias Suits Over English-Only Rules." *New York Times,* April 23, 1997.

Oldfield, Duane Murray. 1996. *The Right and the Righteous: The Christian Right Confronts the Republican Party.* Lanham, MD: Rowman and Littlefield.

Oliver, J. Eric. 1996. "The Effects of Eligibility Restrictions and Party Activity on Absentee Voting and Overall Turnout." *American Journal of Political Science* 40, pp. 498–513.

Oliver, J. Eric. 1999. "The Effects of Metropolitan Economic Segregation on Local Civic Participation." *American Journal of Political Science* 43, pp. 186–212.

Oliver, J. Eric. 2001. *Democracy in Suburbia.* Princeton, NJ: Princeton University Press.

Oliver, J. Eric. and Tali Mendelberg. 2000. "Reconsidering the Environmental Determinates of White Racial Attitudes." *American Journal of Political Science* 44, pp. 574–589.

Oliver, J. Eric and Raymond E. Wolfinger. 1999. "Jury Aversion and Voter Registration." *American Political Science Review* 93, pp. 147–156.

Oliver, Pamela E. and Gerald Marwell. 1992. "Mobilizing Technologies for Collective Action." In *Frontiers in Social Movement Theory,* eds. A. Morris and C. Mueller, pp. 251–272. New Haven, CT: Yale University Press.

Oliver, Pamela E. and Daniel J. Meyers. 1998. "Diffusion Models of Cycles of Protest as a Theory of Social Movements." Paper presented at the International Sociological Association (Montreal).

Oliver, Pamela E. and Daniel J. Meyers. 1999. "How Events Enter the Public Sphere: Conflict, Location and Sponsorship in Local Newspaper Coverage of Public Events." *American Journal of Sociology* 105, pp. 38–87.

Oliverio, Annamarie. 1997. "The State of Injustice: The Politics of Terrorism and the Production of Order." *International Journal of Comparative Sociology* 38, pp. 48–63.

Olsen, Marvin E. 1970. "Social and Political Participation of Blacks." *American Sociological Review* 35, pp. 682–697.

Olsen, Marvin E. and Martin Margar, eds. 1993. *Power in Modern Societies.* Boulder, CO: Westview Press.

Olsen, Marvin E. and Judy C. Tully. 1972. "Socioeconomic Ethnic Status Inconsistency and Preference for Political Change." *American Sociological Review* 37, pp. 560–574.

Olson, Marcur. 1965. *The Logic of Collective Action: Public Goods and the Theory of Groups.* Cambridge, MA: Harvard University Press.

Olson, Paulette Olson and Dell Champlin. 1998. "Ending Corporate Welfare as We Know It: An Institutional Analysis of the Dual Structure of Welfare." *Journal of Economic Issues* 32, pp. 759–771.

Olzak, Susan. 1989. "Labor Unrest, Immigration and Ethnic Conflict in Urban America, 1880–1914." *American Journal of Sociology* 94, pp. 1303–1333.

Olzak, Susan. 1990. "The Political Context of Competition: Lynching and Urban Racial Violence, 1882–1914." *Social Forces* 69, pp. 395–422.

Olzak, Susan and Johan L. Olivier. 1998. "Racial Conflict and Protest in South Africa and the United States." *European Sociological Review* 14, pp. 255–278.

Olzak, Susan, Suzanne Shanahan, and Elizabeth McEneaney. 1996. "Poverty, Segregation, and Race Riots, 1960 to 1993." *American Sociological Review* 61, pp. 590–613.

Omi, Michael and Howard Winant. 1994. *Racial Formation in the United States.* New York: Routledge.

O'Neill, Barry. 1995. "Weak Models, Nil Hypotheses, and Decorative Statistics." *Journal of Conflict Resolution.* 39, pp. 731–749.

Ong, Aihwa and Donald Nonini, eds. 1997. *Underground Empires: The Cultural-politics of Modern Chinese Transnationalism.* New York: Routledge.

Opp, Karl-Dieter and Christiane Gern. 1993. "Dissident Groups, Personal Networks, and Spontaneous Cooperation: The East German Revolution of 1989." *American Sociological Review* 58, pp. 659–680.

Orfield, Gary. 2001. "Schools More Separate: Consequences of a Decade of Resegregation." Harvard Civil Rights Project, Research Report, http://www.civilrightsproject.harvard.edu/research/deseg/call_separateschools.php?Page=2#fullreport.

Orfield, Gary and Susan Eaton. 1996. *Dismantling Desegregation: The Quiet Reversal of Brown v. Board of Education.* New York: New Press.

Orfield, Gary and John Yun. 1999. "Resegregation in American Schools." Harvard Civil Rights Project, Research Report, http://www.civilrightsproject.harvard.edu/research/deseg/reseg_schools99.php.

Orloff, Ann Shola. 1996. "Gender in the Welfare State." *Annual Review of Sociology* 22, pp. 51–78.

Orloff, Ann Shola. 1988. "The Political Origins of America's Belated Welfare State." In *Politics of Social Policy in the United States,* eds. M. Weir, A. S. Orloff, and T. Skocpol, pp. 37–80. Princeton, NJ: Princeton University Press.

Orloff, Ann Shola. 1993a. "Gender and Social Rights of Citizenship." *American Sociological Review* 58, pp. 303–328.

Orloff, Ann Shola. 1993b. *The Politics of Pensions: A Comparative Analysis of Britain, Canada and the United States, 1880–1940.* Madison, WI: University of Wisconsin Press.

Orloff, Ann Shola and Eric Parker. 1990. "Business and Social Policy Canada and the United States, 1920–1940." *Comparative Social Research* 12, pp. 295–339.

Orloff, Ann Shola and Theda Skocpol. 1984. "Why Not Equal Protection? Explaining the Politics of Public Social Spending in Britain 1900–1911, and the United States 1880s–1920." *American Sociological Review* 49, pp. 726–750.

Orr, James R. and Scott G. McNall. 1991. "Fraternal Orders and Working Class Formation in 19th Century Kansas." In *Bringing Class Back In,* eds. S. McNall, R. Levine, and R. Fantasia, pp. 101–118. Boulder, CO: Westview.

Orren, Karen. 1994. "Labor Regulation and Constitutional Theory in the United States and England." *Political Theory* 22, pp. 98–123.

Orren, Karen. 1995. "The Primacy of Labor in American Constitutional Development." *American Political Science Review* 89, pp. 377–389.

Orren, Karen and Stephen Skowronek. 1999. "Regimes and Regime Building in American Government: A Review of Literature on the 1940s." *Political Science Quarterly* 113, pp. 689–702.

Orum, Anthony M. 1966. "A reappraisal of the social and political participation of Negroes." *American Journal of Sociology* 72, pp. 32–46.

Orum, Anthony M. 1972. "Black Students in Protest." Washington, DC: American Sociological Association.

Orum, Anthony M. 1974. "On Participation in Political Protest Movements." *Journal of Applied Behavioral Science* 10, pp. 181–207.

Orum, Anthony M. 1996. "Almost a Half Century of Political Sociology: Trends in the United States." *Current Sociology* 44, pp. 132–151.

Orum, Anthony M. 2001. *Introduction to Political Sociology,* 4th ed. Upper Saddle River, NJ: Prentice Hall.

Ostrander, Susan A. 1984. *Women of the Upper Class.* Philadelphia PA: Temple University Press.

Ostrom, Elinor. 1998. "A Behavioral Approach to the Rational Choice Theory of Collective Action." *American Political Science Review* 92, pp. 1–22.

Owens, John R. and Larry L. Wade. 1988. "Constituency Voting in Great Britain." *Political Studies* 36, pp. 30–51.

P

Pacek, Alexander and Benjamin Radcliff. 1995. "Turnout and the Vote for Left-of-centre Parties: A Cross-national Analysis." *British Journal of Political Science* 25, pp. 137–142.

Page, Ann and Donald Clelland. 1978. "The Kanawha County Textbook Controversy: A Study in the Politics of Lifestyle." *Social Forces* 57, pp. 265–281.

Page, Benjamin I. and Robert Y. Shapiro. 1992. *The Rational Public: Fifty Years of Trends in American's Policy Preferences.* Chicago: University of Chicago Press.

Paige, Jeffrey M. 1971. "Political Orientation and Riot Participation." *American Sociological Review* 36, pp. 810–820.

Paige, Jeffrey M. 1975. *Agrarian Revolution.* New York: Free Press.

Pakulski, Han and Malcom Waters. 1996. "The Reshaping and Dissolution of Social Class in Advanced Society." *Theory and Society* 25, pp. 667–691.

Palast, Greg. 2003. *The Best Democracy Money Can Buy.* New York: Plume, Penguin.

Pampel, Fred C. and John B. Williamson. 1989. *Age, Class, Politics and the Welfare State.* New York: Cambridge University Press.

Pan, Zhongdang and Gerald Kosicki. 1994. "Voters' Reasoning Processes and Media Influence During the Persian Gulf War." *Political Behavior* 16, pp. 117–156.

Panitch, Leo. 1979. "The Development of Corporatism in Liberal Democracies." In *Trends in Corporatist Intermediation,* eds. P. Schmitter and G. Lehmbruch, pp. 119–146. Beverly Hills, CA: Sage.

Papadopoulos, Yannis. 1995. "Analysis of the Functional and Dysfunctions of Direct Democracy: Top Down and Bottom up Perspectives." *Politics and Society* 23, pp. 421–448.

Parker, Suzanne L. 1995. "Toward Understanding of 'Rally' Effects: Public Opinion in the Persian Gulf War." *Public Opinion Quarterly* 59, pp. 526–546.

Parker-Gwin, Rachel and William G. Roy. 1996. "Corporate Law and the Organization of Property in the United States." *Politics and Society* 24, pp. 111–135.

Parry, Geraint. 1969. *Political Elites.* New York: Praeger.

Parsa, Misagh. 1995. "Conversion or Coalition? Ideology in the Iranian and Nicaraguan Revolutions." *Political Power and Social Theory* 9, pp. 23–60.

Pateman, Carole. 1970. *Participation and Democratic Theory.* New York: Cambridge University Press.

Pateman, Carole. 1989. *The Disorder of Women: Democracy, Feminism and Democratic Theory.* Stanford, CA: Stanford University Press.

Pavalko, Eliza K. 1989. "State Timing of Policy Adoption: Workmen's Compensation in the United States, 1909–1929." *American Journal of Sociology* 95, pp. 592–615.

Paxton, Pamela. 1999. "Is Social Capital Declining in the United States? A Multiple Indicator Assessment." *American Journal of Sociology* 105, pp. 88–127.

Paxton, Robert O. 1998. "The Five Stages of Fascism." *Journal of Modern History* 70, pp. 1–23.

Payne, Stanely G. 1980. *Fascism: Comparison and Definition.* Madison, WI: University of Wisconsin Press.

Perlman, Selig and Philip Taft. 1935. *History of Labor in the United States, 1896–1932.* New York: Macmillan.

Perry, H. W. 1991. *Deciding to Decide: Agenda Setting in the United States Supreme Court.* Cambridge, MA.: Harvard University Press.

Perry, Martin, Lily Kong, and Brenda Yeoh. 1997. *Singapore: A Developmental City State.* New York: Wiley.

Peschek, Joseph. 1987. *Policy Planning Organizations, Elite Agendas and America's Rightward Turn.* Philadelphia: Temple University Press.

Peters, B. Guy and Martin Heisler. 1983. "Thinking About Public Sector Growth." In *Why Governments Grow,* ed. C. L. Taylor, pp. 175–197. Newbury Park, CA: Sage.

Peterson, Iver. 1997. "Press, Politics and Consensus in the New Old South." *New York Times,* February 24, 1997.

Peterson, Paul E. 1990–1991. "The Rise and Fall of Special Interest Politics." *Political Science Quarterly* 105, pp. 539–556.

Petras, James and Christian Davenport. 1991. "Crime and the Transformation of Capitalism." *Crime, Law and Social Change* 16, pp. 155–175.

Pettigrew, Thomas. 1998. "Reactions Toward Minorities in Western Europe." *Annual Review of Sociology* 24, pp. 77–103.

Pettit, Becky and Bruce Western. 2004. "Mass Imprisonment and the Life Course." *American Sociological Review* 69, pp. 151–170.

Pfaff, Steven. 1996. "Collective Identity and Informal Groups in Revolutionary Mobilization: East Germany in 1989." *Social Forces* 75, pp. 91–117.

Pfaff, Steven and Guobin Yang. 2001. "Double-edged Rituals and the Symbolic Resources of Collective Action: Political Commemorations and the Mobilization of Protest in 1989." *Theory and Society* 30, pp. 539–589.

Pfau-Effinger, Brigit. 1999. "Change of Family Policies in the Socio-cultural Context of European Societies." *Comparative Social Research* 18, pp. 135–159.

Phelan, Jo, Bruce Link, Ann Stueve, and Robert Moore. 1995. "Education, Social Liberalism and Economic Conservatism: Attitudes toward Homeless People." *American Sociological Review* 60, pp. 126–140.

Pichardo, Nelson. 1988. "Resource Mobilization: An Analysis of Conflicting Theoretical Variations." *Sociological Quarterly* 29, pp. 97–110.

Pichardo, Nelson. 1997. "New Social Mobilizations: A Critical Review." *Annual Review of Sociology* 23, pp. 411–430.

Pierson, Christopher. 1996. *The Modern State.* New York: Routledge.

Pierson, Paul. 1994. *Dismantling the welfare state?* New York: Cambridge University Press.

Pierson, Paul. 1996. "The New Politics of the Welfare State." *World Politics* 48, pp. 143–179.

Pierson, Paul. 2000. "Three Worlds of Welfare State Research." *Comparative Political Studies* 33, pp. 791–821.

Pierson, Paul. 2001. "Coping with Permanent Austerity." In *The New Politics of the Welfare State,* ed. P. Pierson, pp. 410–456. New York: Oxford University Press.

Piven, Frances Fox. 1998. "Welfare and the Transformation of Electoral Politics." In *Social Policy and the Conservative Agenda,* eds. C. Lo and M. Schwartz, pp. 21–36. New York: Blackwell.

Piven, Frances Fox. 2001. "Globalization, American Politics, and Welfare Policy." *Annals of the American Academy of Political and Social Science* 577, pp. 26–37.

Piven, Frances Fox and Richard A. Cloward. 1971. *Regulating the Poor.* New York: Pantheon Books.

Piven, Frances Fox and Richard A. Cloward. 1977. *Poor People's Movements: Why They Succeed and Why They Fail.* New York: Vintage.

Piven, Frances Fox and Richard A. Cloward. 1988. *Why Americans Don't Vote.* New York: Pantheon.

Piven, Frances Fox and Richard A. Cloward. 1992. "Normalizing Collective Protest." In *Frontiers in Social Movement Theory,* eds. A. Morris and C. M. Mueller, pp. 301–325. New Haven, CT: Yale University Press.

Piven, Frances Fox and Richard A. Cloward. 2000. *Why Americans Still Don't Vote: And Why Politicians Want It That Way.* Boston: Beacon.

Plutzer, Eric and John F. Zipp. 1996. "Identity Politics, Partisanship and Voting for Women Candidates." *Public Opinion Quarterly* 60, pp. 30–57.

Plutzer, Eric, Ardith Maney, and Robert E. O'Connor. 1998. "Ideology and Elites' Perceptions of the Safety of New Technologies." *American Journal of Political Science* 42, pp. 190–209.

Poggi, Gianfranco. 1973. "Political Sociology." *Cambridge Review* 9, pp. 33–37.

Poggi, Gianfranco. 1978. *The Development of the Modern State: A Sociological Introduction.* Stanford, CA: Stanford University Press.

Polletta, Francesca and James M. Jasper. 2001. "Collective Identity and Social Movements." *Annual Review of Sociology* 27, pp. 283–305.

Polsby, Nelson W. 1963. *Community Power and Political Theory.* New Haven, CT: Yale University Press.

Pomper, Gerald M. and Loretta A. Sernekos. 1991. "Bake Sales and Voting." *Society* 28, pp. 10–16.

Porter, Theodore M. 1995. *Trust in Numbers: The Pursuit of Objectivity in Social Science and Public Life.* Princeton, NJ: Princeton University Press.

Portes, Alejandro. 1971. "Political Primitivism, Differential Socialization and Lower-class Leftist Radicalism." *American Sociological Review* 36, pp. 820–835.

Portes, Alejandro. 1998. "Social Capital: Its Origins and Application in Modern Sociology." *Annual Review of Sociology* 24, pp. 1–24.

Poster, Mark. 1984. *Foucault, Marxism and History: Mode of Production versus Mode of Information.* New York: Polity Press.

Poulantzas, Nicos. 1973. *Political Power and Social Classes,* trans. Timothy O'Hagan. London: New Left Books.

Poulantzas, Nicos. 1974. *Fascism and Dictatorship.* trans. Judith White. London: New Left Books.

Poulantzas, Nicos. 1975. *Classes in Contemporary Capitalism,* trans. David Fernbach. Atlantic Highlands, NJ: Humanities Press.

Poulantzas, Nicos. 1976. "The Capitalist State." *New Left Review* 95, pp. 63–83.

Poulantzas, Nicos. 1978. *State, Power, Socialism,* trans. P. Camiller. London: New Left Books.

Poulantzas, Nicos. 1979. "The Political Crisis and the Crisis of the State." In *Critical Sociology.* ed. J. W. Freiburg, pp. 357–393. New York: Halsted.

Poveda, Tony G. 1992. "White Collar Crime and the Justice Department: The Institutionalization of a Concept." *Crime, Law and Social Change* 17, pp. 235–252.

Powell, G. Bingham. 1986. "American Voter Turnout in Comparative Perspective." *American Political Science Review* 80, pp. 17–43.

Powell, Walter W. 1987. "The Blockbuster Decade: The Media As Big Business." In *American Media and Mass Culture: Left Perspectives,* ed. D. Lazere, pp. 53–63. Berkeley, CA: University of California Press.

Powell, Walter W. and Paul J. Dimaggio. 1991. *The New Institutionalism in Organizational Analysis.* Chicago: University of Chicago Press.

Pratto, Felicia and Anthony F. Lemieux. 2001. "The Psychological Ambiguity of Immigration and Its Implications for Promoting Immigration Policy." *Journal of Social Issues* 57, pp. 413–430.

Pratto, Felicia, J. Liu, S. Levin, J. Sidanius, M. Shih, H. Bachrach, and P. Hegarty. 2000. "Social Dominance Orientation and the Legitimation of Inequality Across Cultures." *Journal of Cross-Cultural Psychology* 31, pp. 369–409.

Prechel, Harland. 1990. "Steel and the State: Industry Politics and Business Policy Formation, 1940–1989." *American Sociological Review* 55, pp. 648–668.

Prechel, Harland. 2000. *Big Business and the State: Historical Transitions and Corporate Transformation, 1880s–1990s.* Albany, NY: State University of New York Press.

Prechel, Harland. 2003. "Historical Contingency Theory, Policy Paradigm Shifts, and Corporate Malfeasance at the Turn of the 21st Century." *Research in Political Sociology* 14, pp. 311–340.

Prechel, Harland and John Boies. 1998. "Capital Dependence, Financial Risk, and Change from the Multidivisional to the Multilayered Subsidiary Form." *Sociological Forum* 13, pp. 321–362.

Press, Eyal and Jennifer Washburn. 2000. "The Kept University." *Atlantic Monthly* (March), pp. 39–52.

Pressen, Edward. 1984. *The Log Cabin Myth: The Social Backgrounds of the Presidents.* New Haven, CT: Yale University Press.

Preston, William, Jr. 1963. *Aliens and Dissenters: Federal Suppression of Radicals, 1903–1933.* Cambridge, MA: Harvard University Press.

Pring, George. W. and Penelope Canan. 1996. *SLAPPS: Getting Sued for Speaking Out.* Philadelphia: Temple University Press.

Przeworski, Adam. 1985. *Capitalism and Social Democracy.* New York: Cambridge University Press.

Pultzer, Eric. 1987. "Determinates of Leftist Racial Belief in the United States." *Social Forces* 65, pp. 1002–1019.

Puri, Jyoti. 2004. *Encountering Nationalism.* Malden, MA: Blackwell.

PuruShotam, Nirmala. 1997. *Negotiating Language, Constructing Race: Disciplining Difference in Singapore.* New York: Mouton de Gruyter.

Putnam, Robert D. 1993. *Making Democracy Work: Civil Traditions in Modern Italy.* Princeton, NJ: Princeton University Press.

Putnam, Robert D. 1995. "Bowling Alone." *Journal of Democracy* 6, pp. 65–78.

Pye, Lucien. 1971. "The Concept of Political Development." In *Political Development and Social Change,* eds. J. Finkle and R. Gable, pp. 43–51. New York: John Wiley.

Q

Quadagno, Jill. 1984. "Welfare Capitalism and the Social Security Act of 1935." *American Sociological Review* 49, pp. 632–648.

Quadagno, Jill. 1987. "Theories of the Welfare State." *Annual Review of Sociology* 13, pp. 109–128.

Quadagno, Jill. 1988. *The Transformation of Old Age Security: Class and Politics in the American Welfare State.* Chicago: University of Chicago Press.

Quadagno, Jill. 1990. "Race, Class and Gender in the U.S. Welfare State." *American Sociological Review* 55, pp. 11–28.

Quadagno, Jill. 1992. "Social Movements and State Transformation: Labor Unions and Racial Conflict in the War on Poverty." *American Sociological Review* 57, pp. 616–634.

Quadagno, Jill. 1994. *The Color of Welfare: How Racism Undermined the War on Poverty.* New York: Oxford University Press.

Quadagno, Jill. 1998. "Social Security Policy and the Entitlement Debate: The New American Exceptionalism." In *Social Policy and the Conservative Agenda,* eds. C. Lo and M. Schwartz, pp. 72–94. Malden, MA: Blackwell.

Quadagno, Jill. 1999. "Creating a Capital Investment Welfare State: The New American Exceptionalism." *American Sociological Review* 64, pp. 1–11.

Quadagno, Jill. 2000. "Another Face of Inequality: Racial and Ethnic Exclusion in the Welfare State." *Social Politics* 7, pp. 229–237.

Quigley, Fran. 1995. "United States Nonvoters: Assessing the Potential Impact of National Voter Registration Act of 1993." *Journal of Military and Political Sociology* 23, pp. 213–229.

Quigley, Margaret. 1995. "The Roots of the IQ Debate." In *Eyes Right,* ed. C. Berlet, pp. 210–223. Boston, MA: South End Press.

Quinn, Dennis and Robert Y. Shapiro. 1991a. "Economic Growth Strategies: The Effects of Ideological Partisanship on Interest Rates and Business Taxation in the United States." *American Journal of Political Science* 35, pp. 656–685.

Quinn, Dennis and Robert Y. Shapiro. 1991b. "Business Political Power: The Case of Taxation." *American Political Science Review* 85, pp. 851–874.

Quinney, Richard. 1974. "A Critical Theory of Criminal Law." In *Criminal Justice in America,* ed. R. Quinney, pp. 2–25. Boston: Little, Brown.

Quinney, Richard. 1977. *Class, State and Crime: On the Theory and Practice of Criminal Justice.* New York: David McKay.

R

Radcliff, Benjamin. 1992. "The Welfare State, Turnout, and the Economy: A Comparative Analysis." *American Political Science Review* 86, pp. 444–455.

Radcliff, Benjamin. 1994. "Turnout and the Democratic Vote." *American Politics Quarterly* 22, pp. 259–277.

Radcliff, Benjamin. 2001. "Organized Labor and Electoral Participation in American National Elections." Journal of Labor Research 22, pp. 405–414.

Radcliff, Benjamin and Patricia Davis. 2000. "Labor Organization and Electoral Participation in Industrial Democracies." *American Journal of Political Science* 44, pp. 132–141.

Radcliff, Benjamin and Martin Saiz. 1995. "Race, Turnout, and Public Policy In the American States." *Political Research Quarterly* 48, pp. 775–794.

Radelet, Michael L. and Marian J. Borg. 2000. "The Changing Nature of Death Penalty Debates." *Annual Review of Sociology* 26, pp. 43–61.

Rae, Nicol C. 1992. "Class and Culture: American Political Cleavages in the Twentieth Century." *Western Political Quarterly* 45, pp. 629–649.

Ragin, Charles C. 1994. "A Qualitative Comparative Analysis of Pensions Systems." In *The Comparative Political Economy of the Welfare State,* eds. T. Janoski and A. Hicks, pp. 320–345. New York: Cambridge University Press.

Ragsdale, Lyn and Jerrold G. Rusk. 1993. "Who Are Nonvoters? Profiles from the 1990 Senate Elections." *American Journal of Political Science* 37, pp. 721–746.

Ralph, John H. and Richard Rubinson. 1980. "Immigration and the Expansion of Schooling in the United States, 1890–1970." *American Sociological Review* 45, pp. 943–954.

Ramirez, Bruno. 1978. *When Workers Fight: The Politics of Industrial Relations in the Progressive Era, 1898–1916.* Westport, CT: Greenwood Press.

Ramirez, Francisco and John Boli. 1987. "The Political Construction of Mass Schooling: European Origins and Worldwide Institutionalization." *Sociology of Education* 60, pp. 2–17.

Ramirez, Francisco O., Yasemin Soysal, and Suzanne Shanahan. 1997. "The Changing Logic of Political Citizenship: Cross-national Acquisition of Women's Suffrage Rights, 1890–1990." *American Sociological Review* 62, pp. 735–745.

Rampton, Sheldon and John Stauber. 2003. *Weapons of Mass Deception: The Uses of Propaganda in Bush's War on Iraq.* New York: Tarcher/Putnam.

Ranger, Terence. 1983. "The Invention of Tradition in Colonial Africa.". In *The Invention of Tradition,* eds. E. Hobsbawn and T. Ranger, pp. 211–262. New York: Cambridge University Press.

Ransford, H. Edward. 1968. "Isolation, Powerlessness, and Violence: A Study of Attitudes and Participation in the Watts Riot." *American Journal of Sociology* 73, pp. 581–591.

Rapoport, Ronald, Walter Stone, and Alan Abramowitz. 1990. "Sex and the Caucus Participant: The Gender Gap and the Presidential Nominations." *American Journal of Political Science* 34, pp. 725–770.

Rasler, Karen. 1996. "Concessions, Repression, and Political Protest in the Iranian Revolution." *American Sociological Review* 61, pp. 132–152.

Ratcliff, Richard. 1980. "Declining Cities and Capitalist Class Structure." In *Power Structure Research,* ed. G. Domhoff, pp. 115–138. Beverly Hills, CA: Sage.

Reese, Ellen. 2001. "The Politics of Motherhood: The Restriction of Poor Mothers' Welfare Rights in the United States, 1949–1960." *Social Politics* 8, pp. 65–112.

Regnerus, Mark D., David Sikkink, and Christian Smith. 1999. "Voting with the Christian Right: Contextual and Individual Patterns of Electoral Influence." *Social Forces* 77, pp. 1375–1401.

Reiman, Jeffrey. 1990. *The Rich Get Richer and the Poor Get Prison: Ideology, Crime and Criminal Justice.* 4th ed. Needham Heights, MA: Allyn and Bacon.

Reimann, Kim D. 2001. "Building Networks from the Outside In: International Movements, Japanese NGOs, and the Kyoto Climate Change Conference." *Mobilization* 6, pp. 69–82.

Reinarman, Craig. 1988. "The Social Construction of an Alcohol Problem: The Case of Mothers against Drunk Drivers and Social Control in the 1980s." *Theory and Society* 17, pp. 91–120.

Rempel, Michael. 1998. "Expanding the Class Politics Debate: The Social Origins of Urban Political Cleavages in the United States." *Research in Political Sociology* 8, pp. 241–278.

Rhoades, Gary and Sheila Slaughter. 1991. "Professors, Administrators, and Patents: The Negotiation of Technology Transfer." *Sociology of Education* 64, pp. 265–277.

Rhoades, Gary and Sheila Slaughter. 1997. "Academic Capitalism, Managed Professionals, and Supply-Side Higher Education." *Social Text* 51, pp. 9–38.

Rice, Bradley R. 1977. *Progressive Cities: The Commission Government Movement in America, 1901–1920.* Austin, TX: University of Texas Press.

Rich, Andrew and R. Kent Weaver. 2000. "Think Tanks in the U.S. Media." *Harvard International Journal of Press/Politics* 5, pp. 81–103.

Richardson, Diane. 1998. "Sexuality and Citizenship." *Sociology* 32, pp. 83–100.

Rimlinger, Gaston. 1971. *Welfare Policy and Industrialization in Europe, America and Russia.* New York: Wiley.

Rivkin, Steven G. 1994. "Residential Segregation and School Integration." *Sociology of Education* 67, pp. 279–292.

Roberts, Julian V. and Loretta J. Stalans. 2000. *Public Opinion, Crime and Criminal Justice.* Boulder, CO: Westview.

Roberts, Ron E. and Robert M. Kloss. 1974. *Social Movements: Between the Balcony and the Barricade.* St. Louis: Mosby.

Robin, Ron Theodore. 2001. *Making of the Cold War Enemy.* Princeton, NJ: Princeton University Press.

Robinson, Michael. 1993. "Enduring Anxieties: Cultural Nationalism and Modern East Asia." In *Cultural Nationalism in East Asia: Representation and Identity,* ed. H. Befu, pp. 167–186. Berkeley, CA: University of California at Berkeley.

Robinson, Richard. 1986. "Class Formation Politics, and Institutions: Schooling in the United States." *American Journal of Sociology* 92, pp. 519–548.

Robinson, William L. 2001. "Social Theory and Globalization." *Theory and Society* 30, pp. 157–200.

Robnett, Belinda. 1996. "African-American Women in the Civil Rights Movement, 1954–1965: Gender, Leadership and Micromobilization." *American Journal of Sociology* 101, pp. 1661–1693.

Roche, Maurice. 1987. "Citizenship, Social Theory and Social Change." *Theory and Society* 16, pp. 363–399.

Roche, Maurice. 1992. *Rethinking Citizenship: Welfare, Ideology and Change in Modern Society.* Cambridge, UK: Polity Press.

Roche, Maurice. 1995. "Citizenship and Modernity." *British Journal of Sociology* 46, pp. 715–733.

Rochon, Thomas R. and Daniel A. Mazmanian. 1993. "Social Movements and the Policy Process." *Annals of the American Association of Public and Social Science* 528, pp. 75–87.

Rockman, Bert A. 1994. "The New Institutionalism and the Old Institutions." In *New Perspectives on American Politics,* eds. L. Dodd and C. Jillson, pp. 143–161. Washington, DC: Congressional Quarterly Press.

Rocscigno, Vincent J. and William F. Danaher. 2001. "Media and Mobilization: The Case of Radio and the Southern Textile Worker Insurgency, 1929 to 1934." *American Sociological Review* 66, pp. 21–48.

Rodan, Garry, ed, 2001. *Singapore.* Burlington, VT: Ashgate.

Rodriquez, Clara E. 2002. *Changing Race: Latinos, the Census and the History of Ethnicity in the United States.* New York: New York University Press.

Roemer, John E. 1994. "The Strategic Role of Party Ideology When Voters are Uncertain About How the Economy Works." *American Political Science Review* 88, pp. 327–335.

Rogin, Michael 1967. *The Intellectuals and McCarthy.* Cambridge: M.I.T. Press.

Rogowski, Ronald. 1989. *Commerce and Coalitions: How Trade Affects Domestic Political Alignments.* Princeton, NJ: Princeton University Press.

Romer, Thomas and James Snyder, Jr. 1994. "An Empirical Investigation of the Dynamics of PAC Contributions." *American Journal of Political Science* 38, pp. 745–769.

Roper, Brian S. 1991. "From the Welfare State to the Free Market: Explaining the Transition. Part II: Crisis, Class Ideology and the State." *New Zealand Sociology* 6, pp. 135–176.

Rose, Arnold. 1967. *The Power Structure: Political Process in American Society.* New York: Oxford University Press.

Rose, Richard. 1983. "Disaggregating the Concept of Government." In *Why Governments Grow,* ed. C. Taylor, pp. 157–176. Newbury Park, CA: Sage.

Rosenbaum, H. Jon and Peter Sederberg. 1976. *Vigilante Politics.* Philadelphia: University of Pennsylvania Press.

Rosenstone, Steven J. 1982. "Economic Adversity and Voter Turnout." *American Journal of Political Science* 26, pp. 25–46.

Rosenstone, Steven J. and John Mark Hansen. 1993. *Mobilization, Participation and Democracy in America.* New York: Macmillan.

Rosenstone, Steven J., Roy Behr, and Edward Lazarus. 1984. *Third Parties in America: Citizen Response to Major Party Failure.* Princeton, NJ: Princeton University Press.

Rosenthal, Uriel. 1983. "Welfare State or State of Welfare: Repression and Welfare in the Modern State." *Comparative Social Research* 6, pp. 279–297.

Rosenzweig, Roy and David Thelen. 1998. *The Presence of the Past: Popular Uses of History in American Life.* New York: Columbia University Press.

Ross, Dorothy. 1991. *The Origins of American Social Science.* New York: Cambridge University Press.

Ross, Jeffrey Ian. 1998. "Situating the Academic Study of Controlling State Crime." *Crime, Law and Social Change,* 1998, 29, pp. 331–340.

Rostow, W. W. 1960. *The Stages of Economic Growth: A Non-Communist Manifesto.* New York: Cambridge University Press.

Rotberg, Robert I. and Dennis Thompson, eds. 2000. *Truth v. Justice.* Princeton, NJ: Princeton University Press.

Rothstein, Bo. 1992. "Social Justice and State Capacity." *Politics and Society* 20, pp. 101–126.

Roundtree, Pamela Wilson and Kenneth C. Land. 1996. "Perceived Risk vs. Fear of Crime." *Social Forces,* 74, pp. 1353–1376.

Roy, William G. 1981. "The Vesting of Interests and Determinants of Political Power." *American Journal of Sociology* 81, pp. 1287–1310.

Roy, William G. 1991. "The Organization of the Corporate Class Segment of the U.S. Capitalist Class at the Turn of this Century.". In *Bringing Class Back In,* eds. S. McNall, R. Levin, and R. Fantasia, pp. 139–163. Boulder, CO: Westview.

Roy, William G. 1997. *Socializing Capital: The Rise of the Large Industrial Corporation in America.* Princeton, NJ: Princeton University Press.

Roy, William G. and Philip Bonacich. 1988. "Interlocking Directorates and Communities of Interest Among American Railroad Companies." *American Sociological Review* 53, pp. 368–379.

Rozell, Mark J. and Clyde Wilcox. 1996. *Second Coming: The New Christian Right in Virginia Politics.* Baltimore: Johns Hopkins University Press.

Rozell, Mark J., Clyde Wilcox, and John C. Green. 1998. "Religious Constituencies and Support for the Christian Right in the 1990s." *Social Science Quarterly* 79, pp. 815–827.

Rubin, Beth A. 1995. "Flexible Accumulation: The Decline of the Contract and Social Transformation." *Research in Social Stratification and Mobility* 14, pp. 297–323.

Rubin, Beth A. 1996. *Shifts in the Social Contract: Understanding Change in American Society.* Thousand Oaks, CA: Pine Forge Press.

Rubin, Steve. 1996. "Manhattan Institute." *Human Events* 52, p. 16.

Rubinson, Richard. 1986. "Class Formation, Politics, and Institutions: Schooling in the United States." *American Journal of Sociology* 92, pp. 519–48.

Rucht, Dieter. 1996. "The Impact of National Contexts on Social Movement Structures." In *Comparative Perspectives on Social Movements,* eds. D. McAdam, J. McCarthy, and M. Zald, pp. 185–204. New York: Cambridge University Press.

Rueschemeyer, Dietrich, Evelyne Huber Stephens, and John D. Stephens. 1992. *Capitalist Development and Democracy.* Chicago: University of Chicago Press.

Rusche, Georg and Otto Kirchheimer. 1939. *Punishment and Social Structure.* New York: Russell and Russell.

Rush, Gary. 1967. "Status Consistency and Rightwing Extremism." *American Sociological Review* 32, pp. 86–92.

Rush, Mark. 1994. "Gerrymandering: Out of the Political Thicket and into the Quagmire." *PS* 27, pp. 682–685.

Rusk, Jerrold G. 1970. "The Effect of the Australian Ballot Reform on Split Ticket Voting, 1876–1908." *American Political Science Review* 64, pp. 1220–1238.

Russell, Gregory. 1994. *The Death Penalty And Racial Bias: Overturning Supreme Court Assumptions.* Westport: Greenwood Press.

S

Sabato, Larry J. 1984. *PAC Power: Inside the World of Political Action Committees.* New York: W.W. Norton.

Sabato, Larry J. 1989. "Realignment: Reality or Reverie?" In *American Politics: Class and Contemporary Readings,* eds. A. Cigler and B. Loomis, pp. 235–246. New York: Houghton Mifflin.

Sabato, Larry J. 1996. *Dirty Little Secrets: The Persistence of Corruption in American Politics.* New York: Times Books.

Sacco, Vincent. 1995. "Media Construction of Crime." *Annals of American Academy of Political and Social Science* 539, pp. 141–154.

Sachs, Susan. 1999. "Pressed by Backlog, U.S. Rethinks Citizenship Test." *New York Times,* July 5, 1999.

Sainsbury, Diane, ed. 1996. *Gender, Equality, and Welfare States.* New York: Cambridge University Press.

Salamini, Leonardo. 1974. "Gramsci and Marxist Sociology of Knowledge." *Sociological Quarterly.* 15, pp. 359–380.

Salamon, Lester and John J. Siegfried. 1977. "Economic Power and Political Influence." *American Political Science Review* 71, pp. 1026–1043.

Sale, Kirkpatrick. 1975. *Power Shift: The Rise of the Southern Rim and Its Challenge to the Eastern Establishment.* New York: Vintage.

Salisbury, Robert H. 1979. "Why No Corporatism in America?" In *Trends in Corporatist Intermediation,* eds. P. Schmitter and G. Lehmbruch, pp. 213–230. Beverly Hills, CA: Sage.

Sallach, David L. 1974. "Class Domination and Ideological Hegemony." *Sociological Quarterly* 15, pp. 38–50.

Salopek, Phillip A. and Christopher Vanderpool. 1976. "Status Inconsistency and Democratic Party Preference: A Replication and Critique." *Journal of Political and Military Sociology* 4, pp. 29–38.

Saltzstein, Alan L. 1986. "Did Proposition 13 Change Spending Preferences?" *Research in Urban Policy* 2, pp. 145–157.

Sampedro, Victor. 1997. "The Media Politics of Social Protest." *Mobilization* 2, pp. 185–205.

Samuels, Richard J. 1994. *Rich Nation Strong Army.* Ithaca, NY: Cornell University Press.

Sanchez, Samantha. 1996. "How the West Was Won: Astroturf Lobbying and the 'Wise Use' Movement." *American Prospect* 25, pp. 37–42.

Sanders, Elizabeth. 1986. "Industrial Concentration, Sectoral Competition, and Antitrust Politics in America, 1880–1980." *Studies in American Political Development* 1, pp. 142–214.

Santoro, Wayne A. 1995. "Black Politics and Employment Policies: The Determinants of Local Government Affirmative Action." *Social Science Quarterly* 76, pp. 794–806.

Santoro, Wayne A. 1999. "Conventional Politics Takes Center Stage: The Latino Struggle Against English-only Laws." *Social Forces* 77, pp. 887–909.

Santoro, Wayne A. and Gail M. McGuire. 1997. "Social Movement Insiders: The Impact of Institutional Activists on Affirmative Action and Comparable Worth Policies." *Social Problems* 44, pp. 503–519.

Saporito, Salvatore. 2003. "Private Choices, Public Consequences: Magnet School Choice and Segregation by Race and Poverty." *Social Problems* 46, pp. 418–439.

Saporito, Salvatore and Annette Lareau. 1999. "School Selection as a Process: The Multiple Dimensions of Race in Framing Educational Choice." *Social Problems* 46, pp. 418–439.

Sarat, Austin. 1998. *The Killing State: Capital Punishment in Law, Politics and Culture.* New York: Oxford University Press.

Sarat, Austin and Joel Grossman. 1975. "Courts, Conflict Resolution: Problems of the Mobilization of Adjudication." *American Political Science Review* 69, pp. 1200–1217.

Sargent, Lyman Tower. 1987. *Contemporary Political Ideologies,* 7th ed. Chicago: Dorsey.

Sassen, Sasaki. 1999. *Globalization and Its Discontents.* New York: New Press.

Sassen, Sasaki. 2000. *The Global City, 2nd ed.* Princeton, NJ: Princeton University Press.

Sassen, Sasaki. 2001. *Global Networks, Linked Cities.* New York: Routledge.

Sasson, Anne Showstack. 1987. *Gramsci's Politics,* 2nd ed. London: Hutchinson.

Savage, J. A. 1995. "Astroturf Lobbying Replaces Grassroots Organizing." *Business and Society Review* 95, pp. 8–11.

Savage, James D. 1999. *Funding Science in America: Congress, Universities, and the Politics of the Academic Pork Barrel.* New York: Cambridge University Press.

Savelsberg, Joachim J. 1992. "Law That Does Not Fit Society: Sentencing Guidelines as a Neoclassical Reaction to the Dilemmas of Substantivized Law." *American Journal of Sociology* 97, pp. 1346–1415.

Savelsberg, Joachim J. 1994. "Knowledge, Domination and Criminal Punishment." *American Journal of Sociology* 99, pp. 911–943.

Savelsberg, Joachim J., Ryan King, and Lara Cleveland. 2002. "Politicized Scholarship? Science on Crime and the State." *Social Problems* 49, pp. 327–348.

Sawyers, Traci M. and David S. Meyer. 1999. "Missed Opportunities: Social Movement Abeyance and Public Policy." *Social Problems* 46, pp. 187–206.

Scattschneider, E. E. 1960. *The Semisovereign People: A Realist's View of Democracy in America.* New York: Holt, Rinehart and Winston.

Schaeffer, Robert K. 1997. *Understanding Globalization.* Lanham, MD: Rowman and Littlefield.

Scheb, John M. II and William Lyons. 2000. "The Myth of Legality and Public Evaluation of the Supreme Court." *Social Science Quarterly* 81, pp. 928–941.

Scheingold, Stuart A. 1991. *The Politics of Street Crime.* Philadelphia: Temple University Press.

Scheingold, Stuart A. 1995. "Politics, Public Policy, and Street Crime." *Annals of the American Association of Political and Social Science* 539, pp. 155–168.

Scheppele, Kim Lane. 1994. "Legal Theory and Social Theory." *Annual Review of Sociology* 20, pp. 383–406.

Schiesl, Martin J. 1977. *The Politics of Efficiency, Municipal Administration, and Reform in America, 1880–1920.* Berkeley, CA: University of California Press.

Schiller, Herbert I. 1989. *Culture, Inc: The Corporate Takeover of Public Expression.* New York: Oxford University Press.

Schlesinger, Jacob M. 1999. *Shadow Shoguns: The Rise and Fall of Japan's Postwar Political System.* Stanford, CA: Stanford University Press.

Schlosser, Eric. 1998. "The Prison-Industrial Complex." *Atlantic Monthly* (December), pp. 51–77.

Schlozman, Kay Lehman, Nancy Burns, Sidney Verba, and Jesse Donahue. 1995. "Gender and Citizen Participation: Is There a Different Voice?" *American Journal of Political Science* 39, pp. 267–291.

Schmidt, Manfred G. 1983. "The Growth of the Tax State: The Industrial Democracies, 1950–1978." In *Why Governments Grow,* ed. C. L. Taylor, pp. 261–285. Newbury Park, CA: Sage.

Schmidt, Vivien A. 2002. "Does Discourse Matter in the Politics of Welfare State Adjustment?" *Comparative Political Studies* 35, pp. 168–193.

Schmitt, Eric. 1996. "House Approves Measure on Official U.S. Language." *New York Times,* August 2, 1996.

Schmitter, Philippe. 1974. "Still the Century of Corporatism?" *Review of Politics* 36, pp. 85–130.

Schneider, Anne and Helen Ingram. 1993. "Social Construction of Target Populations: Implications for Politics and Policy." *American Political Science Review* 87, pp. 334–347.

Schneider, Anne and Helen Ingram. 1995. "Response." *American Political Science Review* 89, pp. 441–446.

Schneider, Paul Teske, Melissa Marshall, and Christine Roch. 1998. "Shopping for Schools: In the Land of the Blind, The One-Eyed Parent May Be Enough." *American Journal of Political Science* 42, pp. 769–793.

Schneider, Paul Teske, Christine Roch, and Melissa Marshall. 1997. "Networks to Nowhere: Segregation and Stratification in Networks of Information About Schools." *American Journal of Political Science* 41, pp. 1201–1223.

Schneider, Saundra K. 1982. "The Sequential Development of Social Programs in Eighteen Welfare States." *Comparative Social Research* 5, pp. 195–219.

Schram, Sanford F. 1995. *Words of Welfare: The Poverty of Social Science and the Social Science of Poverty.* Minneapolis: University of Minnesota Press.

Schram, Sanford F. and Joe Soss. 2001. "Success Stories: Welfare Reform, Policy Discourse, and the Politics of Research." *Annals of the American Academy of Political and Social Science* 577, pp. 49–65.

Schram, Sanford F. and J. Patrick Turbett. 1983. "Civil Disorder and the Welfare Explosion: A Two-Step Process." *American Sociological Review* 48, pp. 408–414.

Schram, Sanford F., Lawrence Nitz, and Gary Krueger. 1998. "Without Cause or Effect: Reconsidering Welfare Migration as a Policy Problem." *American Journal of Political Science* 42, pp. 210–230.

Schrecker, Ellen W. 1986. *No Ivory Tower: McCarthyism and the Universities.* New York: Oxford University Press.

Schudson, Michael. 1978. *Discovering the News: A Social History of American Newspapers.* New York: Basic Books.

Schudson, Michael. 1995. *The Power of News.* Cambridge, MA: Harvard University Press.

Schultz, Bud and Ruth Schultz, eds. 1989. *It Did Happen Here: Recollections of Political Repression in America.* Berkeley, CA: University of California Press.

Schultz, Kenneth A. 1995. "The Politics of the Political Business Cycle." *British Journal of Political Science* 25, pp. 79–99.

Schuman, Howard. 1972. "Two Sources of Antiwar Sentiment in America." *American Journal of Sociology* 78, pp. 513–536.

Schuman, Howard and Lawrence Bobo. 1988. "Survey-based Experiments on White Racial Attitudes towards Residential Integration." *American Journal of Sociology* 94, pp. 273–299.

Schuman, Howard and Maria Krysan. 1999. "A Historical Note on Whites' Beliefs about Racial Inequality." *American Sociological Review* 64, pp. 847–855.

Schuman, Howard, Lawrence Bobo, and Maria Krysan. 1992. "Authoritarianism in the General Population: The Education Interaction Hypothesis." *Social Psychology Quarterly* 55, pp. 379–387.

Schuman, Howard, Charles Steeh, and Lawrence Bobo. 1985. *Racial Attitudes in America.* Cambridge, MA: Harvard University Press.

Schumpeter, Joseph A. 1950. *Capitalism, Socialism and Democracy,* 3rd ed. New York: Harper and Row.

Schwartz, Barry. 1987. *George Washington: The Making of an American Symbol.* Ithaca, NY: Cornell University Press.

Schwartz, Barry. 1991a. "Social Change and Collective Memory: The Democratization of George Washington." *American Sociological Review* 56, pp. 221–236.

Schwartz, Barry. 1991b. "Iconography and Collective Memory: Lincoln's Image in the American Mind." *Sociological Quarterly* 32, pp. 301–320.

Schwartz, Barry. 1995. "Deconstruction and Reconstructing the Past." *Qualitative Sociology* 18, p. 263.

Schwartz, Barry. 1996a. "Introduction: The Expanding Past." *Qualitative Sociology* 19, pp. 275–282.

Schwartz, Barry. 1996b. "Memory as a Cultural System: Abraham Lincoln in World War II." *American Sociological Review* 61, pp. 908–928.

Schwartz, Barry. 1997. "Collective Memory and History: How Abraham Lincoln Became a Symbol of Racial Equality." *Sociological Quarterly* 38, pp. 469–495.

Schwartz, Barry. 1998. "Postmodernity and Historical Reputation: Abraham Lincoln in Late Twentieth-century American Memory." *Social Forces* 77, pp. 63–104.

Schwartz, Barry and Todd Bayma. 1999. "Commemoration and the Politics of Recognition." *American Behavioral Scientist* 42, pp. 946–968.

Schwartz, Michael and Shuva Paul. 1992. "Resource Mobilization versus the Mobilization of People." In *Frontiers in Social Movement Theory,* eds. A. Morris and C. M. Mueller, pp. 205–223. New Haven, CT: Yale University Press.

Schwartz, Mildred. 1981. "Politics and Moral Causes in Canada and the United States." *Comparative Social Research* 4, pp. 65–90.

Schwartzman, Kathleen C. 1998. "Globalization And Democracy." *Annual Review of Sociology* 24, pp. 159–181.

Schwendinger, Herman and Julia R. Schwendinger. 1974. *The Sociologists of the Chair: A Radical Analysis of the Formative Years of North American Sociology.* New York: Basic.

Scott, Jacqueline and Howard Schuman. 1988. "Attitude Strength and Social Action in the Abortion Dispute." *American Sociological Review* 53, pp. 785–793.

Scott, Janny. 1997. "Intellectuals Who Became Influential." *New York Times,* May 12, 1997.

Scott, John. 1991. *Who Rules Britain?* Cambridge, MA: Polity Press.

Scott, John. 1996. *Corporate Business and Capitalist Classes.* New York: Oxford University Press.

Sears, David, and Jack Citrin. 1982. *Tax Revolt.* Cambridge, MA: Harvard University Press.

Sears, David O. 1988. "Symbolic Racism." In *Eliminating Racism: Means and Controversies,* eds. P. Katz and D. Taylor, pp. 53–84. New York: Plenum.

Sears, David O. and Carolyn Funk. 1999. "Evidence of the Long-term Persistence of Adults' Political Predispositions." *Journal of Politics* 61, pp. 1–28.

Sears, David O. and Nicholas A. Valentino. 1997. "Politics Matters: Political Events as Catalysts for Pre-adult Socialization." *American Political Science Review* 91, pp. 45–66.

Sears, David O., Colette Van Laar, Mary Carrillo, and Rick Kosterman. 1997. "Is It Really Racism? The Origins of White Americans' Opposition to Race-targeted Policies." *Public Opinion Quarterly* 61, pp. 16–53.

See, Katherine O'Sullivan. 1986. *First World Nationalisms: Class and Ethnic Politics in Northern Ireland and Quebec.* Chicago: University of Chicago Press.

Seelye, Katharine. "Americans Take a Dim View of Government, Survey Finds." *New York Times,* March 10, 1998.

Seelye, Katharine. 1997. "Lott Calls Gifts the 'American Way.'" *New York Times,* February 21, 1997.

Segal, David. 1969. "Status Inconsistency, Cross Pressures, and American Political Behavior." *American Sociological Review* 34, pp. 352–358.

Segal, David and David Knoke. 1968. "Social Mobility, Status Inconsistency and the Partisan Realignment of the United States." *Social Forces* 47, pp. 154–157.

Segal, David and David Knoke. 1972. "The Impact of Social Stratification, Social Mobility and Status Inconsistency on German Party Infrastructure." *Journal of Political and Military Sociology* 1, pp. 18–37.

Segal, Jeffrey A. and Harold J. Spaeth. 1993. *The Supreme Court and the Attitudinal Model.* New York: Cambridge University Press.

Segal, Jeffrey A. and Harold J. Spaeth. 1996. "The Influence of *Stare Decisis* on the Votes of Supreme Court Justices." *American Journal of Political Science* 40, pp. 971–1003.

Segal, Jeffrey A., Lee Epstein, and Charles Cameron. 1995. "Ideological Values and the Votes of U.S. Supreme Court Justices Revisited," *Journal of Politics* 57, pp. 812–823.

Seidel, Gill. 1986. "Culture, Nation and 'Race' in the British and French New Right." In *The Ideology of the New Right,* ed. R. Levitas, pp. 107–135. New York: Polity Press.

Selznick, Philip. 1996. "Institutionalism 'Old' and 'New'." *Administrative Science Quarterly* 41, pp. 270–277.

Seron, Carroll and Frank Munger. 1996. "Law and Inequality." *Annual Review of Sociology* 22, pp. 187–212.

Seton-Watson, Hugh. 1977. *Nations and States: An Inquiry into the Origins of Nations and the Politics of Nationalism.* London: Metheun.

Sewell, William H., Jr. 1980. *Work and Revolution in France: The Language of Labor from the Old Regime to 1848.* New York: Cambridge University Press.

Shaffer, Tim S., Larry Reynolds, and David Gruenenfelder. 1982. "Liberal Bias and Conservative Capitulation: A Case Study of Government Pressure and Mass Media Response." *Quarterly Journal of Ideology* 5, pp. 27–31.

Shalev, Michael. 1983. "The Social Democratic Model and Beyond: Two Generations of Comparative Research on the Welfare State." *Comparative Social Research* 6, pp. 315–351.

Shamir, Jacob and Michael Shamir. 1997. "Pluralistic Ignorance Across Issues and Over Time." *Public Opinion Quarterly* 61, pp. 227–260.

Shanahan, Suzanne. 1997. "Different Standards and Standard Differences: Contemporary Citizenship and Immigration Debates." *Theory and Society* 26, pp. 421–448.

Shapiro, Robert Y. and Harpert Mahajan. 1986. "Gender Differences in Policy Preferences." *Public Opinion Quarterly* 50, pp. 42–61.

Shapiro, Virginia and Pamela Johnson Conover. 1997. "The Variable Gender Basis of Electoral Politics: Gender and Context in the 1992 U.S. Election." *British Journal of Political Science* 27, pp. 497–523.

Shaver, Sheila. 2002. "Gender, Welfare, Regimes, and Agency." *Social Politics* 9, pp. 203–211.

Shaw, Daron, Rodolfo del la Garza, and Jongho Lee. 2000. "Examining Latino Turnout in 1996: A Three-State, Validated Survey Approach." *American Journal of Political Science* 44, pp. 338–340.

Shaw, Greg M., Robert Y. Shapiro, Shmuel Lock, and Lawrence Jacobs. 1998. "Trends: Crime, the Police, and Civil Liberties." *Public Opinion Quarterly* 62, pp. 405–426.

Shea, Dorothy C. 2000. *The South African Truth Commission: The Politics of Reconciliation.* Washington, DC: U.S. Institute of Peace Press.

Shearing, Clifford and Philip Stenning. 1983. "Private Security: Implications for Social Control." *Social Problems* 30, pp. 493–506.

Shearing, Clifford and Philip Stenning, eds. 1987. *Private Policing.* Newbury Park, CA: Sage Publications.

Shefter, Martin. 1979. "Party Bureaucracy and Political Change in the United States." In *Development of Political Parties* Vol. 4, eds. L. Maisela and J. Cooper, Sage Electoral Studies Yearbook, pp. 211–265. Beverly Hills, CA: Sage.

Shefter, Martin. 1985. *Political Crisis, Fiscal Crisis: The Collapse and Revival of New York City.* New York: Basic Books.

Shefter, Martin. 1993. "Regional Receptivity to Reform: Legacy of the Progressive Era." *Political Science Quarterly* 98, pp. 459–483.

Shenon, Philip. 1998. "Senators Keep Gay Nominee for Luxembourg Post in Limbo." *New York Times,* March 8, 1998.

Shepsle, Kenneth A. and Barry R. Weingast. 1981. "Political Preferences for the Pork Barrel: A Generalization." *American Journal of Political Science* 25, pp. 96–111.

Sheridan, Alan. 1980. *Michel Foucault: The Will to Truth.* New York: Tavistock.

Sherkat, Darren E. and Jean Blocker. 1994. "The Political Development of Sixties' Activists: Identifying the Influence of Class, Gender and Socialization on Protest Participation." *Social Forces.* 72, pp. 821–842.

Sherkat, Darren E. and Jean Blocker. 1997. "Explaining the Political and Personal Consequences of Protest." *Social Forces* 75, pp. 1049–1070.

Sherkat, Darren E. and Alfred Darnell. 1999. "The Effect of Parents' Fundamentalism on Children's Educational Attainment." *Journal for the Scientific Study of Religion* 38, pp. 23–35.

Shichor, David. 1995. *Punishment for Profit: Private Prisons/Public Concerns.* Thousand Oaks, CA: Sage.

Shingles, Richard D. 1981. "Black Consciousness and Political Participation: The Missing Link." *American Political Science Review* 75, pp. 76–91.

Shoch, Jim. 1994. "The Politics of the U.S. Industrial Policy Debate, 1981–1984." In *Social structures of accumulation,* ed. D. Kotz, T. McDonough, and M. Reich, pp. 173–190. New York: Cambridge University Press.

Shonfield, Andrew. 1965. *Modern Capitalism: The Changing Balance of Public and Private Power.* New York: Oxford University Press.

Short, James F., Jr. 1997. "The Place of Rational Choice in Criminology and Risk Analysis." *American Sociologist* 28, pp. 61–72.

Shoup, Laurence H. and William Minter. 1979. *Imperial Brain Trust: The Council on Foreign Relations and American Foreign Policy.*

Sidanius, Jim and Felicia Pratto. 1999. *Social Dominance: An Intergroup Theory of Social Hierarchy and Oppression.* New York: Cambridge University Press.

Sidanius, Jim, Felicia Pratto, and Lawrence Bobo. 1996. "Racism, Conservatism, Affirmative Action and Intellectual Sophistication." *Journal of Personality and Social Psychology* 70, pp. 476–490.

Sigelman, Carol K. and Lee Sigelman. 1995. "Black Candidates, White Voters: Understanding Racial Bias in Political Perceptions." *American Journal of Political Science* 39, pp. 241–265.

Sigelman, Lee, Clyde Wilcox, and Emmett Buell, Jr. 1987. "An Unchanging Minority: Popular Support for the Moral Majority, 1980 and 1984." *Social Science Quarterly* 68, pp. 876–884.

Sikkink, David. 1999. "The Social Sources of Alienation from Public Schools." *Social Forces* 78, pp. 51–86.

Silberman, Bernard S. 1993. *Cages of Reason: The Rise of the Rational State in France, Japan, the United States and Great Britain.* Chicago: University of Chicago Press.

Silva, Eduardo. 1993. "Capitalist Coalitions, the State, and Neoliberal Economic Restructuring: Chile, 1973–88." *World Politics* 45, pp. 526–559.

Silva, Edward T. and Sheila A. Slaughter. 1980. "Prometheus Bound: The Limits of Social Science Professionalization in the Progressive Period." *Theory and Society* 9, pp. 781–819.

Silva, Edward T. and Sheila A. Slaughter. 1984. *Serving Power: The Making of the Academic Social Science Expert.* Westport, CT: Greenwood.

Simon, Herbert A. 1986. "Rationality in Psychology and Economics." *Journal of Business* 59, pp. 209–224.

Simon, Jonathan. 1999. "Paramilitary Features of Contemporary Penalty." *Journal of Political and Military Sociology* 27, pp. 279–290.

Simon, Roger. 1982. *Gramsci's Political Thought.* London: Lawrence and Wishart.

Simpson, John H. 1983. "Moral Issues and Status Politics." In *The New Christian Right: Mobilization and Legitimation,* eds. R. Liebman and R. Wuthnow, pp. 187–205. New York: Aldine.

Simpson, Sally S. 1986. "The Decomposition of Antitrust: Testing a Multi-level, Longitudinal Model of Profit Squeeze." *American Sociological Review* 51, pp. 859–875.

Simpson, Sally S. 1987. "Cycles of Illegality: Antitrust Violations in Corporate America." *Social Forces* 65, pp. 943–963.

Simpson, Sally S. and Nicole Leeper Piquero. 2002. "Low Self-control, Organizational Theory, and Corporate Crime." *Law & Society Review* 36, pp. 509–547.

Skerry, Peter. 2000. *Counting on the Census? Race, Group Identity, and the Evasion of Politics.* Washington, DC: Brookings Institution Press.

Skidmore, Dan and Davita Silfen Glasberg. 1996. "State Theory and Corporate Welfare: The Crisis and Bailout of the Savings and Loan Industry from a Contingency Perspective." *Political Power and Social Theory* 10, pp. 149–191.

Sklar, Holly, ed. 1980. *Trilateralism: The Trilateral Commission and Elite Planning for World Management.* Boston: South End Press.

Sklar, Martin J. 1992. *The United States as a Developing Country: Studies in U.S. History in the Progressive Era and the 1920s.* New York: Cambridge University Press.

Skocpol, Theda. 1979. *States and Revolutions.* New York: Cambridge University Press.

Skocpol, Theda. 1980. "Political Responses to Capitalist Crisis: Neo-Marxist Theories of the State and the Case of the New Deal." *Politics and Society* 10, pp. 155–202.

Skocpol, Theda. 1985. "Bringing the State Back In: Strategies of Analysis in Current Research." In *Bringing the State Back In,* eds. P. Evans, D. Rueschemeyer, and T. Skocpol, pp. 3–35. Princeton, NJ: Princeton University Press.

Skocpol, Theda. 1988. "The Limits of the New Deal System and the Roots of Contemporary Welfare Dilemmas." In *Politics of Social Policy in the United States,* eds. M. Weir, A. S. Orloff, and T. Skocpol, pp. 293–311. Princeton, NJ: Princeton University Press.

Skocpol, Theda. 1992a. *Protecting Soldiers & Mothers: The Political Origins of Social Policy in the United States.* Cambridge, MA: Harvard University Press.

Skocpol, Theda. 1992b. "State Formation and Social Policy in the United States." *The American Behavioral Scientist* 35, pp. 559–584.

Skocpol, Theda. 1993. "America's First Social Security System: The Expansion of Benefits for Civil War Veterans." *Political Science Quarterly* 108, pp. 85–116.

Skocpol, Theda. 1995a. "Why I Am an Historical Institutionalist." *Polity* 28, pp. 103–106.

Skocpol, Theda. 1995b. *Social Policy in the United States: Future Possibilities in Historical Perspective.* Princeton, NJ: Princeton University Press.

Skocpol, Theda. 1996. "Unravelling From Above," *The American Prospect* 25 (March–April), pp. 20–25.

Skocpol, Theda. 1997. "The GI Bill and U.S. Social Policy, Past and Future." In *The Welfare State,* eds. E. Paul, F. Miller, and J. Paul, pp. 95–115. New York: Cambridge University Press.

Skocpol, Theda and Edwin Amenta. 1985. "Did Capitalists Shape Social Security?" *American Sociological Review* 50, pp. 572–578.

Skocpol, Theda and Edwin Amenta. 1986. "States and Social Policies." *Annual Review of Sociology* 12, pp. 131–157.

Skocpol, Theda and John Ikenberry. 1983. "The Political Formation of the American Welfare State." *Comparative Social Research* 6, pp. 87–148.

Skocpol, Theda and Kenneth Finegold. 1982. "State Capacity and Economic Intervention in the Early New Deal." *Political Science Quarterly* 97, pp. 255–278.

Skocpol, Theda, Marjorie Abend-Wein, Christopher Howard, and Susan Lehmann. 1993. "Women's Associations and the Enactment of Mother's Pensions in the United States." *American Political Science Review* 87, pp. 686–701.

Skowronek, Steven. 1981. "National Railroad Regulation and the Problems of State-Building." *Politics and Society* 10, pp. 225–250.

Skowronek, Steven. 1982. *Building A New American State: The Expansion of National Administrative Capacities, 1877–1920.* Cambridge University Press.

Skrentny, John David. 1998. "The Effect of the Cold War on African-American Civil Rights: America and the World Audience, 1945–1968." *Theory and Society* 27, pp. 237–285.

Slater, Phil. 1977. *Origin and Significance of the Frankfurt School.* Routledge and Kegan Paul.

Slaughter, Shelia. 1988. "Academic Freedom and the State: Reflections on the Uses of Knowledge." *Journal of Higher Education* 59, pp. 241–262.

Slaughter, Shelia. 1990. *The Higher Learning and High Technology: Dynamics of Higher Education Policy Formation.* Albany, NY: State University of New York Press.

Slaughter, Sheila and Edward Silva. 1983. "Making Hegemony Problematic for the Professoriate: Power, Knowledge and the Concurrent Center in America's Higher Learning." *Educational Theory* 33, pp. 79–90.

Slaughter, Sheila and Edward Silva. 1985. "Towards a Political Economy of Retrenchment: The American Public Research Universities." *Review of Higher Education* 8, pp. 295–318.

Smart, Barry. 1985. *Michel Foucault.* New York: Tavistock.

Smelser, Neil J. 1963. *The Theory of Collective Behavior.* New York: Free Press.

Smelser, Neil J. 1992. "The Rational Choice Perspective." *Rationality and Society* 4, pp. 381–411.

Smith, A. Wade. 1981a. "Racial Tolerance as a Function of Group Position." *American Sociological Review* 46, pp. 558–573.

Smith, A. Wade. 1981b. "Tolerance of School Desegregation." *Social Forces* 59, pp. 1256–1274.

Smith, Anthony. 1980. *The Geopolitics of Information: How Western Culture Dominates the World.* New York: Oxford University Press.

Smith, Anthony D. 1979. *Nationalism in the 20th Century.* Oxford, UK: Martin Robertson.

Smith, Anthony D. 1986. *The Ethnic Origins of Nations.* New York: Basil Blackwell.

Smith, Anthony D. 1990. "The Suppression of Nationalism." *International Journal of Comparative Sociology* 31, pp. 1–31.

Smith, Jackie, John McCarthy, Clark McPhail, and Boguslaw Augustyn. 2001. "From Protest to Agenda Building: Descriptions of Bias in Media Coverage of Protest Events in Washington DC." *Social Forces* 79, pp. 1397–1424.

Smith, James Allen. 1990. *The Idea Brokers: Think Tanks and the Rise of the New Policy Elite.* New York: Free Press.

Smith, Kevin B. 1997. "Explaining Variation in State-Level Homicide Rates: Does Crime Policy Pay?" *Journal of Politics* 59, pp. 350–367.

Smith, Richard A. 1979. "Decision-making and Non-decision Making in Cities." *American Sociological Review* 44, pp. 147–161.

Smith, Robert B. 1997."Ideology, Partisanship, and the New Political Continuum. "*Society* 34, no. 3, pp. 13–18.

Smith, Tom W. 1987. "That Which We Call Welfare by Any Other Name Would Smell Sweeter." *Public Opinion Quarterly* 51, pp. 75–83.

Sniderman, Paul M. and Michael Gray Hagen. 1985. *Race and Inequality: A Study in American Values.* Chatham, NJ: Chatham House.

Sniderman, Paul M. and Philip E. Tetlock. 1986. "Symbolic Racism: Problems of Motive Attribution in Political Analysis." *Journal of Social Issues* 42, pp. 129–150.

Sniderman, Paul M., Richard A. Brody, and James Kuklinski. 1984. "Policy Reasoning and Political Values: The Problem of Racial Equality." *American Journal of Political Science* 28, pp. 75–94.

Sniderman, Paul M., Richard A. Brody, and Philip E. Tetlock. 1991. *Reasoning and choice.* New York: Cambridge University Press.

Sniderman, Paul M., Thomas Piazza, Philip E. Tetlock, and Ann Kendrick. 1991. "The New Racism." *American Journal of Political Science* 35, pp. 423–447.

Snow, David A. and Robert D. Benford. 1988. "Master Frames and Cycles of Protest." Paper presented at the "Workshop on Frontiers in Social Movement Theory." University of Michigan, Ann Arbor, Michigan.

Snow, David A. and Robert D. Benford. 1992. "Master Frames and Cycles of Protest." In *Frontiers in Social Movement Theory,* eds. A. Morris and C. M. Mueller, pp. 133–155. New Haven, CT: Yale University Press.

Snow, David A. and Robert D. Benford. 2000. "Clarifying the Relationship between Framing and Ideology." *Mobilization* 5, pp. 55–60.

Snow, David A. and Doug McAdam. 1999. "Identity Work Process in the Context of Social Movements." In *Self, Identity and Social Movements,* eds. S. Stryker, T. Owens, and R. White, pp. 41–67. Minneapolis: University of Minnesota.

Snow, David A., Louis Zurcher, Jr., and Sheldon Ekland-Olson. 1980. "Social Networks and Social Movements: Microstructural Approach to Differential Recruitment." *American Sociological Review* 45, pp. 787–801.

Snow, David A., E. Burke Rochford, Jr., Steven K. Worden, and Robert D. Benford. 1986. "Frame Alignment Processes, Micromobilization, and Movement Participation." *American Sociological Review* 51, pp. 464–481.

Sochen, June. 1981. *Herstory: A Record of Women's Past.* Palo Alto, CA: Mayfield.

Soley, Lawrence C. "Heritage Clones in the Heartland." *EXTRA!* (September/October, 1998).

Soley, Lawrence C. 1992. *The News Shapers: The Sources Who Explain the News.* New York: Praeger.

Soley, Lawrence C. 1995. *Leasing the Ivory Tower: The Corporate Takeover of Academia.* Boston, MA: South End Press.

Solinger, Dorthy J. 1999. *Contesting Citizenship in Urban China.* Berkeley, CA: University of California Press.

Solomon, Lawrence S., Donald Tomashovic-Devy, and Barbara Risman. 1989. "The Gender Gap and Nuclear Power: Attitudes in a Politicized Environment." *Sex Roles* 21, pp. 401–422.

Solomon, Norman. "The Manhattan Institute: Launch Pad for Conservative Authors." *EXTRA!* (March/April, 1998a).

Solomon, Norman. "Media Moguls on the Board: Murdoch, Malone and the Cato Institute." *EXTRA!* (January/February, 1998b).

Solomon, William S. 1993. "Framing Violence: Press Coverage of the L.A.P.D./Rodney King Beating and First Trial." *New Political Science* 27, pp. 85–104.

Somers, Margaret R. 1993. "Citizenship and the Place of the Public Sphere: Law, Community and Political Culture in the Transition to Democracy." *American Sociological Review* 58, pp. 587–620.

Somin, Ilya. 1998. "Voter Ignorance and the Democratic Ideal." *Critical Review* 12, pp. 413–458.

Somma, Mark. 1992. "The Gender Gap and Attitudes Toward Economic Development Strategies among Midwestern Adults." *Women and Politics* 12, pp. 41–57.

Soskice, David. 1999. "Divergent Production Regimes." In *Continuity and Change in Contemporary Capitalism,* eds. H. Kitschelt, P. Lange, G. Marks, and J. Stephens, pp. 101–134. New York: Cambridge University Press.

Soule, Sarah. 1992. "Populism and Black Lynching in Georgia, 1890–1900." *Social Forces* 71, pp. 431–450.

Soule, Sarah and Yvonne Zylan. 1997. "Runaway Train? The Diffusion of State-Level Reform in ADC/AFDC Eligibility Requirements, 1950–1967." *American Journal of Sociology* 103, pp. 733–762.

Southwell, Priscilla. 1986. "Alienation and Non-voting in the United States: The Crucial Interactive Effects among Independent Variables." *Journal of Political and Military Sociology* 14, pp. 249–361.

Southwell, Priscilla. 1987. "The Registered Non-voter: Alienation or Aberrance?" *Journal of Political and Military Sociology* 15, pp. 187–196.

Southwell, Priscilla. 1995. "Alienation and Non-voting in the 1992 Presidential Election." *Journal of Political and Military Sociology* 23, pp. 99–117.

Southwell, Priscilla. 1996. "Economic Salience and Differential Abstention in Presidential Elections." *American Politics Quarterly* 24, pp. 221–237.

Spector, Malcolm and John I. Kituse. 1977. *Constructing Social Problems.* Menlo Park, CA: Cummings Publishing.

Spitzer, Steven. 1975. "Towards a Marxian Theory of Deviance." *Social Problems* 22, pp. 638–651.

Spitzer, Steven. 1979. "The Rationalization of Crime Control in Capitalist Society." *Contemporary Crises* 3, pp. 187–206.

Spitzer, Steven. 1983. "Marxist Perspectives in the Sociology of Law." *Annual Review of Sociology* 9, pp. 101–124.

Spitzer, Steven and Andrew Scull. 1977. "Privatization and Capitalist Development: The Case of the Private Police." *Social Problems* 25, pp. 18–29.

Squire, Peverill, Raymond E. Wolfinger, and David P. Glass. 1987. "Residential Mobility and Voter Turnout." *American Political Science Review* 81, pp. 45–65.

Staggenborg, Suzanne. 1988. "The Consequences of Professionalization and Formalization in the Pro-choice Movement." *American Sociological Review* 53, pp. 585–606.

Staggenborg, Suzanne. 1989. "Organizational and Environmental Influences on the Development of the Pro-choice Movement." *Social Forces* 68, pp. 204–240.

Staggenborg, Suzanne. 1991. *The Pro-choice Movement: Organization and Activism in the Abortion Conflict.* New York: Oxford University Press.

Staggenborg, Suzanne. 1998. "Social Movement Communities and Cycles of Protest: The Emergence and Maintenance of a Local Women's Movement." *Social Problems* 45, pp. 180–204.

Stanger, Jeffrey D. and Douglas G. Rivlin. 1998. "Issue Advocacy Advertising During the 1997–1998 Election Cycle." University Park, PA: Anneberg Public Policy Center, University of Pennsylvania.

Stanley, Jay. 1996. "Harold Lasswell and the Idea of the Garrison State," *Society* 33, pp. 46–52.

Staples, William G. 1997. *The Culture Of Surveillance: Discipline and Social Control in the United States.* New York: St. Martin's Press.

Stark, Margaret, Walter Raine, Stephen Burbeck, and Keith Davison. 1974. "Some Empirical Patterns in a Riot Process." *American Sociological Review* 39, pp. 865–876.

Stearns, Linda B. and Kenneth Allan. 1996. "Economic Behavior in Institutional Environments: The Corporate Merger Wave of the 1980s." *American Sociological Review* 61, pp. 699–718.

Steedman, Carolyn. 1984. *Policing the Victorian Community.* London, Routledge, Kegan and Paul.

Steel, Brent S. and Nicholas P. Lovrich. 1998. "Determinants of Public Support for Tax and Expenditure Initiatives: An Oregon and Washington Case Study." *Social Science Journal* 35, pp. 213–229.

Steele, Janet E. 1995. "Experts and the Operational Bias of Television News: The Case of the Persian Gulf War." *Journalism and Mass Communication Quarterly* 72, pp. 799–812.

Stein, Robert M. and Kenneth N. Bickers. 1994. "Congressional Elections and the Pork Barrel." *Journal of Politics* 56, pp. 377–399.

Steinberger, Peter J. 1999. "Public and Private." *Political Studies* 67, pp. 292–313.

Steingold, Stuart A. 1995. "Political, Public Policy and Street Crime." *Annals of the American Academic of Political and Social Science* 539, pp. 155–168.

Steinmetz, George. 1999. "Introduction: Culture and the State." In *State/Culture: State Formation after the Cultural Turn,* ed. G. Steinmetz, pp. 1–50. Ithaca, NY: Cornell University Press.

Stephens, John D., E. Huber, and L. Ray. 1999. "The Welfare State in Hard Times." In *Continuity and Change in Contemporary Capitalism,* eds. H. Kitschelt, P. Lange, G. Markes, and J. Stephens, pp. 164–193. New York: Cambridge University Press.

Stevens, Beth. 1988. "Blurring Boundaries: How the Federal Government Has Influenced Welfare Benefits in the Private Sector." In *The Policy of Social Policy in the United States,* eds. M. Weir, A. S. Orloff, and T. Skocpol, pp. 123–148. Princeton, NJ: Princeton University Press.

Stevenson, David Lee and David P. Baker. 1991. "State Control of the Curriculum and Classroom Instruction." *Sociology of Education* 64, pp. 1–10.

Stewart, Angus. 1995. "Two Conceptions of Citizenship." *British Journal of Sociology* 46, pp. 63–78.

Stier, Haya, Noah Lewin-Epstein, and Michael Braun. 2001. "Welfare Regimes, Family-Supportive Policies, and Women's Employment along the Life-Course." *American Journal of Sociology* 106, pp. 1731–1760.

Stimson, James A. 1975. "Belief Systems: Constraint, Complexity and the 1972 Election." *American Journal of Political Science* 19, pp. 393–417.

Stimson, James A., Michael B. MacKuen, and Robert Erikson. 1995. "Dynamic Representation." *American Political Science Review* 89, pp. 543–565.

Stinchcombe, Arthur L. 1997. "On the Virtues of the Old Institutionalism." *Annual Review of Sociology* 23, pp. 1–18.

Stoecker, Randy. 1995. "Community, Movement, Organization: The Problem of Identity Convergence in Collective Action." *Sociological Quarterly* 36, pp. 111–130.

Stockwin, J. A. A. 1999. *Governing Japan,* 3rd ed. Malden, MA: Blackwell.

Stoker, Laura and M. Kent Jennings. 1995. "Life-cycle Transitions and Political Participation: The Case of Marriage." *American Political Science Review* 89, pp. 421–433.

Storper, Michael and Robert Salais. 1997. *Worlds of Production: The Action Frameworks of the Economy.* Cambridge, MA: Harvard University Press.

Stouffer, Samuel. 1955. *Communism, Conformity and Civil Liberties.* New York: Doubleday.

Stowers, Genie N. L. 1990. "Political Participation, Ethnicity, and Class Status: The Case of Cubans in Miami." *Ethnic Groups* 8, pp. 73–90.

Straits, Bruce C. 1990. "The Social Context of Voter Turnout." *Public Opinion Quarterly* 54, pp. 64–73.

Streeck, Wolfgang. 2001. "Introduction: Explorations into the Origins of Nonliberal Capitalism in Germany and Japan." In *The Origins of Non-liberal Capitalism,* eds. W. Streeck and K. Yamamura, pp. 1–38. Ithaca, NY: Cornell University Press.

Stretton, Hugh and Lionel Orchard. 1994. *Public Goods, Public Enterprise, Public Choice.* New York: Macmillan.

Stryker, Robin. 1989. "Limits on Technocratization of the Law: The Elimination of the National Labor Relation Board's Division of Economic Research." *American Sociological Review* 54, pp. 341–358.

Stryker, Robin. 1990a. "Law, Science and the Welfare State: A Class-Centered Functional Account." *American Journal of Sociology* 96, pp. 684–726.

Stryker, Robin. 1990b. "A Tale of Two Agencies: Class, Political-institutional and Organizational Factors Affecting State Reliance on Social Science." *Politics and Society* 18, pp. 101–141.

Stryker, Robin. 1994. "Rules, Resources, and Legitimacy Processes: Some Implications for Social Conflict, Order, and Change." *American Journal of Sociology* 99, pp. 847–910.

Stryker, Sheldon, Timothy Owens, and Robert White. 2000. "Social Psychology and Social Movements: Cloudy Past and Bright Future." In *Self, Identity and Social Movements,* eds. S. Stryker, T. Owens, and R. White, pp. 1–17. Minneapolis: University of Minnesota Press.

Studlar, Donley T., Ian McAllister, and Bernadette C. Hayes. 1998. "Explaining the Gender Gap in Voting: A Cross-National Analysis." *Social Science Quarterly* 79, pp. 779–799.

Su, Tie ting, Alan Neustadtl, and Dan Clawson. 1993. "Corporate PACs and Conservative Realignment: Comparison of 1980 and 1984." *Social Science Research* 22, pp. 33–71.

Su, Tie ting, Alan Neustadtl, and Dan Clawson. 1995. "Business and the Conservative Shift: Corporate PAC Contributions, 1976–1986." *Social Science Quarterly* 76, pp. 20–40.

Sugarman, David. 1983. "Introduction and Overview." In *Legality, Ideology and the State,* ed. D. Sugarman, pp. 1–11. New York: Academic Press.

Suh, Doowon. 2001. "How Do Political Opportunities Matter for Social Movements?" *Sociological Quarterly* 42, pp. 437–460.

Sullivan, John L. and George E. Marcus. 1988. "A Note on Trends in Political Tolerance." *Public Opinion Quarterly* 52, pp. 26–32.

Sullivan, John L., James Piereson, and George E. Marcus. 1979. "An Alternative Conceptualization of Illusory Increases, 1950s–1970s." *American Political Science Review* 73, pp. 781–794.

Sullivan, John L., James Piereson, and George E. Marcus. 1982. *Political Tolerance and American Democracy.* Chicago: University of Chicago Press.

Sumner, Colin. 1979. *Reading Ideologies: An Investigation into the Marxist Theory of Ideology and Law.* New York: Academic Press.

Sumner, Colin. 1983. "Law, Legitimation and the Advanced Capitalist State: The Jurisprudence and Social Theory of Jurgen Habermas." In *Legality, Ideology and the State,* ed. D. Sugarman, pp. 119–158. New York: Academic Press.

Sundquist, James L. 1973. *Dynamics of the Party System.* Washington, DC: Brookings Institution.

Sutton, John R. 1987. "Doing Time: Dynamics of Imprisonment in the Reformist State." *American Sociological Review* 52, pp. 612–630.

Sutton, John R. 1990. "Bureaucrats and Entrepreneurs: Institutional Responses to Deviant Children in the United States, 1890–1920s." *American Journal of Sociology* 95, pp. 1367–1400.

Sutton, John R. 1991. "The Political Economy of Madness: The Expansion of the Asylum in Progressive America." *American Sociological Review* 56, pp. 665–678.

Sutton, John R. 2000. "Imprisonment and Social Classification in Five Common-Law Democracies, 1955–1985." *American Journal of Sociology* 106, pp. 350–386.

Sutton, John R. 2004. "The Political Economy of Imprisonment in Affluent Western Democracies, 1960–1990." *American Sociological Review* 69, pp. 171–189.

Suzuki, Motoshi and Henry Chappell, Jr. 1996. "The Rationality of Economic Voting Revisited." *Journal of Politics* 58, pp. 224–236.

Svalifors, Stefan. 1997. "Worlds of Welfare and Attitudes to Redistribution: A Comparison of Eight Western Nations." *European Sociological Review* 13, pp. 283–304.

Swank, Duane. 1992. "Politics and the Structural Dependence of the State in Democratic Capitalism Nations." *American Political Science Review* 86, pp. 38–54.

Swank, Duane. 2001. "Political Institutions and Welfare State Restructuring." In *The New Politics of the Welfare State,* ed. P. Pierson, pp. 197–237. New York: Oxford University Press.

Swank, Duane. 2002. *Global Capital, Political Institutions, and Policy Change in Developed Welfare States.* New York: Cambridge University Press.

Swart, William J. 1995. "The League of Nations and the Irish Question: Master Frames, Cycles of Protest, and Master Frame Alignment." *Sociological Quarterly* 36, pp. 465–481.

Swartz, David. 1997. *Culture and Power: The Sociology of Pierre Bourdieu.* Chicago: University of Chicago Press.

Swedberg, Richard. 1997. "New Economic Sociology: What Has Been Accomplished, What is Ahead?" *Acta Sociologica* 40, pp. 161–182.

Swenson, Peter. 1997. "Arranged Alliance: Business Interests in the New Deal." *Politics and Society* 25, pp. 66–116.

Sykes, Charles J. 1988. *Profscam: Professors and the Demise of Higher Education.* New York: St. Martins.

Szalay, Lorand B., and Rita Mae Kelly. 1982. "Political Ideology and Subjective Culture: Conceptualization and Empirical Assessment." *American Political Science Review* 76, pp. 585–602.

Szasz, Andrew. 1984. "Industrial Resistance to Occupational Health and Safety Legislation, 1971–1981." *Social Problems* 32, pp. 103–116.

Szasz, Andrew. 1986. "The Reversal of Federal Policy toward Worker Safety and Health." *Science and Society* 50, pp. 25–51.

Szasz, Andrew. 1992. "Progress through Mischief: The Social Movement Alternative to Secondary Associations." *Politics and Society* 20, pp. 521–529.

T

Tarde, Gabriel. 1890. *The Laws of Imitation.* New York: Holt.

Tarrow, Sidney. 1988. "National Politics and Collective Action: Recent Theory and Research in Western Europe and the United States." *Annual Review of Sociology* 14, pp. 421–440.

Tarrow, Sidney. 1991. "Cycles of Collective Action: Between Moments of Madness and the Repertoire of Contention." *Social Science History* 17, pp. 291–308.

Tarrow, Sidney. 1992. "Mentalities, Political Cultures and Collective Action Frames." In *Frontiers in Social Movement Theory,* eds. A. Morris and C. M. Mueller, pp. 174–205. New Haven, CT: Yale University Press.

Tarrow, Sidney. 1993. "Modular Collective Action and the Rise of the Social Movement: Why the French Revolution Was Not Enough." *Politics and Society* 21, pp. 69–90.

Tarrow, Sidney. 1994. *Power in Movement.* New York: Cambridge University Press.

Tarrow, Sidney. 1996. "States and Opportunities." In *Comparative Perspectives on Social Movements,* eds. D. McAdam, J. McCarthy, and M. Zald, pp. 41–61. New York: Cambridge University Press.

Tarrow, Sidney. 1998a. " 'The Very Excess of Democracy." In *Social Movements and American Political Institutions,* eds. A. Costain and A. McFarland, pp. 20–38. Lanham, MD: Rowman and Littlefield.

Tarrow, Sidney. 1998b. "Social Protest and Policy Reform: May 1968 and the *Loi d'Orienation* in France." In *From Contention to Democracy,* eds. M. Giugni, D. McAdam, and C. Tilly, pp. 31–56. Landam, MD: Rowman and Littlefield.

Tatalovich, Raymond. 1995. *Nativism Reborn? The Official English Language Movement and the American States.* Lexington, KY: University of Kentucky Press.

Tate, Katherine. 1991. "Black Political Participation in the 1984 and 1988 Presidential Elections." *American Political Science Review* 85, pp. 1159–1176.

Tate, Katherine. 1994. *From Protest to Politics: The New Black Voters in American Politics,* enlarged ed. Cambridge, MA: Harvard University Press.

Taub, James. 1994. "Intellectual Stock Picking." *New Yorker* 69 (February 7, 1994), pp. 36–43.

Taylor, Charles Lewis (ed.). 1983. *Why Governments Grow. Measuring Public Sector Size.* Beverly Hills, CA: Sage.

Taylor, Marylee C. 1995. "White Backlash to Workplace Affirmative Action: Peril or Myth?" *Social Forces* 73, pp. 1385–1414.

Taylor, Verta. 1989. "Social Movement Continuity: The Women's Movement in Abeyance." *American Sociological Review* 54, pp. 761–775.

Taylor, Verta and Nancy E. Whittler. 1992. "Collective Identity in Social Movement Communities: Lesbian Feminist Mobilization." In *Frontiers in Social Movement Theory,* ed. A. Morris and C. M. Mueller, pp. 104–129. New Haven, CT: Yale University Press.

Teixeira, Ruy A. 1987. *Why American's Don't Vote: Turnout Decline in the United States, 1960–1984.* Westport, CT: Greenwood Press.

Teixeira, Ruy A. 1992. *The Disappearing American Voter.* Washington, DC: Brookings.

Terkildsen, Nayda. 1993. "When White Voters Evaluate Black Candidates." *American Journal of Political Science* 37, pp. 1032–1053.

Terry, Don. "Arizona Court Strikes Down Law Requiring English Use." *New York Times,* April 28, 1998.

Thelen, David. 1995. "History after the Enola Gay Controversy: An Introduction." *Journal of American History* 82, pp. 1029–1036.

Theoharis, Athan. 1978. *Spying on Americans: Political Surveillance from Hoover to the Huston Plan.* Philadelphia: Temple University Press.

Therborn, Göran. 1977. "The Rule of Capital and the Rise of Democracy." *New Left Review* 103, pp. 3–42.

Therborn, Göran. 1978. *What Does the Ruling Class Do When It Rules?* London: New Left Books.

Therborn, Göran. 1980. *The Ideology of Power and the Power of Ideology.* New York: Verso.

Therborn, Göran. 1987. "Welfare States and Capitalist Markets." *Acta Sociologica* 30, pp. 237–254.

Therborn, Göran. 1997. "The Rule of Capital and the Rise of Democracy." In *Classes and Elites in Democracy and Democratization,* ed. E. Etzioni-Halevy, pp. 134–149. New York: Garland.

Thistle, Susan. 2002. "Gender, Class and Welfare State Formation in the 21st Century." *Current Perspectives in Social Theory* 21, pp. 115–142.

Thomas, George M. 1989. *Revivalism and Cultural Change.* Chicago: University of Chicago Press.

Thomas, George M. and John W. Meyer. 1984. "The Expansion of the State." *Annual Review of Sociology* 10, pp. 461–482.

Thomas, Michael and Charles Flippen. 1972. "American Civil Religion: An Empirical Study." *Social Forces* 51, pp. 218–225.

Thompson, E. P. 1975. *Whigs and Hunters.* New York: Pantheon.

Thompson, Joel A. 1986. "Bringing Home the Bacon: The Politics of Pork Barrel in the North Carolina Legislature?" *Legislative Studies Quarterly* 11, pp. 91–108.

Thompson, John B. 1984. *Studies in the Theory of Ideology.* Berkeley, CA: University of California Press.

Thompson, Kenneth. 1986. *Beliefs and Ideology.* New York: Tavistock.

Thompson, Kenneth. 1998. *Moral Panics.* New York: Routledge.

Tigar, Michael E. and Madeleine R. Levy. 1977. *Law and the Rise of Capitalism.* New York: Monthly Review.

Tilly, Charles. 1975. "Reflections on the History of European State-making." In *The Formation of Nation States in Western Europe,* ed. C. Tilly, pp. 3–83. Princeton, NJ: Princeton University Press.

Tilly, Charles. 1975. *The Formation of Nation States in Western Europe.* Princeton, NJ: Princeton University Press.

Tilly, Charles. 1978. *From Mobilization to Revolution.* Reading, MA: Addison-Wesley.

Tilly, Charles. 1984. "Social Movements and National Politics." In *State Making and Social Movements,* eds. C. Bright and S. Harding, pp. 297-237. Ann Arbor, MI: University of Michigan Press.

Tilly, Charles. 1986. *The Contentious French: Four Centuries of Popular Struggles.* Cambridge, MA: Harvard University Press.

Tilly, Charles. 1996a. "Nationalism and the State." *Critical Review* 10, pp. 229–306.

Tilly, Charles. 1996b. "Citizenship, Identity and Social History." In *Citizenship, Identity and Social History,* ed. C. Tilly, pp. 1–18. New York: Cambridge University Press.

Tilly, Charles. 1997. "The Top-down and Bottom-up Construction of Democracy." In *Classes and Elites in Democracy and Democratization,* ed. E. Etzioni-Halevy, pp. 275–284. New York: Garland Publishers.

Tilly, Charles. 1999. "From Interactions to Outcomes in Social Movements." In *How Social Movements Matter,* eds. M. Giugni, D. McAdam, and C. Tilly, pp. 253–270. Minneapolis: University of Minnesota Press.

Timberlake, Jeffrey M., Kenneth Rasinski, and Eric Lock. 2001. "Effects of Conservative Sociopolitical Attitudes on Public Support for Drug Rehabilitation Spending." *Social Science Quarterly* 82, pp. 184–197.

Timpone, Richard J. 1995. "Mass Mobilization or Government Intervention? The Growth of Black Registration in the South." *Journal of Politics* 57, pp. 425–442.

Timpone, Richard J. 1998. "Structure, Behavior and Voter Turnout in the United States." *American Political Science Review* 92, pp. 145–158.

Tocqueville, Alexis de, [1831] 1964. *Democracy in America,* edited and intro. by Andrew Hacker. New York, Washington Square Press.

Tolbert, Pamela S. and Lynne G. Zucker. 1983. "Institutional Sources of Change in the Formal Structure of Organizations: The Diffusion of Civil Service Reform, 1880–1935." *Administrative Science Quarterly,* 28, pp. 22–39.

Tolnay, Steward E. and E. M. Beck. 1992. "Racial Violence and Black Migration in the American South, 1900." *American Sociological Review* 57, pp. 103–116.

Tolnay, Stewart E., E. M. Beck, and James L. Massey. 1989. "Black Lynchings: The Power Threat Hypothesis Revisited." *Social Forces* 67, pp. 605–623.

Tolnay, Stewart E., E. M. Beck, and James L. Massey. 1992. "Black Competition and White Vengeance: Legal Execution of Blacks as Social Control in the Cotton South, 1890–1929." *Social Science Quarterly* 73, pp. 627–643.

Tolnay, Steward E., Glenn Deane, and E. M. Beck. 1996. "Vicarious Violence: Spatial Effects on Southern Lynchings, 1890–1919." *American Journal of Sociology* 102, pp. 788–815.

Tomlins, Christopher. 1985. *The State and the Unions: Labor Relations, Law, and the Organized Labor Movement in America, 1880–1960.* New York: Cambridge University Press.

Torpey, John. 2000. *The Invention of the Passport: Surveillance, Citizenship and the State.* New York: Cambridge University Press.

Trevor, Margaret C. 1999. "Political Socialization, Party Identification and the Gender Gap." *Public Opinion Quarterly* 63, pp. 62–89.

Tremewan, Christopher. 1996. *The Political Economy of Social Control in Singapore.* New York: St. Martins.

Trimberger, Ellen Kay. 1978. *Revolution from Above: Military Bureaucrats and Development in Japan, Turkey, Egypt, and Peru.* New Brunswick, NJ: Transaction.

Tu, Wei-ming. 1994. "Cultural China: The Periphery as Center." In *The Living Tree: The Changing Meaning of Being Chinese Today,* ed. Tu Wei-ming, pp. 1–34. Stanford, CA: Stanford University Press.

Tuch, Steven A. 1987. "Urbanism, Region, and Tolerance Revisited: The Case of Racial Prejudice." *American Sociological Review* 52, pp. 504–510.

Tuchman, Gaye. 1973. "Making News by Doing Work: Routinizing the Unexpected." *American Journal of Sociology* 79, pp. 110–131.

Tuchman, Gaye. 1978. *Making News.* New York: Free Press.

Tuchman, Gaye. 1980. "Facts of the Moment: The Study of News." *Symbolic-Interaction* 3, pp. 9–20.

Turk, Austin T. 1976. "Law as a Weapon in Social Conflict." *Social Problems* 23, pp. 276–291.

Turk, Austin. T. 1982. *Political Criminality: The Defiance and Defense of Authority.* Beverly Hills, CA: Sage.

Turk, Austin. T. 2004. "The Sociology of Terrorism." *Annual Review of Sociology* 30, pp. 271–286.

Turner, Bryan S. 1986. *Citizenship and Capitalism.* London: Allyn and Unwin.

Turner, Bryan S. 1990. "Outline of a Theory of Citizenship." *Sociology* 21, pp. 189–217.

Turner, Bryan S. 1993a. "Contemporary Problems in the Theory of Citizenship." In *Citizenship and Social Theory,* ed. B. Turner, pp. 1–18. Newbury Park, CA: Sage.

Turner, Bryan S. 1993b. "Outline of a Theory of Human Rights." In *Citizenship and Social Theory,* ed. B. Turner, pp. 162–190. Newbury Park, CA: Sage.

Turner, Ralph H. 1969. "The Public Perception of Protest." *American Sociological Review* 34, pp. 815–830.

Turner, Stephen Park and Jonathan H. Turner. 1990. *The Impossible Science: An Institutional Analysis of American Sociology.* Newbury Park, CA: Sage.

U

Uggen, Christopher and Jeff Manza. 2002. "Democratic Contraction? Political Consequences of Felon Disenfranchisement in the United States." *American Sociological Review* 67, pp. 777–803.

Ungar, Sheldon. 1990. "Moral Panics, the Military-industrial Complex, and the Arms Race." *Sociological Quarterly* 31, pp. 165–185.

United Nations Children's Fund. 2002. "League Table on Child Poverty." Florence Italy: UNICEF Innocenti Research Centre.

Useem, Bert. 1980. "Solidarity Model, Breakdown Model, and the Boston Anti-busing Movement." *American Sociological Review* 45, pp. 357–369.

Useem, Bert. 1997. "The State and Collective Disorders: The Los Angeles Riot/Protest of April, 1992." *Social Forces* 76, pp. 357–378.

Useem, Michael. 1980. "Corporations and the Corporate Elite." *Annual Review of Sociology* 6, pp. 41–77.

Useem, Michael. 1983. "Business and Politics in the United States and the United Kingdom." *Theory and Society* 12, pp. 281–308.

Useem, Michael. 1984. *The Inner Circle: Large Corporations and the Rise of Business Political Activity in the U.S. and U.K.* New York: Oxford University Press.

Useem, Michael. 1987. "The Inner Circle and the Political Voice of Business." In *The Business Elite as a Ruling Class*, ed. M. Schwartz, pp. 143–153. New York: Holmes and Meier.

Useem, Michael and Jerome Karabel. 1986. "Pathways to Top Corporate Management." *American Sociological Review* 51, pp. 184–200.

Usui, Chikako. 1993. "The Origin and Development of Modern Welfare State Policies in 60 Countries, 1880–1975." *Research in Political Sociology* 6, pp. 39–69.

Usui, Chikako. 1994. "Welfare State Development in a World System Context." In *The Comparative Political Economy of the Welfare State*, eds. T. Janoski and A. Hicks, pp. 254–277. New York: Cambridge University Press.

V

Van Dyke, Nella. 1998. "Hotbeds of Activism: Locations of Student Protest." *Social Problems* 45, pp. 205–220.

Vago, Steven. 1991. *Law and Society*, 3rd ed. Englewood Cliffs, NJ: Prentice Hall.

Valelly, Richard M. 1993. "Party, Coercion, and Inclusion: The Two Reconstructions and the South's Electoral Politics." *Politics and Society* 21, pp. 37–67.

Valocchi, Steve. 1989. "The Relative Autonomy of the State and the Origins of British Welfare Policy." *Sociological Forum* 4, pp. 349–366.

Valocchi, Steve. 1990. "The Unemployed Workers Movement of the 1930s: A Reexamination of the Piven and Cloward Thesis." *Social Problems* 37, pp. 191–205.

Van Hear, Nicholas. 1998. *New Diasporas.* Seattle: University of Washington Press.

Van Natta, Don and Jane Fritsch. 1997. "$250,000 Buys 'The Best Access to Congress.'" *New York Times* (January 27, 1997).

van Steenbergen, Bart. 1994. "The Condition of Citizenship: An Introduction." In *The Condition of Citizenship* edited by B. van Steenberger, pp. 1–9. Thousand Oaks, CA: Sage.

Van Voorhis, Rebecca. 2002. "Different Types of Welfare States?" *Journal of Sociology and Social Welfare.* 29, pp. 3–18.

Verba, Sidney and Norman H. Nie. 1972. *Participation in America: Political Democracy and Social Equality.* New York: Harper and Row.

Verba, Sidney and Gary R. Orren. 1985. *Equality in America: The View From the Top.* Cambridge, MA: Harvard University Press.

Verba, Sidney, Norman Nie and Jae-on Kim. 1978. *Participation and Political Equality.* New York: Cambridge University Press.

Verba, Sidney, Kay Lehman Scholzman, and Henry Brady. 1993. "Race, Ethnicity and Political Resources: Participation in the United States." *British Journal of Political Science* 23, pp. 453–497.

Verba, Sidney, Kay Lehman Scholzman, Henry Brady and Norman H. Nie. 1993. "Citizen Activity: Who Participates? What Do They Say?" *American Political Science Review* 87, pp. 303–318.

Verber, Jean. 2001. "Falling Through the Safety Net." *Social Politics* 8, pp. 197–202.

Vincent, Andrew. 1987. *Theories of the State.* New York: Basil Blackwell.

Vito, Gennaro and Thomas Keil. 2000. "The Powell Hypothesis: Race and Non-Capital Sentences for Murder in Kentucky, 1976–1991." *American Journal of Criminal Justice* 24, pp. 287–300.

Vogel, David. 1978. "Why Businessmen Distrust Their State: The Political Consciousness of American Corporate Executives." *British Journal of Political Science* 8, pp. 45–78.

Vogel, David. 1981. "The 'New' Social Regulation in Historical and Comparative Perspective." In *Regulation in Perspective*, ed. T. McCraw, pp. 155–186. Cambridge, MA: Harvard University Press.

Vogel, David. 1983. "The Power of Business in America: A Reappraisal." *British Journal of Political Science* 13, pp. 19–43.

Vogel, David. 1996. *Kindred Strangers: The Uneasy Relationship Between Politics and Business in America.* Princeton, NJ: Princeton University Press.

Vogel, Ursula. 1991. "Is Citizenship Gender-specific?" In *The Frontiers of Citizenship*, eds. U. Vogel and M. Moranl, pp. 58–85. London: Macmillan.

Vogel, Ursula. 1994. "Marriage and the Boundaries of Citizenship." In *The Condition of Citizenship*, ed. B. van Steenbergen, pp. 76–89. Thousand Oaks, CA: Sage.

von Hayek, Friedrich A. 1994 [1944]. *Freedom from Serfdom.* Chicago: University of Chicago Press.

Voss, Kim. 1996. "The Collapse of a Social Movement." In *Comparative Perspectives on Social Movements*, eds. D. McAdam, J. McCarthy, and M. Zald, pp. 227–260. New York: Cambridge University Press.

W

Waddell, Brian. 1999. "Corporate Influence and World War II: Resolving the New Deal Political Stalemate." *Journal of Policy History* 11, pp. 223–256.

Wade, Robert. 1990. *Governing the Market.* Princeton, NJ: Princeton University Press.

Wadsworth, Nancy D. 1997. "Reconciliation Politics: Conservative Evangelicals and the New Race Discourse." *Politics and Society* 25, pp. 341–376.

Wagner, David and Marcia B. Cohen. 1991. "The Power of the People: Homeless Protesters in the Aftermath of Social Movement Participation." *Social Problems* 38, pp. 543–561.

Wagner-Pacifici, Robin and Barry Schwartz. 1991. "The Vietnam Veterans Memorial: Commemorating a Difficult Past." *American Journal of Sociology* 97, pp. 376–420.

Walby, Sylvia. 1994. "Is Citizenship Gendered?" *Sociology* 28, pp. 379–395.

Wald, Kenneth D., James W. Button, and Barbara Rienzo. 1996. "The Politics of Gay Rights in American Communities: Explaining Antidiscrimination Ordinances and Policies." *American Journal of Political Science* 40, pp. 1152–1178.

Wald, Kenneth D., Dennis Owen, and Samuel Hill. 1988. "Churches as Political Communities." *American Journal of Political Science* 82, pp. 531–548.

Waldmeir, Patti. 1998. *Anatomy of a Miracle: The End of Apartheid and the Birth of the New South Africa.* New Brunswick, NJ: Rutgers University Press.

Waldner, David. 1999. *State Building and Late Development.* Ithaca, NY: Cornell University Press.

Walker, Martin. 2000. "What Europeans Think of America." *World Policy Journal* 17, pp. 26–38.

Wallace, Anthony. 1956. "Revitalization Movements." *American Anthropologist* 58, pp. 264–281.

Wallerstein, Immanuel. 1976. *The Modern World System.* New York: Academic Press.

Wallerstein, Immanuel. 1991. *Geopolitics and Geoculture.* New York: Cambridge University Press.

Walters, Pamela Barnhouse. 1984. "Occupation and Labor Market Effects on Secondary and Postsecondary Educational Expansion in the United States: 1922–1979." *American Sociological Review* 49, pp. 659–671.

Walters, Pamela Barnhouse and Philip J. O'Connell. 1988. "The Family Economy, Work and Educational Participation in the United States, 1890–1940." *American Journal of Sociology* 93, pp. 1116–1152.

Walters, Pamela Barnhouse and Philip J. O'Connell. 1990. "Post-World War II Higher Educational Expansion, the Organization of Work, and Changes in Labor Productivity in the U.S." *Research in Sociology of Education & Socialization* 9, pp. 1–23.

Walters, Pamela Barnhouse and Richard Rubinson. 1983. "Educational Expansion and Economic Output in the United States, 1890–1969." *American Sociological Review* 48, pp. 480–493.

Walters, Pamela Barnhouse, David R. James, and Holly J. McCammon. 1997. "Citizenship and Public Schools: Accounting for Racial Inequality and Education in the Pre- and Post-disfranchisement South." *American Sociological Review* 62, pp. 34–52.

Walzer, Michael. 1988. "Socializing the Welfare State." In *Democracy and the Welfare State,* ed. Amy Gutmann, pp. 13–26. Princeton, NJ: Princeton University Press.

Wanta, Wayne and Yu-Wei Hu. 1994. "Time-lag Differences in the Agenda Setting Process: An Examination of Five News Media." *International Journal of Public Opinion Research* 6, pp. 225–240.

Warren, Mark E. 1996. "Deliberative Democracy and Authority." *American Political Science Review* 90, pp. 46–60.

Wasserman, Ira. 1979. "A Reanalysis of the Wallace Movement." *Journal of Political and Military Sociology.* 7, pp. 243–356.

Wasserman, Ira. 1990. "Status Politics and Economic Class Interests: The 1918 Prohibition Referendum in California." *Sociological Quarterly* 31, pp. 475–484.

Watanabe, Tsutomu. 2000. "Cross-national Analysis of Social Movements-effectiveness of the Concept of Political Opportunity Structure." (in Japanese). *Riron to Hoho / Sociological Theory and Methods* 15, pp. 135–148.

Waters, Malcolm. 1995. *Globalization.* New York: Routledge.

Wattenberg, Martin P. and Craig L. Brians. 1999. "Negative Campaign Advertising: Demobilizing or Mobilizer?" *American Political Science Review* 93, pp. 891–899.

Watts, Mark D., David Domke, and Dhavan V. Shah. 1999. "Elite Cues and Media Bias in Presidential Campaigns: Explaining Public Perceptions of a Liberal Press." *Communication Research* 26, pp. 44–75.

Wayne, Leslie. 1996. "Business is Biggest Campaign Spender, Study Says." *New York Times,* October 18, 1996.

Wayne, Leslie. 1997a. "Broadcast Lobby's Formula: Airtime + Money = Influence." *New York Times,* May 5, 1997.

Wayne, Leslie. 1997b. "A Back Door for the Conservative Donor." *New York Times,* May 22, 1997.

Weakliem, David L. 1993. "Class Consciousness and Political Change: Voting and Political Attitudes in the British Working Class, 1964–1970." *American Sociological Review* 58, pp. 382–397.

Weakliem, David L. 1997. "Race versus Class? Racial Composition and Class Voting, 1936–1992." *Social Forces,* pp. 939–956.

Weakliem, David L. and Anthony E. Heath. 1994. "Rational Choice and Class Voting." *Rationality and Society* 6, pp. 243–270.

Weale, Albert. 1991. "Citizenship Beyond Borders." In *The Frontiers of Citizenship*, eds. U. Vogel and M. Moranl, pp. 155–165. London: Macmillan.

Weatherford, M. Stephen. 1982. "Interpersonal Networks and Political Behavior." *American Journal of Political Science* 26, pp. 117–143.

Weaver, David H. 1996. "What Voters Learn from Media." *Annals of the American Association of Political and Social Science* 546, pp. 34–46.

Webber, Michael J. and G. William Domhoff. 1996. "Myth and Reality in Business Support for Democrats and Republicans in the 1936 Presidential Election." *American Political Science Review* 90, pp. 824–833.

Weber, Max. 1968. *Economy and Society* (2 volumes), eds. Guenther Roth and Claus Wittich. New York: Bedminster Press.

Weed, Frank J. 1989. "The Impact of Support Resources on Local Chapter Operations in the Antidrunk-driving Movement." *Sociological Quarterly* 30, pp. 77–91.

Weed, Frank J. 1990. "The Victim-activist Role in the Anti-drunk Driving Movement." *Sociological Quarterly* 31, pp. 459–473.

Weed, Frank J. 1991. "Organizational Mortality in the Anti-drunk-driving Movement: Failure among Local MADD Chapters." *Social-Forces,* 69, pp. 851–868.

Weglyn, Michi. 1976. *Years of Infamy: The Untold Story of America's Concentration Camps.* New York: Morrow.

Weil, Frederick D. 1982. "Tolerance of Free Speech in the United States and West Germany, 1970–79." *Social Forces* 60, pp. 973–992.

Weil, Frederick D. 1985. "The Variable Effects of Education on Liberal Attitudes." *American Sociological Review* 50, pp. 458–474.

Weingast, Barry R. 1995. "A Rational Choice Perspective on the Role of Ideas: Shared Belief Systems and State Sovereignty in International Cooperation." *Politics and Society* 23, pp. 449–464.

Weinstein, James. 1962. "Organized Business and the Commission and Manager Movements." *Journal of Southern History* 28, pp. 166–182.

Weinstein, James. 1968. *The Corporate Ideal in the Liberal State: 1900–1918.* Boston: Beacon.

Weir, Margaret. 1994. "Urban Poverty and Defensive Localism." *Dissent* 41 (Summer), pp. 337–342.

Weir, Margaret, Ann Shola Orloff, and Theda Skocpol, eds. 1988. *The Politics of Social Policy in the United States.* Princeton, NJ: Princeton University Press.

Weiss, Linda. 1998. *The Myth of the Powerless State.* Ithaca, NY: Cornell University Press.

Weissberg, Robert. 1998. *Political Tolerance: Balancing Community and Diversity.* Thousand Oaks, CA: Sage.

Welch, Michael. 2000. *Flag Burning: Moral Panic and the Criminalization of Protest.* New York: Aldine de Gruyter.

Welch, Michael and Jennifer Bryan. 1996. "Flag Desecration in American Culture: Offenses against Civil Religion and a Consecrated Symbol of Nationalism." *Crime, Law and Social Change* 26, pp. 77–93.

Welch, Michael and Jennifer Bryan. 1998. "Reactions to Flag Desecration in American Society: Exploring the Contours of Formal and Informal Social Control." *American Journal of Criminal Justice* 22, pp. 151–168.

Welch, Michael and Melissa Fenwick. 1997. "Primary Definitions of Crime and Moral Panic." *Journal of Research in Crime and Delinquency* 34, pp. 474–495.

Welch, Michael, Lisa Weber, and Walter Edwards. 2000. " 'All the News That's Fit to Print': A Content Analysis of Correctional Debate in the New York Times." *Prison Journal* 80, pp. 245–265.

Welch, Susan and Lee Sigelman. 1989. "A Black Gender Gap?" *Social Science Quarterly* 70, pp. 120–133.

Welch, Susan and Lee Sigelman. 1992. "A Gender Gap among Hispanics? A Comparison with Blacks and Anglos." *Western Political Quarterly* 45, pp. 181–199.

Welch, Susan and Lee Sigelman. 1993. "The Politics of Hispanic Americans: Insights from National Surveys, 1980–1988." *Social Science Quarterly* 76, pp. 76–94.

Welch, Susan, John Comer, and Michael Steinman. 1975. "Ethnic Differences in Social and Political Participation: A Comparison of Some Anglo and Mexican Americans." *Pacific Sociological Review* 18, pp. 361–382.

Wendt, Alexander. 1994. "Collective Identity Formation and the International State." *American Political Science Review* 88, pp. 384–396.

Western, Bruce. 1997. *Between Class and Market.* Princeton, NJ: Princeton University Press.

Wheeler, Mark. 1997. *Politics and the Mass Media.* Cambridge, MA: Basil Blackwell.

White, Gordon and Roger Goodman. 1998. "Welfare Orientalism and the Search for an East Asian Welfare Model." In *The East Asian Welfare Model*, eds. R. Goodman, G. White, and H. Kwon, pp. 3–24. New York: Routledge.

White, James Boyd. 1985. *Heracles' Bow: Essays on the Rhetoric and Poetics of the Law.* Madison, WI: University of Wisconsin Press.

Whitt, Hugh P. 1983. "Status Inconsistency: A Body of Negative Evidence or a Statistical Artifact?" *Social Forces* 62, pp. 201–233.

Whitt, J. Allen. 1979. "Toward a Class-dialectical Model of Power." *American Sociological Review* 44, pp. 81–99.

Whitt, J. Allen. 1982. *Urban Elites and Mass Transportation: The Dialectics of Power.* Princeton, NJ: Princeton University Press.

Whittier, Nancy. 1997. "Political Generations, Micro-cohorts, and the Transformation of Social Movements." *American Sociological Review* 62, pp. 760–778.

Wiebe, Robert H. 1967. *The Search for Order, 1877–1920.* New York: Hill and Wang.

Wielhouwer, Peter W. and Brad Lockerbie. 1994. "Party Contacting and Political Participation, 1952–1990." *American Journal of Political Science* 38, pp. 211–230.

Wiggershaus, Rolf. 1994. *The Frankfurt School: Its History, Theories and Political Significance,* trans. Michael Robertson. Cambridge, MA: M.I.T. Press.

Wilcox, Clyde. 1987. "America's Radical Right Revisited: A Comparison of the Activists in Christian Right Organizations from the 1960s to the 1980s." *Sociological Analysis* 48, pp. 46–57.

Wilcox, Clyde. 1989. "Popular Support for the New Christian Right." *Social Science Journal* 26, pp. 55–63.

Wilcox, Clyde. 1992. *God's Warriors: The Christian Right in Twentieth Century.* Baltimore: Johns Hopkins University Press.

Wilcox, Clyde. 1994. "Premillennialists at the Millennium: Some Reflections on the Christian Right in the Twenty-First Century." *Sociology of Religion* 55, pp. 243–261.

Wilcox, Clyde. 1997. "The Diverse Paths to Understanding Public Opinion." In *Understanding Public Opinion,* eds. B. Norrander and C. Wilcox, pp. 1–15. Washington, DC: Congressional Quarterly Press.

Wilcox, Clyde and Leopoldo Gomez. 1990. "Religion, Group Identification and Politics and American Blacks." *Sociological Analysis* 51, pp. 271–285.

Wilcox, Clyde and Lee Sigelman. 2001. "Political Mobilization in the Pews." *Social Science Quarterly* 82, pp. 524–535.

Wilcox, Clyde, Clifford W. Brown Jr., and Lynda Powell. 1993. "Sex and the Political Contributor: The Gender Gap among Contributors to Presidential Candidates in 1988." *Political Research Quarterly* 46, pp. 355–369.

Wilcox, Clyde, Matthew DeBell, and Lee Sigelman. 1999. "The Second Coming of the New Christian Right: Patterns of Popular Support in 1984 and 1996." *Social Science Quarterly* 80, pp. 181–192.

Wilcox, Clyde, Mark J. Rozell, and Roland Gunn. 1996. "Religious Coalitions in the New Christian Right." *Social Science Quarterly* 77, pp. 543–558.

Wilensky, Harold L. 1975. *The Welfare State and Equality.* Berkeley, CA: University of California Press.

Wilensky, Harold L. and Charles N. Lebeaux. 1958. *Industrial Society and Social Welfare.* New York: Russell Sage Foundation.

Wilkes, Christopher. 1991. "The Future of the State and the State of the Future in New Zealand." *Economic and Industrial Democracy* 12, pp. 535–544.

Wilkinson, Patrick. 1999. "The Selfless and the Helpless: Maternalist Origins of the U.S. Welfare State." *Feminist Studies* 25, pp. 571–597.

Williams, David S., James Jackon, and Tony Brown. 1999. "Traditional and Contemporary Prejudice and Urban White's Support for Affirmative Action and Government Help." *Social Problems* 46, pp. 503–527.

Williams, Katherine and Craig Johnson. 2000. "The Politics of the Selective Gaze: Closed Circuit Television and Policing the Public Space." *Crime, Law and Society* 34, pp. 183–210.

Williams, Paul and Julie Dickinson. 1993. "Fear of Crime: Read All about It." *Journal of Criminology* 33, pp. 33–56.

Williams, Rhys H. 1995. "Constructing the Public Good: Social Movements and Cultural Resources." *Social Problems.* 42, pp. 124–145.

Williams, Rhys H. and Susan Alexander. 1994. "Religious Rhetoric in American Populism: Civil Religion as a Movement Ideology." *Journal for the Scientific Study of Religion* 33, pp. 1–15.

Williams, Rhys H. and N. J. Demerath III. 1991. "Religion and Political Process in an American City." *American Sociological Review* 56, pp. 417–431.

Williams, William Applebaum. 1964. *The Great Evasion.* Chicago: Quadrangle.

Williamson, John B. and Joseph W. Weiss. 1979. "Egalitarian Political Movements, Social Welfare Effort, and Convergence Theory." *Comparative Social Research* 2, pp. 289–302.

Williamson, Peter J. 1985. *Varieties of Corporatism: Theory and Practice.* New York: Cambridge University Press.

Wilson, Richard A., Chris Arup, Martin Chanock, Pat O'Malley, Sally Engle Merry and Susan Silbey. 2001. *The Politics of Truth and Reconciliation in South Africa: Legitimizing the Post-apartheid State.* New York: Cambridge University Press.

Wilson, James Q. 1974. "The Politics of Regulation." In *Social Responsibility and the Business Predicament,* ed. J. McKie, pp. 135–168. Washington, DC: Brookings.

Wilson, James Q. 1980. "The Politics of Regulation." In *The Politics of Regulation,* ed. J. Wilson, pp. 357–394. New York: Basic Books.

Wilson, John. 1973. *Introduction to Social Movements.* New York: Basic Books.

Wilson, Kenneth L. 1979. "Status Inconsistency and the Hope Technique, I: The Grounds for a Resurrection." *Social Forces* 57, pp. 1229–1247.

Wilson, Thomas C. 1985. "Urbanism and Tolerance: A Test of Some Hypotheses Draw from Wirth and Stouffer." *American Sociological Review* 50, pp. 117–123.

Wilson, Thomas C. 1986. "Community Population Size and Social Heterogeneity: An Empirical Test." *American Journal of Sociology* 91, pp. 1154–1169.

Wilson, Thomas C. 1991. "Urbanism, Migration, and Tolerance: A Reassessment." *American Sociological Review* 56, pp. 117–123.

Wilson, Thomas C. 1992. "Urbanism and Nontraditional Opinion: Another Look at the Data." *Social Science Quarterly* 73, pp. 610–612.

Wilson, Thomas C. 1995. "Urbanism and Unconventionality: The Case of Sexual Behavior." *Social Science Quarterly* 76, pp. 346–363.

Wilson, Thomas C. 1996. "Cohort and Prejudice: White's Attitudes Toward Blacks, Hispanics, Jews and Asians." *Public Opinion Quarterly* 60, pp. 253–274.

Wilson, Thomas M. and Hastings Donnan. 1998. "Nation, State and Identity at International Borders." In *Border Identities,* eds. T. Wilson and H. Donnan, pp. 1–30. New York: Cambridge University Press.

Wilson, William Julius. 1994. "Citizenship and the Inner-city Ghetto Poor." In *The Condition of Citizenship*, ed. B. van Steenbergen, pp. 49–65. Thousand Oaks, CA: Sage.

Wilson, William Julius. 1996. *When Work Disappears: The World of the New Urban Poor*. New York: Vintage.

Wiltfang, Gregory and Doug McAdam. 1991. "The Costs and Risks of Social Activism: A Study of Sanctuary Movement Activism." *Social Forces* 69, pp. 987–1010.

Wimberly, Ronald C. 1979. "Continuity in the Measurement of Civil Religion." *Sociological Analysis* 40, pp. 59–62.

Wimberly, Ronald C. and James C. Christenson. 1980. "Civil Religion and Church and State." *Sociological Quarterly* 21, pp. 35–40.

Wimberly, Ronald C. and James C. Christenson. 1982. "Civil Religion, Social Indicators and Public Policy." *Social Indicators Research* 10, pp. 211–223.

Wimmer, Andreas. 2002. *Nationalist Exclusion and Ethnic Conflict: Shadows of Modernity*. New York: Cambridge University Press.

Winders, Bill. 1999. "The Roller Coaster of Class Conflict: Class Segments, Mass Mobilization and Voter Turnout in the U.S., 1840–1996." *Social Forces* 77, pp. 833–860.

Winkler, J. T. 1976. "Corporatism." *European Journal of Sociology* 17, pp. 100–136.

Wirls, Daniel. 1986. "Reinterpreting the Gender Gap." *Public Opinion Quarterly* 50, pp. 316–330.

Wirth, Louis. 1936. "Preface." In *Ideology and Utopia*, by Karl Mannheim. New York: Harcourt, Brace and Janovitch.

Wisler, Dominique and Marco Giugni. 1999. "Under the Spotlight: The Impact of Media Attention on Protest Policing." *Mobilization* 4, pp. 171–187.

Witte, John F. 2000. *The Market Approach to Education: An Analysis of America's First Voucher Program*. Princeton, NJ: Princeton University Press.

Wolf, Charlotte. 1992. "Constructions of Lynching" *Sociological Inquiry* 62, pp. 83–97.

Wolf, Eric R. 1969. *Peasant Wars of the Twentieth Century*. New York: Harper and Row.

Wolf, Eric R. 1999. *Envisioning Power: Ideologies of Dominance and Crisis*. Berkeley, CA: University of California Press.

Wolfe, Alan. 1973. *The Seamy Side of Democracy*. New York: David McKay.

Wolfinger, Raymond E. and Steven J. Rosenstone. 1980. *Who Votes?* New Haven, CT: Yale University Press.

Wolfson, Mark. 1995. "The Legislative Impact of Social Movement Organizations." *Social Science Quarterly* 76, pp. 311–327.

Wollstonecraft, Mary. 1796. *A Vindication of the Rights of Woman: with Strictures on Moral and Political Subjects*. Philadelphia PA: printed and sold by William Gibbons.

Wonders, Nancy and Frederic Solop. 1993. "Understanding the Emergence of Law and Public Policy: Toward a Relational Model of the State." In *Making Law*, eds. W. Chambliss and M. Zatz, pp. 204–225. Bloomington, IN: Indiana University Press.

Wong, Sandra L. 1991. "Evaluating the Content of Textbooks: Public Interests and Professional Authority." *Sociology of Education* 64, pp. 11–18.

Woo-Cummings, Meredith. 1991. *Race to the Swift*. New York: Columbia University Press.

Woo-Cummings, Meredith. 1999. ed. *The Developmental State*. Ithaca, NY: Cornell University Press.

Wood, B. Dan and James E. Anderson. 1993. "The Politics of U.S. Antitrust Enforcement." *American Journal of Political Science* 37, pp. 1–39.

Wood, James L. and Maurice Jackson. 1982. *Social Movements: Development, Participation, and Dynamics*. Belmont, CA: Wadsworth.

Wood, Michael and Michael Hughes. 1984. "The Moral Basis of Moral Reform." *American Sociological Review* 49, pp. 86–99.

Woodberry, Robert D. and Christian S. Smith. 1998. "Fundamentalism et al: Conservative Protestantism in America." *Annual Review of Sociology* 24, pp. 25–56.

Wright, Erik Olin. 1985. *Classes*. New York: Verso.

Wright, Erik Olin. 1991. "The Conceptual Status of Class Structure in Class Analysis." In *Bringing Class Back In: Contemporary and Historical Perspectives*, eds. S. McNall, R. Levine, and R. Fantasia, pp. 17–38. Boulder, CO: Westview.

Wright, Erik Olin. 2000. "Working-class Power, Capitalist-class Interests, and Class Compromise." *American Journal of Sociology* 105, pp. 957–1002.

Wright, Erik Olin and Donmoon Cho. 1992. "State Employment, Class Location and Ideological Orientation: A Comparative Analysis of the United States and Sweden." *Politics and Society* 20, pp. 167–196.

Wright, James D. 1976. *Dissent of the Governed*. New York: Academic Press.

Wrigley, Julia. 1982. *Class Politics and Public Schools: Chicago, 1900–1950*. New Brunswick, NJ: Rutgers University Press.

Wrong, Dennis. 1979. *Power: Its Forms, Bases and Uses*. New York: Harper and Row.

Wuthnow, Robert. 1987. *Meaning and Moral Order*. Berkeley, CA: University of California Press.

Wysong, Earl, Richard Aniskiewicz, and David Wright. 1994. "Truth and DARE: Tacking Drug Education to Graduation as Symbolic Politics." *Social Problems*, 41, pp. 448–472.

Y

Yasui, Minoru. 1989. "In Defense of the Constitution." In *It Did Happen Here: Recollections of Political Repression in America*, eds. B. Schultz and R. Schultz, pp. 347–359. Berkeley, CA: University of California Press.

Yeager, Peter C. 1987. "Structural Bias in Regulatory Law Enforcement: The Case of the U.S. Environmental Protection Agency." *Social Problems* 34, pp. 330–344.

Yeager, Peter C. 1991. *The Limits of Law: The Public Regulation of Private Pollution.* New York: Cambridge University Press.

Yee, Albert S. 1997. "Thick Rationality and the Missing 'Brute Fact': The Limits of Rationalist Incorporations of Norms and Ideas." *Journal of Politics.* 59, pp. 1001–1039.

Yoshino, Kosaku. 1992. *Cultural Nationalism in Contemporary Japan.* New York: Routledge.

Young, Richard P. and Jerome Burstein. 1995. "Federalism and the Demise of Prescriptive Racism in the United States." *Studies in American Political Development* 9, pp. 1–54.

Young, Robert L. 1985. "Perceptions of Crime, Racial Attitudes and Firearms Ownership." *Social Forces* 64, pp. 473–487.

Z

Zafirovski, Milan. 1999a. "Political Behavior in the Social Milieu: Toward Rehabilitation of the Classical Tradition of Political Sociology." *International Review of Sociology* 9, pp. 41–73.

Zafirovski, Milan. 1999b. "Public Choice Theory for Political Sociology." *International Journal of Politics, Culture and Society* 12, pp. 465–502.

Zald, Mayer, N. 1985. "Political Change, Citizenship Rights, and the Welfare State." *Annals of the American Academy of Political and Social Science* 479, pp. 48–66.

Zald, Mayer, N. 1996. "Culture, Ideology, and Strategic Framing." In *Comparative Perspectives on Social Movements,* eds. D. McAdam, J. McCarthy, and M. Zald, pp. 261–274. New York: Cambridge University Press.

Zald, Mayer N. and Michael A. Berger. 1978. "Social Movements in Organizations: Coup d'Etat, Insurgency, and Mass Movements." *American Journal of Sociology* 83, pp. 823–861.

Zaller, John R. 1992. *The Nature and Origins of Mass Opinion.* New York: Cambridge University Press.

Zaret, David. 1996. "Petitions and the 'Invention' of Public Opinion in the English Revolution." *American Journal of Sociology* 101, pp. 1497–1555.

Zeitlin, Maurice. 1974. "Corporate Ownership and Control: The Large Corporation and the Capitalist Class." *American Journal of Sociology* 70, pp. 1073–1119.

Zeitlin, Maurice. 1980, ed. *Classes, Class Conflict and the State: Empirical studies in Class Analysis.* Cambridge, MA: Winthrop.

Zeitlin, Maurice and Richard Earl Ratcliff. 1988. *Landlords and Capitalists the Dominant Class of Chile.* Princeton, NJ: Princeton University Press.

Zeitlin, Maurice, W. Lawrence Neuman, and Richard E. Ratcliff. 1976. "Class Segments: Agrarian Property and Representative Political Activity in the Capitalist Class of Chile." *American Sociological Review* 41, pp. 1006–1029.

Zelditch, Morris, Jr., William Harris, George M. Thomas, and Henry A. Walker. 1983. "Decisions, Non-decisions and Metadecisions." *Research in Social Movements Conflict and Change* 5, pp. 1–32.

Zey, Mary. 1998. "Embeddedness of Interorganizational Corporate Crime in the 1980s: Securities Fraud of Banks and Investment Banks." *Research in the Sociology of Organizations* 15, pp. 111–159.

Zey, Mary and Tami Swenson, 1998. "Corporate Tax Laws, Corporate Restructuring, and Subsidiarization of Corporate Form, 1981–1995." *Sociological Quarterly* 39, pp. 555–581.

Zey, Mary and Tami Swenson. 1999. "The Transformation of the Dominant Corporate Form from Multidivisional to Multisubsidiary: The Role of the 1986 Tax Reform Act." *Sociological Quarterly* 40, pp. 241–267.

Zey, Mary and Tami Swenson. 2001. "Survival of Fortune 500 Industrial Corporations through Mergers and Acquisition, 1981–1995." *Sociological Quarterly* 42, pp. 461–486.

Zhang, Baohui. 1994. "Corporatism, Totalitarianism, and Transitions to Democracy." *Comparative Political Studies* 27, pp. 108–137.

Zimmermann, Ekkart. 1978. "Bringing Common Sense Back In: Some Neglected Assumptions in Status Inconsistency Theory and Research." *European Journal of Sociology* 19, pp. 53–73.

Zipp, John F. 1985. "Perceived Representatives and Voting: An Assessment of the Impact of 'Choices vs. Echoes.'" *American Political Science Review* 79, pp. 50–61.

Zipp, John F. and Joel Smith. 1982. "A Structural Analysis of Class Voting." *Social Forces* 60, pp. 738–759.

Zipp, John F., Richard Landerman, and Paul Luebke. 1982. "Political Parties and Political Participation: A Reexamination of the Standard Socioeconomic Model." *Social Forces* 60, pp. 1140–1153.

Zipper, Ben. 1999. "From Slapps to Astroturf Groups." *Arena Magazine* 41, p. 270.

Zurcher, Louis A., Jr. and R. George Kirkpatrick. 1976. *Citizens for Decency: Antipornography Crusades as Status Defense.* Austin, TX: University of Texas Press.

Zunz, Oliver. 1990. *Making American Corporate, 1870–1920.* Chicago: University of Chicago Press.

Zuo, Jiping and Robert D. Benford. 1995. "Mobilization Processes and the 1989 Chinese Democracy Movement." *Sociological Quarterly* 36, pp. 131–156.

Zweigenhaft, Richard L. 1993. "Prep School and Public School Graduates of Harvard." *Journal of Higher Education* 64, pp. 211–225.

Zweigenhaft, Richard L. and G. William Domhoff. 1991. *Blacks in the White Establishment?: A Study of Race and Class in America.* New Haven, CT: Yale University Press.

Name Index

SUBJECT INDEX